myPerspectives™

ENGLISH LANGUAGE ARTS

Pearson

NEW YORK, NEW YORK • BOSTON, MASSACHUSETTS
CHANDLER, ARIZONA • GLENVIEW, ILLINOIS

Photo locators denoted as follows: Top (T), Center (C), Bottom (B), Left (L), Right (R), Background (Bkgd)

COVER: (Bkgd) © Efks/123RF, (C) © Robert F. Balazik/Shutterstock; T3: londoneye/Getty Images; T4: Artishok/ Shutterstock; T5B: Derek Latta/E+/Getty Images; T5B: OJO Images Ltd/Alamy T5B: PathDoc/Shutterstock; T5B: Franck Boston/Shutterstock; T19: Victoria Kisel/Shutterstock; T20: karandaev/fotolia; T23: Jojje/Shutterstock; T25: Nikada/Getty Images; T26B: Creativa Images/Shutterstock; T32: Monkey Business Images/Shutterstock; T33: Hocus Focus Studio/Getty Images; T34: artagent/Fotolia;

Acknowledgments of third-party content appear on page R73, which constitutes an extension of this copyright page.

Copyright © 2017 by Pearson Education, Inc., or its affiliates. All Rights Reserved. Printed in the United States of America. This publication is protected by copyright, and permission should be obtained from the publisher prior to any prohibited reproduction, storage in a retrieval system, or transmission in any form or by any means, electronic, mechanical, photocopying, recording, or otherwise. For information regarding permissions, request forms, and the appropriate contacts within the Pearson Education Global Rights & Permissions department, please visit www.pearsoned.com/permissions.

This work is solely for the use of instructors and administrators for the purpose of teaching courses and assessing student learning. Unauthorized dissemination, publication, or sale of the work, in whole or in part (including posting on the internet) will destroy the integrity of the work and is strictly prohibited.

PEARSON, ALWAYS LEARNING, and myPerspectives are exclusive trademarks owned by Pearson Education, Inc. or its affiliates, in the U.S. and/or other countries.

Unless otherwise indicated herein, any third-party trademarks that may appear in this work are the property of their respective owners and any references to third-party trademarks, logos, or other trade dress are for demonstrative or descriptive purposes only. Such references are not intended to imply any sponsorship, endorsement, authorization, or promotion of Pearson's products by the owners of such marks, or any relationship between the owner and Pearson Education, Inc. or its affiliates, authors, licensees, or distributors.

Common Core State Standards: © Copyright 2010. National Governors Association Center for Best Practices and Council of Chief State School Officers. All rights reserved.

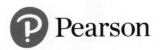

ISBN-13: 978-0-13-333864-5
ISBN-10:   0-13-333864-9
18 19

Welcome!

*my*Perspectives™ *English Language Arts* is a student-centered learning environment where you will analyze text, cite evidence, and respond critically about your learning. You will take ownership of your learning through goal-setting, reflection, independent text selection, and activities that allow you to collaborate with your peers.

Each unit of study includes selections of different genres—including multimedia—all related to a relevant and meaningful Essential Question. As you read, you will engage in activities that inspire thoughtful discussion and debate with your peers allowing you to formulate, and defend, your own perspectives.

*my*Perspectives *ELA* offers a variety of ways to interact directly with the text. You can annotate by writing in your print consumable, or you can annotate in your digital Student Edition. In addition, exciting technology allows you to access multimedia directly from your mobile device and communicate using an online discussion board!

We hope you enjoy using *my*Perspectives *ELA* as you develop the skills required to be successful throughout college and career.

Authors' Perspectives

*my*Perspectives is informed by a team of respected experts whose experiences working with students and study of instructional best practices have positively impacted education. From the evolving role of the teacher to how students learn in a digital age, our authors bring new ideas, innovations, and strategies that transform teaching and learning in today's competitive and interconnected world.

> "The teaching of English needs to focus on engaging a new generation of learners. How do we get them excited about reading and writing? How do we help them to envision themselves as readers and writers? And, how can we make the teaching of English more culturally, socially, and technologically relevant? Throughout the curriculum, we've created spaces that enhance youth voice and participation and that connect the teaching of literature and writing to technological transformations of the digital age."

Ernest Morrell, Ph.D.

is the Macy professor of English Education at Teachers College, Columbia University, a class of 2014 Fellow of the American Educational Research Association, and the Past-President of the National Council of Teachers of English (NCTE). He is also the Director of Teachers College's Institute for Urban and Minority Education (IUME). He is an award-winning author and in his spare time he coaches youth sports and writes poems and plays. Dr. Morrell has influenced the development of *my*Perspectives in Assessment, Writing & Research, Student Engagement, and Collaborative Learning.

Elfrieda Hiebert, Ph.D.

is President and CEO of TextProject, a nonprofit that provides resources to support higher reading levels. She is also a research associate at the University of California, Santa Cruz. Dr. Hiebert has worked in the field of early reading acquisition for 45 years, first as a teacher's aide and teacher of primary-level students in California and, subsequently, as a teacher and researcher. Her research addresses how fluency, vocabulary, and knowledge can be fostered through appropriate texts. Dr. Hiebert has influenced the development of *my*Perspectives in Vocabulary, Text Complexity, and Assessment.

> " The signature of complex text is challenging vocabulary. In the systems of vocabulary, it's important to provide ways to show how concepts can be made more transparent to students. We provide lessons and activities that develop a strong vocabulary and concept foundation—a foundation that permits students to comprehend increasingly more complex text."

Kelly Gallagher, M.Ed.

teaches at Magnolia High School in Anaheim, California, where he is in his thirty-first year. He is the former co-director of the South Basin Writing Project at California State University, Long Beach. Mr. Gallagher has influenced the development of *my*Perspectives in Writing, Close Reading, and the Role of Teachers.

> " The *my*Perspectives classroom is dynamic. The teacher inspires, models, instructs, facilitates, and advises students as they evolve and grow. When teachers guide students through meaningful learning tasks and then pass them ownership of their own learning, students become engaged and work harder. This is how we make a difference in student achievement—by putting students at the center of their learning and giving them the opportunities to choose, explore, collaborate, and work independently."

> " It's critical to give students the opportunity to read a wide range of highly engaging texts and to immerse themselves in exploring powerful ideas and how these ideas are expressed. In *my*Perspectives, we focus on building up students' awareness of how academic language works, which is especially important for English language learners."

Jim Cummins, Ph.D.

is a Professor Emeritus in the Department of Curriculum, Teaching and Learning of the University of Toronto. His research focuses on literacy development in multilingual school contexts as well as on the potential roles of technology in promoting language and literacy development. In recent years, he has been working actively with teachers to identify ways of increasing the literacy engagement of learners in multilingual school contexts. Dr. Cummins has influenced the development of *my*Perspectives in English Language Learner and English Language Development support.

Each unit focuses on an engaging topic related to the Essential Question.

UNIT 1 Childhood

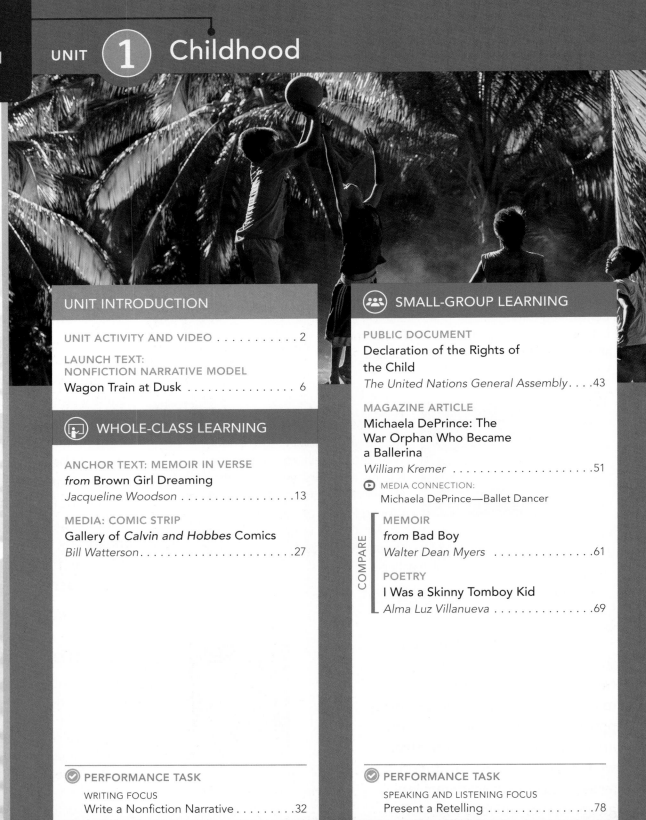

© Pearson Education, Inc., or its affiliates. All rights reserved.

vi

ESSENTIAL QUESTION: What are some of the challenges and triumphs of growing up?

An Essential Question frames all unit activities and discussions.

 INDEPENDENT LEARNING

These selections can be accessed via the Interactive Student Edition.

 PERFORMANCE-BASED ASSESSMENT PREP

PERFORMANCE-BASED ASSESSMENT

UNIT REFLECTION

All unit activities are backwards-designed to the Performance-Based Assessment.

DIGITAL PERSPECTIVES

SCAN FOR MULTIMEDIA Use the BouncePage app whenever you see "Scan for Multimedia" to access:

- Unit Introduction Videos
- Media Selections
- Modeling Videos
- Selection Audio Recordings

Additional digital resources can be found in:

- Interactive Student Edition
- *my*Perspectives+

© Pearson Education, Inc., or its affiliates. All rights reserved.

UNIT 2 Animal Allies

The Launch Text introduces a perspective on the unit topic.

UNIT INTRODUCTION

WHOLE-CLASS LEARNING

Teachers lead the shared reading experience, providing modeling and support, as students begin exploring perspectives on the unit topic.

Students encounter diverse perspectives on the unit topic, working in collaborative teams.

SMALL-GROUP LEARNING

© Pearson Education, Inc., or its affiliates. All rights reserved.

Students self-select a text to explore an aspect of the unit topic and share their learning with the class.

INDEPENDENT LEARNING

NOVEL EXCERPT
from The Wind in the Willows
Kenneth Grahame

FABLE
How the Camel Got His Hump
from Just So Stories
Rudyard Kipling

NEWS ARTICLE
The Girl Who Gets Gifts
From Birds
Katy Sewall

NEWS ARTICLE
Pet Therapy:
How Animals and Humans
Heal Each Other
Julie Rovner

These selections can be accessed via the Interactive Student Edition.

PERFORMANCE-BASED ASSESSMENT

UNIT REFLECTION

DIGITAL PERSPECTIVES

 Use the BouncePage app whenever you see "Scan for Multimedia" to access:

- Unit Introduction Videos
- Media Selections
- Modeling Videos
- Selection Audio Recordings

Additional digital resources can be found in:

- Interactive Student Edition
- *my*Perspectives+

© Pearson Education, Inc., or its affiliates. All rights reserved.

UNIT $\boxed{3}$ Modern Technology

The Launch Text models the mode of writing that will be at the core of the Performance-Based Assessment.

A rich array of media selections engage students in multi-modal learning.

Performance Tasks build toward and prepare students for the Unit Performance-Based Assessment.

© Pearson Education, Inc., or its affiliates. All rights reserved.

x

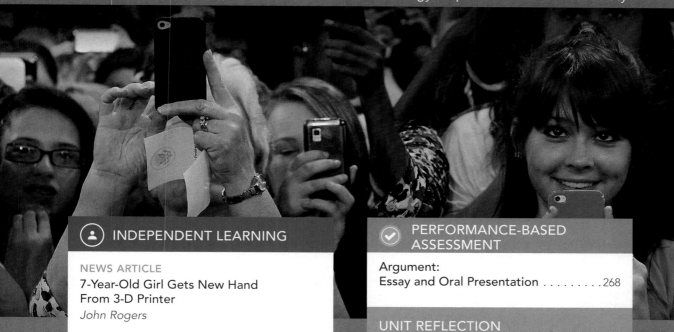

ESSENTIAL QUESTION: How is modern technology helpful and harmful to society?

INDEPENDENT LEARNING

These selections can be accessed via the Interactive Student Edition.

PERFORMANCE-BASED ASSESSMENT

UNIT REFLECTION

DIGITAL PERSPECTIVES

 SCAN FOR MULTIMEDIA

Use the BouncePage app whenever you see "Scan for Multimedia" to access:

- Unit Introduction Videos
- Media Selections
- Modeling Videos
- Selection Audio Recordings

Additional digital resources can be found in:

- Interactive Student Edition
- *my*Perspectives+

Students pull together their notes, evidence, completed activities, and Performance Tasks to prepare for the Performance-Based Assessment.

© Pearson Education, Inc., or its affiliates. All rights reserved.

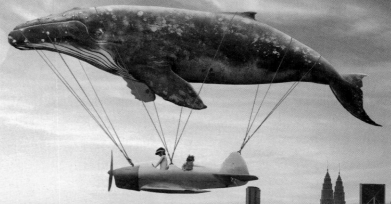

UNIT Imagination

Comparing a text and media version of classic literature deepens the learning experience and develops critical skills.

© Pearson Education, Inc., or its affiliates. All rights reserved.

INDEPENDENT LEARNING

These selections can be accessed via the Interactive Student Edition.

 PERFORMANCE-BASED
ASSESSMENT PREP

© Pearson Education, Inc., or its affiliates. All rights reserved.

 PERFORMANCE-BASED
ASSESSMENT

UNIT REFLECTION

DIGITAL
PERSPECTIVES

 SCAN FOR
MULTIMEDIA

Use the BouncePage app whenever you see "Scan for Multimedia" to access:

- Unit Introduction Videos
- Media Selections
- Modeling Videos
- Selection Audio Recordings

Additional digital resources can be found in:
- Interactive Student Edition
- *my*Perspectives+

Access multimedia resources directly from print by using your mobile or tablet device.

Digital resources, including editable worksheets, can be found in *my*Perspectives+.

xiii

T13

UNIT 5 Exploration

Graphic novels brings relevance and engagement to the classroom.

© Pearson Education, Inc., or its affiliates. All rights reserved.

xiv

T14

INDEPENDENT LEARNING

OPINION PIECE
Mars Can Wait. Oceans Can't.
Amitai Etzioni

NONFICTION NARRATIVE
from Shipwreck at the Bottom of the World
Jennifer Armstrong

HISTORICAL FICTION
from Sacajawea
Joseph Bruchac

EXPOSITORY NONFICTION
The Legacy of Arctic Explorer Matthew Henson
James Mills

INFORMATIVE ARTICLE
Should Polar Tourism Be Allowed?
Emily Goldberg

These selections can be accessed via the Interactive Student Edition.

 PERFORMANCE-BASED ASSESSMENT PREP

PERFORMANCE-BASED ASSESSMENT

UNIT REFLECTION

> Unit Reflection allows students to revisit learning goals and review skills and content learned.

DIGITAL PERSPECTIVES

SCAN FOR MULTIMEDIA | Use the BouncePage app whenever you see "Scan for Multimedia" to access:

- Unit Introduction Videos
- Media Selections
- Modeling Videos
- Selection Audio Recordings

Additional digital resources can be found in:

- Interactive Student Edition
- *my*Perspectives+

© Pearson Education, Inc., or its affiliates. All rights reserved.

xv

Student-Centered Learning

*my*Perspectives promotes student-centered learning through a unit organization that:

▶ gives students increasing responsibility for the learning process as they understand expectations, set goals, use self-assessment measures, and monitor and reflect on their learning.

▶ supports active learning in which students annotate texts, answer questions, pose questions of their own, and construct knowledge as they search for meaning.

▶ promotes social collaboration and interaction among learners in ways that strengthen positive interdependence and individual accountability.

▶ engages students in making choices in their learning and work they are producing.

▶ provides flexibility for teachers to manage resources to match learner needs.

UNIT INTRODUCTION

▶ An open-ended Essential Question is posed to stimulate thoughtful student inquiry into the richness of a topic.

▶ The Launch Text, unit opener video, and discussion board engage students by provoking and generating interest in the unit topic.

▶ Unit goals link directly to the demands of the Performance-Based Assessment.

WHOLE-CLASS LEARNING

▶ Teachers model, instruct, and support with anchor texts as the class broadens its perspective of the unit topic.

▶ Activities focus on making meaning, language development, and effective expression.

▶ Students develop and share their perspectives on the unit topic through writing in a targeted mode.

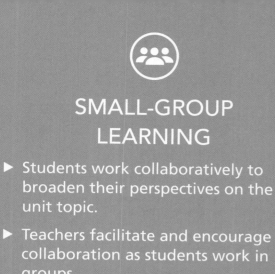

SMALL-GROUP LEARNING

▶ Students work collaboratively to broaden their perspectives on the unit topic.

▶ Teachers facilitate and encourage collaboration as students work in groups.

▶ Students develop presentations, participate in group discussions and debates, and share their learning with the class in an array of speaking and listening activities.

INDEPENDENT LEARNING

▶ Students select one online text to read independently.

▶ Teachers advise and encourage students as they implement close-reading strategies.

PERFORMANCE-BASED ASSESSMENT

Students are required to demonstrate their learning by pulling together the content knowledge, process skills, and learning habits they acquired, practiced, and engaged in throughout the unit.

Interactive Student Edition

Whether your students use the print or digital version, the Student Edition is interactive!

Provides easy access to background, author, and standards information.

Integrated notebook captures student responses to activities and allows for easy submission to the teacher.

Inline annotation tools allow students to highlight text and write comments as they apply close-reading strategies.

Embedded, interactive graphic organizers and activities allow for

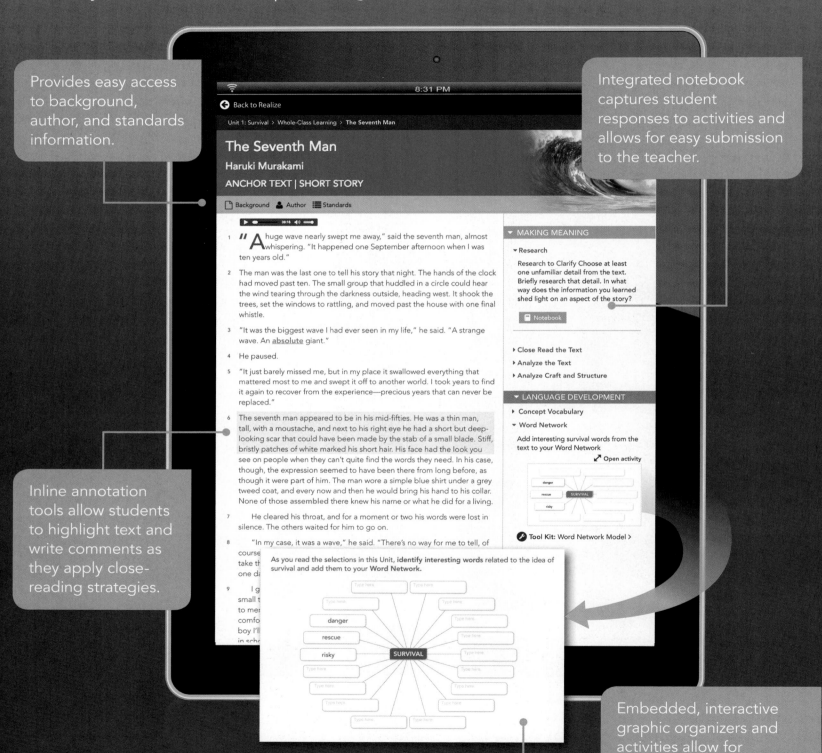

Download the Pearson BouncePages App to access audio, video, and multimedia selections through your mobile device!

About the Author

In 1978, **Haruki Murakami** (b. 1949) was attending a baseball game in Japan where the American player Dave Hilton hit a double. In that moment, Murakami had a flash of inspiration during which he decided he could write a novel. He began writing that evening. Since then, his numerous novels and short stories have been translated more than the works of any other Japanese writer of his generation.

Tool Kit
First-Read Guide and Model Annotation

STANDARDS
Reading Literature
By the end of grade 9, read and comprehend literature, including stories, dramas, and poems, in the grades 9–10 text complexity band proficiently, with scaffolding as needed at the high end of the range.

The Seventh Man

Concept Vocabulary

You will encounter the following words as you read "The Seventh Man." Before reading, note how familiar you are with each word. Then, rank the words in order from most familiar (1) to least familiar (6).

WORD	YOUR RANKING
desperate	1
entranced	4
hallucination	2
premonition	3
profound	5
meditative	6

After completing the first read, come back to the concept vocabulary and review your rankings. Mark changes to your original rankings as needed.

First Read FICTION

Apply these strategies as you conduct your first read. You will have an opportunity to complete the close-read notes after your first read.

NOTICE whom the story is about, what happens, where and when it happens, and why those involved react as they do.

ANNOTATE by marking vocabulary and key passages you want to revisit.

First Read

CONNECT ideas within the selection to what you already know and what you have already read.

RESPOND by completing the Comprehension Check and by writing a brief summary of the selection.

© Pearson Education, Inc., or its affiliates. All rights reserved.

ANCHOR TEXT | SHORT STORY

The Seventh Man

Haruki Murakami

SCAN FOR MULTIMEDIA

BACKGROUND

Hurricanes that originate in the northwest Pacific Ocean are called typhoons. They can stretch up to 500 miles in diameter and produce high winds, heavy rains, enormous waves, and severe flooding. On average, Japan is hit by three severe typhoons each year due to its location and climatic conditions.

1 "A huge wave nearly swept me away," said the seventh man, almost whispering. "It happened one September afternoon when I was ten years old."

2 The man was the last one to tell his story that night. The hands of the clock had moved past ten. The small group that huddled in a circle could hear the wind tearing through the darkness outside, heading west. It shook the trees, set the windows to rattling, and moved past the house with one final whistle.

3 "It was the biggest wave I had ever seen in my life," he said. "A strange wave. An absolute giant."

4 He paused.

5 "It just barely missed me, but in my place it swallowed everything that mattered most to me and swept it off to another world. I took years to find it again and to recover from the experience—precious years that can never be replaced."

6 The seventh man appeared to be in his mid-fifties. He was a thin man, tall, with a moustache, and next to his right eye he had a short but deep-looking scar that could have been made by the stab of a small blade. Stiff, bristly patches of white marked his short hair. His face had the look you see on people when they can't quite find the words they need. In his case, though, the expression seemed to have

NOTES

CLOSE READ
ANNOTATE: Mark details in paragraph 2 that describe where the action takes place.

QUESTION: What can you tell about the story's setting?

The mood was very dark and dreary. There was a sense of doom.

A write-in Student Edition allows students to annotate the

Close-Reading Routine

myPerspectives motivates students to read a text thoughtfully, apply strategies as they read, and critically examine the text.

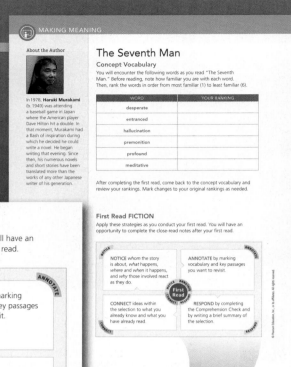

First Read FICTION

Apply these strategies as you conduct your first read. You will have an opportunity to complete the close-read notes after your first read.

NOTICE *whom* the story is about, *what* happens, *where* and *when* it happens, and *why* those involved react as they do.

ANNOTATE by marking vocabulary and key passages you want to revisit.

CONNECT ideas within the selection to what you already know and what you have already read.

RESPOND by completing the Comprehension Check and by writing a brief summary of the selection.

First Read

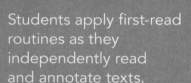

Students apply first-read routines as they independently read and annotate texts.

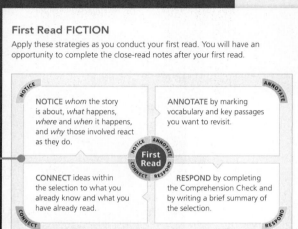

Students close read complex and rich text passages, studying structures, diction, and other elements of author's craft.

Close Read the Text

1. The model, from paragraph 5 of the story, shows two sample annotations, along with questions and conclusions. Close read the passage, and find another detail to annotate. Then, write a question and your conclusion.

Close Read

ANNOTATE: This phrase describes the wave in almost human terms.

QUESTION: What effect does this word choice create?

CONCLUDE: This description makes the wave seem alive and evil.

ANNOTATE: This word is repeated.

QUESTION: Why does the author repeat the word *years*?

CONCLUDE: The repetition emphasizes how long it takes the man to recover from the experience.

Models show students how to close read the text.

"It just barely missed me, but in my place it swallowed everything that mattered most to me and swept it off to another world. I took years to find it again and to recover from the experience—precious years that can never be replaced."

sc...ething. I was sure I had yelled loud enough, but my voice did not seem to have reached him. He might have been so absorbed in whatever it was he had found that my call made no impression on him. K. was like that. He would get involved with things to the point of forgetting everything else. Or possibly I had not yelled as loudly as I had thought. I do recall that my voice sounded strange to me, as though it belonged to someone else.

29 Then I heard a deep rumbling sound. It seemed to shake the earth.

NOTES

CLOSE READ
ANNOTATE: In paragraph 27, mark the details the author uses to describe the waves.

QUESTION: Why does the author include so many contrasting descriptions?

CONCLUDE: In what ways is the author preparing you for what comes next?

Closer Look notes, found only in the Teacher's Edition, provide additional close-reading opportunities.

Digital Annotation Highlights focus on passages in the Interactive Teacher's Edition.

NOTES

CLOSER LOOK

Analyze Character

Students may have marked paragraph 10 during their first read. Use this paragraph to help students understand the seventh man's friendship with K.

ANNOTATE: Have students mark details in the paragraph that describe K.'s appearance and personality.

QUESTION: What overall impression does the author create of K.? How does the author characterize the relationship between K. and the seventh man?

Possible response: K. is an artistic, sensitive boy who is often picked on because he is physically different from most boys his age. His speech impediment and difficulty with academics lead most people to think something is wrong with him. K. and the seventh man are best friends. The seventh man feels protective of K., and often stands up for him when he is picked on by others.

CONCLUDE: How does the author's characterization of K. and his friendship with the seventh man help you understand the impact of K.'s death?

Possible response: The seventh man viewed himself as K.'s protector. When K. was lost to the wave the seventh man lost his best friend, and he blamed himself for failing to protect K., carrying that guilt with him for most of his life.

Remind students that there are two types of characterization. In **direct characterization**, [...] a character's traits. [...]ion, an author [...]aracter by describing [...]e, does, and says, as [...]ers react to him or [...] draw conclusions [...] this indirect[...]

looks like, feels like, or sounds like. You may wish to model the close read using the following think-aloud format. Possible responses to questions on the student page are included. You may also want to print copies of the Close-Read Guide for students to use.

ANNOTATE: As I read paragraph 2, I notice and highlight the details *the hands of the clock had moved past ten* and *the wind tearing through the darkness outside.* These details suggest to me that the story is set at night during a storm.

💬 Hide Annotation Highlights

▶ ━━━━ 36:18 🔊 ━━━━

1 "A huge wave nearly swept me away," said the seventh man, almost whispering. "It happened one September afternoon when I was ten years old."

2 The man was the last one to tell his story that night. *The hands of the clock had moved past ten.* The small group that huddled in a circle could hear *the wind tearing through the darkness outside,* heading west. It shook the trees, set the windows to rattling, and moved past the house with one final whistle.

3 "It was the biggest wave I had ever seen in my life," he said. "A strange wave. An absolute giant."

4 He paused.

5 "It just barely missed me, but in my place it swallowed everything that mattered most to me and swept it off to another world. I took years to find it again and to recover from the experience—precious years that can never be replaced."

6 The seventh man appeared to be in his mid-fifties. He was a thin man, tall, with a moustache, and next to his right eye he had a short but deep-looking scar that could have been made by the stab of a small blade. Stiff, bristly patches of white marked his short

Building Literacy

For each selection, students **Make Meaning** through first- and close-read routines and by analyzing author's craft and structure. Students also complete **Language Development** activities with concept vocabulary and conventions practice tasks. **Effective Expression** activities provide students with opportunities to share their learning through written and oral projects.

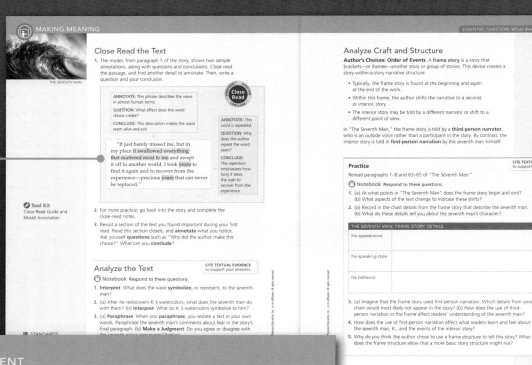

MAKING MEANING

Students make meaning of the text through close reading and analysis.

MAKING MEANING

ESSENTIAL QUESTION: What does it take to survive?

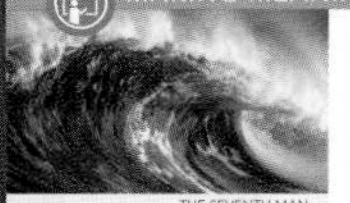

THE SEVENTH MAN

Close Read the Text

1. The model, from paragraph 5 of the story, shows two sample annotations, along with questions and conclusions. Close read the passage, and find another detail to annotate. Then, write a question and your conclusion.

Close Read — ANNOTATE, QUESTION, CONCLUDE

ANNOTATE: This phrase describes the wave in almost human terms.

QUESTION: What effect does this word choice create?

CONCLUDE: This description makes the wave seem alive and evil.

"It just barely missed me, but in my place it swallowed everything that mattered most to me and swept it off to another world. I took years to find it again and to recover from the experience—precious years that can never be replaced."

ANNOTATE: This word is repeated.

QUESTION: Why does the author repeat the word *years*?

CONCLUDE: The repetition emphasizes how long it takes the man to recover from the experience.

Tool Kit
Close-Read Guide and Model Annotation

2. For more practice, go back into the story and complete the close-read notes.
3. Revisit a section of the text you found important during your first read. Read this section closely, and **annotate** what you notice. Ask yourself **questions** such as "Why did the author make this choice?" What can you **conclude**?

Analyze the Text

CITE TEXTUAL EVIDENCE to support your answers.

Notebook **Respond to these questions.**

1. **Interpret** What does the wave **symbolize,** or represent, to the seventh man?
2. (a) After he rediscovers K.'s watercolors, what does the seventh man do with them? (b) **Interpret** What do K.'s watercolors symbolize to him?
3. (a) **Paraphrase** When you **paraphrase**, you restate a text in your own words. Paraphrase the seventh man's comments about fear in the story's final paragraph. (b) **Make a Judgment** Do you agree or disagree with the seventh man's comments? Explain.

STANDARDS

Pearson Education, Inc., or its affiliates. All rights reserved.

Analyze Craft and Structure

Author's Choices: Order of Events A **frame story** is a story that brackets—or *frames*—another story or group of stories. This device creates a story-within-a-story narrative structure.

- Typically, the frame story is found at the beginning and again at the end of the work.
- Within this frame, the author shifts the narrative to a second, or interior, story.
- The interior story may be told by a different narrator or shift to a different point of view.

In "The Seventh Man," the frame story is told by a **third-person narrator**, who is an outside voice rather than a participant in the story. By contrast, the interior story is told in **first-person narration** by the seventh man himself.

Practice

CITE TEXTUAL EVIDENCE to support your answers.

Reread paragraphs 1–8 and 63–65 of "The Seventh Man."

Notebook **Respond to these questions.**

1. (a) At what points in "The Seventh Man" does the frame story begin and end? (b) What aspects of the text change to indicate these shifts?
2. (a) Record in the chart details from the frame story that describe the seventh man. (b) What do these details tell you about the seventh man's character?

THE SEVENTH MAN: FRAME STORY DETAILS	
his appearance	
his speaking style	
his behavior	

3. (a) Imagine that the frame story used first-person narration. Which details from your chart would most likely not appear in the story? (b) How does the use of third-person narration in the frame affect readers' understanding of the seventh man?
4. How does the use of first-person narration affect what readers learn and feel about the seventh man, K., and the events of the interior story?
5. Why do you think the author chose to use a frame structure to tell this story? What does the frame structure allow that a more basic story structure might not?

Pearson Education, Inc., or its affiliates. All rights reserved.

The Seventh Man **147**

LANGUAGE DEVELOPMENT

THE SEVENTH MAN

Concept Vocabulary

desperate	hallucination	profound
entranced	premonition	meditative

Why These Words? These concept words help to reveal the emotional state of the seventh man. For example, when the wave approaches, the seventh man is *entranced*, waiting for it to attack. After the wave hits, the seventh man believes he sees his friend K. in the wave and claims that this experience was no *hallucination*. Notice that both words relate to experiences that occur only in the mind of the seventh man.

1. How does the concept vocabulary sharpen the reader's understanding of the mental or emotional state of the seventh man?
2. What other words in the selection connect to this concept?

LANGUAGE DEVELOPMENT

Concept Vocabulary words are taught in conjunction with each text. The selected words enable students to study words within meaningful clusters.

EFFECTIVE EXPRESSION

Students are provided with frequent opportunities to practice writing within the unit's focus mode.

Throughout the unit, students participate in speaking and listening, writing, and research activities that enable them to share learning.

EFFECTIVE EXPRESSION

THE SEVENTH MAN

Writing to Sources

Critical writing is a type of argumentation in which you explain your insights about a literary work and persuade others to share your point of view. Like any argument, critical writing requires you to state a claim, or position, and to support it with strong evidence.

Assignment

Write a **critical review** of "The Seventh Man" that could appear in your school paper or website. State specific reasons why you either recommend or do not recommend the story to other readers.

Your review should include:

- Title and author of the work being reviewed
- A brief summary of the work
- A clear statement o
- Valid reasoning tha

Vocabulary and Conve
including several of the c
infinitive phrases to add v

desperate

entranced

Reflect on Your Writ
After you have written yo

1. How do you think writ
   understanding of the s

2. What evidence and su
   did they help support y

3. **Why These Words?**
   your writing. Which w
   your critical review?

STANDARDS

Writing
Introduce precise claim(s), distinguish the claim(s) from alternate or opposing claims, and create an organization that establishes clear relationships among the claim(s), counterclaims, reasons, and evidence.

Speaking and Listening
Present information, findings, and supporting evidence clearly, concisely, and logically such that listeners can follow the line of reasoning and the organization, development, substance, and style are appropriate to purpose, audience, and task.

150 UNIT 2 • SURVIVAL

Speaking and Listening

Assignment

With a partner, prepare a **retelling** of "The Seventh Man" from another point of view. For example, you may choose to retell the story from K.'s parents' point of view, or from that of a hidden onlooker. Refresh your memory by rereading the selection. Then, follow these steps to complete the assignment.

1. **Identify Your Character** Choose your character and determine how he or she fits into the original story. Decide what important information you will need to tell your audience to clarify the character's background and motivations.

2. **Plan Your Retelling** Once you've identified your character, think about his or her perspective on the events in the story. As you plan your retelling, keep the following in mind:

   - How does your character see the story differently from the seventh man? What fresh perspective does he or she offer?
   - Make a list of the story events, as experienced by your character. Then, weave those events into a coherent retelling.
   - Choose language that is appropriate to the character you chose. For example, a child would choose simple words and sentences and may not fully understand what is he or she is observing.

3. **Prepare Your Delivery** Practice your retelling with your partner. Include the following performance techniques to help you achieve the desired effect.

   - Vary your intonation to reflect the emotions of your character. Avoid speaking in a flat, monotone style.
   - As you speak, use facial expressions and gestures that help convey your character's personality.
   - Make eye contact with your audience to engage them in the story.

4. **Evaluate Retellings** As your classmates deliver their retellings, listen attentively. Use an evaluation guide like the one shown to analyze their delivery.

EVALUATION GUIDE

Rate each statement on a scale of 1 (not demons
to 4 (demonstrated).

☐ The character was clearly identified.

☐ The speaker communicated clearly

☐ The speaker used a variety of sp

☐ The speaker used effective ges

EVIDENCE LOG

Before moving on to a
selection, go to your
Log and record
learned from
Man."

th Man **151**

© Pearson Education, Inc., or its affiliates. All rights reserved.

Assessments to Inform Instruction

Assessments can be administered in print and/or online.

Pearson Realize™ provides powerful data reporting.

Balanced Opinion/Argumentative Performance Task

Excerpt from *Pride and Prejudice*

This story recounts the first meeting between Mr. Darcy and Elizabeth Bennet, who later marry each other.

Excerpt from *Pride and Prejudice*
by Jane Austen

Mr. Bingley was good-looking and gentleman-like; he had a pleasant countenance, and easy, unaffected manners. His sisters were fine women, with an air of decided fashion. His brother-in-law, Mr. Hurst, merely looked the gentleman; but his friend Mr. Darcy soon drew the attention of the room by his fine, tall person, handsome features, noble mien, and the report, which was in general circulation within five minutes after his entrance, of his having ten thousand a year. The gentlemen pronounced him to be a fine figure of a man, the ladies declared he was much handsomer than Mr. Bingley, and he was looked at with great admiration for about half the evening, till his manners gave a disgust which turned the tide of his popularity; for he was discovered to be proud, to be

2. In "Excerpt from *Pride and Prejudice*," the author reveals the viewpoints of **three** distinct characters—Mr. Bingley, Mr. Darcy, and Elizabeth Bennet. Write a one or two paragraph response in which you evaluate which of the three characters' opinions is **most** credible or believable. Use evidence from the excerpt to support your response.

Browse Programs

Teachers can instantly access student and class data that shows standards mastery on assessments, Online activity, and overall progress.

Data overview

Mastery | Average score on completed tests. Select a bar to see how well your class mastered this standard.

75%
Average scores on assessments

- 80% - 100%
- 60% - 79%
- 0% - 59%
- Test average

Progress | Class completion of assignments including tests. Select a bar to get each student's percent completion of the assignment.

88%
Class average on all completed assignments

- 80% - 100%
- 60% - 79%
- 0% - 59%
- Average progress

Usage | Average time spent by the class on assignments including tests. Select a bar to see each student's time on the assignment.

20:00
Average minutes per assignment

- Time spent
- Average time spent

PEARSON

YEAR-LONG ASSESSMENT

Beginning-of-Year Test

▶ Tests all standards that will be taught in the school year.

▶ Allows you to use test data to plan which standards need focus.

Mid-Year Test

▶ Tests mastery of standards taught in the first half of the year.

▶ Provides an opportunity to remediate; if administered online, remediation is assigned automatically.

End-of-Year Test

▶ Allows you to use results to determine mastery of standards, place students in classes for the following school year, and to capture final assessment data.

UNIT-LEVEL ASSESSMENT

Selection Activities

▶ Instructional activities can be used to assess students' grasp of critical concepts.

Formative Assessments

▶ Selection activities can be used as formative checks.

▶ Notes in the Teacher's Edition offer suggestions for reteaching.

Selection Tests

▶ Test items track student progress toward mastering standards taught with the selection.

Performance Tasks

▶ Each unit includes both a writing and a speaking and listening performance task.

▶ Performance Tasks prepare students for success on the end-of-unit Performance-Based Assessment.

Unit Tests

▶ Students apply standards taught in the unit with new texts.

▶ These tests provide an opportunity to remediate; if administered online, remediation is assigned automatically.

Performance-Based Assessments

▶ All unit activities are backwards-mapped to the end-of-unit Performance-Based Assessment.

▶ Students use their notes, knowledge, and skills learned to complete a project.

Technology-enhanced items allow students to experience next-generation assessment formats.

Personalize for Learning

The Teacher's Edition provides support before, during, and after each selection to help you personalize learning for your students.

A continuous improvement loop is built in to help teachers perform formative assessment and remediation.

A full range of reading supports is provided for each text, based on text complexity rubrics.

WHOLE

Reading Support

Text Complexity Rubric: The Seventh Man	
Quantitative Measures	
Lexile: 910 Text Length: 5,860 words	
Qualitative Measures	
Knowledge Demands ①—❷—③—④—⑤	Life experience demands: The situations may be unfamiliar to some readers (experiencing a typhoon, tragedy of losing someone in a natural disaster), but the situations and emotions are clearly explained.
Structure ①—❷—③—④—⑤	Use of flash-back, flash-forward (transitions from narration in third person and the seventh man's story told in first person)
Language Conventionality and Clarity ①—②—❸—④—⑤	Figurative language; complex descriptions
Levels of Meaning/Purpose ①—②—❸—④—⑤	Multiple levels of meaning (events are described that also signify emotions of guilt or of self-forgiveness); concepts and meanings are mostly explained and easy to grasp.

DECIDE AND PLAN

English Language Support
Provide English Learners with support for context and vocabulary as they read the selection. **PI.8; PI.12**

Knowledge Demands Tell students that this short story is about an event that occurred during a typhoon. They should expect to see language that describes weather and the sea. (high tide, low tide,...)

Language Conventiality and Clarity Students may find the use of sensory language difficult to grasp. Explain that the author often uses words in a figurative way to create feelings or sensations. Figurative language is language that is used imaginatively rather than literally. Such expressions can be difficult for second-language learners.

Strategic Support
Provide students with strategic support to ensure that they can successfully read the text.

Knowledge Demands Use the background information to discuss typhoons. Determine students' prior knowledge and experience with natural disasters. Provide additional background if needed.

Structure Discuss what it means to flash-back or flash-forward in a text. Point out that a story might switch back and forth to different time periods. If students continue to have difficulty with the time sequence, point out clues to transitions between past and present; for example, sentences that say that the man is telling a story, or use of first and third person. When students reread, have them note each transition from past to present.

Challenge
Provide students who need to be challenged with ideas for how they can go beyond a simple interpretation of the text.

Text Analysis For students that grasp the time transitions, have them identify the use of first person when the seventh man is speaking, and descriptions in third person when the story moves to the present.

Written Response Ask students to speculate on what might have happened if the seventh man had made different choices in his life. Have them analyze each choice he made and determine how his life might have differed if he had chosen differently. Have them rewrite the story with reflection the choices.

TEACH

Read and Respond
Have the class do their first read of the selection. Then have them complete their close read. Finally, work with them on the Making Meaning, Language Development, and Effective Expression activities.

Text complexity rubrics provide targeted suggestions for learner levels, including English Language supports that are based on the demands of the text.

Standards Support Through

IDENTIFY NEEDS
Analyze results of the Beginning-of-Year Assessment, focusing on the items relating to Unit 2. Also take into consideration student performance to this point and your observations of where particular students struggle.

- If students have per scaffolds before ass
- If students have do keep progressing ar
- Use the Selection R students continually

Instructional Stand		
	Catching	
Reading	Review co students t understan have diffe different c You may the Order to help stu the basic s narrative.	
Writing	You may the Reteac Anecdotes students u anecdote an argume	
Speaking and Listening	You may the Reteac worksheet help stude to plan an excerpt.	
Language	You may the Clause help stude function o Review co students t understan have diffe different c	

ANALYZE AND REVISE
- Analyze student work for evidence of student learning.
- Identify whether or not students have met the expectations in the standards.
- Identify implications for future instruction.

TEACH
Implement the planned lesson, and gather evidence of student learning.

Challenge
Encourage interested students to expand the Research to Explore
activity by learning about the motto of other branches of the U.S.
military, including the Air Force, Army, Coast Guard, and Navy, in
addition to the Marines. Students can also c[...]
branch and present their results in a poster [...]

PERSONALIZE FOR LEARNING

English Language Support
Idioms Explain to students that *eye of the storm* in paragraph 15 is
an idiomatic expression—the words used are not meant literally. If
students struggle to understand idioms, encourage them to look for
context clues. Instruct students to keep reading to get clues about
the meaning of this expression (*No such "eye" existed, of course: we
were just in that momentary quiet spot at the center of the pool of
whirling air*). Make sure students understand that eye of the storm
means "a calm in the middle of a turbulent situation. **ALL LEVELS**

English Language Support
notes provide support for
skills and concepts such as
idioms, figurative language,
and multiple-meaning words.

Practical and easy-to-
implement supports
ensure that all students'
needs are met as they
practice and apply
standards with each text.

Customize and Enrich

nd Learning Cycle

DIGITAL PERSPECTIVES

Enriching the Text In 2013, the environmental
scientist Tim Jarvis re-created Shackleton's
voyage from Elephant Island to South Georgia
in a replica of the *James Caird*. Jarvis and
his crew used the same clothing, food, and
navigational equipment that Shackleton had.
The documentary *Shackleton: Death or Glory*
chronicles the journey. Find a clip from the

documentary online and show students (after
previewing it yourself). Then, have students write
a paragraph explaining how the clip enhances
their understanding of the selection "The Voyage
of the *James Caird*." For example, students might
gain a better understanding of the size of the
boat and the harsh conditions Shackleton and his
men endured.

Digital Perspectives offers suggestions for using digital
resources to strengthen concepts being taught.

AND PLAN

s matching these standards, then provide selection
el lesson provided in the Student Edition.

g-of-Year Assessment, then challenge them to
em opportunities to practice the skills in depth.

lanning Pages for The Seventh Man to help
master the standards.

an

Year	Looking Forward
-10.4 Determine the ning of words and phrases ey are used in the text.	Have students analyze the subtleties and nuances of various word choices.
-10.5 Analyze how an or's choices concerning to structure a text, events within it, and pulate time create such ts as mystery, tension, or ise.	Have students recast the beginning of the story without the frame and analyze the impact on the story as a whole.
10.3.a-e Write narratives evelop real or imagined riences or events using tive technique, well- en details, and well- tured event sequences.	Encourage students to incorporate both real and fictional anecdotes in their writing.
-10.4.b Plan, memorize present a recitation conveys the meaning e selection and includes opriate performance niques (e.g., tone, rate, modulation) to achieve esired aesthetic effect.	You may wish to challenge students to memorize and recite increasingly longer or more complex selections.
0.1.B Use various types rases to convey specific nings and add variety nterest to writing or entations.	You may wish to challenge students to use increasingly complex phrases and clauses in their writing.
10.4a Use context as a to the meaning of a word rase.	Have students analyze the subtleties and nuances of various word choices in different contexts.

AUTHOR'S PERSPECTIVE   Jim Cummins

Importance of Background Knowledge It is
important for all students, and especially English
Language Learners, to tap into background
knowledge when they read a text. It is incumbent
on teachers to help students access this
knowledge and integrate it with new textual
information. One way to do this is to encourage
groups to share what they know about the topic
of the text before they begin reading. For example,

on a superficial level, some students may have
prior knowledge about sailing, which can help
to scaffold understanding of "The Voyage of the
James Caird." On a deeper level, more students
may be able to relate to the idea of forcing oneself
to go to extremes or taking risks in order to help
others. After students have completed their first
read, have them discuss how their background
knowledge helped them understand the text.

Author's Perspective notes offer expert insights
on topics, including incorporating first-language
knowledge, building background knowledge, and
academic and conversational vocabulary.

FORMATIVE ASSESSMENT
Analyze Craft and Structure 📄
• **If** students fail to identify the frame, **then** have
  them look for clues that indicate the point of
  view. For example, the person narrating the
  frame may not be involved in the interior story.
• **If** students are unable to identify the point of

A formative assessment
opportunity with
recommended prescriptive
activities is provided with

English Language Support

myPerspectives provides supports for English Language Learners at the Emerging, Expanding, and Bridging levels. Various resources can be used flexibly in print and online to meet your students' individual needs.

Selection audio can be found in the Interactive Student Edition and via BouncePages in the print Student Edition.

Glossary terms are defined at point of use and include English and Spanish audio.

Concept and Academic Vocabulary words are defined in Spanish.

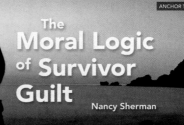

ANCHOR TEXT | OPINION PIECE

The Moral Logic of Survivor Guilt
Nancy Sherman

The Moral Logic of Survivor Guilt
Nancy Sherman
ANCHOR TEXT | OPINION PIECE

📄 Background 👤 Author ☰ Standards

▶ ●———————— 11:44 🔊 ———

 If there is one thing we have learned from returning war veterans—especially those of the last decade—it's that the emotional reality of the soldier at home is often at odds with that of the civilian public they left behind. And while friends and families of returning service members may be experiencing gratefulness or relief this holiday,[1] many of those they've welcomed home are likely struggling with other emotions.

Is the sense of responsibility soldiers feel toward each other irrational?

[2] High on that list of emotions is guilt. Soldiers often carry this <u>burden</u> home—survivor guilt being perhaps the kind most familiar to us. In war, standing here rather than there can save your life but cost a buddy his. It's flukish luck, but you feel responsible. The guilt begins an endless loop of counterfactuals—thoughts that you could have or should have done otherwise, though in fact you did nothing wrong. The feelings are, of course, not restricted to the battlefield. But given the magnitude[2] of loss in war, they hang

---

BACKGROUND
Traumatic events take a toll on the physical and mental well-being of the individuals who must endure them. Survivors of the Holocaust, rescue workers, and war veterans, for example, might wonder how they were able to make it out alive when others did not. The term "survivor guilt" is used to describe these feelings.

© Pearson Education, Inc., or its affiliates. All rights reserved

SCAN FOR MULTIMEDIA

[1] If there is one thing we have learned from returning war veterans—especially those of the last decade—it's that the emotional reality of the soldier at home is often at odds with that of the civilian public they left behind. And while friends and families of returning service members may be experiencing gratefulness or relief this holiday,[1] many of those they've welcomed home are likely struggling with other emotions.

Is the sense of responsibility soldiers feel toward each other irrational?

[2] High on that list of emotions is guilt. Soldiers often carry this burden home—survivor guilt being perhaps the kind most familiar to us. In war, standing here rather than there can save your life but cost a buddy his. It's flukish luck, but you feel responsible. The guilt begins an endless loop of counterfactuals—thoughts that you could have or should have done otherwise, though in fact you did nothing wrong. The feelings are, of course, not restricted to the battlefield. But given the magnitude[2] of loss in war, they hang heavy there and are pervasive. And they raise the question of just how irrational those feelings are, and if they aren't, of what is the basis of their reasonableness.

1. **this holiday** This essay was originally published the day before the 4th of July (Independence Day).
2. **magnitude** *n.* great size or extent.

NOTES

burden (BURD n) *n.* something that is carried with difficulty or obligation

CLOSE READ
ANNOTATE: Mark words in paragraph 1 that show opposites.

QUESTION: What groups of people are being contrasted by using these opposites?

CONCLUDE: What does this contrast suggest about the two groups?

The Moral Logic of Survivor Guilt **33**

GLOSARIO: VOCABULARIO ACADÉMICO

VOCABULARIO ACADÉMICOS/ VOCABULARIO DE CONCEPTOS

El vocabulario académico está en letra azul.

Pronunciation Key

Symbol	Sample Words	Symbol	
a	*at, catapult, Alabama*	ihr	
a	*father, charms, argue*	o	
ahr	*far, archaic, argument*	oh	
ar	*marry, various, arrogant*	o͞o [lig]	*would, pull, foot*
aw	*law, maraud, caution*	o͞o	*boot, soup, crucial*
awr	*pour, organism, forewarn*	ow	*now, stout, flounder*
ay	*ape, sails, implication*	oy	*boy, toil, oyster*
ayr	*Mary, compare, hair*	u	*us, disrupt, understand*
ee	*even, teeth, really*	uh	*ago, focus, contemplation*
eer	*sneer, veneer, sincere*	uhr	*under, guttural, discolor*
eh	*ten, repel, elephant*	ur	*bird, urgent, perforation*
ehr	*merry, verify, terribly*	y	*by, delight, identify*
ih	*is, continue, fugitive*		

A

abash / avergonzar *v.* apenar

ambiguity / ambigüedad *s.* estado o cualidad de ser indefinido; vago

El Septimo Hombre
Haruki Murakami
CUENTO | RESUMEN AUDIO

00:00/04:27

English / Inglés

Online selection summaries with both English and Spanish audio and text are assignable.

El séptimo hombre de Haruki Murakami empieza con una introducción del narrador y protagonista, llamado el "séptimo hombre", puesto que es el último de un grupo de siete en contar su historia. No hay explicación sobre este grupo. Su objetivo sólo se puede adivinar por el tipo de historia que cuenta el séptimo hombre y por el entorno.

La historia en sí misma empieza en la infancia del séptimo hombre, en una población costera de Japón, y se centra en la relación de amistad con un niño al que se refiere como K. K es algo más joven que el narrador, y frágil, necesitado del apoyo y la protección del narrador. K tiene un gran talento artístico que el narrador admira.

Unit 2: Survival > Whole-Class Learning: The Seventh Man

85%

36:18

looks like, feels like, or sounds like. You may wish to model the close read using the following think-aloud format. Possible responses to questions on the student page are included. You may also want to print copies of the Close-Read Guide for students to use.

1   "A huge wave nearly swept me away," said the seventh man, almost whispering. "It happened one September afternoon when I was ten years old."

2   The man was the last one to tell his story that night. *The hands of the clock had moved past ten.* The small group that huddled in a circle could hear *the wind tearing through the darkness outside,* heading west. It shook the trees, set the windows to rattling, and moved past the house with one final whistle.

3   "It was the biggest wave I had ever seen in my life," he said. "A strange wave. An absolute giant."

4   He paused.

5   "It just barely missed me, but in my place it swallowed everything that mattered most to me and swept it off to another world. I took years to find it again and to recover from the experience—precious years that can never be replaced."

6   The seventh man appeared to be in his mid-fifties. He was a thin man, tall, with a mustache, and next to his right eye he had a short but deep-looking scar that could have been made by the stab of a small blade. Stiff, bristly patches of white marked his short

ANNOTATE: As I read paragraph 2, I notice and highlight the details *the hands of the clock had moved past ten* and *the wind tearing through the darkness outside.* These details suggest to me that the story is set at night during a storm.

💬 Hide Annotation Highlights

Highlighted passages in the Interactive Teacher's Edition focus on a key element of the text type or illustrate how language choices develop cohesion and link ideas, events, and concepts within a text.

ENGLISH LANGUAGE SUPPORT LESSON

The Seventh Man
Analyze Craft and Structure

Author's Choices: Order of Events
Objective Students will learn to describe a sequence of events using a variety of words and sentence structures.

JUMP START

Tell students to listen as you describe the following order of events. *My friend Julio came to my house. Then we walked to the pizza shop. Then we played soccer. Then we went home.*

Ask students for their evaluation of the sentences. Point out that your description used the word *then* many times to describe sequence. Ask: *How can we put more variety into our language when we're talking about sequence of events?*

TEACH

Display this sample sentence:

First, the sky began to change. Next, the wind began to howl and the rain began to beat against the house.

Ask students which words indicate the order of events.

Next, display the second sample sentence. Point out that it's a variation of the first sentence.

After the sky began to change, the wind began to howl and the rain began to beat against the house.

Ask students which word tells about the order of events.

Introduce these other words that show time order: *last, afterward, subsequently, when, before, before long, as soon as, later, finally.*

To challenge students, have them rewrite the sentence one more time to show a different sequence.

Possible response: *When the sky began to change, the wind began to howl and the rain began to beat against the house.*

Remind students that when they read, it's important to pay attention to the order of events. The order of events presented in the story may not be the order in which the events actually happened. Stories can flash back and flash forward.

For example, read aloud the following events from "The Seventh Man."

a. The Seventh Man is telling his story.

b. K. was swept off by a wave.

c. The Seventh Man got past his guilt.

Ask students in what order the events are told in the story. (a, b, c) Then ask in what order the events happened. (b, c, a) Point out that the events are told in that order because "The Seventh Man" is a frame story—a story within a story. In "The Seventh Man," the narrator is telling his story, which occurred at an

Printable English Language Support Lessons provide additional instructional opportunities.

Personalize for Teaching

Lesson planning is easy and efficient with clearly labeled support at point of use in the Teacher's Edition.

A trade book alignment with suggestions for integrating longer works within the unit is provided. Lesson plans for recommended titles are available online.

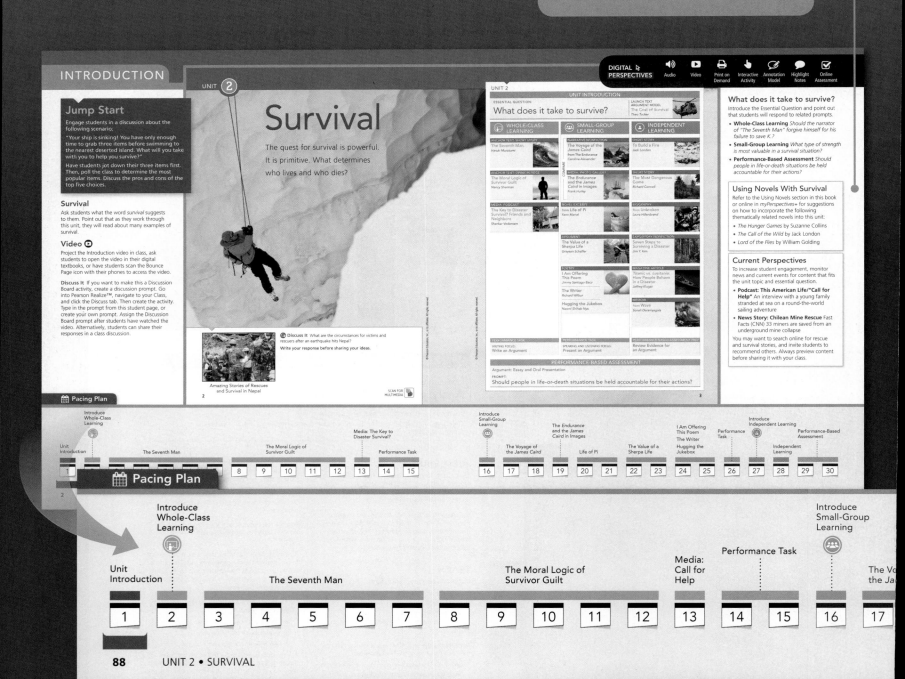

The Seventh Man

◆)) AUDIO SUMMARIES
Audio summaries of "The Seventh Man" are available in both English and Spanish and can be assigned to students in Pearson Realize™. Assigning these summaries prior to reading the selection may help students build additional background knowledge and set a context for their first read.

Summary

"The Seventh Man" begins on a stormy night in a house where a group of people is sharing stories. The unnamed seventh man tells his story last and describes a huge wave that changed his life forever. He explains that he grew up in a seaside town in Japan, where he and his best friend, described only as K., were as close as brothers. A typhoon strikes and when the eye of the storm passes over, the seventh man's father allows the boys to go outside. They go down to the beach to play. When the a tsunami strikes, the seventh man runs for his life, leaving K. behind. He struggles with guilt for into his adult life. Forty years later, the seventh man makes an important realization.

Insight

The choices survivors make are not always easy or clear. Reading "The Seventh Man" will help students begin their reflections on how complicated survival can be. Although a survivor may have escaped with his or her life, that life may never be the same.

Some students may find "The Seventh Man" disturbing. The realization that a childhood decision might color someone's whole life is sobering and may require support.

Digital Perspectives identifies online resources.

DIGITAL �ˊ₂ PERSPECTIVES Audio Video Print on Demand Interactive Activity Annotation Model ● Highlight Notes ☑ Online Assessment

Planning pages provide essential information, including selection summaries, insights, and links to the Essential Question.

Lesson Resources provides at-a-glance listings of standards, student-facing resources, on-level and reteaching support, and even a place for you to write in your own resources!

LESSON RESOURCES

	Making Meaning	Language Development	Effective Expression
Lesson	First Read Close Read Analyze the Text Analyze Craft and Structure	Concept Vocabulary Word Study Conventions	Writing to Sources Speaking and Listening
Instructional Standards	RL.9–10.4 RL.9–10.5 PI.5 PI.6a	L.9–10.1b L.9–10.4a PII.3, PII.4, PII.5	W.9–10.3.a–e SL.9–10.4.b PI.1, PI.5, PI.11
⌲ STUDENT RESOURCES	Search for these resources in myPerspectives Digital Student Edition or myPerspectives+		
Selection Resources	◆) Audio Selection ▶ Student Modeling Video ▤ Close–Read Guide ▤ First–Read Guide	▤ Word Network	▤ Evidence Log
⌲ TEACHER RESOURCES	Search for these resources in myPerspectives Digital Teacher's Edition or myPerspectives+		
Selection Resources	✎ Annotation Model ◆) Audio Summaries ◆) Additional English Language Support ▤ Analyze Text ✎ Frame Story Graphic Organizer ▤ Order of Events	✎ Dependent Clause Tree ▤ Concept Vocabulary ▤ Suffixes ▤ Clauses	▤ Anecdotes ▤ Recitations
Reteach and Practice	▤ Analyze the Text ▤ Frame Story	▤ Concept Vocabulary ▤ Suffixes ▤ Clauses	▤ Anecdotes ▤ Recitations
Assessment			▤ ☑ Selection Test
My Resources*	• Map of Japan • _____ • _____ • _____	• Sentence Strips • Tree diagram for dependent clauses • _____ • _____	• _____ • _____ • _____ • _____

* These resources are suggested at point of use in this lesson.

Whole-Class Learning 98B

e *Endurance* d the *James* aird in Images

from Life of Pi

The Value of a Sherpa Life

I Am Offering This Poem
The Writer
Hugging the Jukebox

Performance Task

Introduce Independent Learning

Independent Learning

Performance-Based Assessment

| 19 | 20 | 21 | 22 | 23 | 24 | 25 | 26 | 27 | 28 | 29 | 30 |

A Pacing Plan provides recommended pacing.

Unit Introduction **89**

Resources for Flexibility

myPerspectives+ includes hundreds of additional teacher resources you can use to customize your lessons. Interactive lessons, grammar tutorials, digital novels, and more are student-facing to allow students to work independently.

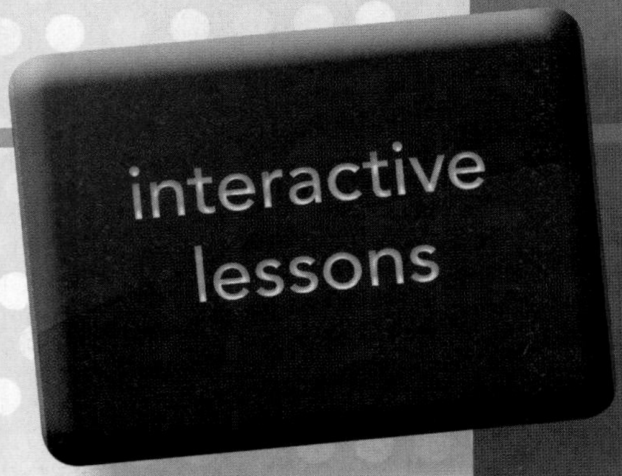

interactive lessons

grammar tutorials

graphic organizers and rubrics

trade book lesson plans

digital novels

*my*Perspectives™

- Digital novels, including classics such as *Great Expectations, Pride and Prejudice, The Adventures of Tom Sawyer, Alice in Wonderland, The Scarlet Letter,* and *Romeo and Juliet*

- Novel lesson plans for over 100 titles, including those aligned to each unit

- Interactive lessons to help students develop critical writing, speaking, and listening skills

- High-interest readings and resources for struggling students

- Engaging grammar and academic vocabulary tutorials

- Writing Whiteboard Activities for an interactive and engaging classroom experience

- Editable grammar worksheets for extra practice with this crucial skill

- Generic graphic organizers and rubrics that can be used with any lesson

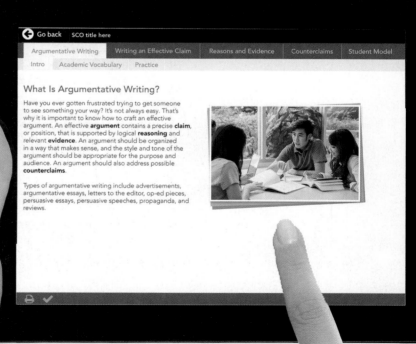

PEARSON
realize™

Pearson Realize™ is your online destination for digital resources, assessments, and data. Flexible classroom management tools give you an amazing amount of freedom and control.

Easily manage your classes and data.

YOU HAVE THE POWER

Customize the program to make it your own.

- Rearrange content
- Upload your own content
- Add links to online media
- Edit resources and assessment

All program-specific resources, flexible agnostic resources, and assessments are available in one location for easy lesson planning and presentation.

Selection resources are available at point of use!

DIGITAL ⟲ PERSPECTIVES

🔊 Audio
▶ Video
📄 Document
✏ Annotation Highlights
💬 EL Highlights
☑ Online Assessment

Digital Perspectives in the Teacher's Edition identifies digital resources available for each lesson.

UNIT 1: Childhood

Integrating Trade Books With *my*Perspectives

These titles provide students with another perspective on the topic of childhood, touching upon many of the ideas found within the unit selections.

Depending on your objectives for the unit, as well as your students' needs, you may choose to integrate the trade book into the unit in several ways, including:

- **Supplement the Unit** Form literature circles and have students read one of the trade books throughout the course of the unit as a supplement to the selections and activities.

- **Substitute for Unit Selections** If you replace unit selections with a trade book, review the standards taught with those selections. Teacher Resources that provide practice with all standards are available.

- **Extend Independent Learning** Extend the unit by replacing independent reading selections with one of these trade books.

- **Pacing** However you choose to integrate trade books, the Pacing Guide below offers suggestions for aligning the trade books with this unit.

Trade Book Lesson Plans

Trade book lesson plans for *The Secret Garden; Bud, Not Buddy;* and *The Young Landlords* are available online in *my*Perspectives+.

Childhood UNIT 1

📅 Pacing Guide: Unit Supplement

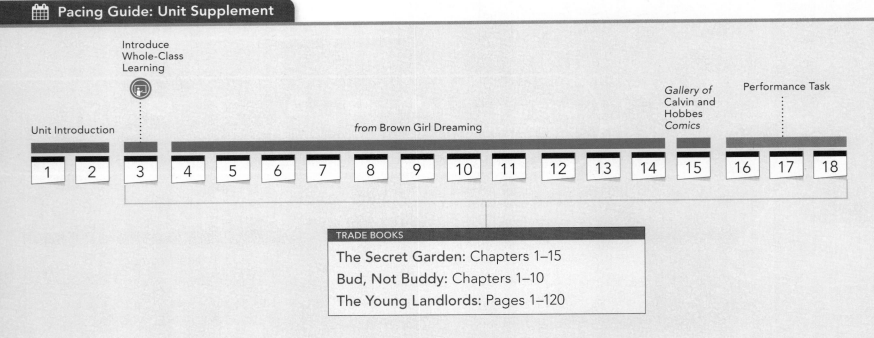

Introduce Whole-Class Learning

Unit Introduction

from Brown Girl Dreaming

Gallery of Calvin and Hobbes Comics

Performance Task

| 1 | 2 | 3 | 4 | 5 | 6 | 7 | 8 | 9 | 10 | 11 | 12 | 13 | 14 | 15 | 16 | 17 | 18 |

TRADE BOOKS

The Secret Garden: Chapters 1–15

Bud, Not Buddy: Chapters 1–10

The Young Landlords: Pages 1–120

Suggested Trade Books

The Secret Garden

Frances Hodgson Burnett

Lexile: 970

A selfish and spoiled girl moves to England and discovers that she has a young cousin who uses a wheelchair, whom she secretly nurses back to health in a mysterious garden.

Connection to Essential Question

Mary Lennox finds the ability to be selfless when she helps her young cousin learn to walk after years spent in a wheelchair. Mary matures through the difficult process of caring for someone other than herself. Her experiences provide insight into the Essential Question: *What are some of the challenges and triumphs of growing up?*

Bud, Not Buddy

Christopher Paul Curtis

Lexile: 950

During the Great Depression, a young orphan runs away from his foster family with a friend, crosses the country, and discovers that his favorite musician is actually his grandfather.

Connection to Essential Question

Bud's problems often stem from what he doesn't know yet. Still, he learns from his mistakes. Though Bud is treated unkindly by nearly everyone he meets, he perseveres, finds family, and feels hopeful about a future in music. Through his struggles, readers see the connection to the Essential Question: *What are some of the challenges and triumphs of growing up?*

The Young Landlords

Walter Dean Myers

Lexile: 820

After a developer tricks them into buying his dilapidated building, a group of kids try to clean up their neighborhood, and learn just what it takes to run a building.

Connection to Essential Question

Since none of their tenants pay rent, the kids learn to run fundraisers. They use this money to improve the squalid conditions of their building and improve the lives of the people who live there. By taking responsibility for their community, they help us understand the Essential Question: *What are some of the challenges and triumphs of growing up?*

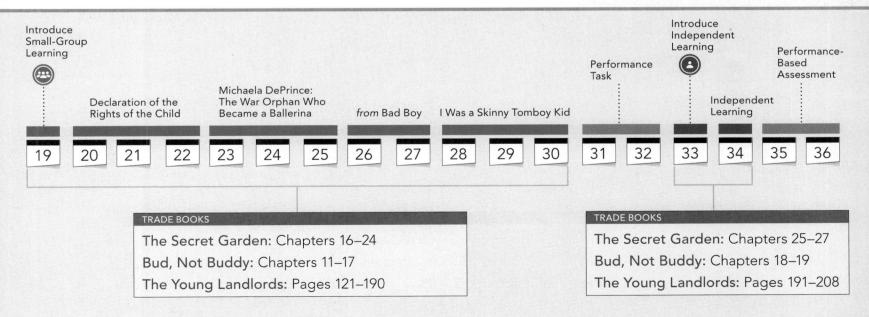

Introduce Small-Group Learning

Declaration of the Rights of the Child

Michaela DePrince: The War Orphan Who Became a Ballerina

from Bad Boy

I Was a Skinny Tomboy Kid

Performance Task

Introduce Independent Learning

Independent Learning

Performance-Based Assessment

19 20 21 22 23 24 25 26 27 28 29 30 31 32 33 34 35 36

TRADE BOOKS

The Secret Garden: Chapters 16–24

Bud, Not Buddy: Chapters 11–17

The Young Landlords: Pages 121–190

TRADE BOOKS

The Secret Garden: Chapters 25–27

Bud, Not Buddy: Chapters 18–19

The Young Landlords: Pages 191–208

UNIT 2: Animal Allies

Integrating Trade Books With *my*Perspectives

These titles provide students with another perspective on the topic of animal allies, touching upon many of the ideas found within the unit selections.

Depending on your objectives for the unit, as well as your students' needs, you may choose to integrate the trade book into the unit in several ways, including:

- **Supplement the Unit** Form literature circles and have students read one of the trade books throughout the course of the unit as a supplement to the selections and activities.
- **Substitute for Unit Selections** If you replace unit selections with a trade book, review the standards taught with those selections. Teacher Resources that provide practice with all standards are available.
- **Extend Independent Learning** Extend the unit by replacing independent reading selections with one of these trade books.
- **Pacing** However you choose to integrate trade books, the Pacing Guide below offers suggestions for aligning the trade books with this unit.

Animal Allies UNIT 2

Trade Book Lesson Plans

Trade book lesson plans for *The Jungle Book, Where the Red Fern Grows,* and *Black Beauty* are available online in *my*Perspectives+.

📅 Pacing Guide: Unit Supplement

Introduce Whole-Class Learning

Performance Task

Unit Introduction   *from* My Life With the Chimpanzees   Hachiko: The True Story of a Loyal Dog

| 1 | 2 | 3 | 4 | 5 | 6 | 7 | 8 | 9 | 10 | 11 | 12 | 13 | 14 | 15 | 16 | 17 | 18 |

TRADE BOOKS

The Jungle Book: Chapters 1–7

Where the Red Fern Grows: Chapters 1–10

Black Beauty: Chapters 1–25

Suggested Trade Books

The Jungle Book

Rudyard Kipling

Lexile: 1020

A young boy is raised by wild animals in India but eventually must prepare to return to human civilization.

Connection to Essential Question

The animals teach laws of the jungle to keep individuals and communities safe. Mowgli's adventures teach him both self-reliance and teamwork. The heart of the book explores the Essential Question: *How can people and animals relate to each other?* In the end, Mowgli realizes the importance of being part of a human community.

Where the Red Fern Grows

Wilson Rawls

Lexile: 700

After years of saving money, a boy earns enough to buy a pair of puppies. He raises them and they explore the woods together.

Connection to Essential Question

Through Billy's experiences with his puppies, students gain insight into the Essential Question: *How can people and animals relate to each other?* Billy and his dogs form close bonds, and they use their complementary talents to win a hunting championship.

Black Beauty

Anna Sewell

Lexile: 1010

The life of a horse reveals both human kindness and human cruelty.

Connection to Essential Question

Sewell uses an animal's perspective to examine human morality. Messages of kindness and sympathy are woven through the book. The detailed, vivid descriptions of Black Beauty's experiences build empathy. This work helped lead to animal-welfare reforms, making it a vivid exploration of the Essential Question: *How can people and animals relate to each other?*

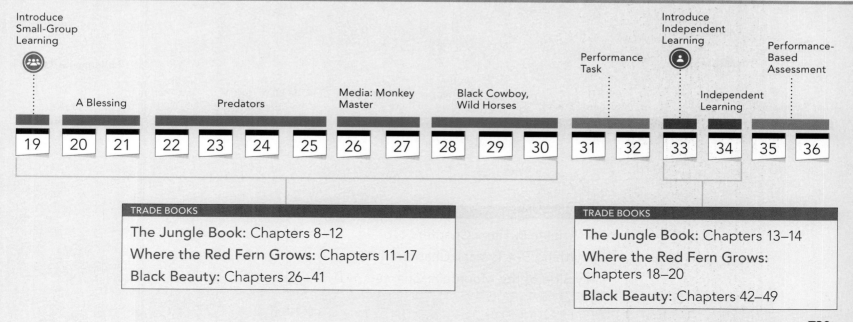

Introduce Small-Group Learning

A Blessing — 20 21

Predators — 22 23 24 25

Media: Monkey Master — 26 27

Black Cowboy, Wild Horses — 28 29 30

Performance Task — 31 32

Introduce Independent Learning

Independent Learning — 33 34

Performance-Based Assessment — 35 36

19

TRADE BOOKS

The Jungle Book: Chapters 8–12

Where the Red Fern Grows: Chapters 11–17

Black Beauty: Chapters 26–41

TRADE BOOKS

The Jungle Book: Chapters 13–14

Where the Red Fern Grows: Chapters 18–20

Black Beauty: Chapters 42–49

UNIT 3: Modern Technology

Integrating Trade Books With *my*Perspectives

These titles provide students with another perspective on the topic of modern technology, touching upon many of the ideas found within the unit selections.

Depending on your objectives for the unit, as well as your students' needs, you may choose to integrate the trade book into the unit in several ways, including:

- **Supplement the Unit** Form literature circles and have students read one of the trade books throughout the course of the unit as a supplement to the selections and activities.
- **Substitute for Unit Selections** If you replace unit selections with a trade book, review the standards taught with those selections. Teacher Resources that provide practice with all standards are available.
- **Extend Independent Learning** Extend the unit by replacing independent reading selections with one of these trade books.
- **Pacing** However you choose to integrate trade books, the Pacing Guide below offers suggestions for aligning the trade books with this unit.

Modern Technology UNIT 3

Trade Book Lesson Plans

Trade book lesson plans for *A Wrinkle in Time, Anything But Typical,* and *My Side of the Mountain* are available online in *my*Perspectives+.

📅 Pacing Guide: Unit Supplement

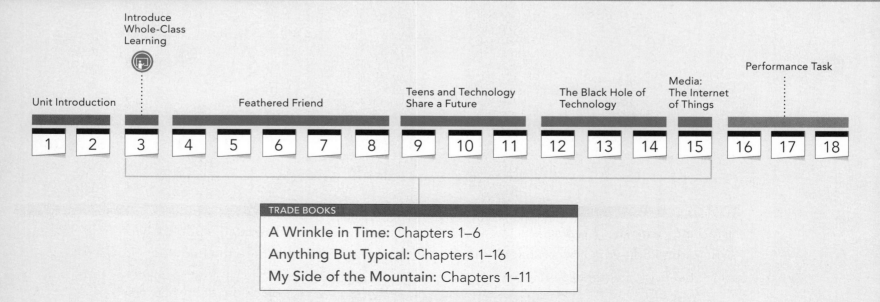

Introduce Whole-Class Learning

Performance Task

| Unit Introduction | | Feathered Friend | | | | | Teens and Technology Share a Future | | | The Black Hole of Technology | | | Media: The Internet of Things | Performance Task | | |
| 1 | 2 | 3 | 4 | 5 | 6 | 7 | 8 | 9 | 10 | 11 | 12 | 13 | 14 | 15 | 16 | 17 | 18 |

TRADE BOOKS

A Wrinkle in Time: Chapters 1–6

Anything But Typical: Chapters 1–16

My Side of the Mountain: Chapters 1–11

Suggested Trade Books

A Wrinkle in Time

Madeleine L'Engle

Lexile: 740

Meg, a thirteen-year-old girl, travels across space and time to try to save her father, a scientist who has mysteriously disappeared.

Connection to Essential Question

L'Engle portrays science as useful for both good and evil. In Meg's time travels, both the utopian society of Uriel and the totalitarian society of Camazotz use remarkable technology. The difference lies in whether they use their technology out of love or out of desire for power. As a result, the work provides a useful, balanced perspective on the Essential Question: *How is modern technology helpful and harmful to society?*

Anything But Typical

Nora Raleigh Baskin

Lexile: 640

Through the Internet, an autistic boy makes his first real friend.

Connection to Essential Question

Modern technology lets Jason make a friend without having to worry about the difficulties with body language and social expectations that bedevil his in-person interactions. Thus, this novel provides an optimistic answer to the Essential Question: *How is modern technology helpful and harmful to society?*

My Side of the Mountain

Jean Craighead George

Lexile: 810

Sam runs away from home and is torn between wanting to fend for himself and wanting to be with the people he loves.

Connection to Essential Question

At first glance, one might not expect a book about living in the woods in the 1950s to give insight into the Essential Question: *How is modern technology helpful and harmful to society?* Sam tries to avoid recent technology—but without a library book, he never would have learned the survival skills he needed to survive in the woods

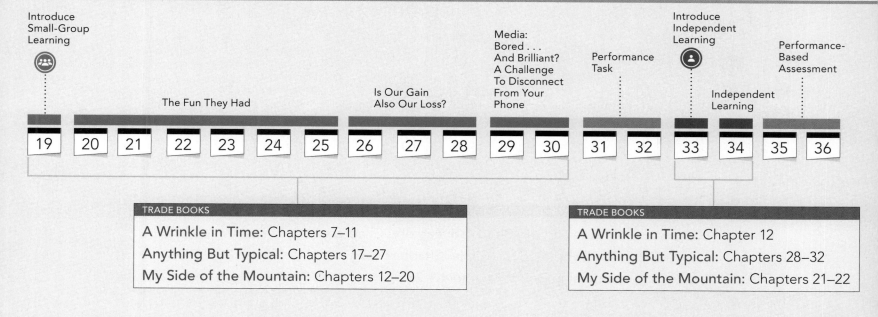

Introduce Small-Group Learning

The Fun They Had

Is Our Gain Also Our Loss?

Media: Bored . . . And Brilliant? A Challenge To Disconnect From Your Phone

Performance Task

Introduce Independent Learning

Independent Learning

Performance-Based Assessment

19 20 21 22 23 24 25 26 27 28 29 30 31 32 33 34 35 36

TRADE BOOKS

A Wrinkle in Time: Chapters 7–11

Anything But Typical: Chapters 17–27

My Side of the Mountain: Chapters 12–20

TRADE BOOKS

A Wrinkle in Time: Chapter 12

Anything But Typical: Chapters 28–32

My Side of the Mountain: Chapters 21–22

UNIT 4: Imagination

Integrating Trade Books With *my*Perspectives

These titles provide students with another perspective on the topic of imagination and where it can lead, touching upon many of the ideas found within the unit selections.

Depending on your objectives for the unit, as well as your students' needs, you may choose to integrate the trade book into the unit in several ways, including:

- **Supplement the Unit** Form literature circles and have students read one of the trade books throughout the course of the unit as a supplement to the selections and activities.

- **Substitute for Unit Selections** If you replace unit selections with a trade book, review the standards taught with those selections. Teacher Resources that provide practice with all standards are available.

- **Extend Independent Learning** Extend the unit by replacing independent reading selections with one of these trade books.

- **Pacing** However you choose to integrate trade books, the Pacing Guide below offers suggestions for aligning the trade books with this unit.

Imagination UNIT 4

Trade Book Lesson Plans

Trade book lesson plans for *Charlie and the Chocolate Factory, The Sword and the Circle,* and *Watership Down* are available online in *my*Perspectives+.

📅 Pacing Guide: Unit Supplement

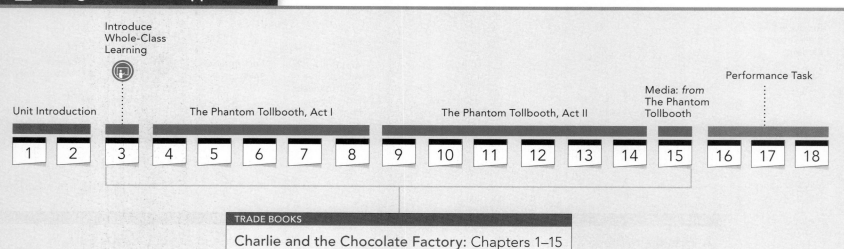

Introduce Whole-Class Learning

Performance Task

Media: *from* The Phantom Tollbooth

Unit Introduction	The Phantom Tollbooth, Act I	The Phantom Tollbooth, Act II	

| 1 | 2 | 3 | 4 | 5 | 6 | 7 | 8 | 9 | 10 | 11 | 12 | 13 | 14 | 15 | 16 | 17 | 18 |

TRADE BOOKS

Charlie and the Chocolate Factory: Chapters 1–15

The Sword and the Circle: Chapters 1–7

Watership Down: Chapters 1–26

Suggested Trade Books

Charlie and the Chocolate Factory

Roald Dahl

Lexile: 810

Charlie leads a life of poverty but finds a golden ticket that allows him to enter Willy Wonka's magical chocolate factory. His innocence and honesty reward him.

Connection to Essential Question

Charlie leads a life of poverty but finds a golden ticket that allows him to enter Willy Wonka's magical chocolate factory. His innocence and honesty reward him. This classic children's story celebrates the imagination of a candy maker. Willy Wonka makes innovative chocolates and warns readers about the dangers of undisciplined children's behaviors. By considering the best and the worst, Dahl's book provides two angles on the answer to the Essential Question: *Where can imagination lead?*

The Sword and the Circle

Rosemary Sutcliff

Lexile: 1210

Arthur becomes a legendary king of England and embarks on adventures with his famous Knights of the Round Table.

Connection to Essential Question

The book strays from the usual Arthurian stories by incorporating new tales. Even seemingly ancient and static stories have room for new interpretations and new additions. Students may see that going beyond the well-known texts helps us see the meaning behind the Essential Question: *Where can imagination lead?*

Watership Down

Richard Adams

Lexile: 880

A clairvoyant rabbit named Fiver convinces a small group of friends to leave their warren in search of a new home where they will be safe.

Connection to Essential Question

The rabbits have their own imaginatively written language, history, and myths. The novel's unique setting illustrates the Essential Question: *Where can imagination lead?* but so do its characters. The folk hero they hold up as an exemplar is distinguished by cleverness and devotion, using his creativity to protect friends and home.

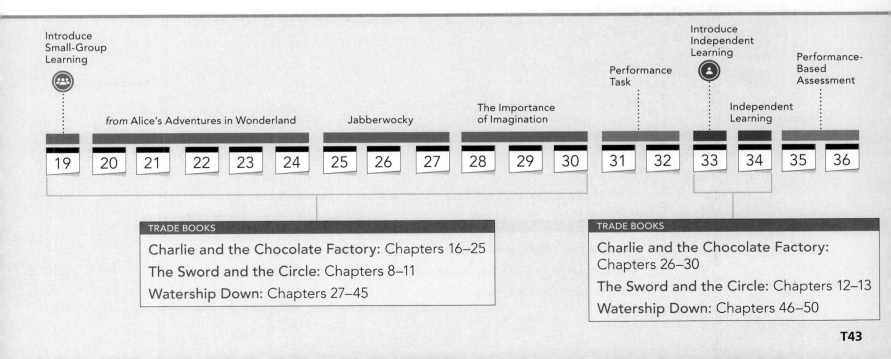

Introduce Small-Group Learning

from Alice's Adventures in Wonderland

Jabberwocky

The Importance of Imagination

Performance Task

Introduce Independent Learning

Independent Learning

Performance-Based Assessment

19 | 20 | 21 | 22 | 23 | 24 | 25 | 26 | 27 | 28 | 29 | 30 | 31 | 32 | 33 | 34 | 35 | 36

TRADE BOOKS

Charlie and the Chocolate Factory: Chapters 16–25

The Sword and the Circle: Chapters 8–11

Watership Down: Chapters 27–45

TRADE BOOKS

Charlie and the Chocolate Factory: Chapters 26–30

The Sword and the Circle: Chapters 12–13

Watership Down: Chapters 46–50

UNIT 5: Exploration

Integrating Trade Books With *my*Perspectives

These titles provide students with another perspective on the topic of exploration, touching upon many of the ideas found within the unit selections.

Depending on your objectives for the unit, as well as your students' needs, you may choose to integrate the trade book into the unit in several ways, including:

- **Supplement the Unit** Form literature circles and have students read one of the trade books throughout the course of the unit as a supplement to the selections and activities.
- **Substitute for Unit Selections** If you replace unit selections with a trade book, review the standards taught with those selections. Teacher Resources that provide practice with all standards are available.
- **Extend Independent Learning** Extend the unit by replacing independent reading selections with one of these trade books.
- **Pacing** However you choose to integrate trade books, the Pacing Guide below offers suggestions for aligning the trade books with this unit.

Exploration UNIT 5

Trade Book Lesson Plans

Trade book lesson plans for *Around the World in 80 Days*, *The House of Dies Drear*, and *Maniac Magee* are available online in *my*Perspectives+.

📅 Pacing Guide: Unit Supplement

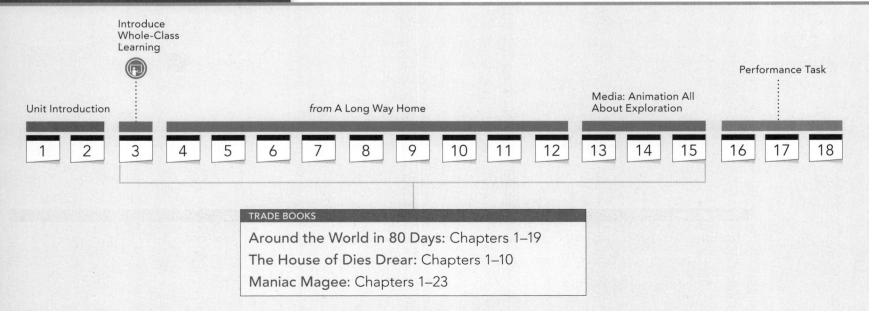

Introduce Whole-Class Learning

Performance Task

Unit Introduction | *from* A Long Way Home | Media: Animation All About Exploration

| 1 | 2 | 3 | 4 | 5 | 6 | 7 | 8 | 9 | 10 | 11 | 12 | 13 | 14 | 15 | 16 | 17 | 18 |

TRADE BOOKS

Around the World in 80 Days: Chapters 1–19

The House of Dies Drear: Chapters 1–10

Maniac Magee: Chapters 1–23

Suggested Trade Books

Around the World in 80 Days

Jules Verne

Lexile: 1070

A wealthy Englishman attempts to circumnavigate Earth in less than eighty days, after his friends bet him a fortune that he can't.

Connection to Essential Question

Phileas Fogg sets out on his adventure because of the money at stake, but Verne makes it clear that Fogg has long been curious about proving that such a feat is possible. This gives readers two answers to the Essential Question: *What drives people to explore?*

The House of Dies Drear

Virginia Hamilton

Lexile: 670

Thomas moves into a house riddled with tunnels that were once part of the Underground Railroad. He suspects it may be haunted.

Connection to Essential Question

Curiosity drives Thomas—he wonders about both history and his neighbors' motives. This text offers a strong, straightforward inquiry into the Essential Question: *What drives people to explore?*

Maniac Magee

Jerry Spinelli

Lexile: 820

A fearless homeless boy explores a new town, and he crosses both physical and racial boundaries.

Connection to Essential Question

Jeffrey's sense of justice drives him to explore, but so does his desire to find a home. This novel provides both emotional and practical answers to the Essential Question: *What drives people to explore?*

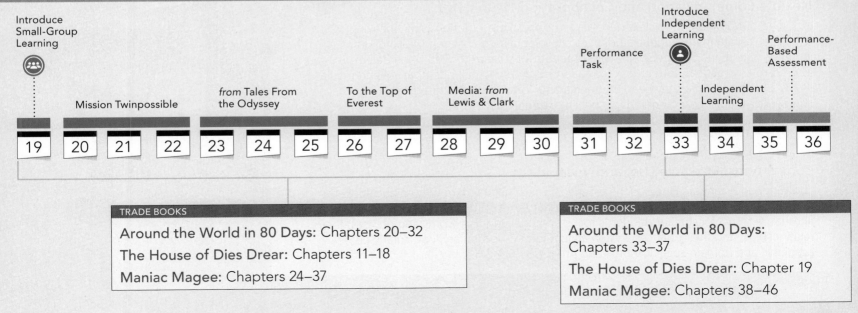

Introduce Small-Group Learning

Mission Twinpossible

from Tales From the Odyssey

To the Top of Everest

Media: *from* Lewis & Clark

Performance Task

Introduce Independent Learning

Independent Learning

Performance-Based Assessment

19 | 20 | 21 | 22 | 23 | 24 | 25 | 26 | 27 | 28 | 29 | 30 | 31 | 32 | 33 | 34 | 35 | 36

TRADE BOOKS

Around the World in 80 Days: Chapters 20–32

The House of Dies Drear: Chapters 11–18

Maniac Magee: Chapters 24–37

TRADE BOOKS

Around the World in 80 Days: Chapters 33–37

The House of Dies Drear: Chapter 19

Maniac Magee: Chapters 38–46

Standards Correlation

Key Features of the Standards

The following summary of key features is from the Introduction to the Common Core State Standards for English Language Arts © 2010, National Governors Association for Best Practices and Council of Chief State School Officers. All rights reserved.

Reading

Text Complexity and the Growth of Comprehension

The Reading standards place equal emphasis on the sophistication of what students read and the skill with which they read. Standard 10 defines a grade-by-grade "staircase" of increasing text complexity that rises from beginning reading to the college and career readiness level. Whatever they are reading, students must also show a steadily growing ability to discern more from and make fuller use of text. This process should include making an increasing number of connections among ideas and between texts, considering a wider range of textual evidence, and becoming more sensitive to inconsistencies, ambiguities, and poor reasoning in texts.

Writing

Text Types, Responding to Reading, and Research

The Standards acknowledge the fact that whereas some writing skills, such as the ability to plan, revise, edit, and publish, are applicable to many types of writing, other skills are more properly defined in terms of specific writing types: arguments, informative/explanatory texts, and narratives. Standard 9 stresses the importance of the writing-reading connection by requiring students to draw upon and write about evidence from literary and informational texts. Because of the centrality of writing to most forms of inquiry, research standards are prominently included in this strand, though skills important to research are infused throughout the document.

Speaking and Listening

Flexible Communication and Collaboration

Including but not limited to skills necessary for formal presentations, the Speaking and Listening standards require students to develop a range of broadly useful oral communication and interpersonal skills. Students must learn to work together, express and listen carefully to ideas, integrate information from oral, visual, quantitative, and media sources, evaluate what they hear, use media and visual displays strategically to help achieve communicative purposes, and adapt speech to context and task.

Language

Conventions, Effective Use, and Vocabulary

The Language standards include the essential "rules" of standard written and spoken English, but they also approach language as a matter of craft and informed choice among alternatives. The vocabulary standards focus on understanding words and phrases, their relationships, and their nuances and on acquiring new vocabulary, particularly general academic and domain-specific words and phrases.

Correlation to *myPerspectives*™ *English Language Arts*

The following correlation shows points at which focused standards instruction is provided in the Student Edition. The Teacher's Edition provides further opportunity to address standards through Personalize for Learning notes and additional resources available only in the Interactive Teacher's Edition.

Standards for Reading

College and Career Readiness Anchor Standards for Reading

Key Ideas and Details

1. Read closely to determine what the text says explicitly and to make logical inferences from it; cite specific textual evidence when writing or speaking to support conclusions drawn from the text.

2. Determine central ideas or themes of a text and analyze their development; summarize the key supporting details and ideas.

3. Analyze how and why individuals, events, and ideas develop and interact over the course of a text.

Craft and Structure

4. Interpret words and phrases as they are used in a text, including determining technical, connotative, and figurative meanings, and analyze how specific word choices shape meaning or tone.

5. Analyze the structure of texts, including how specific sentences, paragraphs, and larger portions of the text (e.g., a section, chapter, scene, or stanza) relate to each other and the whole.

6. Assess how point of view or purpose shapes the content and style of a text.

Integration of Knowledge and Ideas

7. Integrate and evaluate content presented in diverse formats and media, including visually and quantitatively, as well as in words.

8. Delineate and evaluate the argument and specific claims in a text, including the validity of the reasoning as well as the relevance and sufficiency of the evidence.

9. Analyze how two or more texts address similar themes or topics in order to build knowledge or to compare the approaches the authors take.

Range of Reading and Level of Text Complexity

10. Read and comprehend complex literary and informational texts independently and proficiently.

Standards Correlation

Grade 6 Reading Standards for Literature

STANDARD CODE	Standard	Print and Interactive Editions
Key Ideas and Details		
RL.6.1	Cite textual evidence to support analysis of what the text says explicitly as well as inferences drawn from the text.	**SE/TE:** "Gallery of 'Calvin and Hobbes' Comics," 30; "I Was a Skinny Tomboy Kid," 74; "Feathered Friend," 200; *Alice's Adventures in Wonderland*, 368; Students will address this standard in *Analyze the Text* features which appear with every literature selection.
RL.6.2	Determine a theme or central idea of a text and how it is conveyed through particular details; provide a summary of the text distinct from personal opinions or judgments.	**SE/TE:** "I Was a Skinny Tomboy Kid," 74; "Hachiko," 122; "Feathered Friend," 200; "The Fun They Had," 244; *Tales From the Odyssey*, 460
RL.6.3	Describe how a particular story's or drama's plot unfolds in a series of episodes as well as how the characters respond or change as the plot moves toward a resolution.	**SE/TE:** "Hachiko," 122; "Black Cowboy, Wild Horses," 168; *The Phantom Tollbooth*, Act I, 308; *Alice's Adventures in Wonderland*, 368
Craft and Structure		
RL.6.4	Determine the meaning of words and phrases as they are used in a text, including figurative and connotative meanings; analyze the impact of a specific word choice on meaning and tone.	**SE/TE:** *Brown Girl Dreaming*, 22; "A Blessing," 142; "Predators," 149; "Jabberwocky," 376, 378; *Tales From the Odyssey*, 459
RL.6.5	Analyze how a particular sentence, chapter, scene, or stanza fits into the overall structure of a text and contributes to the development of the theme, setting, or plot.	**SE/TE:** *Brown Girl Dreaming*, 20; "I Was a Skinny Tomboy Kid," 74; "Hachiko," 122; "Predators," 148; "Feathered Friend," 200; "The Fun They Had," 244; *The Phantom Tollbooth*, Act I, 308; *The Phantom Tollbooth*, Act II, 340; *Tales From the Odyssey*, 460
RL.6.6	Explain how an author develops the point of view of the narrator or speaker in a text.	**SE/TE:** *Brown Girl Dreaming*, 20; *The Phantom Tollbooth*, Act I, 308
Integration of Knowledge and Ideas		
RL.6.7	Compare and contrast the experience of reading a story, drama, or poem to listening to or viewing an audio, video, or live version of the text, including contrasting what they "see" and "hear" when reading the text to what they perceive when they listen or watch.	**SE/TE:** *The Phantom Tollbooth*, / *The Phantom Tollbooth* (media), 351; *Alice's Adventures in Wonderland*, 371; "Jabberwocky," 374, 379
RL.6.8	(Not applicable to literature)	
RL.6.9	Compare and contrast texts in different forms or genres (e.g., stories and poems; historical novels and fantasy stories) in terms of their approaches to similar themes and topics.	**SE/TE:** *Bad Boy* / "I Was a Skinny Tomboy Kid," 76; *Tales From the Odyssey* / "To the Top of Everest," 474
Range of Reading and Level of Text Complexity		
RL.6.10	By the end of the year, read and comprehend literature, including stories, dramas, and poems, in the grades 6–8 text complexity band proficiently, with scaffolding as needed at the high end of the range.	**SE/TE:** *Brown Girl Dreaming*, 12; "Gallery of 'Calvin and Hobbes' Comics," 26; "I Was a Skinny Tomboy Kid," 68; First-Read Guide, Unit 1: 82, Unit 2: 176, Unit 3: 264, Unit 4: 392, Unit 5: 488; Close-Read Guide, Unit 1: 83, Unit 2: 177, Unit 3: 265, Unit 4: 393, Unit 5: 489; "Hachiko," 118; "A Blessing," 138; "Predators," 144; "Black Cowboy, Wild Horses," 162; "Feathered Friend," 194; "The Fun They Had," 238; *The Phantom Tollbooth*, Act I, 282; *The Phantom Tollbooth*, Act II, 312; *The Phantom Tollbooth* (media)," 346; *Alice's Adventures in Wonderland*, 362; "Jabberwocky," 372; *Tales From the Odyssey*, 452; *Lewis & Clark*, 476

Grade 6 Reading Standards for Informational Text

STANDARD CODE	Standard	Print and Interactive Editions
Key Ideas and Details		
RI.6.1	Cite textual evidence to support analysis of what the text says explicitly as well as inferences drawn from the text.	**SE/TE:** *Bad Boy,* 66; *My Life With the Chimpanzees,* 112; "Teens and Technology Share a Future," 210; "Is Our Gain Also Our Loss?", 252; "The Importance of Imagination," 384; *A Long Way Home,* 424; "All About Exploration," 432; Students will address this standard in *Analyze the Text* features which appear with every informational text selection.
RI.6.2	Determine a central idea of a text and how it is conveyed through particular details; provide a summary of the text distinct from personal opinions or judgments.	**SE/TE:** *Bad Boy,* 66; "The Importance of Imagination," 384; *A Long Way Home,* 424; "To the Top of Everest," 472
RI.6.3	Analyze in detail how a key individual, event, or idea is introduced, illustrated, and elaborated in a text (e.g., through examples or anecdotes).	**SE/TE:** "Declaration of the Rights of the Child," 46; "Michaela DePrince: The War Orphan Who Became a Ballerina," 57; "Is Our Gain Also Our Loss?", 252; "The Importance of Imagination," 384; *A Long Way Home,* 426; "To the Top of Everest," 472
Craft and Structure		
RI.6.4	Determine the meaning of words and phrases as they are used in a text, including figurative, connotative, and technical meanings.	**SE/TE:** "Teens and Technology Share a Future," 212; "The Black Hole of Technology," 218, 220
RI.6.5	Analyze how a particular sentence, paragraph, chapter, or section fits into the overall structure of a text and contributes to the development of the ideas.	**SE/TE:** *Brown Girl Dreaming,* 20; "Declaration of the Rights of the Child," 46; "Michaela DePrince: The War Orphan Who Became a Ballerina," 57; *Bad Boy,* 66; "Teens and Technology Share a Future," 210; "Is Our Gain Also Our Loss?", 252; *A Long Way Home,* 424
RI.6.6	Determine an author's point of view or purpose in a text and explain how it is conveyed in the text.	**SE/TE:** *Brown Girl Dreaming,* 20; *My Life With the Chimpanzees,* 112; "Teens and Technology Share a Future," 210; "The Black Hole of Technology," 218
Integration of Knowledge and Ideas		
RI.6.7	Integrate information presented in different media or formats (e.g., visually, quantitatively) as well as in words to develop a coherent understanding of a topic or issue.	**SE/TE:** "Monkey Master," 160; *Lewis & Clark,* 483
RI.6.8	Trace and evaluate the argument and specific claims in a text, distinguishing claims that are supported by reasons and evidence from claims that are not.	**SE/TE:** "Teens and Technology Share a Future," 210; "The Black Hole of Technology," 218; "Teens and Technology Share a Future" / "The Black Hole of Technology," 222–223
RI.6.9	Compare and contrast one author's presentation of events with that of another (e.g., a memoir written by and a biography on the same person).	**SE/TE:** *Bad Boy* / "I Was a Skinny Tomboy Kid," 76; "Teens and Technology Share a Future" / "The Black Hole of Technology," 222–223
Range of Reading and Level of Text Complexity		
RI.6.10	By the end of the year, read and comprehend literary nonfiction in the grades 6–8 text complexity band proficiently, with scaffolding as needed at the high end of the range.	**SE/TE:** *Brown Girl Dreaming,* 12; "Declaration of the Rights of the Child," 42; "Michaela DePrince: The War Orphan Who Became a Ballerina," 50; *Bad Boy,* 60; First-Read Guide, Unit 1: 82, Unit 2: 176, Unit 3: 264, Unit 4: 392, Unit 5: 488; Close-Read Guide, Unit 1: 83, Unit 2: 177, Unit 3: 265, Unit 4: 393, Unit 5: 489; *My Life With the Chimpanzees,* 100; "Monkey Master," 152; "Teens and Technology Share a Future," 206; "The Black Hole of Technology," 214; "The Internet of Things," 224; "Is Our Gain Also Our Loss?", 248; "Bored . . . and Brilliant?", 256; "The Importance of Imagination," 380; *A Long Way Home,* 410; "All About Exploration," 430; "Mission Twinpossible," 444; "To the Top of Everest," 462

Standards Correlation

Standards for Writing

College and Career Readiness Anchor Standards for Writing

Text Types and Purposes

1. Write arguments to support claims in an analysis of substantive topics or texts, using valid reasoning and relevant and sufficient evidence.

2. Write informative/explanatory texts to examine and convey complex ideas and information clearly and accurately through the effective selection, organization, and analysis of content.

3. Write narratives to develop real or imagined experiences or events using effective technique, well-chosen details, and well-structured event sequences.

Production and Distribution of Writing

4. Produce clear and coherent writing in which the development, organization, and style are appropriate to task, purpose, and audience.

5. Develop and strengthen writing as needed by planning, revising, editing, rewriting, or trying a new approach.

6. Use technology, including the Internet, to produce and publish writing and to interact and collaborate with others.

Research to Build and Present Knowledge

7. Conduct short as well as more sustained research projects based on focused questions, demonstrating understanding of the subject under investigation.

8. Gather relevant information from multiple print and digital sources, assess the credibility and accuracy of each source, and integrate the information while avoiding plagiarism.

9. Draw evidence from literary or informational texts to support analysis, reflection, and research.

Range of Writing

10. Write routinely over extended time frames (time for research, reflection, and revision) and shorter time frames (a single sitting or a day or two) for a range of tasks, purposes, and audiences.

Grade 6 Writing Standards

STANDARD CODE	Standard	Print and Interactive Editions
Text Types and Purposes		
W.6.1	Write arguments to support claims with clear reasons and relevant evidence.	**SE/TE:** "Feathered Friend," 204; "Teens and Technology Share a Future" / "The Black Hole of Technology," 222–223; *A Long Way Home,* 428; Whole-Class Performance Task, Unit 3: 228–232, Unit 5: 434–438; Small-Group Performance Task, Unit 3: 260–261, Unit 5: 484; Performance-Based Assessment, Unit 3: 267–268, Unit 5: 491–493
W.6.1.a	Introduce claim(s) and organize the reasons and evidence clearly.	**SE/TE:** "Feathered Friend," 204; "Teens and Technology Share a Future" / "The Black Hole of Technology," 222–223; *A Long Way Home,* 428; Whole-Class Performance Task, Unit 3: 229, Unit 5: 435, 438; Small-Group Performance Task, Unit 3: 260–261; Performance-Based Assessment, Unit 3: 267
W.6.1.b	Support claim(s) with clear reasons and relevant evidence, using credible sources and demonstrating an understanding of the topic or text.	**SE/TE:** "Feathered Friend," 204; "Teens and Technology Share a Future" / "The Black Hole of Technology," 222–223; *A Long Way Home,* 428; Whole-Class Performance Task, Unit 3: 229, 232, Unit 5: 435, 438; Small-Group Performance Task, Unit 3: 260–261, Unit 5: 484; Performance-Based Assessment, Unit 3: 269, Unit 5: 491
W.6.1.c	Use words, phrases, and clauses to clarify the relationships among claim(s) and reasons.	**SE/TE:** "Feathered Friend," 204; "Teens and Technology Share a Future" / "The Black Hole of Technology," 222–223; *A Long Way Home,* 428; Whole-Class Performance Task, Unit 3: 231–232, Unit 5: 438; Performance-Based Assessment, Unit 3: 269
W.6.1.d	Establish and maintain a formal style.	**SE/TE:** "Feathered Friend," 204; "Teens and Technology Share a Future" / "The Black Hole of Technology," 222–223; *A Long Way Home,* 428; Whole-Class Performance Task, Unit 3: 232, Unit 5: 437; Performance-Based Assessment, Unit 3: 269
W.6.1.e	Provide a concluding statement or section that follows from the argument presented.	**SE/TE:** "Feathered Friend," 204; "Teens and Technology Share a Future" / "The Black Hole of Technology," 222–223; *A Long Way Home,* 428; Whole-Class Performance Task, Unit 3: 230, Unit 5: 436; Performance-Based Assessment, Unit 3: 269
W.6.2	Write informative/explanatory texts to examine a topic and convey ideas, concepts, and information through the selection, organization, and analysis of relevant content.	**SE/TE:** "Declaration of the Rights of the Child," 49; *Bad Boy* / "I Was a Skinny Tomboy Kid," 77; *My Life With the Chimpanzees,* 116; "A Blessing" / "Predators," 151; "The Internet of Things," 227; "Bored . . . and Brilliant?", 259; *The Phantom Tollbooth,* / *The Phantom Tollbooth* (media)," 351; *Alice's Adventures in Wonderland,* 371; "The Importance of Imagination," 387; "All About Exploration," 433; "Mission Twinpossible," 451; *Tales From the Odyssey* / "To the Top of Everest," 474–475; Whole-Class Performance Task, Unit 2: 128–130, 132; Performance-Based Assessment, Unit 2: 179–181
W.6.2.a	Introduce a topic; organize ideas, concepts, and information, using strategies such as definition, classification, comparison/contrast, and cause/effect; include formatting (e.g., headings), graphics (e.g., charts, tables), and multimedia when useful to aiding comprehension.	**SE/TE:** "Declaration of the Rights of the Child," 49; *Bad Boy* / "I Was a Skinny Tomboy Kid," 77; *My Life With the Chimpanzees,* 116; "A Blessing" / "Predators," 151; *The Phantom Tollbooth* / *The Phantom Tollbooth* (media), 351; *Alice's Adventures in Wonderland,* 371; "The Importance of Imagination," 387; "Mission Twinpossible," 451; *Tales From the Odyssey* / "To the Top of Everest," 475; Whole-Class Performance Task, Unit 2: 130; Performance-Based Assessment, Unit 2: 179–181
W.6.2.b	Develop the topic with relevant facts, definitions, concrete details, quotations, or other information and examples.	**SE/TE:** "Declaration of the Rights of the Child," 49; *Bad Boy* / "I Was a Skinny Tomboy Kid," 77; *My Life With the Chimpanzees,* 116; "A Blessing" / "Predators," 151; "The Importance of Imagination," 387; "All About Exploration," 433; "Mission Twinpossible," 451; *Tales From the Odyssey* / "To the Top of Everest," 474; Whole-Class Performance Task, Unit 2: 129; Performance-Based Assessment, Unit 2: 179–181

Standards Correlation

Grade 6 Writing Standards (continued)

STANDARD CODE	Standard	Print and Interactive Editions
Text Types and Purposes (continued)		
W.6.2.c	Use appropriate transitions to clarify the relationships among ideas and concepts.	**SE/TE:** "Declaration of the Rights of the Child," 49; *Bad Boy* / "I Was a Skinny Tomboy Kid," 77; *My Life With the Chimpanzees,* 116; "A Blessing" / "Predators," 151; "The Importance of Imagination," 387; "Mission Twinpossible," 451; *Tales From the Odyssey* / "To the Top of Everest," 475; Whole-Class Performance Task, Unit 2: 132; Performance-Based Assessment, Unit 2: 179–181
W.6.2.d	Use precise language and domain-specific vocabulary to inform about or explain the topic.	**SE/TE:** "Declaration of the Rights of the Child," 49; *Bad Boy* / "I Was a Skinny Tomboy Kid," 77; *My Life With the Chimpanzees,* 116; "A Blessing" / "Predators," 151; "The Importance of Imagination," 387; Whole-Class Performance Task, Unit 2: 129; Performance-Based Assessment, Unit 2: 179–181
W.6.2.e	Establish and maintain a formal style.	**SE/TE:** "Declaration of the Rights of the Child," 49; *Bad Boy* / "I Was a Skinny Tomboy Kid," 77; *My Life With the Chimpanzees,* 116; "A Blessing" / "Predators," 151; "The Importance of Imagination," 387; Whole-Class Performance Task, Unit 2: 132; Performance-Based Assessment, Unit 2: 179–181
W.6.2.f	Provide a concluding statement or section that follows from the information or explanation presented.	**SE/TE:** "Declaration of the Rights of the Child," 49; *Bad Boy* / "I Was a Skinny Tomboy Kid," 77; *My Life With the Chimpanzees,* 116; "A Blessing" / "Predators," 151; "The Importance of Imagination," 387; Whole-Class Performance Task, Unit 2: 130; Performance-Based Assessment, Unit 2: 179–181
W.6.3	Write narratives to develop real or imagined experiences or events using effective technique, relevant descriptive details, and well-structured event sequences.	**SE/TE:** *Brown Girl Dreaming,* 24; "Hachiko," 126; "The Fun They Had," 247; *The Phantom Tollbooth,* Act II, 344; Whole-Class Performance Task, Unit 1: 32–36, Unit 4: 352–354, 356; Small-Group Performance Task, Unit 4: 388; Performance-Based Assessment, Unit 1: 85–87, Unit 4: 395–397
W.6.3.a	Engage and orient the reader by establishing a context and introducing a narrator and/or characters; organize an event sequence that unfolds naturally and logically.	**SE/TE:** "Hachiko," 126; "The Fun They Had," 247; *The Phantom Tollbooth,* Act II, 344; Whole-Class Performance Task, Unit 1: 34, Unit 4: 354, 356; Small-Group Performance Task, Unit 4: 388; Performance-Based Assessment, Unit 1: 85–87
W.6.3.b	Use narrative techniques, such as dialogue, pacing, and description, to develop experiences, events, and/or characters.	**SE/TE:** *Brown Girl Dreaming,* 24; "Hachiko," 126; "The Fun They Had," 247; *The Phantom Tollbooth,* Act II, 344; Whole-Class Performance Task, Unit 1: 33, 36, Unit 4: 353, 356; Small-Group Performance Task, Unit 4: 388; Performance-Based Assessment, Unit 1: 85–87
W.6.3.c	Use a variety of transition words, phrases, and clauses to convey sequence and signal shifts from one time frame or setting to another.	**SE/TE:** "Hachiko," 126; Whole-Class Performance Task, Unit 1: 34, Unit 4: 356; Performance-Based Assessment, Unit 1: 85–87
W.6.3.d	Use precise words and phrases, relevant descriptive details, and sensory language to convey experiences and events.	**SE/TE:** *Brown Girl Dreaming,* 24; "Hachiko," 126; "The Fun They Had," 247; Whole-Class Performance Task, Unit 1: 33, 35–36, Unit 4: 353; Small-Group Performance Task, Unit 4: 388; Performance-Based Assessment, Unit 1: 85–87, Unit 4: 395–397
W.6.3.e	Provide a conclusion that follows from the narrated experiences or events.	**SE/TE:** "Hachiko," 126; Whole-Class Performance Task, Unit 1: 34, 36, Unit 4: 354; Performance-Based Assessment, Unit 1: 85–87

Grade 6 Writing Standards (continued)

STANDARD CODE	Standard	Print and Interactive Editions
Production and Distribution of Writing		
W.6.4	Produce clear and coherent writing in which the development, organization, and style are appropriate to task, purpose, and audience.	**SE/TE:** Whole-Class Performance Task, Unit 1, Unit 2, Unit 3, Unit 4, Unit 5; Small-Group Performance Task, Unit 5: 484
W.6.5	With some guidance and support from peers and adults, develop and strengthen writing as needed by planning, revising, editing, rewriting, or trying a new approach.	**SE/TE:** "A Blessing" / "Predators," 151; "The Importance of Imagination," 387; Whole-Class Performance Task, Unit 1, Unit 2, Unit 3, Unit 4, Unit 5
W.6.6	Use technology, including the Internet, to produce and publish writing as well as to interact and collaborate with others; demonstrate sufficient command of keyboarding skills to type a minimum of three pages in a single sitting.	**SE/TE:** "Feathered Friend," 205; "Bored . . . and Brilliant?", 259; "Black Cowboy, Wild Horses," 171; "Jabberwocky," 379; Small-Group Performance Task, Unit 1: 79; Whole-Class Performance Task, Unit 1: 37, Unit 2: 133, Unit 3: 233, Unit 5: 439
Research to Build and Present Knowledge		
W.6.7	Conduct short research projects to answer a question, drawing on several sources and refocusing the inquiry when appropriate.	**SE/TE:** "Gallery of 'Calvin and Hobbes' Comics," 30; "Monkey Master," 160; "Black Cowboy, Wild Horses," 171; "Feathered Friend," 204; *Alice's Adventures in Wonderland,* 371; "All About Exploration," 433; "Mission Twinpossible," 451; *Lewis & Clark,* 483; Small-Group Performance Task, Unit 3: 260–261
W.6.8	Gather relevant information from multiple print and digital sources; assess the credibility of each source; and quote or paraphrase the data and conclusions of others while avoiding plagiarism and providing basic bibliographic information for sources.	**SE/TE:** "Monkey Master," 160; "Black Cowboy, Wild Horses," 171; "Bored . . . and Brilliant?", 259; *Alice's Adventures in Wonderland,* 371; "Mission Twinpossible," 451; *Lewis & Clark,* 483
W.6.9	Draw evidence from literary or informational texts to support analysis, reflection, and research.	**SE/TE:** *Brown Girl Dreaming,* 24; *Bad Boy* / "I Was a Skinny Tomboy Kid," 77; "Hachiko," 126; "A Blessing" / "Predators," 151; "Teens and Technology Share a Future" / "The Black Hole of Technology," 222–223; *Tales From the Odyssey* / "To the Top of Everest," 474; Whole-Class Performance Task, Unit 3: 230, Unit 5: 434; Performance-Based Assessment, Unit 3: 268
W.6.9.a	Apply *grade 6 Reading standards* to literature (e.g., "Compare and contrast texts in different forms or genres [e.g., stories and poems; historical novels and fantasy stories] in terms of their approaches to similar themes and topics").	**SE/TE:** *Brown Girl Dreaming,* 24; *Bad Boy* / "I Was a Skinny Tomboy Kid," 77; "Hachiko," 126; "A Blessing" / "Predators," 151; *Tales From the Odyssey* / "To the Top of Everest," 474; Whole-Class Performance Task, Unit 3: 230; Performance-Based Assessment, Unit 3: 268
W.6.9.b	Apply *grade 6 Reading standards* to literary nonfiction (e.g., "Trace and evaluate the argument and specific claims in a text, distinguishing claims that are supported by reasons and evidence from claims that are not").	**SE/TE:** *Bad Boy* / "I Was a Skinny Tomboy Kid," 77; "Teens and Technology Share a Future" / "The Black Hole of Technology," 222–223; Whole-Class Performance Task, Unit 3: 230, Unit 5: 434; Performance-Based Assessment, Unit 3: 268
Range of Writing		
W.6.10	Write routinely over extended time frames (time for research, reflection, and revision) and shorter time frames (a single sitting or a day or two) for a range of discipline-specific tasks, purposes, and audiences.	**SE/TE:** Whole-Class Performance Task, Unit 1: 32, Unit 2: 128, Unit 3: 228, Unit 4: 352, Unit 5: 434; Performance-Based Assessment, Unit 2: 180, Unit 3: 268, Unit 4: 396, Unit 5: 492

Standards Correlation

Standards for Speaking and Listening

College and Career Readiness Anchor Standards for Speaking and Listening

Comprehension and Collaboration

1. Prepare for and participate effectively in a range of conversations and collaborations with diverse partners, building on others' ideas and expressing their own clearly and persuasively.

2. Integrate and evaluate information presented in diverse media and formats, including visually, quantitatively, and orally.

3. Evaluate a speaker's point of view, reasoning, and use of evidence and rhetoric.

Presentation of Knowledge and Ideas

4. Present information, findings, and supporting evidence such that listeners can follow the line of reasoning and the organization, development, and style are appropriate to task, purpose, and audience.

5. Make strategic use of digital media and visual displays of data to express information and enhance understanding of presentations.

6. Adapt speech to a variety of contexts and communicative tasks, demonstrating command of formal English when indicated or appropriate.

Grade 6 Speaking and Listening Standards

STANDARD CODE	Standard	Print and Interactive Editions
Comprehension and Collaboration		
SL.6.1	Engage effectively in a range of collaborative discussions (one-on-one, in groups, and teacher-led) with diverse partners on *grade 6 topics, texts, and issues,* building on others' ideas and expressing their own clearly.	**SE/TE:** *Brown Girl Dreaming,* 25; "Gallery of 'Calvin and Hobbes' Comics," 30; *My Life With the Chimpanzees,* 117; "Hachiko," 126; "Monkey Master," 160; "Black Cowboy, Wild Horses," 171; "Is Our Gain Also Our Loss?", 255; "Jabberwocky," 379; *A Long Way Home,* 429; Share Your Independent Learning, Unit 2: 178, Unit 5: 490; Small-Group Performance Task, Unit 4: 389
SL.6.1.a	Come to discussions prepared, having read or studied required material; explicitly draw on that preparation by referring to evidence on the topic, text, or issue to probe and reflect on ideas under discussion.	**SE/TE:** *Brown Girl Dreaming,* 25; "Gallery of 'Calvin and Hobbes' Comics," 30; *My Life With the Chimpanzees,* 117; "Hachiko," 126 "Is Our Gain Also Our Loss?", 255; "Jabberwocky," 379; *A Long Way Home,* 429
SL.6.1.b	Follow rules for collegial discussions, set specific goals and deadlines, and define individual roles as needed.	**SE/TE:** *Brown Girl Dreaming,* 25; *My Life With the Chimpanzees,* 117; "Hachiko," 126; "Black Cowboy, Wild Horses," 171; "Is Our Gain Also Our Loss?", 255; "Jabberwocky," 379; Small-Group Performance Task, Unit 4: 389; Students will address this standard in *Working as a Team* features which appear in the Small Group Learning Overview lessons.
SL.6.1.c	Pose and respond to specific questions with elaboration and detail by making comments that contribute to the topic, text, or issue under discussion.	**SE/TE:** *Brown Girl Dreaming,* 25; "Gallery of 'Calvin and Hobbes' Comics," 30; *My Life With the Chimpanzees,* 117; "Monkey Master," 160; Students will address this standard in *Launch Activity* features which appear in the Unit Introduction and in *Working as a Team* features which appear in the Small Group Learning Overview lessons.
SL.6.1.d	Review the key ideas expressed and demonstrate understanding of multiple perspectives through reflection and paraphrasing.	**SE/TE:** *Brown Girl Dreaming,* 25; "Gallery of 'Calvin and Hobbes' Comics," 30; *My Life With the Chimpanzees,* 117; *A Long Way Home,* 429
SL.6.2	Interpret information presented in diverse media and formats (e.g., visually, quantitatively, orally) and explain how it contributes to a topic, text, or issue under study.	**SE/TE:** "Calvin and Hobbes," 30; "The Internet of Things," 227; *The Phantom Tollbooth* (media), 349; *The Phantom Tollbooth / The Phantom Tollbooth* (media), 351; *A Long Way Home,* 429; *Lewis & Clark,* 483; Students will address this standard in *Launch Activity* features which appear in the Unit Introduction, in *Working as a Team* features which appear in the Small Group Learning Overview lessons, and *Group Discussion Tips* which appear throughout the program.
SL.6.3	Delineate a speaker's argument and specific claims, distinguishing claims that are supported by reasons and evidence from claims that are not.	**SE/TE:** Small-Group Performance Task, Unit 3: 260–261, Unit 5: 485

Standards Correlation

Grade 6 Speaking and Listening Standards (continued)

STANDARD CODE	Standard	Print and Interactive Editions
Presentation of Knowledge and Ideas		
SL.6.4	Present claims and findings, sequencing ideas logically and using pertinent descriptions, facts, and details to accentuate main ideas or themes; use appropriate eye contact, adequate volume, and clear pronunciation.	**SE/TE:** "Michaela DePrince: The War Orphan Who Became a Ballerina," 59; "Hachiko," 126; "Feathered Friend," 204; "The Internet of Things," 227; "Jabberwocky," 379; Small-Group Performance Task, Unit 1: 78, Unit 2: 172, Unit 3: 260–261, Unit 4: 389, Unit 5: 485; Performance-Based Assessment, Unit 2: 182, Unit 3: 270, Unit 4: 398, Unit 5: 494
SL.6.5	Include multimedia components (e.g., graphics, images, music, sound) and visual displays in presentations to clarify information.	**SE/TE:** "Black Cowboy, Wild Horses," 171; "Feathered Friend," 204; "Bored . . . and Brilliant?", 259; "Jabberwocky," 379; *A Long Way Home,* 429; "All About Exploration," 433; *Lewis & Clark,* 483; Small-Group Performance Task, Unit 1: 78, Unit 2: 172, Unit 3: 261, Unit 4: 389, Unit 5: 485; Performance-Based Assessment, Unit 3: 270
SL.6.6	Adapt speech to a variety of contexts and tasks, demonstrating command of formal English when indicated or appropriate.	**SE/TE:** *The Phantom Tollbooth,* Act II, 345; Small-Group Performance Task, Unit 1: 78, Unit 2: 173; Performance-Based Assessment, Unit 1: 88, Unit 4: 398, Unit 5: 494

Standards for Language

Conventions of Standard English

1. Demonstrate command of the conventions of standard English grammar and usage when writing or speaking.

2. Demonstrate command of the conventions of standard English capitalization, punctuation, and spelling when writing.

Knowledge of Language

3. Apply knowledge of language to understand how language functions in different contexts, to make effective choices for meaning or style, and to comprehend more fully when reading or listening.

Vocabulary Acquisition and Use

4. Determine or clarify the meaning of unknown and multiple-meaning words and phrases by using context clues, analyzing meaningful word parts, and consulting general and specialized reference materials, as appropriate.

5. Demonstrate understanding of figurative language, word relationships, and nuances in word meanings.

6. Acquire and use accurately a range of general academic and domain-specific words and phrases sufficient for reading, writing, speaking, and listening at the college and career readiness level; demonstrate independence in gathering vocabulary knowledge when considering a word or phrase important to comprehension or expression.

Standards Correlation

Grade 6 Language Standards

STANDARD CODE	Standard	Print and Interactive Editions
Conventions of Standard English		
L.6.1	Demonstrate command of the conventions of standard English grammar and usage when writing or speaking.	**SE/TE:** "Declaration of the Rights of the Child," 48; "Michaela DePrince: The War Orphan Who Became a Ballerina," 58; *Bad Boy*, 67; "A Blessing," 143; "Black Cowboy, Wild Horses," 170; "Feathered Friend," 202; "Teens and Technology Share a Future," 212; "The Black Hole of Technology," 220; "The Fun They Had," 246; "Is Our Gain Also Our Loss?", 254; *The Phantom Tollbooth*, Act I, 310; *The Phantom Tollbooth*, Act II, 342; *Alice's Adventures in Wonderland*, 370; "Jabberwocky," 378; "The Importance of Imagination," 386; "Mission Twinpossible," 450; *Tales From the Odyssey*, 461; "To the Top of Everest," 473; Whole-Class Performance Task, Unit 2: 131, Unit 4: 355, Unit 5: 439
L.6.1.a	Ensure that pronouns are in the proper case (subjective, objective, possessive).	**SE/TE:** "Declaration of the Rights of the Child," 48; Whole-Class Performance Task, Unit 2: 131
L.6.1.b	Use intensive pronouns (e.g., *myself, ourselves*).	**SE/TE:** "Michaela DePrince: The War Orphan Who Became a Ballerina," 58; Grammar Handbook, R57
L.6.1.c	Recognize and correct inappropriate shifts in pronoun number and person.	**SE/TE:** "Michaela DePrince: The War Orphan Who Became a Ballerina," 58; "The Importance of Imagination," 386; Whole-Class Performance Task, Unit 2: 131
L.6.1.d	Recognize and correct vague pronouns (i.e., ones with unclear or ambiguous antecedents).	**SE/TE:** "The Importance of Imagination," 386
L.6.1.e	Recognize variations from standard English in their own and others' writing and speaking, and identify and use strategies to improve expression in conventional language.	**SE/TE:** "Jabberwocky," 378; Whole-Class Performance Task, Unit 2: 131, Unit 5: 439
L.6.2	Demonstrate command of the conventions of standard English capitalization, punctuation, and spelling when writing.	**SE/TE:** *Brown Girl Dreaming*, 22; *Bad Boy* / "I Was a Skinny Tomboy Kid," 77; *My Life With the Chimpanzees*, 114; "Hachiko," 124; "Teens and Technology Share a Future," 212; "The Black Hole of Technology," 220; *Alice's Adventures in Wonderland*, 370
L.6.2.a	Use punctuation (commas, parentheses, dashes) to set off nonrestrictive/parenthetical elements.	**SE/TE:** *My Life With the Chimpanzees*, 114; "Teens and Technology Share a Future," 212; "The Black Hole of Technology," 220
L.6.2.b	Spell correctly.	**SE/TE:** *Bad Boy* / "I Was a Skinny Tomboy Kid," 77; "Hachiko," 124
Knowledge of Language		
L.6.3	Use knowledge of language and its conventions when writing, speaking, reading, or listening.	**SE/TE:** *Brown Girl Dreaming*, 22; *The Phantom Tollbooth*, Act II, 342; Whole-Class Performance Task, Unit 1: 35, Unit 4: 355, Unit 5: 437; Performance-Based Assessment, Unit 5: 492
L.6.3.a	Vary sentence patterns for meaning, reader/listener interest, and style.	**SE/TE:** *The Phantom Tollbooth*, Act II, 342; Whole-Class Performance Task, Unit 1: 35, Unit 4: 355
L.6.3.b	Maintain consistency in style and tone.	**SE/TE:** Whole-Class Performance Task, Unit 5: 437; Small-Group Performance Task, Unit 5: 485; Performance-Based Assessment, Unit 5: 492

Grade 6 Language Standards (continued)

STANDARD CODE	Standard	Print and Interactive Editions
Vocabulary Acquisition and Use		
L.6.4	Determine or clarify the meaning of unknown and multiple-meaning words and phrases based on *grade 6 reading and content,* choosing flexibly from a range of strategies.	**SE/TE:** "Declaration of the Rights of the Child," 42, 46; "Michaela DePrince: The War Orphan Who Became a Ballerina," 50, 56; *Bad Boy,* 60, 65; "I Was a Skinny Tomboy Kid," 68, 73; *My Life With the Chimpanzees,* 114; "Hachiko," 124; "A Blessing," 138, 141; "Predators," 144, 147; "Monkey Master," 152, 160; "Black Cowboy, Wild Horses," 162, 168; "Feathered Friend," 202; "Teens and Technology Share a Future," 212; "The Black Hole of Technology," 220; "The Fun They Had," 238, 244; "Is Our Gain Also Our Loss?", 248, 252; *The Phantom Tollbooth,* Act II, 342; *Alice's Adventures in Wonderland,* 362; "Jabberwocky," 372, 376, 378; "The Importance of Imagination," 380, 384; *A Long Way Home,* 426; "Mission Twinpossible," 444, 448; *Tales From the Odyssey,* 452, 459; "To the Top of Everest," 462, 471
L.6.4.a	Use context (e.g., the overall meaning of a sentence or paragraph; a word's position or function in a sentence) as a clue to the meaning of a word or phrase.	**SE/TE:** "I Was a Skinny Tomboy Kid," 68; "A Blessing," 138; "Predators," 144; "Black Cowboy, Wild Horses," 162; "The Black Hole of Technology," 220; "The Fun They Had," 238; *Alice's Adventures in Wonderland,* 362; "Jabberwocky," 372, 378; "The Importance of Imagination," 380; *Tales From the Odyssey,* 452
L.6.4.b	Use common, grade-appropriate Greek or Latin affixes and roots as clues to the meaning of a word (e.g., *audience, auditory, audible*).	**SE/TE:** "Declaration of the Rights of the Child," 46; *Bad Boy,* 65; *My Life With the Chimpanzees,* 114; "Predators," 147; "Monkey Master," 160; "Feathered Friend," 202; "Teens and Technology Share a Future," 212; "The Fun They Had," 244; "Is Our Gain Also Our Loss?", 252; *The Phantom Tollbooth,* Act II, 342; "The Importance of Imagination," 384; *A Long Way Home,* 426; "Mission Twinpossible," 448; *Tales From the Odyssey,* 459; "To the Top of Everest," 471
L.6.4.c	Consult reference materials (e.g., dictionaries, glossaries, thesauruses), both print and digital, to find the pronunciation of a word or determine or clarify its precise meaning or its part of speech.	**SE/TE:** "Michaela DePrince: The War Orphan Who Became a Ballerina," 56; *Bad Boy,* 65; "A Blessing," 141; "Monkey Master," 152; "Jabberwocky," 376; "Mission Twinpossible," 448; *Tales From the Odyssey,* 459; "To the Top of Everest," 471
L.6.4.d	Verify the preliminary determination of the meaning of a word or phrase (e.g., by checking the inferred meaning in context or in a dictionary).	**SE/TE:** "Michaela DePrince: The War Orphan Who Became a Ballerina," 56; "Hachiko," 124; "Monkey Master," 160; "The Black Hole of Technology," 220; "To the Top of Everest," 471
L.6.5	Demonstrate understanding of figurative language, word relationships, and nuances in word meanings.	**SE/TE:** *Brown Girl Dreaming,* 22; "Michaela DePrince: The War Orphan Who Became a Ballerina," 56; "I Was a Skinny Tomboy Kid," 75; *My Life With the Chimpanzees,* 114; "Hachiko," 124; "Predators," 149; "Feathered Friend," 202; *The Phantom Tollbooth,* Act I, 310; *Alice's Adventures in Wonderland,* 368; "Jabberwocky," 378; "Mission Twinpossible," 444
L.6.5.a	Interpret figures of speech (e.g., personification) in context.	**SE/TE:** "I Was a Skinny Tomboy Kid," 75; "The Black Hole of Technology," 218
L.6.5.b	Use the relationship between particular words (e.g., cause/effect, part/whole, item/category) to better understand each of the words.	**SE/TE:** "Michaela DePrince: The War Orphan Who Became a Ballerina," 56; *My Life With the Chimpanzees,* 114; "Hachiko," 124; *Alice's Adventures in Wonderland,* 368; "Jabberwocky," 378; "Mission Twinpossible," 444
L.6.5.c	Distinguish among the connotations (associations) of words with similar denotations (definitions) (e.g., *stingy, scrimping, economical, unwasteful, thrifty*).	**SE/TE:** "Predators," 149; *The Phantom Tollbooth,* Act I, 310
L.6.6	Acquire and use accurately grade-appropriate general academic and domain-specific words and phrases; gather vocabulary knowledge when considering a word or phrase important to comprehension or expression.	**SE/TE:** Unit Goals, Unit 1: 4, Unit 2: 92, Unit 3: 186, Unit 4: 274, Unit 5: 402; "Calvin and Hobbes," 26; "The Internet of Things," 224; "Bored . . . and Brilliant?", 256; *The Phantom Tollbooth* (media), 346, 349; "All About Exploration," 430; "Mission Twinpossible," 444, 448; *Lewis & Clark,* 476

Jump Start

Engage students in a discussion about what it means to grow up—both the challenges and triumphs. Have students jot down three things that they look forward to in adulthood. Then, have them note three things that they think they'll miss about being a kid. Next, poll the class to determine what students look forward to about becoming adults and what they might miss about childhood. Explain that in this unit, students will explore the pros and cons of growing up and what the term *childhood* means to them on a personal level.

Childhood

Ask students what the word *childhood* suggests to them. Point out that as they work through this unit, they will read many examples about the challenges and triumphs of growing up.

Video ▶

Project the introduction video in class, ask students to open the video in their interactive textbooks, or have students scan the Bounce Page icon with their phones to access the video.

Discuss It If you want to make this a digital activity, go online and navigate to the Discussion Board. Alternatively, students can share their responses in a class discussion.

Block Scheduling

Each day in this pacing calendar represents a 40–50 minute class period. Teachers using block scheduling may combine days to reflect their class schedule. In addition, teachers may revise pacing to differentiate and support core instruction by integrating components and resources as students require.

📅 **Pacing Plan**

Childhood

You face challenges every day, but learning how to deal with them is part of growing up.

© Pearson Education, Inc. or its affiliates. All rights reserved.

Best of the Bee

💬 **Discuss It** Do you think competition should be part of everyone's childhood?

Write your response before sharing your ideas.

SCAN FOR MULTIMEDIA

2

Unit Introduction

Introduce Whole-Class Learning

from Brown Girl Dreaming

Gallery of Calvin and Hobbes Comics

Performance Task

| 1 | 2 | 3 | 4 | 5 | 6 | 7 | 8 | 9 | 10 | 11 | 12 | 13 | 14 | 15 | 16 | 17 | 18 |

UNIT 1

UNIT INTRODUCTION

ESSENTIAL QUESTION:

What are some of the challenges and triumphs of growing up?

LAUNCH TEXT NONFICTION NARRATIVE MODEL
Wagon Train at Dusk

WHOLE-CLASS LEARNING

ANCHOR TEXT: MEMOIR IN VERSE

from Brown Girl Dreaming
Jacqueline Woodson

MEDIA: COMIC STRIP

Gallery of *Calvin and Hobbes* Comics
Bill Watterson

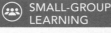 SMALL-GROUP LEARNING

PUBLIC DOCUMENT

Declaration of the Rights of the Child
The United Nations General Assembly

MAGAZINE ARTICLE

Michaela DePrince: The War Orphan Who Became a Ballerina
William Kremer

▶ MEDIA CONNECTION: Michaela DePrince— Ballet Dancer

COMPARE

MEMOIR

from Bad Boy
Walter Dean Myers

POETRY

I Was a Skinny Tomboy Kid
Alma Luz Villanueva

 INDEPENDENT LEARNING

NOVEL EXCERPT

from Peter Pan
J. M. Barrie

POETRY

Oranges
Gary Soto

ESSAY

The Boy Nobody Knew
Faith Ringgold

SHORT STORY

Raymond's Run
Toni Cade Bambara

SHORT STORY

Eleven
Sandra Cisneros

PERFORMANCE TASK

WRITING FOCUS:
Write a Nonfiction Narrative

PERFORMANCE TASK

SPEAKING AND LISTENING FOCUS:
Present a Retelling

PERFORMANCE-BASED ASSESSMENT PREP

Review Evidence for a Nonfiction Narrative

PERFORMANCE-BASED ASSESSMENT

Narration: Nonfiction Narrative and Oral Recitation

PROMPT:
When did a challenge lead to a triumph?

3

What are some of the challenges and triumphs of growing up?

Introduce the Essential Question and point out that students will respond to related prompts.

- **Whole-Class Learning** *When did you have to use your imagination to find another way to do something?*
- **Small-Group Learning** *Deliver a retelling of the childhood challenges presented in one of the stories.*
- **Performance-Based Assessment** *When did a challenge lead to a triumph?*

Using Trade Books

Refer to the Teaching with Trade Books section for suggestions on how to incorporate the following thematically related titles into this unit:

- *The Secret Garden* by Frances Hodgson Burnett
- *Bud, Not Buddy* by Christopher Paul Curtis
- *The Young Landlords* by Walter Dean Myers

Current Perspectives

To increase student engagement, search online for stories about childhood and the challenges of growing up, and invite your students to recommend stories they find. Always preview content before sharing it with your class.

- **Article: "Teens Obsessed With Facebook May Struggle With Anxiety, Sleep Problems" (*Huffington Post*)** Children face problems because of social media.
- **Video: "My Philosophy for a Happy Life" (TEDx Talks)** Sam Berns talks about living happily, despite suffering from progeria.

© Pearson Education, Inc., or its affiliates. All rights reserved.

Introduce Small-Group Learning

Introduce Independent Learning

Performance-Based Assessment

Declaration of the Rights of the Child

Michaela DePrince: The War Orphan Who Became a Ballerina

from Bad Boy

I Was a Skinny Tomboy Kid

Performance Task

Independent Learning

| 19 | 20 | 21 | 22 | 23 | 24 | 25 | 26 | 27 | 28 | 29 | 30 | 31 | 32 | 33 | 34 | 35 | 36 |

About the Unit Goals

These unit goals were backward designed from the Performance-Based Assessment at the end of the unit and the Whole-Class and Small-Group Performance Tasks. Students will practice and become proficient in many more standards over the course of this unit.

Unit Goals ▶

Review the goals with students and explain that as they read and discuss the selections in this unit, they will improve their skills in reading, writing, research, language, and speaking and listening.

• Have students watch the video on Goal Setting.

• A video on this topic is available online in the Professional Development Center.

Reading Goals Tell students they will read and evaluate nonfiction narratives. They will also read arguments, explanatory essays, and fiction to better understand the ways writers express ideas.

Writing and Research Goals Tell students that they will learn the elements of nonfiction narrative writing. They will also conduct research to clarify and explore ideas.

Language Goal Tell students that they will develop a deeper understanding of the conventions of standard English grammar and usage, including correct usage of different types of nouns. They will then practice using nouns correctly in their own writing.

Speaking and Listening Explain to students that they will work together to build on one another's ideas, develop consensus, and communicate with one another. They will also learn to incorporate audio, visuals, and text in presentations.

HOME Connection ✉

A Home Connection letter to students' parents or guardians is available in the Interactive Teacher's Edition. The letter explains what students will be learning in this unit and how they will be assessed.

STANDARDS

Language
Acquire and use accurately grade-appropriate general academic and domain-specific words and phrases; gather vocabulary knowledge when considering a word or phrase important to comprehension or expression.

4 UNIT 1 • CHILDHOOD

Unit Goals

Throughout this unit, you will deepen your understanding of the stage of life known as childhood through reading, writing, speaking, listening, and presenting. These goals will help you succeed on the Unit Performance-Based Assessment.

Rate how well you meet these goals right now. You will revisit your ratings later when you reflect on your growth during this unit.

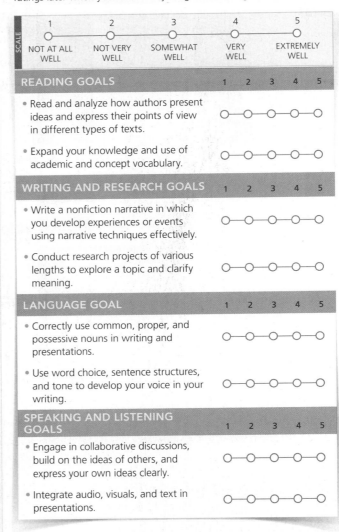

SCALE	1	2	3	4	5
	NOT AT ALL WELL	NOT VERY WELL	SOMEWHAT WELL	VERY WELL	EXTREMELY WELL

READING GOALS	1	2	3	4	5
• Read and analyze how authors present ideas and express their points of view in different types of texts.					
• Expand your knowledge and use of academic and concept vocabulary.					

WRITING AND RESEARCH GOALS	1	2	3	4	5
• Write a nonfiction narrative in which you develop experiences or events using narrative techniques effectively.					
• Conduct research projects of various lengths to explore a topic and clarify meaning.					

LANGUAGE GOAL	1	2	3	4	5
• Correctly use common, proper, and possessive nouns in writing and presentations.					
• Use word choice, sentence structures, and tone to develop your voice in your writing.					

SPEAKING AND LISTENING GOALS	1	2	3	4	5
• Engage in collaborative discussions, build on the ideas of others, and express your own ideas clearly.					
• Integrate audio, visuals, and text in presentations.					

© Pearson Education, Inc. or its affiliates. All rights reserved.

SCAN FOR MULTIMEDIA

AUTHOR'S PERSPECTIVE: **Ernest Morrell, Ph.D.**

Why Goal Setting Matters Establishing goals helps students take responsibility for their own learning and become independent scholars and thinkers. One way to encourage students to set, follow, and achieve goals is to have them write their goals down. Students can use the following process for crafting well-defined and measurable goals:

• *Decide What You Want*: Have students skim the Unit 1 Table of Contents and decide what they most want to learn from the unit. Guide students to set specific, realistic goals, such as "learn and correctly use five new concept words from the unit."

• *Write the Goals Down*: Have students draft the goals in clear, precise language. Students should also include a way to measure results so they can assess their progress.

• *Set a Time Frame*: Have students include a realistic schedule for completion, using the length of the selections in Unit 1 as a guide. As necessary, have students break large goals into smaller ones to make the goal more likely to be completed.

When students take more responsibility for their learning, they may learn to rely more on themselves and take more interest in their success.

Academic Vocabulary: Nonfiction Narrative

Understanding and using academic terms can help you read, write, and speak with precision and clarity. Here are five academic words that will be useful to you in this unit as you analyze and write nonfiction narratives.

Complete the chart.

1. Review each word, its root, and the mentor sentences.

2. Use the information and your own knowledge to predict the meaning of each word.

3. For each word, list at least two related words.

4. Refer to the dictionary or other resources if needed.

> **TIP**
> **FOLLOW THROUGH**
> Study the words in this chart, and mark them or their forms wherever they appear in the unit.

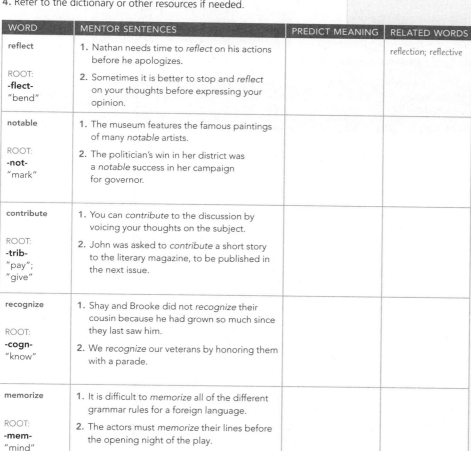

WORD	MENTOR SENTENCES	PREDICT MEANING	RELATED WORDS
reflect ROOT: **-flect-** "bend"	1. Nathan needs time to *reflect* on his actions before he apologizes. 2. Sometimes it is better to stop and *reflect* on your thoughts before expressing your opinion.		reflection; reflective
notable ROOT: **-not-** "mark"	1. The museum features the famous paintings of many *notable* artists. 2. The politician's win in her district was a *notable* success in her campaign for governor.		
contribute ROOT: **-trib-** "pay"; "give"	1. You can *contribute* to the discussion by voicing your thoughts on the subject. 2. John was asked to *contribute* a short story to the literary magazine, to be published in the next issue.		
recognize ROOT: **-cogn-** "know"	1. Shay and Brooke did not *recognize* their cousin because he had grown so much since they last saw him. 2. We *recognize* our veterans by honoring them with a parade.		
memorize ROOT: **-mem-** "mind"	1. It is difficult to *memorize* all of the different grammar rules for a foreign language. 2. The actors must *memorize* their lines before the opening night of the play.		

© Pearson Education, Inc., or its affiliates. All rights reserved.

Academic Vocabulary: Nonfiction Narrative

Introduce the blue academic vocabulary words in the chart on the student page. Point out that the root of each word provides a clue to its meaning. Discuss the mentor sentences to ensure students understand each word's usage. Students should also use the mentor sentences as context to help them predict the meaning of each word. Check that students are able to fill the chart in correctly. Complete pronunciations, parts of speech, and definitions are provided for you. Students are only expected to provide the definition.

Possible responses:

reflect *v.* (rih FLEHKT)
Meaning: to think carefully about
Related words: reflects, reflected
Additional words related to the root *-flect-*: reflection, reflective, inflection, deflect

notable *adj.* (NOH tuh buhl)
Meaning: important, worthy of notice
Related word: notably
Additional words related to the root *-not-*: note, notation, denote, denotation, connotation

contribute *v.* (kuhn TRIHB yoot)
Meaning: to give; to write for a publication
Related words: contribution, contributor
Additional words related to the root *-trib-*: distribute, attribute, tribute, tributary, tribune

recognize *v.* (REHK uhg nyz)
Meaning: to acknowledge or be aware of someone or something
Related words: recognition, recognizable
Additional words related to the root *-cogn-*: cognition, cognizant

memorize *v.* MEHM uh ryz
Meaning: to learn something by heart
Related words: memorizing, memorized
Additional words related to the root *-mem-*: memory, memento, remember, memorial

PERSONALIZE FOR LEARNING

English Language Support
Cognates Many of the academic words have Spanish cognates. Use these cognates with students whose home language is Spanish.

reflect – reflexionar   notable – notable

contribute – contribuir   recognize – reconocer

Not all English learners will recognize and use these cognates automatically. Help students build their cognate awareness by pointing out that these cognates share the same root in both English and Spanish. **ALL LEVELS**

INTRODUCTION

Purpose of the Launch Text

The Launch Text provides students with a common starting point to address the unit topic. After reading the Launch Text, all students will be able to participate in discussions about childhood.

Lexile: 740 The easier reading level of this selection makes it perfect to assign for homework. Students will need little or no support to understand it.

Additionally, "Wagon Train at Dusk" provides a writing model for the Performance-Based Assessment students complete at the end of the unit

Launch Text: Nonfiction Narrative Model

Point out to students how the author begins the narrative with "Sometimes you just have to laugh," grabbing the reader's attention right away. Have students note the way the author recounts the story in chronological order, describing people, places, and things using specific and descriptive words. Ask students to pay attention to the author's use of dialogue and to the lesson that's woven into the conclusion.

Encourage students to read this text on their own and annotate unfamiliar words and sections of text they think are particularly important.

🔊 AUDIO SUMMARIES

Audio summaries of "Wagon Train at Dusk" are available in both English and Spanish in the Interactive Teacher's Edition or Unit Resources. Assigning these summaries before students read the Launch Text may help them build additional background knowledge and set a context for their reading.

LAUNCH TEXT | NONFICTION NARRATIVE

Wagon Train at Dusk

This selection is an example of a **nonfiction narrative**, a type of writing in which an author tells a true story. This is the type of writing you will develop in the Performance-Based Assessment at the end of the unit.

As you read, look at the way the author describes events and experiences. Mark the text to help you answer this question: What descriptive details make this narrative realistic and memorable?

NOTES

1 "Sometimes you just have to laugh," I tell my daughter, who is having an especially bad day. She's lost her favorite bracelet, she turned in the wrong homework assignment, and she just found out she would be playing Marshmallow #2 in the class play.

2 "Oh, you wouldn't understand," Sarah says, sulkily.

3 I ask her if I've ever told her the story of the diorama.

4 "Yes, Dad. More than once," she says.

5 That doesn't stop me. "When I was in the sixth grade," I say in my storyteller's voice, "we had to make shoebox dioramas of a scene from American history. I decided to do a wagon train traveling across the Great Plains in the mid-1800s."

6 Sarah pretends she isn't rolling her eyes, but I keep going. "I wanted it to be great. A diorama to end all dioramas! I wanted to be famous. I wanted to be on the local news. But what I really wanted was to show up Jorge Nuñez," I say.

7 "Jorge and I had been in the same class since fourth grade. We were pretty evenly matched when it came to test scores and homework, but for hands-on projects, there was no one like Jorge. He always came up with these unique creations, beautifully conceived and executed. Jorge's mom and dad were architects, so maybe he had a leg up, but who knows."

8 Sarah shrugs in sympathy—which I take as permission to continue. "As soon as I heard Jorge announce that he was making a shoebox diorama of a log cabin, I decided to go one better. I'd

© Pearson Education, Inc., or its affiliates. All rights reserved.

SCAN FOR MULTIMEDIA

CROSS-CURRICULAR PERSPECTIVES

Social Studies Tell students that children traveled in wagon trains that crossed the Great Plains in the 18th and 19th centuries. Have students look for information about what life was like for these children and write a short report. They should include information about the obstacles they faced and what was expected of them on the journey.

© Pearson Education, Inc., or its affiliates. All rights reserved.

create a fleet of Conestoga wagons in a circle formation around a campfire at dusk, with miniature people and horses and dogs made of pipe cleaners, and children running around playing hoops. It would be a masterpiece. And that's just how it turned out: a masterpiece! I carried it upstairs to my room and that night I went to sleep with a smile on my face, imagining Jorge's reaction."

9   "Then," I go on, "in the middle of the night I was jolted awake by a ripping sound. My heart stopped. I felt sick. *I know that sound,* I thought. There was no mistaking what it was—Lucy was demolishing my masterpiece! You couldn't even tell what it was supposed to be! I lay there in a stupor of self-pity and the sense that nothing in the world would ever be right again. *The dog ate my diorama,* I thought, and I pictured myself saying this in class. I pictured the hoots and guffaws and hollers. I pictured my teacher's puzzled expression as she tried to work out if I was being serious." I make the expression myself, and Sarah smiles.

10   "Then I said it out loud: *The dog ate my diorama.* It was funny, actually. The more I said it, the funnier it got. I started laughing. I laughed until my sides hurt. I couldn't stop laughing."

11   "And then?" Sarah says, knowing what comes next.

12   "Well," I say, "I picked up all the pieces and put them in the box and took the whole thing to school. I called it 'Wagon Train After a Tornado.' The teacher loved it. Everyone enjoyed my story. I think Jorge was actually jealous."

13   Sarah gives a reluctant smile, like she's supposed to. "So," she says, remembering that there's a lesson in there somewhere, "you learned to laugh at bad things. Right?"

14   I shake my head. "Nope," I tell her. "I learned that some things aren't so bad." ❧

NOTES

WORD NETWORK FOR CHILDHOOD

Vocabulary A Word Network is a collection of words related to a topic. As you read the selections in this unit, identify interesting words related to childhood, and add them to your Word Network. For example, you might begin by adding words from the Launch Text, such as *sulkily*, *diorama,* and *homework.* Continue to add words as you complete this unit.

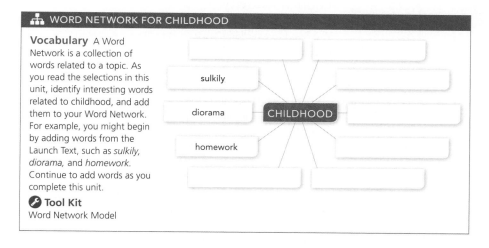

🔧 **Tool Kit**
Word Network Model

DIGITAL
PERSPECTIVES 🔊 📄

Word Network for Childhood 📄

Tell students that they can fill in the Word Network as they read texts in the unit, or they can record the words elsewhere and add them later. Point out to students that people may have personal associations with some words. A word that one student thinks is related to the concept of childhood might not be a word another student would pick. However, students should feel free to add any word they personally think is relevant to their Word Network. Each person's Word Network will be unique. If you choose to print the Word Network, distribute it to students at this point so they can use it throughout the rest of the unit.

AUTHOR'S PERSPECTIVE: **Elfrieda Hiebert, Ph.D.**

Word Networks Vocabulary word networks enable students to learn, use, and retain a large number of useful words related to a particular concept. In addition, generating vocabulary in this way can help students appreciate the subtleties of an author's word choice and evaluate the effectiveness of an author's style. Using vocabulary word networks also helps students choose more precise words when they write and edit. Finally, forging connections among related words, as opposed to teaching the words individually, allows students to approach new words with confidence and knowledge.

When students discuss the unit's theme, they can choose from a wide variety of related words, each with its own connotation, to create a word network. While students may not know more complex words at first, they do know common conversation words and words that get at the big idea. These words can serve as a gateway to the more complex words they will encounter in these selections.

Summary

Have students read the introductory paragraph. Provide them with tips for writing a summary:

- Write in the present tense.
- Make sure to include the title of the work.
- Be concise: a summary should not be equal in length to the original text.
- If you need to quote the words of the author, use quotation marks.
- Don't put your own opinions, ideas, or interpretations into the summary. The purpose of writing a summary is to accurately represent what the author says, not to provide a critique.

If necessary, students can refer to the Tool Kit for help in understanding the elements of a good summary.

See possible Summary on the student page.

Launch Activity

Explain to students that as they work on this unit they will have many opportunities to discuss how challenges may lead to triumphs and whether learning new things has to be challenging. Students may rely on their personal opinions as they choose their initial response to the questions. Remind students that they will need to support their position with facts. Group summaries will vary but should include the main points of discussion.

Summary

Write a summary of "Wagon Train at Dusk." A **summary** is a concise, complete, and accurate overview of a text. It should not include a statement of your opinion or an analysis.

Possible response: Wagon Train at Dusk

In this nonfiction narrative, a father comforts his daughter, who just had a tough day at school. He tells her a story from his own school days, one which she's heard many times before. Back in sixth grade, he had a project to make a diorama, a three-dimensional model, of a historic scene. Driven by rivalry with a classmate, he made a masterpiece. But while he was in bed that night, his dog Lucy attacked his diorama. He was horrified and sad, but then realized how funny the situation sounded. And from there, he figured out a way to salvage the situation.

Launch Activity

Participate in a Group Discussion Consider this statement:
You need to overcome obstacles to learn new things.

Prepare for the discussion by thinking about the topic:

- Have you ever faced a challenge that led to success? Do you know someone who has had this experience?
- Does learning new things have to be challenging?

Decide your position, and record a brief explanation.

☐ Strongly Agree ☐ Agree ☐ Disagree ☐ Strongly Disagree

_____

_____

Form a small group with other students. Then, discuss your responses to the prompt and the questions. When you have finished your conversation, write a summary of the main points you covered. Share your summary with the class.

© Pearson Education, Inc., or its affiliates. All rights reserved.

QuickWrite

Consider class discussions, the video, and the Launch Text as you think about the prompt. Record your first thoughts here.

PROMPT: **When did a challenge lead to a triumph?**

Possible response: In "Wagon Train at Dusk," the narrator tells his daughter about a challenge he faced when his dog destroyed his diorama of a wagon train. He felt awful until he realized how funny the situation was. Then he titled his diorama "Wagon Train After a Tornado." His creativity helped turn the challenge into a success, and everyone loved his project.

EVIDENCE LOG FOR CHILDHOOD

Review your QuickWrite. Summarize your thoughts in one sentence to record in your Evidence Log. Then, record textual details or evidence from "Wagon Train at Dusk" that support your thinking.

Prepare for the Performance-Based Assessment at the end of the unit by completing the Evidence Log after each selection.

Tool Kit
Evidence Log Model

| Title of Text: _____ | | Date: _____ |
CONNECTION TO PROMPT	TEXT EVIDENCE/DETAILS	ADDITIONAL NOTES/IDEAS

How does this text change or add to my thinking?   Date: _____

SCAN FOR
MULTIMEDIA

© Pearson Education, Inc., or its affiliates. All rights reserved.

QuickWrite

In this QuickWrite, students should present their own response to the prompt based on the material they have read and viewed in the Unit Overview and Introduction. This initial response will help inform their work when they complete the Performance-Based Assessment at the end of the unit. Students should make sure their response includes examples that reflect both the challenges and the triumphs that they have read about and discussed so far.

See possible QuickWrite on the student page.

Evidence Log for Childhood

Students should record their initial thinking in their Evidence Logs. Then they should record evidence from "Wagon Train at Dusk" that supports this thinking.

If you choose to print the Evidence Log, distribute it to students at this point so they can use it throughout the rest of the unit.

Performance-Based Assessment: Refining Your Thinking

- Have students watch the video on Refining Your Thinking
- A video on this topic is available online in the Professional Development Center.

PERSONALIZE FOR LEARNING

Challenge

Description In "Wagon Train at Dusk," the narrator describes a shoebox diorama that he created in sixth grade, using details such as the materials he used and what it looked like. Have students write a two- to three-paragraph description of a project, for school or another purpose, that was particularly challenging. Remind them to include details about the project, including the materials they used, the challenges they faced, how the project turned out, and how they felt about it.

Draw students' attention to the narrator's description of his motivations for choosing this particular project, including the details about his competition with Jorge Nuñez. Students should be similarly descriptive in explaining why they chose their project and how they went about completing it.

WHOLE-CLASS LEARNING

What are some of the challenges and triumphs of growing up?

Childhood may pose challenges, such as difficulty in school or problems with friends. But it is also a time of learning and having fun. Taken together, the experiences of childhood help prepare us for adulthood. During Whole-Class Learning, students will read selections about childhood.

Whole-Class Learning Strategies ⏵

Review the Learning Strategies with students and explain that as they work through Whole-Class Learning they will develop strategies to work in large-group environments.

- Have students watch the video on Whole-Class Learning Strategies.
- A video on this topic is available online in the Professional Development Center.

You may wish to discuss some action items to add to the chart as a class before students complete it on their own. For example, for "Listen actively," you might solicit the following from students:

- Take notes so that you remember details.
- Ask questions if you need clarification.

Block Scheduling

Each day in this Pacing Plan represents a 40–50 minute class period. Teachers using block scheduling may combine days to reflect their class schedule. In addition, teachers may revise pacing to differentiate and support core instruction by integrating components and resources as students require.

📅 **Pacing Plan**

OVERVIEW: WHOLE-CLASS LEARNING

ESSENTIAL QUESTION:

What are some of the challenges and triumphs of growing up?

You deal with challenges every day. Some are big challenges, while others are small. Whatever the challenge is, you learn and grow from that experience. As you read, you will work with your whole class to explore the ways that people can learn from and triumph over childhood challenges.

Whole-Class Learning Strategies

Throughout your life, in school, in your community, and in your career, you will continue to learn and work in large-group environments.

Review these strategies and the actions you can take to practice them as you work with your whole class. Add ideas of your own for each strategy. Get ready to use these strategies during Whole-Class Learning.

STRATEGY	ACTION PLAN
Listen actively	• Eliminate distractions. For example, put your cellphone away. • Keep your eyes on the speaker. •
Clarify by asking questions	• If you're confused, other people probably are, too. Ask a question to help your whole class. • If you see that you are guessing, ask a question instead. •
Monitor understanding	• Notice what information you already know and be ready to build on it. • Ask for help if you are struggling. •
Interact and share ideas	• Share your ideas and answer questions, even if you are unsure. • Build on the ideas of others by adding details or making a connection. •

© Pearson Education, Inc., or its affiliates. All rights reserved.

SCAN FOR MULTIMEDIA

Introduce Whole-Class Learning

Unit Introduction

from Brown Girl Dreaming

Gallery of Calvin and Hobbes *Comics*

Performance Task

| 1 | 2 | 3 | 4 | 5 | 6 | 7 | 8 | 9 | 10 | 11 | 12 | 13 | 14 | 15 | 16 | 17 | 18 |

WHOLE-CLASS LEARNING

CONTENTS

ANCHOR TEXT: MEMOIR IN VERSE

from Brown Girl Dreaming
Jacqueline Woodson

An author relates her childhood experiences in a memorable new way—through poetry.

MEDIA: COMIC STRIP

Gallery of *Calvin and Hobbes* Comics
Bill Watterson

For Calvin and his tiger Hobbes, childhood is an adventure.

PERFORMANCE TASK

WRITING FOCUS

Write a Nonfiction Narrative

The Whole-Class readings illustrate ways in which young people navigate the challenges of growing up. After reading, you will write a nonfiction narrative about a time when you used your imagination to find a new way to do something.

© Pearson Education, Inc., or its affiliates. All rights reserved.

Contents

Anchor Texts Preview the anchor text and comic strip with students to generate interest. Encourage students to discuss other texts they may have read or movies or television shows they may have seen that deal with the issues of becoming an adult.

You may wish to conduct a poll to determine which selection students think looks more interesting and discuss the reasons for their preference. Students can return to this poll after they have read the selections to see if their preference changed.

Performance Task

Write a Nonfiction Narrative Explain to students that after they have finished reading the selections, they will write nonfiction narratives about how children use their imagination to find new ways to do things. To help them prepare, encourage students to think about the topic as they progress through the selections and as they participate in the Whole-Class Learning experience.

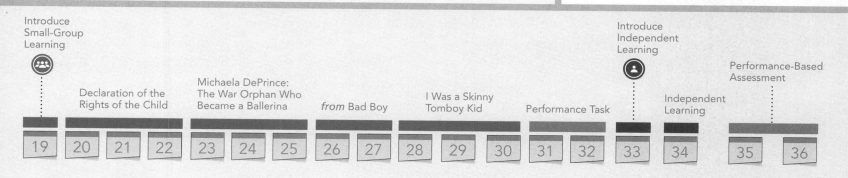

Introduce Small-Group Learning

Declaration of the Rights of the Child

Michaela DePrince: The War Orphan Who Became a Ballerina

from Bad Boy

I Was a Skinny Tomboy Kid

Performance Task

Introduce Independent Learning

Independent Learning

Performance-Based Assessment

19 20 21 22 23 24 25 26 27 28 29 30 31 32 33 34 35 36

from Brown Girl Dreaming

🔊 **AUDIO SUMMARIES**

Audio summaries of the excerpt from *Brown Girl Dreaming* are available online in both English and Spanish in the Interactive Teacher's Edition or Unit Resources. Assigning these summaries prior to reading the selection may help students build additional background knowledge and set a context for their first read.

Summary

This excerpt comes from Jacqueline Woodson's memoir *Brown Girl Dreaming*. In verse, Woodson tells of her childhood, describing the joys and hardships of her life. Some of the important themes that weave through the memoir are the challenge of moving from the South to the North, the bonds and rivalry among family members, and the importance of imagination. Woodson beautifully expresses the roots of her interest in language and storytelling: the desire to "catch words one day."

Insight

Beyond the beauty and humanity of the memoir itself, this selection helps us see how young people develop the interests that they will one day build their lives around. Note that the discussion of dead or absent fathers in "sometimes" may be difficult for students who have experienced similar situations.

ESSENTIAL QUESTION:
What are some of the challenges and triumphs of growing up?

Connection to Essential Question

There are several milestones we can see in this section, including moving, losing a parent, and discovering one's passions.

WHOLE-CLASS LEARNING PERFORMANCE TASK
When did you have to use your imagination to find another way to do something?

UNIT PERFORMANCE-BASED ASSESSMENT
When did a challenge lead to a triumph?

Connection to Performance Tasks

Whole-Class Learning Performance Task In this Performance Task, students will explore imagination and how we use it to find new ways to do something. In the poem "another way," the speaker and her brother use their imagination to enjoy games with rules they don't understand. The poems can help inspire students to discuss similar experiences in their lives.

Unit Performance-Based Assessment In these poems, the speaker faces the challenges of living in a new place and having rivalry with her sister. She tries to triumph over the challenges by making up stories.

LESSON RESOURCES

	Making Meaning	Language Development	Effective Expression
Lesson	**First Read** **Close Read** **Analyze the Text** **Analyze Craft and Structure**	**Concept Vocabulary** **Word Study** **Conventions**	**Writing to Sources** **Speaking and Listening**
Instructional Standards	**RL.10** By the end of the year, read and comprehend literature . . . **RI.10** By the end of the year, read and comprehend literary nonfiction . . . **RL.5** Analyze how a particular sentence, chapter, scene, or stanza . . . **RL.6** Explain how an author develops the point of view . . . **RI.5** Analyze how a particular sentence, paragraph, chapter, or section . . . **RI.6** Determine an author's point of view or purpose in a text . . .	**RL.4** Determine the meaning of words and phrases . . . **L.2** Demonstrate command of the conventions . . . **L.3** Use knowledge of language and its conventions . . . **L.5** Demonstrate understanding of figurative language . . .	**W.3** Write narratives to develop real or imagined . . . **W.3.b** Use narrative techniques . . . **W.3.d** Use precise words and phrases . . . **W.9** Draw evidence from literary or informational texts . . . **W.9.a** Apply *grade 6 Reading standards* . . . **SL.1** Engage effectively in a range of collaborative discussions . . . **SL.1.a** Come to discussions prepared . . . **SL.1.b** Follow rules for collegial discussions . . . **SL.1.c** Pose and respond to specific questions . . . **SL.1.d** Review the key ideas expressed . . .
STUDENT RESOURCES			
Available online in the Interactive Student Edition or Unit Resources	Selection Audio First-Read Guide: Nonfiction First-Read Guide: Poetry Close-Read Guide: Nonfiction Close-Read Guide: Poetry	Word Network	Evidence Log
TEACHER RESOURCES			
Selection Resources Available online in the Interactive Teacher's Edition or Unit Resources	Audio Summaries Annotation Highlights EL Highlights English Language Support Lesson: Poetic Elements Analyze Craft and Structure: Memoir and Poetry	Concept Vocabulary and Word Study Conventions: Common, Proper, and Possessive Nouns	Writing to Sources: Poem Speaking and Listening: Partner Discussion
Reteach/Practice (RP) Available online in the Interactive Teacher's Edition or Unit Resources	Analyze Craft and Structure: Memoir and Poetry (RP)	Word Study: Onomatopoeia (RP) Conventions: Common, Proper, and Possessive Nouns (RP)	Writing to Sources: Poem (RP) Speaking and Listening: Partner Discussion (RP)
Assessment Available online in Assessments	Selection Test		
My Resources	A Unit 1 Answer Key is available online and in the Interactive Teacher's Edition.		

Reading Support

Text Complexity Rubric: *from* Brown Girl Dreaming	
Qualitative Measures	
Lexile: NP **Text Length:** 186 lines	
Quantitative Measures	
Knowledge Demands ① — ② — **❸** — ④ — ⑤	Knowing background of author's life is helpful to understanding poems. Poems explore themes of varying complexity and abstraction, but some of the pieces portray common experiences.
Structure ① — ② — **❸** — ④ — ⑤	Seven separate poems, all in free verse; a combination of sentences and phrases makes structure unpredictable; all are in first person narrated by same character, creating a thread between pieces.
Language Conventionality and Clarity ① — ② — ③ — **❹** — ⑤	Poems contain a lot of figurative language and abstract phrases; vocabulary is mostly contemporary and familiar; there is a mix of full sentences and poetic phrases.
Levels of Meaning/Purpose ① — ② — ③ — **❹** — ⑤	Poems contain multiple meanings that are sometimes hard to identify. Themes are subtle. Reader must infer situations by piecing together multiple phrases and descriptive images.

DECIDE AND PLAN

English Language Support

Provide English Learners with support for knowledge demands and language as they read the selection.

Knowledge Demands Refer to the background information and ask students about South Carolina and Brooklyn, New York. Point out the phrase in line 11: "*people below me move fast, heads bent.*" Ask *Does that sound like the country or the city? (the city).* Point out that the author moved from the country to the city.

Language Guide students to the language needed to understand the meaning of the poems. For example, for *brooklyn rain,* help them to identify phrases that describe life in the country in Greenville—*smell of honeysuckle, squish of pine, slide through grass.* Then have them look for phrases describing the city: *gray sidewalk, people below me move fast.*

Strategic Support

Provide students with strategic support to ensure that they can successfully read the text.

Knowledge Demands Make sure students understand the subject of each poem. For example, for *brooklyn rain* refer to the background information and ask students where the author moved (from the country to the city).

Meaning Help students piece together meaning by making connections between phrases. For example, point out that the first line in *sometimes* says there is *one other house* without a father, which means that the speaker does not have a father. Then she says *I lie* and *He died.* Ask *If it's a lie that he died, then what could be the truth about her father?* (he left) The sister says they *don't have a father anymore,* so they did have one once.

Challenge

Provide students who need to be challenged with ideas for how they can go beyond a simple interpretation of the text.

Text Analysis Pair students. Ask each partner to choose one of the poems. Ask them to describe to their partner what the poem is about and what feelings the author is expressing in the poem. Then ask partners to tell the class about the poems their partners described.

Written Response Have students read more selections from the book *Brown Girl Dreaming.* Ask them to choose several of their favorite selections and write what those poems were about, why they liked them the best, and what feelings the author was expressing in the poems.

TEACH

Read and Respond

Have students do their first read of the selection. Then, have them complete their close read. Finally, work with them on the Making Meaning, Language Development, and Effective Expression activities.

Standards Support Through Teaching and Learning Cycle

IDENTIFY NEEDS

Analyze results of the Beginning-of-Year Assessment, focusing on the items relating to Unit 1. Also take into consideration student performance to this point and your observations of where particular students struggle.

ANALYZE AND REVISE

- Analyze student work for evidence of student learning.
- Identify whether or not students have met the expectations in the standards.
- Identify implications for future instruction.

TEACH

Implement the planned lesson, and gather evidence of student learning.

DECIDE AND PLAN

- If students have performed poorly on items matching these standards, then provide selection scaffolds before assigning them the on-level lesson provided in the Student Edition.
- If students have done well on the Beginning-of-Year Assessment, then challenge them to keep progressing and learning by giving them opportunities to practice the skills in depth.
- Use the Selection Resources listed on the Planning pages for "*from* Brown Girl Dreaming" to help students continually improve their ability to master the standards.

Instructional Standards: *from* Brown Girl Dreaming

	Catching Up	This Year	Looking Forward
Reading	You may wish to administer the **Analyze Craft and Structure: Memoir and Poetry (RP)** worksheet to help students understand how an author conveys his or her purpose.	**RL.6** Explain how an author develops the point of view of the narrator or speaker in a text. **RI.6** Determine an author's point of view or purpose in a text and explain how it is conveyed in the text.	Challenge students to rewrite part of a text from an alternative point of view and discuss how this changes the text.
Writing	You may wish to administer the **Writing to Sources: Poem (RP)** worksheet to help students organize their narrative in verse.	**W.3.b** Use narrative techniques, such as dialogue, pacing, and description, to develop experiences, events, and/or characters.	Challenge students to peer edit a partner's narrative, focusing specifically on the sequence of events, pacing, characterization, and descriptive language.
Speaking and Listening	You may wish to administer the **Speaking and Listening: Partner Discussion (RP)** worksheet to help students organize their opinions and positions.	**SL.1.c** Pose and respond to specific questions with elaboration and detail by making comments that contribute to the topic, text, or issue under discussion.	Challenge students to argue their opposition's side of the argument.
Language	You may wish to administer the **Conventions: Common, Proper, and Possessive Nouns (RP)** worksheet to help students understand noun forms. You may wish to administer the **Word Study: Onomatopoeia (RP)** worksheet to help students understand imitative sounds.	**L.2** Demonstrate command of the conventions of standard English capitalization, punctuation, and spelling when writing. **L.5** Demonstrate understanding of figurative language, word relationships, and nuances in word meanings.	Have students analyze the subtleties and nuances of various word choices in different contexts. Challenge students to use onomatopoeia in their narrative verse.

Jump Start

FIRST READ Prior to students' first read, tell them that they are going to read poetry. Engage students in a discussion of what topics poetry covers and then point out that these poems each tell about a different memory, a different event, of a young girl's life. Point out that together, the poems make up a memoir.

from Brown Girl Dreaming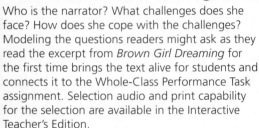

Who is the narrator? What challenges does she face? How does she cope with the challenges? Modeling the questions readers might ask as they read the excerpt from *Brown Girl Dreaming* for the first time brings the text alive for students and connects it to the Whole-Class Performance Task assignment. Selection audio and print capability for the selection are available in the Interactive Teacher's Edition.

Concept Vocabulary

Support students as they rank their words. Ask if they've ever heard, read, or used them. Reassure them that the definitions for these words are listed in the selection.

⬤ FIRST READ

As they read, students should perform the steps of the first read:

NOTICE: You may want to encourage students to notice what has changed recently in the speaker's life and what she says and does that show how she feels about that change.

ANNOTATE: Remind students to mark passages that include repetition and words that are particularly descriptive. For example, students might want to notice which words appeal to the senses of sight, sound, and touch.

CONNECT: Encourage students to go beyond the text to make connections. If they cannot make connections to their own lives or other texts, have them consider stories they have heard from relatives or friends, or perhaps movies they've seen.

RESPOND: Students will answer questions and write a summary to demonstrate understanding.

Point out to students that while they will always complete the Respond step at the end of the first read, the other steps will probably happen somewhat concurrently. You may wish to print copies of the **First-Read Guide: Nonfiction** or **First-Read Guide: Poetry** for students to use. 📄

About the Author

Jacqueline Woodson (b. 1964) was born in Columbus, Ohio. She recalls being happiest as a child when she was writing: "I wrote on paper bags and my shoes and denim binders." A 2008 Newbery Honor winner, Woodson believes that writers need to be honest and to listen to the voices of young people.

🔧 **Tool Kit**
First-Read Guide and Model Annotation

📋 **STANDARDS**

Reading Literature
By the end of the year, read and comprehend literature, including stories, dramas, and poems, in the grades 6–8 text complexity band proficiently, with scaffolding as needed at the high end of the range.

Reading Informational Text
By the end of the year, read and comprehend literature, including stories, dramas, and poems, in the grades 6–8 text complexity band proficiently, with scaffolding as needed at the high end of the range.

12 UNIT 1 • CHILDHOOD

from Brown Girl Dreaming

Concept Vocabulary

You will encounter the following words as you read the excerpt from *Brown Girl Dreaming*. Before reading, note how familiar you are with each word. Then, rank the words in order from most familiar (1) to least familiar (6).

WORD	YOUR RANKING
squish	
humming	
twist	
twirl	
shushes	
feathery	

After completing the first read, come back to the concept vocabulary and review your rankings. Mark changes to your original rankings as needed.

First Read MEMOIR IN VERSE

Apply these strategies as you conduct your first read. You will have an opportunity to complete the close-read notes after your first read.

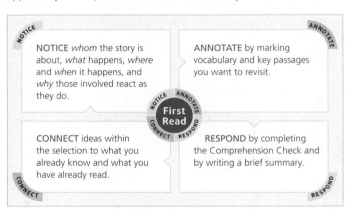

NOTICE *whom* the story is about, *what* happens, *where* and *when* it happens, and *why* those involved react as they do.

ANNOTATE by marking vocabulary and key passages you want to revisit.

CONNECT ideas within the selection to what you already know and what you have already read.

RESPOND by completing the Comprehension Check and by writing a brief summary.

© Pearson Education, Inc., or its affiliates. All rights reserved.

AUTHOR'S PERSPECTIVE   **Kelly Gallagher, M.Ed.**

Teacher as the Best Reader in the Class
Rather than being the wizard behind the curtain, use modeling to do the work of reading in front of students. When students see that even good readers wrestle with difficult text, they gain confidence. Use these methods:

• **Using think-alouds.** Choose a passage from this unit and model read alouds/think alouds to

show students what effective readers do when they are confused. The *Annotate Question Conclude* feature and the teacher edition support highlight the importance of this work.

• **Marking the text.** If students say they don't understand, have them use a yellow highlighter (or sticky notes) for parts they understand and a pink highlighter for those they don't.

from Brown Girl Dreaming

Jacqueline Woodson

BACKGROUND
As a child in the 1960s, Jacqueline Woodson moved with her family from Greenville, South Carolina, to Brooklyn, in New York City. Her memoir *Brown Girl Dreaming* tells of her childhood experiences growing up in both places. In a memoir, an author recalls important events in his or her life. *Brown Girl Dreaming* is unique as a memoir because it is written in verse, or as poetry.

SCAN FOR MULTIMEDIA

brooklyn rain

The rain here is different than the way
it rains in Greenville. No sweet smell of honeysuckle.
No soft squish of pine. No slip and slide through grass.
Just Mama saying, *Stay inside today. It's raining,*
5   and me at the window. Nothing to do but
watch
the gray sidewalk grow darker,
watch
the drops slide down the glass pane,
10 watch
people below me move fast, heads bent.

Already there are stories
in my head. Already color and sound and words.

NOTES

squish (skwihsh) *n.* spongy, cushioned feeling when walking on a flexible surface

from Brown Girl Dreaming **13**

© Pearson Education, Inc., or its affiliates. All rights reserved.

 CLOSER LOOK

Analyze Line Breaks

Students may have marked the word *watch* on lines 6, 8, and 10 during their first read. Use this stanza to help students understand how line breaks help shape a poem's meaning. Encourage them to talk about the annotations that they marked. You may want to model a close read with the class based on the highlights shown in the text.

ANNOTATE: Have students mark details that show that the author intends to emphasize certain words or phrases, or have students participate while you highlight them.

QUESTION: Guide students to consider what these details might tell them. Ask what a reader can infer from the word *No* in lines 2–3 and the word *watch* in lines 6, 8, and 10.

Possible response: The narrator repeats *No* to describe what she misses about rain in Greenville. *Watch* is repeated to show what she sees from her window in Brooklyn when it rains.

CONCLUDE: Help students to formulate conclusions about the importance of these details in the text. Ask students why the author might have included these details.

Possible response: The author breaks the lines as she does to emphasize the last word on each line and the single word *watch*. Doing so draws the reader's attention to the importance of these words and helps the reader draw meaning from the poem.

Remind students that unlike prose, poems are usually written in stanzas with **line breaks**. Though punctuation doesn't necessarily appear at the end of a line, the reader is forced to pause at a line break, and this pause helps emphasize the last word on the line. This same text written in prose would lose much of its meaning, as the emphasis on the words that describe what she sees from her Brooklyn window would be lost.

- **Using sentence starters.** To identify where students are having comprehension problems, have them complete this sentence starter: "I don't understand . . ." Then, as a class, work to resolve the issues. Use these additional sentence starters:

I noticed . . .; I wonder . . .; I think . . .; I'm surprised that . . .; I realized . . .; I'm not sure . . .

- It is also important for students to know that applying tools like these doesn't always work: sometimes, readers decide to live with ambiguity.

 Additional **English Language Support** is available in the Interactive Teacher's Edition.

© Pearson Education, Inc., or its affiliates. All rights reserved.

NOTES

humming (HUHM ihng) v.
singing with closed lips
and without words

Already I'm
15 drawing circles on the glass, **humming**
myself someplace far away from here.

Down south, there was always someplace else to go
you could step out into the rain and
Grandma would let you
20 lift your head and stick out your tongue
be happy.

Down south already feels like a long time ago
but the stories in my head
take me back there, set me down in Daddy's garden
25 where the sun is always shining.

* * *

another way

While our friends are watching TV or playing outside,
we are in our house, knowing that begging our mother
to turn the television on is useless, begging her for
ten minutes outside will only mean her saying,
5 *No.* Saying,
You can run wild with your friends anytime. Today
I want you to find another way to play.

And then one day my mother
comes home with two shopping bags
10 filled with board games—Monopoly, checkers, chess,
Ants in the Pants, Sorry, Trouble,
just about every game we've ever seen
in the commercials between
our Saturday morning cartoons.

15 So many games, we don't know
where to begin playing, so we let Roman choose.
And he chooses Trouble
because he likes the sound the die makes
when it pops inside
20 its plastic bubble. And for days and days,
it is Christmas in November,
games to play when our homework is done,
Monopoly money to count
and checkers to slam down on boards, ants to flip
25 into blue plastic pants,
chess pieces to practice moving until we understand
their power
and when we don't, Roman and I argue
that there's another way to play

14 UNIT 1 • CHILDHOOD

PERSONALIZE FOR LEARNING

Strategic Support

Description Lead students in reviewing how the narrator reacts to staying inside in "brooklyn rain." As a class, reread lines 14–16. Then lead students in reviewing how the narrator reacts to staying inside in "another way." As a class, reread lines 15–29 and discuss what they learn about the narrator from the first poem, and how the second poem gives them a different view of her character. Talk about the specific words and phrases the author uses to indicate joy, such as line 15: "So many games, we don't know/ where to begin playing" and line 21: "it is Christmas in November."

called *Our Way*. But Hope and Dell tell us
that we're too immature to even begin to understand
then bend over the chessboard in silence, each becoming
the next chess champ of the house, depending on the day
and the way the game is played.

35 Sometimes, Roman and I leave Hope and Dell alone
go to another corner of the room and become
what the others call us—*the two youngest*,
playing games we know the rules to
tic-tac-toe and checkers,
40 hangman and connect the dots

but mostly, we lean over their shoulders
as quietly as we can, watching
waiting
wanting to understand
45 how to play another way.

* * *

gifted

Everyone knows my sister
is brilliant. The letters come home folded neatly
inside official-looking envelopes that my sister proudly
hands over to my mother.
5 Odella has achieved
Odella has excelled at
Odella has been recommended to
Odella's outstanding performance in

She is gifted
10 we are told.
And I imagine presents surrounding her.

I am not gifted. When I read, the words **twist**
twirl across the page.
When they settle, it is too late.
15 The class has already moved on.

I want to catch words one day. I want to hold them
then blow gently,
watch them float
right out of my hands.

* * *

NOTES

CLOSE READ
ANNOTATE: In "gifted," mark the words that are repeated in lines 5–7.

QUESTION: Why has the poet chosen to repeat these words?

CONCLUDE: What effect does this repetition have on the reader?

twist (twihst) *v.* wind or spin around one another
twirl (twurl) *v.* turn around and around quickly

© Pearson Education, Inc., or its affiliates. All rights reserved.

from Brown Girl Dreaming **15**

CLOSE READ

As students look for examples of repetition in lines 5–8 of "gifted," remind them to mark phrases that are repeated. You may wish to model the Close Read using the following think-aloud format. Possible responses to questions on the student page are included. You may also want to print copies of the **Close-Read Guide: Nonfiction** or **Close-Read Guide: Poetry** for students to use.

ANNOTATE: As I read the first stanza of "gifted," I notice and highlight the repetition of a phrase in lines 5–7.

QUESTION: I notice that the author finishes the phrase with some accomplishment, for example, "achieved" and "excelled at." The words are repeated to draw attention to what Odella has done.

CONCLUDE: The repetition is rhythmic; it sounds as if the author is repeating what she has heard, just as a child would mimic someone in a mocking voice. The effect of the repetition is to reinforce the idea that the author's sister is brilliant and that her achievements overshadow anything the author has done.

VOCABULARY DEVELOPMENT

Multiple Meanings Tell students that the word *gifted* has two meanings. Discuss the following sentences with students.

1. She was a gifted piano player. (She was very talented.)
2. She gifted him with flowers. (She gave him a gift of flowers.)

Have students reread lines 9–11 of "gifted." Ask students to identify which meaning of *gifted* is meant here, and why the author has alluded to the second meaning of gifted. Discuss how to use context clues and ask students which words in the first stanza are clues to the meaning of *gifted*.

⬤ CLOSE READ ✎

Remind students to look for special treatment of the text that indicates someone is speaking. You may wish to model the Close Read using the following think-aloud format. Possible responses to questions on the student page are included.

ANNOTATE: As I read the first stanza, I notice that the boy is talking and that his words are in italics. Then I see that in the second stanza, the author and her sister are speaking. I look for and mark the words in italics in the second stanza.

QUESTION: When I reread what the author says, it makes me think that maybe she's sad or embarrassed that they don't have a father. It also makes me wonder if she maybe believes what she says. When I read the sister's words, it makes me think she is more mature, maybe a little bossy and critical of the author.

CONCLUDE: I can conclude that when the sister corrects the author and says that she's making up stories, the sister is more sensible and realistic while the author seems immature and not quite understanding of their situation.

NOTES

CLOSE READ
ANNOTATE: Mark words that indicate the exact words of Woodson and her sister in lines 9–23 of "sometimes."

QUESTION: What can you tell about Woodson from these lines? What can you tell about her sister?

CONCLUDE: How does this dialogue help you understand the differences between Woodson and her sister?

shushes (SHUHSH ihz) *v.* tells or signals someone to be quiet

sometimes

There is only one other house on our block
where a father doesn't live. When somebody asks why,
the boy says, *He died.*
The girl looks off, down the block, her thumb
5 slowly rising to her mouth. The boy says,
I was a baby. Says, *She doesn't remember him*
and points to his silent sister.

Sometimes, I lie about my father.
He died, I say, *in a car wreck* or
10 *He fell off a roof* or maybe
He's coming soon.
Next week and
next week and
next week . . . but
15 if my sister's nearby
she shakes her head. Says,
She's making up stories again.
Says,
We don't have a father anymore.
20 Says,
Our grandfather's our father now.
Says,
Sometimes, that's the way things happen.

* * *

uncle robert

Uncle Robert has moved to New York City!

I hear him taking the stairs
two at a time and then
he is at our door, knocking loud until our mother
opens it,
5 curlers in her hair, robe pulled closed, whispering,
It's almost midnight, don't you wake my children!

But we are already awake, all four of us, smiling
and jumping around
my uncle: *What'd you bring me?*

Our mama **shushes** us, says,
10 *It's too late for presents and the like.*
But we want presents and the like.
And she, too, is smiling now, happy to see her
baby brother who lives all the way over
in Far Rockaway where the ocean is right there
if you look out your window.

16 UNIT 1 • CHILDHOOD

© Pearson Education, Inc., or its affiliates. All rights reserved.

CROSS-CURRICULAR PERSPECTIVES

Art Have students interpret "sometimes" or "uncle robert" through artistic expression. Students can create drawings, collages, or graphic designs that represent the ideas that the author is trying to convey in the poem. Remind students that color, as well as images, can help convey the mood, or feeling of the poem and that they may find that certain words or phrases bring to mind images they want to illustrate. As students conduct a gallery walk of the artwork, have them discuss how each artist interpreted the poem. **(Research to Clarify)**

15   Robert opens his hand to reveal a pair of silver earrings,
    says to my sister, *This is a gift for how smart you are.*
    I want
    to be smart like Dell, I want
    someone to hand me silver and gold
20   just because my brain clicks into thinking whenever
    it needs to but
    I am not smart like Dell so I watch her press
      the silver moons into her ears
    I say, *I know a girl ten times smarter than her. She gets*
      diamonds every time she gets a hundred on a test.
      And Robert looks at me, his dark eyes smiling, asks,
      Is that something you made up? Or something real?
    In my own head,
25   it's real as anything.

    In my head
    all kinds of people are doing all kinds of things.
    I want to tell him this, that
    the world we're living in right here in Brownsville isn't
30   the only place. But now my brothers are asking,

    What'd you bring me, and my uncle is pulling gifts
      from his pockets,
    from his leather briefcase, from inside his socks.
      He hands
    my mother a record, a small 45—James Brown,[1]
      who none of us
    like because he screams when he sings. But my mother
      puts it on the record player, turned way down low
      and then even us kids are dancing around—
      Robert showing us the steps he learned
      at the Far Rockaway parties. His feet are magic
35   and we all try to slide across the floor like he does,
    our own feet, again and again,
    betraying us.

    Teach us, Robert! we keep saying. *Teach us!*

             ❊ ❊ ❊

---

1. **James Brown** (1933–2006) American singer and dancer, and founding father of funk
music. He is often referred to as the "Godfather of Soul."

from Brown Girl Dreaming **17**

NOTES

CLOSE READ
ANNOTATE: Mark details in lines 15–23 of "uncle robert" that show what the poet is thinking.

QUESTION: Why might the poet have included these details?

CONCLUDE: What do these details suggest about the poet's character?

 CLOSE READ

Remind students to focus on what the author says and how this reflects what she is thinking. You may wish to model the Close Read using the following think-aloud format. Possible responses to questions on the student page are included.

ANNOTATE: As I read lines 15–23, I notice and highlight what the speaker says she wants, what she believes about herself, and what she says to her uncle. The phrase that begins *I know a girl ten times smarter* is in italics, which tells me that this is something that is said or thought.

QUESTION: I notice that the poet admits that she wishes she would get attention for being smart, as her sister does, but she doesn't believe that she is as smart. Also, she wants to point out to her uncle that there are other people smarter than her sister. This tells me that she is jealous of her sister and insecure about her own intelligence.

CONCLUDE: The details show me that the speaker believes her life would be better if she were "smart like Dell" and explain part of her motivation to cope by making up stories.

© Pearson Education, Inc., or its affiliates. All rights reserved.

DIGITAL PERSPECTIVES

Illuminating the Text Review lines 30-35. Show students a video of James Brown singing and dancing. Ask them if they picture the narrator and her family dancing like James Brown dances in the video. Then have students compare the way James Brown sings to the way the narrator describes his singing. Encourage them to discuss whether the narrator's description helps them better visualize the scene in "uncle robert."

⬤ **CLOSE READ** ✐

Remind students to mark details that refer to things you can touch and to things you can feel or think but that you cannot touch. You may wish to model the Close Read using the following think-aloud format. Possible responses to questions on the student page are included.

ANNOTATE: As I read the poem "wishes," I notice details related to things you can touch, including *swings, sliding boards, hands,* and *eyes.* Details that describe things you cannot touch include *wishes, dream,* and *universe.*

QUESTION: I see that the poet uses different kinds of details to connect feelings and ideas to the physical images.

CONCLUDE: The different details connect the dandelion puffs and the children to the "universe." They show how big even a small moment like this can be to a child.

NOTES

feathery (FEH<u>TH</u> uhr ee) *adj.* light and airy, like the touch of a feather

CLOSE READ
ANNOTATE: Mark details in lines 4-8 of "wishes" that refer to things you can touch. Mark other words that refer to things you can feel or think, but cannot touch.

QUESTION: Why does the poet use these different kinds of details?

CONCLUDE: How do these details help the reader understand what the wishes mean to the children?

---

wishes

When he takes us to the park, Uncle Robert tells us,
If you catch a dandelion puff, you can make a wish.
Anything you want will come true, he says as
we chase the feathery wishes around swings,
5 beneath sliding boards,
until we can hold them in our hands,
close our eyes tight, whisper our dream
then set it floating out into the universe hoping
our uncle is telling the truth,
10 hoping each thing we wish for
will one day come true.

* * *

believing

The stories start like this—

Jack and Jill went up a hill, my uncle sings.
I went up a hill yesterday, I say.
What hill?
5 *In the park.*
What park?
Halsey Park.
Who was with you?
Nobody.
10 *But you're not allowed to go to the park without anyone.*
I just did.
Maybe you dreamed it, my uncle says.
No, I really went.

And my uncle likes the stories I'm making up.

15 *. . . Along came a spider and sat down beside her.*
I got bit by a spider, I say.
When?
The other day.
Where?
20 *Right on my foot.*
Show us.
It's gone now.

But my mother accuses me of lying.
If you lie, she says, *one day you'll steal.*

25 *I won't steal.*
It's hard to understand how one leads to the other,
how stories could ever
make us criminals.

© Pearson Education, Inc., or its affiliates. All rights reserved.

PERSONALIZE FOR LEARNING

English Language Support
Building Background Direct students to lines 2 and 15 in the poem "believing." Tell students that each of these lines is the beginning of a different nursery rhyme or a simple traditional song that small children sing. Point out that the uncle is probably telling the author the nursery rhyme because she is a young child, and that instead of saying the nursery rhyme with her uncle, the author responds with a story. Point out that nursery rhymes usually include a story that is fantastical, much like the stories the author makes up. **ALL LEVELS**

It's hard to understand
30 the way my brain works—so different
from everybody around me.
How each new story
I'm told becomes a thing
that happens,
35 in some other way
to me . . . !

Keep making up stories, my uncle says.
You're lying, my mother says.

Maybe the truth is somewhere in between
40 all that I'm told
and memory.

"another way," "believing," "brooklyn rain," "gifted," "sometimes," "uncle robert," "wishes" and "believing" from *Brown Girl Dreaming* by Jacqueline Woodson, copyright © 2014 by Jacqueline Woodson. Used by permission of Nancy Paulsen Books, an imprint of Penguin Young Readers Group, a division of Penguin Random House LLC.

NOTES

CLOSE READ

ANNOTATE: In lines 23–38 of "believing," mark words that show how the poet's mother reacts to her stories. Then, mark words that show how her uncle reacts.

QUESTION: Why does the poet include these different reactions?

CONCLUDE: How does this contrast help the reader better understand the poet's struggle?

Comprehension Check

Complete the following items after you finish your first read.

1. In "brooklyn rain," what does Woodson's mother say?

2. In "gifted," what does the poet hope she will one day be able to do with words?

3. In "uncle robert," what do Woodson and her siblings want their uncle to teach them?

4. 📓 **Notebook** Write a mini-summary (one or two sentences) of each poem in the excerpt from *Brown Girl Dreaming*.

- -

RESEARCH

Research to Clarify Choose at least one unfamiliar detail from the excerpt. Briefly research that detail. In what way does the information you learned help you better understand an aspect of the memoir?

from Brown Girl Dreaming **19**

© Pearson Education, Inc., or its affiliates. All rights reserved.

🔴 **CLOSE READ**

Remind students that they should look for special treatment of the text to indicate that the mother and the uncle are speaking. Model the Close Read using the following think-aloud format.

ANNOTATE: As I read the poem "believing," I mark lines in italics in lines 23–38 that indicate that the mother and uncle are speaking. I notice in line 25 that the author herself is speaking in response to what her mother says.

QUESTION: The mother discourages the author's stories by telling her she's lying and will become a criminal, but the uncle thinks she should continue making up stories. He encourages her.

CONCLUDE: The poet must decide whether to listen to her uncle, who encourages her storytelling, or her mother, who discourages it.

Comprehension Check

Possible Responses:

1. The author's mother says, "Stay inside today. It's raining."
2. She hopes she will be able to catch and control them and then let them go.
3. They want him to teach them the dance steps.
4. **brooklyn rain:** In Greenville, the narrator got to play outside when it rained. In Brooklyn, she has to stay inside and watch the rain through the window.

another way: The narrator and Roman, the youngest siblings, do not understand the rules of all the games their mother brought home. They either try to make up their own rules, play easier games on their own, or watch their older siblings play the harder games.
gifted: The narrator wishes she was gifted like her sister. She has trouble with reading.
sometimes: When people ask the narrator about her father, she sometimes lies, telling them that her father died or that he'll be coming home soon.
uncle robert: Uncle Robert moves to New York City and brings gifts for the narrator's family.
wishes: Uncle Robert takes the children to a park and tells them that if they catch a dandelion puff, they can make a wish.
believing: Uncle Robert sings nursery rhymes to the narrator, and she makes up stories about the events in the rhymes happening to her.

Research to Clarify If students struggle to come up with a detail to research, suggest that they focus on one of the following topics: Brooklyn, Greenville, dyslexia, the rules of chess.

Jump Start

CLOSE READ Have students close read the excerpt from *Brown Girl Dreaming*. Ask students why they think the author gave this title to her **memoir,** or nonfiction book about her life. Have them discuss what she does in the poem that indicates she is "dreaming." Point out that dreaming can refer to daydreams as well as to aspirations. Ask students what kind of dreaming Jacqueline Woodson does in her poems.

Close Read the Text ✐

Walk students through the annotation model. Encourage them to complete items 2 and 3 on their own. Review and discuss the sections students have marked. If needed, continue to model close reading by using the Annotation Highlights in the Interactive Teacher's Edition.

Analyze the Text

Possible responses:

1. (a) In lines 12–13 in "brooklyn rain," she says "Already there are stories / in my head." In "gifted," she says, "When I read, the words twist/ twirl across the page. / When they settle, it is too late." In "sometimes," she says, "Sometimes I lie about my father." **DOK 2** (b) The first example suggests that Woodson is imaginative, the second suggests that she struggles with reading, and the third suggests that she is embarrassed that her father is gone. **DOK 3**

2. She likes to make up stories because she is dissatisfied with her life and she therefore likes to imagine all the different places she could be and the different lives she could lead. **DOK 3**

3. No, it's not. Lots of people make up stories, and they don't steal. All writers make up stories, or "lie," as the narrator's mother puts it. There's no reason to think that someone who likes to make up stories would necessarily steal. **DOK 3**

4. This memoir explores many challenges in Woodson's childhood, such as having parents who are separated, trying to find outlets for one's creativity, moving to a new city, and sibling rivalry and jealousy. **DOK 3**

FORMATIVE ASSESSMENT
Analyze the Text

• **If** students fail to cite evidence, **then** remind them to support their ideas with specific information.

• **If** students struggle to speculate why Woodson likes to make up stories, **then** discuss when she makes up stories and what the reactions are of those around her.

 MAKING MEANING

from BROWN GIRL DREAMING

Close Read the Text

1. This model, from lines 1–6 of "brooklyn rain," shows two sample annotations, along with questions and conclusions. Close read the passage, and find another detail to annotate. Then, write a question and your conclusion.

Close Read
ANNOTATE • QUESTION • CONCLUDE

> **ANNOTATE:** These phrases appeal to the senses of smell and touch.
>
> **QUESTION:** Why does Woodson use language that appeals to the senses?
>
> **CONCLUDE:** These phrases create images for readers of how Woodson experienced the rain in Greenville.

> **ANNOTATE:** The word *No* repeats.
>
> **QUESTION:** Why does Woodson repeat the word *No*?
>
> **CONCLUDE:** The repetition emphasizes the ways in which Woodson's life in Brooklyn is different from her life in Greenville.

> The rain here is different than the way/it rains in Greenville. No sweet smell of honeysuckle./No soft squish of pine. No slip and slide through grass./Just mama saying, *Stay inside today. It's raining,/*and me at the window. Nothing to do but/watch . . .

2. For more practice, go back into the text, and complete the close-read notes.

3. Revisit a section of the text you found important during your first read. Read this section closely, and **annotate** what you notice. Ask yourself **questions** such as "Why did the author make this choice?" What can you **conclude**?

Analyze the Text

CITE TEXTUAL EVIDENCE to support your answers.

📓 **Notebook** Respond to these questions.

1. (a) List three details from the poems that connect to an aspect of Woodson's personality. (b) **Make Inferences** What do these details suggest about Woodson as a child?

2. **Speculate** Why do you think Woodson likes to make up stories so much?

3. **Make a Judgment** Woodson's mother worries that if Woodson lies, one day she will steal. Do you think this is a reasonable concern? Explain.

4. **Essential Question:** *What are some of the challenges and triumphs of growing up?* What have you learned about the challenges and triumphs of growing up from reading this selection?

🔧 **Tool Kit**
Close-Read Guide and Model Annotation

☰ **STANDARDS**

Reading Literature
• Analyze how a particular sentence, chapter, scene, or stanza fits into the overall structure of a text and contributes to the development of the theme, setting, or plot.
• Explain how an author develops the point of view of the narrator or speaker in a text.

Reading Informational Text
• Analyze how a particular sentence, paragraph, chapter, or section fits into the overall structure of a text and contributes to the development of the ideas.
• Determine an author's point of view or purpose in a text and explain how it is conveyed in the text.

© Pearson Education, Inc., or its affiliates. All rights reserved.

DIGITAL PERSPECTIVES

Enriching the Text To give students a better understanding of how Jacqueline Woodson writes stories and develops characters, show them an interview with the author in which she addresses the writing process. Be sure to preview the interview before sharing it with the class.

What does Woodson think makes a good story? How does she develop her characters? Ask students what they think of Woodson based on the interview. Is she like they imagined? What have they learned about the writing process from the interview?

Discuss why Woodson thinks that reading is an essential part of writing and how she came to determine that her stories were important and should be told.

Analyze Craft and Structure

Memoir and Poetry In a **memoir,** an author tells a true story of an important time in his or her life. Most memoirs are written in **first-person point of view,** or from the author's perspective. The author tells what happened and what he or she thought and felt about it. Memoirs are usually written in **prose,** or complete sentences and paragraphs. Most also use dialogue to show how people speak and what they are like. In this memoir, Jacqueline Woodson takes a different approach. Instead of prose, she tells her story in a series of poems that include these elements:

- **stanzas,** or sections, rather than paragraphs
- complete sentences that are broken up into separate lines
- language that breaks certain rules— for example, Woodson sometimes uses sentence fragments and nonstandard capitalization (see the sentence fragment in lines 32–36 of "believing")

Woodson's choice to tell her story through poems affects how readers understand it. It allows Woodson to emphasize certain words, phrases, and ideas. She also uses storytelling elements, such as dialogue. This combination of poetry and storytelling helps Woodson immerse readers even more deeply into her childhood world.

Practice

CITE TEXTUAL EVIDENCE
to support your answers.

Notebook Respond to these questions.

1. (a) Identify one example of a private thought or feeling Woodson shares in her memoir. (b) Explain how the use of first-person point of view allows her to share this detail.

2. (a) Identify the sentence fragments in lines 2–3 of "brooklyn rain." (b) Explain how these fragments help to create a vivid picture of the rain in Greenville.

3. (a) In lines 4–11 of "brooklyn rain," what word appears on its own line three times? (b) Read the lines aloud. Why do you think Woodson chose to set this word apart in this way?

4. (a) In line 23 of "sometimes," Woodson's sister says "Sometimes, that's the way things happen." What does this tell you about her sister's feelings about life? (b) How might the stories of Woodson's childhood be different if they were told from her sister's point of view?

from Brown Girl Dreaming **21**

© Pearson Education, Inc., or its affiliates. All rights reserved.

PERSONALIZE FOR LEARNING

Strategic Support

Point of View If students struggle to understand how point of view affects the way a story is told, ask them to role-play a conversation that might have happened, based on the poem "believing."

Have pairs of students play the narrator and her mother, explaining the narrator's storytelling and the reaction to it from each perspective. Then ask students to discuss whether they felt differently about the narrator or her mother after the exercise.

Analyze Craft and Structure

Memoir and Poetry Discuss with students how reading a memoir in verse may affect the way readers feel about the narrator and the events in the story. Ask them to consider if reading and understanding the thoughts and feelings of a narrator as poetry makes the narrator's story more compelling, even more human. In contrast, ask them to think about how the stories in each poem would be different if they had been written in prose. Students should recognize that poetry allows the reader to gain insight about specific moments and the narrator's feelings. For more support, **see Analyze Craft and Structure: Memoir and Poetry.**

Practice

Possible responses:

1. (a) In "brooklyn rain," lines 12 and 13, the poet writes, "Already there are stories / in my head . . . . (b) First-person point of view allows the poet to share her thoughts directly with the reader.

2. (a)"No sweet smell of honeysuckle"; "No soft squish of pine"; and "No slip and slide through grass." (b) The fragments convey a vivid sensory description of the rain in Greenville, accentuated by alliteration.

3. (a) *watch* (b) Woodson may have chosen to set the word on its own line so that the reader would slow down while reading about the things the narrator describes seeing.

4. (a) This line suggests that the narrator's sister possibly has a more mature outlook than the narrator. She understands that parents sometimes split up, and that it doesn't reflect badly on the children, nor is it something to be ashamed of. (b) The stories would focus on the sister's thoughts and feelings. The reader wouldn't get to know about this narrator's inner life. She might just be presented as somebody's annoying and childish little sister.

FORMATIVE ASSESSMENT

Analyze Craft and Structure

- **If** students are unable to identify the elements of the excerpt that are typical of a memoir, **then** have them look for the pronouns *I* and *me* that indicate first-person point of view.

- **If** students are unable to understand how the memoir can be categorized as poetry, **then** have them look for repeated words and nonstandard use of language, capitalization, and punctuation. For Reteach and Practice, see **Analyze Craft and Structure: Memoir and Poetry (RP).**

Concept Vocabulary

Why These Words?

Possible responses:

1. The concept vocabulary allows the reader to vividly imagine what the poet is seeing, smelling, hearing, touching, or tasting.

2. slip (line 3 of "brooklyn rain"), slide (line 3 of "brooklyn rain"), whispering (line 5 of "uncle robert")

Practice

Possible responses:

1. There is no pine here. I wish I was someplace far away. It is hard for me to follow along with the words when I try to read. Our mother tells us to be quiet. We run after the dandelion puffs.

2. The original sentences are stronger. Taking away the figurative language and imagery makes the sentences less fun to read. Rewriting the sentences made me think about the precise meaning of the vocabulary words.

Word Network

Possible words: *immature, achieved, memory*

Word Study

For more support, see **Concept Vocabulary and Word Study.** 📄

Possible responses

1. My shoes *squish* on the grass. The girl was *humming* a song. The teacher *shushes* a loud student.

2. *crash, hiss, boom, fizzle, bang, cluck, neigh*

FORMATIVE ASSESSMENT

Concept Vocabulary

If students fail to see the connection between the words, **then** have them make a three-column chart with columns labeled "sight," "sound," and "touch."

Word Study

If students don't understand the definition of onomatopoeia, **then** have them create a list of animal sounds, pointing out that each sound is an example of onomatopoeia. For Reteach and Practice, see **Word Study: Onomatopoeia (RP).** 📄

from BROWN GIRL DREAMING

🔗 WORD NETWORK

Add words related to childhood from the text to your Word Network.

▤ STANDARDS

Reading Literature
Determine the meaning of words and phrases as they are used in a text, including figurative and connotative meanings; analyze the impact of a specific word choice on meaning and tone.

Language
• Demonstrate command of the conventions of standard English capitalization, punctuation, and spelling when writing.
• Use knowledge of language and its conventions when writing, speaking, reading, or listening.
• Demonstrate understanding of figurative language, word relationships, and nuances in word meanings.

🖥 LANGUAGE DEVELOPMENT

Concept Vocabulary

squish	twist	shushes
humming	twirl	feathery

Why These Words? These concept words are all examples of **sensory language**, or words that appeal to the five senses: touch, sight, smell, hearing, and taste. In *Brown Girl Dreaming,* Woodson uses these sensory words to create **imagery**, or vivid word pictures. Imagery helps readers understand ideas in a deeper way than plain explanations might allow. For example, the words *twist* and *twirl* help the reader understand Woodson's difficulty with reading: "the words twist / twirl across the page."

1. How does the concept vocabulary sharpen the reader's understanding of Woodson's feelings?

2. What other words in the selection are examples of sensory language?

Practice

📝 **Notebook** The concept vocabulary words appear in *Brown Girl Dreaming.*

1. Find each concept vocabulary word in the text, and write down the sentence in which it appears. Then, rewrite each sentence without using any sensory language. Make sure the sentence has the same basic meaning. For example, "When I read, the words twist / twirl across the page" might become "When I read, I have trouble following the words."

2. How did your changes affect the meaning of the sentences? Did removing the sensory language improve your understanding of the concept vocabulary? If so, how?

Word Study

📝 **Notebook Onomatopoeia** The concept vocabulary words *squish, humming,* and *shushes* are examples of **onomatopoeia,** or words that imitate the sounds they mean. Animal sounds—such as *woof, moo,* and *meow*—are other examples of onomatopoeia.

1. Use each onomatopoeic concept vocabulary word in a sentence of your own.

2. Jot down other examples of onomatopoeia that you have come across in your own experience or in the selection.

© Pearson Education, Inc., or its affiliates. All rights reserved.

AUTHOR'S PERSPECTIVE Elfrieda Hiebert, Ph.D.

Author's Word Choice In a text, authors may or may not explicitly state the underlying theme. When the theme of a text is left unstated, readers will have to put together clues in the text to infer the author's overarching message. Among the most useful clues are the author's choice of words, and understanding how vocabulary functions in this way can help students identify the selection's theme.

Teachers can convey the power of vocabulary to convey theme by selecting a narrative from Unit 1 and guiding students to find words and phrases that are part of a network. The words should be related because of their denotations, connotations, or imagery, for example. Model for students how to choose words that belong in a network. For example, if the passage describes cooking, students

can select words from the passage as *warm, clean, fragrant,* and *sweetness.* Be sure the list is narrowly focused and students can explain the relationship among the words and why they chose each word. Then have students explore the effect of the words and explain how they convey the author's theme and make the story richer.

Conventions

Common, Proper, and Possessive Nouns A **noun** names a person, a place, a thing, or an idea. Here are several types of nouns:

- A **common noun** names any one of a class of people, places, things, or ideas. Common nouns are not capitalized.

- A **proper noun** names a specific person, place, thing, or idea. Proper nouns are capitalized. However, a poet may sometimes choose not to capitalize a proper noun, for effect or for style. For example, Jacqueline Woodson doesn't capitalize *brooklyn*, even though it is the name of a specific place.

- A **possessive noun** shows ownership. Possessive nouns function as adjectives by modifying a noun or pronoun in a sentence. Most singular possessive nouns end in an apostrophe and the letter *s* (*'s*). An example is *sister's*. Most plural possessive nouns end in the letter *s* and an apostrophe (*s'*). An example is *sisters'*.

The chart shows examples of common, proper, and possessive nouns from the excerpt from *Brown Girl Dreaming*.

COMMON NOUNS	PROPER NOUNS	POSSESSIVE NOUNS
And my uncle likes the stories I'm making up. ("believing," line 14)	*. . . Robert showing us the steps he learned / at the Far Rockaway parties.* ("uncle robert," lines 33–34)	*. . . stories in my head / take me back there, set me down in Daddy's garden. . . .* ("brooklyn rain," lines 23–24)

Read It

1. In each sentence, mark proper nouns that should be capitalized. Add an apostrophe to possessive nouns where needed.

   a. hopes home in south carolina is very different from ericas home in new york.

   b. jacquelines plans for the weekend include hiking in smith park and calling her grandmother in arizona.

   c. uncle roberts silly songs and dance lessons make us smile and laugh.

2. Reread "brooklyn rain." Then, mark at least one common noun, one proper noun, and one possessive noun in the poem.

Write It

Notebook Write a paragraph about the similarities and the differences between Woodson and her sister Odella. Include at least two proper nouns and one possessive noun. Label all common nouns.

from Brown Girl Dreaming **23**

Conventions

Common, Proper, and Possessive Nouns Discuss the different types of nouns with students. As you review examples of each type of noun, explain that singular common nouns are usually preceded by an article (*a, an, the*) and that plural common nouns may also be preceded by an article (for example, *the cities*). Then point out that possessive nouns may also be proper nouns (for example, *Julio's bike*). In this case, the proper noun must be capitalized and contain an apostrophe. For more support, see **Conventions: Common, Proper, and Possessive Nouns.**

Read It

1. (a) hope's home in south carolina is very different from erica's home in new york.
   (b) jacqueline's plans for the weekend include hiking in smith park and calling her grandmother in arizona.
   (c) uncle robert's silly songs and dance lessons make us smile and laugh.

2. **Possible response:** common noun: rain; proper noun: Greenville; possessive noun: Daddy's

Write It

Possible response: Like her sister Odella, Jacqueline is smart. But whereas Odella is traditionally smart, doing well in school, Jacqueline is creative and imaginative. She does not do as well in school as Odella. She also tends to get in trouble more than Odella, partly because of her storytelling. Jacqueline's made-up stories upset their mother, whereas Odella's good grades make their mother happy.

FORMATIVE ASSESSMENT

Conventions

- **If** students can't locate nouns, **then** remind them to look for any word that stands for a person, place, thing, or idea.

- **If** students can't distinguish between types of nouns, **then** remind them to look for articles, which indicate common nouns, capital letters, which often indicate proper nouns, and apostrophes, which often indicate possessive nouns.

For Reteach and Practice, see **Conventions: Common, Proper, and Possessive Nouns (RP).**

PERSONALIZE FOR LEARNING

English Language Support

Parts of Speech Review the definitions of the different types of nouns. Begin a list of each type of noun for students, then have them add to the list, encouraging them to look through books and magazines, identifying the nouns in the pictures or text to add to their list. Remind them to look for clues that help them identify the type of noun, for example, indefinite pronouns that indicate common nouns, capital letters that indicate proper nouns, and apostrophes that indicate possessive nouns. **ALL LEVELS**

© Pearson Education, Inc., or its affiliates. All rights reserved.

Writing to Sources

Explain to students that when they write a poem, they should begin by planning their narrative. Have them think about how they will describe their experience by brainstorming descriptive words and phrases for the setting, the people involved in the experience, and what the experience felt like. They may want to use a chart like this one to record their ideas:

Descriptive Words and Phrases
Setting:
People:
How It Felt:

Point out that poetry generally uses fewer words than prose but that each word or phrase is carefully chosen to paint a colorful picture or evoke an emotion in the reader. Suggest that students review the words and phrases they came up with and choose only the most powerful sensory words to include in their poem. For more support, see **Writing to Sources: Poem.** 📄

Reflect on Your Writing

1. Responses will vary. If students need support, ask them to think about which part of the assignment took the longest.

2. Responses will vary. Be sure that students make connections between the techniques they used and the effectiveness of their poem.

3. Responses will vary. Have students list specific examples of words they have chosen that add power to their poem.

FORMATIVE ASSESSMENT

Writing to Sources

If students struggle to use descriptive language in their poems, **then** have them review "brooklyn rain" and identify the way the author uses repetition and onomatopoeia to describe the scene. For Reteach and Practice, see **Writing to Sources: Poem (RP).** 📄

24   UNIT 1 • CHILDHOOD

📷 EFFECTIVE EXPRESSION

from BROWN GIRL DREAMING

Writing to Sources

In *Brown Girl Dreaming,* Jacqueline Woodson tells stories in poem form about specific moments from her childhood. In each poem, she also shares her thoughts and feelings about the moment she describes. The separate poems work together to tell the story of Woodson's childhood.

> **Assignment**
> Write a brief **poem** in which you use Woodson's memoir as inspiration. Follow these steps:
>
> • Choose a single moment on which to focus. It can be something small or seemingly unimportant. For example, you might write about what you see from your window in the morning, or about eating lunch at school. Then, write a regular prose paragraph in which you describe the moment. Include details that show what the moment looked and felt like.
>
> • Change your paragraph into a poem by applying elements of poetry such as the ones Woodson uses. For example, break up sentences to make poetic lines. Consider repeating important words or setting them on their own lines. You may even play with incomplete sentences or fragments. Try to make the moment you described in your paragraph even more vivid as a poem.
>
> • Once your poem is organized, consider adding dialogue or more descriptive details. Alternatively, you may need to cut some details. Work to make your poem capture the moment and make it fresh and alive for readers.

Vocabulary Connection Consider using several of the concept vocabulary words in your writing.

squish	twist	shushes
humming	twirl	feathery

STANDARDS
Writing
• Write narratives to develop real or imagined experiences or events using effective technique, relevant descriptive details, and well-structured event sequences.
  b. Use narrative techniques, such as dialogue, pacing, and description, to develop experiences, events, and/or characters.
  d. Use precise words and phrases, relevant descriptive details, and sensory language to convey experiences and events.
• Draw evidence from literary or informational texts to support analysis, reflection, and research.
  a. Apply *grade 6 Reading standards* to literature.

Reflect on Your Writing

After you have written your poem, answer the following questions.

1. What was the most challenging part of the assignment?

2. What poetic and narrative techniques did you use in your writing? How did they help you bring your ideas to life?

3. **Why These Words?** The words you choose make a difference in your writing. Which words did you choose to create a vivid picture for your readers?

24 UNIT 1 • CHILDHOOD

© Pearson Education, Inc., or its affiliates. All rights reserved.

PERSONALIZE FOR LEARNING

English Language Support

Writing a Poem Have students write 3 to 5 descriptive words that describe their lives, character traits, or dreams. Encourage students to choose words that are interesting and vivid. **EMERGING**

Have students write a short poem that reveals something about their lives, experiences, or personalities. Remind students that poems are meant to convey information in non-standard ways. **EXPANDING**

Have students write a poem about themselves, choosing words that are rhythmic and vivid, and that convey information in meaningful or unusual ways. **BRIDGING**

An expanded **English Language Support Lesson** on Poetic Elements is available in the Interactive Teacher's Edition. 📄

Speaking and Listening

Assignment

In the last three lines of the excerpt, Woodson questions the differences between the ideas in her head and reality: *"Maybe the truth is somewhere in between / all that I'm told / and memory."* Woodson also discusses how her mother often says she is lying. In telling stories, do you think Woodson is lying or just using her imagination? Is there a point at which the use of imagination becomes a lie? Take a position on these questions, and participate in a brief **partner discussion** in which you express your views. Use examples from the text and from your own experience to support your ideas. After you and your partner talk, regroup with the class and share highlights of your discussion.

1. **Prepare for the Discussion** Decide whether you think Woodson's use of imagination as a child goes so far it could be considered lying. Then, determine why you feel this way. Note examples from the text and your own experience to support your reasons.

2. **Discuss With Your Partner** Use your notes as you and your partner talk about the issue. Consider the following questions:

   - Do you and your partner agree on your basic position?
   - If so, do you have similar or different reasons and examples that support your position?
   - If not, do the reasons and examples your partner offers change your opinion?

3. **Discuss With Your Class** Begin the class discussion by having each set of partners take turns offering a different idea about Woodson's use of imagination. Do not repeat an idea that was already introduced by your classmates; try to come up with a new idea even if it was not the one you had originally planned on sharing. Once each set of partners has contributed, discuss the ways in which your ideas are similar and different.

4. **Reflect on the Discussion** After both the partner and group discussions, consider how talking about ideas helped you better understand your own thinking. Did your initial position change as a result of the discussions? Why or why not?

© Pearson Education, Inc., or its affiliates. All rights reserved.

EVIDENCE LOG

Before moving on to a new selection, go to your Evidence Log, and record what you learned from *Brown Girl Dreaming*.

STANDARDS

Speaking and Listening
Engage effectively in a range of collaborative discussions with diverse partners on *grade 6 topics, texts, and issues,* building on others' ideas and expressing their own clearly.

a. Come to discussions prepared, having read or studied required material; explicitly draw on that preparation by referring to evidence on the topic, text, or issue to probe and reflect on ideas under discussion.
b. Follow rules for collegial discussions, set specific goals and deadlines, and define individual roles as needed.
c. Pose and respond to specific questions with elaboration and detail by making comments that contribute to the topic, text, or issue under discussion.
d. Review the key ideas expressed and demonstrate understanding of multiple perspectives through reflection and paraphrasing.

from Brown Girl Dreaming **25**

Speaking and Listening

1. **Prepare for the Discussion** You may wish to guide students in choosing a position by asking them how they define lying and what they thought of the author when they first read about her storytelling.

2. **Discuss With Your Partner** Tell students that they will work individually to come up with reasons to support their argument. Point out that the evidence can refer to what the author herself says about her storytelling as well as to what Uncle Robert and the author's mother say about it. After collecting their evidence, they can use their notes in their discussion with their partner.

3. **Discuss With Your Class** Encourage partners to allow each speaker the opportunity to finish, but remind them of any time constraints. Point out that speakers should refer to their talking points when debating.

4. **Reflect on the Discussion** Encourage students to make supportive comments about different sets of partners' contributions and to note the most persuasive points in the opposing argument. For more support, see **Speaking and Listening: Partner Discussion.**

Evidence Log Support students in completing their Evidence Log. This paced activity will help prepare them for the Performance-Based Assessment at the end of the unit.

FORMATIVE ASSESSMENT

Speaking and Listening

- **If** students struggle to identify evidence from the text, **then** point out that they should focus on the poems "sometimes," "uncle robert," and "believing."

- **If** students struggle with the partner discussion format, **then** allow each student two or three minutes to present his or her argument, and allow each partner the same amount of time to rebut the opposing point of view.

For Reteach and Practice, see **Speaking and Listening: Partner Discussion (RP).**

Selection Test

Administer the "*from* Brown Girl Dreaming" Selection Test, which is available in both print and digital formats online in Assessments.

WriteNow Express and Reflect

Describe Students have participated in a discussion about whether Woodson's storytelling was lying or just imaginative thinking. Now have them consider how Woodson's description of truth (*"Maybe the truth is somewhere in between / all that I'm told / and memory"*) may relate to their own memories. Have students write about a time when their memory of an event was not quite the way others remembered it. Ask them to explain why they think they remembered the event as they did and whether or not, like Woodson, the truth of the event was somewhere between what they were told and their own memory of the event.

Gallery of *Calvin and Hobbes* Comics

🔊 AUDIO SUMMARIES

Audio summaries of the Gallery of *Calvin and Hobbes* Comics are available online in both English and Spanish in the Interactive Teacher's Edition or Unit Resources. Assigning these summaries prior to reading the selection may help students build additional background knowledge and set a context for their first read.

Summary

This media selection consists of three *Calvin and Hobbes* comic strips by Bill Watterson. The main characters are Calvin, a six-year-old boy, and Hobbes, a stuffed tiger who is Calvin's best friend. In the first two of these strips, Calvin and Hobbes accidentally terrify each other on a campout, and they get into a dispute over feelings—the kind of friendly argument common in some friendships. In the third strip, Calvin has built an army of snowmen that block his father's road to work.

Insight

These comic strips provide entertaining, accessible insight into common types of childhood experiences—such as facing fear, dealing with unwanted feelings, and having disputes with parents or guardians—that are part of growing up. At the same time, they portray close friendship, love, and the determination to do something desirable. The emotional depth of Watterson's comics may explain why their popularity endures.

ESSENTIAL QUESTION:
What are some of the challenges and triumphs of growing up?

Connection to Essential Question

This selection gives dramatized examples of some common problems and joys of childhood. While most kids probably haven't built dozens of snowmen, the emotional tone of the situations shown is easily recognizable.

WHOLE-CLASS LEARNING PERFORMANCE TASK
When did you have to use your imagination to find another way to do something?

Connection to Performance Tasks

Whole-Class Learning Performance Task
Calvin's vivid imagination brings him both joy and trouble. With Hobbes, he has a friend who can help him do things in a unique way.

UNIT PERFORMANCE-BASED ASSESSMENT
When did a challenge lead to a triumph?

Unit Performance-Based Assessment
Calvin's imagination can sometimes cause problems for him. However, it also gives him Hobbes, which may lead him to triumph.

LESSON RESOURCES

	Making Meaning	Effective Expression
Lesson	**First Review** **Close Review** **Analyze the Media**	**Media Vocabulary** **Research**
Instructional Standards	**RL.10** By the end of the year, read and comprehend literature . . . **L.6** Acquire and use accurately grade-appropriate general academic and domain-specific words and phrases . . . **RL.1** Cite textual evidence to support analysis . . .	**W.7** Conduct short research projects . . . **SL.1** Engage effectively in a range of collaborative discussions . . . **SL.1.a** Come to discussions prepared . . . **SL.1.c** Pose and respond to specific questions . . . **SL.1.d** Review the key ideas expressed . . . **SL.2** Interpret information presented in diverse media and formats . . .

STUDENT RESOURCES

Available online in the Interactive Student Edition or Unit Resources	Selection Audio First-Review Guide: Media: Art and Photography Close-Review Guide: Media: Art and Photography	Evidence Log

TEACHER RESOURCES

Selection Resources Available online in the Interactive Teacher's Edition or Unit Resources	Audio Summaries Media Vocabulary	Research: Class Discussion
My Resources	A Unit 1 Answer Key is available online and in the Interactive Teacher's Edition.	

Media Complexity Rubric: Gallery of Calvin and Hobbes Comics

Qualitative Measures

Format and Length Three comic strips with speech bubbles and titles

Quantitative Measures

Knowledge Demands ①—**❷**—③—④—⑤	Some previous familiarity with Calvin and Hobbes as characters is helpful in order to fully appreciate the characters in the cartoons.
Structure **❶**—②—③—④—⑤	Traditional and familiar comic format with graphics in one or more frames and speech bubbles makes it very easy for readers of any age to grasp.
Language Conventionality and Clarity **❶**—②—③—④—⑤	Speech bubbles have very simple conversational language (phrases and questions) and basic vocabulary. The comic strip includes one sign abbreviation for crossing (*Xing*), and the language corresponds to the visuals.
Levels of Meaning/Purpose ①—②—**❸**—④—⑤	The cartoons use ironic humor, subtle meaning, and meaning that must be inferred from knowledge of the characters, such as knowing that the name Calvin refers to a child in the third cartoon.

Jump Start

FIRST REVIEW Prior to students' first review, engage them in a discussion about childhood stuffed animals and imaginary friends to help them make connections between the text and their own experiences.

Gallery of *Calvin and Hobbes* Comics 🔊 🖨

Who are Calvin and Hobbes? How does Calvin use his imagination? Is this comic strip an accurate representation of childhood? Modeling questions such as these will help students connect to *Calvin and Hobbes* and to the Whole-Class Performance Task assignment. Selection audio and print capability for the selection are available in the Interactive Teacher's Edition.

Media Vocabulary

Encourage students to discuss the media vocabulary. Have they seen the terms in texts before? Do they use any of them in their speech and writing?

Point out that students may have seen these words in other contexts, but that they have different and specific meanings when referring to comic strips. A panel, for instance, can refer to a group of people gathered for a discussion, or a portion of a surface. When referring to comic strips, *panel* refers specifically to an individual frame of a comic.

⬤ FIRST REVIEW

As they review, students should perform the steps of the first review:

LOOK: Students should focus on the setting, characters, and the basic actions depicted in the panels to ensure they understand what is happening.

NOTE: Students should mark any panels or speech bubbles they wish to revisit during their close review.

CONNECT: Students should increase their understanding by connecting the events depicted in the comic to their own personal imaginative childhood experiences.

RESPOND: Students will answer questions and write a summary to demonstrate their understanding.

Point out to students that while they will always complete the Respond step at the end of the first review, the other steps will probably happen concurrently. You may wish to print copies of the **First-Review Guide: Media: Art and Photography** for students to use. 🖨

About the Artist

The cartoonist **Bill Watterson** (b. 1958) is the creator of the popular *Calvin and Hobbes* comic strip and a two-time recipient of the Reuben Award for Outstanding Cartoonist of the Year. He graduated from Kenyon College in Ohio, and he had his first *Calvin and Hobbes* strip published at the age of twenty-seven. Watterson fought against the commercialization and merchandising of his comics.

Gallery of *Calvin and Hobbes* Comics

Media Vocabulary

The following words will be useful to you as you analyze, discuss, and write about the comic strips.

panel: individual frame of a comic, depicting a single moment	• Panels work together to tell a story. • Panels cannot show everything that happens, so readers must use their imaginations to fill in the blanks.
encapsulation: choice of important scenes to display in each panel	• The layout of the scenes influences the readers' interpretations. • Authors and cartoonists can use size and shape to give more or less weight, or importance, to scenes.
speech balloon: display of what a character is speaking or thinking	• The size, shape, and color of the speech balloon can show the emotion of the speaker. • Speech balloons can also show emotion or meaning through the use of punctuation marks.

First Review MEDIA: ART AND PHOTOGRAPHY

Apply these strategies as you conduct your first review. You will have an opportunity to complete a close review after your first review.

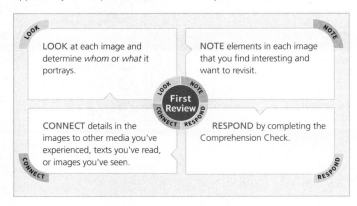

LOOK at each image and determine *whom* or *what* it portrays.

NOTE elements in each image that you find interesting and want to revisit.

CONNECT details in the images to other media you've experienced, texts you've read, or images you've seen.

RESPOND by completing the Comprehension Check.

☰ STANDARDS

Reading Literature
By the end of the year, read and comprehend literature, including stories, dramas, and poems, in the grades 6–8 text complexity band proficiently, with scaffolding as needed at the high end of the range.

Language
Acquire and use accurately grade-appropriate general academic and domain-specific words and phrases; gather vocabulary knowledge when considering a word or phrase important to comprehension or expression.

© Pearson Education, Inc., or its affiliates. All rights reserved.

DIGITAL PERSPECTIVES

Enriching the Text *Dear Mr. Watterson* is a 2013 documentary that follows the career of Bill Watterson and the enduring influence of *Calvin and Hobbes*. After students complete their close read, show clips from the documentary. Engage students in a discussion about how the interviews in the documentary add to their understanding of the comic. Preview all clips before showing them in class.

Gallery of *Calvin and Hobbes* Comics

Bill Watterson

BACKGROUND

Calvin and Hobbes was a highly popular comic strip that ran from 1985 to 1995. It follows the adventures of Calvin, a clever six-year-old with a wild imagination, and his stuffed tiger and imaginary friend, Hobbes. *Calvin and Hobbes* has appeared in thousands of newspapers worldwide and has attracted fans of all ages.

SCAN FOR MULTIMEDIA

NOTES

© Pearson Education, Inc., or its affiliates. All rights reserved.

Gallery of *Calvin and Hobbes* Comics **27**

⬤ CLOSER REVIEW

Interpret Images ⊘

Students may have noted the photograph of Bill Watterson during their first review. Use this photograph to help students understand the process of creating a comic strip. Encourage them to talk about what they noted. You may want to model a close review with the class based on the notes below.

NOTE: Have students note the details in the photograph that reveal what it might be like to work as a comic strip creator, or have students participate while you note them.

QUESTION: Guide students to consider what these details might tell them. Ask how the photograph might help readers to better understand Calvin and Hobbes, Bill Watterson, or the process of creating comics.

Possible response: Bill Watterson is shown sitting at a desk in what is probably a quiet room in his house. He also has two rulers on his desk. It looks like creating comic strips requires a lot of attention to detail. Watterson is smiling, so he probably enjoyed creating the comic strip.

CONCLUDE: Help students to formulate conclusions about the importance of these details in the photograph. Ask students why the photographer might have included these details. What does the photograph tell you about the comic strip?

Possible response: The photograph shows the contrast between the creator of the comic strip (an adult working hard at a desk) and the subject of the comic (a child engaging in imaginative play). Watterson's apparent happiness might suggest that he enjoys reliving happy childhood memories through his comic.

Remind students that **images** included with a selection, such as this photograph, can still be helpful even if they do not explicitly reveal information about the selection itself. A photograph of an artist or writer at work can provide valuable insight into the process of creation.

VOCABULARY DEVELOPMENT

Media Vocabulary Reinforcement Reinforce student's comprehension of media vocabulary with "show-you-know" sentences. The first sentence, or the first part of the sentence, uses the vocabulary word in an appropriate context. The second part or sentence—the "show-you-know" part—clarifies or gives more information about the first. Model the strategy with this example:

The cartoonist varies the design of the speech balloons according to the dialogue. In "Do You Like Her?" the *speech balloon* with the word *No!* is jagged and huge.

Then give students these sentence prompts and coach them to talk about the comic strips using the media vocabulary:

1. The [1st, 2nd, etc.] *panel* of cartoon [1, 2, or 3] is interesting to me because _____.
2. In this panel, Watterson *encapsulates* [a feeling, action, or event] by showing _____.

Whole-Class Learning **27**

● CLOSER REVIEW

Analyze Character

Students may have noted Calvin's response to Hobbes at the end of Cartoon 2, "Do You Like Her?" during their first review. Use the cartoons on this page to help students understand the characterization of Calvin. Encourage them to talk about what they noted. You may want to model a close review with the class based on the notes below.

NOTE: Have students note the details in the cartoons that reveal information about Calvin's personality, or have students participate while you note them.

QUESTION: Guide students to consider what these details might tell them. Ask what a reader can infer from these details about Calvin's personality, and accept student responses.

Possible response: In Cartoon 1, Calvin is imaginative because he convinces himself that there are ghosts around when he and Hobbes are camping. In Cartoon 2, he seems childish because he pretends to be completely disinterested in the new girl in class.

CONCLUDE: Help students formulate conclusions about the importance of these details in the comic strips. Ask students why the cartoonist might have included these details.

Possible response: The cartoonist might have characterized Calvin in this way to remind readers of what it's like to be a child. Children often have very active imaginations, but it's also a very confusing time because they have all these feelings that they don't know how to manage.

Remind students that there are two types of **characterization:** direct and indirect. With direct characterization, a writer directly states what a character is like. With indirect characterization, the writer *shows* what a character is like through the character's actions, thoughts, and speech. Since there are very few words in Calvin and Hobbes, most of the characterization is indirect. Most cartoons rely on indirect characterization.

CARTOON 1: Ghosts

NOTES

CARTOON 2: Do You Like Her?

NOTES

© Pearson Education, Inc., or its affiliates. All rights reserved.

PERSONALIZE FOR LEARNING

English Language Support

Cultural Context Review the comic strips and point out Hobbes, the tiger. In certain cultures, children are less likely to have imaginary friends. The concept of imaginary friends might, therefore, be unfamiliar to some students. Explain to students that Hobbes is Calvin's stuffed tiger and imaginary friend. Ask students if they know what an imaginary friend is, and ask them what term, if any, they use to refer to imaginary friends in their first language. Encourage students to talk about their own knowledge of other imaginary friends in movies, TV shows, or literature. **ALL LEVELS**

CARTOON 3: Snowman Xing

NOTES

Comprehension Check

Possible responses:

1. They are camping in a tent outdoors.
2. Calvin strongly denies having any interest whatsoever in the new girl, despite having started the conversation about her.
3. Calvin built several snowmen across the driveway, preventing his father from driving to work.
4. **Ghosts:** Calvin and Hobbes get scared of ghosts while they are camping in a tent.

   Do You Like Her?: Calvin mentions that there is a new girl in class but denies any interest in her when Hobbes persistently questions him.

   Snowman Xing: Calvin's father cannot go to work because Calvin has built a horde of snowmen across the driveway.

Comprehension Check

Complete the following items after you finish your first review.

1. In "Ghosts," where are Calvin and Hobbes?

2. In "Do You Like Her?" how does Calvin respond when Hobbes asks him whether he likes the new girl in his class?

3. In "Snowman Xing," why does Calvin's dad yell to Calvin that he's late for work?

4. 📓 **Notebook** Write a one-sentence description of each comic strip.

Gallery of *Calvin and Hobbes* Comics **29**

© Pearson Education, Inc., or its affiliates. All rights reserved.

PERSONALIZE FOR LEARNING

Challenge

Creating a Comic Strip Invite students to create their own comic strip depicting a humorous or otherwise memorable event from their own childhood. Begin by asking students to identify the essential elements of a comic (e.g., characters, dialogue, plot, speech bubbles). Remind students that since comics usually have few words, it is necessary to use indirect characterization to reveal the characters' personalities. Discuss ways to develop characters using few words. Have students share their comic strips with their classmates and discuss how the process of creating a comic compared to their expectations.

Jump Start

CLOSE REVIEW Ask students to consider the following question: *If you were asked to encapsulate the experience of childhood in a single drawing, or panel of a comic strip, what would you draw? What are the most important and defining aspects of childhood?* Have students discuss the prompt in a whole-class discussion.

Close Review

If needed, model close reviewing by using the Closer Review notes in the Interactive Teacher's Edition. You may wish to print the **Close-Review Guide: Media: Art and Photography** for students to use. 📄

Analyze the Media

Possible Responses:

1. (a) Calvin and Hobbes scare themselves talking about ghosts, so they cannot sleep. **DOK 2**
(b) I base my inference on the fact that the two seem to be going to sleep peacefully until one asks the other "Do you believe in ghosts?" In the fourth panel, the sun is coming up and the two look terrified, so I assume they've been talking about scary things all night. **DOK 2**

2. I think Calvin likes the new girl in his class, but he's too embarrassed to admit it. **DOK 2**

3. Calvin and Hobbes seem to be best friends who do almost everything together. Hobbes knows when Calvin is hiding something from him, and he's not afraid to ask questions that make Calvin uncomfortable. For example, in "Do You Like Her?" Hobbes asks Calvin if he likes the new girl. **DOK 2**

4. The challenges of growing up include embarrassment over crushes and being afraid of things like ghosts. The triumphs include being able to do fun things, like sleeping in a tent, rolling down a hill on a wagon, and building lots of snowmen. **DOK 2**

Media Vocabulary

For more support, see **Media Vocabulary.** 📄

Possible Responses:

1. I think he included only one panel in "Snowmen Xing" because it's not necessary to show Calvin building the snowmen. It is more interesting to see his father's reaction.

2. The lettering gets bigger and darker. In the last panel of "Do You Like Her?" the speech balloon is big and jagged, and it shows that Calvin is denying his interest in the girl.

3. I think he used the panels with no dialogue to show that time has passed. In the first case, the two may be falling asleep. In the second case, they are too tired and scared to talk.

MAKING MEANING

GALLERY OF *CALVIN AND HOBBES* COMICS

Close Review

Revisit the comic strips and your first-review notes. Write down any new observations that seem important. What **questions** do you have? What can you **conclude**?

- -

Analyze the Media

📓 **Notebook** Respond to these questions.

1. **Make Inferences** An **inference** is a conclusion you draw about something that is not directly stated or shown. **(a)** In "Ghosts," what do you think happens between the third and fourth panels? **(b)** What details in the comic support your inference?

2. **Speculate** Why do you think Calvin refuses to answer Hobbes's questions about the new girl in class? Explain.

3. **Draw Conclusions** What can you tell about the relationship between Calvin and Hobbes ? Explain, citing details from the comics that you used to draw your conclusion.

4. **Essential Question: *What are some of the challenges and triumphs of growing up?*** What have you learned about the challenges and triumphs of growing up by reading these comic strips?

LANGUAGE DEVELOPMENT

Media Vocabulary

panel	encapsulation	speech balloon

Respond to these questions.

1. Why might Watterson have included only one panel in "Snowman Xing"?

2. In "Do You Like Her?" how does Watterson indicate that a character is speaking with emotion?

3. In "Ghosts," some of the panels include dialogue, whereas others do not. Why do you think Watterson chose to have panels without dialogue in this comic strip?

© Pearson Education, Inc., or its affiliates. All rights reserved.

📋 **STANDARDS**

Reading Literature
Cite textual evidence to support analysis of what the text says explicitly as well as inferences drawn from the text.

Writing
Conduct short research projects to answer a question, drawing on several sources and refocusing the inquiry when appropriate.

Speaking and Listening
• Engage effectively in a range of collaborative discussions with diverse partners on *grade 6 topics, texts, and issues,* building on others' ideas and expressing their own clearly.
  a. Come to discussions prepared, having read or studied required material; explicitly draw on that preparation by referring to evidence on the topic, text, or issue to probe and reflect on ideas under discussion.
  c. Pose and respond to specific questions with elaboration and detail by making comments that contribute to the topic, text, or issue under discussion.
  d. Review the key ideas expressed and demonstrate understanding of multiple perspectives through reflection and paraphrasing.
• Interpret information presented in diverse media and formats and explain how it contributes to a topic, text, or issue under study.

30 UNIT 1 • CHILDHOOD

FORMATIVE ASSESSMENT

Media Vocabulary

- **If** students struggle to explain how the speech balloons vary, **then** have them review the definition of *speech balloon* and then describe how the speech balloons in different panels look.

Research

Assignment

Calvin and Hobbes was a very popular comic strip, which appeared in newspapers for more than ten years. Conduct research in preparation for a **class discussion** about what made this comic strip so popular. In your research, look for examples of the comic strip from different years, information about Bill Watterson, and comments by fans in response to the comics.

Conduct Research To prepare for the class discussion, consider these questions, and perform research to answer them.

- What did fans like about the comic strip?
- Why did Watterson create *Calvin and Hobbes*? What were his influences?
- What qualities do you think made the comic strip successful for so long?
- Do you think the comic strip would still be popular today? Why or why not?

As you conduct your research, follow these guidelines.

- Consult multiple reliable sources of information—both print and digital. Ask yourself questions like the ones in the chart to make sure the sources you consult are reliable.

MAIN QUESTION	RELATED QUESTIONS
Does the source have a good reputation?	• Who is responsible for the information? Is it a person, a publisher, or another organization? • Do people generally agree that the source is trustworthy?
Does the source present solid facts?	• Does the source present mostly facts or mostly opinions? • If it expresses opinions, does it clearly say so?
Does the source avoid bias—prejudice or an unfair opinion?	• Does the source ignore any facts that are important? • Does the source twist the meaning of any facts?

- Jot down relevant details and examples to support your ideas during the class discussion.
- Write down any additional questions that your research raises and that you would like to discuss with the class.

Hold a Discussion As a class, discuss the findings of your research. Keep the following tips in mind:

- Support your ideas by citing specific details from the selection and your research.
- If you are unsure of what other classmates are trying to say, ask questions to help them expand on their ideas.
- Reflect on new ideas that other classmates express, and paraphrase their ideas to confirm your understanding of them. To paraphrase, restate their ideas in your own words.

EVIDENCE LOG

Before moving on to a new selection, go to your Evidence Log, and record what you learned from the gallery of *Calvin and Hobbes* comics.

Gallery of *Calvin and Hobbes* Comics **31**

© Pearson Education, Inc., or its affiliates. All rights reserved.

Research

Conduct Research Discuss with students the importance of using reliable research sources. Ask students to explain how they can tell if a source is reliable. Point out that government, educational, and professional organizations are likely to be good sources of information. Website URLs that end with *.gov* or *.edu* are likely to be reliable online sources. For this particular assignment, encourage students to seek out quotations from Bill Watterson himself. They should also look for articles about the comic strip and why it was so popular.

Hold a Discussion Remind students to use notes from their research as they take part in the discussion. For more support, see **Research and Discuss: Class Discussion.**

Evidence Log Support students in completing their Evidence Log. This paced activity will help prepare them for the Performance-Based Assessment at the end of the unit.

FORMATIVE ASSESSMENT

Research and Discuss

- **If** students struggle with finding relevant sources of information, **then** have them refine the search terms they are using to locate resources.
- **If** students struggle with identifying why the comic strip was and is popular, **then** have them review fans' comments on websites created by and for fans.

CROSS-CURRICULAR PERSPECTIVES

Humanities Explain to students that the characters in the comic strip are named after historical figures. John Calvin was an influential French theologian who lived in the 1500s, while Thomas Hobbes was an English political philosopher who lived in the 1600s. Invite students to choose either John Calvin or Thomas Hobbes and do independent research into his ideas and philosophies. Then have them write a short essay that introduces Calvin's or Hobbes's ideas and explains the connection with the cartoon characters. They should conclude by explaining whether they think the characters' personalities have a meaningful connection with the historical figures, or if Watterson chose the names for more superficial reasons.

Jump Start

Why is it important for children to be imaginative? How can imagination help us find new ways to accomplish something or solve a problem? Ask students to think about what they have learned about childhood imagination from the selections in this unit, and start a class discussion about the importance of imagination. Encourage students to share specific memories from their childhoods to support their ideas.

Write a Nonfiction Narrative

Make sure students understand what they are being asked to do in the assignment. Explain that the writing prompt relates to the selections in this unit because both selections describe children who construct their own imaginative worlds.

Students should complete the assignment using word processing software to take advantage of editing tools and features.

Elements of a Nonfiction Narrative

Remind students that an effective nonfiction narrative, such as "Wagon Train at Dusk," contains all of the listed required elements, retells events that unfold in a natural manner, and uses vivid and varied language choices.

MAKE IT INTERACTIVE

Project "Wagon Train at Dusk" from the Interactive Teacher's Edition and have students identify the elements of a nonfiction narrative, such as a narrator, problem or conflict, dialogue, description, sensory language, and conclusion.

Academic Vocabulary

Invite students to suggest possible sentences that relate to the assignment and include the academic vocabulary.

WRITING TO SOURCES

• *from* BROWN GIRL DREAMING

• GALLERY OF *CALVIN AND HOBBES* COMICS

🔧 **Tool Kit**
Student Model of a Narrative

ACADEMIC VOCABULARY

As you craft your nonfiction narrative, consider using some of the academic vocabulary you learned in the beginning of the unit.

reflect
notable
contribute
recognize
memorize

▤ STANDARDS

Writing
• Write narratives to develop real or imagined experiences or events using effective technique, relevant descriptive details, and well-structured event sequences
• Write routinely over extended time frames and shorter time frames for a range of discipline-specific tasks, purposes, and audiences.

32 UNIT 1 • CHILDHOOD

Write a Nonfiction Narrative

You have read selections in which people use their imaginations in different ways to shape their childhood worlds. In the *Calvin and Hobbes* comics, a young boy experiences life's ups and downs with his constant companion and imaginary friend. In the excerpt from *Brown Girl Dreaming,* Jacqueline Woodson describes how she used her imagination to navigate the challenges of growing up. Now, you will explore this idea by writing a personal narrative in which you tell a story about your own experience with imagination.

> **Assignment**
> In the poem "another day," Jacqueline Woodson's mother tells the children, "Today I want you to find another way to play." Write a **personal narrative** in response to the following prompt:
>
> > When did you have to use your imagination to find another way to do something?
>
> For example, perhaps you found another way to play, solve a problem, make a friend, or learn a new skill. In your narrative, tell the story of your experience and reflect on the ways in which using your imagination made things better.

Elements of a Nonfiction Narrative

A **nonfiction narrative** is a true story. A **personal narrative** is a true story about the writer's own life. In a personal narrative, the writer uses the first-person point of view to relate experiences and events.

A well-written nonfiction narrative contains the following elements:

- a conflict or problem
- people who play a role in the events described in the narrative
- a clear sequence of events with transitional words and phrases that show shifts in time or setting
- narrative techniques, such as dialogue, description, and pacing, that help to convey experiences and events in a memorable way
- precise words, descriptive details, and sensory language that show what settings and people are like
- a conclusion that follows from the experiences and events in the narrative

Model Nonfiction Narrative For a model of a well-crafted nonfiction narrative, see the Launch Text, "Wagon Train at Dusk."

Challenge yourself to find all of the elements of an effective nonfiction narrative in the text. You will have an opportunity to review these elements as you prepare to write your own nonfiction narrative.

LAUNCH TEXT

Wagon Train at Dusk

© Pearson Education, Inc., or its affiliates. All rights reserved.

AUTHOR'S PERSPECTIVE   **Kelly Gallagher, M.Ed.**

Pump Up the Volume of Writing Spend some time talking to kids about why they should write—not just how. Students should write more than the teacher can grade. To help students get the most from their writing, teachers can use techniques such as these:

- **Confer** Teachers can achieve more in a two-minute conference than they can by spending five-to-seven minutes writing comments on a paper. Developing writers need face time with

the most experienced writer in the class—the teacher.

- **Model** Teachers can model how they write by frequently writing in front of students. Show students that effective writing extends far past correctness. Teachers can do this in short bursts, and model authentic writing, whether brainstorming a topic, working to add details, or revising to find the right word. Note: other

times the teacher can bring a model to class that has already been written for the students to study.

- **Share models of excellent writing.** Show students models from professional writers and from other students. As they study mentor texts, students begin to see the moves a writer has made, and they can work to emulate those moves.

Prewriting / Planning

Focus Your Topic Reread the assignment. Consider the experience you would like to describe in your narrative. Summarize what happens in your narrative by completing this sentence starter.

I used my imagination to find another way to do something when _____

_____ .

Explore Setting Vivid, specific descriptions of places in your story can help your readers better understand your experiences and insights. Use the chart to write down the places you want to describe. Then, note sensory details you can use to bring those places to life for readers.

PLACES	SENSORY DETAILS (sights, sounds, smells, tastes, sensations)

Gather Details About People and Events Now that you have thought about the setting of your narrative, gather details about the people and events. To do so, think about these questions:

- **Events:** *What events triggered the need for you to use your imagination? What events occurred as a result?*
- **People:** *Who are the main characters of your narrative? What specific words describe their personalities? How did they respond to the events you are describing?*

Study the Launch Text to identify ways in which the writer uses details to make the people, setting, and events come alive.

Identify the Conflict A successful narrative centers around a clear conflict. Narrow your focus by identifying a specific conflict you will explore in your nonfiction story. To do so, ask yourself these questions:

- What did I want? Why did I have to find another way to get it? Who or what was getting in the way?
- How did using my imagination help me overcome this obstacle?

:= STANDARDS
Writing
Write narratives to develop
real or imagined experiences or
events using effective technique,
relevant descriptive details, and
well-structured event sequences.
  b. Use narrative techniques, such as
  dialogue, pacing, and description,
  to develop experiences, events,
  and/or characters
  d. Use precise language and
  domain-specific vocabulary to
  inform about or explain the topic.

Performance Task: Write a Nonfiction Narrative **33**

© Pearson Education, Inc., or its affiliates. All rights reserved.

Prewriting/Planning

Focus Your Topic Explain to students that the first step in writing a nonfiction narrative is to identify the specific experience that they would like to write about. Encourage students to make a list of ideas for topics, and then to pick the topic that offers the best opportunity for elaboration.

Explore Setting Ask students to recall the most memorable settings from books and stories they have read. Have students identify what made those settings unique, interesting, and memorable.

Gather Details About People and Events Explain that one good way to gather evidence from the people who were involved in the events you are writing about is through an interview. Discuss elements of effective interview questions (for example, open-ended vs. yes-or-no questions). Have pairs of students practice interviewing each other.

Identify the Conflict Ask students to think carefully about the main obstacle they faced in getting what they wanted. Have them describe what inspired the imaginative ideas that helped them to resolve the conflict.

- **Use a Rubric.** Experiment with changing the rubric. Encourage students to help you build it. This creates buy-in when the students see that each rubric is personalized to some degree to their needs.

PERSONALIZE FOR LEARNING

English Language Support
Writing a Nonfiction Narrative Support students as they write a topic sentence for their nonfiction narrative.

Have students review the definition of a nonfiction narrative. Encourage them to write a short, complete sentence that states their main idea. **EMERGING**

Have students review the definition of a nonfiction narrative. Encourage them to write their claim in a complete sentence, and to think about how their narrative might be organized. **EXPANDING**

Remind students to write a clear and complete sentence that explains their main idea. Encourage them to think about details and evidence that support their main idea. **BRIDGING**

Whole-Class Learning   **33**

Drafting

Organize a Sequence of Events Explain to students that although narratives are *usually* organized in chronological order, they are not *always* organized this way. Some writers use time sequences inventively, for instance by including flashbacks or a story within a story. Point out that the Launch Text, "Wagon Train at Dusk," has a story within a story. Both the Launch Text itself and the story that Dad tells Sarah within the Launch Text have their own distinct timelines. Point out that the organizer will help students place the events in order and see what is important to include in their narratives.

Signal Shifts Emphasize the importance of using transition words in a narrative to create clarity and cohesion. If students are having trouble using time-order transitions, have them go back to their Chronological Sequence of Events and revise the transition words to work better with the events in the timeline (e.g., replacing *Next* with *Then* for number 3, *Later* for number 4, and *Finally* for number 5.)

Write a First Draft Remind students that the purpose of the first draft is simply to get all their ideas on paper. At this stage, they should not worry about creating the perfect turn of phrase or producing error-free prose. Their focus should be on including all the basic elements of a nonfiction narrative: characters, a problem or conflict, and a clear sequence of events. They will refine their writing in the revising and editing stages.

☰ STANDARDS

Writing
Write narratives to develop real or imagined experiences or events using effective technique, relevant descriptive details, and well-structured event sequences.
   a. Engage and orient the reader by establishing a context and introducing a narrator and/or characters; organize an event sequence that unfolds naturally and logically.
   c. Use a variety of transition words, phrases, and clauses to convey sequence and signal shifts from one time frame or setting to another.
   e. Provide a conclusion that follow from the narrated experiences or events.

34 UNIT 1 • CHILDHOOD

Drafting

Organize a Sequence of Events Narratives are often organized in **chronological order**, so that one event leads to the next in the order in which they actually happened. Use the organizer to list the events of your story in chronological order. Fill out the "First" line and the "Next" lines. Add more lines, if necessary.

CHRONOLOGICAL SEQUENCE OF EVENTS
1. First:
2. Next:
3. Next:
4. Next:
5. Next:

Signal Shifts Think about places in your story where the sequence of events might be more complicated. Consider these questions:

- Does the story start out in one setting and move to another?
- Does a new person enter the story?
- Does something happen either before or after the main events?

Time-order transitions, such a *first, then, next, earlier,* and *later* can help you establish a clear order of events. **Spatial-order transitions** such as *in front of, in the distance, beyond,* and *nearby* can help you make settings clearer. Determine which transition words to use, and where in your narrative to use them.

Write a First Draft Use your chronological list as a guide as you draft your story. Add an introduction in which you describe the setting and people involved. Add a conclusion in which you reflect on what the experiences you describe meant to you or what you learned from them.

© Pearson Education, Inc., or its affiliates. All rights reserved.

Jim Cummins, Ph.D.

Writing Enhances Student Identity Writing is an expression of oneself, and writing projects that self into the new social spheres. However, students learning English are often defined by what they are missing rather than by what they possess. While teaching writing through the Performance Tasks in *myPerspectives,* you may want to supplement the writing instruction and practice for English learners by using *identity texts*. These texts allow students to invest their identities into their writing. The results hold a mirror up to students and reflect their identities in a positive light. Teachers can use this process:

1. Encourage students to have a hand in picking the topic to ensure they are writing about something that reflects themselves or their identities. Have students write their drafts in English, illustrate them, and work with various sources, such as parents and older students fluent in their home language, to translate the drafts into their home language.

2. Publish these texts. Help students share identity texts with multiple audiences including peers, teachers, parents, grandparents, sister classes,

LANGUAGE DEVELOPMENT

Author's Style: Voice

Voice A writer's **voice** is the personality that comes through his or her language. It is the quality that makes your writing sound like you. These literary elements help to create a writer's voice:

- **Word Choice:** the words a writer chooses
- **Sentence Structure:** the way the writer constructs sentences
- **Tone:** the writer's attitude toward the subject

Read It

This chart identifies some of the elements that create the voice of the author of the Launch Text.

Vivid Words	*jolted awake by a ripping sound*
Short and Long Sentences	• *That doesn't stop me.* • *He always came up with these unique creations, beautifully conceived and executed.*
Casual Tone	*"Nope," I tell her.*

Write It

Ask yourself the following questions to help develop your voice.

- Am I using words with which I am comfortable, even as I try to stretch my vocabulary?
- Do my descriptions really show how I see things?
- Does my writing seem true and authentic?

Also, make sure to consider your readers by varying your sentence structures. For example, avoid beginning too many sentences with the word *I*. Instead, develop your voice by trying out different types of sentences. The chart shows some options.

ORIGINAL	HOW TO ADD VARIETY	REVISION
I was happy to see my father at the airport.	Start your sentence with a word that describes your emotion or mood.	Delighted, I watched my father emerge from behind the sliding glass door into the baggage claim area.
I excitedly waved to him as soon as he noticed me.	Move another part of the sentence to the beginning.	As soon as he noticed me, I excitedly waved to him.
He told me he had some good news to share with me.	Start with a direct quotation instead of writing that someone said something.	"Katie," he started, "I've been waiting all week to tell you this."

TIP

STYLE
Use sensory language to make your descriptions come alive. Don't just tell readers that a noise was loud—use precise words to show them.

STANDARDS

Writing
Write narratives to develop real or imagined experiences or events using effective technique, relevant descriptive details, and well-structured event sequences.

d. Use precise words and phrases, relevant descriptive details, and sensory language to convey experiences and events.

Language
Use knowledge of language and its conventions when writing, speaking, reading, or listening.

a. Vary sentence patterns for meaning, reader/listener interest, and style.

© Pearson Education, Inc., or its affiliates. All rights reserved.

Author's Style: Voice

Read It

Explain that voice is a subjective aspect of writing—it's not simply a matter of right or wrong. Some writers and readers prefer sparse, concise prose, while others prefer more flowery, ornate prose. Point out that developing their own voice is one way that writers can let their individuality and personality show through their work.

MAKE IT INTERACTIVE
Project "Wagon Train at Dusk" from the Interactive Teacher's Edition and ask students to identify additional examples of ways in which the author develops his voice.

- Vivid Words: *demolishing my masterpiece, hoots and guffaws and hollers*
- Short and Long Sentences: *I'd create a fleet of Conestoga wagons in a circle formation around a campfire at dusk, with miniature people and horses and dogs made of pipe cleaners, and children running around playing hoops.* (long and descriptive); *It would be a masterpiece.* (short and to the point)

Write It

For additional practice, consider inviting students to suggest alternative revisions for the example sentences in this section. You might also display individual sentences from the Launch Text and encourage students to suggest possible ways to make them stronger. For example:

- I ask her if I've told her the story of the diorama.
- Sarah pretends she isn't rolling her eyes, but I keep going.
- I make the expression myself, and Sarah smiles.

---

and the media. It is critical that students share their writing with broad audiences to build this positive experience. Students are likely to receive positive feedback and affirmation of self by providing true audiences with which to share their work.

3. Writing and publishing identity texts helps ELL students take active control and ownership of the learning process and invest their identities in their drafts.

PERSONALIZE FOR LEARNING

Strategic Support
Voice Some students may require additional support in developing their voice and adding variety to their writing. Pair students together and have them review each other's nonfiction narratives. Encourage them to point out areas that would benefit from adding variety in word choice and sentence structure. Have pairs of students work together to revise each other's sentences. Remind students that it is ultimately their choice whether or not to accept their partner's suggestions.

Revising

Evaluating Your Draft Before students begin revising their writing, they should first evaluate their draft to make sure it contains all of the essential elements of narrative nonfiction, effectively uses narrative techniques, and follows the norms and conventions of narrative writing.

Revising for Focus and Organization

Add Narrative Techniques Explain to students that dialogue in a narrative can move the action forward. Suggest that students review "Wagon Train at Dusk" to see how the author uses dialogue. Point out that the narrator tells the whole story of the model train in dialogue to his daughter. Encourage students to experiment with sentence length to improve pacing.

Revising for Evidence and Elaboration

Use Precise Language Remind students that the purpose of a narrative is not simply to retell an event, but also to entertain the reader. Students can use much more lively and creative language than they would in a more formal piece of writing, such as a research paper. Encourage students to choose words that are not just precise, but also engaging and fun (if appropriate). They can have fun with language for this assignment.

Revising

Evaluating Your Draft

Use the following checklist to evaluate the effectiveness of your first draft. Then, use the checklist and the instruction on this page to guide your revision.

FOCUS AND ORGANIZATION	EVIDENCE AND ELABORATION	CONVENTIONS
☐ Provides an introduction that establishes the setting and introduces the people being described.	☐ Effectively uses narrative techniques, such as dialogue, pacing, and description.	☐ Is free of grammar and spelling errors.
☐ Presents a clear chronological sequence of events that are linked by a variety of transitions.	☐ Uses descriptive details, sensory language, and precise words and phrases.	☐ Uses a variety of sentence lengths and avoids beginning too many sentences with *I*.
☐ Provides a conclusion that follows from the events and experiences in the narrative.	☐ Establishes the writer's voice through word choice, sentence structure, and tone.	

🔗 WORD NETWORK

Include words from your Word Network in your narrative.

☰ STANDARDS

Writing
Write narratives to develop real or imagined experiences or events using effective technique, relevant descriptive details, and well-structured event sequences.

b. Use narrative techniques, such as dialogue, pacing, and description, to develop experiences, events, and/or characters.

d. Use precise words and phrases, relevant descriptive details, and sensory language to convey experiences and events.

e. Provide a conclusion that follows from the narrated experiences or events.

Revising for Evidence and Elaboration

Add Narrative Techniques Scan your draft and note places where the story seems dull. Bring those sections to life by using dialogue or pacing.

* **Dialogue** refers to spoken conversations in a text. Find explanations in your narrative that would be more exciting as dialogue. Make sure your dialogue accurately reflects what people really said. Use quotation marks to set off dialogue from the rest of the text.

* **Pacing** is the sense of speed with which a story moves forward. Look for places where a series of short sentences would speed up the action. Use longer, descriptive sentences to show a person or setting.

Use Precise Language To write a lively narrative that holds your readers' interest, avoid vague words and phrases that leave the reader with questions such as *What kind? How? In what way? How often?* and *To what extent?* As you review and revise your work, replace vague words with precise words that convey your ideas more vividly and accurately. Here are some examples:

Instead of...

noun: stuff	*use*	toys, postcards, t-shirts
verb: said	*use*	exclaimed, shouted, asked
adjective: nice	*use*	friendly, generous, kind
adverb: slowly	*use*	lazily, casually, carefully

© Pearson Education, Inc., or its affiliates. All rights reserved.

HOW LANGUAGE WORKS

Voice As students revise their nonfiction narratives, remind them to use creative word choices, varied sentence structures, and tone to develop their voice. Encourage them to ask themselves questions such as: *Will readers be able to easily visualize what I have described in this sentence? What is the tone of my narrative—does it convey what I wish to convey? Have I used a variety of sentence structures and lengths? How many of my sentences begin with the pronoun I?*

PEER REVIEW

Exchange narratives with a classmate. Use the checklist to evaluate your classmate's narrative and provide supportive feedback.

1. Are the setting and people developed using descriptive details?

☐ yes ☐ no If no, suggest how the writer can revise to strengthen his or her descriptions.

2. Is there a clear sequence of events that is clarified by transitions?

☐ yes ☐ no If no, explain what confused you.

3. Does the narrative end with a memorable conclusion that reflects on the experiences described in the narrative?

☐ yes ☐ no If no, tell the writer what you think might be missing.

4. What is the strongest part of your classmate's narrative? Why?

_____

_____

Editing and Proofreading

As students proofread they should check for grammar, spelling, and punctuation errors. Remind them that computer spellchecks are useful, but not perfect. They still need to get in the habit of manually checking for spelling and grammar errors. Remind students to check for commonly misspelled words and homophones, such as *your/you're* and *they're/there/their.*

Publishing and Presenting

Remind students that the final draft of their narrative should be error-free, neat, and legible. Encourage them to choose a font that is easy to read and moderately sized (such as Times New Roman or Arial, size 12). Each paragraph should be indented, and the narrative should have a title and a byline.

Reflecting

Students should write a short journal entry reflecting both on the process of writing their nonfiction narrative and on the feedback they received from their peers.

Editing and Proofreading

Edit for Conventions Reread your draft, and correct errors in grammar and word usage. Be sure you have included a variety of sentence types.

Proofread for Accuracy As you proofread, make sure that any dialogue is enclosed in quotation marks. Refer to the Launch Text for examples of how to punctuate dialogue.

Publishing and Presenting

Create a final version of your narrative in a digital format. Use a class or school Web site, a class whiteboard, or email to share and comment on other classmates' narratives. As you comment, consider the ways in which your narratives are similar and different. Remember to be polite and respectful when commenting on the work of others.

Reflecting

Reflect on what you learned as you wrote your narrative. How did writing about a personal experience help you better understand its significance? What was the hardest part of this assignment? What did you learn from reviewing the work of others?

▤ STANDARDS

Writing
• Produce clear and coherent writing in which the development, organization, and style are appropriate to task, purpose, and audience.
• With some guidance and support from peers and adults, develop and strengthen writing as needed by planning, revising, editing, rewriting, or trying a new approach.
• Use technology, including the Internet, to produce and publish writing as well as to interact and collaborate with others; demonstrate sufficient command of keyboarding skills to type a minimum of three pages in a single sitting.

Performance Task: Write a Nonfiction Narrative **37**

© Pearson Education, Inc., or its affiliates. All rights reserved.

PERSONALIZE FOR LEARNING

Challenge

Different Forms Encourage students to rewrite their narrative in another form. For example, they might retell their story in verse, as Woodson does in *Brown Girl Dreaming*. Or they might create a comic book version of their story, similar to *Calvin and Hobbes*. Before they begin, ask students to identify the essential elements of their chosen form. Remind students that comics and poems use fewer words than prose narratives, so they will need to omit certain details. When they have finished writing, have them share their new stories with their classmates and reflect on how the process was similar to and different from the process of writing a prose narrative.

OVERVIEW

SMALL-GROUP LEARNING

What are some of the challenges and triumphs of growing up?

Children may sometimes feel that the challenges they face are overwhelming or insurmountable. Without the life experience and the perspective that comes from having lived through difficult times or overcome challenges, it can be difficult to see that perseverance can make a person stronger and more mature. During Small-Group Learning, students will read selections that deal with the difficult process of becoming an adult.

Small-Group Learning Strategies ▶

Review the Learning Strategies with students and explain that as they work through Small-Group Learning they will develop strategies to work in small-group environments.

- Have students watch the video on Small-Group Learning Strategies.
- A video on this topic is available online in the Professional Development Center.

You may wish to discuss some action items to add to the chart as a class before students complete it on their own. For example, for "Support others," you might solicit the following from students:

- Offer criticism that is constructive and helps your classmates succeed.
- Be respectful if you disagree with a point being made.

Block Scheduling

Each day in this Pacing Plan represents a 40–50 minute class period. Teachers using block scheduling may combine days to reflect their class schedule. In addition, teachers may revise pacing to differentiate and support core instruction by integrating components and resources as students require.

📅 **Pacing Plan**

👥 OVERVIEW: SMALL-GROUP LEARNING

ESSENTIAL QUESTION:

What are some of the challenges and triumphs of growing up?

Growing up isn't always easy. Some challenges are difficult to overcome, but learning how to persevere through hardships is a triumph in itself. It is a triumph because every new experience is a lesson learned. You will work in a group to continue your exploration of some of these challenges and triumphs.

Small-Group Learning Strategies

Throughout your life, in school, in your community, and in your career, you will continue to learn and work with others.

Review these strategies and the actions you can take to practice them as you work in teams. Add ideas of your own for each step. Use these strategies during Small-Group Learning.

STRATEGY	ACTION PLAN
Prepare	• Complete your assignments so that you are prepared for group work. • Organize your thinking so you can contribute to your group's discussion. •
Participate fully	• Make eye contact to signal that you are listening and taking in what is being said. • Use text evidence when making a point. •
Support others	• Build on ideas from others in your group. • Invite others who have not yet spoken to do so. •
Clarify	• Paraphrase the ideas of others to ensure that your understanding is correct. • Ask follow-up questions. •

SCAN FOR MULTIMEDIA

© Pearson Education, Inc., or its affiliates. All rights reserved.

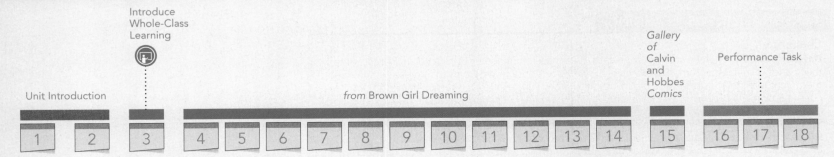

Unit Introduction | Introduce Whole-Class Learning | *from* Brown Girl Dreaming | *Gallery of Calvin and Hobbes Comics* | Performance Task

1 | 2 | 3 | 4 | 5 | 6 | 7 | 8 | 9 | 10 | 11 | 12 | 13 | 14 | 15 | 16 | 17 | 18

CONTENTS

© Pearson Education, Inc., or its affiliates. All rights reserved.

Contents

Selections Circulate among groups as they preview the selections. You might encourage groups to discuss any knowledge they already have about any of the selections or the situations and settings shown in the photographs. Students may wish to take a poll within their group to determine which selections look the most interesting.

Remind students that communicating and collaborating in groups is an important skill that they will use throughout their lives—in school, in their careers, and in their community.

Performance Task

Present a Retelling Give groups time to read about and briefly discuss the retelling they will present after reading. Encourage students to do some preliminary thinking about the types of challenges they expect to find. This may help focus their subsequent reading and group discussion.

Introduce Small-Group Learning

Introduce Independent Learning

Performance-Based Assessment

	Declaration of the Rights of the Child			Michaela DePrince: The War Orphan Who Became a Ballerina			*from* Bad Boy		I Was a Skinny Tomboy Kid			Performance Task			Independent Learning		

| 19 | 20 | 21 | 22 | 23 | 24 | 25 | 26 | 27 | 28 | 29 | 30 | 31 | 32 | 33 | 34 | 35 | 36 |

SMALL-GROUP LEARNING

Small-Group Learning **39**

SMALL-GROUP LEARNING

Working as a Team

1. **Take a Position** Remind groups to let all members share their responses. You may wish to set a time limit for this discussion.

2. **List Your Rules** You may want to have groups share their lists of rules and consolidate them into a master list to be displayed and followed by all groups.

3. **Apply the Rules** As you circulate among the groups, ensure that students are staying on task. Consider a short time limit for this step.

4. **Name Your Group** This task can be creative and fun. If students have trouble coming up with a name, suggest that they think of something related to the unit topic. Encourage groups to share their names with the class.

5. **Create a Communication Plan** Encourage groups to include in their plans agreed-upon times during the day to share ideas. They should also devise a method for recording and saving their communications.

Accountable Talk

Remind students that groups should communicate politely. You can post these Accountable Talk suggestions and encourage students to add their own. Students should:

Remember to . . .
Ask clarifying questions.

Which sounds like . . .
Can you please repeat what you said?
Would you give me an example?
I think you said _____. Did I understand you correctly?

Remember to . . .
Explain your thinking.

Which sounds like . . .
I believe _____ is true because _____.
I feel _____ because _____.

Remember to . . .
Build on the ideas of others.

Which sounds like . . .
When _____ said _____, it made me think of _____.

Working as a Team

1. **Take a Position** In your group, discuss the following question:

   > What ideas and experiences about growing up can young people share with one another?

   As you take turns sharing your ideas, be sure to provide reasons and examples. After all group members have shared, discuss the ideas and what they mean to you.

2. **List Your Rules** As a group, decide on the rules that you will follow as you work together. Two samples are provided. Add two more of your own. You may add or revise rules based on your experience together.

   - Everyone should participate in group discussions.
   - People should not interrupt.

   - _____
     _____

   - _____
     _____

3. **Apply the Rules** Share what you have learned about growing up. Make sure each person in the group contributes. Take notes and be prepared to share with the class one thing that you heard from another member of your group.

4. **Name Your Group** Choose a name that reflects the unit topic.

   Our group's name: _____

5. **Create a Communication Plan** Decide how you want to communicate with one another. For example, you might use online collaboration tools, email, or instant messaging.

   Our group's decision: _____
   _____

© Pearson Education, Inc., or its affiliates. All rights reserved.

AUTHOR'S PERSPECTIVE **Kelly Gallagher, M.Ed.**

Meaningful Talk Instead of asking teacher-directed questions that lead students to see specific elements, give the power back to the students. Help them find their own big ideas and support them by building in talk opportunities. Use these two strategies to help students achieve deeper comprehension.

- _See the Relevance in Reading:_ Teachers have students read great works of literature to give students an opportunity to think

deeply about issues that will affect their lives. Asking students "What is worth talking about here?" helps them find themes and interpretations and get to the heart of the unit theme.

- _One Question; One Comment Strategy:_ To get students to revisit a chapter or passage they find particularly challenging and generate an in-depth discussion of the text, teachers can

Making a Schedule

First, find out the due dates for the Small-Group activities. Then, preview the texts and activities with your group and make a schedule for completing the tasks.

SELECTION	ACTIVITIES	DUE DATE
Declaration of the Rights of the Child		
Michaela DePrince: The War Orphan Who Became a Ballerina		
from Bad Boy		
I Was a Skinny Tomboy Kid		

Working on Group Projects

Different projects require different roles. As your group works together, you'll find it more effective if each person has a specific role. Before beginning a project, discuss the necessary roles, and choose one for each group member. Here are some possible roles; add your own ideas.

Project Manager: monitors the schedule and keeps everyone on task

Researcher: organizes research activities

Recorder: takes notes during group meetings

_____

_____

_____

_____

_____

_____

_____

© Pearson Education, Inc., or its affiliates. All rights reserved.

 SCAN FOR
MULTIMEDIA

Making a Schedule

Encourage groups to preview the reading selections and to consider how long it will take them to complete the activities accompanying each selection. Point out that they can adjust the due dates for particular selections as needed as they work on their small-group projects; however, they must complete all assigned tasks before the group Performance Task is due. Encourage groups to review their schedules upon completing the activities for each selection to make sure they are on track to meet the final due date.

Working on Group Projects

Point out to groups that the roles they assign can also be changed later. Students might have to make changes based on who is best at doing what. Try to make sure that there is no favoritism, cliquishness, or stereotyping by gender or other means in the assignment of roles.

Also, you should review the roles each group assigns to its members. Based on your understanding of students' individual strengths, you might find it necessary to suggest some changes.

ask students to come to class with one question and one comment generated from their reading assignment. During the class discussion, have the first student share one comment or question. The next student can answer the question, respond to the comment, or build on the discussion with his or her own question or comment. Continue the process until everyone in class has participated.

• *Silent Talk*: Students write their thoughts quietly for four minutes and then rotate their papers to the next student. The next student then continues the "conversation."

Using these strategies will lessen student dependence on the teacher and so help to build independence.

😊 FACILITATING SMALL-GROUP LEARNING

Forming Groups You may wish to form groups for Small-Group Learning so that each consists of students with different learning abilities. Some students may be adept at organizing information whereas others may have strengths related to generating or synthesizing information. A good mix of abilities can make the experience of Small-Group Learning dynamic and productive.

Declaration of the Rights of the Child

🔊 **AUDIO SUMMARIES**
Audio summaries of "Declaration of the Rights of the Child" are available in both English and Spanish and can be assigned to students in the Interactive Teacher's Edition or Unit Resources. Assigning these summaries prior to reading the selection may help students build additional background knowledge and set a context for their first read.

Summary

In this public document created by the United Nations, the member states proclaim that children must be guaranteed certain rights so that they may have happy childhoods—for their own good and for the good of society. These rights include social services to guarantee adequate food, housing, and medical attention; special care for children with disabilities; and education. The declaration emphasizes that these rights should be provided without discrimination.

Insight

This selection helps give insight into some of the challenges of childhood and what can be done to support children as they encounter them. Note that point number six may be sensitive for adopted children.

ESSENTIAL QUESTION:
What are some of the challenges and triumphs of growing up?

Connection to Essential Question

Everyone faces some challenges while growing up. Many children need support to help them meet these challenges. As a society, we can help by ensuring that basic rights and protections are put in place for all children as they face the challenges of their world.

SMALL-GROUP LEARNING PERFORMANCE TASK
Deliver a retelling of the childhood challenges presented in one of the texts you have read in this section.

Connection to Performance Tasks

Small-Group Learning Performance Task As students prepare to retell challenges they read about in one of the texts in this section, they may look at whether those involved could have been affected—or have been affected—by not receiving the rights stated in this document.

UNIT PERFORMANCE-BASED ASSESSMENT
When did a challenge lead to a triumph?

Unit Performance-Based Assessment These guidelines take on a range of challenges and seek to guarantee children certain rights that enable them to succeed—particularly in education.

LESSON RESOURCES

	Making Meaning	Language Development	Effective Expression
Lesson	First Read Close Read Analyze the Text Analyze Craft and Structure	Conventions Concept Vocabulary Word Study	Writing to Compare
Instructional Standards	**RI.10** By the end of the year, read and comprehend literary nonfiction . . . **L.4** Determine or clarify the meaning of unknown and multiple-meaning words and phrases . . . **RI.3** Analyze in detail how a key individual, event, or idea . . . **RI.5** Analyze how a particular sentence, paragraph, chapter, or section . . .	**L.4** Determine or clarify the meaning of unknown and multiple-meaning words and phrases . . . **L.4.b** Use common, grade-appropriate Greek or Latin affixes and roots . . . **L.1** Demonstrate command of the conventions . . . **L.1.a** Ensure that pronouns are in the proper case . . .	**W.2** Write informative/explanatory texts to examine a topic and convey ideas, concepts, and information . . .

STUDENT RESOURCES

Available online in the Interactive Student Edition or Unit Resources	Selection Audio First-Read Guide: Nonfiction Close-Read Guide: Nonfiction	Word Network	Evidence Log

TEACHER RESOURCES

Selection Resources Available online in the Interactive Teacher's Edition or Unit Resources	Audio Summaries Annotation Highlights EL Highlights Declaration of the Rights of the Child: Text Questions Analyze Craft and Structure: Development of Ideas	Concept Vocabulary and Word Study Conventions: Pronoun Case English Language Support Lesson: Nouns and Pronouns	Writing to Sources Informational Article, Essay
Reteach/Practice (RP) Available online in the Interactive Teacher's Edition or Unit Resources	Analyze Craft and Structure: Development of Ideas (RP)	Conventions: Pronoun Case (RP) Word Study: Latin Root –puls– (RP)	Writing to Sources Informational Article, Essay
Assessment Available online in Assessments	Selection Test		
My Resources	A Unit 1 Answer Key is available online and in the Interactive Teacher's Edition.		

Reading Support

Text Complexity Rubric: Declaration of the Rights of the Child

Quantitative Measures

Lexile 1380L   **Text Length** 658 words

Qualitative Measures

Knowledge Demands ①—②—③—**❹**—⑤	The background information and opening paragraphs clearly explain the overall concept, but the rights cover a wide range of content, from recognizable ideas to less familiar, complex concepts.
Structure ①—②—**❸**—④—⑤	Each of the ten rights are in separate paragraphs, making navigation easier; Organization is evident and logical, but covers a wide range of ideas that are separate and distinct.
Language Conventionality and Clarity ①—②—③—**❹**—⑤	Formal legal language is used, containing lengthy sentences with multiple clauses, above-level vocabulary, and syntax and phrases that will be unfamiliar to most readers at this grade level.
Levels of Meaning/Purpose ①—②—③—**❹**—⑤	Purpose is explicit and clearly stated in beginning; Document as a whole has specific focus (rights of children), but the individual rights cover a wide range of content; ideas are expressed in complex language.

DECIDE & PLAN

English Language Support

Provide English Learners with support for language and meaning as they read the selection.

Language Point out the use of *shall* (*will, will be able to*). Explain phrases that are likely to be unfamiliar, for example *a child of tender years* means *a young child*. Ask students to identify difficult sentences and help to rephrase language as needed. For example, the last sentence of #2 could be rephrased as *When laws are made, it is important to think about the needs of the children.*

Meaning/Purpose Guide students to highlight or copy key words or phrases in each paragraph that help to identify the main ideas. For example, in paragraph 2, students might highlight *discrimination, race, color, sex, language, religion,* and *political or other opinion.*

Strategic Support

Provide students with strategic support to ensure that they can successfully read the text.

Knowledge Demands Before reading, make a list of the topics that students will find in each paragraph about rights, for example *discrimination, physical and mental health, name and nationality, free education.* Have students copy the list. As they read, ask them to write notes about anything they do not understand about each topic. Discuss students' questions and then have them reread.

Meaning/Purpose For each paragraph, make the meaning concrete by giving examples. Ask students to help come up with scenarios that clarify the rights. For example, for paragraph 8, students might say, "If children did not have the right to recreation, it would be legal to never have any gym or recess."

Challenge

Provide students who need to be challenged with ideas for how they can go beyond a simple interpretation of the text.

Text Analysis Ask students to make a list of categories that are covered in the Declaration, for example *education, special needs, health, emotional needs,* etc. Then ask them to summarize in their own words what the Declaration says in each of these areas.

Written Response Ask students to choose three of the rights in the Declaration. For each choice, have them give an example of why it would be important to protect that right, or what the danger would be to a society if the right were not protected.

TEACH

Read and Respond

Have groups read the selection and complete the Making Meaning, Language Development, and Effective Expression activities.

Standards Support Through Teaching and Learning Cycle

IDENTIFY NEEDS

Analyze results of the Beginning-of-Year Assessment, focusing on the items relating to Unit 1. Also take into consideration student performance to this point and your observations of where particular students struggle.

DECIDE AND PLAN

- If students have performed poorly on items matching these standards, then provide selection scaffolds before assigning them the on-level lesson provided in the Student Edition.
- If students have done well on the Beginning-of-Year Assessment, then challenge them to keep progressing and learning by giving them opportunities to practice the skills in depth.
- Use the Selection Resources listed on the Planning pages for "Declaration of the Rights of the Child" to help students continually improve their ability to master the standards.

Instructional Standards: Declaration of the Rights of the Child

	Catching Up	This Year	Looking Forward
Reading	You may wish to administer the **Analyze Craft and Structure: Development of Ideas (RP)** worksheet to help students understand how authors organize text and ideas.	**RI.5** Analyze how a particular sentence, paragraph, chapter, or section fits into the overall structure of a text and contributes to the development of the ideas.	Challenge students to critique the organization of other important documents, such as the Declaration of Independence. Have them discuss how the document is organized and what makes the organization effective.
Language	You may wish to administer the **Conventions: Pronoun Case (RP)** worksheet to help students understand subjective, objective, and possessive case pronouns. You may wish to administer the **Word Study: Latin Root -puls- (RP)** worksheet to help students understand the meaning of words with the root -puls-.	**L.1** Demonstrate command of the conventions of standard English grammar and usage when writing or speaking. **L.4.b** Use common, grade-appropriate Greek or Latin affixes and roots as clues to the meaning of a word.	Challenge students to replace nouns with pronouns in the correct case. Have students identify and define other words that have the Latin root –puls–.

ANALYZE AND REVISE

- Analyze student work for evidence of student learning.
- Identify whether or not students have met the expectations in the standards.
- Identify implications for future instruction.

TEACH

Implement the planned lesson, and gather evidence of student learning.

© Pearson Education, Inc., or its affiliates, All rights reserved.

Jump Start

FIRST READ Are children different from adults? How? What rights should children have? Do children need special protections? Engage students in a discussion of childhood, what distinguishes it from adulthood, and what unique rights and protections should be granted to children. The discussion should provide context for reading "Declaration of the Rights of the Child." As students share their thoughts, guide them to identify specific factors that affected their thinking.

Declaration of the Rights of the Child 🔊 📄

What special challenges do children face? Why might it be especially important for governments and organizations like the United Nations to protect children? What protections should be put in place? Modeling questions such as these will help students connect to the "Declaration of the Rights of the Child" and to the Small-Group Performance Task assignment. Selection audio and print capability for the selection are available in the Interactive Teacher's Edition.

Concept Vocabulary

Ask groups to identify unfamiliar words and any base words they contain. Encourage groups to use their knowledge of base words to determine the meanings of the unfamiliar words.

⬤ FIRST READ

Have students perform the steps of the first read independently.

NOTICE: Encourage students to notice the main ideas, including the rights protected.

ANNOTATE: Remind students to mark key details, such as the specific, unique needs of children.

CONNECT: Encourage students to compare the rights protected by the document to their own lives and the rights they enjoy.

RESPOND: Students will answer questions and identify the rights to demonstrate understanding.

Point out to students that while they will always complete the Respond step at the end of the first read, the other steps will probably happen somewhat concurrently. You may wish to print copies of the **First-Read Guide: Nonfiction** for students to use. 📄

MAKING MEANING

About the United Nations
The **United Nations** (UN) is an international organization that is made up of 193 member states from around the world. All 193 member states collectively form the General Assembly. The **General Assembly** meets every year to discuss, address, and make policies that protect fundamental human rights and maintain global peace. One of these policies was to adopt and expand Eglantyne Jebb's document, the Geneva Declaration of the Rights of the Child.

STANDARDS
Reading Informational Text
By the end of the year, read and comprehend literary nonfiction in the grades 6–8 text complexity band proficiently, with scaffolding as needed at the high end of the range.

Language
Determine or clarify the meaning of unknown and multiple-meaning words and phrases based on *grade 6 reading and content*, choosing flexibly from a range of strategies.

Declaration of the Rights of the Child

Concept Vocabulary

As you perform your first read, you will encounter these words.

entitled	enactment	compulsory

Base Words If these words are unfamiliar, look for base words you know. Use your knowledge of the "inside" word, along with context, to determine meaning. Here is an example of how to apply the strategy.

> **Unfamiliar Word:** *complimentary*
>
> **Context:** She made **complimentary** remarks about the <u>tasty</u> food.
>
> **Familiar "Inside" Word:** *compliment*, meaning "something good to say about someone or something"
>
> **Conclusion:** The food was tasty, which is a good thing. *Complimentary* may mean "expressing good comments."
>
> **Confirm:** Use a dictionary to verify the meaning you infer.

Apply your knowledge of base words and other vocabulary strategies to determine the meanings of unfamiliar words you encounter during your first read.

First Read NONFICTION

Apply these strategies as you conduct your first read. You will have an opportunity to complete a close read after your first read.

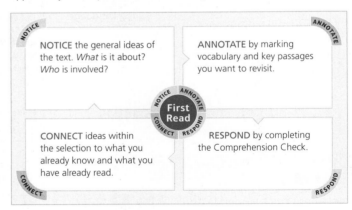

NOTICE the general ideas of the text. *What* is it about? *Who* is involved?

ANNOTATE by marking vocabulary and key passages you want to revisit.

CONNECT ideas within the selection to what you already know and what you have already read.

RESPOND by completing the Comprehension Check.

First Read — NOTICE, ANNOTATE, CONNECT, RESPOND

PERSONALIZE FOR LEARNING

English Language Support
Formal Diction Many of the choices in this document may be unfamiliar and especially challenging for English Language Learners. For instance, the word *shall* is not commonly used in everyday speech, but most native speakers will be familiar with it. Tell students that *shall* means "will." Then, read the document aloud as students follow along to aid comprehension. Then, encourage students to use context clues to determine the meanings of unfamiliar words. Have students highlight words and phrases that they do not understand and guide them in using context clues to understand them.

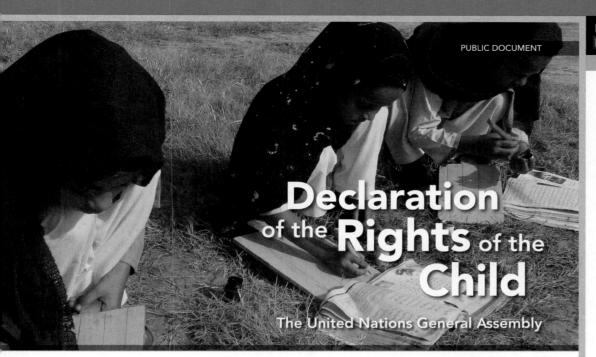

Declaration of the Rights of the Child

The United Nations General Assembly

Concept Vocabulary

ENTITLED If groups are struggling to define *entitled* in paragraph 2, point out that the word has the base word *title*, which can mean "a legally just cause" or "a legal right." Draw students' attention to the context clue *these rights* and use it to help define the word.

Possible response: In this context, *entitled* means "allowed be given a legal right."

BACKGROUND

In the late nineteenth century, many countries began to officially recognize that children need special legal protection. The Declaration of the Rights of the Child, which was adopted by the United Nations in 1959, is the first major international agreement on children's rights. It was inspired by the original declaration written by Eglantyne Jebb, a British activist.

SCAN FOR MULTIMEDIA

1   THIS DECLARATION OF THE RIGHTS OF THE CHILD to the end that he may have a happy childhood and enjoy for his own good and for the good of society the rights and freedoms herein set forth, and calls upon parents, upon men and women as individuals, and upon voluntary organizations, local authorities and national governments to recognize these rights and strive for their observance by legislative and other measures progressively taken in accordance[1] with the following principles:

2   The child shall enjoy all the rights set forth in this Declaration. Every child, without any exception whatsoever, shall be **entitled** to these rights, without distinction or discrimination on account of race, color, sex, language, religion, political or other opinion, national or social origin, property, birth or other status, whether of himself or of his family.

> NOTES
>
> Mark base words or indicate another strategy you used that helped you determine meaning. Confirm the definition by consulting a dictionary.
>
> **entitled** (ehn TY tuhld) *v.*
> MEANING:

_____

1. **accordance** (uh KAWRD uhns) *n.* agreement.

© Pearson Education, Inc., or its affiliates. All rights reserved.

AUTHOR'S PERSPECTIVE: **Jim Cummins, Ph.D.**

Literacy Engagements The more students are engaged with print texts, the more they can develop their academic language proficiency. Conversational fluency is faster to achieve than academic proficiency, so students working in small groups can build language. To support academic language growth and help enhance student engagement with literacy, use these methods:

- **Increase access to print:** To build academic vocabulary, reading is key. Encourage students to

read the texts in *myPerspectives* as well as other selections of their choice.

- **Scaffold Meaning:** Teachers can support students' understanding by using visuals such as illustrations and graphic organizers in the text. Next, teachers can use students' first language to help them understand content in their second language by using electronic translators and bilingual dictionaries.

- **Connect to Students' Lives:** Students' background knowledge is activated by the instruction. This may

or may not occur through a student's first language. Help students build off what they already know.

- **Extend Language:** Use instructional strategies across the curriculum to expand students' language base. For example, make an effort to call out new words, unusual syntax, or other language challenges when the opportunities arise.

Concept Vocabulary

ENACTMENT If groups are struggling to define *enactment* in paragraph 3, point out that the word has the base word *enact*, which can mean "to establish by legal act." Draw students' attention to the context clue *laws for this purpose* and use it to help define the word.

Possible response: In this context, *enactment* means "establishment of by legal act."

COMPULSORY If groups are struggling to define *compulsory* in paragraph 8, point out that the word has the base word, or "inside word," *compulsion*, which can mean "the act of being compelled or forced." Draw students' attention to the context clue *receive education* and use it to help define the word.

Possible response: In this context, *compulsory* means "mandatory."

Additional **English Language Support** is available in the Interactive Teacher's Edition.

© Pearson Education, Inc., or its affiliates. All rights reserved.

NOTES
Mark base words or indicate another strategy you used that helped you determine meaning. Confirm the definition by consulting a dictionary.

enactment (ehn AKT muhnt) *n.*

MEANING:

Mark base words or indicate another strategy you used that helped you determine meaning. Confirm the definition by consulting a dictionary.

compulsory (kuhm PUHL suhr ee) *adj.*

MEANING:

3   The child shall enjoy special protection, and shall be given opportunities and facilities,[2] by law and by other means, to enable him to develop physically, mentally, morally, spiritually and socially in a healthy and normal manner and in conditions of freedom and dignity. In the **enactment** of laws for this purpose, the best interests of the child shall be the paramount consideration.

4   The child shall be entitled from his birth to a name and a nationality.

5   The child shall enjoy the benefits of social security. He shall be entitled to grow and develop in health; to this end, special care and protection shall be provided both to him and to his mother, including adequate pre-natal and post-natal care.[3] The child shall have the right to adequate nutrition, housing, recreation and medical services.

6   The child who is physically, mentally or socially handicapped shall be given the special treatment, education and care required by his particular condition.

7   The child, for the full and harmonious development of his personality, needs love and understanding. He shall, wherever possible, grow up in the care and under the responsibility of his parents, and, in any case, in an atmosphere of affection and of moral and material security; a child of tender years shall not, save in exceptional circumstances, be separated from his mother. Society and the public authorities shall have the duty to extend particular care to children without a family and to those without adequate means of support. Payment of State and other assistance towards the maintenance of children of large families is desirable.

8   The child is entitled to receive education, which shall be free and **compulsory**, at least in the elementary stages. He shall be given an education which will promote his general culture and enable him, on a basis of equal opportunity, to develop his abilities, his individual judgment, and his sense of moral and social responsibility, and to become a useful member of society. The best interests of the child shall be the guiding principle of those responsible for his education and guidance; that responsibility lies in the first place with his parents. The child shall have full opportunity for play and recreation, which should be

2. **facilities** (fuh SIHL uh teez) *n.* buildings designed for a specific purpose.
3. **pre-natal and post-natal care** care given to women before and after the birth of a child.

44 UNIT 1 • CHILDHOOD

👥 FACILITATING SMALL GROUP CLOSE READING

CLOSE READ: Nonfiction As groups perform the close read, circulate and offer support as needed.

• Remind groups that when they read nonfiction, they should be sure to identify the main ideas and key details.

• If a group is confused about why particular ideas are important, remind them to think about how the ideas are related to the Declaration's purpose.

• Challenge groups to paraphrase the text using more familiar language.

directed to the same purposes as education; society and the public authorities shall endeavor to promote the enjoyment of this right.

9 The child shall in all circumstances be among the first to receive protection and relief.

10 The child shall be protected against all forms of neglect, cruelty and exploitation. He shall not be the subject of traffic, in any form. The child shall not be admitted to employment before an appropriate minimum age; he shall in no case be caused or permitted to engage in any occupation or employment which would prejudice his health or education, or interfere with his physical, mental or moral development.

11 The child shall be protected from practices which may foster racial, religious and any other form of discrimination. He shall be brought up in a spirit of understanding, tolerance, friendship among peoples, peace and universal brotherhood, and in full consciousness⁴ that his energy and talents should be devoted to the service of his fellow men. ❧

---

4. **consciousness** (KON shuhs nihs) *n.* awareness or understanding.

NOTES

Comprehension Check

Possible responses:

1. According to the document, every child is entitled to these rights.
2. special protection; education
3. They should be given "the special treatment, education, and care required by his particular condition."

Research to Clarify If groups struggle to identify their research topics, you might want to suggest one of the following topics: child labor laws, laws governing school attendance or school attendance rates, literacy rates among boys and girls, malnutrition in children, or the laws governing the protection of refugee children. Encourage students to research different countries.

Comprehension Check

Complete the following items after you finish your first read. Review and clarify details with your group.

1. Which children are entitled to the rights this document sets forth?

2. Identify two rights defined or described in this document.

3. According to the document, what should children who are physically or mentally disabled be given?

- -

RESEARCH

Research to Clarify Choose at least one unfamiliar detail from the text. Briefly research that detail. In what way does the information you learned shed light on an aspect of the Declaration?

Declaration of the Rights of the Child **45**

© Pearson Education, Inc., or its affiliates. All rights reserved.

PERSONALIZE FOR LEARNING

Challenge

Text-to-World Connection Have students research children who have campaigned for the rights of other children. Then, have each student choose one child activist and create a brief multimedia presentation that tells about the life of the child, how he or she became an activist and why, and what he or she has accomplished. Students should share their presentations with the class. Potential research subjects include Malala Yousafzai, Iqbal Masih, and Severn Cullis-Suzuki.

Jump Start

CLOSE READ Ask students to consider what challenges faced by children are addressed by the "Declaration of the Rights of the Child" and which are not. As students discuss in their groups, have them identify any protections they think should be added to the Declaration.

Close Read the Text

If needed, model close reading by using the Annotation Highlights in the Interactive Teacher's Edition.

Remind students to use Accountable Talk in their discussions and to support one another as they complete the close read.

Analyze the Text

1. **Possible response:** According to the document, all children are entitled to a free and compulsory education. The U.N. hoped this education would help the child become a useful member of society.

2. Passages will vary by group. Students should participate in discussion.

3. Responses will vary by group.

Concept Vocabulary

Why These Words? Possible response: The words are all related to laws and rights.

Practice

Sample response: Children are *entitled* to human rights. The *enactment* of laws protects these rights. For instance, laws in many countries make elementary education *compulsory*.

Word Network

Possible responses: *pre-natal, post-natal, development*

Word Study

Possible response: *compulsory* means "pushing," or enforcing, people to do something. Another word formed from the root is *expulsion*, which means "to force people out."

For more support, see **Concept Vocabulary and Word Study.** 📄

MAKING MEANING

DECLARATION OF THE RIGHTS OF THE CHILD

TIP

GROUP DISCUSSION
When your group rereads paragraph 8, read it aloud, with each person taking turns to read one sentence. Doing so may give you a stronger sense of what the writers of the document had in mind.

WORD NETWORK
Add words related to childhood from the text to your Word Network.

STANDARDS
Reading Informational Text
• Analyze in detail how a key individual, event, or idea is introduced, illustrated, and elaborated in a text.
• Analyze how a particular sentence, paragraph, chapter, or section fits into the overall structure of a text and contributes to the development of the ideas.
Language
Determine or clarify the meaning of unknown and multiple-meaning words and phrases based on *grade 6 reading and content*, choosing flexibly from a range of strategies.
  b. Use common, grade-appropriate Greek or Latin affixes and roots as a clue to the meaning of a word or phrase.

46 UNIT 1 • CHILDHOOD

Close Read the Text

With your group, revisit sections of the text you marked during your first read. **Annotate** details that you notice. What **questions** do you have? What can you **conclude**?

Close Read — ANNOTATE QUESTION CONCLUDE

Analyze the Text

CITE TEXTUAL EVIDENCE to support your answers.

📄 Notebook **Complete the activities.**

1. **Review and Clarify** With your group, reread paragraph 8 of the Declaration. Discuss the kind of education to which all children are entitled, according to the document. What did the UN General Assembly hope education would accomplish for children?

2. **Present and Discuss** Now, work with your group to share passages from the selection that you found especially important. Take turns presenting your passages. Discuss what you noticed in the selection, what questions you asked, and what conclusions you reached.

3. **Essential Question:** *What are some of the challenges and triumphs of growing up?* What has this text taught you about childhood? Discuss with your group.

LANGUAGE DEVELOPMENT

Concept Vocabulary

entitled	enactment	compulsory

Why These Words? The concept vocabulary words from the text are related. With your group, determine what the words have in common. Write your ideas, and add another word that fits the category.

Practice

📄 Notebook Check your understanding of the concept vocabulary words by using them in sentences. In each sentence, provide context clues that hint at the vocabulary word's meaning.

Word Study

📄 Notebook **Latin Root: -puls-** The Declaration states that education for children should be free and compulsory. The word *compulsory* is formed from the Latin root *-puls-* (also spelled *-pel-*), which means "push," "drive," or "force." Write a definition of *compulsory* that shows how the root *-puls-* contributes to its meaning. Find another word formed from this root. Write the word and its meaning.

© Pearson Education, Inc., or its affiliates. All rights reserved.

FORMATIVE ASSESSMENT

Analyze the Text 📄

If students struggle to close read the document, **then** provide the **Declaration of the Rights of the Child: Text Questions** available online in the Interactive Teacher's Edition or Unit Resources. Answers and DOK levels are also available.

Concept Vocabulary

If students struggle to identify the concept, **then** have them look up the definition of each word and consider what is similar about them.

Word Study

If students fail to correctly use the word in a sentence, **then** suggest they fill in the blank in the following sentence. *I'm glad that _____ is not compulsory because I don't like it.* For Reteach and Practice, see **Word Study: Latin Root -puls- (RP).** 📄

Analyze Craft and Structure

Development of Ideas: Structure The Declaration of the Rights of the Child expresses its ideas using a simple structure. Paragraph 1 explains the purpose and goal of the Declaration. Paragraph 2 explains the scope of the Declaration, or the people and rights that it covers. Paragraphs 3–11 list and describe specific rights.

Practice

© Pearson Education, Inc., or its affiliates. All rights reserved.

CITE TEXTUAL EVIDENCE to support your answers.

📓 **Notebook** Work together to answer the questions and complete the activities.

1. Reread paragraph 1. What are the purpose and goal of the Declaration?

2. Reread paragraph 2. Whose rights does the Declaration set forth?

3. Choose three paragraphs from paragraphs 3–11. In the chart, identify the paragraphs you have chosen. List the rights that each paragraph describes. Then, state whether you think the rights are described in a way that is confusing or clear. Explain why.

PARAGRAPH	RIGHTS LISTED	CLEAR OR CONFUSING? WHY?
4	name and nationality	clear because it states exactly what the rights are and gives no other details
5	social security, including health care for mother and child; adequate food, housing, recreation	confusing if you don't know the meaning of *social security* or *pre-natal* and *post-natal*
6	child who is physically, socially, or mentally handicapped has the right to special treatment, education, and care	clear, although the term *disabled* is more commonly used than *handicapped* today.

4. As a group, discuss whether the text is organized effectively. Would the issues being presented have been clearer or more powerful if statistics, charts, or personal stories had been included? Why or why not?

5. Why do you think the United Nations General Assembly organized the information in this way? Discuss with your group. Come to an agreement about at least two reasons. Write them here.

Declaration of the Rights of the Child **47**

DIGITAL PERSPECTIVES

Analyze Craft and Structure

Development of Ideas: Structure Remind students than an author's **purpose** is his or her reason for writing and that an author can have more than one purpose. For instance, a writer might want to inform and persuade readers that children should have a specific right, like the right to an education. For more support, see **Analyze Craft and Structure: Development of Ideas.** 🔘

Practice

1. The purpose and goal of the Declaration is to set forth the rights and freedoms all children should have, so that parents, organizations, and governments will ensure that children will have them.

2. The rights are set forth for every child.

3. See possible responses in chart on student page.

4. The organization makes sense because each paragraph focuses on one main idea and has one purpose. The issues being presented would not have been clearer if statistics or charts were used, as data may change over time. Personal stories might draw attention to one area or problem, which would make the document seem less universal.

5. The information is organized in this way for clarity and because statistics or charts would become inaccurate over time.

FORMATIVE ASSESSMENT

Analyze Craft and Structure

If students are unable to identify the rights in the paragraphs, **then** have them circle key words and then identify main ideas. For Reteach and Practice, see **Analyze Craft and Structure: Development of Ideas (RP).** 🔘

CROSS-CURRICULAR PERSPECTIVES

Art Challenge students to create art that depicts or is inspired by each of the rights of the child described in the document. Students can then work in their small groups to create collages that include all the rights. Groups could then present or display their collages.

FACILITATING

Conventions

Pronoun Case Tell students that pronouns can take the place of nouns as subjects or objects of sentences. They can also replace possessive nouns.

- <u>Her</u> books are too heavy to carry in a backpack. (possessive)
- <u>She</u> tried to give a chair to the man. (subjective)
- The librarian recommended some plays to <u>them</u>. (objective)

For more support, see **Conventions: Pronoun Case.**

Read It

Responses:

1a. <u>their</u> - possessive

  b. <u>he</u>, <u>she</u> - subjective

  c. <u>we</u> - subjective; <u>them</u> - objective

  d. <u>his</u> - possessive

Write It

Possible responses:

1. Her goal was to help children.

2. As a result, she founded an organization.

3. The name of it is Save the Children.

FORMATIVE ASSESSMENT

Conventions

If students are unable to identify pronouns used as subjects, objects, or in the possessive, **then** have them practice by using the following pronouns in sentences: *he, she, them, her.* For Reteach and Practice, see **Conventions: Pronoun Case (RP).**

LANGUAGE DEVELOPMENT

DECLARATION OF THE RIGHTS OF THE CHILD

Conventions

Pronoun Case Effective writing involves correct usage of pronouns. A **pronoun** is a word that takes the place of one or more nouns or other pronouns. **Pronoun case** is the form a pronoun takes to show whether it is being used as a subject, an object, or a possessive. Writers use pronouns to avoid repetition of nouns in their writing, and the case they use depends on the pronoun's function in a sentence.

There are three pronoun cases, as shown in the chart.

PRONOUN CASE	EXAMPLES
Nominative (or **Subjective**) **Case:** names the subject of a verb or is used in the predicate after a linking verb nominative pronouns: I, you, he, she, it, we, you, they	He likes the sound of the train on the tracks. They searched online for the article. The singers of the duet will be <u>she</u> and <u>I</u>.
Objective Case: names the direct object of a verb, the indirect object of a verb, or the object of a preposition objective pronous: me, you, him, her, it, us, you, them	Domingo sent <u>it</u> to Mel. Please give <u>me</u> the earrings. The cafeteria chefs had prepared a meal for <u>us</u>.
Possessive Case: shows ownership possessive pronouns: my, your, his, her, its, our, their, mine, yours, hers, ours, theirs	After an hour of running, <u>my</u> legs ached. Please stick out <u>your</u> tongue for the doctor. Theo works during <u>his</u> summer breaks.

Read It

1. Mark the pronouns in each sentence. Label the case of each pronoun.

   a. Children are not responsible for their own education.

   b. When a child is born, he or she will be entitled to special human rights.

   c. Children are important, and we protect them from discrimination.

   d. The child shall be entitled from his birth to a name and a nationality.

Write It

Notebook Read the example. Notice that the underlined text has been replaced with a pronoun. Do the same for the sentences in items 1–3.

> **Original:** The writer of the first declaration is <u>Eglantyne Jebb</u>.
>
> **Revision:** The writer of the first declaration is **she.**

1. <u>Eglantyne Jebb's</u> goal was to help children.

2. As a result, <u>Eglantyne Jebb</u> founded an organization.

3. The name of <u>the organization</u> is Save the Children.

≡ STANDARDS

Language
Demonstrate command of the conventions of standard English grammar and usage when writing or speaking.
  a. Ensure that pronouns are in the proper case.

48 UNIT 1 • CHILDHOOD

© Pearson Education, Inc., or its affiliates. All rights reserved.

PERSONALIZE FOR LEARNING

English Language Support
Practicing with Nouns and Pronouns Ask students to write a few sentences about their pet or a pet they would like to have. Tell them to make two columns—one that lists the nouns that they use and one that lists the pronouns. **EMERGING**

Ask students to write a paragraph about their pet or a pet they would like to have. Tell them to make two columns—one that lists the nouns that they use and one that lists the pronouns. In the pronoun column, have them write the nouns that each of the pronouns refers to. **EXPANDING**

Ask students to write a paragraph about their pet or a pet they would like to have. Tell them to make two columns—one that lists the nouns that they use and one that lists the pronouns. Then have them list which nouns each of the pronouns refer to. Have them read their paragraph to a partner without using any of the pronouns and discuss how the paragraph is different from their original **BRIDGING**

An expanded **English Language Support Lesson** on Practicing with Nouns and Pronouns is available in the Interactive Teacher's Edition.

Writing to Sources

Assignment

Choose one of the options and write a response. If necessary, conduct brief research to support or develop your ideas. Work with your group to discuss and plan, but do your own writing.

☐ **Option 1:** Write an **informational article** that describes the purposes for which the Declaration of the Rights of the Child was written. What do you think the writers wanted to achieve? Make sure readers understand the main ideas of the Declaration by including a summary.

☐ **Option 2:** Choose two of the rights listed in the Declaration that you feel are most important. Then, write a brief **essay** in which you explain the reasons for your choices. Why do these rights matter matter so much? Include details from the text as well as your own opinions and any examples you might find through research.

Project Plan Before you begin, meet as a group to discuss each student's choice of project and to share ideas. Go back to the Declaration and work together to clarify any sections that might be confusing. Then, work independently to write.

Finding Examples Choose passages from the Declaration that clearly support your ideas. Make sure you quote them accurately. Use a chart like this one to keep track of your examples. Remember to include appropriate citations.

EXAMPLE	IDEA IT SUPPORTS	CITATION INFORMATION

Present Organize a brief presentation in which you explain the different main ideas each member of your group expressed. Share your presentation with the class.

VOCABULARY DEVELOPMENT

Word Analysis If groups are struggling with the concept of a *declaration,* tell them that it is derived from the Latin verb *clarare,* meaning "to make clear." Have groups discuss the various ideas that the "Declaration of the Rights of the Child" makes clear.

EVIDENCE LOG

Before moving on to a new selection, go to your Evidence Log and record what you learned from the Declaration of the Rights of the Child.

STANDARDS

Writing
Write informative/explanatory texts to examine a topic and convey ideas, concepts, and information through the selection, organization, and analysis of relevant content.

Writing to Sources

Tell students that regardless of which prompt they choose to address, they will be writing paragraphs whose purpose is to inform. Provide these criteria for effective informational writing:

- an engaging introductory sentence that grabs the reader's attention
- a clear statement of the central idea
- specific, relevant details and evidence from the text
- logical organization
- language appropriate to audience and purpose
- transitional words and phrases, such as those that show comparison and contrast: *likewise, similarly, in contrast,* and *however.*

For more support, see **Writing to Sources: Informational Article, Essay.**

Project Plan Encourage students to talk about which prompt they are addressing. Then have them discuss the parts of the Declaration that they have questions about, sharing ideas and explanations.

Finding Examples Remind students that different people can interpret examples in different ways. Encourage the students in each group to discuss the examples they gather. Encourage them to give each other feedback about how well they believe the examples support the main points.

Evidence Log Support students in completing their Evidence Log. This paced activity will help prepare them for the Performance-Based Assessment at the end of the unit.

FORMATIVE ASSESSMENT

Writing to Sources

If students are unable to write to inform, **then** have them use the criteria outlined above to revise their paragraph(s). For Reteach and Practice, see **Writing to Sources: Informational Article, Essay (RP).**

Selection Test

Administer the "Declaration of the Rights of the Child" Selection Test, which is available in both print and digital formats online in Assessments.

© Pearson Education, Inc., or its affiliates. All rights reserved.

Michaela DePrince: The War Orphan Who Became a Ballerina

AUDIO SUMMARIES

Audio summaries of "Michaela DePrince: The War Orphan Who Became a Ballerina" are available in both English and Spanish and can be assigned to students in the Interactive Teacher's Edition or Unit Resources. Assigning these summaries prior to reading the selection may help students build additional background knowledge and set a context for their first read.

Summary

The article "Michaela DePrince: The War Orphan Who Became a Ballerina," by William Kremer, follows an incredible life. DePrince grew up in Sierra Leone and lost her parents to war. During her difficult life in an orphanage, she saw an image of a ballerina and was struck by the hope and love she saw there. Because of a skin condition, she feared people would think she was ugly and would never adopt her. But a woman who met DePrince did adopt her, and she brought DePrince to a safer place. There, DePrince was able to pursue ballet as she'd dreamed of doing. She is now a professional dancer.

Insight

This article teaches us the importance of inspiration and goals for overcoming adversity. It also deals with the issue of being self-conscious about one's appearance, which is common among young people. The difficulties that DePrince went through include losing her parents, being teased for her appearance, and coping with violence done to people she cared about (a teacher). Be sensitive to students who may have gone through similar trials.

ESSENTIAL QUESTION:
What are some of the challenges and triumphs of growing up?

Connection to Essential Question

DePrince's story reflects many aspects of childhood. Most young people are conscious about their appearance at some point, and many find the inspiration that leads them to be who they want to be as an adult.

SMALL-GROUP LEARNING PERFORMANCE TASK
Deliver a retelling of the childhood challenges presented in one of the texts you have read in this section.

UNIT PERFORMANCE-BASED ASSESSMENT
When did a challenge lead to a triumph?

Connection to Performance Tasks

Small-Group Learning Performance Task Students may choose to retell DePrince's challenges, including cruelty she experienced at the orphanage. Many children may relate to the hard work DePrince must endure in order to find success.

Unit Performance-Based Assessment This selection will contribute to students' understanding of the challenges we face in childhood by showing how DePrince faced a great deal of adversity in her young life. She overcame such difficulties in part because she aspired to a goal and took the necessary steps to achieve it.

LESSON RESOURCES

	Making Meaning	**Language Development**	**Effective Expression**
Lesson	**First Read** **Close Read** **Analyze the Text** **Analyze Craft and Structure**	**Concept Vocabulary** **Word Study** **Conventions**	**Speaking and Listening**
Instructional Standards	**RI.10** By the end of the year, read and comprehend literary nonfiction . . . **L.4** Determine or clarify the meaning of unknown and multiple-meaning words and phrases . . . **L.4.a** Use context as a clue . . . **RI.3** Analyze in detail how a key individual, event, or idea . . . **RI.5** Analyze how a particular sentence, paragraph, chapter, or section . . .	**L.4** Determine or clarify the meaning of unknown and multiple-meaning words and phrases . . . **L.4.c** Consult reference materials to find the pronunciation . . . **L.4.d** Verify the preliminary determination . . . **L.5** Demonstrate understanding of figurative language . . . **L.5.b** Use the relationship between particular words . . . **L.1** Demonstrate command of the conventions . . . **L.1.b** Use intensive pronouns . . .	**SL.4** Present claims and findings, sequencing ideas logically and using pertinent descriptions, facts, and details . . .

▶ STUDENT RESOURCES

Available online in the Interactive Student Edition or Unit Resources	Selection Audio 🖹 First-Read Guide: Nonfiction 🖹 Close-Read Guide: Nonfiction	🖹 Word Network	🖹 Evidence Log

▶ TEACHER RESOURCES

Selection Resources Available online in the Interactive Teacher's Edition or Unit Resources	🔊 Audio Summaries ✏ Annotation Highlights 💬 EL Highlights 🖹 Michaela DePrince: Text Questions 🖹 Analyze Craft and Structure: Biographical Writing	🖹 Concept Vocabulary and Word Study 🖹 Conventions: Reflexive and Intensive Pronouns 🖹 English Language Support Lesson: Planning a Profile	🖹 Speaking and Listening: Oral Presentation
Reteach/Practice (RP) Available online in the Interactive Teacher's Edition or Unit Resources	🖹 Analyze Craft and Structure: Biographical Writing (RP)	🖹 Word Study: Synonyms and Antonyms (RP) 🖹 Conventions: Reflexive and Intensive Pronouns (RP)	🖹 Speaking and Listening: Oral Presentation (RP)
Assessment Available online in Assessments	🖹 ☑ Selection Test		
My Resources	🖹 A Unit 1 Answer Key is available online and in the Interactive Teacher's Edition.		

Reading Support

Text Complexity Rubric: Michaela DePrince: The War Orphan Who Became a Ballerina

Quantitative Measures

Lexile 1040   **Text Length** 890 words

Qualitative Measures

Knowledge Demands ①—②—③—❹—⑤	Experiences portrayed include the following: life in orphanage in Sierre Leone, adoption into U.S. studying and performing ballet
Structure ①—❷—③—④—⑤	Story spans many years, but is told clearly and chronologically; told in journalistic style, going between narration and quotations from Michaela DePrince.
Language Conventionality and Clarity ①—②—③—❹—⑤	Language is explicit and literal, but with a lot of above-level vocabulary; Sentence structure is often complex, and there are many lengthy sentences with multiple clauses.
Levels of Meaning/Purpose ①—②—❸—④—⑤	Purpose is explicitly stated, clear, and concrete, and content is narrowly focused, but understanding of meaning at times is dependent on reader's prior knowledge and ability to understand language.

DECIDE AND PLAN

English Language Support

Provide English Learners with support for knowledge demands and language as they read the selection.

Knowledge Demands Before students read, review some of the background information they will need to understand the text. Ask them to locate Sierra Leone in West Africa on a map or globe. Write the words *orphan, orphanage, adopt, adoption* and determine if students know the meanings. Explain or have them look up words if necessary.

Language Help students to understand complex sentences by breaking them down into parts. For example, (paragraph 7) *The other girls were told not to play with DePrince; DePrince became friends with child number 26; The girl was called Mabinty; the Aunties disliked her because she was left-handed.*

Strategic Support

Provide students with strategic support to ensure that they can successfully read the text.

Knowledge Demands Have students read the title and background and tell you what they learned so far. For example, *Michaela DePrince was a war orphan. She lost both parents in a war in Sierra Leone.* Tell students Sierra Leone is in West Africa. Check understanding as they read. *Where was she born? Where did she go when her parents died? What does it mean when she became a number? (they called her number 27).*

Language Help students to unpack lengthy sentences by asking questions about each part. For example, (paragraph 7) *Who became DePrince's friend? (a girl named Mabinty) Why did the Aunties dislike her? (she was left-handed).*

Challenge

Provide students who need to be challenged with ideas for how they can go beyond a simple interpretation of the text.

Text Analysis After reading, ask students to comment on the aspects of life in the orphanage that would have been most difficult for the children. Have them describe the feelings DePrince had while in the orphanage, when she was adopted, and how she feels now as a dancer.

Written Response Ask students to look up Michaela DePrince on the Internet and find information about her book, *Taking Flight*. Ask them to read that book or look up other biographical information about the dancer's life. Have them write what they found most interesting about the dancer.

TEACH

Read and Respond

Have groups read the selection and complete the Making Meaning and Language Development activities.

Standards Support Through Teaching and Learning

IDENTIFY NEEDS

Analyze results of the Beginning-of-Year Assessment, focusing on the items relating to Unit 1. Also take into consideration student performance to this point and your observations of where particular students struggle.

ANALYZE AND REVISE

- Analyze student work for evidence of student learning.
- Identify whether or not students have met the expectations in the standards.
- Identify implications for future instruction.

TEACH

Implement the planned lesson, and gather evidence of student learning.

DECIDE AND PLAN

- If students have performed poorly on items matching these standards, then provide selection scaffolds before assigning them the on-level lesson provided in the Student Edition.
- If students have done well on the Beginning-of-Year Assessment, then challenge them to keep progressing and learning by giving them opportunities to practice the skills in depth.
- Use the Selection Resources listed on the Planning pages for "Michaela DePrince: The War Orphan Who Became a Ballerina" to help students continually improve their ability to master the standards.

Instructional Standards: Michaela DePrince: The War Orphan Who Became a Ballerina

	Catching Up	This Year	Looking Forward
Reading	You may wish to administer the **Analyze Craft and Structure: Biographical Writing (RP)** worksheet to help students understand how authors organize ideas in a logical order.	**RI.3** Analyze in detail how a key individual, event, or idea is introduced, illustrated, and elaborated in a text.	Challenge students to analyze and discuss another selection, noting how the author uses facts, details, examples, and quotations to organize the text.
Speaking and Listening	You may wish to administer the **Speaking and Listening: Oral Presentation (RP)** worksheet to help students plan and organize their presentations.	**SL.4** Present claims and findings, sequencing ideas logically and using pertinent descriptions, facts, and details to accentuate main ideas or themes; use appropriate eye contact, adequate volume, and clear pronunciation.	Challenge students to research other individuals who have overcome significant obstacles to achieve success. Then have students give oral presentations about the individuals they select.
Language	You may wish to administer the **Conventions: Reflexive and Intensive Pronouns (RP)** worksheet to help students understand how these pronouns are used. You may wish to administer the **Word Study: Synonyms and Antonyms (RP)** worksheet to help students understand how to better understand a word by finding other words that mean the same thing or have the opposite meaning.	**L.1.b** Use intensive pronouns. **L.5.b** Use the relationship between particular words to better understand each of the words.	Challenge students to use reflexive and intensive pronouns in a writing assignment. Challenge students to rewrite a few paragraphs of text using antonyms or synonyms for some of the words. Encourage students to use reference materials to find additional words.

Jump Start

FIRST READ Have students discuss these questions: What can inspire children to overcome obstacles? What support can help them to accomplish their goals? The discussion should provide context for reading "Michaela DePrince: The War Orphan Who Became a Ballerina." As students share their thoughts, guide them to identify specific factors and personal experiences that shape their responses to these questions.

Michaela DePrince: The War Orphan Who Became a Ballerina 🔊 📄

Have you ever faced a situation in which you felt isolated, abandoned, or alone? What helped you? Modeling questions such as these will help students connect to the "Michaela DePrince: The War Orphan Who Became a Ballerina" and to the Small-Group Performance Task assignment. Selection audio and print capability for the selection are available in the Interactive Teacher's Edition.

Concept Vocabulary

Ask groups to look closely at the three types of context clues—synonym, restatement of an idea, and contrast of ideas and topics—and discuss how these types of clues can help clarify meaning. Encourage groups to think of one other type of context clue that they might encounter in a text. Possibilities include examples, antonyms, and definitions.

⬤ FIRST READ

Have students perform the steps of the first read independently.

NOTICE: Encourage students to notice the sequence of events.

ANNOTATE: Remind students to mark key details, such as those that give insight into Michaela's feelings.

CONNECT: Encourage students to compare Michaela's dreams of becoming a ballerina to their own aspirations.

RESPOND: Students will answer questions and write a summary to demonstrate understanding.

Point out to students that while they will always complete the Respond step at the end of the first read, the other steps will probably happen somewhat concurrently. You may wish to print copies of the **First-Read Guide: Nonfiction** for students to use. 📄

About the Author
William Kremer is a feature writer at the British Broadcasting Corporation (BBC), a major radio, television, and media company.

Michaela DePrince: The War Orphan Who Became a Ballerina

Concept Vocabulary

As you perform your first read of "Michaela DePrince: The War Orphan Who Became a Ballerina," you will encounter these words.

antagonism	refugee	distraught

Context Clues To find the meaning of an unfamiliar word, look for **context clues**—other words and phrases that appear nearby in the text. There are various types of context clues that can help you as you read.

> **Context:** Rather than wearing **leotards** during dance class, she covered herself with sweatshirts.
>
> **Conclusion:** The girl covers herself with sweatshirts instead of leotards during dance class. *Leotards* must be another type of clothing. Perhaps they are a type of clothing worn by dancers in particular.

Apply your knowledge of context clues and other vocabulary strategies to determine the meanings of unfamiliar words you encounter during your first read.

First Read NONFICTION

Apply these strategies as you conduct your first read. You will have an opportunity to complete a close read after your first read.

NOTICE the general ideas of the text. *What* is it about? *Who* is involved?

ANNOTATE by marking vocabulary and key passages you want to revisit.

CONNECT ideas within the selection to what you already know and what you have already read.

RESPOND by completing the Comprehension Check and by writing a brief summary of the selection.

STANDARDS
Reading Informational Text
By the end of the year, read and comprehend literary nonfiction in the grades 6–8 text complexity band proficiently, with scaffolding as needed at the high end of the range.

Language
Determine or clarify the meaning of unknown and multiple-meaning words and phrases based on *grade 6 reading and content,* choosing flexibly from a range of strategies.
   a. Use context as a clue to the meaning of a word or phrase.

© Pearson Education, Inc., or its affiliates. All rights reserved.

PERSONALIZE FOR LEARNING

Strategic Support

Sequence of Events If students have difficulty understanding the sequence of events, have them work in pairs to create a timeline. If students still need additional support, provide a timeline with some of the events already added, such as the following.

1995		2012
Michaela is born	parents die	Michaela tours with Dance Theatre of Harlem
Students should add at least three more events to the timeline.		

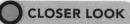
MAGAZINE ARTICLE

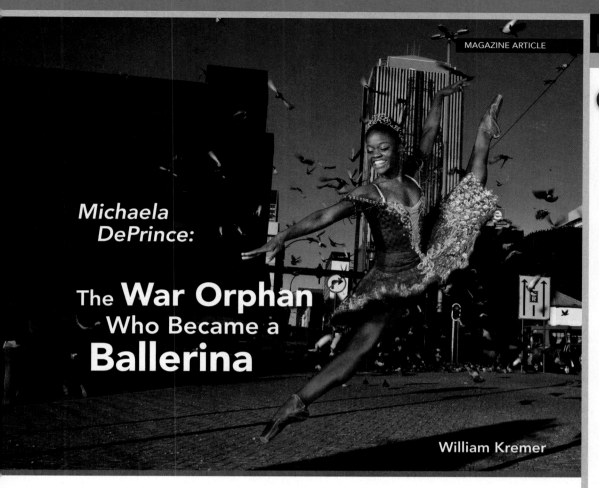

Michaela DePrince:

The **War Orphan**
Who Became a
Ballerina

William Kremer

© Pearson Education, Inc., or its affiliates. All rights reserved.

BACKGROUND

From 1991 to 2002, Sierra Leone went through a violent civil war. During this decade, life in Sierra Leone was extremely dangerous due to a near complete lack of law in the country. Tens of thousands of people lost their lives, and countless families were torn apart. Children who lost their parents during the war became known as "war orphans."

SCAN FOR
MULTIMEDIA

1 A professional stage debut is a huge event in the life of any ballerina, but Michaela DePrince's recent tour of South Africa also marked the end of an extraordinary journey from her childhood as a war orphan in Sierra Leone.

NOTES

2 "I got out of a terrible place," says DePrince. "I had no idea I would be here—I'm living my dream every single day."

3 She was born in Sierra Leone in 1995. Her parents named her Mabinty, but after they both died during the civil war, she was sent to an orphanage, where she became a number.

Michaela DePrince: The War Orphan Who Became a Ballerina **51**

● **CLOSER LOOK**

Analyze Sequence of Events

Circulate among groups as students conduct their close read. Suggest that groups close read paragraphs 1–3. Encourage them to talk about the annotations that they mark. If needed, provide the following support.

ANNOTATE: Have students highlight important events in Michaela's life. For instance, students might highlight *professional stage debut, born in Sierra Leone in 1995,* and *parents…died during the civil war.*

QUESTION: Guide students to consider the sequence of events. Ask what event happened most recently, and accept student responses.

Possible responses: The most recent event is Michaela's professional stage debut.

CONCLUDE: Help students formulate conclusions about the importance of sequence of events in the article. Ask students why the author begins the article with the professional stage debut.

Possible responses: By mentioning the stage debut first, the author highlights its importance in Michaela's life.

Remind students that writers of nonfiction magazine articles often use narrative techniques such as **sequence of events**, flashback, and flash forward. Presenting events in a specific order can engage readers in the same way that the plot of a well-crafted short story compels readers.

CROSS-CURRICULAR PERSPECTIVES

Social Studies Challenge students to work in small groups to locate Sierra Leone on a map of the world and to briefly research that country's civil war. Have students answer these questions:

Where is Sierra Leone? What caused its civil war? How many people were killed during the war? What are conditions like now for people in Sierra Leone? Groups could then present their findings to the class.

Concept Vocabulary

ANTAGONISM If groups are struggling to define the word *antagonism* in paragraph 5, remind them to look for context clues. Ask them what *fierce* suggests and have them read the paragraph from the top. Ask students if DePrince's skin condition qualifies her for special care from the Aunties. If they think she's possessed by an evil spirit, are they likely to feel any fondness to her? Have students look for the answer in paragraph 5. If not fondness, then what is their fierce feeling toward the girl?

Possible response: *Antagonism* means "hatred" or "hostility."

REFUGEE If groups are having trouble working out the meaning of the word *refugee* in paragraph 13, remind them that it sometimes works to look for a familiar word inside the larger, unfamiliar word. Ask them what "refuge" means. Where have they seen the *-ee* ending? Who answers an interviewer's questions? Who is employed by an employer? If *-ee* suggests a person directly affected by or acted on by the verb (not noun) at the core of the word, then ask students for a definition of *refugee*.

Possible response: *Refugee* means "a person searching for a place of safety" or "a person fleeing from harm."

DISTRAUGHT If groups are struggling to define *distraught* in paragraph 14, have them look at context clues. To whom does the word apply directly? Ask students what reason Michaela has to be *distraught*. Do they think she wishes to be left behind—and if not, how does she feel?

Possible response: *Distraught* means "anxious" or "very distressed."

 Additional **English Language Support** is available in the Interactive Teacher's Edition.

NOTES

Mark context clues or indicate another strategy you used that helped you determine meaning.

antagonism (an TAG uh nihz uhm) *n.*

MEANING:

Mark context clues or indicate another strategy you used that helped you determine meaning.

refugee (rehf yoo JEE) *n.*

MEANING:

distraught (dihs TRAWT) *adj.*

MEANING:

---

4   "They named us from one to 27," she recalls. "One was the favorite child of the orphanage and 27 was the least favorite."

5   DePrince was number 27, because she suffers from vitiligo, a condition in which patches of skin lose pigmentation.[1] To the "Aunties" who ran the orphanage, it was evidence of the evil spirit within the three-year-old. She still recalls the fierce **antagonism** of the women.

6   "They thought of me as a devil's child. They told me every day how I wasn't going to get adopted, because nobody would want a devil's child," she says.

7   Although the other girls in the orphanage were encouraged not to play with her, DePrince formed a close friendship with child number 26, also called Mabinty, who was disliked by the Aunties because she was left-handed.

8   The pair shared a sleeping mat. At night, when Michaela had bad dreams, her "mat-mate" would soothe her with kind words and stories.

* * *

9   Her memories of early childhood are fragmentary—moments of piercing clarity which have been reassembled in date order. She believes it was soon after witnessing the killing of her teacher that she stumbled upon something that was to shape the rest of her life—a discarded magazine.

10   "There was a lady on it, she was on her tippy-toes, in this pink, beautiful tutu. I had never seen anything like this—a costume that stuck out with glitter on it, with just so much beauty. I could just see the beauty in that person and the hope and the love and just everything that I didn't have.

11   "And I just thought: 'Wow! This is what I want to be.'"

12   DePrince ripped the photograph out of the magazine and, for the lack of anywhere else to keep it, stuffed the treasured scrap in her underwear.

13   One day, the orphanage was warned it would be bombed and the children were marched to a distant **refugee** camp. Here DePrince learned that her beloved mat-mate was to be adopted.

14   An American woman, Elaine DePrince, had come to the camp to adopt child number 26, now called Mia. For a moment, Michaela was **distraught** because she believed that all the other children would be taken to new homes and she would be left behind.

---

1. **pigmentation** (pihg muhn TAY shuhn) *n.* natural coloring.

© Pearson Education, Inc., or its affiliates. All rights reserved.

PERSONALIZE FOR LEARNING

English Language Support

Unfamiliar Words Review paragraph 5 with students. Many of the words in this article may be unfamiliar and especially challenging for English Language Learners. For instance, the words *vitiligo* and *pigmentation* in paragraph 5 are not commonly used in everyday speech. Encourage students to use context clues to determine the meanings of unfamiliar words. Have students highlight words and phrases that they do not understand and guide them in using context clues to understand them. Guide them also to the footnote that explains the meaning of *pigmentation*.

15   But abruptly there was a change of plan. When the Aunties told Elaine DePrince that Michaela was unlikely to find another home, she decided to adopt both girls.

16   Michaela remembers struggling to understand what was happening. She was intoxicated[2] by the American woman with her dazzling blonde hair, but there was something else on her mind too.

17   "I was looking at people's feet because I thought: 'Everyone has to have [ballet] pointe shoes, they have to have pointe shoes because these are people from the US!'"

18   Not only was Elaine not wearing any pointe shoes, but as Michaela found when she looked through her suitcase that night, she had none in her luggage either.

19   Her new mother quickly noticed Michaela's obsession with ballet.

20   "We found a *Nutcracker*[3] video and I watched it 150 times," Michaela says.

21   When they finally went to see a stage performance, she was able to point out to her mother the places where dancers had missed their steps.

22   Elaine enrolled five-year-old Michaela in the Rock School of Dance in Philadelphia, making the 45-minute drive from New Jersey every day.

23   But DePrince remained a shy girl, painfully self-conscious of her vitiligo. "That was all I would think about when I was on stage. I had trouble looking at myself in the mirror," she says.

24   Instead of glorying in the glittery tutus and bodices that had drawn her to ballet, she covered herself up whenever possible with turtleneck sweaters.

25   One day, DePrince asked one of her ballet teachers if she thought her skin condition might hold back her career. The teacher asked her what she was talking about. She hadn't even noticed the pale patches on her skin—she'd just been watching her steps. That was a significant moment for her.

26   But, she says, being a black ballet dancer is hard, even in the US. She thinks the problem is that in the corps de ballet—the group of ballerinas who are not soloists—girls are supposed to look the same.

---

2. **intoxicated** (ihn TOK sih kay tihd) *adj.* overwhelmed and excited.
3. **[The] Nutcracker** popular ballet with music by the famous Russian composer Peter Illyich Tchaikovsyk (1840–1893).

© Pearson Education, Inc., or its affiliates. All rights reserved.

FACILITATING SMALL-GROUP LEARNING

CLOSE READ: Magazine Article As groups perform the close read, circulate and offer support as needed.

- Remind groups that when they read nonfiction, they should be sure to identify the main ideas, events, and the key details.

- If a group is confused about the sequence of events, guide them in creating a timeline of events.

- Challenge groups to paraphrase the text in more familiar language.

MEDIA CONNECTION ▶

Project the media connection video in class, ask students to open the video in their interactive textbooks, or have students scan the Bounce Page icon with their phones to access the video.

Discuss It

Possible response: The contrast between the pain in Michaela's story and the beauty of her dancing powerfully depicts her triumphant ability to rise above her circumstances.

NOTES

27   "It is a challenge," she says. "If you look at [ballet] companies you won't really see any black girls. You might see a mixed-race girl but there are only one or two black soloists in the whole U.S."

28   Now 17, DePrince recently completed a tour with the Dance Theater of Harlem, many of whose dancers are African American, or mixed-race.

29   "I have become more upbeat—I used to be very shy," she says.

30   "Now I've grown up and I'm so happy with the way things are turning out." ❧

MEDIA CONNECTION

💬 **Discuss It** How does viewing this video add to your understanding of the difficulties Michaela faced as a child?

Write your response before sharing your ideas.

Michaela DePrince—Ballet Dancer

SCAN FOR MULTIMEDIA

© Pearson Education, Inc., or its affiliates. All rights reserved.

DIGITAL PERSPECTIVES

Illuminating the Media Have students work in their small groups to create Venn diagrams that compare and contrast the video and the magazine article. Tell them to consider these points of comparison:

- information given
- purpose
- effect on reader/viewer

(Research to Clarify)

Comprehension Check

Complete the following items after you finish your first read. Review and clarify details with your group.

1. Why did the Aunties at the orphanage dislike Michaela?

2. How did Michaela first learn about ballet and ballerinas?

3. How did Michaela finally leave the orphanage?

4. 🗐 **Notebook** Confirm your understanding of the selection by writing a brief summary of what happened to Michaela after she left the orphanage.

- -

RESEARCH

Research to Clarify Choose at least one unfamiliar detail from the text. Briefly research that detail. In what way does the information you learned shed light on an aspect of the article?

Michaela DePrince: The War Orphan Who Became a Ballerina **55**

© Pearson Education, Inc., or its affiliates. All rights reserved.

Comprehension Check

Possible responses:

1. Michaela had a condition in which patches of skin lack color. Because of this, the Aunties thought Michaela was unnatural.

2. She found a picture of a ballerina in a magazine.

3. She was adopted by an American woman named Elaine DePrince.

4. After Michaela left the orphanage, she was taken to the United States by Elaine DePrince. When Elaine learned how much Michaela loved ballet, she enrolled her in ballet school. The young girl was afraid her skin condition would get in the way of her career, but her teacher showed her this wasn't true. Michaela recently performed with the Dance Theatre of Harlem.

Research to Clarify If groups struggle to identify their research topics, you might want to suggest one of the following topics: children affected by war, Sierra Leone and its civil war, African American ballerinas, and international adoption.

PERSONALIZE FOR LEARNING

Challenge

Text-to-World Connection Have students research more about children around the world affected by war. In which places around the world are children currently affected by war? Choose one country whose children are affected and write a brief research report describing the conflict, the effect on the nation's children, and the steps being taken to help them. If possible, include information about how readers can help.

Jump Start

CLOSE READ Ask groups to consider the following prompt: *Do you think the challenges faced by Michaela made her more passionate about becoming a ballerina? Why or why not?* As students discuss the questions in their groups, ask them to consider the challenges she faced and how she overcame them.

Close Read the Text

If needed, model close reading by using the Annotation Highlights in the Interactive Teacher's Edition.

Remind students to use Accountable Talk in their discussions and to support one another as they complete the close read.

Analyze the Text

1. **Possible response:** Michaela's world revolved around ballet. She had not been to the U.S, and had no access to media or the Internet. She did not have very accurate ideas about the U.S.

2. **Passages will vary.**

3. **Responses will vary by group.**

Concept Vocabulary

Why These Words? Possible response: The words are all related to difficulties or to difficult situations, such as war.

Practice

Possible response: Due to *antagonism* between groups of people in her native Sierra Leone, Michaela became a *refugee* and an orphan. She bonded with another girl at the orphanage but was *distraught* when she learned the other girl would be adopted. Luckily, she was also adopted.

Word Network

Possible responses: *orphanage, adopted*

Word Study

For more support, see **Concept Vocabulary and Word Study.**

Possible responses:

antagonism—synonyms: *opposition*: "contrary action." The army faced fierce *opposition* as it charged up the hill. *hatred*: "profound aversion." *Hatred* can cause some people to treat others cruelly.

antagonism—antonyms: *agreement*: "harmony of opinion, action, or character." After the committee met, there was general *agreement* on what it should do next. *approval*: "the expression of a favorable opinion." The candidate's suggestion that taxes should be lowered was met with *approval*.

MAKING MEANING

MICHAELA DEPRINCE: THE WAR ORPHAN WHO BECAME A BALLERINA

TIP

GROUP DISCUSSION
As you discuss the article, make sure everyone in your group has a chance to speak. Take turns expressing your ideas.

WORD NETWORK
Add words related to childhood from the text to your Word Network.

STANDARDS
Language
• Determine or clarify the meaning of unknown and multiple-meaning words and phrases based on *grade 6 reading and content*, choosing flexibly from a range of strategies.
  c. Consult reference materials, both print and digital, to find the pronunciation of a word or determine or clarify its precise meaning or its part of speech.
  d. Verify the preliminary determination of the meaning of a word or phrases.
• Demonstrate understanding of figurative language, word relationships, and nuances in word meanings.
  b. Use the relationship between particular words to better understand each of the words.

56 UNIT 1 • CHILDHOOD

Close Read the Text

With your group, revisit sections of the text you marked during your first read. **Annotate** details that you notice. What **questions** do you have? What can you **conclude**?

Analyze the Text

CITE TEXTUAL EVIDENCE to support your answers.

Notebook Complete the activities.

1. **Review and Clarify** With your group, reread paragraph 17 of the selection. Why do you think Michaela thought that everyone from the United States had to have pointe shoes? What does this tell you about Michaela and her ideas about the United States?

2. **Present and Discuss** Now, work with your group to share passages from the selection that you found especially important. Take turns presenting your passages. Discuss what you noticed in the selection, what questions you asked, and what conclusions you reached.

3. **Essential Question:** *What are some of the challenges and triumphs of growing up?* What has this article taught you about challenges that some children face and how they overcome them? Discuss with your group.

LANGUAGE DEVELOPMENT

Concept Vocabulary

antagonism	refugee	distraught

Why These Words? The concept vocabulary words from the text are related. With your group, determine what the words have in common. Write your ideas and add another word that fits the category.

Practice

Notebook Check your understanding of the concept vocabulary words by using them in a paragraph. Include context clues that hint at each word's meaning. Share and discuss your paragraph with your group.

Word Study

Notebook Synonyms and Antonyms One way to better understand a word is to find **synonyms**, or words that have a same or similar meaning, and **antonyms**, words that have an opposite meaning. For example, one synonym of *antagonism* is *hostility*. One antonym is *friendship*.

Using a dictionary, determine and verify the precise meaning of *antagonism*. Then, find two more synonyms and two more antonyms for *antagonism* in a thesaurus. Write a sentence for each word you find.

© Pearson Education, Inc., or its affiliates. All rights reserved.

FORMATIVE ASSESSMENT

Analyze the Text

If students struggle to close read the text, **then** provide the **Michaela DePrince: Text Questions** available online in the Interactive Teacher's Edition or Unit Resources. Answers and DOK levels are also available.

Concept Vocabulary

If students struggle to identify the connection between the words, **then** have them think about the feelings associated with the words.

Word Study

If students have difficulty understanding synonyms and antonyms, **then** provide examples using simpler words.

For Reteach and Practice, see **Word Study: Synonyms and Antonyms (RP).**

Analyze Craft and Structure

Biographical Writing When a nonfiction text tells a story, it is a work of **narrative nonfiction.** Biographical writing is one type of narrative nonfiction. In **biographical writing,** an author tells the story of another person's life. This type of writing has specific features:

- The subject is a real-life person. The work presents facts and actual events from the subject's life.
- The writer uses **direct quotations,** or the subject's exact words, to show his or her thoughts and feelings.
- The writer may describe other people's views of the subject. He or she may use quotations from people who know the subject well.

Authors of biographies use these elements to develop a portrait in words and to tell the story of the person about whom they are writing.

Practice

CITE TEXTUAL EVIDENCE
to support your answers.

Notebook Work independently to answer the questions and complete the activity. Then, share and discuss your responses with your group.

1. (a) What information about Michaela DePrince does the writer include in paragraphs 1 and 2? (b) Why might this information interest readers in her story?

2. Use the chart to identify examples of each element of biographical writing used in paragraphs 2–8. Explain how the author uses each item to add to the reader's understanding of DePrince.

ELEMENT OF BIOGRAPHY	EXAMPLES	READER'S UNDERSTANDING
Facts	She was born in Sierra Leone in 1995.	age and background of DePrince
Actual Events	Her parents died in the civil war in Sierra Leone.	She was an orphan in a war-torn country.
Direct Quotations	"They named us from one to 27"	She was treated like a number in the orphanage.
Other People's Views	The women thought of her as a devil's child.	She had a very difficult early childhood.

3. (a) What turning point, or major change, does the author describe in paragraph 10? (b) Why is this moment so important to DePrince? (c) What other moment described in the biography is a turning point in DePrince's life? Explain your choice.

4. (a) Describe the struggles DePrince faced after she started studying ballet. (b) Cite specific examples of a fact, an actual event, and a direct quotation that help readers understand those struggles.

© Pearson Education, Inc., or its affiliates. All rights reserved.

STANDARDS
Reading Informational Text
• Analyze in detail how a key individual, event, or idea is introduced, illustrated, and elaborated in a text.
• Analyze how a particular sentence, paragraph, chapter, or section fits into the overall structure of a text and contributes to the development of the ideas.

Michaela DePrince: The War Orphan Who Became a Ballerina **57**

Analyze Craft and Structure

Biographical Writing Remind students that authors often organize stories, including biographical writing, in chronological order. However, this does not mean that the author presents events strictly in the order in which they happened. Authors can use flashbacks or flash forwards to move backwards or forwards in time. They can also emphasize a turning point in the subject's story, highlighting that particular event or realization, see **Analyze Craft and Structure: Biographical Writing.**

Possible responses:

1. (a) The writer includes that Michaela DePrince was a war orphan in Sierra Leone who made her debut as a ballerina and toured South Africa. He also includes a quotation from DePrince, who says she is living her dream. (b) This information might interest readers because it shows the extremes of her life experience.

2. See possible responses in chart on student page.

3. (a) DePrince tells about when she saw a picture of a ballerina in a magazine. (b) From that moment, she wanted to be a ballerina. (c) Elaine DePrince decided to adopt her as well as Mia. This made it possible for Michaela to realize her dreams.

4. (a) After she started studying ballet, DePrince worried about her skin condition but learned that her teacher didn't even notice it. (b) Fact: DePrince would wear turtlenecks to cover her skin condition. Actual event: she asked her teacher if her skin condition would hold back her career. Direct quotation: "I had trouble looking at myself in the mirror."

FORMATIVE ASSESSMENT

Analyze Craft and Structure

If students are unable to identify how the author develops ideas, **then** have them reread the relevant paragraphs and circle key words. For Reteach and Practice, see **Analyze Craft and Structure: Biographical Writing (RP).**

CROSS-CURRICULAR PERSPECTIVES

Art Challenge students to work in small groups to research some of the ballet-related terminology in the article. For instance, students might research pointe shoes, soloists, and the corps de ballet. They might also research the Dance Theatre of Harlem, Alvin Ailey, and other African American dancers in the United States. Have students explain how the information they find illuminates the information in the article. Groups could then present their findings to the class.

Conventions

Reflexive and Intensive Pronouns Explain to students that to detect whether a pronoun is reflexive or intensive, they can look at the part of speech of the word it follows. Reflexive pronouns follow verbs or prepositions, while intensive pronouns follow nouns or pronouns. For more support, see **Conventions: Reflexive and Intensive Pronouns.** 📄

Read It

Possible responses:
1. myself—reflexive
2. herself—reflexive

Write It

Possible responses:
1. Michaela didn't realize that she herself would be adopted, too.
2. She was self-conscious about the vitiligo itself.
3. The Aunties themselves were not kind to Michaela.

FORMATIVE ASSESSMENT

Conventions

If students are unable to use intensive pronouns in sentences, give them sentence starters, such as: *She _____ read the book. We _____ had scarcely heard of it. Should I _____ go to the party?* Then, have students fill in the blanks in the sentences. For Reteach and Practice, see **Conventions: Reflexive and Intensive Pronouns (RP).** 📄

MICHAELA DEPRINCE: THE WAR ORPHAN WHO BECAME A BALLERINA

Conventions

Reflexive and Intensive Pronouns A **pronoun** is a word that takes the place of one or more nouns or other pronouns. Reflexive pronouns and intensive pronouns are forms of pronouns that end with *-self* or *-selves*. These pronoun forms look the same, but they function differently within a sentence.

	SINGULAR	PLURAL
First Person	myself	ourselves
Second Person	yourself	yourselves
Third Person	himself, herself, itself	themselves

A **reflexive pronoun** reflects, or directs, the action of a verb back on its subject. It indicates that the person or thing performing the action of the verb is also receiving the action. A reflexive pronoun is essential to the meaning of its sentence.

An **intensive pronoun** simply emphasizes the noun or pronoun to which it refers. It usually appears very close to the noun or pronoun it emphasizes. An intensive pronoun can be removed from a sentence without changing its meaning. In the chart, subjects are underlined and pronouns are set in italics.

EXAMPLES OF REFLEXIVE PRONOUNS	EXAMPLES OF INTENSIVE PRONOUNS
I bought *myself* a new paintbrush.	I *myself* chose the paintbrush I wanted.
Luke made *himself* late for school.	Luke *himself* should have known better.
Emil and Maria were mad at *themselves* for losing the cat.	Emil and Maria *themselves* searched for the lost cat.

Read It

Mark the reflexive or intensive pronoun in each of these passages from "Michaela DePrince: The War Orphan Who Became a Ballerina." Then, write whether the pronoun is reflexive or intensive.

1. "That was all I would think about when I was on stage. I had trouble looking at myself in the mirror," she says.

2. Instead of glorying in the glittery tutus and bodices that had drawn her to ballet, she covered herself up whenever possible with turtleneck sweaters.

Write It

Write three sentences about Michaela DePrince's life using intensive pronouns. Use a different intensive pronoun in each sentence.

▥ STANDARDS
Language
Demonstrate command of the conventions of standard English grammar and usage when writing or speaking.
  b. Use intensive pronouns.

© Pearson Education, Inc., or its affiliates. All rights reserved.

PERSONALIZE FOR LEARNING

English Language Support

Reflexive and Intensive Pronouns Tell students to avoid using *hisself* or *theirselves*. Remind them that these are nonstandard forms of English and should be avoided. You might help them practice by giving them sentences like the following to correct.

He had to do it all hisself.

When the students were asked to mark their own papers, they gave theirselves good grades. **ALL LEVELS**

Speaking and Listening

Assignment

With your group, write and deliver an **oral presentation**. Choose from the following options:

☐ **Option 1:** Michaela DePrince talks about the difficulties of being an African American ballerina. Conduct research on another African American dancer. Then, prepare and deliver a **personality profile** of the dancer you chose. Compare and contrast his or her experience with DePrince's. Include descriptive details and a logical sequence of ideas so that the points of comparison and contrast are clear to your audience.

☐ **Option 2:** Becoming a ballet dancer takes hard work and many years of training. Research to learn about the challenges aspiring dancers face. Then, write and deliver an **informative report** in which you talk about why DePrince's success is so impressive. Include facts, descriptive details, and ideas that are ordered in a way that will make sense to readers.

Make an Outline Creating an outline will help your group organize ideas in an order that makes sense. An outline is a list of the main ideas in your presentation. If your group is doing a personality profile, your ideas will be points of comparison and contrast between DePrince and another dancer. If your group is doing an informative report, your ideas will focus on the importance of DePrince's success.

Work with your group to create an outline by using the following structure. Write a sentence for each line of the outline.

I. Thesis Statement: _____

II. Body of Presentation

A. First Idea: _____

B. Second Idea: _____

C. Third Idea: _____

III. Conclusion (Importance of Ideas): _____

Practice and Present Practice your presentation before you deliver it to the class. Use the following tips while delivering your presentation.

- Speak clearly and comfortably without rushing.
- Vary the tone and pitch of your voice to help your audience understand your points and to add interest. Avoid speaking flatly and without emotion.
- Use appropriate and varied body language. Maintain eye contact to keep your audience's attention.

TIP

GROUP DISCUSSION
If your group cannot agree on which project to complete, work together to resolve the issue so that most of the group is happy. Agree beforehand that everyone will go along with the decision.

EVIDENCE LOG

Before moving on to a new selection, go to your Evidence Log and record what you've learned from "Michaela DePrince: The War Orphan Who Became a Ballerina."

STANDARDS

Speaking and Listening
Present claims and findings, sequencing ideas logically and using pertinent descriptions, facts, and details to accentuate main ideas or themes; use appropriate eye contact, adequate volume, and clear pronunciation.

Michaela DePrince: The War Orphan Who Became a Ballerina **59**

© Pearson Education, Inc., or its affiliates. All rights reserved.

Speaking and Listening

Tell students that regardless of which prompt they choose to address, they will be giving an informational presentation. Provide these criteria for effective informational presentations:

- an engaging opening that grabs the audience's attention
- a clear central idea
- specific, relevant details and evidence from the text
- logical organization, such as compare and contrast for the profile or main idea and supporting details for the report
- language appropriate to audience and purpose

For more support, see **Speaking and Listening: Oral Presentation.**

Make an Outline Suggest to groups that they conduct initial research before they create their outline.

Practice and Present Encourage the members of each group to practice before the group, with the members giving feedback after each student's practice presentation. Remind students to make their feedback constructive and positive.

Evidence Log Support students in completing their Evidence Log. This paced activity will help prepare them for the Performance-Based Assessment at the end of the unit.

FORMATIVE ASSESSMENT

Speaking and Listening

If groups struggle to identify African American dancers, **then** provide them with the following suggestions: Lauren Anderson, Janet Collins, Misty Copeland, Ashley Murphy, Ebony Williams, and Raven Wilkinson. For Reteach and Practice, see **Speaking and Listening: Oral Presentation (RP).**

Selection Test

Administer the "Michaela DePrince: The War Orphan Who Became a Ballerina" Selection Test, which is available in both print and digital formats online in Assessments.

PERSONALIZE FOR LEARNING

English Language Support

Planning a Profile Have pairs of students work together to write a list of questions that they would ask the subject of a personality profile.

Have pairs of students work together to write a list of questions that they would ask the subject of a personality profile. Remind students to write mostly open-ended questions.

Have pairs of students work together to plan a profile of a famous figure. Tell them to write a list of open-ended questions and list other people they might speak to for the profile.

An expanded **English Language Support Lesson** on Planning a Profile is available in the Interactive Teacher's Edition.

Small-Group Learning **59**

from Bad Boy

🔊 **AUDIO SUMMARIES**
Audio summaries of the excerpt from *Bad Boy* are available in both English and Spanish and can be assigned to students in the Interactive Teacher's Edition or Unit Resources. Assigning these summaries prior to reading the selection may help students build additional background knowledge and set a context for their first read.

Summary

In this excerpt from the memoir *Bad Boy*, author Walter Dean Myers talks about his favorite activities during his childhood. He played different sports with his friends, watched other sports, and read at the library. Myers discusses his love of books and what they meant to him on a personal level. He also discusses the importance placed on gender roles when he was growing up and how he had to keep activities such as reading, writing poems, and dancing a secret to avoid teasing from other kids.

Insight

This selection helps students understand that, at times, peer pressure can have a negative impact on their lives. In spite of this pressure, they should feel free to pursue activities for which their friends might make fun of them.

ESSENTIAL QUESTION:
What are some of the challenges and triumphs of growing up?

Connection to Essential Question

Reconciling your interests with the interests that your social circle expects you to have is a challenge for everyone. And sticking with what you love despite social pressures is a triumph.

SMALL-GROUP LEARNING PERFORMANCE TASK
Deliver a retelling of the childhood challenges presented in one of the texts you have read in this section.

Connection to Performance Tasks

Small-Group Learning Performance Task In this Performance Task, students will retell a challenge that they read about in one of the texts. In this selection, students will read about the social pressure Walter Dean Myers faced when he pursued interests that were not popular with other boys.

UNIT PERFORMANCE-BASED ASSESSMENT
When did a challenge lead to a triumph?

Unit Performance-Based Assessment This selection will contribute to students' understanding of the variety of challenges individuals face and triumphs they experience in their own lives. Myers had to hide some of his interests from his friends to avoid being teased for them. But he was able to fulfill his interests in reading and dance.

LESSON RESOURCES

	Making Meaning	Language Development
Lesson	**First Read** **Close Read** **Analyze the Text** **Analyze Craft and Structure**	**Concept Vocabulary** **Word Study** **Conventions**
Instructional Standards	**RI.10** By the end of the year, read and comprehend literary nonfiction . . . **L.4** Determine or clarify the meaning of unknown and multiple-meaning words and phrases . . . **L.4.a** Use context as a clue . . . **RI.1** Cite textual evidence to support analysis of what the text says . . . **RI.2** Determine a central idea of a text and how it is conveyed . . . **RI.5** Analyze how a particular sentence, paragraph, chapter, or section . . .	**L.4** Determine or clarify the meaning of unknown and multiple-meaning words and phrases . . . **L.4.b** Use common, grade-appropriate Greek or Latin affixes and roots as clues . . . **L.4.c** Consult reference materials . . . **L.1** Demonstrate command of the conventions of standard English grammar and usage . . .

▶ STUDENT RESOURCES

Available online in the Interactive Student Edition or Unit Resources	🔊 Selection Audio 📄 First-Read Guide: Nonfiction 📄 Close-Read Guide: Nonfiction	📄 Word Network

▶ TEACHER RESOURCES

Selection Resources Available online in the Interactive Teacher's Edition or Unit Resources	🔊 Audio Summaries ✏️ Annotation Highlights 💬 EL Highlights 📄 *from* Bad Boy: Text Questions 📄 Analyze Craft and Structure: Central Idea	📄 Concept Vocabulary and Word Study 📄 Conventions: Adjectives and Adverbs 📄 English Language Support Lesson: Adjectives and Adverbs
Reteach/Practice (RP) Available online in the Interactive Teacher's Edition or Unit Resources	📄 Analyze Craft and Structure: Central Idea (RP)	📄 Word Study: Latin Root *-spec-* (RP) 📄 Conventions: Adjectives and Adverbs (RP)
Assessment Available online in Assessments	📄 ☑️ Selection Test	
My Resources	📄 Unit 1 Answer Key is available online and in the Interactive Teacher's Edition.	

Reading Support

Text Complexity Rubric: *from* Bad Boy	
Quantitative Measures	
Lexile 1000 Text Length 830 words	
Qualitative Measures	
Knowledge Demands ①—②—❸—④—⑤	Story takes place in Harlem in the 1950s; the time period and location may not be familiar but the themes will be to most readers (social situations in school, girls' and boys' expected roles).
Structure ①—❷—③—④—⑤	Story is told chronologically; organization is clear and logical; there is a little bit of dialogue which helps to break up the long sections of text.
Language Conventionality and Clarity ①—②—❸—④—⑤	Language is conversational and contemporary; some sentences have complex or awkward constructions; vocabulary is mostly on-level with a few above-level words.
Levels of Meaning/Purpose ①—②—❸—④—⑤	Meaning is partly explicit, but revealed more over entirety of text; some characters' feelings are explained but some need to be inferred by actions or by reader relating to experiences.

DECIDE AND PLAN

English Language Support

Provide English Learners with support for language and meaning as they read the selection.

Language Some sentence constructions may be difficult for English language learners, for example (paragraph 2): *With school out and me not having access to . . . books, I rediscovered the library.* Rephrase if necessary to clarify subject and verbs: *School was over. I didn't have access to books, so I went to the library.*

Meaning Make sure students understand what the author is saying about gender role expectations. Ask them to read the first three sentences of paragraph 4. Discuss the third sentence: *It was, they made it clear, not what boys did.* Ask, *What does* it *refer to?* (reading) *What did the older kids think about reading?* (Boys should not read.)

Strategic Support

Provide students with strategic support to ensure that they can successfully read the text.

Language Ask volunteers to read aloud sentences that may be confusing, for example, several of the sentences in paragraph 2. For each sentence, ask students if they can think of another way to say the same thing. Pair students and have them reread together, highlighting unclear sentences and helping each other to rephrase them.

Meaning Ask questions to help students understand the meaning of the selection. For example, (paragraph 4) *What does it mean that reading had to be a secret vice?* (He thought he had to hide the fact that he was reading.) *Why did the older kids tease him?* (They thought reading was something boys should not do.)

Challenge

Provide students who need to be challenged with ideas for how they can go beyond a simple interpretation of the text.

Text Analysis Ask students to comment on the feelings the boy has at different times in the story, for example when he is hiding his books in paper bags, or when he is watching the girls dance. Ask volunteers to tell about times when they have felt that they or people they knew did not fit into the gender roles that were expected of them.

Written Response Have students read more of the book *Bad Boy*, from which this selection is excerpted. Ask each student to select a section of the book to write about. They may give a summary of what they have read, including the emotions of the character in different situations.

TEACH

Read and Respond

Have groups read the selection and complete the Making Meaning and Language Development activities.

Standards Support Through Teaching and Learning Cycle

IDENTIFY NEEDS

Analyze results of the Beginning-of-Year Assessment, focusing on the items relating to Unit 1. Also take into consideration student performance to this point and your observations of where particular students struggle.

ANALYZE AND REVISE

- Analyze student work for evidence of student learning.
- Identify whether or not students have met the expectations in the standards.
- Identify implications for future instruction.

TEACH

Implement the planned lesson, and gather evidence of student learning.

DECIDE AND PLAN

- If students have performed poorly on items matching these standards, then provide selection scaffolds before assigning them the on-level lesson provided in the Student Edition.
- If students have done well on the Beginning-of-Year Assessment, then challenge them to keep progressing and learning by giving them opportunities to practice the skills in depth.
- Use the Selection Resources listed on the Planning pages for the excerpt from *Bad Boy* to help students continually improve their ability to master the standards.

Instructional Standards: *from* Bad Boy

	Catching Up	This Year	Looking Forward
Reading	You may wish to administer the **Analyze Craft and Structure: Central Idea (RP)** worksheet to help students identify the key ideas in the selection.	**RI.2** Determine a central idea of a text and how it is conveyed through particular details; provide a summary of the text distinct from personal opinions or judgments.	Challenge students to identify and note the ideas in another selection of their choice. What details does the writer use to convey the central idea? Have students share their analysis with a partner.
Language	You may wish to administer the **Conventions: Adjectives and Adverbs (RP)** worksheet to help students identify and understand their use. Review context clues with students to ensure they understand that words can have different meanings in different contexts.	**L.1** Demonstrate command of the conventions of standard English grammar and usage when writing or speaking. **L.4.a** Use context as a clue to the meaning of a word or phrase.	Challenge students to identify adverbs and the words they modify and adjectives and the words they modify in additional selections. Have students analyze the nuances and subtleties of various word choices in different contexts.

© Pearson Education, Inc., or its affiliates. All rights reserved.

Jump Start

FIRST READ Engage students in a discussion of expectations placed on them by parents, friends, teachers, and society as a whole. Then, ask students to evaluate whether or not these expectations are helpful. As students share their thoughts, guide them to be as specific as possible in identifying the expectations and the reasons for their evaluations of them.

from Bad Boy

What expectations does society have for me based on my age, gender, race, or other aspect of my identity? How do I feel about these expectations? Modeling questions such as these will help students connect to the excerpt from *Bad Boy* and to the Small-Group Performance Task assignment. Selection audio and print capability for the selection are available in the Interactive Teacher's Edition.

Concept Vocabulary

Have groups discuss the three concept vocabulary words. Are the words connected? To what or whom do they apply? Remind students that the search for meaning is twofold: first, they should try to identify any helpful roots, prefixes, or suffixes. Second, they should check the word's context.

● FIRST READ

Have students perform the steps of the first read independently.

NOTICE: Encourage students to notice the expectations, or rules for behavior, that the narrator feels are imposed by those around him.

ANNOTATE: Remind students to mark key details, such as how the narrator feels.

CONNECT: Encourage students to compare the expectations imposed on the narrator to those imposed on them.

RESPOND: Students will answer questions and write a summary to demonstrate understanding.

Point out to students that while they will always complete the Respond step at the end of the first read, the other steps will probably happen somewhat concurrently. You may wish to print copies of the **First-Read Guide: Nonfiction** for students to use. ●

Comparing Texts

from BAD BOY

In this lesson, you will read a memoir excerpt and a poem expressing a similar theme. The work you do with your group on this memoir will prepare you to compare it with the poem.

I WAS A SKINNY TOMBOY KID

About the Author

By the age of five, **Walter Dean Myers** (1937–2014) was reading daily newspapers. Despite this impressive start with words, Myers did not think writing would be his career. However, in his twenties, he won a writing contest and went on to find success as an author of young adult books. Myers often wrote about his African American heritage and his life growing up in Harlem, a part of New York City.

☰ STANDARDS

Reading Informational Text
By the end of the year, read and comprehend literary nonfiction in the grades 6–8 text complexity band proficiently, with scaffolding as needed at the high end of the range.

Language
Determine or clarify the meaning of unknown and multiple-meaning words and phrases based on *grade 6 reading and content*, choosing flexibly from a range of strategies.
  a. Use context as a clue to the meaning of a word or phrase.

60 UNIT 1 • CHILDHOOD

from Bad Boy

Concept Vocabulary

As you perform your first read of the excerpt from *Bad Boy,* you will encounter these words.

respected	desperate	disgusted

Context Clues To find the meaning of an unfamiliar word, look for **context clues**—other words and phrases that appear nearby in the text. There are various types of context clues that can help you as you read.

> **Context:** Marcus hid the **trove** of baseball cards he'd collected for many years under his bed.
>
> **Conclusion:** Marcus collected baseball cards for many years and hid them. Perhaps *trove* means "valuable, hidden collection."

Apply your knowledge of context clues and other vocabulary strategies to determine the meanings of unfamiliar words you encounter during your first read.

First Read NONFICTION

Apply these strategies as you conduct your first read. You will have an opportunity to complete a close read after your first read.

NOTICE the general ideas of the text. *What* is it about? *Who* is involved?

ANNOTATE by marking vocabulary and key passages you want to revisit.

First Read

CONNECT ideas within the selection to what you already know and what you have already read.

RESPOND by completing the Comprehension Check and by writing a brief summary of the selection.

HOW LANGUAGE WORKS

Concept Vocabulary Reinforcement To test theories on vocabulary meaning, ask students to use each of the words in a sentence related to societal expectations. Students should write a sentence that identifies each of the following:

• someone who is *respected* in their community

• something that helps them when they are feeling *desperate*

• something that they are *disgusted* by

Encourage students to check for context clues when they encounter these words as they read the selection.

MEMOIR

from **Bad Boy**

Walter Dean Myers

© Pearson Education, Inc., or its affiliates. All rights reserved

BACKGROUND

In his memoir, Walter Dean Myers describes his childhood growing up in Harlem, New York, in the 1940s and 1950s. This excerpt takes place when Myers is in elementary school. Earlier in the chapter, his teacher, Mrs. Conway, lent him books to read after noticing his interest in reading.

SCAN FOR
MULTIMEDIA

1   There were two categories of friends in my life: those with whom I played ball and everyone else. Athletes were highly **respected** in the black community, and boys my age were encouraged to play some sport. I loved playing ball. I would play basketball in the mornings with the boys who were just reaching

NOTES

Mark context clues or indicate another strategy you used that helped you determine meaning.

respected (rih SPEHK tihd) *adj.*

MEANING:

from Bad Boy **61**

Concept Vocabulary

RESPECTED If groups are struggling to define *respected*, have them examine the word's context in paragraph 1. Are athletes admired in the black community? Is that why promising young athletes are encouraged? Help them use context clues to suggest a likely meaning for *respected*.

Possible response: In this context, *respected* means "admired," or "looked up to."

PERSONALIZE FOR LEARNING

English Language Support

Colloquialisms Provide students with some context for the many types of *ball* that the narrator mentions in the first paragraph of the selection. Explain that *ball* refers to any game played with a ball. While students will probably be familiar with basketball, they may not know what *stoop ball* is. Explain or have a student explain that *stoop* refers to the front steps of a row house, and stoop ball involves hitting the ball against the concrete stoop. *Punch ball,* on the other hand, is a form of street baseball. Have students highlight words and phrases that they do not understand and guide them in using context clues to understand them. **ALL LEVELS**

Concept Vocabulary

DESPERATE If groups are struggling to define *desperate*, point out that the word has several meanings. Ask students to look at paragraph 3 so that they can see the word in context and judge its meaning. Ask students if "spaces of my life" are cheerful or bleak. Have students look a few lines above and ask how books affect the writer's life. How does the writer feel when books are not available to him? Ask students for the meaning of *desperate*.

Possible response: *Desperate* means "in dire need" or "hopeless."

💬 Additional **English Language Support** is available in the Interactive Teacher's Edition.

NOTES

their teens, and then stoop ball or punchball on the block with boys my age. Sometimes Eric and I would go down to the courts on Riverside Drive and play there. And I was a bad, bad loser. Most of my prayers, when they weren't for the Dodgers,[1] were quick ones in the middle of a game, asking God to let me win. I liked other sports as well and even followed the New York Rangers hockey team in the papers for a while until I found out that all the references to ice meant just that, that they were skating on ice. There wasn't any ice to skate on in Harlem, so I gave up hockey.

2   With school out and me not having access to Mrs. Conway's cache[2] of books, I rediscovered the George Bruce Branch of the public library on 125th Street. Sometimes on rainy days I would sit in the library and read. The librarians always suggested books that were too young for me, but I still went on a regular basis. I could never have afforded to buy the books and was pleased to have the library with its free supply.

3   Being a boy meant to me that I was not particularly like girls. Most of the girls I knew couldn't play ball, and that excluded them from most of what I wanted to do with my life. Dorothy Dodson, daughter of the Wicked Witch,[3] read books, and I knew she did, but she couldn't stand me and was more than happy to tell me so on a number of occasions. Sometimes I would see other children on the trolley with books under their arms and suspected that they were like me somehow. I felt a connection with these readers but didn't know what the connection was. I knew there were things going on in my head, a fantasy life, that somehow corresponded to the books I read. I also felt a kind of comfort with books that I did not experience when I was away from them. Away from books I was, at times, almost **desperate** to fill up the spaces of my life. Books filled those spaces for me.

4   As much as I enjoyed reading, in the world in which I was living it had to be a secret vice.[4] When I brought a book home from the library, I would sometimes run into older kids who would tease me about my reading. It was, they made it clear, not what boys did. And though by now I was fighting older boys and didn't mind that one bit, for some reason I didn't want to fight about books. Books were special and said something about me that I didn't want to reveal. I began taking a brown paper bag to the library to bring my books home in.

Mark context clues or indicate another strategy you used that helped you determine meaning.

desperate (DEHS puhr iht) *adj.*

MEANING:

---

1. **Dodgers** Brooklyn Dodgers, an American professional baseball team, which moved to Los Angeles, California, after the 1957 season.
2. **cache** (kash) *n.* hidden supply.
3. **Wicked Witch** Walter's nickname for Mrs. Dodson, a neighbor he dislikes.
4. **vice** (vys) *n.* bad habit.

© Pearson Education, Inc., or its affiliates. All rights reserved.

👥 FACILITATING SMALL-GROUP CLOSE READING

CLOSE READ: Memoir As groups perform the close read, circulate and offer support as needed.

- Remind groups that when they read nonfiction, they should be sure to identify the central ideas and key details.
- If a group is confused about why particular ideas are important, remind them to think about how the ideas are related to the development of ideas about societal expectations.

- Challenge groups to paraphrase the text in more familiar language.

DIGITAL

PERSPECTIVES

5   That year I learned that being a boy meant that I was supposed to do certain things and act in a certain way. I was very comfortable being a boy, but there were times when the role was uncomfortable. We often played ball in the church gym, and one rainy day, along with my brother Mickey and some of "my guys," I went to the gym, only to find a bevy of girls exercising on one half of the court. We wanted to run a full-court game, so we directed a few nasty remarks to the other side of the small gym. Then we saw that the girls were doing some kind of dance, so we imitated them, cracking ourselves up.

6   When the girls had finished their dancing, they went through some stretching exercises. A teenager, Lorelle Henry, was leading the group, and she was pretty, so we sent a few *woo-woo*s her way.

7   "I bet you guys can't even do these stretching exercises," Lorelle challenged.

8   We scoffed, as expected.

9   "If you can do these exercises, we'll get off the court," Lorelle said. "If not, you go through the whole dance routine with us."

10   It was a way to get rid of the girls, and we went over to do the exercises. Not one of us was limber[5] enough to do the stretching exercises, and soon we were all trying to look as disgusted as we could while we hopped around the floor to the music.

11   They danced to music as a poem was being read. I liked the poem, which turned out to be "The Creation" by James Weldon Johnson. I liked dancing, too, but I had to pretend that I didn't like it. No big deal. I was already keeping reading and writing poems a secret; I would just add dancing.

___

5. **limber** (LIHM buhr) *adj.* flexible.

NOTES

Mark context clues or indicate another strategy you used that helped you determine meaning.

disgusted (dihs GUHS tihd) *adj.*

MEANING:

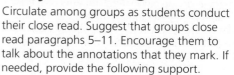

from Bad Boy **63**

© Pearson Education, Inc., or its affiliates. All rights reserved.

Concept Vocabulary

DISGUSTED If groups are struggling to define the word *disgusted* in paragraph 10, ask them to consider the dramatic context in which the word is used. Have them read the episode with the girls described in paragraphs 5–11. Do students think the girls got the better of the dispute with the writer and his friends? How did the boys feel about having to do the girls' exercises? How did they try to keep their dignity and show the girls what a waste of time they thought the exercises were? Ask students to offer possible meanings for *disgusted*.

Possible response: *Disgusted* means "very displeased," "nauseated."

CLOSER LOOK

Analyze Details

Circulate among groups as students conduct their close read. Suggest that groups close read paragraphs 5–11. Encourage them to talk about the annotations that they mark. If needed, provide the following support.

ANNOTATE: Have students mark details related to feelings. Work with small groups to have students participate while you highlight details related to feelings. Tell students that many of these details will be adjectives, such as *comfortable*.

QUESTION: Guide students to consider why the author might have included all these details about the narrator's feelings. Ask what central idea the details suggest, and accept student responses.

Possible response: The many details about the narrator's feelings suggest that his feelings are complex and confusing to him.

CONCLUDE: Help students to formulate conclusions about the importance of the author's use of details to describe feelings, and how the feelings are related to the idea of expectations.

Possible response: Details about the narrator's feelings, such as being comfortable, uncomfortable, and disgusted suggest that the narrator is aware of societal expectations and feels uncomfortable when he does not meet them.

Remind students that authors develop their central ideas and themes with specific **details** that accrue to develop the author's message.

CROSS-CURRICULAR PERSPECTIVES

Social Studies Gender roles and expectations vary from country to country. In some cultures, dancing is very important among men, and male dancing is the norm. Challenge students to research such a culture and report their findings to the class. Cultures in which men traditionally dance include many Native American groups, the Wodaabe of Nigeria and Cameroon, Celts in Ireland, and men in the southwestern Indian state of Kerala, who dance Kathakali. Have students conclude their reports with speculation about why dance is considered a masculine pursuit in some cultures and less so in others.

Comprehension Check

Possible responses:

1. The two categories of friends in young Myers's life are people with whom he plays ball and everyone else.

2. Young Myers keeps his love of reading books secret because older kids would tease him about his reading.

3. His other two secrets are writing poems and his enjoyment of dancing.

4. As a boy growing up in Harlem, Walter Myers liked to read books, but he kept this secret because older kids would tease him about it. He learned that boys were supposed to do certain things and act in certain ways. One of the things he was "supposed to" do was not like girls. One day when Walter Myers and his friends were at a gym, they made fun of a group of girls who were dancing. The leader of the group challenged them to do the girls' stretching exercises. If they couldn't, they would have to join the girls and dance. The boys couldn't do the exercises and had to dance. That day, Walter Myers discovered he liked to dance. But he had to keep this secret, too.

Research

Research to Clarify If groups struggle to identify their research topics, you might want to suggest one of the following topics: the Dodgers, the New York Rangers, Harlem, the New York Public Library system, "The Creation" by James Weldon.

Comprehension Check

Complete the following items after you finish your first read. Review and clarify details with your group.

1. What are the two categories of friends in young Myers's life?

2. Why does young Myers keep his love of reading books secret?

3. What two other secrets does young Myers have?

4. 🖥 **Notebook** Confirm your understanding of the selection by writing a brief summary.

- -

RESEARCH

Research to Clarify Choose at least one unfamiliar detail from the text. Briefly research that detail. In what way does the information you learned shed light on an aspect of the memoir?

© Pearson Education, Inc., or its affiliates. All rights reserved.

PERSONALIZE FOR LEARNING

Challenge

Relating to Personal Experiences Have students write an autobiographical essay of two or three paragraphs in which they identify things expected of them by their community. How do they feel about these expectations and how do they deal with them? Remind students that since they will be sharing their essays, they should not write about anything of a highly personal nature. Have students share and discuss their essays in their small groups.

Close Read the Text

With your group, revisit sections of the text you marked during your first read. **Annotate** what you notice. What **questions** do you have? What can you **conclude**?

(ANNOTATE · QUESTION · Close Read · CONCLUDE)

from BAD BOY

Analyze the Text

> CITE TEXTUAL EVIDENCE
> to support your answers.

📓 **Notebook** Complete the activities.

1. **Review and Clarify** With your group, reread paragraph 4 of the selection. Why do you think young Myers decides he doesn't want to fight about books? What does this tell you about Myers and what books mean to him?

2. **Present and Discuss** Now, work with your group to share passages from the selection that you found especially important. Take turns presenting your passages. Discuss what you noticed in the selection, what questions you asked, and what conclusions you reached.

3. **Essential Question:** *What are some of the challenges and triumphs of growing up?* What has this memoir taught you about childhood? Discuss with your group.

LANGUAGE DEVELOPMENT

Concept Vocabulary

respected	desperate	disgusted

Why These Words? The concept vocabulary words from the text are related. With your group, determine what the words have in common. Write your ideas, and add another word that fits the category.

Practice

📓 **Notebook** Check your understanding of these words from the text by using them in a brief paragraph. Make sure to include context clues that hint at each word's meaning.

Word Study

Latin Root: -spec- The word *respected* is formed from the Latin prefix *re-*, which means "back," and the Latin root *-spec-*, which means "look" or "see." With this information, you can make an inference about the meaning of the word.

Check the exact meaning of *respected* in a dictionary, and use the word in a sentence. Then, find two other words formed from the root *-spec-*. Explain how each word you found relates to looking or seeing.

© Pearson Education, Inc., or its affiliates. All rights reserved.

💡 TIP

GROUP DISCUSSION

There may be times when you don't understand what your classmate is saying. If that happens, politely ask your classmate to clarify his or her idea. You can say something like, "I don't understand what you mean. Will you please explain that?"

🔗 WORD NETWORK

Add words related to childhood from the text to your Word Network.

▤ STANDARDS

Language
Determine or clarify the meaning of unknown and multiple-meaning words and phrases based on *grade 6 reading and content*, choosing flexibly from a range of strategies.
 b. Use common, grade-appropriate Greek or Latin affixes and roots as clues to the meaning of a word.
 c. Consult reference materials, both print and digital, to find the pronunciation of a word or determine or clarify its precise meaning or its part of speech.

from Bad Boy **65**

Jump Start

CLOSE READ Ask groups to consider the following prompt: *What challenges did Walter Myers face? How are they similar to or different from ones you face or have faced?* As students discuss in their groups, ask them to consider how Walter Myers dealt with the challenges he faced.

Close Read the Text 🌐

If needed, model close reading by using the Annotation Highlights in the Interactive Teacher's Edition.

Remind students to use Accountable Talk in their discussions and to support one another as they complete the close read.

Analyze the Text

1. **Possible response:** Walter's reluctance to fight about books suggests that he considers them very important and even worthy of reverence.

2. **Passages will vary by group.** Remind students to explain why they chose the passage they presented to group members.

3. **Responses will vary by group.**

Concept Vocabulary

Why These Words? Possible response: The words all convey states of mind, or attitudes, of different kinds and intensities.

Practice

Sample response: There are many expectations placed on children by parents and other *respected* adults. Sometimes, children feel *desperate* to meet these expectations. They are afraid people will be *disgusted* with them if they don't.

Word Network

Possible responses: *friends, boys, playing, teens, school*

Word Study

For more support, see **Concept Vocabulary and Word Study.** 📄

Possible responses:

I *respect* anyone who finishes what he or she starts out to do.

inspect: "to look at carefully."

spectator: "a person who watches something."

FORMATIVE ASSESSMENT

Analyze the Text 📄

If students struggle to close read the document, **then** provide the *from Bad Boy: Text Questions* available online in the Interactive Teacher's Edition or Unit Resources. Answers and DOK levels are also available.

Concept Vocabulary

If students struggle to identify the concept, **then** have them look up the definition of each word and work out what is similar about them.

Word Study

If students fail to use the word correctly in a sentence, **then** suggest they fill in the blank in the following sentence.

I _____ my grandmother for her strength and sense of humor.

For Reteach and Practice, see **Word Study: Latin root -spec- (RP).**

Analyze Craft and Structure

Central Idea Tell students that an author's word choice can be used to help determine his or her point of view about a subject. For instance, read this sentence from the selection: *As much as I enjoyed reading, in the world in which I was living it had to be a secret vice.*

Confirm that groups understand that a *vice* is a bad habit or practice. Point out that the author's choice of the words "secret vice" is ironic—as reading is not usually considered a vice or something that needs to be a secret. This choice of words suggests that the author's point of view toward the expectation that boys should not be caught reading is silly—but that the author felt he still had to conform to this silly expectation. Ask them to determine how this choice of words helps develop the author's central idea. For more support, see **Analyze Craft and Structure: Central Idea.**

Practice

1. See possible responses in chart on student page.
2. Answers will vary. Students should include evidence from the text to support their answer.
3. Answers will vary.

FORMATIVE ASSESSMENT

Analyze Craft and Structure

If students are unable to identify quotations that support the and central idea, **then** have them reread paragraph 5, underlining the statement of the central idea and circling words and phrases that imply the same idea.

For Reteach and Practice, see **Analyze Craft and Structure: Central Idea (RP).**

MAKING MEANING

from BAD BOY

TIP

CLARIFICATION
Pay careful attention to specific details that will help you clarify the central idea. Keep in mind that not every detail supports the central idea.

STANDARDS
Reading Informational Text
• Cite textual evidence to support analysis of what the text says explicitly as well as inferences drawn from the text.
• Determine a central idea of a text and how it is conveyed through particular details; provide a summary of the text distinct from personal opinions or judgments.
• Analyze how a particular sentence, paragraph, chapter, or section fits into the overall structure of a text and contributes to the development of the ideas.

Analyze Craft and Structure

Central Idea A **central idea** is the main message or idea expressed in a nonfiction text. A central idea is always related to the **author's purpose,** or the reason that an author writes a text. In most essays, the author states the central idea directly. However, in narrative nonfiction, such as memoirs, the author suggests the central detail through details. To identify the central idea, readers examine the details in a text and then decide what they think the central idea is.

In the excerpt from *Bad Boy,* the central idea is that society wrongly expects boys to act a certain way.

Practice

CITE TEXTUAL EVIDENCE
to support your answers.

Work with your group to complete the following activities.

1. Identify specific details from the excerpt from *Bad Boy* that help build the central idea. Use the chart to capture your notes.

CENTRAL IDEA: BOYS ARE SUPPOSED TO ACT A CERTAIN WAY	
DETAIL	**HOW IT CONNECTS TO CENTRAL IDEA**
Myers got teased for reading.	Myers finds out there is pressure as a boy to do some things and not others.
Myers hides his books from his friends.	Myers continues to read, in spite of social pressure to stop.
The boys imitate the girls dancing.	The boys seem to think dancing is silly and not something boys should do.
Myers finds that he likes dancing.	He decides he will dance and keep it secret from others, like his reading.

2. Which detail do you think is most effective in supporting the central idea? Explain your choice.

3. If you were writing a text with the same central idea as *Bad Boy,* what examples or types of evidence would you use as support?

© Pearson Education, Inc., or its affiliates. All rights reserved.

Conventions

Adjectives and Adverbs Writers use adjectives and adverbs to make their writing more precise and lively. An **adjective** is a word that describes a noun or pronoun. An adjective answers one of these questions: *What kind? Which one? How many?* or *How much?* This chart shows examples of adjectives and the questions they answer.

WHAT KIND?	WHICH ONE?	HOW MANY?	HOW MUCH?
<u>brick</u> house	<u>that</u> judge	<u>one</u> lion	<u>no</u> time
<u>white</u> paper	<u>each</u> answer	<u>several</u> roses	<u>enough</u> sugar
<u>American</u> cheese	<u>my</u> sister	<u>both</u> brothers	<u>some</u> milk

An **adverb** is a word that modifies a verb, an adjective, or another adverb. An adverb answers one of these questions: *Where? When? In what way?* or *To what extent?* This chart shows examples of adverbs and the questions they answer.

WHERE?	WHEN?	IN WHAT WAY?	TO WHAT EXTENT?
pushed <u>down</u>	will leave <u>soon</u>	works <u>carefully</u>	<u>nearly</u> won
stand <u>nearby</u>	went <u>yesterday</u>	smiled <u>happily</u>	<u>fully</u> agrees
will walk <u>there</u>	swims <u>often</u>	chewed <u>noisily</u>	<u>barely</u> ate

Read It

Read each of these sentences from the excerpt from *Bad Boy*. Working individually, label each underlined word as an adjective or an adverb. Then, discuss with your group what question each one is answering.

1. <u>Sometimes</u> on <u>rainy</u> days I would sit in the library and read.
2. The librarians <u>always</u> suggested books that were <u>too</u> <u>young</u> for me. . . .
3. We wanted to run a <u>full-court</u> game, so we directed a <u>few</u> <u>nasty</u> remarks to the <u>other</u> side of the <u>small</u> gym.

Write It

Write a paragraph about the excerpt from *Bad Boy*. Include at least four adjectives and four adverbs. Label each adjective or adverb. Then, mark the word it describes or modifies.

TIP

CLARIFICATION

Adverbs that answer the question *In what way?* are called adverbs of manner. Adverbs of manner are easy to recognize because they usually end with *-ly*. Refer to the Grammar Handbook to learn more about adjectives and adverbs.

✏ EVIDENCE LOG

Before moving on to a new selection, go to your Evidence Log and record what you learned from *Bad Boy*.

☰ STANDARDS
Language
Demonstrate command of the conventions of standard English grammar and usage when writing or speaking.

from Bad Boy **67**

© Pearson Education, Inc., or its affiliates. All rights reserved.

DIGITAL
PERSPECTIVES

Conventions

Adjective and Adverbs Remind students that most adjectives come before the noun they modify, while adverbs may occur before or after the verbs they modify. For more support, see **Conventions: Adjectives and Adverbs.**

Read It

1. <u>sometimes</u> - adverb. It answers *When*?; <u>rainy</u> - adjective. It answers *What kind*?
2. <u>always</u> - adverb. It answers When?; <u>too</u> - adverb. It answers *To what extent*?; <u>young</u> - adjective. It answers *What kind*?
3. <u>full-court</u> - adjective. It answers *What kind*?; <u>few</u> - adjective. It answers *How many*?; <u>nasty</u> - adjective. It answers *What kind*?; <u>other</u> - adjective. It answers *Which one*?; <u>small</u> - adjective. It answers *What kind*?

Write It

Paragraphs should include four adjectives and four adverbs. Students should demonstrate that they know how to use each part of speech correctly.

FORMATIVE ASSESSMENT

Conventions

If students are unable to identify adjectives and adverbs and the words they modify, refer them to the Clarification Tip on the SE page. For Reteach and Practice, see **Conventions: Adjectives and Adverbs (RP).**

Selection Test

Administer the "Bad Boy" Selection Test, which is available in both print and digital formats online in Assessments.

Evidence Log Support students in completing their Evidence Log. This paced activity will help prepare them for the Performance-Based Assessment at the end of the unit.

PERSONALIZE FOR LEARNING

English Language Support

Using Adjectives and Adverbs Ask pairs of students to choose adjectives and adverbs to describe the following nouns and verbs: *sunset, painting, jump, eat.* **EMERGING**

List the following nouns and verbs on the board: *sunset, painting, jump, eat.* Ask students to write a sentence using each of the words, using adjectives or adverbs to describe them. **EXPANDING**

Ask students to write a paragraph about how Mrs. Conway's books impacted Walter Dean Myers. Remind them to use a variety of adjectives and adverbs to describe the nouns and verbs that they use. **BRIDGING**

An expanded **English Language Support Lesson** on Adjectives and Adverbs is available in the Interactive Teacher's Edition.

I Was a Skinny Tomboy Kid

◄)) AUDIO SUMMARIES
Audio summaries of "I Was a Skinny Tomboy Kid" are available in both English and Spanish and can be assigned to students in the Interactive Teacher's Edition or Unit Resources. Assigning these summaries prior to reading the selection may help students build additional background knowledge and set a context for their first read.

Summary

In Alma Villanueva's poem "I Was a Skinny Tomboy Kid," the speaker describes how she acted when she was young, when she wandered around her neighborhood and leaped from roof to roof. She tells how she biked to the ocean dressed as a boy, went fishing, and sold her catches. She didn't want to grow up and be a woman because she associated it with helplessness. At the time, she didn't see the inner strength her mother had. At the end of the poem, she notes that even to this day, she still sometimes wakes up in the tense state of mind she had then.

Insight

Navigating gender roles can be a very difficult part of childhood, especially in communities with restrictive social norms. Villanueva handles the topic with a delicate touch, incorporating the protagonist's gender-nonconforming behavior in youth and how she feels about that time in her life as she looks back.

ESSENTIAL QUESTION:
What are some of the challenges and triumphs of growing up?

Connection to Essential Question

This selection can support students as they consider this unit's essential question—What are some of the challenges and triumphs of growing up? The way the speaker navigates the difficulties of her childhood made her feel happy and strong.

SMALL-GROUP LEARNING
PERFORMANCE TASK
Deliver a retelling of the childhood challenges presented in one of the texts you have read in this section.

Connection to Performance Tasks

Small-Group Learning Performance Task This poem provides examples of a young person who tries to address a feeling of helplessness. Athletic tests such as fishing and traversing long distances without walking on the ground are common for kids to try out.

UNIT PERFORMANCE-BASED
ASSESSMENT
When did a challenge lead to a triumph?

Unit Performance-Based Assessment Most of the challenges the narrator faces here are self-imposed, such as staying off the ground. Some may see these as a way of avoiding a challenge that she didn't want to face at the time—growing up as a woman. Yet, she overcame every challenge we see her face, including that one.

LESSON RESOURCES

	Making Meaning	Language Development	Effective Expression
Lesson	**First Read** **Close Read** **Analyze the Text** **Analyze Craft and Structure**	**Author's Style** **Concept Vocabulary** **Word Study**	**Writing to Compare**
Instructional Standards	**RL.10** By the end of the year, read and comprehend literature . . . **L.4** Determine or clarify the meaning of unknown and multiple-meaning words and phrases . . . **L.4.a** Use context as a clue . . . **RL.1** Cite textual evidence to support analysis of what the text says . . . **RL.2** Determine a theme or central idea of a text . . . **RL.5** Analyze how a particular sentence, chapter, scene, or stanza . . .	**L.4** Determine or clarify the meaning of unknown and multiple-meaning words and phrases . . . **L.5** Demonstrate understanding of figurative language . . . **L.5.a** Interpret figures of speech in context . . .	**RL.9** Compare and contrast texts in different forms or genres . . . **RI.9** Compare and contrast one author's presentation of events . . . **W.2** Write informative/explanatory texts . . . **W.2.a** Introduce a topic . . . **W.2.b** Develop the topic . . . **W.2.c** Use appropriate transitions . . . **W.9** Draw evidence from literary or informational texts . . . **W.9.a** Apply *grade 6 reading standards* . . . **W.9.b** Apply *grade 6 reading standards* . . . **L.1** Demonstrate command of the conventions . . . **L.1.b** Spell correctly . . .

▷ STUDENT RESOURCES

Available online in the Interactive Student Edition or Unit Resources	🔊 Selection Audio 📄 First-Read Guide: Poetry 📄 Close-Read Guide: Poetry	📄 Word Network	📄 Evidence Log

▷ TEACHER RESOURCES

Selection Resources Available online in the Interactive Teacher's Edition or Unit Resources	🔊 Audio Summaries ✏️ Annotation Highlights 💬 EL Highlights 📄 English Language Support Lesson: Using Imagery 📄 I Was a Skinny Tomboy Kid: Text Questions 📄 Analyze Craft and Structure: Theme	📄 Concept Vocabulary and Word Study 📄 Author's Style: Figurative Language	📄 Writing to Compare: Compare-and-Contrast Essay
Reteach/Practice (RP) Available online in the Interactive Teacher's Edition or Unit Resources	📄 Analyze Craft and Structure: Theme (RP)	📄 Word Study: Anglo-Saxon Suffix: *-ness* (RP) 📄 Author's Style: Figurative Language (RP)	
Assessment Available online in Assessments	📄 ☑️ Selection Test		
My Resources	📄 A Unit 1 Answer Key is available online and in the Interactive Teacher's Edition.		

Reading Support

Text Complexity Rubric: I Was a Skinny Tomboy Kid

Qualitative Measures

Lexile: NP   Text Length: 87 lines

Qualitative Measures

Knowledge Demands ①—②—**❸**—④—⑤	To understand the poem, reader must know the meaning of the word *tomboy* and have some understanding of gender perceptions that author portrays.
Structure ①—②—③—**❹**—⑤	Poem is written in free verse with no separation of stanzas; ideas flow from one to another in style of stream of consciousness.
Language Conventionality and Clarity ①—②—**❸**—④—⑤	Contemporary and conversational, with some figurative language; free verse has mix of full sentences and fragments; sentences are not all punctuated and separate; tense switches from past to present.
Levels of Meaning/Purpose ①—②—**❸**—④—⑤	Meaning is subtle and assumes understanding of gender expectations; meaning must be inferred by actions and images representing gender (clenched fists, running on roof, army jacket, fishing tackle).

DECIDE AND PLAN

English Language Support

Provide English Learners with support for structure and meaning as they read the selection.

Structure After reading once, help students to divide the poem into sections to read again. Have them mark sentences that are punctuated. Then have them try to identify additional sentences.

Point out the change of tense in the poem (lines 1-69 in past, rest in present) that indicates a change from the speaker talking about things in the past and switching to portray feelings she has in the present.

Meaning Use the background information to discuss the meaning of *tomboy*. Point out references to gender: (line 35) *disguised as a boy*, (line 54) *grow up to be a woman*. Together, make a list of actions in the poem, for example, fishing, running on roofs, dressing in army jacket.

Strategic Support

Provide students with strategic support to ensure that they can successfully read the text.

Knowledge demands Ask students to read the background information. Discuss their understanding of the word *tomboy*. Tell students that as they read, they should look for descriptions of what the girl does that the author associates with being a tomboy—how she dresses, moves, or chooses activities. Ask them to list what they find and have volunteers read aloud the items.

Language Discuss the figurative language the author uses, making sure students understand the meaning. For example, say *The author says she liked to fly from roof to roof. What was she doing?* (running and jumping fast)

Challenge

Provide students who need to be challenged with ideas for how they can go beyond a simple interpretation of the text.

Text Analysis Pair students. Assign one of the following phrases from the poem to each pair: *believing in my own myth, transforming my reality, creating a legendary self*. Ask pairs to discuss the meaning of the phrases and to tell the group what they concluded.

Written Response Have students write their thoughts on the "tomboy" behaviors in the poem. Ask them to give their opinions on whether, in their experience, each of the behaviors (for example, fishing or wearing army jackets) are more typical of males than females. Then have them write their opinion about whether the word *tomboy* is a useful term or if it contributes to gender stereotyping.

TEACH

Read and Respond

Have groups read the selection and complete the Making Meaning, Language Development, and Effective Expression activities.

Standards Support Through Teaching and Learning Cycle

IDENTIFY NEEDS

Analyze results of the Beginning-of-Year Assessment, focusing on the items relating to Unit 1. Also take into consideration student performance to this point and your observations of where particular students struggle.

ANALYZE AND REVISE

- Analyze student work for evidence of student learning.
- Identify whether or not students have met the expectations in the standards.
- Identify implications for future instruction.

TEACH

Implement the planned lesson, and gather evidence of student learning.

DECIDE AND PLAN

- If students have performed poorly on items matching these standards, then provide selection scaffolds before assigning them the on-level lesson provided in the Student Edition.
- If students have done well on the Beginning-of-Year Assessment, then challenge them to keep progressing and learning by giving them opportunities to practice the skills in depth.
- Use the Selection Resources listed on the Planning pages for "I Was a Skinny Tomboy Kid" to help students continually improve their ability to master the standards.

Instructional Standards: I Was a Skinny Tomboy Kid

	Catching Up	This Year	Looking Forward
Reading	You may wish to administer the **Analyze Craft and Structure: Determine Theme (RP)** worksheet to help students understand how an author develops a message, or theme, when writing.	**RL.2** Determine a theme or central idea of a text and how it is conveyed through particular details; provide a summary of the text distinct from personal opinions or judgments.	Invite students to think of expectations or limits they have felt in their own lives. Then have students create a theme chart with details that could be used to organize an essay on the topic.
Writing	You may wish to administer the **Writing to Compare: Compare-and-Contrast Essay (RP)** worksheet to help students organize their comparison-and-contrast essays.	**W.2.a** Introduce a topic; organize ideas, concepts, and information, using strategies such as definition, classification, comparison/contrast, and cause/effect; include formatting, graphics, and multimedia when useful to aiding comprehension.	Challenge students to compare and contrast two selections of their choosing. Encourage students to write a 3–4 paragraph essay that includes relevant quotations and examples, as well as clear transitions and a concluding statement.
Language	You may wish to administer the **Author's Style: Figurative Language (RP)** worksheet to help students understand how writers use words to create sensory word pictures for readers.	**L.5.a** Interpret figures of speech in context.	Challenge students to write a short descriptive essay about a favorite place, memory, or person which includes at least four examples of figurative language.

© Pearson Education, Inc., or its affiliates. All rights reserved.

Jump Start

FIRST READ Do young people sometimes feel like "outsiders"? What are some things that can make a young person feel like they're different? Engage students in a discussion that sets the context for reading "I Was a Skinny Tomboy Kid." As students share their thoughts, focus on ideas that relate to the poem.

I Was a Skinny Tomboy Kid 🔊 📄

In what ways might boys and girls feel different from other boys and girls? Can feeling different be a good thing? Modeling the questions readers might ask as they read "I Was a Skinny Tomboy Kid" for the first time brings the text alive for students and connects it to the Small-Group Performance Task assignment. Selection audio and print capability for the selection are available in the Interactive Teacher's Edition.

Concept Vocabulary

Encourage groups to discuss the concept vocabulary words. Ask groups to look closely at the example of a context clue and discuss how these types of clues can help clarify meaning. Encourage groups to discuss how words surrounding an unknown word can help them discover the word's meaning.

⬤ FIRST READ

As they read, students should perform the steps of the first read:

NOTICE: You may want to encourage students to notice words and phrases that relate to the poem's main characters or key events.

ANNOTATE: Remind students to mark parts of the poem they feel express an important idea or express something in an interesting way.

CONNECT: Encourage students to go beyond the text to make connections to their own lives, people they know, books they have read, or films they have seen.

RESPOND: Students will answer questions and write a summary to demonstrate understanding. Point out to students that while they will always complete the Respond step at the end of the first read, the other steps will probably happen somewhat concurrently. You may wish to print copies of the **First-Read Guide: Poetry** for students to use. 📄

---

from BAD BOY

Comparing Texts

Now, you will read the poem "I Was a Skinny Tomboy Kid." After reading, you will compare and contrast the theme of this poem with that of the excerpt from *Bad Boy*.

I WAS A SKINNY TOMBOY KID

About the Poet

Alma Luz Villanueva (b. 1944) was raised in the Mission District of San Francisco by her maternal grandmother, a Yaqui Indian healer. Although Villanueva now writes in English, the inspiration for her works is rooted in the Spanish language and in the Yaqui prayers her grandmother used to sing every morning.

I Was a Skinny Tomboy Kid

Concept Vocabulary

As you perform your first read of "I Was a Skinny Tomboy Kid," you will encounter these words.

clenched	stubborn	tenseness

Context Clues If these words are unfamiliar to you, try using **context clues**—other words and phrases in nearby text—to help you determine their meanings.

> **Context:** Marta **deceptively** hid the winning card in her hand until the end, so that no one would suspect she had it.
>
> **Conclusion:** The word *hid* and the clause *so that no one would suspect she had it* tell you Marta is doing something in a secretive way to prevent others from guessing she has the card. *Deceptively* may mean "in a way meant to mislead others."

Apply your knowledge of context clues and other vocabulary strategies to determine the meanings of unfamiliar words you encounter during your first read.

First Read POETRY

Apply these strategies as you conduct your first read. You will have an opportunity to complete a close read after your first read.

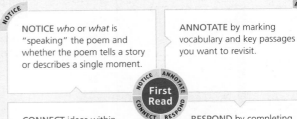

NOTICE who or what is "speaking" the poem and whether the poem tells a story or describes a single moment.

ANNOTATE by marking vocabulary and key passages you want to revisit.

First Read

CONNECT ideas within the selection to what you already know and what you have already read.

RESPOND by completing the Comprehension Check and by writing a brief summary of the poem.

☰ STANDARDS

Reading Literature
By the end of the year, read and comprehend literature, including stories, dramas, and poems, in the grades 6–8 text complexity band proficiently, with scaffolding as needed at the high end of the range.

Language
Determine or clarify the meaning of unknown and multiple-meaning words and phrases based on *grade 6 reading and content*, choosing flexibly from a range of strategies.
  a. Use context as a clue to the meaning of a word or phrase.

68 UNIT 1 • CHILDHOOD

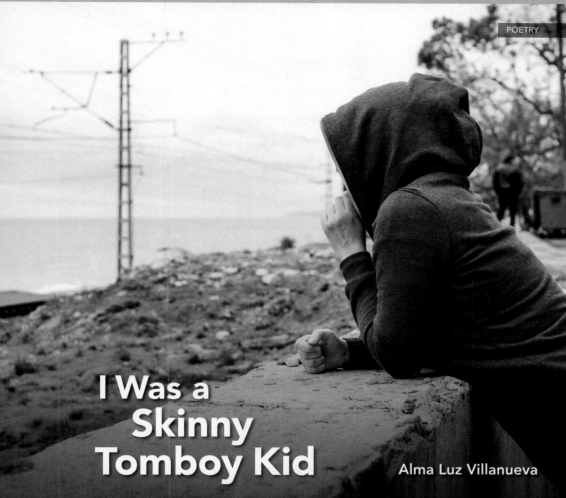

 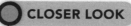
I Was a Skinny Tomboy Kid

Alma Luz Villanueva

© Pearson Education, Inc., or its affiliates. All rights reserved.

BACKGROUND

Although the word *tomboy* was originally defined as "a rude or noisy boy," it grew to be a label for a girl whose behavior and appearance were not considered to be traditionally feminine. In this poem, the speaker relates her experiences growing up in San Francisco, California, as a self-described tomboy.

SCAN FOR
MULTIMEDIA

I was a skinny tomboy kid
who walked down the streets
with my fists clenched into
        tight balls.

NOTES

Mark context clues or indicate another strategy you used that helped you determine meaning.

clenched (klehncht) *adj.*

MEANING:

I Was a Skinny Tomboy Kid **69**

CLOSE READ: Poetry Monitor groups as they conduct their close read. Offer support as needed.

- Discuss differences between poetry and prose. Help students see that poems tend to be short, and poets use fewer words than writers of prose. Rather than write a long description of someone or something, a poet might use a word or phrase that paints a picture for the reader.

- Encourage students to look for details that help them see the images the author creates.

- Encourage students to consider the author's word choice so they might be able to infer the speaker's message.

CLOSER LOOK

Analyze Character

Circulate among groups as students conduct their close read. Suggest that groups close read the first four lines of the poem. Encourage them to talk about the annotations they mark. If needed, provide the following support.

ANNOTATE: In lines 1-4 of the poem, have students mark details that reveal something about the speaker's character, or work with small groups to have students participate while you highlight them together.

QUESTION: Guide students to consider what these details might tell them. Ask them what words or phrases in the text tell them something about the speaker in the poem, and accept student responses.

Possible response: The poem's speaker is unhappy, angry, or tense.

CONCLUDE: Help students to draw conclusions about the importance of these details. Ask students why the author might have included these details so early in the poem.

Possible response: The author might have included these details early in the poem so readers immediately form an impression of the poem's speaker.

Remind students that authors can use both **direct characterization** and **indirect characterization.** In direct characterization, the author directly states a person's traits; in indirect characterization, the author provides clues about a person by describing his or her actions, appearance, and the reactions of others. Point out that in these lines the author is using the words "a skinny tomboy kid" which is a direct characterization, but the details about clenched fists are indirect characterization.

Concept Vocabulary

CLENCHED If groups are struggling to define the word *clenched*, point out the context clues "fists" and "into tight balls." Then ask students to define the word.

Possible response: *Clenched* must mean "held something tightly."

 Additional **English Language Support** is available in the Interactive Teacher's Edition.

NOTES

5 I knew all the roofs
And back yard fences,
      I liked traveling that way
            sometimes
      not touching
10   the sidewalks
      for blocks and blocks
            it made
                  me feel

                  victorious
15   somehow
over the streets.
I liked to fly
      from roof
            to roof
20   the gravel
                  falling
                        away
beneath my feet,
      I liked
25   the edge
            of almost
not making it.
      and the freedom
            of riding
30   my bike
            to the ocean
and smelling it
      long before
I could see it,
35   and I traveled disguised
            as a boy
            (I thought)
            in an old army jacket
                  carrying my
40   fishing tackle
            to the piers, and
                  bumming[1] bait
            and a couple of cokes
and catching crabs
45   sometimes and
      selling them
to some chinese guys

---

1. **bumming** getting by asking.

© Pearson Education, Inc., or its affiliates. All rights reserved.

VOCABULARY DEVELOPMENT

Word Forms Review lines 7–14. Model other forms of the word *victorious* in sentences: Winning the race was a great *victory* for Caleb. After the debate, the *victor* was applauded by the audience. Jessie raised her arms *victoriously* after she won the spelling bee.

Word	Part of Speech	Meaning
victory	noun	achievement of mastery or success
victor	noun	one that defeats an enemy or opponent
victoriously	adverb	of, relating to, or characteristic of victory

and i'd give
          the fish away,
50 I didn't like fish
      I just liked to fish—
          and I vowed
              to never
                  grow up
55   to be a woman and
          be helpless like
              my mother,
      but then I didn't realize
          the kind of guts
60   it often took
              for her to just keep
                  standing
      where she was.

      I grew like a thin, **stubborn** weed
65 watering myself whatever way I could
      believing in my own myth
          transforming my reality
              and creating a
                  legendary/self
70 every once in a while
          late at night
              in the deep
              darkness of my sleep
              I wake
75   with a **tenseness**
      in my arms
          and I follow
              it from my elbow to
                  my wrist
80 and realize
          my fists are tightly clenched
      and the streets come grinning
          and I forget who I'm protecting
      and I coil up
85   in a self/mothering fashion
              and tell myself
      it's o.k.

© Pearson Education, Inc., or its affiliates. All rights reserved.

NOTES

Mark context clues or indicate
another strategy you used that
helped you determine meaning.

stubborn (STUHB uhrn) *adj.*

MEANING:

Mark context clues or indicate
another strategy you used that
helped you determine meaning.

tenseness (TEHNS nihs) *n.*

MEANING:

I Was a Skinny Tomboy Kid **71**

Concept Vocabulary

STUBBORN If groups are struggling to define the word *stubborn*, encourage them to look for context clues in line 64. Ask what "a thin, stubborn weed" suggests. Ask students to list the chief characteristics of weeds. Guide students to see that weeds grow all over and are hard to kill. Encourage students to close read the way the speaker compares herself to a weed, and then have them give possible meanings of stubborn.

Possible response: *Stubborn* means "determined" or "persistent."

TENSENESS If groups are struggling to define the word *tenseness*, point out that the suffix *-ness* means "the state or condition of being." Ask them to read through line 81. Remind students that if their fists are clenched, the muscles in their arms must be tight, too. Have students check the way tenseness is used in line 75—it refers to a muscular *tension* produced by anxiety dreams. Ask students to define the word.

Possible response: *Tenseness* means "the state or condition of being tense" or "not at ease."

PERSONALIZE FOR LEARNING

Strategic Support

Theme Have students review the poem. Students may require support to identify the theme of a poem because it is often implied rather than directly stated. Remind students that a poem's theme is not the topic of the poem, but the "big idea" about life that the poet is trying to convey. Have students list three or four important ideas in the poem. Then have them write one sentence that sums up these ideas and expresses a concept about life. If students continue to need support, ask them to think about how the ideas on their list relate to one another.

Comprehension Check

Possible responses:

1. The speaker gets a sense of freedom from riding her bike to the ocean and smelling the ocean before she sees it.

2. She does not want to be a helpless woman like her mother.

3. She does not like fish. She just likes fishing.

4. Responses will vary. Students should mention that the speaker is a girl living in a city who views herself as a tomboy; she likes traveling over the city on rooftops, riding her bike to the ocean, and fishing from the city's piers; when she travels through the city, she dresses like a boy; she doesn't want to grow up to be a helpless woman like her mother; sometimes she wakes up late at night with her fists clenched; when that happens, she tells herself it's going to be O.K.

Research

Research to Clarify If groups struggle to choose a detail to research, you may want to suggest one of the following: tomboys, pier fishing.

Comprehension Check

Complete the following items after you finish your first read. Review and clarify details with your group.

1. What gives the speaker a sense of freedom?

2. What does the speaker not want to be when she grows up?

3. Why does the speaker give away the fish she catches?

4. ⊟ **Notebook** Confirm your understanding of the poem by writing a brief summary.

- -

RESEARCH

Research to Clarify Choose at least one unfamiliar detail from the text. Briefly research that detail. In what way does the information you learned shed light on an aspect of the poem?

© Pearson Education, Inc., or its affiliates. All rights reserved.

PERSONALIZE FOR LEARNING

Challenge

Research Encourage students to conduct research and write brief reports about places in San Francisco mentioned in the poem: beaches at the ocean; what neighborhood houses and buildings look like; city piers. Reports should include images of San Francisco to give students a fuller sense of the city and what it's like to live there.

© Pearson Education, Inc. or its affiliates. All rights reserved.

MAKING MEANING

Close Read the Text

With your group, revisit sections of the text you marked during your first read. **Annotate** details that you notice. What **questions** do you have? What can you **conclude**?

Close Read — ANNOTATE QUESTION CONCLUDE

I WAS A SKINNY TOMBOY KID

Analyze the Text

CITE TEXTUAL EVIDENCE to support your answers.

📓 **Notebook** Complete the activities.

1. **Review and Clarify** With your group, reread lines 52–63 of the poem. Why do you think the speaker says her mother had "guts"? What does this suggest about the speaker's family and her life?

2. **Present and Discuss** Now, work with your group to share passages from the selection that you found especially important. Take turns presenting your passages. Discuss what you noticed in the selection, what questions you asked, and what conclusions you reached.

3. **Essential Question:** *What are some of the challenges and triumphs of growing up?* What has this poem taught you about childhood? Discuss with your group.

TIP

GROUP DISCUSSION

As you discuss the poem with your group, build upon the ideas of others, and cite text examples to support your ideas.

LANGUAGE DEVELOPMENT

Concept Vocabulary

clenched	stubborn	tenseness

Why These Words? The concept vocabulary words from the text are related. With your group, determine what the words have in common. Write your ideas, and add two more words that fit the category.

Practice

📓 **Notebook** Check your understanding of the concept vocabulary words by completing the following activities:

- Describe a situation in which someone might have *clenched* teeth.
- Describe what a person might do if he or she were *stubborn*.
- Describe what someone might do to relieve a feeling of *tenseness*.

Share your sentences with your group. Discuss whether each vocabulary word has been used correctly.

Word Study

📓 **Notebook Anglo-Saxon Suffix: -ness** The speaker of the poem describes waking up with a tenseness in her arms. The Anglo-Saxon suffix *-ness* means "the condition, state, or quality of being" and changes an adjective, such as *tense*, into a noun. Find two additional words that end with the suffix *-ness*. Write a sentence that contains each of those words.

⊞ **WORD NETWORK**

Add words related to childhood from the text to your Word Network.

☰ STANDARDS

Language
Determine or clarify the meaning of unknown and multiple-meaning words and phrases based on *grade 6 reading and content*, choosing flexibly from a range of strategies.

I Was a Skinny Tomboy Kid **73**

FORMATIVE ASSESSMENT

Analyze the Text 📄

If students struggle to close read the text, then provide the **I Was a Skinny Tomboy Kid: Text Questions** available online in the Interactive Teacher's Edition or Unit Resources. Answers and DOK levels are also available.

Concept Vocabulary

If students fail to see the connection between the words or don't understand how they relate to childhood, **then** have them use each word in a sentence and think about similarities between the sentences.

Word Study

If students are unable to locate words with the suffix *-ness*, **then** have them list several adjectives that describe a person (happy; sad; silly) and try adding *-ness* to these words. For Reteach and Practice, see **Word Study: Anglo-Saxon Suffix -ness (RP).** 📄

DIGITAL PERSPECTIVES ✏️ 📄

Jump Start

CLOSE READ Ask groups to consider the following prompt: *What makes people feel the need to act tougher than they might be?* As students have discussions in their groups, remind them to consider the speaker in this poem and how she might answer the question.

Close Read the Text 🌐

If needed, model close reading by using the Annotation Highlights in the Interactive Teacher's Edition. Remind students to use Accountable Talk in their discussions and to support one another as they complete the close read.

Analyze the Text

1. **Possible response:** The speaker's mother had "guts" because she kept going and refused to quit. This suggests that the speaker and her family did not have an easy life.

2. **Responses will vary by group.** Remind students to explain why they chose the parts of the poem they presented to group members.

3. **Responses will vary by group.**

Concept Vocabulary

Why These Words? Possible response: Each of the words describes a state or a response related to a negative feeling. Two other words that fit the category are *helpless* and *coil*.

Practice
Possible response:

- I might *clench* my teeth when feeling anxious in a new place.
- He or she might be *stubborn* and refuse to try a new way to do something.
- To get rid of feelings of *tenseness*, someone could exercise.

Word Network
Possible words: *kid, bike, boy, mother*

Word Study

For more support, see **Concept Vocabulary and Word Study.** 📄

Possible responses:

tenseness—"the condition of being nervous or uneasy"

rudeness—The teacher was amazed by the student's *rudeness* as he refused to answer her questions.

darkness—As the evening wore on, *darkness* fell.

Small-Group Learning **73**

Analyze Craft and Structure

Theme Remind students that an author doesn't always state a theme directly, and that this is particularly common with poetry. Help students understand this concept through reference to the following: Imagine you read a poem about a man who is forever rolling a huge stone up a hill and never gives up, even though every time he's almost at the top the stone rolls down to the bottom. What might be the theme of that poem? (Never give up.) For more support, see **Analyze Craft and Structure: Theme**. 📄

Practice

1. See possible responses in the chart on the student page.

2. **Possible responses:** The poem suggests that sometimes people resist following the rules that govern how a girl or boy should act. The speaker challenges the rules. She dresses like a boy and acts like a "tomboy" because she does not want to be helpless, which is how she has viewed her mother.

FORMATIVE ASSESSMENT

Analyze Craft and Structure

If students are unable to identify the theme of the poem, **then** have them list three things the poet reveals about the speaker of the poem. Using these details, students should write one sentence describing this person. For Reteach and Practice, see **Analyze Craft and Structure: Theme (RP)**. 📄

👥 MAKING MEANING

I WAS A SKINNY TOMBOY KID

Analyze Craft and Structure

Theme The **theme** of a literary work is the insight or message about life that it expresses. Sometimes, the theme of a literary work is stated directly. More often, it is only implied, or hinted at.

When a theme is not stated directly, readers must use details in the text to draw their own conclusions. To determine an implied theme, group together details that seem connected. Then, try to figure out what message the writer is expressing with those details.

One possible theme of "I Was a Skinny Tomboy Kid," is that being different can be difficult. The poet does not state this theme directly. Instead, she suggests the theme through the thoughts, feelings, and actions of the speaker. She also suggests the theme through the way she organizes the lines of the poem to emphasize certain words and phrases.

Practice

CITE TEXTUAL EVIDENCE to support your answers.

📓 **Notebook** Work with your group to complete the following activities.

1. Use the chart to list details from the poem that imply the possible theme. Consider details that relate to the speaker's thoughts and feelings, appearance, and actions.

POSSIBLE THEME: BEING DIFFERENT CAN BE DIFFICULT
Speaker's Thoughts and Feelings: The speaker has "fists clenched," which suggests she is tense.
Speaker's Appearance: She is a "skinny tomboy" who disguises herself as a boy.
Speaker's Actions: She wakes up tense, believing she is back in that time.

2. With your group, discuss the following questions, and then share your thoughts with the rest of the class.

   • What does this poem suggest about the "rules" that govern how a girl or boy should act?

   • Does the speaker challenge or break these rules? Explain.

📋 STANDARDS
Reading Literature
• Cite textual evidence to support analysis of what the text says explicitly as well as inferences drawn from the text.
• Determine a theme or central idea of a text and how it is conveyed through particular details; provide a summary of the text distinct from personal opinions or judgments.
• Analyze how a particular sentence, chapter, scene, or stanza fits into the overall structure of a text and contributes to the development of the theme, setting, or plot.

74 UNIT 1 • CHILDHOOD

© Pearson Education, Inc., or its affiliates. All rights reserved.

PERSONALIZE FOR LEARNING

English Language Support

Using Imagery To help students practice developing imagery, provide them with a picture of a historical event and have them write down words that describe the picture and appeal to one of the five senses. **EMERGING**

Provide students with a picture of a historical event and have them write three sentences describing it using sensory language. **EXPANDING**

Have students choose a historical event and then write a paragraph describing it using sensory language. Discuss how the words students chose make an impact on the description. **BRIDGING**

An expanded **English Language Support Lesson** on Using Imagery is available in the Interactive Teacher's Edition. 📄

Author's Style

Figurative Language Language that is not meant to be taken literally is called **figurative language.** Figurative language often takes the form of a comparison that represents a fresh, new way of looking at something. The chart shows three types of figurative language, along with examples: simile, metaphor, and personification.

TYPE OF FIGURATIVE LANGUAGE	EXAMPLE
A **simile** compares two unlike things using a word such as *like* or *as.*	He roared through the house <u>like a storm</u>.
A **metaphor** compares two unlike things without using a word such as *like* or *as.*	He <u>was a storm</u> roaring though the house.
Personification involves giving human qualities to nonhuman things.	The ocean waves <u>kissed the shores</u> of the sandy beach.

Read It

Reread lines 64–87 of "I Was a Skinny Tomboy Kid." In the middle column of the chart, identify one simile and one use of personification. In the right-hand column, write in your own words the literal meaning of each example you found.

TYPE OF FIGURATIVE LANGUAGE	EXAMPLE	MEANING
simile	I grew like a thin, stubborn weed.	The speaker grew up to be tough and strong.
personification	the streets come grinning	The speaker imagines the streets beckoning to her.

Write It

🖉 **Notebook** Write a paragraph that tells a story. Include at least two examples of figurative language in your story—at least one simile and one use of personification. Then, label each example as either simile or personification.

▤ STANDARD
Language
Demonstrate understanding of figurative language, word relationships, and nuances in word meanings.
  a. Interpret figures of speech in context.

I Was a Skinny Tomboy Kid **75**

© Pearson Education, Inc., or its affiliates. All rights reserved.

HOW LANGUAGE WORKS

Figurative Language Review similes, metaphors, and personification by providing the following examples. Ask students to identify which type of figurative language is used in each sentence, and to discuss how the image works.

The computer was brilliant as it spat out its answers. (Personification—gives human traits to a nonhuman thing.)

She was a whirlwind of determination. (Metaphor—compares two things without *like* or *as*.)

The piece of wood was as brittle as an egg shell. (Simile—uses *as* to compare two things.)

Author's Style

Figurative Language Remind students that they have to use their imagination to best understand what an author means when he or she uses figurative language. One way to do this is to deliberately imagine exactly what is being described. For example, when they read "The plane was a screaming streak as it flashed across the sky," what do students immediately imagine? For more support, see **Author's Style: Figurative Language.** ▤

Read It

See possible responses on the chart on the student page.

Write It

Possible Response:
The old house stood in the forest, quiet as a whisper. It was an empty shell, abandoned long ago by those who once lived in it. But it was willing to wait, sure that one day someone would walk through its patient door. "quiet as a whisper"—simile; "It was an empty shell,"—metaphor; "It was willing to wait, . . . "—personification.

FORMATIVE ASSESSMENT

Author's Style

If students are unable to identify similes, **then** have students look for text that contains the words *like* or *as* and ask them if anything is being compared. For Reteach and Practice, see **Author's Style: Figurative Language (RP).** ▤

Selection Test

Administer the "I Was a Skinny Tomboy Kid" Selection Test, which is available in both print and digital formats online in Assessments. ▤ ☑

Small-Group Learning **75**

Writing to Compare

As students prepare to compare the excerpt from the memoir *Bad Boy* with the poem "I Was a Skinny Tomboy Kid," they will consider the themes of the two selections.

Prewriting

Encourage groups to begin by discussing what the themes of the selections are. Remind them that the theme is the central idea revealed in a literary work. Tell them to provide evidence from the text for what the themes are. This evidence can serve as a starting point for the charts they are to fill out. Also remind students that figurative language often consists of imaginative descriptions like imagery and metaphors.

See possible response in chart on student page.

Possible responses:

1. A memoir allows a writer to develop ideas in great detail. The writer can provide many types of supporting evidence.

2. A poem allows a writer to use poetic devices, such as figurative language and rhythm, to develop ideas.

3. Answers will vary. Students should support their ideas with evidence from the text.

from BAD BOY

I WAS A SKINNY TOMBOY KID

:≡ STANDARDS

Reading Literature
Compare and contrast texts in different forms or genres in terms of their approaches to similar themes and topics.

Reading Informational Text
Compare and contrast one author's presentation of events with that of another.

EFFECTIVE EXPRESSION

Writing to Compare

The memoir *Bad Boy* and the poem "I Was a Skinny Tomboy Kid" share a central idea or theme: Being different can be difficult. Both texts share insights about being oneself and about fitting in.

Assignment

Write a **compare-and-contrast essay** in which you analyze the ways in which the memoir and the poem present ideas about how boys and girls are "supposed" to act. Also, discuss similarities and differences in how the form of each text allows those ideas to be presented. Work with your group to analyze the texts. Then, work independently to write your essay.

Prewriting

Analyze the Texts When you compare two texts, you note how they are alike. When you contrast them, you note how they are different. With your group, compare and contrast the memoir and poem, and make notes in the chart. As you work, consider the major parts of each text, such as structure, word choice, and use of figurative language. For example, you might use one row to compare and contrast word choice in each text and another row to compare and contrast figurative language.

from BAD BOY	I WAS A SKINNY TOMBOY KID
Word choice: "a bad, bad loser," "I felt a connection with these readers," "reading had to be a secret vice"	Word choice: "fists clenched into tight balls," "bumming bait," "creating a legendary / self"
Figurative language: "desperate to fill up the spaces in my life," "a bevy of girls exercising"	Figurative language: "fly from roof to roof," "I grew like a thin, stubborn weed," "the streets come grinning"
Disguised actions: Carries books in a brown paper bag	Disguised actions: "I traveled disguised as a boy"

⊖ **Notebook** Answer the questions.

1. What are the advantages of a memoir for expressing ideas?

2. What are the advantages of a poem for expressing ideas?

3. Which text do you think does a better job of expressing ideas about how boys and girls are "supposed" to act? Why?

© Pearson Education, Inc., or its affiliates. All rights reserved.

WriteNow Inform and Explain

Process Explanation Have students write a paragraph explaining how they arrived at identifying the themes in *Bad Boy* and "I Was a Skinny Tomboy Kid."

Drafting

Create an Organizational Plan Now that you have analyzed the texts with your group, write your essay on your own. First, review the chart you filled in with your group, and choose the information you will use in your essay. Also, consider whether there is any additional material your group may have missed.

Next, think about how you will present your information. Will you write about each selection separately, and then compare and contrast them? Or will you compare and contrast the selections category by category, perhaps starting with word choice in both selections and then moving on to figurative language? Either plan is fine as long as you follow it consistently.

Provide Support Make sure you support your ideas with examples from both selections. Use quotation marks for examples that you copy word for word, even if they are just phrases. Review each example to make sure it is directly related to the idea you want to express.

Use Transitions Your essay will read more smoothly if you use transitional words and phrases to show connections among ideas. Some of the most common transitions are shown in the chart:

for example	therefore	on the other hand
for instance	as a result	however
specifically	similarly	in contrast

Review, Revise, and Edit

After writing your essay, review it and look for ways to improve it.

- Have you discussed how the selections present ideas about how boys and girls are "supposed to" act?
- Have you expressed your ideas clearly?
- Have you used transitions to connect your ideas?
- Have you supported your ideas with details from both selections?
- Did you check your grammar, punctuation, and spelling? Did you correct any errors you found?

© Pearson Education, Inc., or its affiliates. All rights reserved.

EVIDENCE LOG

Before moving on to a new selection, go to your Evidence Log and record what you've learned from the excerpt from *Bad Boy* and "I Was a Skinny Tomboy Kid."

STANDARDS

Writing
- Write informative/expository texts to examine a topic and convey ideas, concepts, and information through the selection, organization, and analysis of relevant content.
  a. Introduce a topic; organize ideas, concepts, and information, using strategies such as definition, classification, comparison/contrast, and cause/effect; include formatting, graphics, and multimedia when useful to aiding comprehension.
  b. Develop the topic with relevant facts, definitions, concrete details, quotations, or other information and examples.
  c. Use appropriate transitions to clarify the relationships among ideas and concepts.
- Draw evidence from literary or informational texts to support analysis, reflection, and research.
  a. Apply *grade 6 Reading standards* to literature.
  b. Apply *grade 6 Reading standards* to literary nonfiction.

Language
Demonstrate command of the conventions of standard English capitalization, punctuation, and spelling when writing.
  b. Spell correctly.

I Was a Skinny Tomboy Kid **77**

Drafting

Create an Organizational Plan Clarify for students that at this point they are working individually on compare-and-contrast essays. Encourage them to reread the Assignment box on the previous page to make sure they are providing the correct content for the essay.

Provide Support Remind students to make sure their supporting evidence is clearly related to one of their ideas. Have them use quotations marks for evidence that is taken word-for-word from a text.

Use Transitions Tell students that transitions are often used at the starts of paragraphs to introduce new ideas.

Review, Revise, and Edit

As students revise, encourage them to review their draft to be sure they have clearly identified a theme for each selection. Ask them to check that they have organized their ideas into separate paragraphs. Finally, remind students to check for grammar, usage, and mechanics.

For more support, see **Writing to Compare: Compare-and-Contrast Essay.**

Evidence Log Support students in completing their Evidence Log. This paced activity will help prepare them for the Performance-Based Assessment at the end of the unit.

FORMATIVE ASSESSMENT

Writing to Compare

If groups struggle to identify the advantages and disadvantages of each genre, **then** ask them to imagine if they would rather write about themselves in a memoir or a poem, and why.

Selection Test

Administer the "I Was a Skinny Tomboy Kid (*with an excerpt from Bad Boy*)" Selection Test, which is available in both print and digital formats online in Assessments.

PERSONALIZE FOR LEARNING

Strategic Support

Theme Some students may need additional help distinguishing theme from topic. Review with students that the topic is what a text is generally about, while a theme is an idea about life that an author wants to communicate. For example, the topic of "The Tortoise and the Hare" is a race. The theme might be expressed as: Having too much confidence can stop someone from succeeding.

Present a Retelling

Assignment Before groups begin work on their projects, have them clearly differentiate the role each group member will play. Remind groups to consult the schedule for Small-Group Learning to guide their work during the Performance Task.

Students should complete the assignment using presentation software to take advantage of text, graphics, and sound features.

Plan With Your Group

Analyze the Text Have students review the readings and make notes in the right-hand column of the chart. Tell them to note not only the challenges faced but also the ways the children (and others) faced and overcame the challenges. Remind students that they will be sharing their presentations with an audience and guide them away from referencing challenges that are emotionally-charged or sensitive.

Gather Evidence and Media Examples Have students include specific details and references to the text. Remind them to jot down page numbers so that they can easily find information when drafting their presentation. Explain that they should copy links to any Web-based sources and paste them into a document for future reference.

SOURCES

- DECLARATION OF THE RIGHTS OF THE CHILD
- MICHAELA DEPRINCE: THE WAR ORPHAN WHO BECAME A BALLERINA
- *from* BAD BOY
- I WAS A SKINNY TOMBOY KID

Present a Retelling

Assignment
A retelling is a new version of a text that keeps the content recognizable but also changes it. A retelling may show a story from a different perspective or move it to a different setting. Deliver a **retelling** of the childhood challenges presented in either the magazine article, the memoir excerpt, or the poem from this section. In your retelling, you may wish to refer to one or more of the rights set forth in the Declaration of the Rights of the Child. Enhance your presentation with media.

Plan With Your Group

Analyze the Text With your group, review the texts you have read during Small-Group Learning. Consider the ways in which childhood challenges are presented in each text. Capture your ideas and observations in the chart.

SELECTION	CHILDHOOD CHALLENGES
Declaration of the Rights of the Child	
Michaela DePrince: The War Orphan Who Became a Ballerina	
from Bad Boy	
I Was a Skinny Tomboy Kid	

▤ STANDARDS

Speaking and Listening
- Present claims and findings, sequencing ideas logically and using pertinent descriptions, facts, and details to accentuate main ideas or themes; use appropriate eye contact, adequate volume, and clear pronunciation.
- Include multimedia components and visual displays in presentations to clarify information.
- Adapt speech to a variety of contexts and tasks, demonstrating command of formal English when indicated or appropriate.

78 UNIT 1 • CHILDHOOD

As a group, choose one text on which to focus. Then, divide the text into sections, and have each group member focus on a different section. As you plan your retelling, keep this idea in mind: A successful retelling is true to the ideas in the original text but presents them in way that is new or fresh.

Gather Evidence and Media Examples Reread the text to find the points you wish to emphasize and to figure out where adding media would have the biggest impact. Work as a group to locate video, audio, or images that will clarify your ideas and make your retelling come alive. For example, if you want to make clear for an audience how difficult it was for Michaela DePrince to become a ballerina, you might find a video that shows the sweat and hard work of a ballet class.

© Pearson Education, Inc., or its affiliates. All rights reserved.

AUTHOR'S PERSPECTIVE: Ernest Morrell, Ph.D.

How to Package a Speech/Oral Presentation The small-group speaking and listening activity will help students learn how to engage an audience during a presentation. This is important for students as they prepare for careers, public service, and higher education. Help students learn to become better speakers by reminding them to ask themselves these questions as they practice and rehearse their speeches and oral presentations:

- *Posture*: Does my posture convey authority and ease? Do I look relaxed and comfortable as I'm presenting?
- *Body language*: How do I connect physically with my audience? For instance, do I make eye contact, lean forward at key points to show emphasis, and use appropriate gestures?
- *Voice*: Am I changing my voice by varying my pitch and volume to show emotion and convey

meaning? Does my voice project to the back rows?
- *Humor*: How do I add humor when it suits my audience and purpose? Do I tell jokes or anecdotes, for instance?
- *Tone*: Do I speak with passion to engage my audience?

Organize Your Ideas With your group, brainstorm for ways to organize your presentation, including ways to integrate multimedia. Make sure that you think of your audience and organize materials in a way that will make sense to a first-time viewer.

Rehearse With Your Group

Practice With Your Group Before you present your retelling to the class, practice delivering it as a group. Make sure that each member uses a an appropriate tone. Also, work to make eye contact with viewers, and to speak clearly and loudly so that you can be heard and understood by everyone in the audience.

As you practice your presentation, use this checklist to evaluate the effectiveness of your group's first run-through. Then, use your evaluation and the instruction here to guide your revision.

CONTENT	USE OF MEDIA	PRESENTATION TECHNIQUES
☐ The retelling is true to the ideas expressed in the text the group has chosen.	☐ The media are relevant to the ideas expressed in the text the group has chosen.	☐ The media are visible and audible.
☐ The retelling expresses the ideas from the text in a way that is new or fresh.	☐ The media add interest and contribute new ideas to the spoken portion of the retelling.	☐ The transitions between speakers are smooth. ☐ Each presenter speaks clearly.

Fine-Tune the Content Check to be sure you have emphasized key events in the original text. Also, review details that describe characters and situations. Add descriptive details as needed.

Improve Your Use of Media Make sure you are using media that add in meaningful ways to your ideas. Also, make sure that all media choices work well with the spoken portions of your presentation.

Brush Up on Your Presentation Techniques Avoid speaking in a flat, uninterested, or bored tone. Instead, vary your tone and speak with enthusiasm and liveliness.

Present and Evaluate

Remember that you are giving this presentation as a group. Everyone is equally important, and each person represents the entire group. Don't let your attention wander when other members of your group are giving their parts of the presentation. In addition, give other groups your full attention when they are giving their presentations.

© Pearson Education, Inc., or its affiliates. All rights reserved.

Organize Your Ideas Remind groups that they will need to create transitions between the different sections of their presentations. Since the presentations include media, students could use both transitional words and phrases and images that serve as transitions between ideas.

Rehearse With Your Group

Practice With Your Group Consider allowing students to videotape their presentations using their phones or some other digital recording device. Students can then play back and watch the videos to see which elements of the presentations need improvement.

Improve Your Use of Media Point out to students that when they rehearse, they should not just run through the spoken part of the presentation, but should include all the different elements.

Brush Up on Your Presentation Techniques Point out to students that strong presenters identify places in a presentation where they will change tone of voice or add more emotion to their voices.

Present and Evaluate

To ensure students listen actively as others deliver their presentations, provide them with a set of questions to answer about each presentation. Questions could include the following:

- What childhood challenge does the presentation focus on?
- Which portion of the presentation did you find most engaging and why?
- Which multimedia elements were most effective?

PERSONALIZE FOR LEARNING

Strategic Support
Listening Sensitively Some of the challenging experiences touched upon in the presentations might be emotionally charged for some students. Remind students to listen respectfully and to respond to others' experiences and feelings with sensitivity.

INDEPENDENT LEARNING

What are some of the challenges and triumphs of growing up?

Encourage students to think carefully about what they have already learned and what more they want to know about the unit topic of childhood. This is a key first step to previewing and selecting the text they will read in Independent Learning.

Independent Learning Strategies ▶

Review the Learning Strategies with students and explain that as they work through Independent Learning they will develop strategies to work on their own.

- Have students watch the video on Independent Learning Strategies.
- A video on this topic is available online in the Professional Development Center.

Students should include any favorite strategies that they might have devised on their own during Whole-Class and Small-Group Learning. For example, for the strategy "Take notes," students might include:

- If you are unclear about something, make a note of it so you can ask a question for clarification.
- Compare notes with classmates.

Block Scheduling

Each day in this Pacing Plan represents a 40–50 minute class period. Teachers using block scheduling may combine days to reflect their class schedule. In addition, teachers may revise pacing to differentiate and support core instruction by integrating components and resources as students require.

📅 **Pacing Plan**

👤 OVERVIEW: INDEPENDENT LEARNING

ESSENTIAL QUESTION:
What are some of the challenges and triumphs of growing up?

Young people have different points of view about growing up. In this section, you will choose one additional selection about childhood for your final reading experience in this unit. Follow these steps to help you choose.

Look Back Think about the selections you have already read. What more do you want to know about the topic of childhood?

Look Ahead Preview the selections by reading the descriptions. Which one seems most interesting and appealing to you?

Look Inside Take a few minutes to scan through the text you chose. Make another selection if this text doesn't meet your needs.

Independent Learning Strategies

Throughout your life, in school, in your community, and in your career, you will need to rely on yourself to learn and work on your own. Review these strategies and the actions you can take to practice them during Independent Learning. Add ideas of your own for each category.

STRATEGY	ACTION PLAN
Create a schedule	• Understand your goals and deadlines. • Make a plan for what to do each day. •
Practice what you've learned	• Use First-Read and Close-Read Strategies to deepen your understanding. • Evaluate the usefulness of the evidence to help you understand the topic. • Consider the quality and reliability of the source. •
Take notes	• Record important ideas and information. • Review your notes before preparing to share with a group. •

© Pearson Education, Inc., or its affiliates. All rights reserved.

SCAN FOR MULTIMEDIA

Introduce Whole-Class Learning

Unit Introduction

from Brown Girl Dreaming

Gallery of Calvin and Hobbes Comics

Performance Task

| 1 | 2 | 3 | 4 | 5 | 6 | 7 | 8 | 9 | 10 | 11 | 12 | 13 | 14 | 15 | 16 | 17 | 18 |

Choose one selection. Selections are available online only.

CONTENTS

 SCAN FOR MULTIMEDIA

© Pearson Education, Inc., or its affiliates. All rights reserved.

Contents

Selections Encourage students to scan and preview the selections before choosing the one they would like to read. Suggest that they consider the genre and subject matter of each one before making their decision. You can use the information on the following planning pages to advise students in making their choice.

> Remind students that the selections for Independent Learning are only available in the Interactive Student Edition. Allow students who do not have digital access at home to preview the selections using classroom or computer lab technology. Then either have students print the selection they choose or provide a printout for them.

Performance Based-Assessment Prep

Review Evidence for a Nonfiction Narrative Point out to students that collecting evidence during Independent Learning is the last step in completing their Evidence Log. After they finish their independent reading, they will synthesize all the evidence they have compiled in the unit.

The evidence students collect will serve as the primary source of information they will use to complete the writing and oral presentation for the Performance-Based Assessment at the end of the unit.

Introduce Small-Group Learning

Introduce Independent Learning

Performance-Based Assessment

Declaration of the Rights of the Child

Michaela DePrince: The War Orphan Who Became a Ballerina

from Bad Boy

I Was a Skinny Tomboy Kid

Performance Task

Independent Learning

| 19 | 20 | 21 | 22 | 23 | 24 | 25 | 26 | 27 | 28 | 29 | 30 | 31 | 32 | 33 | 34 | 35 | 36 |

INDEPENDENT LEARNING

SELECTION RESOURCES

- First-Read Guide: Fiction
- Close-Read Guide: Fiction
- *from* Peter Pan: Text Questions
- Audio Summaries
- Selection Audio
- Selection Test

from Peter Pan

Summary

This selection is an excerpt from the novel *Peter Pan*, by J.M. Barrie. In it, a group of children on an island play an extended game, play-acting as though they were a family. Wendy is the only girl and she pretends to be the mother of the group. Peter plays the father. Wendy tells the story of children who have left to live in Neverland and the parents at home who miss them. When Peter argues with the story, Wendy decides it is time to go back home. Wendy invites the boys and some want to go. Only Peter says he wants to stay. Their trip is delayed, however, when the others on the island attack them in battle.

Insight

This story is in large part a meditation on what it means to be a child. Paradoxically, the characters worry about grown-up concerns as they play the role. Note that the story uses "redskin" a few times, a term for Native Americans that students may consider derogatory.

Connection to Essential Question

This story is more concerned with what it means to grow up than with specific trials or triumphs. Students should nonetheless be able to draw answers to the question "What are some of the challenges and triumphs of growing up?"

Connection to Performance-Based Assessment

The question here is "When did a challenge lead to a triumph?" The children here must make a number of tricky choices, including how (and, for them, whether) to grow up.

Text Complexity Rubric: *from* Peter Pan

Quantitative Measures

Lexile: 800   Text Length: 3,928 words

Qualitative Measures

Knowledge Demands ①—②—③—**④**—⑤	To fully understand the excerpt, reader should have background of the story of Peter Pan, the characters, and nuances of their personalities presented in preceding chapters.
Structure ①—②—**③**—④—⑤	Story is told chronologically, but has some time shifts and a story within a story (Wendy tells a story to the boys). Abundant dialogue makes the story a little easier to follow.
Language Conventionality and Clarity ①—②—③—**④**—⑤	Language has formal archaic style (British, written in early 1900s); some sentences are complex or have unfamiliar syntax; vocabulary is mostly on-level with some more difficult words.
Levels of Meaning/Purpose ①—②—③—**④**—⑤	There are multiple levels of meaning. Relationships and characters' feelings are not always explicit and need to be inferred from the narrator's descriptions, characters' actions, and dialogue.

Oranges

SELECTION RESOURCES

- 📄 First-Read Guide: Poetry
- 📄 Close-Read Guide: Poetry
- 📄 Oranges: Text Questions
- 🔊 Audio Summaries
- 🔊 Selection Audio
- ☑️📄 Selection Test

Summary

In the poem "Oranges" by Gary Soto, the speaker talks about the first time he went for a walk with a girl that he liked. He describes the winter cold and a dog barking at him as he waits in front of her house. They go to a small shop together, where she wants a piece of candy that costs a dime. The boy doesn't have enough money, but the salesperson lets him pay with the nickel he has and one of two oranges he is carrying. They go back outside to eat together.

Insight

First love is a vivid part of adolescence. For many people, it ends up no more than a vague pleasant memory. For others, the outcomes affect their lives for years to come.

Connection to Essential Question

The essential question for this unit is "What are some of the challenges and triumphs of growing up?" The slice of a relationship we see here includes a challenge caused by a lack of money and a fortunate triumph.

Connection to Performance-Based Assessment

The question here is "When did a challenge lead to a triumph?" The poem presents a child's lack of access as a challenge. He uses his wits to overcome this challenge and experiences the triumph of a budding romance.

Text Complexity Rubric: Oranges

Quantitative Measures

Lexile: NP   **Text Length:** 27 lines

Qualitative Measures

Knowledge Demands ①—**②**—③—④—⑤	The poem explores a single theme (friendship / young love). The experience of a walk to the candy store is familiar and common to most readers.
Structure ①—②—**③**—④—⑤	This free verse poem contains a mix of sentences and sentence fragments. It has no breaks of stanzas, and not all sentences are punctuated. The poem tells a chronological story.
Language Conventionality and Clarity ①—②—**③**—④—⑤	The language is largely explicit and easy to understand. The poem contains contemporary and familiar language, and some figurative language is used.
Levels of Meaning/Purpose ①—②—**③**—④—⑤	The theme is explicit and revealed early in text. The meaning is mostly clear, but in some places, it needs to be inferred by characters' actions or is expressed in figurative language.

SELECTION RESOURCES

- 📄 First-Read Guide: Nonfiction
- 📄 Close-Read Guide: Nonfiction
- 📄 The Boy Nobody Knew: Text Questions
- 🔊 Audio Summaries
- 🔊 Selection Audio
- ☑ 📄 Selection Test

The Boy Nobody Knew

Summary

In the reflective essay "The Boy Nobody Knew," Faith Ringgold tells about an experience she had while growing up in Harlem in the 1930s. One evening, her family has to flee their apartment building because of a fire. Fortunately, the fire does not do serious damage. While outside, they see a boy in a wheelchair. No one seems to recognize him. They learn that he is part of a family that lives on the fifth floor. The fire evacuation changes his life.

Insight

The story ends encouragingly: Everyone gets to know Kenneth, the boy with the disability. His parents hid him away, but going outside brings new experiences.

Connection to Essential Question

The essential question for this unit is "What are some of the challenges and triumphs of growing up?" Making friends is a common difficulty. This story addresses challenges that students might not have considered—the isolation of a physical condition that sets a child apart from his peers.

Connection to Performance-Based Assessment

The question here is "When did a challenge lead to a triumph?" In the essay, the challenge of a fire leads to one positive outcome—a formerly hidden boy is accepted by the neighborhood.

Text Complexity Rubric: The Boy Nobody Knew

Quantitative Measures

Lexile: 820   Text Length: 845 words

Qualitative Measures

Knowledge Demands ①—②—❸—④—⑤	Several themes are explored, such as life in Harlem in 1937 and awareness of special needs, but they are communicated through a child's point of view and everyday experiences.
Structure ①—②—❸—④—⑤	The essay is clearly organized and chronological. It is narrated in first person, but it has some dialogue that breaks up the text.
Language Conventionality and Clarity ①—②—❸—④—⑤	The style is personal narrative, with contemporary and conversational language. Some sentences are lengthy with multiple clauses. Vocabulary is mostly on-level.
Levels of Meaning/Purpose ①—②—❸—④—⑤	Some of the themes of the story (attitudes towards people with special needs, relationships in a community) are subtle and are not revealed until the end of the text.

Raymond's Run

SELECTION RESOURCES

📄 First-Read Guide: Fiction

📄 Close-Read Guide: Fiction

📄 Raymond's Run: Text Questions

🔊 Audio Summaries

🔊 Selection Audio

📄 ☑ Selection Test

Summary

This selection is a short story called "Raymond's Run," by Toni Cade Bambara. The narrator is a girl nicknamed Squeaky, an excellent runner. She has a number of worries on her mind: other girls at school, upcoming races, and the well-being of her brother Raymond, who is developmentally disabled. Squeaky is very confident and unafraid of confrontation. During a race she's been looking forward to, Squeaky competes against a rival named Gretchen. Squeaky is distracted when she realizes that her brother, despite his disability, might make an excellent competitor himself. The story ends with a surprising twist in Squeaky's attitude.

Insight

This story follows an assertive and aggressive protagonist. Some readers will think she's inspiring; others will think she's mean. The story offers a compelling angle on this young woman's complex personality.

Connection to Essential Question

The essential question for this unit is "What are some of the challenges and triumphs of growing up?" Squeaky is great at athletics and confrontation, but she is also under a lot of stress, and the story leads readers to see her growth.

Connection to Performance-Based Assessment

The prompt is "When did a challenge lead to a triumph?" Through Squeaky's story, students will find that, although caring for a developmentally challenged relative may provide challenges during childhood, it also may provide triumphs.

Text Complexity Rubric: Raymond's Run

Quantitative Measures

Lexile: 1280   Text Length: 3,737 words

Qualitative Measures

Knowledge Demands ①—②—③—**④**—⑤	Experiences depicted are familiar, but several themes are explored with varying levels of complexity, including identity, gender issues, and attitudes toward people with special needs.
Structure ①—②—③—**④**—⑤	The narrative structure is in the first person with some sequential storytelling interspersed with commentary about friends and family. Organization is difficult to predict.
Language Conventionality and Clarity ①—②—③—**④**—⑤	This first-person narrative is written using vernacular. There are many very long, complex sentences and sentence fragments. Some figurative language is used.
Levels of Meaning/Purpose ①—②—③—**④**—⑤	There are multiple levels of meaning that are difficult to identify and interpret. Meaning is revealed throughout the text.

SELECTION RESOURCES

📄 First-Read Guide: Fiction

📄 Close-Read Guide: Fiction

📄 Eleven: Text Questions

🔊 Audio Summaries

🔊 Selection Audio

📄 ☑ Selection Test

Eleven

Summary

The short story "Eleven," by Sandra Cisneros, starts with a reflection on what it feels like to be eleven years old. The narrator, Rachel, argues that a person is a combination of all the ages he or she has lived before: ten years old, nine years old, and so on. This is a way of explaining how one acts at different times. The narrator has an uncomfortable experience in school, having to take ownership of a sweater that isn't hers when she isn't assertive enough to tell the teacher that it isn't hers. She feels bad and ends up crying. The story ends with Rachel wishing that she weren't eleven years old.

Insight

Everyone has tough days, and sometimes it's hard to cope with growing older. Rachel's experiences are relatable.

Connection to Essential Question

The essential question is "What are some of the challenges and triumphs of growing up?" This story focuses on a few of the social and emotional challenges of moving through childhood.

Connection to Performance-Based Assessment

The question here is "When did a challenge lead to a triumph?" In this story, there is no triumph, only moving past the challenge.

Text Complexity Rubric: Eleven

Quantitative Measures

Lexile: 980   Text Length: 3,928 words

Qualitative Measures

Knowledge Demands ①—❷—③—④—⑤	The selection depicts situations that are familiar and commonplace (events during a school day), but it covers themes that are at times complex and abstract.
Structure ①—②—❸—④—⑤	The story is a first-person narrative of a day at school that is told chronologically, but it is preceded by stream-of-consciousness abstract ideas before the events are explained. Dialogue is included in the text.
Language Conventionality and Clarity ①—②—❸—④—⑤	The story is written in the voice of an eleven-year-old, with lengthy run-on sentences and some fragments. Vocabulary is on-level. The story is about events in the past, but it uses present tense for both past events and reflection.
Levels of Meaning/Purpose ①—②—❸—④—⑤	The selection explores multiple themes (identity, embarrassment, fairness, and relationships with classmates and teachers). Its meaning is mostly explicit, but with some subtlety.

MY NOTES

You may wish to direct students to use the generic **First-Read** and **Close-Read Guides** in the Print Student Edition. Alternatively, you may wish to print copies of the genre-specific **First-Read** and **Close-Read Guides** for students. These are available online in the Interactive Student Edition or Unit Resources. 📄

● FIRST READ

Students should perform the steps of the first read independently.

NOTICE: Students should focus on the basic elements of the text to ensure they understand what is happening.

ANNOTATE: Students should mark any passages they wish to revisit during their close read.

CONNECT: Students should increase their understanding by connecting what they've read to other texts or personal experiences.

RESPOND: Students will write a summary to demonstrate their understanding.

Point out to students that while they will always complete the Respond step at the end of the first read, the other steps will probably happen somewhat concurrently. Remind students that they will revisit their first-read annotations during the close read.

> After students have completed the First-Read Guide, you may wish to assign the Text Questions for the selection that are available in the Interactive Teacher's Edition.

Anchor Standards

In the first two sections of the unit, students worked with the whole class and in small groups to gain topical knowledge and greater understanding of the skills required by the anchor standards. In this section, they are asked to work independently, applying what they have learned and demonstrating increased readiness for college and career.

👤 INDEPENDENT LEARNING

First-Read Guide

Use this page to record your first-read ideas.

Selection Title: _____

🔧 **Tool Kit**
First-Read Guide and
Model Annotation

NOTICE new information or ideas you learn about the unit topic as you first read this text.

ANNOTATE by marking vocabulary and key passages you want to revisit.

First Read

CONNECT ideas within the selection to other knowledge and the selections you have read.

RESPOND by writing a brief summary of the selection.

≣ STANDARD

Reading Read and comprehend complex literary and informational texts independently and proficiently.

82 UNIT 1 • CHILDHOOD

© Pearson Education, Inc., or its affiliates. All rights reserved.

PERSONALIZE FOR LEARNING

English Language Support
Skim, Predict, and Use KWL Chart Use the Text Complexity Rubrics to help students select a text appropriate for their proficiency level. Help students identify the genre of the selection they chose. Then have them skim the selection to notice text features, such as headings or visuals. They can also look for quotation marks and words that stand out to them. Explain to students that when they skim, they should focus on understanding the general idea and not stop to figure out unfamiliar words. Next, have students work with a partner to predict what their selection is about. Instruct them to ask and answer *Wh-* questions. Provide sample questions. Finally, help partners complete a KWL chart.
ALL LEVELS

Close-Read Guide

Use this page to record your close-read ideas.

Tool Kit
Close-Read Guide and
Model Annotation

Selection Title: _____

Close Read the Text

Revisit sections of the text you marked during your first read. Read these sections closely and **annotate** what you notice. Ask yourself **questions** about the text. What can you **conclude**? Write down your ideas.

Analyze the Text

Think about the author's choices of patterns, structure, techniques, and ideas included in the text. Select one and record your thoughts about what this choice conveys.

QuickWrite

Pick a paragraph from the text that grabbed your interest. Explain the power of this passage.

_____
_____
_____
_____
_____
_____
_____
_____
_____

© Pearson Education, Inc., or its affiliates. All rights reserved.

STANDARD

Reading Read and comprehend complex literary and informational texts independently and proficiently.

Overview: Independent Learning **83**

 CLOSE READ

Students should begin their close read by revisiting the annotations they made during their first read. Then, students should analyze one of the author's choices regarding the following:

- **patterns,** such as repetition or parallelism
- **structure,** such as cause-and-effect or problem-solution
- **techniques,** such as description or dialogue
- **ideas,** such as the author's main idea or claim

MAKE IT INTERACTIVE
Group students according to the selection they have chosen. Then, have students meet to discuss the selection in depth. Their discussions should be guided by their insights and questions.

PERSONALIZE FOR LEARNING

English Language Support
Read Aloud and Confirm Predictions Pair students or put them in groups so they can take turns reading aloud to one another. Each student can read one paragraph, or you can split up the text in any other way that makes sense. For example, for a short story, you may wish to assign different characters and the role of the narrator to individual students to take turns reading aloud.

Have students make predictions as they listen, and then have partners or groups discuss, compare, and confirm the predictions they made. Ask: *Did anything surprise you? Were any predictions correct? Which ones?* Finally, have partners or groups work together to add more details about what they learned to the Close Read the Text box on their Close-Read Guide. **ALL LEVELS**

Independent Learning **83**

Share Your Independent Learning

Prepare to Share

Explain to students that sharing what they learned from their Independent Learning selection provides classmates who read a different selection with an opportunity to consider the text as a source of evidence during the Performance-Based Assessment. As students prepare to share, remind them to highlight how their selection contributed to their knowledge of the concept of childhood as well as how the selection connects to the question, *What are some of the challenges and triumphs of growing up?*

Learn From Your Classmates

As students discuss the Independent Learning selections, direct them to take particular note of how their classmates' chosen selections align with their current position on the Performance-Based Assessment question.

Reflect

Students may want to add their reflection to their Evidence Log, particularly if their insight relates to a specific selection from the unit.

MAKE IT INTERACTIVE

Group students based on the selection they read, and have them discuss briefly what they liked and disliked about it. Then, tell students to imagine that they are going to make a movie version, video presentation, or audio reading of the selection they read. Who would they hire to play the parts or perform the reading? What visual images would they use? Why? How would they have the actors or readers convey the insights they gained from their reading and discussion? Have groups share their ideas with the class.

Evidence Log Support students in completing their Evidence Log. This paced activity will help prepare them for the Performance-Based Assessment at the end of the unit.

✎ EVIDENCE LOG

Go to your Evidence Log and record what you learned from the text you read.

Share Your Independent Learning

Prepare to Share

What are some of the challenges and triumphs of growing up?

Even when you read or learn something independently, you can continue to grow when you share what you have learned with others. Reflect on the text you explored independently, and write notes about its connection to the unit. In your notes, consider why this text belongs in this unit.

Learn From Your Classmates

◗ Discuss It Share your ideas about the text you explored on your own. As you talk with others in your class, jot down a few ideas that you learned from them.

Reflect

Review your notes, and mark the most important insight you gained from these writing and discussion activities. Explain how this idea adds to your understanding of childhood challenges and triumphs.

© Pearson Education, Inc., or its affiliates. All rights reserved.

AUTHOR'S PERSPECTIVE   **Ernest Morrell, Ph.D.**

How to Package a Speech/Oral Presentation
The small-group speaking and listening activity will help students learn how to engage an audience during a presentation. This is important for students as they prepare for careers, public service, and higher education. Help students learn to become better speakers by reminding them to ask themselves these questions as they practice and rehearse their speeches and oral presentation:

- *Posture*: Does my posture convey authority and ease? Do I look relaxed and comfortable as I'm presenting?
- *Body language*: How do I connect physically with my audience? For instance, do I make eye contact, lean forward at key point to show emphasis, and use appropriate gestures?
- *Voice*: Am I changing my voice by varying my pitch and volume to show emotion and convey meaning? Does my voice project to the back rows?

- *Humor*: How do I add humor when it suits my audience and purpose? Do I tell jokes or anecdotes, for instance?
- *Tone*: Do I speak with passion to engage my audience?

Remind students that the way the present their information is often just as important as what they are saying.

Review Evidence for a Nonfiction Narrative

At the beginning of this unit, you wrote your first thoughts about a life experience that might answer the following question:

When did a challenge lead to a triumph?

✎ EVIDENCE LOG

Review your Evidence Log and your QuickWrite from the beginning of the unit. Did you learn anything new?

NOTES

Identify at least three pieces of evidence that interested you about the challenges and triumphs of growing up.

1.

2.

3.

Identify a real-life experience that illustrates one of your ideas about childhood challenges and triumphs.

_____

Develop your thoughts into a topic sentence for a nonfiction narrative. Complete this sentence starter:
Although it was challenging when _____

_____ ,

the end result was a triumph in that _____

_____

Evaluate the Strength of Your Details Do you have enough details to write a well-developed and engaging narrative about real-life events? If not, make a plan.

☐ Brainstorm for details to add   ☐ Talk with my classmates

☐ Reread a selection   ☐ Ask an expert

☐ Other: _____

_____

© Pearson Education, Inc., or its affiliates. All rights reserved.

≔ STANDARDS
Writing
Write narratives to develop real or imagined experiences or events using effective technique, relevant descriptive details, and well-structured event sequences.
a. Engage and orient the reader by establishing a context and introducing a narrator and/or characters; organize an event sequence that unfolds naturally and logically.

Review Evidence for Nonfiction Narrative

Evidence Log Explain that through reading the selections, they should have more ideas about how to answer the question *When did a challenge lead to a triumph?* Students may choose to develop a narrative about a personal experience they thought of earlier, or they may choose to develop a narrative based on a new idea.

Evaluate the Strength of Your Details
Remind students that they can take steps to make sure they have many strong details. For example, they can:

• talk to other people who were involved in the event to get their recollections

• check their own personal records

• spend time quietly concentrating so that they can fully picture the event as it happened, including sensory details.

ASSESSING

Writing to Sources: Nonfiction Narrative

Students should complete the Performance-Based Assessment independently, with little to no input or feedback during the process. Students should use word processing software to take advantage of editing tools and features.

Prior to beginning the Assessment, ask students to think about examples of when a challenge led to a triumph.

Review the Elements of Effective Nonfiction Narrative Students can review the work they did earlier in the unit as they complete the Performance-Based Assessment. They may also consult other resources such as:

- the elements of an effective nonfiction narrative, including a description of the setting, a clear sequence of events, and a conclusion that follows from the events in the narrative, available in Whole-Class Learning.
- their Evidence Log
- their Word Network

Encourage students to collect additional details, such as sensory details and dialogue from their own experience.

© Pearson Education, Inc., or its affiliates. All rights reserved.

PERFORMANCE-BASED ASSESSMENT

SOURCES

- WHOLE-CLASS SELECTIONS
- SMALL-GROUP SELECTIONS
- INDEPENDENT-LEARNING SELECTION

🔧 WORD NETWORK

As you write and revise your nonfiction narrative, use your Word Network to help vary your word choices.

☰ STANDARDS

Writing
Write narratives to develop real or imagined experiences or events using effective technique, relevant descriptive details, and well-structured event sequences.

PART 1

Writing to Sources: Nonfiction Narrative

In this unit, you have read about different challenges and triumphs of growing up. Some of the selections described hardships and confusing changes, whereas other selections described the joys of discovery.

Assignment

Write a **nonfiction narrative** in which you tell about a real-life experience that answers this question:

> When did a challenge lead to a triumph?

The experience may be yours, or it may be that of someone you know. Begin by giving your reader background about the experience. Then, present a natural, logical series of events that shows how a challenge led to a triumph. Conclude by reflecting on the importance of the experience.

Reread the Assignment Review the assignment to be sure you fully understand it. The task may reference some of the academic words presented at the beginning of the unit. Be sure you understand each of the words here in order to complete the assignment correctly.

Academic Vocabulary

reflect	contribute	memorize
notable	recognize	

Review the Elements of Nonfiction Narrative Before you begin writing, read the Nonfiction Narrative Rubric. Once you have completed your first draft, check it against the rubric. If one or more of the elements are missing or not as strong as they could be, revise your narrative to add or strengthen those components.

AUTHOR'S PERSPECTIVE: Kelly Gallagher, M. Ed.

Building a Writing Portfolio With Students Teachers can create a portfolio that enables students to demonstrate the variety of writing they complete over the year. There are three elements of keeping a portfolio—collection of all the writing a student has done, selection of the best pieces, and reflection to evaluate growth.

Teachers can set the criteria using such categories as *Best Argument, Best Narrative Piece, Best Informative Piece, Best On-Demand Writing, Best Poetry, Best Blended Genre, Best Writing from Another Class, Best Model of Revision,* and *Best Single Line You Wrote this Year.* Students should also include a reflective letter at the end of the year. To help them learn to reflect, use questions like this throughout the year.

- Where does your writing still need improvement? How will you improve?
- Reflect on a struggle you faced during this unit. How did you overcome it?
- Discuss a specific writing strategy you used and how it worked for you.

Nonfiction Narrative Rubric

	Focus and Organization	Evidence and Elaboration	Conventions
4	The introduction is engaging and introduces the characters and situation in a way that appeals to readers. Events in the narrative progress in logical order and are linked by clear transitions. The conclusion effectively follows from the narrated experiences or events.	The narrative effectively includes techniques such as dialogue and description to add interest and to develop the characters and events. The narrative effectively includes precise words and phrases, relevant descriptive details, and sensory language to convey experiences and events. The narrative effectively establishes voice through word choice, sentence structure, and tone.	The narrative consistently uses standard English conventions of usage and mechanics. The narrative effectively varies sentence patterns for meaning, reader interest, and style.
3	The introduction is somewhat engaging and clearly introduces the characters and situation. Events in the narrative progress logically and are often linked by transition words. The conclusion mostly follows from the narrated experiences or events.	The narrative mostly includes dialogue and description to add interest and develop experiences and events. The narrative mostly includes precise words and sensory language to convey experiences and events. The narrative mostly establishes voice through word choice, sentence structure, and tone.	The narrative mostly demonstrates accuracy in standard English conventions of usage and mechanics. The narrative mostly varies sentence patterns for meaning, reader interest, and style.
2	The introduction occasionally introduces characters. Events in the narrative progress somewhat logically and are sometimes linked by transition words. The conclusion adds very little to the narrated experiences or events.	The narrative includes some dialogue and descriptions. The words in the narrative vary between vague and precise, and some sensory language is included. The narrative occasionally establishes voice through word choice, sentence structure, and tone.	The narrative demonstrates some accuracy in standard English conventions of usage and mechanics. The narrative occasionally varies sentence patterns for meaning, reader interest, and style.
1	The introduction does not introduce characters and an experience, or there is no clear introduction. The events in the narrative do not progress logically. The ideas seem disconnected and the sentences are not linked by transitional words and phrases. The conclusion does not connect to the narrative or there is no conclusion.	Dialogue and descriptions are not included in the narrative. The narrative does not incorporate sensory language or precise words to convey experiences and to develop characters. The narrative does not establish voice through word choice, sentence structure, and tone.	The narrative contains mistakes in standard English conventions of usage and mechanics. The narrative does not vary sentence patterns for meaning, reader interest, and style.

© Pearson Education, Inc., or its affiliates. All rights reserved.

Performance-Based Assessment **87**

Nonfiction Narrative Rubric

As you review the **Nonfiction Narrative** Rubric with students, remind them that the rubric is a resource that can guide their revisions. Students should pay particular attention to the differences between a nonfiction narrative that effectively includes techniques such as dialogue and description to develop characters and events (a score of 4) and one that only does so adequately (a score of 3).

- What strengths have you developed as a writer? Where are those strengths found in this portfolio?
- Where can you demonstrate in this portfolio that you have improved as a reader and as a writer?

At the end of the year, students can review these pieces to see their growth as writers.

PERSONALIZE FOR LEARNING

English Language Support

Order of Events Help English Learners describe a series of events by displaying or providing words that tell about the order of events, such as *first, next, then, afterward, before, subsequently, as soon as, later,* and *finally.* If necessary, have students to work with a partner to revise their work to include a clear series of events using transitional words and phrases such as these. Remind students also to pay careful attention to the tenses of verbs to describe past, present, future, and ongoing events.

Speaking and Listening: Recitation

Students should annotate their written nonfiction narrative in preparation for the recitation, marking the important elements (description, dialogue, a clear series of events, and precise language) as well as sensory details and voice.

Remind students that the effectiveness of an oral nonfiction narrative relies on how the speaker establishes credibility with his or her audience. If a speaker comes across as confident and lively, it will be easier to engage the audience and sustain their interest.

Review the Rubric As you review the rubric with students, remind them that it is a valuable tool that can help them plan their presentation. They should strive to include all of the criteria required to achieve a score of 3. Draw their attention to some of the subtle differences between scores of 2 and 3.

PART 2
Speaking and Listening: Recitation

Assignment
After completing the final draft of your nonfiction narrative, plan and present a **recitation,** in which you tell the story to classmates.

Do not simply read your narrative aloud. Examine what you have written, and adapt it for a listening audience. Follow these steps to make your recitation lively and engaging.

- Go back to your narrative, and annotate key events or descriptions that you want to emphasize.
- Mark places in the narrative where you intend to slow down or speed up.
- Add transitions as needed, to help a listening audience follow along.
- Use appropriate eye contact. Make sure to speak loudly enough for people to hear you, and pronounce words clearly.

Review the Rubric The criteria by which your recitation will be evaluated appear in the rubric below. Review these criteria before presenting to ensure that you are prepared.

STANDARDS

Speaking and Listening
Adapt speech to a variety of contexts and tasks, demonstrating command of formal English when indicated or appropriate.

	Content	Presentation Techniques
3	The presentation has an engaging introduction, a logical sequence of events, and a meaningful conclusion.	The speaker maintains effective eye contact and speaks clearly and with adequate volume.
	The presentation effectively includes narrative techniques and a variety of transitions for clarity.	The speaker varies tone and volume to create an engaging presentation.
	The presentation effectively includes descriptive details relevant to the story.	
2	The presentation has an introduction, a somewhat logical sequence of events, and a conclusion.	The speaker sometimes maintains effective eye contact and speaks somewhat clearly and with adequate volume.
	The presentation includes some narrative techniques and some transitions for clarity.	The speaker sometimes varies tone and emphasis to create an engaging presentation.
	The presentation includes some descriptive details.	
1	The presentation does not have a logical sequence of events, and lacks an introduction or conclusion.	The speaker does not maintain effective eye contact or speak clearly with adequate volume.
	The presentation does not include narrative techniques and transitions.	The speaker does not vary tone and emphasis to create an engaging presentation.
	The presentation does not include descriptive details.	

© Pearson Education, Inc., or its affiliates. All rights reserved.

DIGITAL PERSPECTIVES

Preparing for the Assignment To help students understand what an effective oral nonfiction narrative looks and sounds like, find examples on the Internet of students or adults presenting nonfiction narratives. Project the examples for the class, and have students note the techniques that make each speaker successful (gesture, emotion, facial expressions, pacing, tone, and so on). Suggest that students record themselves prior to presenting their nonfiction narratives to the class so that they can practice incorporating some of the elements they saw in the examples.

Reflect on the Unit

Now that you've completed the unit, take a few moments to reflect on your learning.

Reflect on the Unit Goals

Look back at the goals at the beginning of the unit. Use a different-colored pen to rate yourself again. Think about readings and activities that contributed the most to the growth of your understanding. Record your thoughts.

Reflect on the Learning Strategies

💬 **Discuss It** Write a reflection on whether you were able to improve your learning based on your Action Plans. Think about what worked, what didn't, and what you might do to keep working on these strategies. Record your ideas before a class discussion.

Reflect on the Text

Choose a selection that you found challenging, and explain what made it difficult.

Explain something that surprised you about a text in the unit. Which activity taught you the most about childhood? What did you learn?

© Pearson Education, Inc., or its affiliates. All rights reserved.

SCAN FOR
MULTIMEDIA

Reflect on the Unit ▶

- Have students watch the video on Reflecting on Your Learning.
- A video on this topic is available online in the Professional Development Center.

Reflect on the Unit Goals

Students should re-evaluate how well they met the unit goals now that they have completed the unit. You might ask them to provide a written commentary on the goal they made the most progress with as well as the goal they feel warrants continued focus.

Reflect on the Learning Strategies

Discuss It If you want to make this a digital activity, go online and navigate to the Discussion Board. Alternatively, students can share their learning strategies reflections in a class discussion.

Reflect on the Text

Consider having students share their text reflections with one another.

MAKE IT INTERACTIVE

Have each student use presentation software to prepare a slide that summarizes his or her reflections on this unit. Students should be prepared to give a 30-second oral summary of their slide. Collate student slides into a presentation that can be viewed by the class. If appropriate, set the presentation to music related to the theme of the unit—childhood.

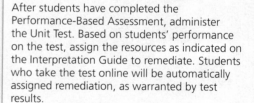

Unit Test and Remediation 📄 ☑

After students have completed the Performance-Based Assessment, administer the Unit Test. Based on students' performance on the test, assign the resources as indicated on the Interpretation Guide to remediate. Students who take the test online will be automatically assigned remediation, as warranted by test results.

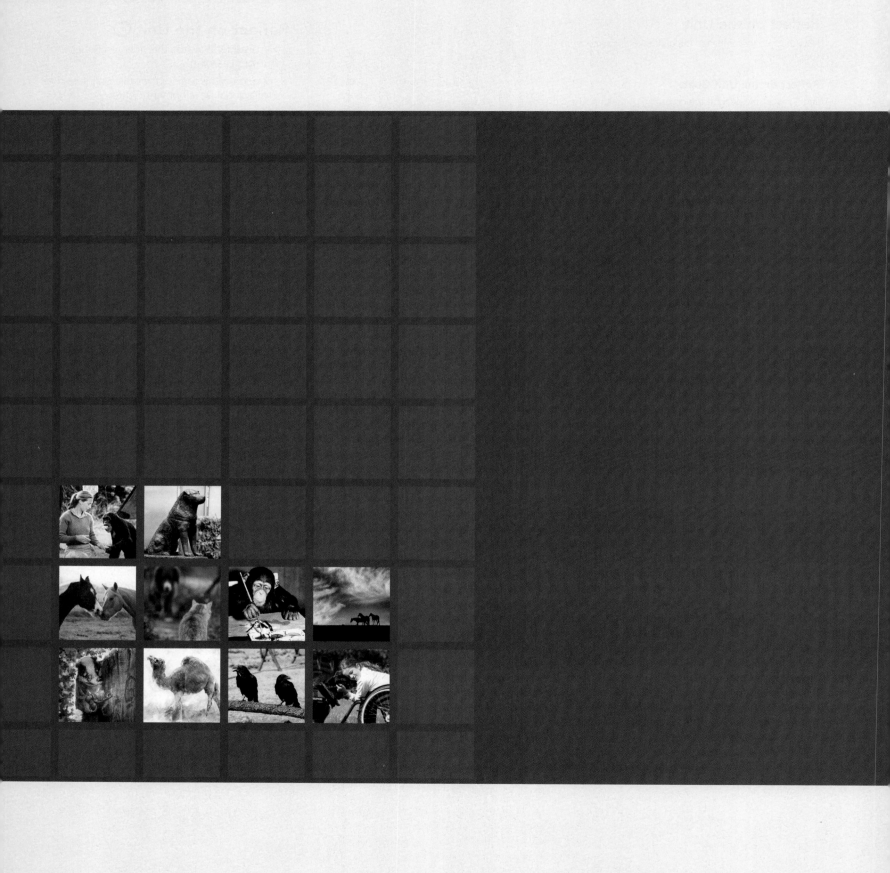

UNIT  2

Animal Allies

Jump Start

Engage students in a discussion about their relationships with pets and other animals. Ask the following questions:

Can pets be our friends? Can we be friends to our pets?

Have students write the name of the animal they feel closest to and the main reason why. Then poll the class. Which kind of animal is most popular? Why?

Animal Allies

Ask students what the phrase *Animal Allies* suggests to them. Point out that as they work through this unit, they will read many examples about animals that have gone to extraordinary lengths to help humans in need.

Video ▶

Project the introduction video in class, ask students to open the video in their interactive textbooks, or have students scan the BouncePage icon with their phones to access the video.

Discuss It If you want to make this a digital activity, go online and navigate to the Discussion Board. Alternatively, students can share their responses in a class discussion.

Block Scheduling

Each day in this pacing calendar represents a 40–50 minute class period. Teachers using block scheduling may combine days to reflect their class schedule. In addition, teachers may revise pacing to differentiate and support core instruction by integrating components and resources as students require.

Animals and people can form unique relationships. How can these relationships affect both the animal and the person?

© Pearson Education, Inc. or its affiliates. All rights reserved.

People of the Horse: Special Bond

90

💬 **Discuss It** Is the relationship between animals and people truly a special bond?

Write your response before sharing your ideas.

SCAN FOR MULTIMEDIA

📅 **Pacing Plan**

 Pacing Plan

Introduce Whole-Class Learning

Performance Task

Unit Introduction   *from* My Life With the Chimpanzees   Hachiko: The True Story of a Loyal Dog

| 1 | 2 | 3 | 4 | 5 | 6 | 7 | 8 | 9 | 10 | 11 | 12 | 13 | 14 | 15 | 16 | 17 | 18 |

Audio　**Video**　**Document**　**Annotation Highlights**　**EL Highlights**　**Online Assessment**

UNIT 2

UNIT INTRODUCTION

ESSENTIAL QUESTION:

How can people and animals relate to each other?

LAUNCH TEXT
INFORMATIVE/
EXPLANATORY MODEL
Reading Buddies

WHOLE-CLASS LEARNING

ANCHOR TEXT: MEMOIR

from My Life With the Chimpanzees
Jane Goodall

ANCHOR TEXT: HISTORICAL FICTION

Hachiko: The True Story of a Loyal Dog
Pamela S. Turner

▶ MEDIA CONNECTION:
The Secret Life of the Dog

SMALL-GROUP LEARNING

COMPARE

POETRY

A Blessing
James Wright

POETRY

Predators
Linda Hogan

ESSAY

Monkey Master
Waldemar Januszczak

SHORT STORY

Black Cowboy, Wild Horses
Julius Lester

INDEPENDENT LEARNING

NOVEL EXCERPT

from The Wind in the Willows
Kenneth Grahame

FABLE

How the Camel Got His Hump
from Just So Stories
Rudyard Kipling

NEWS ARTICLE

The Girl Who Gets Gifts From Birds
Katy Sewall

NEWS ARTICLE

Pet Therapy: How Animals and Humans Heal Each Other
Julie Rovner

PERFORMANCE TASK

WRITING FOCUS:
Write an Explanatory Essay

PERFORMANCE TASK

SPEAKING AND LISTENING FOCUS:
Deliver an Informative Presentation

PERFORMANCE-BASED ASSESSMENT PREP

Review Evidence for an Explanatory Essay

PERFORMANCE-BASED ASSESSMENT

Explanatory Text: Essay and Informative Presentation

PROMPT:

How can animals and people help one another?

© Pearson Education, Inc., or its affiliates. All rights reserved.

91

How can people and animals relate to each other?

Introduce the Essential Question and point out that students will respond to related prompts.

- **Whole-Class Learning** *What qualities do Goodall and Turner believe people and animals share?*
- **Small-Group Learning** *How can the bonds between people and animals be surprising?*
- **Performance-Based Assessment** *How can animals and people help one another?*

Using Trade Books

Refer to the Teaching with Trade Books section in this book or online in the Interactive Teacher's Edition for suggestions on how to incorporate the following thematically-related novels into this unit.

- *The Jungle Book* by Rudyard Kipling
- *Where the Red Fern Grows* by Wilson Rawls
- *Black Beauty* by Anna Sewell

Current Perspectives

To increase student engagement, search online for stories about humans and animals that work together to help each other, and invite your students to recommend stories they find. Always preview content before sharing it with your class.

- **Article: Relating Animals to Humans Could Help Conservation Projects (*Science Daily*)** When humans are able to relate to animals, they are more likely to participate in conservation efforts.
- **Video: Dogs and People Bond Through Eye Contact (*CBS News*)** Dogs bond with humans in the same way as babies bond with their parents.

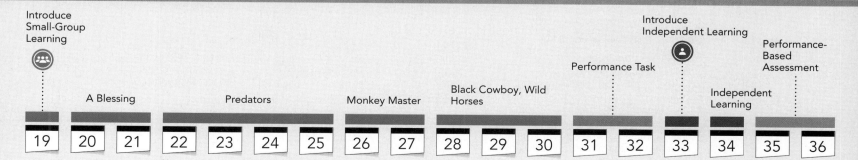

Introduce
Small-Group
Learning

A Blessing　Predators　Monkey Master　Black Cowboy, Wild Horses　Performance Task

Introduce
Independent Learning

Performance-Based Assessment

Independent Learning

19　20　21　22　23　24　25　26　27　28　29　30　31　32　33　34　35　36

About the Unit Goals

These unit goals were backward designed from the Performance-Based Assessment at the end of the unit and the Whole-Class and Small-Group Performance Tasks. Students will practice and become proficient in many more standards over the course of this unit.

Unit Goals ▶

Review the goals with students and explain that as they read and discuss the selections in this unit, they will improve their skills in reading, writing, research, language, and speaking and listening.

• Have students watch the video on Goal Setting.

• A video on this topic is available online in the Professional Development Center.

Reading Goals Tell students they will read and evaluate informative essays. They will also read arguments, fictional narratives, and nonfiction narratives.

Writing and Research Goals Tell students that they will learn the elements of explanatory essay writing. They will also write their own informative essays. They will conduct research to clarify and explore ideas.

Language Goal Tell students that they will develop a deeper understanding of command of the conventions of standard English grammar and usage. They will then practice correct usage of pronouns in their own writing.

Speaking and Listening Goals Explain to students that they will work together to build on one another's ideas, develop consensus, and communicate with one another. They will also learn to incorporate audio, visuals, and text in presentations.

HOME Connection ✉

A Home Connection letter to students' parents or guardians is available in the Interactive Teacher's Edition. The letter explains what students will be learning in this unit and how they will be assessed.

Unit Goals

Throughout this unit, you will deepen your understanding of the ways that people and animals can relate to each other by reading, writing, speaking, listening, and presenting. These goals will help you succeed on the Unit Performance-Based Assessment.

Rate how well you meet these goals right now. You will revisit your ratings later when you reflect on your growth during this unit.

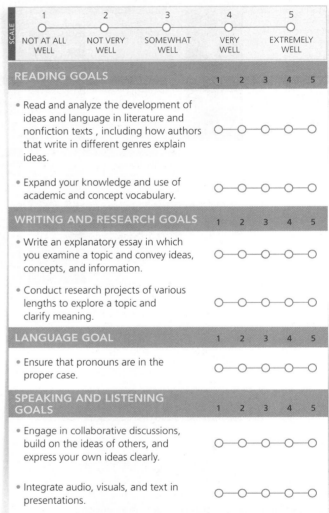

■ STANDARDS

Language
Acquire and use accurately grade-appropriate general academic and domain-specific words and phrases; gather vocabulary knowledge when considering a word or phrase important to comprehension or expression.

92 UNIT 2 • ANIMAL ALLIES

© Pearson Education, Inc., or its affiliates. All rights reserved.

SCAN FOR MULTIMEDIA

AUTHOR'S PERSPECTIVE **Ernest Morrell, Ph. D.**

Self-Assessing Progress The Unit Goals will help students share responsibility for their learning. This is an important ownership for students as they prepare for life in higher education, in their professional career, and as leaders in their families and communities. One way to encourage students to practice monitoring their own learning is to give them guiding questions

like these to help them assess their progress as they work through the unit. Remind students to ask themselves such questions as they complete each selection or activity in the unit so they can track their progress.

• Do I have a better understanding of an explanatory essay and how to recognize them when reading and using them when writing?

• Do I have a better understanding of the differences between academic and concept vocabulary?

• Am I recognizing and using pronouns correctly?

• Am I effective when I collaborate with others?

ESSENTIAL QUESTION: How can people and animals relate to each other?

DIGITAL
PERSPECTIVES

Academic Vocabulary: Informative/ Explanatory Text

Understanding and using academic terms can help you read, write, and speak with precision and clarity. Here are five academic words that will be useful to you in this unit as you analyze and write informative and explanatory texts.

Complete the chart.

1. Review each word, its root, and mentor sentences.

2. Use the information and your own knowledge to predict the meaning of each word.

3. For each word, list at least two related words.

4. Refer to the dictionary or other resources if needed.

TIP

FOLLOW THROUGH
Study the words in this chart, and mark them or their forms wherever they appear in the unit.

WORD	MENTOR SENTENCES	PREDICT MEANING	RELATED WORDS
exclude ROOT: -clud- "shut"	1. He prefers to invite his entire class to his birthday party rather than *exclude* anyone. 2. To *exclude* people from the club based on their age would be unfair.		include; conclusive
illustrate ROOT: -lus- "shine"	1. Can you give me an example to *illustrate* that idea? I'm confused. 2. I gathered pictures of my family to *illustrate* my autobiographical narrative.		
community ROOT: -commun- "common"	1. *Community* leaders regularly meet to discuss the town's issues. 2. The business *community* is important to the growth of the town.		
elaborate ROOT: -lab- "work"	1. Because Sara's instructions were hard to understand, Frank asked her to *elaborate* in detail. 2. You may first create an outline to list the key points, but then you must support and *elaborate* on your ideas with examples.		
objective ROOT: -ject- "throw"	1. The *objective* in a soccer game is to score goals by putting the ball in the other team's net. 2. When Mike drafted his resume, he made sure to state his *objective* for career success.		

© Pearson Education, Inc., or its affiliates. All rights reserved.

Academic Vocabulary: Informative/Explanatory Text

Introduce the blue academic vocabulary words in the chart on the student page. Point out that the root of each word provides a clue to its meaning. Discuss the mentor sentences to ensure students understand each word's usage. Students should also use the mentor sentences as context to help them predict the meaning of each word. Check that students are able to fill the chart in correctly. Complete pronunciations, parts of speech, and definitions are provided for you. Students are only expected to provide the definition.

Possible responses:
exclude *v.* (ehk SKLOOD)
Meaning: shut out; keep from entering, happening, or being
Related words: exclusion, exclusionary
Additional words related to root -clud-: include, conclude, conclusion, secluded

illustrate *v.* (IHL uh strayt)
Meaning: to explain by adding information like graphs, images, or examples
Related words: illustration, illustrator
Additional words related to root -lustr-: lustrous, illustrative, lackluster

community *n.* (kuh MYOO nih tee)
Meaning: a group of people who live in the same area; a group of people who have the same interests, religion, etc.
Related words: communicate, communicator
Additional words related to root -commun-: communal, communion

elaborate *adj.* or *v.* (ih LAB uhr iht)
Meaning: something done with great detail or to explain by adding more details
Related words: elaboration, elaborator
Additional words related to root -lab-: labor, laborious, collaborate

objective *n.* (uhb JEHK tihv)
Meaning: aim or goal
Related words: object, objector
Additional words related to root -ject-: project, reject, interject

---

PERSONALIZE FOR LEARNING

English Language Support
Cognates Many of the academic words have Spanish cognates. Use these cognates with students whose home language is Spanish.
ALL LEVELS

objective – objetivo	exclude – excluir
illustrate – ilustrar	communicate – comunicar
elaborate – elaborar	

Purpose of the Launch Text

The Launch Text provides students with a common starting point to address the unit topic. After reading the Launch Text, all students will be able to participate in discussions about animal allies.

Lexile: 890 The easier reading level of this selection makes it perfect to assign for homework. Students will need little or no support to understand it.

Additionally, "Reading Buddies" provides a writing model for the Performance-Based Assessment students complete at the end of the unit.

Launch Text: Informative/ Explanatory Text Model

Remind students that the point of an informative/ explanatory text is to present facts in a logical and objective way. Point to the title of the essay and explain that the title is a clue to the topic. Then ask students to pay attention to the structure of the text. They should note that the author explains the topic of the essay and presents the thesis statement in the first couple of paragraphs. In the remainder of the essay, the author provides background, examples, and anecdotes that expand on the topic further. The author then restates the thesis in the concluding paragraph.

Encourage students to read this text on their own and annotate unfamiliar words and sections of text they think are particularly important.

🔊 AUDIO SUMMARIES

Audio summaries of "Reading Buddies" are available in both English and Spanish in the Interactive Teacher's Edition or Unit Resources. Assigning these summaries before students read the Launch Text may help them build additional background knowledge and set a context for their reading.

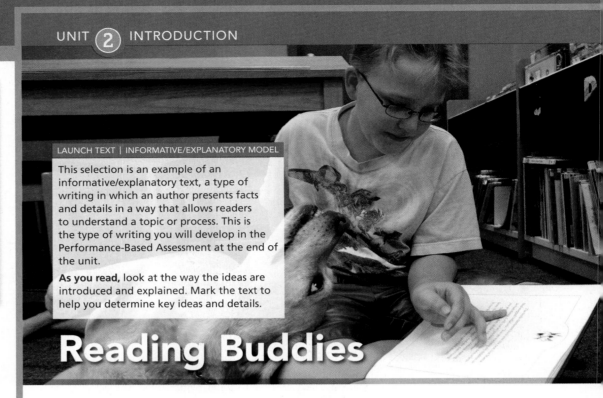

LAUNCH TEXT | INFORMATIVE/EXPLANATORY MODEL

This selection is an example of an informative/explanatory text, a type of writing in which an author presents facts and details in a way that allows readers to understand a topic or process. This is the type of writing you will develop in the Performance-Based Assessment at the end of the unit.

As you read, look at the way the ideas are introduced and explained. Mark the text to help you determine key ideas and details.

Reading Buddies

NOTES

1   In a school library across town, a third-grade boy is reading his favorite book to a dog named Theo. The boy is petting the dog as he reads, and the dog has its paw on the boy's foot. Both seem relaxed and happy, but what is a dog doing in a school library?

2   Theo, a five-year-old border collie, is one of more than 2,300 dogs around the country that have been trained to listen to people read aloud. He is part of a program that began in Utah in 1999. Through this program, teams of dogs and their handlers were sent out to schools and libraries to serve as reading companions for kids who were having trouble reading. Since then, similar reading programs have popped up in every region of the United States. They have helped thousands of kids improve not only their reading skills but also their attitudes about reading.

3   There are many reasons kids can have trouble reading. Some have learning disabilities. Some think it's boring. Some are new to English. Others just haven't found a book they like.

4   Whatever the cause, struggling readers have one thing in common: They lack confidence. Learning to read is often less about reading skills than it is about confidence. To a struggling reader, an animal listener can produce less anxiety than a human listener.

© Pearson Education, Inc., or its affiliates. All rights reserved.

94 UNIT 2 • ANIMAL ALLIES

SCAN FOR MULTIMEDIA

English Language Support

Noun Phrases Direct students' attention to paragraph 2. Point out that "five-year-old" is an adjective and "border collie" is a kind of dog. Point out that "one of more than 2,300 dogs around the country that have been trained to listen to people read aloud" also describes the border collie. Explain that the "Arizona Animal Welfare League & Society for Prevention of Cruelty to Animals" is the name of such an organization. **ALL LEVELS**

5   Dogs are the ideal reading companions. They aren't in a hurry, so you can read at your own pace. They won't stop you when you've pronounced something wrong. They won't laugh at you or make you feel self-conscious. When you read to a dog, you are not as likely to feel judged. You get a chance to focus on the book you're reading rather than your performance.

6   "I never finished a whole book before," said a 10-year-old girl who participated in the program. She had been reading at a first-grade level and hardly ever practiced, because she was too shy to read aloud. But after a few weeks of reading to a dog companion, she finished the book. She was proud of herself for having overcome such a major hurdle!

7   Reading is like any other skill—the more you practice, the better you get. But it's hard to find someone who has the time to sit down and listen. Readers can also feel nervous about making mistakes. "But if you're practicing with a dog," said one reading specialist, "you don't mind making the mistake. In fact, you'll probably correct it."

8   More and more libraries and schools are using dogs to help kids improve their reading skills and confidence level. Sometimes, when people read to dogs, it's the *dogs* that benefit. For example, the Arizona Animal Welfare League & Society for Prevention of Cruelty to Animals is using reading as a tool to help shelter animals become happier, more well-adjusted pets. Program volunteers spend time reading to dogs and cats who are waiting to be adopted. Reading calms the animals down and makes them more comfortable around people.

9   Through the experience of reading, humans and animals are helping each other develop the skills they need to take on life's challenges—whatever those challenges happen to be. ❧

NOTES

© Pearson Education, Inc., or its affiliates. All rights reserved.

⚓ WORD NETWORK FOR ANIMAL ALLIES

Vocabulary A Word Network is a collection of words related to a topic. As you read the selections in this unit, identify interesting words related to the relationships between animals and people, and add them to your Word Network. For example, you might begin by adding words from the Launch Text, such as *participated, handlers,* and *well-adjusted.* Continue to add words as you complete this unit.

🔧 **Tool Kit** Word Network Model

participated

handlers

well-adjusted

ANIMAL/HUMAN RELATIONSHIPS

Reading Buddies **95**

Word Network for Animal Allies

Tell students that they can fill in the Word Network as they read texts in the unit, or they can record the words elsewhere and add them later. Point out to students that people may have personal associations with some words. A word that one student thinks is related to animal/human relationships might not be a word another student would pick. However, students should fell free to add any word they personally think is relevant to their Word Network. Each person's Word Network will be unique. If you choose to print the Word Network, distribute it to students at this point so they can use it throughout the rest of the unit.

AUTHOR'S PERSPECTIVE: Elfrieda Hiebert, Ph.D.

Generative Vocabulary Rare words are the words that typically account for only 10 percent of all the words in a text, compared to the more common vocabulary words that students know better. Generative vocabulary strategies can help students build their rare vocabulary.

Generative refers to the way students can apply knowledge of how words work — morphologically and conceptually — when encountering new words. Building off of a big idea like this unit's animal allies, words can be taught as networks of ideas rather than as single, unrelated but grade-appropriate words. Studying words in conceptual groupings enables students to learn more words while reading.

Although some "animal allies" words may be unfamiliar to students, the overarching concept will not be. Students may not know every word related to the idea of animal allies, but the concept of connections between people and animals should be familiar to them. Word networks help students build vocabulary as they see a wide variety of words can relate to one concept.

Summary

Have students read the introductory paragraph. Provide them with tips for writing a summary:

- Write in the present tense.
- Make sure to include the title of the work.
- Be concise: a summary should not be equal in length to the original text.
- If you need to quote the words of the author, use quotation marks.
- Don't put your own opinions, ideas, or interpretations into the summary. The purpose of writing a summary is to accurately represent what the author says, not to provide a critique.

If necessary, students can refer to the Tool Kit for help in understanding the elements of a good summary.

See possible summary on student page.

Launch Activity

Explain to students that as they work on this unit they will have many opportunities to discuss the topic of animal allies. Remind them that there is no right or wrong position, but that they should be able to support their positions with evidence from the material they've read, viewed, and seen so far in the unit, as well as their prior knowledge.

Encourage students to listen to their classmates' opinions and to keep an open mind throughout the discussion.

Summary

Write a summary of "Reading Buddies." A **summary** is a concise, complete, and accurate overview of a text. It should not include a statement of your opinion or an analysis.

Possible response: In this informative/explanatory text, "Reading Buddies," we learn about an unusual way for kids who have trouble reading to gain confidence and read better. They read aloud to dogs. This is less stressful than reading aloud to people, making it easier for kids to concentrate, avoid making mistakes, and correct the mistakes they make. It also helps the dogs calm down and makes them more comfortable around people. People and animals can make each other happy and relaxed; and this method just so happens to help kids with learning disabilities and animals from shelters.

Launch Activity

Conduct a Discussion Consider this question: **Is using animal reading buddies a good way to improve reading skills?**

- Record your position on the statement and explain your thinking.

☐ Strongly Agree ☐ Agree ☐ Disagree ☐ Strongly Disagree

- Form small groups to share your opinions. Give examples from stories you have heard or read, including the Launch Text.
- Listen respectfully and carefully to the ideas expressed, and reflect on each other's perspectives thoughtfully.
- Finally, write a short paragraph stating whether the discussion changed your opinion. Explain the reasons your opinion either changed or stayed the same.

© Pearson Education, Inc., or its affiliates. All rights reserved.

QuickWrite

Consider class discussions, the video, and the Launch Text as you think about the prompt. Record your first thoughts here.

PROMPT: **How can animals and people help one another?**

> **Possible response:** People and animals can't help each other in the ways people would help people (like giving advice), or in the ways animals would help animals (like physically cooperating on a task). Instead, they can help each other through how they make each other feel. When someone trains a dog, he or she rewards it for doing the right thing and chide it for doing the wrong thing. The latter might not always be nice, but it does help the dog learn what's right. Similarly, growing up with pets can teach kids how to be kind and respectful of feelings, from how their pet reacts to their behavior.

✍ EVIDENCE LOG FOR ANIMAL ALLIES

Review your QuickWrite. Summarize your thoughts in one sentence to record in your Evidence Log. Then, record evidence from "Reading Buddies" that supports your thinking.

Prepare for the Performance-Based Assessment at the end of the unit by completing the Evidence Log after each selection.

🔧 **Tool Kit**
Evidence Log Model

Title of Text: _____ Date: _____

CONNECTION TO PROMPT	TEXT EVIDENCE/DETAILS	ADDITIONAL NOTES/IDEAS

How does this text change or add to my thinking? Date: _____

SCAN FOR
MULTIMEDIA

Unit Introduction **97**

© Pearson Education, Inc., or its affiliates. All rights reserved.

QuickWrite

In this QuickWrite, students should present their own response to the prompt based on the material they have read and viewed in the Unit Overview and Introduction. This initial response will help inform their work when they complete the Performance-Based Assessment at the end of the unit. Students should consider all the examples they've seen of how animals and people interact positively, using accurate details.

See possible QuickWrite on student page.

Evidence Log for Animal Allies 🗎

Students should record their initial thinking in their Evidence Logs along with evidence from "Reading Buddies" that support this thinking.

If you choose to print the Evidence Log, distribute it to students at this point so they can use it throughout the rest of the unit.

Performance-Based Assessment: Refining Your Thinking ▶

- Have students watch the video on Refining Your Thinking.
- A video on this topic is available online in the Professional Development Center.

DIGITAL PERSPECTIVES

Enriching the Text To give students a better idea of how assist animals help people, show them a video clip of an assist animal with the person it helps. Be sure to preview the clip before you show it to students.

Once students have viewed the video, have them compare what the service animal in the video does with the role of the dogs in the launch text. Direct their discussion by asking them what the service animal is trained to do and how it assists people. Invite them to comment on how the animal and the person it assists interact. Then ask them if they can tell in the video how the person feels about the animal. Have students discuss what they learned from the video about the ways that assist animals interact with people and how it helped them understand the launch text.

Reading Buddies **97**

OVERVIEW

WHOLE-CLASS LEARNING

How can people and animals relate to each other?

Engage students in a discussion about how they interact with their pets and other animals. Point out that humans have always lived with animals, and that animals have been used for work or service or kept as pets. What is the difference between a service animal and a pet? During Whole-Class Learning, students will read selections about the close relationships that often develop between people and animals.

Whole-Class Learning Strategies ▶

Review the Learning Strategies with students and explain that as they work through Whole-Class Learning they will develop strategies to work in large-group environments.

- Have students watch the video on Whole-Class Learning Strategies.
- A video on this topic is available online in the Professional Development Center.

You may wish to discuss some action items to add to the chart as a class before students complete it on their own. For example, for "Listen actively," you might solicit the following from students:

- Take notes when something seems particularly important.
- Ask questions after the speaker has finished.

Block Scheduling

Each day in this Pacing Plan represents a 40–50 minute class period. Teachers using block scheduling may combine days to reflect their class schedule. In addition, teachers may revise pacing to differentiate and support core instruction by integrating components and resources as students require.

OVERVIEW: WHOLE-CLASS LEARNING

ESSENTIAL QUESTION:

How can people and animals relate to each other?

Over thousands of years humans and animals have formed important relationships. For example, humans rely on some animals to help with farmwork, rescue, or transportation; some animals rely on humans for protection, shelter, and food. The selections you are going to read present insights into the bonds that exist between people and animals.

Whole-Class Learning Strategies

Throughout your life, in school, in your community, and in your career, you will continue to learn and work in large-group environments.

Review these strategies and the actions you can take to practice them as you work with your whole class. Add ideas of your own for each strategy. Get ready to use these strategies during Whole-Class Learning.

STRATEGY	ACTION PLAN
Listen actively	• Eliminate distractions. For example, put your cellphone away. • Keep your eyes on the speaker. •
Clarify by asking questions	• If you're confused, other people probably are, too. Ask a question to help your whole class. • If you see that you are guessing, ask a question instead. •
Monitor understanding	• Notice what information you already know and be ready to build on it. • Ask for help if you are struggling. •
Interact and share ideas	• Share your ideas and answer questions, even if you are unsure. • Build on the ideas of others by adding details or making a connection. •

© Pearson Education, Inc., or its affiliates. All rights reserved.

SCAN FOR MULTIMEDIA

98 UNIT 2 • ANIMAL ALLIES

Introduce Whole-Class Learning

Performance Task

Unit Introduction

from My Life With the Chimpanzees

Hachiko: The True Story of a Loyal Dog

| 1 | 2 | 3 | 4 | 5 | 6 | 7 | 8 | 9 | 10 | 11 | 12 | 13 | 14 | 15 | 16 | 17 | 18 |

WHOLE-CLASS LEARNING

CONTENTS

ANCHOR TEXT: MEMOIR

from My Life With the Chimpanzees
Jane Goodall

Jane Goodall was only twenty-six years old when she moved to Tanzania to live with and study chimpanzees in the wild—it became the focus of her life's work.

ANCHOR TEXT: HISTORICAL FICTION

Hachiko: The True Story of a Loyal Dog
Pamela S. Turner

A dog becomes beloved by an entire nation for his loyalty.

▶ MEDIA CONNECTION: The Secret Life of the Dog

PERFORMANCE TASK

WRITING FOCUS
Write an Explanatory Essay

The Whole-Class readings present animals as intelligent creatures with unique personalities. After reading, you will write an explanatory essay in which you explain the traits these authors believe people and animals share.

© Pearson Education, Inc., or its affiliates. All rights reserved.

Contents

Anchor Texts Preview the anchor texts and media with students to generate interest. Encourage students to discuss other texts they may have read or movies or television shows they may have seen that deal with the issues of people and our strong bond with animals.

You may wish to conduct a poll to determine which selection students think looks more interesting and discuss the reasons for their preference. Students can return to this poll after they have read the selections to see if their preference changed.

Performance Task

Write an Explanatory Essay Explain to students that after they have finished reading the selections, they will write an explanatory essay that examines the ways that the authors present people and animals as having things in common. To help them prepare, encourage students to think about the topic as they progress through the selections and as they participate in the Whole-Class Learning experience.

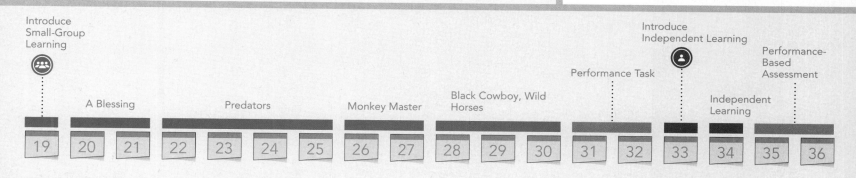

Introduce
Small-Group
Learning

Introduce
Independent Learning

Performance-
Based
Assessment

Performance Task

A Blessing   Predators   Monkey Master   Black Cowboy, Wild Horses   Independent Learning

| 19 | 20 | 21 | 22 | 23 | 24 | 25 | 26 | 27 | 28 | 29 | 30 | 31 | 32 | 33 | 34 | 35 | 36 |

from My Life With the Chimpanzees

🔊 **AUDIO SUMMARIES**

Audio summaries of from My Life With the Chimpanzees are available online in both English and Spanish in the Interactive Teacher's Edition or Unit Resources. Assigning these summaries prior to reading the selection may help students build additional background knowledge and set a context for their first read.

Summary

from My Life with the Chimpanzees is an excerpt from a memoir written by Jane Goodall, who revolutionized our understanding of humanity's closest living relatives. She describes her first few months observing chimpanzees in the wild. It was a challenge, of course— the conditions were dangerous, and the chimps feared humans and often ran and hid. But Goodall found ways to observe the chimps, which became easier and easier as they got used to her presence. She observed them making tools, something scientists had long believed only humans did, and she learned about the ways in which the chimps communicated. As it became possible to learn more and more, Goodall went from just observing these remarkable animals to directing a research center for animal study.

Insight

This selection takes a nuanced and clear-eyed view of chimpanzees, revealing how they are both similar to and different than humans. More broadly, it shows how hard work and dedication to a task—research—paid off.

ESSENTIAL QUESTION:
How can people and animals relate to each other?

Connection to Essential Question

One of Goodall's most important contributions to the field was making scientific observations of ways chimp behavior was analogous to human behavior, including fear and jockeying for social status.

WHOLE-CLASS LEARNING PERFORMANCE TASK
What qualities do Goodall and Turner believe people and animals share?

Connection to Performance Tasks

Whole-Class Learning Performance Task Dr. Goodall compares chimp and human gestures, tool use, and emotional responses.

UNIT PERFORMANCE-BASED ASSESSMENT
How can animals and people help one another?

Unit Performance-Based Assessment As students read this text, they may gather evidence to address the prompt. A possible response is that humans can help keep chimps safe, and chimps can help us understand the human condition.

LESSON RESOURCES

Lesson	Making Meaning	Language Development	Effective Expression
Lesson	**First Read** **Close Read** **Analyze the Text** **Analyze Craft and Structure**	**Concept Vocabulary** **Word Study** **Conventions**	**Writing to Sources** **Speaking and Listening**
Instructional Standards	**RI.1** Cite textual evidence to support analysis . . . **RI.6** Determine an author's point of view . . . **RI.10** By the end of the year, read and comprehend literary nonfiction . . .	**L.2** Demonstrate command of the conventions . . . **L.2.a** Use punctuation . . . **L.4** Determine or clarify the meaning of unknown and multiple-meaning words and phrases . . . **L.4.b** Use common, grade-appropriate Greek or Latin affixes and roots . . . **L.5** Demonstrate understanding of figurative language . . . **L.5.b** Use the relationship between particular words . . .	**W.2** Write informative/explanatory texts . . . **W.2.a** Introduce a topic . . . **W.2.b** Develop the topic . . . **W.2.c** Use appropriate transitions . . . **W.2.d** Use precise language and domain-specific vocabulary . . . **SL.1** Engage effectively in a range of collaborative discussions . . . **SL.1.a** Come to discussions prepared . . . **SL 1.b** Follow rules for collegial discussions . . . **SL.1.c** Pose and respond to specific questions . . . **SL.1.d** Review the key ideas expressed . . .

▶ STUDENT RESOURCES

Available online in the Interactive Student Edition or Unit Resources	🔊 Selection Audio 📄 First-Read Guide: Nonfiction 📄 Close-Read Guide: Nonfiction	📄 Word Network	📄 Evidence Log

▶ TEACHER RESOURCES

Selection Resources Available online in the Interactive Teacher's Edition or Unit Resources	🔊 Audio Summaries ✏️ Annotation Highlights 💬 EL Highlights 📄 Analyze Craft and Structure: Author's Purpose	📄 Concept Vocabulary and Word Study 📄 Conventions: Commas, Parentheses, and Dashes 📄 English Language Support Lesson: Commas	📄 Writing to Sources: How-to Essay 📄 Speaking and Listening: Class Discussion
Reteach/Practice (RP) Available online in the Interactive Teacher's Edition or Unit Resources	📄 Analyze Craft and Structure: Author's Purpose (RP)	📄 Word Study: Latin suffix *–able* (RP) 📄 Conventions: Commas, Parentheses, and Dashes (RP)	📄 Writing to Sources: How-to Essay (RP) 📄 Speaking and Listening: Class Discussion (RP)
Assessment Available online in Assessments	📄 ☑️ Selection Test		
My Resources	📄 A Unit 2 Answer Key is available online and in the Interactive Teacher's Edition.		

Reading Support

Text Complexity Rubric: *from* My Life With the Chimpanzees

Quantitative Measures

Lexile: 860   Text Length: 4,237 words

Qualitative Measures

Knowledge Demands (1—2—**3**—4—5)	The situation may be unfamiliar to some readers (chimpanzee research in Tanzania), but the situations and emotions are clearly explained. Some geographical context may be helpful.
Structure (1—2—**3**—4—5)	Organization is evident and sequential. Paragraphs are not broken up with any headings, but the information is presented in a clear manner.
Language Conventionality and Clarity (1—2—**3**—4—5)	Vocabulary is mostly on level and syntax is generally simple. There are several complex sentences with extensive use of dashes. Language is clear.
Levels of Meaning/Purpose (1—**2**—3—4—5)	Selection has only one level of meaning. The main concept and supporting ideas are clearly stated when reading or listening.

DECIDE AND PLAN

English Language Support

Provide English Learners with support for knowledge demands and language as they read the selection.

Knowledge Demands Before reading the text, have students summarize the background information. Provide students with a map that details where Jane Goodall carried out her research. Making notes of what they know so far will help them as they read the text.

Language If students have difficulty with complex sentences, work together to break down sentences into smaller chunks in order to understand their meaning. Ask students to highlight words or phrases that they don't understand. As a group, help to define some of the terms they find difficult.

Strategic Support

Provide students with strategic support to ensure that they can successfully read the text.

Knowledge Demands Use the background information to discuss Jane Goodall and her work in Tanzania. Determine students' prior knowledge. Provide additional background if needed.

Language / Clarity For students that may have difficulty with difficult and complex sentences, encourage them to break the sentences down into smaller chunks or identify the meaning of unfamiliar words or phrases. Then have them reread the whole sentences.

Challenge

Provide students who need to be challenged with ideas for how they can go beyond a simple interpretation of the text.

Text Analysis Ask students to describe what Goodall learned about the ability of chimpanzees to use tools. What was David Greybeard able to do? Ask them to discuss why this discovery was so exciting for Goodall and her colleagues.

Written Response Ask students to read more about Jane Goodall and her work with chimpanzees. Have them write a page explaining aspects of her research that they found most interesting. Ask students to share their findings with the class.

TEACH

Read and Respond

Have students do their first read of the selection. Then have them complete their close read. Finally, work with them on the Making Meaning, Language Development, and Effective Expression activities.

Standards Support Through Teaching and Learning Cycle

IDENTIFY NEEDS

Analyze results of the Beginning-of-Year Assessment, focusing on the items relating to Unit 2. Also take into consideration student performance to this point and your observations of where particular students struggle.

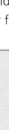

ANALYZE AND REVISE

- Analyze student work for evidence of student learning.
- Identify whether or not students have met the expectations in the standards.
- Identify implications for future instruction.

TEACH

Implement the planned lesson, and gather evidence of student learning.

DECIDE AND PLAN

- If students have performed poorly on items matching these standards, then provide selection scaffolds before assigning them the on-level lesson provided in the Student Edition.
- If students have done well on the Beginning-of-Year Assessment, then challenge them to keep progressing and learning by giving them opportunities to practice the skills in depth.
- Use the Selection Resources listed on the Planning pages for the excerpt from *My Life With the Chimpanzees* to help students continually improve their ability to master the standards.

Instructional Standards: *from* My Life with the Chimpanzees

	Catching Up	This Year	Looking Forward
Reading	You may wish to administer the **Analyze Craft and Structure: Author's Purpose (RP)** worksheet to help students identify why the author is writing and from what point of view.	**RI.6** Determine an author's point of view or purpose in a text and explain how it is conveyed in the text.	Challenge students to find three details from the text that help them identify the point of view and three details that help them identify the author's purpose.
Writing	You may wish to administer the **Writing to Sources: How-to Essay (RP)** worksheet to help students organize and write their explanatory essays.	**W.2** Write informative/explanatory texts to examine a topic and convey ideas, concepts, and information through the selection, organization, and analysis of relevant content. **W.2.d** Use precise language and domain-specific vocabulary to inform about or explain the topic.	Ask students to incorporate and cite specific facts to back up their ideas.
Speaking and Listening	You may wish to administer the **Speaking and Listening: Class Discussion (RP)** worksheet to help students prepare and conduct a group discussion.	**SL.1.a** Come to discussions prepared, having read or studied required material; explicitly draw on that preparation by referring to evidence on the topic, text, or issue to probe and reflect on ideas under discussion.	Have students each take a turn leading a group discussion. Challenge each student to ask a follow-up question.
Language	You may administer the **Conventions: Commas, Parentheses, and Dashes (RP)** worksheet to help students understand this punctuation.	**L.2.a** Use punctuation to set off nonrestrictive/parenthetical elements.	Ask students to write two sentences using each type of punctuation mark. Then have students peer edit.

Jump Start

FIRST READ Ask students to consider the following questions: *What do you already know about chimpanzee behavior? What do you think you will learn about chimpanzees through reading about Jane Goodall's time living with and observing them?*

from My Life With the Chimpanzees 🔊 📄

What does Goodall learn about chimpanzees? Modeling questions a reader might ask brings the text alive and connects to the Performance Task question. Selection audio and print capability for the selection are available in the Interactive Teacher's Edition.

Concept Vocabulary

Reassure students that the definitions for these words are listed in the selection.

⬤ FIRST READ

Students should perform the steps of the first read independently.

NOTICE: You may want to encourage students to notice what Goodall observed in Gombe.

ANNOTATE: Remind students to mark passages they feel are informative or worthy of analysis in their close read.

CONNECT: Suggest connections such as other texts and personal experiences.

RESPOND: Students will answer questions and write a summary to demonstrate understanding.

Students will always complete the Respond step at the end of the first read. Other steps can happen concurrently. You may wish to print copies of the **First-Read Guide: Nonfiction** for students to use. 📄

Remind students that during their first read, they should not answer the close-read questions that appear in the selection.

About the Author

Dame **Jane Goodall** (b. 1934) is the most celebrated primatologist, or researcher of primates (which includes apes, chimpanzees, and monkeys), of the twentieth century. She spent extended periods living with and observing chimpanzees in the wild. Dr. Goodall did most of her research in Tanzania at the Gombe Stream Game Reserve (now a national park), where she lived from 1960 to 1975. In 1977, she co-founded the Jane Goodall Institute for Wildlife Research, Education, and Conservation.

🔧 **Tool Kit**
First-Read Guide and Model Annotation

📇 STANDARDS
Reading Informational Text
By the end of the year, read and comprehend literary nonfiction in the grades 6–8 text complexity band proficiently, with scaffolding as needed at the high end of the range.

from My Life With the Chimpanzees

Concept Vocabulary

You will encounter the following words as you read this excerpt from *My Life With the Chimpanzees*. Before reading, note how familiar you are with each word. Then, rank the words in order from most familiar (1) to least familiar (6).

WORD	YOUR RANKING
vanished	
miserable	
irritable	
threateningly	
impetuous	
dominate	

After completing the first read, come back to the concept vocabulary and review your rankings. Mark changes to your original rankings as needed.

First Read NONFICTION

Apply these strategies as you conduct your first read. You will have an opportunity to complete the close-read notes after your first read.

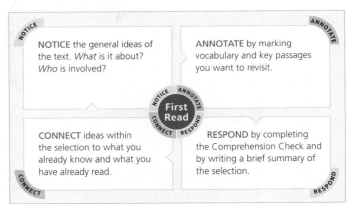

NOTICE the general ideas of the text. *What* is it about? *Who* is involved?

ANNOTATE by marking vocabulary and key passages you want to revisit.

CONNECT ideas within the selection to what you already know and what you have already read.

RESPOND by completing the Comprehension Check and by writing a brief summary of the selection.

© Pearson Education, Inc., or its affiliates. All rights reserved.

AUTHOR'S PERSPECTIVE Kelly Gallagher, M.Ed.

First Read Strategies As students encounter unfamiliar and challenging text for the first time, some may hit a frustration point early. Students often think that if they don't understand something on the first try that they will never understand. Comprehension when reading is not an all-or-nothing situation. Share these strategies for getting through the gray areas:

• ***Read on With Uncertainty*** Students who are "a little bit lost" may be able to read a little further to resolve confusion. Model this mindset with the opening paragraphs of a novel or long work. Read the text, and show students what questions you already have. Demonstrate that many questions arise at the beginning as readers place themselves in the world the writer has created. Good readers can live with this confusion

because within a few paragraphs or pages, key ideas often become more clear.

• ***Monitor Comprehension*** To make their comprehension more concrete for students, have them use two different colors to mark the text: one color for text they understand, and another color to highlight the text that is challenging to them. This will help pinpoint areas of confusion and show how much of the text they understand.

ANCHOR TEXT | MEMOIR

from
My Life With the **Chimpanzees**

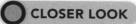

Jane Goodall

BACKGROUND

Gombe Stream National Park in Tanzania, Africa, is best known as the site of Jane Goodall's groundbreaking chimpanzee research. The park covers only about 20 square miles, but is home to a great variety of animals. Dr. Goodall's research in Gombe was supported by the famous paleontologist Louis Leakey. In this account, Dr. Goodall occasionally refers to Dr. Leakey by his first name only.

SCAN FOR
MULTIMEDIA

1   July 16, 1960, was a day I shall remember all my life. It was when I first set foot on the shingle and sand beach of Chimpanzee Land—that is, Gombe National Park. I was twenty-six years old.

2   Mum and I were greeted by the two African game scouts who were responsible for protecting the thirty square miles of the park. They helped us to find a place where we could put up our old ex-army tent.

3   We chose a lovely spot under some shady trees near the small, fast-flowing Kakombe Stream. In Kigoma (before setting out), we had found a cook, Dominic. He put up his little tent some distance from ours and quite near the lake.

4   When camp was ready I set off to explore. It was already late afternoon, so I could not go far. There had been a grass fire not long before, so all the vegetation of the more open ridges and peaks had burned away. This made it quite easy to move around, except that the slopes above the valley were very steep in places, and I slipped several times on the loose, gravelly soil.

NOTES

from My Life With the Chimpanzees **101**

© Pearson Education, Inc., or its affiliates. All rights reserved.

CLOSER LOOK

Analyze First-Person Narrative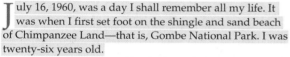

Students may have marked paragraph 1 during their first read. Use this paragraph to help students understand the characteristics of the first-person narrative. Encourage them to talk about the annotations that they marked. You may want to model a close read with the class based on the highlights shown in the text.

ANNOTATE: Have students mark details in paragraph 1 that demonstrate that an event is being described as it was perceived by the narrator, or have students participate while you highlight them.

QUESTION: Guide students to consider what these details might tell them. Ask what a reader can infer from the author's first-person narrative, and accept student responses.

Possible response: The narrator, in this case the author, is describing an event that happened long ago but is very important to her.

CONCLUDE: Help students to formulate conclusions about the importance of these details in the text. Ask students why the author might have included these details.

Possible response: The author included these details because she wants readers to understand how arriving in Gombe changed her life. She also wants readers to know how her story began.

Remind students that in a **first-person narrative**, events are told from the narrator's point of view. Nonfiction first-person narration is a feature of memoirs or personal narratives. Point out that first-person narration allows authors to reveal their thoughts and feelings about experiences that were meaningful to them.

• *Apply Fix-It Strategies* Students who are struggling with comprehension may use fix-it strategies to start by rereading at the word level and decoding words they don't know. They can then move to the sentence level to make sure that they are following the text.

When students have the tools to monitor their comprehension, they may feel more empowered to get through their first read. Once they can get past the literal interpretation of text, they can then move toward uncovering deeper meaning.

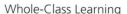

CLOSE READ

As students look for repetition in paragraph 8, remind them to look for phrases that are repeated for effect. You may wish to model the Close Read using the following think-aloud format. Possible responses to questions on the student page are included. You may also want to print copies of the **Close-Read Guide: Nonfiction** for students to use.

ANNOTATE: As I read paragraph 8, I notice and highlight details that tell me what Dr. Goodall saw when she went out to view the chimps.

QUESTION: I notice that Dr. Goodall had at first seen chimps. But then she went out to search for them and saw nothing, over and over. I think she repeats the phrase because she wants to emphasize the repetition she felt in searching and seeing nothing.

CONCLUDE: From the details Dr. Goodall provides, I can tell that she felt frustrated. She continued to go out searching for chimpanzees but continued to find no trace of them.

○ Additional **English Language Support** is available in the Interactive Teacher's Edition.

NOTES

CLOSE READ
ANNOTATE: In paragraph 8, mark the repetition of words that describe Dr. Goodall's experience with the chimps after the first day.

QUESTION: Why do you think Dr. Goodall has chosen to repeat these words?

CONCLUDE: How does this repetition help communicate Goodall's experience to the reader?

vanished (VAN ihsht) *v.* disappeared

---

5   I shall never forget the thrill of that first exploration. Soon after leaving camp I met a troop of baboons. They were afraid of the strange, white-skinned creature (that was I) and gave their barking alarm call, "Waa-hoo! Waa-hoo!" again and again. I left them, hoping that they would become used to me soon—otherwise, I thought, all the creatures of Gombe would be frightened. As I crossed a narrow ravine crowded with low trees and bushes I got very close to a beautiful red-gold bushbuck—a forest antelope about the size of a long-legged goat. I knew it was female because she had no horns. When she scented me she kept quite still for a moment and stared toward me with her big dark eyes. Then, with a loud barking call, she turned and bounded away.

6   When I got to one of the high ridges I looked down into the valley. There the forest was dark and thick. That was where I planned to go the next day to look for chimpanzees.

7   When I got back to camp it was dusk. Dominic had made a fire and was cooking our supper. That evening, and for the next four days, we had fresh food from Kigoma, but after that we ate out of cans. Louis had not managed to find very much money for our expedition, so our possessions were few and simple—a knife, fork, and spoon each, a couple of tin plates and tin mugs. But that was all we needed. After supper, Mum and I talked around our campfire, then snuggled into our two cots in the tent.

8   Early the next morning I set out to search for chimpanzees. I had been told by the British game ranger in charge of Gombe not to travel about the mountains by myself—except near camp. Otherwise, I had to take one of the game scouts with me. So I set off with Adolf. That first day we saw two chimps feeding in a tall tree. As soon as they saw us they leapt down and **vanished**. The next day we saw no chimps at all. Nor the day after. Nor the day after that.

9   A whole week went by before we found a very big tree full of tiny round red fruits that Adolf told me were called *msulula*. From the other side of the valley we could watch chimps arriving at the tree, feeding, then climbing down and vanishing into the forest. I decided to camp in the best viewing site so that I could see them first thing in the morning. I spent three days in that valley and I saw a lot of chimps. But they were too far away and the foliage of the tree was too thick. It was disappointing and frustrating, and I didn't have much to tell Mum when I got back.

10   There was another problem that I had to cope with—Adolf was very lazy. He was almost always late in the morning. I decided to try another man, Rashidi. He was far better and helped me a lot, showing me the trails through the forests and the best ways to move from one valley to the next. He had sharp eyes and spotted chimps from far away.

102 UNIT 2 • ANIMAL ALLIES

© Pearson Education, Inc., or its affiliates. All rights reserved.

HOW LANGUAGE WORKS

Commas, Parentheses, and Dashes Call student attention to paragraph 5. As students perform their close read, they will note that the author frequently uses parentheses and dashes in the text. Point out that like commas, both parentheses and dashes tell a reader when to pause. But unlike a comma, a dash indicates a sharp interruption in thought, as in paragraph 5, and is generally used to emphasize something.

Explain that parentheses, on the other hand, can be thought of as a sidenote, as in the third line of paragraph 5. Have students complete sentences like these by adding a dash or parentheses.

For five years (some say longer) the scientist studied the forest creatures.

She hiked up the mountain—in a raging snowstorm—for nearly three hours.

11 But even after several months, the chimps had not become used to us. They ran off if we got anywhere near to them. I begged the game ranger to let me move about the forests by myself. I promised that I would always tell Rashidi in which direction I was going, so that he would know where to look for me if I failed to turn up in the evening. The game ranger finally gave in. At last I could make friends with the chimpanzees in my own way.

12 Every morning I got up when I heard the alarm clock at 5:30 A.M. I ate a couple of slices of bread and had a cup of coffee from the Thermos flask. Then I set off, climbing to where I thought the chimps might be.

13 Most often, I went to the Peak. I discovered that from this high place I had a splendid view in all directions. I could see chimps moving in the trees and I could hear if they called. At first I watched from afar, through my binoculars, and never tried to get close. I knew that if I did, the chimps would run silently away.

14 Gradually I began to learn about the chimps' home and how they lived. I discovered that, most of the time, the chimps wandered about in small groups of six or less, not in a big troop like the baboons. Often a little group was made up of a mother with her children, or two or three adult males by themselves. Sometimes many groups joined together, especially when there was delicious ripe fruit on one big tree. When the chimps got together like that, they were very excited, made a lot of noise, and were easy to find.

15 Eventually I realized that the chimps I watched from the Peak were all part of one group—a community. There were about fifty chimps belonging to this community. They made use of three of the valleys to the north of the Kakombe Valley (where our tent was) and two valleys to the south. These valleys have lovely sounding names: Kasakela, Linda, and Rutanga in the north, Mkenke and Nyasanga in the south.

16 From the Peak I noted which trees the chimps were feeding in and then, when they had gone, I scrambled down and collected some of the leaves, flowers, or fruits so they could be identified later. I found that the chimps eat mostly fruits but also a good many kinds of leaves, blossoms, seeds, and stems. Later I would discover that they eat a variety of insects and sometimes hunt and kill prey animals to feed on meat.

17 During those months of gradual discovery, the chimps very slowly began to realize that I was not so frightening after all. Even so, it was almost a year before I could approach to within one hundred yards, and that is not really very close. The baboons got used to me much more quickly. Indeed, they became a nuisance around our camp by grabbing any food that we accidentally left lying on the table.

NOTES

CLOSE READ

ANNOTATE: In paragraph 17, mark details that show how the chimps behave. Mark other details that show how the baboons behave.

QUESTION: Why does Goodall contrast the chimps' and baboons' behavior?

CONCLUDE: What does this contrast reveal about the chimps?

from My Life With the Chimpanzees **103**

CLOSE READ

As they read paragraph 17, remind students to focus on phrases that show that the chimps are reacting differently to Dr. Goodall. You may wish to model the Close Read using the following think-aloud format. Possible responses to questions on the student page are included.

ANNOTATE: As I read paragraph 17, I notice and highlight the details that tell me how the chimpanzees are responding to Dr. Goodall now. I notice that these details include adjectives and adverbs that help describe how her relationship with the chimps changed.

QUESTION: Dr. Goodall describes the baboons as unafraid of people and almost intrusive, whereas the chimps were a lot more tentative at first.

CONCLUDE: I think this contrast reveals that the chimps are less trusting than the baboons, at least at first, but that they seem a lot more thoughtful and careful. The chimps are intelligent and take their time in letting anyone get close.

PERSONALIZE FOR LEARNING

English Language Support

Idioms Tell students that the expressions "turn up" and "gave in" in paragraph 11 are idioms. Remind students that an idiom is a commonly used expression that is not meant literally.

Explain that "turn up" means to arrive. Have students look at the part of the

sentence that reads, "so that he would know where to look for me.. . ." Point out that this supports the meaning of the idiom. Someone looks for you because you have not appeared.

Explain that "gave in" means to surrender. Have students look at the sentence that

follows the idiom, "At last I could make friends with the chimpanzees in my own way." Point out that this sentence, too, supports the meaning of the idiom. When the ranger "gave in," or surrendered, Dr. Goodall was able to do what she wanted to do. **ALL LEVELS**

© Pearson Education, Inc., or its affiliates. All rights reserved.

NOTES

18   I began to learn more about the other creatures that shared the forests with the chimpanzees. There were four kinds of monkeys in addition to the baboons, and many smaller animals such as squirrels and mongooses. There was also a whole variety of nocturnal (nighttime) creatures: porcupines and civets (creatures looking rather like raccoons) and all manners of rats and mice. Only a very few animals in the forests at Gombe were potentially dangerous—mainly buffalo and leopards. Bush pigs can be dangerous too, but only if you threaten them or their young. And, of course, there are poisonous snakes—seven different kinds.

19   Once, as I arrived on the Peak in the early morning before it was properly light, I saw the dark shape of a large animal looming in front of me. I stood quite still. My heart began to beat fast, for I realized it was a buffalo. Many hunters fear buffalo more than lions or elephants.

20   By a lucky chance the wind was blowing from him to me, so he couldn't smell me. He was peacefully gazing in the opposite direction and chewing his cud. He hadn't heard my approach—always I try to move as quietly as I can in the bush. So, though I was only ten yards from him, he had no idea I was there. Very slowly I retreated.

21   Another time, as I was sitting on the Peak, I heard a strange mewing sound. I looked around and there, about fifteen yards away, a leopard was approaching. I could just see the black and white tip of its tail above the tall grass. It was walking along the little trail that led directly to where I sat.

22   Leopards are not usually dangerous unless they have been wounded. But I was frightened of them in those days—probably as a result of my experience with the leopard and the wolfhound[1] two years before. And so, very silently, I moved away and looked for chimps in another valley.

23   Later I went back to the Peak. I found that, just like any cat, that leopard had been very curious. There, in the exact place where I had been sitting, he had left his mark—his droppings.

24   Most of the time, though, nothing more alarming than insects disturbed my vigils on the Peak. It began to feel like home. I carried a little tin trunk up there. In it I kept a kettle, some sugar and coffee, and a tin mug. Then, when I got tired from a long trek to another valley, I could make a drink in the middle of the day. I kept a blanket up there, too, and when the chimps slept near the Peak, I slept there, so that I could be close by in the morning. I loved to be up there at night, especially when there was a moon. If I heard the coughing grunt of a leopard, I just prayed and pulled the blanket over my head!

1. **leopard and the wolfhound** Previously, Goodall saw a leopard kill a large hunting dog.

© Pearson Education, Inc., or its affiliates. All rights reserved.

VOCABULARY DEVELOPMENT

Multiple-Meanings Words Call student attention to the word *manner* in paragraph 18. Tell students that the word *manners* is a noun and that it has multiple meanings. Discuss the following sentences with students.

1. She always showed good manners, saying "please" and "thank you" without fail. (behavior in the presence of others)
2. The committee found all manners of problems. (sort or kind)
3. The young woman had a gracious manner. (way of acting or comporting oneself)

Have students read the following sentence in paragraph 18. *There was also a whole variety of nocturnal (nighttime) creatures: porcupines and civets (creatures looking rather like raccoons) and all manners of rats and mice.* Guide them to identify which meaning of the word *manners* is used in the sentence. Discuss how to use context clues to define a word with multiple meanings.

25 Chimps sleep all night, just as we do. From the Peak I often watched how they made their nests, or beds. First the chimp bent a branch down over some solid foundation, such as a fork or two parallel branches. Holding it in place with his feet, he then bent another over it. Then he folded the end of the first branch back over the second. And so on. He often ended up by picking lots of small, soft, leafy twigs to make a pillow. Chimps like their comfort! I've learned over the years that infants sleep in their nest with their mothers until they are about five years old or until the next baby is born and the older child has to make its own bed.

26 I never returned to camp before sunset. But even when I slept on the Peak, I first went down to have supper with Mum and tell her what I had seen that day. And she would tell me what she had been doing.

27 Mum set up a clinic. She handed out medicine to any of the local Africans, mostly fishermen, who were sick. Once she cured an old man who was very ill indeed. Word about this cure spread far and wide, and sometimes patients would walk for miles to get treatment from the wonderful white woman-doctor.

28 Her clinic was very good for me. It meant that the local people realized we wanted to help. When Mum had to go back to England after four months to manage things at home, the Africans wanted, in turn, to help me.

29 Of course, Mum worried about leaving me on my own. Dominic was a wonderful cook and great company. He was not really reliable. So Louis Leakey asked Hassan to come all the way from Lake Victoria to help with the boat and engine. It was lovely to see his handsome, smiling face again, and his arrival relieved Mum's mind no end.

30 Of course, I missed her after she'd gone, but I didn't have time to be lonely. There was so much to do.

31 Soon after she'd left, I got back one evening and was greeted by an excited Dominic. He told me that a big male chimp had spent an hour feeding on the fruit of one of the oil-nut palms growing in the camp clearing. Afterward he had climbed down, gone over to my tent, and taken the bananas that had just been put there for my supper.

32 This was fantastic news. For months the chimps had been running off when they saw me—now one had actually visited my camp! Perhaps he would come again.

33 The next day I waited, in case he did. What a luxury to lie in until 7:00 A.M. As the hours went by I began to fear that the chimp wouldn't come. But finally, at about four in the afternoon, I heard a rustling in the undergrowth opposite my tent, and a black shape appeared on the other side of the clearing.

NOTES

CLOSE READ

ANNOTATE: In paragraph 32, mark the punctuation that Dr. Goodall uses to describe her reaction to the news about the chimpanzee visit.

QUESTION: Why might she have chosen to use this punctuation?

CONCLUDE: What does the punctuation reveal about her reaction?

from My Life With the Chimpanzees **105**

CLOSE READ

As they read paragraph 32, remind students to focus on the punctuation the author uses to show how she reacted to the news that a big male chimp had visited the camp. You may wish to model the Close Read using the following think-aloud format. Possible responses to questions on the student page are included.

ANNOTATE: As I read paragraph 32, I notice and mark the dash and the exclamation point that Dr. Goodall uses in the second sentence of the paragraph.

QUESTION: Dr. Goodall begins the paragraph with the phrase "This was fantastic news," so I know that she is happy. The dash helps show a contrast between what happened before and what was happening now. It helps draw attention to the change in the chimps' behavior. The exclamation point at the end of the sentence shows that the author is excited about this change.

CONCLUDE: From Dr. Goodall's use of a dash and an exclamation point, I can conclude that she is trying to show that the appearance of the chimp in camp is a significant development. The punctuation draws attention to the sentence. It says, "Look at this—this is important."

© Pearson Education, Inc., or its affiliates. All rights reserved.

CROSS-CURRICULAR PERSPECTIVES

Science Dr. Goodall's research takes place in Gombe Stream National Park in Tanzania, Africa, a wildlife preserve that protects chimpanzees while allowing scientists the opportunity to study them. Have interested students conduct research into why these protected areas are necessary and prepare a brief presentation for the class. Ask them to describe the dangers facing chimpanzees and what places like Gombe are doing to help keep population levels from declining. Encourage students to identify dangers beyond hunting and deforestation to such problems as illnesses contracted from contact with humans. **(Research to Explore)**

CLOSER LOOK

Infer Key Ideas

Students may have marked paragraphs 38 and 39 during their first read. Use these paragraphs to help students understand a key idea of the selection—that Dr. Goodall made certain observations that changed our understanding of chimpanzee behavior. Encourage them to talk about the annotations that they marked. You may want to model a close read with the class based on the highlights shown in the text.

ANNOTATE: Have students mark details in paragraphs 38 and 39 that show what Dr. Goodall observed and that hint at the significance of her observation, or have students participate while you highlight them.

QUESTION: Guide students to consider what these details might tell them. Ask what a reader can infer from Dr. Goodall's reaction to observing the chimpanzee fishing for termites, and accept student responses.

Possible response: Dr. Goodall's excitement in seeing the chimp fishing for termites and making a twig into a tool, as well as her mention that scientists had not observed this behavior before and that they did not realize chimpanzees could make tools, leads the reader to infer that this observation changed the way scientists understood chimpanzees.

CONCLUDE: Help students to formulate conclusions about the importance of these details in the text. Ask students why the author might have included these details.

Possible response: The description of the chimpanzee's use of tools shows the careful observations that Dr. Goodall made, and her reaction to what she saw shows how much it added to scientists' understanding of chimpanzee behavior. By including the details about the chimp behavior and explaining how she felt about the observation, Dr. Goodall is highlighting how important the discovery was and how significant it was to her research.

Remind students that authors include details and anecdotes to help build the **key ideas** in text.

Dr. Goodall was the first person to observe chimps like this one using grass and sticks to "fish" for termites.

NOTES

34   I recognized him at once. It was the handsome male with the dense white beard. I had already named him David Greybeard. Quite calmly he climbed into the palm and feasted on its nuts. And then he helped himself to the bananas I had set out for him.

35   There were ripe palm nuts on that tree for another five days, and David Greybeard visited three more times and got lots of bananas.

36   A month later, when another palm tree in camp bore ripe fruit, David again visited us. And on one of those occasions he actually took a banana from my hand. I could hardly believe it.

37   From that time on things got easier for me. Sometimes when I met David Greybeard out in the forest, he would come up to see if I had a banana hidden in my pocket. The other chimps stared with amazement. Obviously I wasn't as dangerous as they had thought. Gradually they allowed me closer and closer.

38   It was David Greybeard who provided me with my most exciting observation. One morning, near the Peak, I came upon him squatting on a termite mound. As I watched, he picked a blade of grass, poked it into a tunnel in the mound, and then withdrew it. The grass was covered with termites all clinging on with their jaws. He picked them off with his lips and scrunched them up. Then he fished for more. When his piece of grass got bent, he dropped it, picked up a little twig, stripped the leaves off it, and used that.

39   I was really thrilled. David had used objects as tools! He had also changed a twig into something more suitable for fishing termites. He had actually *made* a tool. Before this observation, scientists had thought that only humans could make tools. Later I would learn that chimpanzees use more objects as tools than any creature except for us. This finding excited Louis Leakey more than any other.

40   In October the dry season ended and it began to rain. Soon the golden mountain slopes were covered with lush green grass. Flowers appeared, and the air smelled lovely. Most days it rained just a little. Sometimes there was a downpour. I loved being out in the forest in the rain. And I loved the cool evenings when I could lace the tent shut and make it cozy inside with a storm lantern. The only trouble was that everything got damp and grew mold.

© Pearson Education, Inc., or its affiliates. All rights reserved.

PERSONALIZE FOR LEARNING

Challenge

Interview Draw students' attention to paragraph 34. Encourage interested students to create a brief video in which they imagine that they are a news crew interviewing Dr. Goodall about chimpanzees' use of tools right after she made her observation of David Greybeard. What questions should students ask Dr. Goodall? How will Dr. Goodall respond? Students can write scripts upon which to base their interviews.

Scorpions and giant poisonous centipedes sometimes appeared in the tent—even, a few times, a snake. But I was lucky—I never got stung or bitten.

41   The chimpanzees often seemed **miserable** in the rain. They looked cold, and they shivered. Since they were clever enough to use tools, I was surprised that they had not learned to make shelters. Many of them got coughs and colds. Often, during heavy rain, they seemed **irritable** and bad tempered.

42   Once, as I walked through thick forest in a downpour, I suddenly saw a chimp hunched in front of me. Quickly I stopped. Then I heard a sound from above. I looked up and there was a big chimp there, too. When he saw me he gave a loud, clear wailing *wraaaah*—a spine-chilling call that is used to threaten a dangerous animal. To my right I saw a large black hand shaking a branch and bright eyes glaring **threateningly** through the foliage. Then came another savage *wraaaah* from behind. Up above, the big male began to sway the vegetation. I was surrounded. I crouched down, trying to appear as nonthreatening as possible.

43   Suddenly a chimp charged straight toward me. His hair bristled with rage. At the last minute he swerved and ran off. I stayed still. Two more chimps charged nearby. Then, suddenly, I realized I was alone again. All the chimps had gone.

44   Only then did I realize how frightened I had been. When I stood up my legs were trembling! Male chimps, although they are only four feet tall when upright, are at least three times stronger than a grown man. And I weighed only about ninety pounds. I had become very thin with so much climbing in the mountains and only one meal a day. That incident took place soon after the chimps had lost their initial terror of me but before they had learned to accept me calmly as part of their forest world. If David Greybeard had been among them, they probably would not have behaved like that, I thought.

45   After my long days in the forests I looked forward to supper. Dominic always had it ready for me when I got back in the evenings. Once a month he went into Kigoma with Hassan. They came back with new supplies, including fresh vegetables and fruit and eggs. And they brought my mail—that was something I really looked forward to.

46   After supper I would get out the little notebook in which I had scribbled everything I had seen while watching the chimps during the day. I would settle down to write it all legibly into my journal. It was very important to do that every evening, while it was all fresh in my mind. Even on days when I climbed back to sleep near the chimps, I always wrote up my journal first.

47   Gradually, as the weeks went by, I began to recognize more and more chimpanzees as individuals. Some, like Goliath, William,

NOTES

miserable (MIHZ uhr uh buhl) *adj.* extremely unhappy or uncomfortable

irritable (IHR uh tuh buhl) *adj.* easily annoyed or angered

threateningly (THREHT uhn ihng lee) *adv.* in a frightening or alarming way

from My Life With the Chimpanzees **107**

© Pearson Education, Inc., or its affiliates. All rights reserved.

PERSONALIZE FOR LEARNING

English Language Support
False Cognates False cognates can interfere with a student's understanding of the text. Point out that *took place* in paragraph 44 means happened, and does not have the same meaning as *placer* in Spanish. Then point to *Once* at the beginning of paragraph 42. Explain that the word means "at one time" and not the number eleven, as in Spanish. Similarly, explain that *large* in paragraph 42 means big, not simply long, as *largo* in Spanish. Remind students that when they read a word that they think might be a cognate, they should think about whether the word makes sense in the context. **ALL LEVELS**

CLOSE READ

As students look for words that describe the chimps' behavior, remind them to look for words and phrases that tell what the chimps did and how the author perceived it. You may wish to model the Close Read using the following think-aloud format. Possible responses to questions on the student page are included.

ANNOTATE: As I read paragraphs 48–49, I notice and highlight the details that describe how the chimps looked and behaved.

QUESTION: I think that Dr. Goodall chose these descriptions to show that the chimps have distinct physical traits as well as personalities. The words and phrases she chose to describe the chimps' behavior could easily be used to describe human behavior.

CONCLUDE: I think that Dr. Goodall's descriptions help the reader to understand that the chimps are unique individuals and that their behavior is almost human. The descriptions make the reader relate to the chimps almost as you would to a person.

NOTES

CLOSE READ
ANNOTATE: In paragraphs 48–49, mark the words that describe how the chimps look and behave.

QUESTION: Why do you think Dr. Goodall chose to include these descriptions of the chimps and their behavior?

CONCLUDE: How do these descriptions help the reader better understand the chimps?

impetuous (ihm PEHCH yoo uhs) *adj.* acting suddenly with little thought

---

and old Flo, I got to know well, because David Greybeard sometimes brought them with him when he visited camp. I always had a supply of bananas ready in case the chimps arrived.

48 Once you have been close to chimps for a while they are as easy to tell apart as your classmates. Their faces look different, and they have different characters. David Greybeard, for example, was a calm chimp who liked to keep out of trouble. But he was also very determined to get his own way. If he arrived in camp and couldn't find any bananas, he would walk into my tent and search. Afterward, all was chaos. It looked as though some burglar had raided the place! Goliath had a much more excitable, impetuous temperament. William, with his long-shaped face, was shy and timid.

49 Old Flo was easy to identify. She had a bulbous nose and ragged ears. She came to camp with her infant daughter, whom I named Fifi, and her juvenile son, Figan. Sometimes adolescent Faben came, too. It was from Flo that I first learned that in the wild, female chimps have only one baby every five or six years. The older offspring, even after they have become independent, still spend a lot of time with their mothers, and all the different family members help one another.

50 Flo also taught me that female chimps do not have just one mate. One day she came to my camp with a pink swelling on her rump. This was a sign that she was ready for mating. She was followed by a long line of suitors. Many of them had never visited my camp before, and they were scared. But they were so attracted to Flo that they overcame their fear in order to keep close to her. She allowed them all to mate with her at different times.

51 Soon after the chimps had begun to visit my camp, the National Geographic Society, which was giving Louis money for my research, sent a photographer to Gombe to make a film. Hugo van Lawick was a Dutch baron. He loved and respected animals just as I did, and he made a wonderful movie. One year later, in England, we got married.

52 By then I had left Gombe for a while, to start my own studies at Cambridge University. I hated to leave, but I knew I would soon be back. I had promised Louis that I would work hard and get my Ph.D. degree.

53 After I got the degree, Hugo and I went back to Gombe together. It was a very exciting time, as Flo had just had a baby, little Flint. That was the first wild chimpanzee infant that I ever saw close up, nearly four years after I had begun my research.

54 Flo came very often to camp looking for bananas. Fifi, now six years old, and Figan, five years older, were still always with her. Fifi loved her new baby brother. When he was four months old

© Pearson Education, Inc., or its affiliates. All rights reserved.

DIGITAL PERSPECTIVES

Enriching the Text Call student attention to the description of Old Flo in paragraphs 49–50. To help students understand how chimpanzee family members help one another, share one of the videos from the Jane Goodall Institute website. Ask students to compare the behavior of the chimpanzees in the video to the author's description of chimpanzee behavior. Discuss with students how the video adds to their understanding of the text. What information did the video contain that the text did not? Which scene in the video was particularly interesting or surprising? Did the chimpanzees behave like humans in any way? How? Preview the video before showing it to the class.

she was allowed to play with and groom him. Sometimes Flo let her carry him when they moved through the forest. During that time, Fifi learned a lot about how to be a good mother.

NOTES

55   Flint learned to walk and climb when he was six months old. And he learned to ride on his mother's back during travel, instead of always clinging on underneath. He gradually spent more time playing with his two older brothers. They were always very gentle with him. So were other youngsters of the community. They had to be, for if Flo thought any other chimps were too rough, she would charge over and threaten or even attack them.

> Gradually, as the weeks went by, I began to recognize more and more chimpanzees as individuals.

56   I watched how Flint gradually learned to use more and more of the different calls and gestures that chimpanzees use to communicate with each other. Some of these gestures are just like ours—holding hands, embracing, kissing, patting one another on the back. They mean about the same, too. And although they do not make up a language the way human words do, all the different calls do help the chimpanzees know what is happening, even if they are far away when they hear the sounds. Each call (there are at least thirty, perhaps more) means something different.

57   Flo was the top-ranked female of her community and could **dominate** all the others. But she could not boss any of the males. In chimpanzee society, males are the dominant sex. Among the males themselves, there is a social order, and one male at the top is the boss.

dominate (DOM uh nayt) *v.* rule or control

58   The first top-ranking male I knew was Goliath. Then, in 1964, Mike took over. He did this by using his brain. He would gather up one or two empty kerosene cans from my camp and hit and kick them ahead of him as he charged toward a group of adult males. It was a spectacular performance and made a lot of noise. The other chimps fled. So Mike didn't need to fight to get to the top—which was just as well, as he was a very small chimp. He was top male for six years.

59   The adult males spend a lot of time in each other's company. They often patrol the boundaries of their territory and may attack chimpanzees of different communities if they meet. These conflicts are very brutal, and the victim may die. Only young females can move from one community to another without being hurt. In fact, the big males sometimes go out looking for such females and try to take them back into their own territory.

© Pearson Education, Inc., or its affiliates. All rights reserved.

from My Life With the Chimpanzees **109**

CLOSER LOOK

Analyze Repetition

Students may have marked paragraphs 60 and 61 during their first read. Use this paragraph to help students understand why the author repeats certain words and phrases. Encourage them to talk about the annotations that they marked. You may want to model a close read with the class based on the highlights shown in the text.

ANNOTATE: Have students mark details that show repetition of words and phrases in paragraphs 60 and 61, or have students participate while you highlight them.

QUESTION: Guide students to consider what these details might tell them. Ask what a reader can infer from the repetition of the word *more* and accept student responses.

Possible response: Readers can infer that Dr. Goodall's responsibilities were growing, as was the staff of people to help her with those responsibilities.

CONCLUDE: Help students to formulate conclusions about the importance of these details in the text. Ask students why the author might have included these details.

Possible response: By repeating the word *more* and the phrase *more and more*, Dr. Goodall wants to communicate the idea of growth: how quickly the research center grew and how successful it had become. Through the author's use of repetition, she is able to communicate how much her work had changed since her arrival in Gombe.

Remind students that **repetition** can be used to help authors emphasize or stress a particular point. It can also be used to help make an idea clearer.

This photo from 1965 shows Dr. Goodall in her Gombe Stream camp with the chimp she named David Greybeard.

NOTES

60 As the months went by, I learned more and more. I recorded more and more details when I watched the chimpanzees. Instead of writing the information in notebooks, I started to use a little tape recorder. Then I could keep my eyes on the chimps all the time. By the end of each day there was so much typing to be done that I found I couldn't do it all myself. I needed an assistant to help. Soon, with even more chimps coming to camp, I needed other people to help with the observations.

61 There were always more fascinating things to watch and record, more people to help write everything down. What had started as a little camp for Mum and me ended up, six years later, as a research center, where students could come and collect information for their degrees. I was the director. ❧

Reprinted with the permission of Simon & Schuster Books for Young Readers, an imprint of Simon & Schuster Children's Publishing Division from *My Life With the Chimpanzees* by Jane Goodall. Copyright 1988, 1996 Byron Preiss Visual Publications, Inc. Text copyright © 1998, 1996 Jane Goodall.

© Pearson Education, Inc., or its affiliates. All rights reserved.

110 UNIT 2 • ANIMAL ALLIES

PERSONALIZE FOR LEARNING

Strategic Support

Background Draw students' attention to paragraph 61. Students may have trouble understanding what a research center is. Explain that the research center that Dr. Goodall started is located in a national park where the chimpanzees are protected. Explain that the center itself is a place where both college students and scientists go to learn more about chimpanzees by observing them, much like Dr. Goodall did. Point out that the Gombe Research Center is still operating today.

Comprehension Check

Complete the following items after you finish your first read.

1. Why have Jane Goodall and her mother come to Gombe National Park?

2. At first, how do the chimpanzees react to Goodall?

3. What type of service does Goodall's mother set up for the local people?

4. Why does Goodall leave Gombe?

5. How does Goodall's camp become a research center?

⊙ **Notebook** Write a brief summary of the excerpt from *My Life With the Chimpanzees* to demonstrate your understanding.

- -

RESEARCH

Research to Clarify Choose at least one unfamiliar detail from the text. Briefly research that detail. In what way does the information you learned shed light on an aspect of the memoir?

Research to Explore Choose something that interested you from the text, and formulate a research question.

© Pearson Education, Inc., or its affiliates. All rights reserved.

from My Life With the Chimpanzees **111**

Comprehension Check

Possible responses
1. Goodall is there to study the chimpanzees, and her mother is there to set up a clinic and treat sick people.
2. The chimpanzees run away at first whenever Goodall and her team get close to them.
3. Goodall's mother sets up a clinic where the locals can come for medicine and treatment.
4. She leaves Gombe to get married and to attend Cambridge University to get her Ph.D.
5. More and more chimpanzees come to the camp and Dr. Goodall needs assistants. Students work as assistants and collect information for their degrees.

Summaries will vary, but students should demonstrate understanding of Jane Goodall's life and work with the chimpanzees.

Research

Research to Clarify If students struggle to come up with a detail to research, you may want to suggest that they focus on one of the following topics: how chimpanzees use tools, chimpanzee communication, chimpanzee aggression or violence toward other chimpanzees, or family bonds among chimpanzees.

Research to Explore If students aren't sure how to go about formulating a research question, suggest that they use their findings from Research to Clarify as a starting point. For example, if students researched how chimpanzees use tools, they might formulate questions such as "What do chimpanzees use tools for?"

PERSONALIZE FOR LEARNING

Challenge
Research Encourage interested students to extend the Research to Explore activity by learning about other wild animals that use tools, including certain birds, other great apes, dolphins, and octopuses. Students can view video clips from the Internet of some of these animals using tools and can write a brief report. They might also include photographs or drawings of the animals in their reports.

Jump Start

CLOSE READ Have students discuss the title of Dr. Goodall's memoir, *My Life With the Chimpanzees.* Ask students to consider why she did not title the book *My Life Studying the Chimpanzees* or something similar. Have them think about what the phrase "with the chimpanzees" suggests about the way Dr. Goodall views her interaction with them and how she wants the reader to think about them.

Close Read the Text ✏

Walk students through the annotation model on the student page. Encourage them to complete items 2 and 3 on their own. Review and discuss the sections students have marked. If needed, continue to model close reading by using the Annotation Highlights in the Interactive Teacher's Edition.

Analyze the Text

Possible responses

1. The visits show that the chimps are getting used to her and that when they do not feel threatened, they can learn to trust humans. **DOK 3**

2. It may help people to realize that chimpanzees are more intelligent and complex than we previously knew. **DOK 2**

3. The selection suggests that people and animals can learn from each other and can get along when there is no threat. **DOK 3**

FORMATIVE ASSESSMENT

Analyze the Text

- **If** students fail to cite evidence, **then** remind them to support their ideas with specific information.

- **If** students fail to recognize that David Greybeard's visits to Dr. Goodall's camp signaled a change in the way the chimpanzees reacted to her, **then** discuss how they behaved toward her before he began to approach her camp and then after.

from MY LIFE WITH THE CHIMPANZEES

MAKING MEANING

Close Read the Text

1. This model, from paragraph 42 of the text, shows two sample annotations, along with questions and conclusions. Close read the passage, and find another detail to annotate. Then, write a question and conclusion.

> **ANNOTATE:** The writer has included a series of words that describe her actions.
>
> **QUESTION:** What effect is created by this word choice?
>
> **CONCLUDE:** The words help to create a feeling of suspense.

ANNOTATE: This passage contains a lot of descriptive details.

QUESTION: What effect does this use of language create?

CONCLUDE: The word choice, including the onomatopoeic *wraaaah*, brings to life a scary incident.

> Once, as I walked through thick forest in a downpour, I suddenly saw a chimp hunched in front of me. Quickly I stopped. Then I heard a sound from above. I looked up and there was a big chimp there, too. When he saw me he gave a loud, clear wailing *wraaaah*—a spine-chilling call that is used to threaten a dangerous animal.

🔧 **Tool Kit**
Close-Read Guide and Model Annotation

2. For more practice, go back into text and complete the close-read notes.

3. Revisit a section of the text you found important during your first read. Read this section closely and **annotate** what you notice. Ask yourself **questions** such as "Why did the author make this choice?" What can you **conclude**?

Analyze the Text

CITE TEXTUAL EVIDENCE to support your answers.

📓 **Notebook** Respond to these questions.

1. **Make Inferences** What do David Greybeard's visits to Dr. Goodall's camp show about the chimpanzees' changing response to her presence?

2. **Speculate** How might understanding the chimpanzees' system of gestures and calls change the way people think about the animals?

3. **Essential Question:** *How can people and animals relate to each other?* What have you learned from this memoir about how people and animals interact?

STANDARDS

Reading Informational Text
- Cite textual evidence to support analysis of what the text says explicitly as well as inferences drawn from the text.
- Determine an author's point of view or purpose in a text and explain how it is conveyed in the text.

© Pearson Education, Inc., or its affiliates. All rights reserved.

CROSS-CURRICULAR PERSPECTIVES

Science Point out to students that Jane Goodall did groundbreaking research into chimpanzee behavior at a time when few women worked in the sciences. Suggest that students research another celebrated female scientist from the twentieth century, such as Dian Fossey, Margaret Meade, or Rachel Carson, and learn more about that scientist's life. As a class, discuss the ways in which the achievements of these women have contributed positively to society.

Analyze Craft and Structure

Author's Purpose *My Life With the Chimpanzees* is a **memoir,** a type of nonfiction in which an author tells about a memorable time in his or her own life. A memoir, then, is a type of true story.

Like all narratives, authors of memoir have a purpose for writing. An **author's purpose** is his or her main reason for writing. For example, an author's purpose may be to inform, persuade, entertain, describe, or express feelings. In many cases, an author has more than one purpose. For example an author may write about the impacts of an oil spill to both inform readers as well as to persuade them to take action. To determine an **author's purpose,** make inferences, or educated guesses, based on the details he or she includes in the text.

Practice

CITE TEXTUAL EVIDENCE
to support your answers.

Notebook Complete the following activity, and then respond to the questions.

1. Reread the passages from the memoir shown in the chart, and mark important details in each. Then, explain what each passage shows about Goodall's experiences.

PASSAGE FROM TEXT	WHAT IT SHOWS
I shall never forget the thrill of that first exploration. Soon after leaving camp I met a troop of baboons. They were afraid of the strange, white-skinned creature (that was I) and gave their barking alarm call, "Waa-hoo! Waa-hoo!" again and again. I left them, hoping that they would become used to me soon—otherwise, I thought, all the creatures of Gombe would be frightened. (paragraph 5)	This passage shows Goodall's feelings of excitement and hope for successful work in Gombe.
Only a very few animals in the forests at Gombe were potentially dangerous—mainly buffalo and leopards. Bush pigs can be dangerous too, but only if you threaten them or their young. And, of course, there are poisonous snakes—seven different kinds. (paragraph 18)	This passage shows that Goodall was trying to give a sense of the environment in which she was living and working and describe potential hazards.
There were always more fascinating things to watch and record, more people to help write everything down. What had started as a little camp for Mum and me ended up, six years later, as a research center, where students could come and collect information for their degrees. I was the director. (paragraph 61)	This passage shows how Goodall was still completely dedicated to her work and was proud of how the research center came to be.

2. Review the notes you entered into the chart. What might be Goodall's overall purpose for writing?

3. (a) Does the title of this memoir, *My Life With the Chimpanzees,* help to indicate the writer's main purpose? (b) If not, what might be a better title?

from My Life With the Chimpanzees **113**

Analyze Craft and Structure

Author's Purpose Explain to students that the author's purpose is his or her reason for writing, which can be to entertain, to inform, or to persuade. Ask students to think about why they think Dr. Goodall wrote her memoir. Point out how Dr. Goodall shares her feelings about some of the people who worked for her or her feelings of frustration at going for weeks without seeing chimpanzees. Then explain that understanding why an author writes a particular work helps readers determine how best to evaluate the information. For more support, see **Analyze Craft and Structure: Author's Purpose.**

Practice

Possible responses

1. See possible responses in chart on student page.

2. I think Goodall not only wants to educate readers about the chimpanzees, but she also describes her life with the chimps and expresses her feelings about her experiences.

3. (a) I think the title explains enough to know that this is going to inform the reader about her life with the chimps. (b) Responses will vary.

FORMATIVE ASSESSMENT
Analyze Craft and Structure

- **If** students are unable to identify the author's purpose from the passages in the chart, **then** have them look for other passages in the text that contain feelings, descriptions, or reflections about living with the chimpanzees.

For Reteach and Practice, see **Analyze Craft and Structure: Author's Purpose (RP).**

Whole-Class Learning **113**

© Pearson Education, Inc., or its affiliates. All rights reserved.

Concept Vocabulary

Why These Words?

Possible responses:

1. The concept vocabulary helps to show how the chimpanzees interact with each other and with Dr. Goodall.

2. *amazement, clever, bad tempered, rage, determined, excitable, shy, timid, brutal*

Practice

Possible responses:

1. Dr. Goodall could not see the chimpanzees; they had *vanished* into the forest. Synonym: *disappeared*; antonym: *arrived*

2. The animals were *miserable* as they looked for shelter from the gloomy, cold rain. Synonym: *unhappy*; antonym: *content*

3. The chimpanzees fought because hunger made them *irritable*. Synonym: *grouchy*; antonym: *friendly*

4. The dog growled *threateningly* and bared its teeth. Synonym: *menacingly*; antonym: *encouragingly*

5. The boy's *impetuous* behavior often got him into trouble. Synonym: *impulsive*; antonym: *thoughtful*

6. She noticed that the older, bigger chimpanzees seemed to *dominate* the younger, smaller ones. Synonym: *control*; antonym: *follow*

Word Network

Possible words: *fear, frightened, retreated, accept, calmly*

Word Study

For more support, see **Concept Vocabulary and Word Study.** 📄

Possible responses:

1. The addition of the suffix *-able* to the word *misery* helps me understand that the word *miserable* is an adjective and means "given to misery."

2. *Excitable* (excite): easily upset or inspired

FORMATIVE ASSESSMENT

Concept Vocabulary

If students do not see a connection between the words, **then** have them use each word in a sentence about chimpanzees and think about what is similar about the sentences.

Word Study

If students fail to identify the root word, **then** point out that when adding a suffix, the last letter is sometimes dropped from a root word. For Reteach and Practice, see **Word Study: Latin Suffix -able (RP).** 📄

from MY LIFE WITH THE CHIMPANZEES

🔀 WORD NETWORK

Add words related to people and animals from the text to your Word Network.

☰ STANDARDS

Language

• Demonstrate command of the conventions of standard English capitalization, punctuation, and spelling when writing.

  a. Use punctuation to set off nonrestrictive/parenthetical elements.

• Determine or clarify the meaning of unknown and multiple-meaning words and phrases based on *grade 6 reading and content,* choosing flexibly from a range of strategies.

  b. Use common, grade-appropriate Greek or Latin affixes and roots as clues to the meaning of a word.

• Demonstrate understanding of figurative language, word relationships, and nuances in word meanings.

  b. Use the relationship between particular words to better understand each of the words.

Concept Vocabulary

vanished	irritable	impetuous
miserable	threateningly	dominate

Why These Words? The six concept words describe different aspects of the chimpanzees' behavior. For example, the chimpanzees appear *miserable* and *irritable* in the rain. Notice that both words describe what the chimpanzees seem to be feeling.

1. How does the concept vocabulary sharpen the reader's understanding of chimpanzees' behavior?

2. What other words in the selection connect to this concept?

Practice

📝 **Notebook** The words listed above appear in *My Life With the Chimpanzees.* Use each concept vocabulary word in a sentence that shows the word's meaning. Then, find at least one **synonym,** or word with a similar meaning, and one **antonym,** or word with an opposite meaning, for each word.

Word Study

Latin Suffix: -able The Latin suffix *-able* means "capable of, given to, or tending to," and it usually indicates that a word is an adjective. In *My Life With the Chimpanzees,* the word *irritable* means "tending to be irritated," or "tending to be easily annoyed." Knowing the **base word,** or "inside" word, along with the suffix can help you determine the meaning of an unfamiliar word. For example, in the word *irritable,* the base word is *irritate.*

1. How does the definition of the suffix *-able* help you understand the meaning of the vocabulary word *miserable*?

2. Review paragraph 48 and find a word with the suffix *-able.* Identify the base word. Then, write a definition for the word.

© Pearson Education, Inc., or its affiliates. All rights reserved.

AUTHOR'S PERSPECTIVE   Elfrieda Hiebert, Ph.D.

Collecting Sentences To help students become more adept with words, give them the experience of working with them. By studying sentences that use new vocabulary well, students can build their vocabulary strength. Encourage students to collect model sentences using two strategies:

• **Find sentences in the text.** Help students locate sentences that use new vocabulary, or have students identify sentences where

word choice truly packs power into the text. Discuss how the words are used, and have students emulate the writer by writing similar sentences.

• **Find sentences in online vocabulary resources.** When students are learning new words, it is useful to see the word used correctly in a variety of contexts. Many

Conventions

Commas, Parentheses, and Dashes Punctuation marks help writers organize their thoughts and divide sentences into meaningful parts.

A **comma** signals readers to pause. It is used to separate words or groups of words in a list or series.

EXAMPLE: *The chimps ate bananas, seeds, flowers, stems, and meat.*

Commas are also used to set off nonessential elements in a sentence, such as phrases or clauses. A **nonessential, or nonrestrictive, element** is one that is not needed to convey the main idea of a sentence. It can be deleted without affecting the sentence's basic meaning.

SET OFF NONESSENTIAL APPOSITIVE PHRASE	SET OFF NONESSENTIAL PARTICIPIAL PHRASE	SET OFF NONESSENTIAL RELATIVE CLAUSE
David Greybeard, <u>the boldest chimp</u>, was the first she met.	The chimps, <u>hidden in the treetops</u>, watched her every move.	The chimps, <u>whom Goodall named</u>, have unique personalities.

> **TIP**
> CLARIFICATION
> Refer to the Grammar Handbook to learn more about these terms.

Like commas, **parentheses** also set apart nonessential elements from the rest of a sentence. However, parentheses suggest the information they contain is even less important than information set off by commas.

EXAMPLE: *The chimps made tools (twigs or grass blades) to gather food.*

Dashes are another type of punctuation mark used to set apart nonessential elements. They have the added effect of indicating a sudden or strong interruption in thought.

EXAMPLE: *Jane Goodall was young—surprisingly so—when she first went to Africa to study chimpanzees.*

Read It

1. Each of the following sentences should contain one or more commas, parentheses, or dashes. Add the indicated punctuation correctly.
   a. The many supplies Jane and her mother brought included food medicines writing materials blankets and pillows. (commas)
   b. Chimpanzees eat mostly fruits bananas especially but also plants, stems, seeds, blossoms, and leaves. (parentheses)
   c. Jane discovered that chimps enjoy sleeping in comfort just as people do. (dash)
2. Reread paragraph 15. Mark one example each of a comma, parentheses, and a dash. Then, explain the purpose of each mark.

Write It

🗐 **Notebook** Punctuate this paragraph correctly.

Jane Goodall first began her work in the 1950s and despite the years that have gone by remains well-known for her study of chimpanzees. She was first to learn that chimpanzees are not strictly vegetarians they eat meat, too. She was also one of the first scientists to give names to the chimpanzees she studied usually the chimps were numbered.

from My Life With the Chimpanzees **115**

© Pearson Education, Inc., or its affiliates. All rights reserved.

Conventions

Commas, Parentheses, and Dashes Discuss the nonessential, or nonrestrictive phrase. Then point out that commas are the most widely used way to separate nonrestrictive phrases. Explain that dashes tend to be used in more informal writing and to make sentences stronger or more interesting. Parentheses are used to enclose extra material. For more support, see **Conventions: Commas, Parentheses, and Dashes.** 🗐

Read It

Possible responses:
1. **a.** The many supplies Jane and her mother brought included medicines, writing materials, blankets, and pillows.
   b. Chimpanzees eat mostly fruits (but also plants, stems, seeds, blossoms, and leaves).
   c. Jane discovered that chimps enjoy sleeping in comfort—just as people do.
2. Comma: . . . Kasakela, Linda, and Rutanga . . .; parentheses: (where our tent was); dash: one group—a community. The purpose of the comma is to separate the names in a list; the parentheses are used just to point out additional information for the reader; the dash is used to emphasize that the group was a community.

Write It

Possible response:

Jane Goodall first began her work in the 1950s and, despite the years that have gone by, remains well known for her study of chimpanzees. She was the first to learn chimpanzees are not strictly vegetarians—they eat meat, too. She was also one of the first scientists to name the chimpanzees in her writing (usually the chimps were numbered).

FORMATIVE ASSESSMENT

Conventions

If students cannot use a comma to separate introductory clauses or items in a series, **then** have them read the sentences without commas and ask them what is confusing. For Reteach and Practice, see **Conventions: Commas, Parentheses, and Dashes (RP).** 🗐

online dictionaries provide contemporary and cross-curricular examples to help learners see the words in action.

There are several benefits of this approach. First, a study of words and the way they are used can help students appreciate and understand writers. Second, looking closely at vocabulary and the spectrum of related words can help students improve their own writing.

PERSONALIZE FOR LEARNING

English Language Support

Punctuating Nonrestrictive Elements Write the following sentence from the selection and have students re-write it without a nonrestrictive element: *Soon after the chimps had begun to visit my camp, the National Geographic Society, which was giving Louis money for my research, sent a photographer to Gombe to make a film.*

(Possible answer: Soon after the chimps had begun to visit my camp, the National Geographic Society sent a photographer to Gombe to make a film.) **ALL LEVELS**

An expanded **English Language Support Lesson** on Commas is available in the Interactive Teacher's Edition.

Writing to Sources

Explain to students that when they write an explanatory essay that describes a process of how to do or make something, they should make sure that they explain the steps in the order they occur. Suggest that students write a brief outline of the steps that Dr. Goodall takes before beginning their essay.

Remind students to use facts and examples from the text to support each step. For more support, see **Writing to Sources: How-to Essay.** 📄

Reflect on Your Writing

1. Responses will vary. If students need support, ask them to consider the insights they gained in writing their how-to essay.

2. Responses will vary. Make sure that students make connections between each step and the detail(s) they chose from the selection.

3. Responses will vary. Have students list specific examples of words they have chosen that clearly show the steps in the process.

FORMATIVE ASSESSMENT

Writing to Sources

If students fail to use precise language to explain what Dr. Goodall did, **then** ask them to think about where they could replace common nouns for precise nouns and where they could replace "to be" verbs for strong, active verbs. For Reteach and Practice, see **Writing to Sources: How-to Essay (RP).** 📄

🖥 EFFECTIVE EXPRESSION

from MY LIFE WITH THE CHIMPANZEES

Writing to Sources

A **how-to essay** is a type of explanatory essay that provides step-by-step instructions for how to do or make something.

Assignment

Dr. Goodall describes the process, or steps, by which she earned the chimpanzees' trust. Review the text, and record concrete details and other information related to the process Goodall used to gain the chimpanzees' friendship. Then, write a brief **how-to essay** that describes the process.

- State and explain each step clearly, and support your explanation with details from the text.
- Use formatting, such as boldface headings, to distinguish each step in the process. Describe each step in complete sentences.
- Use transitions, such as *first, next, then,* and *finally,* to clarify the position of each step in the process.
- Use precise language to explain exactly what Dr. Goodall did in each step.

Vocabulary and Conventions Connection Try to include several of the concept vocabulary words in your essay. Also, remember to use commas, parentheses or dashes to set off nonessential sentence elements.

vanished	irritable	impetuous
miserable	threateningly	dominate

Reflect on Your Writing

📓 **Notebook** After you have written your explanatory essay, answer the following questions.

1. How did explaining the steps in Dr. Goodall's process help you to understand her research?

2. Which details from the excerpt did you include in your writing? How did they help you to convey the steps of the process?

3. **Why These Words?** The words you choose make a difference in your writing. Which words did you specifically choose to explain the steps in the process clearly?

© Pearson Education, Inc., or its affiliates. All rights reserved.

☰ STANDARDS

Writing
Write informative/explanatory texts to examine a topic and convey ideas, concepts, and information through the selection, organization, and analysis of relevant content.

a. Introduce a topic; organize ideas, concepts, and information using strategies such as definition, classification, comparison/contrast, and cause/effect; include formatting, graphics, and multimedia when useful to aiding comprehension.
b. Develop the topic with relevant facts, definitions, concrete details, quotations, or other information and examples.
c. Use appropriate transitions to clarify the relationships among ideas and concepts.
d. Use precise language and domain-specific vocabulary to inform about or explain the topic.

116 UNIT 2 • ANIMAL ALLIES

PERSONALIZE FOR LEARNING

English Language Support

Transition Words Display transition words (*first, next, then,* and *finally*), and then have students practice using the transition words by asking them to explain what they did when they got up this morning. As students become more comfortable using the transition words, ask them to review the selection and list and number the steps that

Dr. Goodall takes to earn the chimpanzees' trust. Finally, have students go back through the numbered steps and add a transition word to the beginning of each step. Point out that their numbered steps can act as an outline for their essay as they fill in the details for each step. **ALL LEVELS**

Speaking and Listening

Assignment

Dr. Goodall describes several chimpanzee behaviors that are similar to human behaviors. Participate in a **class discussion** in which you compare and contrast these behaviors.

1. **Explore the Topic** Think about details from the text as you explore the topic. Cite passages from the memoir as evidence. Also, include relevant examples from your own experience. To prepare for the discussion, consider the following questions.

   • What chimpanzee behaviors does Dr. Goodall describe that are similar to human behaviors?

   • What makes the chimpanzee behavior seem like that of humans?

   • Do these similarities help you better understand chimpanzees? Why, or why not?

2. **Conduct the Discussion** As your classmates contribute their ideas about the topic, give your full attention to each speaker. If you disagree with a statement, express your reasons respectfully and politely. Do not interrupt other classmates when they are speaking. When it is your turn to contribute, speak clearly and loudly enough to be heard by the entire class.

3. **Evaluate the Discussion** During the discussion, listen closely as your classmates share their ideas. Use a guide like the one shown to evaluate the group discussion.

EVALUATION GUIDE

Rate each statement on a scale of 1 (not demonstrated) to 5 (demonstrated).

☐ Each class member had the opportunity to contribute his or her ideas.

☐ Class members listened closely as each person spoke and did not interrupt one other.

☐ Class members expressed disagreements respectfully.

Reflect Write a few sentences in which you reflect on what you have learned from the discussion. In what ways has this knowledge increased your understanding of the relationship between humans and animals?

⬚ EVIDENCE LOG

Before moving on to a new selection, go to your Evidence Log, and record what you learned from *My Life With the Chimpanzees*.

⬛ STANDARDS

Speaking and Listening
Engage effectively in a range of collaborative discussions with diverse partners on *grade 6 topics, texts, and issues,* building on others' ideas and expressing their own clearly.
a. Come to discussions prepared, having read or studied required material; explicitly draw on that preparation by referring to evidence on the topic, text, or issue to probe and reflect on ideas under discussion.
b. Follow rules for collegial discussions, set specific goals and deadlines, and define individual roles as needed.
c. Pose and respond to specific questions with elaboration and detail by making comments that contribute to the topic, text, or issue under discussion.
d. Review the key ideas expressed and demonstrate understanding of multiple perspectives through reflection and paraphrasing.

from My Life With the Chimpanzees **117**

Speaking and Listening

1. **Explore the Topic** Tell students that they should focus on behaviors that Dr. Goodall describes are human-like. Ask students to think about how the chimpanzees act and how they interact with each other. Students should remember to cite specific examples and quotations from the selection to support the points they will make during the discussion.

2. **Conduct the Discussion** Suggest that students listen closely to each speaker and when it is their turn to speak, respond to or otherwise tie in their ideas with the contributions of their classmates.

3. **Evaluate the Discussion** Encourage students to make a least one supportive comment about the discussion. For more support, see **Speaking and Listening: Class Discussion.** ⬚

Evidence Log Support students in completing their Evidence Log. This paced activity will help prepare them for the Performance-Based Assessment at the end of the unit.

FORMATIVE ASSESSMENT

Speaking and Listening

• **If** students struggle to identify behaviors that are similar to human behaviors, **then** have them list all the behaviors that they read about and underline the ones that seem the most like human behaviors.

• **If** students struggle to speak in front of the whole class, **then** have them practice discussing the topic with a small group of students. For Reteach and Practice, see **Speaking and Listening: Class Discussion (RP).** ⬚

Selection Test

Administer the *from* My Life With the Chimpanzees Selection Test, which is available in both print and digital formats online in Assessments. ⬚ ⬚

PERSONALIZE FOR LEARNING

Strategic Support

Finding Evidence Point out that Dr. Goodall suggests that some of the chimpanzees' behaviors are human-like by using specific verbs associated with human behavior. Suggest that students skim the text for verbs that are generally associated with humans (such as *kissing, embracing,* and so on) but that Dr. Goodall uses to describe chimpanzee behavior. Discuss with them how Dr. Goodall's word choice helps shape the reader's perception of chimpanzee behavior.

© Pearson Education, Inc., or its affiliates. All rights reserved.

Hachiko: The True Story of a Loyal Dog

🔊 **AUDIO SUMMARIES**

Audio summaries of "Hachiko: The True Story of a Loyal Dog" are available online in both English and Spanish in the Interactive Teacher's Edition or Unit Resources. Assigning these summaries prior to reading the selection may help students build additional background knowledge and set a context for their first read.

Summary

"Hachiko: The True Story of a Loyal Dog" is a historical fiction story by Pamela S. Turner. In the story, a boy named Kentaro tells of how he moved to Tokyo near a train station. While Kentaro and his mother are waiting at the station one day for his father to arrive, Kentaro spots a dog sitting alone. Kentaro learns that the dog is named Hachiko and that his owner is a professor named Dr. Ueno. Hachiko waits faithfully at the train station every day for Dr. Ueno to arrive, and Kentaro begins to go to the station each day so he can visit Hachiko. One day Dr. Ueno does not arrive at the station, and Kentaro learns Dr. Ueno has died. Hachiko continues to visit the station each day for many years, waiting for his master. As his story spread, Hachiko became a nationwide symbol of loyalty in Japan.

Insight

Hachiko's loyalty to his master is the center of the story. However, one should also note Kentaro's attachment to Hachiko and how Kentaro cared for the dog each day.

ESSENTIAL QUESTION:
How can people and animals relate to each other?

Connection to Essential Question

Hachiko's great care for his master, and the empathy and admiration people felt for him in return, show how people and animals can relate to one another.

WHOLE-CLASS LEARNING PERFORMANCE TASK
What qualities do Goodall and Turner believe people and animals share?

Connection to Performance Tasks

Whole-Class Learning Performance Task This text will provide students with ideas that may help them address the prompt. The author portrays Hachiko as very loyal, which is a quality that many people share.

UNIT PERFORMANCE-BASED ASSESSMENT
How can animals and people help one another?

Unit Performance-Based Assessment The story of Hachiko will give students an opportunity to prepare for the prompt. They will see that people fed and cared for Hachiko, and Hachiko inspired people.

LESSON RESOURCES

	Making Meaning	Language Development	Effective Expression
Lesson	**First Read** **Close Read** **Analyze the Text** **Analyze Craft and Structure**	**Concept Vocabulary** **Word Study** **Conventions**	**Writing to Sources** **Speaking and Listening**
Instructional Standards	**RL.2** Determine a theme or central idea of a text . . . **RL.3** Describe how a particular story's or drama's plot unfolds . . . **RL.5** Analyze how a particular sentence, chapter, scene, or stanza fits into the overall structure of a text . . . **RL.10** By the end of the year, read and comprehend literature . . .	**L.2** Demonstrate command of the conventions . . . **L.2.b** Spell correctly. **L.4** Determine or clarify the meaning of unknown and multiple-meaning words and phrases . . . **L.4.d** Verify the preliminary determination . . . **L.5** Demonstrate understanding of figurative language . . . **L.5.b** Use the relationship between particular words . . .	**W.3** Write narratives . . . **W.3.a** Engage and orient the reader . . . **W.9** Draw information from literary or informational texts . . . **W.9.a** Apply *grade 6 Reading standards* . . . **SL.1** Engage effectively in a range of collaborative discussions . . . **SL.1.a** Come to discussions prepared . . . **SL.1.b** Follow rules for collegial discussions . . . **SL.4** Present claims and findings . . .

▶ STUDENT RESOURCES

Available online in the Interactive Student Edition or Unit Resources	🔊 Selection Audio 📄 First-Read Guide: Fiction 📄 Close-Read Guide: Fiction	📄 Word Network	📄 Evidence Log

▶ TEACHER RESOURCES

Selection Resources Available online in the Interactive Teacher's Edition or Unit Resources	🔊 Audio Summaries ✏️ Annotation Highlights 💬 EL Highlights 📄 English Language Support Lesson: Historical Fiction 📄 Analyze Craft and Structure: Historical Fiction	📄 Concept Vocabulary and Word Study 📄 Conventions: Spelling and Capitalization	📄 Writing to Sources: Story Adaptation 📄 Speaking and Listening: Partner Discussion
Reteach/Practice (RP) Available online in the Interactive Teacher's Edition or Unit Resources	📄 Analyze Craft and Structure: Historical Fiction (RP)	📄 Word Study: Anglo-Saxon Suffix *-ly* (RP) 📄 Conventions: Spelling and Capitalization (RP)	📄 Writing to Sources: Story Adaptation (RP) 📄 Speaking and Listening: Partner Discussion (RP)
Assessment Available online in Assessments	📄 ☑ Selection Test		
My Resources	📄 A Unit 2 Answer Key is available online and in the Interactive Teacher's Edition.		

Reading Support

Text Complexity Rubric: Hachiko: The True Story of a Loyal Dog

Quantitative Measures

Lexile: 690   Text Length: 1,221 words

Qualitative Measures

Knowledge Demands ①—**②**—③—④—⑤	The central situation (the unwavering loyalty of a dog) may not be familiar to all students, but the concept is explained clearly through the eyes of the story's main character.
Structure ①—**②**—③—④—⑤	The story is told in a conventional, straightforward, linear way.
Language Conventionality and Clarity ①—②—**❸**—④—⑤	The syntax is generally simple. The selection contains on-level vocabulary and fairly simple dialogue.
Levels of Meaning/Purpose ①—**②**—③—④—⑤	Selection has only one level of meaning. The main concept and supporting ideas are clearly stated when reading or listening.

DECIDE AND PLAN

English Language Support

Provide English Learners with support for knowledge demands and language as they read the selection.

Knowledge Demands Point out paragraph 27. Have students tell why they think people cared so much about Hachiko.

Language Help students reword sentences that contain words students might not know. Using the language from the selection, suggest simpler sentences that convey the same meaning. For example, for paragraph 4: The dog ran over to the man, his whole body shaking with happiness. Ask students to read the new sentences and discuss.

Strategic Support

Provide students with strategic support to ensure that they can successfully read the text.

Language If students have difficulty with complex sentences, work together to break down sentences into smaller chunks in order to understand their meaning. Ask students to highlight words or phrases that they don't understand. As a group, help to define some of the terms they find difficult.

Levels of Meaning / Purpose To help students to sort out the events and ideas in the story, suggest that they keep a log of the main events, stating them in their own words.

Challenge

Provide students who need to be challenged with ideas for how they can go beyond a simple interpretation of the text.

Text Analysis Ask students to read aloud the paragraph about how the statue of Hachiko became a famous meeting place (paragraph 31). Ask students to explain why they think "Today Hachiko is a place where friends and family long separated come together again."

Written Response Ask students to write an informative paragraph about an example of loyalty from their own lives, whether the loyalty of a pet or a person. Ask students to read their work to a partner and discuss the situations they wrote about.

TEACH

Read and Respond

Have students do their first read of the selection. Then have them complete their close read. Finally, work with them on the Making Meaning, Language Development, and Effective Expression activities.

Standards Support Through Teaching and Learning Cycle

IDENTIFY NEEDS

Analyze results of the Beginning-of-Year Assessment, focusing on the items relating to Unit 2. Also take into consideration student performance to this point and your observations of where particular students struggle.

ANALYZE AND REVISE

- Analyze student work for evidence of student learning.
- Identify whether or not students have met the expectations in the standards.
- Identify implications for future instruction.

TEACH

Implement the planned lesson, and gather evidence of student learning.

DECIDE AND PLAN

- If students have performed poorly on items matching these standards, then provide selection scaffolds before assigning them the on-level lesson provided in the Student Edition.
- If students have done well on the Beginning-of-Year Assessment, then challenge them to keep progressing and learning by giving them opportunities to practice the skills in depth.
- Use the Selection Resources listed on the Planning pages for "Hachiko: The True Story of a Loyal Dog" to help students continually improve their ability to master the standards.

Instructional Standards: Hachiko: The True Story of a Loyal Dog

	Catching Up	This Year	Looking Forward
Reading	You may wish to administer the **Analyze Craft and Structure: Historical Fiction (RP)** worksheet to help students understand what the main elements are of the genre.	**RL.3** Describe how a particular story's or drama's plot unfolds in a series of episodes as well as how the characters respond or change as the plot moves toward a resolution.	Challenge students to think of other examples of historical fiction.
Writing	You may wish to administer the **Writing to Sources: Story Adaptation (RP)** worksheet to help students organize and write their adaptation of the story.	**W.3** Write narratives to convey real or imagined experiences using effective technique, relevant descriptive details, and well-structured event sequences.	Encourage students to find another story to adapt. Students may select a narrative and retell it from another character's perspective.
Speaking and Listening	You may wish to administer the **Speaking and Listening: Partner Discussion (RP)** worksheet to help students prepare for the class discussion.	**SL.4**. Present claims and findings, sequencing ideas logically and using pertinent descriptions, facts, and details to accentuate main ideas or themes; use appropriate eye contact, adequate volume, and clear pronunciation.	Challenge students to write down three questions they have about the connections between the book and Hachiko. Encourage students to incorporate the questions into the discussion.
Language	You may wish to administer the **Word Study: Anglo-Saxon Suffix -ly (RP)** worksheet to help students understand suffixes and how they affect a word's meaning.	**L.4** Determine or clarify the meaning of unknown and multiple-meaning words and phrases based on *Grade 6 reading and content*, choosing flexibly from a range of strategies.	Ask students to find three additional words that have the Anglo-Saxon suffix -ly and use each word in a sentence.

Jump Start

FIRST READ Students might have a dog, or they probably know someone who does. Engage them in a discussion about the qualities that make dogs good pets. Then ask them if they have seen movies or read stories about dogs that have an extraordinary connection with their owners, or that go to great lengths to save a person or be with a person. Talk about what makes the connection between dogs and people so powerful. This can set the context for reading "Hachiko: The True Story of a Loyal Dog."

Hachiko: The True Story of a Loyal Dog 🔊 📄

Why do some dogs grow so attached to their owners? How can a dog find its way around a busy city? How can a dog know what time it is? Modeling the questions a reader might ask as they read "Hachiko: The True Story of a Loyal Dog" for the first time brings the text alive for students and connects it to the Whole-Class Performance Task assignment. Selection audio and print capability for the selection are available in the Interactive Teacher's Edition.

Concept Vocabulary

Support students as they rank their words. Ask if they've ever heard, read, or used them. Reassure them that the definitions for these words are listed in the selection.

⬤ FIRST READ

Students should perform the steps of the first read independently.

NOTICE: You may want to encourage students to notice what happened to the professor and where Hachiko went as a result.

ANNOTATE: Remind students to mark passages that include repetition to help them see the pattern that emerges in the life of Hachiko.

CONNECT: Encourage students to think about dogs they have seen or heard about. What kind of a connection do they have to their owners? Have these dogs shown such loyalty to their owners? How?

RESPOND: Students will answer questions and write a summary to demonstrate understanding.

Point out to students that while they will always complete the Respond step at the end of the first read, the other steps will probably happen somewhat concurrently. You may wish to print copies of the **First-Read Guide: Fiction** for students to use. 📄

About the Author

Pamela S. Turner (b. 1957) grew up in Southern California. She has always been interested in writing, and has said that the very first thing she remembers wanting to be was a children's author. Turner has lived all over the world. While living in Japan, she heard the story of Hachiko. When she returned to the United States, she wrote her first book, *Hachiko: The True Story of a Loyal Dog*. Since then, she has written many other books for children, and has won numerous awards for her writing.

🔧 **Tool Kit** First-Read Guide and Model Annotation

▤ STANDARDS

Reading Literature
By the end of the year, read and comprehend literature, including stories, dramas, and poems, in the grades 6–8 text complexity band proficiently, with scaffolding as needed at the high end of the range.

Hachiko: The True Story of a Loyal Dog

Concept Vocabulary

You will encounter the following words as you read this work of historical fiction. Before reading, note how familiar you are with each word. Then, rank the words in order from most familiar (1) to least familiar (5).

WORD	YOUR RANKING
timidly	
anxiously	
patiently	
thoughtfully	
silently	

After completing the first read, come back to the concept vocabulary and review your rankings. Mark changes to your original rankings as needed.

First Read FICTION

Apply these strategies as you conduct your first read. You will have an opportunity to complete the close-read notes after your first read.

NOTICE *whom* the story is about, *what* happens, *where* and *when* it happens, and *why* those involved react as they do.

ANNOTATE by marking vocabulary and key passages you want to revisit.

First Read

CONNECT ideas within the selection to what you already know and what you have already read.

RESPOND by completing the Comprehension Check and by writing a brief summary of the selection.

© Pearson Education, Inc., or its affiliates. All rights reserved.

PERSONALIZE FOR LEARNING

Strategic Support
If students struggle to comprehend the text during the first read, have a partner conduct a think aloud to explain the thought process as he or she works through the NOTICE, ANNOTATE, CONNECT, and RESPOND steps. For example, the student can isolate the key details and explain what they reveal.

Hachiko:
The True Story of a Loyal Dog

Pamela S. Turner

DIGITAL PERSPECTIVES

SCAN FOR MULTIMEDIA

NOTES

1   When I was six years old, my family moved to a little house in Tokyo near the Shibuya train station. At first the trains frightened me. But after a while, I grew to enjoy their power and the furious noises they made. One day I begged Mama to take me to meet Papa as he came home on the afternoon train. She laughed and said, "Kentaro, you have become big and brave, just like a samurai!" Together we walked to the station. Mama and I had stopped near the station entrance when I noticed the dog.

2   He was sitting quietly, all alone, by a newspaper stand. He had thick, cream-colored fur, small pointed ears, and a broad, bushy tail that curved up over his back. I wondered if the dog was a stray, but he was wearing a nice leather harness and looked healthy and strong.

3   His brown eyes were fixed on the station entrance.

4   Just then, Papa appeared. He was chatting with an older man. The dog bounded over to the man, his entire body wiggling and quivering with delight. His eyes shone, and his mouth curled up into something that looked, to me, just like a smile.

5   "Ah, Kentaro! You see, Dr. Ueno, you are not the only one who has someone to welcome him," said Papa. He introduced us to the older man. "Dr. Ueno works with me at Tokyo Imperial University."

6   "What is your dog's name?" I asked **timidly**. The dog was beautiful, but his sharp face reminded me of a wolf's. I grabbed Mama's kimono and stepped behind her, just in case.

7   "Don't be afraid," said Dr. Ueno kindly. "This is Hachiko. He is big, but still a puppy. He walks me to the station every morning and waits for me to come home every afternoon. I think Hachiko stores up all his joy, all day long, and then lets it all out at once!"

8   Hachiko stood wagging his tail next to Dr. Ueno. I reached to touch him, and he bounced forward and sniffed my face. I yelped and jumped back behind Mama.

9   They all laughed. "Oh, Kentaro, don't worry—he just wants to get to know you," said Dr. Ueno. "Dogs can tell a lot about people just by smelling them. Why, Hachiko probably knows what you ate for lunch!"

10   From that day on, I went to the train station almost every afternoon. But I no longer went to see the trains. I went to see

timidly (TIHM ihd lee) *adv.* in a shy or fearful way; cautiously

CLOSE READ

ANNOTATE: In paragraphs 4 and 5, mark details that indicate Dr. Ueno's age. Mark details in paragraph 7 that indicate Hachiko's age.

QUESTION: Why does the author include these details?

CONCLUDE: How do these details help set up the situation that occurs in the story?

 CLOSE READ

As students read paragraphs 4 and 5, remind them to focus on details that indicate Dr. Ueno's age. As they read paragraph 7, have students focus on details that hint at Hachiko's age. You may wish to model the Close Read using the following think-aloud format. Possible responses to questions on the student page are included. You may also want to print copies of the **Close-Read Guide: Fiction** for students to use.

ANNOTATE: As I read paragraphs 4 and 5, I notice and mark details that indicate Dr. Ueno's age. As I read paragraph 7, I notice and mark details that indicate Hachiko's age.

QUESTION: The author includes these details to give the reader a picture of both Dr. Ueno and Hachiko when Kentaro first meets them.

CONCLUDE: The author establishes the idea that Dr. Ueno is elderly and Hachiko is just a puppy. This helps explain Dr. Ueno's death and the years Hachiko spends waiting for him at the train station.

Additional **English Language Support** is available in the Interactive Teacher's Edition.

© Pearson Education, Inc., or its affiliates. All rights reserved.

Hachiko: The True Story of a Loyal Dog   **119**

CLOSER LOOK

Infer Key Ideas 🖉

Students may have marked paragraph 22 during their first read. Use these paragraphs to help students understand Hachiko's loyalty to Dr. Ueno. Encourage them to talk about the annotations that they marked. You may want to model a close read with the class based on the highlights shown in the text.

ANNOTATE: Have students mark details in paragraph 22 that tell what Hachiko does even though Dr. Ueno is gone, or have students participate while you highlight them.

QUESTION: Guide students to consider what these details might tell them. Ask what a reader can infer from these details, and accept student responses.

Possible response: Hachiko shows loyalty to his master by sleeping at his master's house and going to the station each day.

CONCLUDE: Help students to formulate conclusions about the importance of these details in the text. Ask students why the author might have included these details.

Possible response: People found the story of Hachiko amazing because stories about pets and their loyalty to their owners are fascinating to most people, regardless of age.

Remind students that authors often make readers **infer key ideas.** Point out that readers use logical thinking to analyze details the author provides, combined with what they already know, to infer important ideas in a selection.

NOTES

anxiously (ANGK shuhs lee)
adv. in a worried, uneasy manner; nervously

patiently (PAY shuhnt lee)
adv. bearing annoyance, hardship, or pain calmly and without complaint or anger

---

Hachiko. He was always there, waiting near the newspaper stand. I often saved a morsel from my lunch and hid it in one of my pockets.

11   Hachiko would sniff me all over, wagging his tail, until he found a sticky bit of fish or soybean cake. Then he would nudge me with his nose, as if to say, "Give me my prize!" When it was cold, I would bury my face in the thick ruff of creamy fur around his neck.

12   One day in May, I was waiting at the station with Hachiko. The moment I saw Papa, I knew something was wrong. He was alone, and he walked hunched over, staring sadly at the gray pavement under his feet.

13   "What's the matter, Papa?" I asked him **anxiously,** standing with one hand on Hachiko's broad head. He sighed. "Kentaro, let's go home." Hachiko's bright brown eyes followed us as we walked away, but he stayed behind, waiting for Dr. Ueno.

14   When we got home, Papa told us that Dr. Ueno had died that morning at the university. I was stunned. "But what will happen to Hachiko?" I asked, blinking hard to keep the tears back. "What will he do?"

15   The next day, I went back to check on Hachiko, but he was not there. Papa told me that Hachiko had been taken several miles away to live with some of Dr. Ueno's relatives. "But I'll never see him again!" I cried. "Why can't he live with us?"

16   "We don't have room for a dog," protested Papa. "And Hachiko really belongs to Dr. Ueno's relatives, now that Dr. Ueno is dead. Hachiko is better off having a home than sitting in a train station."

17   But Hachiko had other ideas. A few days later he was back at Shibuya Station, **patiently** waiting, his brown eyes fixed on the entrance. Hachiko had run back to his old home, and from there to Shibuya Station.

18   Mama and Papa let me take food and water to Hachiko every day. Other people at the station took an interest in Hachiko. Men and women who rode Papa and Dr. Ueno's train stopped by to scratch his ears and say a few kind words. One day I saw an old man filling Hachiko's water bowl as Hachiko licked his hand. The old man's hair was streaked with gray, and he was stooped, as if he had spent most of his life bent over the ground. But his eyes were as sharp and bright as Hachiko's.

19   "Are you young Kentaro?" the old man asked. I nodded. "I am Mr. Kobayashi. I was Dr. Ueno's gardener."

20   "Dr. Ueno told me that you and Hachiko often wait for the afternoon train together."

21   "Do you still take care of the house where Dr. Ueno lived?" I asked.

22   "Yes," said Mr. Kobayashi. "Hachiko comes back to the house every night to sleep on the porch. But in the morning, he walks to the station just like he did with Dr. Ueno. When the last train leaves the station, he returns home."

© Pearson Education, Inc., or its affiliates. All rights reserved.

VOCABULARY DEVELOPMENT

Concept Vocabulary Reinforcement Students will benefit from additional examples and practice with the concept vocabulary. Reinforce their comprehension with "show-you-know" sentences. The first part of the sentence uses the vocabulary word in an appropriate context. The second part of the sentence—the "show-you-know" part—clarifies the first.

Model the strategy with this example for *timidly.*

Kentaro asked *timidly;* he was unsure how the dog would behave.

Then give students these sentence prompts and coach them in creating the clarification part:

1. Hachiko sat *patiently* at the train station; _____.

Possible response: he was content to sit and wait for his master's return.

2. Papa greeted me *silently;* _____.

Possible response: he was unsure of what he should say to me.

© Pearson Education, Inc., or its affiliates. All rights reserved.

23   We were both silent. Then I asked, "Do you think Hachiko knows that Dr. Ueno died?"

24   Mr. Kobayashi said **thoughtfully**, "I don't know, Kentaro. Perhaps he still hopes that Dr. Ueno will return someday. Or perhaps he knows Dr. Ueno is dead, but he waits at the station to honor his master's memory."

25   As the years passed and Hachiko got older, he became very stiff and could barely walk to Shibuya Station. But still he went, every day. People began collecting money to build a statue of Hachiko at the station. Papa, Mama, and I all gave money, and we were very happy when the statue was placed next to the spot where Hachiko had waited for so many years.

26   One chilly morning I woke to the sound of Mama crying. "What's wrong?" I asked as I stumbled into the kitchen. Papa sat **silently** at the table, and Mama turned her tear-stained face to me. "Hachiko died last night at Shibuya Station," she choked. "Still waiting for Dr. Ueno."

27   Later that day we all went to the station. To our great surprise, Hachiko's spot near the newspaper stand was covered in flowers placed there by his many friends.

28   Old Mr. Kobayashi was there. He shuffled over to me and put a hand on my shoulder.

29   "Hachiko didn't come back to the house last night," he said quietly. "I walked to the station and found him. I think his spirit is with Dr. Ueno's, don't you?"

30   "Yes," I whispered.

31   The big bronze statue of Hachiko is a very famous meeting place. Shibuya Station is enormous now, and hundreds of thousands of people travel through it every day. People always say to each other, "Let's meet at Hachiko." Today Hachiko is a place where friends and family long separated come together again. ⁂

NOTES

thoughtfully (THAWT fuhl lee) *adv.* showing careful consideration or attention

silently (SY luhnt lee) *adv.* without noise

SCAN FOR MULTIMEDIA

MEDIA CONNECTION

The Secret Life of the Dog

Discuss It How does viewing this video add to your understanding of the relationship between dogs and people? Write your response before sharing your ideas.

Comprehension Check

Complete the following items after you finish your first read.

1. How does Kentaro first meet Hachiko?

2. According to the story, what do people say today when they want to meet at Shibuya Station?

3. **Notebook** Write a three-sentence summary of the selection.

RESEARCH
Research to Clarify
Formulate a research question that you might use to find out more about the real-life Hachiko.

Comprehension Check

Possible responses:

1. Kentaro first meets Hachiko when Kentaro and his parents see Dr. Ueno at the train station.

2. Today people who want to meet at Shibuya Station say, "Let's meet at Hachiko," because everyone knows the statue.

3. Summaries will vary, but students should include a description of why the dog returned to the train station each day, how people felt about Hachiko, and what happened to Hachiko in the end.

Research

Research to Clarify If students struggle to come up with a research question, suggest that they focus on words that might tell them about Hachiko's life, such as *Who was Hachiko?* or a question about Hachiko's loyalty to his owner.

PERSONALIZE FOR LEARNING

Challenge
Domesticating Dogs Encourage interested students to research the history of domesticated dogs. When did people first start keeping dogs as pets? Why? What were the first dogs like? How did they help people? Students should also include information about which modern-day dogs most closely resemble those first dogs that people kept as pets. Students can present their results as a timeline or as a poster.

MAKING MEANING

HACHIKO: THE TRUE STORY OF A LOYAL DOG

Jump Start

CLOSE READ Dogs are often called "man's best friend." Engage students in a discussion about how dogs are portrayed in the media and in literature, and why dogs are one of the most popular pets in the world. Ask students to consider whether or not people have a special bond with dogs, and if so, how that bond helps both people and dogs.

Close Read the Text 🖉

Walk students through the annotation model on the student page. Encourage them to complete items 2 and 3 on their own. Review and discuss the sections students have marked. If needed, continue to model close reading by using the Annotation Highlights in the Interactive Teacher's Edition.

Analyze the Text

Possible responses:

1. The statue of Hachiko represents reuniting with friends or loved ones after being separated. **DOK 2**

2. Kentaro grew attached to Hachiko and the two formed a bond, just like Hachiko had with Dr. Ueno. I think Kentaro was loyal to Hachiko because Hachiko was so loyal to Dr. Ueno. **DOK 3**

3. I have learned that some pets can form very strong and long-lasting attachments to their owners. **DOK 3**

FORMATIVE ASSESSMENT

Analyze the Text

• **If** students fail to cite evidence, **then** remind them to support their ideas with specific information.

• **If** students struggle to determine why Hachiko symbolizes loyalty, **then** discuss the term *symbolize* and illustrate with examples.

Close Read the Text

1. This model, from paragraph 4, shows two sample annotations, along with questions and conclusions. Close read the passage, and find another detail to annotate. Then, write a question and conclusion.

> **Close Read**
> ANNOTATE · QUESTION · CONCLUDE

> **ANNOTATE:** The author uses vivid language to describe Hachiko's movements.
>
> **QUESTION:** Why does the author choose these words to describe Hachiko's movements?
>
> **CONCLUDE:** These vivid words create a word picture of Hachiko's joy.

> **ANNOTATE:** Thie idea of a dog smiling is interesting.
>
> **QUESTION:** Why does the author describe Hachiko in this way?
>
> **CONCLUDE:** This description makes Hachiko's feelings seem like strong human emotions.

> Just then, Papa appeared. He was chatting with an older man. The dog bounded over to the man, his entire body wiggling and quivering with delight. His eyes shone, and his mouth curled up into something that looked, to me, just like a smile.

🔧 **Tool Kit**
Close-Read Guide and Model Annotation

2. For more practice, go back into the text and complete the close-read note.

3. Revisit a section of the text you found important during your first read. Read this section closely and **annotate** what you notice. Ask yourself **questions** such as "Why did the author make this choice?" What can you **conclude**?

▦ **STANDARDS**
Reading Literature
• Determine a theme or central idea of a text and how it is conveyed through particular details; provide a summary of the text distinct from personal opinions or judgments.
• Describe how a particular story's or drama's plot unfolds in a series of episodes as well as how the characters respond or change as the plot moves toward a resolution.
• Analyze how a particular sentence, chapter, scene, or stanza fits into the overall structure of a text and contributes to the development of the theme, setting, or plot.

Analyze the Text

CITE TEXTUAL EVIDENCE to support your answers.

📓 **Notebook** Respond to these questions.

1. **Interpret** What does the statue of Hachiko **symbolize,** or represent, to the people of Japan?

2. **Compare and Contrast** How does Kentaro's loyalty to Hachiko compare with Hachiko's loyalty to Dr. Ueno?

3. **Essential Question:** *How can people and animals relate to each other?* What have you learned about the connection between people and animals from reading this selection?

122 UNIT 2 • ANIMAL ALLIES

© Pearson Education, Inc., or its affiliates. All rights reserved.

DIGITAL PERSPECTIVES

Enriching the Text Locate and project one or more Internet resources related to the Akita breed of dogs.

Use search terms such as "Akita" or "The American Kennel Club." Be sure to preview websites before displaying them to students. As you review these sites with students, engage them in a discussion about how the information about the Akita on the sites corresponds to the qualities the author attributes to Hachiko.

Analyze Craft and Structure

Historical Fiction When writers base fictional stories on real events from the past, it is called **historical fiction.** Historical fiction uses facts, but blends them with elements from the author's imagination. Historical fiction shows what the past *might* have been like. Certain literary elements are especially important in this type of fiction:

- **Setting** is the time and place in which a story occurs. In historical fiction, the setting must accurately show real places. In addition, made-up places have to be believable.

- **Conflict** is the struggle or problem characters face. A story shows how a conflict begins, increases, and ends. In historical fiction, the conflict may show how a situation or character (such as a dog) became famous or important.

- **Theme** is a message about life or human nature that a story reveals. Historical fiction combines real and imaginative elements to express a theme.

In this story, Hachiko and Dr. Ueno are real. They lived in Tokyo, Japan, in the early twentieth-century. Shibuya Station is also a real place. Dr. Ueno's death and Hachiko's actions really happened. However, Kentaro and his parents are fictional. Their actions are also fictional, although they are likely based on things real people felt and did.

Practice

CITE TEXTUAL EVIDENCE to support your answers.

📝 **Notebook** Respond to these questions.

1. How does the setting at the beginning of the story compare with the description of Shibuya Station at the end? Explain how this change shows the importance of Hachiko's story to the people of Tokyo.

2. (a) In the chart, record details that show the loyalty shown between Hachiko and other characters in the story. (b) What possible theme do these details suggest?

	LOYALTY TO HACHIKO	LOYALTY FROM HACHIKO
Dr. Ueno	keeps Hachiko healthy	Hachiko waits for Dr. Ueno
Kentaro	gives Hachiko water and treats	meets Kentaro each day
Mr. Kobayashi	cares for Hachiko	licks Kobayashi's hand, sleeps at house
others	speak kindly to dog; build statue	demonstrated love and loyalty
THEME	These details suggest that both animals and people are capable of loyalty to one another.	

3. Both Hachiko and Kentaro face conflicts following Dr. Ueno's death. (a) How do they deal with these conflicts? (b) What results from their efforts? Explain.

4. Focus on paragraphs 18–24, in which Kentaro meets Mr. Kobayashi. How does this scene relate to the story as a whole?

Hachiko: The True Story of a Loyal Dog **123**

© Pearson Education, Inc., or its affiliates. All rights reserved.

Analyze Craft and Structure

Historical Fiction Tell students that in historical fiction, the stories are made up and set in the past, with realistic settings and historical events but often with some fictional characters.

Historical fiction also has an element of conflict in which the main character or characters struggle with an opposing force. The conflict helps reveal the characters' motivations and the point or purpose of the story. For more support, see **Analyze Craft and Structure: Historical Fiction.** 📄

Practice

1. In the beginning of the story, the station is the focal point of the setting and is where Hachiko faithfully waits for his master, day after day, year after year. At the end of the story, Shibuya Station is described as a meeting place that everyone knows, because everyone knows the story of Hachiko and his loyalty.

2. See responses in chart on student page.

3. (a) Hachiko continues to wait at the station in spite of Dr. Ueno's absence. Kentaro meets Hachiko at the station each day and cares for him. (b) Kentaro becomes very attached to Hachiko and is loyal to him. Other people besides Kentaro notice Hachiko's loyalty to his master and build a statue in Hachiko's honor after his death.

4. I think this scene shows how both people and animals can show loyalty to each other and also show it in different ways, for example, even after someone dies.

PERSONALIZE FOR LEARNING

English Language Support

Elements of Historical Fiction Tell students that historical fiction most often includes real places and events, but can have both real and fictional characters. Ask students to write a sentence that includes the real setting of the story, one real character, and one fictional character.

Have students explain why they think the author chose to tell the story of Hachiko from Kentaro's point of view. **ALL LEVELS**

An expanded **English Language Support Lesson** on Historical Fiction is in the Interactive Teacher's Edition.

FORMATIVE ASSESSMENT

Analyze Craft and Structure

If students are unable to identify the specific elements that contribute to historical fiction, **then** have them go back through the text and underline realistic details about the setting of the story and about Hachiko. For Reteach and Practice, see **Analyze Craft and Structure: Historical Fiction. (RP)** 📄

Whole-Class Learning **123**

Concept Vocabulary

Why These Words?

Possible responses:

1. The words tell the way the characters do things or how they react to each other or to situations.

2. *quietly, kindly*

Practice

Possible responses:

timidly: synonym: nervously; antonym: boldly;
anxiously: synonym: fearfully; antonym: confidently;
patiently: synonym: calmly; antonym: restlessly;
thoughtfully: synonym: carefully; antonym: inconsiderately;
silently: synonym: quietly; antonym: loudly

Word Network

Possible words: *stray, smelling, master*

Word Study

For more support, see **Concept Vocabulary and Word Study.** 📄

Possible responses:

1. *Timidly:* timid; *anxiously:* anxious; *patiently:* patient; *thoughtfully:* thoughtful; *silently:* silent

2. *quietly:* something done without words or sound; *kindly:* in a kind of sympathetic manner

---

FORMATIVE ASSESSMENT

Concept Vocabulary

If students are unable identify other words in the selection that connect to the concept, **then** have them look for other adjectives in the story that could be made adverbs by adding *-ly*.

Word Study

If students struggle with modifying words using *-ly*, **then** remind them to focus on how *-ly* changes a word's meaning. For Reteach and Practice, see **Word Study: Anglo-Saxon Suffix -ly. (RP)** 📄

HACHIKO: THE TRUE STORY OF A LOYAL DOG

⊞ WORD NETWORK

Add words related to people and animals from the text to your Word Network.

☰ STANDARDS

Language

• Demonstrate command of the conventions of standard English capitalization, punctuation, and spelling when writing.
  b. Spell correctly.
• Determine or clarify the meaning of unknown and multiple-meaning words and phrases based on *grade 6 reading and content*, choosing flexibly from a range of strategies.
  d. Verify the preliminary determination of the meaning of a word or phrase.
• Demonstrate understanding of figurative language, word relationships, and nuances in word meanings.
  b. Use the relationship between particular words to better understand each of the words.

🔲 LANGUAGE DEVELOPMENT

Concept Vocabulary

timidly	anxiously	patiently
thoughtfully	silently	

Why These Words? The five concept vocabulary words all show how people act and react to one another. For example, when Kentaro first meets Hachiko, he asks the dog's name *timidly*, with shyness and caution.

1. How does the concept vocabulary convey the characters' emotional responses to important events in the story?

2. What other words in the selection relate to this concept?

Practice

🔘 **Notebook** The concept vocabulary words appear in the selection. Use a thesaurus to find at least one **synonym,** or word with a similar meaning, and one **antonym,** or word with an opposite meaning, for each concept vocabulary word. Then, use a dictionary to determine the precise meaning of each synonym and antonym.

Word Study

Anglo-Saxon Suffix: -ly Each of the concept vocabulary words ends with *-ly*. The Anglo-Saxon suffix *-ly* can be added to an adjective to form an adverb that modifies a verb. An adverb ending in *-ly* is called an **adverb of manner** because it describes the manner or way in which an action takes place.

1. Review each concept vocabulary word as Turner uses it in the selection. Identify the verb each concept word modifies by showing the way in which it takes place.

2. Scan paragraphs 2 and 7, and find two more words with the suffix *-ly*. Then, write a definition for each word that shows your understanding of the suffix *-ly*.

© Pearson Education, Inc., or its affiliates. All rights reserved.

VOCABULARY DEVELOPMENT

Concept Vocabulary Reinforcement To increase familiarity with the concept vocabulary, ask students to use each of the words in a sentence. Encourage students to include context clues in their own sentences to demonstrate their knowledge of the word. If students are still struggling with the words, encourage them to identify the base word in each term, look up the base word in the dictionary, and then use the definition to come up with the meaning of the concept vocabulary word.

Conventions

Spelling and Capitalization Most nouns follow straightforward spelling rules when changing from singular to plural. For example, you simply add -s or -es to the end of the singular word. The nouns *train, watch,* and *hero* are singular. The plural forms are *trains, watches,* and *heroes.* Other nouns need additional spelling changes to go from singular to plural. For these **irregular plurals,** follow these rules.

SPELLING OF SINGULAR NOUN	RULE	EXAMPLES
Ends with a consonant plus -y	Change the y to i and add -es	story, stories memory, memories
Ends in -f or -fe	Change the f to v and add -es or -s	life, lives yourself, yourselves

It is also important to follow rules for correct capitalization. Here are some capitalization rules to use:

CAPITALIZE	EXAMPLE
the first word in a sentence	Just then, Papa appeared.
the first word in a line of dialogue	"But what will happen to Hachiko?" I asked.
the pronoun I	I went to see Hachiko.
a proper noun or adjective	Shibuya Station is enormous now.
a person's title if used as part of the name	Dr. Ueno said, "His name is Hachiko."

Read It

1. Correct the capitalization in each of the following sentences. Explain the reasons for your corrections.

   a. hachiko was born in japan in november of 1923.

   b. the loyal dog walked from his home to shibuya station each day.

   c. "are you kentaro?" the old man asked. "i am mr. kobayashi."

2. Reread paragraph 5 of "Hachiko: The True Story of a Loyal Dog." Mark the proper nouns.

Write It

Notebook Write a paragraph about Hachiko. Spell plural nouns correctly, and observe the rules of capitalization.

Hachiko: The True Story of a Loyal Dog **125**

© Pearson Education, Inc., or its affiliates. All rights reserved.

HOW LANGUAGE WORKS

Irregular Plural Nouns Point out to students that there are actually several rules for creating the plural form of irregular nouns. Explain that some nouns become plural by changing the vowel, for example, *tooth* and *teeth; man* and *men; foot* and *feet.* Then point out that some nouns form the plural by changing endings, for example, *cactus* and *cacti.* Tell students that there is yet another category of irregular plural nouns—those that do not change their form at all, for example, *scissors, deer,* and *sheep.* Encourage students to create their own list of words that follow each rule.

Conventions

Spelling and Capitalization Display the following list of irregular plural nouns for students:

ox, oxen
copy, copies
loaf, loaves

Explain that though these nouns do not form the plural by adding -s or -es, they do follow certain rules for forming the plural. Ask students if they can identify what those rules are.

Then explain that knowing how an irregular plural is spelled takes practice.

Next, provide the following models:
Adam had lunch with Uncle Robert at the Buzz Cafe.
The boy had lunch with his uncle at the restaurant.

Point out that the first example includes proper nouns, which are capitalized. The second example includes only common nouns, which are not capitalized. For more support, see **Conventions: Spelling and Capitalization.**

Read It

1. (a) Hachiko was born in Japan in November of 1923. (I capitalized Hachiko, Japan, and November because they are all proper nouns.) (b) The loyal dog walked from his home to Shibuya Station each day. (I capitalized the first word of the sentence as well as Shibuya Station because it is a proper noun.) (c) "Are you Kentaro?" the old man asked. "I am Mr. Kobayashi." (I capitalized the first word in the sentence, Kentaro because it is a name, and Mr. Kobayashi because it is a title and name.)

2. Kentaro, Dr. Ueno, Papa, Tokyo Imperial University

Write It

Students' paragraphs will vary but should include several plural nouns, both regular and irregular. Paragraphs should also contain no spelling or capitalization errors.

FORMATIVE ASSESSMENT

Conventions

- **If** students fail to identify words that need to be capitalized, **then** remind them to look for nouns that name *specific* things or people.
- **If** students struggle to spell irregular plural nouns, **then** have them think of other nouns that are spelled similarly and ask them to recall how those nouns form the plural.

For Reteach and Practice, see **Conventions: Spelling and Capitalization. (RP)**

Whole-Class Learning **125**

Writing to Sources

Explain to students that when they write their own version, or adaptation, of the story, they should think about what they will need to change in order to tell the story from Hachiko's point of view. As students are rereading the story, remind them to make notes about how Hachiko relates to the people in the story and how he might express his thoughts about his life experiences. For more support, see **Writing to Sources: Story Adaptation.** 📄

Reflect on Your Writing

1. Responses will vary, but students should give examples of how they told the adaptation and what was challenging about rewriting the story.

2. Responses will vary.

Why These Words? Students should list specific words they used to detail the thoughts, feelings, and senses Hachiko experienced throughout the story.

FORMATIVE ASSESSMENT

Writing to Sources

• **If** students are unable to relate the story from Hachiko's point of view, **then** have them work with a partner to review the selection, listing each of Hachiko's experiences with the humans in the story and how he might have expressed what was happening around him. For Reteach and Practice, see **Writing to Sources: Story Adaptation. (RP)** 📄

EFFECTIVE EXPRESSION

HACHIKO: THE TRUE STORY OF
A LOYAL DOG

STANDARDS

Writing
• Write narratives to convey real or imagined experiences or events using effective technique, relevant descriptive details, and well-structured event sequences.
  a. Engage and orient the reader by establishing a context and introducing a narrator and/or characters; organize an event sequence that unfolds naturally and logically.

• Draw evidence from literary or informational texts to support analysis, reflection, and research.
  a. Apply *grade 6 Reading standards* to literature.

Speaking and Listening
• Engage effectively in a range of collaborative discussions with diverse partners on *grade 6 topics, texts, and issues,* building on others' ideas and expressing their own clearly.
  a. Come to discussions prepared, having read or studied required material; explicitly draw on that preparation by referring to evidence on the topic, text, or issue to probe and reflect on ideas under discussion.
  b. Follow rules for collegial discussions, set specific goals and deadlines, and define individual roles as needed.

• Present claims and findings, sequencing ideas logically and using pertinent descriptions, facts, and details to accentuate main ideas or themes; use appropriate eye contact, adequate volume, and clear pronunciation

Writing to Sources

"Hachiko: The True Story of a Loyal Dog" tells the story of a boy and a dog. This story is narrated by Kentaro, a character in the story. Readers get to learn about Hachiko through Kentaro's eyes.

> **Assignment**
>
> Write your own version, or **story adaptation,** of "Hachiko: The True Story of a Loyal Dog." In your adaptation, change the narrator, and tell the story through Hachiko's eyes. Follow these steps:
>
> • Reread the story, and identify main plot events.
>
> • Take careful note of Hachiko's actions. Also, note his relationships with Dr. Ueno, Mr. Kobayashi, and other human beings in the story.
>
> • Then, relate the story from Hachiko's point of view. As Hachiko tells the story, use details that show what he saw, smelled, heard, and felt as he lived through his experiences.

Vocabulary and Conventions Connection Consider including several of the concept vocabulary words. Also, remember to follow spelling and capitalization rules when writing.

timidly	anxiously	patiently
thoughtfully	silently	

- -

Reflect on Your Writing

After you have written your story adaptation, answer the following questions.

1. What was the most challenging part of the assignment?

2. How might you revise your story to improve it?

3. **Why These Words?** The words you choose make a difference in your writing. Which words did you specifically choose to bring your narrator to life?

© Pearson Education, Inc., or its affiliates. All rights reserved.

DIGITAL PERSPECTIVES

Illuminating the Text Find and show images of service dogs working with the disabled, for example service dogs for the blind or the wheelchair-bound. Ask students to notice whether any of the dogs look like Hachiko or whether they all seem to be of a similar size and breed. You might want to note that German Shepherds and Labrador Retrievers are frequently used as service dogs because they have the kinds of characteristics that are needed for such work. Discuss with students why loyalty and intelligence would be necessary characteristics for service dogs and why people likely form close bonds with their service dogs.

Speaking and Listening

The unique relationship between dogs and people is important in many stories you may have heard or read.

Assignment

Briefly research a real-life account of a dog who performed a heroic act. Then, hold a **partner discussion** with a classmate. During the discussion, share the story you researched, and discuss similarities and differences between the dog heroes you learned about and Hachiko.

Follow these steps as a guide.

1. **Perform Research** Locate a story of a heroic dog that you enjoy. If you are researching online, choose specific keywords to narrow your search. For example, you might use the keywords "dog" and "hero." When you find a story you like, make a copy of it.

2. **Read Your Stories Aloud** Choose a partner, and take turns reading your stories aloud to each other. Read clearly, and vary your tone to give expression to the reading.

3. **Listen Closely** Listen attentively as your partner reads aloud. Take notes as you listen to use in your discussion.

4. **Discuss Your Observations** Once you have finished reading your stories aloud, talk about the similarities and differences you see between the dogs you researched and Hachiko.

5. **Evaluate** Use an evaluation guide like the one shown to evaluate your partner discussion.

DISCUSSION EVALUATION GUIDE

Rate each statement on a scale of 1 (not demonstrated) to 5 (demonstrated).

☐ Each partner was prepared to share stories, information, and observations.

☐ Each partner presented a story and related ideas in a focused way.

☐ Each partner listened closely and provided feedback and comments.

☐ Partners took turns speaking, and built on each other's ideas.

© Pearson Education, Inc., or its affiliates. All rights reserved.

✒ EVIDENCE LOG

Before moving on to a new selection, go to your Evidence Log and record what you learned from "Hachiko: The True Story of a Loyal Dog."

Hachiko: The True Story of a Loyal Dog **127**

Speaking and Listening

1. **Perform Research** Tell students that they will be researching a real-life story of a dog that performed a heroic act. Remind students to choose specific key words if there's a certain dog or act of heroism they wish to write about.

2. **Read Your Stories Aloud** Remind partners to read slowly and to vary their intonation to avoid reading in a flat, monotone style. Tell students that if the story they have found is particularly long, they might summarize the story for their partner.

3. **Listen Closely** Tell students that to better understand the main idea of a story that is read aloud, they should listen for transition words, such as *first, then,* and *finally*.

4. **Discuss Your Observations** Have students point out what they learned about the dog heroes they researched and how those dogs compare with Hachiko.

5. **Evaluate** Encourage students to make at least one supportive comment.

For more support, see **Speaking and Listening: Partner Discussion.** 📄

Evidence Log Support students in completing their Evidence Log. This paced activity will help prepare them for the Performance-Based Assessment at the end of the unit.

FORMATIVE ASSESSMENT

Speaking and Listening

If students struggle to find a story to read and discuss, **then** provide them with a list of simple search terms, such as "lifesaving dogs," "heroic dogs," or "true dog stories." For Reteach and Practice, see **Speaking and Listening: Partner Discussion. (RP)** 📄

Selection Test

Administer the "Hachiko: The True Story of a Loyal Dog" Selection Test, which is available in both print and digital formats online in Assessments. 📄 ☑

PERSONALIZE FOR LEARNING

Strategic Support

Compare and Contrast If students have difficulty discussing similarities and differences between the story they found and Hachiko's story, encourage them to create a graphic organizer, such as a chart or a Venn diagram, before their discussion to help them compare the stories. Suggest that they list the basic details of their story, such as the breed of dog they researched, what the dog did, and what happened to the dog, in one column and then list similar details about Hachiko in the other. Encourage students to use the chart to remind them of their talking points as they conduct their discussion.

Jump Start

Ask students to consider this question: *Why are people interested in animal behavior?*

Point out that stories about animals, both domesticated and wild, are all over television and the Internet. Ask students to think about why they might find these stories interesting or even amazing. Then guide students to consider the same question as it applies to the texts they just read. Have them share their ideas, citing specific examples from both selections of why animal behavior intrigues us.

Write an Explanatory Essay

Help students understand the assignment. Explain that they will answer a question about how the authors of the two selections portray the animals as intelligent individuals.

Students should complete the assignment using word processing software to take advantage of editing tools and features.

Elements of an Explanatory Essay

Remind students that an effective informative/explanatory text, such as "Reading Buddies," contains all of the listed required elements.

MAKE IT INTERACTIVE

Project "Reading Buddies" from the Interactive Teacher's Edition and have students identify the elements of an explanatory essay, such as introduction, thesis statement, reasons, evidence, and conclusion.

Academic Vocabulary

Ask students to review the concept vocabulary words in their notebooks. Reviewing their work on the academic vocabulary will help them think about how the selection authors portrayed the animals.

WRITING TO SOURCES

• *from* MY LIFE WITH THE CHIMPANZEES

• HACHIKO: THE TRUE STORY OF A LOYAL DOG

🔧 Tool Kit
Student Model of an Explanatory Essay

ACADEMIC VOCABULARY

As you craft your explanatory essay, consider using some of the academic vocabulary you learned in the beginning of the unit.

exclude
illustrate
community
elaborate
objective

☰ STANDARDS

Writing
• Write informative/explanatory texts to examine a topic and convey ideas, concepts, and information through the selection, organization, and analysis of relevant content.
• Write routinely over extended time frames and shorter time frames for a range of discipline-specific tasks, purposes, and audiences.

Write an Explanatory Essay

You have read an excerpt from a memoir and a work of historical fiction that demonstrate ways in which people and animals interact. In the excerpt from *My Life With the Chimpanzees,* Dr. Jane Goodall describes what she learned about chimpanzees, including how intelligent they are and how they behave in a group. In "Hachiko: The True Story of a Loyal Dog," Pamela S. Turner tells the story of a dog's loyalty to his owner.

Assignment

Use your knowledge of the excerpt from *My Life With the Chimpanzees* and "Hachiko: The True Story of a Loyal Dog" to consider qualities that human beings and animals seem to share. Write an **explanatory essay** that answers the question:

> What qualities do Goodall and Turner believe people and animals share?

Think about the experiences Goodall has with the chimpanzees and the way Turner describes Dr. Ueno and Hachiko. Identify feelings and ways of behaving that the two authors suggest animals and people have in common.

Elements of an Explanatory Essay

An **explanatory essay** uses facts, examples, and other information to explain a subject or topic. The purpose of an explanatory essay is to help readers better understand a topic.

A successful explanatory essay contains these elements:

• an introduction that states a clear central idea, or thesis
• a logical organization that helps readers follow the explanation
• concrete details, quotations, and examples that support the explanation
• transitions that connect ideas and show the relationships among them
• precise language and vocabulary to explain a topic
• a formal style
• a concluding statement that completes the explanation given in the essay

Model Informative/Explanatory Text For a model of a well-crafted informative/explanatory text, see the Launch Text, "Reading Buddies."

Challenge yourself to find all of the elements of an explanatory essay in the text. You will have an opportunity to review these elements as you prepare to write your own essay.

LAUNCH TEXT

Reading Buddies

© Pearson Education, Inc., or its affiliates. All rights reserved.

Kelly Gallagher, M.Ed.

The Best Writer in the Room Intensive modeling is one of the most effective ways to improve writing instruction. When teachers model at every stage of the writing process, they stop *assigning* writing and start *teaching* it. While you are teaching writing through this Performance Task, show your students

how you attack these parts of the assignment:
Prewriting Brainstorm reasons and facts and ask students to add their own ideas to your list. List types of evidence you could use.
Drafting Outline the explanatory essay and draft alongside students.

Revising Use your model or a student model as an example.
Do this work in front of students each time. While it may seem more efficient to follow the same steps with each class or show a perfectly polished essay, don't take this path. If you authentically model the work of writing, students may be more open to the work of writing.

Prewriting / Planning

Write a Working Thesis Now that you have read and thought about the selections, write a sentence in which you state your **thesis**, or central idea. As you continue to write your essay, you may revise your thesis or even change it entirely. For now, it will help guide you in developing ideas and choosing supporting details from the selections.

Working Thesis: _____

_____ .

Gather Evidence From Sources After you have crafted a working thesis, look for evidence from the two texts to support it. Take notes on the following types of evidence you may want to use:

- **facts:** information that can be proved true

- **examples:** descriptions of specific people, things, or situations that support a general idea

Connect Across Texts The excerpt from *My Life With the Chimpanzees* includes facts about many different chimpanzees. In contrast, "Hachiko: The True Story of a Loyal Dog" focuses on one dog and his relationships with the people who care for him. The two texts offer different kinds of evidence, but they are both valuable. As you write, work to include details from both texts. Incorporate that evidence in different ways; for example, consider using both paraphrases and direction quotations.

- **Direct quotations** are an author's exact words. Use direct quotations when the precise words an author uses are especially interesting or important.

- If the author's ideas are valuable, but the specific words are not as important, **paraphrase** the information by restating it in your own words. Be careful to choose precise language and vocabulary when you paraphrase to be sure you accurately communicate the author's ideas.

Incorporating evidence in different ways will help you to express and support your ideas about the topic with accuracy and precision.

EVIDENCE LOG

Review your Evidence Log and identify key details you may want to cite in your essay.

STANDARDS
Writing
Write informative/explanatory texts to examine a topic and convey ideas, concepts, and information through the selection, organization, and analysis of relevant content.
b. Develop the topic with relevant facts, definitions, concrete details, quotations, or other information and examples.
d. Use precise language and domain-specific vocabulary to inform about or explain the topic.

Performance Task: Write an Explanatory Essay **129**

© Pearson Education, Inc., or its affiliates. All rights reserved.

Prewriting/Planning

Write a Working Thesis Explain to students that the first step in writing an explanatory essay is to come up with a controlling idea. Point out that a thesis statement gives an essay purpose and direction and that their thesis statement should be a response to the question: *What qualities do Goodall and Turner believe people and animals share?*

Gather Evidence From Sources Have students review their Evidence Log to find possible support for their thesis statement. If they do not have sufficient evidence in their Evidence Log, encourage them to review the selections to look for details, both facts about the animals and examples from the events the authors relay, that support their thesis statement.

Connect Across Texts Remind students that they may repeat a fact or an example from the selections and paraphrase it or put it in their own words. But point out that if they want to repeat a statement by one of the authors, they must enclose the statement in quotation marks and attribute it to the author to avoid plagiarizing.

PERSONALIZE FOR LEARNING

Strategic Support

Finding Evidence Some students may need additional support to complete the planning process. Be prepared to support students in looking for evidence to support their thesis statement. Pair students with a partner and have them create a chart in which they list the evidence from each text that supports their thinking. For example:

Thesis statement: Dr. Goodall and Turner describe animal behavior using words associated with human behavior.	
Evidence from *My Life With the Chimpanzees*	Evidence from "Hachiko"
The chimpanzees *kiss and embrace*.	Hachiko was *patiently waiting*.

Drafting

Organize Your Essay Point out to students that the organization of any essay is essentially the same. There is an introduction, a body, and a conclusion, and through it all runs the common thread of the thesis statement. Explain that completing an Explanatory Essay Outline of their own will help them recognize what is required in each part of the essay.

Write a First Draft Remind students that the main goal of the first draft is to get their ideas on paper, incorporating all the elements of an explanatory essay. As students write their first draft, remind them to refer back to their outline to ensure a logical organization.

Encourage students to begin their essay with a question or a quotation that gets the reader's attention.

STANDARDS
Writing

Write informative/explanatory texts to examine a topic and convey ideas, concepts, and information through the selection, organization, and analysis of relevant content.

a. Introduce a topic; organize ideas, concepts, and information, using strategies such as definition, classification, comparison/contrast, and cause/effect; include formatting, graphics, and multimedia when useful to aiding comprehension.

f. Provide a concluding statement or section that follows from the information or explanation presented.

Drafting

Organize Your Essay As you write your essay, organize your ideas and evidence into three main sections:

- the **introduction** in which you introduce your topic and your thesis, and identify the main points you will make in the essay
- the **body** in which you explain the main points in more detail
- the **conclusion** in which you circle back to your thesis and restate it in a new way

Each paragraph in the body of your essay should have a clear main idea that relates to your thesis. State the main idea in a **topic sentence**. Then, explain the main idea and use details from the text to show how it is accurate or correct. The outline shows how the Launch Text is organized. Notice how each body paragraph includes a main idea that supports the thesis of the essay. Use it as a model to create an outline for your essay.

LAUNCH TEXT

Model: "Reading Buddies" Outline

INTRODUCTION
Paragraph 1 introduces the topic. Paragraph 2 introduces the thesis: *Reading programs that team up dogs and children help kids improve their reading skills.*

BODY
Paragraphs 3 and 4 provide background information: *There are many reasons kids struggle with reading.*

Paragraph 5 supports the thesis: *Dogs are the ideal reading companions for many reasons.*

Paragraph 6 provides an example to support the point made in paragraph 5: *One girl finished reading a whole book to a dog.*

Paragraph 7 supports the thesis: *Dogs enable kids to practice their reading skills in a nonthreatening way.*

Paragraph 8 supports the thesis: *Visiting schools and libraries helps dogs become more well-adjusted.*

CONCLUSION
Paragraph 9 restates the thesis: *The reading program helps both children and dogs.*

Explanatory Essay Outline

INTRODUCTION

_____

_____

BODY

_____

_____

CONCLUSION

Write a First Draft Use your outline to write your first draft. Remember to state your thesis in your introduction and to provide a strong conclusion. Cite details and examples from the texts to support your thesis.

© Pearson Education, Inc., or its affiliates. All rights reserved.

Jim Cummins, Ph.D.

Sentence Frames Students learning English may be challenged by a blank page. Support them with scaffolding to help them organize their explanatory essays and flesh out their outlines. They may benefit from using sentence frames like the following to help them map out their writing.

Introduction: Dr. Goodall and Turner believe people and animals share these qualities: _____.

Evidence from the text: My point of view is supported by the fact that _____.

Counterclaim: Others may not say that animals and people have things in common because _____, but this view is problematic because _____.

Remind students that the writing process is recursive, and they will be able to refine their outlines and sentence frames as they draft. These are simply tools to help them organize their thoughts before they begin writing.

LANGUAGE DEVELOPMENT: CONVENTIONS

Revising for Correct Pronoun Case

A **pronoun** is a word that takes the place of a noun or another pronoun. English has three cases, or forms, of pronouns. **Nominative, or subjective, case** is used for the subjects of verbs and for subject predicates. **Objective case** is used for direct and indirect objects and for objects of prepositions. **Possessive case** is used to show ownership.

Read It

This chart shows personal pronouns grouped by case.

CASE	PRONOUNS	FUNCTION IN A SENTENCE	EXAMPLE
Nominative/ Subjective	I, we, you, he, she, it, they	Subject of a verb	*She* told a story.
		Subject predicate	The storyteller was *she*.
Objective	me, us, you, him, her, it, them	Direct object	Amy told *it* to Anthony.
		Indirect object	Amy told *him* the story.
		Object of a preposition	Amy told the story to *him*.
Possessive	my, mine, our, ours, your, yours, his, her hers, its, their, theirs,	To show ownership	Amy told *her* story to Anthony.

Write It

Pronoun case can be confusing when you use compound subjects or objects. To make sure you have chosen the correct case, try using the pronoun alone with the verb. If it sounds wrong, it probably is.

1. **Compound Subject / Example Sentence:** The <u>dog and *me*</u> wait by the station.
   Pronoun Used Alone: *Me* wait by the station.
   Conclusion: The objective case sounds wrong. The nominative case is needed. The sentence should read: The <u>dog and *I*</u> wait by the station.

2. **Compound Object / Example Sentence:** The chimps play with <u>Jane and *I*</u>.
   Pronoun Used Alone: The chimps play with *I*.
   Conclusion: The nominative case sounds wrong. The objective case is needed. The sentence should read: The chimps play with <u>Jane and *me*</u>.

⊞ STANDARDS
Language
Demonstrate command of the conventions of standard English grammar and usage when writing or speaking.
  a. Ensure that pronouns are in the proper case.
  e. Recognize variations from standard English in their own and others' writing and speaking, and identify and use strategies to improve expression in conventional language.

© Pearson Education, Inc., or its affiliates. All rights reserved.

Revising for Correct Pronoun Case

Read It

Point out that using the correct pronoun case can be tricky. For example, it is not uncommon for people to say, "Between you and I" when the correct pronoun should be "me." Emphasize that using the correct pronoun case is a matter of following a couple of simple rules.

MAKE IT INTERACTIVE

Project "Reading Buddies" from the Interactive Teacher's Edition and ask students to identify additional examples of pronouns in the nominative/subjective, objective, and possessive case.

- <u>He</u> is part of a program that began in Utah. (nominative/subjective)

- And some just haven't found a book that grabs <u>them</u>. (objective)

- <u>They</u> aren't in a hurry, so <u>you</u> can read at <u>your</u> own pace. (nominative/subjective, nominative/subjective, possessive)

- Reading calms the animals down and makes <u>them</u> more comfortable around people. (objective)

Write It

As students revise their draft, they should make sure that they have used pronouns where necessary to avoid repeating a name. Point out that the chart is a handy tool for checking that they have used the correct pronoun case in their essay.

Consider reviewing additional examples of pronoun use and the methods for testing that those cases are correct. For example,

- <u>She</u> and the chimps lived in Gombe.
  TEST: Block out the rest of the subject: She lived in Gombe.

- The scientist is <u>she</u>.
  TEST: Switch the noun and pronoun: She is the scientist.

- No one was a more loyal dog than <u>he</u>.
  TEST: Complete the phrase: No one was a more loyal dog than he (was).

PERSONALIZE FOR LEARNING

English Language Support

Pronouns Pronoun case can be confusing for English Language Learners. Explain to students that the nominative/subjective case pronouns perform the action in a sentence. For example, <u>She</u> walks to the store. Then point out that the objective case is the one receiving the action. For example, Amal likes <u>him</u>. To support students as they revise their essays, pair them with a partner and have them identify places in their essays where they could add or correct personal pronouns. **ALL LEVELS**

Revising

Evaluating Your Draft Before students begin revising their writing, they should first evaluate their draft to make sure it contains all the required elements, is organized well, and adheres to the norms and conventions of explanatory essays.

Revising for Focus and Organization

Use Transitions As students revise their drafts, encourage them to review their writing to make sure that the organization is logical. Have them check to make sure that they use a variety of transitions to connect ideas, and that paragraphs flow from one to the other in a way that makes sense.

Revising for Evidence and Elaboration

Use a Formal Style Remind students that evidence should be supported by facts and concrete examples that support their thesis. Encourage students to use academic vocabulary if possible, and to avoid using superlative adjectives, words that suggest opinion or bias, and informal language that is not appropriate for the classroom.

Revising

Evaluating Your Draft

Use the following checklist to evaluate the effectiveness of your first draft. Then, use your evaluation and the instruction on this page to guide your revision.

FOCUS AND ORGANIZATION	EVIDENCE AND ELABORATION	CONVENTIONS
☐ Provides an introduction that includes a thesis statement.	☐ Develops main ideas with strong facts and relevant details from the texts.	☐ Uses correct pronoun case.
☐ Establishes a logical organization that is easy for readers to follow.	☐ Provides examples for each major point.	☐ Establishes and maintains a formal style.
☐ Provides a conclusion that follows from the ideas presented earlier in the essay.	☐ Uses precise language to express and support ideas.	
☐ Uses transitions that show clear relationships among ideas.		

🔧 WORD NETWORK

Include words from your Word Network in your explanatory essay.

Revising for Focus and Organization

Use Transitions Reread your draft, paying careful attention to the organization of your ideas. Note any places where the relationship of one idea to the next is not clear. Consider using transitions to improve the flow of your ideas.

TO SHOW . . .	TRANSITIONS
Similarities	*equally important, moreover, as well as, similarly, in addition*
Differences	*however, on the other hand, although, despite, in contrast, yet*
Examples	*for instance, including, for example, especially, in other words*

Revising for Evidence and Elaboration

Use a Formal Style An explanatory essay uses facts and examples to support a central idea. It should not include informal statements of your opinion. As you revise your essay, review your word choices. Avoid the following types of words or statements:

- words that suggest a bias, such as *excellent* or *awful,* unless supported by factual evidence
- superlative adjectives, such as *most, least, best,* and *worst,* unless supported by factual evidence

▤ STANDARDS
Writing
Write informative/explanatory texts to examine a topic and convey ideas, concepts, and information through the selection, organization, and analysis of relevant content.
  c. Use appropriate transitions to clarify the relationships among ideas and concepts.
  e. Establish and maintain a formal style.

© Pearson Education, Inc., or its affiliates. All rights reserved.

HOW LANGUAGE WORKS

Personal Pronouns As students revise their explanatory essays, remind them to use personal pronouns to avoid repeating nouns and to check to make sure that the pronouns they have used are in the correct case. Make a chart like the one below available for students as they revise:

PERSONAL PRONOUN CASES

Number	Subjective	Objective	Possessive
Singular	I, you, he, she, it	me, you, him, her, it	mine, yours, his, hers, its
Plural	we, you, they	us, you, them	ours, yours, theirs

PEER REVIEW

Exchange essays with a classmate. Use the checklist to evaluate your classmate's essay and provide supportive feedback.

1. Is the thesis clear?

☐ yes ☐ no   If no, explain what confused you.

2. Are ideas clearly stated and supported by facts and examples?

☐ yes ☐ no   If no, point out which points need more support.

3. Does the conclusion logically wrap up the essay?

☐ yes ☐ no   If no, suggest information that you feel is missing.

4. What is the strongest part of your classmate's essay?

_____

Editing and Proofreading

Edit for Conventions Reread your draft for accuracy and consistency. Correct errors in grammar and word usage. Review your essay to be sure the pronouns you use are in the proper case. Refer to the strategies given in the Language Development section to identify and correct errors in pronoun case.

Proofread for Accuracy Read your draft carefully, correcting errors in spelling and punctuation. Remember to check the selection texts for the correct spelling of proper names.

Publishing and Presenting

Create a final version of your essay. Then, using the information from your essay and computer software, develop, design, and present an **informative booklet** about human and animal interaction. Choose a font or style that is easy to read and creates an attractive text. Then, exchange booklets with your classmates and give one another feedback. Take turns noting which booklets contained information that was similar to the information in yours, and which suggested very different ideas. Contribute in positive, supportive ways to the discussion, and listen closely when it is someone else's turn to speak.

Reflecting

Think about what you learned by writing your essay and what you learned from reading the essays and booklets of your classmates. What could you do differently the next time you need to write an explanatory essay that might make it stronger?

:≡ STANDARDS

Writing
• Produce clear and coherent writing in which the development, organization, and style are appropriate to task, purpose, and audience.

• With some guidance and support from peers and adults, develop and strengthen writing as needed by planning, revising, editing, rewriting, or trying a new approach.

• Use technology, including the Internet, to produce and publish writing as well as to interact and collaborate with others; demonstrate sufficient command of keyboarding skills to type a minimum of three pages in a single sitting.

Performance Task: Write an Explanatory Essay **133**

© Pearson Education, Inc., or its affiliates. All rights reserved.

Peer Review

As students read their peers' work, remind them that the focus is on clarity and completeness. Tell students that the purpose of the peer review is to help one another write more clearly. Students should make note of places in the essay where the writer could use more detail to add interest or to clarify a point.

Editing and Proofreading

Remind students that proper names must be capitalized. Point out, for example, some of the proper names in the selections: Jane Goodall, Gombe, Tanzania, David Greybeard, Hachiko, and Japan. Then remind students that their spell checks on their computer will likely note some of the names, such as Gombe and Hachiko, are misspelled. Suggest that students verify the spelling by checking it against the selections.

Publishing and Presenting

As students prepare their informative booklets about human and animal interaction, suggest that they add graphics or images to the design. Encourage them to look closely at the final product on the computer before printing, adding boldface to titles when necessary and making sure that paragraph breaks are clear.

Before students review their classmate's informative booklet, remind them to point out the booklet's strong points as well as areas that could use improvement. Have students be sure to use formal language when making comments.

Reflecting

Suggest that students jot down at least one piece of information they learned from reading the peer's work.

PERSONALIZE FOR LEARNING

English Language Support

Some English Language Learners may be reluctant to elaborate on what they found similar or different in another classmate's informative booklet. Encourage these students by asking them questions that require them to elaborate or by having a partner ask them questions, such as "How is that idea similar to one you wrote?"

Ensure that they feel encouraged to speak by nodding and otherwise noting that they are being heard and that they have sufficient time to formulate their response. **ALL LEVELS**

SMALL-GROUP LEARNING

How can people and animals relate to each other?

People and animals have long formed extremely close bonds. For almost as long as humans have existed, we have lived and depended on animals. During Small-Group Learning, students will read selections that explore the strong ties between people and animals.

Small-Group Learning Strategies ▶

Review the Learning Strategies with students and explain that as they work through Small-Group Learning they will develop strategies to work in small-group environments.

- Have students watch the video on Small-Group Learning Strategies.
- A video on this topic is available online in the Professional Development Center.

You may wish to discuss some action items to add to the chart as a class before students complete it on their own. For example, for "Support others," you might solicit the following from students:

- Share notes with your group.
- Encourage others in your group to share and develop their ideas.

Block Scheduling

Each day in this Pacing Plan represents a 40–50 minute class period. Teachers using block scheduling may combine days to reflect their class schedule. In addition, teachers may revise pacing to differentiate and support core instruction by integrating components and resources as students require.

📅 **Pacing Plan**

OVERVIEW: SMALL-GROUP LEARNING

ESSENTIAL QUESTION:

How can people and animals relate to each other?

Sometimes animals communicate with other kinds of animals. Other times, they communicate with people. How is the relationship between animal species similar to and different from the relationship between animals and people? You will work in a group to continue your exploration of these relationships.

Small-Group Learning Strategies

Throughout your life, in school, in your community, and in your career, you will continue to learn and work with others.

Review these strategies and the actions you can take to practice them as you work in teams. Add ideas of your own for each step. Use these strategies during Small-Group Learning.

STRATEGY	ACTION PLAN
Prepare	• Complete your assignments so that you are prepared for group work. • Organize your thinking so you can contribute to your group's discussion. •
Participate fully	• Make eye contact to signal that you are listening and taking in what is being said. • Use text evidence when making a point. •
Support others	• Build on ideas from others in your group. • Invite others who have not yet spoken to join the discussion. •
Clarify	• Paraphrase the ideas of others to ensure that your understanding is correct. • Ask follow-up questions. •

© Pearson Education, Inc., or its affiliates. All rights reserved.

SCAN FOR MULTIMEDIA

Introduce Whole-Class Learning

Performance Task

Unit Introduction

from My Life With the Chimpanzees

Hachiko: The True Story of a Loyal Dog

| 1 | 2 | 3 | 4 | 5 | 6 | 7 | 8 | 9 | 10 | 11 | 12 | 13 | 14 | 15 | 16 | 17 | 18 |

CONTENTS

PERFORMANCE TASK

SPEAKING AND LISTENING FOCUS
Deliver an Informative Presentation

The Small-Group readings explore ways in which people and animals relate to or communicate with one another. After reading, your group will create an informative multimedia presentation about the ideas presented in these texts.

Overview: Small-Group Learning **135**

Contents

Selections Circulate among groups as they preview the selections. You might encourage groups to discuss any knowledge they already have about any of the selections or the situations and settings shown in the photographs. Students may wish to take a poll within their group to determine which selections look the most interesting.

Remind students that communicating and collaborating in groups is an important skill that they will use throughout their lives—in school, in their careers, and in their community.

Performance Task

Deliver an Informative Presentation Give groups time to read about and briefly discuss the informative multimedia presentation they will create after reading. Encourage students to do some preliminary thinking about the types of media they may want to use. This may help focus their subsequent reading and group discussion.

© Pearson Education, Inc., or its affiliates. All rights reserved.

Introduce
Small-Group
Learning

Introduce
Independent Learning

Performance Task

Performance-Based
Assessment

A Blessing

Predators

Monkey Master

Black Cowboy, Wild Horses

Independent
Learning

| 19 | 20 | 21 | 22 | 23 | 24 | 25 | 26 | 27 | 28 | 29 | 30 | 31 | 32 | 33 | 34 | 35 | 36 |

SMALL-GROUP LEARNING

SMALL-GROUP LEARNING

Working as a Team

1. **Take a Position** Remind groups to let all members share their responses. You may wish to set a time limit for this discussion.

2. **List Your Rules** You may want to have groups share their lists of rules and consolidate them into a master list to be displayed and followed by all groups.

3. **Apply the Rules** As you circulate among the groups, ensure that students are staying on task. Consider a short time limit for this step.

4. **Name Your Group** This task can be creative and fun. If students have trouble coming up with a name, suggest that they think of something related to the unit topic. Encourage groups to share their names with the class.

5. **Create a Communication Plan** Encourage groups to include in their plans agreed-upon times during the day to share ideas. They should also devise a method for recording and saving their communications.

Accountable Talk

Remind students that groups should communicate politely. You can post these Accountable Talk suggestions and encourage students to add their own. Students should:

Remember to . . .
Ask clarifying questions.

Which sounds like . . .
Can you please repeat what you said?
Would you give me an example?
I think you said _____. Did I understand you?

Remember to . . .
Explain your thinking.

Which sounds like . . .
I believe _____ is true because _____.
I feel that _____ because _____.

Remember to . . .
Build on the ideas of others.

Which sounds like . . .
When _____ said _____, it made me think of _____.

Working as a Team

1. **Take a Position** In your group, discuss the following question:

   What are some ways that animals can communicate with each other and with other animal species?

   As you take turns sharing your ideas, be sure to provide examples that illustrate them. After all group members have shared, discuss the ways in which animal communication is similar to and different from human communication.

2. **List Your Rules** As a group, decide on the rules that you will follow as you work together. Two examples are provided. Add two more of your own. You may add or revise rules based on your experience together.

   • Everyone should participate in group discussions.

   • People should not interrupt.

   • _____
     _____

   • _____
     _____

3. **Apply the Rules** Practice working as a group. Share what you have learned about the ways in which people and animals relate to one another. Make sure each person in the group contributes. Take notes and be prepared to share with the class one thing that you heard from another member of your group.

4. **Name Your Group** Choose a name that reflects the unit topic.

   Our group's name: _____

5. **Create a Communication Plan** Decide how you want to share information with one another. For example, you might use online collaboration tools, email, or instant messaging.

   Our group's decision: _____
   _____

© Pearson Education, Inc., or its affiliates. All rights reserved.

FACILITATING SMALL-GROUP LEARNING

Forming Groups You may wish to form groups for Small-Group Learning so that each consists of students with different learning abilities. Some students may be adept at organizing information whereas other may have strengths related to generating or synthesizing information. A good mix of abilities can make the experience of Small-Group Learning dynamic and productive.

Making a Schedule

First, find out the due dates for the Small-Group activities. Then, preview the texts and activities with your group and make a schedule for completing the tasks.

SELECTION	ACTIVITIES	DUE DATE
A Blessing		
Predators		
Monkey Master		
Black Cowboy, Wild Horses		

Working on Group Projects

As your group works together, you'll find it more effective if each person has a specific role. Different projects require different roles. Before beginning a project, discuss the necessary roles, and choose one for each group member. Here are some possible roles; add your own ideas.

Project Manager: monitors the schedule and keeps everyone on task

Researcher: organizes research activities

Recorder: takes notes during group meetings

_____

_____

_____

_____

© Pearson Education, Inc., or its affiliates. All rights reserved.

SCAN FOR
MULTIMEDIA

Overview: Small-Group Learning **137**

Making a Schedule

Encourage groups to preview the reading selections and to consider how long it will take them to complete the activities accompanying each selection. Point out that they can adjust the due dates for particular selections as needed as they work on their small-group projects. However, they must complete all assigned tasks before the group Performance Task is due. Encourage groups to review their schedules upon completing the activities for each selection to make sure they are on track to meet the final due date.

Working on Group Projects

Point out to groups that the roles they assign can also be changed later. Students might have to make changes based on who is best at doing what. Try to make sure that there is no favoritism, cliquishness, or stereotyping by gender or other means in the assignment of roles.

Also, you should review the roles each group assigns to its members. Based on your understanding of students' individual strengths, you might find it necessary to suggest some changes.

AUTHOR'S PERSPECTIVE   Ernest Morrell, Ph.D.

Supporting Small-Group Learning Because the dominant mode of discourse in classrooms has historically been teacher-led, many students may not be immediately comfortable discussing and collaborating in groups. The first few times students meet in their groups, you may need to provide additional support by setting expectations for collaborative behavior and discussions.

Remind students that it is important for all group members to contribute to discussion, but that no one member of the group should monopolize discussion. Whether students are speaking or listening, they should be active participants. Visit groups to explain that even when students aren't speaking, they should be listening to other group members and noting important points that they would like to build upon when it is their turn to speak.

Small-Group Learning   **137**

A Blessing

🔊 AUDIO SUMMARIES
Audio summaries of "A Blessing" are available online in both English and Spanish in the Interactive Teacher's Edition or Unit Resources. Assigning these summaries prior to reading the selection may help students build additional background knowledge and set a context for their first read.

Summary

The poem "A Blessing," by James Wright, involves a mystical, spiritually-tinged meeting between humans and animals. A pair of travelers are driving near Rochester, Minnesota. They encounter a pair of ponies in a fenced pasture by the road. The ponies come out from the trees welcomingly, and the travelers step into their pasture. They feel affection for each other. The ponies' shyness and affection perhaps mirrors that of the narrator and his friend.

Insight

This poem portrays the animals as straightforwardly positive and kind. The ponies seem delicate, friendly, and loving.

ESSENTIAL QUESTION:
How can people and animals relate to each other?

Connection to Essential Question

"A Blessing" offers an evocative response to the Essential Question, "How can people and animals relate to each other?" The loveliness and solitude of the horses inspire the poem's speaker, while the animals' welcoming nature and nuzzling affection seem to set an example of kindness and love. Wright's poem leaves an impression of the special relationship that has long existed between people and horses.

SMALL-GROUP LEARNING PERFORMANCE TASK
How can the bonds between people and animals be surprising?

Connection to Performance Tasks

Small-Group Learning Task The relationship between the ponies and the visitors will help students address the prompt. The ponies are welcoming, accepting, and calm when they are approached by two travelers, and the ponies share a quiet affection with their temporary visitors.

UNIT PERFORMANCE-BASED ASSESSMENT
How can animals and people help one another?

Unit Performance-Based Assessment Students may chose to cite this text as they prepare for the assessment. The love and kindness the animals seem to radiate gives the narrator an emotional and peaceful experience.

LESSON RESOURCES

	Making Meaning	**Language Development**
Lesson	**First Read** **Close Read** **Analyze the Text** **Analyze Craft and Structure**	**Concept Vocabulary** **Word Study** **Conventions**
Instructional Standards	**RL.4** Determine the meaning of words and phrases . . . **RL.10** By the end of the year, read and comprehend literature . . . **L.4** Determine or clarify the meaning of unknown and multiple-meaning words and phrases . . . **L.4.a** Use context as a clue . . .	**L.1** Demonstrate command of the conventions . . . **L.4** Determine or clarify the meaning of unknown and multiple-meaning words and phrases . . . **L.4.c** Consult reference materials . . .

▶ STUDENT RESOURCES

Available online in the Interactive Student Edition or Unit Resources	🔊 Selection Audio 📄 First-Read Guide: Poetry 📄 Close-Read Guide: Poetry	📄 Word Network

▶ TEACHER RESOURCES

Selection Resources Available online in the Interactive Teacher's Edition or Unit Resources	🔊 Audio Summaries ✎ Annotation Highlights 💬 EL Highlights 📄 English Language Support Lesson: Repetition and Alliteration 📄 A Blessing: Text Questions 📄 Analyze Craft and Structure: Elements of Poetry	📄 Concept Vocabulary and Word Study 📄 Conventions: Verbs and Verb Tenses
Reteach/Practice (RP) Available online in the Interactive Teacher's Edition or Unit Resources	📄 Analyze Craft and Structure: Elements of Poetry	📄 Word Study: Multiple-Meaning Words (RP) 📄 Conventions: Verbs and Verb Tenses (RP)
Assessment Available online in Assessments	📄 ☑ Selection Test	
My Resources	📄 A Unit 2 Answer Key is available online and in the Interactive Teacher's Edition.	

Reading Support

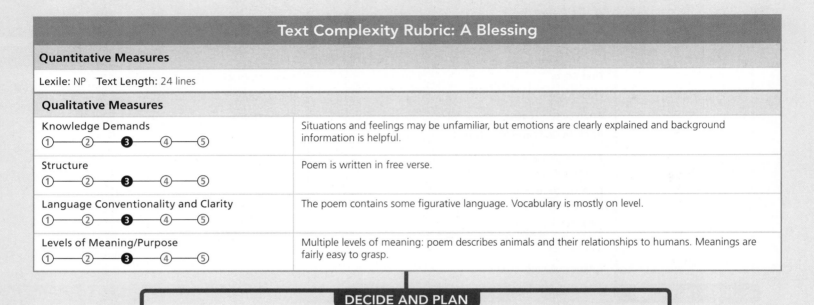

Text Complexity Rubric: A Blessing

Quantitative Measures

Lexile: NP   **Text Length:** 24 lines

Qualitative Measures

Knowledge Demands ①—②—**❸**—④—⑤	Situations and feelings may be unfamiliar, but emotions are clearly explained and background information is helpful.
Structure ①—②—**❸**—④—⑤	Poem is written in free verse.
Language Conventionality and Clarity ①—②—**❸**—④—⑤	The poem contains some figurative language. Vocabulary is mostly on level.
Levels of Meaning/Purpose ①—②—**❸**—④—⑤	Multiple levels of meaning: poem describes animals and their relationships to humans. Meanings are fairly easy to grasp.

DECIDE AND PLAN

English Language Support

Provide English learners with support for language and meaning as they read the selection.

Language Students may need help not only with the metaphors and similes themselves, but also with the structure of the language and the vocabulary. For example, in "A Blessing" point out that the author uses the pronouns *they, she,* and *her* instead of *the ponies* or *the pony* throughout the poem. Ask students to reread some of the phrases making this replacement in order to make sure they understand them. Then have them reread with the poem's original language.

Meaning Work with students to help them understand the meaning of figurative language by first understanding the literal meaning. For example, discuss the line "They bow shyly as wet swans." Make sure students understand what image the writer is trying to convey.

Strategic Support

Provide students with strategic support to ensure that they can successfully read the text.

Language Remind students that in the poem they are about to read, they may find metaphors and similes. Discuss the difference—similes use the word *like* or *as* to compare, whereas metaphors do not. Give an example from the poem, such as *delicate as the skin over a girl's wrist,* or *I would break Into blossom,* and ask students to be on the lookout for other such similes or metaphors.

Meaning For students who have difficulty understanding metaphors and similes, have them underline or list the phrases that they don't understand. Then have them read those phrases again and work with a partner to try to figure out the comparison the poet is making.

Challenge

Provide students who need to be challenged with ideas for how they can go beyond a simple interpretation of the text.

Text Analysis Ask students to make a list of all the metaphors and similes they find in the poem. Pair students and have one say a simile or metaphor (for example, *They bow shyly as wet swans).* and the other describe the image conveyed by these words and give their analysis of what they think the poet is trying to describe.

Written Response Using the similes and metaphors in the poem, ask students to write their own. For example, ask them what other images they could use to convey the connection between humans and animals.

TEACH

Read and Respond

Have groups read the selection and complete the Making Meaning and Language Development activities.

Standards Support Through Teaching and Learning Cycle

IDENTIFY NEEDS

Analyze results of the Beginning-of-Year Assessment, focusing on the items relating to Unit 2. Also take into consideration student performance to this point and your observations of where particular students struggle.

ANALYZE AND REVISE

- Analyze student work for evidence of student learning.
- Identify whether or not students have met the expectations in the standards.
- Identify implications for future instruction.

TEACH

Implement the planned lesson, and gather evidence of student learning.

DECIDE AND PLAN

- If students have performed poorly on items matching these standards, then provide selection scaffolds before assigning them the on-level lesson provided in the Student Edition.
- If students have done well on the Beginning-of-Year Assessment, then challenge them to keep progressing and learning by giving them opportunities to practice the skills in depth.
- Use the Selection Resources listed on the Planning pages for "A Blessing" to help students continually improve their ability to master the standards.

Instructional Standards: A Blessing

	Catching Up	This Year	Looking Forward
Reading	You may wish to administer the **Analyze Craft and Structure: Elements of Poetry (RP)** worksheet to help students understand and identify the author's choice of words and tone.	**RL.4** Determine the meaning of words and phrases as they are used in a text, including figurative and connotative meanings; analyze the impact of a specific word choice on meaning and tone.	Challenge students to make a list of words that impact the tone and meaning of the poems. Then have them discuss the list with a partner. What effect does each word have? Why did the author choose each word?
Language	You may wish to administer the **Conventions: Verbs and Verb Tenses (RP)** worksheet to help students understand verbs. You may wish to administer the **Word Study: Multiple-Meaning Words (RP)** worksheet to help students understand words that have more than one meaning.	**L.1** Demonstrate command of the conventions of standard English grammar and usage when writing or speaking. **L.4** Determine or clarify the meaning of unknown and multiple-meaning words and phrases based on *grade 6 reading and content,* choosing flexibly from a range of strategies.	Challenge students to use three verbs in sentences with the past tense, present tense, and future tense. Challenge students to create a list of five multiple-meaning words and write a sentence using each of their words.

Jump Start

FIRST READ Ask students to consider the following question: *Can animals and humans share an emotional connection?* Engage students in a classroom discussion about emotional connections between humans and animals. Remind them to offer specific reasons and evidence to back up their opinions. Encourage students to share their own personal experiences of connecting with animals.

A Blessing 🔊 📄

How do the horses respond to their human visitors? What effect does the female horse have on the speaker? Modeling questions such as these will help students connect to "A Blessing" and to the Small-Group Performance Task assignment. Selection audio and print capability for the selection are available in the Interactive Teacher's Edition.

Concept Vocabulary

Ask students to read the section on context clues and study the example sentence for synonyms. Have them discuss how synonyms can be used to help determine the meaning of unfamiliar words. Then encourage groups to think of other types of context clues they might encounter in a poem. Possibilities include elaborating details, contrast of ideas, and antonyms.

🔘 FIRST READ

Students should perform the steps of the first read independently.

NOTICE: You may want to encourage students to notice the words used to describe the ponies.

ANNOTATE: Remind students to mark any lines that include sound devices (such as onomatopoeia) or figurative language (such as metaphor).

CONNECT: Have students compare the encounter described in the poem with a meaningful encounter that they have had with an animal.

RESPOND: Students will answer questions to demonstrate understanding.

Point out to students that while they will always complete the Respond step at the end of the first read, the other steps will probably happen somewhat concurrently. You may wish to print copies of the **First-Read Guide: Poetry** for students to use. 📄

Comparing Texts

A BLESSING

In this lesson, you will read and compare two poems. First, you will complete the first-read and close-read activities for "A Blessing." The work you do with your group on this title will help prepare you for the comparing task.

PREDATORS

About the Author

James Wright (1927–1980) was a Pulitzer Prize–winning American poet born in Martins Ferry, Ohio. He was known as a master of a variety of writing styles, and for the beauty and emotional quality of his work. His early poems often focused on isolation and loneliness. However, his later poetry often praised the joy and comfort that could be found in the natural world.

📋 STANDARDS

Reading Literature
By the end of the year, read and comprehend literature, including stories, dramas, and poems, in the grades 6–8 text complexity band proficiently, with scaffolding as needed at the high end of the range.

Language
Determine or clarify the meaning of unknown and multiple-meaning words and phrases based on *grade 6 reading and content,* choosing flexibly from a range of strategies.
a. Use context as a clue to the meaning of a word or phrase.

138 UNIT 2 • ANIMAL ALLIES

A Blessing

Concept Vocabulary

As you perform your first read of "A Blessing" you will encounter these words.

| shyly | loneliness | blossom |

Context Clues To find the meaning of unfamiliar words, look for clues in the context, which is made up of words and punctuation that surround the unknown word. There are various types of context clues that may help you as you read. Here are two examples:

Synonyms: The horses <u>searched</u> and **foraged** for grass on the sandy field with little success.

Contrast of Ideas: Petra is **shrewd,** but her twin sister is very <u>foolish.</u>

Apply your knowledge of context clues and other vocabulary strategies to determine the meanings of unfamiliar words you encounter during your first read.

First Read POETRY

Apply these strategies as you conduct your first read. You will have an opportunity to complete a close read after your first read.

NOTICE *who* or *what* is "speaking" the poem and whether the poem tells a story or describes a single moment.

ANNOTATE by marking vocabulary and key passages you want to revisit.

First Read

CONNECT ideas within the selection to what you already know and what you have already read.

RESPOND by completing the Comprehension Check.

© Pearson Education, Inc, or its affiliates. All rights reserved.

AUTHOR'S PERSPECTIVE **Jim Cummins, Ph.D.**

Importance of Background Knowledge It is important for all students, and especially for English learners, to learn to tap into their background knowledge when they read a text. Teachers can help students access this knowledge and integrate it with new textual information. One way to do this is to encourage groups to share what they know about the topic of the text before they begin reading. For example, on a superficial level, some students may have prior knowledge about horses, which can help to scaffold understanding of "A Blessing." On a deeper level, more students may be able to relate to the idea of communicating with pets or other animals. After students have completed their first read, have them discuss how their background knowledge helped them understand the text.

A Blessing

James Wright

© Pearson Education, Inc. or its affiliates. All rights reserved.

BACKGROUND
For thousands of years, people have relied on horses to carry their belongings, plow fields, and to take them farther and faster than they could go on their own two feet. But the relationship with horses is not only about work—we can share a deep emotional connection with these graceful animals.

SCAN FOR MULTIMEDIA

Just off the highway to Rochester, Minnesota,
Twilight bounds softly forth on the grass.
And the eyes of those two Indian ponies
Darken with kindness.
5 They have come gladly out of the willows
To welcome my friend and me.
We step over the barbed wire into the pasture
Where they have been grazing all day, alone.
They ripple tensely, they can hardly contain their happiness
10 That we have come.
They bow **shyly** as wet swans. They love each other.
There is no **loneliness** like theirs.

NOTES

Mark context clues or indicate another strategy you used that helped you determine meaning.

shyly (SHY lee) *adv.*
MEANING:

loneliness (LOHN lee nihs) *n.*
MEANING:

A Blessing **139**

DIGITAL PERSPECTIVES

Concept Vocabulary

SHYLY If groups are struggling to define the word *shyly* in line 11, point out that they can use context clues to infer the meaning of the word. Draw students' attention to the sentence "They bow shyly as wet swans" and encourage them to use these context clues to define the word.

Possible response: *Shyly* means "in a bashful or timid manner."

LONELINESS If groups are struggling to define the word *loneliness* in line 12, point out that they can use context clues to infer the meaning of the word. Draw students' attention to the words *they have been grazing all day, alone* in line 8 and encourage them to use these context clues to define the word.

Possible response: *Loneliness* contains the words *lone* and *lonely*. In this context, loneliness means "feeling of being alone or isolated."

Additional **English Language Support** is available in the Interactive Teacher's Edition.

DIGITAL PERSPECTIVES

Enriching the Text To help students better understand horse–human interactions, show them a clip from a movie about horses (for example, *The Man from Snowy River* or *The Black Stallion*). Before students watch the clip, ask them to take note of how the horse is depicted, how the human character interacts with it, and how the character is affected by the interaction. Discuss how the horse–human interaction in the movie clip is similar to and different from the interaction described in "A Blessing." Preview the clip before showing it in class. **(Research to Clarify)**

FACILITATING

Concept Vocabulary

BLOSSOM Groups may struggle to define the word *blossom* in line 24 and to understand its figurative meaning in the poem. Tell students that *blossom* means "flower." Invite them to employ the alternative strategy of examining connotations, or a word's emotional associations. Then, ask them whether the speaker is referring to a literal flower.

Possible response: The word *blossom* suggests beauty, freshness, and growth. I think the speaker does not mean a literal flower. Instead, the speaker is suggesting a feeling of beauty, growth, and joy.

Comprehension Check

Possible responses:

1. The poem takes place in a pasture during springtime.
2. The speaker and the speaker's friend are greeted by two Indian ponies.
3. The "slenderer one" walks over to the speaker and nuzzles the speaker's hand.

Research

Research to Clarify If groups struggle to narrow their research topic, suggest they research the setting (a rural area near Rochester, Minnesota), social relationships between horses, or horse–human relationships.

NOTES

Mark context clues or indicate another strategy you used that helped you determine meaning.

blossom (BLOS uhm) *n.*

MEANING:

At home once more,
They begin munching the young tufts[1] of spring in the darkness.
15 I would like to hold the slenderer one in my arms,
For she has walked over to me
And nuzzled my left hand.
She is black and white,
Her mane falls wild on her forehead,
20 And the light breeze moves me to caress her long ear
That is delicate as the skin over a girl's wrist.
Suddenly I realize
That if I stepped out of my body I would break
Into blossom.

_____

1. **tufts** (tuhfts) *n.* bunches of soft material, such as grass.

Comprehension Check

Complete the following items after you finish your first read. Review and clarify details with your group.

1. Where does the poem take place?

2. Who greets the speaker and the speaker's friend?

3. What does the "slenderer one" do that moves the speaker?

- -

RESEARCH

Research to Clarify Choose at least one unfamiliar detail from the poem. Briefly research that detail. In what way does the information you learned shed light on an aspect of the poem?

© Pearson Education, Inc., or its affiliates. All rights reserved.

PERSONALIZE FOR LEARNING

Challenge

Writing a Poem Invite students to write a poem based on "A Blessing" from the perspective of one of the ponies. Encourage them to think about how the pony felt about the encounter: was it a moving experience for the pony too, or perhaps a more mundane experience?

Remind students to include figurative and sensory language, symbolism, and sound devices.

After students have written their poems, have them share with their classmates and discuss the themes and poetic techniques in the poems.

Close Read the Text

With your group, revisit sections of the text you marked during your first read. **Annotate** details that you notice. What **questions** do you have? What can you **conclude**?

ANNOTATE · QUESTION · Close Read · CONCLUDE

Analyze the Text

CITE TEXTUAL EVIDENCE
to support your answers.

📓 Notebook Complete the activities.

1. **Review and Clarify** With your group, reread "A Blessing." What are some words or phrases that help you visualize, or picture in your mind, the setting of the poem?

2. **Present and Discuss** Now, work with your group to share lines from the poem that you found especially important. Take turns presenting the lines you chose. Discuss what you noticed in the poem, what questions you asked, and what conclusions you reached.

3. **Essential Question:** *How can people and animals relate to each other?* What has this poem taught you about the ways people and animals can relate to each other? Discuss with your group.

LANGUAGE DEVELOPMENT

Concept Vocabulary

shyly	loneliness	blossom

Why These Words? The three concept vocabulary words from the poem are related. With your group, determine what the words have in common. How do these word choices enhance the impact of the text?

Practice

📓 Notebook The concept vocabulary words appear in "A Blessing." For each word, write a sentence in which you use the word correctly.

Word Study

Multiple-Meaning Words Many words in English have multiple meanings, or more than one definition. For example, the word *blossom*, which appears in the poem "A Blessing," has several meanings, and can be a verb or a noun. With your group, write a definition of *blossom* as it is used in the poem. Then, use a dictionary to find another definition for *blossom*. Finally, find two more multiple-meaning words in the poem. Record the words and two definitions for each word.

© Pearson Education, Inc., or its affiliates. All rights reserved.

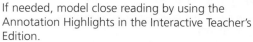

A BLESSING

TIP

GROUP DISCUSSION
Your group members might have different opinions of the poem. When you discuss your opinions, be supportive of other members' views. Remember to cite evidence from the poem to support your opinions.

🔗 **WORD NETWORK**

Add words related to people and animals from the text to your Word Network.

☰ **STANDARDS**
Language
Determine or clarify the meaning of unknown and multiple-meaning words and phrases based on grade 6 reading and content, choosing flexibly from a range of strategies.
 c. Consult reference materials, both print and digital, to find the pronunciation of a word or determine or clarify its precise meaning or its part of speech.

A Blessing **141**

Jump Start

CLOSE READ Invite groups to discuss the following prompts: *Is it right or wrong to assign human qualities and emotions to animals? Do animals experience feelings like love and loneliness like we do?* As students discuss this in their groups, ask them to cite reasons and evidence from the poem, their personal experience, and what they know about animal behavior.

Close Read the Text

If needed, model close reading by using the Annotation Highlights in the Interactive Teacher's Edition.

Remind students to use Accountable Talk in their discussions and to support one another as they complete the close read.

Analyze the Text

1. **Possible response:** "Just off the highway," "Twilight bounds softly forth on the grass," "out of the willows," "barbed wire into the pasture," "young tufts of spring"

2. Lines will vary by group. Remind students to explain why they chose the lines they presented to group members.

3. Responses will vary by group.

Concept Vocabulary

Why These Words? Possible response: The words all relate to emotions the speaker is feeling or horses' emotions or behaviors.

Practice

Possible responses: The new student stood **shyly** by the door before the teacher invited him into the classroom. She felt a strong sense of **loneliness** after her best friend moved away. Now that it was spring, the gardener couldn't wait for his flowers to **blossom**.

Word Network

Possible words: *kindness, welcome, nuzzled*

Word Study

For more support, see **Concept Vocabulary and Word Study.**

Possible Response:
Blossom means "the state of flowering" in the poem. Another definition is "the flower of a plant." *Spring* refers to the season of spring or "to leap or move suddenly." *Break* means "to smash or split" or "an abrupt or marked change."

FORMATIVE ASSESSMENT

Analyze the Text

• **If** students struggle to close read the text, **then** provide the **A Blessing: Text Questions** available online in the Interactive Teacher's Edition or Unit Resources. Answers and DOK levels are also available.

Concept Vocabulary

If students struggle to identify how the words are related, **then** have them review the poem and look for similarities in how the three words are used in context.

Word Study

If students struggle to identify other examples of multiple-meaning words, **then** ask them for words they use every day that have different meanings. For Reteach and Practice, see **Word Study: Multiple-Meaning Words (RP).**

Analyze Craft and Structure

Elements of Poetry Discuss the differences between poems and other types of writing. Encourage students to consider why poets are particularly likely to be very careful about word choice and to use sound devices, such as repetition or alliteration, and figurative language. Point out that since poems usually have fewer words than prose, each word is worth more. Ask students to identify another type of writing that is similar to poetry in this respect (songwriting, for example). For more support, see **Analyze Craft and Structure: Elements of Poetry: Word Choice and Tone.** 📄

Practice

1. In line 9, the poet uses repetition of the word *they*.

2. (a) In lines 23–24, the poet uses figurative language. (b) The speaker feels he will "break into blossom," which adds to the poem's emotional effect.

3. (a) "As" is used to create a simile. (b) The shy ponies are compared to wet swans. (c) I think the poet uses this simile to put an image in the reader's mind of the ponies' behavior. It gives the ponies a quality of being accepting and a bit submissive at the arrival of the humans.

4. (a) In lines 20–21, the poet compares one of the pony's ears to the delicate skin of a girl's wrist. (b) The simile gives a gentle quality to the pony it describes.

5. The tone of this poem is peaceful and happy. The poet's use of *kindness, gladly, happiness, nuzzled,* and *caress* help create the tone.

FORMATIVE ASSESSMENT

Analyze Craft and Structure

If students have trouble identifying examples of literary devices in the poem, **then** provide them with examples of each type of literary device before having students search for them in the poem. For Reteach and Practice, see **Analyze Craft and Structure: Elements of Poetry (RP).** 📄

👥 **MAKING MEANING**

A BLESSING

Analyze Craft and Structure

Elements of Poetry "A Blessing" is a **lyric poem,** which is a short work about a moment in time or a single insight. Most lyric poems use literary devices to add meaning and beauty. For example, a poet may use **sound devices,** or groups of words that create sound patterns. These are two types of sound devices:

- **Repetition:** the use of any part of language more than once—it could be a letter, a word, a phrase, or a sentence.
- **Alliteration:** repetition of the same consonant sound at the beginning of words that are close together—in this line, the "l" sound creates alliteration: "leave me a little love."

Sound devices may make a line of poetry sound like flowing water, banging drums, or anything in between.

Poets also use **figurative language,** which are imaginative descriptions. One common type of figurative language is the simile. A **simile** is a comparison of two unlike things that uses a comparing word, such as "like" or "as." This line is a simile: *papers fill the room like hay in a barn.*

A poem's subject and language combine to create a certain **tone,** or attitude. You can describe tone with the same words you use to name emotions, such as *sad, peaceful,* or *loving.*

Practice

CITE TEXTUAL EVIDENCE
to support your answers.

📓 **Notebook** Read the poem or individual lines aloud to help you hear the poet's use of literary devices. Then, work with your group to answer the questions.

1. What sound device appears in line 9? Explain.

2. (a) What sound device appears in lines 23–24? (b) How does this sound device add to the poem's effect? For example, how does it help emphasize important words?

3. (a) What comparing word is used to create a simile in line 11? (b) What two unlike things are compared? (c) Why do you think the poet uses this simile? What quality does it give to the two ponies?

4. Explain the simile that appears in lines 20–21: (a) What two unlike things are compared? (b) What quality does this simile give to the pony it describes?

5. How would you describe the tone of this poem? Identify specific words that help create that tone.

⠿ STANDARDS
Reading Literature
Determine the meaning of words and phrases as they are used in a text, including figurative and connotative meanings; analyze the impact of a specific word choice on meaning and tone.

142 UNIT 2 • ANIMAL ALLIES

© Pearson Education, Inc., or its affiliates. All rights reserved.

PERSONALIZE FOR LEARNING

English Language Support
Using Alliteration Ask pairs of students to write a noun for each of the following adjectives in order to create phrases that feature alliteration: better, every, little, silly. **EMERGING**

Have students write an adjective and a noun with the same beginning sound for each of the following letters: A, N, S, T. **EXPANDING**

Have students write an adjective and a noun with the same beginning sound for each of the following letters: A, N, S, T. Then have them write sentences with each of the phrases that they wrote. **BRIDGING**

An expanded **English Language Support Lesson** on Repetition and Alliteration is available in the Interactive Teacher's Edition.

Conventions

Verbs and Verb Tenses A **verb** expresses an action or a state of being. Every complete sentence includes at least one verb. There are two main types of verbs: action verbs and linking verbs.

- An **action verb** refers to physical or mental activity. *Jump* and *run* are action verbs. *Guess* and *wish* are also action verbs even though they refer to ways of thinking or feeling rather than physical activities.

- A **linking verb** connects a noun or a pronoun to a word that identifies, renames, or describes it. Linking verbs include all forms of the verb *be* (such as *am, is, were,* or *will be*), and certain other verbs such as *seem* and *become.*

Examples:

They *were* hungry.
She *became* interested.

When a verb is used in a sentence, it has a **tense.** A verb tense shows when the action takes place. The three simple tenses are **present tense, past tense,** and **future tense.** To form the past tense of regular verbs—such as *march, bake,* and *talk*—add *-ed* or *-d.* Some verbs, such as *go,* are irregular. Their forms in different tenses do not follow a set pattern. For irregular verbs, you need to memorize the tense changes.

TENSE	REGULAR VERB: *bake*	IRREGULAR VERB: *be*
Present	I bake	He is
Past	I baked	He was
Future	I will bake	He will be

Read It

1. Identify the verb in each line from the poem. State whether it is an action verb or a linking verb. Then, identify its tense.

   a. They bow shyly as wet swans.

   b. And nuzzled my left hand.

   c. There is no loneliness like theirs.

2. Reread lines 18–21 from the poem. Mark each verb. State whether it is an action verb or a linking verb. Then, identify its tense.

Write It

Notebook Rewrite each line. Change the tense of the verb to the one indicated in parentheses.

1. And the eyes of those two Indian ponies darken with kindness. (future tense)

2. Twilight bounds softly forth on the grass. (past tense)

3. And nuzzled my left hand (present tense)

EVIDENCE LOG

Before moving on to a new selection, go to your Evidence Log and record what you learned from "A Blessing."

STANDARDS

Language
Demonstrate command of the conventions of standard English grammar and usage when writing or speaking.

A Blessing **143**

Conventions

Verbs and Verb Tenses Verbs express an action or state of being and are a necessary part of a complete sentence. Point out the difference between action verbs and linking verbs to students.

As you review the three simple verb tenses, consider providing additional examples of irregular verbs to reinforce the idea that irregular verbs do not follow a predictable pattern in forming the past tense.

- I swim / I swam / I will swim
- He has / he had / he will have
- We choose / we chose / we will choose
- They find / they found / they will find

For more support, see **Conventions: Verbs and Verb Tenses.**

Read It

Possible responses:

1. a. bow; action; present tense
   b. nuzzled; action; past tense
   c. is; linking; present tense

2. She **is** black and white, (present, linking)
   Her mane **falls** wild on her forehead, (present, action)
   And the light breeze **moves** me to **caress** her long ear (both verbs are action, present)
   That **is** delicate as the skin over a girl's wrist. (linking, present)

Write It

Possible responses:

1. And the eyes of those two Indian ponies **will darken** with kindness.

2. Twilight **bounded** softly forth on the grass.

3. And **nuzzles** my left hand.

Evidence Log Support students in completing their Evidence Log. This paced activity will help prepare them for the Performance-Based Assessment at the end of the unit.

FORMATIVE ASSESSMENT

Conventions

If students have trouble identifying verb tenses, **then** ask them to explain whether the action the verb describes is taking place now, if it happened in the past, or if it will happen in the future. For Reteach and Practice, see **Conventions: Verbs and Verb Tenses (RP).**

Selection Test

Administer the "A Blessing" Selection Test, which is available in both print and digital formats online in Assessments.

© Pearson Education, Inc., or its affiliates. All rights reserved.

PERSONALIZE FOR LEARNING

English Language Support

Past, Present, and Future Put pairs of students together and have them interview each other about what they have done in the past, what they are doing now, and what they have planned for the future. Provide students with examples of questions they might ask and sentence starters for answers. For example: *What did you do last weekend? Last weekend, I _____. What are you going to do next summer? Next summer, I will _____.* Remind students to choose the appropriate verb tense for each time period. **ALL LEVELS**

Small-Group Learning **143**

Predators

◉))) AUDIO SUMMARIES
Audio summaries of "Predators" are available in both English and Spanish and can be assigned to students in the Interactive Teacher's Edition or Unit Resources. Assigning these summaries prior to reading the selection may help students build additional background knowledge and set a context for their first read.

Summary

"Predators" is a poem by Linda Hogan. The speaker thinks about the contact between wild and domestic animals. The speaker is working in the garden and thinking about what the land was like before she came there. The speaker explores how a wild fox comes near and how it behaves toward the speaker's cat and dogs. The speaker imagines how the animals feel about sharing the same space by describing their thoughts and behaviors toward one another.

Insight

"Predators" takes a somewhat uncertain attitude toward nature. It portrays nature as consuming, wild, and impossible for domesticated people and animals to understand.

ESSENTIAL QUESTION:
How can people and animals relate to each other?

Connection to Essential Question

"Predators" considers the interaction of wild animals with humans and domesticated animals. The poet suggests that wild animals might teach people, who think they may have become "domesticated," about themselves.

SMALL-GROUP LEARNING PERFORMANCE TASK
How can the bonds between people and animals be surprising?

Connection to Performance Tasks

Small-Group Learning Performance Task In "Predators," the foxes seem content to be near the speaker and the speaker's pets without causing any disturbance to them.

UNIT PERFORMANCE-BASED ASSESSMENT
How can animals and people help one another?

Unit Performance-Based Assessment In "Predators," the narrator's domestic animals seem pleasant, but the wild foxes are more ambiguous. They seem to acknowledge the domestic animals' "rule" over the land, and may be looking for an opportunity to coexist peacefully.

LESSON RESOURCES

	Making Meaning	Language Development	Effective Expression
Lesson	**First Read** **Close Read** **Analyze the Text** **Analyze Craft and Structure**	**Concept Vocabulary** **Word Study** **Author's Style**	**Writing to Compare**
Instructional Standards	**RL.5** Analyze how a particular sentence, chapter, scene, or stanza fits into the overall structure of a text . . . **RL.10** By the end of the year, read and comprehend literature . . . **L.4** Determine or clarify the meaning of unknown and multiple-meaning words and phrases . . . **L.4.a** Use context as a clue . . .	**RL.4** Determine the meaning of words and phrases . . . **L.4** Determine or clarify the meaning of unknown and multiple-meaning words and phrases . . . **L.4.b** Use common, grade-appropriate Greek or Latin affixes and roots . . . **L.5** Demonstrate understanding of figurative language . . . **L.5.c** Distinguish among the connotations . . .	**W.2** Write informative/explanatory texts . . . **W.2.a** Introduce a topic . . . **W.2.b** Develop the topic . . . **W.2.f** Provide a concluding statement or section . . . **W.5** With some guidance and support from peers and adults, develop and strengthen writing . . . **W.9** Draw evidence from literary or informational texts . . . **W.9.a** Apply *grade 6 Reading standards* . . .

⇱ STUDENT RESOURCES

Available online in the Interactive Student Edition or Unit Resources	🔊 Selection Audio 📄 First-Read Guide: Poetry 📄 Close-Read Guide: Poetry	📄 Word Network	📄 Evidence Log

⇱ TEACHER RESOURCES

Selection Resources Available online in the Interactive Teacher's Edition or Unit Resource	🔊 Audio Summaries ✏️ Annotation Highlights 💬 EL Highlights 📄 English Language Support Lesson: Word Choice 📄 Predators: Text Questions 📄 Analyze Craft and Structure: Poetic Structures	📄 Concept Vocabulary and Word Study 📄 Author's Style: Word Choice and Tone	📄 Writing to Compare: Comparison-and-Contrast Essay
Reteach/Practice (RP) Available online in the Interactive Teacher's Edition or Unit Resources	📄 Analyze Craft and Structure: Poetic Structures (RP)	📄 Word Study: Latin Root *-dom-* (RP) 📄 Author's Style: Word Choice and Tone (RP)	
Assessment Available online in Assessments	📄 ☑️ Selection Test		
My Resources	📄 A Unit 2 Answer Key is available online and in the Interactive Teacher's Edition.		

Reading Support

Text Complexity Rubric: Predators

Quantitative Measures

Lexile: NP   Text Length: 15 lines

Qualitative Measures

Knowledge Demands ①——②——**❸**——④——⑤	Situations may be unfamiliar and use of figurative language will likely make it difficult to grasp. Background information will be helpful.
Structure ①——②——**❸**——④——⑤	The poem is written in free verse.
Language Conventionality and Clarity ①——②——③——**❹**——⑤	The poem contains figurative language and some above-level vocabulary. Lengthy, broken sentence structure will likely be challenging.
Levels of Meaning/Purpose ①——②——③——**❹**——⑤	Multiple levels of meaning: poem describes animals and their relationships to humans and the human relationship to nature, but the meaning is not always clearly stated.

DECIDE AND PLAN

English Language Support

Provide English Learners with support for language and meaning as they read the selection.

Language Students may need help not only with the metaphorical language, but also with the structure of the language and the vocabulary. Help students reword long and complex sentences. Suggest that students read the sentences in smaller pieces. For example, in lines 6–9: *I hoe and cultivate, find my dead aim in the trust that many tales spun this tract long before I came.*

Meaning Work with students to help them understand the meaning of figurative language by first understanding the literal meaning. For example, discuss the lines *The dogs do not understand wild nature. I also was domesticated,* from "Predators." Make sure students understand how a human might be domesticated.

Strategic Support

Provide students with strategic support to ensure that they can successfully read the text.

Language If students have difficulty with complex sentences, work together to break down sentences into smaller chunks in order to understand their meaning. Ask students to highlight words or phrases that they don't understand. As a group, help to define some of the terms they find difficult.

Meaning For students who have difficulty understanding metaphors, have them underline or list the phrases that they don't understand. Then have them read those phrases again and work with a partner to try to figure out the comparison the poet is making.

Challenge

Provide students who need to be challenged with ideas for how they can go beyond a simple interpretation of the text.

Text Analysis Ask students to read aloud lines 10–11: *The dogs do not understand wild nature. I also was domesticated.* Ask students to discuss what the author means. Why don't the dogs understand wild nature? What does it mean to be domesticated, as a human?

Written Response Using the writing style in the poem, ask students to write their own free verse poem. Ask them what other images they could use to convey the connection between humans and animals, or humans and nature.

TEACH

Read and Respond

Have groups read the selection and complete the Making Meaning, Language Development, and Effective Expression activities.

Standards Support Through Teaching and Learning Cycle

IDENTIFY NEEDS

Analyze results of the Beginning-of-Year Assessment, focusing on the items relating to Unit 2. Also take into consideration student performance to this point and your observations of where particular students struggle.

ANALYZE AND REVISE

- Analyze student work for evidence of student learning.
- Identify whether or not students have met the expectations in the standards.
- Identify implications for future instruction.

TEACH

Implement the planned lesson, and gather evidence of student learning.

DECIDE AND PLAN

- If students have performed poorly on items matching these standards, then provide selection scaffolds before assigning them the on-level lesson provided in the Student Edition.
- If students have done well on the Beginning-of-Year Assessment, then challenge them to keep progressing and learning by giving them opportunities to practice the skills in depth.
- Use the Selection Resources listed on the Planning pages for "Predators" to help students continually improve their ability to master the standards.

Instructional Standards: "Predators"

	Catching Up	This Year	Looking Forward
Reading	You may wish to administer the **Analyze Craft and Structure: Poetic Structures (RP)** worksheet to help students understand the author's choices.	**RL.5** Analyze how a particular sentence, chapter, scene, or stanza fits into the overall structure of a text and contributes to the development of the theme, setting, or plot.	Challenge students to write sentences that imitate the structure, punctuation, and spacing of the sentences in one of the poems. Have them share their sentences with a partner.
Writing	You may wish to administer the **Writing to Compare: Comparison-and-Contrast Essay** worksheet to help students organize and write their comparison-and-contrast essays.	**W.2** Write informative/explanatory texts to examine a topic and convey ideas, concepts, and information through the selection, organization, and analysis of relevant content.	Challenge students to analyze the transitions in their comparison-and-contrast essay. Have students revise text that does not logically transition from one idea to the next.
Language	You may wish to administer the **Word Study: Latin Root -dom- (RP)** worksheet to help students understand words with this root. You may wish to administer the **Author's Style: Word Choice and Tone (RP)** worksheet to help students understand diction and word choice that is part of poetic style.	**L.4.b** Use common, grade-appropriate Greek or Latin affixes and roots as clues to the meaning of a word. **L.5** Demonstrate understanding of figurative language, word relationships, and nuances in word meanings.	Challenge students to find three words with the Latin root -dom- and use each one in a sentence. Challenge students to make a list of words that affect the tone and meaning of the poems. Then have them discuss the list with a partner. What effect does each word have? Why did the author choose each word?

Jump Start

FIRST READ What happens to wildlife when humans destroy their habitat to build homes and businesses? How do humans and domesticated animals interact with wild animals when their paths converge? Use these prompts to start a classroom discussion that will set the context for reading "Predators." Encourage students to talk about their own encounters with wild animals.

Predators 🔊 📄

What are the different animals in the poem doing? How does the speaker feel at the end of the poem? Modeling questions such as these will help students connect to "Predators" and to the Small-Group Performance Task assignment. Selection audio and print capability for the selection are available in the Interactive Teacher's Edition.

Concept Vocabulary

Ask groups to look closely at the type of context clue discussed on the page—restatement of an idea—and discuss how this context clue can be used to help clarify meaning. Encourage groups to look for other types of context clues when they encounter unfamiliar words in "Predators."

⬤ FIRST READ

Students should perform the steps of the first read independently.

NOTICE: You may want to encourage students to notice how wild and domesticated animals are contrasted.

ANNOTATE: Remind students to mark lines that include symbolism.

CONNECT: Have students compare the situation described in "Predators" with their own experience of wildlife in an urban or suburban area.

RESPOND: Students will answer questions and write a summary to demonstrate understanding.

Point out to students that while they will always complete the Respond step at the end of the first read, the other steps will probably happen somewhat concurrently. You may wish to print copies of the **First-Read Guide: Poetry** for students to use. 📄

👥 MAKING MEANING

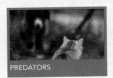

Comparing Texts

Complete the first-read and close-read activities for "Predators." Then, compare this poem with "A Blessing."

A BLESSING

PREDATORS

About the Author

Linda Hogan (b. 1947) is an award-winning Chickasaw novelist, essayist, environmentalist, and poet. Her writing often addresses topics such as the environment and Native American history. An activist and educator, Hogan has been a featured speaker at numerous international conferences and events on the environment and literature. She lives in the Colorado mountains and is currently the Chickasaw Nation's writer-in-residence.

⊟ **STANDARDS**

Reading Literature
By the end of the year, read and comprehend literature, including stories, dramas, and poems, in the grades 6–8 text complexity band proficiently, with scaffolding as needed at the high end of the range.

Language
Determine or clarify the meaning of unknown and multiple-meaning words and phrases based on *grade 6 reading and content,* choosing flexibly from a range of strategies.
  a. Use context as a clue to the meaning of a word or phrase.

144 UNIT 2 • ANIMAL ALLIES

Predators

Concept Vocabulary

As you perform your first read of "Predators," you will encounter these words.

| cultivate | wild | domesticated |

Context Clues To find the meaning of unfamiliar words, look for clues in the context, which is made up of the words and punctuation that surround the unknown word in a text. There are different types of context clues that may help you as you read. Here are two examples:

> **Synonym:** The dogs **gazed**, or watched, as the foxes walked into the woods.
>
> **Elaborating Details:** The faded colors and **indistinct** shapes show that the artist was losing his sight.

Apply your knowledge of context clues and other vocabulary strategies to determine the meanings of unfamiliar words you encounter during your first read.

First Read POETRY

Apply these strategies as you conduct your first read. You will have an opportunity to complete a close read after your first read.

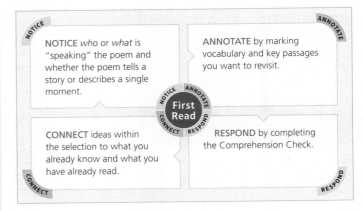

NOTICE who or what is "speaking" the poem and whether the poem tells a story or describes a single moment.

ANNOTATE by marking vocabulary and key passages you want to revisit.

CONNECT ideas within the selection to what you already know and what you have already read.

RESPOND by completing the Comprehension Check.

First Read

© Pearson Education, Inc., or its affiliates. All rights reserved.

👥 FACILITATING SMALL-GROUP CLOSE READING

CLOSE READ: Poetry As groups perform the close read, circulate and offer support as needed.

- Remind groups that when they read poetry, they should pay particular attention to figurative and sensory language.
- If a group is confused about the poem's meaning, suggest that they consider each

word the poet uses and think about every possible meaning the word may have. Remind them to consider both connotative and denotative meanings.

- Challenge group members to debate with each other the poem's meaning to develop a deeper understanding of the theme.

Predators

Linda Hogan

Concept Vocabulary

CULTIVATE If groups are struggling to define the word *cultivate* in line 7, point out that they can use context clues to clarify the meaning of the word. Explain that the word appears in tandem with the word *hoe*. If students know what a hoe is, or the verb to *hoe*, they can use this context clue to infer what *cultivate* may mean.

Possible response: *Cultivate* means "to work and prepare the land for growing plants."

© Pearson Education, Inc., or its affiliates. All rights reserved.

BACKGROUND

Habitat loss is a major threat to wildlife in the United States. As people use more land and alter natural environments, wild animals are forced to move into places where people and domestic animals live. Foxes are one type of wild animal that has been seen in residential neighborhoods in increasing numbers. The female fox is called a "vixen."

SCAN FOR MULTIMEDIA

I cannot smell the scent of the cat
who slept on this sweater, but do know
how the garden swells with old
and pungent* herb art. In sun the fox

NOTES

---

*pungent (PUHN juhnt) *adj.* strong-smelling

Predators **145**

PERSONALIZE FOR LEARNING

English Language Support

Figurative Language English language learners might not understand the use of the word *swells* in line 3 of "Predators." Explain that this is an example of figurative language, or language that is used imaginatively rather than literally in order to create an effect. The literal meaning of the word *swells* is to grow in size, but the poet does not mean the garden literally, or actually, grew bigger. Explain that the poet uses figurative language here to create a powerful mental image of the garden being completely overtaken by the herbs. The reader can imagine the herbs filling and practically bursting out of the garden.

FACILITATING

Concept Vocabulary

WILD If groups are struggling to define the word *wild* in line 10, point out that they can use context clues to clarify the meaning of the word. The word *wild* appears in the line before the word *domesticated*. If students think about why domesticated dogs "do not understand wild nature," they can infer what *wild* may mean in this context.

Possible response: *Wild* here means "not tamed or domesticated."

DOMESTICATED If groups are struggling to define the word *domesticated* in line 11, point out the sentence "The dogs do not understand wild nature." Have them use this context clue to write a definition for *domesticated*.

Possible response: *Domesticated* means "tamed; not wild."

Comprehension Check

Possible responses:

1. The setting is in and around the speaker's garden.
2. The fox reacts to the cats and dogs with acceptance that the cat and dogs "rule" this space.
3. The vixens are devouring a small animal.

Research

Research to Clarify If students struggle to come up with a detail to research, you may want to suggest that they use one of the following topics: fox behavior, gardening, the domestication of cats and dogs.

Research to Explore If students aren't sure how to go about formulating a research question, suggest that they use their findings from Research to Clarify as a starting point. For example, if students researched the domestication of cats and dogs, they might formulate a question such as *How have dogs changed since they were domesticated?*

NOTES

Mark context clues or indicate another strategy you used that helped you determine meaning.

cultivate (KUHL tuh vayt) *v.*

MEANING:

wild (wyld) *adj.*

MEANING:

domesticated (duh MEHS tuh kay tihd) *adj.*

MEANING:

5 bows to my feline and her good
dog friends who rule this land. I hoe
and **cultivate**, find my dead aim
in the trust that many tales spun

this tract long before I came.
10 The dogs do not understand **wild** nature.
I also was **domesticated**.
Oh, give me strength to watch their sorry
looks as a bevy of vixen

feed on a much smaller body
15 not the cat's . . . But it could be.

Comprehension Check

Complete the following items after you finish your first read. Review and clarify details with your group.

1. What is the setting of the poem?

2. According to the speaker, how does the fox react to the cat and dogs?

3. What are the vixens doing at the end of the poem?

- -

RESEARCH

Research to Clarify Choose at least one unfamiliar detail from the poem. Briefly research that detail. In what way does the information you learned shed light on an aspect of the poem?

Research to Explore Choose something from the text that interests you, and formulate a research question.

© Pearson Education, Inc., or its affiliates. All rights reserved.

PERSONALIZE FOR LEARNING

Challenge

Illuminating the Text To help students better understand the context of the poem, have them conduct research on habitat loss. Encourage them to find statistics on how many wild animals are displaced or killed as a result of human development. They can also research what the effects are of animals losing their natural habitats, how wild animals adapt to their new environments, and how wild animals interact with humans. Then encourage small groups to talk about what, if anything, people should do to protect the habitats of wild animals.

© Pearson Education, Inc., or its affiliates. All rights reserved.

MAKING MEANING

Close Read the Text

With your group, revisit sections of the text you marked during your first read. **Annotate** details that you notice. What **questions** do you have? What can you **conclude**?

Close Read

Analyze the Text

CITE TEXTUAL EVIDENCE to support your answers.

📓 **Notebook** Complete the activities.

1. **Review and Clarify** With your group, reread "Predators." Why might the speaker say dogs do not understand wild nature?

2. **Present and Discuss** Now, work with your group to share lines from the poem that you found especially important. Take turns presenting the lines you chose. Discuss what you noticed in the text, what questions you asked, and what conclusions you reached.

3. **Essential Question: *How can people and animals relate to each other?*** What has this poem taught you about the ways people and animals can relate to each other? Discuss with your group.

LANGUAGE DEVELOPMENT

Concept Vocabulary

| cultivate | wild | domesticated |

Why These words? The three concept vocabulary words from the text are related. With your group, determine what the words have in common. How do these word choices enhance the impact of the text?

Practice

📓 **Notebook** The concept vocabulary words appear in "Predators." Work together as a group to write a sentence for each word.

Word Study

Latin Root: *-dom-* The speaker in "Predators" describes both herself and dogs as domesticated. The word *domesticated* is formed from the Latin root *-dom-*, which may mean "house" or "home," but which may also mean "lord" or "master."

Write a definition of *domesticated* that shows how the root *-dom-* contributes to its meaning. Then, find three other words formed from the same root. Write the words and their meanings.

PREDATORS

💡 TIP

GROUP DISCUSSION
Be sure to identify specific lines or words from the poem so your group members can follow your thinking.

🔗 **WORD NETWORK**

Add words related to people and animals from the text to your Word Network.

≡ STANDARDS

Language
Determine or clarify the meaning of unknown and multiple-meaning words and phrases based on *grade 6 reading and content*, choosing flexibly from a range of strategies.
 b. Use common, grade-appropriate Greek or Latin affixes and roots as clues to the meaning of a word.

Predators **147**

Jump Start

CLOSE READ How are wild animals and domesticated animals juxtaposed in "Predators"? Ask students to specifically consider line 10 from the poem: *"The dogs do not understand wild nature."* Engage students in a discussion about what this line means and why it is important.

Close Read the Text

If needed, model close reading by using the Annotation Highlights in the Interactive Teacher's Edition.

Remind students to use Accountable Talk in their discussions and to support one another as they complete the close read.

Analyze the Text

Possible responses:

1. The speaker probably thinks that dogs, being domesticated, behave a certain way and wouldn't be able to understand why wild animals behave the way they do.

2. Lines will vary by group. Remind students to explain why they chose the lines they presented to group members.

3. Responses will vary by group.

Concept Vocabulary

Why These Words? Possible response: These words are all related to gardening or nature, which helps to establish the setting of the poem.

Practice

Sandra is trying to **cultivate** the practice of playing the piano daily. My brother pointed out the **wild** turkeys walking on the side of the road. Our teacher said we should keep only **domesticated** animals as pets.

Word Network

Possible words: *scent, feline, vixen*

Word Study

For more support, see **Concept Vocabulary and Word Study.** 📄

Possible responses:
Domesticated – no longer wild; tamed.;
domicile – a place of residence; house or home;
dominant – having rule or control over others;
domestic – relating to the home, household, or family

FORMATIVE ASSESSMENT

Analyze the Text 📄

If students struggle to close read the text, **then** provide the **Predators: Text Questions** available online in the Interactive Teacher's Edition or Unit Resources. Answers and DOK levels are also available.

Concept Vocabulary

If students struggle to make a connection between the concept vocabulary words, **then** have them review the poem and look at how the words are used in context.

Word Study

If students struggle to find words containing *-dom-*, **then** assist them with fine-tuning their search terms. For Reteach and Practice, **see Word Study: Latin Root *-dom-* (RP).**

Analyze Craft and Structure

Poetic Structures Engage students in a discussion about the differences between poetry and prose. Have students identify as many differences as they can (e.g., line length, stanzas, punctuation). Ask students to consider why a writer might prefer writing poetry to prose, and vice versa. For more support, see **Analyze Craft and Structure: Poetic Structures** 📄

Practice

1. The first two stanzas are both quatrains; each stanza contains four lines.

2. (a) The final stanza is made up of two lines. (b) This type of stanza is called a couplet.

3. a. lines 9, 10, 11, and 15
   b. line 6
   c. line 9
   d. line 15.

4. **Possible responses:** (a) Each line is structured as a complete declarative sentence that ends with a period. This helps the reader take each statement as a simple fact. (b) The poet ends each stanza in the middle of a sentence, which is completed in the next stanza. This creates a seamless flow that leads the reader to continue through the poem.

FORMATIVE ASSESSMENT

Analyze Craft and Structure

If students struggle to analyze the structure of the poem, **then** point to specific lines or stanzas in the poem and ask students what they notice. For Reteach and Practice, see **Analyze Craft and Structure: Poetic Structures**. 📄

PREDATORS

Analyze Craft and Structure

Poetic Structures Poetry features certain structures, or ways of being organized, that are different from prose. These structures include lines and stanzas.

- A **line** is a group of words arranged into a row. The point at which a line ends, or breaks, is important. It is a choice the poet makes for specific reasons. For example, the poet may want a line to include a certain number of syllables or have a certain rhythm. In some cases, a line break happens at the end of a sentence or in a place where a reader would naturally pause. In other cases, the line ends but the sentence continues onto the next line.

- A **stanza** is a group of lines. Like paragraphs in prose, each stanza in a poem may focus on a single main idea. **Stanza structure** refers to the way a poet organizes the stanzas. A poet may make all the stanzas in a poem the same length or different lengths. Stanzas are named by the number of lines they contain:

two lines: *couplet*   **four lines:** *quatrain*
six lines: *sestet*   **eight lines:** *octave*

All of the choices a poet makes about line lengths, line breaks, and stanzas add to the effect and meaning of a poem. They are tools that help the poet emphasize certain words or phrases, give a poem a particular shape and order, and add to its emotional impact on readers.

Practice

CITE TEXTUAL EVIDENCE to support your answers.

📓 **Notebook** Work with your group to answer the questions.

1. The poem includes four stanzas. What type of stanza is used in stanzas 1 and 2? Explain.

2. **(a)** How many lines make up the poem's final stanza? **(b)** What is the name for this type of stanza?

3. Complete the chart to analyze the line breaks in this poem. Identify lines by number.

See possible responses in Teacher's Editions.

Which lines in the poem break at the end of a sentence?	a.
Where does the sentence that begins in the middle of line 4 end?	b.
Where does the sentence that begins at the end of line 6 end?	c.
Where does the sentence that begins on line 12 end?	d.

4. Use the analysis you did in question three to answer these questions: **(a)** In lines 10 and 11, the speaker simply states an observation. How does the structure of each line add to the statement-like quality? **(b)** How does the poet use line breaks to create a flow from stanza to stanza? Explain.

© Pearson Education, Inc., or its affiliates. All rights reserved.

≣ STANDARDS
Reading Literature
Analyze how a particular sentence, chapter, scene, or stanza fits into the overall structure of a text and contributes to the development of the theme, setting, or plot.

148 UNIT 2 • ANIMAL ALLIES

PERSONALIZE FOR LEARNING

Strategic Support

Poetry and Prose If students have trouble analyzing poetic structures, rewrite the poem in plain, simple prose. Share your prose version of the poem with students, and engage students in a discussion about what was lost. Ask students to consider how a poetic structure and evocative word choices enhanced the meaning of the poem. Point out that poets use figurative and sensory language so that readers can experience the setting and events of the poem.

Author's Style

Word Choice and Tone Word choice, or **diction,** is an important part of a poet's style. A poet's diction may have many different qualities. For example, it might be simple, old-fashioned, modern, formal, or informal. Often, a poet will use different types of diction, even within a single poem.

When making specific word choices, a poet will consider the word's meaning and the emotional qualities it conveys. These two elements of word meaning are called denotation and connotation:

- **Denotation** is a word's definition. You will find a word's denotation in a dictionary.
- **Connotations** are a word's emotional associations. Even if words are synonyms that share denotations, their connotations may be very different. For example, the word *car* has no connotation—it is a neutral word. *Junker* is a synonym for *car,* but it suggests a broken-down vehicle. *Classic* is also a synonym for *car* but it suggests a vehicle worthy of showing in a parade.

Read It

In her poem "Predators," Linda Hogan uses simple words that may be familiar to even young children. She also mixes in sophisticated words that may be unfamiliar to many readers. Complete the chart by adding words from "Predators" that fit the two categories. Work independently. Then, share and discuss your responses with your group. Two words have been done for you.

SIMPLE DICTION	SOPHISTICATED DICTION
Cat	Pungent
Garden	Swells
Fox	Feline
Dog	Cultivate
Nature	Bevy
Body	Vixen

Write It

📓 **Notebook** Choose one of the words from the "sophisticated" column of the chart. Use a dictionary to identify the word's meaning. Then, use a thesaurus to find a synonym. Rewrite the line from Hogan's poem, replacing it with a synonym. Explain how this revision changes the meaning or emotional quality of the line.

© Pearson Education, Inc., or its affiliates. All rights reserved.

STANDARDS

Reading Literature
Determine the meaning of words and phrases as they are used in a text, including figurative and connotative meanings; analyze the impact of a specific word choice on meaning and tone.

Language
Demonstrate understanding of of figurative language, word relationships, and nuances in word meanings.
  c. Distinguish among the connotations of words with similar denotations.

Predators **149**

Author's Style

Word Choice and Tone Start a discussion about why poetic styles are so different and what tools a poet might use to develop his or her own style. A poet's diction, or word choice, is one element that makes his or her poetic style unique. A poet's diction can also help to set the tone of the poem. Encourage students to rearead "Predators" and consider the type of diction, or word choice, the poet uses. Ask students to consider particular words, such as the concept vocabulary, and each word's denotation and connotations. For more support, see **Author's Style: Word Choice and Tone.** 📄

See possible responses in chart on student page.

Write It

Responses will vary, but students should make sure they chose a word from the "sophisticated" column of the chart and included its meaning. Once they have found a synonym and rewritten a line from the poem, they should be able to explain how the line changed because of the revision.

FORMATIVE ASSESSMENT
Author's Style

If students have trouble expressing how diction lends itself to the poet's style in "Predators," **then** remind them to review their notes from their group's discussion and use them as a starting point. For Reteach and Practice, see **Author's Style: Word Choice and Tone (RP).** 📄

PERSONALIZE FOR LEARNING

English Language Support
Analyzing Word Choice and Tone Have pairs of students look at the poem "Predators" together. Have them write down two or three words they don't recognize and use a dictionary to find the words' meanings. Ask students to write a synonym for each of the words to confirm their understanding of what each word means. Have them reread the lines with the "problem" words again and explain why the poet might have chosen these words to convey a feeling or to make a description more vivid. **ALL LEVELS**

An expanded **English Language Support Lesson** on Word Choice is available in the Interactive Teacher's Edition.

FACILITATING

Writing to Compare

As students prepare to compare the poem "A Blessing" with the poem "Predators," they will consider the animals in the poems and people's interactions with or observations of the animals.

Planning and Prewriting

Analyze the Texts

While groups begin working on the planning and prewriting chart, remind them that they should think about similarities and differences between the tame and wild animals in the poems and how the humans interact with the animals. Have students think about the speakers' feelings and attitudes about the animal encounters in each of the poems.

See possible response in chart on student page.

Possible responses:

1. Responses will vary, but students might think that "A Blessing" is more positive because both the people and the ponies in the poem seem so happy and have such a peaceful interaction. Some students might thing "Predators" is more positive because the speakers observes both tame and wild animals just being how they are and marvels at how they interact with each other.

2. Responses will vary. Students might choose "A Blessing" because the speaker gives such human behaviors and emotions to the ponies. Some students might choose "Predators" because of the focus on the fox looking in on the garden and the foxes devouring the small animal at the end of the poem.

A BLESSING

PREDATORS

Writing to Compare

In "A Blessing" and "Predators," two different poets describe encounters with or observations of animals. Deepen your understanding of the poems by comparing them. Then, share your insights in writing.

Assignment

Write a **comparison-and-contrast essay** in which you discuss similarities and differences in how the two poems present people and animals. In your essay, discuss the following questions:

- The animals: Are the animals wild, tame, or both?
- The speakers' feelings: Does the speaker feel peaceful, troubled, or both? Why?
- The title: What do the titles suggest about the speakers' attitudes?
- The conclusions: What new understanding does each speaker gain?

Work together as a group to analyze the poems. Then, work independently to write your essay.

Planning and Prewriting

Analyze the Texts With your group, discuss the questions as they relate to each poem on its own. Use the chart to write your notes and to identify relevant details from the poems.

	A BLESSING	PREDATORS
What animals are presented? Are they wild, tame, or both?	Two Indian ponies are presented. They are tame.	This poem presents a fox that is wild and a cat and dogs that are tame.
How does the speaker feel in the presence of the animals?	The speaker feels joyful, peaceful, and loving.	The speaker seems to be humbled by the fox but also cautious.
What does the title suggest about the speaker's attitude?	The title suggests the speaker is respectful and feels privileged to be there.	The title suggests that the speaker realizes the foxes' "wild nature" when they devour an animal.
At the end of the poem, what does the speaker learn or understand?	The speaker seems to understand he has had a rare, beautiful experience in nature.	The speaker realizes that the cat could have been the foxes' prey.

📓 **Notebook** Respond to these questions.

1. Which poem is more positive about the role of animals in the world? Explain.

2. Which poem conveys a stronger sense about what the animals' experience is like? Explain.

© Pearson Education, Inc., or its affiliates. All rights reserved.

WriteNow Express and Reflect

Imagery The imagery and figurative language in "A Blessing" and "Predators" bring the animal encounters described in these poems alive. Ask students to think of another encounter between a person and an animal. It can be a real one from their personal experience or an imagined one. Then have students write a few sentences using imagery and figurative language to describe the encounter.

Drafting

Determine Your Central Idea In one sentence state the central idea or thesis that you will explain in your essay:

Central Idea/Thesis: _____

_____

As you write, your ideas may change. After you write each paragraph, revisit your thesis to make sure it expresses your ideas.

Choose a Structure Decide how you want to organize your essay. Will you discuss one poem in full before moving on to the second poem? Or will you discuss one important idea at a time, drawing examples from both poems?

Decide on the main idea you will develop in each paragraph of your essay. Consider stating that idea clearly in a topic sentence at the beginning of each paragraph. Double check that the main idea of each paragraph supports the central idea of the essay as a whole as stated in your thesis. Include at least two pieces of evidence from the texts to support each main idea. Make sure the quotations you choose from the poems strongly support your thesis and main ideas.

Reviewing and Revising

Review the Criteria Once you are done drafting, share your essay with your group. As you review one another's work, look for the following elements:

- [ ] stays on subject and addresses both poems effectively

- [ ] identifies clear similarities and differences between the two poems

- [ ] includes details and quotations from the poems that clearly relate to the thesis and main ideas.

- [ ] ends with a strong conclusion that refers back to the thesis

- [ ] is clearly written and uses correct punctuation, capitalization, spelling, and grammar

Give Feedback Each member of your group may have different strengths and weaknesses in their writing. For example, one person may need to clarify the thesis, another might need help with organization, and still another may need to choose details more effectively. Provide suggestions to one another in a positive way, but make sure each person finds his or her own solutions.

© Pearson Education, Inc., or its affiliates. All rights reserved.

EVIDENCE LOG

Before moving on to a new selection, go to your Evidence Log and record what you've learned from "Predators."

STANDARDS
Writing
• Write informative/explanatory texts to examine a topic and convey ideas, concepts, and information through the selection, organization, and analysis of relevant content.
a. Introduce a topic; organize ideas, concepts, and information, using strategies such as definition, classification, comparison/contrast, and cause/effect; include formatting, graphics, and multimedia when useful to aiding comprehension.
b. Develop the topic with relevant facts, definitions, concrete details, quotations, or other information and examples.
f. Provide a concluding statement or section that follows from the information or explanation presented.
• With some guidance and support from peers and adults, develop and strengthen writing as needed by planning, revising, editing, rewriting, or trying a new approach.
• Draw evidence from literary or informational texts to support analysis, reflection, and research.
a. Apply grade 6 Reading standards to literature.

A Blessing • Predators **151**

Drafting

Determine Your Central Idea Clarify for students that while they worked in groups to complete the prewriting activity, they will now work individually on the actual drafting of the essay. Encourage them to return to the poems for additional supporting evidence as they develop their central idea while drafting.

Choose a Structure As students develop a structure for the essay, have them reread the Assignment box in the previous page. Remind them that they must discuss animals and setting as part of the essay. Point out that setting includes time as well as place.

Reviewing and Revising

Review the Criteria After working individually on their drafts, students will return to their groups for the review stage. If you are dealing with time constraints, divide the group into pairs of students to make the feedback stage more efficient.

Give Feedback Encourage students to give constructive feedback as well as positive feedback. Demonstrate how to give constructive feedback in a polite way.

For more support, see **Writing to Compare: Comparison-and-Contrast Essay.**

Evidence Log Support students in completing their Evidence Log. This paced activity will help prepare them for the Performance-Based Assessment at the end of the unit.

FORMATIVE ASSESSMENT

Writing to Compare

If students struggle to explain how a speaker develops a point of view, **then** have them review the word choice in the poem and think about how the speaker seems to feel about the animals.

Selection Test

Administer the "Predators" Selection Test, which is available in both print and digital formats online in Assessments.

PERSONALIZE FOR LEARNING

Strategic Support

Thesis Some students might need additional support in developing a thesis. Explain that a thesis statement is usually a single sentence that appears near the beginning of an essay. The thesis should explain the overall point, or the main idea, the writer is making about the two poems. It should explain the significance of the comparisons and contrasts made in the essay.

Suggest that students review their evidence from the texts first, and then decide what overall point they want to make and draft it into a thesis statement. Point out that they should return to their thesis after they've written their first drafts and adjust it if necessary: the process of writing the essay might have taken their thoughts in new and unexpected directions.

Monkey Master

Summary

In this essay, "Monkey Master," art critic Waldemar Januszczak writes about art painted by a number of apes—most notably a chimpanzee named Congo. Januszczak notes that comparing someone's painting to a monkey's would normally be an insulting joke, but some of Congo's art is legitimately excellent abstract art. What Januszczak learns about Congo's painting method also makes him think of an artist. Januszczak also cites a few example of famous twentieth-century arguments comparing artists' work to animals'. Januszczak argues for the importance of finding meaning and pleasure in this art.

Insight

This essay suggests that some animals may have a deeper intelligence than we give them credit for. It also introduces students to the concept of abstract art, which many may not have encountered yet.

🔊 **AUDIO SUMMARIES**
Audio summaries of "Monkey Master" are available in both English and Spanish and can be assigned to students in the Interactive Teacher's Edition or Unit Resources. Assigning these summaries prior to reading the selection may help students build additional background knowledge and set a context for their first read.

ESSENTIAL QUESTION:
How can people and animals relate to each other?

Connection to Essential Question

Art, in the sense of creating things for other people to see, is an important way that people relate to one another. There are also apparent examples of art in the animal kingdom, like the decorated nests bowerbirds make. But here we learn that animals can make art for people!

SMALL-GROUP LEARNING PERFORMANCE TASK
How can the bonds between people and animals be surprising?

UNIT PERFORMANCE-BASED ASSESSMENT
How can animals and people help one another?

Connection to Performance Tasks

Small-Group Learning Task This text can help students to prepare to address the prompt. Congo's paintings impress Januszczak and change how Januszczak he sees apes.

Unit Performance-Based Assessment In this selection, we seem to see people teaching an animal how to do something it enjoyed, which in turn made it possible for the animal to produce art that people enjoy seeing.

DIGITAL PERSPECTIVES

 Audio

 Video

 Document

 Annotation Highlights

 EL Highlights

 Online Assessment

LESSON RESOURCES

	Making Meaning	Language Development	Effective Expression
Lesson	**First Read** **Close Read** **Analyze the Text**	**Concept Vocabulary** **Word Study**	**Research and Discuss**
Instructional Standards	**RI.7** Integrate information presented . . . **RI.10** By the end of the year, read and comprehend literary nonfiction . . . **L.4** Determine or clarify the meaning of unknown and multiple-meaning words and phrases . . . **L.4.c** Consult reference materials . . .	**L.4** Determine or clarify the meaning of unknown and multiple-meaning words and phrases . . . **L.4.b** Use common, grade-appropriate Greek or Latin affixes and roots . . . **L.4.d** Verify the preliminary determination . . .	**W.7** Conduct short research projects . . . **W.8** Gather relevant information . . . **SL.1** Engage effectively in a range of collaborative discussions . . . **SL.1.c** Pose and respond to specific questions . . .
STUDENT RESOURCES Available online	Selection Audio First-Read Guide: Nonfiction Close-Read Guide: Nonfiction	Word Network	Evidence Log
TEACHER RESOURCES Selection Resources Available online	Audio Summaries Annotation Highlights Monkey Master: Text Questions	Concept Vocabulary and Word Study Word Study: Greek Suffix *-ist* (RP)	Research and Discuss: Group Discussion Research and Discuss: Group Discussion (RP) English Language Support Lesson: Taking Notes for a Discussion
Assessment and Resources	Selection Test available online in Assessments A Unit 2 Answer Key is available online and in the Interactive Teacher's Edition.		

Text Complexity Rubric: Monkey Master

Quantitative Measures

Lexile: 1050   Word Count: 1,299

Qualitative Measures

Knowledge Demands ① — ② — ❸ — ④ — ⑤	To fully understand the text and paintings, some prior knowledge is needed about the animals that create art. Background information is provided.
Structure ① — ② — ❸ — ④ — ⑤	The visuals are interspersed with lengthy text that explains the art.
Language Conventionality and Clarity ① — ② — ③ — ❹ — ⑤	The syntax in the text includes many complex sentences that have several subordinate clauses or phrases, above–level vocabulary, and frequent difficult art references ("The mood is pure Kandinsky...").
Levels of Meaning/Purpose ① — ② — ❸ — ④ — ⑤	The reader needs to study details of the text and analyze explanations in order to appreciate the paintings.

Jump Start

FIRST READ Ask groups to consider and discuss the following prompts: *What does it take to be an artist? What is art, and who decides if something is a work of art? Can a child become a famous artist? How about an animal?*

Monkey Master ▶ 🖹

For an animal to become an artist, what part would a person need to play? Can the animal create without the influence of a person? Modeling questions such as these will help students connect to "Monkey Master" and to the Small-Group Performance Task assignment. Selection audio and print capability for the selection are available in the Interactive Teacher's Edition.

Concept Vocabulary

Encourage groups to discuss the concept vocabulary. Have they seen the terms in texts before? Do they use any of them in their speech and writing?

Have groups consider how the three terms are related and share their ideas with the class.

⬤ FIRST READ

Students should perform the steps of the first read independently.

NOTICE: Encourage students to make note of some general ideas about the text, including the main ideas of the text and which people and animals it is about.

ANNOTATE: Remind students to mark any vocabulary and passages that are unclear or that they wish to know more about.

CONNECT: Encourage students to make connections beyond the selection and the art created by Congo. If they cannot make connections to their own lives, have them consider stories or news reports of other animals who have become noteworthy for their artistic creations.

RESPOND: Students will answer questions and write a summary to demonstrate understanding. Point out to students that while they will always complete the Respond step at the end of the first read, the other steps will probably happen somewhat concurrently. You may wish to print copies of the **First-Read Guide: Nonfiction** for students to use. 🖹

About the Author

Waldemar Januszczak (b. 1954) is the longest-serving art critic in the British national press. The son of Polish immigrants, Januszczak studied the History of Art at Manchester University and in 1977 published his first piece of art criticism. From 1979 to 1987, he served as the chief art critic for the *Guardian,* a British newspaper. In 1993, he became the art critic for another British newspaper called the *Sunday Times,* a position he still holds today. He has also made numerous movies about art.

📋 **STANDARDS**

Reading Informational Text
By the end of the year, read and comprehend literary nonfiction in the grades 6–8 text complexity band proficiently, with scaffolding as needed at the high end of the range.

Language
Determine or clarify the meaning of unknown and multiple-meaning words and phrases based on *grade 6 reading and content,* choosing flexibly from a range of strategies.
  c. Consult reference materials, both print and digital, to find the pronunciation of a word or determine or clarify its precise meaning or its part of speech.

Monkey Master
Concept Vocabulary

As you perform your first read of "Monkey Master," you will encounter these words.

purist	aesthetic	abstract

Using a Specialized Dictionary Some words have multiple meanings, especially when they are used in different fields of study. Consider the word *composition*:

> **Customary Meanings:** the way in which something is made up of different parts or elements; the act of combining parts or elements to form a whole
>
> **Specialized Meaning:** the way in which artistic elements, including color, lines, shapes, and space, are arranged in a work of art

To find the precise meanings of such terms, consult a specialized dictionary. A **specialized dictionary** is a reference source that provides information about words as they are used in a particular field of study, such as art or geography. As you read "Monkey Master," use a print or online art dictionary to determine the meanings of unfamiliar art terms you encounter.

First Read NONFICTION

Apply these strategies as you conduct your first read. You will have an opportunity to complete a close read after your first read.

NOTICE the general ideas of the text. *What* is it about? *Who* is involved?

ANNOTATE by marking vocabulary and key passages you want to revisit.

First Read

CONNECT ideas within the selection to what you already know and what you have already read.

RESPOND by completing the Comprehension Check and by writing a brief summary of the selection.

© Pearson Education, Inc., or its affiliates. All rights reserved.

Monkey Master

Waldemar Januszczak

© Pearson Education, Inc., or its affiliates. All rights reserved.

BACKGROUND

SCAN FOR MULTIMEDIA

In this essay, the author describes and analyzes paintings created by a chimpanzee-artist named Congo during the 1950s. The author draws parallels between Congo's paintings and the works of some famous modern artists, such as Pablo Picasso and Wassily Kandinsky. These artists were considered pioneers of abstract art, which does not portray subjects as they appear in real life. Instead, abstract artists emphasize the process of making art as well as the formal elements of color and shape separate from realistic portrayals. They often work to express emotions and ideas in ways that challenge viewers' perceptions.

1   Can a monkey paint a good picture? It's a question that has come up a few times during my tenure as an art critic, as a result of various modern art jokes, scams, cons, and the like.

2   Normally, I would waste no time on the issue. It is, or was, my firmly held view that, in the field of art, monkeys do whatever they do by accident or coercion. Monkeys cannot paint.

3   Then along comes a fascinating and slightly worrying exhibition at London's Mayor Gallery, Ape Artists of the 1950s, and I am no longer so certain. In particular, along comes the artistic work of a talented chimpanzee named Congo.

NOTES

Monkey Master **153**

CLOSER LOOK

Analyze Opinion

Circulate among groups as students conduct their close read. Suggest that groups close read paragraph 2. If needed, provide the following support.

ANNOTATE: Have students mark details in paragraph 2 that reveal the author's initial opinion about monkeys and art.

QUESTION: Guide students to consider what these details might tell them. Ask what a reader can infer from these details and accept student responses.

Possible response: When he first thought about whether a monkey could paint a good picture, the author was doubtful. He thought if monkeys painted, it was not by their own choice.

CONCLUDE: Help students to formulate conclusions about the importance of these details in the text. Ask students why the author might have included these details.

Possible response: The author of this essay at first seems to have a definite opinion that monkeys can't paint, but his essay is called "Monkey Master," which makes the reader think the author might change his opinion.

Remind students that an **opinion** is someone's own view or belief about a subject and is not supported by facts. Sometimes people will change their opinions if they are presented with more information about a subject that make them view the subject differently.

NOTES

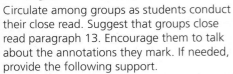

CLOSER LOOK

Analyze Simile ⊘

Circulate among groups as students conduct their close read. Suggest that groups close read paragraph 13. Encourage them to talk about the annotations they mark. If needed, provide the following support.

ANNOTATE: Have students mark details in paragraph 13 that demonstrate the use of a simile, or work with small groups to have students participate as you highlight them together.

QUESTION: Guide students to consider what these details might tell them. Ask what a reader can infer from these details and accept student responses.

Possible response: The author is comparing Congo's best paintings to stained glass, writing that the paintings "shine."

CONCLUDE: Help students to formulate conclusions about the importance of these details in the text. As students why the author might have included these details.

Possible response: The author likely included this simile to give the reader a better picture of how good the author thinks Congo's paintings are.

Remind students that a **simile** is a figure of speech that makes a comparison between two different things and shows similarities between the two.

4 Having carefully examined Congo's paintings, all of which might best be described as examples of lyrical abstract expressionism,[1] I find myself assailed by doubts. I like Congo's paintings. A couple of them I love.

5 I am less sure of the output of the show's gorilla. And not much taken with the orangutan's pictures, either. But in all their cases, something of interest is undoubtedly being attempted, and for the whole show the feeling persists that the lessons being taught here pertain not only to monkeys, but also to us.

6 Congo was born in 1954 and produced about 400 paintings from the age of two to four. He died of tuberculosis in 1964. He appeared on television in the late 1950s, the star turn on *Zootime,* an animal magazine show presented live from London Zoo by animal behavioralist[2] and *The Naked Ape* author Desmond Morris.

7 Apparently, the experiments with Congo began by accident. One day, he picked up a pencil and drew a line. Then he drew more, until it was clear to Morris that the chimp's actions were deliberate.

8 After a short drawing phase, it was decided to move him on to painting. Morris had a baby's highchair and tray adapted to create a seating arrangement at which Congo could work.

9 There are photographs of Congo in action, in which particular attention is drawn to the grip with which he held the brush. It's similar to the way you or I might hold a pen, and was absolutely Congo's invention, apparently. If so, that is already a remarkable development.

10 Congo would be given a piece of paper and, in conditions of considerable concentration, would begin painting. The choice of colors was his, red being a particular favorite, blue being a color he disliked.

11 Fascinatingly, if you tried to take a picture away from Congo before he had finished with it, he would scream and throw fits. However, if he considered the picture done, no amount of cajoling would persuade him to continue. The master's work was complete. That was that.

12 The results have been placed in functional wooden frames and hung in a line in the no-frills exhibition box of the Mayor Gallery. The exhibition comes on the heels of a recent auction of some of Congo's works in London, at which an American collector paid $25,000 for one painting, 20 times the expected price.

13 But not even the Mayor Gallery's charmless presentation can dim the disquieting beauty of Congo's best pictures. They shine off the walls like stained glass.

---

1. **abstract expressionism** post–World War II American art movement in which artists reinvented abstract art to create a distinctly American style; characterized by rich expressions of emotion with an emphasis on the unplanned nature of the creative act or process.
2. **animal behavioralist** person who studies the behavior of animals to understand its causes, functions, and development; also called an animal behaviorist.

© Pearson Education, Inc., or its affiliates. All rights reserved.

154 UNIT 2 • ANIMAL ALLIES

PERSONALIZE FOR LEARNING

English Language Support
Domain-Specific Vocabulary The domain-specific vocabulary that appears in "Monkey Master" may present challenges to English learners. Support them in understanding the photo essay by reviewing the following terms:

Art:

Lyrical: *shows direct feeling*

Abstract: *concerned with the lines, colors, or shapes and their relationship to one another*

Expressionism: *contemporary art that often has bold, bright colors or thick sometimes black lines*

Science:

Animal behavioralist: *a scientist who examines and learns from the actions of animals*

Have students locate these terms in paragraphs 4 and 6 and read the sentence containing the term. Then, have them paraphrase the sentence in their groups.
ALL LEVELS

< In this photograph, Congo is
at work on one of his many
paintings. Notice how he holds
his brush.

NOTES

^ The paintings that illustrate this essay are examples of Congo's artwork.
Here is one of Congo's many paintings called simply *Composition*.

14 There's a cracker[3] called *Composition on White Card,* painted on
August 17, 1958, which is dramatically, even shockingly, sparse.

15 An audacious pink splodge at the center plays a delicate game
of tag across the paper with a couple of different blues. That's
it. And it really works. For Congo to have finished this picture
as he finished it—for a monkey to be this minimal—is deeply
disconcerting.

3. **cracker** British slang term for a thing or person that is especially good or exciting.

Monkey Master **155**

© Pearson Education, Inc., or its affiliates. All rights reserved.

😊 FACILITATING SMALL-GROUP CLOSE READING

CLOSE READ: Essay As groups perform their
close read, circulate and offer support as needed.

- Remind groups as they read "Monkey Master,"
they should also examine the images as they
are being described.

- Remind groups as they read, they may
encounter domain-specific words that are
unfamiliar to them.

- Challenge groups to use context clues and
examples from the images to support their
understanding of unfamiliar words
or concepts.

Concept Vocabulary

PURIST If groups are struggling to define the word *purist* in paragraph 17, call student attention to the word *pure* at the base of the word. Congo does not mix colors. Ask students to use this knowledge, and the context of the paragraph to define the word.

Possible response: In this context, *purist* means "someone who follows the rules."

AESTHETIC If groups are struggling to define the word *aesthetic* in paragraph 19, call student attention to the details in the paragraph related to the quality and color of the paper. Ask students to use this knowledge, and the context of the paragraph to define the word.

Possible response: In this context, *aesthetic* means "related to beauty."

∧ This painting is another example of Congo's artwork. Notice that the brush strokes are deliberate.

NOTES

Use a specialized dictionary or indicate another strategy you used that helped you determine meaning.

purist (PYOOR ihst) *n.*

MEANING:

16   *Composition on Buff Paper,* painted on October 31, 1957, is perhaps Congo's masterpiece. Built compositionally around a central expanse of Congo's beloved crimson, it features an array of blacks and pale greens soaring around the red like vultures around a mountain. The mood is pure Kandinsky, the achievement profound. Not all of Congo's paintings get it as right. His range of painting gestures is narrow: The brush has a tendency to go round and round. He is as guilty as any monkey might be of overdoing things, and most of the paintings lack the specific character of the ones I have described. But the display never stops being remarkable.

17   What is really spooky is the care Congo always brings to working within the paper. Only rarely does the brush stray over the edge. And he clearly understands the notion of balance, too. If a pink has a blue on one side of it, and needs another blue on the other side, he will add one. The absence of muddiness, of colors mixed to sludge through mindless scrubbing, is also spectacular. When it comes to pigments, Congo is a **purist**.

18   So much so that there is some small room for doubt about the role played by Morris. It seems that although the paintings were made for *Zootime,* Congo was not often filmed painting them, because the studio activity put him off. Morris's experiments were mostly conducted off camera, which is a shame.

© Pearson Education, Inc., or its affiliates. All rights reserved.

VOCABULARY DEVELOPMENT

Concept Vocabulary Reinforcement
Paragraph 17 uses the concept vocabulary word *purist* to describe how Congo used color in his paintings. Point out to students that the base word for *purist* is *pure.* Review the meaning of the word as it applies to the Congo and his paintings. Ask why the author describes Congo as a *purist.*

Possible response: The author writes that Congo's paintings have no muddiness, meaning that they were not mixed together mindlessly. That he describes Congo as a *purist* tells me that Congo liked and chose specific, "pure" colors for his paintings.

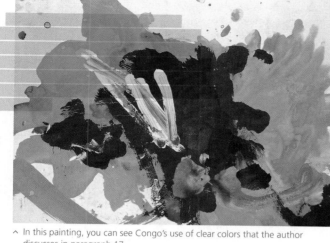

^ In this painting, you can see Congo's use of clear colors that the author discusses in paragraph 17.

NOTES

19   Not for a moment do I question the authenticity of the images, or the methods used to produce them, but it would have been interesting to see the extent of Morris's involvement in important **aesthetic** matters such as the choice of colored paper for Congo to work on. This use of red, orange, green paper has a considerable decorative impact on the final image. Congo may have selected the colors, but who came up with the original wheeze[4] of using impactful colored paper? How much guidance was Congo receiving?

20   I ask only because this intriguing show could profitably have been bigger, fuller, packed with more information.

21   I read, too, that Pablo Picasso was a collector of Congo's work. This does not surprise me. The notion of a painting monkey would have appealed to the devil in him. What's more, Congo, as an ape, could not reasonably have mounted any sort of challenge to the ultra-competitive Picasso's self-esteem.

22   Morris tells an excellent story of a journalist asking Picasso his opinion of Congo's work. Picasso left the room and returned, his arms swinging like an ape's and clutching his Congo painting, then jumped on the journalist and bit him. Artists and monkeys are brothers in arms, seemed to be the message.

23   On a similar tack, Salvador Dali is said to have quipped: "The hand of the chimpanzee is quasi-human; the hand of Jackson Pollock is totally animal."

24   Apart from Congo, there are works on show by Betsy, another chimpanzee, a gorilla named Sophie, and Alexander the

_____
4. **wheeze** British slang term for a trick, idea, or plan.

Use a specialized dictionary or indicate another strategy you used that helped you determine meaning.

aesthetic (ehs THEHT ihk) *adj.*

MEANING:

© Pearson Education, Inc., or its affiliates. All rights reserved.

Monkey Master **157**

CLOSER LOOK

Interpret Quotation

Circulate among groups as students conduct their close read. Suggest that groups close read paragraph 23. If needed, provide the following support.

ANNOTATE: Have students mark details in paragraph 23 that demonstrate use of a quotation, or work with small groups to have students participate while you highlight them together.

QUESTION: Guide students to consider what these details might tell them. Ask what they think Salvador Dali meant by what he said, and accept student responses.

Possible response: I think what Salvador Dali meant in the quotation was that he thought the chimpanzee's art looked good enough to be done by a person and that he thought Jackson Pollock's art looked more like it was done by an animal.

CONCLUDE: Help students to formulate conclusions about the importance of these details in the text. Ask students why the artist might have included these details.

Possible response: The author probably included this quotation to show that he was not the only one who appreciated Congo's art. Some famous artists also thought Congo could paint and enjoyed his paintings.

Remind students that a **quotation** is something that a person has said or written that is used by someone else in writing or speech. Quotations are indicated in text by the author's use of quotation marks.

CROSS-CURRICULAR PERSPECTIVES

Art Paragraphs 21–23 mention several contemporary artists. Have groups select and research one of the following artists: Pablo Picasso, Salvador Dali, Jackson Pollock.

Encourage students to copy or download an image from their chosen artist and compare it to the work of Congo. Have groups share the images and their findings with the class. Encourage them to use media vocabulary words when appropriate in their presentation.

FACILITATING

Concept Vocabulary

ABSTRACT If groups are struggling to define the word *abstract* in paragraph 26, call student attention to the clue of shapes and the meaning or intent of the paragraph. Ask students to use this context to define the word.

Possible response: In this context, *abstract* means "without concrete meaning" or "separated from meaning." Abstract art uses shape, color and texture without recreating a recognizable image.

^ In this composition, Congo has painted on a different-colored background.

NOTES

Use a specialized dictionary or indicate another strategy you used that helped you determine meaning.

abstract (AB strakt) *adj.*

MEANING:

orangutan. With so few examples included, it is difficult to come to any worthwhile conclusions about these other simian maestros, though certainly it is surprising to see how fragile and even nervous are the touches of the huge gorilla.

25   Morris has attempted to give the display a truly gigantic story line by insisting on the importance of ape art to our general understanding of the aesthetic impulse. "It is the work of these apes, not that of prehistoric cave artists," he writes, "that can truly be said to represent the birth of art."

26   If that were so, then this would count as one of the most important exhibitions anyone has put on. I am moved to see it the other way round, from the point of view of the visitor, not the creator: Confronted by a pleasing assortment of **abstract** shapes, we humans have a wondrous ability to find meaning in them and to gain pleasure from them. Art, after all, is only as important as its audience. ❧

158 UNIT 2 • ANIMAL ALLIES

© Pearson Education, Inc., or its affiliates. All rights reserved.

PERSONALIZE FOR LEARNING

English Language Support

Background Knowledge Students may struggle with the rigor of the informational text included in the essay "Monkey Master." Encourage students to share experiences regarding apes or monkeys, whether personal (as in a trip to the zoo) or from news stories or personal reading.

Draw students' attention to paragraph 24. Ask students to look up the meaning of *simian* or share with them that *simian* means "ape" or "monkey." Have students to predict and discuss what Januszczak means by "other *simian maestros.*" **ALL LEVELS**

158 UNIT 2 • ANIMAL ALLIES

Comprehension Check

Complete the following items after you finish your first read. Review and clarify details with your group.

1. What is the name of the exhibition that the author discusses in the essay?

2. What does the author think of the paintings done by the gorilla and the orangutan?

3. Who is Desmond Morris?

4. According to the author, what color does Congo like? What color does he dislike?

5. According to the author, how much did an American art collector pay for one of Congo's paintings?

6. ⊟ **Notebook** Confirm your understanding of the text by writing a brief summary.

- -

RESEARCH

Research to Clarify Choose at least one unfamiliar detail from the text. Briefly research that detail. In what way does the information you learned shed light on an aspect of the essay?

© Pearson Education, Inc., or its affiliates. All rights reserved.

Monkey Master **159**

Comprehension Check

Possible responses:

1. The name of the exhibition is Ape Artists of the 1950s.
2. The author is not impressed with paintings done by either the gorilla or the orangutan.
3. Desmond Morris is an animal behaviorist and author who first worked with Congo.
4. The author writes that Congo likes red and dislikes blue.
5. The American art collector paid $25,000.
6. Summaries will vary, but students should include details about Congo and his paintings, and how the author's initial skepticism about Congo's doing paintings turned into admiration for Congo's artistic talent.

Research

Research to Clarify If students struggle to come up with a detail to research, you may want to suggest that they focus on one of the following topics: animal artwork, Congo the chimpanzee, the Mayor Gallery, abstract art.

Challenge

Media Have groups select one human or animal artist mentioned in "Monkey Master." Have groups collect images from the artist and create a montage to present to the class. They should include captions, either student-created or those given to the piece of art, and prepare to discuss the composition of the art. Allow groups to present in smaller settings or to the entire class. When all groups have presented, have them discuss and compare their group's artist with the work of other artists that were presented.

MAKING MEANING

Jump Start

CLOSE READ Ask students to consider the following questions: *Can an animal be an artist? Does the person who assists the animal influence the art? How do you think the animal might choose how to do the art?* As students discuss these questions in their groups, encourage them to consider the influence people and animals have on each other in the creation of art.

Close Read the Text

If needed, model close reading by using the Closer Look notes in the Interactive Teacher's Edition.

Remind students to use Accountable Talk in their discussions and to support one another as they complete the close review.

Analyze the Text

Possible responses:

1. The author was doubtful of the animals' ability to paint, but he changed his mind after learning about Congo the chimpanzee and the paintings Congo created.

2. Presentations will vary by group, but students should have included details from the text, questions, and conclusions.

3. Answers will vary by group.

Concept Vocabulary

Why These Words? Possible response: All of these words have to do with art or the critique of art.

Practice

Possible responses:
The chef was a purist when it came to how the food should be prepared and would not try any other method.; My sister appreciates the *aesthetic* view of the ocean outside her kitchen window.; The students couldn't tell the *abstract* drawing was of an elephant.

Word Study

For more support, see **Concept Vocabulary and Word Study.** 📄

Possible responses:

purist = person who adheres strictly to tradition; humorist = person skilled in telling or writing funny stories; naturalist = person who studies nature; realist = person who understands the reality and possibilities of a situation

---

MONKEY MASTER

STANDARDS

Reading Informational Text
Integrate information presented in different media or formats as well as in words to develop a coherent understanding of a topic or issue.

Writing
• Conduct short research projects to answer a question, drawing on several sources and refocusing the inquiry when appropriate.
• Gather relevant information from multiple print and digital sources; assess the credibility of each source; and quote or paraphrase the data and conclusions of others while avoiding plagiarism and providing basic bibliographic information for sources.

Speaking and Listening
Engage effectively in a range of collaborative discussions with diverse partners on *grade 6 topics, texts, and issues,* building on others' ideas and expressing their own clearly.
 c. Pose and respond to specific questions with elaboration and detail by making comments that contribute to the topic, text, or issue under discussion.

Language
Determine or clarify the meaning of unknown and multiple-meaning words and phrases based on *grade 6 reading and content,* choosing flexibly from a range of strategies.
 b. Use common, grade-appropriate Greek or Latin affixes and roots as clues to the meaning of a word.
 d. Verify the preliminary determination of the meaning of a word or phrase.

160 UNIT 2 • ANIMAL ALLIES

Close Read the Text

With your group, revisit sections of the text you marked during your first read. **Annotate** details that you notice. What **questions** do you have? What can you **conclude**?

Analyze the Text

CITE TEXTUAL EVIDENCE to support your answers.

Complete the activities.

1. **Review and Clarify** Review the essay with your group. According to the author, before attending the exhibition, how did he view art created by apes or other animals? In what ways have his thoughts on the topic changed?

2. **Present and Discuss** Now, work with your group to share the passages from the text that you found especially important. Take turns presenting your passages. Discuss what you noticed in the text, what questions you asked, and what conclusions you reached.

3. 📝 **Notebook Essential Question:** *How can people and animals relate to each other?* What have you learned from this essay about the interactions between people and animals? Discuss with your group.

LANGUAGE DEVELOPMENT

Concept Vocabulary

purist	aesthetic	abstract

Why These Words? The three concept vocabulary words from the text are related. With your group, determine what the words have in common. Record your ideas, and identify at least one more word that fits the category.

Practice

📝 **Notebook** Confirm your understanding of the concept vocabulary words by using each word in a sentence that shows your understanding of the word's meaning.

Word Study

📝 **Notebook Greek Suffix: *-ist*** The Greek suffix *-ist* means "person who does, makes, practices, is skilled in, or believes in." In the essay, the author says that Congo is a *purist* because he prefers the colors in his paintings to be clear and distinct. Use your knowledge of the suffix *-ist* to write a definition for *purist,* as well as for each of these words: *humorist, naturalist, realist.* Then, use a dictionary to confirm your understanding of the meaning of each word.

© Pearson Education, Inc., or its affiliates. All rights reserved.

FORMATIVE ASSESSMENT

Analyze the Media 📄
If students struggle to review the photograph or paintings, **then** provide the **Monkey Master: Text Questions** available online in the Interactive Teacher's Edition or Unit Resources. Answers and DOK levels are also available.

Concept Vocabulary
If students fail to see a connection between the words, **then** have them use each word in a sentence and think about what is similar about the sentences.

Research and Discuss

Assignment

Conduct research, and then participate in a **group discussion** on one of the following topics:

☐ members of other animal species that create art

☐ Congo's life and why he was unique

Research and Take Notes First, decide as a group which topic you will research. Then, prepare for your discussion by following these steps.

- Use a variety of reliable print and online sources. Websites that end in *.gov* or *.edu* tend to be most reliable, but websites that end with *.org* or *.com* may also have useful information.

- Take notes on each source. First, write down information about the source, such as its title, its author, and how you found it.

- Then, write down relevant facts and ideas that you find in each source. For each fact or idea you write, note its exact location so that you can easily find it again.

- As you research, also look for relevant visuals, such as photographs or videos, that will be interesting to share with your group. Copy, print, or save any visuals that you like, and write down information about them. Look for information about your visuals in captions and in nearby text.

Use this chart to record notes from your research sources.

SOURCE INFORMATION	NOTES

Present and Discuss Share your findings with your group. When it is your turn to speak, consult the notes in your chart, and cite examples from your sources. Also share any visuals you found that are interesting and support your ideas. Respond to questions with details from your research. Listen closely as other group members speak, and ask questions that help other group members elaborate on their ideas about the topic.

Monkey Master **161**

📝 EVIDENCE LOG

Before moving on to a new selection, go to your Evidence Log, and record what you learned from "Monkey Master."

© Pearson Education, Inc., or its affiliates. All rights reserved.

Research and Discuss

Encourage groups to consider which research option they prefer. As a group, would they rather explore new information or extend what they have learned from the selection? Both options will require them to conduct research and find visuals.

Research and Take Notes Remind students that as they do their research, they should make sure that any sources they use are credible. Have students take notes as they research, jotting down information related to the topic as well as information about each source and how they found it. Encourage students to use the chart to record notes as they research.

Present and Discuss Remind groups to refer to their research sources when delivering their presentations. For more support, see **Research and Discuss: Group Discussion.** 📄

Evidence Log Support students in completing their Evidence Log. This paced activity will help prepare them for the Performance-Based Assessment at the end of the unit.

💬 An expanded **English Language Support Lesson** on Taking Notes for a Discussion is available in the Interactive Teacher's Edition. 📄

FORMATIVE ASSESSMENT
Research and Discuss

If groups struggle to research their topics, **then** remind them to use credible online and print sources.

PERSONALIZED FOR LEARNING

Strategic Support

Concept Vocabulary If group members struggle to describe the art encountered in their research, have each group select a word from the Concept Vocabulary: *purist, aesthetic,* or *abstract.* Have groups find a specific example of the word, define it for the class, and share and discuss their examples. Encourage groups to apply their vocabulary word to each group's example in the class discussion.

Black Cowboy, Wild Horses

🔊 AUDIO SUMMARIES

Audio summaries of "Black Cowboy, Wild Horses" are available online in both English and Spanish in the Interactive Teacher's Edition or Unit Resources. Assigning these summaries prior to reading the selection may help students build additional background knowledge and set a context for their first read.

Summary

"Black Cowboy, Wild Horses," a folk literature selection by Julius Lester, tells the story of Bob Lemmons, a cowboy in the West who is very skilled at taming horses. Bob was a slave who had been deprived of a formal education. But he had great practical knowledge and special skill at bringing valuable wild horses in to be tamed. Bob is patient and clever. In the vast wilderness, he braves a storm, rattlesnakes, and the dangerous, wild horses. Bob and his horse, Warrior, ride with the mustangs day and night, and are challenged by the herd's stallion as Bob and Warrior try to round up the herd and lead them into a corral.

Insight

Bob takes control of the herd by manipulating their hierarchical structure. He arranges circumstances to make the lead stallion vulnerable, then successfully takes charge.

ESSENTIAL QUESTION:
How can people and animals relate to each other?

Connection to the Essential Question

This story explores a deep connection between man and animal, addressing the Essential Question, "How can people and animals relate to each other?" Bob understands the feelings and motivations of the horses, and they in turn follow his lead.

SMALL-GROUP LEARNING PERFORMANCE TASK
How can the bonds between people and animals be surprising?

UNIT PERFORMANCE-BASED ASSESSMENT
How can animals and people help one another?

Connection to Performance Tasks

Small-Group Learning Performance Task This story shows the capture of animals. However, Bob seems to feel great empathy for the horses, and he hopes to see them riding free across the plains again.

Unit Performance-Based Assessment This selection will contribute to the students' understanding of interactions between people and animals and how they might help one another by illustrating Bob's patience and gentle perseverance in getting the mustangs to accept him before he leads them to the corral.

LESSON RESOURCES

	Making Meaning	Language Development	Effective Expression
Lesson	**First Read** **Close Read** **Analyze the Text** **Analyze Craft and Structure**	**Concept Vocabulary** **Word Study** **Conventions**	**Research**
Instructional Standards	**RL.3** Describe how a particular story's or drama's plot unfolds . . . **RL.10** By the end of the year, read and comprehend literature . . . **L.4** Determine or clarify the meaning of unknown and multiple-meaning words and phrases . . . **L.4.a** Use context as a clue . . .	**L.1** Demonstrate command of the conventions . . . **L.4** Determine or clarify the meaning of unknown and multiple-meaning words and phrases . . .	**W.7** Conduct short research projects . . . **W.8** Gather relevant information from multiple print and digital sources . . . **SL.1** Engage effectively in a range of collaborative discussions . . . **SL.1.b** Follow rules for collegial discussions . . . **SL.5** Include multimedia components and visual displays . . .

▷ STUDENT RESOURCES

Available online in the Interactive Student Edition or Unit Resources	🔊 Selection Audio 📄 First-Read Guide: Fiction 📄 Close-Read Guide: Fiction	📄 Word Network	📄 Evidence Log

▷ TEACHER RESOURCES

Selection Resources Available online in the Interactive Teacher's Edition or Unit Resources	🔊 Audio Summaries ✒ Annotation Highlights 💬 EL Highlights 📄 Black Cowboy, Wild Horses: Text Questions 📄 Analyze Craft and Structure: Story Structure: Plot	📄 Concept Vocabulary and Word Study 📄 Conventions: Perfect Tenses of Verbs 📄 English Language Support Lesson: Using Verb Tenses	📄 Research: Informative Multimedia Presentation
Reteach/Practice (RP) Available online in the Interactive Teacher's Edition or Unit Resources	📄 Analyze Craft and Structure: Story Structure: Plot (RP)	📄 Word Study: Multiple-Meaning Words (RP) 📄 Conventions: Perfect Tenses of Verbs (RP)	📄 Research: Informative Multimedia Presentation (RP)
Assessment Available online in Assessments	📄 ☑ Selection Test		
My Resources	📄 A Unit 2 Answer Key is available online and in the Interactive Teacher's Edition.		

Reading Support

Text Complexity Rubric: Black Cowboy, Wild Horses

Quantitative Measures

Lexile 710   Text Length 1,745 words

Qualitative Measures

Knowledge Demands ①——②——**❸**——④——⑤	The situations may be unfamiliar to some readers (a cowboy rounding up horses), but the situations and emotions are clearly explained.
Structure ①——**❷**——③——④——⑤	Linear story; the only dialogue is the character's conversations with his horse.
Language Conventionality and Clarity ①——②——**❸**——④——⑤	Selection contains figurative language and complex descriptions.
Levels of Meaning/Purpose ①——②——**❸**——④——⑤	Multiple levels of meaning; events are described that also signify the human connection with the natural world; concepts and meanings are mostly explained and easy to grasp.

DECIDE AND PLAN

English Language Support

Provide English Learners with support for language and levels of meaning/purpose as they read the selection.

Language Students may get confused reading passages with figurative language; for example, from paragraph 1, *stared at the land stretching as wide as love in every direction.... a hawk was suspended on cold threads of unseen winds.* Ask questions to guide students to understand that these are figurative rather than literal phrases.

Levels of Meaning/Purpose To help students sort out the events and ideas in the story, suggest that they keep a log of the main events, stating them in their own words. For example, for paragraphs 4–6, *Bob is tracking a herd of horses. He is able to look at the tracks and figure out how many horses are in the herd and how long ago they had been there.*

Strategic Support

Provide students with strategic support to ensure that they can successfully read the text.

Language For students who have difficulty understanding metaphors and similes, have them underline or list the phrases that they don't understand. Then have them read those phrases again and work with a partner to try to figure out the comparison the writer is making.

Levels of Meaning/Purpose If students have difficulty understanding the multiple levels of meaning, focus on individual paragraphs. Ask students to first state the events that happen. Then ask them to reread the paragraph to determine what feelings or ideas are conveyed about Bob's relationship to animals and nature.

Challenge

For students who need to be challenged, provide ideas for how they can go beyond a simple interpretation of the text.

Text Analysis Ask students to analyze paragraph 23, in which Bob comes across a rattlesnake. What does this encounter say about Bob's relationship with nature? The writer uses the simile *as beautiful as a necklace.* Why did he choose this comparison? What are some other similes that would evoke a different feeling about the snake?

Written Response After discussing Bob's ability to have empathy for the snake, ask students to write a paragraph about how this relationship helps him to gain control of the wild horses. How does thinking like a horse help Bob with his task?

TEACH

Read and Respond

Have groups read the selection and complete the Making Meaning, Language Development, and Effective Expression activities.

Standards Support Through Teaching and Learning Cycle

IDENTIFY NEEDS

Analyze results of the Beginning-of-Year Assessment, focusing on the items relating to Unit 2. Also take into consideration student performance to this point and your observations of where particular students struggle.

ANALYZE AND REVISE

- Analyze student work for evidence of student learning.
- Identify whether or not students have met the expectations in the standards.
- Identify implications for future instruction.

TEACH

Implement the planned lesson, and gather evidence of student learning.

DECIDE AND PLAN

- If students have performed poorly on items matching these standards, then provide selection scaffolds before assigning them the on-level lesson provided in the Student Edition.
- If students have done well on the Beginning-of-Year Assessment, then challenge them to keep progressing and learning by giving them opportunities to practice the skills in depth.
- Use the Selection Resources listed on the Planning pages for "Black Cowboy, Wild Horses" to help students continually improve their ability to master the standards.

Instructional Standards: "Black Cowboy, Wild Horses"

	Catching Up	This Year	Looking Forward
Reading	You may wish to administer the **Analyze Craft and Structure: Story Structure: Plot (RP)** worksheet to help students understand the plot structure in the text.	**RL.3** Describe how a particular story's or drama's plot unfolds in a series of episodes as well as how the characters respond or change as the plot moves toward a resolution.	Have students discuss what conflict was solved. How does the ending compare to that of other stories about folk heroes they have read?
Speaking and Listening	You may wish to administer the **Research: Informative Multimedia Presentation (RP)** worksheet to help students organize their multimedia presentations.	**SL.5** Include multimedia components and visual displays in presentations to clarify information.	You may wish to challenge students to create their own artwork to accompany their presentations.
Language	You may wish to administer the **Word Study: Multiple-Meaning Words (RP)** worksheet to help students understand that some words have more than one meaning. You may wish to administer the **Conventions: Perfect Tenses of Verbs (RP)** worksheet to help students understand how to form the past perfect, present perfect, and future perfect of verbs.	**L.4** Determine or clarify the meaning of unknown and multiple-meaning words and phrases based on *grade 6 reading and content*, choosing flexibly from a range of strategies. **L.1** Demonstrate command of the conventions of standard English grammar and usage when writing or speaking.	Have students analyze the subtleties and nuances of various word choices in the texts that they read.

Jump Start

FIRST READ Ask students to consider the following questions: *Why are some people better at interacting with animals than other people are? What causes an animal to like or "take to" one person, while it is afraid of someone else?* Engage students in a discussion about the interaction between people and animals to help them make connections between their own experiences and "Black Cowboy, Wild Horses."

Black Cowboy, Wild Horses 🔊 📄

What makes Bob better at his job than other cowboys? What do Bob's choices show about his understanding of the mustangs? Modeling questions such as these will help students connect to "Black Cowboy, Wild Horses" and to the Small-Group Performance Task assignment. Selection audio and print capability for the selection are available in the Interactive Teacher's Edition.

Concept Vocabulary

Ask groups to look closely at the base words in the example and discuss how looking at the familiar word helps to determine the meaning of the unfamiliar word. Encourage groups to discuss other vocabulary strategies they could use if they are unfamiliar with the base word. Possibilities include context clues such as synonyms, elaborating details, or contrast of details.

● FIRST READ

Students should perform the steps of the first read independently.

NOTICE: You may want to encourage students to notice the speed or pace that Bob takes throughout the story.

ANNOTATE: Remind students to mark passages that include language that helps to create an especially vivid description.

CONNECT: Encourage students to discuss personal encounters with animals, either wild or domestic. Ask them to identify lessons that they have learned from their personal encounters or from those in news reports or other media sources.

RESPOND: Students will answer questions to demonstrate understanding.

Point out to students that while they will always complete the Respond step at the end of the first read, the other steps will probably happen somewhat concurrently. You may wish to print copies of the **First-Read Guide: Fiction** for students to use. 📄

About the Author

Julius Lester (b. 1939), a native of St. Louis, Missouri, has been a folk singer, a civil rights photographer, a writer, and a professor of African American Studies and Judaic Studies. His works include novels, stories, poetry, nonfiction, and a memoir.

☰ STANDARDS

Reading Literature
By the end of the year, read and comprehend literature, including stories, dramas, and poems, in the grades 6–8 text complexity band proficiently, with scaffolding as needed at the high end of the range.

Language
Determine or clarify the meaning of unknown and multiple-meaning words and phrases based on *grade 6 reading and content,* choosing flexibly from a range of strategies.
  a. Use context as a clue to the meaning of a word or phrase.

Black Cowboy, Wild Horses

Concept Vocabulary

As you perform your first read of "Black Cowboy, Wild Horses," you will encounter these words.

milled	skittered	quivering

Context Clues If these words are unfamiliar to you, try using **context clues**—other words and phrases that appear nearby in a text—to help you determine their meanings. There are various types of context clues that may help you as you read. Here are some examples:

Synonyms: The passengers **griped** and <u>complained</u> when the bus got stuck in traffic.

Elaboration of Ideas: Her music was an **amalgam** of genres, <u>mixing jazz, rock, and hip-hop</u>.

Contrast of Ideas: <u>Instead of</u> **balking** at the challenge, we <u>bravely accepted</u> it.

Apply your knowledge of base words and other vocabulary strategies to determine the meanings of unfamiliar words you encounter during your first read.

First Read FICTION

Apply these strategies as you conduct your first read. You will have an opportunity to complete a close read after your first read.

NOTICE whom the story is about, *what* happens, *where* and *when* it happens, and *why* those involved react as they do.

ANNOTATE by marking vocabulary and key passages you want to revisit.

First Read

CONNECT ideas within the selection to what you already know and what you have already read.

RESPOND by completing the Comprehension Check.

© Pearson Education, Inc., or its affiliates. All rights reserved.

CLOSE READ: Short Story As groups perform the close read, circulate and offer support as needed.

- Remind students that characters may be people or animals.
- If a group struggles with the lack of dialogue in the selection, encourage them to think

about what the events say about the main character.

- Challenge the group to examine the impact that the main character has on the horses and the impact that the horses have on the main character.

SHORT STORY

Black Cowboy, Wild Horses

Julius Lester

BACKGROUND

When Spanish explorers came to the Americas, they brought domesticated horses with them. Over time, some of these horses escaped into the wild, where they formed untamed herds and eventually spread west across the Great Plains. These wild horses became known as mustangs.

SCAN FOR
MULTIMEDIA

1 First Light. Bob Lemmons rode his horse slowly up the rise. When he reached the top, he stopped at the edge of the bluff.[1] He looked down at the corral[2] where the other cowboys were beginning the morning chores, then turned away and stared at the land stretching as wide as love in every direction. The sky was curved as if it were a lap on which the earth lay napping like a curled cat. High above, a hawk was suspended on cold threads of unseen winds. Far, far away, at what looked to be the edge of the world, land and sky kissed.

NOTES

2 He guided Warrior, his black stallion, slowly down the bluff. When they reached the bottom, the horse reared, eager to run across the vastness of the plains until he reached forever. Bob smiled and patted him gently on the neck. "Easy. Easy," he whispered. "We'll have time for that. But not yet."

---

1. **bluff** *n.* cliff.
2. **corral** (kuh RAL) *n.* fenced area for horses and cattle.

© Pearson Education, Inc., or its affiliates. All rights reserved.

CLOSER LOOK

Understand Figurative Language

Circulate among groups as students conduct their close read. Suggest that groups close read paragraph 1. Encourage them to talk about the annotations they mark. If needed, provide the following support.

ANNOTATE: Have students mark details in paragraph 1 that the author used in a figurative rather than literal sense, or work with small groups as you highlight them together.

QUESTION: Guide students to consider what these details might tell them. Ask what a reader can infer from the use of figurative language in these phrases. Ask what they might suggest about Bob Lemmons's thoughts about nature, and accept student responses.

Possible response: He sees the land stretching a wide as love; he sees the earth napping; he sees the land and sky kiss. These are all examples of figurative language that show that Bob sees nature as peaceful and beautiful.

CONCLUDE: Help students to formulate conclusions about the importance of these details in the text. Ask students why the author might have included these details.

Possible response: In paragraph 1, by using the simile, "the land stretching as wide as love," the author shows that Bob loves the wide-open spaces. It helps readers begin to see a man who is not afraid, but who feels calm.

Remind students that authors use **figurative language,** phrases and clauses that are not meant to be taken literally, to achieve a specific effect. Figurative language often allows writers to create more vivid descriptions and add layers of meaning.

Additional **English Language Support** is available in the Interactive Teacher's Edition.

PERSONALIZE FOR LEARNING

English Language Support

Figurative Language Note this sentence in paragraph 1: *The sky was curved as if it were a lap on which the earth lay napping like a curled cat.* Explain to students that this sentence contains examples of a simile, which compares one thing to an unlike thing to show their similarities. Similes use words such as *like* or *as* to help readers better understand the author's meaning.

Ask students what things are being compared in the sentence. Make sure that they understand that the sky is being compared to a lap and the earth is being compared to a curled up and napping cat.
Ask students why they think the author chose to use this image. Encourage students to draw from their own experiences and share their stories with others to help them better understand this and other examples of figurative language.

NOTES

3   He let the horse trot for a while, then slowed him and began peering intently at the ground as if looking for the answer to a question he scarcely understood.

4   It was late afternoon when he saw them—the hoofprints of mustangs, the wild horses that lived on the plains. He stopped, dismounted, and walked around carefully until he had seen all the prints. Then he got down on his hands and knees to examine them more closely.

5   Some people learned from books. Bob had been a slave and never learned to read words. But he could look at the ground and read what animals had walked on it, their size and weight, when they had passed by, and where they were going. No one he knew could bring in mustangs by themselves, but Bob could make horses think he was one of them—because he was.

6   He stood, reached into his saddlebag, took out an apple, and gave it to Warrior, who chewed with noisy enthusiasm. It was a herd of eight mares, a colt, and a stallion. They had passed there two days ago. He would see them soon. But he needed to smell of sun, moon, stars, and wind before the mustangs would accept him.

7   The sun went down and the chilly night air came quickly. Bob took the saddle, saddlebag, and blanket off Warrior. He was cold, but could not make a fire. The mustangs would smell the smoke in his clothes from miles away. He draped a thick blanket around himself, then took the cotton sack of dried fruit, beef jerky, and nuts from his saddlebag and ate. When he was done, he lay his head on his saddle and was quickly asleep. Warrior grazed in the tall, sweet grasses.

8   As soon as the sun's round shoulders came over the horizon, Bob awoke. He ate, filled his canteen, and saddling Warrior, rode away. All day he followed the tracks without hurrying.

9   Near dusk, clouds appeared, piled atop each other like mountains made of fear. Lightning flickered from within them like candle flames shivering in a breeze. Bob heard the faint but distinct rumbling of thunder. Suddenly lightning vaulted from cloud to cloud across the curved heavens.

10   Warrior reared, his front hooves pawing as if trying to knock the white streaks of fire from the night sky. Bob raced Warrior to a nearby ravine[3] as the sky exploded sheets of light. And there, in the distance, beneath the ghostly light, Bob saw the herd of mustangs. As if sensing their presence, Warrior rose into the air once again, this time not challenging the heavens but almost in greeting. Bob thought he saw the mustang stallion rise in response as the earth shuddered from the sound of thunder.

11   Then the rain came as hard and stinging as remorse. Quickly Bob put on his poncho, and turning Warrior away from the wind

3. **ravine** (ruh VEEN) *n.* narrow canyon with steep sides.

© Pearson Education, Inc., or its affiliates. All rights reserved.

PERSONALIZE FOR LEARNING

English Language Support

Characterization English Language Learners may struggle with characterization because there is little dialogue to show what others think or how they react to the main character. Have English learners describe the ways in which they learn about a character. Encourage students to create a chart to capture examples from the selection of *direct* and *indirect* characterization. **ALL LEVELS**

Direct Characterization *(what is stated about Bob)*	Indirect Characterization *(what Bob's actions show)*
Bob had been a slave and never learned to read words. (paragraph 5)	Careful
. . . he could look at the ground and read what animals had walked on it . . . (paragraph 5)	Thoughtful
	Moves slowly
. . . Bob could make horses think he was one of them—because he was. (paragraph 5)	Pays attention
	Plans ahead

After creating the chart, have groups discuss their notations and write a few sentences to describe Bob.

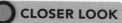

and the rain, waited. The storm would pass soon. Or it wouldn't. There was nothing to do but wait.

12   Finally the rain slowed and then stopped. The clouds thinned, and there, high in the sky, the moon appeared as white as grief. Bob slept in the saddle while Warrior grazed on the wet grasses.

13   The sun rose into a clear sky and Bob was awake immediately. The storm would have washed away the tracks, but they had been going toward the big river. He would go there and wait.

14   By mid-afternoon he could see the ribbon of river shining in the distance. He stopped, needing only to be close enough to see the horses when they came to drink. Toward evening he saw a trail of rolling, dusty clouds.

15   In front was the mustang herd. As it reached the water, the stallion slowed and stopped. He looked around, his head raised, nostrils flared, smelling the air. He turned in Bob's direction and sniffed the air again.

16   Bob tensed. Had he come too close too soon? If the stallion smelled anything new, he and the herd would be gone and Bob would never find them again. The stallion seemed to be looking directly at him. Bob was too far away to be seen, but he did not even blink his eyes, afraid the stallion would hear the sound. Finally the stallion began drinking and the other horses followed. Bob let his breath out slowly. He had been accepted.

17   The next morning he crossed the river and picked up the herd's trail. He moved Warrior slowly, without sound, without dust. Soon he saw them grazing. He stopped. The horses did not notice him. After a while he moved forward, slowly, quietly. The stallion raised his head. Bob stopped.

18   When the stallion went back to grazing, Bob moved forward again. All day Bob watched the herd, moving only when it moved but always coming closer. The mustangs sensed his presence. They thought he was a horse.

19   So did he.

20   The following morning Bob and Warrior walked into the herd. The stallion eyed them for a moment. Then, as if to test this newcomer, he led the herd off in a gallop. Bob lay flat across Warrior's back and moved with the herd. If anyone had been watching, they would not have noticed a man among the horses.

21   When the herd set out early the next day, it was moving slowly. If the horses had been going faster, it would not have happened.

22   The colt fell to the ground as if she had stepped into a hole and broken her leg. Bob and the horses heard the chilling sound of the rattles. Rattlesnakes didn't always give a warning before they struck. Sometimes, when someone or something came too close, they bit with the fury of fear.

NOTES

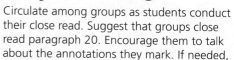

CLOSER LOOK

Analyze Conflict

Circulate among groups as students conduct their close read. Suggest that groups close read paragraph 20. Encourage them to talk about the annotations they mark. If needed, provide the following support.

ANNOTATE: Have students mark details in paragraph 20 that demonstrate the relationship between Bob and the mustangs, or work with small groups as you highlight them together.

QUESTION: Guide students to consider what these details might tell them. Ask what a reader can infer from the way that Bob interacts with the herd of mustang. Students may consider what steps Bob had to take to make this happen. Accept student responses.

Possible response: The horses were not afraid of Bob. He was accepted by the mustangs because he was patient and moved slowly until they recognized him as one of the horses.

CONCLUDE: Help students to formulate conclusions about the importance of these details in the text. Ask students why the author might have included these details.

Possible response: Bob knew that if he approached too quickly, they would smell something new and run from him. The author writes that if "anyone had been watching, they would not have noticed a man among the horses." Because he understood the behavior of the mustangs and was patient, Bob was able to ride unnoticed among the horses.

Remind students that the **conflict** in the story is the problem that needs to be resolved. This paragraph escalates the conflict because Bob has moved into the herd. Readers will continue to track what happens next in the text.

© Pearson Education, Inc., or its affiliates. All rights reserved.

Concept Vocabulary

MILLED If groups are struggling to define the word *milled* in paragraph 25, point out that the base word is *mill*. Draw students' attention to the additional context clue *aimlessly* and have them use the base word and context clue to define *milled*.

Possible response: In this context, *milled* means "moved around in a disorganized way."

SKITTERED If groups are struggling to define the word *skittered* in paragraph 25, point out that the base word is *skitter*. Draw student attention to the sentence to examine the additional context clue, *She skittered away*, and have them use the base word and context clue to define *skittered*.

Possible response: In this context, *skittered* means "moved in a quick manner."

QUIVERING If groups are struggling to define the word *quivering* in paragraph 32, point out the base word, *quiver*. Draw their attention to the context clue, *the rippling of muscles*. Point out that this is a context clue that restates an idea. Have students use the base word and the context clue to define *quivering*.

Possible response: In this context, *quivering* means "shaking" or "shivering."

 Additional **English Language Support** is available in the Interactive Teacher's Edition.

NOTES

Mark context clues or indicate another strategy you used that helped you determine meaning.

milled (mihld) *v.*

MEANING:

skittered (SKIHT uhrd) *v.*

MEANING:

quivering (KWIHV uhr ihng) *n.*

MEANING:

---

23   The horses whinnied and pranced nervously, smelling the snake and death among them. Bob saw the rattler, as beautiful as a necklace, sliding silently through the tall grasses. He made no move to kill it. Everything in nature had the right to protect itself, especially when it was afraid.

24   The stallion galloped to the colt. He pushed at her. The colt struggled to get up, but fell to her side, shivering and kicking feebly with her thin legs. Quickly she was dead.

25   Already vultures circled high in the sky. The mustangs **milled** aimlessly. The colt's mother whinnied, refusing to leave the side of her colt. The stallion wanted to move the herd from there, and pushed the mare with his head. She refused to budge, and he nipped her on the rump. She **skittered** away. Before she could return to the colt, the stallion bit her again, this time harder. She ran toward the herd. He bit her a third time, and the herd was off. As they galloped away, Bob looked back. The vultures were descending from the sky as gracefully as dusk.

26   It was time to take over the herd. The stallion would not have the heart to fight fiercely so soon after the death of the colt. Bob galloped Warrior to the front and wheeled around, forcing the stallion to stop quickly. The herd, confused, slowed and stopped also.

27   Bob raised Warrior to stand high on his back legs, fetlocks pawing and kicking the air. The stallion's eyes widened. He snorted and pawed the ground, surprised and uncertain. Bob charged at the stallion.

28   Both horses rose on hind legs, teeth bared as they kicked at each other. When they came down, Bob charged Warrior at the stallion again, pushing him backward. Bob rushed yet again.

29   The stallion neighed loudly, and nipped Warrior on the neck. Warrior snorted angrily, reared, and kicked out with his forelegs, striking the stallion on the nose. Still maintaining his balance, Warrior struck again and again. The mustang stallion cried out in pain. Warrior pushed hard against the stallion. The stallion lost his footing and fell to the earth. Warrior rose, neighing triumphantly, his front legs pawing as if seeking for the rungs on which he could climb a ladder into the sky.

30   The mustang scrambled to his feet, beaten. He snorted weakly. When Warrior made as if to attack again, the stallion turned, whinnied weakly, and trotted away.

31   Bob was now the herd's leader, but would they follow him? He rode slowly at first, then faster and faster. The mustangs followed as if being led on ropes.

32   Throughout that day and the next he rode with the horses. For Bob there was only the bulging of the horses' dark eyes, the **quivering** of their flesh, the rippling of muscles and bending of

© Pearson Education, Inc., or its affiliates. All rights reserved.

166 UNIT 2 • ANIMAL ALLIES

DIGITAL PERSPECTIVES

Illuminating the Text To help students better understand and visualize the sense of community and the movements of wild horses, have groups research and locate photos and videos of wild horses. Display the photos and videos for students after they have finished reading, and have groups discuss how the images enhance their understanding of "Black Cowboy, Wild Horses." Encourage them to consider how or if their view of the lead mustang and his actions changed in reaction to the photos and videos. **(Research to Clarify)**

Segbones in their bodies. He was now sky and plains and grass and river and horse.

33   When his food was almost gone. Bob led the horses on one last ride, a dark surge of flesh flashing across the plains like black lightning. Toward evening he led the herd up the steep hillside, onto the bluff, and down the slope toward the big corral. The cowboys heard him coming and opened the corral gate. Bob led the herd, but at the last moment he swerved Warrior aside, and the mustangs flowed into the fenced enclosure. The cowboys leaped and shouted as they quickly closed the gate.

34   Bob rode away from them and back up to the bluff. He stopped and stared out onto the plains. Warrior reared and whinnied loudly.

35   "I know," Bob whispered. "I know. Maybe someday."

36   Maybe someday they would ride with the mustangs, ride to that forever place where land and sky kissed, and then ride on. Maybe someday. ❧

NOTES

Comprehension Check

Complete the following items after you finish your first read. Review and clarify details with your group.

1. Who is Warrior?

2. What do Bob and Warrior dream of doing someday?

3. 📔 **Notebook** Confirm your understanding of the text by making a set of sketches, or quick drawings, of the story's most important events.

- -

RESEARCH

Research to Clarify Choose at least one unfamiliar detail from the text. Briefly research that detail. In what way does the information you learned shed light on an aspect of the story?

Research to ClarifyBlack Cowboy, Wild Horses **167**

Pearson Education, Inc., or its affiliates. All rights reserved.

DIGITAL PERSPECTIVES

Comprehension Check

Possible responses:

1. Warrior is Bob's horse.
2. Bob and Warrior dream of living among the mustangs rather than capturing them.
3. Sketches will vary but should include these events: Bob tracks mustangs. Rainstorm occurs. Bob slowly gains mustangs' trust and is accepted. Snake bites colt. Colt dies and stallion tries to move herd. Bob and Warrior challenge stallion and win. Bob and Warrior lead the mustangs into captivity.

Research

Research to Clarify If groups struggle to narrow and choose one unfamiliar detail from the story, encourage students to focus on the dangers of the mustangs' natural environment or on the life of a cowboy.

PERSONALIZED FOR LEARNING

Challenge

Research Encourage interested students to research the laws surrounding wild mustangs in the United States. Which states have wild mustangs? How has the mustang population changed over years? What impact do the laws regarding wild mustangs have on their population? Have students create a map showing areas of concentration and ask students to share their findings with their groups.

Small-Group Learning   **167**

Jump Start

CLOSE READ Ask groups to consider the following prompts: *Why do you think Bob was able to capture the wild mustangs when others would have failed? Was his success based on the careful steps he took, was it purely by chance, or was it a combination of factors?* As students discuss in their groups, ask them to consider how the elements of nature impacted Bob and how he reacted to them.

BLACK COWBOY, WILD HORSES

Close Read the Text

With your group, revisit sections of the text you marked during your first read. **Annotate** details that you notice. What **questions** do you have? What can you **conclude**?

Close Read the Text

If needed, model close reading by using the Annotation Highlights in the Interactive Teacher's Edition.

Remind students to use Accountable Talk in their discussions and to support one another as they complete the close read.

Analyze the Text

CITE TEXTUAL EVIDENCE to support your answers.

📓 **Notebook** Complete the activities.

1. **Review and Clarify** With your group, reread paragraph 5 of the selection. What can Bob "read"? Having read the entire selection, why do you think the author describes Bob as one of the horses?

2. **Present and Discuss** Now, work with your group to share the passages from the text that you found especially important. Take turns presenting your passages. Discuss what you noticed in the text, what questions you asked, and what conclusions you reached.

3. **Essential Question:** *How can people and animals relate to each other?* What has this story taught you about how people and animals can relate to each other? Discuss with your group.

Analyze the Text

1. **Possible response:** Bob could "read" the ground for signs of animals that walked there and know all kinds of information about them. I think the author described Bob as being one of the horses because Bob was so in tune with animals and the way they would behave.

2. Remind students to explain why they chose the passage they presented to group members.

3. Responses will vary by group.

Concept Vocabulary

Why These Words? Possible response: All of these words have to do with movement which helps the reader visualize the natural behaviors of the horses.

Practice

Possible responses:

- The anxious shopper **milled** around the entrance waiting for the store to open.
- The frightened kitten **skittered** away and sat **quivering** under the chair because the small child approached too quickly.

Word Study

For more support, see **Concept Vocabulary and Word Study.** 📄
Possible responses:
mill, *noun:* 1. a building that has machinery to grind grain; 2. a machine that grinds material; *verb:* 1. to process materials by grinding; 2. to move about without direction

Word Network

Possible response: *mustang, trot, hoofprints, dismounted, saddlebag, whinnied, fetlocks, neighed, mares*

TIP

GROUP DISCUSSION
When you work in your group to answer the Analyze the Text questions, be sure to support your opinions and ideas with evidence from the text.

⊞ WORD NETWORK
Add words related to people and animals from the text to your Word Network.

⬛ STANDARDS
Reading Literature
Describe how a particular story's or drama's plot unfolds in a series of episodes as well as how the characters respond or change as the plot moves toward a resolution.

Language
Determine or clarify the meaning of unknown and multiple-meaning words and phrases based on *grade 6 reading and content,* choosing flexibly from a range of strategies.

168 UNIT 2 • ANIMAL ALLIES

LANGUAGE DEVELOPMENT

Concept Vocabulary

milled	skittered	quivering

Why These Words? The three concept vocabulary words from the text are related. With your group, determine what the words have in common. How do these word choices enhance the impact of the text?

Practice

📓 **Notebook** Confirm your understanding of these words by using them in sentences. Be sure to include context clues that hint at each word's meaning. If necessary, look up the precise meanings of the vocabulary words in a dictionary.

Word Study

Multiple-Meaning Words Some words have more than one meaning. For instance, the word *mill* has many different meanings and is used as several different parts of speech. Use a dictionary to look up two meanings for the noun *mill* and two meanings for the verb *mill*. Record your findings.

© Pearson Education, Inc., or its affiliates. All rights reserved.

FORMATIVE ASSESSMENT

Analyze the Text

If students struggle to close read the text, **then** provide the **Black Cowboy, Wild Horses: Text Questions** available online in the Interactive Teacher's Edition or Unit Resources. Answers and DOK levels are also available.

Concept Vocabulary

If students fail to see a connection between the words, **then** have them use each word in a sentence and think about what is similar about the sentences.

Word Study

If students do not see a difference in the meaning of *mill* as a noun, **then** have them explain each meaning to a partner and use the correct definition in a sentence. For Reteach and Practice, see **Word Study: Multiple-Meaning Words (RP).** 📄

Analyze Craft and Structure

Story Structure: Plot A **plot** is the sequence of related events in a story. All plots center on a **conflict,** which is a struggle or problem the characters face. In some stories, the conflict comes from an outside force, such as nature or another character. In other stories, the conflict comes from within a character, who may have a desire or a goal that is difficult to achieve. Every plot follows a set of steps, or stages, in which the conflict is introduced, developed, and finally resolved.

- **Exposition:** The characters, setting, and basic situation are introduced.
- **Rising Action:** The conflict begins and starts to get more intense.
- **Climax:** The conflict reaches its point of greatest drama or tension.
- **Falling Action:** The eventual outcome of the story becomes clear. The tension in the story decreases.
- **Resolution:** The conflict comes to an end, and any loose ends are tied up.

Practice

CITE TEXTUAL EVIDENCE to support your answers.

📝 **Notebook** Work independently to answer the questions. Then, share your responses with your group and discuss any differences.

1. (a) In this story, what does Bob Lemmons want to achieve? (b) Identify at least two problems Bob solves in order to achieve his goal. Explain your choices.

2. (a) What information about the setting, Bob Lemmons, and Warrior appears in the first two paragraphs? (b) To which stage of the story's plot do these paragraphs belong? Explain.

3. (a) What important information appears in paragraph 4? (b) Why is this information important? (c) To which stage of the story's plot do you think this paragraph belongs? Explain your thinking.

4. At what point do you think the story reaches its climax, or point of greatest tension? Explain your choice.

5. (a) At the end of the story, what unfulfilled longing does Bob express? (b) Why do you think the author ends with this open issue, rather than with Bob's successful achievement of his goal? Explain your thinking.

© Pearson Education, Inc., or its affiliates. All rights reserved.

Black Cowboy, Wild Horses **169**

Analyze Craft and Structure

Story Structure: Plot Explain that the conflict is the driving force in most short stories. Discuss with students the difference between the *external conflicts* and *internal conflicts* that Bob encounters. Ask students to consider how these conflicts influence him and impact the plot. Examples of external conflict may include the storm, the rattlesnake, and the death of the colt. Examples of internal conflict may include Bob's potential remorse over leaving the horses in captivity. For more support, see **Analyze Craft and Structure: Story Structure: Plot.** 🔊

Practice

Possible responses:

1. (a) Bob Lemmons wanted to bring in and corral a herd of mustangs by himself. (b) Bob and Warrior would spook the herd if they moved too quickly, so they had to move slowly and quietly in order to be accepted by the herd's stallion. Bob had to overtake the mustang stallion in order to become the herd's leader. In order to bring in the herd, he had to be stronger than the stallion.

2. (a) Bob Lemmons is a cowboy and Warrior is his horse. They live and work in a wide open space in the plains. (b) These paragraphs belong to the exposition stage of the plot because the characters and setting are introduced.

3. (a) Bob first sees the mustangs' hoofprints. (b) This information is important because the hoofprints show that wild mustangs are nearby. That Bob spots the hoofprints sets up the story. (c) This paragraph belongs in the rising action part of the plot because the plot starts to get more intense.

4. The story reaches its greatest point of tension when Bob and Warrior overtake the mustang stallion. Bob is not sure the stallion will back down.

5. (a) Bob expresses a longing to ride with the mustangs someday. (b) The author ends with this unfulfilled longing, probably to express that he understands the mustangs' wild nature even though he corralled them.

FORMATIVE ASSESSMENT

Analyze Craft and Structure

If students are unable to analyze the plot structure, **then** have them list the key events and explain how they impact the story. Allow them to skim the selection if needed. For Reteach and Practice, see **Analyze Craft and Structure: Story Structure: Plot (RP).** 🔊

Small-Group Learning **169**

Conventions

Perfect Tenses of Verbs Before discussing the definition of *present perfect, past perfect,* and *future perfect* verbs, remind students of the definition of a past participle of a verb. It is the form of a verb typically ending in *-ed*. It is used to build the perfect tenses of verbs. You may choose to use the concept vocabulary word *skittered* as an additional example.

> Present Perfect: The toddler has skittered around the room.
>
> Past Perfect: The inexperienced player had skittered away from the ball.
>
> Future Perfect: Her paper will have skittered away in the breeze before she catches it.

For more support, see **Conventions: Perfect Tenses of Verbs.**

Read It

Possible responses:
1. (a) had been (b) had walked, had passed
2. Responses will vary, but students should explain that the story is about Bob Lemmons reflecting back on specific events rather than speaking about the present or about his future plans.

Write It

Possible response:
I have talked to the teacher. I had talked to the teacher before I did my homework. I will have talked to the teacher before the grading period is over. She has read the book. She had read the book before she saw the movie. She will have read the book before the test.

FORMATIVE ASSESSMENT

Conventions

If students can't form the correct perfect tense of a verb, **then** remind them to begin by using the correct form of *have* and then add the past participle of the verb. For Reteach and Practice, see **Conventions: Perfect Tenses of Verbs (RP).**

BLACK COWBOY, WILD HORSES

Conventions

Perfect Tenses of Verbs The three **perfect tenses** of a verb are used to tell when an action or condition was or will be completed.

- The **present perfect tense** shows an action or condition that began in the past and has consequences that continue into the present.
- The **past perfect tense** shows a past action or condition that ended before another past action began.
- The **future perfect tense** shows a future action or condition that will have ended before another begins.

To form one of the perfect tenses, combine a form of the helping verb *have* with the past participle of the main verb. This chart shows how to form the three perfect tenses.

PRESENT PERFECT TENSE	PAST PERFECT TENSE	FUTURE PERFECT TENSE
have, has + past participle	*had* + past participle	*will have* + past participle
She *has voted* in every election.	She *had voted* by the time we arrived.	I *will have voted* by the time the polls close tomorrow.

Read It

1. In these sentences from "Black Cowboy, Wild Horses," mark all of the verbs in the past perfect tense.
   a. Bob had been a slave and never learned to read words.
   b. But he could look at the ground and read what animals had walked on it, their size and weight, when they had passed by, and where they were going.

2. "Black Cowboy, Wild Horses" has several examples of verbs in the past perfect tense. However, there are no verbs in the present perfect tense or the future perfect tense. Discuss with your group why this is so. If needed, review the definitions of the three perfect tenses.

Write It

📓 **Notebook** Write three sentences for each of the following verbs: *talk, read.* Use the past perfect tense once, the present perfect tense once, and the future perfect tense once.

📋 STANDARDS
Language
Demonstrate command of the conventions of standard English grammar and usage when writing or speaking.

© Pearson Education, Inc., or its affiliates. All rights reserved.

PERSONALIZE FOR LEARNING

English Language Support

Using Verb Tenses Ask pairs of students to write three sentences about the selection, each using a different verb tense. **EMERGING**

Ask students to write three sentences about the selection, each using a different verb tense. **EXPANDING**

Have students write a paragraph about how the mustangs affected life in America on the Great

Plains in the eighteenth and nineteenth centuries. Tell them to include sentences with each of the verb tenses—present, past, future. **BRIDGING**

An expanded **English Language Support Lesson** on Verb Tenses is available in the Interactive Teacher's Edition. 📄

Research

Assignment

Work with your group to research and create an **informative multimedia presentation** on one of the following topics:

☐ the real-life Bob Lemmons, including his life and work as a "mustanger" and cowboy

☐ another legendary cowboy, including his or her life and the reasons he or she became a famous figure

Incorporate text and a variety of multimedia to highlight the main ideas in your presentation. Conclude your presentation by comparing your topic to Julius Lester's portrayal of the legendary figure of Bob Lemmons in "Black Cowboy, Wild Horses."

Conduct Research Work with your group to decide on a topic, and determine a research assignment for each group member. For example, have some group members find text sources and others look for multimedia. As you conduct research, use notecards like the one shown to record important bibliographic information about your sources, both print and digital:

☐ Print   ☐ Digital   ☐ Text   ☐ Media

Title: _____

Author/Publisher: _____

Date of Access/Copyright Date: _____

URL/Other Location Information: _____

Organize Your Presentation After you have finished your research, work with your group to organize your presentation so that multimedia elements highlight the main points of your presentation. Rehearse with your group, and rearrange the elements of your presentation as necessary so that text and media are integrated and flow smoothly.

Include a Works-Cited List Plagiarism is the act of presenting someone else's ideas or research as your own—the equivalent of academic stealing, or fraud. Even if you restate the ideas in your own words, you still must credit the source that provides them. To avoid plagiarism, you must cite all your sources accurately. Use the notecards from your research to create a **Works-Cited list,** or **bibliography,** in which you credit all your sources according to the citation style your teacher prefers. Your Works-Cited list should appear at the end of your presentation.

EVIDENCE LOG

Before moving on to a new selection, go to your Evidence Log, and record what you learned from "Black Cowboy, Wild Horses."

STANDARDS

Writing
• Conduct short research projects to answer a question, drawing on several sources and refocusing the inquiry when appropriate.
• Gather relevant information from multiple print and digital sources; assess the credibility of each source; and quote or paraphrase the data and conclusions of others while avoiding plagiarism and providing basic bibliographic information for sources.

Speaking and Listening
• Engage effectively in a range of collaborative discussions with diverse partners on *grade 6 topics, texts, and issues,* building on others' ideas and expressing their own clearly.
  b. Follow rules for collegial discussions, set specific goals and deadlines, and define individual roles as needed.
• Include multimedia components and visual displays in presentations to clarify information.

© Pearson Education, Inc., or its affiliates. All rights reserved.

PERSONALIZE FOR LEARNING

Strategic Support

Multimedia Presentation Some students have less experience and may require additional time and support in gathering digital resources and creating the presentation. Prior to forming groups, you may want to identify those who have digital expertise and balance groups accordingly to include a digital leader as an identified role in each group.

Research

Remind students that before they choose a topic that they will be researching the real-life Bob Lemmons or another legendary cowboy or cowgirl. Students should make sure to include different types of multimedia in their presentation to help support their main ideas. For more support, see **Research: Informative Multimedia Presentation.**

Conduct Research Have students decide which group members will do the various research tasks before they start doing research on their topic. Encourage them to record bibliographic information and to refer to the example on the student page.

Organize Your Presentation Remind students that they should make sure any multimedia they use makes sense with the main points they are presenting. Encourage students to practice their presentation with their group so that the presentation runs smoothly when presented to the class.

Include a Works-Cited List Have students make sure to keep track of any sources they used for their research topic. Remind them of the importance of citing sources to avoid plagiarizing any information they obtained.

Encourage students to make supportive comments about each speaker's multimedia selections, words, ideas, and delivery.
Evidence Log Support students in completing their Evidence Log. This paced activity will help prepare them for the Performance-Based Assessment at the end of the unit.

FORMATIVE ASSESSMENT

Research

If some students are unable to present in front of the class for any reason, **then** have them record their multimedia presentation and transcribed script to be shared digitally with the class or a small group. For Reteach and Practice, see **Research: Informative Multimedia Presentation (RP).**

Selection Test

Administer the "Black Cowboy, Wild Horses" Selection Test, which is available in both print and digital formats online in Assessments.

Deliver an Informative Presentation

Assignment Before groups begin work on their projects, have them clearly differentiate the role each group member will play. Remind groups to consult the schedule for Small-Group Learning to guide their work during the Performance Task.

Students should complete the assignment using presentation software to take advantage of text, graphics, and sound features.

Plan With Your Group

Analyze the Text Remind students that although some of the selections may be more robust in terms of offering support for the prompt, it is important that they include evidence from all the selections. Encourage students to include examples of surprising aspects of bonds between people and animals. They should also think about differences in the bonds the people and animals in the selections had and how the people and animals related to each other.

Gather Evidence and Media Examples If students have trouble coming up with ideas for media examples, offer some suggestions. For example, a video clip of an emotionally charged interaction between a person and a horse might be good support for "A Blessing" or for "Black Cowboy, Wild Horses." Remind students that all media examples should be chosen strategically.

SOURCES

- A BLESSING
- PREDATORS
- MONKEY MASTER
- BLACK COWBOY, WILD HORSES

Deliver an Informative Presentation

Assignment

You have read poems, an essay, and a short story that explore relationships between animals and people. With your group, plan and deliver an **informative multimedia presentation** that examines this topic:

> **How can the bonds between people and animals be surprising?**

Use images or other media to illustrate, emphasize, and clarify key points in your presentation. End with a brief question-and-answer session.

Plan With Your Group

Analyze the Text With your group, review the selections in Small-Group learning. Discuss how the people and animals relate to one another. In what ways are those relationships unexpected or surprising? Use the chart to list your ideas. Try to come to an agreement on the most important points in each selection.

TITLE	SURPRISING ASPECTS
A Blessing	
Predators	
Monkey Master	
Black Cowboy, Wild Horses	

Gather Evidence and Media Examples Go back over the selections to record specific examples that support your group's ideas about surprising connections between people and animals. Then, brainstorm for types of media you can use to illustrate each example. Consider photographs, illustrations, music, and video clips. Allow each group member to make suggestions.

© Pearson Education, Inc., or its affiliates. All rights reserved.

☰ STANDARDS

Speaking and Listening
• Present claims and findings, sequencing ideas logically and using pertinent descriptions, facts, and details to accentuate main ideas or themes; use appropriate eye contact, adequate volume, and clear pronunciation.

• Include multimedia components and visual displays in presentations to clarify information.

172 UNIT 2 • ANIMAL ALLIES

AUTHOR'S PERSPECTIVE Ernest Morrell, Ph.D.

Strategic Use of Media Media is becoming more important as a communication tool, but teachers need to guide students to understand media's value. As groups plan their presentation, remind them that it is important to use media and visuals strategically so that they support the presentation but don't dominate it. Share these suggestions:

- Students should ensure that each piece of media has a specific purpose and is not mere "filler."
- Encourage students to let the content of their slideshow drive their decisions about which media support to include, rather than finding appealing media and trying to force them into a presentation where they might not work.

- Remind groups that although media and visuals can enhance a presentation, the content of what students say during the presentation is what is most important.

Ultimately, the presentation should be able to stand alone without media support and still make sense.

Organize Your Presentation As a group, work together to plan of your presentation. Organize everyone's work into a logical sequence. Then, make choices about your delivery. For example, decide who will introduce the presentation, who will read or present the text, who will handle the visuals or other media, who will present a conclusion, and who will be in charge of taking questions from the audience.

Rehearse With Your Group

Practice With Your Group Before delivering your presentation for the class, practice it as a group. Use this checklist to evaluate the effectiveness of your first run-through. Then, use your evaluation and these instructions to apply changes that will improve your content, use of media, and delivery techniques.

CONTENT	USE OF MEDIA	PRESENTATION TECHNIQUES
☐ The presentation clearly addresses the prompt.	☐ Images and other media clearly illustrate the ideas and information.	☐ Presenters make eye contact and speak clearly with adequate volume.
☐ Ideas and information are organized in a logical sequence.	☐ Images and other media are well-chosen and add interest to the presentation.	☐ Presenters use formal English.

Fine-Tune the Content If your presentation does not adequately address the prompt, work as a group to focus the content. Delete or revise any ideas or information that do not clearly connect to the topic.

Improve Your Use of Media Make sure you have enough media, but not too much. If you have long stretches without any media, consider adding some. Remove or replace any media that is not that interesting or relevant.

Brush Up on Your Presentation Techniques Practice a few times until your group is comfortable. Make sure everyone uses formal English and clearly pronounces words so that listeners can understand them.

Present and Evaluate

When you present as a group, be sure that each member has taken into account each of the checklist items. As you watch other groups' presentations, think about their content, media, and presentation techniques and how well they meet the criteria of the checklist. Listen attentively and politely. Did other presentations provide you with another way to view the topic?

© Pearson Education, Inc., or its affiliates. All rights reserved.

⚏ STANDARDS
Speaking and Listening
Adapt speech to a variety of contexts and tasks, demonstrating command of formal English when indicated or appropriate.

Performance Task: Deliver an Informative Presentation **173**

Organize Your Presentation If students have trouble locating relevant media examples, help them narrow their search terms. For example, "horse" is too broad. "Horse person interaction" may yield more relevant results.

Rehearse With Your Group

Improve Your Use of Media Suggest that students be prepared to justify the inclusion of every piece of media in their presentation. If they can't think of a convincing answer to "Why is this piece of media used here?" they should delete or replace the media.

Brush Up on Your Presentation Techniques Remind students to ensure that all members know the order in which they are presenting. Students should make a note of the last phrase or sentence that the preceding speaker says, and use that as a cue that it is their turn to present.

MAKE IT INTERACTIVE
Suggest that groups video record their rehearsal and then watch it together as a way to improve their presentation.

Present and Evaluate

Before beginning the presentations, set the expectations for the audience. You may wish to have students consider these questions as groups present.

- What is the presenting group's main idea?
- What evidence did they provide to support their main idea?
- Did their use of media support their ideas? Which pieces of media were most effective?
- What presentation skills did this group excel at, and how can they improve?

As students provide feedback to the presenting group, remind them that it is important to both praise the group for what they did well, and provide constructive criticism on what they could do better.

PERSONALIZE FOR LEARNING

Strategic Support

Transitions Some groups may require additional support in using transitions effectively. Have one student in the group read the whole presentation aloud, while other group members identify places where transition words and phrases might clarify the message or improve the flow of ideas. Provide students with a list of transitions that are particularly relevant to explanatory essays. Examples: *such as, notably, significantly, in general, for instance, to demonstrate, whereas, however, in contrast, in conclusion.*

INDEPENDENT LEARNING

How can people and animals relate to each other?

Encourage students to think carefully about what they have already learned and what more they want to know about the unit topic of Animal Allies. This is a key first step to previewing and selecting the text they will read in Independent Learning.

Independent Learning Strategies ▶

Review the Learning Strategies with students and explain that as they work through Independent Learning they will develop strategies to work on their own.

- Have students watch the video on Independent Learning Strategies.
- A video on this topic is available online in the Professional Development Center.

Students should include any favorite strategies that they might have devised on their own during Whole-Class and Small-Group Learning. For example, for the strategy "Create a schedule," students might include:

- Make an outline of the topics you'd like to discuss.
- Allocate your available time to the topics, in order to ensure that you'll be able to finish your presentation.

Block Scheduling

Each day in this Pacing Plan represents a 40–50 minute class period. Teachers using block scheduling may combine days to reflect their class schedule. In addition, teachers may revise pacing to differentiate and support core instruction by integrating components and resources as students require.

📅 **Pacing Plan**

👤 OVERVIEW: INDEPENDENT LEARNING

ESSENTIAL QUESTION:

How can people and animals relate to each other?

Animals and people learn from each other in different ways. In this section, you will complete your study of the relationship between people and animals by exploring an additional selection related to the topic. You'll then share what you learn with classmates. To choose a text, follow these steps.

Look Back Think about the selections you have already studied. What more do you want to know about the relationships between people and animals?

Look Ahead Preview the texts by reading the descriptions. Which one seems most interesting and appealing to you?

Look Inside Take a few minutes to scan the text you chose. Choose a different one if this text doesn't meet your needs.

Independent Learning Strategies

Throughout your life, in school, in your community, and in your career, you will need to rely on yourself to learn and work on your own. Review these strategies and the actions you can take to practice them during Independent Learning. Add ideas of your own for each category.

STRATEGY	ACTION PLAN
Create a schedule	• Understand your goals and deadlines. • Make a plan for what to do each day. •
Practice what you have learned	• Use first-read and close-read strategies to deepen your understanding. • After you read, evaluate the usefulness of the evidence to help you understand the topic. • Consider the quality and reliability of the source. •
Take notes	• Record important ideas and information. • Review notes before preparing to share with a group. •

© Pearson Education, Inc., or its affiliates. All rights reserved.

SCAN FOR MULTIMEDIA

174 UNIT 2 • ANIMAL ALLIES

Introduce Whole-Class Learning

Performance Task

Unit Introduction

from My Life With the Chimpanzees

Hachiko: The True Story of a Loyal Dog

| 1 | 2 | 3 | 4 | 5 | 6 | 7 | 8 | 9 | 10 | 11 | 12 | 13 | 14 | 15 | 16 | 17 | 18 |

CONTENTS

Choose one selection. Selections are available online only.

NOVEL EXCERPT

from The Wind in the Willows
Kenneth Grahame

In this story, animal nature is a lot like human nature.

FABLE

How the Camel Got His Hump
from Just So Stories
Rudyard Kipling

Did you ever wonder why some animals look the way they do?

NEWS ARTICLE

The Girl Who Gets Gifts From Birds
Katy Sewall

People aren't the only ones to give presents.

NEWS ARTICLE

Pet Therapy: How Animals and Humans Heal Each Other
Julie Rovner

Some types of medicine might bark or neigh.

PERFORMANCE-BASED ASSESSMENT PREP

Review Evidence for an Explanatory Essay

Complete your Evidence Log for the unit by evaluating what you have learned and synthesizing the information you have recorded.

 SCAN FOR MULTIMEDIA

Overview: Independent Learning **175**

Contents

Selections Encourage students to scan and preview the selections before choosing the one they would like to read. Suggest that they consider the genre and subject matter of each one before making their decision. You can use the information on the following Planning pages to advise students in making their choice.

> Remind students that the selections for Independent Learning are only available in the digital edition of the Interactive Student Edition. Allow students who do not have digital access at home to preview the selections using classroom or computer lab technology. Then either have students print the selection they choose or provide a printout for them.

Performance Based-Assessment Prep
Review Evidence for an Explanatory Essay
Point out to students that collecting evidence during Independent Learning is the last step in completing their Evidence Log. After they finish their independent reading, they will synthesize all the evidence they have compiled in the unit.

The evidence students collect will serve as the primary source of information they will use to complete the writing and oral presentation for the Performance-Based Assessment at the end of the unit.

© Pearson Education, Inc., or its affiliates. All rights reserved.

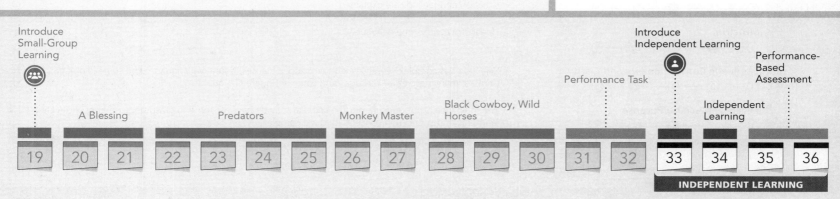

Introduce
Small-Group
Learning

Introduce
Independent Learning

Performance Task

Performance-
Based
Assessment

A Blessing   Predators   Monkey Master   Black Cowboy, Wild Horses   Independent Learning

| 19 | 20 | 21 | 22 | 23 | 24 | 25 | 26 | 27 | 28 | 29 | 30 | 31 | 32 | 33 | 34 | 35 | 36 |

INDEPENDENT LEARNING

from The Wind in the Willows

SELECTION RESOURCES

📄 First-Read Guide: Fiction

📄 Close-Read Guide: Fiction

📄 *from* The Wind in the Willows: Text Questions

🔊 Audio Summaries

🔊 Selection Audio

☑📄 Selection Test

Summary

from The Wind in the Willows is an excerpt from a novel by Kenneth Grahame. In this chapter, various small creatures meet up to exchange news and take care of each other. Mole and Rat pay a visit to Badger for shelter on a cold night. Badger receives them kindly and takes care of an injury Mole has sustained. They discuss their mutual friend Toad's reckless driving and plan to make him see reason. Afterwards, surrounded by the comfort of Badger's home, they go off to rest.

Insight

This selection functions as a sort of fable of hospitality and kindness. It portrays characters helping each other. The characters make plans to help a friend who may not necessarily want (but probably does need) their intervention.

Connection to Essential Question

The Essential Question is "How can people and animals relate to each other?" While there are no human characters in this selection, it shows characters empathizing and planning to help each other in ways that are universal.

Connection to Performance-Based Assessment

The Performance-Based Assessment prompt is "How can animals and people help one another?" The characters here feed, shelter, and care for each other in ways that are universal.

Text Complexity Rubric: *from* The Wind in the Willows

Quantitative Measures

Lexile: 1170   Text Length: 1,816 words

Qualitative Measures

Knowledge Demands ①—②—**❸**—④—⑤	Unfamiliar and fantastical situation. Though students will not be able to relate own experiences, the situation and feelings are explained.
Structure ①—**❷**—③—④—⑤	Linear story with some dialogue.
Language Conventionality and Clarity ①—②—③—**❹**—⑤	Selection has complex sentences with embedded clauses, figurative language, and some idiomatic phrases; many descriptive passages and some antiquated language.
Levels of Meaning/Purpose ①—②—**❸**—④—⑤	The main idea is not difficult, but the concept may be hard for some to grasp because of sophisticated language and supporting concepts that are complex.

How the Camel Got His Hump

SELECTION RESOURCES

📄 First-Read Guide: Fiction

📄 Close-Read Guide: Fiction

📄 How the Camel Got His Hump: Text Questions

🔊 Audio Summaries

🔊 Selection Audio

☑ 📄 Selection Test

Summary

In "How the Camel Got His Hump," a fable from Rudyard Kipling's collection *Just So Stories*, the Camel lived in the middle of the desert because he didn't want to work. Other animals, including a dog, a horse, and an ox, visit Camel, and urge him to take up their way of life, but he ignores them. The animals are upset because Man says they must work twice as hard if Camel won't help them work. A Djinn gives Camel his hump, which enables him to work for days without eating. The camel is forced to work to make up for his idleness.

Insight

This fable expresses Kipling's ideals—particularly unrestrained rulership and putting the "idle" to work for their "betters." It is worth pointing out how this links into colonialism.

Connection to Essential Question

The Essential Question is "How can people and animals relate to each other?" Kipling portrays Man as sympathetic to the animals, but nonetheless pushing them hard.

Connection to Performance-Based Assessment

The prompt is "How can animals and people help one another?" Students who read this fable will be able to consider the ways horses, dogs, and oxen help people.

Text Complexity Rubric: How the Camel Got His Hump

Quantitative Measures

Lexile: 940   **Text Length:** 1,099 words

Qualitative Measures

Knowledge Demands ①—②—❸—④—⑤	Unfamiliar and fantastical situation; though students will not be able to relate to their own experiences, the situation is explained.
Structure ①—❷—③—④—⑤	Linear story broken up with dialogue.
Language Conventionality and Clarity ①—②—③—❹—⑤	Selection has complex sentences with embedded clauses, above level vocabulary; many descriptive passages; unconventional spelling and syntax. (*'scruciating, made a-purpose, long towelly-thing*)
Levels of Meaning/Purpose ①—②—❸—④—⑤	Multiple levels of meaning; concepts are not hard, but may be difficult to grasp due to sophisticated language.

SELECTION RESOURCES

- First-Read Guide: Nonfiction
- Close-Read Guide: Nonfiction
- The Girl Who Gets Gifts from Birds: Text Questions
- Audio Summaries
- Selection Audio
- Selection Test

The Girl Who Gets Gifts From Birds

Summary

In this news article, "The Girl Who Gets Gifts from Birds," Katy Sewall tells us about a young girl who has forged a unique relationship with the crows who live in her garden. Gabi Mann has fed these birds for years. After she started feeding them every day, the crows began leaving gifts for her—anything shiny and small enough for a crow to carry. A wildlife scientist advises that crows and ravens may bond with people who give them consistent rewards. There are other cases of crows and people communicating and forming personal relationships. Most exciting for Gabi's mom, a crow brought her back a piece of her camera, which she'd lost.

Insight

The article emphasizes a two-way exchange; crows seem to be grateful to people who consistently help them, and bring them rewards in return. It also points out how our actions are often watched by animals, some of which are smart enough to count on them.

Connection to Essential Question

This article sheds a new light on the Essential Question "How can people and animals relate to each other?" The crows of course don't totally understand what humans *want*, but we can see their good intentions when they bring us rusty screws or dead baby birds.

Connection to Performance-Based Assessment

The prompt is "How can animals and people help one another?" People feed the crows, and in return the crows give them mostly-pleasing gifts. Emotional bonds may be a truer reward than the gifts themselves.

Text Complexity Rubric: The Girl Who Gets Gifts From Birds

Quantitative Measures

Lexile: 830   Text Length: 1,018 words

Qualitative Measures

Knowledge Demands ①—❷—③—④—⑤	The situations may be unfamiliar to some readers (a girl with a special connection with birds), but the situations and emotions are clearly explained.
Structure ①—②—❸—④—⑤	Organization is mostly sequential; quotes break up the text somewhat.
Language Conventionality and Clarity ①—②—❸—④—⑤	Some sentences in the explanation are complex, with multiple clauses, unconventional sentence structure, and difficult vocabulary, but the selection also has many quotations using conversational language.
Levels of Meaning/Purpose ①—❷—③—④—⑤	Meaning and concepts are straightforward. The main purpose of the selection is to convey the details of an amazing relationship between a girl and birds.

Pet Therapy: How Animals and Humans Heal Each Other

SELECTION RESOURCES

- 📄 First-Read Guide: Nonfiction
- 📄 Close-Read Guide: Nonfiction
- 📄 Pet Therapy: How Animals and Humans Heal Each Other: Text Questions
- 🔊 Audio Summaries
- 🔊 Selection Audio
- ☑ 📄 Selection Test

Summary

In the news article "Pet Therapy: How Animals and Humans Heal Each Other," Julie Rovner explains how animals can be used in many settings to make people happier and healthier. Being happy and relaxed doesn't just happen in the mind—these qualities can be seen in the body, like lower blood pressure (a sign of lower stress), and certain chemical changes in the brain. The article discusses several places where animals help provide a kind of therapy to people. People have seen positive results when they pet a dog or work with a horse. Animals can also help people exercise, which is often helpful with rehabilitation. This also helps the animals because it gives them a chance to be around people. Researchers are collecting data to prove the relationship between animals and humans can be medically helpful to both.

Insight

While students may enjoy interacting with animals, this article develops several examples of how animals make people live healthier lives.

Connection to Essential Question

This article provides many answers to the Essential Question, "How can people and animals relate to each other?" In this article, the writer describes the therapeutic value of pets and other animals.

Connection to Performance-Based Assessment

This text provides a strong connection to the Performance-Based Prompt, "How can animals and people help one another?" Animals seem to speed patients' recovery, and spending time with patients makes shelter animals more likely to get adopted.

Text Complexity Rubric: Pet Therapy: How Animals and Humans Heal Each Other

Quantitative Measures

Lexile: 1190　Text Length: 1,157 words

Qualitative Measures

Knowledge Demands	①—②—**❸**—④—⑤	The central concept, that animals can help in therapeutic settings, may not be familiar to all students, but the concepts are explained clearly.
Structure	①—②—**❸**—④—⑤	Organization is evident and sequential, but paragraphs contain a lot of information that is not broken up with any headings or graphics to organize.
Language Conventionality and Clarity	①—②—③—**❹**—⑤	Some sentences in the explanation are complex, with multiple clauses and difficult vocabulary. Selection contains several clinical references.
Levels of Meaning/Purpose	①—②—**❸**—④—⑤	The main idea is revealed early, but the concept may be hard for some to grasp because of sophisticated language and supporting concepts that are complex.

MY NOTES

You may wish to direct students to use the generic **First-Read** and **Close-Read Guides** in the Print Student Edition. Alternatively, you may wish to print copies of the genre-specific **First-Read** and **Close-Read Guides** for students. These are available online in the Interactive Student Edition or Unit Resources. 📖

FIRST READ

Students should perform the steps of the first read independently.

NOTICE: Students should focus on the basic elements of the text to ensure they understand what is happening.

ANNOTATE: Students should mark any passages they wish to revisit during their close read.

CONNECT: Students should increase their understanding by connecting what they've read to other texts or personal experiences.

RESPOND: Students will write a summary to demonstrate their understanding.

Point out to students that while they will always complete the Respond step at the end of the first read, the other steps will probably happen somewhat concurrently. Remind students that they will revisit their first-read annotations during the close read.

> After students have completed the First-Read Guide, you may wish to assign the Text Questions for the selection that are available in the Interactive Teacher's Edition

Anchor Standards

In the first two sections of the unit, students worked with the whole class and in small groups to gain topical knowledge and greater understanding of the skills required by the anchor standards. In this section, they are asked to work independently, applying what they have learned and demonstrating increased readiness for college and career.

INDEPENDENT LEARNING

First-Read Guide

Use this page to record your first-read ideas.

Selection Title: _____

Tool Kit
First-Read Guide and Model Annotation

NOTICE new information or ideas you learn about the unit topic as you first read this text.

ANNOTATE by marking vocabulary and key passages you want to revisit.

First Read — NOTICE · ANNOTATE · CONNECT · RESPOND

CONNECT ideas within the selection to other knowledge and the selections you have read.

RESPOND by writing a brief summary of the selection.

© Pearson Education, Inc., or its affiliates. All rights reserved.

▤ STANDARD
Reading Read and comprehend complex literary and informational texts independently and proficiently.

176 UNIT 2 • ANIMAL ALLIES

PERSONALIZE FOR LEARNING

Strategic Support
Text Preview Remind students who struggle with independent reading to preview the text by looking at the title along with visuals, captions, and headings. Ask them to track their ideas about the topic or genre of the text, along with their thoughts about the author's purpose for writing. Encourage students to consider what they already know about the topic or genre they think they will encounter.

During the First Read, students should annotate words that are unfamiliar or stand out to them as possible clues to the meaning of the text.

When First- and Close-Read Guide entries are completed by students independently, and students learn the meaning of all their annotated words, encourage students to compile the vocabulary words into a class dictionary that everyone can consult.

Close-Read Guide

Use this page to record your close-read ideas.

🔧 Tool Kit
Close-Read Guide and
Model Annotation

Selection Title: _____

Close Read the Text

Revisit sections of the text you marked during your first read. Read these sections closely and **annotate** what you notice. Ask yourself **questions** about the text. What can you **conclude**? Write down your ideas.

Analyze the Text

Think about the author's choices of patterns, structure, techniques, and ideas included in the text. Select one, and record your thoughts about what this choice conveys.

QuickWrite

Pick a paragraph from the text that grabbed your interest. Explain the power of this passage.

▤ STANDARD

Reading Read and comprehend complex literary and informational texts independently and proficiently.

© Pearson Education, Inc., or its affiliates. All rights reserved.

● CLOSE READ

Students should begin their close read by revisiting the annotations they made during their first read. Then, students should analyze one of the author's choices regarding the following elements:

- **patterns**, such as repetition or parallelism
- **structure,** such as cause-and-effect or problem-solution
- **techniques,** such as description or dialogue
- **ideas,** such as the author's main idea or claim

MAKE IT INTERACTIVE
Group students according to the selection they have chosen. Then, have students meet to discuss the selection in depth. Their discussions should be guided by their insights and questions.

PERSONALIZE FOR LEARNING

Strategic Support
Annotations Reinforce the strategies of close reading for students who struggle with its benefits. After they complete the Close-Read Guide, review the experience. Have students choose a first-read annotation that helped them understand the text more deeply during the close read. Discuss the following questions with students:

- How did a revisit of the first-read annotation help you better understand the text during your close read?
- What did you learn about that passage during the close read? What strategies did you use to study the passage you marked?

- What can you conclude about the text, based on the passage you selected?

Ask for student volunteers to discuss how using the First-Read and Close-Read Guides helped them understand the text better.

Share Your Independent Learning

Prepare to Share

Explain to students that sharing what they learned from their Independent Learning selection provides classmates who read a different selection with an opportunity to consider the text as a source of evidence during the Performance-Based Assessment. As students prepare to share, remind them to highlight how their selection contributed to their knowledge of the concept of survival as well as how the selection connects to the question *How can people and animals relate to each other?*

Learn From Your Classmates

As students discuss the Independent Learning selections, direct them to take particular note of how their classmates' chosen selections align with their current position on the Performance-Based Assessment question.

Reflect

Students may want to add their reflection to their Evidence Log, particularly if their insight relates to a specific selection from the unit.

MAKE IT INTERACTIVE

Have students create a list of animals that they might see in their daily lives—such as domesticated dogs or cats, squirrels, pigeons, and so on—and a list of animals that live in remote or protected wild areas. Then, have them consider their lists as you prompt them with questions related to the difference between these types of animals, such as *Does being in close proximity to people help or hurt animals? Why or why not? What do wild animals represent to us? Why?*

Evidence Log Support students in completing their Evidence Log. This paced activity will help prepare them for the Performance-Based Assessment at the end of the unit.

INDEPENDENT LEARNING

EVIDENCE LOG

Go to your Evidence Log, and record what you learned from the text you read.

Share Your Independent Learning

Prepare to Share

How can people and animals relate to each other?

Even when you read something independently, your understanding continues to grow when you share what you have learned with others. Reflect on the text you explored independently and write notes about its connection to the unit. In your notes, consider why this text belongs in this unit.

Learn From Your Classmates

Discuss It Share your ideas about the text you explored on your own. As you talk with others in your class, jot down a few ideas that you learn from them.

Reflect

Mark the most important insight you gained from these writing and discussion activities. Explain how this idea adds to your understanding of the relationship between people and animals.

STANDARDS
Speaking and Listening
Engage effectively in a range of collaborative discussions with diverse partners on *grade 6 topics, texts, and issues,* building on others' ideas and expressing their own clearly.

© Pearson Education, Inc., or its affiliates. All rights reserved.

AUTHOR'S PERSPECTIVE Ernest Morrell, Ph.D.

Active Listening and Learning It's important to support students as they learn and develop the skills of participating in small-group discussions. As students discuss their Independent Learning selection with classmates, remind them that it is important to be an active, but not dominant, participant. Explain that an active participant is one who speaks confidently, but also listens carefully to others, while a dominant participant is one who

takes over and does not allow others to contribute. Remind students that being an active listener involves these strategies:

- **Taking notes** Students who take useful notes capture the speaker's main points and note ideas to contribute once the speaker is done talking.

- **Restating others' ideas to show understanding** Encourage students to use such

language as "This is what I heard you saying . . ." and "I think this is what you meant when you said . . ."

- **Asking clarifying questions** When they don't understand, or if they want to move the conversation forward, students might ask peers questions like, "Could you explain what you meant when you said . . ."

Review Evidence for an Explanatory Essay

At the beginning of this unit, you expressed an idea about the following statement:

How can animals and people help one another?

✍ EVIDENCE LOG

Review your Evidence Log and your QuickWrite from the beginning of the unit. Did you learn anything new?

NOTES

Identify three pieces of evidence from the texts you have read that show the unique relationships between people and animals.

1. _____

2. _____

3. _____

Identify a real-life example that illustrates one of your ideas about the relationship between people and animals:

_____

_____

Develop your thoughts into a starter sentence for an explanatory essay. Complete this sentence starter: *I learned that one of the ways that people and animals can relate to each other is*

_____

_____

Evaluate the Strength of Your Evidence Consider your central ideas. Do you have enough evidence to support your central ideas? If not, make a plan.

☐ Do more research   ☐ Talk with my classmates

☐ Reread a selection   ☐ Ask an expert

☐ Other: _____

☰ STANDARDS
Writing
Write informative/explanatory texts to examine a topic and convey ideas, concepts, and information through the selection, organization, and analysis of relevant content.
  b. Develop the topic with relevant facts, definitions, concrete details, quotations, or other information and examples.

© Pearson Education, Inc., or its affiliates. All rights reserved.

DIGITAL PERSPECTIVES

Review Evidence for an Explanatory Essay

Evidence Log Students should understand that their position on an issue could evolve as they learn more about the subject and are exposed to additional points of view. Point out that just because they took an initial position on the question *How can animals and people help one another?* doesn't mean that their position can't change after careful consideration of their learning and evidence.

Evaluate the Strength of Your Evidence
Remind students that there are many different types of evidence they can use to support their thesis statement.

In addition to ensuring they have sufficient evidence to support their thesis, students should evaluate the reliability of their evidence. Discuss what might make evidence more credible, and suggest these questions:

- Did the evidence come from a reliable source, such as a government, educational, or professional organization?
- Has it been reviewed by experts for accuracy?
- Does it include references to other sources?

Performance-Based Assessment Prep **179**

Writing to Sources: Explanatory Essay

Students should complete the Performance-Based Assessment independently, with little to no input or feedback during the process. Students should use word processing software to take advantage of editing tools and features.

Prior to beginning the Assessment, ask students to think about the ways people and animals interact with each other—and depend on each other.

Review the Elements of Effective Explanatory Essays Students can review the work they did earlier in the unit as they complete the Performance-Based Assessment. They may also consult other resources such as:

- the elements of an explanatory essay, including a precise thesis statement, valid reasoning and evidence, and appropriate transitions, as well as how to organize an explanatory essay, available in Whole-Class Learning
- their Evidence Log
- their Word Network

Although students will use evidence from unit selections for their essay, they may need to collect additional evidence, including facts, statistics, anecdotes, quotations from authorities, or examples.

SOURCES

- WHOLE-CLASS SELECTIONS
- SMALL-GROUP SELECTIONS
- INDEPENDENT-LEARNING SELECTION

⛓ WORD NETWORK

As you write and revise your explanatory essay, use your Word Network to help vary your word choices.

≡ STANDARDS

Writing
- Write informative/explanatory texts to examine a topic and convey ideas, concepts, and information through the selection, organization, and analysis of relevant content
- Write routinely over extended time frames and shorter time frames for a range of discipline-specific tasks, purposes, and audiences.

PART 1
Writing to Sources: Explanatory Essay

In this unit, you read about the different relationships between animals and people. In some cases, animals revealed a new way of looking at the world. In others, people and animals educated each other.

> **Assignment**
>
> Write an **explanatory essay** in which you answer the following question:
>
> How can animals and people help one another?
>
> Use evidence from the selections in this unit to elaborate on your explanation. Explain your ideas thoughtfully, and use transitions to make connections among them. Make sure that you use a formal style, and organize your essay in a logical way so that it is easy for readers to follow.

Reread the Assignment Review the assignment to be sure you fully understand it. The assignment may reference some of the academic words presented at the beginning of the unit. Be sure you understand each of the words given below in order to complete the assignment correctly.

Academic Vocabulary

objective	exclude	illustrate
community	elaborate	

Review the Elements of Effective Explanatory Essays Before you begin writing, read the Explanatory Essay Rubric. Once you have completed your first draft, check it against the rubric. If one or more of the elements is missing or not as strong as it could be, revise your essay to add or strengthen that component.

© Pearson Education, Inc., or its affiliates. All rights reserved.

AUTHOR'S PERSPECTIVE   Kelly Gallagher, M.Ed.

Building a Writing Portfolio with Students You can create a portfolio to show the variety of writing students complete over the year. You can set the criteria using such categories as *Best Argument, Best Narrative Piece, Best On-Demand Writing, Best Informative Piece, Best Poetry, Best Writing from Another*

Class, Best Model of Revision, and Best Single Line. You might also ask students to include a reflective letter at the end of the year. To help them learn to reflect, use questions like these throughout the year:

- Where does your writing still need improvement? How will you improve?

- Reflect on a struggle you faced during this unit. How did you overcome it?
- Discuss a specific writing strategy you used and how it worked for you.

At the end of the year, students can review these pieces to see their growth as writers.

Explanatory Essay Rubric

	Focus and Organization	Evidence and Elaboration	Language Conventions
4	The introduction is clear, engaging, and establishes the topic in a compelling way. Ideas are well organized and progress logically. A variety of transitions are included to create cohesion and show the relationships among ideas. The conclusion follows from and supports the information presented in the essay.	The topic is developed with relevant facts, definitions, details, quotations, and other examples. The style of the essay is formal. The vocabulary is precise and relevant to the topic, audience, and purpose.	The essay always uses standard English conventions of usage and mechanics and has no errors.
3	The introduction is clear and engaging. Ideas are well organized. Transitions are included to show the relationships among ideas. The conclusion mostly follows from the information provided in the essay.	The topic is developed with some relevant facts, definitions, details, quotations, and other examples. The style of the essay is mostly formal. The vocabulary is generally appropriate for the topic, audience, and purpose.	The essay mostly uses standard English conventions of usage and mechanics and has few errors.
2	The introduction establishes the topic. Ideas are somewhat organized. A few transitions are included that show the relationships among ideas. The conclusion is related to the topic of the essay.	The topic is developed with a few facts, details, and examples. The style of the essay is sometimes formal and sometimes informal. The vocabulary is somewhat appropriate for the topic, audience, and purpose.	The essay often uses standard English conventions of usage and mechanics but also has many errors.
1	The topic is not clearly stated. Ideas are disorganized, and do not follow a logical sequence. Transitions are not included. The conclusion is not related to the essay topic or is nonexistent.	The topic is not developed with relevant evidence. The style is informal. The vocabulary is not appropriate for the topic, audience, and purpose.	The essay does not use standard English conventions of usage and mechanics.

© Pearson Education, Inc., or its affiliates. All rights reserved.

Explanatory Essay Rubric

As you review the Explanatory Essay Rubric with students, remind them that the rubric is a resource that can guide their revisions. Students should pay particular attention to the differences between an explanatory essay that contains all of the required elements (a score of 3) and one that is compelling and engaging and uses precise, formal language. (a score of 4).

Performance-Based Assessment **181**

PERSONALIZE FOR LEARNING

English Language Support

Connecting Ideas Some English learners may need additional support in connecting their ideas in logical, natural manner. Suggest that students create an outline for their essay before they begin writing. Provide students with an outline template for a 3–5 paragraph essay. Remind students that their essays will need to include an introduction and a conclusion. Help students organize their reasons and evidence in the body of their essay outline. Suggest that each body paragraph focus on either one idea or one selection. Ideas should not "jump around"—each idea or detail should logically connect to the last. Provide students with a list of transition words and phrases. Pair students together and have them read their essays aloud to each other and identify areas where the sequence of ideas is unclear. **ALL LEVELS**

Speaking and Listening: Informative Presentation

Students should annotate their written explanatory essay in preparation for the informative presentation, marking the important elements (thesis statement, details and examples that relate to the thesis, and concluding statement) as well as specific examples from the selections.

Remind students that the effectiveness of an informative presentation relies on how the speaker establishes credibility with his or her audience. If a speaker comes across as confident and authoritative, it will be easier for the audience to give credence to the speaker's presentation.

Review the Rubric As you review the Rubric with students, remind them that it is a valuable tool that can help them plan their presentation. They should strive to include all of the criteria required to achieve a score of 3. Draw their attention to some of the subtle differences between scores of 2 and 3.

PART 2
Speaking and Listening: Informative Presentation

Assignment
After completing the final draft of your essay, use it as the foundation for a brief **informative presentation.**

Do not simply read your essay aloud. Instead, take the following steps to make your presentation lively and engaging.

- Go back to your essay and annotate the most important ideas and supporting details from your introduction, body paragraphs, and conclusion.
- Refer to your annotated essay to guide your presentation and keep it focused.
- Speak clearly and make eye contact with your audience.

Review the Rubric Before you deliver your presentation, check your plans against the criteria listed in this rubric. If one or more of the elements is missing or not as strong as it could be, revise your presentation to meet all the criteria of the rubric.

STANDARDS

Speaking and Listening
Present claims and findings, sequencing ideas logically and using pertinent descriptions, facts, and details to accentuate main ideas or themes; use appropriate eye contact, adequate volume, and clear pronunciation.

	Content	Organization	Presentation
3	The introduction is engaging and clearly establishes the topic in a compelling way. The speaker points to key details and evidence to support his or her ideas. The conclusion is clear and reflects the information presented.	The presentation uses time effectively, devoting the right amount of time to each idea. Ideas progress logically, and transitions are used to connect ideas. Listeners can follow the presentation.	The speaker presents clearly and loudly enough for the audience to hear. The speaker maintains effective eye contact.
2	The introduction clearly establishes the topic. The speaker uses some evidence to support his or her ideas. The conclusion reflects the information presented.	The presentation mostly uses time effectively, but may spend too much or too little time on one part. Ideas progress somewhat logically, and a few transitions are used to connect ideas. Listeners can mostly follow the presentation.	The speaker presents clearly most of the time. The speaker makes some eye contact.
1	The introduction does not establish the topic. The speaker does not support his or her ideas with evidence. The conclusion is not related to the topic.	The presentation does not use time effectively. Ideas do not progress logically, and transitions are not used. Listeners have difficulty in following presentation.	The speaker presents too quickly or too slowly or not clearly. The speaker does not make eye contact with the audience.

© Pearson Education, Inc., or its affiliates. All rights reserved.

DIGITAL PERSPECTIVES

Preparing for the Assignment To help students understand what an effective informative presentation looks and sounds like, find videos on the Internet of students or adults giving informative talks or presentations. Play the examples for the class, and have students take notes on and discuss the techniques that make each speaker successful (or unsuccessful).

Suggest that students record themselves rehearsing their presentations so that they can practice incorporating some of the elements from the examples. Consider having students share their recordings with a partner so that they can provide each other with constructive criticism before the final presentation.

UNIT ② REFLECTION

DIGITAL
PERSPECTIVES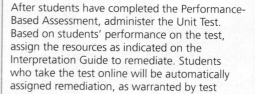

Reflect on the Unit

Now that you have completed the unit, take a few moments to reflect on your learning.

Reflect on the Unit Goals

Look back at the goals at the beginning of the unit. Use a different colored pen to rate yourself again. Then, think about readings and activities that contributed the most to the growth of your understanding. Record your thoughts.

Reflect on the Learning Strategies

💬 Discuss It Write a reflection on whether you were able to improve your learning based on your Action Plans. Think about what worked, what didn't, and what you might do to keep working on these strategies. Record your ideas before joining a class discussion.

Reflect on the Text

Choose a selection that you found challenging, and explain what made it difficult.

Describe something that surprised you about a text in the unit.

Which activity taught you the most about the relationships between people and animals? What did you learn?

SCAN FOR
MULTIMEDIA

© Pearson Education, Inc., or its affiliates. All rights reserved.

Reflect on the Unit

- Have students watch the video on Reflecting on Your Learning.
- A video on this topic is available online in the Professional Development Center.

Reflect on the Unit Goals

Students should re-evaluate how well they met the unit goals now that they have completed the unit. You might ask them to provide a written commentary on the goal they made the most progress with as well as the goal they feel warrants continued focus.

Reflect on the Learning Strategies

Discuss It If you want to make this a digital activity, go online and navigate to the Discussion Board. Alternatively, students can share their learning strategies reflections in a class discussion.

Reflect on the Text

Consider having students share their text reflections with one another.

MAKE IT INTERACTIVE

Have each student prepare a single slideshow slide about one of the selections in the unit. The slide should summarize the student's reflections on their chosen selection.

Put students' slides together and project the entire slideshow for the class. Ask students to discuss whether seeing each other's slides brought up any interesting ideas that they had not thought about.

Unit Test and Remediation 📄 ☑

After students have completed the Performance-Based Assessment, administer the Unit Test. Based on students' performance on the test, assign the resources as indicated on the Interpretation Guide to remediate. Students who take the test online will be automatically assigned remediation, as warranted by test results.

Modern Technology

INTRODUCTION

© Pearson Education, Inc. or its affiliates. All rights reserved.

Jump Start

Ask the students what their favorite technology is and why is it important to them. Engage them in a discussion about the positives and negatives of modern technology.

Modern Technology

Ask students what the phrase *modern technology* suggests to them. Point out that as they work through this unit, they will read about many examples of modern technology and how it has helped and harmed society.

Video

Project the introduction video in class, ask students to open the video in their interactive textbooks, or have students scan the BouncePage icon with their phones to access the video.

Discuss It If you want to make this a digital activity, go online and navigate to the Discussion Board. Alternatively, students can share their responses in a class discussion.

Block Scheduling

Each day in this pacing calendar represents a 40–50 minute class period. Teachers using block scheduling may combine days to reflect their class schedule. In addition, teachers may revise pacing to differentiate and support core instruction by integrating components and resources as students require.

 Pacing Plan

UNIT (3)

Modern Technology

Technology has become an important part of our lives, creating solutions but also new problems.

Dog Receives Prosthetic Legs Made by 3-D Printer

184

Discuss It How does modern technology help us solve problems in new ways?

Write your response before sharing your ideas.

SCAN FOR MULTIMEDIA

Introduce Whole-Class Learning

Unit Introduction		Feathered Friend					Teens and Technology Share a Future			The Black Hole of Technology			Media: The Internet of Things	Performance Task		
1	2	3	4	5	6	7	8	9	10	11	12	13	14	15	16	17	18

UNIT 3

UNIT INTRODUCTION

ESSENTIAL QUESTION:

How is modern technology helpful and harmful to society?

LAUNCH TEXT
ARGUMENT MODEL
That's Not Progress!

WHOLE-CLASS LEARNING

SMALL-GROUP LEARNING

INDEPENDENT LEARNING

ANCHOR TEXT: SHORT STORY
Feathered Friend
Arthur C. Clarke

SHORT STORY
The Fun They Had
Isaac Asimov

NEWS ARTICLE
7-Year-Old Girl Gets New Hand From 3-D Printer
John Rogers

ANCHOR TEXT: BLOG POST
Teens and Technology Share a Future
Stefan Etienne

BLOG POST
Is Our Gain Also Our Loss?
Cailin Loesch

NEWS ARTICLE
Screen Time Can Mess With the Body's "Clock"
Andrew Bridges

ANCHOR TEXT: BLOG POST
The Black Hole of Technology
Leena Khan

MEDIA: PODCAST
Bored . . . and Brilliant? A Challenge to Disconnect From Your Phone
NPR

POETRY COLLECTION
All Watched Over by Machines of Loving Grace
Richard Brautigan

Sonnet, without Salmon
Sherman Alexie

MEDIA: VIDEO
The Internet of Things
IBM Social Media

NEWS ARTICLE
Teen Researchers Defend Media Multitasking
Sumathi Reddy

PERFORMANCE TASK
WRITING FOCUS:
Write an Argument

PERFORMANCE TASK
SPEAKING AND LISTENING FOCUS:
Deliver a Multimedia Presentation

PERFORMANCE-BASED ASSESSMENT PREP
Review Evidence for an Argument

PERFORMANCE-BASED ASSESSMENT

Argument: Essay and Oral Presentation

PROMPT:
Do we rely on technology too much?

185

How is modern technology helpful and harmful to society?

Introduce the Essential Question and point out that students will respond to related prompts.

- **Whole-Class Learning** *Which blogger made a better case for his or her argument?*
- **Small-Group Learning** *Do the benefits of technology outweigh the disadvantages of technology?*
- **Performance-Based Assessment** *Do we rely on technology too much?*

Using Trade Books

Refer to the Teaching with Trade Books section for suggestions on how to incorporate the following thematically related titles into this unit:

- *A Wrinkle in Time* by Madeleine L'Engle
- *Anything but Typical* by Nora Raleigh Baskin
- *My Side of the Mountain* by Jean Craighead George

Current Perspectives

To increase student engagement, search online for stories about modern technology, and invite your students to recommend stories they find. Always preview content before sharing it with your class.

- **News Story: As Technology Gets Better, Will Society Get Worse? (The New Yorker)** An article by Tim Wu about the trade-off between technology's being helpful and the harm it can do to society.
- **Video: What Do Mobile Phones Do to Teenage Brains? (CBS News)** A video by Alphonso Van Marsh about a London school that will monitor the effects of cell phone use on 3,000 teenagers over the next three years.

Introduce Small-Group Learning

Introduce Independent Learning

The Fun They Had

Is Our Gain Also Our Loss?

Media: Bored... and Brilliant? A Challenge to Disconnect From Your Phone

Performance Task

Performance-Based Assessment

Independent Learning

| 19 | 20 | 21 | 22 | 23 | 24 | 25 | 26 | 27 | 28 | 29 | 30 | 31 | 32 | 33 | 34 | 35 | 36 |

About the Unit Goals

These unit goals were backward designed from the Performance-Based Assessment at the end of the unit and the Whole-Class and Small-Group Performance Tasks. Students will practice and become proficient in many more standards over the course of this unit.

Unit Goals ▶

Review the goals with students and explain that as they read and discuss the selections in this unit, they will improve their skills in reading, writing, research, language, and speaking and listening.

- Have students watch the video on Goal Setting.
- A video on this topic is available in the Professional Development Center.

Reading Goals Tell students they will read and evaluate an argument. They will also read news articles, short stories, blog posts, and poetry to better understand the ways writers express ideas.

Writing and Research Goals Tell students that they will learn the elements of argumentative writing. They will also write their own arguments and conduct research to clarify and explore ideas.

Language Goal Tell students that they will develop a deeper understanding of how to clarify the relationships among claims and reasons by using words, phrases, and clauses.

Speaking and Listening Explain to students that they will work together to build on one another's ideas, develop consensus, and communicate. They will also learn to incorporate audio, visuals, and text in presentations.

HOME Connection ✉

A Home Connection letter to students' parents or guardians is available in the Interactive Teacher's Edition. The letter explains what students will be learning in this unit and how they will be assessed.

⊟ STANDARDS

Language
Acquire and use accurately grade-appropriate general academic and domain-specific words and phrases; gather vocabulary knowledge when considering a word or phrase important to comprehension or expression.

Unit Goals

Throughout this unit, you will deepen your understanding of the impact of modern technology on society by reading, writing, speaking, listening, and presenting. These goals will help you succeed on the Unit Performance-Based Assessment.

Rate how well you meet these goals right now. You will revisit your ratings later when you reflect on your growth during this unit.

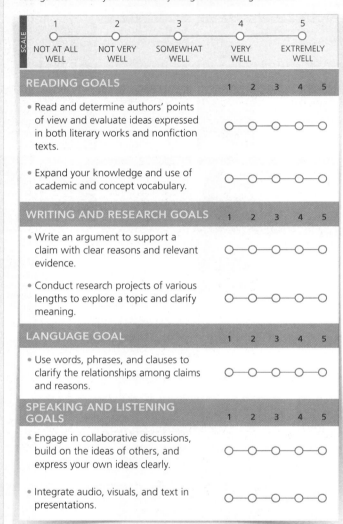

SCALE	1	2	3	4	5
	NOT AT ALL WELL	NOT VERY WELL	SOMEWHAT WELL	VERY WELL	EXTREMELY WELL

READING GOALS	1	2	3	4	5

- Read and determine authors' points of view and evaluate ideas expressed in both literary works and nonfiction texts.
- Expand your knowledge and use of academic and concept vocabulary.

WRITING AND RESEARCH GOALS	1	2	3	4	5

- Write an argument to support a claim with clear reasons and relevant evidence.
- Conduct research projects of various lengths to explore a topic and clarify meaning.

LANGUAGE GOAL	1	2	3	4	5

- Use words, phrases, and clauses to clarify the relationships among claims and reasons.

SPEAKING AND LISTENING GOALS	1	2	3	4	5

- Engage in collaborative discussions, build on the ideas of others, and express your own ideas clearly.
- Integrate audio, visuals, and text in presentations.

© Pearson Education, Inc., or its affiliates. All rights reserved.

SCAN FOR MULTIMEDIA

AUTHOR'S PERSPECTIVE   Ernest Morrell, Ph.D.

When Students Feel They Can't Reach Their Goals People often get discouraged when they can't reach their goals, and this feeling can be especially difficult for students. Teachers can help students overcome their pessimism about setting and meeting goals with these strategies:

- **Offer occasions for students to revisit and revise their goals.** Explain that this step in the process is common and important. Remind students that sometimes the goals we set are unrealistic and they will need to be revised.
- **Help break down the goals into smaller steps.** Building intermediate steps into goals

may make them more manageable. For example, when students are setting long-term goals, have them identify a first step. Ask them what they can do immediately, over the next few days. Help students identify the steps they'll need to take to achieve a goal and encourage them to take them one at a time.

Academic Vocabulary: Argument

Understanding and using academic terms can help you read, write, and speak with precision and clarity. Here are five academic words that will be useful in this unit as you analyze and write argumentative texts.

Complete the chart.

1. Review each word, its root, and the mentor sentences.

2. Use the information and your own knowledge to predict the meaning of each word.

3. For each word, list at least two related words.

4. Refer to the dictionary or other resources if needed.

> **TIP**
>
> **FOLLOW THROUGH**
> Study the words on this chart, and mark them or their forms wherever they appear in the unit.

WORD	MENTOR SENTENCES	PREDICT MEANING	RELATED WORDS
convince ROOT: **-vict-/-vinc-** "conquer"	1. To *convince* the jury, the lawyer presented evidence of the woman's innocence. 2. I will try to *convince* my mother that I need new clothes, even though she bought me a new shirt last week.		convincingly; unconvincing
certain ROOT: **-cert-** "sure"	1. The band became famous for having a *certain* jangly sound in their music. 2. I will be *certain* to study before the next test.		
sufficient ROOT: **-fic-/-fac-** "make"; "do"	1. We brought a *sufficient* amount of food and water for a week's worth of camping. 2. Studying an hour a day during the week before the test is *sufficient* to do well.		
declare ROOT: **-clar-** "clear"	1. Many officials will *declare* their support of the mayor's campaign by speaking at the press conference. 2. Ruthie was about to *declare* her innocence, but the chocolate stain on her face and the empty cookie jar told the truth.		
various ROOT: **-var-** "different"	1. There are *various* tips for effective public speaking, including speaking clearly and making eye contact. 2. We discussed *various* places to host the event—many of which were close to home.		

© Pearson Education, Inc., or its affiliates. All rights reserved.

Unit Introduction **187**

Academic Vocabulary: Argument

Introduce the blue academic vocabulary words in the chart on the student page. Point out that the root of each word provides a clue to its meaning. Discuss the mentor sentences to ensure students understand each word's usage. Students should also use the mentor sentences as context to help them predict the meaning of each word. Check that students are able to fill the chart in correctly. Complete pronunciations, parts of speech, and definitions are provided for you. Students are only expected to provide the definition.

Possible responses

convince *v.* (kuhn VIHNS)
Meaning: to persuade
Related words: convinced, convincing, convincer
Additional words related to root *-vict-/-vinc-:* victor, conviction, evict

certain *adj.* (SUR tuhn)
Meaning: free from doubt; definite or particular
Related words: certainly, certainty
Additional words related to root *-cert-:* concert, concerted, disconcerting

sufficient *adj.* (suh FIHSH uhnt)
Meaning: adequate, enough
Related words: insufficient, sufficiently
Additional words related to root *-fic-/-fac-:* artifice, deficit, sacrifice, specific

declare *v.* (dih KLAYIR)
Meaning: to make a statement; announce
Related words: declared, declaration, declarative
Additional words related to root *-clar-:* clarify, clarification, clarinet

various *adj.* (VAR ee uhs)
Meaning: different from one another
Related words: vary, variously
Additional words related to root *-var-:* variable, variant, variety

---

PERSONALIZE FOR LEARNING

English Language Support

Cognates Many of the academic words have Spanish cognates. Use these cognates with students whose home language is Spanish.

ALL LEVELS

convince – convencer   declare – declarar

certain – cierto   various – varios

sufficient – suficiente

INTRODUCTION

Purpose of the Launch Text

The Launch Text provides students with a common starting point to address the unit topic. After reading the Launch Text, all students will be able to participate in discussions about modern technology.

Lexile: 910 The easier reading level of this selection makes it perfect to assign for homework. Students will need little or no support to understand it.

Additionally, "That's Not Progress!" provides a writing model for the Performance-Based Assessment students complete at the end of the unit.

Launch Text: Argument Model

Remind students to determine what the author's claim is and how the author supports that claim.

Have students note the structure of the text. Point out that author introduces the topic and takes a position on it in the first and second paragraphs: Social networking can lead to anxiety, low self-confidence, and loneliness. Then explain that the paragraphs that follow provide reasons and evidence that support the position. The concluding paragraph sums up the author's argument.

Encourage students to read this text on their own and annotate unfamiliar words and sections of text they think are particularly important.

🔊 AUDIO SUMMARIES

Audio summaries of "That's Not Progress!" are available in both English and Spanish in the Interactive Teacher's Edition or Unit Resources. Assigning these summaries before students read the Launch Text may help them build additional background knowledge and set a context for their reading.

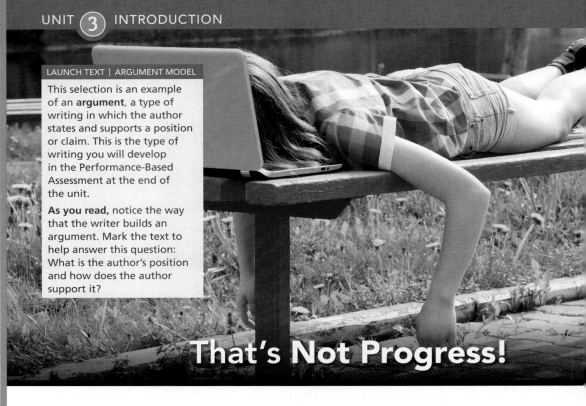

LAUNCH TEXT | ARGUMENT MODEL

This selection is an example of an **argument**, a type of writing in which the author states and supports a position or claim. This is the type of writing you will develop in the Performance-Based Assessment at the end of the unit.

As you read, notice the way that the writer builds an argument. Mark the text to help answer this question: What is the author's position and how does the author support it?

That's Not Progress!

NOTES

1   Social networking has become a big part of our lives, and its negative effects can be overlooked. But mental health experts are starting to notice—and what they are finding is disturbing.

2   As the popularity of social media skyrockets, so do reports of "Facebook depression." Like other kinds of depression, its common signs are anxiety, low self-confidence, and loneliness.

3   This form of depression hits those who worry too much about what others think. It largely affects young people because they tend to worry most about others' opinions. The constant need to see how they're "measuring up" can cause people to feel huge amounts of stress.

4   Studies have found that people who get their sense of self-worth from others are more likely to keep checking their status. They want to monitor their updates, wall posts, and photos to see how well or how poorly they're measuring up. The feeling that they're missing out on something makes it hard to take a break. And they don't have to—smartphones have made it possible to log in from any place at any time. The result is more stress.

5   Social networking can cause serious emotional problems. Everyone knows the effects of online bullying. There are other ways to damage a person's self-confidence. "When 'friends'

© Pearson Education, Inc., or its affiliates. All rights reserved.

188 UNIT 3 • MODERN TECHNOLOGY

SCAN FOR MULTIMEDIA

AUTHOR'S PERSPECTIVE   **Elfrieda Hiebert, Ph.D.**

Word Networks Vary by Word Type Concept maps or nets—the graphic organizers that help students understand the essential attributes, qualities, or characteristics of a word's meaning –vary depending on the type of word they help capture. For example, maps for concepts that explain phenomenon about the physical world and those that describe features of people and social situations can be different.

Concept maps about people and social situations contain words that have subtle differences in meaning and cannot necessarily be substituted for one another. For example, for a network built around the word *depression, loneliness, sadness,* and *anxiety* carry similar meanings but are not interchangeable.

In concept maps related to physical phenomenon, the words are typically not synonyms; rather, they

are connected by topic. For example, for the topic *technology*, the words *satellite, device, smartphone,* and *television* all have different meanings, but each could be used in a word network.

To help students build their word knowledge, help them understand the power of word networks. Often, especially in narratives, the concepts represented by rare words are known by

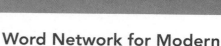

DIGITAL
PERSPECTIVES

upload unflattering photos and post mean comments, it can seriously damage a person's self-image," says one mental health expert. In additiion, getting no response to a post or not being "friended" can also be very painful.

6   The effects can be physical, too. Frequent users of social media often suffer from pain in their fingers and wrists. Blood vessels in their eyes and necks can narrow. Their backs can ache from being hunched over phones and computers for hours at a time.

7   Texting is another problem created by technology. Half the nation's youth send 50 or more text messages a day. One study found that young people send an average of 34 texts a night after they get into bed! This loss of sleep can affect the ability to concentrate, problem-solve, and learn.

8   Not all experts agree with this analysis. Some point to the benefits of social media. Dr. Megan Moreno is an assistant professor of pediatrics and adolescent medicine. She believes that social networking helps develop a young person's sense of community. She also believes that it can be used to identify youth who are most at risk for depression. "Our studies have found that adolescents often share feelings of depression on Facebook," she says. "Social media is a tool; it cannot in and of itself cause mental illness," says Dr. Moreno. She insists that young people had problems before computers came into being.

9   Maybe so. In the past, however, young people found ways to escape from their problems. Now, smartphones and other high-tech devices have made escape impossible. Is that progress?

10   Technology should simplify life, not complicate it. The danger of social media is that young users can eventually lose their ability to focus on what is most important in life—no matter what path they choose to follow. ❧

NOTES

Word Network for Modern Technology

Tell students that they can fill in the Word Network as they read texts in the unit, or they can record the words elsewhere and add them later. Point out to students that people may have personal associations with some words. A word that one student thinks is related to modern technology might not be a word another student would pick. However, students should feel free to add any word they personally think is relevant to their Word Network. Each person's Word Network will be unique. If you choose to print the Word Network, distribute it to students at this point so they can use it throughout the rest of the unit.

⚓ WORD NETWORK FOR MODERN TECHNOLOGY

Vocabulary A Word Network is a collection of words related to a topic. As you read the selections in this unit, identify interesting words related to the impact of modern technology, and add them to your Word Network. For example, you might begin by adding words from the Launch Text, such as *stress*, *status*, and *community*. Continue to add words as you complete this unit.

stress

status

community

MODERN TECHNOLOGY

🔧 **Tool Kit** Word Network Model

© Pearson Education, Inc., or its affiliates. All rights reserved.

That's Not Progress! **189**

---

common words that most students understand. In part, that's because in describing traits of characters or features of a problem or context, an author will use a number of different words to describe the same concept rather than repeating the same word over and over. For example, *announcement, missive,* and *communication* are all more complex words for *message*.

PERSONALIZE FOR LEARNING

English Language Support

Domain-specific Vocabulary The domain-specific words that appear in the text may challenge English Learners. Support them by reviewing the following mental health terms.

Depression medical condition marked by deep sadness

Anxiety fear or nervousness

Self-confidence trust in your own abilities

Have students locate these terms and read the sentences where they appear. Then, have them paraphrase the sentences, replacing the term with its definition. **ALL LEVELS**

Summary

Have students read the introductory paragraph. Provide them with tips for writing a summary:

- Write in the present tense.
- Make sure to include the title of the work.
- Be concise: a summary should not be equal in length to the original text.
- If you need to quote the words of the author, use quotation marks.
- Don't put your own opinions, ideas, or interpretations into the summary. The purpose of writing a summary is to accurately represent what the author says, not to provide a critique.

If necessary, students can refer to the Tool Kit for help in understanding the elements of a good summary.

See possible Summary on student page.

Launch Activity

Explain to students that as they work on this unit they will have many opportunities to discuss the topic of modern technology and its effects on young people. Remind them that there is no right or wrong position but that they must be able to support whichever position they take with strong reasons and evidence from the material they've read and analyzed so far in the unit, as well as from their prior knowledge.

Encourage students to listen to their classmates' reasoning and to weigh whether or not their arguments are persuasive. Point out that they may choose to change their own position based on what they hear.

Summary

Write a summary of "That's Not Progress!" A **summary** is a concise, complete, and accurate overview of a text. It should not include a statement of your opinion or an analysis.

> Possible response: In this argument, the author claims that social media sites can make people depressed. Constantly comparing your life to those of people you see bragging online can be very stressful. Unwanted interactions, or not getting interactions you'd hoped for, can also be painful. And then there are negative physical effects, like loss of sleep, or back pain from hunching over a computer or phone all day. An expert argues that social media can't cause mental illness, and that plenty of people had problems before computing was so common. But smartphones and similar technologies are more pervasive than other, previous forms of social interaction. Their constant presence creates opportunities to damage mental health.

Launch Activity

Conduct a Walk-Around Debate Consider this statement: Technology improves our lives by providing us with access to large amounts of information quickly.

- Prepare for the debate by thinking about the topic. Consider how access to smartphones and the Internet affects your life and the lives of people you know.
- Jot down your ideas about the topic.
- Decide whether you agree or disagree with the statement, and write your opinion on a sticky note that you stick to your clothes.
- Walk around the room, and share your ideas about the topic with at least two people who do not hold your opinion.
- At the end of the debate, determine how many people in the room changed their opinions, and why.

© Pearson Education, Inc., or its affiliates. All rights reserved.

VOCABULARY DEVELOPMENT

Academic Vocabulary Reinforcement Students will benefit from additional examples and practice with the academic vocabulary. Reinforce their comprehension with "show-you-know" sentences. The first part of the sentence uses the vocabulary word in an appropriate context. The second part

of the sentences—the "show-you-know" part—clarifies the first. Model this example for *convince:*

We need to convince the coach that we're ready; she will be persuaded by our demonstration.

Then give students these prompts and coach them in creating the clarification part.

1. Maria likes the *concept;* _____. Possible response: it is a new idea but one that appeals to her.
2. We can *declare* our support at the meeting; _____. Possible response: student council should hear that we like the proposal.

QuickWrite

Consider class discussions, the video, and the Launch Text as you think about the prompt. Record your first thoughts here.

PROMPT: **Do we rely on technology too much?**

Possible response: Some chimpanzees use stone tools to crack nuts open for food. I'm sure that the chimps who don't do this think the chimps who do rely on technology too much.

It's true that relying on technology might make us lose some skills. I know that I got worse at navigating after I got a phone with a maps app. But that doesn't matter. I keep my phone charged and don't go places where the maps don't work. I'm never going to need the navigational skills I've lost. Technology makes things easier, and if it's reliable there's no point in worrying about what'll happen if it doesn't work. People don't spend much time worrying about whether we're too reliant on farming, sewer systems, and concrete.

EVIDENCE LOG FOR MODERN TECHNOLOGY

Review your QuickWrite. Summarize your point of view in one sentence to record in your Evidence Log. Then, record evidence from "That's Not Progress!" that supports your point of view.

After each selection, you will continue to use your Evidence Log to record the evidence you gather and the connections you make. This graphic shows what your Evidence Log looks like.

 Tool Kit
Evidence Log Model

Title of Text: _____ Date: _____

CONNECTION TO PROMPT	TEXT EVIDENCE/DETAILS	ADDITIONAL NOTES/IDEAS

How does this text change or add to my thinking? Date: _____

SCAN FOR
MULTIMEDIA

Unit Introduction **191**

QuickWrite

In this QuickWrite, students should present their own answer to the question based on the material in the Unit Opener. This initial response will help inform their work when they complete the Performance-Based Assessment at the end of the unit. Students should make sure that they present their position clearly and that they support it with logical reasons and thoughtful examples.

See possible QuickWrite on student page.

Evidence Log for Modern Technology

Students should record their initial position in their Evidence Logs along with evidence from "That's Not Progress!" that support this position.

If you choose to print the Evidence Log, distribute it to students at this point so they can use it throughout the rest of the unit.

Performance-Based Assessment: Refining Your Thinking

- Have students watch the video on Refining Your Thinking.
- A video on this topic is available online in the Professional Development Center.

© Pearson Education, Inc., or its affiliates. All rights reserved.

OVERVIEW

WHOLE-CLASS LEARNING

How is modern technology helpful and harmful to society?

People have benefited from technology and become dependent on technology. There are positive and negative impacts that modern technology has on our lives. During Whole-Class Learning, students will read selections about the impact of modern technology.

Whole-Class Learning Strategies ▶

Review the Learning Strategies with students and explain that as they work through Whole-Class Learning they will develop strategies to work in large-group environments.

- Have students watch the video on Whole-Class Learning Strategies.
- A video on this topic is available online in the Professional Development Center.

You may wish to discuss some action items to add to the chart as a class before students complete it on their own. For example, for "Listen actively," you might solicit the following from students:

- Eliminate distractions.
- Keep your eyes on the speaker.

Block Scheduling

Each day in this Pacing Plan represents a 40–50 minute class period. Teachers using block scheduling may combine days to reflect their class schedule. In addition, teachers may revise pacing to differentiate and support core instruction by integrating components and resources as students require.

 OVERVIEW: WHOLE-CLASS LEARNING

ESSENTIAL QUESTION:

How is modern technology helpful and harmful to society?

Technology and social media have become central parts of today's world—but are they truly improving our lives? You will work with your whole class to explore the impact of modern technology on society. The selections you will read present insights into its positive and negative effects.

Whole-Class Learning Strategies

Throughout your life, in school, in your community, and in your career, you will continue to learn and work in large-group environments.

Review these strategies and the actions you can take to practice them as you work with your whole class. Add ideas of your own for each step. Get ready to use these strategies during Whole-Class Learning.

STRATEGY	ACTION PLAN
Listen actively	• Eliminate distractions. For example, put your cellphone away. • Keep your eyes on the speaker. •
Clarify by asking questions	• If you're confused, other people probably are, too. Ask a question to help your whole class. • If you see that you are guessing, ask a question instead. •
Monitor understanding	• Notice what information you already know and be ready to build on it. • Ask for help if you are struggling. •
Interact and share ideas	• Share your ideas and answer questions, even if you are unsure. • Build on the ideas of others by adding details or making a connection. •

© Pearson Education, Inc., or its affiliates. All rights reserved.

SCAN FOR MULTIMEDIA

📅 **Pacing Plan**

Introduce Whole-Class Learning

Unit Introduction

Feathered Friend

Teens and Technology Share a Future

The Black Hole of Technology

Media: The Internet of Things

Performance Task

| 1 | 2 | 3 | 4 | 5 | 6 | 7 | 8 | 9 | 10 | 11 | 12 | 13 | 14 | 15 | 16 | 17 | 18 |

WHOLE-CLASS LEARNING

CONTENTS

COMPARE

PERFORMANCE TASK

WRITING FOCUS

Write an Argument

The Whole-Class selections illustrate ways in which technology has affected our everyday lives. After reading the texts and watching the video, you will write an argument in the form of an editorial about the impact of modern technology.

© Pearson Education, Inc., or its affiliates. All rights reserved.

Contents

Anchor Texts Preview the anchor texts and media with students to generate interest. Encourage students to discuss other texts they may have read or movies or television shows they may have seen that deal with the issues of modern technology.

You may wish to conduct a poll to determine which selection students think looks more interesting and discuss the reasons for their preference. Students can return to this poll after they have read the selections to see if their preference changed.

Performance Task

Write an Argument Explain to students that after they have finished reading the selections, they will write an argument in the form of an editorial about the impact of modern technology. To help them prepare, encourage students to think about the topic as they progress through the selections and as they participate in the Whole-Class Learning experience.

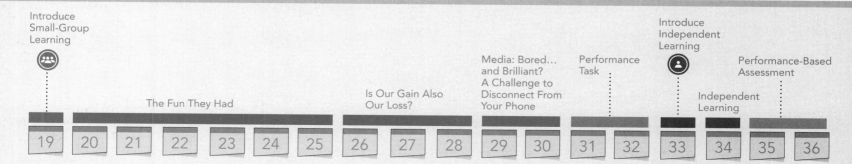

Introduce Small-Group Learning

The Fun They Had

Is Our Gain Also Our Loss?

Media: Bored... and Brilliant? A Challenge to Disconnect From Your Phone

Performance Task

Introduce Independent Learning

Independent Learning

Performance-Based Assessment

19 20 21 22 23 24 25 26 27 28 29 30 31 32 33 34 35 36

Feathered Friend

🔊 **AUDIO SUMMARIES**

Audio summaries of "Feathered Friend" are available online in both English and Spanish in the Interactive Teacher's Edition or Unit Resources. Assigning these summaries prior to reading the selection may help students build additional background knowledge and set a context for their first read.

Summary

"Feathered Friend," a science fiction short story by Arthur C. Clarke, is about a space-station worker and his coworker's pet canary. The canary is allowed to move freely about the station, hovering and floating instead of using her wings. She quickly becomes a favorite with all the crew members. They keep her hidden from visitors who might think it isn't appropriate to have a bird on a space station. However, the canary helps the narrator avoid a disaster, and changes how the narrator views technology.

Insight

The bird lets the workers know that oxygen levels in the station have gotten too low when the alarm fails to warn them. This is similar to a safety precaution mines used to protect miners from high levels of carbon monoxide. The story illustrates how simple approaches can be just as effective or dependable as high-tech ones.

ESSENTIAL QUESTION:
How is modern technology helpful and harmful to society?

Connection to Essential Question

Living on a space station is incredible, and of course it wouldn't be possible without advanced technology. However, relying exclusively on technology can have negative effects. This story illustrates what can happen when technology fails.

WHOLE-CLASS LEARNING PERFORMANCE TASK
Do electronic devices and online access really improve our lives?

Connection to Performance Tasks

Whole-Class Learning Performance Task This selection sets the stage for the blog posts in selections 2 and 3. It introduces the concept that the benefits of technology should be weighed with the risks of what happens when it fails.

UNIT PERFORMANCE-BASED ASSESSMENT
Do we rely on technology too much?

Unit Performance-Based Assessment The selection addresses the question of whether we rely too much on technology alone. In this situation, the workers would have died if they had relied solely on the alarm system.

LESSON RESOURCES

	Making Meaning	Language Development	Effective Expression
Lesson	**First Read** **Close Read** **Analyze the Text** **Analyze Craft and Structure**	**Concept Vocabulary** **Word Study** **Conventions**	**Writing to Sources** **Speaking and Listening**
Instructional Standards	**RL.10** By the end of the year, read and comprehend literature . . . **RL.1** Cite textual evidence to support analysis . . . **RL.2** Determine a theme or central idea of a text . . . **RL.5** Analyze how a particular sentence, chapter, scene, or stanza fits into the overall structure of a text . . .	**L.1** Demonstrate command of the conventions . . . **L.4** Determine or clarify the meaning of unknown and multiple-meaning words and phrases . . . **L.4.b** Use common, grade-appropriate Greek or Latin affixes and roots . . . **L.5** Demonstrate understanding of figurative language . . .	**W.1** Write arguments . . . **W.1.a** Introduce claim(s) . . . **W.1.b** Support claim(s) . . . **W.1.c** Use words, phrases, and clauses . . . **W.1.e** Provide a concluding statement . . . **W.7** Conduct short research projects . . . **SL.4** Present claims and findings . . . **SL.5** Include multimedia components . . .
STUDENT RESOURCES Available online in the Interactive Student Edition or Unit Resources	Selection Audio First-Read Guide: Fiction Close-Read Guide: Fiction	Word Network	Evidence Log
TEACHER RESOURCES **Selection Resources** Available online in the Interactive Teacher's Edition or Unit Resources	Audio Summaries Annotation Highlights EL Highlights English Language Support Lesson: Greek Root *-path-* Analyze Craft and Structure: Determine Theme	Concept Vocabulary and Word Study Conventions: Compound Words	Writing to Sources: Argument Speaking and Listening: Multimedia Presentation
Reteach/Practice (RP) Available online in the Interactive Teacher's Edition or Unit Resources	Analyze Craft and Structure: Determine Theme (RP)	Word Study: Greek Root *-path-* (RP) Conventions: Compound Words (RP)	Writing to Sources: Argument (RP) Speaking and Listening: Multimedia Presentation (RP)
Assessment Available online in Assessments	Selection Test		
My Resources	A Unit 3 Answer Key is available online and in the Interactive Teacher's Edition.		

Reading Support

Text Complexity Rubric: Feathered Friend	
Quantitative Measures	
Lexile: 1100 Text Length: 1,281 words	
Qualitative Measures	
Knowledge Demands ①—②—**③**—④—⑤	The experiences that are portrayed in the story (life in a space station) are uncommon to readers, but are explained. Some knowledge about space travel is needed (weightlessness, the need for oxygen).
Structure ①—②—**③**—④—⑤	The story is told chronologically, but the situation is not fully revealed right away. The text includes both narration (in first person) and dialogue, which makes it easier to follow.
Language Conventionality and Clarity ①—②—**③**—④—⑤	The language is clear and concrete. Some sentences are very long, with complex structure and multiple clauses. Vocabulary is mostly on-level, with some more difficult words.
Levels of Meaning/Purpose ①—②—**③**—④—⑤	The situations and meaning of the story are not revealed until the end, but once they are revealed, they are explicit and easy to understand.

DECIDE AND PLAN

English Language Support

Provide English Learners with support for knowledge demands and language as they read the selection.

Knowledge Demands Present the situation in the story. Explain that it takes place in a space station and that one of the needs in space is to have oxygen. Ask students to be looking for what the characters learn from the canary.

Language Encourage students to break apart long sentences into smaller chunks in order to understand them. Ask them to write short sentences to summarize each piece of information they get from a long sentence. For example, for the first sentences in paragraph 3, they might write: *Sven was a construction man. He excelled at his work. Construction men did tricky, specialized work. They collected girders as they floated around.*

Strategic Support

Provide students with strategic support to ensure that they can successfully read the text.

Knowledge Demands Determine how much students know about life in a space station. Ask students if they know why objects float around (there is no gravity). Then ask what might need to be controlled so that people can breathe (the oxygen levels).

Meaning After reading the text, review the basics of the story by asking questions. For example, *Where are the characters?* (in a space station) *What happens to the canary?* (It is unconscious and it almost dies.) *Why did this happen to the canary?* (There wasn't enough oxygen.) *What does the narrator think every space station needs?* (a canary as a backup to instruments measuring oxygen)

Challenge

Provide students who need to be challenged with ideas for how they can go beyond a simple interpretation of the text.

Text Analysis Ask students to write what they think of the idea of using animals the way the author suggested using the canary—as a safety alarm for loss of oxygen. Have them give their opinion about whether it is humane to use an animal for this purpose and explain why, or why not.

Written Response Ask students to write a short story about a trip in space with any kind of animal. Ask them to include information of what the animal did and how its presence in space affected the animal or the people. Encourage them to give detailed examples of the animal and human behavior.

TEACH

Read and Respond

Have the class do their first read of the selection. Then have them complete their close read. Finally, work with them on the Making Meaning, Language Development, and Effective Expression activities.

Standards Support Through Teaching and Learning Cycle

IDENTIFY NEEDS

Analyze results of the Beginning-of-Year Assessment, focusing on the items relating to Unit 3. Also take into consideration student performance to this point and your observations of where particular students struggle.

ANALYZE AND REVISE

- Analyze student work for evidence of student learning.
- Identify whether or not students have met the expectations in the standards.
- Identify implications for future instruction.

TEACH

Implement the planned lesson, and gather evidence of student learning.

DECIDE AND PLAN

- If students have performed poorly on items matching these standards, then provide selection scaffolds before assigning them the on-level lesson provided in the Student Edition.
- If students have done well on the Beginning-of-Year Assessment, then challenge them to keep progressing and learning by giving them opportunities to practice the skills in depth.
- Use the Selection Resources listed on the Planning pages for "Feathered Friend" to help students continually improve their ability to master the standards.

Instructional Standards: Feathered Friend

	Catching Up	This Year	Looking Forward
Reading	You may wish to administer the **Analyze Craft and Structure: Determine Theme (RP)** worksheet to familiarize students with central idea.	**RL.2** Determine a theme or central idea of a text and how it is conveyed through particular details; provide a summary of the text distinct from personal opinions or judgments.	Challenge students to determine the themes of other works they are familiar with.
Writing	You may wish to administer the **Writing to Sources: Argument (RP)** worksheet to help students better understand constructing argument.	**W.7** Conduct short research projects to answer a question, drawing on several sources and refocusing the inquiry when appropriate.	Challenge students to begin considering *counterarguments* to their claims.
Speaking and Listening	You may wish to administer the **Speaking and Listening: Multimedia Presentation (RP)** worksheet to help students better understand diction.	**SL.5** Include multimedia components and visual displays in presentations to clarify information.	Have students search for sample multimedia presentations on the Internet for ideas on how to elevate theirs.
Language	Review the **Word Study: Greek Root *-path-* (RP)** worksheet with students to better familiarize them with the root word. Review the **Conventions: Compound Words (RP)** worksheet with students to better familiarize them with compound words.	**L.4.b** Use common, grade-appropriate Greek or Latin affixes and roots as clues to the meaning of a word. **L.5** Demonstrate understanding of figurative language, word relationships, and nuances in word meanings.	Challenge students to create their own words using the root *-path-*. Challenge students to create their own compound words.

Jump Start

FIRST READ We all know that humans cannot survive in outer space without technology. Spacecraft contain equipment to help astronauts breathe, to protect them from radiation, and to keep them warm, among other things. But what happens if technology fails? Engage students in a discussion about the advantages, and limits, of technology when life depends on it.

Feathered Friend 🔊 📄

Why is a bird in a space station? What might cause sluggishness and a headache in space? Modeling questions such as these will help students connect to "Feathered Friend" and to the Performance Task assignment. Selection audio and print capability for the selection are available in the Interactive Teacher's Edition.

Concept Vocabulary

Support students as they rank their words. Ask if they've ever heard, read, or used them. Reassure them that the definitions for these words are listed in the selection.

⬤ FIRST READ

As they read, students should perform the steps of the first read:

NOTICE: You may want to encourage students to notice that the narrator is one of the people on the space station, along with someone named Sven, who is a construction man.

ANNOTATE: Remind students to mark passages that they feel are particularly descriptive or worthy of analysis in their close read.

CONNECT: Encourage students to make connections to their own lives or to the lives of people they know. If they are unable to make connections to the lives of those around them, have them consider stories they've seen on the news, in books and movies, or on television.

RESPOND: Students will answer questions and write a summary to demonstrate understanding. Point out to students that while they will always complete the Respond step at the end of the first read, the other steps will probably happen somewhat concurrently. You may wish to print copies of the **First-Read Guide: Fiction** for students to use. 📄

Remind students that during their first read, they should not answer the close-read questions that appear in the selection.

About the Author

With more than one hundred million copies of his books in print worldwide, **Arthur C. Clarke** (1917–2008) may have been the most successful science-fiction writer of all time. He is known for combining his knowledge of technology and science with touches of poetry. Clarke once said, "The only way of finding the limits of the possible is by going beyond them into the impossible."

🔧 Tool Kit

First-Read Guide and Model Annotation

☰ STANDARDS

Reading Literature
By the end of the year, read and comprehend literature, including stories, dramas, and poems, in the grades 6–8 text complexity band proficiently, with scaffolding as needed at the high end of the range.

Feathered Friend

Concept Vocabulary

You will encounter the following words as you read "Feathered Friend." Before reading, note how familiar you are with each word. Then, rank the words in order from most familiar (1) to least familiar (5).

WORD	YOUR RANKING
pathetically	
distressed	
mournfully	
apologetically	
lamented	

After completing the first read, come back to the concept vocabulary and review your rankings. Mark changes to your original rankings as needed.

First Read FICTION

Apply these strategies as you conduct your first read. You will have an opportunity to complete the close-read notes after your first read.

NOTICE *whom* the story is about, *what* happens, *where* and *when* it happens, and *why* those involved react as they do.

ANNOTATE by marking vocabulary and key passages you want to revisit.

First Read

CONNECT ideas within the selection to what you already know and what you have already read.

RESPOND by completing the Comprehension Check and by writing a brief summary of the selection.

© Pearson Education, Inc., or its affiliates. All rights reserved.

Kelly Gallagher, M.Ed.

The Value of Rereading To get the most out of a text, it is important for students to move beyond surface-level comprehension into deeper, inferential meaning. Give students re-reading strategies such as having them ask themselves the following four questions, in order, as they read:

1. What does it say?
2. What does it mean?
3. How is it said?
4. Why does it matter?

Question 1 taps literal comprehension. Question 2 requires students to return to the text to provide specific details and passages. Question 3 asks students to think about the author's technique. Question 4 gives students the opportunity to think deeply about the issues.

Feathered Friend

Arthur C. Clarke

© Pearson Education, Inc., or its affiliates. All rights reserved.

BACKGROUND

This story was written during the 1950s, a time of growth and technological advancement in the United States. The possibility of space exploration created a feeling of immense potential. This optimism about the future influenced all areas of the arts, especially popular literature, in what is now called the Golden Age of Science Fiction.

SCAN FOR
MULTIMEDIA

1   To the best of my knowledge, there's never been a regulation that forbids one to keep pets in a space station. No one ever thought it was necessary—and even had such a rule existed, I am quite certain that Sven Olsen would have ignored it.

2   With a name like that, you will picture Sven at once as a six-foot-six Nordic giant, built like a bull and with a voice to match. Had this been so, his chances of getting a job in space would have been very slim. Actually he was a wiry little fellow, like most of the early spacers, and managed to qualify easily for the 150-pound bonus that kept so many of us on a reducing diet.

3   Sven was one of our best construction men, and excelled at the tricky and specialized work of collecting assorted girders as they floated around in free fall, making them do the slow-motion, three-dimensional ballet that would get them into their right positions, and fusing the pieces together when they were precisely dovetailed into the intended pattern: It was a skilled and difficult job, for a spacesuit is not the most convenient of garbs in which to work. However, Sven's team had one great advantage over the construction gangs you see putting up skyscrapers down on

NOTES

CLOSER LOOK

Analyze Description

Students may have marked paragraph 2 during their first read. Use this paragraph to help students understand how the author's description helps them picture the character. Encourage them to talk about the annotations that they marked. You may want to model a close read with the class based on the highlights shown in the text.

ANNOTATE: Have students mark details in paragraph 2 that describe Sven Olsen, or have students participate while you highlight them.

QUESTION: Guide students to consider what these details might tell them. Ask what a reader can infer from details that contrast the description of the character to a giant and a bull and accept student responses.

Possible response: The author explains that a typical reader might picture a man with the name Sven Olsen to be a "six-foot-six Nordic giant." However, Olsen was actually a small man. That description changes the reader's mental image of the character.

CONCLUDE: Help students to formulate conclusions about the importance of these details in the text. Ask students why the author might have included these details.

Possible response: These details help the reader create a mental picture of Sven and help the reader understand that most of the men on the station were, like Sven, small.

Explain to students that a **description** is a portrait in words of a person, place, or thing. Descriptive writing uses images that appeal to the senses: sight, hearing, taste, smell, and touch.

   Additional **English Language Support** is available in the Interactive Teacher's Edition.

PERSONALIZE FOR LEARNING

English Language Support

Idiom Tell students that the expression *to the best of my knowledge* in the first sentence in paragraph 1 is an idiom. Remind students that an idiom is a commonly used expression that is not meant literally.

Explain that *to the best of my knowledge* means "I think but I am not completely sure." Have students look at the rest of the paragraph: ". . . and even if such a rule existed . . . " Point out

that this supports the meaning of the idiom. It expresses that the narrator thinks but is not completely certain that there is no rule regarding pets.

Remind students that when they come across an idiom in their reading, they may be able to find context clues to help them figure out the idiom's meaning. **ALL LEVELS**

CLOSE READ

As students read paragraph 6, guide them to look for descriptive details. Remind them to find the words that tell what something looks like, feels like, or sounds like. You may wish to model the close read using the following think-aloud format. Possible responses to questions on the student page are included. You may also want to print copies of the **Close-Read Guide: Fiction** for students to use. 📄

ANNOTATE: As I read paragraph 6, I notice and highlight the details that tell what the canary looks like and how it moves in the absence of gravity.

QUESTION: The descriptive detail helps me see that the bird looks like a normal canary but that it hovers rather than flies, without flapping its wings. It also helps me see that the bird can move easily in space and seems to feel comfortable doing so.

CONCLUDE: I think this description helps readers imagine what it's like to be weightless in space.

NOTES

CLOSE READ
ANNOTATE: Mark details in paragraph 6 that describe the canary's appearance and movements.

QUESTION: Why does the author include so much descriptive detail about the canary?

CONCLUDE: What aspects of life in space does this description help readers imagine?

Earth. They could step back and admire their handiwork without being abruptly parted from it by gravity. . . .

4 Don't ask me why Sven wanted a pet, or why he chose the one he did. I'm not a psychologist, but I must admit that his selection was very sensible. Claribel weighed practically nothing, her food requirements were tiny—and she was not worried, as most animals would have been, by the absence of gravity.

5 I first became aware that Claribel was aboard when I was sitting in the little cubbyhole laughingly called my office, checking through my lists of technical stores to decide what items we'd be running out of next. When I heard the musical whistle beside my ear, I assumed that it had come over the station intercom, and waited for an announcement to follow. It didn't; instead, there was a long and involved pattern of melody that made me look up with such a start that I forgot all about the angle beam just behind my head. When the stars had ceased to explode before my eyes, I had my first view of Claribel.

6 She was a small yellow canary, hanging in the air as motionless as a hummingbird—and with much less effort, for her wings were quietly folded along her sides. We stared at each other for a minute; then, before I had quite recovered my wits, she did a curious kind of backward loop I'm sure no earthbound canary had ever managed, and departed with a few leisurely flicks. It was quite obvious that she'd already learned how to operate in the absence of gravity, and did not believe in doing unnecessary work.

7 Sven didn't confess to her ownership for several days, and by that time it no longer mattered, because Claribel was a general pet. He had smuggled her up on the last ferry from Earth, when he came back from leave—partly, he claimed, out of sheer scientific curiosity. He wanted to see just how a bird would operate when it had no weight but could still use its wings.

8 Claribel thrived and grew fat. On the whole, we had little trouble concealing our guest when VIPs from Earth came visiting. A space station has more hiding places than you can count; the only problem was that Claribel got rather noisy when she was upset, and we sometimes had to think fast to explain the curious peeps and whistles that came from ventilating shafts and storage bulkheads. There were a couple of narrow escapes—but then who would dream of looking for a canary in a space station?

9 We were now on twelve-hour watches, which was not as bad as it sounds, since you need little sleep in space. Though of course there is no "day" and "night" when you are floating in permanent sunlight, it was still convenient to stick to the terms. Certainly when I woke that "morning" it felt like 6:00 A.M. on Earth. I had

© Pearson Education, Inc., or its affiliates. All rights reserved.

WriteNow Express and Reflect

Description In paragraph 6, the narrator describes the canary as it hovers and then darts off into space. Have students write a one-paragraph description of an animal, either a pet or a wild animal that they have seen, like a squirrel or a bird. Remind students to include details about the animal that reveal what it looks like and how it moves. Point out that the narrator uses a simile ("hanging in the air as motionless as a hummingbird") to describe the effortless way the canary moves aboard the space station. These techniques help draw a picture of the canary.

Draw students' attention to the fact that the narrator adds analysis of the canary's behavior: "It was quite obvious that she'd already learned how to operate in the absence of gravity, and did not believe in doing unnecessary work." Students should similarly provide analysis or commentary on their animal's movements or behavior.

a nagging headache, and vague memories of fitful, disturbed dreams. It took me ages to undo my bunk straps, and I was still only half awake when I joined the remainder of the duty crew in the mess. Breakfast was unusually quiet, and there was one seat vacant.

10   "Where's Sven?" I asked, not very much caring.

11   "He's looking for Claribel," someone answered. "Says he can't find her anywhere. She usually wakes him up."

12   Before I could retort that she usually woke me up, too, Sven came in through the doorway, and we could see at once that something was wrong. He slowly opened his hand, and there lay a tiny bundle of yellow feathers, with two clenched claws sticking **pathetically** up into the air.

13   "What happened?" we asked, all equally **distressed**.

14   "I don't know," said Sven **mournfully**. "I just found her like this."

15   "Let's have a look at her," said Jock Duncan, our cook-doctor-dietitian. We all waited in hushed silence while he held Claribel against his ear in an attempt to detect any heartbeat.

16   Presently he shook his head. "I can't hear anything, but that doesn't prove she's dead. I've never listened to a canary's heart," he added rather **apologetically**.

17   "Give her a shot of oxygen," suggested somebody, pointing to the green-banded emergency cylinder in its recess beside the door. Everyone agreed that this was an excellent idea, and Claribel was tucked snugly into a face mask that was large enough to serve as a complete oxygen tent for her.

18   To our delighted surprise, she revived at once. Beaming broadly, Sven removed the mask, and she hopped onto his finger. She gave her series of "Come to the cookhouse, boys" trills—then promptly keeled over again.

19   "I don't get it," **lamented** Sven. "What's wrong with her? She's never done this before."

20   For the last few minutes, something had been tugging at my memory. My mind seemed to be very sluggish that morning, as if I was still unable to cast off the burden of sleep. I felt that I could do with some of that oxygen—but before I could reach the mask, understanding exploded in my brain. I whirled on the duty engineer and said urgently:

21   "Jim! There's something wrong with the air! That's why Claribel's passed out. I've just remembered that miners used to carry canaries down to warn them of gas."

22   "Nonsense!" said Jim. "The alarms would have gone off. We've got duplicate circuits, operating independently."

© Pearson Education, Inc., or its affiliates. All rights reserved.

NOTES

pathetically (puh THEHT ihk lee) *adv.* in a way that causes someone to feel pity

distressed (dih STREHST) *adj.* troubled; upset

mournfully (MAWRN fuh lee) *adv.* in a way that expresses grief or sadness

apologetically (uh pol uh JEHT ihk lee) *adv.* in a way that shows someone is sorry for having done or said something; regretfully

lamented (luh MEHN tihd) *v.* said in a way that showed sadness or sorrow

Feathered Friend **197**

CLOSER LOOK

Analyze First-Person Narrative

Students may have marked paragraph 20 during their first read. Use this paragraph to help students understand the characteristics of the first-person narrative. Encourage them to talk about the annotations that they marked. You may want to model a close read with the class based on the highlights shown in the text.

ANNOTATE: Have students mark details in paragraph 20 that demonstrate that events are being described as they were perceived by the narrator, or have students participate while you highlight them.

QUESTION: Guide students to consider what these details might tell them. Ask what a reader can infer from these details of the first-person narrative, and accept student responses.

Possible response: The narrator suddenly connects how he has been feeling all morning—tired and unable to think properly—to the canary's condition.

CONCLUDE: Help students to formulate conclusions about the importance of these details in the text. Ask students why the author might have included these details.

Possible response: In showing the effects of the lack of oxygen on the narrator by describing his sluggishness, the author implies that the others felt the same way. The details enable the author to show how the people on the spacecraft feel and allow the narrator to solve the problem—a problem that the reader had also probably solved at around the same time.

Remind students a **first-person narrator** is a character who tells the story, speaking in the first person (using the pronoun *I*). With a first-person narrator, the reader sees, hears, and understands only what this character sees, hears, and understands—and only what this character chooses to reveal.

VOCABULARY DEVELOPMENT

Concept Vocabulary Reinforcement To increase familiarity with the concept vocabulary, ask students to use each of the words in a sentence. Encourage students to include context clues in their own sentences to demonstrate their knowledge of the word. If students are still struggling with the words, encourage them to identify the base word in each term, look up the base word in the dictionary, and then use the definition to come up with the meaning of the concept vocabulary word.

© Pearson Education, Inc., or its affiliates. All rights reserved.

⬤ CLOSER LOOK

Analyze Irony 🧭

Students may have marked paragraphs 24 and 25 during their first read. Use these paragraphs to help students understand the characteristics of irony in literature. Encourage them to talk about the annotations that they marked. You may want to model a close read with the class based on the highlights shown in the text.

ANNOTATE: Have students mark details in paragraphs 24 and 25 that demonstrate that events did not turn out as the narrator had thought they would, or have students participate while you highlight them.

QUESTION: Guide students to consider what these details might tell them. Ask what a reader can infer from these two conflicting sets of details, and accept student responses.

Possible response: The narrator implies that despite hundreds of thousands of dollars of equipment to protect the workers, space stations may now rely on canaries to protect people.

CONCLUDE: Help students to formulate conclusions about the importance of these details in the text. Ask students why the author might have included these details.

Possible response: In noting that the workers were not protected by technology and instead were saved by a bird, the narrator is questioning the value of technology. He seems to be suggesting that sometimes, old, proven methods work best.

Remind students that **irony** is a discrepancy or contradiction between appearance and reality, between expectation and outcome, or between meaning and intention. There are three main types of irony. In this situational irony (or irony of situation), something happened that directly contradicted the expectations of the characters, the readers, or the audience.

NOTES

23 "Er—the second alarm circuit isn't connected up yet." His assistant reminded him. That shook Jim; he left without a word, while we stood arguing and passing the oxygen bottle around like a pipe of peace.

24 He came back ten minutes later with a sheepish expression. It was one of those accidents that couldn't possibly happen; we'd had one of our rare eclipses by Earth's shadow that night: Part of the air purifier had frozen up, and the single alarm in the circuit had failed to go off. Half a million dollars' worth of chemical and electronic engineering had let us down completely. Without Claribel, we should soon have been slightly dead.

25 So now, if you visit any space station, don't be surprised if you hear an inexplicable snatch of birdsong. There's no need to be alarmed; on the contrary, in fact. It will mean that you're being doubly safeguarded, at practically no extra expense. ❧

CROSS-CURRICULAR PERSPECTIVES

Science In paragraph 24, it is revealed that the problem on the space station was caused by "one of our rare eclipses by Earth's shadow" that caused the air purifier to freeze. Tell students that presumably the Earth was between the sun and the space station, casting a shadow on the space station. Ask them to consider why the air purifier might have frozen, given this scenario. (With the sun blocked, the space station would have gotten colder.)

Have students research the NASA website about eclipses and answer these questions:

- What are the two kinds of eclipses and what happens during each?
- How frequently do eclipses occur?
- How big a temperature drop is there when a solar eclipse occurs?

Have volunteers share their responses with the class.

Comprehension Check

Complete the following items after you complete your first read.

1. Where does the story take place?

2. How does the narrator discover Claribel's presence?

3. Why does Sven bring Claribel onboard?

4. What causes Claribel to pass out?

5. 🔖 **Notebook** Confirm your understanding of the story by writing a summary.

- -

RESEARCH

Research to Clarify Choose at least one unfamiliar detail from the text. Briefly research that detail. In what way does the information you learned shed light on an aspect of the story?

Research to Explore Choose something from the text that interests you, and formulate a research question. For example, you may want to learn more about canaries or space stations.

© Pearson Education, Inc., or its affiliates. All rights reserved.

Comprehension Check

Possible responses:

1. The story takes place on a space station.
2. He heard a whistling and looked up.
3. He wanted to see how a bird would operate in zero gravity, with no weight but with the use of its wings.
4. A lack of oxygen causes her to pass out.
5. Summaries will vary; however, students should include a description of Claribel's condition, how the crew tried to revive her, and how the narrator determined what the problem was.

Research

Research to Clarify If students struggle to come up with a detail to research, you may want to suggest that they focus on one of the following topics: space stations, animals in space, canaries in coal mines.

Research to Explore If students aren't sure how to go about formulating a research question, suggest that they use their findings from Research to Clarify as a starting point. For example, if students researched space stations, they might formulate a question such as *What are some examples of discoveries or advancements in science that have come from experiments on the International Space Station?*

PERSONALIZE FOR LEARNING

Challenge

Research This story is a work of science fiction, written in the 1950s. This was before humans ever went to space, but during a period of time when technology was rapidly advancing. Encourage interested students to find and read another science fiction short story from the 1950s, either by Clarke or by another author, such as Isaac Asimov or Algis Budrys, and write a short report on the story. Encourage them to note how the story they read was similar to or different from "Feathered Friend" and how each story deals with the concept of technology.

Jump Start

CLOSE READ Ask students to consider the following prompt: *Do people tend to rely on technology too much? What happens when technology lets us down?* As students discuss these questions, ask them to consider the position of the narrator in "Feathered Friend." Would he say that technology is overrated? Why or why not?

Close Read the Text 🌐

Walk students through the annotation model on the student page. Encourage them to complete items 2 and 3 on their own. Review and discuss the sections students have marked. If needed, continue to model close reading by using the Annotation Highlights in the Interactive Teacher's Edition.

Analyze the Text

Possible responses:

1. (a) They are all fond of her. **DOK 2** (b) Having a pet makes people less lonely and perks up their spirits. **DOK 3**

2. (a) He hasn't slept well, had bad dreams, has a headache, and feels groggy and sleepy, as if he needs oxygen. **DOK 2** (b) Both are responsible. If it hadn't been for Claribel losing consciousness, the narrator would never have made the connection that led to the discovery that the equipment was broken. **DOK 3**

3. (a) The first alarm didn't go off, and the back-up alarm hadn't been connected yet. **DOK 1** (b) The canary might get sick from something else or otherwise mislead them into thinking something has gone wrong. **DOK 3** (c) I think an electronic system is generally more reliable because it is not usually affected by problems that might affect a living thing. **DOK 3**

FORMATIVE ASSESSMENT

Analyze the Text

- **If** students fail to cite evidence, **then** remind them to support their ideas with specific information.

- **If** students struggle to identify who saved the crew's lives, **then** remind them that there is no right or wrong answer, as long as they provide an explanation.

MAKING MEANING

FEATHERED FRIEND

Close Read the Text

1. This model, from paragraph 3 of the story, shows two sample annotations, along with questions and conclusions. Close read the passage, and find another detail to annotate. Then, write a question and your conclusion.

ANNOTATE QUESTION
Close Read
CONCLUDE

> **ANNOTATE:** Some of these details are very technical, but others are very poetic.
>
> **QUESTION:** Why does Clarke use different types of language to describe Sven's movements?
>
> **CONCLUDE:** These details suggest that working in space is both freeing and beautiful, and exacting and scientific.

Sven was one of our best construction men, and excelled at the tricky and specialized work of collecting assorted girders as they floated around in free fall, making them do the slow-motion, three-dimensional ballet that would get them into their right positions, and fusing the pieces together when they were precisely dovetailed into the intended pattern. . . .

> **ANNOTATE:** The author combines familiar details of construction work with unfamiliar details of zero gravity.
>
> **QUESTION:** Why does the author make this choice?
>
> **CONCLUDE:** The combination of Earth-like details and space-related details creates a startling setting.

🔧 Tool Kit
Close-Read Guide and Model Annotation

STANDARDS
Reading Literature
• Cite textual evidence to support analysis of what the text says explicitly as well as inferences drawn from the text.

• Determine a theme or central idea of a text and how it is conveyed through particular details; provide a summary of the text distinct from personal opinions or judgments.

• Analyze how a particular sentence, chapter, scene, or stanza fits into the overall structure of a text and contributes to the development of the theme, setting, or plot.

2. For more practice, go back into the story, and complete the close-read notes.

3. Revisit a section of the text you found important during your first read. Read this section closely, and **annotate** what you notice. Ask yourself **questions** such as "Why did the author make this choice?" "What can you **conclude**?"

- -

Analyze the Text

CITE TEXTUAL EVIDENCE to support your answers.

📓 **Notebook** Respond to these questions.

1. (a) **Infer** How do the crew members feel about Claribel? (b) **Draw Conclusions** What is the benefit of having a pet in the space station?

2. (a) **Synthesize** What events or factors help the narrator figure out that something is wrong with the air? (b) **Make a Judgment** Who is responsible for saving the crew's lives: Claribel or the narrator? Explain.

3. (a) What causes the failure of the alarm that was intended to warn about air quality? (b) **Speculate** What are some potential problems with using a canary instead of an electronic alarm system? (c) **Evaluate** Which is a more reliable form of alarm? Explain.

© Pearson Education, Inc., or its affiliates. All rights reserved.

PERSONALIZE FOR LEARNING

English Language Support

Cognates English learners might be overwhelmed by the task of answering questions to test their understanding of a short story. To help them tackle the "Analyze the Text" questions, suggest that they take one question at a time and look for cognates or words that are similar to those in their native language that might help them understand the question and then formulate the answer. For example, in Spanish, member is *miembro*, space is *espacio*, station is *estación*, and potential is *potencial*. When students read a word that they think might be a cognate, remind them to consider if the word makes sense in the context. **ALL LEVELS**

Analyze Craft and Structure

Determine Theme The **theme** of a short story is the message or insight about life that it expresses. Sometimes, the narrator states the theme directly. More often, the theme is implied, or suggested by details in the text. To figure out the **implied theme** of a story, look closely at details, think about how they fit together, and consider what larger meaning they convey. To determine the theme of "Feathered Friend," focus on the following elements:

- the story's title
- the characters' thoughts and feelings
- the **setting** of the story, or when and where the story takes place
- the knowledge and insights that characters gain in the course of the story
- the outcome of the conflict and the effect the outcome has on the characters

Readers may interpret a story's theme in different ways. In order for an interpretation to be valid, it must take into account all of the story's important details.

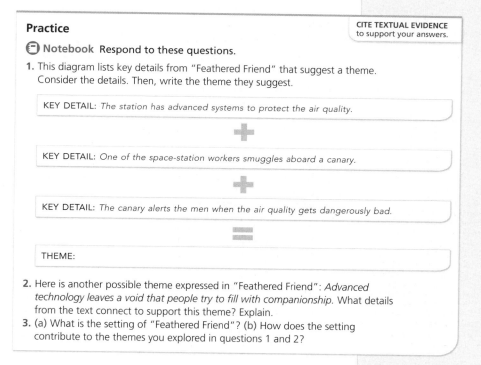

Practice

CITE TEXTUAL EVIDENCE
to support your answers.

🔲 **Notebook** Respond to these questions.

1. This diagram lists key details from "Feathered Friend" that suggest a theme. Consider the details. Then, write the theme they suggest.

> KEY DETAIL: *The station has advanced systems to protect the air quality.*

➕

> KEY DETAIL: *One of the space-station workers smuggles aboard a canary.*

➕

> KEY DETAIL: *The canary alerts the men when the air quality gets dangerously bad.*

═

> THEME:

2. Here is another possible theme expressed in "Feathered Friend": *Advanced technology leaves a void that people try to fill with companionship.* What details from the text connect to support this theme? Explain.
3. (a) What is the setting of "Feathered Friend"? (b) How does the setting contribute to the themes you explored in questions 1 and 2?

Feathered Friend **201**

Analyze Craft and Structure

Determine Theme Remind students that unlike a main idea, which is what a work is mostly about, a theme is a message or an understanding a reader should get from the story. Point out that in "Feathered Friend," the author does not tell you the themes; he helps you infer these messages through the story events and the narrator's analysis of those events. Explain to students that often in a story with first-person narration, the narrator's insights and what the narrator learns are keys to understanding the story's themes. Remind students, too, that there is often more than one theme in a story. For more support, see **Analyze Craft and Structure: Determine Theme.** 🔲

Practice

Possible responses:

1. Theme: Sometimes people rely too much on technology when nature serves them better.
2. It's clear that Claribel is a pet that provides companionship. For example, the crew tries to hide her presence from visitors so she won't be taken away, and Sven is upset when Claribel goes missing because she usually wakes him up in the morning.
3. (a) The setting is a space station orbiting Earth. (b) The setting contributes to the theme because it requires technology to keep people alive, and the technology that was in place failed.

FORMATIVE ASSESSMENT

Analyze Craft and Structure

- **If** students fail to identify the setting, **then** explain that this is where the story takes place and that it is described in the first paragraph of the story.

- **If** students fail to identify a theme, **then** have them think about how the overall story might change if some of the main details changed, for example, if nothing had happened to the equipment.

For Reteach and Practice, see **Analyze Craft and Structure: Determine Theme (RP).** 🔲

Whole-Class Learning   **201**

PERSONALIZE FOR LEARNING

Challenge

Theme Have interested students think about a recent movie or book that they have all either seen or read, perhaps a blockbuster. Then ask them to write a short paragraph describing the theme, noting the story details that led them to infer the theme. Invite students to share their ideas with the class and encourage students who came up with different themes or who noted story details that were different from ones others noted to explain their choices. Encourage debate about the theme, but remind students that there is usually more than one theme in a story.

© Pearson Education, Inc., or its affiliates. All rights reserved.

Concept Vocabulary

Why These Words

Possible responses:

1. It shows how the crew members respond when Claribel is found unconscious.

2. *sad, miserable, pitiful, sorry, woeful*

Practice

Possible responses:

1. correct; *pathetically* properly modifies mewed

2. correct; *lamented* appropriately describes a loss

3. incorrect; grinning and clapping hands indicate the baby is happy, not *distressed*

4. correct; *mournfully* properly explains how one cries after a death

5. incorrect; Kara is boasting, so *apologetically* does not appropriately describe how she cheered.

Word Network

Possible words: *space station, oxygen tent, circuit*

Word Study

For more support, see **Concept Vocabulary and Word Study.** 📄

Possible responses:

1. *sympathy:* to feel compassion and sorrow for others.

2. *empathy:* the ability to understand others' feelings.

FORMATIVE ASSESSMENT

Concept Vocabulary

If students fail to see a connection between the words, **then** have them use each word in a sentence and think about the similarities.

Word Study

If students struggle to write a sentence containing the word *sympathy,* **then** suggest they try using another form, such as *sympathize* or *sympathetic.* For Reteach and Practice, see **Word Study: Greek Root -*path*- (RP).** 📄

🔲 LANGUAGE DEVELOPMENT

FEATHERED FRIEND

🔗 WORD NETWORK

Add words related to modern technology from the text to your Word Network.

▤ STANDARDS

Language

• Demonstrate command of the conventions of standard English grammar and usage when writing or speaking.

• Determine or clarify the meaning of unknown and multiple-meaning words and phrases based on *grade 6 reading and content,* choosing flexibly from a range of strategies.
  b. Use common, grade-appropriate Greek or Latin affixes and roots as clues to the meaning of a word.

• Demonstrate understanding of figurative language, word relationships, and nuances in word meanings.

202 UNIT 3 • MODERN TECHNOLOGY

Concept Vocabulary

pathetically	mournfully	lamented
distressed	apologetically	

Why These Words? These concept vocabulary words all relate to feelings of sadness, suffering, or regret. For example, when something is wrong with Claribel, the crew members are *distressed,* and her owner speaks *mournfully.*

1. How does the concept vocabulary help readers appreciate Claribel's importance to the crew?

2. What other words do you know that connect to this concept?

Practice

🖥 **Notebook** Indicate whether the concept vocabulary word is used correctly in each sentence. Explain your answers.

1. The frightened cat hid in the corner and mewed *pathetically.*

2. We *lamented* the loss of our favorite teacher when she moved to another state.

3. The baby was so *distressed* by the attention that she grinned widely and clapped her hands.

4. The dog was old and sick, but I still cried *mournfully* when she died.

5. "I'm so happy that I won!" Kara cheered *apologetically.*

Word Study

Greek Root: -*path*- The Greek root -*path*- means "feeling" or "suffering." In "Feathered Friend," when Claribel is unwell, her claws stick up *pathetically* in the air. Claribel's claws are sticking up in a way that causes the crew members to feel sadness for her suffering.

1. Write a definition of the word *sympathy* that shows your understanding of the Greek root -*path*-. Then, use the word *sympathy* correctly in a sentence.

2. Use a dictionary to find the meaning of the word *empathy.* Write the definition. Then, explain how the definition connects to the meaning of the Greek root.

© Pearson Education, Inc., or its affiliates. All rights reserved.

AUTHOR'S PERSPECTIVE   **Elfrieda Hiebert, Ph.D.**

Frequency of Concepts in Narrative Texts In describing character traits or problems, skilled authors rarely repeat the same word, other than to achieve unity through repetition. Instead, authors use different words to create an interesting style. For instance, authors use a variety of words to describe setting, such as *lagoon, swales, bog.* Specifically, in *The Wizard of Oz,* L. Frank Baum describes what Dorothy and her companions see on arriving in the Emerald City with these words: *brilliance, dazzled, glittering.* Word variety also helps authors build characterization in jobs (*actor, lawyer, expert*) and roles (*adult/relative, female, male*). Especially in stories, the concepts represented by rare words are often known by common words that most students understand, such as *down* and *blah* for the rare words *lethargic, listless, slothful,* and *sluggish.* However, the more complex the text, the rarer the words that describe a particular concept will be. For instance, in a complex text, rather than describing a character as *calm,* the author might use *phlegmatic.* However, be sure that students understand that words such as these in a concept network have subtle differences in meaning and cannot necessarily be substituted for one another.

Conventions

Compound Words "Feathered Friend" contains a wide assortment of **compound words,** words that are made up of two or more other words. They sometimes appear in closed form as a single word, as in *heartbeat.* In other cases, they are hyphenated, as in *three-dimensional.* Some compound words appear in open form as two separate words, as in *free fall.*

Compound words can function as various parts of speech, depending on how they are being used. Here are some examples:

PART OF SPEECH	EXAMPLES
noun	The **space station** was running low on supplies.
	Skyscrapers were visible from far away.
verb	The engineer **dovetailed** the girders.
	Alarms **safeguarded** the crew from danger.
adjective	**Earthbound** passengers boarded the shuttle.
	The technicians worked in **twelve-hour** shifts.
adverb	The bird jumped **sideways** when startled.

Read It

1. Reread paragraph 3 of "Feathered Friend," and mark the compound words you see. List the words.

2. Read each passage from "Feathered Friend," and mark the compound word or words. Then, identify each compound word's part of speech.

PASSAGE	PART OF SPEECH
1. . . . you will picture Sven at once as a six-foot-six Nordic giant, built like a bull and with a voice to match.	six-foot-six (adjective)
2. She was a small yellow canary, hanging in the air as motionless as a hummingbird. . . .	hummingbird (noun)
3. So now, . . . don't be surprised if you hear an inexplicable snatch of birdsong.	birdsong (noun)

Write It

three-dimensional	bulkhead	spacesuit
breakfast	headache	doorway

📓 **Notebook** Write three sentences in which you use compound words. You may use the words in the chart, which appear in "Feathered Friend," or come up with words of your own.

© Pearson Education, Inc., or its affiliates. All rights reserved.

Conventions

Compound Words Point out to students that they use compound words every day; for example, words like *toothpaste, hairbrush, classroom, textbook,* and *breakfast* are all compound words. Explain that there is no hard and fast rule for the spelling of compound words. Rather, students must memorize whether the words are written as one word, as a hyphenated word, or as two words. Remind students that if they are in doubt, they should consult a dictionary.

Point out that students should be able to decode compound words by chunking them—breaking them into recognizable parts. For more support, see **Conventions: Compound Words.** 📄

MAKE IT INTERACTIVE
Provide each student with a compound word card that lists a part of a compound word. Have students move around the room to find the other half of their compound word.

Read It

Possible responses:
1. *free fall, slow-motion, three-dimensional, dovetailed, spacesuit, skyscrapers, handiwork*
2. **See possible responses in the chart on the student page.**

Write It

Possible responses:
1. I had a headache this morning so I didn't eat breakfast.
2. They have to wear a spacesuit when they go for a space walk.
3. Our outdoor cat eats and sleeps on the porch, but he is not allowed through the doorway.

FORMATIVE ASSESSMENT

Conventions

- **If** students can't identify compound words, **then** tell them to look for words with smaller words in them or to look for hyphenated words.

- **If** students struggle to write sentences with the listed compound words, **then** have them think about their morning routine and create sentences with compound words based on that.

For Reteach and Practice, see **Conventions: Compound Words (RP).** 📄

PERSONALIZE FOR LEARNING

English Language Support
Greek and Latin Affixes Ask students to work in pairs to write a list of five words they know with Greek or Latin affixes. **EMERGING**

Ask students to write a short paragraph using at least four words with the following affixes: *techno-, anthro-, mono-,* and *–ology.* **EXPANDING**

Ask students to choose a topic, make a list of words with Greek or Latin affixes they may need

to use to develop that particular subject, and then use the words in a paragraph. **BRIDGING**

An expanded **English Language Support Lesson** on Greek Root *-path-* is available in the Interactive Teacher's Edition. 📄

Writing to Sources

Explain to students that a written argument includes an opinion and reasons, evidence, and examples to support it. Note that other forms of written arguments, such as letters to the editor, advertisements, and even blogs, take a position on a subject. Remind students that the purpose of an argument is to get readers to understand and agree with your point of view. For more support, see **Writing to Sources: Argument.**

Reflect on Your Writing

1. **Responses will vary.** If students need support, ask them to think about what they learned about the story while writing their argument.

2. **Responses will vary.** If students struggle to evaluate the logic of their argument, have them exchange essays with a partner for a peer review.

3. **Responses will vary.** Have students list examples of words they have chosen to make their argument powerful and convincing.

FORMATIVE ASSESSMENT

Writing to Sources

If students struggle to take a position on the theme, **then** remind them of the answers they developed in the "Analyze Craft and Structure" activity. For Reteach and Practice, see **Writing to Sources: Argument (RP).**

FEATHERED FRIEND

Writing to Sources

An argument is a form of writing in which a writer states a claim, develops it with reasons, and supports it with evidence. The purpose of an argument is to convince readers to agree with the claim.

Assignment

One theme of "Feathered Friend" is that it is risky for people to become dependent on technology. Write a brief **argumentative essay** in which you take a position on that theme. Do you think the story expresses valid concerns about the risks of technology? Use details from the story, as well as your own observations and insights, to support your claim and craft a convincing argument.

Your essay should include:

- a claim, or clear statement of your position
- a logical organization, with words and phrases that show how your claim, reasons, and evidence connect
- relevant details from the story that support your claim
- a concluding statement that emphasizes the strength of your claim

Vocabulary and Conventions Connection In your argument, consider using several of the concept vocabulary words. If you use any compound words, look them up in a dictionary to see whether they should be hyphenated.

| pathetically | mournfully | lamented |
| distressed | apologetically | |

Reflect on Your Writing

After you have written your argument, answer the following questions.

1. How did writing your argument strengthen your understanding of the story's theme?

2. Is your argument clear and easy to follow? If not, how might you improve the organization and support?

3. **Why These Words?** The words you choose make a difference in your writing. Which words did you specifically choose to make your argument persuasive, or convincing?

© Pearson Education, Inc., or its affiliates. All rights reserved.

STANDARDS
Writing
• Write arguments to support claims with clear reasons and relevant evidence.
  a. Introduce claim(s) and organize the reasons and evidence clearly.
  b. Support claim(s) with clear reasons and relevant evidence, using credible sources and demonstrating an understanding of the topic or text.
  c. Use words, phrases, and clauses to clarify the relationship among claim(s) and reasons.
  e. Provide a concluding statement or section that follows from the argument presented.
• Conduct short research projects to answer a question, drawing on several sources and refocusing the inquiry when appropriate.
Speaking and Listening
• Present claims and findings, sequencing ideas logically and using pertinent descriptions, facts, and details to accentuate main ideas or themes; use appropriate eye contact, adequate volume, and clear pronunciation.
• Include multimedia components and visual displays in presentations to clarify information.

PERSONALIZE FOR LEARNING

Challenge

Counterclaim Most well-written arguments include a **counterclaim**. A counterclaim notes the opposing point of view, along with the reasons and evidence to support that point of view. Write a one-page counterclaim in which you argue a point of view that is the opposite of the one you took in the assignment. Include logic, reasoning, and support that is used, or would likely be used, to back up that claim. Then explain why the counterclaim is not accurate, based on your research.

Speaking and Listening

Canaries were used in coal mines as a low-tech way to detect deadly gases, before the invention of high-tech devices. In "Feathered Friend," Arthur C. Clarke shows the benefits of high-tech and low-tech methods working together.

Assignment

Work with a partner to create a **multimedia presentation**. In your presentation, explain another way in which high-tech and low-tech methods can work well together. Conclude your presentation by reflecting on whether your research has changed your opinions about modern technology.

1. **Research the Topic** Research ways in which high-tech and low-tech methods can work together. Then, identify one example to be the focus of your presentation.

2. **Organize Your Multimedia** Your presentation should explain how high-tech and low-tech methods work together in the example you present. Make sure you present your multimedia components in the order that makes the most sense. They should help clarify the information you present.

3. **Consider Your Conclusion** Consider the new knowledge you have gained from your research. What have you learned? Have your opinions about modern technology changed? Share your thoughts with the class at the end of your presentation.

4. **Prepare Your Delivery** Practice delivering your presentation with your partner. Remember to do the following:
   - maintain eye contact with your audience
   - speak with enough volume that everyone can hear you
   - speak with clear pronunciation

5. **Evaluate Multimedia Presentations** Listen closely as your classmates deliver their presentations. Use an evaluation guide like the one shown to rate their deliveries.

EVALUATION GUIDE

Rate each statement on a scale of 1 (not demonstrated) to 5 (well demonstrated).

☐ The information and media were placed in a logical order.

☐ The presentation clearly addressed both high- and low-tech methods.

☐ The presentation ended with a strong conclusion.

☐ The speakers maintained eye contact and spoke clearly and with enough volume.

✎ EVIDENCE LOG

Before moving on to a new selection, go to your Evidence Log and record what you learned from "Feathered Friend."

Feathered Friend **205**

© Pearson Education, Inc., or its affiliates. All rights reserved.

PERSONALIZE FOR LEARNING

Strategic Support

Finding Sources If students have difficulty finding information about the ways that low-tech and high-tech methods work together, suggest they refine their search terms and use respected databases such as those that index respected newspapers, magazines, and journals.

Speaking and Listening

1. **Research the Topic** You may wish to introduce the research component by suggesting ways in which apps allow people to shop, go to meetings and doctor's appointments, even tour places remotely. Note that people also use computers to generate drawings and plans. Encourage students to list other ways that high-tech methods are used in place of or in conjunction with low-tech methods.

2. **Organize Your Multimedia** Encourage students to consider what kinds of components are considered high-tech (computer graphics, computer animation and video) and which are considered low-tech (posters, drawings, audio recordings, speeches). Direct students to consider in what order they will present each component as they put their presentation together.

3. **Consider Your Conclusion** Have students prepare their remarks, explaining whether or not they feel differently about high and low technology after completing the presentation.

4. **Prepare Your Delivery** Suggest that partners practice by video recording each other's presentations and then evaluating them to determine what they need to do differently.

5. **Evaluate Multimedia Presentations** Encourage students to make at least one supportive comment about each presentation.

For more support, see **Speaking and Listening: Multimedia Presentation.** 📄

Evidence Log Support students in completing their Evidence Log. This paced activity will help prepare them for the Performance-Based Assessment at the end of the unit.

FORMATIVE ASSESSMENT

Speaking and Listening

- **If** students struggle to organize their multimedia, **then** suggest they choose one high-tech and one low-tech component for their presentation.

- **If** students are unable to speak in front of the entire class without significant distress, **then** suggest they have their partner record their presentation and use that as part of the high-tech component.

For Reteach and Practice, see **Speaking and Listening: Multimedia Presentation (RP).** 📄

Selection Test

Administer the "Feathered Friend" Selection Test, which is available in both print and digital formats online in Assessments. 📄 ☑

Teens and Technology Share a Future

🔊 **AUDIO SUMMARIES**

Audio summaries of "Teens and Technology Share a Future" are available online in both English and Spanish in the Interactive Teacher's Edition or Unit Resources. Assigning these summaries prior to reading the selection may help students build additional background knowledge and set a context for their first read.

Summary

In this blog post, "Teens and Technology Share a Future," 17-year-old writer Stefan Etienne argues that technology is, and should be, very important to young people. He talks about the excitement of finding things out. The sense of control and responsibility that comes from controlling information is important to him. He explains that it is easy to get overwhelmed by the large amount of useless or misleading information on the Internet, but with a little work, people can find what's most useful. And you can find pretty much any information you want. If young people read carefully and make good choices about what to study, they can be the best-informed generation ever.

Insight

This article argues for the value of modern technology. The greatest value of the Internet is that it provides an easy way to find and share a wide variety of information.

ESSENTIAL QUESTION:
How is modern technology helpful and harmful to society?

Connection to Essential Question

Etienne emphasizes the ability to find out important information. But he doesn't shy away from discussing the problems of inaccuracy and distraction on the Internet.

WHOLE-CLASS LEARNING PERFORMANCE TASK
Do electronic devices and online access really improve our lives?

UNIT PERFORMANCE-BASED ASSESSMENT
Do we rely on technology too much?

Connection to Performance Tasks

Whole-Class Learning Performance Task Etienne makes a pro-technology argument. Students should consider Etienne's point of view in light of their own knowledge and experiences, as well as the ideas expressed in the other selections in this section.

Unit Performance-Based Assessment Etienne argues that technology can make us more informed and responsible. He does not think we rely too much on it, but he does warn against using technology for harm and allowing ourselves to become distracted by meaningless content.

LESSON RESOURCES

	Making Meaning	Language Development
Lesson	**First Read** **Close Read** **Analyze the Text** **Analyze Craft and Structure**	**Technical Vocabulary** **Word Study** **Conventions**
Instructional Standards	**RI.10** By the end of the year, read and comprehend literary nonfiction . . . **RI.1** Cite textual evidence to support analysis of what the text says . . . **RI.5** Analyze how a particular sentence . . . **RI.6** Determine an author's point of view . . . **RI.8** Trace and evaluate the argument and specific claims in a text . . .	**RI.4** Determine the meaning of words and phrases . . . **L.1** Demonstrate command of the conventions . . . **L.2** Demonstrate command of the conventions . . . **L.2.a** Use punctuation . . . **L.4** Determine or clarify the meaning of unknown and multiple-meaning words and phrases . . . **L.4.b** Use common, grade-appropriate Greek or Latin affixes and roots . . .

⌨ STUDENT RESOURCES

Available online in the Interactive Student Edition or Unit Resources	🔊 Selection Audio 📄 First-Read Guide: Nonfiction 📄 Close-Read Guide: Nonfiction	📄 Word Network

⌨ TEACHER RESOURCES

Selection Resources Available online in the Interactive Teacher's Edition or Unit Resources	🔊 Audio Summaries ✏ Annotation Highlights 💬 EL Highlights 📄 English Language Support Lesson: Appositives and Appositive Phrases 📄 Analyze Craft and Structure: Argument	📄 Concept Vocabulary and Word Study 📄 Conventions: Appositives and Appositive Phrases
Reteach/Practice (RP) Available online in the Interactive Teacher's Edition or Unit Resources	📄 Analyze Craft and Structure: Argument (RP)	📄 Word Study: Greek Suffix -*metry* (RP) 📄 Conventions: Appositives and Appositive Phrases (RP)
Assessment Available online in Assessments	📄 ☑ Selection Test	
My Resources	📄 A Unit 3 Answer Key is available online and in the Interactive Teacher's Edition.	

Reading Support

Text Complexity Rubric: Teens and Technology Share a Future	
Quantitative Measures	
Lexile: 1100 **Text Length:** 586 words	
Qualitative Measures	
Knowledge Demands ①—**②**—③—④—⑤	The selection is centered around information that is familiar and requires only everyday knowledge of Internet use.
Structure ①—②—**③**—④—⑤	The structure is mostly easy to follow, but organization and connection between ideas are not always immediately apparent.
Language Conventionality and Clarity ①—②—**③**—④—⑤	The language is conversational and familiar. Some sentences are long and complex with multiple ideas. At times referents are unclear (for example, what pronouns refer to). Many idioms are used.
Levels of Meaning/Purpose ①—②—**③**—④—⑤	The meaning is somewhat hard to determine throughout text, but it is more clearly stated by the end. Some points are implied by use of rhetorical questions or metaphors.

DECIDE AND PLAN

English Language Support

Provide English learners with support for language and meaning as they read the selection.

Language Students may have difficulty with sentences in which it is not clear what the pronoun refers to. For example, (paragraph 2) in the sentence *Then, search for it online...* the pronoun *it* refers to something you are curious about, mentioned in the previous sentence.

Meaning Point out that some questions are *rhetorical questions*—a question that makes a statement. For example, (paragraph 7) *What superpower could one possibly want when we have technology...?* This is the author's way of saying that having technology is as good as having superpowers.

Strategic Support

Provide students with strategic support to ensure that they can successfully read the text.

Language Pair students. Have them take turns reading paragraphs aloud. Ask them to copy words or phrases they don't understand. Encourage them to try to figure out the meanings from context or by looking up words. If needed, help explain difficult words or phrases.

Meaning Discuss the author's use of metaphors and similes (both are comparisons, but a simile uses *like* or *as*). Give an example: (paragraph 3) . . . *a little like Indiana Jones.* Discuss the meaning. Then ask students to find a metaphor in paragraph 4 (the polar vortex and the sun breaking through the clouds). Ask them to read the whole paragraph. Discuss the meaning of that comparison.

Challenge

Provide students who need to be challenged with ideas for how they can go beyond a simple interpretation of the text.

Text Analysis Pair students. Ask them to discuss paragraphs 4 and 8. Have them write statements that summarize the author's opinion about the negative and positive aspects of the Internet. Discuss as a group. Then ask students what they think the author means by being prepared to take charge in an informed, responsible, and powerful manner.

Written Response Ask students to write their ideas about the best use of the Internet in their own experience or for people in general. Encourage them to be specific and to use examples. Ask volunteers to share their writing with the class.

TEACH

Read and Respond

Have the class do their first read of the selection. Then, have them complete their close read. Finally, work with them on the Making Meaning and Language Development activities.

Standards Support Through Teaching and Learning Cycle

IDENTIFY NEEDS

Analyze results of the Beginning-of-Year Assessment, focusing on the items relating to Unit 3. Also take into consideration student performance to this point and your observations of where particular students struggle.

DECIDE AND PLAN

- If students have performed poorly on items matching these standards, then provide selection scaffolds before assigning them the on-level lesson provided in the Student Edition.
- If students have done well on the Beginning-of-Year Assessment, then challenge them to keep progressing and learning by giving them opportunities to practice the skills in depth.
- Use the Selection Resources listed on the Planning pages for "Teens and Technology Share a Future" to help students continually improve their ability to master the standards.

Instructional Standards: Teens and Technology Share a Future

	Catching Up	This Year	Looking Forward
Reading	You may wish to administer the **Analyze Craft and Structure: Argument (RP)** worksheet to help students better understand how to construct an argument.	**RI.6** Determine an author's point of view or purpose in a text and explain how it is conveyed in the text.	Challenge students to think of other ways they may determine an author's purpose or point of view.
Language	Review the **Word Study: Greek Suffix -metry (RP)** worksheet with students to better familiarize them with the root word. Review the **Conventions: Appositives and Appositive Phrases (RP)** worksheet with students help them better understand the convention.	**L.4.b** Use common, grade-appropriate Greek or Latin affixes and roots as clues to the meaning of a word. **L.2.a** Use punctuation to set off nonrestrictive/parenthetical elements.	Challenge students to think of other words that use the suffix -metry. Challenge students to locate uses of appositives and appositive phrases in other selections they have read.

ANALYZE AND REVISE

- Analyze student work for evidence of student learning.
- Identify whether or not students have met the expectations in the standards.
- Identify implications for future instruction.

TEACH

Implement the planned lesson, and gather evidence of student learning.

Jump Start

FIRST READ You've probably heard that too much technology is bad for kids. In fact, there is a lot of focus on the negative side of technology. But can kids benefit from technology? Engage students in a discussion about kids using information technology—and how the ways they use it can help them and the world.

Teens and Technology Share a Future

In what ways can accessing information through the Internet be difficult? How has the Internet made access to information easy? Modeling questions such as these will help students connect to "Teens and Technology Share a Future" and to the Performance Task assignment. Selection audio and print capability for the selection are available in the Interactive Teacher's Edition.

Technical Vocabulary

Support students as they rank their words. Ask if they've ever heard, read, or used them. Reassure them that the definitions for these words are listed in the selection.

FIRST READ

As they read, students should perform the steps of the first read:

NOTICE: You may want to encourage students to notice the author's main claim or argument about the role of technology in the lives of today's teens.

ANNOTATE: Remind students to mark passages that include the author's reasons for the position he takes, as well as the examples he gives to support his reasons.

CONNECT: Encourage students to go beyond the text to make connections. Point out that they can connect to their own lives, to the lives of people they know, or to television shows, movies, or stories they've seen or read.

RESPOND: Students will answer questions and write a summary to demonstrate understanding.

Point out to students that while they will always complete the Respond step at the end of the first read, the other steps will probably happen somewhat concurrently. You may wish to print copies of the **First-Read Guide: Nonfiction** for students to use.

Comparing Texts

In this lesson, you will read and compare two arguments, in the form of blog posts, about the impact of modern technology. First, you will complete the first-read and close-read activities for "Teens and Technology Share a Future."

TEENS AND TECHNOLOGY SHARE A FUTURE

THE BLACK HOLE OF TECHNOLOGY

About the Author

Stefan Etienne (b. 1997) was born in Miami and now lives in New York City. At age twelve, he founded a technology blog called LaptopMemo.com. Etienne blogs about consumer technology.

🔧 Tool Kit
First-Read Guide and Model Annotation

☰ STANDARDS
Reading Informational Text
By the end of the year, read and comprehend literary nonfiction in the grades 6–8 text complexity band proficiently, with scaffolding as needed at the high end of the range.

Teens and Technology Share a Future

Technical Vocabulary

You will encounter the following words as you read "Teens and Technology Share a Future." Before reading, rate how familiar you are with each word. Rank the words in order from most familiar (1) to least familiar (3).

WORD	YOUR RANKING
microchips	
trigonometry	
pixels	

After completing the first read, come back to the technical vocabulary and review your rankings. Mark changes to your original rankings as needed.

First Read NONFICTION

Apply these strategies as you conduct your first read. You will have an opportunity to complete the close-read notes after your first read.

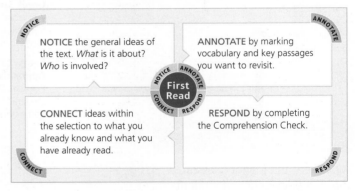

NOTICE the general ideas of the text. *What* is it about? *Who* is involved?

ANNOTATE by marking vocabulary and key passages you want to revisit.

CONNECT ideas within the selection to what you already know and what you have already read.

RESPOND by completing the Comprehension Check.

© Pearson Education, Inc., or its affiliates. All rights reserved.

CROSS-CURRICULAR PERSPECTIVES

Social Studies Though the Internet has grown substantially since the 1990s, its development began much earlier than that. Have students research and write a short report on the history of the Internet. Provide the following research questions: *When was it first conceived or invented? Who invented it? What was it first used for? How did it change into the Internet we* *know today?* As students conduct their research, remind them that information from *.gov, .edu,* and *.org* sites is generally more reliable than from *.com* sites. However, explain that reputable news (*.com*) sites may provide good information. Encourage interested students to create a timeline to go with their report and present their findings to the class.

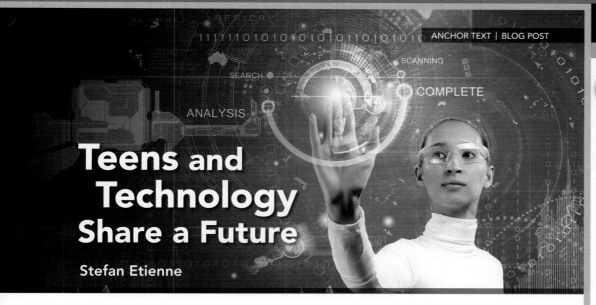

ANCHOR TEXT | BLOG POST

Teens and Technology Share a Future

Stefan Etienne

CLOSE READ

As students read paragraph 3, guide them to look for an extended comparison describing the process of getting information on the Internet. You may wish to model the close read using the following think-aloud format. Possible responses to questions on the student page are included. You may also want to print copies of the **Close-Read Guide: Nonfiction** for students to use.

ANNOTATE: As I read paragraph 3, I notice and highlight the details that tell how difficult but rewarding it is to find information you're looking for on the Internet.

QUESTION: I see that finding information is compared to being on a search similar to the character Indiana Jones, and also to turning over a small stone in a river with millions of other stones. I think the author included the comparisons because he knows that people who use the Internet often, especially teens, will know what he's talking about and understand the feeling he describes.

CONCLUDE: The first comparison makes me feel like I'm on an adventure or a quest. The second comparison makes me picture turning over a stone in a riverbed of millions of stones. The effect is that I feel that I've accomplished something and added something of value, no matter how small that accomplishment may feel. It also makes me feel like I am part of a larger community of people who are turning over similar "stones" through their own research.

BACKGROUND

The Internet puts an enormous amount of information at your fingertips. However, it only became widely available in the 1990s. It was first developed by the United States Defense Department as a communication tool in the 1970s. By the 2000s, about 360 million people, or 6% of the world's population, were connected to the Internet. This blog post discusses the impact of those changes.

SCAN FOR MULTIMEDIA

1   Perhaps it is the years of experience I've had in front of a computer, a laptop, or some sort of device with a screen. Talking about technology, attending press events in NYC,[1] and meeting the industry's most interesting people—all older than me, but all with the same childish hunger to see what comes next.

2   With its **microchips**, input methods, operating systems,[2] and everything in between, technology of the twenty-first century is a window into a new world for all of humanity, but especially for teenagers. Are you curious about something no one you know has even heard of? Then, search for it online—and maybe even come across the wrong answer, initially.

3   You do more research and eventually uncover the truth. Inside, you feel a little like Indiana Jones,[3] finding information that you believe will make you a more complete human being. In the grand scheme of things, you've done us all a great service: You've turned over a small stone of information, one in a river of millions. With every stone turned, our picture of the world becomes clearer.

NOTES

microchips (MY kroh chihps) *n.* small pieces of computer technology that have integrated circuits

CLOSE READ

ANNOTATE: In paragraph 3, mark the two comparisons the author makes.

QUESTION: Why does the author use these comparisons?

CONCLUDE: How do these comparisons help readers understand the writer's ideas?

1. **NYC** New York City.
2. **operating systems** basic software that allow devices to run applications.
3. **Indiana Jones** classic movie character, known for being an explorer and archaeologist.

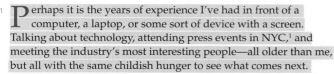
Additional **English Language Support** is available in the Interactive Teacher's Edition.

© Pearson Education, Inc., or its affiliates. All rights reserved.

Teens and Technology Share a Future **207**

DIGITAL PERSPECTIVES

Enriching the Text Explain to students that while teens have latched on to technology, using it often and for many purposes, some people, especially older people who did not grow up using technology, are not as comfortable with it. To bridge the gap, programs have sprung up around the world to encourage teens to teach seniors how to use technology. Show students a trailer of the documentary *Cyber-Seniors*. After students have viewed the clip, engage them in a discussion about the ways that teens can use technology to enrich the lives of others. You might also note how the Internet can be a frustrating place, as the author notes, for new users like the ones in the video. Preview the video before showing the class. **(Research to Explore)**

TEACHING

CLOSER LOOK

Analyze Persuasive Techniques ✐

Students may have marked paragraphs 6 and 7 during their first read. Use these paragraphs to help students understand the different methods that writers use to persuade their audience. Encourage them to talk about the annotations that they marked. You may want to model a close read with the class based on the highlights shown in the text.

ANNOTATE: Have students mark details in paragraphs 6 and 7 that show that the author is trying to get the reader to think in a certain way, or have students participate while you highlight them.

QUESTION: Guide students to consider what these details might tell them. Ask what a reader can infer from the questions the author asks the reader or his reference to a well-known writer, and accept student responses.

Possible response: The author wants the reader to agree that the Internet has great power to allow people to do a number of things, including helping others.

CONCLUDE: Help students to formulate conclusions about the importance of these details in the text. Ask students why the author might have included these details.

Possible response: By asking the reader questions that have obvious answers and by quoting a famous writer, the author is trying to persuade the reader. These devices are a way of getting the reader to see not only the author's point of view but that it is the correct point of view.

Remind students that **persuasive techniques** (or persuasive devices) are methods a writer or speaker uses to persuade a reader or listener to think or act in a particular way. Persuasive techniques may include **appeals to authority,** which are generally based on the position, experience, or stature of the person whose opinions are being quoted, and **rhetorical questions,** or questions with obvious answers. Rhetorical questions can make the audience feel personally and even emotionally involved, or they can suggest that an argument is obvious because the alternative is unthinkable.

NOTES

trigonometry (trihg uh NOM uh tree) *n.* field of math that deals with the relationships between the sides and angles of triangles

pixels (PIHK suhlz) *n.* smallest elements of an image that can be individually processed in a video display system

4   It's similar to my experience with the polar vortex[4] that has been plaguing New York for more than a month: Only when the sun breaks out for a moment do I realize how beautiful the snow can be. That's what computer technology can do—like sunshine breaking through the cold, it changes how we see things. When you filter out the useless Facebook messages, out-of-context tweets, and all the GIFs from Reddit,[5] you see that you—yes, you—are in control of your own information network. Best of all, you can do *anything* you want to do with it. There's no excuse to be confused by that math problem in **trigonometry,** or lack a source to cite in an essay. It's all on you now.

5   Of course, right off the bat, you may be thinking: "Here comes a geek, obsessed with technology, preaching about its effectiveness and adaptability, and how it's great for everyone who is currently a teenager."

6   You're absolutely right. But even if you are not as much of a geek as I am, you are still immersed in technology. How else would you be reading this blog? How else would you understand what "LOL" means, or be able to send a text message without even thinking about it?

7   The world is facing many problems, but young people—using the power of technology—have the opportunity to solve them. Technology connects us in ways no one has ever been connected before. As Henry David Thoreau[6] put it in an age before the Internet, "Could a greater miracle take place than for us to look through each other's eyes, for just an instant?" If only Thoreau had known that we would be able to look into another person's eyes—even if they are actually just **pixels** on a screen—thousands of miles away! What superpower could one possibly want when we have technology that lets us meet new people, invent new things, and help others?

8   Today's teenagers (as of 2014) have the potential to be the most influential and informed generation of human beings ever seen. But that will only happen if we step up to the challenge, wake up, and be prepared to take charge in an informed, responsible, and powerful way. (Hopefully, we will not make our problems worse.)

9   What is better than a will to do great things? The actual actions that will make those great things happen. ❧

---
4. **polar vortex** extremely cold wind near the North or South Pole. When this blog post was written, the cold air from the north polar vortex was affecting New York.
5. **GIFs . . . Reddit** animated digital images from an entertainment- and news-based social-networking website.
6. **Henry David Thoreau** nineteenth-century writer, known for his love of nature and living simply.

208 UNIT 3 • MODERN TECHNOLOGY

PERSONALIZE FOR LEARNING

English Language Support

Idioms Call student attention to paragraphs 4–8. Idioms can be confusing to English learners, and there are several on this page. First, explain that the phrase *it's all on you* in paragraph 4 means "you have the responsibility." Then tell students that the phrase *right off the bat* in paragraph 5 means "right away or immediately." Point out the idioms in paragraph 8: *step up to the challenge, wake up, take charge.* Explain that *step up to the challenge* means "to respond to the challenge," *wake up* means "to be aware," and *take charge* means "to assume control." Remind students that context clues can sometimes help them understand the general meaning or tone of idioms. For example, the idioms in paragraph 8 relate to being "informed, responsible, and powerful." **ALL LEVELS**

© Pearson Education, Inc., or its affiliates. All rights reserved.

208 UNIT 3 • MODERN TECHNOLOGY

Comprehension Check

Complete the following items after you finish your first read.

1. According to the author, how is technology a "window into a new world"?

2. What does the author suggest people need to do to be in control of their own information network?

3. According to the author, in what way is technology like a superpower?

4. According to the author, what must this generation do to fulfill the potential it has to influence the world in a positive way?

5. What does the author say is better than wanting to do great things?

6. 🗐 **Notebook** List three important ideas from the selection to show your understanding.

RESEARCH

Research to Clarify Choose at least one unfamiliar detail from the text. Briefly research that detail. In what way does the information you learned shed light on an aspect of the blog post?

Research to Explore Choose something that interested you from the text, and formulate a research question.

Teens and Technology Share a Future **209**

© Pearson Education, Inc., or its affiliates. All rights reserved.

Comprehension Check

Possible responses:

1. It allows people to get information that would have otherwise been difficult to get.
2. They need to filter out all the useless information.
3. The author suggests that technology is like a superpower because it allows us to meet new people, invent new things, help others, and even solve problems.
4. This generation must be informed and willing to take charge.
5. The author says that actions that cause great things to happen are better than just having the will to do great things.
6. Students' ideas will vary; however, students should include the author's points about the potential of both the Internet and the way teens use the Internet.

Research

Research to Clarify If students struggle to come up with a detail to research, you may want to suggest that they focus on one of the following topics: Facebook, computers, communication technology.

Research to Explore If students aren't sure how to go about formulating a research question, suggest that they use their findings from Research to Clarify as a starting point. For example, if students researched communication technology, they might formulate a question such as *What is the history of the cell phone?*

PERSONALIZE FOR LEARNING

Challenge

Speculate Guide students to reread paragraph 8 of the selection. Then ask them to consider what the future would look like according to Etienne's scenario. Have them write a two- to three-paragraph essay speculating how teens today, with their potential to be the most informed generation, can change the world for the better. Guide students to cite specific examples of changes that their generation could make. Encourage students to share their ideas with the class.

Jump Start

CLOSE READ Ask students to consider the following prompt: *Does your generation have a responsibility to make life better for future generations?* As students discuss in groups, ask them to consider how technology can help achieve this goal and whether or not technology also has the capacity to make the future worse for future generations.

Close Read the Text

Walk students through the annotation model on the student page. Encourage them to complete items 2 and 3 on their own. Review and discuss the sections students have marked. If needed, continue to model close reading by using the Annotation Highlights in the Interactive Teacher's Edition.

Analyze the Text

Possible responses:

1. (a) The blogger suggests that the snow of a swirling winter storm is information and the Internet helps you see the information. **DOK 2** (b) The blogger goes on to explain what he means, but it is initially unclear what the snow represents and what the sun represents. **DOK 3**

2. He may direct his argument toward teens because he is a teen himself, because he knows teens use technology, or because teens will be in charge one day. **DOK 3**

3. He means that teens must educate themselves by taking advantage of technology to access information. **DOK 2**

4. Technology is powerful, so it can help people by providing information, allowing people to solve difficult problems. But it can also hurt people by providing incorrect information. **DOK 3**

FORMATIVE ASSESSMENT

Analyze the Text

- **If** students fail to cite evidence, **then** remind them to support their ideas with specific information.

- **If** students struggle to paraphrase, **then** explain that paraphrasing is simply stating something in their own words.

MAKING MEANING

TEENS AND TECHNOLOGY
SHARE A FUTURE

Tool Kit
Close-Read Guide and
Model Annotation

STANDARDS

Reading Informational Text
• Cite textual evidence to support analysis of what the text says explicitly as well as inferences drawn from the text.
• Analyze how a particular sentence, paragraph, chapter, or section fits into the overall structure of a text and contributes to the development of the ideas.
• Determine an author's point of view or purpose in a text and explain how it is conveyed in the text.
• Trace and evaluate the argument and specific claims in a text, distinguishing claims that are supported by reasons and evidence from claims that are not.

Close Read the Text

1. This model, from paragraph 4 of the text, shows two sample annotations, along with questions and conclusions. Close read the passage, and find another detail to annotate. Then, write a question and your conclusion.

> **ANNOTATE:** These are all very specific examples of different kinds of information we get from computer technology.
>
> **QUESTION:** Why does the author mention such specific items?
>
> **CONCLUDE:** Using specific terms helps make a connection to readers—they may recognize their own use of technology in these examples.

> **ANNOTATE:** The author repeats the word *you*.
>
> **QUESTION:** Why does the author put so much emphasis on *you*?
>
> **CONCLUDE:** He is stressing the idea that we are all personally responsible for our uses of technology.

> When you filter out the useless Facebook messages, out-of-context tweets, and all the GIFs from Reddit, you see that you—yes, you—are in control of your own information network. Best of all, you can do *anything* you want to do with it.

2. For more practice, go back into the text, and complete the close-read notes.

3. Revisit a section of the text you found important during your first read. Read this section closely, and **annotate** what you notice. Ask yourself **questions** such as "Why did the blogger make this choice?" What can you **conclude**?

Analyze the Text

CITE TEXTUAL EVIDENCE to support your answers.

Notebook Respond to these questions.

1. (a) **Paraphrase** Explain the blogger's comparison of technology to the polar vortex. (b) **Evaluate** Is his comparison effective? Explain.

2. **Speculate** Why do you think he specifically addresses teens?

3. **Interpret** What does the blogger mean when he says that teens must "take charge in an informed, responsible, and powerful way"?

4. **Essential Question:** *How is modern technology helpful and harmful to society?* What have you learned about the ways that technology can help or harm society from reading this blog post?

© Pearson Education, Inc., or its affiliates. All rights reserved.

PERSONALIZE FOR LEARNING

English Language Support

Asking Questions Conducting a second close read of a nonfiction article can be a demanding task for English learners. To help them understand the more complex parts of the article, suggest that when they annotate details, they go back and reread those details. Suggest that they jot down questions, for example, *"What does the author mean by turning over a stone?"*

When students have finished the selection, suggest they return to the questions. Point out that sometimes, the answer to the question becomes clearer the more they read. Suggest that if the question was not answered in the reading that the students work with a partner and discuss the questions they have. **ALL LEVELS**

Analyze Craft and Structure

Author's Perspective: Argument This blog post is an example of an **argument**, a type of writing in which an author tries to persuade readers to think or do something specific. All persuasive writing presents a main **claim**, which is the author's position or opinion. The writer may include other claims that relate to the main one. Most writers use different types of details to support their claims. These supporting details are called *evidence*, and they may be any of the following types:

- logical reasons
- facts, or statements that can be proved true
- quotations from experts
- examples that help illustrate ideas

The author's claim reflects his or her **perspective**, or viewpoint. An author's perspective relates to his or her attitudes and experiences. For example, this blogger enjoys technology. His claim shows that perspective.

Practice

CITE TEXTUAL EVIDENCE to support your answers.

🔵 **Notebook** Answer the following questions.

1. (a) What is Etienne's main claim? (b) Identify two reasons he offers to support his claim.

2. (a) Identify a quotation from another author that Etienne uses to support his claim. (b) How does the quotation help strengthen his argument?

3. (a) Note two points at which Etienne says that technology can cause harm. (b) Why does he admit something that goes against his claim? (c) How does this actually strengthen his argument?

4. Etienne compares computer technology to a variety of different things. Use the chart to analyze whether each comparison makes his ideas clearer or has another effect.

COMPARISON	EFFECT
windows into a new world	The comparison creates an image that expresses the power of being able to see and learn new things on the Internet.
stones in a river	The comparison has the effect of illustrating the limitless choices and amounts of information available to us. It also demonstrates that individuals must be active learners and turn over each stone.
superpowers	The comparison makes readers realize the tremendous, untapped power available to them.

© Pearson Education, Inc., or its affiliates. All rights reserved.

Teens and Technology Share a Future **211**

WriteNow Express and Reflect

Comment The author of the blog post "Teens and Technology Share a Future" makes the claim that technology enables teens to solve problems and make the world a better place. Point out that most blogs give readers an opportunity to comment. Have students write a two- to three- paragraph comment to Stefan Etienne, explaining whether or not they agree with his position and why. Remind students to include details that help reveal their point of view about the subject, just as Etienne included details to establish his point of view.

Analyze Craft and Structure

Author's Perspective: Argument Guide students to distinguish the main claim of the selection from some of the other claims, which may be compelling and interesting but do not necessarily constitute the main claim. Suggest that students identify descriptive words chosen by the author that highlight the importance of certain claims. Or suggest that students reread the blog post and write the main idea for each paragraph and then analyze any patterns or repetition in the main ideas as a way of deciding on the main claim of the argument. For more support see **Analyze Craft and Structure: Argument.** 🔵

MAKE IT INTERACTIVE

Project the digital version of "Teens and Technology Share a Future" and read paragraphs 2–3. Model how to evaluate how the tone, word choice, and sense of address can be evaluated as indicators of the author's main claim. For example, ask the students why the author may have chosen to use the second-person in paragraph 3, and identify who the intended "you" might be.

Practice

Possible responses:

1. (a) The younger generation has both the responsibility to take charge of technology and improve society. (b) The younger generation is immersed in technology, and the Internet provides the power to access any information or perspective.

2. The Thoreau quote links to the claim that the Internet provides the opportunity to search for and discover any kind of information.

3. (a) Unnecessary information and the ability to inflict harm are two harmful uses of technology. (b) His argument is more credible if he shows all sides of the issue.

4. See possible responses in the chart on the student page.

FORMATIVE ASSESSMENT

Analyze Craft and Structure

- **If** students are unable to identify that the blog post is an argument, **then** ask them to find one thing they agree with and one thing they disagree with in the post.

- **If** students struggle to explain how well the author argues his point, **then** ask them to consider whether or not he persuaded them.

For Reteach and Practice, see **Analyze Craft and Structure: Argument (RP).** 🔵

Whole-Class Learning **211**

Technical Vocabulary

Why These Words?

Possible responses:

1. The blogger's use of technical vocabulary suggests he has an interest in and knowledge of technology, which helps the reader infer that the author's opinion is a positive one.

2. *methods, industry, network*

Practice

Possible responses:

1. *Microchips* in my cell phone keep it working. The teacher gave us homework today in *trigonometry* class. The number of *pixels* on my computer screen helps determine how good the resolution is.

2. *cell phones, computers, photographs, pictures, monitor, math*

Word Network

Possible words: *operating systems, tweets, GIF, LOL*

Word Study

For more support, see **Concept Vocabulary and Word Study.** 📄

Possible responses:

1. A clock, stopwatch, or any other device that measures time would be used by someone in the field of *horometry*.

2. A person would go to someone who practices *optometry* to have eyes examined and measured to gauge their health and to get glasses or contact lenses to correct vision problems.

FORMATIVE ASSESSMENT

Technical Vocabulary

If students fail to see the connection between words, **then** have them think about what is similar about the sentences they wrote for each word.

Word Study

If students are unable to determine the definition of *chronometer* and *optometry*, **then** use each word in a sentence. For example, *The chronometer was broken, so I lost track of time. When I had blurry vision, I went to see a doctor of optometry.*

For Reteach and Practice, see **Word Study: Greek Suffix: -metry (RP).** 📄

TEENS AND TECHNOLOGY SHARE A FUTURE

WORD NETWORK

Add words related to modern technology from the text to your Word Network.

STANDARDS

Reading Informational Text
Determine the meaning of words and phrases as they are used in a text, including figurative, connotative, and technical meanings.

Language
• Demonstrate command of the conventions of standard English grammar and usage when writing or speaking.
• Demonstrate command of the conventions of standard English capitalization, punctuation, and spelling when writing.
  a. Use punctuation to set off nonrestrictive/parenthetical elements.

• Determine or clarify the meaning of unknown and multiple-meaning words and phrases based on *grade 6 reading and content*, choosing flexibly from a range of strategies.
  b. Use common, grade-appropriate Greek or Latin affixes and roots as clues to the meaning of a word.

212 UNIT 3 • MODERN TECHNOLOGY

Technical Vocabulary

microchips	trigonometry	pixels

Why These Words? Like other fields, the technology industry has its own specialized vocabulary. These three technical vocabulary words are part of this specialized vocabulary.

1. How does the technical vocabulary sharpen the reader's understanding of the blogger's opinion about technology?

2. What other words in the blog post connect to this concept?

Practice

📔 **Notebook** The technical vocabulary words appear in "Teens and Technology Share a Future."

1. Use each technical word in a sentence that demonstrates your understanding of the word's meaning.

2. With a partner, take turns listing as many words related to the technical vocabulary words as you can.

Word Study

Greek Suffix: -metry The Greek suffix *-metry* means "process of measuring." *Trigonometry* is a type of mathematics that uses the properties of triangles to determine unknown angles and lengths. Knowing the meaning of *-metry* can help you determine the meanings of other words.

1. The Greek root *-hor-* means "time." What kind of tool or device might someone use in the field of *horometry*?

2. The Greek root *-opt-* means "eye" or "sight." Why might someone visit a person who practices *optometry*?

© Pearson Education, Inc., or its affiliates. All rights reserved.

VOCABULARY DEVELOPMENT

Domain-Specific Vocabulary Many students may not be familiar with all of the the technical vocabulary in the blog. To reinforce comprehension, pair students and have them find domain-specific terms and define them. Terms include: *input methods, operating systems, tweets, text message*. Once students have defined the terms, ask them to use each term in a sentence to demonstrate their understanding.

Conventions

Appositives and Appositive Phrases Writers use appositives to add information that helps the reader understand certain nouns. An **appositive** is a noun or pronoun that identifies, renames, or explains another noun or pronoun next to it. An **appositive phrase** includes an appositive and its modifiers.

- If the information in an appositive or appositive phrase is restrictive, which means that it is essential to understanding the sentence, *do not* set it off with commas or dashes.
- If the information in the appositive or appositive phrase is nonrestrictive, or nonessential, *do* set it off with commas or dashes.

APPOSITIVE	APPOSITIVE PHRASE
My friend _Marcos_ is great at using technology. (essential)	I bought clothes from the website, _an online shop_. (nonessential)

Read It

1. Read these sentences. Mark each example of an appositive or an appositive phrase. Label each as essential or nonessential.

   a. Examples of texting symbols include emoticons, picture portrayals of the writer's mood.

   b. We replay GIFs—funny images of cats, usually—and laugh every single time.

   c. The reference book _Oxford English Dictionary_ added new words in September 2015.

2. Read this passage from the selection. Mark the appositive or appositive phrase, and label it as essential or nonessential.

   You've turned over a small stone of information, one in a river of millions.

Write It

📓 **Notebook** Write a paragraph explaining when and how you usually use the Internet. Use at least two appositives or appositive phrases.

TIP

CLARIFICATION
Refer to the Grammar Handbook to learn more about these terms.

✏️ **EVIDENCE LOG**

Before moving on to a new selection, go to your Evidence Log and record what you've learned from "Teens and Technology Share a Future."

Teens and Technology Share a Future **213**

© Pearson Education, Inc., or its affiliates. All rights reserved.

Conventions

Appositives and Appositive Phrases Explain to students that an appositive helps tell more about the noun it modifies. Point out that they can determine whether or not the information in the appositive is essential by reading the sentence without the appositive. If the sentence is unclear without it, the information is essential and the appositive should not be set off with commas. If the sentence is clear without the appositive, they should set it off with commas. Provide students with the following example:

> My friend Jason gave a speech on space technology in class.

> My friend gave a speech on space technology in class.

Ask them which sentence is clearer. Point out that Jason is essential to understanding the sentence because without it, the reader would be left wondering which friend the writer was talking about. Explain that because *Jason* is essential information, it should not be set off with commas. For more support, see **Conventions: Appositives and Appositive Phrases.** 📄

Read It
Possible responses:
1. (a) Examples of texting symbols include emoticons, picture symbols of the writer's mood. (nonessential)
   (b) We play GIFs—funny images of cats, usually—and laugh every single time. (nonessential)
   (c) The reference source _Oxford English Dictionary_ added new words in September 2015. (essential)
2. You've turned over a small stone of information, one in a river of millions. (nonessential)

Write It

Students' paragraphs will vary but should reflect an understanding of how appositives are used and how they are punctuated.

Evidence Log Support students in completing their Evidence Log. This paced activity will help prepare them for the Performance-Based Assessment at the end of the unit.

FORMATIVE ASSESSMENT

Conventions

If students struggle to use appositives in their paragraphs, **then** have them list synonyms for the nouns they use, and point out that these can be used as appositives. For Reteach and Practice, see **Conventions: Appositives and Appositive Phrases (RP).** 📄

Selection Test

Administer the "Teens and Technology Share a Future" Selection Test, which is available in both print and digital formats online in Assessments. 📄 ☑

Whole-Class Learning **213**

PERSONALIZE FOR LEARNING

English Language Support
Appositives and Appositive Phrases Ask students to work in pairs to write a sentence, then add an appositive or an appositive phrase. **EMERGING**

Ask students to write two sentences—one with an appositive, and the other with an appositive phrase. **EXPANDING**

Ask students to write four sentences using appositives and appositive phrases. Tell them to use nonessential appositives in at least two of them. **BRIDGING**

An expanded **English Language Support Lesson** on Appositives and Appositive Phrases is available in the Interactive Teacher's Edition. 📄

The Black Hole of Technology

Summary

In this blog post, called "The Black Hole of Technology," Leena Khan argues that overusing modern technology is making us less aware and less happy. The amount of information you read is less important than the quality. She tells the story of a visit she paid to a temple in Cambodia, where her phone distracted her from the sight of a beautiful ancient temple. She noticed that the people nearby, though poor, seemed far happier than her friends back home. Digesting useless information distracts us from what's really significant and keeps us from being happy.

Insight

This blog post argues that we need to use modern technology moderately. Spending too much time with technology can distract us from what's really important.

🔊 AUDIO SUMMARIES
Audio summaries of "The Black Hole of Technology" are available online in both English and Spanish in the Interactive Teacher's Edition or Unit Resources. Assigning these summaries prior to reading the selection may help students build additional background knowledge and set a context for their first read.

ESSENTIAL QUESTION:
How is modern technology helpful and harmful to society?

WHOLE-CLASS LEARNING PERFORMANCE TASK
Do electronic devices and online access really improve our lives?

UNIT PERFORMANCE-BASED ASSESSMENT
Do we rely on technology too much?

Connection to Essential Question

Khan notes that a vast amount of news and information is available online. However, she argues that when we read too much online, we don't retain much of what we read. Thus, overusing modern technology can waste our time. It can also make us less happy.

Connection to Performance Tasks

Whole-Class Learning Performance Task The author argues for more moderate use of technology. Students should read critically, apply their own observations and knowledge, and consider the author's ideas in relationship to those expressed by other writers in this section.

Unit Performance-Based Assessment Khan argues that spending too much time on technology distracts us from what we really care about. She uses the example of nearly missing out on the unusual experience of visiting a Cambodian town and temple because she was thinking more about the meaningless information she could get from her smartphone than she was about her surroundings.

LESSON RESOURCES

	Making Meaning	Language Development	Effective Expression
Lesson	**First Read** **Close Read** **Analyze the Text** **Analyze Craft and Structure**	**Concept Vocabulary** **Word Study** **Conventions**	**Writing to Compare**
Instructional Standards	**RI.10** By the end of the year, read and comprehend literary nonfiction . . . **RI.4** Determine the meanings of words and phrases . . . **RI.6** Determine an author's point of view or purpose . . . **RI.8** Trace and evaluate the argument and specific claims in a text . . . **L.5.a** Interpret figures of speech . . .	**RI.4** Determine the meaning of words and phrases . . **L.1** Demonstrate command of the conventions . . . **L.2** Demonstrate command of the conventions . . . **L.2.a** Use punctuation . . . **L.4** Determine or clarify the meaning of unknown and multiple-meaning words and phrases . . . **L.4.a** Use context as a clue . . . **L.4.d** Verify the preliminary determination . . .	**RI.8** Trace and evaluate the argument . . . **RI.9** Compare and contrast one author's presentation of events . . . **W.1** Write arguments . . . **W.1.a** Introduce claim(s) . . . **W.1.b** Support claim(s) . . . **W.1.e** Provide a concluding statement . . . **W.9** Draw evidence from literary or informational texts . . .
STUDENT RESOURCES Available online in the Interactive Student Edition or Unit Resources	Selection Audio First-Read Guide: Nonfiction Close-Read Guide: Nonfiction	Word Network	Evidence Log
TEACHER RESOURCES **Selection Resources** Available online in the Interactive Teacher's Edition or Unit Resources	Audio Summaries Annotation Highlights EL Highlights English Language Support Lesson: Argumentative Essay Analyze Craft and Structure: Persuasive Techniques	Concept Vocabulary and Word Study Conventions: Independent and Dependent Clauses	Writing to Compare: Argumentative Essay
Reteach/Practice (RP) Available online in the Interactive Teacher's Edition or Unit Resources	Analyze Craft and Structure: Persuasive Techniques (RP)	Word Study: Multiple-Meaning Words (RP) Conventions: Independent and Dependent Clauses (RP)	
Assessment Available online in Assessments	Selection Test		
My Resources	A Unit 3 Answer Key is available online and in the Interactive Teacher's Edition.		

Reading Support

Text Complexity Rubric: The Black Hole of Technology

Quantitative Measures

Lexile: 980   Text Length: 821 words

Qualitative Measures

Knowledge Demands ①—❷—③—④—⑤	The selection is mostly centered around themes and situations that are common to most readers. Though the author's travel experiences are specific, no prior knowledge about them is needed.
Structure ①—❷—③—④—⑤	The selection begins with statement of opinion, and then the author backs it up with the story of a personal experience. The organization is clear and explicit, with clear connection between events and ideas.
Language Conventionality and Clarity ①—❷—③—④—⑤	The language is straightforward and clear, with conversational and contemporary tone. There is some use of metaphors and idioms. Sentences generally have simple construction.
Levels of Meaning/Purpose ①—❷—③—④—⑤	The opinion is clearly stated at beginning and at the end. Throughout the piece, concepts supporting the author's opinion are clear and straightforward. The metaphor of the *black hole of technology* is used throughout.

DECIDE AND PLAN

English Language Support

Provide English Learners with support for structure and meaning as they read the selection.

Structure Help students to understand the organization of the selection. Point out that the piece begins with a statement of the author's opinion. In the second paragraph there is an example of an event that helps to make the point. The next four paragraphs tell a longer story about an experience while traveling. The last paragraph concludes the piece with the author's view.

Meaning Discuss the ideas that are stated in the first and last paragraphs. As a group, have students help you to make a list of the author's ideas. Rephrase ideas or explain as necessary. For example, *It's more important to look at your surroundings instead of just texting.*

Strategic Support

Provide students with strategic support to ensure that they can successfully read the text.

Structure Ask students to make an outline showing the structure of the selection. Ask questions to help them do this: *What does the author do in the first paragraph? (states the opinion). In which paragraphs does the author describe personal experiences? (2–6) How does the author end the piece? (with a concluding paragraph stating the opinions and plans).*

Meaning Discuss the meaning of the metaphor that technology is a *black hole*. If necessary, explain that in space, a black hole has gravity that pulls objects in. Ask why students think the author used that metaphor. Then go through the selection with students to help them to pull out the main ideas of each section of the text.

Challenge

Provide students who need to be challenged with ideas for how they can go beyond a simple interpretation of the text.

Text Analysis Pair students. Ask them to think about the positive and negative opinions about the use of technology in this selection and the last. Ask students to list the authors' viewpoints. Then as a group, ask students to explain why they agree or disagree.

Written Response Have students write about a time that they felt that using their phone or computer got in the way of doing other things they wanted to do. Or, they may write about their opinions about the use of devices and whether their parents share their views. Encourage them to use examples and specific details. Invite volunteers to share their writing.

TEACH

Read and Respond

Have the class do their first read of the selection. Then have them complete their close read. Finally, work with them on the Making Meaning, Language Development, and Effective Expression activities.

Standards Support Through Teaching and Learning Cycle

IDENTIFY NEEDS

Analyze results of the Beginning-of-Year Assessment, focusing on the items relating to Unit 3. Also take into consideration student performance to this point and your observations of where particular students struggle.

ANALYZE AND REVISE

- Analyze student work for evidence of student learning.
- Identify whether or not students have met the expectations in the standards.
- Identify implications for future instruction.

TEACH

Implement the planned lesson, and gather evidence of student learning.

DECIDE AND PLAN

- If students have performed poorly on items matching these standards, then provide selection scaffolds before assigning them the on-level lesson provided in the Student Edition.
- If students have done well on the Beginning-of-Year Assessment, then challenge them to keep progressing and learning by giving them opportunities to practice the skills in depth.
- Use the Selection Resources listed on the Planning pages for "The Black Hole of Technology" to help students continually improve their ability to master the standards.

Instructional Standards: The Black Hole of Technology

	Catching Up	This Year	Looking Forward
Reading	You may wish to administer the **Analyze Craft and Structure: Persuasive Techniques (RP)** worksheet to help students better understand how to determine author's purpose.	**RI.6** Determine an author's point of view or purpose in a text and explain how it is conveyed in the text.	Challenge students to think of other ways they may determine an author's purpose or point of view.
Language	Review the **Word Study: Multiple-Meaning Words (RP)** worksheet with students to better familiarize them with how to use context. Review the **Conventions: Independent and Dependent Clauses (RP)** worksheet with students to familiarize them with the types of clauses.	**RI.4** Determine the meaning of words and phrases as they are used in a text, including figurative, connotative, and technical meanings. **L.1** Demonstrate command of the conventions of standard English grammar and usage when writing or speaking.	Have students look up words they are familiar with to determine if they have multiple meanings they were not aware of. Challenge students to consider the effects different types of clauses have on a sentence's meaning.

Jump Start

FIRST READ Prior to students' first read, ask them this question: What is the biggest complaint you hear parents and other adults make about kids and their smartphones? Engage students in a discussion about the drawbacks of constant access to smartphones.

The Black Hole of Technology 🔊 📄

Why does the author think people don't stop to process information anymore? Why does the author's dad take away her cell phone? Modeling questions such as these will help students connect to "The Black Hole of Technology" and to the Performance Task assignment. Selection audio and print capability for the selection are available in the Interactive Teacher's Edition.

Concept Vocabulary

Support students as they rank their words. Ask if they've ever heard, read, or used them. Reassure them that the definitions for these words are listed in the selection.

🔘 FIRST READ

As they read, students should perform the steps of the first read:

NOTICE: You may want to encourage students to notice how the author says she interacts with the world now.

ANNOTATE: Remind students to mark passages that contrast how the author interacted with the world before and after her father took away her phone.

CONNECT: Encourage students to think about their own cell phone and computer use or that of people they know. Are they also consumed by their devices? Do they also forget when to stop using them?

RESPOND: Students will answer questions and write a summary to demonstrate understanding.

Point out to students that while they will always complete the Respond step at the end of the first read, the other steps will probably happen somewhat concurrently. You may wish to print copies of the **First-Read Guide: Nonfiction** for students to use. 📄

Remind students that during their first read, they should not answer the close-read questions that appear in the selection.

🖥 MAKING MEANING

Comparing Texts

Read this blog post and complete the first-read and close-read activities. Then, compare the blogger's argument to the one expressed in "Teens and Technology Share a Future."

TEENS AND TECHNOLOGY SHARE A FUTURE

THE BLACK HOLE OF TECHNOLOGY

About the Author

Leena Khan (b. 2001) is an aspiring author. Khan lives in Saudi Arabia.

The Black Hole of Technology

Concept Vocabulary

You will encounter the following words as you read "The Black Hole of Technology." Before reading, rate how familiar you are with each word. Rank the words in order from most familiar (1) to least familiar (5).

WORD	YOUR RANKING
devouring	
absorbing	
process	
consumed	
digesting	

After completing the first read, come back to the concept vocabulary and review your rankings. Mark changes to your original rankings as needed.

First Read NONFICTION

Apply these strategies as you conduct your first read. You will have an opportunity to complete the close-read notes after your first read.

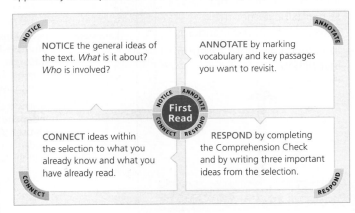

NOTICE the general ideas of the text. *What* is it about? *Who* is involved?

ANNOTATE by marking vocabulary and key passages you want to revisit.

First Read

CONNECT ideas within the selection to what you already know and what you have already read.

RESPOND by completing the Comprehension Check and by writing three important ideas from the selection.

© Pearson Education, Inc., or its affiliates. All rights reserved.

☰ STANDARDS
Reading Informational Text
By the end of the year, read and comprehend literary nonfiction in the grades 6–8 text complexity band proficiently, with scaffolding as needed at the high end of the range.

214 UNIT 3 • MODERN TECHNOLOGY

VOCABULARY DEVELOPMENT

Concept Vocabulary Reinforcement To increase familiarity with the concept vocabulary, ask students to use each of the words in a sentence. Encourage students to include context clues in their own sentences to demonstrate their knowledge of the word. If students are still struggling with the words, encourage them to identify the base word in each term, look up the base word in the dictionary, and then use the definition to come up with the meaning of the concept vocabulary word.

The Black Hole of Technology

Leena Khan

 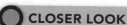

CLOSER LOOK

Analyze Repetition

Students may have marked paragraph 1 during their first read. Use this paragraph to help students understand why the author repeats certain phrases. Encourage them to talk about the annotations that they marked. You may want to model a close read with the class based on the highlights shown in the text.

ANNOTATE: Have students mark examples in paragraph 1 of repetition of a word or phrase, or have students participate while you highlight them.

QUESTION: Guide students to consider what these details might tell them. Ask what a reader can infer from the author's repetition of the phrase "no one" or the author's repetition of "go" and accept student responses.

Possible response: The author wants to point out that people aren't processing information or appreciating personal interaction anymore. She also wants to show how fast-paced everything is.

CONCLUDE: Help students to formulate conclusions about the importance of these details in the text. Ask students why the author might have included these details.

Possible response: The repetition of "no one" emphasizes how widespread this behavior is. The "go, go, go" contrasts with the sentence that follows it: "Not once do we stop."

Remind students that **repetition** is the repeated use of any element of language—a sound, a word, a phrase, a clause, or a sentence. Point out that repetition is used for emphasis and to create musical effects.

BACKGROUND

The first smartphone was introduced in 1993. Since then, smartphones have become the fastest-selling devices in history. By 2013, 22% of the world's total population owned a smartphone. Although many people also own personal computers, the smartphone is a portable device that allows people to stay connected wherever they go.

SCAN FOR MULTIMEDIA

1 The black hole of endless, unimportant streams of technology-enabled information is **devouring** everyone living in the twenty-first century. No matter how much people may look at information, it does not mean they are **absorbing** it. Equating quality with speed and volume, people may read thousands of news headlines broadcasted across the world daily, yet they will forget them in a couple of hours. No one stops to **process** information anymore to determine its significance or importance. No one appreciates the value of personal interaction or nature. Everything is go, go, go. Not once do we stop. Before being introduced to my phone and computer, I had been more appreciative of the world around me. Now, I'm always **consumed** by my "tech," and I never stop to take a break.

2 "Did you guys see what Miley Cyrus[1] posted?" My friend Fouly only peeled her eyes away from her iPhone screen to ask us that question. I glanced around at my friends, and they all quickly checked Instagram[2] in the hopes that they hadn't missed Miley's latest update. I, on the other hand, glanced out the window separating us from the beautiful weather outside. We were 15 friends sitting inside under artificial lighting and with our hands

NOTES

devouring (dih VOW rihng) *v.* taking in greedily

absorbing (ab ZAWR bihng) *v.* learning; fully taking in

process (PROS ehs) *v.* gain an understanding of

consumed (kuhn SOOMD) *adj.* absorbed; occupied

---

1. **Miley Cyrus** celebrity who has achieved fame as an actress and a singer.
2. **Instagram** online social-media platform.

 Additional **English Language Support** is available in the Interactive Teacher's Edition.

© Pearson Education, Inc., or its affiliates. All rights reserved.

PERSONALIZE FOR LEARNING

Strategic Support

First Read Support If students struggle to comprehend the text during the first read, have a partner conduct a think-aloud to explain the thought process as he or she works through the NOTICE, ANNOTATE, CONNECT, and RESPOND steps. For example, in paragraph 2, the student might notice that the author describes how her friends are all on their smartphones as they sit together. The student might annotate "I glanced around at my friends, and they all quickly checked Instagram in the hopes that they hadn't missed Miley's latest update" to return to in the close read to see what it reveals about the author's perspective.

CLOSE READ 🖉

Remind students that poems and songs often contain alliteration, a technique that appeals to the sense of sound. You may wish to model the close read using the following think-aloud format. Possible responses to questions on the student page are included. You may also want to print copies of the **Close-Read Guide: Nonfiction** for students to use.

ANNOTATE: As I read paragraph 3, I notice and highlight sensory words and descriptions.

QUESTION: I think these details emphasize the physical world in which the author exists during this scene.

CONCLUDE: The details help to create a feeling of separation between how we exist in the real world and the virtual world on our technology devices.

NOTES

CLOSE READ
ANNOTATE: In paragraph 3, mark sensory words and phrases. These are details that relate to the senses (sight, hearing, taste, touch, or smell).

QUESTION: Why does the blogger use these sensory details?

CONCLUDE: What mood or feeling do these details help create?

digesting (dih JEH stihng) *v.* thinking over; mentally taking in

glued to our phones on a Friday, when the enticing warmth of the sun and delicate breeze were begging us to run around outside. Of course, our ears were deaf to nature's pleas, just like any other teenager nowadays. I put my phone down to shut the curtains, then I continued to mindlessly scroll through Miley's Instagram page.

3 I found myself longing for that Instagram page a week later, in an entirely different country. The scorching sun baked the back of my neck as my family and I walked along the wide, crowded dirt path on our way to visit yet another Cambodian temple. I slipped my phone out of my bag to check for a signal, but before I could even unlock it, it was snatched out of my hands.

4 "Leena, you're heading toward one of the most well preserved ancient wonders in the world. It would do you well to appreciate your surroundings!" my dad scolded.

5 My phone was wailing at me from the tight grip his hands had on it, but I had no choice but to ignore it, like I had been forced to do for the entire fall break. Huffing, I looked up and drank in our surroundings. There were tents perched on the sides of the sandy roads, and a couple of half-naked boys were jumping into a murky lake nearby. A toddler was laughing her head off, playing with an old man who I assumed was her grandfather. I missed all of this liveliness, the beauty of a community, because I was trapped in the black hole of technology. Everyone around me was smiling, despite having to live their lives in poverty. Then I noticed something I hadn't before: no one had a cellphone on them. There were no TVs, no radios, and their music came from live instruments instead of mp3 players and iPods. These people had nothing. Some of them were even walking around without shoes! How could they look so happy? Then I thought . . . Maybe it's because they don't have all that modern technology. They aren't subjected to the black hole of endless information.

6 I carried my insightful observations all the way to the temple, and my breath caught in my throat when we got there. It was stunning. When the guide started a long speech about the origin of the temple, I turned to face him. Then I realized I was inside of the black hole again. I was paying attention to the information the guide was throwing at me instead of also recognizing this once-in-a-lifetime experience. When would I be able to visit one of the seven wonders of the world again? The answer was pretty clear, so keeping one ear with the guide, and turning the rest of myself to the temple, I soaked in the extraordinary sight before me. For once, I wasn't **digesting** useless information. I wasn't typing into my phone, or watching any screen at all. In a life of go, go, go I had finally stopped.

© Pearson Education, Inc., or its affiliates. All rights reserved.

PERSONALIZE FOR LEARNING

English Language Support
Syntax Point students to the second sentence in paragraph 4: "'It would do you well to appreciate your surroundings!' my dad scolded." Explain that *well* is an adverb and that adverbs usually appear at the beginning of a sentence or right before or after the verb they modify. For example,

You would do well to learn the poem. Tell students that the construction in paragraph 4 is a formal construction with the same meaning as "You would do well to appreciate your surroundings." It is worth noting that another reason this construction might be difficult for English

Language Learners is that the subject "it" refers to something that is understood but perhaps not clear to someone deconstructing a sentence.

Remind them that in this sentence, the context and the verb "scolded" is a clue to the sentence's meaning. **ALL LEVELS**

7   It was then that I vowed that the next time my friends and I are absorbed in our phones on a sunny day, I won't close the curtains. Next time I'm walking along any road, I'll value my surroundings instead of texting on a device. From now on, I will make sure that the endless information flying my way won't go in one ear and out the other. I will find the significance in things and recognize it, because that's something many people fail to do—by falling into the technology trap. Escape the black hole of technology, because when you do . . . you feel free. ✎

NOTES

Comprehension Check

Complete the following items after you finish your first read.

1. What does the author do when a friend points out a new Miley Cyrus post?

2. Where do the author and her family go on vacation?

3. Why does the author's father take away her cellphone?

4. ⊟ **Notebook** Write three important ideas from the selection.

- -

RESEARCH

Research to Clarify Choose at least one unfamiliar detail from the text. Briefly research that detail. In what way does the information you learned shed light on an aspect of the blog post?

© Pearson Education, Inc., or its affiliates. All rights reserved.

The Black Hole of Technology **217**

Comprehension Check

Possible responses:
1. She first looked out the window, then she checked Miley Cyrus's Instagram page for the latest post.
2. She and her family go to Cambodia to visit ancient temples.
3. He wants her to appreciate her surroundings.
4. Students' ideas will vary; however, they should include a variation of the claim that technology keeps people from noticing and attending to the things around them.

Research

Research to Clarify If students struggle to come up with a detail to research, you may want to suggest that they focus on one of the following topics: smartphones, Cambodia, teen blogs, teens and technology.

PERSONALIZE FOR LEARNING

Challenge
Relating to Personal Experience Explain to students that what Leena describes in her blog is the constant distraction of computers and smartphones. Have students think of a time when they or someone they know was distracted from an important conversation, from participating in an interesting or exciting event, or from experiencing something new and unusual, because they were distracted by a smartphone, computer, television, or some other form of technology. Students should write a paragraph describing what happened and how it made them feel.

Jump Start

CLOSE READ Take an impromptu poll by asking students if they think people have become too dependent on technology, namely smartphones and computers. Encourage students who have different points of view to share their ideas.

Close Read the Text

Walk students through the annotation model on the student page. Encourage them to complete items 2 and 3 on their own. Review and discuss the sections students have marked. If needed, continue to model close reading by using the Annotation Highlights in the Interactive Teacher's Edition.

Analyze the Text

Possible responses:

1. She could not focus on what was around her. **DOK 2**

2. (a) She notes that she is not paying attention to her surroundings. **DOK 2** (b) I agree that it is difficult to look around when you are paying attention to what the guide says. But to really appreciate the surroundings, she needed the information that the guide had. **DOK 3**

3. No, it will not be easy because everyone else will be engrossed in technology. **DOK 3**

4. Technology can prevent us from seeing what's real and what's around us. It can prevent us from connecting with other people. It also provides us a steady stream of information, but we do not have time to process it all. **DOK 3**

FORMATIVE ASSESSMENT

Analyze the Text

• **If** students fail to cite evidence, **then** remind them to support their ideas with specific information.

• **If** students struggle to identify how listening to the guide is like accessing technology-enabled information, **then** discuss with them what both activities prevent the blogger from doing.

 MAKING MEANING

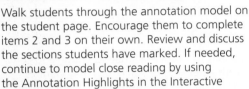

THE BLACK HOLE OF TECHNOLOGY

Close Read the Text

1. This model, from paragraph 5 of the text, shows two sample annotations, along with questions and conclusions. Close read the passage, and find another detail to annotate. Then, write a question and your conclusion.

> **ANNOTATE:** This concept is repeated.
>
> **QUESTION:** Why does the blogger repeat this concept?
>
> **CONCLUDE:** The repetition emphasizes how startled the blogger is when she notices people without technology.

> **ANNOTATE:** The blogger ends a paragraph with an exclamation and a question.
>
> **QUESTION:** Why does the blogger use these punctuation marks?
>
> **CONCLUDE:** The punctuation emphasizes her emotions. She is both startled and amazed.

> There were no TVs, no radios, and their music came from live instruments instead of mp3 players and iPods. These people had nothing. Some of them were even walking around without shoes! How could they look so happy?

Close Read

2. For more practice, go back into the text, and complete the close-read notes.

3. Revisit a section of the text you found important during your first read. Read this section closely, and **annotate** what you notice. Ask yourself **questions** such as "Why did the blogger make this choice?" What can you **conclude**?

🔧 Tool Kit
Close-Read Guide and Model Annotation

Analyze the Text

CITE TEXTUAL EVIDENCE to support your answers.

📓 **Notebook** Respond to these questions.

1. **Analyze** Why does Leena Khan feel the urge to check her cellphone for a signal when she is walking toward a temple in Cambodia?

2. (a) **Analyze** Why does she draw a connection between listening to the guide and accessing data on her cellphone? (b) **Evaluate** Do you agree that the two things are similar? Why or why not?

3. **Speculate** Leena Khan vows to "find the significance in things." Explain whether you think this will be easy to do once she returns home.

4. **Essential Question:** *How is modern technology helpful and harmful to society?* What have you learned about the ways that technology can harm society from reading this blog post?

≡ STANDARDS

Reading Informational Text
• Determine the meaning of words and phrases as they are used in a text, including figurative, connotative, and technical meanings.
• Determine an author's point of view or purpose in a text and explain how it is conveyed in the text.
• Trace and evaluate the argument and specific claims in a text, distinguishing claims that are supported by reasons and evidence from claims that are not.

Language
Interpret figures of speech in context.

© Pearson Education, Inc., or its affiliates. All rights reserved.

VOCABULARY DEVELOPMENT

Word Analysis Point out that the blogger uses the word *technology-enabled* to describe information. Tell students that *technology-enabled* is a compound adjective and that compound adjectives express a single idea. Point out that without the hyphen, the meaning might be unclear (as in *man-eating shark* vs. *man eating shark*). Point out that students can determine the meaning of the word and of others like it by analyzing its parts. Explain that *enabled* means "to make something happen." *Technology-enabled*, then, refers to information that is made available by technology.

Analyze Craft and Structure

Persuasive Techniques In a persuasive text, a writer attempts to convince readers to see a topic in a new way. The writer states a position, or **claim,** and then includes facts and other evidence to support it. Persuasive writers also use a variety of techniques to make their ideas more convincing. Here are some of those techniques:

- **Repetition:** *Repeating a word or phrase*—this emphasizes the word or idea and makes it more memorable.

- **Appeal to Emotion:** *Words, phrases, or stories that make readers feel something*—readers can be influenced by words that create positive feelings for the author's position and ones that create negative feelings for an opposing position.

- **Appeal to Reason:** *Facts and reasons that are organized in a clear way*—readers can follow a writer's thought process and be convinced by strong, well-connected logic.

Each of these techniques has strengths and weaknesses, so writers often use them in combination. Also, some techniques may be more effective for certain types of ideas or readers than others.

Practice

CITE TEXTUAL EVIDENCE to support your answers.

⊙ **Notebook** Respond to these questions.

1. (a) What does Leena Khan want readers to do or think? (b) What position, or claim, does she express?

2. (a) Give three examples of words or phrases from the blog post that have positive associations. Explain your choices. (b) Note three examples of words or phrases that have negative associations. Explain your choices. (c) How do these word choices help Khan make her argument?

3. Besides emotional appeals, what other types of techniques from the list above are present in the blog post? Provide examples, and explain each choice.

4. (a) In your opinion, how well does Khan support her claim? Use details from the text to support your answer. (b) Do you think her argument would work as well for adults as it does for teenagers? Why or why not?

© Pearson Education, Inc., or its affiliates. All rights reserved.

FORMATIVE ASSESSMENT

Analyze Craft and Structure

- **If** students fail to understand examples of appeals to emotion, **then** have them identify words in the selection that arouse the strongest feelings in themselves.

- **If** students are unable to determine the effectiveness of the blogger's appeal, **then** have students write their own opinion on the subject in one subject.

For Reteach and Practice, see **Analyze Craft and Structure: Persuasive Techniques (RP).** ⊕

Analyze Craft and Structure

Persuasive Techniques To help students distinguish between appeals to emotion and appeals to reason, lead the class in inventing an appeal about some local or school issue; for example: a later start to the school day. Brainstorm reasons in favor of a late start and write them on the board. Then lead the class in categorizing the reasons as appealing more to emotion or to reason. For example, an appeal to emotion might be: *Everyone wants to be able to sleep later.* An appeal to reason might be: *Studies show that student performance improves when they get more sleep.* For more support, see **Analyze Craft and Structure: Persuasive Techniques.** ⊕

MAKE IT INTERACTIVE

Project the digital version of "The Black Hole of Technology" and read paragraph 1. As you read each sentence, ask students to explain whether each sentence appears to be part of an appeal to reason or an appeal to emotion. Prompt students to detect which sentences are fact- or logic-driven (appeals to reason), and which use language and images that arouse feelings (appeals to emotion). Then guide students to draw conclusions about the type of appeal the paragraph represents.

Practice

Possible responses:

1. She wants readers to use technology less and to experience the real world more. Her position is that we are sacrificing our real life experience in favor of time-wasting digital activities.

2. Positive: *appreciative; enticing warmth of the sun; appreciate your surroundings.* These phrases all represent positive aspects of life that we should pay more attention to. Negative: *black hole; artificial lighting; mindlessly scroll.* These phrases all emphasize the worthless nature of most digital experiences.

3. Appeal to Reason: In paragraph 5, she explains the logical sequence of thoughts she had in the temple as she observed the people around her and came to the conclusion that they were happy because they were not connected to technology. Repetition: She repeats the phrase "black hole of technology" several times to emphasize how difficult it is to resist the enticement to engage with technology and shut out the real world.

4. Responses will vary. Students should support their responses with evidence from the text.

Concept Vocabulary

Why These Words?
Possible responses:

1. The concept vocabulary words mostly project images of being consumed or controlled by technology, which represents the blogger's attitude.

2. *endless, wailing, mindlessly*

Practice
Possible responses:

1. Paragraphs will vary but should show an understanding of the concept vocabulary words.

2. *devouring:* exhausting, ravaging
   absorbing: consuming, soaking up
   process: operation, system
   consumed: depleted, spent
   digesting: swallowing, dissolving

Word Network
Possible words: *broadcasted, tech, iPhone, Instagram, cellphone, mp3 players, iPods*

Word Study

For more support, see **Concept Vocabulary and Word Study.** 📄
Possible responses:

1. The water-purification plant uses a careful, step-by-step process to ensure the community has safe drinking water. These days, most people use digital cameras, so it's hard to find a store that will process film and make prints.

2. If you could speak more slowly, I'll be able to assimilate all the data you're giving me. Eating local foods is one way many people assimilate after moving to a new country.

FORMATIVE ASSESSMENT

Concept Vocabulary
If students fail to identify synonyms, **then** have them look for antonyms for the content vocabulary words.

Word Study
If students struggle to write sentences for different meanings of multiple-meaning words, **then** have them use other forms or tenses of the words. For Reteach and Practice, see **Word Study: Multiple-Meaning Words (RP).** 📄

THE BLACK HOLE OF TECHNOLOGY

Concept Vocabulary

| devouring | process | digesting |
| absorbing | consumed | |

Why These Words? These concept words all relate to eating and taking in nutrients, but also apply to the way we take in information. For example, the same person who is *devouring* a plate of scrambled eggs in the morning could be later *devouring* an article about why people should limit the number of eggs they eat each week.

1. How does the concept vocabulary sharpen the reader's understanding of the blogger's attitude toward technology?

2. What other words in the selection connect to this concept?

🔧 WORD NETWORK

Add words related to modern technology from the text to your Word Network.

☰ STANDARDS

Reading Informational Text
Determine the meaning of words and phrases as they are used in a text, including figurative, connotative, and technical meanings.

Language
• Demonstrate command of the conventions of standard English grammar and usage when writing or speaking.
• Demonstrate command of the conventions of standard English capitalization, punctuation, and spelling when writing.
  a. Use punctuation to set off nonrestrictive/parenthetical elements.
• Determine or clarify the meaning of unknown and multiple-meaning words and phrases based on *grade 6 reading and content,* choosing flexibly from a range of strategies.
  a. Use context as a clue to the meaning of a word or phrase.
  d. Verify the preliminary determination of the meaning of a word or phrase.

Practice

🔵 **Notebook** The concept vocabulary words appear in "The Black Hole of Technology."

1. Use as many concept words as you can in a paragraph about the blog to demonstrate your understanding of each word's meaning.

2. Use a thesaurus to find two synonyms for each word.

Word Study

Multiple-Meaning Words A multiple-meaning word has more than one definition. In this text, Leena Khan uses the word *process,* which has more than one meaning. She describes how "no one stops to *process* information anymore," meaning "understand" or "make sense of." You most likely determined which meaning she intended by using context clues. You could also verify a word's meaning by using a dictionary.

1. Using the dictionary, find two more meanings of *process.* Then, use the word in two sentences that reflect the two meanings.

2. *Assimilate* is another multiple-meaning word that relates to the other concept vocabulary words. Use a dictionary to identify two meanings of *assimilate.* Then, write two sentences that use the word and reflect its distinct meanings.

© Pearson Education, Inc., or its affiliates. All rights reserved.

WriteNow Express and Reflect

Description Leena Khan wrote a description of a scene that she witnessed in Cambodia. She described what people were doing and how they were interacting, as well as her own impressions of the scene. Have students write a one-page description of a scene that they witnessed recently. Remind students to include details about the scene like the blogger did. Point out that the blogger draws attention to what the boys were wearing (half-naked, no shoes), as well as to what the water in the lake looked like (murky). Draw students' attention to the fact that she includes her thoughts as she observed the scene. (How could they look so happy?) Students should convey their thoughts about the scene in a similar way, using powerful words that reveal their attitude about what they have observed.

Conventions

Independent and Dependent Clauses Understanding clauses is key to well-structured writing because clauses are used to build sentences. A **clause** is a group of words with its own subject and verb. The two major types of clauses are independent clauses and dependent clauses. An **independent clause** expresses a complete thought and can stand alone as a sentence. A **dependent clause**—also known as a **subordinate clause**—cannot stand alone as a complete sentence.

Many dependent clauses begin with subordinating conjunctions, such as *when* and *if*. A **relative clause** is one kind of dependent clause and begins with a relative pronoun, such as *who* or *that*.

TIP

CLARIFICATION
Refer to the Grammar Handbook to learn more about these terms.

KEY WORDS	EXAMPLES OF CLAUSES
Subordinating Conjunctions *after, although, because, before, if, since, unless, until, when, whether*	after we got home since I bought my new phone
Relative Pronouns *that, which, who, whom, whose*	whom I met at the airport that we often ignore

Place a comma after a dependent clause that opens a sentence. If the dependent clause is **nonrestrictive**, or not necessary to understand the main idea of the sentence, set it off with commas, dashes, or parentheses.

EXAMPLE: <u>When I have time</u>, I'll check her social media for any updates.

EXAMPLE: She wrote an opinion piece, <u>which was posted online</u>.

Read It

Notebook Mark the dependent, or subordinate, clause in each sentence. Label the ones that are relative clauses.

1. I will find the significance in things, because many other people will fail to do so.
2. I was digesting information that was completely useless.
3. When the guide started a long speech on the origin of the temple, I turned to face him.

Write It

Notebook Write a paragraph about the selection using subordinate clauses, including one or more relative clauses. Remember to set off nonrestrictive clauses with commas, dashes, or parentheses.

The Black Hole of Technology **221**

© Pearson Education, Inc., or its affiliates. All rights reserved.

PERSONALIZE FOR LEARNING

Challenge

Response Invite students to write a response to Leena Khan's blog. Their responses should include two to three paragraphs in which they explain whether or not they agree with the blogger's point of view, and why. Remind them to be specific in their critiques, referencing the author's reasoning in their responses. Tell them that they should also be descriptive in explaining their own reaction to the blog. Remind them that dependent clauses can help make their writing more expressive.

Conventions

Independent and Dependent Clauses Explain to students that knowing how and when to punctuate a sentence depends on identifying independent and dependent clauses when they see them. Explain that when an independent clause is combined with another independent clause, it requires a semicolon or a comma along with a coordinating conjunction (and, but, or, for, yet, so) to separate the clauses.

Remind students of the rules for punctuating dependent clauses. Then explain that they can determine whether or not a clause is restrictive by figuring out if the clause gives information about an otherwise general noun. For more support, see **Conventions: Independent and Dependent Clauses.**

Read It

Possible responses:

1. I will find the significance in things, <u>because many other people will fail to do so.</u>
2. I was digesting information <u>that was completely useless.</u> (relative)
3. <u>When the guide started a long speech on the origin of the temple</u>, I turned to face him.

Write It

Paragraphs will vary but should reflect accurate use of subordinate clauses, including relative clauses.

FORMATIVE ASSESSMENT

Conventions

- **If** students struggle to identify the subordinate clause, **then** direct them to the chart on the student page.

- **If** students fail to set off nonrestrictive clauses with commas, **then** remind them that if they would likely take a slight pause in speaking the sentence aloud, the pause should probably be represented with a comma in writing.

For Reteach and Practice, see **Conventions: Independent and Dependent Clauses (RP).**

Writing to Compare

As students prepare to compare the blog posts "Teens and Technology Share the Future" and "The Black Hole of Technology," they will evaluate the effectiveness of each post.

Prewriting

Analyze Arguments Encourage students to begin by thinking about the titles of the two blog posts and what these titles might say about the writers' points of view. Remind them that their goal during prewriting is to gather information so that they can evaluate which blog post presents a more effective argument.

See possible responses in chart on student page.
Possible responses:
Answers will vary, but students should support their responses with evidence from the texts.

EFFECTIVE EXPRESSION

TEENS AND TECHNOLOGY
SHARE A FUTURE

THE BLACK HOLE OF TECHNOLOGY

TIP

Your classmates might have a different opinion about which point of view was more persuasive. Your goal is not to convince each other, but to examine the effectiveness of each argument.

Writing to Compare

You have read two blog posts that express different views of technology. Consider the arguments conveyed in "Teens and Technology Share a Future" and "The Black Hole of Technology." Which one presents a stronger case?

Assignment

Write an **argumentative essay** in which you compare and contrast the two blog posts and decide which one is more convincing. It does not need to be the blog you agree with personally, but the one you believe presents a stronger case. Consider the following questions:

- Which blogger presents stronger supporting evidence?
- Which blogger makes better use of persuasive techniques, including repetition and appeals to emotion and reason?
- Which blogger makes a stronger connection with the reader?
- Which blogger does a better job dealing with opposing opinions?

Prewriting

Analyze Arguments With a partner, take notes on each blogger's perspective, and discuss what you notice. Use the chart to capture your observations.

	TEENS AND TECHNOLOGY SHARE A FUTURE	THE BLACK HOLE OF TECHNOLOGY
strongest reasons	lists many ways in which technology is helpful	gives examples of things people miss out on when they are glued to their smartphones
persuasive techniques used	multiple examples, allusion to Thoreau	examples of both useless information on the Internet and valuable experiences away from technology
opposing opinions addressed	mentions social media and other uses of technology that are of controversial value	describes how being away from technology was uncomfortable at first
weaknesses	absence of statistics and other data, not much logical reasoning	uses overgeneralizations such as statements beginning with "no one" and "everything"

© Pearson Education, Inc., or its affiliates. All rights reserved.

PERSONALIZE FOR LEARNING

English Language Support
Mind Maps Participating in a whole-class discussion can be intimidating for English learners. Even after organizing notes in a chart, students may have difficulty accessing key words and ideas to participate confidently. To help students prepare for the discussion, encourage them to create a mind map of key words and phrases that relate to each argument. **ALL LEVELS**

Drafting

Organization After you have finished your discussion, decide on a position statement, or thesis, stating which blog post you found to be more effective. Then, plan how you will present your judgment. When you are writing about two subjects, block and point-by-point are two effective ways to organize your ideas.

Block Organization

I. Topic: "Teens and Technology Share a Future"
   A. Blogger's perspective and the reasons and examples used to support it
   B. Strengths and weaknesses of the argument

II. Topic: "The Black Hole of Technology"
   A. Blogger's perspective and the reasons and examples used to support it
   B. Strengths and weaknesses of the argument

III. Topic: Judgment
   A. Which blog is more effective
   B. Reasons for your judgment

Point-by-Point Organization

I. Topic: Points of View
   A. Blogger's point of view in "Teens and Technology Share a Future" and the reasons and examples used to support it
   B. Blogger's point of view in "The Black Hole of Technology" and the reasons and examples used to support it

II. Topic: Strengths and Weaknesses
   A. Strengths and weaknesses of "Teens and Technology Share a Future"
   B. Strengths and weaknesses of "The Black Hole of Technology"

III. Topic: Judgment
   A. Which blog is more effective
   B. Reasons for your judgment

Review, Revise, and Edit

Once you have finished writing, review and revise your essay. Refer back to your thesis. Make sure you have supported your thesis with solid reasons. Also, make sure you have included details from the blogs to support your reasons. If you see any weaknesses in your reasons or supporting evidence, go back and clarify your ideas or add more convincing details. Once you have finished, reread your essay to make sure you have spelled words correctly and used proper grammar.

© Pearson Education, Inc., or its affiliates. All rights reserved.

✏ EVIDENCE LOG

Before moving on to a new selection, go to your Evidence Log and record what you learned from "The Black Hole of Technology."

☰ STANDARDS

Reading Informational Text
• Trace and evaluate the argument and specific claims in a text, distinguishing claims that are supported by reasons and evidence from claims that are not.
• Compare and contrast one author's presentation of events with that of another.

Writing
• Write arguments to support claims with clear reasons and relevant evidence.
   a. Introduce claim(s) and organize the reasons and evidence clearly.
   b. Support claim(s) with clear reasons and relevant evidence, using credible sources and demonstrating an understanding of the topic or text.
   e. Provide a concluding statement or section that follows from the argument presented.
• Draw evidence from literary or informational texts to support analysis, reflection, and research.
   b. Apply *grade 6 Reading standards* to literary nonfiction.

Teens and Technology Share a Future • The Black Hole of Technology **223**

Drafting

Organization Encourage students to draw on their prewriting chart as they begin drafting. Regardless of which organization option they use, they should provide plenty of support from the texts for their evaluations.

Review, Revise, and Edit

As students revise, encourage them to review their draft to be sure they have evaluated persuasive techniques. Ask them to review their word choice. Finally, remind students to check for grammar, usage, and mechanics.

For more support, see **Writing to Compare: Argumentative Essay.** 🔲

Evidence Log Support students in completing their Evidence Log. This paced activity will help prepare them for the Performance-Based Assessment at the end of the unit.

PERSONALIZE FOR LEARNING

English Language Development

Supporting Claims Read aloud the following sentences from the selection: "The black hole of endless, unimportant streams of technology-enabled information is devouring everyone living in the twenty-first century." "No one appreciates the value of personal interaction or nature."

Ask students to work in pairs to determine whether these two statements are sufficiently supported in the selection. **EMERGING**

Ask students to write down the passages in the selection where the above statements are supported by either reasons or evidence. **EXPANDING**

Ask students to write a paragraph explaining why it may be so difficult to support statements including words such as "everyone," "no one," or "unimportant." **BRIDGING**

An expanded **English Language Development Lesson** on Argumentative Essay is available in the Interactive Teacher's Edition. 🔲

FORMATIVE ASSESSMENT

Writing to Compare

If students struggle to find supporting evidence, **then** suggest they return to the selections and look for the reasons the writers provide for their opinions.

Selection Test

Administer the "The Black Hole of Technology" Selection Test, which is available in both print and digital formats online in Assessments. 🔲 ☑

The Internet of Things

🔊 **AUDIO SUMMARIES**

Audio summaries of "The Internet of Things" are available online in both English and Spanish in the Interactive Teacher's Edition or Unit Resources. Assigning these summaries prior to reading the selection may help students build additional background knowledge and set a context for their first read.

Summary

This video, "The Internet of Things" from IBM, discusses how it is becoming possible to collect data from an enormous number of different things on Earth. Passing data back and forth between different devices could be very helpful to us. It could save us a lot of time and thought, and it could make our use of power more efficient. If cities and houses could respond to problems without human intervention, it would make our lives easier. The narrators describe this change in grand terms, such as giving us information that only the universe had before or a planet-wide nervous sytem.

Insight

This video argues that networking more devices together will greatly change our lives for the better. It is a useful jumping-off point for students to consider what they think will happen in the future because of increased connectivity.

ESSENTIAL QUESTION:
How is modern technology helpful and harmful to society?

Connection to Essential Question

This video discusses the positive sides of linking up systems of data. Humans with access to this data can more efficiently use their time, and cities can make more efficient use of data. However, this video does not address the issue that connected devices have associated risks, such as making people's lives more vulnerable to hackers and identity thieves.

WHOLE-CLASS LEARNING PERFORMANCE TASK
Do electronic devices and online access really improve our lives?

Connection to Performance Tasks

Whole-Class Learning Performance Task This selection provides a useful backdrop to the blog posts about whether teen use of technology is a good thing or not. The extension of the argument is whether widespread data sharing among all people is helpful or harmful.

UNIT PERFORMANCE-BASED ASSESSMENT
Do we rely on technology too much?

Unit Performance-Based Assessment People around the world depend on technology to a large degree already, and this video calls for embracing and increasing that dependence. Students may make arguments for or against whether this is a good idea or a bad idea.

LESSON RESOURCES

	Making Meaning	Effective Expression
Lesson	**First Review** **Close Review** **Analyze the Media** **Media Vocabulary**	**Writing to Sources** **Speaking and Listening**
Instructional Standards	**RI.10** By the end of the year, read and comprehend literary nonfiction . . . **L.6** Acquire and use accurately grade-appropriate general academic and domain-specific words and phrases . . .	**W.2** Write informative/explanatory texts . . . **SL.2** Interpret information presented in diverse media and formats . . . **SL.4** Present claims and findings . . .

⇡ STUDENT RESOURCES

Available online in the Interactive Student Edition or Unit Resources	Selection Audio First-Review Guide: Media Video Word Network	Evidence Log

⇡ TEACHER RESOURCES

Selection Resources Available online in the Interactive Teacher's Edition or Unit Resources	Audio Summaries Media Vocabulary	Writing to Sources: Objective Summary Speaking and Listening: Oral Report
My Resources	A Unit 3 Answer Key is available online and in the Interactive Teacher's Edition.	

Media Complexity Rubric: The Internet of Things

Quantitative Measures

Format and Length Video, 5 minutes, 24 seconds

Qualitative Measures

Knowledge Demands ①——②——**❸**——④——⑤	Many situations are everyday. Some references may not be as familiar.
Structure ①——②——**❸**——④——⑤	Video has multiple graphic images and multiple voices.
Language Conventionality and Clarity ①——②——**❸**——④——⑤	Language is conversational and mostly easy to understand. Sentences are not overly complex.
Levels of Meaning/Purpose ①——②——**❸**——④——⑤	Many concepts are clear, but some may be abstract.

TEACHING

Jump Start

FIRST REVIEW Point out to students that the Internet not only connects people around the world, it also connects "things" or machines. Ask them what they think this means and how it might work.

The Internet of Things ▶ ◀

How do we gather data from things? How might connecting things to the Internet help people organize their days? How might it help people in a city? Modeling questions such as these will help students connect to "The Internet of Things" and to the Performance Task assignment. Selection audio is available in the Interactive Teacher's Edition.

Media Vocabulary

Encourage students to discuss the media vocabulary. Have they seen or used these words before? Do they use any of them in their speech or writing?

Have students look closely at the words and discuss their use and meanings. Students should notice that some of the words (such as *animation* and *voiceover*) are closely tied to videos or movies, while others (such as *images or graphics* and *narrator*) have much wider usage. Have students discuss whether the words' meanings change in different contexts.

● FIRST REVIEW

As they review, students should perform the steps of the first review:

WATCH: Remind students to watch the way graphics are used to illustrate concepts as the narrators describe each one.

NOTE: Encourage students to listen to the narrators to note key ideas.

CONNECT: Encourage students to make connections beyond the video. If they cannot make connections to their own lives, have them consider news stories or movies that feature data derived from different systems around the world.

RESPOND: Students will answer questions and write a summary to demonstrate understanding.

Point out to students that while they will always complete the Respond step at the end of the first review, the other steps will probably happen concurrently. You may wish to print copies of the **First-Read Guide: Media Video** for students to use. ⊟

About IBM

International Business Machines Corporation (IBM) is one of the world's largest companies, employing nearly half a million people. In 1953, the company introduced its first computer, and in 1981 it introduced its version of the personal computer, a landmark event in the era of desktop computing.

≡ STANDARDS

Reading Informational Text
By the end of the year, read and comprehend literary nonfiction in the grades 6–8 text complexity band proficiently, with scaffolding as needed at the high end of the range.
Language
Acquire and use accurately grade-appropriate general academic and domain-specific words and phrases; gather vocabulary knowledge when considering a word or phrase important to comprehension or expression.

The Internet of Things

Media Vocabulary

These words will be useful to you as you analyze, discuss, and write about videos.

images or graphics: representations of a person or thing	• Images or graphics, such as a map of a country, show a visual representation of what people, objects, or ideas look like.
animation: process of making films or cartoons from drawings, computer graphics, or photos	• Animation can make certain scenes more lively or help an audience understand a process.
audio: recorded sound	• Listening to audio in a video or on a website allows listeners to hear actual sound effects or voices.
voiceover: voice commenting on the action or narrating a film off-camera	• Voiceovers may provide additional background information for viewers or listeners.
narrator: person who tells a story	• In an informational video, the narrator reads or relates descriptions or explanations.

First Review MEDIA: VIDEO

Apply these strategies as you watch the video.

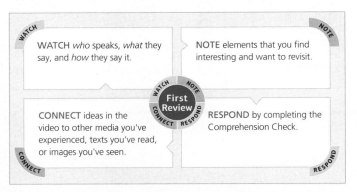

WATCH who speaks, *what* they say, and *how* they say it.

NOTE elements that you find interesting and want to revisit.

CONNECT ideas in the video to other media you've experienced, texts you've read, or images you've seen.

RESPOND by completing the Comprehension Check.

⊟ **Notebook** As you watch, write down your observations and questions, making sure to note time codes so you can easily revisit sections later.

© Pearson Education, Inc., or its affiliates. All rights reserved.

VOCABULARY DEVELOPMENT

Domain-specific Vocabulary Reinforce students' comprehension of media vocabulary by modeling the example and giving the students time to practice.

The *voiceover* was of two different *narrators* describing how the Internet of Things works, as graphs and pictures on the screen illustrated what they were talking about.

Then give students these sentence prompts and coach them to create the clarification part:

1. The *images* help the viewer understand the ideas by _____.
2. The video used *animation* to show _____.
3. Besides the images, the video included *audio*, which _____.

MEDIA | VIDEO

The Internet of Things
IBM Social Media

BACKGROUND

The IBM "Smarter Planet" program promotes and discusses how global leaders can use new technologies and types of data to create a "smarter planet"—a world in which the smart use of information can matter as much as any other natural resource. This video was produced as part of their "Smarter Planet" series.

SCAN FOR MULTIMEDIA

NOTES

The Internet of Things **225**

© Pearson Education, Inc., or its affiliates. All rights reserved.

CLOSER LOOK

Analyze Evidence

Suggest that students close review 3:30 to 4:18 in the video. Circulate among them as they conduct their reviews. Encourage students to take notes about their observations in order to share them later in writing and discussion.

NOTE: Have students note the details in the video that describe the narrators' claim and the evidence used to support it, or have students participate while you note them together.

QUESTION: Guide students to consider what these details might tell them. Ask what viewers can infer from these details, and accept student responses.

Possible response: Different systems in a city all constantly send messages to keep those systems running smoothly.

CONCLUDE: Help students formulate conclusions about the importance of these details in the video. Ask students why the narrators might have included these details.

Possible response: Providing examples of how "The Internet of Things" works helps people visualize what the term means. It also helps people see the real-world applications of these communications systems and how dependent people have become on them.

Remind students that even oral claims should be supported with reasons and **evidence**.

CROSS-CURRICULAR PERSPECTIVES

Science Point out to students that IBM, the company that produced the video, helped popularize the personal computer. The device brought computer technology into the home and allowed people to use computers for many different things. Encourage students to find out more about the history of the personal computer, from when it was first introduced in the late 1970s to now. Have them create a timeline with images that show the evolution of the personal computer from a large, clunky device to today's versions. Encourage students to share their findings with the class.

Comprehension Check

Possible responses

1. Everything is now instrumented, enabling us to capture data.

2. Wisdom is the ultimate goal.

3. Sensors can be found in the water main and taxis.

4. "The Internet of Things" can create a smarter planet by allowing us to be more effective and efficient.

Close Review

If needed, model close reviewing by using the Closer Review notes in the Interactive Teacher's Edition.

Analyze the Media

Possible responses:

1. The video offers a great deal of information. At first, it isn't clear what "Internet of Things" refers to. Then the narrators clarify by explaining systems and interconnectedness. **DOK 3**

2. (a) It helps viewers visualize what the narrators mean by "The Internet of Things." **DOK 2** (b) The images of the map and the pyramid are effective because they help explain what people hope to achieve with connectivity. **DOK 3**

3. It means that, like a human central nervous system, the instruments connected through the Internet of things communicate with each other and operate efficiently. **DOK 2**

4. The connectivity of different devices makes systems more efficient and helps people learn and understand more about the world. **DOK 3**

Word Network

Possible words: *interconnectedness, systems, matrices*

Media Vocabulary

For more support, see **Media Vocabulary**. 📄

FORMATIVE ASSESSMENT

Analyze the Media

- **If** students fail to cite evidence, **then** remind them to support their ideas with specific information from the video.

- **If** students struggle to identify the most effective images, **then** ask them which images they remember and to explain why those images stick with them.

Comprehension Check

Complete the following items after you finish your first review.

1. What enables us to capture data from natural and human systems?

2. According to the pyramid graphic, what is the ultimate goal of the data we get from the many sensors that stream information?

3. Where are some of the sensors that we might find in a city?

4. According to the video, how can connectivity, or "The Internet of Things," help create a smarter planet?

MEDIA VOCABULARY

Use these words as you discuss and write about the video.

images
graphics
animation
audio
voiceover
narrator

🔗 **WORD NETWORK**

Add words related to modern technology from the text to your Word Network.

Close Review

Watch the video or parts of it again. Write any new observations that seem important. What **questions** do you have? What can you **conclude**?

Analyze the Media

🔘 **Notebook** Respond to these questions.

1. **Evaluate** Do the narrators explain the concept of "The Internet of Things" clearly? Explain your position.

2. (a) **Analyze** Revisit the scene that shows the world map made up of devices. What does this scene add to the video? (b) **Evaluate** In your opinion, which images are most effective in helping the viewer understand the important ideas? Explain.

3. **Interpret** The narrator explains that the planet has "grown a central nervous system." What does this statement mean?

4. **Essential Question:** *How is modern technology helpful and harmful to society?* What have you learned about how technology helps or hurts society from watching this video?

© Pearson Education, Inc., or its affiliates. All rights reserved.

PERSONALIZE FOR LEARNING

Challenge

Research Encourage interested students to research devices that now exist that allow appliances in the home to communicate with each other. Encourage students to explain how they work and what systems they connect. Suggest that students write a brief report and include a diagram that explains the concept. Then ask volunteers to share their findings in a brief presentation to the class.

Writing to Sources

Writing a summary can help you identify the most important points in an informational video.

Assignment

Write a brief **objective summary** of the video. An objective summary is a retelling of the most important ideas in an unbiased way.

To write an objective summary, follow these steps:

1. Watch the video, and take notes on the most important ideas.

2. Put the ideas in the correct order, and restate them in your own words.

3. Include important details from the video that help explain each main idea.

4. Use an objective tone in your writing. *Objective* means that you do not include your opinion.

Speaking and Listening

The video is a brief description of the concept of "The Internet of Things" and shows how being electronically interconnected benefits society.

Assignment

Prepare and deliver an **oral report** about the video.

To prepare your oral report, take notes on the following:

• Identify the source of the video. *Who* is delivering the information, and *what* is the purpose of the message?

• Determine whether the information presented in the video is supported by facts or opinions. A **fact** is something that can be proved. An **opinion** can be supported, but not proved.

• Consider the message the video conveys: What do the video makers want viewers to think or do? Is this message convincing?

Once you have taken notes, organize your information into **talking points**—a list of brief statements you can refer to while sharing your findings. Then, practice delivering your talking points. To do so, glance at your talking points, but then make eye contact with your audience. In addition, speak expressively, pausing to emphasize key words.

THE INTERNET OF THINGS

✍ EVIDENCE LOG

Before moving on to a new selection, go to your Evidence Log and record what you learned from the video.

☰ STANDARDS

Writing
Write informative/explanatory texts to examine a topic and convey ideas, concepts, and information through the selection, organization, and analysis of relevant content.

Speaking and Listening
• Interpret information presented in diverse media and formats and explain how it contributes to a topic, text, or issue under study.
• Present claims and findings, sequencing ideas logically and using pertinent descriptions, facts, and details to accentuate main ideas or themes; use appropriate eye contact, adequate volume, and clear pronunciation.

The Internet of Things **227**

Writing to Sources

Explain to students that writing a summary can help them identify the main ideas and the evidence used to support those ideas. Point out to students that to help them determine the main ideas in the video, they should note terms that are repeated both in the images and by the narrators.

MAKE IT INTERACTIVE

Have students write the main ideas they noted in their summaries on sentence strips and post them around the room. Ask students to walk around the room and note the most important ideas their classmates inferred from the video.

For more support, see **Writing to Sources: Objective Summary.** 🖹

Speaking and Listening

Tell students that considering the narrators' word choice will help them identify the purpose. Remind them that word choice also shapes the tone or attitude that a narrator has toward the subject. Ask them to consider how the words the narrators use to describe the Internet of Things makes them feel about this concept.

Suggest that students note the most powerful audio or visual elements in the video that they thought were delivered by the author or producer's message and then feature those elements in their report as aids to illustrate students' points.

Remind students that they should speak with appropriate phrasing and to avoid a flat, monotone delivery. Suggest that they practice their delivery by taking videos of each other and then analyzing the videos. For more support, see **Speaking and Listening: Oral Report.** 🖹

Evidence Log Support students in completing their Evidence Log. This paced activity will help prepare them for the Performance-Based Assessment at the end of the unit.

© Pearson Education, Inc., or its affiliates. All rights reserved.

PERSONALIZE FOR LEARNING

English Language Support

Reviewing Video Support English learners as they watch the video. Pair students with a partner and have them watch the video in 30-second increments. Students should take notes on the keys ideas and details in each segment. Remind them that the illustrations help explain some of the more complex ideas. After watching for 30 seconds, have partners compare their notes. Repeat the process until students have watched the entire video. **ALL LEVELS**

FORMATIVE ASSESSMENT

Writing to Sources

If students are unable to identify the main ideas, **then** have them watch the video again, pausing to take notes on the content.

Speaking and Listening

If students struggle to evaluate the delivery of the video, **then** ask them whether they were left with the idea that the interconnectedness of systems is good or bad for people.

Jump Start

Create a T-chart on the board and ask students to note what they have learned about how technology can both help and hurt us. As students share, ask them to cite specific examples from the texts or video to support their ideas.

Write an Argument

Make sure students understand what they are being asked to do in the Assignment. Explain that an editorial is an argument that appears in some form of media.

Students should complete the assignment using word processing software to take advantage of editing tools and features.

Elements of an Editorial

Point out that an editorial is written to be published in a particular format and address a specific audience. For this reason, writers of editorials choose language and tone carefully. Student editorials should evaluate writing and make an argument clarifying how and why one of the bloggers made a stronger case than the other.

MAKE IT INTERACTIVE

Project "That's Not Progress!" from the Interactive Teacher's Edition and have students identify the elements of an argument, such as the claim, counterclaim, reasons, evidence, and concluding statement.

Academic Vocabulary

Consider asking students which academic vocabulary words might be especially useful in writing their editorials.

WRITING TO SOURCES

- FEATHERED FRIEND
- TEENS AND TECHNOLOGY SHARE A FUTURE
- THE BLACK HOLE OF TECHNOLOGY
- THE INTERNET OF THINGS

🔧 **Tool Kit**
Student Model of an Argument

ACADEMIC VOCABULARY

As you craft your argument, consider using some of the academic vocabulary you learned in the beginning of the unit.

convince
certain
sufficient
declare
various

≡ STANDARDS
Writing
• Write arguments to support claims with clear reasons and relevant evidence.
• Write routinely over extended time frames and shorter time frames for a range of discipline-specific tasks, purposes, and audiences.

228 UNIT 3 • MODERN TECHNOLOGY

Write an Argument

In this section, you have examined four perspectives on technology. "Feathered Friend" shows the advantages of both high-tech and low-tech safety measures. In "Teens and Technology Share a Future," blogger Stefan Etienne argues that technology improves our lives. In "The Black Hole of Technology," blogger Leena Khan argues the opposite. "The Internet of Things" examines the complex systems that have resulted from improvements in technology.

> **Assignment**
>
> Write a brief argument, in the form of an **editorial**, in which you state and support your position on this question:
>
> > Do electronic devices and online access really improve our lives?
>
> Draw evidence from the texts in this section to support your ideas.

Elements of an Editorial

An **editorial** is a kind of argument that is published in a print or digital newspaper or magazine. In an editorial, an author offers an opinion about an issue. A well-written editorial uses valid reasons and evidence to convince readers to agree with the author's position.

An effective editorial contains these elements:

- a precise claim, or position
- clear reasons and evidence that support the claim
- a logical organization that makes clear connections among claims, reasons, and evidence
- a concluding statement or section that logically completes the argument
- a formal and objective language and tone
- use of transitions to show the relationships between ideas

Model Argument For a model of a well-crafted argument, see the Launch Text, "That's Not Progress!"

Challenge yourself to find all of the elements of an effective argument in the text. You will have an opportunity to review these elements as you prepare to write your own editorial.

© Pearson Education, Inc., or its affiliates. All rights reserved.

AUTHOR'S PERSPECTIVE   **Kelly Gallagher, M.Ed.**

Revision E. B. White once said, "The best writing is rewriting." Unfortunately, many students come to us with the "I wrote it once; I'm done" philosophy. Demonstrate the importance of *revision*—making writing better by looking at it again—through teacher modeling. First, write with the class for eight minutes on a specific topic. Then, complete the activity with the class.

1. Display your first draft on the screen. Use think alouds as you use RADaR strategies for revision: REPLACE; ADD; DELETE; REORDER. For each change you implement, mark the type of change you made.
2. Have students use the same process on their first drafts. Remind students that they will work on making their papers

correct later; for now, they are to revise with the goal of being able to point out places where their second draft is better than their first.

Last, have students hold their two drafts side-by-side as you modeled, and indicate which RADaR strategies they used to revise their first drafts.

Prewriting / Planning

Write a Claim After you have reviewed the selections, write a thesis statement—one sentence in which you state your claim. As you continue to write, you may revise your claim or even change it. For now, it will help you choose reasons and supporting evidence.

Claim: _____

_____.

Plan Your Argument An effective argument successfully addresses counterclaims, or opposing positions. Plan to include evidence to show why those counterclaims are not strong enough to change your position. Complete these sentences to address a counterclaim.

An opposing view is _____.

The evidence that supports this is _____.

The reason I don't find the opposing view convincing is _____.

Gather Evidence From Sources You can use different types of evidence to support your argument:

- **facts:** statements that can be proved true
- **statistics:** facts presented in the form of numbers
- **anecdotes:** brief stories that illustrate a point
- **quotations from experts:** statements from people with special knowledge of a subject
- **examples:** facts, ideas, or events that illustrate a general idea

A variety of evidence can make your argument stronger. For example, in the Launch Text, the writer uses facts and statistics:

> *Half the nation's youth send 50 or more text messages a day. One study found that young people send an average of 34 texts a night after they get into bed! This loss of sleep can affect the ability to concentrate, problem-solve, and learn.*
> —from "That's Not Progress!"

Take notes on the sources of your information. You will need to give credit to any words or ideas that are not your own.

© Pearson Education, Inc., or its affiliates. All rights reserved.

EVIDENCE LOG

Review your Evidence Log and identify key details you may want to cite in your argument.

STANDARDS
Writing
Write arguments to support claims with clear reasons and relevant evidence.
a. Introduce claim(s) and organize the reasons and evidence clearly.
b. Support claim(s) with clear reasons and relevant evidence, using credible sources and demonstrating an understanding of the topic or text.

Performance Task: Write an Argument **229**

Prewriting/Planning

Write a Claim Remind students that the first step in writing an argument is to take a position on the subject. The thesis statement should be clear, unambiguous, and defensible but should not list reasons or evidence.

Plan Your Argument Explain that including a counterclaim in their editorial is useful for multiple reasons. Anticipating an objection that a reader might make shows that the writer is thoughtful and has considered the issue fully. In addition, directly addressing the counterclaim gives the editorial persuasive force.

Gather Evidence From Sources Have students review their Evidence Log to find possible support for their claim. Remind them that if they have sufficient evidence in their Evidence Log, they may want to go back and review the selections to identify additional or stronger evidence for their argument. Because the claim of the editorial is related only to the two blog posts, the majority of evidence should come from those sources. Students may use additional sources to introduce counterclaims or to support their interpretation of the source texts. Make sure students know to include direct quotes in quotation marks and to cite their sources. Remind them to paraphrase, or use their own words to explain, ideas that they do not put in quotation marks.

PERSONALIZE FOR LEARNING

Strategic Support

Finding Evidence If students are having difficulty finding outside sources about the effects of technology on teens, suggest they refine their search terms and use respected databases such as those that end in *.edu*, *.gov*, and *.org*. Point out that there are also respected journals that might provide information on the topic. Remind them as they skim the sources that they are looking for evidence and examples that support the position of the blogger that they think made a better case.

Drafting

Organize Your Editorial Explain to students the difference between the elements of an argument (claim, counterclaims, reasoning, and evidence) and the organization of an argument (introduction, body, and conclusion). Point out that they will develop the body of the argument to support their claim, noting the reasons they have developed and the evidence they have identified to support their position.

Write a First Draft Tell students that their outline should act as a roadmap for their first draft. They should refer to it to determine what they will write next. Remind them that as they write, they should assume that their audience knows nothing about the topic and include as much explanation and detail as they can.

Point out that good editorials often begin with a quotation or some interesting statistic that grabs the reader's attention.

PERFORMANCE TASK: WRITING FOCUS

Drafting

Organize Your Editorial To keep your organization simple and easy to follow, your editorial should include three parts:

- **the introduction,** in which you state your claim
- **the body,** in which you provide analysis, reasons, and evidence
- **the conclusion,** in which you summarize or restate your claim

Each part of your editorial should build on the part that came before, and every point should connect directly to your main claim. This outline shows the key sections of the Launch Text. Notice how the author traces the argument from its introduction through its conclusion. Note specific claims and evidence that support the argument. Create your outline.

STANDARDS
Writing
- Write arguments to support claims with clear reasons and relevant evidence.
  e. Provide a concluding statement or section that follows from the argument presented.
- Draw evidence from literary or informational texts to support analysis, reflection, and research.
  a. Apply *grade 6 Reading standards* to literature.
  b. Apply *grade 6 Reading standards* to literary nonfiction.

LAUNCH TEXT

Model: "That's Not Progress!" Outline

INTRODUCTION
Paragraphs 1 and 2 introduce topic and state claim: *Social networking can lead to anxiety, low self-confidence, and loneliness in teens.*

BODY
Paragraphs 3–6 present support for claim: *Social networking affects mostly teens because they tend to worry about what others think. It also causes stress and lack of confidence.*

Paragraphs 7 and 8 present additional information: *Frequent users of social media may experience aches in areas such as fingers and eyes, as well as loss of sleep.*

Paragraphs 9 and 10 present a counterargument: *Social media can help prevent and identify depression.*

Paragraph 11 refutes, or disproves, counterargument: *Before social media, teens found ways to escape from their problems.*

CONCLUSION
Paragraph 12 restates claim: *Social media has negative effects for teenagers.*

Argument Outline

INTRODUCTION

BODY

CONCLUSION

Write a First Draft Use your outline to help organize your first draft. Include a precise claim in your introduction and offer evidence and support in the body of the editorial. Provide a strong conclusion that follows from your claim. As you write, make sure to keep your readers in mind. Define words they may not know. Also, explain situations or summarize texts so that your readers have the information they need to understand your ideas.

230 UNIT 3 • MODERN TECHNOLOGY

© Pearson Education, Inc., or its affiliates. All rights reserved.

AUTHOR'S PERSPECTIVE   **Jim Cummins, Ph.D.**

The Importance of Frequent Writing
Writing develops a different awareness from reading. Second-language learners need abundant opportunities to write for varied audiences and purposes to determine what they do and do not know. Frequent writing can be accomplished through a combination of low-stakes (informal, ungraded) and high-stakes (formal, revised, graded) writing. Using this approach allows the teacher to nurture writing without needing to grade everything. Here are some suggestions for fostering regular writing:

- Do QuickWrites daily to review lessons and learning.

- Assign public writing, aimed at real audiences.
- Include personal writing, such as journals and diaries.
- Have students write reactions in response to their readings. Students can upload their reviews to class or school webpages.

LANGUAGE DEVELOPMENT: STYLE

Transitions

Transitions are words and phrases that show how ideas relate to one another. Transitional words and phrases perform an essential function in an editorial because they help guide readers through the writer's thinking.

Read It

These sentences about the Launch Text use transitional expressions to show specific connections among ideas.

- *Also, she believes that it can be used to identify youth who are most at risk for depression.* **(shows addition)**
- *Facebook depression, however, has its own features.* **(shows contrast)**
- *For one thing, it hits those who worry too much about what others think; for another, it mostly affects young people.* **(illustrates or shows)**

Write It

As you draft your argument, choose transitional words and phrases that accurately show specific relationships among your ideas. Transitions are especially important when connecting one paragraph to the next.

If you want to . . .	consider using one of these transitions
list or add ideas	*first, finally, next, lastly, also, in addition*
show similarity	*similarly, likewise*
show contrast	*however, in contrast, although, on the other hand*
emphasize	*indeed, in fact, of course*
show effect	*therefore, consequently, thus, as a result*
illustrate or show	*for example, for instance, specifically*

TIP

PUNCTUATION
Punctuate transitions correctly.

- Use a comma after most transitions at the beginning of a sentence.
- Use a comma before and after a transition in the middle of a sentence unless the transition follows a semicolon. In that case, add a comma only *after* the transition.

STANDARDS
Writing
Write arguments to support claims with clear reasons and relevant evidence.
  c. Use words, phrases, and clauses to clarify the relationships among claim(s) and reasons.

Transitions

Read It

Tell students that transition words help the reader know where they are in an argument. They act like road signs, signaling where the reader is and where the reader is headed as they navigate through the claims, counterclaims, and reasoning of a well-developed argument.

MAKE IT INTERACTIVE
Project "That's Not Progress!" from the Interactive Teacher's Edition and ask students to identify additional examples of transitions.

- Similar: *Like other kinds of depression, its common signs are anxiety, low self-confidence, and loneliness.* (paragraph 2)
- Contrast: *But there are other, less obvious ways to damage a person's self-confidence.* (paragraph 5)

Write It

As students write their draft, ask them to think about the relationship between ideas and to use the suggested transitions to help them clarify their argument. Remind them to punctuate transitions correctly. Commas should set off independent clauses, introductory clauses that begin sentences such as *Because the evidence was strongly linked to the claim*, and nonrestrictive clauses that add nonessential information to sentences.

© Pearson Education, Inc., or its affiliates. All rights reserved.

Performance Task: Write an Argument **231**

- Have students write across genres. Try each one, having students pay attention to the conventions of each genre, such as stage directions in drama and dialogue in fiction. All genres have value; for example, poetry is powerful and likely easier for ESL students because of its condensed vocabulary. These assignments can be linked to word networks, too.

TEACHING

Revising

Evaluating Your Draft Before students begin revising their writing, they should evaluate their draft and make sure it contains the elements and organization of an argument.

Revising for Focus and Organization

Identify and Support Claim Tell students that not only will their claim help them maintain focus in their essay but also it will help the reader understand their purpose for writing.

Explain that some writers preview in their claim the main reasons for the position they have taken. Point out that if they decide to write a claim that includes reasons, the claim should still be clear and direct and should leave no doubt what their position is. You might suggest that students read aloud their position statement to a partner, evaluating the strength and clarity of each other's claims.

Revising for Evidence and Elaboration

Clarify Relationships As students revise their arguments for elaboration, have them highlight the evidence they provide for each reason using a different color. When they have finished, have them look over their arguments. Is there far more of one color than of any other? If so, they should consider adding more examples and evidence to support their ideas.

Use Formal Style Tell students that there are levels of formal and informal language, using examples of the style of address they might use in conversation with their friends compared to conversation with their parents or conversations with public authority figures, such as a principal or police officer. Guide students to understand how more formal language can be more persuasive for different audiences.

PERFORMANCE TASK: WRITING FOCUS

Revising

Evaluating Your Draft

Use the following checklist to evaluate the effectiveness of your first draft. Then, use your evaluation and the instruction on this page to guide your revision.

FOCUS AND ORGANIZATION	EVIDENCE AND ELABORATION	CONVENTIONS
☐ Provides an introduction that leads to the argument.	☐ Cites facts from credible and reliable sources to support the argument.	☐ Attends to the norms and conventions of the discipline, especially the correct use and punctuation of transitions.
☐ Introduces a precise claim.	☐ Demonstrates an understanding of the topic by providing adequate examples for each central idea.	
☐ Supports the claim with clear reasons and relevant evidence.		
☐ Provides a conclusion that follows from the argument.	☐ Uses vocabulary that is appropriate for the audience and purpose.	
☐ Establishes a logical organization and develops a progression throughout the argument.	☐ Establishes and maintains a formal style and an objective tone.	
☐ Uses transitional words and phrases to clarify the relationships between and among ideas.		

🔀 WORD NETWORK

Include interesting words from your Word Network in your editorial.

☰ STANDARDS

Writing
Write arguments to support claims with clear reasons and relevant evidence.
  b. Support claim(s) with clear reasons and relevant evidence, using credible sources and demonstrating an understanding of the topic or text.
  c. Use words, phrases, and clauses to clarify the relationships among claim(s) and reasons.
  d. Establish and maintain a formal style.

232 UNIT 3 • MODERN TECHNOLOGY

Revising for Focus and Organization

Identify and Support Claim Reread your editorial, and make sure your claim is clear and specific. Ask yourself: *What do I want to convince readers to do or think?* If necessary, rewrite your claim to make it clearer. Then, make sure all your reasons and evidence relate directly to your claim and support it. If you see any ideas or evidence that do not have strong, clear connections to your main claim, rewrite or delete them.

Revising for Evidence and Elaboration

Clarify Relationships If any of the connections between your ideas are vague, add or replace transitional words or expressions to make them clearer. Consider using these transitional phrases: *in addition, on the other hand, as a result,* or *in fact.*

Use Formal Style Editorials are more persuasive when they are written in a formal style. When presenting evidence and examples, mix in longer sentences and harder words. Avoid slang or informal language that will take away from the force of your argument.

Informal language: Technology is really messing up our lives.

Formal language: Technology is having a negative impact on our lives.

HOW LANGUAGE WORKS

Transitions As students revise their arguments, remind them to use transitional words and phrases to connect and show relationships among ideas and create cohesion in their writing. Explain that using transitions is a key element in a logically organized argument. You may want to suggest students consider the following types of transitions as they revise their argument:

When . . .	Transition Type
Considering possible counterclaims	Contrast
Providing reasons to support your claim	Show effect; compare
Using evidence to support your reasons	Show effect; compare
Concluding your argument	Emphasize

© Pearson Education, Inc., or its affiliates. All rights reserved.

PEER REVIEW

Exchange editorials with a classmate. Use the checklist to evaluate your classmate's editorial and provide supportive feedback.

1. Is the claim clear?

☐ yes ☐ no If no, explain what confused you.

2. Is the claim supported with clear reasons and relevant evidence?

☐ yes ☐ no If no, point out what is missing.

3. Does the conclusion logically follow from the claim?

☐ yes ☐ no If no, suggest how the writer might improve it.

4. What is the strongest part of your classmate's editorial?

_____

_____

Editing and Proofreading

Edit for Conventions Reread your draft for accuracy and consistency. Correct errors in grammar and word usage. Be sure that you have included transitional words and phrases that clarify the relationships among the claims and reasons in your editorial.

Proofread for Accuracy Read your draft carefully, looking for errors in spelling and punctuation. If you have any short sentences with related ideas, consider combining them with coordinating conjunctions such as *and, so, but,* and *or.*

Publishing and Presenting

Create a final version of your essay. Share it with your class so that your classmates can read it and make comments. In turn, review and comment on your classmates' work. Consider other students' editorials and the claims they express. Think about how theirs are similar to and different from your own. Remember to maintain a polite and respectful tone when commenting.

Reflecting

Think about what you learned by writing your editorial. What could you do differently the next time you need to write an editorial to make it easier and to make your argument stronger?

© Pearson Education, Inc., or its affiliates. All rights reserved.

☰ STANDARDS

Writing
• With some guidance and support from peers and adults, develop and strengthen writing as needed by planning, revising, editing, rewriting, or trying a new approach.
• Use technology, including the Internet, to produce and publish writing as well as to interact and collaborate with others; demonstrate sufficient command of keyboarding skills to type a minimum of three pages in a single sitting.

Performance Task: Write an Argument **233**

Editing and Proofreading

Remind students to use the spell check and grammar check but not to rely on them. Proper names, like those of the bloggers they are writing about, will not be caught by the spell check. Tell students to read through their editorials, looking for errors in punctuation, too. Remind them that some transition words and phrases require a comma before or after the word.

Publishing and Presenting

Remind students that they should be mindful of appropriate formatting as they publish their editorials. Explain that this includes paying attention to top and bottom margins, to font size and style, to spacing, and to tabs.

Before students review their classmates' editorials, remind them to keep their comments positive and to use formal language. Point out that their purpose in reviewing their classmates' editorials is not to note whether or not they took the same position. Instead, their purpose is to evaluate the strength of their classmates' editorials by determining whether they used adequate reasons and strong evidence to support their claims.

Reflecting

Remind students to think about the comments they received from classmates as they reflect on the process for writing their editorial.

PERSONALIZE FOR LEARNING

Challenge

Building Understanding Point out that for this unit students read a short science fiction story and two arguments and that they viewed a video about technology. Then conduct a quick poll. Ask students which genre they found most thought-provoking. Once students have voted, discuss the results. Have students explain why they voted for the genre they did and what was confusing or difficult or not quite as interesting about the other genres. Remind students that one genre is no better than another. Work with students to create a list or chart of genre traits and examples from the selections in this unit. Allow students to refer to and add to or revise the chart as they encounter new selections.

OVERVIEW

SMALL-GROUP LEARNING

How is modern technology helpful and harmful to society?

Some people claim that modern technology has had some negative effects on our society. During Small-Group Learning, students will read selections that explain how modern technology has changed our lives.

Small-Group Learning Strategies

Review the Learning Strategies with students and explain that as they work through Small-Group Learning they will develop strategies to work in small-group environments.

- Have students watch the video on Small-Group Learning Strategies.
- A video on this topic is available online in the Professional Development Center.

You may wish to discuss some action items to add to the chart as a class before students complete it on their own. For example, for "Participate fully," you might solicit the following action from students:

- Ignore distractions to focus on the discussion.
- Challenge yourself to add an idea to the discussion every day.

Block Scheduling

Each day in this Pacing Plan represents a 40–50 minute class period. Teachers using block scheduling may combine days to reflect their class schedule. In addition, teachers may revise pacing to differentiate and support core instruction by integrating components and resources as students require.

👥 OVERVIEW: SMALL-GROUP LEARNING

ESSENTIAL QUESTION:

How is modern technology helpful and harmful to society?

Modern technology has made our lives easier in many ways. It has also raised our expectations about how quickly tasks can be completed. You will read selections that examine the presence of modern technology and social media in our daily lives. You will work in a group to continue your exploration of living in a world that is increasingly dependent on technology.

Small-Group Learning Strategies

Throughout your life, in school, in your community, and in your career, you will continue to learn and work with others.

Review these strategies and the actions you can take to practice them as you work in teams. Add ideas of your own for each step. Use these strategies during Small-Group Learning.

STRATEGY	ACTION PLAN
Prepare	• Complete your assignments so that you are prepared for group work. • Organize your thinking so you can contribute to your group's discussion. •
Participate fully	• Make eye contact to signal that you are listening and taking in what is being said. • Use text evidence when making a point. •
Support others	• Build on ideas from others in your group. • Invite others who have not yet spoken to join the conversation •
Clarify	• Paraphrase the ideas of others to ensure that your understanding is correct. • Ask follow-up questions. •

© Pearson Education, Inc., or its affiliates. All rights reserved.

234 UNIT 3 • MODERN TECHNOLOGY

SCAN FOR MULTIMEDIA

Introduce Whole-Class Learning

Unit Introduction	Feathered Friend	Teens and Technology Share a Future	The Black Hole of Technology	Media: The Internet of Things	Performance Task

| 1 | 2 | 3 | 4 | 5 | 6 | 7 | 8 | 9 | 10 | 11 | 12 | 13 | 14 | 15 | 16 | 17 | 18 |

CONTENTS

Overview: Small-Group Learning **235**

© Pearson Education, Inc., or its affiliates. All rights reserved.

Contents

Selections Circulate among groups as they preview the selections. You might encourage groups to discuss any knowledge they already have about any of the selections or the situations and settings shown in the photographs. Students may wish to take a poll within their group to determine which selections look the most interesting.

Remind students that communicating and collaborating in groups is an important skill that they will use throughout their lives—in school, in their careers, and in their community.

Performance Task

Deliver a Multimedia Presentation Give groups time to read about and briefly discuss the benefits or disadvantages of modern technology. They will return to this discussion before delivering a multimedia presentation after reading. Encourage students to do some preliminary thinking about the types of media they may want to use. This may help focus their subsequent reading and group discussion.

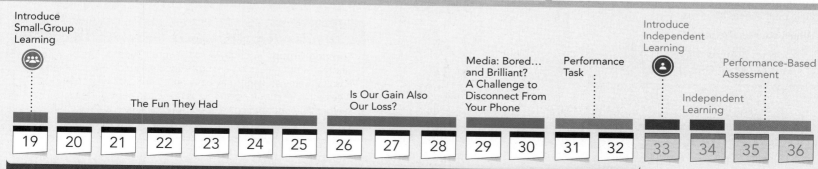

Introduce Small-Group Learning

The Fun They Had

Is Our Gain Also Our Loss?

Media: Bored... and Brilliant? A Challenge to Disconnect From Your Phone

Performance Task

Introduce Independent Learning

Independent Learning

Performance-Based Assessment

| 19 | 20 | 21 | 22 | 23 | 24 | 25 | 26 | 27 | 28 | 29 | 30 | 31 | 32 | 33 | 34 | 35 | 36 |

SMALL-GROUP LEARNING

SMALL-GROUP LEARNING

Working as a Team

1. **Take a Position** Remind groups to let all members share their responses. You may wish to set a time limit for this discussion.

2. **List Your Rules** You may want to have groups share their lists of rules and consolidate them into a master list to be displayed and followed by all groups.

3. **Apply the Rules** As you circulate among the groups, ensure that students are staying on task. Consider a short time limit for this step.

4. **Name Your Group** This task can be creative and fun. If students have trouble coming up with a name, suggest that they think of something related to the unit topic. Encourage groups to share their names with the class.

5. **Create a Communication Plan** Encourage groups to include in their plans agreed-upon times during the day to share ideas. They should also devise a method for recording and saving their communications.

Accountable Talk

Remind students that groups should communicate politely. You can post these Accountable Talk suggestions and encourage students to add their own. Students should:

Remember to . . .
Ask clarifying questions.

Which sounds like . . .
Can you please repeat what you said?
Would you give me an example?
I think you said _____. Did I understand you correctly?

Remember to . . .
Explain your thinking.

Which sounds like . . .
I believe _____ is true because _____.
I feel _____ because _____.

Remember to . . .
Build on the ideas of others.

Which sounds like . . .
When _____ said _____, it made me think of _____.

Working as a Team

1. **Take a Position** In your group, discuss the following question:

   Does having instant access to information always make our lives easier?

   As you take turns sharing your positions, be sure to provide examples or other support for your ideas. After all group members have shared, discuss the the ways in which instant access to information changes people's expectations.

2. **List Your Rules** As a group, decide on the rules that you will follow as you work together. Two samples are provided. Add two more of your own. You may add or revise rules based on your experience together.

   • Everyone should participate in group discussions.
   • People should not interrupt.

   • _____
     _____

   • _____
     _____

3. **Apply the Rules** Share what you have learned about technology. Make sure each person in the group contributes. Take notes and be prepared to share with the class one thing that you heard from another member of your group.

4. **Name Your Group** Choose a name that reflects the unit topic.

   Our group's name: _____

5. **Create a Communication Plan** Decide how you want to communicate with one another. For example, you might use online collaboration tools, email, or instant messaging.

   Our group's decision: _____

   _____

© Pearson Education, Inc., or its affiliates. All rights reserved.

FACILITATING SMALL-GROUP LEARNING

Forming Groups You may wish to form groups for Small-Group Learning so that each consists of students with different learning abilities. Some students may be adept at organizing information whereas other may have strengths related to generating or synthesizing information. A good mix of abilities can make the experience of Small-Group Learning dynamic and productive.

Making a Schedule

First, find out the due dates for the small-group activities. Then, preview the texts and activities with your group, and make a schedule for completing the tasks.

SELECTION	ACTIVITIES	DUE DATE
The Fun They Had		
Is Our Gain Also Our Loss?		
Bored . . . and Brilliant? A Challenge to Disconnect From Your Phone		

Working on Group Projects

As your group works together, you'll find it more effective if each person has a specific role. Different projects require different roles. Before beginning a project, discuss the necessary roles, and choose one for each group member. Here are some possible roles; add your own ideas.

Project Manager: monitors the schedule and keeps everyone on task

Researcher: organizes research activities

Recorder: takes notes during group meetings

_____

_____

_____

_____

© Pearson Education, Inc., or its affiliates. All rights reserved.

SCAN FOR MULTIMEDIA

Making a Schedule

Encourage groups to preview the reading selections and to consider how long it will take them to complete the activities accompanying each selection. Point out that they can adjust the due dates for particular selections as needed as they work on their small-group projects. However, they must complete all assigned tasks before the group Performance Task is due. Encourage groups to review their schedules upon completing the activities for each selection to make sure they are on track to meet the final due date.

Working on Group Projects

Point out to groups that the roles they assign can also be changed later. Students might have to make changes based on who is best at doing what. Try to make sure that there is no favoritism, cliquishness, or stereotyping by gender or other means in the assignment of roles.

Also, you should review the roles each group assigns to its members. Based on your understanding of students' individual strengths, you might find it necessary to suggest some changes.

AUTHOR'S PERSPECTIVE | **Kelly Gallagher, M.Ed.**

The Teacher's Role After the ability to read and write with fluency, the skill that employers value most is the ability to collaborate successfully. Talking with other people can help us all learn more, change our opinions, and make us more thoughtful because we are exposed to ideas that we may not have previously considered. Student collaboration also serves as a useful formative assessment tool. To find out what students think about their reading, an effective strategy is to ask, "What is worth talking about?" Hearing what they get and pinpointing what they've missed informs further instruction. Here are some additional strategies for encouraging effective collaboration:

• _Flow in and out of groups_ as students work, modeling and encouraging meaningful talk.

• _Take notes_ on what is being said outright and what is being implied. See what background individuals contribute.

• _Plan pathways for subsequent lessons_ from what you've heard and observed.

The Fun They Had

◀)) AUDIO SUMMARIES
Audio summaries of "The Fun They Had" are available online in both English and Spanish in the Interactive Teacher's Edition or Unit Resources. Assigning these summaries prior to reading the selection may help students build additional background knowledge and set a context for their first read.

Summary

In Isaac Asimov's science fiction short story "The Fun They Had," Margie and Tommy, two young children from 2155, look at a book from the past. They find it strange because they are used to getting information from television screens. The old book states that students used to have teachers and learn together in classrooms. In 2155, students are taught by mechanical teachers, which are robots that stay in the children's homes. When she is alone, Margie fondly imagines what it must have been like to be in the classrooms of the past.

Insight

In this story, technology offers tailored education for every student; however, the social interaction is now missing. Tommy does not seem to mind the technological advances, but the end of the story suggests that Margie wishes she had a classroom education.

ESSENTIAL QUESTION:
How is modern technology helpful and harmful to society?

Connection to Essential Question

This story examines some advantages and drawbacks of electronics. Human teachers aren't vulnerable to malfunction, and learning in person gives more of a sense of community than learning alone.

SMALL-GROUP LEARNING PERFORMANCE TASK
Do the benefits of technology outweigh the disadvantages of technology?

UNIT PERFORMANCE-BASED ASSESSMENT
Do we rely on technology too much?

Connection to Performance Tasks

Small-Group Learning Performance Task Students will be asked to create a multimedia presentation regarding the advantages and disadvantages of technology. Their groups can refer to the ideas presented in this speculative fiction text to support their positions.

Unit Performance-Based Assessment Students will be asked to take a position on whether we have come to rely too much on technology. While this Isaac Asmiov story is science fiction, it does predict how cold and impersonal a future with solely technology-based education would look compared to what we have today. Students may refer to this story's speculation as reference in their arguments.

DIGITAL PERSPECTIVES

 Audio

 Video

 Document

Annotation Highlights

EL Highlights

 Online Assessment

LESSON RESOURCES

	Making Meaning	Language Development	Effective Expression
Lesson	**First Read** **Close Read** **Analyze the Text** **Analyze Craft and Structure**	**Concept Vocabulary** **Word Study** **Conventions**	**Writing to Sources**
Instructional Standards	**RL.10** By the end of the year, read and comprehend literature . . . **L.4** Determine or clarify the meaning of unknown and multiple-meaning words and phrases . . . **L.4.a** Use context as a clue . . . **RL.2** Determine a theme or central idea of a text . . . **RL.5** Analyze how a particular sentence, chapter, scene, or stanza . . .	**L.4** Determine or clarify the meaning of unknown and multiple-meaning words and phrases . . . **L.4.b** Use common, grade-appropriate Greek or Latin affixes and roots . . . **L.1** Demonstrate command of the conventions . . .	**W.3** Write narratives . . . **W.3.a** Engage and orient the reader . . . **W.3.b** Use narrative techniques . . . **W.3.d** Use precise words and phrases . . .
STUDENT RESOURCES			
Available online in the Interactive Student Edition or Unit Resources	Selection Audio First-Read Guide: Fiction Close-Read Guide: Fiction	Word Network	Evidence Log
TEACHER RESOURCES			
Selection Resources Available online in the Interactive Teacher's Edition or Unit Resources	Audio Summaries Annotation Highlights EL Highlights English Language Support Lesson: Action Verbs and Linking Verbs The Fun They Had: Text Questions Analyze Craft and Structure: Science-Fiction Writing	Concept Vocabulary and Word Study Conventions: Action Verbs and Linking Verbs	Writing to Sources: Dialogue
Reteach/Practice (RP) Available online in the Interactive Teacher's Edition or Unit Resources	Analyze Craft and Structure: Science-Fiction Writing (RP)	Word Study: Anglo-Saxon Suffix -ful (RP) Conventions: Action Verbs and Linking Verbs (RP)	Writing to Sources: Dialogue (RP)
Assessment Available online in Assessments	Selection Test		
My Resources	A Unit 3 Answer Key is available online and in the Interactive Teacher's Edition.		

Reading Support

Text Complexity Rubric: The Fun They Had

Quantitative Measures

Lexile: 750   Text Length: 1,049 words

Qualitative Measures

Knowledge Demands ① —**❷**— ③ —④— ⑤	Selection is based in the future; experiences depicted are unfamiliar because they are descriptions of the future, but they are described in everyday, familiar ways that are easy to understand.
Structure ① —**❷**— ③ —④— ⑤	Story contains a lot of dialogue, making it easy to follow. Events in story are described chronologically.
Language Conventionality and Clarity ① —**❷**— ③ —④— ⑤	The language is mostly explicit and easy to understand with some occasions for more complex meaning and irony. Sentences are mostly simple and compound; vocabulary in dialogue is conversational.
Levels of Meaning/Purpose ① —②— **❸** —④— ⑤	The story has multiple levels of meaning. The theme is implicit and is revealed over the entirety of the text. Reader must infer meaning by the characters' responses to their future world and what they think about the past one.

DECIDE AND PLAN

English Language Support

Provide English learners with support for knowledge demands and meaning as they read the selection.

Knowledge Demands Ask students to look in the first paragraph for the year the story takes place (2155). Then ask them to read the first two paragraphs. Ask what the line "Today Tommy found a real book" and the information in the second paragraph tell them about the story. (There are no more paper books used in the year 2155.)

Meaning Ask questions that help students understand the meaning of the story. For example, *How does the girl feel about school?* (In paragraph 10, she says she hates it.) *What does she imagine people thought of school in the past when there were real teachers?* (She thinks that school used to be fun.)

Strategic Support

Provide students with strategic support to ensure that they can successfully read the text.

Language Have students work in groups of three. Have each group read aloud the story, with one being the narrator, and the other two reading the dialogue of Margie and Tommy. Encourage them to read with expression.

Meaning Have students reread sections of the text and write down what they learn about the characters or the time they are living in. For example, have them read paragraphs 1–10 and write the facts about the future that they learn. (The year is 2155. People don't use paper books anymore. There are mechanical teachers. The mechanical teachers assign homework and tests.)

Challenge

Provide students who need to be challenged with ideas for how they can go beyond a simple interpretation of the text.

Text Analysis Point out that Asimov wrote this story in 1951, and set the future date in his story about 200 years later. Ask students to analyze which aspects of education he thought would stay the same, and which would change (for example, in his future school, there are tests and homework, but not teachers). Ask which aspects of his imagined future are already true or partially true today (for example, we already have electronic books).

Written Response Ask students to write what they think would be the pros or cons of having a mechanical teacher instead of a human one. Encourage them to be specific and give examples in their responses.

TEACH

Read and Respond

Have groups read the selection and complete the Making Meaning, Language Development, and Effective Expression activities.

Standards Support Through Teaching and Learning Cycle

IDENTIFY NEEDS

Analyze results of the Beginning-of-Year Assessment, focusing on the items relating to Unit 3. Also take into consideration student performance to this point and your observations of where particular students struggle.

ANALYZE AND REVISE

- Analyze student work for evidence of student learning.
- Identify whether or not students have met the expectations in the standards.
- Identify implications for future instruction.

TEACH

Implement the planned lesson, and gather evidence of student learning.

DECIDE AND PLAN

- If students have performed poorly on items matching these standards, then provide selection scaffolds before assigning them the on-level lesson provided in the Student Edition.
- If students have done well on the Beginning-of-Year Assessment, then challenge them to keep progressing and learning by giving them opportunities to practice the skills in depth.
- Use the Selection Resources listed on the Planning pages for "The Fun They Had" to help students continually improve their ability to master the standards.

Instructional Standards: The Fun They Had

	Catching Up	This Year	Looking Forward
Reading	You may wish to administer the **Analyze Craft and Structure: Science-Fiction Writing (RP)** worksheet to familiarize students with science-fiction writing.	**RL.2** Determine a theme or central idea of a text and how it is conveyed through particular details; provide a summary of the text distinct from personal opinions or judgments.	Challenge students to compare and contrast the science fiction genre to other genres to show how they may overlap.
Writing	You may wish to administer the **Writing to Sources: Dialogue (RP)** worksheet to help students better understand how the technique works.	**W.3.b** Use narrative techniques, such as dialogue, pacing, and description, to develop experiences, events, and/or characters.	Encourage students to add dialogue to other writing they have produced.
Language	Review the **Word Study: Anglo-Saxon Suffix -ful (RP)** worksheet with students to familiarize them with the prefix. You may wish to administer the **Conventions: Action Verbs and Linking Verbs (RP)** worksheet to help students better understand action verbs and linking verbs.	**L.4.b** Use common, grade-appropriate Greek or Latin affixes and roots as clues to the meaning of a word. **L.1** Demonstrate command of the conventions of standard English grammar and usage when writing or speaking.	Ask students to look for other suffixes in the texts that they read. Challenge students to come up with sentences that use action verbs and linking verbs.

Jump Start

FIRST READ *What will schools be like one or two hundred years from now? What role will technology play in the schools of the future?* Invite students to share their predictions, and engage students in a discussion about the future that sets the context for reading this short story by Isaac Asimov.

The Fun They Had 🔊 📄

What are the advantages and disadvantages of human teachers? What are the benefits and drawbacks of Margie and Tommy's robot teachers? Modeling questions such as these will help students connect "The Fun They Had" to the Small-Group Performance Task assignment. Selection audio and print capability for the selection are available in the Interactive Teacher's Edition.

Concept Vocabulary

Encourage groups to study the types of context clues presented on the student page and to discuss how these types of clues can help clarify meaning. Ask students to think of another type of context clue that they might encounter in a short story, such as elaborating details or contrast of ideas.

⬤ FIRST READ

As they read, students should perform the steps of the first read:

NOTICE: You may want to encourage students to notice how Margie and Tommy's schooling is different from modern schooling.

ANNOTATE: Remind students to mark words that provide information about the characters' attitudes, thoughts, and feelings.

CONNECT: Encourage students to compare the future described in this short story with the future described in other science fiction texts, movies, or television shows that they have read or watched.

RESPOND: Students will answer questions and write a summary to demonstrate understanding.

Point out to students that while they will always complete the Respond step at the end of the first read, the other steps will probably happen somewhat concurrently. You may wish to print copies of the **First-Read Guide: Fiction** for students to use. 📄

About the Author

Isaac Asimov (1920–1992) became a science-fiction fan after reading fantastic stories in magazines. Asimov's father discouraged his son's early interest, and described the magazines he loved as "junk." Still, Asimov's interest in science fiction continued, and he started writing his own stories at age eleven. At first, his stories were rejected, but Asimov developed into a visionary writer and became one of the most influential science-fiction authors of the twentieth century.

📋 STANDARDS

Reading Literature
By the end of the year, read and comprehend literature, including stories, dramas, and poems, in the grades 6–8 text complexity band proficiently, with scaffolding as needed at the high end of the range.

Language
Determine or clarify the meaning of unknown and multiple-meaning words and phrases based on *grade 6 reading and content,* choosing flexibly from a range of strategies.

  a. Use context clues as a clue to the meaning of a word or phrase.

238 UNIT 3 • MODERN TECHNOLOGY

The Fun They Had

Concept Vocabulary

As you perform your first read of "The Fun They Had," you will encounter these words.

sorrowfully	loftily	nonchalantly

Context Clues To find the meanings of unfamiliar words, look for clues in the context, which is made up of other words and phrases that surround the unknown word. There are different types of context clues that may help you as you read. Consider these examples:

> **Synonyms:** The director <u>blamed</u> and **criticized** Andre and Gaby for missing band rehearsal.

> **Elaborating Details:** Terry could be **arrogant**—<u>he really thought he was superior</u>—when he had the right answer.

Apply your knowledge of context clues and other vocabulary strategies to determine the meanings of unfamiliar words you encounter during your first read.

First Read FICTION

Apply these strategies as you conduct your first read. You will have an opportunity to complete a close read after your first read.

NOTICE *whom* the story is about, *what* happens, *where* and *when* it happens, and *why* those involved react as they do.

ANNOTATE by marking vocabulary and key passages you want to revisit.

First Read

CONNECT ideas within the selection to what you already know and what you have already read.

RESPOND by completing the Comprehension Check and by writing a brief summary of the selection.

© Pearson Education, Inc., or its affiliates. All rights reserved.

AUTHOR'S PERSPECTIVE   Jim Cummins, Ph.D.

Critical Literacies Recent research shows that even early-stage English learners can use higher-order thinking skills and engage with complex social issues with the appropriate instructional support. The following questions illustrate how teachers can support the development of critical thinking:

Step 1: Textual Dimension In order to help students read deeply to understand how the language and multimodal dimensions of the text construct meaning, ask, "When, where, and how did it happen?" and "Who did it? Why?"

Step 2: Personal Dimension Encourage students to reflect critically on the text in relation to their experiences and emotions. Ask, "Have you ever seen, felt, or experienced something like this?" or "Have you ever wanted something similar?"

The Fun They Had

Isaac Asimov

CLOSER LOOK

Analyze Narrator

Circulate among groups as students conduct their close read. Suggest that groups close read paragraphs 1–2. Encourage them to talk about the annotations they mark. If needed, provide the following support.

ANNOTATE: Have students mark details in the first two paragraphs that reveal the type of narrator, or work with small groups as you highlight them together.

QUESTION: Guide students to consider what these details might tell them. Ask what a reader can infer about the narrator from these details (Who is telling the story? How much does the narrator know about each character?), and accept student responses.

Possible response: The story has a third-person narrator because the narration uses pronouns like *he/she/they* instead of *I* or *you*. The narrator seems to know a lot about Margie because the story includes details that only Margie would know about, such as what she wrote in her diary. The narrator doesn't give any information about Tommy, except through Margie's thoughts about him.

CONCLUDE: Help students to formulate conclusions about the importance of these details in the text. Ask students why the author might have chosen this type of narrator.

Possible response: The author might have chosen this type of narrator so he could provide a lot of information—the actions, words, thoughts, memories, and feelings—about one particular character. The character of Margie is probably more important to the story than any other character.

Discuss types of **narrators** with students. In a fictional work, a limited third-person narrator is a voice outside the story who speaks in the third person (using the pronouns he, she, they, and so on). This narrator is neither a character nor an all-knowing voice, but instead sees the world through a single character's eyes and reveals only what that character is experiencing, thinking, and feeling. Stories told by a limited third-person narrator are told from the limited third-person point of view.

BACKGROUND

New methods of learning have been influenced by changes in technology. During ancient times, the Romans wrote on wax tablets. Children in the 1700s read and practiced writing on slates, or blackboards. In the 1900s, educational radio programs were introduced. In today's society, online education has become popular.

SCAN FOR MULTIMEDIA

1   Margie even wrote about it that night in her diary. On the page headed May 17, 2155, she wrote, "Today Tommy found a real book."

2   It was a very old book. Margie's grandfather once said that when he was a little boy, his grandfather told him that there was a time when all stories were printed on paper.

3   They turned the pages, which were yellow and crinkly, and it was awfully funny to read words that stood still instead of moving the way they were supposed to—on a screen, you know. And then, when they turned back to the page before, it had the same words on it that it had had when they read it the first time.

NOTES

The Fun They Had **239**

Step 3: Critical Dimension Engage students in critical analysis of issues in the text by asking questions such as: "Is what this person said valid? Always? Under what conditions? Are there any alternatives to this situation?"

Step 4: Creative/Transformative Dimension Engage students in creative, constructive actions that address the social realities discussed. Ask, "How can the problem or issues be resolved?" and "What role can we play in helping resolve the problem?" Projects can involve drama, role play, art, poetry, stories, and newsletter publication.

© Pearson Education, Inc., or its affiliates. All rights reserved.

Concept Vocabulary

SORROWFULLY If groups are struggling to define the word *sorrowfully* in paragraph 10, ask students if there are any roots or suffixes in this word that they recognize. Point out that *sorrowfully* can be broken into three parts—*sorrow*, *ful*, and *ly*. The suffix *-ly* turns an adjective into an adverb and means "to do something in a certain manner." Encourage students to use this clue to infer the meaning of the word and write a possible definition.

Possible response: *Sorrowfully* means "to do something in a sad manner."

NOTES

Mark context clues or indicate another strategy you used that helped you determine meaning.

sorrowfully (SAWR oh fuhl ee) *adv.*

MEANING:

4   "Gee," said Tommy, "what a waste. When you're through with the book, you just throw it away, I guess. Our television screen must have had a million books on it and it's good for plenty more. I wouldn't throw it away."

5   "Same with mine," said Margie. She was eleven and hadn't seen as many telebooks as Tommy had. He was thirteen.

6   She said, "Where did you find it?"

7   "In my house." He pointed without looking, because he was busy reading. "In the attic."

8   "What's it about?"

9   "School."

10 Margie was scornful. "School? What's there to write about school? I hate school." Margie always hated school, but now she hated it more than ever. The mechanical teacher had been giving her test after test in geography, and she had been doing worse and worse until her mother had shaken her head **sorrowfully** and sent for the county inspector.

11 He was a round little man with a red face and a whole box of tools with dials and wires. He smiled at her and gave her an apple, then took the teacher apart. Margie had hoped he wouldn't know how to put it together again, but he knew how all right and, after an hour or so, there it was again, large and ugly, with a big screen on which all the lessons were shown and the questions were asked. That wasn't so bad. The part she hated most was the slot where she had to put homework and test papers. She always had to write them out in a punch code[1] they made her learn when she was six years old, and the mechanical teacher calculated the mark in no time.

> **Why would anyone write about school?**

12 The inspector had smiled after he was finished and patted her head. He said to her mother, "It's not the little girl's fault, Mrs. Jones. I think the geography sector was geared a little too quick. Those things happen sometimes. I've slowed it up to an average ten-year level. Actually, the overall pattern of her progress is quite satisfactory." And he patted Margie's head again.

13 Margie was disappointed. She had been hoping they would take the teacher away altogether. They had once taken Tommy's teacher away for nearly a month because the history sector had blanked out completely.

14 So she said to Tommy, "Why would anyone write about school?"

15 Tommy looked at her with very superior eyes. "Because it's not our kind of school, stupid. This is the old kind of school that

---

1. **punch code** card containing data that was used to program computers during the 1940s, when this story was written.

© Pearson Education, Inc., or its affiliates. All rights reserved.

VOCABULARY DEVELOPMENT

Word Forms Model using other forms of the word *sorrowfully* in paragraph 10 in these sentences:

- The week after my grandmother's funeral consisted of days of sorrow.
- After losing the hockey game, the team formed a sorrowful line to shake hands with the winners.
- Both the judge and jury were outraged by the criminal's sorrowless confession.

Word	Part of Speech	Meaning
sorrow	noun	a feeling of great sadness
sorrowful	adjective	full of sorrow or grief
sorrowless	adjective	a lack of sadness or grief

they had hundreds and hundreds of years ago." He added **loftily**, pronouncing the word carefully, "*Centuries* ago."

16   Margie was hurt. "Well, I don't know what kind of school they had all that time ago." She read the book over his shoulder for a while, then said, "Anyway, they had a teacher."

17   "Sure they had a teacher, but it wasn't a *regular* teacher. It was a man."

18   "A man? How could a man be a teacher?"

19   "Well, he just told the boys and girls things and gave them homework and asked them questions."

20   "A man isn't smart enough."

21   "Sure he is. My father knows as much as my teacher."

22   "He can't. A man can't know as much as a teacher."

23   "He knows almost as much I betcha."

24   Margie wasn't prepared to dispute that. She said, "I wouldn't want a strange man in my house to teach me."

25   Tommy screamed with laughter, "You don't know much, Margie. The teachers didn't live in the house. They had a special building and all the kids went there."

26   "And all the kids learned the same thing?"

27   "Sure, if they were the same age."

28   "But my mother says a teacher has to be adjusted to fit the mind of each boy and girl it teaches and that each kid has to be taught differently."

29   "Just the same, they didn't do it that way then. If you don't like it, you don't have to read the book."

30   "I didn't say I didn't like it," Margie said quickly. She wanted to read about those funny schools.

31   They weren't even half finished when Margie's mother called, "Margie! School!"

32   Margie looked up. "Not yet, Mamma."

33   "Now," said Mrs. Jones. "And it's probably time for Tommy, too."

34   Margie said to Tommy, "Can I read the book some more with you after school?"

35   "Maybe," he said, **nonchalantly**. He walked away whistling, the dusty old book tucked beneath his arm.

36   Margie went into the schoolroom. It was right next to her bedroom, and the mechanical teacher was on and waiting for her. It was always on at the same time every day except Saturday and Sunday, because her mother said little girls learned better if they learned at regular hours.

37   The screen was lit up, and it said: "Today's arithmetic lesson is on the addition of proper fractions. Please insert yesterday's homework in the proper slot."

© Pearson Education, Inc., or its affiliates. All rights reserved.

NOTES

Mark context clues or indicate another strategy you used that helped you determine meaning.

loftily (LAWF tih lee) *adv.*

MEANING:

Mark context clues or indicate another strategy you used that helped you determine meaning.

nonchalantly (non shuh LONT lee) *adv.*

MEANING:

Concept Vocabulary

LOFTILY If groups are struggling to define the word *loftily* in paragraph 15, point out that they can use context clues to help them define the word. Remind students to look for other descriptive details in the paragraph about how Tommy talks to Margie. These details reveal his attitude and may help students define the word *loftily*.

Possible response: *Loftily* might mean "arrogantly" or "in a way that shows a feeling of superiority."

NONCHALANTLY If groups are struggling to define the word *nonchalantly* in paragraph 35, point out that they can use context clues to help them define the word. Remind students to look at the dialogue before the use of this word, as well as Tommy's actions immediately after. These details reveal the manner in which Tommy is acting and may help students define the word *nonchalantly*.

Possible response: *Nonchalantly* might mean "in a way that suggests one does not care about what is happening."

 Additional **English Language Support** is available in the Interactive Teacher's Edition.

The Fun They Had **241**

PERSONALIZE FOR LEARNING

English Language Support

Formal vs. Informal English Draw students' attention to the word *betcha* in paragraph 23. Explain that this is an *informal contraction*. A contraction is a word that is formed by combining two or more words together and leaving out some of the letters. Provide examples such as *I'm*, *won't*, *isn't*, and *they're*. Explain that spoken English sometimes uses informal contractions, such as *wanna*, *gonna*, *gotta*, and *whatcha*.

Explain to students that using informal contractions is acceptable in casual writing and speech, but that they should be avoided in formal writing, such as homework assignments. Add that, despite being a piece of formal writing, the story uses the word *betcha* because the author wants to show how the character of Tommy would actually talk in a casual conversation. **ALL LEVELS**

NOTES

38   Margie did so with a sigh. She was thinking about the old schools they had when her grandfather's grandfather was a little boy. All the kids from the whole neighborhood came, laughing and shouting in the schoolyard, sitting together in the schoolroom, going home together at the end of the day. They learned the same things so they could help one another on the homework and talk about it.

39   And the teachers were people. . . .

40   The mechanical teacher was flashing on the screen: "When we add the fractions ½ and ¼ . . . "

41   Margie was thinking about how the kids must have loved it in the old days. She was thinking about the fun they had. ❧

© Pearson Education, Inc., or its affiliates. All rights reserved.

242 UNIT 3 • MODERN TECHNOLOGY

CROSS-CURRICULAR PERSPECTIVES

Humanities Call student attention to paragraph 5. Point out that the "telebooks" predicted in Asimov's "The Fun They Had" share a lot of similarities with today's e-books. Have students conduct research into e-books and make lists of the pros and cons of both e-books and paper books. Then encourage groups to debate the following question: *Is the growing popularity of e-books good or bad for society?*

Comprehension Check

Complete the following items after you finish your first read. Review and clarify details with your group.

1. What does Tommy find in the attic?

2. Why does Margie hate school now more than ever?

3. Why does Margie's mother send for the county inspector?

4. What surprises Margie about teachers of the past?

5. 🖹 **Notebook** Write three to five sentences to summarize the story.

- -

RESEARCH

Research to Clarify Choose at least one unfamiliar detail from the text. Briefly research that detail. In what way does the information you learned shed light on an aspect of the story?

Research to Explore Choose something that interested you from the text, and formulate a research question that you might use to find out more about the topic.

The Fun They Had **243**

Comprehension Check

Possible responses:

1. Tommy finds an old book made from paper in the attic.
2. Margie hates school because she's been doing poorly on her geography tests.
3. Margie's mother sends for the county inspector because Margie has been getting bad grades, and her mother wants to find out if there is something wrong with the "mechanical teacher."
4. Margie is surprised that humans used to be teachers. She thinks that a human can't know as much or be as smart as a robot teacher.
5. Margie and Tommy are children in the year 2155. Tommy finds an old book in his attic, and the children talk about how strange it is compared to their modern "telebooks." Tommy then tells Margie about the schools of the past, which had human teachers and physical schoolrooms instead of robot teachers that teach in children's homes. Margie thinks about how much fun it must have been to go to school with other kids.

Research

Research to Clarify If students struggle to come up with a detail to research, you may want to suggest that they focus on one of the following topics: e-books, robots, how schools have changed.

Research to Explore If students aren't sure how to go about formulating a research question, suggest that they use their findings from Research to Clarify as a starting point. For example, if students researched robots, they might formulate a question such as *Will robots replace humans in certain jobs some day?*

© Pearson Education, Inc. or its affiliates. All rights reserved.

PERSONALIZE FOR LEARNING

Challenge

Creative Writing Assign students the following creative writing prompt: *Write about a character who time travels to the year 2155. What do they see? Whom do they meet? What do they talk about with the people of 2155? What new technologies do they encounter?* Encourage students to use rich descriptions, figurative and sensory language, and dialogue. Remind students to organize the events of their story in a logical manner. After students have finished writing, invite them to share their stories with their small-group members and discuss each other's work.

Jump Start

CLOSE READ *What would it be like to live in a world where robots and humans live side by side? How would humans and robots interact and get along? What problems might arise? As students discuss these questions in their groups, encourage them to refer to details from "The Fun They Had."*

Close Read the Text ✏

If needed, model close reading by using the Annotation Highlights in the Interactive Teacher's Edition.

Remind students to use Accountable Talk in their discussions and to support one another as they complete the close read.

Analyze the Text

Possible responses:
1. Margie's school is different because she learns from home and has a robot teacher, instead of going to a physical school and having a human teacher.
2. Passages will vary by group. Remind students to explain why they chose the passage they presented to group members.
3. Responses will vary by group.

Concept Vocabulary

Why These Words? Possible response: These words all describe attitudes and behavior. They help to develop the characters' personalities.

Practice

Possible response: "I guess this is something only a high-schooler like me would understand," Cassie sneered *loftily* to her younger brother. Alex looked at the ground and mumbled *sorrowfully,* "Sorry I messed up." "Whatever. Tell mom I won't be home for dinner," Cassie shot back as she *nonchalantly* grabbed her coat and walked out the door.

Word Network

Possible words: *telebooks, sector, mechanical*

Word Study

For more support, see **Concept Vocabulary and Word Study.** 📄

Possible responses:
1. full of sadness
2. Responses will vary.

👥 MAKING MEANING

THE FUN THEY HAD

💡 TIP

GROUP DISCUSSION
It's important to keep an open mind during group discussions. Be open to the possibility that some of your opinions may change.

🔗 WORD NETWORK

Add words related to modern technology from the text to your Word Network.

☰ STANDARDS

Reading Literature
• Determine a theme or central idea of a text and how it is conveyed through particular details; provide a summary of the text distinct from personal opinions or judgments.
• Analyze how a particular sentence, chapter, scene, or stanza fits into the overall structure of a text and contributes to the development of the theme, setting, or plot.
Language
Determine or clarify the meaning of unknown and multiple-meaning words and phrases based on *grade 6 reading and content,* choosing flexibly from a range of strategies.
b. Use common, grade-appropriate Greek or Latin affixes and roots as clues to the meaning of a word.

244 UNIT 3 • MODERN TECHNOLOGY

Close Read the Text

With your group, revisit sections of the text you marked during your first read. **Annotate** details that you notice. What **questions** do you have? What can you **conclude**?

Analyze the Text

CITE TEXTUAL EVIDENCE
to support your answers.

📧 Complete the activities.

1. **Review and Clarify** With your group, review the selection. How is Margie's school different from schools of the past?

2. **Present and Discuss** Share with your group the passages from the selection that you found especially important. Take turns presenting your passages. Discuss what you noticed in the selection, what questions you asked, and what conclusions you reached.

3. **Essential Question:** *How is modern technology helpful and harmful to society?* What has this article taught you about the impact of modern technology on society? Discuss with your group.

LANGUAGE DEVELOPMENT

Concept Vocabulary

| sorrowfully | loftily | nonchalantly |

Why These Words? The three concept vocabulary words from the text are related. With your group, determine what the words have in common. How do these word choices add to the impact of the text?

Practice

📓 **Notebook** Write a paragraph using the three concept vocabulary words. Your paragraph can be based on Asimov's characters and setting or it can be completely new.

Word Study

Anglo-Saxon Suffix: -*ful* The suffix *-ful* means "full of" or "having the qualities of." When added to a noun that names an emotion, the suffix creates an adjective that describes someone who feels that emotion. Use your knowledge of the suffix *-ful* to complete these activities.

1. When the suffix *-ly* is removed from the adverb *sorrowfully,* it becomes the adjective *sorrowful.* Define *sorrowful.*

2. Write three other words that end in *-ful* or *-fully.* Write their meanings.

© Pearson Education, Inc., or its affiliates. All rights reserved.

FORMATIVE ASSESSMENT

Analyze the Text 📄
If groups struggle to close read the text, **then** provide the **The Fun They Had: Text Questions** available online in the Interactive Teacher's Edition or Unit Resources. Answers and DOK levels are also available.

Concept Vocabulary
If groups have trouble making a connection between the words, **then** have them review how the words were used in the story.

Word Study
If groups struggle to identify words starting with *non-,* **then** help them look up words starting with *non-* in the dictionary. For Reteach and Practice, see **Word Study: Anglo-Saxon Suffix -*ful* (RP).** 📄

Analyze Craft and Structure

Science-Fiction Writing Science fiction is a form, or genre, of fiction that imagines the technology and science of the future. Science-fiction stories balance technological and scientific ideas with realistic elements—characters, events, and situations that are true to life. These realistic details help readers relate to a story that may take place in very unfamiliar places. Most science fiction includes these types of elements:

- scientific ideas
- imaginary beings, such as futuristic robots or aliens from distant planets
- settings that are different from Earth or from Earth right now—These may be non-Earthly places, such as spaceships, other planets, or alternate universes. Or, they may be Earth, but in the future.
- plots that reflect issues in society today, such as the impact of technology or even political ideas—Science-fiction writers often place familiar issues into unfamiliar settings in order to explore their complexities and understand them better.

Like all other types of literature, science fiction conveys **themes,** or insights into life. These themes may relate to science and technology, or they may simply relate to human nature and society.

Practice

CITE TEXTUAL EVIDENCE
to support your answers.

1. Use the chart to identify passages from "The Fun They Had" that reflect each element of science fiction. Work individually, and then share your responses with your group.

THE FUN THEY HAD	
SCIENCE-FICTION ELEMENT	EXAMPLE FROM STORY
Scientific Ideas	paper reading materials replaced by "telebooks"
Imaginary Beings	mechanical teachers
Alternate Setting	set in the year 2155
Comment on Issues in Society Today	advancement of technology has not yet replaced human interaction

Notebook Answer the questions.

2. Consider this possible theme for the story: *Nothing, not even great technology, can replace human interaction.* Which story details support this theme? Explain.

3. In what ways might this story be considered a warning about the future? Explain your response.

The Fun They Had **245**

Analyze Craft and Structure

Science-Fiction Writing Some students may confuse science-fiction writing with fantasy writing. Remind groups that these are two different genres, although they share some similarities. Explain that science fiction makes predictions based on current scientific knowledge, whereas fantasy is usually not based on scientifically viable ideas. Science fiction explores a future that the writer believes could actually happen (however unlikely it may be). A writer of fantasy does not expect his or her ideas to ever actually come true. For more support, see **Analyze Craft and Structure: Science-Fiction Writing.**

Possible responses:

1. See possible responses in the chart on the student page.

2. Margie hates the impersonal nature of her technology-driven education and thinks fondly of the old-fashioned ways schools were run with human teachers and students attending school together, in the same classrooms.

3. The story could be warning us that if we allow technology to grow too much, our humanity will be threatened. For example, if we replace the human interaction we receive in school, we may lose much of the value of education itself.

FORMATIVE ASSESSMENT

Analyze Craft and Structure

If groups struggle to identify the theme of the story, **then** ask them what they think the author wanted readers to learn from reading the story. For Reteach and Practice, see **Analyze Craft and Structure: Science-Fiction Writing (RP).**

VOCABULARY DEVELOPMENT

Vocabulary Reinforcement Students will benefit from additional examples and practice with some of the vocabulary on this page. Reinforce their comprehension with "show-you-know" sentences. The first part of the sentence uses the vocabulary word in an appropriate context. The second part of the sentence—the "show-you-know" part—clarifies the first. Model the strategy with this example for *convey*:

Toby wanted to *convey* the gravity of his news; he looked her in the eyes and told her she'd better sit down for this.

Then give students these sentence prompts and coach them in creating the clarification part:

1. The story takes place in an *alternate* universe; _____.

Possible response: one where every person has a clone.

2. She was very *inventive* as a child; _____.

Possible response: she was always fiddling with electronics and coming up with new uses for them.

3. The writer makes many *predictions* about the future; _____.

Possible response: for instance, that one day robots will rule the world.

© Pearson Education, Inc., or its affiliates. All rights reserved.

Conventions

Action Verbs and Linking Verbs As you review the examples of action verbs and linking verbs in the chart, guide groups to identify other examples of action and linking verbs from the selection. For example, from paragraph 11:

Linking Verb: *He was a round little man with a red face and a whole box of tools with dials and wires.*

Action Verb: *He smiled at her and gave her an apple, then took the teacher apart.*

Have groups discuss the purpose and effect of the verbs and identify more examples of each type of verb. For more support, see **Conventions: Action Verbs and Linking Verbs (RP).**

Read It

Possible responses:
1. wrote (action)
2. was (linking)
3. is (linking)
4. insert (action)

Write It

Paragraphs will vary, but make sure that students use descriptive words and create a vivid picture of their character's feelings.

FORMATIVE ASSESSMENT

Conventions

If groups have trouble differentiating verb forms, **then** have them attempt to pantomime verbs physically and judge whether the ability to act out a verb helps determine if it's an action verb or a linking verb. For Reteach and Practice, see **Conventions: Action Verbs and Linking Verbs (RP).**

THE FUN THEY HAD

Conventions

Action Verbs and Linking Verbs Verbs are an essential element of all sentences and clauses. A **verb** expresses action or indicates a state or condition.

An **action verb** can express a physical action, such as *shake* or *laugh*, or a mental action, such as *hope* or *learn*.

A **linking verb** connects a subject to a word in the predicate that renames, identifies, or describes it. The most common linking verb is *be*, with forms such as *are, was, were, is being,* and *have been*. Other common linking verbs include *appear, become, feel, look,* and *seem*.

ACTION VERBS	LINKING VERBS
Her mother *had shaken* her head. (The action is *shaking*.)	Tommy and Margie *are* students. (*Are* links *Tommy and Margie* to *students*. *Students* renames *Tommy and Margie*.)
All the kids *laughed* in the schoolyard. (The action is *laughing*.)	The girl *became* curious about the old book. (*Became* links *girl* to *curious*. *Curious* describes the *girl*.)

Read It

Identify the verb(s) in each sentence from the selection. Then, label each verb as an action verb or a linking verb.

1. Margie even wrote about it that night in her diary.

2. He was a round little man with a red face and a whole box of tools with dials and wires.

3. ". . . Actually, the overall pattern of her progress is quite satisfactory."

4. "Please insert yesterday's homework in the proper slot."

Write It

 Notebook Imagine that you are Margie's friend in the year 2155. Write a journal entry describing your feelings about your mechanical teacher. Use at least three action verbs and two linking verbs in your writing.

STANDARDS

Language
Demonstrate command of the conventions of standard English grammar and usage when writing or speaking.

© Pearson Education, Inc., or its affiliates. All rights reserved.

PERSONALIZE FOR LEARNING

English Language Support

Action Verbs and Linking Verbs Ask students to write a list of three action verbs and three linking verbs. **EMERGING**

Ask students to work in pairs to write a list of three action verbs and three linking

verbs, and then write six sentences, each using one of the verbs properly. **EXPANDING**

Ask students to write a paragraph describing some aspect of what they think school will be like one hundred years in the future. Have them use at least three

different action verbs and three different linking verbs in the paragraph. **BRIDGING**

An expanded **English Language Support Lesson** on Action Verbs and Linking Verbs is available in the Interactive Teacher's Edition.

Writing to Sources

Dialogue is the conversations that take place among characters in literary works. Authors use dialogue to move the plot forward, as well as to provide insights into characters' personalities and the ways they change.

Assignment

With your group, write a **scene with dialogue** in which Margie describes finding the old book to one of her friends. Choose one of the following options:

☐ Write the scene in dramatic form with characters' names appearing at the beginning of each new line of dialogue. Place in brackets any descriptions or lines not spoken by the characters.

☐ Write the scene in short-story form. All descriptions will appear in paragraphs. Indicate who is speaking, and set lines of dialogue in quotation marks.

Project Plan First, discuss Margie's character and what one of Margie's friends would be like. Then, describe how other aspects of this future time might be different from today and how to pull these ideas into the scene. Brainstorm for a few sample lines of dialogue that feel true to Margie's character and how you think her friend would react. Take notes during the discussion.

Then, use your discussion notes and the story as background to develop the scene. Decide on a logical sequence of events. Use narrative techniques, such as *pacing*. Pacing is similar to rhythm. You can either slow down the action of the scene or speed it up. Slow down action by adding more description and longer sentences. Speed up action by using short sentences that make things seem to happen quickly. When writing your scene, use precise words, vivid details, and descriptive language to show the setting and action.

Revise and Edit Work together to revise and edit the scene. Keep the following elements in mind:

- Are the events arranged in a logical order?
- Are the word choices descriptive, and do they capture the futuristic setting in which the conversation takes place?
- Does the dialogue contribute to the reader's understanding of the characters and plot?
- Do you use appropriate pacing to point out an important idea or to build suspense?

Present and Discuss Present your group's scene to the class and answer any questions your classmates may have.

© Pearson Education, Inc., or its affiliates. All rights reserved.

🖉 EVIDENCE LOG

Before moving on to a new selection, go to your Evidence Log and record what you learned from "The Fun They Had."

☰ STANDARDS

Writing

Write narratives to develop real or imagined experiences or events using effective technique, relevant descriptive details, and well-structured event sequences.

a. Engage and orient the reader by establishing a context and introducing a narrator and/or characters; organize an event sequence that unfolds naturally and logically.

b. Use narrative techniques, such as dialogue, pacing, and description, to develop experiences, events, and/or characters.

d. Use precise words and phrases, relevant descriptive details, and sensory language to convey experiences and events.

Writing to Sources

Explain to groups that because dialogue serves many crucial purposes, authors make careful decisions about word choice, punctuation, and other techniques to help create dialogue that helps build characters and advance the plot. For example, in paragraphs 26–29 the author of this selection ceases using any narration to frame a continuous exchange of dialogue, yet readers likely have no problem understanding which characters are saying the dialogue. This is because the author established a pattern and a rhythm to the conversation, and the characters maintain their characteristic styles of conversation.

Project Plan Emphasize to groups that they have to use their imaginations for this project. They must not only identify a scenario in which to build their scene, they must invent new dialogue that expresses the characters' personalities. While they can refer to the selection for models of how to write effective dialogue, they cannot copy or mimic material from the selection.

Revise and Edit Remind groups to make sure that their characters and plot—in addition to their dialogue—are convincing. Explain that readers of fiction expect to be convinced by the story: they want to believe that it could really happen. Characters should be multidimensional and they should say things that real people might say. For more support, see **Writing to Sources: Dialogue. 📄**

Evidence Log Support students in completing their Evidence Log. This paced activity will help prepare them for the Performance-Based Assessment at the end of the unit.

FORMATIVE ASSESSMENT

Writing to Sources

If groups have trouble creating original dialogue for Margie, **then** have them improvise brief scenarios in which group members take on the parts of the characters. For Reteach and Practice, see **Writing to Sources: Dialogue (RP). 📄**

Selection Test

Administer the "The Fun They Had" Selection Test, which is available in both print and digital formats online in Assessments. 📄 ☑

Is Our Gain Also Our Loss?

◆》 AUDIO SUMMARIES
Audio summaries of "Is Our Gain Also Our Loss?" are available online in both English and Spanish and can be assigned to students in the Interactive Teacher's Edition or Unit Resources. Assigning these summaries prior to reading the selection may help students build additional background knowledge and set a context for their first read.

Summary

In this blog post, Cailin Loesch considers the advantages and disadvantages of modern technology. Her father tells her about how when he was growing up, he had to patiently wait and watch TV weather reports at a particular time to know when he could swim. Cailin realizes that there are experiences her parents have had that she will never have and that she has had experiences that her children will never have. However, she isn't certain that the way she lives today will result in the same kind of nostalgia her father feels. She wonders how future generations will look back on their childhoods.

Insight

This selection focuses on lived experience and how technology affects the small details of our lives. It questions whether the experiences of a particular generation are really preferable to those of a previous generation.

ESSENTIAL QUESTION:
How is modern technology helpful and harmful to society?

Connection to Essential Question

This blog post focuses on how the technology we have access to affects our experiences. The author feels great uncertainty about whether modern technology is really helping or harming us.

SMALL-GROUP LEARNING PERFORMANCE TASK
Do the benefits of technology outweigh the disadvantages of technology?

UNIT PERFORMANCE-BASED ASSESSMENT
Do we rely on technology too much?

Connection to Performance Tasks

Small-Group Learning Performance Task In this selection, it seems as though modern technology makes our experiences less memorable. Is that true? If so, is it a problem?

Unit Performance-Based Assessment Relying too much on technology might prevent us from having experiences that build character. For example, having to wait for the weather report may have taught the author's father to be patient.

LESSON RESOURCES

	Making Meaning	**Language Development**	**Effective Expression**
Lesson	**First Read** **Close Read** **Analyze the Text** **Analyze Craft and Structure**	**Concept Vocabulary** **Word Study** **Conventions**	**Speaking and Listening**
Instructional Standards	**RI.10** By the end of the year, read and comprehend literary nonfiction . . . **L.4** Determine or clarify the meaning of unknown and multiple-meaning words and phrases . . . **RI.1** Cite textual evidence . . . **RI.3** Analyze in detail . . . **RI.5** Analyze how a particular sentence . . .	**L.4** Determine or clarify the meaning of unknown and multiple-meaning words and phrases . . . **L.4.b** Use common, grade-appropriate Greek or Latin affixes and roots . . . **L.1** Demonstrate command of the conventions . . .	**SL.1** Engage effectively in a range of collaborative discussions . . . **SL.1.a** Come to discussions prepared . . . **SL.1.b** Follow rules for collegial discussions . . .

▸ STUDENT RESOURCES

Available online in the Interactive Student Edition or Unit Resources	🔊 Selection Audio 📄 First-Read Guide: Nonfiction 📄 Close-Read Guide: Nonfiction	📄 Word Network	📄 Evidence Log

▸ TEACHER RESOURCES

Selection Resources Available online in the Interactive Teacher's Edition or Unit Resources	🔊 Audio Summaries 🖋 Annotation Highlights 💬 EL Highlights 📄 English Language Support Lesson: Comparative and Superlative Degrees 📄 Is Our Gain Our Loss?: Text Questions 📄 Analyze Craft and Structure: Reflective Writing	📄 Concept Vocabulary and Word Study 📄 Conventions: Comparative and Superlative Degrees	📄 Speaking and Listening: Group Discussion
Reteach/Practice (RP) Available online in the Interactive Teacher's Edition or Unit Resources	📄 Analyze Craft and Structure: Reflective Writing (RP)	📄 Word Study: Latin Suffix -ation (RP) 📄 Conventions: Comparative and Superlative Degrees (RP)	📄 Speaking and Listening: Group Discussion (RP)
Assessment Available online in Assessments	📄 ☑ Selection Test		
My Resources	📄 A Unit 3 Answer Key is available online and in the Interactive Teacher's Edition.		

Reading Support

Text Complexity Rubric: Is Our Gain Also Our Loss?

Quantitative Measures

Lexile: 1180   Text Length: 978 words

Qualitative Measures

Knowledge Demands ①—**❷**—③—④—⑤	Selection relies mostly on everyday knowledge and familiar situations. Some references to technology of the past may be unfamiliar, but most are explained.
Structure ①—②—**❸**—④—⑤	Selection covers a wide range of subjects that are explained with a lot of detailed examples. The connection between ideas and the ways the examples connect to them are not always immediately apparent.
Language Conventionality and Clarity ①—②—③—**❹**—⑤	Language is contemporary and conversational, but somewhat complex. Many sentences are long, with complex construction. Questions posing possibilities for the future may be difficult for some readers.
Levels of Meaning/Purpose ①—②—**❸**—④—⑤	Selection covers a wide range of ideas, and the main concept is not easy to grasp right away. Many ideas are introduced as questions. The main idea is stated explicitly and simply at the end.

DECIDE AND PLAN

English Language Support

Provide English learners with support for language and meaning as they read the selection.

Language Help students understand lengthy sentences by showing them how to break them down into smaller parts. Together, analyze some of the questions about possibilities in the future. Rephrase to clarify if needed. For example, *Today, we use long easily-tangled wires. Maybe in the future, we won't need those anymore and other people won't be able to imagine we ever used them* (paragraph 9, sentence 3).

Meaning Direct students to sentences that help them understand the main concepts. For example, paragraph 5 talks about how technology and our way of life is changing. Paragraphs 11–12 summarize the author's questions about how technology will affect the future.

Strategic Support

Provide students with strategic support to ensure that they can successfully read the text.

Meaning After a first reading, ask a volunteer to read aloud paragraph 5 and another to read paragraphs 11–12. Explain that the blog post is about the way technology is changing. As students read or reread, they should look for examples of how technology is changing.

Language Point out that the author gives examples about changing technology by posing questions about the future. Pair students and ask them to reread the questions in paragraphs 9–10 and to make a list of some technologies that the author thinks might change. Ask them to note any of the questions they find confusing. As a group, discuss their lists, explaining any concepts if needed.

Challenge

Provide students who need to be challenged with ideas for how they can go beyond a simple interpretation of the text.

Text Analysis Have students work in pairs to discuss some of the changes in technology the author suggests might take place. Why might the author believe that these devices will change or become obsolete?

Written Response Ask students to write about a day fifty years ago, describing a character's activities from morning to night, including the technology he or she uses. For example, the character might watch TV and make a call from a phone booth. Students should research which technologies existed at the time.

TEACH

Read and Respond

Have the groups read the selection and complete the Making Meaning, Language Development, and Effective Expression activities.

Standards Support Through Teaching and Learning Cycle

IDENTIFY NEEDS

Analyze results of the Beginning-of-Year Assessment, focusing on the items relating to Unit 3. Also take into consideration student performance to this point and your observations of where particular students struggle.

ANALYZE AND REVISE

- Analyze student work for evidence of student learning.
- Identify whether or not students have met the expectations in the standards.
- Identify implications for future instruction.

TEACH

Implement the planned lesson, and gather evidence of student learning.

DECIDE AND PLAN

- If students have performed poorly on items matching these standards, then provide selection scaffolds before assigning them the on-level lesson provided in the Student Edition.
- If students have done well on the Beginning-of-Year Assessment, then challenge them to keep progressing and learning by giving them opportunities to practice the skills in depth.
- Use the Selection Resources listed on the Planning pages for "Is Our Gain Also Our Loss?" to help students continually improve their ability to master the standards.

Instructional Standards: Is Our Gain Also Our Loss?

	Catching Up	This Year	Looking Forward
Reading	You may wish to administer the **Analyze Craft and Structure: Reflective Writing (RP)** worksheet to familiarize students with reflective essays.	**RI.1** Cite textual evidence to support analysis of what the text says explicitly as well as inferences drawn from the text.	Challenge students to think of ways the author could have strengthened her claims.
Speaking and Listening	You may wish to administer the **Speaking and Listening: Group Discussion (RP)** worksheet to help students better prepare for their presentations.	**SL.1** Engage effectively in a range of collaborative discussions with diverse partners on *grade 6 topics, texts, and issues,* building on others' ideas and expressing their own clearly.	Encourage students to apply group discussion tips as they work in groups going forward.
Language	Review the **Word Study: Latin Suffix -*ation* (RP)** worksheet with students to familiarize them with the suffix. Review the **Conventions: Comparative and Superlative Degrees: (RP)** worksheet with students to familiarize them with how these modifiers work.	**L.4.b** Use common, grade-appropriate Greek or Latin affixes and roots as clues to the meaning of a word. **L.1** Demonstrate command of the conventions of standard English grammar and usage when writing or speaking.	Have students think of other suffixes that change verbs to a noun. Challenge students to come up with words that are synonymous, but have different connotations.

Jump Start

FIRST READ What things can you think of—favorite games, useful tools, popular stores—that existed when you were a young child but are no longer a part of our day-to-day lives? What things do you enjoy today that will probably disappear in the next ten years? Engage groups in a discussion about changes that have occurred in our culture because of technological advancements.

Is Our Gain Also Our Loss? 🔊 📄

How has technology changed daily life? Which changes are positive and which changes are negative? If you could, would you reverse any of the changes, and if so, which ones? Modeling questions such as these will help students connect to "Is Our Gain Also Our Loss?" and to the Small-Group Performance Task assignment. Selection audio and print capability for the selection are available in the Interactive Teacher's Edition.

Concept Vocabulary

Ask groups to look closely at the base words in the example and discuss how looking at the familiar word helps to determine the meaning of the unfamiliar word. Encourage groups to discuss other vocabulary strategies they could use if they are unfamiliar with the base word, such as using context clues.

● FIRST READ

Have students perform the steps of the first read independently:

NOTICE: Encourage students to notice the similarities and differences between the blogger's memories and experiences and those of her father.

ANNOTATE: Remind students to mark passages that describe the memories of the author's father and his response to those memories.

CONNECT: Encourage groups to discuss their memories and experiences as they relate to the selection.

RESPOND: Students will answer questions and write a summary to demonstrate understanding.

Point out to students that while they will always complete the Respond step at the end of the first read, the other steps will probably happen somewhat concurrently. You may wish to print copies of the **First-Read Guide: Nonfiction** for students to use. 📄

About the Author

Cailin Loesch (b. 1997) is a web correspondent for *Teen Kids News*, which is an Emmy Award–winning television series.

© Pearson Education, Inc., or its affiliates. All rights reserved.

📋 **STANDARDS**

Reading Informational Text
By the end of the year, read and comprehend literary nonfiction in the grades 6–8 text complexity band proficiently, with scaffolding as needed at the high end of the range.

Language
Determine or clarify the meaning of unknown and multiple-meaning words and phrases based on *grade 6 reading and content*, choosing flexibly from a range of strategies.

Is Our Gain Also Our Loss?

Concept Vocabulary

As you perform your first read of "Is Our Gain Also Our Loss?" you will encounter these words.

gradually	nostalgic	continuation

Base Words If these words are unfamiliar to you, analyze each one to see whether it contains a base word you know. Then, use your knowledge of the base, or "inside," word, along with the context, to determine the meaning of the word. Here is an example of how to apply the strategy.

> **Unfamiliar Word:** *considerate*
>
> **Familiar "Inside" Word:** *consider*, with meanings including "think"
>
> **Context:** When we were too late to catch the bus, our neighbor was kind and **considerate** enough to drive us to the meeting.
>
> **Conclusion:** The neighbor is described in a positive way, and the word *considerate* is paired with the word *kind*. *Considerate* might mean "thinking about the needs or feelings of others."

Apply your knowledge of base words and other vocabulary strategies to determine the meanings of other unfamiliar words you encounter during your first read.

First Read NONFICTION

Apply these strategies as you conduct your first read. You will have an opportunity to complete a close read after your first read.

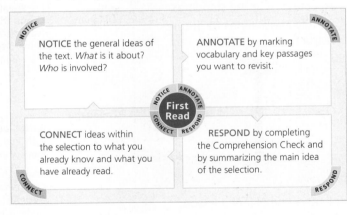

NOTICE the general ideas of the text. *What* is it about? *Who* is involved?

ANNOTATE by marking vocabulary and key passages you want to revisit.

CONNECT ideas within the selection to what you already know and what you have already read.

RESPOND by completing the Comprehension Check and by summarizing the main idea of the selection.

VOCABULARY DEVELOPMENT

Word Forms Expand students' vocabulary by helping them learn related forms of the concept vocabulary words. Word forms often change by adding prefixes or suffixes to the base word. Give students a blank **Word Forms Chart** (available in the Interactive Teacher's Edition) with *gradually, nostalgic,* and *continuation* placed in the correct columns. Work with groups to determine the related forms and discuss their meanings. The final chart should look like this:

Noun	Verb	Adjective	Adverb
gradualness		gradual	**gradually**
nostalgia		**nostalgic**	nostalgically
continuation	continue	continuous	continuously

Is Our Gain Also Our Loss?

Cailin Loesch

BACKGROUND

New technology changes our daily world with ever-increasing speed, often causing things to become obsolete, or out-of-date. These changes can leave older people longing for what they feel was the simpler, less complicated world of their youth. Is every generation destined to long for the past?

SCAN FOR MULTIMEDIA

1 "When I was your age, I had to wait for the hourly report on TV in order to get the information that you have right at your fingertips. That's the problem with the world today."

2 It was the summer of 2012, and I was standing in the kitchen with my dad and sister—holding my iPhone—a towel and bathing suit thrown over my shoulder. I had just finished reading aloud the full-day weather report, and, until my dad spoke, had nothing on my mind but the gleaming pool water that seemed to be calling my name. I waited a moment for his comment to process, then looked down at my phone, analyzing it in a way that I had never before: feeling the cold, hard metal in my palm, and the smooth, sleek screen underneath my thumb.

3 I asked Dad to elaborate on his comment.

4 "When I was a young boy, we had a pool in our backyard. My brothers and I weren't allowed to go swimming until the temperature reached 75 degrees—not one degree less. And so we boys spent our summer mornings waiting by the TV for the hourly report that read the temperature, praying that it would say the number we wanted it to so that we could dive in. I have vivid memories of those mornings."

5 Suddenly, life in the 1970s seemed distant, and people detached. It occurred to me that my dad has experienced life like I will never know it, and that I have experienced life like my children will never know. I even started to think about how things have changed in the years that I've been alive. It's not just technology that's changing, either: It's our way of living. I've seen it with my own eyes, and it's only becoming clearer as the years go by.

NOTES

© Pearson Education, Inc., or its affiliates. All rights reserved.

CLOSER LOOK

Analyze Anecdotes

Circulate among groups as students conduct their close read. Suggest that groups close read paragraphs 1–4. Encourage them to talk about the annotations they mark. If needed, provide the following support.

ANNOTATE: Have students mark details in 1–4 that indicate that the supporting details are part of a story or anecdote, or work with small groups as you highlight them together.

QUESTION: Guide students to consider what these details might tell them. Ask what a reader can infer from the author's use of anecdotes, and accept student responses.

Possible response: The author includes her story and her father's story to show that changes in technology affect people's experiences.

CONCLUDE: Help students to formulate conclusions about the importance of these details in the text. Ask students why the author might have included these details.

Possible response: The author's use of anecdotes helps readers to relate to the stories and begin to consider ways in which technology and our way of living are changing.

Remind students that an **anecdote** is a brief story that illustrates a concept.

Additional **English Language Support** is available in the Interactive Teacher's Edition.

👥 FACILITATING SMALL-GROUP CLOSE READING

CLOSE READ: Blog Post Monitor groups as they conduct their close read. Offer support as needed.

- Ask students to look for the structure of this nonfiction essay, identifying the introduction, claim, support, and conclusion.

- Encourage students to link the writer's anecdotes to the bigger point that the writer is making.

- Ask students to think about the writer's perspective or point of view when it is compared with that of her father and her teachers.

Concept Vocabulary

GRADUALLY If groups are struggling to define the word *gradually* in paragraph 6, point out that the base word is *gradual*. Encourage students to think of other words with the same base word.

Possible response: Based on the context and other words with the same base, *gradually* means "slowly changing or developing."

NOSTALGIC If groups are struggling to define *nostalgic* in paragraph 10, point out that the base part of the word is *nostalgia*. Encourage students to think of other words with the same base word. Draw students' attention to the sentence to examine context clues such as restatement to help define the word.

Possible response: *Nostalgic* and *nostalgia* have the same base word. In the sentence, "Late-Millennials feel *nostalgic* as we look back," the phrase "look back" gives a clue to the meaning. In this context, *nostalgic* means "wanting to return to happy times in the past."

NOTES

Mark base words or indicate another strategy you used that helped you determine meaning.

gradually (GRAJ oo uhl ee) *adv.*

MEANING:

---

6   Gradually, evenings spent doing homework at lamp-lit desks covered in pencils, paper, and textbooks are turning into late nights under bedsheets and blankets, a Google Docs page pulled up, fingers typing aggressively on a keyboard that can barely be seen in the dark. It seems as though I am part of the last generation that will know the satisfied feeling of stapling together a completed research paper, pages still warm from the printer. People of the next generation will never go on a family trip to the local Blockbuster[1] in search of candy and a comedy for movie night. They might miss out on handwritten letters from their grandparents, available to read and reread for years. Do we even realize what we're all leaving behind?

7   This morning, I was sitting at the breakfast table eating cereal when my dad came in to say goodbye before he left for work. When he saw that I was eating Life cereal, a huge smile immediately crept across his face, and he started excitedly reciting a commercial that he remembered from his childhood. He called me into his office, where he threw himself down in front of his desktop computer to search for the ad on YouTube,[2] eager to take me back in time with him.

8   Watching the commercial, my modernly-adjusted ears picked up on a faint hum in the background of the actor's voices. There were no snappy graphics or fast-paced cuts. In fact, the colors were a bit faded and the actors' faces were only highlighted in dim lighting. Then I turned to my dad, who was still beaming, as if all the happy memories from his childhood were flashing before his eyes. Judging by his enthusiastic clapping at the end, he sure didn't seem to miss modern technology during those 30 seconds.

9   In a world of iPhones and missions to Mars, is it even possible that my childhood will ever be looked at in the way that I look at my dad's? By then, will our TV shows be even crisper? Will it be unimaginable that we needed long, easily tangled wires in our ears in order to listen to music? Will my kids marvel at the idea of us old-fashioned teenagers having to wait by wall outlets for our phones to get out of the dreaded red battery zone before heading out for the night? Will they laugh at us for using pieces of green paper to buy things?

10 The thing that has really stayed with me, though, is my dad's comment about how all these new technologies are a "problem." One day, will we late-millennials[3] feel **nostalgic** as we look back on our simpler days, where we sometimes got a 10-minute homework break when our laptops lost battery life, giving us an excuse to sit in peace in front of a warm fire while

nostalgic (nos TAL jihk) *adj.*

MEANING:

---

1. **Blockbuster** chain of stores where people rented movies in the form of physical DVDs or VHS tapes.
2. **YouTube** video-sharing website.
3. **late-millennials** people born between the early 1990s and the early 2000s.

250 UNIT 3 • MODERN TECHNOLOGY

© Pearson Education, Inc., or its affiliates. All rights reserved.

PERSONALIZE FOR LEARNING

English Language Support

Understanding Cultural References Some students may struggle with the meaning of the text if they do not have the same cultural background. Encourage groups to identify cultural references in the text and allow someone who understands the cultural reference to provide an explanation. Encourage students to find a parallel example from their cultural experience and provide an explanation to their group. **ALL LEVELS**

we waited for them to charge? Will a lack of instant-charging mechanisms become the new lack of a weather.com app? Will we pull out our old Nintendo 3DS XLs to smile at what was once the hottest new piece of technology, recalling memories of online play with friends, in the same way that my dad smiled at an old commercial? Will we wish that things had never changed? They say that you should never try to fix what's not broken. Does the charm of the way things are now trump the need for things that are fresher, newer, and more advanced? Will we ever reach a point where there is no possible way to make any more "improvements"? And does this possibly inevitable peak signal impending doom or the **continuation** of tradition?

11   In my last-period sociology[4] class the other day, the teacher ended a class discussion about the impact of changing technology on society with a statement that summarized my thoughts on the matter and left me with something to think about:

12   "I don't know how new technology will affect future generations, and I don't know if it will do more good or bad."

13   I couldn't have said it better myself. ❧

---

4. **sociology** (soh see OL uh jee) *n.* study of social behavior.

NOTES

Mark base words or indicate another strategy you used that helped you determine meaning.

continuation (kuhn tihn yoo AY shuhn) *n.*

MEANING:

Comprehension Check

Complete these items after you finish your first read. Review and clarify details with your group.

1. Why were television weather reports significant to the author's father as a child?

2. 🗐 **Notebook** Summarize the main idea of the selection.

- -

RESEARCH

Research to Clarify Choose at least one unfamiliar detail from the text. Briefly research that detail. In what way does the information you learned shed light on an aspect of the selection?

Is Our Gain Also Our Loss? **251**

Concept Vocabulary

CONTINUATION If groups are struggling to define *continuation* in paragraph 10, point out that it includes the base word *continue*. Draw students' attention to the sentence to examine additional context clues, such as contrasting ideas to help define the word.

Possible response: In the sentence, the author compares "impending doom" and "the continuation of tradition." In this context, *continuation* means "moving forward."

Comprehension Check

Possible responses:

1. The television weather reports were significant to him because he had to wait for the weather report to say it was 75 degrees before he was allowed to go swimming.

2. Technological advancements, for better or worse, are changing the way we live.

Research

Research to Clarify If groups struggle to select an unfamiliar detail to research, you want to suggest that they focus on one of the following topics: Google Docs, missions to Mars, or Nintendo 3DS XL.

PERSONALIZE FOR LEARNING

Challenge

Text-to-World Connection Encourage groups to discuss devices that have become obsolete or that may become obsolete because of technological advancements. Use the text as a prompt to suggest devices students might discuss. Have groups research the devices they discuss.

Encourage them to draw comparisons between their examples and those in "Is Our Gain Also Our Loss?" and make predictions. Have groups share their research with others or with the class.

Jump Start

CLOSE READ Ask groups to consider these questions: *In what ways could technology do more bad for our future than good? In what ways has new technology already had a negative impact? What can be done to minimize these effects?* As students discuss in their groups, ask them to consider how new technologies have directly impacted them.

Close Read the Text

If needed, model close reading by using the Annotation Highlights in the Interactive Teacher's Edition.

Remind groups to use Accountable Talk in their discussions and to support one another as they complete the close read.

Analyze the Text

1. Responses will vary.
2. Passages will vary by group. Remind students to explain why they chose the quote they present to the group members.
3. Responses will vary.

Concept Vocabulary

Why These Words?
Possible response: These words are related to change. Another word that fits this category is *advancement*.

Practice

Possible responses:

Though it may not happen as quickly as some wish, we will *gradually* learn to adapt to the changes.

My older sister grew *nostalgic* about her childhood trinkets as she packed for college.

Today's program is a *continuation* of the one that started yesterday.

Word Network

Possible responses: *app, online*

Word Study

For more support, see **Concept Vocabulary and Word Study.**

Possible responses:

graduate/graduation, participate/participation, evaluate/evaluation, consider/consideration

---

IS OUR GAIN ALSO OUR LOSS?

TIP

GROUP DISCUSSION
Try not to interrupt other speakers. If you must interrupt (for instance, if someone is dominating the discussion), do so politely. For example, ask, "May I please add something?"

WORD NETWORK

Add words related to modern technology from the text to your Word Network.

STANDARDS

Reading Informational Text
• Cite textual evidence to support analysis of what the text says explicitly as well as inferences drawn from the text.
• Analyze in detail how a key individual, event, or idea is introduced, illustrated, and elaborated in a text.
• Analyze how a particular sentence, paragraph, chapter, or section fits into the overall structure of a text and contributes to the development of the ideas.
Language
• Determine or clarify the meaning of unknown and multiple-meaning words and phrases based on *grade 6 reading and content*, choosing flexibly from a range of strategies.
   b. Use common, grade-appropriate Greek or Latin affixes and roots as clues to the meaning of a word.

252 UNIT 3 • MODERN TECHNOLOGY

MAKING MEANING

Close Read the Text

With your group, revisit sections of the text you marked during your first read. **Annotate** details that you notice. What **questions** do you have? What can you **conclude**?

Analyze the Text

CITE TEXTUAL EVIDENCE to support your answers.

Complete the activities.

1. **Review and Clarify** With your group, reread paragraphs 6–9 of the selection. Discuss how the author's conversations with her father changed her perspective on technology. Has reading this selection changed your own perspective on technology?

2. **Present and Discuss** Share with your group the passages from the selection that you found especially important. Take turns presenting your passages. Discuss what you noticed in the selection, what questions you asked, and what conclusions you reached.

3. **Essential Question: *How is modern technology helpful and harmful to society?*** What has this article taught you about the impact of modern technology on society? Discuss with your group.

LANGUAGE DEVELOPMENT

Concept Vocabulary

gradually	nostalgic	continuation

Why These Words? The concept vocabulary words from the text are related. With your group, determine what the words have in common. Write your ideas, and add another word that fits the category.

Practice

Notebook Confirm your understanding of these words by using them in sentences. Give context clues that hint at the word's meaning.

Word Study

Latin Suffix: *-ation* The Latin suffix *-ation* means "the condition or process of." Adding this suffix changes a verb to a noun. In this text, the blogger refers to the "continuation of tradition." Using your knowledge, make an inference about what that phrase means. With your group, brainstorm for other verbs that can be turned into nouns with the suffix *-ation*. Then, find another example of a noun with the suffix *-ation* in the text.

FORMATIVE ASSESSMENT

Analyze the Text

If students struggle, **then** provide the **Is Our Loss Our Gain?: Text Questions** available online in the Interactive Teacher's Edition or Unit Resources. Answers and DOK levels are also available.

Concept Vocabulary

If students struggle to identify the concept, **then** have students use each word in a sentence and think about their similarities.

Word Study

If students are unable to brainstorm other nouns, **then** have them use a dictionary to identify nouns with this suffix. For Reteach and Practice, see **Word Study: Latin Suffix *-ation* (RP).**

© Pearson Education, Inc., or its affiliates. All rights reserved.

Analyze Craft and Structure

Development of Ideas: Reflective Writing A **reflective essay** is a brief prose work in which an author presents his or her thoughts and feelings—or reflections—about an experience or an idea. Most reflective writing includes the following elements:

- descriptions of a specific event, time period, or person that leads to new ways of seeing something

- dialogue and other storytelling elements that convey experiences in vivid ways

- informal language with a thoughtful quality

- discussion of the insights gained from the experience

In "Is Our Gain Also Our Loss?" Cailin Loesch thinks deeply about her father's experiences growing up at a time when technology was not as advanced. She compares and contrasts her father's experiences and attitude toward his childhood with her own feelings about growing up in a world increasingly dependent on technology.

Practice

CITE TEXTUAL EVIDENCE
to support your answers.

Using this chart, list the ways in which Loesch's observations of her father influence her own perspective. Work individually. Then, share your responses with your group.

IS OUR GAIN ALSO OUR LOSS?	
What memories of technology does Loesch's father have from his youth?	He had to wait for hourly news and weather reports. He remembers 30-second, slower-paced television commercials for his favorite cereal.
How do her father's memories contrast with Loesch's experiences during her own childhood?	Her generation has access to news constantly. Her generation is exposed to advertising that is fast-paced and full of snappy graphics. Her generation is shifting from handwriting to digital writing (Google Docs).
What thoughts about the future do these contrasts inspire in Loesch?	She reflects that her generation and future generations will never understand a pre-tech generation like her father's. She wonders if future generations will even have to plug in a phone to charge it, and whether paper money will become digital like everything else.

Notebook Write a one-paragraph response to Loesch's thoughts at the end of the blog. Consider these questions:

- Do you think people will continue to look back fondly on the technology of their youth?
- Will they view current technology as a "problem," as Cailin's father does?

Share your responses with the group.

© Pearson Education, Inc., or its affiliates. All rights reserved.

Analyze Craft and Structure

Development of Ideas: Reflective Writing
Discuss with groups that in this reflective essay, the blogger makes a claim. Discuss the difference between a claim and the reasons and evidence that support a claim. Help students identify the claims that the blogger makes and find the reasons or evidence that supports them. For more support, see **Analyze Craft and Structure: Reflective Writing.**

See possible responses in chart on student page.

NOTEBOOK

Possible responses: Students' paragraphs will vary, but they should address the two questions and include specific details from the text.

FORMATIVE ASSESSMENT

Analyze Craft and Structure

If students struggle identifying the blogger's claim, **then** have them locate reasons or evidence and move backward to identify the claims that they support. For Reteach and Practice, see **Analyze Craft and Structure: Reflective Writing (RP).**

PERSONALIZE FOR LEARNING

English Language Support

Making Connections Have students select one specific event or example from his or her own life that has been influenced by technology and write a reflective paragraph.

Have students review the definition of an argument. Encourage them to write a claim in a short, complete sentence. **EMERGING**

Have students review the definition of an argument. Encourage them to write a claim in a statement that is organized. **EXPANDING**

Ask students to keep in mind that they are writing an argument. Encourage them to write a claim and offer supporting reasons in a brief paragraph. **BRIDGING**

FACILITATING

Conventions

Comparative and Superlative Degrees Review with students the use of adjectives and adverbs in sentences. Discuss adjectives or adverbs that do not follow the typical rules to form comparatives or superlatives. For more support, see **Conventions: Comparative and Superlative Degrees.**

Read It

Possible responses:

1. Will we pull out our old Nintendo 3DS XLs to smile at what was once the <u>hottest</u> new piece of technology. (adjective, superlative)

2. By then, will our TV shows be even <u>crisper</u>? (adjective, comparative)

Write It

Possible responses:

1. Suddenly, life in the 1970s seemed <u>more distant</u>, and people <u>more detached</u>.

2. . . . late nights under bedsheets and blankets, a Google Docs page pulled up, fingers typing <u>more aggressively</u> on a keyboard that can barely be seen in the dark.

FORMATIVE ASSESSMENT

Conventions

If students cannot form the comparative and superlative forms of adjectives and adverbs, **then** review more examples of comparatives and superlatives, focusing on the similarities among the examples. For Reteach and Practice, see **Conventions: Comparative and Superlative Degrees (RP).**

LANGUAGE DEVELOPMENT

IS OUR GAIN ALSO OUR LOSS?

Conventions

Comparative and Superlative Degrees An **adjective** describes a person, a place, a thing, or an idea. An **adverb** describes a verb, an adjective, or another adverb. Adjectives and adverbs can be used to compare two or more items or actions. There are two degrees of comparison: **comparative degree** and **superlative degree**.

DEGREE OF COMPARISON	DEFINITION	ADJECTIVE EXAMPLES	ADVERB EXAMPLES
Comparative	compares two items or actions	*smaller, more frightened*	*more quickly, more easily*
Superlative	compares three or more items or actions	*smallest, most frightened*	*most quickly, most easily*

If an adjective has only one or two syllables, you can often add the suffixes *-er* and *-est* to form the comparative and superlative degrees. If the adjective is a longer word, use the words *more* and *most*. For most adverbs, use *more* and *most*. Do not use both forms (a suffix and the word *more* or *most*) at the same time.

Incorrect: We saw the *most largest* whale model at our local museum.

Correct: We saw the *largest* whale model at our local museum.

Read It

In each item from the text, identify the adjective or adverb used to make a comparison. Label each word as an adverb or an adjective. Then, write whether it is comparative or superlative.

1. Will we pull out our old Nintendo 3DS XLs to smile at what was once the hottest new piece of technology. . . .

2. By then, will our TV shows be even crisper?

Write It

Notebook Rewrite each sentence to include the type of modifier indicated in parentheses.

1. Suddenly, life in the 1970s seemed (distant), and people (detached). **(comparative adjectives)**

2. . . . late nights under bedsheets and blankets, a Google Docs page pulled up, fingers typing (aggressively) on a keyboard that can barely be seen in the dark. **(comparative adverb)**

≡ STANDARDS

Language
Demonstrate command of the conventions of standard English grammar and usage when writing or speaking.

© Pearson Education, Inc., or its affiliates. All rights reserved.

PERSONALIZE FOR LEARNING

English Language Support
Comparative and Superlative Degrees Ask students to work in pairs to write five comparative words ending in *-er* or *-est*. **EMERGING**

Ask students to write four sentences using one comparative word or structure in each. **EXPANDING**

Ask students to write a paragraph comparing their memories of the past to their present lives—

their family, their home, their school, their habits and routine, their pets, their siblings, and their neighborhoods. **BRIDGING**

An expanded **English Language Support Lesson** on **Comparative and Superlative Degrees** is available in the Interactive Teacher's Edition.

Speaking and Listening

At the end of "Is Our Gain Also Our Loss?" Cailin Loesch asks several questions about whether the technology of her own youth will become outdated. Follow up on this question in a group activity.

Assignment

Take part in a **group discussion** about changing technology. Think of an example of an invention or a device you once thought was wonderful, but now think is outdated—like the video-game platform that Loesch mentions at the end of her blog. With your group, compare and contrast your feelings about this example of "progress" with examples offered by other members of the group and with Loesch's blog post.

Discussion Preparation Use the chart to organize your thoughts and plan what you will say during the group discussion.

CHANGING VIEWS TOWARD TECHNOLOGY	
What example of outdated technology will you discuss?	
When was it popular? What purpose did it serve?	
How did you feel when you first heard about it and saw it?	
How do you feel about it now?	
Why have your feelings about it changed?	
Do you feel the technology left a lasting impact on you or on society? Why or why not?	

Assign Tasks Before beginning the discussion, take a moment to assign jobs to individual group members. This could include a moderator to ensure everyone stays on topic and speaks in turn, a timekeeper to ensure the discussion doesn't dwell on a single topic for too long, and a recorder to take notes.

© Pearson Education, Inc., or its affiliates. All rights reserved.

📝 EVIDENCE LOG

Before moving on to a new selection, go to your Evidence Log and record what you learned from "Is Our Gain Also Our Loss?"

⬛ STANDARDS

Speaking and Listening
Engage effectively in a range of collaborative discussions with diverse partners on *grade 6 topics, texts, and issues*, building on others' ideas and expressing their own clearly.

a. Come to discussions prepared, having read or studied required material; explicitly draw on that preparation by referring to evidence on the topic, text, or issue to probe and reflect on ideas under discussion.
b. Follow rules for collegial discussions, set specific goals and deadlines, and define individual roles as needed.

Is Our Gain Also Our Loss? **255**

Speaking and Listening

Discussion Preparation Encourage groups to carefully evaluate their selected invention or device example to ensure that it has the depth to support a substantive group discussion. All group members should have had some experience with the topic so they can participate equally. Be aware of cultural or family-income sensitivities that might cause some students to feel uncomfortable in this discussion. Students should refer to the organization chart for answers to help groups prepare their discussions. For more support, see **Speaking and Listening: Group Discussion.** 📄

Assign Tasks Help groups assign tasks to group members to ensure that all group members have a role in the discussion.

Evidence Log Support students in completing their Evidence Log. This paced activity will help prepare them for the Performance-Based Assessment at the end of the unit.

FORMATIVE ASSESSMENT

Speaking and Listening

If some students struggle to find points to contribute to the group discussion, **then** have groups outline their topic and assign each group member at least one question or point to raise during the discussion. For Reteach and Practice, see **Speaking and Listening: Group Discussion (RP).** 📄

Selection Test

Administer the "Is Our Gain Also Our Loss?" Selection Test, which is available in both print and digital formats online in Assessments. 📄 ☑

PERSONALIZE FOR LEARNING

Strategic Support

Compare and Contrast If groups struggle to identify a device or invention they think is outdated, help them focus their thinking by suggesting a specific single category of technology (e.g., cars, movies, school) or the types of technology typically found in a single room in the home (e.g., living room, kitchen, basement). Then have groups create a two-column chart. In the left column, have groups brainstorm and record examples of current technology associated with those categories. In the right column, have groups describe the same technology five years ago. Finally, have the groups review and evaluate their comparisons and determine which provide the greatest contrast, or change in the last five years.

Bored . . . and Brilliant? A Challenge to Disconnect From Your Phone

🔊 **AUDIO SUMMARIES**

Audio summaries of "Bored... and Brilliant? A Challenge to Disconnect From Your Phone" are available online in both English and Spanish in the Interactive Teacher's Edition or Unit Resources. Assigning these summaries prior to listening to the selection may help students build additional background knowledge and set a context for their first review.

Summary

In the podcast "Bored . . . and Brilliant? A Challenge to Disconnect From Your Phone," the host, Audie Cornish, introduces the topic of smartphone usage and interviews technology podcast host Manoush Zomorodi. In their conversation, Zomorodi describes how boredom can lead to creativity. The podcast also uses interviews with commuters and clips from researchers to explore ideas about smartphone usage and boredom. The podcast ends with a challenge for listeners to observe and rethink their smartphone usage.

Insight

This selection presents the idea that boredom and creativity are linked. Creative thought can take place while someone is doing something that might be considered boring, such as reading a phone book. Zomorodi argues that, instead of cutting out technology all together, people should focus on how to reach a balance between boredom and their tech usage.

ESSENTIAL QUESTION:
How is modern technology helpful and harmful to society?

Connection to Essential Question

This podcast suggests that listeners should think critically about how they use their phones. Technology can be stimulating, but it might distract people from doing their most creative thinking.

SMALL-GROUP LEARNING PERFORMANCE TASK
Do the benefits of technology outweigh the disadvantages of technology?

UNIT PERFORMANCE-BASED ASSESSMENT
Do we rely on technology too much?

Connection to Performance Tasks

Small-Group Learning Performance Task Being more creative and goal-directed may be more beneficial than never being bored.

Unit Performance-Based Assessment This selection makes the case that relying on technology for immediate entertainment prevents us from thinking of more satisfying and useful things.

LESSON RESOURCES

	Making Meaning	Effective Expression
Lesson	**First Review** **Analyze the Media** **Close Review** **Media Vocabulary**	**Research**
Instructional Standards	**RI.10** By the end of the year, read and comprehend literary nonfiction . . . **L.6** Acquire and use accurately grade-appropriate general academic and domain-specific words and phrases . . .	**W.2** Write informative/explanatory texts . . . **W.8** Gather relevant information . . . **SL.5** Include multimedia components and visual displays . . .

▷ STUDENT RESOURCES

Available online in the Interactive Student Edition or Unit Resources	🔊 Selection Audio 📄 First-Review Guide: Media Audio 📄 Close-Review Guide: Media Audio	📄 Word Network 📄 Evidence Log

▷ TEACHER RESOURCES

Selection Resources Available online in the Interactive Teacher's Edition or Unit Resources	🔊 Audio Summaries 📄 Media Vocabulary 📄 Bored . . . and Brilliant: Media Questions	📄 Research: Multimedia Slide Show, Brochure
My Resources	📄 A Unit 3 Answer Key is available online and in the Interactive Teacher's Edition.	

Media Complexity Rubric: Bored . . . and Brilliant? A Challenge to Disconnect From Your Phone

Quantitative Measures

Format and Length: Audio, 5 min 46 sec

Qualitative Measures

Knowledge Demands ①——②——❸——④——⑤	Audio relies mostly on familiar, everyday situations and experiences. However, there are many references made to apps and research projects that will not be familiar.
Structure ①——②——❸——④——⑤	Multiple voices are used and they change back and forth frequently, either in conversations or for quotes taken from many individuals. Changes in voices make it easier to follow, but the fast pace makes it challenging at times.
Language Conventionality and Clarity ①——②——❸——④——⑤	Language is mostly conversational, clear, and concrete. Sentences are mostly simple, with some more complex constructions. Most of the speakers have clear diction, but some speak quickly.
Levels of Meaning/Purpose ①——②——❸——④——⑤	Overall purpose is clear and explicit. However, a lot of detailed information is given, sometimes very quickly. Students may need to listen multiple times to pick up on all necessary details.

Jump Start

FIRST REVIEW Engage students in a discussion about boredom. When was the last time you were really bored? What do you do when you're bored? Have you ever come up with a really good idea when you were bored?

Bored . . . and Brilliant?
A Challenge to Disconnect From Your Phone 🔊 📄

What effect does having constant access to mobile devices have on us? Modeling the questions readers might ask as they listen to "Bored . . . and Brilliant?" brings the text alive for students and connects it to the Small-Group Performance Task assignment. Selection audio for the selection is available in the Interactive Teacher's Edition.

Media Vocabulary

Encourage groups to discuss the media vocabulary. Have they seen the terms in texts before? Do they use any of them in their speech and writing?

Ask groups to study the three terms and identify what they have in common. Students will notice that they are all related to podcasts and radio programs. Encourage students to talk about a podcast or radio program that they listen to and to use some or all of the media vocabulary. For more support, see **Media Vocabulary.** 📄

🔘 FIRST REVIEW

As they review, students should perform the steps of the first review:

LISTEN: Remind students to keep track of who is saying what and to take note of the most important speakers.

NOTE: Encourage students to take notes on Manoush Zomorodi's key ideas.

CONNECT: Encourage students to make connections beyond the podcast. If they cannot make connections to their own lives, have them consider other podcasts or radio programs they may have heard.

RESPOND: Students will answer questions to demonstrate understanding.

Point out to students that while they will always complete the Respond step at the end of the first review, the other steps will probably happen somewhat concurrently. You may wish to print copies of the **First-Read Guide: Media Audio** for students to use. 📄

About the Podcast

All Things Considered began airing in 1971 and was the first news program on National Public Radio (NPR). It has since won numerous awards for excellence. The daily radio show mixes news stories with interviews, analysis, and commentaries on the arts and culture. In 2005, NPR first started making its programs available in the form of podcasts.

Bored . . . and Brilliant?
A Challenge to Disconnect From Your Phone

Media Vocabulary

These words will be useful to you as you analyze, discuss, and write about podcasts.

podcast: digital audio or video file or recording, usually part of a series, that can be downloaded from the Internet	• Many podcasts invite listeners to leave comments or share their thoughts about the shows. • Some podcasts are accompanied by a transcript, or the text of the spoken words.
host: someone who introduces and talks to the guests on a television or radio program	• Most hosts prepare for a program by learning about the background of the guests.
interview: recorded conversation in which someone is asked questions about his or her life, experiences, or opinions	• An interesting interview usually reveals new information about the person being interviewed. • The person conducting an interview typically creates a list of questions prior to the interview, but asks unplanned follow-up questions based on the interviewee's responses.

First Review MEDIA: AUDIO

Apply these strategies as you listen to the podcast.

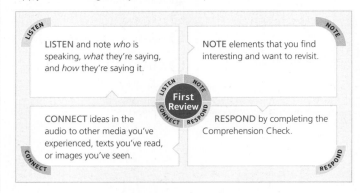

Listening Strategy: Take Notes

📓 **Notebook** As you listen, write down your observations and questions, making sure to note time codes so you can easily visit sections later.

STANDARDS

Reading Informational Text
By the end of the year, read and comprehend literary nonfiction in the grades 6–8 text complexity band proficiently, with scaffolding as needed at the high end of the range.

Language
Acquire and use accurately grade-appropriate general academic and domain-specific words and phrases; gather vocabulary knowledge when considering a word or phrase important to comprehension or expression.

© Pearson Education, Inc., or its affiliates. All rights reserved.

VOCABULARY DEVELOPMENT

Domain-Specific Vocabulary Have each group identify a domain-specific word in the podcast and define it. Words include *reflexively, technophile, stimulation,* and *subconscious,* for example. Have groups share their words with the class. Have one student or group compile the words from each group in a class dictionary that everyone can consult as they discuss the podcast.

Bored . . . and Brilliant?
A Challenge to Disconnect From Your Phone

BACKGROUND

According to a survey by the research group Flurry, which is cited in this podcast, smartphones have taken over television as the most-watched kind of screen in the United States. In 2014, the average American spent almost three hours a day on his or her phone, just a little more than the average American spent watching television.

SCAN FOR MULTIMEDIA

NOTES

Bored . . . and Brilliant? A Challenge to Disconnect From Your Phone **257**

© Pearson Education, Inc., or its affiliates. All rights reserved.

CLOSER REVIEW

Analyze Evidence

Circulate among groups as students conduct their first review. Suggest that groups close review the section of the podcast from 3:22 to 5:13. Encourage them to talk about the notes they make. If needed, provide the following support.

NOTE: Have students note the evidence that Zomorodi uses to support her ideas, or work with small groups to have students participate while you note it together.

Possible response: She references the work of experts, such as psychologists Dr. Sandi Mann and Dr. Marcus Raichle.

QUESTION: Guide students to consider what these details might tell them. Ask what a listener can infer from these details and accept student responses.

Possible response: Zomorodi has done a lot of research into the relationship between smartphone use and boredom.

CONCLUDE: Help students to formulate conclusions about the importance of these details in the podcast. Ask students why Zomorodi might have included these details.

Possible response: Citing scientific research about the effects of boredom provides evidence to support Zomorodi's ideas and to encourage people to use their phones less.

Remind students that podcasts, like written arguments, present main ideas or claims supported by **evidence**.

PERSONALIZE FOR LEARNING

English Language Support

Taking Notes Support students as they listen to the podcast. Pair students together and have them listen to the podcast in one-minute increments. Remind students to take notes on the key ideas and details spoken during each segment. After each segment, have partners share their notes and ask each other questions to confirm their understanding of the podcast. Repeat the process until students have listened to the entirety of the podcast. **ALL LEVELS**

FACILITATING SMALL-GROUP CLOSE-REVIEW

CLOSE REVIEW: Podcast Monitor groups as they conduct the close review. Offer support as needed.

• Ask students to think about the various people's voices represented, and challenge them to explain how each person adds to the main idea of the podcast.

• Encourage students to listen to key sections over again if necessary.

Comprehension Check

Possible responses:

1. Cellphone users spend, on average, almost three hours a day on their phones.
2. We are daydreaming and coming up with our most original ideas.
3. Dr. Sandi Mann researched the connection between boredom and creativity. She made people do something really boring and then do a creative task. They came up with their most creative ideas after they read a phone book—the most boring task of all.

Close Review

If needed, model close reviewing by using the Closer Review notes in the Interactive Teacher's Edition. Remind groups to use Accountable Talk in their discussions and to support one another as they complete the close read.

Analyze the Media

Possible responses:

1. Quotes will vary by group. Remind students to explain why they chose the quote they present to the group members.
2. Yes, I agree. I have noticed that when I spend a lot of time on my phone, I spend less time thinking creatively. If people spent less time on their phones, they would have to entertain themselves with their own imaginations.
3. Responses will vary by group.

Word Network

Possible words: *technophile, smartphone, downloaded, app, check-ins*

FORMATIVE ASSESSMENT

Analyze the Media

If students struggle to close review the podcast, **then** provide the **Bored . . . and Brilliant?: Media Questions** available online in the Interactive Teacher's Edition or Unit Resources. Answers and DOK levels are also available.

Media Vocabulary

If students struggle to understand how the words are related, **then** have them write a sentence using each word and compare the sentences.

Comprehension Check

Complete the following items after you finish your first review. Review and clarify details with your group.

1. On average, about how long do cellphone users spend on their phones each day?

2. What are we really doing "when we think we're doing nothing"?

3. What did Dr. Sandi Mann research? What did she find out?

MEDIA VOCABULARY

Use these words as you discuss and write about the podcast.

podcast
host
interview

WORD NETWORK

Add words related to modern technology from the text to your Word Network.

Close Review

With your group, listen to the podcast again. Write any new observations that seem important. What **questions** do you have? What can you **conclude**?

Analyze the Media

CITE TEXTUAL EVIDENCE to support your answers.

Notebook Respond to these questions.

1. **Present and Discuss** Choose a quote from the podcast that you found interesting or powerful. Explain what you notice, what questions it raises for you, and what conclusions you reached about it.

2. **Review and Synthesize** Do you agree that there is value in being bored? Should we use our cellphones less? Explain.

3. **Essential Question: *How is modern technology helpful and harmful to society?*** What has this podcast taught you about the impact of modern technology on society? Discuss with your group.

© Pearson Education, Inc., or its affiliates. All rights reserved.

Research

Assignment

At the end of the podcast, Manoush Zomorodi issues listeners a challenge: "Start observing your own phone behavior, and get ready to rethink it." With your group, choose from these two options:

Create a **multimedia slide show** to showcase interesting findings of the Bored and Brilliant challenge.

Create a **brochure** to promote implementing the Bored and Brilliant challenge in your classroom.

BORED . . . AND BRILLIANT?
A CHALLENGE TO DISCONNECT
FROM YOUR PHONE

Plan the Project To prepare your slide show or brochure, consider the following:

• Consult at least three credible online or print sources. To find online sources you can trust, consider looking for information published on educational or government sites—those with ".edu" or ".gov" at the end of their Web addresses.

• Conduct research to find relevant information, such as statistics and quotations from experts. Take notes on the sources of your information. You need to give credit to any words or ideas that are not your own.

• Assign everyone in your group a specific job, such as researching, writing, editing, presenting, or organizing multimedia.

Internet Research A search engine is a useful tool for finding information on the Internet. However, with millions of websites available, you can get overwhelmed by long lists of results. Use these tips to narrow down your searches. Note that they may not work for all search engines.

• **Minus Operator (–)** Add a minus sign before a term to indicate that you don't want results that include it. For example, typing "Bat -baseball" will give you information about the flying mammals, but not baseball bats. "NOT" may also be used instead of a minus sign.

• **Exact Phrases** If you want to search for an exact phrase, put it in quotation marks. Searching for "judge a book by its cover" will give you results that have those exact words, but will leave out other sites.

Present and Discuss Share your multimedia slide show or brochure with the rest of the class. Give your classmates an opportunity to ask questions, and support your answers with evidence from both your research and the podcast.

EVIDENCE LOG

Before moving on to a new selection, go to your Evidence Log and record what you learned from "Bored . . . and Brilliant? A Challenge to Disconnect From Your Phone."

STANDARDS

Writing
• Write informative/explanatory texts to examine a topic and convey ideas, concepts, and information through the selection, organization, and analysis of relevant content.
• Gather relevant information from multiple print and digital sources; assess the credibility of each source; and quote or paraphrase the data and conclusions of others while avoiding plagiarism and providing basic bibliographic information for sources.

Speaking and Listening
Include multimedia components and visual displays in presentations to clarify information.

© Pearson Education, Inc., or its affiliates. All rights reserved.

Research

If groups have trouble deciding which research option to choose, encourage them to consider which option plays to their group's strengths the most. For example, if the group is tech savvy, the multimedia slide show might be preferable. If they are talented writers and artists, creating a brochure might be the better option.

Plan the Project Ensure that every student has been assigned a specific role. Emphasize the importance of citing sources. Explain that direct quotations must be enclosed in quotation marks. Add that if students paraphrase someone else's ideas or write them in their own words, they still need to give credit to that person.

Present and Discuss Remind students that all group members should participate in answering questions from the audience, even if they are not one of the presenters. For more support, see **Research: Multimedia Slide Show, Brochure.**

Evidence Log Support students in completing their Evidence Log. This paced activity will help prepare them for the Performance-Based Assessment at the end of the unit.

FORMATIVE ASSESSMENT

Research

If students have trouble finding credible online sources, **then** help them refine their search terms.

PERSONALIZE FOR LEARNING

Strategic Support

Organizing Research Some groups may have difficulty organizing their research and ideas. Encourage students to make a chart like the one below.

Key Idea	Evidence	Source

In the first column, students should list each of the most important key ideas they find in their research about the Bored and Brilliant challenge. In the second column, they should list at least one piece of evidence for each idea (e.g., statistics, quotations, or anecdotes). In the third column, they should list the source for each piece of evidence. They can then decide how to sequence their ideas and evidence in their slide show or brochure.

FACILITATING

Deliver a Multimedia Presentation

Before groups begin work on their projects, have them clearly differentiate the role each group member will play. Remind groups to consult the schedule for Small-Group Learning to guide their work during the Performance Task.

Students should complete the assignment using presentation software to take advantage of text, graphics, and sound features.

Plan With Your Group

Analyze the Text Remind groups to include evidence from the selection. Point out that some of the selections might have been written to promote a particular viewpoint, so groups should evaluate each selection for credibility and balance.

Gather Evidence and Media Examples
Suggest that groups make a list of specific key words to search for when they look for media examples. If students have trouble coming up with ideas for media, offer some suggestions: for example, charts and graphs showing how often people use different types of technology, cartoons related to technology, video clips of experts talking about the effects of technology. Remind groups to provide citations for each source they use.

SOURCES

- THE FUN THEY HAD
- IS OUR GAIN ALSO OUR LOSS?
- BORED . . . AND BRILLIANT? A CHALLENGE TO DISCONNECT FROM YOUR PHONE

Deliver a Multimedia Presentation

Assignment
You have read about the effects of technology in the selections in this section. Work with your group to develop a **multimedia presentation** that addresses this question:

> Do the benefits of technology outweigh its disadvantages?

Plan With Your Group

Analyze the Text With your group, discuss the selections you have read. Take notes on the effects of technology presented in each selection. Then, determine what each selection suggests about the effects of technology on society: Does technology have mostly positive effects? Or, do the disadvantages outweigh the benefits? Record your ideas in a chart like the one shown.

TITLE	BENEFITS OF TECHNOLOGY	DRAWBACKS OF TECHNOLOGY
The Fun They Had		
Is Our Gain Also Our Loss?		
Bored . . . and Brilliant? A Challenge to Disconnect From Your Phone		

Gather Evidence and Media Examples Scan the selections to record specific examples that support your group's claim. Use reliable print and online source materials to find evidence, such as statistics or quotations from experts, that supports your argument. Then, brainstorm for types of media you can use to illustrate and elaborate on each example. Consider including relevant photographs, illustrations, music, charts, graphs, and video clips. Allow each group member to make suggestions.

STANDARDS

Writing
- Write arguments to support claims with clear reasons and relevant evidence.
  a. Introduce claim(s) and organize the reasons and evidence clearly.
  b. Support claim(s) with clear reasons and relevant evidence, using credible sources and demonstrating an understanding of the topic or text.
- Conduct short research projects to answer a question, drawing on several sources and refocusing the inquiry when appropriate.

260 UNIT 3 • MODERN TECHNOLOGY

© Pearson Education, Inc., or its affiliates. All rights reserved.

AUTHOR'S PERSPECTIVE Ernest Morrell, Ph.D.

Mastering Classroom Talk Complex texts can be intimidating and alien to some students, especially those who have had limited exposure to such texts. However, these same students often show deep critical and analytical skills when considering popular culture. Teachers can use their students' background knowledge of popular culture and their enthusiasm for it to increase motivation and classroom talk, especially debate skills, small-group work, and formal public presentations. Start by incorporating elements of popular culture such as rap and hip-hop, movies, or sports into a traditional unit of study. Place popular culture alongside the other historical/literacy periods covered in the unit so students can use their knowledge of the familiar works as a lens through which to evaluate the new ones. Second, have students evaluate one literary work in the program, such as a poem, alongside a contemporary reference of their choice. This approach helps students gain the understanding and confidence they need to discuss classroom texts and enhance their critical perspectives.

Organize Your Ideas To organize your presentation, first, rank your arguments from least important to most important. Once you have a sense of the arguments you want to make, write an introduction that will capture your audience's attention. Clearly state your position in the introduction. Then, explain the reasons for your position, providing at least two pieces of evidence for each reason. Finally, end with a strong restatement of your position. After you have organized your argument, decide the most effective way to incorporate multimedia components into your presentation.

Rehearse With Your Group

Practice With Your Group Rehearse your presentation with your group, and use this checklist to evaluate the effectiveness of your group's first rehearsal. Then, use the evaluation and these instructions to guide revisions to your presentation.

CONTENT	USE OF MEDIA	PRESENTATION TECHNIQUES
☐ The argument begins with a clearly stated claim. ☐ The argument is supported with strong reasons and evidence.	☐ The multimedia components logically connect to and support the argument. ☐ The multimedia components are well-timed and interesting.	☐ The speaker makes eye contact, and speaks clearly. ☐ The speaker adjusts volume and tone as appropriate.

Fine-Tune the Content If your argument does not begin with a clearly stated claim, revise to make your position clear.

Improve Your Use of Media For each piece of multimedia, ask yourself: *What aspect of the argument does this multimedia component support?*

Brush Up on Your Presentation Techniques Practice delivering your portion of the presentation. Then, practice delivering the entire presentation as a group and use feedback to tighten the presentation so that it has a good pace and rhythm.

Present and Evaluate

When it is your group's turn to present, be prepared to respond to questions and comments from your classmates. As you watch the other groups, consider the strength of their reasons and evidence, as well as their use of multimedia.

© Pearson Education, Inc., or its affiliates. All rights reserved.

≣ STANDARDS
Speaking and Listening
• Delineate a speaker's argument and specific claims, distinguishing claims that are supported by reasons and evidence from claims that are not.
• Present claims and findings, sequencing ideas logically and using pertinent descriptions, facts, and details to accentuate main ideas or themes; use appropriate eye contact, adequate volume, and clear pronunciation.
• Include multimedia components and visual displays in presentations to clarify information.

Performance Task: Present an Argument **261**

Organize Your Ideas Suggest that groups save their most compelling reason for last if they want to leave a strong impression in their audience's minds.

Rehearse With Your Group

Practice With Your Group Suggest that each presenter practice individually before practicing with the group. Recommend that groups time their rehearsals to ensure their presentation fits within the time limit allotted to them.

Fine-Tune the Content Explain to groups that the claim should be a brief, single sentence that clearly states whether or not they think the benefits of technology outweigh the disadvantages of technology.

MAKE IT INTERACTIVE
Suggest that groups video record their rehearsal and then watch it together to see where improvements could be made.

Present and Evaluate

Before beginning the presentations, set the expectations for the audience. You may wish to have students consider these questions as groups present.

• What was the presenting group's claim?
• What were some of the strongest supporting reasons and evidence?
• Which multimedia components best illustrated the claim?
• What presentation skills did this group excel at?

As students provide feedback to the presenting group, remind them to balance constructive criticism and praise.

PERSONALIZE FOR LEARNING

Strategic Support
Formulating Reasons Be prepared to help students synthesize their ideas, reasons, and evidence. Use key words such as *because* and *therefore* as you model sentences for students.

• *I think the benefits of technology outweigh the disadvantages of technology* **because**

technology can connect people who would otherwise never get to know each other.

• *Technology reduces the amount of time people spend in face-to-face communication;* **therefore,** *I think the disadvantages of technology outweigh the benefits.*

OVERVIEW

INDEPENDENT LEARNING

How is modern technology helpful and harmful to society?

Encourage students to think carefully about what they have already learned and what more they want to know about the unit topic of modern technology. This is a key first step to previewing and selecting the text or media they will read or review in Independent Learning.

Independent Learning Strategies

Review the Learning Strategies with students and explain that as they work through Independent Learning they will develop strategies to work on their own.

- Have students watch the video on Independent Learning Strategies.
- A video on this topic is available online in the Professional Development Center.

Students should include any favorite strategies that they might have devised on their own during Whole-Class and Small-Group Learning. For example, for the strategy "Practice what you've learned," students might include:

- Use first-read and close-read strategies to strengthen your understanding.
- After reading, evaluate what evidence from the text helps you clearly understand the topic.

Block Scheduling

Each day in this Pacing Plan represents a 40–50 minute class period. Teachers using block scheduling may combine days to reflect their class schedule. In addition, teachers may revise pacing to differentiate and support core instruction by integrating components and resources as students require.

ESSENTIAL QUESTION:

How is modern technology helpful and harmful to society?

People use and rely on technological devices every day in different ways. In this section, you will complete your study of the impact of modern technology by exploring an additional selection related to the topic. You'll then share what you learn with classmates. To choose a text, follow these steps.

Look Back Think about the selections you have already studied. What more do you want to know about the topic of modern technology?

Look Ahead Preview the texts by reading the descriptions. Which one seems most interesting and appealing to you?

Look Inside Take a few minutes to scan through the text you chose. Choose a different one if this text doesn't meet your needs.

Independent Learning Strategies

Throughout your life, in school, in your community, and in your career, you will need to rely on yourself to learn and work on your own. Review these strategies and the actions you can take to practice them during Independent Learning. Add ideas of your own for each category.

STRATEGY	ACTION PLAN
Create a schedule	• Understand your goals and deadlines • Make a plan for what to do each day. •
Practice what you've learned	• Use first-read and close-read strategies to deepen your understanding. • After you read, evaluate the usefulness of the evidence to help you understand the topic. • Consider the quality and reliability of the source. •
Take notes	• Record important ideas and information. • Review your notes before preparing to share with a group. •

© Pearson Education, Inc., or its affiliates. All rights reserved.

SCAN FOR MULTIMEDIA

Pacing Plan:

Unit Introduction — 1 — 2 — 3 (Introduce Whole-Class Learning) — Feathered Friend — 4 — 5 — 6 — 7 — 8 — Teens and Technology Share a Future — 9 — 10 — 11 — The Black Hole of Technology — 12 — 13 — 14 — Media: The Internet of Things — 15 — Performance Task — 16 — 17 — 18

Choose one selection. Selections are available online only.

CONTENTS

 SCAN FOR MULTIMEDIA

Overview: Independent Learning **263**

© Pearson Education, Inc., or its affiliates. All rights reserved.

Contents

Selections Encourage students to scan and preview the selections before choosing the one they would like to read or review. Suggest that they consider the genre and subject matter of each one before making their decision. You can use the information on the following Planning pages to advise students in making their choice.

> Remind students that the selections for Independent Learning are only available in the Interactive Student Edition. Allow students who do not have digital access at home to preview the selections or review the media selection(s) using classroom or computer lab technology. Then either have students print the selection they choose or provide a printout for them.

Performance-Based Assessment Prep

Review Evidence for an Argument Point out to students that collecting evidence during Independent Learning is the last step in completing their Evidence Log. After they finish their independent reading, they will synthesize all the evidence they have compiled in the unit.

The evidence students collect will serve as the primary source of information they will use to complete the writing and oral presentation for the Performance-Based Assessment at the end of the unit.

Introduce
Small-Group
Learning

The Fun They Had

Is Our Gain Also
Our Loss?

Media: Bored...
and Brilliant?
A Challenge to
Disconnect From
Your Phone

Performance
Task

Introduce
Independent
Learning

Independent
Learning

Performance-Based
Assessment

| 19 | 20 | 21 | 22 | 23 | 24 | 25 | 26 | 27 | 28 | 29 | 30 | 31 | 32 | 33 | 34 | 35 | 36 |

INDEPENDENT LEARNING

7-Year-Old Girl Gets New Hand From 3-D Printer

Summary

In the news article "7-Year-Old Girl Gets New Hand From 3-D Printer," reporter John Rogers tells the story of a girl who gets a prosthetic to replace her missing hand. Faith Lennox lost a hand in her first year of life because of an injury during birth. She has grown up without it. Before the new advances in 3-D printing, making artificial limbs for children was difficult. Most prosthetics are heavy, expensive, and need to be adjusted or replaced as kids grow. But using 3-D printing, it is possible to cheaply and quickly make custom-sized prosthetics. They can even be printed in a child's favorite colors.

Insight

This article shows how two technologies—3-D printing and prosthetics—can interact to make wonderful things possible. It also focuses on a physical need.

Connection to Essential Question

Faith's experience is a strong example of a positive answer to the Essential Question, "How is modern technology helpful and harmful to society?" This article explains one way that technology can help people with disabilities by giving them some increased freedoms.

Connection to Performance-Based Assessment

The Performance-Based Assessment prompt is "Do we rely on technology too much?" Technology can help people with disabilities take on tasks they otherwise could not do. On the other hand, personal help can free them from needing to use technology that *isn't* reliable.

Text Complexity Rubric: 7-Year-Old Girl Gets New Hand From 3-D Printer

Quantitative Measures

Lexile: 860   Text Length: 691 words 28 lines; 14 lines

Qualitative Measures

Knowledge Demands ①—②—**❸**—④—⑤	Selection is centered around situations and experiences that are not common to most readers. However, experiences of amputation and prosthetic limbs are explained in everyday, practical terms.
Structure ①—**❷**—③—④—⑤	Ideas are organized clearly. Connection between ideas is clear. Multiple examples are given to explain all ideas.
Language Conventionality and Clarity ①—②—**❸**—④—⑤	Language is clear, straightforward, and explicit. Some sentences are long or have complex construction; vocabulary is mostly familiar, but some more difficult words are used.
Levels of Meaning/Purpose ①—**❷**—③—④—⑤	Purpose of article is clear, explicit, and narrowly focused. Details and examples help to illustrate the concepts that are presented.

Screen Time Can Mess With the Body's "Clock"

SELECTION RESOURCES

- First-Read Guide: Nonfiction
- Close-Read Guide: Nonfiction
- Screen Time Can Mess With the Body's "Clock": Text Questions
- Audio Summaries
- Selection Audio
- Selection Test

Summary

In the news article "Screen Time Can Mess With the Body's 'Clock,'" reporter Andrew Bridges explores how screens from smartphones or other devices can affect sleep. The body has internal systems that regulate when we get hungry, when we sleep, and when we wake up. Daylight regulates this internal clock. But now that artificial light is so common, that clock is easy to disrupt. A research study compared people who read from a tablet screen before going to bed with people who read from a book. The people who read from screens took longer to fall asleep, longer to become alert after waking up, and felt more tired the next day.

Insight

This selection discusses a downside of technology that might surprise people. However, it is evenhanded, and notes that any bright artificial light—not just tablets—could have the same effect.

Connection to Essential Question

This article presents information to support a negative response to the Essential Question, "How is modern technology helpful and harmful to society?" The study the article cites shows how screens can disrupt sleep and thus make people tired, in a way that books don't.

Connection to Performance-Based Assessment

Students may notice that the article emphasizes the challenges of relying on technology. The prompt is "Do we rely on technology too much?" New tech can have surprising and hard-to-notice disadvantages. Too much use of smartphones and new technologies may lead to health problems and actually reduce quality of life.

Text Complexity Rubric: Screen Time Can Mess With the Body's "Clock"

Quantitative Measures

Lexile: 980   Text Length: 702 words

Qualitative Measures

Knowledge Demands ①—②—**❸**—④—⑤	Selection is centered around the everyday experiences of sleep and using technology, but also includes research methods and details of experiments that will be less familiar.
Structure ①—**❷**—③—④—⑤	Organization of ideas is clear, logical, and sequential. Text is broken up by inclusion of quotations by authors and researchers.
Language Conventionality and Clarity ①—②—**❸**—④—⑤	Language is clear and concrete. Sentences have mostly simple construction. Selection contains some academic and subject specific vocabulary.
Levels of Meaning/Purpose ①—**❷**—③—④—⑤	Purpose and main idea of article are clear and explicit. Main idea is supported by detailed examples.

All Watched Over by Machines of Loving Grace • Sonnet, without Salmon

SELECTION RESOURCES

📄 First-Read Guide: Poetry

📄 Close-Read Guide: Poetry

📄 All Watched Over by Machines of Loving Grace • Sonnet, without Salmon: Text Questions

🔊 Audio Summaries

🔊 Selection Audio

☑️ 📄 Selection Test

Summary

Richard Brautigan's poem "All Watched Over by Machines of Loving Grace" describes the environment that the speaker would love to see. His natural scenes are green and lush but include technology, people, and animals harmoniously joined together.

Sherman Alexie's "Sonnet, without Salmon" is a poem that resembles a list. The speaker reflects on his grandmother and her zest for life. He explains how a dam caused a river to become empty of salmon and notes that the electricity was still valuable. Finally, the speaker describes seeing a couple in a cafe communicate by cell phone instead of face to face.

Insight

These two poems examine how technology can interact with nature. Brautigan lays out an idyllic, science-fiction vision of returning to simple lives by integrating the two. Alexie's poem is more realistic and much more jaded.

Connection to Essential Question

Together, these poems present two answers to the Essential Question, "How is modern technology helpful and harmful to society?" Students may say that Brautigan's poem explores the ways technology can create harmony and watch over us. Alexie's poem suggests technology can also alienate us from each other, and destroy the natural world.

Connection to Performance-Based Assessment

The prompt is "Do we rely on technology too much?" Brautigan envisions a future where not just humanity but perhaps all of life relies on technology. Alexie, on the other hand, is more cautious about the costs of technology's benefits.

Text Complexity Rubric: All Watched Over by Machines of Loving Grace • Sonnet, without Salmon

Quantitative Measures

Lexile: NP; NP   Text Length: 28 lines; 14 lines

Qualitative Measures	
Knowledge Demands ①—**②**—③—④—⑤	For "All Watched Over . . ." no prior knowledge is necessary other than the idea of ecology. For "Sonnet, without Salmon," reader needs some understanding of sonnet form to interpret the meaning of the title.
Structure ①—②—**③**—④—⑤	"All Watched Over . . ." has 3 stanzas of the same structure and meter, but no regular rhymes. "Sonnet, without Salmon" is in free verse, numbered lines, in stream of consciousness.
Language Conventionality and Clarity ①—②—**③**—④—⑤	Both poems have descriptive but concrete language, with some figurative imagery; there is a mix of phrases and complete sentences in both poems. Vocabulary is mostly on-level.
Levels of Meaning/Purpose ①—②—③—**④**—⑤	Both poems have multiple levels of meaning, with different interpretations possible. Figurative language is used in both poems, with opportunities for ironic interpretation.

Teen Researchers Defend Media Multitasking

SELECTION RESOURCES

- First-Read Guide: Nonfiction
- Close-Read Guide: Nonfiction
- Teen Researchers Defend Media Multitasking: Text Questions
- Audio Summaries
- Selection Audio
- Selection Test

Summary

The news article "Teen Researchers Defend Media Multitasking" by Sumathi Reddy is about a study two high school students did on the multitasking habits of 400 of their peers. The teenagers decided to conduct this study because they wanted to see whether teenagers who had grown up doing homework, listening to music, and texting were better at multitasking than other people. The researchers found that while most of the people they studied work better when they focus on one thing at a time, a smaller number of people worked better when they multitasked. It was surprising to find that any significant number of persons did better when they multitasked. This is because most research has found that even people who consider themselves good multitaskers perform worse when they do several things at a time.

Insight

Multitasking is *usually* a bad idea, but some people have different learning styles. It is worth considering how modern technology affects the way we study and what distracts us. The article suggests that the brains of "digital natives" may respond differently than those of people who were not always exposed to so many screens.

Connection to Essential Question

This article asks whether different generations may have different responses to the Essential Question: "How is modern technology helpful and harmful to society?" The urge to multitask brought on by modern technology clearly makes things harder for most people, but may help some.

Connection to Performance-Based Assessment

Students may find strong evidence to help them respond to the prompt: "Do we rely on technology too much?" They may argue that it is easy to think that they are doing a lot of useful work when toggling among many activities. However, some may end up working much less efficiently than if they did one thing at a time.

Text Complexity Rubric: Teen Researchers Defend Media Multitasking

Quantitative Measures

Lexile: 1370   Text Length: 1,150 words

Qualitative Measures

Knowledge Demands ①—②—❸—④—⑤	Though selection addresses common experience of multitasking, it focuses more on the research. Some references to brain research will be unfamiliar. Some understanding of research methods is helpful.
Structure ①—②—❸—④—⑤	Text of this selection is dense and filled with a lot of information. However, organization is very clear and logical. Ideas are connected sequentially. Quotations of researchers help to break up the text.
Language Conventionality and Clarity ①—②—③—❹—⑤	Selection contains a lot of highly complex and academic language. Sentences are very lengthy, containing multiple ideas and clauses. Vocabulary is academic, and includes subject specific words associated with brain research.
Levels of Meaning/Purpose ①—②—❸—④—⑤	Purpose of text is clear, concrete, and straightforward. Main concepts are presented and backed up by multiple detailed examples.

MY NOTES

ADVISING

You may wish to direct students to use the generic **First-Read** and **Close-Read Guides** in the Print Student Edition. Alternatively, you may wish to print copies of the genre-specific **First-Read** and **Close-Read Guides** for students. These are available online in the Interactive Student Edition or Unit Resources. 📄

⬤ FIRST READ

Students should perform the steps of the first read independently.

NOTICE: Students should focus on the basic elements of the text to ensure they understand what is happening.

ANNOTATE: Students should mark any passages they wish to revisit during their close read.

CONNECT: Students should increase their understanding by connecting what they've read to other texts or personal experiences.

RESPOND: Students will write a summary to demonstrate their understanding.

   Point out to students that while they will always complete the Respond step at the end of the first read, the other steps will probably happen somewhat concurrently. Remind students that they will revisit their first-read annotations during the close read.

> After students have completed the First-Read Guide, you may wish to assign the Text Questions for the selection that are available in the Interactive Teacher's Edition.

Anchor Standards

In the first two sections of the unit, students worked with the whole class and in small groups to gain topical knowledge and greater understanding of the skills required by the anchor standards. In this section, they are asked to work independently, applying what they have learned and demonstrating increased readiness for college and career.

👤 INDEPENDENT LEARNING

First-Read Guide

🔧 **Tool Kit**
First-Read Guide and
Model Annotation

Use this page to record your first-read ideas.

Selection Title: _____

NOTICE new information or ideas you learn about the unit topic as you first read this text.

ANNOTATE by marking vocabulary and key passages you want to revisit.

First Read

CONNECT ideas within the selection to other knowledge and the selections you have read.

RESPOND by writing a brief summary of the selection.

▤ STANDARD

Reading Read and comprehend complex literary and informational texts independently and proficiently.

264 UNIT 3 • MODERN TECHNOLOGY

© Pearson Education, Inc., or its affiliates. All rights reserved.

PERSONALIZE FOR LEARNING

Strategic Support

Text Connections To help students make connections to the text, remind them that ideas in a text may spark memories in readers. The memories may be connected to real-life experiences or something the student previously read or discovered through media. Point out that these connections tap into what students already

know. They make a text interesting and often help readers better understand what the text means.

To pursue and support the text connections approach, ask students to annotate passages that trigger memories and connections for them. Students can organize their ideas in a chart. One

column ("The text") should show annotated passages, enclosed in quotation marks. In the other column ("My connection"), students can use their own words to describe the connection they made to the text. Students can then use this chart to complete the First-Read Guide.

Close-Read Guide

Use this page to record your first-read ideas.

🔧 **Tool Kit**
Close-Read Guide and
Model Annotation

Selection Title: _____

Close Read the Text

Revisit sections of the text you marked during your first read. Read these sections closely and **annotate** what you notice. Ask yourself **questions** about the text. What can you **conclude**? Write down your ideas.

Analyze the Text

Think about the author's choices of patterns, structure, techniques, and ideas included in the text. Select one and record your thoughts about what this choice conveys.

QuickWrite

Pick a paragraph from the text that grabbed your interest. Explain the power of this passage.

© Pearson Education, Inc., or its affiliates. All rights reserved.

▤ STANDARD

Reading Read and comprehend complex literary and informational texts independently and proficiently.

Overview: Independent Learning **265**

CLOSE READ

Students should begin their close read by revisiting the annotations they made during their first read. Then, students should analyze one of the author's choices regarding the following elements:

- **patterns,** such as repetition or parallelism
- **structure,** such as cause-and-effect or problem-solution
- **techniques,** such as description or dialogue
- **ideas,** such as the author's main idea or claim

MAKE IT INTERACTIVE
Group students according to the selection they have chosen. Then, have students meet to discuss the selection in depth. Their discussions should be guided by their insights and questions.

PERSONALIZE FOR LEARNING

Strategic Support

Analyze the Text Help students complete the Analyze the Text section of the Close-Read Guide. Remind students to study the way that a writer addresses a topic. Suggest that students identify writing-related annotations with these codes:

- **WP:** a writing pattern that is interesting or functional. Remind students to look for word

choice, sentence length, or rhythms in the writing.

- **WS:** writing structures that support the genre. For example, students might note the introduction or conclusion, the claims or main ideas, or the key parts of a plot.
- **L:** literary elements or techniques that bring out the art in the writing. Remind students to

look for figurative language or other devices that reflect the author's style.

- **I:** Ideas that the author addresses. Ask students to think about the message of the writing.

Once students identify a part of the text, they can then focus on thinking about how that section contributes to the whole.

Independent Learning **265**

Share Your Independent Learning

Prepare to Share

Explain to students that sharing what they learned from their Independent Learning selection provides classmates who read a different selection with an opportunity to consider the text as a source of evidence during the Performance-Based Assessment. As students prepare to share, remind them to highlight how their selection contributed to their knowledge of the concept of technology as well as how the selection connects to the question *Do we rely on technology too much?*

Learn From Your Classmates

As students discuss the Independent Learning selections, direct them to take particular note of how their classmates' chosen selections align with their current position on the Performance-Based Assessment question.

Reflect

Students may want to add their reflection to their Evidence Log, particularly if their insight relates to a specific selection from the unit.

MAKE IT INTERACTIVE

Have students create posters featuring the most important sentences or ideas that came out of their discussions and reflections. Conduct a gallery walk and invite students to compare and contrast the insights their classmates generated.

Evidence Log Support students in completing their Evidence Log. This paced activity will help prepare them for the Performance-Based Assessment at the end of the unit.

🖉 EVIDENCE LOG

Go to your Evidence Log and record what you learned from the text you read.

Share Your Independent Learning

Prepare to Share

How is modern technology helpful or harmful to society?

Even if you read something independently, your understanding continues to grow when you share what you have learned with others. Reflect on the text you explored independently, and write notes about its connection to the unit. In your notes, consider why this text belongs in this unit.

Learn From Your Classmates

💬 **Discuss It** Share your ideas about the text that you explored on your own. As you talk with your classmates, jot down ideas that you learn from them.

Reflect

Review your notes, and mark the most important insight you gained from these writing and discussion activities. Explain how this idea adds to your understanding of the impact of modern technology.

© Pearson Education, Inc., or its affiliates. All rights reserved.

AUTHOR'S PERSPECTIVE   Ernest Morrell, Ph.D.

Preparing Students to Be Powerful Speakers Use these suggestions to help students develop the ability to speak confidently in large discussions or presentations:

1. To help students overcome their fear of public speaking, have them visualize success, practice and get feedback on their speech, and exercise briefly before the speech to release stress.

2. Emphasize the importance of speaking loudly and clearly when presenting to the class. The farther away a listener is, the louder a speaker must talk to be heard clearly. Also have students practice speaking with clarity and articulation, paying special attention to not slurring contractions, reversing sounds, omitting letters, and adding letters.

3. As students share in whole groups, remind them to listen carefully and fully before responding, take notes while listening so they can respond on point, and speak with courtesy and respect. They may also wish to draft points for a response quickly before speaking.

4. To field questions, tell students to repeat the question before answering it, as this allows a few seconds to think about a response as well as make sure that everyone hears the question.

Review Evidence for an Argument

At the beginning of this unit you discussed the following statement with your classmates:

> Do we rely on technology too much?

☑ EVIDENCE LOG

Review your Evidence Log and your QuickWrite from the beginning of the unit, and use your own knowledge. Has your position changed?

☐ YES	☐ NO
Identify at least three pieces of evidence that convinced you to change your mind.	Identify at least three pieces of evidence that supported your initial position.
1.	1.
2.	2.
3.	3.

State your position now: _____
_____
_____

Identify a possible counterargument: _____
_____
_____

Evaluate the Strength of Your Evidence Consider your argument. Do you have enough evidence to support your claim? Do you have enough evidence to address a counterargument? If not, make a plan.

☐ Do more research   ☐ Talk with my classmates

☐ Reread a selection   ☐ Ask an expert

☰ STANDARDS
Writing
Write arguments to support claims with clear reasons and relevant evidence.
a. Introduce claim(s) and organize the reasons and evidence clearly.

© Pearson Education, Inc., or its affiliates. All rights reserved.

Review Evidence for an Argument

Evidence Log Students should understand that their position on an issue could evolve as they learn more about the subject and are exposed to additional points of view. Point out that just because they took an initial position on the question *Do we rely on technology too much?* doesn't mean that their position can't change after careful consideration of their learning and evidence.

Evaluate the Strength of Your Evidence

Remind students that there are many different types of evidence they can use to support their argument, including:

- facts
- numbers
- examples

In addition to ensuring they have enough evidence to support their claim and address counterclaims, students should evaluate the reliability of their evidence. Discuss the characteristics that make evidence credible:

- good sources, including government, educational, and professional organizations
- credibility of references and confirmation provided by the source of the evidence

Writing to Sources: Argument

Students should complete the Performance-Based Assessment independently, with little to no input or feedback during the process. Students should use word processing software to take advantage of editing tools and features.

Prior to beginning the Assessment, ask students to think about ways we depend on technology in our everyday lives.

Review the Elements of Effective Argument

Students can review the work they did earlier in the unit as they complete the Performance-Based Assessment. They may also consult other resources such as:

- the elements of an effective argument, including language, tone, and grammar, as well as how to organize an argument, available in Whole-Class Learning
- their Evidence Log
- their Word Network

Although students will use evidence from unit selections for their argument, they may need to collect additional evidence, including facts, statistics, anecdotes, quotations from authorities, and examples.

SOURCES

- WHOLE-CLASS SELECTIONS
- SMALL-GROUP SELECTIONS
- INDEPENDENT-LEARNING SELECTION

🔧 WORD NETWORK

As you write and revise your essay, use your Word Network to help vary your word choices.

⁝ STANDARDS

Writing
- Write arguments to support claims with clear reasons and relevant evidence.
- Draw evidence from literary or informational texts to support analysis, reflection, and research.
  a. Apply *grade 6 Reading standards* to literature.
  b. Apply *grade 6 Reading standards* to literary nonfiction.
- Write routinely over extended time frames and shorter time frames for a range of discipline-specific tasks, purposes, and audiences.

PART 1
Writing to Sources: Argument

In this unit, you read, watched, and listened to selections about modern technology. These texts acknowledged the benefits of technology, but they also address the dangers of being dependent on and consumed by technology.

Assignment

Write an **argumentative essay** in which you state and defend a claim in response to the following question:

> Do we rely on technology too much?

Use convincing evidence from at least three of the selections that you read in this unit to support your claim. Support your ideas with strong reasons and relevant evidence. Organize your ideas effectively so that your argument is easy to follow. Establish and maintain a formal tone. Include a conclusion that clearly relates to the main idea you expressed.

Reread the Assignment Review the assignment to be sure you fully understand it. The assignment may refer to some of the academic words presented at the beginning of the unit. Be sure you understand each of the words given here to complete the assignment correctly.

convince	certain	sufficient
declare	various	

Review the Elements of Effective Argument Before you begin writing, read the Argument Rubric. Once you have completed your first draft, check it against the rubric. If one or more of the elements is missing or not as strong as it could be, revise your essay to add or strengthen that part.

© Pearson Education, Inc., or its affiliates. All rights reserved.

ESSENTIAL QUESTION: How is modern technology helpful and harmful to society?

DIGITAL
PERSPECTIVES

Argument Rubric

	Focus and Organization	Evidence and Elaboration	Conventions
4	The introduction is engaging and states the claim in a compelling way. The claim is supported by clear reasons and relevant evidence, and opposing claims are addressed. Reasons and evidence are logically organized so that the argument is easy to follow. The conclusion clearly follows from the argument presented.	Sources are credible and accurate. The argument demonstrates an understanding of the topic. The tone of the argument is formal and objective.	The argument correctly uses standard English conventions of usage and mechanics.
3	The introduction is somewhat engaging and states the claim clearly. The claim is supported by reasons and evidence and opposing claims are acknowledged. Reasons and evidence are organized so that the argument can be followed. The conclusion mostly follows from the argument presented.	Sources are mostly credible and accurate. The argument mostly demonstrates an understanding of the topic. The tone of the argument is mostly formal and objective.	The argument mostly demonstrates accuracy in standard English conventions of usage and mechanics.
2	The introduction states the claim. The claim is supported by some reasons and evidence, and opposing claims may be briefly acknowledged. Reasons and evidence are organized somewhat logically. The conclusion somewhat follows from the argument presented.	Some sources are credible. The argument somewhat demonstrates an understanding of the topic. The tone of the argument is occasionally formal and objective.	The argument demonstrates some accuracy in standard English conventions of usage and mechanics.
1	The claim is not clearly stated. The claim is not supported by reasons and evidence, and opposing claims are not addressed. Reasons and evidence are disorganized and the argument is difficult to follow. The conclusion does not follow from the argument presented.	There is little or no credible evidence. The argument does not demonstrate an understanding of the topic. The tone of the argument is informal.	The argument contains mistakes in standard English conventions of usage and mechanics.

© Pearson Education, Inc., or its affiliates. All rights reserved.

Argument Rubric

As you review the Argument Rubric with students, remind them that the rubric is a resource that can guide their revisions. Students should pay particular attention to the differences between an argument that contains all of the required elements (a score of 3) and one that is compelling, well-organized, and thoroughly supported by clear reasons and relevant evidence (a score of 4).

ASSESSING

Speaking and Listening: Oral Presentation

Point out that students should not simply repeat the claims and reasons they mark in their written arguments. They should decide how to use presentation techniques to make each mention stand out.

Remind students that the effectiveness of an oral argument relies on how the speaker establishes credibility with his or her audience. If a speaker comes across as confident and authoritative, it will be easier for the audience to give credence to the speaker's presentation.

Review the Rubric As you review the Oral Presentation Rubric with students, remind them that it is a valuable tool that can help them plan their presentation. They should strive to include all of the criteria required to achieve a score of 3. Draw their attention to some of the subtle differences between scores of 2 and 3.

 PERFORMANCE-BASED ASSESSMENT

PART 2
Speaking and Listening: Oral Presentation

> **Assignment**
> After completing the final draft of your argument, use it as the foundation for a brief **oral presentation.**

Do not simply read your argument aloud. Take the following steps to make your presentation lively and engaging.

- Reread your argument and mark the claims and reasons from your introduction, body paragraphs, and conclusion. Refer to the annotations to guide your presentation.
- Use appropriate eye contact. Make sure to speak loudly enough for people to hear you and pronounce words clearly.
- Deliver your argument with confidence.

Review the Rubric Before you deliver your presentation, check your plans against this rubric. If one or more of the elements is missing or not as strong as it could be, revise your presentation.

STANDARDS

Speaking and Listening
- Present claims and findings, sequencing ideas logically and using pertinent descriptions, facts, and details to accentuate main ideas or themes; use appropriate eye contact, adequate volume, and clear pronunciation.
- Include multimedia components and visual displays in presentations to clarify information.

	Content	Organization	Presentation Techniques
3	The introduction is engaging and establishes the claim in a convincing way.	The speaker uses time effectively, spending the right amount on each part.	The speaker maintains appropriate eye contact and speaks clearly and with adequate volume.
	The presentation includes clear reasons and relevant evidence to support the claim.	Ideas progress logically, with clear transitions so that the argument is easy to follow.	The speaker presents the argument with energy and strong conviction.
	The conclusion follows from and restates the claim.		
2	The introduction partially establishes a claim.	The speaker uses time somewhat effectively, spending the right amount of time on most parts.	The speaker sometimes maintains appropriate eye contact and speaks somewhat clearly and with adequate volume.
	The presentation includes some clear reasons and relevant to support the claim.	Ideas progress logically, with some transitions between ideas. Listeners can mostly follow the speaker's argument.	The speaker presents with some energy and confidence.
	The conclusion restates some important information about the claim.		
1	The introduction does not clearly state a claim.	The speaker does not use time effectively and focuses too much time on some parts and too little on others.	The speaker does not maintain appropriate eye contact or speak clearly with adequate volume.
	The presentation does not include reasons or evidence to support a claim.	Ideas do not progress logically. Listeners have trouble following the argument.	The speaker's argument lacks energy or confidence.
	The conclusion does not restate important information about a claim.		

© Pearson Education, Inc., or its affiliates. All rights reserved.

DIGITAL PERSPECTIVES

Preparing for the Assignment To help students understand what an effective oral argument looks and sounds like, encourage students to look for videos on the Internet of people presenting arguments. After previewing all the video clips, choose one or two effective arguments and one or two ineffective arguments to play for the whole class. Have students discuss which techniques worked well and which didn't in each of the clips. Finally, suggest that students record themselves practicing their arguments so that they can practice incorporating some of the techniques from the videos they watched.

Reflect on the Unit

Now that you've completed the unit, take a few moments to reflect on your learning.

Reflect on the Unit Goals

Look back at the goals at the beginning of the unit. Use a different colored pen to rate yourself again. Think about readings and activities that contributed the most to the growth of your understanding. Record your thoughts.

Reflect on the Learning Strategies

Discuss It Write a reflection on whether you were able to improve your learning based on your Action Plans. Think about what worked, what didn't, and what you might do to keep working on these strategies. Record your ideas before a class discussion.

Reflect on the Text

Choose a selection that you found challenging, and explain what made it difficult.

Describe something that surprised you about a text in the unit.

Which activity taught you the most about the impacts of modern technology on society? What did you learn?

SCAN FOR MULTIMEDIA

Reflect on the Unit ▶

- Have students watch the video on Reflecting on Your Learning.
- A video on this topic is available online in the Professional Development Center.

Reflect on the Unit Goals

Students should re-evaluate how well they met the unit goals now that they have completed the unit. You might ask them to provide a written commentary on the goal they made the most progress with as well as the goal they feel warrants continued focus.

Reflect on the Learning Strategies

Discuss It If you want to make this a digital activity, go online and navigate to the Discussion Board. Alternatively, students can share their learning strategies reflections in a class discussion.

Reflect on the Text

Consider having students share their text reflections with one another.

MAKE IT INTERACTIVE
Have each group of students make a 5-minute video summarizing what they learned from the selections in this unit. Encourage students to be creative in their videos. Project each video for the whole class to watch.

Unit Test and Remediation 📄 ☑

After students have completed the Performance-Based Assessment, administer the Unit Test. Based on students' performance on the test, assign the resources as indicated on the Interpretation Guide to remediate. Students who take the test online will be automatically assigned remediation, as warranted by test results.

© Pearson Education, Inc., or its affiliates. All rights reserved.

Imagination

UNIT 4

Jump Start

Engage students in a discussion about the power of imagination by asking them to name a product or device that doesn't exist but that they wish would (regardless of how impossible it might seem), such as a car that lets you fly through the air when there's traffic, a time machine that lets you travel backward or forward in time, or a robot chef that instantly creates any meal you'd like.

Imagination

Ask students what the word *imagination* suggests to them. Point out that they will read texts and watch a video about the power of imagination.

Video ▶

Project the introduction video in class, ask students to open the video in their interactive textbooks, or have students scan the BouncePage icon with their phones to access the video.

Discuss It If you want to make this a digital activity, go online and navigate to the Discussion Board. Alternatively, students can share their responses in a class discussion.

Block Scheduling

Each day in this pacing calendar represents a 40–50 minute class period. Teachers using block scheduling may combine days to reflect their class schedule. In addition, teachers may revise pacing to differentiate and support core instruction by integrating components and resources as students require.

 Pacing Plan

Imagination

What kinds of adventures can you experience when you use your imagination?

Yo Ho Ho and a Rubber Ducky

💬 **Discuss It** Do you think children experience imaginative daydreams more than adults do?

Write your response before sharing your ideas.

272

SCAN FOR MULTIMEDIA

© Pearson Education, Inc., or its affiliates. All rights reserved.

Introduce Whole-Class Learning

Media: *from* The Phantom Tollbooth

Performance Task

Unit Introduction

The Phantom Tollbooth, Act I

The Phantom Tollbooth, Act II

| 1 | 2 | 3 | 4 | 5 | 6 | 7 | 8 | 9 | 10 | 11 | 12 | 13 | 14 | 15 | 16 | 17 | 18 |

UNIT 4

UNIT INTRODUCTION

ESSENTIAL QUESTION:

Where can imagination lead?

LAUNCH TEXT FICTIONAL NARRATIVE MODEL
The Great Universal Undo

WHOLE-CLASS LEARNING

ANCHOR TEXT: DRAMA
The Phantom Tollbooth, Act I
play by Susan Nanus, based on the book by Norton Juster

ANCHOR TEXT: DRAMA
The Phantom Tollbooth, Act II
play by Susan Nanus, based on the book by Norton Juster

COMPARE

MULTIMEDIA
from The Phantom Tollbooth

PERFORMANCE TASK
WRITING FOCUS:
Write a Short Story

SMALL-GROUP LEARNING

NOVEL EXCERPT
from Alice's Adventures in Wonderland
Lewis Carroll

POETRY
Jabberwocky
from Through the Looking-Glass
Lewis Carroll

▶ MEDIA CONNECTION:
Alice in Wonderland (1983)—Jabberwocky

REFLECTIVE ESSAY
The Importance of Imagination
Esha Chhabra

PERFORMANCE TASK
SPEAKING AND LISTENING FOCUS:
Perform a Fictional Narrative

INDEPENDENT LEARNING

NOVEL EXCERPT
from The Wonderful Wizard of Oz
L. Frank Baum

POETRY COLLECTION
Our Wreath of Rose Buds
Corrinne

Fantasy
Gwendolyn Bennett

NOVEL EXCERPT
The Shah of Blah
from Haroun and the Sea of Stories
Salman Rushdie

SHORT STORY
Prince Francis
Roddy Doyle

PERFORMANCE-BASED ASSESSMENT PREP
Review Notes for a Fictional Narrative

PERFORMANCE-BASED ASSESSMENT

Fictional Narrative: Short Story and Storytelling

PROMPT:
What might happen if a fictional character were to come into the real world?

273

Where can imagination lead?

Introduce the Essential Question and point out that students will respond to related prompts.

- **Whole-Class Learning** *One day in the Kingdom of Wisdom . . .*
- **Small-Group Learning** *When Alice finally gets through the door . . .*
- **Performance-Based Assessment** *What might happen if a fictional character were to come into the real world?*

Using Trade Books

Refer to the Teaching with Trade Books section for suggestions on how to incorporate the following thematically related titles into this unit:

- *Charlie and the Chocolate Factory* by Roald Dahl
- *The Sword and the Circle* by Rosemary Sutcliffe
- *Watership Down* by Richard Adams

Current Perspectives

To increase student engagement, search online for stories about the power of imagination, and invite your students to recommend stories they find. Always preview content before sharing it with your class.

- **News Story: So Elon Musk's Hyperloop Is Actually Getting Kinda Serious** *(Wired 2015)* This article is about Elon Musk's concept of a 745-mph passenger train and the plans to make it a reality.
- **Video: Walter Isaacson: This Is the One Trait All Innovators Share** *(Business Insider)* Explains that influential innovators share the ability to be creative and imaginative.

© Pearson Education, Inc., or its affiliates. All rights reserved.

Introduce Small-Group Learning

Performance Task

Introduce Independent Learning

Performance-Based Assessment

from Alice's Adventures in Wonderland   Jabberwocky   The Importance of Imagination   Independent Learning

| 19 | 20 | 21 | 22 | 23 | 24 | 25 | 26 | 27 | 28 | 29 | 30 | 31 | 32 | 33 | 34 | 35 | 36 |

About the Unit Goals

These unit goals were backward designed from the Performance-Based Assessment at the end of the unit and the Whole-Class and Small-Group Performance Tasks. Students will practice and become proficient in many more standards over the course of this unit.

Unit Goals ▶

Review the goals with students and explain that as they read the selections in this unit, they will improve their skills in reading, writing, research, language, and speaking and listening.

Reading Goals Tell students they will read and evaluate fictional narratives. They will also read reflective essays, poetry, and an interview to better understand the ways writers express ideas.

Writing and Research Goals Tell students that they will learn the elements of fictional narrative writing. Students will write for a number of reasons, including reflecting on experiences, and gathering evidence. They will conduct research to clarify and explore ideas.

Language Goal Tell students that they will develop understanding of combining sentences for variety. They will practice combining sentences for variety in their own writing.

Speaking and Listening Explain to students that they will work to build on one another's ideas, and communicate with one another. They will also learn to incorporate audio, visuals, and text in presentations.

HOME CONNECTION ✉

A Home Connection letter to students' parents or guardians is available in the Interactive Teacher's Edtion. The letter explains what students will be learning in this unit and how they will be assessed.

⬛ STANDARDS

Language
Acquire and use accurately grade-appropriate general academic and domain-specific words and phrases; gather vocabulary knowledge when considering a word or phrase important to comprehension or expression.

Unit Goals

Throughout this unit, you will deepen your understanding of imagination by reading, writing, speaking, listening, and presenting. These goals will help you succeed on the Unit Performance-Based Assessment.

Rate how well you meet these goals right now. You will revisit your ratings later when you reflect on your growth during this unit.

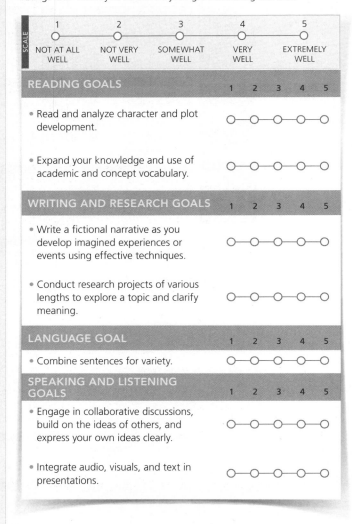

SCALE

	1	2	3	4	5
	NOT AT ALL WELL	NOT VERY WELL	SOMEWHAT WELL	VERY WELL	EXTREMELY WELL

READING GOALS — 1 2 3 4 5

- Read and analyze character and plot development.
- Expand your knowledge and use of academic and concept vocabulary.

WRITING AND RESEARCH GOALS — 1 2 3 4 5

- Write a fictional narrative as you develop imagined experiences or events using effective techniques.
- Conduct research projects of various lengths to explore a topic and clarify meaning.

LANGUAGE GOAL — 1 2 3 4 5

- Combine sentences for variety.

SPEAKING AND LISTENING GOALS — 1 2 3 4 5

- Engage in collaborative discussions, build on the ideas of others, and express your own ideas clearly.
- Integrate audio, visuals, and text in presentations.

SCAN FOR MULTIMEDIA

© Pearson Education, Inc., or its affiliates. All rights reserved.

AUTHOR'S PERSPECTIVE · **Ernest Morrell, Ph.D.**

Taking Responsibility for Learning Teachers can talk to students about becoming motivated learners. Start by having students reflect on things they are good at outside of class, such as sports, music, and video games. Then have students think about how they take responsibility for their own achievement in these areas, such as having the discipline to practice. Help students further understand the value of becoming independent learners by providing tips on how to do so, such as these:

1. **Be self-motivated and persistent.** Don't be discouraged when faced with minor set-backs.

2. **Develop effective time management skills.** Track assignments and deadlines.

3. **Seek help when necessary.** Don't be afraid to get assistance when you need it.

4. **Set realistic goals.** Then plan ways to achieve your goals.

5. **Believe in yourself.** Visualize success. Recognize that you have the ability to soar.

Encourage students to add to this list to help them focus on strategies for taking ownership of their learning.

Academic Vocabulary: Fictional Narrative

Understanding and using academic terms can help you read, write, and speak with precision and clarity. Here are five academic words that will be useful in this unit as you analyze and write fictional narratives.

Complete the chart.

1. Review each word, its root, and the mentor sentences.

2. Use the information and your own knowledge to predict the meaning of each word.

3. For each word, list at least two related words.

4. Refer to the dictionary or other resources if needed.

TIP

FOLLOW THROUGH
Study the words in this chart, and mark them or their forms wherever they appear in the unit.

WORD	MENTOR SENTENCES	PREDICT MEANING	RELATED WORDS
perspective ROOT: **-spec-** "see"	1. When she faces a problem, Lily tries to maintain a positive *perspective*. 2. Sal gained a better *perspective* on the situation by learning more about it.		suspect; inspect
transform ROOT: **-form-** "shape"	1. The clay was soft and easy to *transform* from a lump into the shape of a vase. 2. The caterpillar will *transform* into a butterfly.		
novelty ROOT: **-nov-** "new"	1. Having grown up in the city, riding a horse was a *novelty* for Ben. 2. The shop was full of *novelty* items that tourists would buy.		
consequently ROOT: **-sequ-** "follow"	1. The pothole in the road was fixed, and *consequently* it was much easier to drive. 2. Kayla missed the bus and *consequently* was late for practice.		
inspire ROOT: **-spir-** "breath"	1. The chef tried to *inspire* the students to try out different types of food. 2. I think a day at the museum will *inspire* me to paint again.		

© Pearson Education, Inc., or its affiliates. All rights reserved.

Academic Vocabulary: Fictional Narrative

Introduce the blue academic vocabulary words in the chart on the student page. Point out that the root of each word provides a clue to its meaning. Discuss the mentor sentences to ensure students understand each word's usage. Students should also use the mentor sentences as context to help them predict the meaning of each word. Check that students are able to fill the chart in correctly. Complete pronunciations, parts of speech, and definitions are provided for you. Students are only expected to provide the definition.

Possible responses:

perspective *n.* (pehr SPEHK tihv)
Meaning: a point of view; a way of seeing something
Related words: suspect, inspect
Additional words related to the root -*spec*-: spectacle, spectator, respect, speculate

transform *v.* (trans FAWRM)
Meaning: to change
Related words: transformer, transforming
Additional words related to the root -*form*-: uniform, reform, formula, formulate

novelty *n.* (NOV uhl tee)
Meaning: something new, fresh, or unusual
Related words: novel, novelties
Additional words related to the root -*nov*-: novice, innovate, renovate, novitiate

consequently *adv.* (KON sih kwent lee)
Meaning: as a result
Related words: consequence, consequences, inconsequential
Additional words related to the root -*sequ*-: sequence, consecutive, sequel, subsequent

inspire *v.* (ihn SPY ihr)
Meaning: motivate, push
Related words: inspiration, inspirational
Additional words related to the root -*spir*-: respiration, perspiration, aspirate, aspire, spirit, conspire, conspiracy

---

PERSONALIZE FOR LEARNING

English Language Support
Cognates Many of the academic words have Spanish cognates. Use these cognates with students whose home language is Spanish.
ALL LEVELS

perspective – perspectiva
transform – transformar
novelty – novedad
consequently – consiguente
inspire – inspirar

INTRODUCTION

Purpose of the Launch Text

The Launch Text provides students with a common starting point to address the unit topic. After reading the Launch Text, all students will be able to participate in discussions about imagination.

Lexile: 670 The easier reading level of this selection makes it perfect to assign for homework. Students will need little or no support to understand it.

Additionally, "The Great Universal Undo" provides a writing model for the Performance-Based Assessment students complete at the end of the unit.

Launch Text: Fictional Narrative

Point out the first paragraph of the story, in which the author introduces Alexander, the main character, and his invention, the Great Universal Undo.

Have students pay attention to the structure of the text. They should note the rising action, the climax, and the resolution of the story. They should also pay attention to the dialogue and how it moves the plot along.

Encourage students to read this text on their own and annotate unfamiliar words and sections of text they think are particularly important.

🔊 AUDIO SUMMARIES

Audio summaries of "The Great Universal Undo" are available online in both English and Spanish in the Interactive Teacher's Edition or Unit Resources. Assigning these summaries before students read the Launch Text may help them build additional background knowledge and set a context for their reading.

LAUNCH TEXT | FICTIONAL NARRATIVE

This selection is an example of a **fictional narrative**, a type of writing in which the author tells a story about made-up characters and events. This is the type of writing you will develop in the Performance-Based Assessment at the end of the unit.

As you read, consider how the author makes the characters and situation interesting. Mark the text to help answer this question: How does the author keep the reader interested and make the flow of events clear?

The
Great Universal Undo

NOTES

1   If Alexander Dillahunt wasn't the world's worst typist, he was close. But that was okay. Fixing mistakes on a computer was a snap—especially if you caught them right away. That was the beauty of the Undo, Alexander thought: a tiny backwards arrow at the top of the screen that performed magic, allowing the user to go back to a more perfect, mistake-free moment in time.

2   That's how Alexander Dillahunt got it into his head to create the Universal Undo. The Universal Undo would do nothing short of "taking back" the last thing a person did.

3   Making a working model was simple. All Alexander needed to do was figure out how to take something in 2-D and make it 4-D (skipping over 3-D completely) and then get the whole thing to fit inside his smartphone. Finally, after a few weeks of trial and error, the Universal Undo was ready for a test run.

4   Alexander went into the kitchen and stood in front of the refrigerator. From there he walked to the cupboard. He waited a few seconds, then hit Universal Undo on his smartphone. Presto! Alexander was back at the refrigerator. He walked to the stove. He waited, hit Universal Undo—and there he was, back at the refrigerator again. Action undone!

5   Alexander took his new invention outside. By the traffic lights, he ran into Mrs. Bieberman, who was carrying a bag of groceries and holding the hand of her 3-year-old son Tommy.

© Pearson Education, Inc., or its affiliates. All rights reserved.

SCAN FOR MULTIMEDIA

CROSS-CURRICULAR PERSPECTIVES

Science Point out to students that the premise of the short story is that Alexander's invention allows him to go back in time. Explain that although time travel has long been a popular topic in science fiction, scientific consensus indicates that it is not possible. Suggest that interested students learn more about topics related to time travel, including current theories regarding faster-than-light travel or wormholes. Have them present their findings to the class.

6   "Hello Mrs. Bieberman! Hi Tommy!" Alexander called out. He smiled. "That's a really silly hat you're wearing, Mrs. Bieberman!" Then he tapped his smartphone. If everything worked, his last comment would be Undone.

7   "Hello yourself, Alexander!" exclaimed Mrs. Bieberman.

8   *Good!* thought Alexander. *She hadn't heard it!* Flushed with excitement, he continued. "You know, your little boy looks like a toad." He paused, waiting for a response.

9   "I do *not* not look like a toe!" Tommy wailed and, still blubbering, started to play his video game. Had Alexander tapped Undo—or just imagined it? He couldn't remember.

10   "He can't go long without his game," Mrs. Bieberman said, sighing. "And only three years old." Alexander hadn't started playing video games until he was nine.

11   "I want a cookie!" said Tommy suddenly, tugging at the hem of his mother's skirt. Mrs. Bieberman reached into a bag of cookies and pulled one out. "I'll give you just one, Tommy." Tommy grabbed it and stuffed it in his mouth.

12   "How's your mother?" asked Mrs. Bieberman. "I should call her."

13   Alexander was aware of a *tap tapping* sound.

14   Mrs. Bieberman reached into a bag of cookies and pulled one out. "I'll give you just one, Tommy."

15   Alexander froze. *How could he have missed it?* He'd read all about multiple discovery—the idea that most inventions are made by a number of different people in different places at the same time. *How could he have thought he was the only one?*

16   "'Bye Mrs. Bieberman, Tommy" said Alexander in a shaky voice.

17   Tommy, his mouth crammed with cookie, looked into Alexander's eyes and hit a button on his video game. *Tap, tap-tap.*

18   Mrs. Bieberman reached into a bag of cookies and pulled one out. "I'll give you just one, Tommy." ❧

NOTES

WORD NETWORK FOR IMAGINATION

Vocabulary A Word Network is a collection of words related to a topic. As you read the selections in this unit, identify interesting words related to the idea of imagination and add them to your Word Network. For example, you might begin by adding words from the Launch Text, such as *invention*, *excitement*, and *discovery*. Continue to add words as you complete this unit.

invention

excitement   IMAGINATION

discovery

🔧 **Tool Kit**
Word Network Model

The Great Universal Undo **277**

Word Network for Imagination 🗎

Tell students that they can fill in the Word Network as they read texts in the unit, or they can record the words elsewhere and add them later. Point out to students that people may have personal associations with some words. A word that one student finds is related to the concept of imagination might not be a word another student would pick. However, students should feel free to add any word they personally think is relevant to their Word Network. Each person's Word Network will be unique. If you choose to print the Word Network, distribute it to students at this point so they can use it throughout the rest of the unit.

AUTHOR'S PERSPECTIVE   **Elfrieda Hiebert, Ph.D.**

Words in Complex Texts Reassure students that complex texts will always have some words that they haven't encountered before. This point needs to be reviewed year after year because the texts always get harder and, with harder texts, come more complex words. Share these ideas with students:

• Many words will be familiar, but they may be used in a different way with new topics and meanings.

• Authors choose the more complex words (the rare words) for deliberate effect—not serendipitously—to describe characters and contexts, to develop obstacles or problems, to show ways of solving problems.

Making and reviewing word networks helps students develop multiple words related to a concept, and the multiple meanings or concept applications for words. Also encourage students to study the words in context. Students may wish to use digital tools as they do so.

© Pearson Education, Inc., or its affiliates. All rights reserved.

INTRODUCTION

Summary

Have students read the introductory paragraph. Provide them with tips for writing a summary:

- Write in the present tense.
- Make sure to include the title of the work.
- Be concise: a summary should not be equal in length to the original text.
- If you need to quote the words of the author, use quotation marks.
- Don't put your own opinions, ideas, or interpretations into the summary. The purpose of writing a summary is to accurately represent what the author says, not to provide a critique.

If necessary, students can refer to the Tool Kit for help in understanding the elements of a good summary.

See possible Summary on student page.

Launch Activity

Explain to students that as they work on this unit they will have many opportunities to discuss the topic of imagination. Remind students that there is no right or wrong position, but they should be able to support their positions with well-reasoned arguments and examples from what they have read and analyzed so far in the unit, as well as from their own experiences and their knowledge of history.

Encourage group members to listen to the ideas of their classmates and to build off what others add to the discussion.

Summary

Write a summary of "The Great Universal Undo." A **summary** is a concise, complete, and accurate overview of a text. It should not include a statement of your opinion or an analysis.

Possible response: Alexander is used to making a lot of mistakes while typing on his computer. He has to hit the undo button a lot, to take back errors he makes. And that makes him wonder: what if he could undo things he did out in the world, not just on his computer? He finds a way to do it and starts testing to see how it works. It lets him take back walking somewhere and even take back things he said in conversation. And so, not fearing the consequences of his actions, he acts a little mean.

Launch Activity

Participate in a Group Discussion Consider this statement: **Imagination is more important than knowledge.**

Prepare for the discussion by thinking about the topic.

- What has imagination led people to achieve?
- Do we need imagination to learn about the world?

Decide your position and write down a brief explanation.

☐ Strongly Agree ☐ Agree ☐ Disagree ☐ Strongly Disagree

_____

_____

Form a small group with other students. Then, discuss your responses to the prompt and the questions. When you have finished your conversation, write a summary of the main points you covered. Share your summary with the class.

© Pearson Education, Inc., or its affiliates. All rights reserved.

VOCABULARY DEVELOPMENT

Academic Vocabulary Reinforcement
Students will benefit from additional examples and practice with the academic vocabulary. Reinforce their comprehension with "show-you-know" sentences. The first part of the sentence uses the vocabulary word in an appropriate context. The second part of the sentences—the "show-you-know" part—clarifies the first. Model the strategy with this example for *aspect*:

The class was convinced by one aspect of her argument—that we should be responsible for our actions.

Then give students these sentence prompts and coach them in creating the clarification part.
1. Billy has transformed his bedroom; _____.
   Possible response: he cleaned it thoroughly
2. "This a novelty; _____."
   Possible response: I haven't seen you in the library before.

3. Ms. Lewis didn't like the analogy; _____.
   Possible response: she said it was unfair to compare studying for an exam to working in a coalmine.
4. The resolution came at the end of the meeting; _____
   Possible response: everyone agreed to fund the new club

QuickWrite

Consider class discussions, the video, and the Launch Text as you think about the prompt. Record your first thoughts here.

PROMPT: **What might happen if a fictional character were to come into the real world?**

> **Possible response:** The real world would change in a big way if a fictional character were to arrive. Of course, it depends on the character. If it is a character from a realistic story, that character might change our relationships, our feelings, and our interactions with each other. If it is a character from a fantasy story who has magical powers, our real world would change in different ways: science, nature, and time could be altered!

EVIDENCE LOG FOR IMAGINATION

Review your QuickWrite. Summarize your initial position in one sentence to record in your Evidence Log. Then, record evidence from "The Great Universal Undo" that supports your position.

After each selection, you will continue to use your Evidence Log to record the evidence you gather and the connections you make.

🔧 **Tool Kit**
Evidence Log Model

Title of Text: _____ Date: _____

CONNECTION TO PROMPT	TEXT EVIDENCE/DETAILS	ADDITIONAL NOTES/IDEAS

How does this text change or add to my thinking? Date: _____

SCAN FOR
MULTIMEDIA

QuickWrite

In this QuickWrite, students should present their own response to the prompt based on the material they have read and viewed in the Unit Overview and Introduction. This initial response will help inform their work when they complete the Performance-Based Assessment at the end of the unit. Students should make sure they provide an explanation with examples of how imagination can shape or alter a person's experiences.

See possible QuickWrite on student page.

Evidence Log for Imagination 📄

Students should record their initial thinking in their Evidence Logs along with evidence from "The Great Universal Undo" that supports this thinking.

If you choose to print the Evidence Log, distribute it to students at this point so they can use it throughout the rest of the unit.

> **Performance-Based Assessment: Refining Your Thinking** ▶
> - Have students watch the video on Refining Your Thinking.
> - A video on this topic is available online in the Professional Development Center.

© Pearson Education, Inc., or its affiliates. All rights reserved.

WHOLE-CLASS LEARNING

Where can imagination lead?

Engage students in a discussion about the role that imagination plays in our lives. For example, we use our imagination when we read a book and imagine a setting or character. Imagination gives us the power to leave our lives behind and get immersed in new worlds. During Whole-Class Learning, students will read selections and watch a video about the power of imagination.

Whole-Class Learning Strategies ▶

Review the Learning Strategies with students and explain that as they work through Whole-Class Learning they will develop strategies to work in large-group environments.

- Have students watch the video on Whole-Class Learning Strategies.
- A video on this topic is available online in the Professional Development Center.

You may wish to discuss some action items to add to the chart as a class before students complete it on their own. For example, for "Listen Actively," you might solicit the following from students:

- Take notes and jot down ideas.
- Listen for words or phrases on which the speaker places special emphasis.

Block Scheduling

Each day in this Pacing Plan represents a 40–50 minute class period. Teachers using block scheduling may combine days to reflect their class schedule. In addition, teachers may revise pacing to differentiate and support core instruction by integrating components and resources as students require.

📅 Pacing Plan

OVERVIEW: WHOLE-CLASS LEARNING

ESSENTIAL QUESTION:
Where can imagination lead?

When you use your imagination, the possibilities are endless. You might explore an unusual place or daydream about an exciting activity. But what lessons about yourself and your world did you learn from your imagined experience? You will work with your whole class to explore the concept of imagination. The selections you read will present insights into how people use their sense of imagination.

Whole-Class Learning Strategies

Throughout your life, in school, in your community, and in your career, you will continue to learn and work in large-group environments.

Review these strategies and the actions you can take to practice them as you work with your whole class. Add ideas of your own for each step. Get ready to use these strategies during Whole-Class Learning.

STRATEGY	ACTION PLAN
Listen actively	• Eliminate distractions. For example, put your cellphone away. • Keep your eyes on the speaker. •
Clarify by asking questions	• If you're confused, other people probably are, too. Ask a question to help your whole class. • If you see that you are guessing, ask a question instead. •
Monitor understanding	• Notice what information you already know and be ready to build on it. • Ask for help if you are struggling. •
Interact and share ideas	• Share your ideas and answer questions, even if you are unsure. • Build on the ideas of others by adding details or making a connection. •

SCAN FOR
MULTIMEDIA

© Pearson Education, Inc., or its affiliates. All rights reserved.

Unit Introduction | 1 | 2

Introduce Whole-Class Learning | 3

The Phantom Tollbooth, Act I | 4 | 5 | 6 | 7 | 8

The Phantom Tollbooth, Act II | 9 | 10 | 11 | 12 | 13 | 14

Media: *from* The Phantom Tollbooth | 15

Performance Task | 16 | 17 | 18

WHOLE-CLASS LEARNING

CONTENTS

ANCHOR TEXT: DRAMA

The Phantom Tollbooth, Act I

play by Susan Nanus,

based on the book by Norton Juster

What happens when a mysterious package arrives for a bored young boy named Milo?

COMPARE

ANCHOR TEXT: DRAMA

The Phantom Tollbooth, Act II

play by Susan Nanus,

based on the book by Norton Juster

What new adventures will Milo encounter?

MULTIMEDIA

from The Phantom Tollbooth

Can Milo think of a way to continue his journey?

PERFORMANCE TASK

WRITING FOCUS

Write a Fictional Narrative

The Whole-Class readings focus on one boy's fantastical adventures. After reading the drama and listening to the audio, you will write a short story about fantastical events and characters from your own imagination.

Overview: Whole-Class Learning **281**

© Pearson Education, Inc, or its affiliates. All rights reserved.

Contents

Anchor Texts Preview the anchor texts and media with students to generate interest. Encourage students to discuss other texts they may have read or movies or television shows they may have seen that deal with the power of imagination.

You may wish to conduct a poll to determine which selection students think looks more interesting and discuss the reasons for their preference. Students can return to this poll after they have read the selections to see if their preference changed.

Performance Task

Write a Fictional Narrative Explain to students that after they have finished reading the selections and listening to the audio, they will write a fictional narrative about events and characters from their own imagination. To help them prepare, encourage students to think about the topic as they progress through the selections and as they participate in the Whole-Class Learning experience.

Introduce
Small-Group
Learning

from Alice's Adventures in Wonderland

Jabberwocky

The Importance
of Imagination

Performance
Task

Introduce
Independent
Learning

Performance-
Based
Assessment

Independent
Learning

     19 20 21 22 23 24 25 26 27 28 29 30 31 32 33 34 35 36

The Phantom Tollbooth, Act I

🔊 **AUDIO SUMMARIES**
Audio summaries of *The Phantom Tollbooth*, Act I, are available online in both English and Spanish in the Interactive Teacher's Edition or Unit Resources. Assigning these summaries prior to reading the selection may help students build additional background knowledge and set a context for their first read.

Summary

Based on the book *The Phantom Tollbooth,* this drama was adapted by Susan Nanus. The main character, Milo, begins the story bored and apathetic. When he opens a gift containing a functioning tollbooth and a miniature car, he soon finds himself driving on a road in a strange country. There he meets the Whether Man, almost becomes trapped in the Doldrums, and finds Tock the Watchdog, who accompanies him to Dictionopolis, the city of words. Tock explains that this is the Land of Wisdom, which has been in disorder ever since the Princesses Rhyme and Reason were banished. In Dictionopolis, Milo meets King Azaz, ruler of words, and volunteers to rescue the Princesses from their prison in the Mountains of Ignorance.

Insight

The Phantom Tollbooth uses wordplay and surrealism to present moral and intellectual fables. Treating various ideas, like words and numbers, as objects allows the author to comment on how people use them.

ESSENTIAL QUESTION:
Where can imagination lead?

Connection to Essential Question

In the imaginative setting of *The Phantom Tollbooth,* imagination can lead to a physical realm where ideas and concepts become real. One major theme of the drama is that imagination is necessary to get anywhere in life.

WHOLE-CLASS LEARNING PERFORMANCE TASK
One day in the Kingdom of Wisdom . . .

UNIT PERFORMANCE-BASED ASSESSMENT
What might happen if a fictional character were to come into the real world?

Connection to Performance Tasks

Whole-Class Learning Performance Task This selection introduces the episodic structure of *The Phantom Tollbooth,* and some of the characters who inhabit the Land of Wisdom. A knowledge of the setting and its rules will help students with the prompt.

Unit Performance-Based Assessment In this selection Milo is thrown headlong into a strange world in which he learns about himself and about the power of thinking. The play's storyline may help students consider how they will address the prompt, which requires them to write about a reversed situation.

LESSON RESOURCES

	Making Meaning	Language Development
Lesson	**First Read** **Close Read** **Analyze the Text** **Analyze Craft and Structure**	**Concept Vocabulary** **Word Study** **Conventions**
Instructional Standards	**RL.3** Describe how a particular story's or drama's plot . . . **RL.5** Analyze how a particular sentence, chapter, scene, or stanza . . . **RL.6** Explain how an author develops . . . **RL.10** By the end of the year, read and comprehend literature . . .	**L.1** Demonstrate command of the conventions . . . **L.5** Demonstrate understanding of figurative language . . . **L.5.c** Distinguish among the connotations of words . . .

▶ STUDENT RESOURCES

Available online in the Interactive Student Edition or Unit Resources	🔊 Selection Audio 📄 First-Read Guide: Drama 📄 Close-Read Guide: Drama	📄 Word Network 📄 Evidence Log

▶ TEACHER RESOURCES

Selection Resources Available online in the Interactive Teacher's Edition or Unit Resources	🔊 Audio Summaries ✏️ Annotation Highlights 💬 EL Highlights 📄 Analyze Craft and Structure: Dramatic Structures	📄 Concept Vocabulary and Word Study 📄 English Language Support Lesson: Denotation and Nuance 📄 Conventions: Sentence Parts and Types
Reteach/Practice (RP) Available online in the Interactive Teacher's Edition or Unit Resources	📄 Analyze Craft and Structure: Dramatic Structures (RP)	📄 Word Study: Denotation and Nuance (RP) 📄 Conventions: Sentence Parts and Types (RP)
Assessment Available online in Assessments	📄 ☑ Selection Test	
My Resources	📄 A Unit 4 Answer Key is available online and in the Interactive Teacher's Edition.	

Reading Support

Text Complexity Rubric: *The Phantom Tollbooth*, Act I

Quantitative Measures

Lexile: NP   Text Length: 6,443 words

Qualitative Measures

Knowledge Demands ①—②—**❸**—④—⑤	The selection contains imaginary kingdoms. Characters have descriptive names. Students will encounter humorous writing.
Structure ①—②—③—**❹**—⑤	The selection is in play format. It contains dialogue, stage directions, and descriptions of sets.
Language Conventionality and Clarity ①—②—③—**❹**—⑤	The selection contains dialogue, some challenging vocabulary, wordplay, and long, complex sentences.
Levels of Meaning/Purpose ①—②—**❸**—④—⑤	The concept of the selection is accessible. It explores the value of time and hard work.

DECIDE AND PLAN

English Language Support

Provide English learners with support for structure and language as they read the selection.

Structure If students have difficulty with the format, discuss with them how the playwright uses brackets, italics, boldface, and capital letters to indicate setting and dialogue.

Language To help students understand some of the settings and what they represent, review the suffix: *-poli* (from *Dictionopolis* and *Digitopolis*). Explain that it means "city." Point out how *dict* relates to words, as in "dictionary," so that you can lead them to the idea that *Dictionopolis* is a city of words. Repeat for *Digitopolis*: a city of numbers.

Strategic Support

Provide students with strategic support to ensure that they can successfully read the text.

Structure If students have difficulty understanding the purpose of stage directions, discuss how these features support the dialogue. For instance, review how the Lethargarians are always yawning and falling asleep in the stage directions.

Meaning Discuss the use of puns and other word play with students. Cite how double-meaning words are used throughout the discussion of food at the half-bakery (paragraphs 220–235).

Challenge

Provide students who need to be challenged with ideas for how they can go beyond a simple interpretation of the text.

Text Analysis Assign students to small groups to discuss one of the characters. Have them choose a setting in which the character appears and then have them discuss how to create a set for the stage. Ask students to plan for props that should appear with them on stage.

Written Response Discuss the character names in the selection. Ask students to come up with a list of silly character names, giving them official titles. Ask them to describe their characters' appearances and idiosyncrasies.

TEACH

Read and Respond

Have students do their first read of the selection. Then have them complete their close read. Finally, work with them on the Making Meaning and Language Development activities.

Standards Support Through Teaching and Learning Cycle

IDENTIFY NEEDS

Analyze results of the Beginning-of-Year Assessment, focusing on the items relating to Unit 4. Also take into consideration student performance to this point and your observations of where particular students struggle.

ANALYZE AND REVISE

- Analyze student work for evidence of student learning.
- Identify whether or not students have met the expectations in the standards.
- Identify implications for future instruction.

TEACH

Implement the planned lesson, and gather evidence of student learning.

DECIDE AND PLAN

- If students have performed poorly on items matching these standards, then provide selection scaffolds before assigning them the on-level lesson provided in the Student Edition.
- If students have done well on the Beginning-of-Year Assessment, then challenge them to keep progressing and learning by giving them opportunities to practice the skills in depth.
- Use the Selection Resources listed on the Planning pages for *The Phantom Tollbooth*, Act I, to help students continually improve their ability to master the standards.

Instructional Standards: *The Phantom Tollbooth*, Act I

	Catching Up	This Year	Looking Forward
Reading	You may wish to administer the **Analyze Craft and Structure: Dramatic Structures (RP)** worksheet to familiarize students with drama.	**RL.3** Describe how a particular story's or drama's plot unfolds in a series of episodes as well as how the characters respond or change as the plot moves toward a resolution.	Challenge students to explain how one scene leads into the next, and how each subsequent scene builds on the events and ideas of the others.
Language	You may wish to administer the **Conventions: Sentence Parts and Types (RP)** worksheet to help students understand the different parts and types of sentences You may wish to administer the **Word Study: Denotation and Nuance (RP)** worksheet to help students understand the shades of meaning in words that have similar basic definitions.	**L.1** Demonstrate command of the conventions of standard English grammar and usage when writing or speaking. **L.5.c** Distinguish among the connotations of words with similar denotations.	Have students find a short article online and identify the types of sentences in it. Ask students to create word spectrums that present words with similar denotations and different levels of intensity. For example, one spectrum for words that mean *happy* might be *pleased, happy, thrilled, ecstatic*.

Jump Start

FIRST READ Prior to students' first read, ask them how a play script differs from a novel. Discuss what they should expect to see as they read the play. Then point out that the play takes place in the imaginary lands of Wisdom and Ignorance. Discuss with them what the main character might find in these places.

The Phantom Tollbooth, Act I

Who is the Clock? Why is Milo bored? How does the story connect to the concept of imagination? Modeling questions such as these will help students connect to *The Phantom Tollbooth,* Act I, and to the Performance Task assignment. Selection audio and print capability for the selection are available in the Interactive Teacher's Edition.

Concept Vocabulary

Support students as they rank their words. Ask if they've ever heard, read, or used them. Reassure them that the definitions for these words are listed in the selection.

FIRST READ

As they read, students should perform the steps of the first read:

NOTICE: You may want to encourage students to notice who Milo is and how the tollbooth allows him to travel to an imaginary land.

ANNOTATE: Remind students to mark passages that are particularly descriptive or worthy of analysis in their first read.

CONNECT: If students cannot make connections to their own lives or to the lives of people they know, encourage them to make connections to stories they've read or movies they've seen.

RESPOND: Students will answer questions and write a summary to demonstrate understanding.

Point out to students that while they will always complete the Respond step at the end of the first read, the other steps will probably happen somewhat concurrently. You may wish to print copies of the **First-Read Guide: Fiction** for students to use.

Remind students that during their first read, they should not answer the close-read questions that appear in the selection.

About the Playwright
Susan Nanus has written plays, television scripts, and movie screenplays. Like other dramatists, she sometimes bases her plays or screenplays on novels or other existing works. Her script for *The Phantom Tollbooth* was based on the novel by Norton Juster.

For a biography of Norton Juster, see Act II.

🔑 Tool Kit
First-Read Guide and Model Annotation

☰ STANDARDS
Reading Literature
By the end of the year, read and comprehend literature, including stories, dramas, and poems, in the grades 6–8 text complexity band proficiently, with scaffolding as needed at the high end of the range.

The Phantom Tollbooth, Act I

Concept Vocabulary

You will encounter the following words as you read *The Phantom Tollbooth,* Act I. Before reading, note how familiar you are with each word. Then, rank the words in order from most familiar (1) to least familiar (6).

WORD	YOUR RANKING
ignorance	
surmise	
presume	
speculate	
consideration	
misapprehension	

After completing the first read, come back to the concept vocabulary and review your rankings. Mark changes to your original rankings as needed.

First Read DRAMA

Apply these strategies as you conduct your first read. You will have an opportunity to complete the close-read notes after your first read.

NOTICE *whom* the story is about, *what* happens, *where* and *when* it happens, and *why* those involved react as they do.

ANNOTATE by marking vocabulary and key passages you want to revisit.

CONNECT ideas within the selection to what you already know and what you have already read.

RESPOND by completing the Comprehension Check and by writing a brief summary of the selection.

© Pearson Education, Inc., or its affiliates. All rights reserved.

The Phantom Tollbooth Act I

Susan Nanus • Based on the book by Norton Juster

BACKGROUND

The writer of a drama is called a *playwright* or a *dramatist*. Playwright Susan Nanus adapted Norton Juster's novel *The Phantom Tollbooth* into a drama with two acts, or main sections. You will read Act I in this lesson.

SCAN FOR MULTIMEDIA

Cast (In order of appearance)

- The Clock
- Milo, *A Boy*
- The Whether Man
- Six Lethargarians
- Tock, The Watchdog (same as the Clock)
- Azaz the Unabridged, King of Dictionopolis
- The Mathemagician, King of Digitopolis
- Princess Sweet Rhyme
- Princess Pure Reason
- Gatekeeper of Dictionopolis
- Three Word Merchants
- The Letterman (fourth Word Merchant)
- Spelling Bee
- The Humbug

- The Duke of Definition
- The Minister of Meaning
- The Earl of Essence
- The Count of Connotation
- The Undersecretary of Understanding
- A Page
- Kakafonous A. Dischord, Doctor of Dissonance
- The Awful Dynne
- The Dodecahedron
- Miners of the Numbers Mine
- The Everpresent Wordsnatcher
- The Terrible Trivium
- The Demon of Insincerity
- Senses Taker

The Phantom Tollbooth, Act I **283**

© Pearson Education, Inc., or its affiliates. All rights reserved.

CLOSER LOOK

Analyze Characters

Students may have marked some of the characters in the cast list during their first read. Use this paragraph to help students understand what they might learn about the characters' traits from their names. Encourage them to talk about the annotations that they marked. You may want to model a close read with the class based on the highlights shown in the text.

ANNOTATE: Have students mark details in the cast list that indicate what kinds of characters they might find in the play, or have students participate while you highlight them.

QUESTION: Guide students to consider what these details might tell them. Ask what a reader can infer from the names of some of the characters and accept student responses.

Possible response: The names of some of the characters indicate that they will have something to do with words and numbers. Names like Terrible Trivium and Demon of Insincerity indicate that there will be antagonists in the play.

CONCLUDE: Help students to formulate conclusions about the importance of these details in the text. Ask students why the playwright might have included these details.

Possible response: The names of the characters help identify what the characters are like and reflect the imaginary land that is the setting of the play.

Remind students that **character traits** are the qualities, attitudes, and values that a character possesses—such as dependability, intelligence, selfishness, or stubbornness. Point out that a *dynamic character* develops and learns something during the course of the story—unlike a *static character*, who doesn't change. The protagonist is almost always a dynamic (and round) character—and how this character changes is central to the story's theme and plot.

© Pearson Education, Inc., or its affiliates. All rights reserved.

NOTES

ignorance (IHG nuhr uhns) *n.* state of lacking knowledge, learning, or information

The Sets

1. MILO'S BEDROOM—with shelves, pennants, pictures on the wall, as well as suggestions of the characters of the Land of Wisdom.

2. THE ROAD TO THE LAND OF WISDOM—a forest, from which the Whether Man and the Lethargarians emerge.

3. DICTIONOPOLIS—a marketplace full of open air stalls as well as little shops. Letters and signs should abound.

4. DIGITOPOLIS—a dark, glittering place without trees or greenery, but full of shining rocks and cliffs, with hundreds of numbers shining everywhere.

5. THE LAND OF IGNORANCE—a gray, gloomy place full of cliffs and caves, with frightening faces. Different levels and heights should be suggested through one or two platforms or risers, with a set of stairs that lead to the castle in the air.

⌘ ⌘ ⌘

Act I

Scene i

1 [*The stage is completely dark and silent. Suddenly the sound of someone winding an alarm clock is heard, and after that, the sound of loud ticking is heard.*]

2 [*LIGHTS UP on the* Clock, *a huge alarm clock. The* Clock *reads 4:00. The lighting should make it appear that the* Clock *is suspended in mid-air (if possible). The* Clock *ticks for 30 seconds.*]

3 **Clock.** See that! Half a minute gone by. Seems like a long time when you're waiting for something to happen, doesn't it? Funny thing is, time can pass very slowly or very fast, and sometimes even both at once. The time now? Oh, a little after four, but what that means should depend on you. Too often, we do something simply because time tells us to. Time for school, time for bed, whoops, 12:00, time to be hungry. It can get a little silly, don't you think? Time is important, but it's what you do with it that makes it so. So my advice to you is

© Pearson Education, Inc., or its affiliates. All rights reserved.

SCAN FOR
MULTIMEDIA

to use it. Keep your eyes open and your ears perked. Otherwise it will pass before you know it, and you'll certainly have missed something!

4 Things have a habit of doing that, you know. Being here one minute and gone the next.

5 In the twinkling of an eye.

6 In a jiffy.

7 In a flash!

8 I know a girl who yawned and missed a whole summer vacation. And what about that caveman who took a nap one afternoon, and woke up to find himself completely alone. You see, while he was sleeping, someone had invented the wheel and everyone had moved to the suburbs. And then of course, there is Milo. [*LIGHTS UP to reveal* Milo's *Bedroom. The* Clock *appears to be on a shelf in the room of a young boy—a room filled with books, toys, games, maps, papers, pencils, a bed, a desk. There is a dartboard with numbers and the face of the* Mathemagician, *a bedspread made from* King Azaz's *cloak, a kite looking like the* Spelling Bee, *a punching bag with the* Humbug's *face, as well as records, a television, a toy car, and a large box that is wrapped and has an envelope taped to the top. The sound of FOOTSTEPS is heard, and then enter* Milo *dejectedly. He throws down his books and coat, flops into a chair, and sighs loudly.*] Who never knows what to do with himself—not just sometimes, but always. When he's in school, he wants to be out, and when he's out he wants to be in. [*During the following speech,* Milo *examines the various toys, tools, and other possessions in the room, trying them out and rejecting them.*] Wherever he is, he wants to be somewhere else—and when he gets there, so what. Everything is too much trouble or a waste of time. Books—he's already read them. Games—boring. T.V.—dumb. So what's left? Another long, boring afternoon. Unless he bothers to notice a very large package that happened to arrive today.

9 **Milo.** [*Suddenly notices the package. He drags himself over to it, and disinterestedly reads the label.*] "For Milo, who has plenty of time." Well, that's true. [*Sighs and looks at it.*] No. [*Walks away.*] Well . . . [*Comes back. Rips open envelope and reads.*]

10 **A Voice.** "One genuine turnpike tollbooth,[1] easily assembled at home for use by those who have never traveled in lands beyond."

NOTES

CLOSE READ
ANNOTATE: In paragraphs 4–7, mark expressions that mean "very quickly."

QUESTION: Why does the playwright have the Clock repeat the same idea in different ways?

CONCLUDE: What is the effect of this quick series of expressions?

---

1. **turnpike tollbooth** A turnpike is a road that people pay a fee, or toll, to use. A tollbooth is the booth or gate at which tolls are collected.

The Phantom Tollbooth, Act I **285**

CLOSE READ

You may wish to model the close read using the following think-aloud format. Possible responses to questions on the student page are included. You may also want to print copies of the **Close-Read Guide: Fiction** for students to use.

ANNOTATE: As I read paragraphs 4–7, I notice and highlight expressions that mean quickly or fast.

QUESTION: The playwright may have wanted to emphasize the idea.

CONCLUDE: I think that including all these expressions that mean the same thing increases the pacing and the tension of the scene.

Additional **English Language Support** is available in the Interactive Teacher's Edition.

PERSONALIZE FOR LEARNING

Strategic Support

Hyperbole Some students may have difficulty understanding and interpreting the hyperbole and mixture of clichés in paragraphs 4–8. Guide them to understand that both anecdotes that Clock recounts are told for humorous effect. Point out that sometimes, literature exaggerates an idea or event to make a point, as the playwright does here by suggesting that a girl could sleep through summer vacation or that a caveman could wake up to find that everyone had moved to the suburbs. Discuss with students what idea Clock is trying to get across here in both anecdotes. (the idea that time can go by quickly)

NOTES

2. **precautionary** (prih KAW shuh nehr ee) *adj.* done or made to prevent harm or danger.

11 **Milo.** Beyond what? [*Continues reading.*]

12 **A Voice.** "This package contains the following items:" [Milo *pulls the items out of the box and sets them up as they are mentioned.*] "One (1) genuine turnpike tollbooth to be erected according to directions. Three (3) precautionary[2] signs to be used in a precautionary fashion. Assorted coins for paying tolls. One (1) map, strictly up to date, showing how to get from here to there. One (1) book of rules and traffic regulations which may not be bent or broken. Warning! Results are not guaranteed. If not perfectly satisfied, your wasted time will be refunded."

13 **Milo.** [*Skeptically.*] Come off it, who do you think you're kidding? [*Walks around and examines tollbooth.*] What am I supposed to do with this? [*The ticking of the* Clock *grows loud and impatient.*] Well . . . what else do I have to do. [Milo *gets into his toy car and drives up to the first sign.*]

14 **Voice.** "HAVE YOUR DESTINATION IN MIND."

15 **Milo.** [*Pulls out the map.*] Now, let's see. That's funny. I never heard of any of these places. Well, it doesn't matter anyway. Dictionopolis. That's a weird name. I might as well go there. [*Begins to move, following map. Drives off.*]

16 **Clock.** See what I mean? You never know how things are going to get started. But when you're bored, what you need more than anything is a rude awakening.

17 [*The ALARM goes off very loudly as the stage darkens. The sound of the alarm is transformed into the honking of a car horn, and is then joined by the blasts, bleeps, roars and growls of heavy traffic. When the lights come up, Milo's bedroom is gone and we see a lonely road in the middle of nowhere.*]

Scene ii • The Road to Dictionopolis

1 [*Enter* Milo *in his car.*]

2 **Milo.** This is weird! I don't recognize any of this scenery at all. [*A SIGN is held up before* Milo, *startling him.*] Huh? [*Reads.*] WELCOME TO EXPECTATIONS. INFORMATION, PREDICTIONS AND ADVICE CHEERFULLY OFFERED. PARK HERE AND BLOW HORN. [Milo *blows horn.*]

© Pearson Education, Inc., or its affiliates. All rights reserved.

286 UNIT 4 • IMAGINATION

PERSONALIZE FOR LEARNING

English Language Support

Syntax Review paragraph 12, which describes the contents of the package. The list of items Milo receives might be confusing to English learners. To help students understand what the lines describe, point to the colon and explain that it indicates that a list will follow. Next, review each sentence that begins with a number. Explain that these sentences do not follow the usual subject/verb/object structure. Rather, each refers to an item in the package. Point out that separating the items with periods helps avoid confusion in this case. It also helps indicate where the speaker of the lines should pause. **ALL LEVELS**

3 **Whether Man.** [*A little man wearing a long coat and carrying an umbrella pops up from behind the sign he was holding. He speaks very fast and excitedly.*] My, my, my, my, my, welcome, welcome, welcome, welcome to the Land of Expectations, Expectations, Expectations! We don't get many travelers these days; we certainly don't get many travelers. Now what can I do for you? I'm the Whether Man.

4 **Milo.** [*Referring to the map.*] Uh . . . is this the right road to Dictionopolis?

5 **Whether Man.** Well now, well now, well now, I don't know of any wrong road to Dictionopolis, so if this road goes to Dictionopolis at all, it must be the right road, and if it doesn't, it must be the right road to somewhere else, because there are no wrong roads to anywhere. Do you think it will rain?

6 **Milo.** I thought you were the Weather Man.

7 **Whether Man.** Oh, no, I'm the Whether Man, not the weather man. [*Pulls out a SIGN or opens a FLAP of his coat, which reads: "WHETHER."*] After all, it's more important to know whether there will be weather than what the weather will be.

8 **Milo.** What kind of place is Expectations?

9 **Whether Man.** Good question, good question! Expectations is the place you must always go to before you get to where you are going. Of course, some people never go beyond Expectations, but my job is to hurry them along whether they like it or not. Now what else can I do for you? [*Opens his umbrella.*]

10 **Milo.** I think I can find my own way.

11 **Whether Man.** Splendid, splendid, splendid! Whether or not you find your own way, you're bound to find some way. If you happen to find my way, please return it. I lost it years ago. I imagine by now it must be quite rusty. You did say it was going to rain, didn't you? [*Escorts Milo to the car under the open umbrella.*] I'm glad you made your own decision. I do so hate to make up my mind about anything, whether it's good or bad, up or down, rain or shine. Expect everything, I always say, and the unexpected never happens. Goodbye, goodbye, goodbye, good . . .

NOTES

CLOSE READ

ANNOTATE: In paragraph 9, mark the **pun**, or play on words, that Whether Man makes about Expectations.

QUESTION: Why does the playwright include this pun?

CONCLUDE: What double meaning does the pun have? How does the double meaning add to the scene?

© Pearson Education, Inc., or its affiliates. All rights reserved.

The Phantom Tollbooth, Act I **287**

CLOSE READ

As students look for the pun, or play on words, remind them that they are looking for a common phrase or saying that has been modified or changed. You may wish to model the close read using the following think-aloud format. Possible responses to questions on the student page are included.

ANNOTATE: As I read paragraph 9, I notice and highlight the details that suggest that the Whether Man is making a play on words when he refers to people traveling through Expectations.

QUESTION: I've heard of the phrase "going beyond expectations." I think it means to do something better than people thought you could. I think the Whether Man uses the pun because he is referring to the place Expectations. He is using language in a new way that may cause readers to reconsider the phrase "beyond expectations."

CONCLUDE: The pun is funny, but it also makes the reader wonder if Milo will go beyond Expectations, or if he will have to be hurried along, whether he likes it or not. I think Milo could go beyond expectations by doing something brave or by using his imagination.

WriteNow Express and Reflect

Dialogue Review the Whether Man's speech in paragraph 11. The Whether Man has an interesting, excited way of speaking. Encourage interested students to write a short dialogue between Milo and the Whether Man that would replace paragraph 11. Tell them that instead of Milo replying that he can find his own way, he should say something else, for example, "I have too much time on my hands" or some other expression that could be a play on words. Then ask them to write the Whether Man's response, replicating his use of repetition and puns.

Whole-Class Learning **287**

CLOSE READ

Remind students that playwrights use punctuation to indicate the manner in which lines of dialogue should be spoken. You may wish to model the close read using the following think-aloud format. Possible responses to questions on the student page are included.

ANNOTATE: As I read paragraphs 14 and 15, I notice the punctuation that separates words in the dialogue.

QUESTION: When I read the lines out loud, I know that the ellipses tell me to pause between words and to even draw out the word *Doldrums*.

CONCLUDE: The punctuation helps me see that these characters speak very slowly and without urgency.

NOTES

CLOSE READ
ANNOTATE: In paragraphs 14 and 15, mark the punctuation that separates characters' words.

QUESTION: Why does the author include ellipses in the Lethargarians' dialogue?

CONCLUDE: What does this punctuation show about how the Lethargarians speak?

12 [*A loud CLAP OF THUNDER is heard.*] Oh dear! [*He looks up at the sky, puts out his hand to feel for rain, and RUNS AWAY. Milo watches puzzledly and drives on.*]

13 **Milo.** I'd better get out of Expectations, but fast. Talking to a guy like that all day would get me nowhere for sure. [*He tries to speed up, but finds instead that he is moving slower and slower.*] Oh, oh, now what? [*He can barely move. Behind Milo, the LETHARGARIANS begin to enter from all parts of the stage. They are dressed to blend in with the scenery and carry small pillows that look like rocks. Whenever they fall asleep, they rest on the pillows.*] Now I really am getting nowhere. I hope I didn't take a wrong turn. [*The car stops. He tries to start it. It won't move. He gets out and begins to tinker with it.*] I wonder where I am.

14 **Lethargarian 1.** You're . . . in . . . the . . . Dol . . . drums . . . [*Milo looks around.*]

15 **Lethargarian 2.** Yes . . . the . . . Dol . . . drums . . . [*A YAWN is heard.*]

© Pearson Education, Inc., or its affiliates. All rights reserved.

288 UNIT 4 • IMAGINATION

CROSS-CURRICULAR PERSPECTIVES

Music Call students' attention to paragraphs 14–15. Point out to students that the Whether Man's lines were meant to be spoken rapidly and that in contrast, the Lethargarians' lines are meant to be spoken slowly. Ask students to think about the music they hear in movies and how it helps to set the tone or create a mood or simply ask them to think of music that could be used to accentuate what is happening on screen. Then discuss background for the scene with the Whether Man and music that could be used as background for the scene with the Lethargarians. Ask them how the music will help emphasize both the mood of the scene and the way the characters speak their lines.

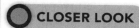
16 **Milo.** [*Yelling.*] WHAT ARE THE DOLDRUMS?

17 **Lethargarian 3.** The Doldrums, my friend, are where nothing ever happens and nothing ever changes. [*Parts of the Scenery stand up or Six People come out of the scenery colored in the same colors of the trees or the road. They move very slowly and as soon as they move, they stop to rest again.*] Allow me to introduce all of us. We are the Lethargarians at your service.

18 **Milo.** [*Uncertainly.*] Very pleased to meet you. I think I'm lost. Can you help me?

19 **Lethargarian 4.** Don't say think. [*He yawns.*] It's against the law.

20 **Lethargarian 1.** No one's allowed to think in the Doldrums. [*He falls asleep.*]

21 **Lethargarian 2.** Don't you have a rule book? It's local ordinance 175389-J. [*He falls asleep.*]

22 **Milo.** [*Pulls out rule book and reads.*] Ordinance 175389-J: "It shall be unlawful, illegal and unethical to think, think of thinking, **surmise**, **presume**, reason, meditate, or **speculate** while in the Doldrums. Anyone breaking this law shall be severely punished." That's a ridiculous law! Everybody thinks.

23 **All The Lethargarians.** We don't!

24 **Lethargarian 2.** And most of the time, you don't, that's why you're here. You weren't thinking and you weren't paying attention either. People who don't pay attention often get stuck in the Doldrums. Face it, most of the time, you're just like us. [*Falls, snoring, to the ground.* Milo *laughs.*]

25 **Lethargarian 5.** Stop that at once. Laughing is against the law. Don't you have a rule book? It's local ordinance 574381-W.

26 **Milo.** [*Opens rule book and reads.*] "In the Doldrums, laughter is frowned upon and smiling is permitted only on alternate Thursdays." Well, if you can't laugh or think, what can you do?

27 **Lethargarian 6.** Anything as long as it's nothing, and everything as long as it isn't anything. There's lots to do. We have a very busy schedule . . .

28 **Lethargarian 1.** At 8:00 we get up and then we spend from 8 to 9 daydreaming.

NOTES

surmise (suhr MYZ) *v.* guess, using only intuition or imagination

presume (prih ZOOM) *v.* take for granted; assume something to be the case

speculate (SPEHK yuh layt) *v.* guess, using information that is uncertain or incomplete

© Pearson Education, Inc., or its affiliates. All rights reserved.

CLOSER LOOK

Analyze Characters

Students may have marked paragraph 24 during their first read. Use these lines to help students understand how playwrights develop a character's personality. Encourage them to talk about the annotations that they marked. You may want to model a close read with the class based on the highlights shown in the text.

ANNOTATE: Have students mark details in paragraph 24 that tell them something about Milo's personality, or have students participate while you highlight them.

QUESTION: Guide students to consider what these details might tell them. Ask what a reader can infer from the Lethargarian's comments about Milo, and accept student responses.

Possible response: Like the Lethargarians, Milo is lazy and avoids thinking too hard about anything.

CONCLUDE: Help students to formulate conclusions about the importance of these details in the text. Ask students why the playwright might have included these details.

Possible response: These details help to show Milo's character. Instead of using only Milo's words and actions to develop his personality, the playwright uses the words and analysis of other characters. By comparing Milo to the Lethargarians, who are slow and lazy, the playwright helps to develop Milo's personality and helps to show his motivation or lack of it.

Remind students that **characterization** is the way a writer develops and reveals a character's personality and temperament. With **direct characterization,** a writer simply tells us what a character is like. With **indirect characterization,** the writer shows us a character's traits, and it is up to the reader to make inferences and draw conclusions.

CLOSER LOOK

Analyze Dialogue

Students may have marked paragraphs 29–36 during their first read. Use these paragraphs to help students understand how playwrights use humor in dialogue. Encourage them to talk about the annotations that they marked. You may want to model a close read with the class based on the highlights shown in the text.

ANNOTATE: Have students mark examples of repeated words or phrases in paragraphs 29–36, or have students participate while you highlight them.

QUESTION: Guide students to consider what these details might tell them. Ask what effect the playwright creates by having the Lethargarians repeatedly saying they take naps, and accept student responses.

Possible response: When the Lethargians keep repeating that they take naps, it makes me think they take a ridiculous number of naps every day.

CONCLUDE: Help students to formulate conclusions about the repetition in the dialogue. Ask students why the playwright might have included these details.

Possible response: The repetition adds humor to the scene and makes the Lethargians seem like strange, funny characters.

Remind students that playwrights use many techniques in **dialogue** for different purposes, including building characters and advancing plot. Repetition in dialogue can create different moods, including intensity, fear, suspense, or, in this case, humor.

NOTES

29 **Lethargarian 2.** From 9:00 to 9:30 we take our early mid-morning nap . . .

30 **Lethargarian 3.** From 9:30 to 10:30 we dawdle and delay . . .

31 **Lethargarian 4.** From 10:30 to 11:30 we take our late early morning nap . . .

32 **Lethargarian 5.** From 11:30 to 12:00 we bide our time and then we eat our lunch.

33 **Lethargarian 6.** From 1:00 to 2:00 we linger and loiter . . .

34 **Lethargarian 1.** From 2:00 to 2:30 we take our early afternoon nap . . .

35 **Lethargarian 2.** From 2:30 to 3:30 we put off for tomorrow what we could have done today . . .

36 **Lethargarian 3.** From 3:30 to 4:00 we take our early late afternoon nap . . .

37 **Lethargarian 4.** From 4:00 to 5:00 we loaf and lounge until dinner . . .

38 **Lethargarian 5.** From 6:00 to 7:00 we dilly-dally . . .

39 **Lethargarian 6.** From 7:00 to 8:00 we take our early evening nap and then for an hour before we go to bed, we waste time.

40 **Lethargarian 1.** [*Yawning.*] You see, it's really quite strenuous doing nothing all day long, and so once a week, we take a holiday and go nowhere.

41 **Lethargarian 5.** Which is just where we were going when you came along. Would you care to join us?

42 **Milo.** [*Yawning.*] That's where I seem to be going, anyway. [*Stretching.*] Tell me, does everyone here do nothing?

43 **Lethargarian 3.** Everyone but the terrible Watchdog. He's always sniffing around to see that nobody wastes time. A most unpleasant character.

44 **Milo.** The Watchdog?

45 **Lethargarian 6.** THE WATCHDOG!

46 **All The Lethargarians.** [*Yelling at once.*] RUN! WAKE UP! RUN! HERE HE COMES! THE WATCHDOG! [*They all run off and ENTER a large dog with the head, feet, and tail of a dog, and the body of a clock, having the same face as the character the Clock.*]

© Pearson Education, Inc., or its affiliates. All rights reserved.

HOW LANGUAGE WORKS

All Uppercase Letters Ask students to look at the text in paragraphs 45–46. Words written in uppercase letters are sometimes used for emphasis. Explain to students that using all uppercase letters has the effect of shouting, as in paragraphs 45–46. Point out that people sometimes use all uppercase letters in emails or in advertisements to call attention to a word or idea.

Ask one volunteer to speak paragraph 45 and a second to speak paragraph 46. Discuss how both the ending punctuation and the treatment of the words in all uppercase changes the way the lines are spoken. Ask students if they think the lines would be interpreted in the same way if only exclamation points were used, without all uppercase letters.

47 **Watchdog.** What are you doing here?

48 **Milo.** Nothing much. Just killing time. You see . . .

49 **Watchdog.** KILLING TIME! [*His ALARM RINGS in fury.*] It's bad enough wasting time without killing it. What are you doing in the Doldrums, anyway? Don't you have anywhere to go?

50 **Milo.** I think I was on my way to Dictionopolis when I got stuck here. Can you help me?

51 **Watchdog.** Help you! You've got to help yourself. I suppose you know why you got stuck.

52 **Milo.** I guess I just wasn't thinking.

53 **Watchdog.** Precisely. Now you're on your way.

54 **Milo.** I am?

55 **Watchdog.** Of course. Since you got here by not thinking, it seems reasonable that in order to get out, you must start thinking. Do you mind if I get in? I love automobile rides. [*He gets in. They wait.*] Well?

56 **Milo.** All right. I'll try. [*Screws up his face and thinks.*] Are we moving?

57 **Watchdog.** Not yet. Think harder.

58 **Milo.** I'm thinking as hard as I can.

59 **Watchdog.** Well, think just a little harder than that. Come on, you can do it.

60 **Milo.** All right, all right . . . I'm thinking of all the planets in the solar system, and why water expands when it turns to ice, and all the words that begin with "q," and . . . [*The wheels begin to move.*] We're moving! We're moving!

61 **Watchdog.** Keep thinking.

62 **Milo.** [*Thinking.*] How a steam engine works and how to bake a pie and the difference between Fahrenheit and Centigrade . . .

63 **Watchdog.** Dictionopolis, here we come.

64 **Milo.** Hey, Watchdog, are you coming along?

65 **Tock.** You can call me Tock, and keep your eyes on the road.

66 **Milo.** What kind of place is Dictionopolis anyway?

NOTES

© Pearson Education, Inc., or its affiliates. All rights reserved.

CLOSE READ ✎

You may wish to model the close read using the following think-aloud format. Possible responses to questions on the student page are included.

ANNOTATE: As I read paragraphs 74–78, I notice and highlight the stage directions that help me see to whom the characters are speaking.

QUESTION: I think the playwright includes these stage directions to help readers understand how the action of the play unfolds. Without the language of prose that tells readers about how a line is said or to whom, the playwright needs a way to share that information.

CONCLUDE: The information in the stage directions helps the actors know how to deliver the lines and brings the text to life for all.

NOTES

CLOSE READ
ANNOTATE: In paragraphs 74–78, mark details that show to whom the characters are speaking.

QUESTION: Why does the playwright include this information?

CONCLUDE: How might these details affect how actors deliver their lines, and how an audience might respond?

67 **Tock.** It's where all the words in the world come from. It used to be a marvelous place, but ever since Rhyme and Reason left, it hasn't been the same.

68 **Milo.** Rhyme and Reason?

69 **Tock.** The two princesses. They used to settle all the arguments between their two brothers who rule over the Land of Wisdom. You see, Azaz is the king of Dictionopolis and the Mathemagician is the king of Digitopolis and they almost never see eye to eye on anything. It was the job of the Princesses Sweet Rhyme and Pure Reason to solve the differences between the two kings, and they always did so well that both sides usually went home feeling very satisfied. But then, one day, the kings had an argument to end all arguments . . .

70 [*The LIGHTS DIM on* Tock *and* Milo, *and come up on* King Azaz *of Dictionopolis on another part of the stage. Azaz has a great stomach, a grey beard reaching to his waist, a small crown, and a long robe with the letters of the alphabet written all over it.*]

71 **Azaz.** Of course, I'll abide by the decision of Rhyme and Reason, though I have no doubt as to what it will be. They will choose *words*, of course. Everyone knows that words are more important than numbers any day of the week.

72 [*The* Mathemagician *appears opposite Azaz. The Mathemagician wears a long flowing robe covered entirely with complex mathematical equations, and a tall pointed hat. He carries a long staff with a pencil point at one end and a large rubber eraser at the other.*]

73 **Mathemagician.** That's what you think, Azaz. People wouldn't even know what day of the week it is without *numbers*. Haven't you ever looked at a calendar? Face it, Azaz. It's numbers that count.

74 **Azaz.** Don't be ridiculous. [*To audience, as if leading a cheer.*] Let's hear it for WORDS!

75 **Mathemagician.** [*To audience, in the same manner.*] Cast your vote for NUMBERS!

76 **Azaz.** A, B, C's!

77 **Mathemagician.** 1, 2, 3's! [*A FANFARE is heard.*]

78 **Azaz and Mathemagician.** [*To each other.*] Quiet! Rhyme and Reason are about to announce their decision.

79 [Rhyme *and* Reason *appear.*]

© Pearson Education, Inc., or its affiliates. All rights reserved.

CROSS-CURRICULAR PERSPECTIVES

Math Tell students that in paragraph 73, the Mathemagician points to calendars as an example of how we use numbers every day. Challenge pairs of students to list all the ways that they use numbers and calculations each day. Remind them to begin in the morning when they wake up and to continue listing the ways they use numbers as they go through their day. Examples might include setting their alarm clock, brushing their teeth for a set amount of time, catching a #10 bus, going to five classes, measuring ingredients for a recipe, stepping out of bounds of a pick-up baseball game, riding a couple of miles on their bike.

80 **Rhyme.** Ladies and gentlemen, letters and numerals, fractions and punctuation marks—may we have your attention, please. After careful **consideration** of the problem set before us by King Azaz of Dictionopolis [*Azaz bows.*] and the Mathemagician of Digitopolis [*Mathemagician raises his hands in a victory salute.*] we have come to the following conclusion:

NOTES

consideration (kuhn sihd uh RAY shuhn) *n.* careful thought

81 **Reason.** Words and numbers are of equal value, for in the cloak of knowledge, one is the warp and the other is the woof.

82 **Rhyme.** It is no more important to count the sands than it is to name the stars.

83 **Rhyme and Reason.** Therefore, let both kingdoms, Dictionopolis and Digitopolis, live in peace.

84 [*The sound of* CHEERING *is heard.*]

85 **Azaz.** Boo! is what I say. Boo and Bah and Hiss!

86 **Mathemagician.** What good are these girls if they can't even settle an argument in anyone's favor? I think I have come to a decision of my own.

87 **Azaz.** So have I.

88 **Azaz and Mathemagician.** [*To the* Princesses.] You are hereby banished from this land to the Castle-in-the-Air. [*To each other.*] And as for you, KEEP OUT OF MY WAY! [*They stalk off in opposite directions.*]

89 [*During this time, the set has been changed to the Market Square of Dictionopolis. LIGHTS come UP on the deserted square.*]

90 **Tock.** And ever since then, there has been neither Rhyme nor Reason in this kingdom. Words are misused and numbers are mismanaged. The argument between the two kings has divided everyone and the real value of both words and numbers has been forgotten. What a waste!

91 **Milo.** Why doesn't somebody rescue the Princesses and set everything straight again?

92 **Tock.** That is easier said than done. The Castle-in-the-Air is very far from here, and the one path which leads to it is guarded by ferocious demons. But hold on, here we are. [*A Man appears, carrying a Gate and a small Tollbooth.*]

93 **Gatekeeper.** AHHHHREMMMM! This is Dictionopolis, a happy kingdom, advantageously located in the foothills of

© Pearson Education, Inc., or its affiliates. All rights reserved.

The Phantom Tollbooth, Act I **293**

CLOSER LOOK

Analyze Structure

Students may have marked the italicized text in paragraph 102 during their first read. Use this paragraph to help students understand how text style is used to indicate stage directions in the structure of a play. Encourage them to talk about the annotations that they marked. You may want to model a close read with the class based on the highlights shown in the text.

ANNOTATE: Have students mark italicized words in paragraph 102 that describe what is happening on stage.

QUESTION: Guide students to consider why these words are italicized.

Possible response: I notice that the playwright has italicized all the directions that tell what the actors are doing and what is happening on stage. I think that the playwright has italicized these words for the same reason—to tell me what is going on in this scene and what the stage looks like.

CONCLUDE: Help students to formulate conclusions the effect of using italicized words for stage directions.

Possible response: The italicized words grab the reader's attention. Italicizing the words on the banner also draws the reader's attention and helps establish what the dialogue is about. The stage directions help me understand what is happening in the scene.

Remind students that a play's **structure** is conveyed both through stage directions and dialogue, and playwrights use tools such as italicized text to convey important information about the structure.

NOTES

Confusion and caressed by gentle breezes from the Sea of Knowledge. Today, by royal proclamation, is Market Day. Have you come to buy or sell?

94 **Milo.** I beg your pardon?

95 **Gatekeeper.** Buy or sell, buy or sell. Which is it? You must have come here for a reason.

96 **Milo.** Well, I . . .

97 **Gatekeeper.** Come now, if you don't have a reason, you must at least have an explanation or certainly an excuse.

98 **Milo.** [*Meekly.*] Uh . . . no.

99 **Gatekeeper.** [*Shaking his head.*] Very serious. You can't get in without a reason. [*Thoughtfully*] Wait a minute. Maybe I have an old one you can use. [*Pulls out on old suitcase from the tollbooth and rummages through it.*] No . . . no . . . no . . . this won't do . . . hmmm . . .

100 **Milo.** [*To* Tock.] What's he looking for? [Tock *shrugs.*]

101 **Gatekeeper.** Ah! This is fine. [*Pulls out a Medallion on a chain. Engraved in the Medallion is: "WHY NOT?"*] Why not. That's a good reason for almost anything . . . a bit used, perhaps, but still quite serviceable. There you are, sir. Now I can truly say: Welcome to Dictionopolis.

102 [*He opens the Gate and walks off.* Citizens *and* Merchants *appear on all levels of the stage, and* Milo *and* Tock *find themselves in the middle of a noisy marketplace. As some people buy and sell their wares, others hang a large banner which reads: WELCOME TO THE WORD MARKET.*]

103 **Milo.** Tock! Look!

104 **Merchant 1.** Hey-ya, hey-ya, hey-ya, step right up and take your pick. Juicy tempting words for sale. Get your fresh-picked "ifs," "ands," and "buts"! Just take a look at these nice ripe "wheres" and "whens."

105 **Merchant 2.** Step right up, step right up, fancy, best-quality words here for sale. Enrich your vocabulary and expand your speech with such elegant items as "quagmire," "flabbergast," or "upholstery."

106 **Merchant 3.** Words by the bag, buy them over here. Words by the bag for the more talkative customer. A pound of "happys" at a very reasonable price. . . . very useful for

© Pearson Education, Inc., or its affiliates. All rights reserved.

"Happy Birthday," "Happy New Year," "happy days," or "happy-go-lucky." Or how about a package of "goods," always handy for "good morning," "good afternoon," "good evening," and "goodbye."

107 **Milo.** I can't believe it. Did you ever see so many words?

108 **Tock.** They're fine if you have something to say. [*They come to a Do-It-Yourself Bin.*]

109 **Milo.** [*To Merchant 4 at the bin.*] Excuse me, but what are these?

110 **Merchant 4.** These are for people who like to make up their own words. You can pick any assortment you like or buy a special box complete with all the letters and a book of instructions. Here, taste an "A." They're very good. [*He pops one into* Milo's *mouth.*]

111 **Milo.** [*Tastes it hesitantly.*] It's sweet! [*He eats it.*]

NOTES

© Pearson Education, Inc., or its affiliates. All rights reserved.

PERSONALIZE FOR LEARNING

English Language Support

Multiple-Meaning Words Direct students' attention to the expressions and greetings in paragraph 106. Explain that while "happy" is a common adjective, it is used in many different contexts. Students will likely know what "Happy Birthday" means and possibly what "Happy New Year" means. But point out that "happy days" and "happy-go-lucky" are not well wishes.

"Happy days" refers to good times and "happy-go-lucky" is an adjective that describes someone who doesn't worry about things. Similarly, point to the wishes that begin with "good." Point out that "good" is also a common adjective, but that it is also used as part of a greeting, as in "good morning." Point out that in this context, the expressions are meant to show the many uses of the two words. **ALL LEVELS**

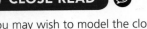
CLOSE READ ✐

You may wish to model the close read using the following think-aloud format. Possible responses to questions on the student page are included.

ANNOTATE: As I read paragraph 117, I notice and mark the works with hyphens.

QUESTION: The playwright presents these words in a different way to indicate that they are not meant to be read as words.

CONCLUDE: The punctuation tells me these words are meant to be spelled out, which makes sense based on the character's name and what he is saying about himself and his skills.

NOTES

CLOSE READ
ANNOTATE: In paragraph 117, mark the words that contain hyphens between the letters.

QUESTION: Why does the playwright present the words in this way?

CONCLUDE: What does the punctuation tell you about what Spelling Bee is doing?

misapprehension (mihs ap ree HEHN shuhn) *n.* incorrect understanding; wrong idea

112 **Merchant 4.** I knew you'd like it. "A" is one of our bestsellers. All of them aren't that good, you know. The "Z," for instance—very dry and sawdusty. And the "X"? Tastes like a trunkful of stale air. But most of the others aren't bad at all. Here, try the "I."

113 **Milo.** [*Tasting.*] Cool! It tastes icy.

114 **Merchant 4.** [*To* Tock] How about the "C" for you? It's as crunchy as a bone. Most people are just too lazy to make their own words, but take it from me, not only is it more fun, but it's also *de*-lightful. [*Holds up a "D."*] *e*-lating. [*Holds up an "E."*] and extremely useful! [*Holds up a "U."*]

115 **Milo.** But isn't it difficult? I'm not very good at making words.

116 [*The* Spelling Bee, *a large colorful bee, comes up from behind.*]

117 **Spelling Bee.** Perhaps I can be of some assistance . . . a-s-s-i-s-t-a-n-c-e. [*The Three turn around and see him.*] Don't be alarmed . . . a-l-a-r-m-e-d. I am the Spelling Bee. I can spell anything. Anything. A-n-y-t-h-i-n-g. Try me. Try me.

118 **Milo.** [*Backing off,* Tock *on his guard.*] Can you spell goodbye?

119 **Spelling Bee.** Perhaps you are under the **misapprehension** . . . m-i-s-a-p-p-r-e-h-e-n-s-i-o-n that I am dangerous. Let me assure you that I am quite peaceful. Now, think of the most difficult word you can, and I'll spell it.

120 **Milo.** Uh . . . o.k. [*At this point,* Milo *may turn to the audience and ask them to help him choose a word or he may think of one on his own.*] How about . . . "Curiosity"?

121 **Spelling Bee.** [*Winking.*] Let's see now . . . uh . . . how much time do I have?

122 **Milo.** Just ten seconds. Count them off, Tock.

123 **Spelling Bee.** [*As* Tock *counts.*] Oh dear, oh dear. [*Just at the last moment, quickly.*] C-u-r-i-o-s-i-t-y.

124 **Merchant 4.** Correct! [ALL *Cheer.*]

125 **Milo.** Can you spell anything?

126 **Spelling Bee.** [*Proudly.*] Just about. You see, years ago, I was an ordinary bee minding my own business, smelling flowers all day, occasionally picking up part-time work in people's bonnets. Then one day, I realized that I'd never amount to anything without an education, so I decided that . . .

© Pearson Education, Inc., or its affiliates. All rights reserved.

127 **Humbug.** [*Coming up in a booming voice.*] BALDERDASH! [*He wears a lavish coat, striped pants, checked vest, spats and a derby hat.*] Let me repeat . . . BALDERDASH! [*Swings his cane and clicks his heels in the air.*] Well, well, what have we here? Isn't someone going to introduce me to the little boy?

128 **Spelling Bee.** [*Disdainfully.*] This is the Humbug. You can't trust a word he says.

129 **Humbug.** NONSENSE! Everyone can trust a Humbug. As I was saying to the king just the other day . . .

130 **Spelling Bee.** You've never met the king. [*To Milo.*] Don't believe a thing he tells you.

131 **Humbug.** Bosh, my boy, pure bosh. The Humbugs are an old and noble family, honorable to the core. Why, we fought in the Crusades with Richard the Lionhearted, crossed the Atlantic with Columbus, blazed trails with the pioneers. History is full of Humbugs.

132 **Spelling Bee.** A very pretty speech . . . s-p-e-e-c-h. Now, why don't you go away? I was just advising the lad of the importance of proper spelling.

133 **Humbug.** BAH! As soon as you learn to spell one word, they ask you to spell another. You can never catch up, so why bother? [*Puts his arm around* Milo.] Take my advice, boy, and forget about it. As my great-great-great-grandfather George Washington Humbug used to say . . .

134 **Spelling Bee.** You, sir, are an impostor i-m-p-o-s-t-o-r who can't even spell his own name!

135 **Humbug.** What? You dare to doubt my word? The word of a Humbug? The word of a Humbug who has direct access to the ear of a King? And the king shall hear of this. I promise you . . .

136 **Voice 1.** Did someone call for the King?

137 **Voice 2.** Did you mention the monarch?

138 **Voice 3.** Speak of the sovereign?

139 **Voice 4.** Entreat the Emperor?

140 **Voice 5.** Hail his highness?

141 [*Five tall, thin gentlemen regally dressed in silks and satins, plumed hats, and buckled shoes appear as they speak.*]

NOTES

The Phantom Tollbooth, Act I **297**

© Pearson Education, Inc., or its affiliates. All rights reserved.

VOCABULARY DEVELOPMENT

Graphic Organizers Point out the word *monarch* in paragraph 137. Have students analyze the word using a four-square diagram, listing the synonyms of the word that appear on the page as well as others that they can think of.

Definition: the head of a country	**Synonyms:** *king, sovereign, emperor, ruler, queen*
Example sentence: The monarch wore a crown when she addressed the people.	**Other forms of the word:** *monarchy, monarchical*

© Pearson Education, Inc., or its affiliates. All rights reserved.

NOTES

3. **unabridged** (uhn uh
BRIHJD) *adj.* complete; not
shortened.

142 **Milo.** Who are they?

143 **Spelling Bee.** The King's advisors. Or in more formal terms, his cabinet.

144 **Minister 1.** Greetings!

145 **Minister 2.** Salutations!

146 **Minister 3.** Welcome!

147 **Minister 4.** Good Afternoon!

148 **Minister 5.** Hello!

149 **Milo.** Uh . . . Hi.

150 [*All the* Ministers, *from here on called by their numbers, unfold their scrolls and read in order.*]

151 **Minister 1.** By the order of Azaz the Unabridged . . .[3]

152 **Minister 2.** King of Dictionopolis . . .

153 **Minister 3.** Monarch of letters . . .

154 **Minister 4.** Emperor of phrases, sentences, and miscellaneous figures of speech . . .

155 **Minister 5.** We offer you the hospitality of our kingdom . . .

156 **Minister 1.** Country.

157 **Minister 2.** Nation.

158 **Minister 3.** State.

159 **Minister 4.** Commonwealth.

160 **Minister 5.** Realm.

161 **Minister 1.** Empire.

162 **Minister 2.** Palatinate.

163 **Minister 3.** Principality.

164 **Milo.** Do all those words mean the same thing?

165 **Minister 1.** Of course.

166 **Minister 2.** Certainly.

167 **Minister 3.** Precisely.

168 **Minister 4.** Exactly.

PERSONALIZE FOR LEARNING

Challenge

Shades of Meaning Point out the synonyms for *kingdom* that appear in paragraphs 156–163. Explain that while each word refers to a state controlled by one governing person or body, these terms each refer to a different kind of state. Have students each choose one of the following terms: *commonwealth, realm, empire, palatinate, principality.* Then have them research the governmental features of their political unit and present their findings to the class. Encourage students to compare the different kinds of states and to name examples of each.

169 **Minister 5.** Yes.

170 **Milo.** Then why don't you use just one? Wouldn't that make a lot more sense?

171 **Minister 1.** Nonsense!

172 **Minister 2.** Ridiculous!

173 **Minister 3.** Fantastic!

174 **Minister 4.** Absurd!

175 **Minister 5.** Bosh!

176 **Minister 1.** We're not interested in making sense. It's not our job.

177 **Minister 2.** Besides, one word is as good as another, so why not use them all?

178 **Minister 3.** Then you don't have to choose which one is right.

179 **Minister 4.** Besides, if one is right, then ten are ten times as right.

180 **Minister 5.** Obviously, you don't know who we are.

181 [*Each presents himself and* Milo *acknowledges the introduction.*]

182 **Minister 1.** The Duke of Definition.

183 **Minister 2.** The Minister of Meaning.

184 **Minister 3.** The Earl of Essence.

185 **Minister 4.** The Count of Connotation.

186 **Minister 5.** The Undersecretary of Understanding.

187 **All Five.** And we have come to invite you to the Royal Banquet.

188 **Spelling Bee.** The banquet! That's quite an honor, my boy. A real h-o-n-o-r.

189 **Humbug.** DON'T BE RIDICULOUS! Everybody goes to the Royal Banquet these days.

190 **Spelling Bee.** [*To the* Humbug] True, everybody does go. But some people are invited and others simply push their way in where they aren't wanted.

191 **Humbug.** HOW DARE YOU? You buzzing little upstart, I'll show you who's not wanted . . . [*Raises his cane threateningly.*]

NOTES

CLOSE READ
ANNOTATE: In paragraphs 182–186, mark the letters that start the two main words of each character's title.

QUESTION: Why do both main words of each character's title begin with the same letters?

CONCLUDE: What effect do these repeated sounds create?

CLOSE READ

You may wish to model the close read using the following think-aloud format. Possible responses to questions on the student page are included.

ANNOTATE: As I read paragraphs 182–186, I notice and highlight the words that the ministers use to identify their titles.

QUESTION: The first word I highlighted in each line sounds official. The second word refers to language. Each word pair uses the same letter. This develops a repeated sound.

CONCLUDE: The playwright's choice to use a repeated sound creates both a rhythm and a musicality. It is also funny.

© Pearson Education, Inc., or its affiliates. All rights reserved.

The Phantom Tollbooth, Act I **299**

© Pearson Education, Inc., or its affiliates. All rights reserved.

NOTES

192 **Spelling Bee.** You just watch it! I'm warning w-a-r-n-i-n-g you! [*At that moment, an ear-shattering blast of TRUMPETS, entirely* off-key, *is heard, and* a page *appears.*]

193 **Page.** King Azaz the Unabridged is about to begin the Royal banquet. All guests who do not appear promptly at the table will automatically lose their place. [*A huge Table is carried out with King Azaz sitting in a large chair, carried out at the head of the table.*]

194 **Azaz.** Places. Everyone take your places. [*All the characters, including the Humbug and the Spelling Bee, who forget their quarrel, rush to take their places at the table. Milo and Tock sit near the king. Azaz looks at Milo.*] And just who is this?

195 **Milo.** Your Highness, my name is Milo and this is Tock. Thank you very much for inviting us to your banquet, and I think your palace is beautiful!

196 **Minister 1.** Exquisite.

197 **Minister 2.** Lovely.

198 **Minister 3.** Handsome.

PERSONALIZE FOR LEARNING

English Language Support
Domain-Specific Vocabulary Review the banquet scene in paragraphs 192–195. Some of the vocabulary that appears in this scene may present challenges to English learners. Support them in understanding the text by reviewing the following terms that relate to a royal event:

Trumpet (paragraph 192): an instrument that is blown before an event

Page (paragraph 192): a person who delivers messages
Banquet (paragraph 193): a grand and formal dinner
Your Highness: (paragraph 195): used when speaking to or about a royal person, such as a king or queen
Palace (paragraph 195): the large, grand home of a royal person

Have students read the lines containing the terms. Then have them paraphrase the sentences, replacing the term with its definition. For example:
Thank you very much for inviting us to your banquet, and I think your palace is beautiful.
Thank you very much for inviting us to your dinner, and I think your home is beautiful. **ALL LEVELS**

© Pearson Education, Inc., or its affiliates. All rights reserved.

199 **Minister 4.** Pretty.

200 **Minister 5.** Charming.

201 **Azaz.** SILENCE! Now tell me, young man, what can you do to entertain us? Sing songs? Tell stories? Juggle plates? Do tumbling tricks? Which is it?

202 **Milo.** I can't do any of those things.

203 **Azaz.** What an ordinary little boy. Can't you do anything at all?

204 **Milo.** Well . . . I can count to a thousand.

205 **Azaz.** AARGH, numbers! Never mention numbers here. Only use them when we absolutely have to. Now, why don't we change the subject and have some dinner? Since you are the guest of honor, you may pick the menu.

206 **Milo.** Me? Well, uh . . . I'm not very hungry. Can we just have a light snack?

207 **Azaz.** A light snack it shall be!

NOTES

The Phantom Tollbooth, Act I **301**

CLOSE READ

You may wish to model the close read using the following think-aloud format. Possible responses to questions on the student page are included.

ANNOTATE: As I read paragraphs 223–226, I notice and mark the words that might sound like they are seasoning for food.

QUESTION: The words are clever and funny, so I think the playwright used them to show how word choices can be clever.

CONCLUDE: The way the playwright introduces these unusual words in the scene has the effect of making the dialogue move quickly and cleverly. It keeps the mood of the play light, but it makes the reader or the audience think about the scene and the words being used.

NOTES

CLOSE READ

ANNOTATE: In paragraphs 223–226, mark the words that sound like but are not actually a seasoning or food.

QUESTION: Why does the playwright use this wordplay?

CONCLUDE: What is the effect of these and other examples of wordplay throughout this scene?

208 [Azaz *claps his hands. Waiters* rush in with covered trays. When they are uncovered, Shafts of Light pour out. The light may be created through the use of battery-operated flashlights which are secured in the trays and covered with a false bottom. The Guests help themselves.]

209 **Humbug.** Not a very substantial meal. Maybe you can suggest something a little more filling.

210 **Milo.** Well, in that case, I think we ought to have a square meal . . .

211 **Azaz.** [*Claps his hands.*] A square meal it is! [*Waiters serve trays of Colored Squares of all sizes. People serve themselves.*]

212 **Spelling Bee.** These are awful. [Humbug *coughs and all the Guests do not care for the food.*]

213 **Azaz.** [*Claps his hands and the trays are removed.*] Time for speeches. [*To* Milo.] You first.

214 **Milo.** [*Hesitantly.*] Your Majesty, ladies and gentlemen, I would like to take this opportunity to say that . . .

215 **Azaz.** That's quite enough. Mustn't talk all day.

216 **Milo.** But I just started to . . .

217 **Azaz.** NEXT!

218 **Humbug.** [*Quickly*] Roast turkey, mashed potatoes, vanilla ice cream.

219 **Spelling Bee.** Hamburgers, corn on the cob, chocolate pudding p-u-d-d-i-n-g. [*Each Guest names two dishes and a dessert.*]

220 **Azaz.** [*The last.*] Pâté de foie gras, soupe à l'oignon, salade endives, fromage et fruits et demi-tasse. [*He claps his hands. Waiters serve each Guest his Words.*] Dig in. [*To* Milo.] Though I can't say I think much of your choice.

221 **Milo.** I didn't know I was going to have to eat my words.

222 **Azaz.** Of course, of course, everybody here does. Your speech should have been in better taste.

223 **Minister 1.** Here, try some somersault. It improves the flavor.

224 **Minister 2.** Have a rigamarole. [*Offers breadbasket.*]

225 **Minister 3.** Or a ragamuffin.

226 **Minister 4.** Perhaps you'd care for a synonym bun.

© Pearson Education, Inc., or its affiliates. All rights reserved.

227 **Minister 5.** Why not wait for your just desserts?

228 **Azaz.** Ah yes, the dessert. We're having a special treat today . . . freshly made at the half-bakery.

229 **Milo.** The half-bakery?

230 **Azaz.** Of course, the half-bakery! Where do you think half-baked ideas come from? Now, please don't interrupt. By royal command, the pastry chefs have . . .

231 **Milo.** What's a half-baked idea?

232 [Azaz *gives up the idea of speaking as a cart is wheeled in and the Guests help themselves.*]

233 **Humbug.** They're very tasty, but they don't always agree with you. Here's a good one. [Humbug *hands one to* Milo.]

234 **Milo.** [*Reads.*] "The earth is flat."

235 **Spelling Bee.** People swallowed that one for years. [*Picks up one and reads.*] "The moon is made of green cheese." Now, there's a half-baked idea.

236 [*Everyone chooses one and eats. They include: "It Never Rains But Pours, "Night Air Is Bad Air," "Everything Happens for the Best," "Coffee Stunts Your Growth."*]

237 **Azaz.** And now for a few closing words. Attention! Let me have your attention! [*Everyone leaps up and Exits, except for* Milo, Tock, *and the* Humbug.] Loyal subjects and friends, once again on this gala occasion, we have . . .

238 **Milo.** Excuse me, but everybody left.

239 **Azaz.** [*Sadly.*] I was hoping no one would notice. It happens every time.

240 **Humbug.** They're gone to dinner, and as soon as I finish this last bite, I shall join them.

241 **Milo.** That's ridiculous. How can they eat dinner right after a banquet?

242 **Azaz.** SCANDALOUS! We'll put a stop to it at once. From now on, by royal command, everyone must eat dinner before the banquet.

243 **Milo.** But that's just as bad.

244 **Humbug.** Or just as good. Things which are equally bad are also equally good. Try to look at the bright side of things.

© Pearson Education, Inc., or its affiliates. All rights reserved.

NOTES

The Phantom Tollbooth, Act I **303**

PERSONALIZE FOR LEARNING

Challenge

Building Understanding Point out the "half-baked ideas" that are mentioned in paragraphs 234–236. Ask students if they have ever heard of these. Point out other half-baked ideas. Then discuss why the playwright calls them "half-baked." Encourage students to dissect the sayings and analyze why people might believe them. Then discuss how sayings like these might actually catch on and get passed down. Encourage interested students to come up with their own lists of half-baked ideas and share them with the class.

TEACHING

● CLOSER LOOK

Understand Alliteration ◉

Students may have highlighted examples of alliteration in paragraph 262 during their first read. Encourage them to talk about the annotations that they marked. You may want to model a close read with the class based on the highlights shown in the text.

ANNOTATE: Have students mark examples of alliteration in paragraph 262. Remind students that alliteration is the repetition of similar consonant sounds at the beginning of words.

QUESTION: Guide students to consider why the playwright used alliteration here.

Possible response: I notice that the words Humbug is using, such as *brave*, *stout*, and *steadfast* are adjectives that are often used to describe heroes, whereas *serviceable* and *small* are a bit more ordinary and practical. I think the playwright is using these examples of alliteration to call attention to the words.

CONCLUDE: Help students draw conclusions about the effect of using alliteration in this dialogue.

Possible response: I think the effect of the alliteration is to create a humorous image—that of a brave hero with a small car. The contrast is funny, though the words sound poetic and important. This fits with Humbug's character, too. He always says things that seem grand or formal.

Remind students that **alliteration** is one of many language techniques playwrights use in dialogue to create humor or to make a point about characterization and theme.

NOTES

245 **Milo.** I don't know which side of anything to look at. Everything is so confusing, and all your words only make things worse.

246 **Azaz.** How true. There must be something we can do about it.

247 **Humbug.** Pass a law.

248 **Azaz.** We have almost as many laws as words.

249 **Humbug.** Offer a reward. [Azaz *shakes his head and looks madder at each suggestion.*] Send for help? Drive a bargain? Pull the switch? Lower the boom? Toe the line?

250 [*As Azaz continues to scowl, the* Humbug *loses confidence and finally gives up.*]

251 **Milo.** Maybe you should let Rhyme and Reason return.

252 **Azaz.** How nice that would be. Even if they were a bother at times, things always went so well when they were here. But I'm afraid it can't be done.

253 **Humbug.** Certainly not. Can't be done.

254 **Milo.** Why not?

255 **Humbug.** [*Now siding with* Milo.] Why not, indeed?

256 **Azaz.** Much too difficult.

257 **Humbug.** Of course, much too difficult.

258 **Milo.** You could, if you really wanted to.

259 **Humbug.** By all means, if you really wanted to, you could.

260 **Azaz.** [*To* Humbug.] How?

261 **Milo.** [*Also to* Humbug.] Yeah, how?

262 **Humbug.** Why . . . uh, it's a simple task for a brave boy with a stout heart, a steadfast dog and a serviceable small automobile.

263 **Azaz.** Go on.

264 **Humbug.** Well, all that he would have to do is cross the dangerous, unknown countryside between here and Digitopolis, where he would have to persuade the Mathemagician to release the Princesses, which we know to

© Pearson Education, Inc., or its affiliates. All rights reserved.

304 UNIT 4 • IMAGINATION

304 UNIT 4 • IMAGINATION

be impossible because the Mathemagician will never agree with Azaz about anything. Once achieving that, it's a simple matter of entering the Mountains of Ignorance from where no one has ever returned alive, an effortless climb up a two thousand foot stairway without railings in a high wind at night to the Castle-in-the-Air. After a pleasant chat with the Princesses, all that remains is a leisurely ride back through those chaotic crags where the frightening fiends have sworn to tear any intruder limb from limb and devour him down to his belt buckle. And finally after doing all that, a triumphal parade! If, of course, there is anything left to parade . . . followed by hot chocolate and cookies for everyone.

NOTES

265 **Azaz.** I never realized it would be so simple.

266 **Milo.** It sounds dangerous to me.

267 **Tock.** And just who is supposed to make that journey?

268 **Azaz.** A very good question. But there is one far more serious problem.

269 **Milo.** What's that?

270 **Azaz.** I'm afraid I can't tell you that until you return.

271 **Milo.** But wait a minute, I didn't . . .

272 **Azaz.** Dictionopolis will always be grateful to you, my boy, and your dog. [Azaz *pats* Tock *and* Milo.]

273 **Tock.** Now, just one moment, sire . . .

274 **Azaz.** You will face many dangers on your journey, but fear not, for I can give you something for your protection. [Azaz *gives* Milo *a box.*] In this box are the letters of the alphabet. With them you can form all the words you will ever need to help you overcome the obstacles that may stand in your path. All you must do is use them well and in the right places.

275 **Milo.** [*Miserably.*] Thanks a lot.

276 **Azaz.** You will need a guide, of course, and since he knows the obstacles so well, the Humbug has cheerfully volunteered to accompany you.

277 **Humbug.** Now, see here . . . !

© Pearson Education, Inc., or its affiliates. All rights reserved.

The Phantom Tollbooth, Act I **305**

PERSONALIZE FOR LEARNING

Strategic Support

Irony Some students may have difficulty understanding and interpreting irony. Guide them through the literal interpretation of the tasks described in paragraph 264. For example, discuss a "climb up a two thousand foot stairway without railings in a high wind at night." Ask students what they think this might be like. Then ask them if Humbug's description of it as "effortless" seems right. Have them consider why the playwright used irony here by considering the character of Humbug and what his motivations are at this point in the play.

CLOSER LOOK

Examine Foreshadowing 📝

Students may have marked paragraphs 281–286 during their first read. Use these paragraphs to help students understand how foreshadowing works to build suspense in literature. Encourage them to talk about the annotations that they marked. You may want to model a close read with the class based on the highlights shown in the text.

ANNOTATE: Have students mark details in paragraphs 281–286 that hint that something will happen later in the play, or have students participate while you highlight them.

QUESTION: Guide students to consider what these details might tell them. Ask what a reader can infer from a loud clap of thunder and Humbug's feeling that something terrible will happen, and accept student responses. **Possible response:** The playwright is using thunder and the characters' fear and nervousness to suggest that they are heading toward danger and that something bad is going to happen.

CONCLUDE: Help students to formulate conclusions about the importance of these details in the text. Ask students why the playwright might have included these details. **Possible response:** By adding these details, the playwright wants the reader or viewer to be scared along with the characters and to wonder what will happen next. The details create suspense.

Remind students that **foreshadowing** is the use of clues that hint at events that are going to occur later in the plot of a narrative. This technique helps create **suspense**, the quality in a literary work that keeps the reader wondering about what will happen next.

NOTES

278 **Azaz.** You will find him dependable, brave, resourceful, and loyal.

279 **Humbug.** [*Flattered.*] Oh, your Majesty.

280 **Milo.** I'm sure he'll be a great help. [*They approach the car.*]

281 **Tock.** I hope so. It looks like we're going to need it.

282 [*The lights darken and the king fades from view.*]

283 **Azaz.** Good luck! Drive carefully! [*The three get into the car and begin to move. Suddenly a thunderously loud NOISE is heard. They slow down the car.*]

284 **Milo.** What was that?

285 **Tock.** It came from up ahead.

286 **Humbug.** It's something terrible, I just know it. Oh, no. Something dreadful is going to happen to us. I can feel it in my bones. [*The NOISE is repeated. They all look at each other fearfully as the lights fade.*] ❧

© Pearson Education, Inc., or its affiliates. All rights reserved.

Comprehension Check

Complete the following items after you finish your first read.

1. What is in the package that Milo receives?

2. Who is Tock and what does he look like?

3. What do the merchants in the marketplace of Dictionopolis sell?

4. What does Azaz send Milo, Tock, and Humbug to do?

5. What does Azaz give Milo?

6. **Notebook** Write a short summary of Act I to show your understanding.

RESEARCH

Research to Clarify Choose at least one unfamiliar detail from the text. Briefly research that detail. In what way does the information you learned shed light on an aspect of the play?

Research to Explore Choose something that interested you from the text and formulate a research question. Write your question here.

The Phantom Tollbooth, Act I **307**

Comprehension Check

Possible responses:

1. A phantom tollbooth is in the package that Milo receives.
2. Tock is a dog with a clock for a body.
3. The merchants in the marketplace sell words.
4. He sends them to convince the Mathemagician to release the princesses and then to bring them back to Dictionopolis.
5. He gives Milo a box containing the letters of the alphabet.
6. Summaries will vary; however, students should include a description of the tollbooth, the Lethargarians, Tock, Humbug, and the mission that Azaz is sending Milo on.

Research

Research to Clarify If students struggle to come up with a detail to research, you may want to suggest that they focus on one of the following topics: tollbooths, clocks, word origins, the alphabet.

Research to Explore If students aren't sure how to go about formulating a research question, suggest that they use their findings from Research to Clarify as a starting point. For example, if students researched the alphabet, they might formulate a question such as *What is the history of the alphabet?*

PERSONALIZE FOR LEARNING

Challenge

Fairy Tale Research Point out to students that *The Phantom Tollbooth* is a kind of modern fairy tale. Encourage interested students to research fairy tales and find out what all fairy tales have in common. Ask them to consider questions such as: *What features does a fairy tale have? What cultures have fairy tales? How long have they been around? What do they teach us?* Students should include short summaries of fairy tales from other cultures that they have read. Suggest that they also create illustrations to go along with the fairy tale. Encourage students to share their findings with the class.

Jump Start

CLOSE READ Have students close read the title "The Phantom Tollbooth." Ask students what *phantom* means, as a noun and as an adjective. Discuss why the author might have described the tollbooth as a "phantom tollbooth" and what it might tell readers about Milo's adventure.

Close Read the Text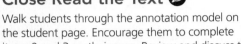

Walk students through the annotation model on the student page. Encourage them to complete items 2 and 3 on their own. Review and discuss the sections students have marked. If needed, continue to model close reading by using the Annotation Highlights in the Interactive Teacher's Edition.

Analyze the Text

Possible responses:

1. The Clock means that when you're bored, you are going to find most things boring. Only something out of the ordinary is going to get you to pay attention. **DOK 2**

2. (a) It symbolizes the need for Milo not to waste time. (b) Milo would probably still be in the Doldrums because he didn't think and that's the only way to get out. **DOK 3**

3. Milo seems interested in the people and things around him. He doesn't seem bored anymore because he is experiencing new things and is being forced to think. **DOK 3**

4. It may mean that it is all happening in his imagination. **DOK 3**

5. Answers will vary. Students may say that imagination and thinking will take you places and will make life more interesting. **DOK 3**

THE PHANTOM TOLLBOOTH,
ACT I

Close Read the Text

1. This model—from Act I, scene ii—shows two sample annotations, along with questions and conclusions. Close read the passage, and find another detail to annotate. Then, write a question and a conclusion.

Close Read

> **ANNOTATE:** These words suggest something easy and stress-free.
>
> **QUESTION:** Why does the playwright use words that make the job sound so easy?
>
> **CONCLUDE:** The contrast shows that Humbug is trying to play down the dangers. It also makes the passage funny.

> **ANNOTATE:** These prepositional phrases add scary details.
>
> **QUESTION:** Why does the playwright add the dangerous details in subordinate phrases?
>
> **CONCLUDE:** The sentence structure shows that Humbug is telling the truth, but also trying to hide it.

> . . . it's a simple matter of entering the Mountains of Ignorance from where no one has ever returned alive, an effortless climb up a two thousand foot stairway without railings in a high wind at night to the Castle-in-the-Air. After a pleasant chat with the Princesses, all that remains is a leisurely ride back through those chaotic crags. . . .

2. For more practice, go back into the text and complete the close-read notes.

3. Revisit a section of the text you found important during your first read. Read this section closely and **annotate** what you notice. Ask yourself **questions** such as "Why did the author make this choice?" What can you **conclude**?

- -

Analyze the Text

CITE TEXTUAL EVIDENCE to support your answers.

📓 **Notebook** Respond to these questions.

1. **Interpret** The Clock says, ". . . when you're bored, what you need more than anything is a rude awakening." Explain what this means.

2. (a) What does the clock on Tock's body represent? (b) **Speculate** If Tock hadn't come along, would Milo still be in the Doldrums? Explain.

3. **Draw Conclusions** At the end of Act I, is Milo still bored? Explain.

4. **Make Inferences** Milo's bedroom contains images of characters from the Land of Wisdom. What might this mean about Milo's adventure?

5. **Essential Question:** *Where can imagination lead?* What have you learned about imagination from reading Act I of the play?

🔧 **Tool Kit**
Close-Read Guide and
Model Annotation

📋 **STANDARDS**

Reading Literature
- Describe how a particular story's or drama's plot unfolds in a series of episodes as well as how the characters respond or change as the plot moves toward a resolution.
- Analyze how a particular sentence, chapter, scene, or stanza fits into the overall structure of a text and contributes to the development of the theme, setting, or plot.
- Explain how an author develops the point of view of the narrator or speaker in a text.

308 UNIT 4 • IMAGINATION

FORMATIVE ASSESSMENT

Analyze the Text

- **If** students fail to cite evidence, **then** remind them to support their ideas with specific information.

- **If** students struggle to determine what the clock symbolizes, **then** discuss the term *symbolize* and provide examples.

PERSONALIZE FOR LEARNING

English Language Support

Asking Questions Conducting a second close read of a drama can be a demanding task for English language learners. To help them understand some of the longer and more complicated lines, suggest that they go back and reread details they annotated. If the meaning is unclear, suggest that they jot down questions, for example, "What was the decision of Rhyme and Reason, and why were the kings upset about it?" When students have finished the selection, suggest they return to the questions. Point out that sometimes, the answer to the question becomes clearer the more they read. Suggest that if their question was not answered in the reading that they pair up with a partner and discuss the questions they have. **ALL LEVELS**

© Pearson Education, Inc., or its affiliates. All rights reserved.

Analyze Craft and Structure

Dramatic Structures A **drama**, or play, is a story that is written to be performed in front of an audience. Dramas are divided into shorter sections called **acts**. Each act may contain several scenes. A **scene** is like a little play by itself. It presents action in a specific situation.

Like a novel or a short story, a drama has characters, settings, and a plot that revolves around conflict. However, in a drama, information about these elements is developed through the actors' words, or **dialogue**. In a **script,** or written form of a play, each character's name appears before his or her dialogue, as in this example:

> **Milo.** I think I was on my way to Dictionopolis when I got stuck here. Can you help me?

> **Watchdog.** Help you! You've got to help yourself. I suppose you know why you got stuck.

When reading a play, think about how each character's **point of view,** or personality and beliefs, is shown through dialogue. Also, notice how the drama provides most of the information about the conflict and moves the story forward.

Practice

CITE TEXTUAL EVIDENCE
to support your answers.

📝 **Notebook** Respond to these questions.

1. Complete this chart to explain what each passage of dialogue tells you about a character, the setting, and an action. An example has been provided.

DIALOGUE	WHAT IT TELLS YOU
Milo. I've never heard of any of these places. Well, it doesn't matter anyway. Dictionopolis. That's a weird name. I might as well go there.	Not caring about where he goes shows that Milo is not fully convinced about the value of this journey. It shows that a change in setting is about to happen. It also moves the action along by having Milo travel to a new place.
Gatekeeper. This is Dictionopolis, a happy kingdom, advantageously located in the foothills of Confusion and caressed by gentle breezes from the Sea of Knowledge.	It reveals the setting of Dictionopolis and suggests what it is like.
Watchdog. KILLING TIME!... It's bad enough wasting time without killing it. What are you doing in the Doldrums, anyway? Don't you have anywhere to go?	It shows that the Watchdog can be impatient and interested in Milo. His questions move the action along.

2. Reread paragraphs 247–274 of Scene ii. How do these lines of dialogue help move the plot forward?

The Phantom Tollbooth, Act I **309**

Analyze Craft and Structure

Dramatic Structures Ask students about a favorite movie or television show they've seen recently. Then ask them to imagine the movie or show if the characters did not speak. Tell students that in movies, television shows, and other dramas, the words spoken by characters are called *dialogue* and that dialogue reveals a lot about what is happening in the story. For more support, see **Analyze Craft and Structure: Dramatic Structures.** 📄

Practice

1. See possible responses in chart on student page.

2. They establish that Milo will have a method for overcoming difficulty. They also show that Humbug is going along as a guide.

FORMATIVE ASSESSMENT

Analyze Craft and Structure

- **If** students struggle to determine how dialogue establishes setting, **then** point them toward descriptive words and phrases and ask them what they describe.

- **If** students fail to see what dialogue reveals about characters, **then** work backwards by asking them what they know about the character and whether the dialogue in question supports that understanding.

For Reteach and Practice, see **Analyze Craft and Structure: Dramatic Structures (RP).** 📄

WriteNow Express and Reflect

Dialogue The dialogue in *The Phantom Tollbooth,* Act I, reveals a lot about the characters, the setting, and the plot of the drama. Have students write one page of dialogue . It can be based on real or imagined events between themselves and someone else, perhaps a friend or sibling. Tell them that the dialogue should reveal something about a problem, about one of the characters in the dialogue, or about the setting. Point out that the dialogue in the drama is clever and fun to read partly because it is not wordy. The lines are short and specific and each line contributes something to the drama.

© Pearson Education, Inc., or its affiliates. All rights reserved.

Concept Vocabulary

Why These Words?

Possible responses:

1. These words focus on confusion. Act I stresses exploration and learning—two strategies for solving problems and reducing confusion.

2. *whether, conclusion, argument, opposite,*

Practice

1. correct; he thought a great deal about it.

2. correct; speculating is guessing but seeing the list would be knowing.

3. correct; misapprehension is a mistaken belief.

4. correct; to surmise is to guess without details. the speaker may not have seen the rain, but instead sees its consequence.

5. incorrect: most people would not be proud of both ignorance and skill.

6. correct: presume is the opposite of knowing for sure.

Word Network

Possible words: *invented, beyond, awakening*

Word Study

For more support, see **Concept Vocabulary and Word Study.** 📄

Possible responses:

Denotation: saves money *Nuances*: stingy—cheap, miserly; economical—sensible with money; thrifty—careful with money

---

FORMATIVE ASSESSMENT

Concept Vocabulary

If students fail to see how the words relate to places in the drama, **then** ask them how the words in the example are used.

Word Study

If students are unable to define the words, **then** have them focus on the prefix *mis-*. For Reteach and Practice, see **Word Study: Denotation and Nuance (RP).** 📄

THE PHANTOM TOLLBOOTH, ACT I

⬡ WORD NETWORK

Add words related to imagination from the text to your Word Network.

⬛ STANDARDS

Language
• Demonstrate command of the conventions of standard English grammar and usage when writing or speaking.

• Demonstrate understanding of figurative language, word relationships, and nuances in word meanings.
  c. Distinguish among the connotations of words with similar denotations.

Concept Vocabulary

ignorance	presume	misapprehension
surmise	speculate	consideration

Why These Words? These concept words relate to people's level of knowledge and how they use their minds. For example, if you are *ignorant,* you lack knowledge. If you hold a *misapprehension,* you are confused about something.

1. How does the concept vocabulary sharpen the reader's understanding of some of the key ideas being explored in *The Phantom Tollbooth,* Act I?

2. What other words in the selection connect to this concept?

Practice

⊜ **Notebook** The six concept vocabulary words appear in the play. Note whether the concept vocabulary word is used correctly in each sentence. Explain your reasoning.

1. Refusing to think about the problem, Monroe gave it all his *consideration.*

2. Rather than *speculate,* let's just wait to see if we made the squad.

3. My *misapprehension* led me to make a lot of mistakes on the test.

4. I *surmise* that it's raining since your coat is soaking wet.

5. Leena was eager to demonstrate her *ignorance* and skill.

6. You should not *presume* where I want to go; you should ask me.

Word Study

Denotation and Nuance The **denotation** of a word is its literal definition, which you would find in a dictionary. Two words that have the same denotation may have different **nuances,** or slight shades of difference in their meanings. For example, the concept vocabulary words *surmise* and *speculate* both mean "guess." However, *surmise* implies that the guessing is based on a hunch, or feeling. In contrast, *speculate* implies that the guessing is based on incomplete information.

Use a dictionary to look up these three words that have the same denotation: *stingy, economical, thrifty.* First, write down the denotation that they share. Then, explain the nuances in their exact meanings.

© Pearson Education, Inc., or its affiliates. All rights reserved.

AUTHOR'S PERSPECTIVE Elfrieda Hiebert, Ph.D.

Concept Vocabulary Teachers can help students expand their word networks by using morphemes and cognates.

• **Morphemes** are the smallest grammatical unit of a language that cannot be subdivided into further such elements. Tell students that morphemes can be words or parts of words, such as the words *as, the, write,* or the *-ed* in *stayed.* Many new words are members of morphological families of three-five words. For example, words that come from the Anglo-Saxon layer of English use inflected endings (such as *-s/-es, -ed, -ing*) and *-er* and *-est* for comparisons (such as *big, bigger, biggest*).

• **Cognates** are words that are descended from the same language, such as the English word *family,* the Spanish *familia,* the French *famille,* the Italian *famiglia,* and the German *familie.* Explain to students that knowing cognates can help build language by introducing multiple words and ways to decode unfamiliar words.

Conventions

Sentence Parts and Types Good writers know how to use sentence parts and sentence variation to make their writing more interesting. A **sentence** consists of a subject and a predicate, and it expresses a complete thought. It always begins with a capital letter.

- A **simple subject** is the single person, place, or thing about which the sentence is written.
- A **complete subject** includes the simple subject and any related words.
- A **simple predicate** is the verb that expresses the sentence's action.
- A **complete predicate** includes the simple predicate and related words, such as adverbs, objects, and prepositional phrases.
- A **compound subject** is made up of two or more nouns that share the same verb and are joined by conjunctions such as *and* or *or*.

Sentences can be classified according to the following functions:

TYPE OF SENTENCE	FUNCTION	END PUNCTUATION	SAMPLE SENTENCE
Declarative	States an idea	Period	We don't like this music.
Interrogative	Asks a question	Question mark	May I play football now?
Imperative	Gives an order or direction	Period or exclamation mark	Put this dish away.
Exclamatory	Expresses strong emotion	Exclamation mark	What a fun game this is!

> **TIP**
>
> **CLARIFICATION**
> Refer to the Grammar Handbook to learn more about these terms.

Read It

 Notebook Read these sentences from the play. Mark the complete subject and complete predicate in each sentence.

1. This package contains the following items.
2. I can count to a thousand.
3. All guests who do not appear promptly at the table will automatically lose their place.

Write It

 Notebook Rewrite each sentence to change it into the type indicated.

1. You can't get in without a reason. (exclamatory)
2. Count them off. (interrogative)
3. May we have a light snack? (imperative)
4. How can they eat dinner right after a banquet? (declarative)

> **EVIDENCE LOG**
>
> Before moving on to a new selection, go to your Evidence Log and record what you learned from *The Phantom Tollbooth*, Act I.

The Phantom Tollbooth, Act I **311**

© Pearson Education, Inc., or its affiliates. All rights reserved.

PERSONALIZE FOR LEARNING

English Language Support

Denotation and Nuance English language learners may struggle to identify nuances of vocabulary meaning. Work with students to practice this important vocabulary skill.

Work with student pairs to explain and identify the difference in English words that students may know: *hard* vs. *impossible*; *big* vs. *enormous*, *tired* vs. *exhausted*. **EMERGING**

Ask students to build off the word pairs presented to add at least one other word with a similar denotation. **EXPANDING**

Ask students to write sentences for each word group to demonstrate the differences in nuance. **BRIDGING**

An expanded **English Language Development Lesson** on Denotation and Nuance is available in the Interactive Teacher's Edition.

Conventions

Sentence Parts and Types Say the following to students:

The dog on the leash.

Ask students if the words make up a sentence, and if not, why. Discuss the fact that while there is a subject, there is no verb and so the words do not express a complete thought. Then ask students how the following sentences differ:

The dog ran away!
Did the dog run away?
The dog ran away.
Make sure the dog doesn't run away.

Point out that while they are similar in subject matter, the punctuation and slight rewording in each sentence suggests a different thought or idea. For more support, see **Conventions: Sentence Parts and Types.**

MAKE IT INTERACTIVE
Have students write each sentence on a sentence strip using a different colored marker for the complete subject and for the complete predicate.

Read It
Possible responses:

1. This package (complete subject) contains the following items. (complete predicate)
2. I (complete subject) can count to a thousand. (complete predicate)
3. All guests who do not appear promptly at the table (complete subject) will automatically lose their place. (complete predicate)

Write It
Possible responses:

1. You can't get in without a reason!
2. Can you count them off?
3. Have a light snack.
4. They can eat dinner right after a banquet.

Evidence Log Support students in completing their Evidence Log. This paced activity will help prepare them for the Performance-Based Assessment at the end of the unit.

FORMATIVE ASSESSMENT

Conventions

- **If** students can't identify the complete predicate, **then** tell them to ask themselves what the subject is doing.

- **If** students struggle to rewrite the sentences into different types, **then** have them first change the end punctuation to the required type and then adjust the sentence so that it fits the end punctuation.

For Reteach and Practice, see **Conventions: Sentence Parts and Types (RP).**

Whole-Class Learning **311**

The Phantom Tollbooth, Act II

🔊 AUDIO SUMMARIES
Audio summaries of *The Phantom Tollbooth*, Act II, are available online in both English and Spanish in the Interactive Teacher's Edition or Unit Resources. Assigning these summaries prior to reading the selection may help students build additional background knowledge and set a context for their first read.

Summary

In the second half of Susan Nanus's adaptation of *The Phantom Tollbooth,* Milo travels towards Digitopolis, city of numbers. On the way he meets Dr. Dischord and the Dynne and the many-faced Dodecahedron. In Digitopolis he convinces the Mathemagician, ruler of numbers, to support his quest to rescue Rhyme and Reason. After explaining the importance of numbers, the Mathemagician sends Milo on to the Land of Ignorance. There, Milo and his friends face a series of demons on their way to the prison of the Princesses Rhyme and Reason. The Princesses escape with them and are chased by the demons. Finally, the forces of Wisdom arrive for the confrontation between the demons and wisdom, and also between Azaz and the Mathemagician.

Insight

In this selection, the story of the Phantom Tollbooth comes to a conclusion with Rhyme and Reason bringing Azaz and the Mathemagician together. Milo's success, though "impossible," is framed as an act of education: the ultimate purpose of his quest was to learn the value of thought and discovery.

ESSENTIAL QUESTION:
Where can imagination lead?

Connection to Essential Question

In this section, the Demons of Ignorance appear, and answer the essential question in a negative sense. The Demons of Ignorance epitomize a lack of imagination and thought.

WHOLE-CLASS LEARNING
PERFORMANCE TASK
One day in the Kingdom of Wisdom . . .

Connection to Performance Tasks

Whole-Class Learning Performance Task This selection provides more examples of the particular style of place that appears in *The Phantom Tollbooth*, as well as characters overcoming literalized intellectual challenges. Students will need to understand the setting and the rules of the Kingdom of Wisdom to address the prompt.

UNIT PERFORMANCE-BASED
ASSESSMENT
What might happen if a fictional character were to come into the real world?

Unit Performance-Based Assessment The extent of the play's imaginary setting is stretched as new characters are introduced to its fictional world. This play will help students consider their own response to the prompt which asks students to consider a reversed premise.

LESSON RESOURCES

	Making Meaning	Language Development	Effective Expression
Lesson	**First Read** **Close Read** **Analyze the Text** **Analyze Craft and Structure**	**Concept Vocabulary** **Word Study** **Conventions**	**Writing to Sources** **Speaking and Listening**
Instructional Standards	**RL.5** Analyze how a particular sentence, chapter, scene, or stanza . . . **RL.10** By the end of the year, read and comprehend literature . . .	**L.1** Demonstrate command of the conventions . . . **L.3** Use knowledge of language and its conventions . . . **L.3.a** Vary sentence patterns for meaning . . . **L.4** Determine or clarify the meaning of unknown and multiple-meaning words and phrases . . . **L.4.b** Use common, grade-appropriate Greek or Latin affixes and roots	**W.3** Write narratives . . . **W.3.a** Engage and orient the reader . . . **W.3.b** Use narrative techniques . . . **SL.6** Adapt speech to a variety of contexts and tasks . . .
▶ **STUDENT RESOURCES**			
Available online in the Interactive Student Edition or Unit Resources	🔊 Selection Audio 📄 First-Read Guide: Drama 📄 Close-Read Guide: Drama	📄 Word Network	📄 Evidence Log
▶ **TEACHER RESOURCES**			
Selection Resources Available online in the Interactive Teacher's Edition or Unit Resources	🔊 Audio Summaries ✏️ Annotation Highlights 💬 EL Highlights 📄 Analyze Craft and Structure: Stage Directions	📄 Concept Vocabulary and Word Study 📄 Conventions: Sentence Structure	📄 Writing to Sources: Narrative Retelling 📄 English Language Support Lesson: Narrative Retelling 📄 Speaking and Listening: Dramatic Reading
Reteach/Practice (RP) Available online in the Interactive Teacher's Edition or Unit Resources	📄 Analyze Craft and Structure: Stage Directions (RP)	📄 Word Study: Latin Suffix *-ity* (RP) 📄 Conventions: Sentence Structure (RP)	📄 Writing to Sources: Narrative Retelling (RP) 📄 Speaking and Listening: Dramatic Reading (RP)
Assessment Available online in Assessments	📄✅ Selection Test		
My Resources	📄 A Unit 4 Answer Key is available online and in the Interactive Teacher's Edition.		

Reading Support

Text Complexity Rubric: *The Phantom Tollbooth*, Act II

Quantitative Measures

Lexile: NP   Text Length: 7,957 words

Qualitative Measures

Knowledge Demands ①—②—**❸**—④—⑤	The selection contains imaginary kingdoms. Characters have descriptive names. Students will encounter humorous writing.
Structure ①—②—③—**❹**—⑤	The selection contains dialogue as well as stage directions and descriptions of sets.
Language Conventionality and Clarity ①—②—③—**❹**—⑤	Selection contains dialogue, some challenging vocabulary, word play, and long, complex sentences.
Levels of Meaning/Purpose ①—②—**❸**—④—⑤	The concept of the selection is accessible. It explores the value of time and hard work.

DECIDE AND PLAN

English Language Support

Provide English learners with support for knowledge demands and language as they read the selection.

Knowledge Demands Before they read Act II, have students summarize what happened in the first Act of *The Phantom Tollbooth* and make a prediction about what will happen in this next part. Then have them read the "Review and Anticipate" section that precedes the second half to see how their summaries and predictions compare.

Language Help students understand the use of onomatopoeia in this selection. Define how the literary device is used to describe sounds, drawing on examples from the beginning section of Act II. Point out the character Kakafonous A. Dischord. Explain how Kakafonous is a phonetic spelling of the word *cacophonous*.

Strategic Support

Provide students with strategic support to ensure that they can successfully read the text.

Language If students are having difficulty with wordplay, discuss how the names *Dynne (din)* and *Dischord (discord)* are related to the word *dissonance*. Have students explain how Dynne and Dischord's dialogue reflects the meaning of their names.

Structure Discuss the playwright's use of "blackout" between scenes and at the last stage direction, in which the "stage goes black." Explain how this feature is indicative of the lights going out or curtains closing during live stage plays. Describe how it is often used to add suspense and drama even here in written language.

Challenge

Provide students who need to be challenged with ideas for how they can go beyond a simple interpretation of the text.

Text Analysis Have students look at the illustration of Dodecahedron that accompanies his appearance in the play and describe the elements that make up his body. Discuss why the illustrator used these elements to create Dodecahedron.

Written Response Ask students to write a short story about a trip to a city of numbers. Have them be creative about naming characters and places with numerals. Have them be especially descriptive about what these names represent.

TEACH

Read and Respond

Have students do their first read of the selection. Then have them complete their close read. Finally, work with them on the Making Meaning, Language Development, and Effective Expression activities.

Standards Support Through Teaching and Learning Cycle

IDENTIFY NEEDS

Analyze results of the Beginning-of-Year Assessment, focusing on the items relating to Unit 4. Also take into consideration student performance to this point and your observations of where particular students struggle.

ANALYZE AND REVISE

- Analyze student work for evidence of student learning.
- Identify whether or not students have met the expectations in the standards.
- Identify implications for future instruction.

TEACH

Implement the planned lesson, and gather evidence of student learning.

DECIDE AND PLAN

- If students have performed poorly on items matching these standards, then provide selection scaffolds before assigning them the on-level lesson provided in the Student Edition.
- If students have done well on the Beginning-of-Year Assessment, then challenge them to keep progressing and learning by giving them opportunities to practice the skills in depth.
- Use the Selection Resources listed on the Planning pages for *The Phantom Tollbooth*, Act II, to help students continually improve their ability to master the standards.

Instructional Standards: *The Phantom Tollbooth*, Act II

	Catching Up	This Year	Looking Forward
Reading	You may wish to administer the **Analyze Craft and Structure: Stage Directions (RP)** worksheet to familiarize students with stage directions.	**RL.5** Analyze how a particular sentence, chapter, scene, or stanza fits into the overall structure of a text and contributes to the development of the theme, setting, or plot.	Ask students to explain how the form of the play contributes to its overall meaning.
Writing	You may wish to administer the **Writing to Sources: Narrative Retelling (RP)** worksheet to prepare students for their writing.	**W.3.b** Use narrative techniques, such as dialogue, pacing, and description, to develop experiences, events, and/or characters.	Challenge students to write their story so that it integrates into the play as a whole.
Speaking and Listening	You may wish to administer the **Speaking and Listening: Dramatic Reading (RP)** worksheet to prepare students for their dramatic readings.	**SL.6** Adapt speech to a variety of contexts and tasks, demonstrating command of formal English when indicated or appropriate.	Challenge students to incorporate other play conventions, such as costumes, props, sets, lighting, and/or music.
Language	You may wish to administer the **Conventions: Sentence Structure (RP)** worksheet to help students understand the differences between simple, compound, and complex sentences. You may wish to administer the **Word Study: Latin Suffix -*ity*** worksheet to help students understand that -*ity* means "the state or quality of."	**L.3.a** Vary sentence patterns for meaning, reader/listener interest, and style. **L.4.b** Use common, grade-appropriate Greek or Latin affixes and roots as clues to the meaning of a word.	Have students find a short article online and identify the types of sentences in it. Have students identify other words in the selection that contain suffixes they recognize.

Jump Start

FIRST READ Before students begin Act II, ask them to predict what they think will happen to Milo, Tock, and Humbug next. Point out that they are leaving Dictionopolis and heading toward Digitopolis. Ask them who and what they think the characters will see there.

The Phantom Tollbooth, Act II 🔊 📄

Who is Dischord? Why do the characters become hungrier as they eat more? Why does the well-dressed man want Milo and his friends to complete tasks with such small tools? Modeling questions such as these will help students connect to *The Phantom Tollbooth*, Act II, and to the Performance Task assignment. Selection audio and print capability for the selection are available in the Interactive Teacher's Edition.

Concept Vocabulary

Support students as they rank their words. Ask if they've ever heard, read, or used them. Reassure them that the definitions for these words are listed in the selection.

⬤ FIRST READ

As they read, students should perform the steps of the first read:

NOTICE: You may want to encourage students to notice who the Dodecahedron and the Mathemagician are.

ANNOTATE: Remind students to mark passages that are particularly descriptive or include some kind of figurative language. For example, students may want to mark passages that include puns or plays on words.

CONNECT: Encourage students to make a connection with the text. If they cannot make a connection to their own lives or to texts they've read, encourage them to think about movies or television shows that feature similar ideas, characters, or events.

RESPOND: Students will answer questions and write a summary to demonstrate understanding.

Point out to students that while they will always complete the Respond step at the end of the first read, the other steps will probably happen somewhat concurrently. You may wish to print copies of the **First–Read Guide: Fiction** for students to use. 📄

MAKING MEANING

About the Author
Norton Juster (b. 1929) designed buildings and other structures during his career as an architect. He took up creative writing in his spare time "as a relaxation" from architecture. When he began writing *The Phantom Tollbooth*, he thought it was just a short story for his own pleasure. Yet before long, Juster says, "it had created its own life, and I was hooked." *The Phantom Tollbooth* has been translated into many languages and adapted for film and audio. You will listen to an audio clip in the next lesson.

🔧 **Tool Kit**
First-Read Guide and Model Annotation

📋 STANDARDS
Reading Literature
By the end of the year, read and comprehend literature, including stories, dramas, and poems, in the grades 6–8 text complexity band proficiently, with scaffolding as needed at the high end of the range.

312 UNIT 4 • IMAGINATION

The Phantom Tollbooth, Act II

Concept Vocabulary

You will encounter the following words as you read *The Phantom Tollbooth*, Act II. Before reading, note how familiar you are with each word. Then, rank the words in order from most familiar (1) to least familiar (6).

WORD	YOUR RANKING
suspiciously	
obstacle	
pessimistic	
malicious	
insincerity	
compromise	

After completing the first read, come back to the concept vocabulary and review your rankings. Mark changes to your original rankings as needed.

First Read DRAMA

Apply these strategies as you conduct your first read. You will have an opportunity to complete the close-read notes after your first read.

NOTICE *whom* the story is about, *what* happens, *where* and *when* it happens, and *why* those involved react as they do.

ANNOTATE by marking vocabulary and key passages you want to revisit.

First Read

CONNECT ideas within the selection to what you already know and what you have already read.

RESPOND by completing the Comprehension Check and by writing a brief summary of the selection.

© Pearson Education, Inc., or its affiliates. All rights reserved.

PERSONALIZE FOR LEARNING

Strategic Support
First–Read Support If a student struggles to comprehend the text during the first read, have a partner conduct a think–aloud to explain the thought process as he or she works through the NOTICE, ANNOTATE, CONNECT, and RESPOND steps. For example, in paragraph 10, the student might notice the question asked by the Voice and annotate it to return to in the close read to see what it reveals about the character whose voice is speaking.

ANCHOR TEXT | DRAMA

The Phantom Tollbooth Act II

Susan Nanus
Based on the book by Norton Juster

© Pearson Education, Inc., or its affiliates. All rights reserved.

REVIEW AND ANTICIPATE

In Act I, Milo is lifted from his boredom into a strange kingdom that is in conflict over the importance of letters and numbers. After traveling through Dictionopolis, he agrees to rescue Princesses Rhyme and Reason, who can settle the conflict. As Act II opens, Milo, Tock, and the Humbug arrive in the city of Digitopolis on their quest to rescue the princesses.

SCAN FOR
MULTIMEDIA

Act II

Scene i

1 *The set of Digitopolis glitters in the background, while Upstage Right near the road, a small colorful Wagon sits, looking quite deserted. On its side in large letters, a sign reads: "KAKAFONOUS A. DISCHORD Doctor of Dissonance."[1] Enter Milo, Tock, and Humbug, fearfully. They look at the wagon.*

NOTES

1. **dissonance** (DIHS uh nuhns)
n. harsh or unpleasant combination of sounds.

The Phantom Tollbooth, Act II **313**

⬤ CLOSER LOOK

Examine Setting

Students may have marked paragraph 1, the italicized text at the beginning of Scene i, during their first read. Use this text to help students understand how setting helps to establish mood. Encourage them to talk about the annotations that they marked. You may want to model a close read with the class based on the highlights shown in the text.

ANNOTATE: Have students mark details in paragraph 1, the italicized text at the beginning of Scene i that suggests the setting of Act II, or have students participate while you highlight them.

QUESTION: Guide students to consider what these details might tell them. Ask what a reader can infer from a glittering city in the background and a small deserted-looking wagon in the foreground and accept student responses.

Possible response: The glittering city suggests that the city is wealthy, but the deserted-looking wagon suggests that not everything is right in this place.

CONCLUDE: Help students to formulate conclusions about the importance of these details in the text. Ask students why the playwright might have included these details.

Possible response: It creates the expectation of abundance and plenty. But the small deserted wagon creates a mood of fear and wariness.

Remind students that the **setting** is the time and place of the action in a literary work. Sometimes the setting merely provides a backdrop for the action, but it can also serve a more important function. Setting can be the force that the protagonist struggles against and thus the source of a story's *conflict*. It can also create an emotional atmosphere, or **mood**. In some works, the setting even serves as a symbol, representing an important theme or motif.

© Pearson Education, Inc., or its affiliates. All rights reserved.

NOTES

2 **Tock.** There's no doubt about it. That's where the noise was coming from.

3 **Humbug.** [*To* Milo.] Well, go on.

4 **Milo.** Go on what?

5 **Humbug.** Go on and see who's making all that noise in there. We can't just ignore a creature like that.

6 **Milo.** Creature? What kind of creature? Do you think he's dangerous?

7 **Humbug.** Go on, Milo. Knock on the door. We'll be right behind you.

8 **Milo.** O.K. Maybe he can tell us how much further it is to Digitopolis.

9 [Milo *tiptoes up to the wagon and KNOCKS timidly. The moment he knocks, a terrible CRASH is heard inside the wagon, and* Milo *and the others jump back in fright. At the same time, the Door Flies Open, and from the dark interior, a Hoarse* Voice *inquires*.]

10 **Voice.** Have you ever heard a whole set of dishes dropped from the ceiling onto a hard stone floor? [*The Others are speechless with fright.* Milo *shakes his head.* Voice *happily.*] Have you ever heard an ant wearing fur slippers walk across a thick wool carpet? [Milo *shakes his head again.*] Have you ever heard a blindfolded octopus unwrap a cellophane-covered bathtub? [Milo *shakes his head a third time.*] Ha! I knew it. [*He hops out, a little man, wearing a white coat, with a stethoscope around his neck, and a small mirror attached to his forehead, and with very huge ears, and a mortar and pestle in his hands. He stares at* Milo, Tock *and* Humbug.] None of you looks well at all! Tsk, tsk, not at all. [*He opens the top or side of his Wagon, revealing a dusty interior resembling an old apothecary shop, with shelves lined with jars and boxes, a table, books, test tubes, and bottles and measuring spoons.*]

11 **Milo.** [*Timidly.*] Are you a doctor?

12 **Dischord.** [Voice.] I am KAKAFONOUS A. DISCHORD. DOCTOR OF DISSONANCE! [*Several small explosions and a grinding crash are heard.*]

13 **Humbug.** [*Stuttering with fear.*] What does the "A" stand for?

14 **Dischord.** AS LOUD AS POSSIBLE! [*Two screeches and a bump are heard.*] Now, step a little closer and stick out your tongues. [Dischord *examines them.*] Just as I expected. [*He opens a large dusty book and thumbs through the pages.*] You're all suffering from a severe lack of noise. [Dischord *begins running around, collecting bottles, reading the labels to himself as he goes along.*] "Loud Cries." "Soft Cries." "Bangs, Bongs, Swishes,

Additional **English Language Support** is available in the Interactive Teacher's Edition.

WriteNow Express and Reflect

Description In paragraph 10, the Voice describes sounds—for example, "an ant wearing fur slippers walking across a thick wool carpet." Have students write a brief description of sounds they have heard either at a recent event, in the park, or there in the classroom as they write. Tell them to record everything they heard, including birdsong, humming machines, and the background noise of people's voices. Then, ask them to describe what they heard, using descriptive language like the Voice uses, or even analogies. For example, they might say that a passing truck outside sounds like thunder or footsteps in the hallway sound like someone tapping their fingers.

Swooshes." "Snaps and Crackles." "Whistles and Gongs." "Squeaks, Squawks, and Miscellaneous Uproar." [*As he reads them off, he pours a little of each into a large glass beaker and stirs the mixture with a wooden spoon. The concoction smokes and bubbles.*] Be ready in just a moment.

15 **Milo.** [**Suspiciously.**] Just what kind of doctor are you?

16 **Dischord.** Well, you might say, I'm a specialist. I specialize in noises, from the loudest to the softest, and from the slightly annoying to the terribly unpleasant. For instance, have you ever heard a square-wheeled steamroller ride over a street full of hard-boiled eggs? [*Very loud CRUNCHING SOUNDS are heard.*]

17 **Milo.** [*Holding his ears.*] But who would want all those terrible noises?

18 **Dischord.** [*Surprised at the question.*] Everybody does. Why, I'm so busy I can hardly fill all the orders for noise pills, racket lotion, clamor salve, and hubbub tonic. That's all people seem to want these days. Years ago, everyone wanted pleasant sounds and business was terrible. But then the cities were built and there was a great need for honking horns, screeching trains, clanging bells, and all the rest of those wonderfully unpleasant sounds we use so much today. I've been working overtime ever since and my medicine here is in great demand. All you have to do is take one spoonful every day, and you'll never have to hear another beautiful sound again. Here, try some.

19 **Humbug.** [*Backing away.*] If it's all the same to you, I'd rather not.

20 **Milo.** I don't want to be cured of beautiful sounds.

21 **Tock.** Besides, there's no such sickness as a lack of noise.

22 **Dischord.** How true. That's what makes it so difficult to cure. [*Takes a large glass bottle from the shelf.*] Very well, if you want to go all through life suffering from a noise deficiency,[2] I'll just give this to Dynne for his lunch. [*Uncorks the bottle and pours the liquid into it. There is a rumbling and then a loud explosion accompanied by smoke, out of which* Dynne, *a smog-like creature with yellow eyes and a frowning mouth, appears.*]

23 **Dynne.** [*Smacking his lips.*] Ahhh, that was good, Master. I thought you'd never let me out. It was really cramped in there.

24 **Dischord.** This is my assistant, the awful Dynne. You must forgive his appearance, for he really doesn't have any.

25 **Milo.** What is a Dynne?

NOTES

suspiciously (suh SPIHSH uhs lee) *adv.* based on a lack of trust or belief; disbelievingly; cautiously

2. **deficiency** (dih FIHSH uhn see) *n.* shortage or lack.

CLOSE READ

ANNOTATE: In paragraphs 22–24, mark details that show what Dynne looks like and how he behaves.

QUESTION: Why does the playwright include these details?

CONCLUDE: What is the effect of these details, especially when added to Dischord's statement that Dynne "doesn't have" an appearance?

The Phantom Tollbooth, Act II **315**

CLOSE READ

You may wish to model the close read using the following think–aloud format. Possible responses to questions on the student page are included.

ANNOTATE: As I read paragraphs 22–24, I notice and highlight the details that describe how Dynne appears and how he behaves.

QUESTION: I think the playwright includes this description of how Dynne appears and what Dynne looks like to help the reader visualize the creature.

CONCLUDE: As I read the description, I can visualize the creature and what I picture in my mind is scary and threatening. The effect, then, is to create a fearful mood.

© Pearson Education, Inc., or its affiliates. All rights reserved.

TEACHING

26 **Dischord.** You mean you've never heard of the awful Dynne? When you're playing in your room and making a great amount or noise, what do they tell you to stop?

27 **Milo.** That awful din.

28 **Dischord.** When the neighbors are playing their radio too loud late at night, what do you wish they'd turn down?

29 **Tock.** That awful din.

30 **Dischord.** And when the street on your block is being repaired and the drills are working all day, what does everyone complain of?

31 **Humbug.** [*Brightly.*] The dreadful row.

32 **Dynne.** The Dreadful Rauw was my grandfather. He perished in the great silence epidemic of 1712. I certainly can't understand why you don't like noise. Why, I heard an explosion last week that was so lovely, I groaned with appreciation for two days. [*He gives a loud groan at the memory.*]

33 **Dischord.** He's right, you know! Noise is the most valuable thing in the world.

34 **Milo.** King Azaz says words are.

35 **Dischord.** NONSENSE! Why, when a baby wants food, how does he ask?

36 **Dynne.** [*Happily.*] He screams!

37 **Dischord.** And when a racing car wants gas?

38 **Dynne.** [*Jumping for Joy.*] It chokes!

39 **Dischord.** And what happens to the dawn when a new day begins?

40 **Dynne.** [*Delighted.*] It breaks!

41 **Dischord.** You see how simple it is? [*To Dynne.*] Isn't it time for us to go?

42 **Milo.** Where to? Maybe we're going the same way.

43 **Dynne.** I doubt it. [*Picking up empty sacks from the table.*] We're going on our collection rounds. Once a day, I travel throughout the kingdom and collect all the wonderfully horrible and beautifully unpleasant sounds I can find and bring them back to the doctor to use in his medicine.

44 **Dischord.** Where are you going?

45 **Milo.** To Digitopolis.

316 UNIT 4 • IMAGINATION

© Pearson Education, Inc., or its affiliates. All rights reserved.

PERSONALIZE FOR LEARNING

English Language Support
Figurative Language Understanding the examples of figurative language that are referred to in paragraphs 37–40 might be challenging for English learners. Explain to students that saying a car chokes when it wants gas is an example of personification, a type of figurative language in which a nonhuman subject is given human characteristics. Point out that the saying is common and that it means that the car isn't working properly. Explain that the expression "dawn is breaking" is an idiom, or an expression that has a different meaning from its literal meaning. Tell students that "dawn is breaking" means that the sun is rising in the morning. Explain that Dischord's use of figurative language in these lines are examples of word play or the different meanings of words. **ALL LEVELS**

316 UNIT 4 • IMAGINATION

46 **Dischord.** Oh, there are a number of ways to get to Digitopolis, if you know how to follow directions. Just take a look at the sign at the fork in the road. Though why you'd ever want to go there, I'll never know.

47 **Milo.** We want to talk to the Mathemagician.

48 **Humbug.** About the release of the Princesses Rhyme and Reason.

49 **Dischord.** Rhyme and Reason? I remember them. Very nice girls, but a little too quiet for my taste. In fact, I've been meaning to send them something that Dynne brought home by mistake and which I have absolutely no use for. [*He rummages through the wagon.*] Ah, here it is . . . or maybe you'd like it for yourself. [*Hands* Milo *a package.*]

50 **Milo.** What is it?

51 **Dischord.** The sounds of laughter. They're so unpleasant to hear, it's almost unbearable. All those giggles and snickers and happy shouts of joy. I don't know what Dynne was thinking of when he collected them. Here, take them to the Princesses or keep them for yourselves, I don't care. Well, time to move on. Goodbye now and good luck! [*He has shut the wagon by now and gets in. LOUD NOISES begin to erupt as* Dynne *pulls the wagon offstage.*]

52 **Milo.** [*Calling after them.*] But wait! The fork in the road . . . you didn't tell us where it is . . .

53 **Tock.** It's too late. He can't hear a thing.

54 **Humbug.** I could use a fork of my own, at the moment. And a knife and a spoon to go with it. All of a sudden, I feel very hungry.

55 **Milo.** So do I, but it's no use thinking about it. There won't be anything to eat until we reach Digitopolis. [*They get into the car.*]

56 **Humbug.** [*Rubbing his stomach.*] Well, the sooner the better is what I say. [*A SIGN suddenly appears.*]

57 **Voice.** [*A strange voice from nowhere.*] But which way will get you there sooner? That is the question.

58 **Tock.** Did you hear something?

59 **Milo.** Look! The fork in the road and a signpost to Digitopolis! [*They read the Sign.*]

60 **Humbug.** Let's travel by miles, it's shorter.

61 **Milo.** Let's travel by half inches. It's quicker.

NOTES

CLOSE READ

ANNOTATE: In paragraph 51, mark terms that identify different kinds of laughter.

QUESTION: Why does the playwright include these details?

CONCLUDE: What is the effect of these details, especially in helping to portray Dischord?

CLOSE READ

Tell students to look for the sentences that tell what Dischord is doing. You may wish to model the close read using the following think–aloud format. Possible responses to questions on the student page are included.

ANNOTATE: As I read paragraph 51, I mark the words that show the different types of laughter.

QUESTION: I think the playwright includes this language to show the many words we have for laughter.

CONCLUDE: These details show that Dischord is unhappy and grumpy. These types of laughter seem pleasant to most people, but Dischord doesn't like them.

© Pearson Education, Inc., or its affiliates. All rights reserved.

© Pearson Education, Inc., or its affiliates. All rights reserved.

NOTES

62 **Tock.** But which road should we take? It must make a difference.

63 **Milo.** Do you think so?

64 **Tock.** Well, I'm not sure, but . . .

65 **Humbug.** He could be right. On the other hand, he could also be wrong. Does it make a difference or not?

66 **Voice.** Yes, indeed, indeed it does, certainly, my yes, it does make a difference.

67 [*The Dodecahedron appears, a 12-sided figure with a different face on each side, and with all the edges labeled with a small letter and all the angles labeled with a large letter. He wears a beret and peers at the others with a serious face. He doffs his cap and recites:*]

68 **Dodecahedron.** *My angles are many.*
My sides are not few.
I'm the Dodecahedron.
Who are you?

318 UNIT 4 • IMAGINATION

DIGITAL PERSPECTIVES

Enriching the Text The Dodecahedron appears in paragraph 67. To help students understand that a dodecahedron is a three–dimensional geometric figure, find images of dodecahedrons and show them to students. You might try to find both still and animated images that show the figure being folded so that they get a better sense of what it looks like. Then encourage students to make their own dodecahedron by cutting out a pattern from paper and folding it. Discuss with students how or whether viewing the images and making the dodecahedron enhances their understanding of the text.

69 **Milo.** What's a Dodecahedron?

70 **Dodecahedron.** [*Turning around slowly.*] See for yourself. A Dodecahedron is a mathematical shape with 12 faces. [*All his faces appear as he turns, each face with a different expression. He points to them.*] I usually use one at a time. It saves wear and tear. What are you called?

71 **Milo.** Milo.

72 **Dodecahedron.** That's an odd name. [*Changing his smiling face to a frowning one.*] And you have only one face.

73 **Milo.** [*Making sure it is still there.*] Is that bad?

74 **Dodecahedron.** You'll soon wear it out using it for everything. Is everyone with one face called Milo?

75 **Milo.** Oh, no. Some are called Billy or Jeffery or Sally or Lisa or lots of other things.

76 **Dodecahedron.** How confusing. Here everything is called exactly what it is. The triangles are called triangles, the circles are called circles, and even the same numbers have the same name. Can you imagine what would happen if we named all the twos Billy or Jeffery or Sally or Lisa or lots of other things? You'd have to say Robert plus John equals four, and if the fours were named Albert, things would be hopeless.

77 **Milo.** I never thought of it that way.

78 **Dodecahedron.** [*With an admonishing face.*] Then I suggest you begin at once, for in Digitopolis, everything is quite precise.

79 **Milo.** Then perhaps you can help us decide which road we should take.

80 **Dodecahedron.** [*Happily.*] By all means. There's nothing to it. [*As he talks, the three others try to solve the problem on a Large Blackboard that is wheeled onstage for the occasion.*] Now, if a small car carrying three people at 30 miles an hour for 10 minutes along a road 5 miles long at 11:35 in the morning starts at the same time as 3 people who have been traveling in a little automobile at 20 miles an hour for 15 minutes on another road exactly twice as long as half the distance of the other, while a dog, a bug, and a boy travel an equal distance in the same time or the same distance in an equal time along a third road in mid-October, then which one arrives first and which is the best way to go?

81 **Humbug.** Seventeen!

82 **Milo.** [*Still figuring frantically.*] I'm not sure, but . . .

NOTES

CLOSER LOOK

Analyze Structure

Students may have highlighted stage directions in paragraphs 82 and 90 during their first read. Use this text to help students understand how stage directions help the reader and the actors better understand characters. Encourage students to talk about the annotations that they marked. You may want to model a close read with the class based on the highlights shown in the text.

ANNOTATE: Have students highlight stage directions in paragraphs 82 and 90 that describe how Milo and Tock respond to the math problem.

QUESTION: Guide students to understand why they think the playwright includes these stage directions.

Possible response: As I read these lines, I see that the two characters work differently at the math problem. Milo is working frantically, while Tock has been working patiently.

CONCLUDE: Help students draw conclusions about the effect of including these stage directions.

Possible response: I can see that the effect of including the stage directions is to provide a clear contrast between the characters' personalities. They approach the math problem—and life—differently.

Remind students that playwrights use stage directions to **structure** the action, physical movement, setting, and props in a play. These elements help to reveal meaning about the characters and theme of a play.

© Pearson Education, Inc., or its affiliates. All rights reserved.

NOTES

83 **Dodecahedron.** You'll have to do better than that.

84 **Milo.** I'm not very good at problems.

85 **Dodecahedron.** What a shame. They're so very useful. Why, did you know that if a beaver 2 feet long with a tail a foot and a half long can build a dam 12 feet high and 6 feet wide in 2 days, all you would need to build Boulder Dam is a beaver 68 feet long with a 51 foot tail?

86 **Humbug.** [*Grumbling as his pencil snaps.*] Where would you find a beaver that big?

87 **Dodecahedron.** I don't know, but if you did, you'd certainly know what to do with him.

88 **Milo.** That's crazy.

89 **Dodecahedron.** That may be true, but it's completely accurate, and as long as the answer is right, who cares if the question is wrong?

90 **Tock.** [*Who has been patiently doing the first problem.*] All three roads arrive at the same place at the same time.

91 **Dodecahedron.** Correct! And I'll take you there myself. [*The blackboard rolls off, and all four get into the car and drive off.*] Now you see how important problems are. If you hadn't done this one properly, you might have gone the wrong way.

92 **Milo.** But if all the roads arrive at the same place at the same time, then aren't they all the right road?

93 **Dodecahedron.** [*Glaring from his upset face.*] Certainly not! They're all the wrong way! Just because you have a choice, it doesn't mean that any of them has to be right. [*Pointing in another direction.*] That's the way to Digitopolis and we'll be there any moment. [*Suddenly the lighting grows dimmer.*] In fact, we're here. Welcome to the Land of Numbers.

94 **Humbug.** [*Looking around at the barren landscape.*] It doesn't look very inviting.

95 **Milo.** Is this the place where numbers are made?

96 **Dodecahedron.** They're not made. You have to dig for them. Don't you know anything at all about numbers?

97 **Milo.** Well, I never really thought they were very important.

98 **Dodecahedron.** NOT IMPORTANT! Could you have tea for two without the 2? Or three blind mice without the 3? And how would you sail the seven seas without the 7?

99 **Milo.** All I meant was . . .

© Pearson Education, Inc., or its affiliates. All rights reserved.

PERSONALIZE FOR LEARNING

English Language Support

Nursery Rhymes English learners will likely be unfamiliar with the references to nursery rhymes in paragraph 98. Explain to them that "Tea for Two" is an old song, and "Three Blind Mice" is a rhyme that people sing to small children. Point out that "the seven seas" is an idiom or expression that has a meaning different from its literal meaning. "The seven seas" usually refers to all the world's oceans. Encourage English learners to think of nursery rhymes or songs from their own language that helped children learn and understand numbers. **ALL LEVELS**

100 **Dodecahedron.** [*Continues shouting angrily.*] If you had high hopes, how would you know how high they were? And did you know that narrow escapes come in different widths? Would you travel the whole world wide without ever knowing how wide it was? And how could you do anything at long last without knowing how long the last was? Why, numbers are the most beautiful and valuable things in the world. Just follow me and I'll show you. [*He motions to them and pantomimes walking through rocky terrain with the others in tow. A Doorway similar to the Tollbooth appears and the* Dodecahedron *opens it and motions the others to follow him through.*] Come along, come along. I can't wait for you all day. [*They enter the doorway and the lights are dimmed very low, as to simulate the interior of a cave. The SOUNDS of scraping and tapping, scuffling and digging are heard around them. He hands them Helmets with flashlights attached.*] Put these on.

101 **Milo.** [*Whispering.*] Where are we going?

102 **Dodecahedron.** We're here. This is the numbers mine. [*LIGHTS UP A LITTLE, revealing Little Men digging and chopping, shoveling, and scraping.*] Right this way and watch your step. [*His voice echoes and reverberates. Iridescent*[3] *and glittery numbers seem to sparkle from everywhere.*]

103 **Milo.** [*Awed.*] Whose mine is it?

104 **Voice of Mathemagician.** By the four million eight hundred and twenty-seven thousand six hundred and fifty-nine hairs on my head, it's mine, of course! [*ENTER the* Mathemagician, *carrying his long staff which looks like a giant pencil.*]

105 **Humbug.** [*Already intimidated.*] It's a lovely mine, really it is.

106 **Mathemagician.** [*Proudly.*] The biggest number mine in the kingdom.

107 **Milo.** [*Excitedly.*] Are there any precious stones in it?

108 **Mathemagician.** Precious stones! [*Then softly.*] By the eight million two hundred and forty-seven thousand three hundred and twelve threads in my robe, I'll say there are. Look here. [*Reaches in a cart, pulls out a small object, polishes it vigorously, and holds it up to the light, where it sparkles.*]

109 **Milo.** But that's a five.

110 **Mathemagician.** Exactly. As valuable a jewel as you'll find anywhere. Look at some of the others. [*Scoops up others and pours them into* Milo's *arms. They include all numbers from 1 to 9 and an assortment of zeros.*]

NOTES

3. **iridescent** (ihr uh DEHS uhnt) *adj.* showing different colors when seen from different angles.

CLOSE READ

ANNOTATE: In paragraph 104 and again in paragraph 108, mark the items the Mathemagician counts.

QUESTION: Why does the playwright indicate that he counts items that are so small and plentiful?

CONCLUDE: What is the effect of these details?

CLOSE READ

You may wish to model the close read using the following think–aloud format. Possible responses to questions on the student page are included.

ANNOTATE: As I read paragraphs 104 and 108, I notice and mark the items the Mathemagician counts.

QUESTION: The objects that he is counting are never counted by average people. This sets up the Mathemagician's attitude and skill.

CONCLUDE: I think these lines show how serious the Mathemagician is about counting. They may also encourage readers or the audience to think about a world where counting becomes as important as it is to this character.

© Pearson Education, Inc., or its affiliates. All rights reserved.

The Phantom Tollbooth, Act II **321**

NOTES

111 **Dodecahedron.** We dig them and polish them right here, and then send them all over the world. Marvelous, aren't they?

112 **Tock.** They are beautiful. [*He holds them up to compare them to the numbers on his clock body.*]

113 **Milo.** So that's where they come from. [*Looks at them and carefully hands them back, but drops a few which smash and break in half.*] Oh. I'm sorry!

114 **Mathemagician.** [*Scooping them up.*] Oh, don't worry about that. We use the broken ones for fractions. How about some lunch? [*Takes out a little whistle and blows it. Two miners rush in carrying an immense cauldron which is bubbling and steaming. The workers put down their tools and gather around to eat.*]

115 **Humbug.** That looks delicious! [Tock *and* Milo *also look hungrily at the pot.*]

116 **Mathemagician.** Perhaps you'd care for something to eat?

117 **Milo.** Oh, yes, sir!

118 **Tock.** Thank you.

119 **Humbug.** [*Already eating.*] Ummm . . . delicious! [*All finish their bowls immediately.*]

120 **Mathemagician.** Please have another portion. [*They eat and finish.* Mathemagician *serves them again.*] Don't stop now. [*They finish.*] Come on, no need to be bashful. [*Serves them again.*]

121 **Milo.** [*To* Tock *and* Humbug *as he finishes again.*] Do you want to hear something strange? Each one I eat makes me a little hungrier than before.

122 **Mathemagician.** Do have some more. [*He serves them again. They eat frantically, until the* Mathemagician *blows his whistle again and the pot is removed.*]

123 **Humbug.** [*Holding his stomach.*] Uggghhh! I think I'm starving.

124 **Milo.** Me, too, and I ate so much.

125 **Dodecahedron.** [*Wiping the gravy from several of his mouths.*] Yes, it was delicious, wasn't it? It's the specialty of the kingdom . . . subtraction stew.

126 **Tock.** [*Weak from hunger.*] I have more of an appetite than when I began.

127 **Mathemagician.** Certainly, what did you expect? The more you eat, the hungrier you get, everyone knows that.

128 **Milo.** They do? Then how do you get enough?

© Pearson Education, Inc., or its affiliates. All rights reserved.

PERSONALIZE FOR LEARNING

Strategic Support

Irony Review paragraphs 114–127. Some students may have trouble interpreting the irony in the meal that Milo, Tock, and Humbug eat in this scene. Guide them in understanding what is happening as the three eat their stew. Point to the name of the stew in paragraph 125—subtraction stew. Ask them how the name of the stew might help explain why the characters feel hungrier as they eat more. Discuss how the playwright incorporates different aspects of math into this scene, which is set in Digitopolis.

129 **Mathemagician.** Enough? Here in Digitopolis, we have our meals when we're full and eat until we're hungry. That way, when you don't have anything at all, you have more than enough. It's a very economical system. You must have been stuffed to have eaten so much.

130 **Dodecahedron.** It's completely logical. The more you want, the less you get, and the less you get, the more you have. Simple arithmetic, that's all. [Tock, Milo *and* Humbug *look at him blankly.*] Now, look, suppose you had something and added nothing to it. What would you have?

131 **Milo.** The same.

132 **Dodecahedron.** Splendid! And suppose you had something and added less than nothing to it? What would you have then?

133 **Humbug.** Starvation! Oh, I'm so hungry.

134 **Dodecahedron.** Now, now, it's not as bad as all that. In a few hours, you'll be nice and full again . . . just in time for dinner.

135 **Milo.** But I only eat when I'm hungry.

136 **Mathemagician.** [*Waving the eraser of his staff.*] What a curious idea. The next thing you'll have us believe is that you only sleep when you're tired.

137 [*The mine has disappeared as well as the Miners.*]

138 **Humbug.** Where did everyone go?

139 **Mathemagician.** Oh, they're still in the mine. I often find that the best way to get from one place to another is to erase everything and start again. Please make yourself at home.

140 [*They find themselves in a unique room, in which all the walls, tables, chairs, desks, cabinets, and blackboards are labeled to show their heights, widths, depths, and distances to and from each other. To one side is a gigantic notepad on an artist's easel, and from hooks and strings hang a collection of rulers, measures, weights and tapes, and all other measuring devices.*]

141 **Milo.** Do you always travel that way? [*He looks around in wonder.*]

142 **Mathemagician.** No, indeed! [*He pulls a plumb line from a hook and walks.*] Most of the time I take the shortest distance between any two points. And of course, when I have to be in several places at once . . . [*He writes $3 \times 1 = 3$ on the notepad with his staff.*] I simply multiply. [Three Figures *looking like the* Mathemagician *appear on a platform above.*]

143 **Milo.** How did you do that?

NOTES

© Pearson Education, Inc., or its affiliates. All rights reserved.

CLOSER LOOK

Analyze Characterization

Students may have highlighted the questions asked by Milo in paragraphs 141 and 143. Encourage students to talk about the annotations that they marked. You may want to model a close read with the class based on the highlights shown in the text.

ANNOTATE: Have students highlight Milo's dialogue in which he asks questions in paragraphs 141 and 143.

QUESTION: Guide students to consider why the playwright has Milo asks questions in this and other scenes in the play.

Possible response: As I read these lines, I see that Milo asks question because he is puzzled by the things he is experiencing.

CONCLUDE: Help students draw conclusions about the effect of Milo asking questions and how this might affect a reader's reaction to Milo as a character.

Possible response: I can conclude that Milo is a curious personality who is continually trying to figure out the world around him. I feel more closely connected to Milo than other characters because he is similar to me: he is confused by the strange environment he's traveling through, and he is trying to figure it out.

Remind students that a playwright's choice of dialogue, such the types of dialogue a character speaks, contributes to **characterization** and helps build a reader's sympathy and other responses to a character.

CLOSE READ 💬

You may wish to model the close read using the following think-aloud format. Possible responses to questions on the student page are included.

ANNOTATE: As I read paragraphs 151 and 158, I notice and mark the stage directions that indicate the characters should speak directly to the audience.

QUESTION: The playwright includes these lines to tell actors and readers about the physical gestures and staging required.

CONCLUDE: I think that this would make the audience feel more involved in the play.

NOTES

CLOSE READ
ANNOTATE: In paragraphs 151 and 158, mark the directions that suggest the characters speak directly to the audience.

QUESTION: Why does the playwright include these directions?

CONCLUDE: If the actors were to follow these directions, how might they affect the audience's response?

---

144 **Mathemagician** and **The Three.** There's nothing to it, if you have a magic staff. [*The Three Figures cancel themselves out and disappear.*]

145 **Humbug.** That's nothing but a big pencil.

146 **Mathemagician.** True enough, but once you learn to use it, there's no end to what you can do.

147 **Milo.** Can you make things disappear?

148 **Mathemagician.** Just step a little closer and watch this. [*Shows them that there is nothing up his sleeve or in his hat. He writes:*]

$$4 + 9 - 2 \times 16 + 1 = 3 \times 6 - 67 + 8 \times 2 - 3 + 26 - 1 - 34 + 3 - 7 + 2 - 5 =$$ [*He looks up expectantly.*]

149 **Humbug.** Seventeen?

150 **Milo.** It all comes to zero.

151 **Mathemagician.** Precisely. [*Makes a theatrical bow and rips off paper from notepad.*] Now, is there anything else you'd like to see? [*At this point, an appeal to the audience to see if anyone would like a problem solved.*]

152 **Milo.** Well . . . can you show me the biggest number there is?

153 **Mathemagician.** Why, I'd be delighted. [*Opening a closet door.*] We keep it right here. It took four miners to dig it out. [*He shows them a huge "3" twice as high as the* Mathemagician.]

154 **Milo.** No, that's not what I mean. Can you show me the longest number there is?

155 **Mathemagician.** Sure. [*Opens another door.*] Here it is. It took three carts to carry it here. [*Door reveals an "8" that is as wide as the "3" was high.*]

156 **Milo.** No, no, that's not what I meant either. [*Looks helplessly at* Tock.]

157 **Tock.** I think what you would like to see is the number of the greatest possible magnitude.

158 **Mathemagician.** Well, why didn't you say so? [*He busily measures them and all other things as he speaks, and marks it down.*] What's the greatest number you can think of? [*Here, an appeal can also be made to the audience or* Milo *may think of his own answers.*]

159 **Milo.** Uh . . . nine trillion, nine hundred and ninety-nine billion, nine hundred ninety-nine million, nine hundred ninety-nine thousand, nine hundred and ninety-nine. [*He puffs.*]

© Pearson Education, Inc., or its affiliates. All rights reserved.

PERSONALIZE FOR LEARNING

Challenge

Research Review paragraphs 152–162. Milo asks the Mathemagician to see the largest number there is. Of course, there is no largest number, but there is a number of the greatest possible magnitude that has been named. Challenge students to research the name of that number and find out why it has been given that name. Have students share their findings with the class and discuss why mathematicians might be inclined to give a name to such a number and what other names might be appropriate for numbers that are even greater.

160 **Mathemagician.** [*Writes that on the pad.*] Very good. Now add one to it. [*Milo or audience does.*] Now add one again. [*Milo or audience does so.*] Now add one again. Now add one again. Now add . . .

161 **Milo.** But when can I stop?

162 **Mathemagician.** Never. Because the number you want is always at least one more than the number you have, and it's so large that if you started saying it yesterday, you wouldn't finish tomorrow.

163 **Humbug.** Where could you ever find a number so big?

164 **Mathemagician.** In the same place they have the smallest number there is, and you know where that is?

165 **Milo.** The smallest number . . . let's see . . . one one-millionth?

166 **Mathemagician.** Almost. Now all you have to do is divide that in half and then divide that in half and then divide that in half and then divide that . . .

167 **Milo.** Doesn't that ever stop either?

168 **Mathemagician.** How can it when you can always take half of what you have and divide it in half again? Look. [*Pointing offstage.*] You see that line?

169 **Milo.** You mean that long one out there?

170 **Mathemagician.** That's it. Now, if you just follow that line forever, and when you reach the end, turn left, you will find the Land of Infinity. That's where the tallest, the shortest, the biggest, the smallest, and the most and the least of everything are kept.

171 **Milo.** But how can you follow anything forever? You know, I get the feeling that everything in Digitopolis is very difficult.

172 **Mathemagician.** But on the other hand, I think you'll find that the only thing you can do easily is be wrong, and that's hardly worth the effort.

173 **Milo.** But . . . what bothers me is . . . well, why is it that even when things are correct, they don't really seem to be right?

174 **Mathemagician.** [*Grows sad and quiet.*] How true. It's been that way ever since Rhyme and Reason were banished. [*Sadness turns to fury.*] And all because of that stubborn wretch Azaz! It's all his fault.

175 **Milo.** Maybe if you discussed it with him . . .

NOTES

CLOSE READ

ANNOTATE: In paragraph 173, mark the ellipses, or punctuation that looks like three periods in a row.

QUESTION: Why does the author use ellipses here?

CONCLUDE: How might this punctuation affect the way in which an actor delivers this line?

CLOSE READ

You may wish to model the close read using the following think–aloud format. Possible responses to questions on the student page are included.

ANNOTATE: As I read paragraph 173, I notice and highlight the ellipses points.

QUESTION: I think these points show a pause. They help to convey Milo's confusion and difficulty with Digitopolis.

CONCLUDE: The punctuation helps an actor know where to pause. I would also expect that the actor would use the punctuation to help him understand Milo's emotional state.

© Pearson Education, Inc., or its affiliates. All rights reserved.

The Phantom Tollbooth, Act II **325**

NOTES

176 **Mathemagician.** He's just too unreasonable! Why just last month, I sent him a very friendly letter, which he never had the courtesy to answer. See for yourself. [*Puts the letter on the easel. The letter reads:*]

177 4738 1919,

667 394107 5841 62589 85371 14

39588 7190434 203 27689 57131 481206.

5864 98053,

62179875073

178 **Milo.** But maybe he doesn't understand numbers.

179 **Mathemagician.** Nonsense! Everybody understands numbers. No matter what language you speak, they always mean the same thing. A seven is a seven everywhere in the world.

180 **Milo.** [*To Tock and* Humbug.] Everyone is so sensitive about what he knows best.

181 **Tock.** With your permission, sir, we'd like to rescue Rhyme and Reason.

182 **Mathemagician.** Has Azaz agreed to it?

183 **Tock.** Yes, sir.

184 **Mathemagician.** THEN I DON'T! Ever since they've been banished, we've never agreed on anything, and we never will.

185 **Milo.** Never?

186 **Mathemagician.** NEVER! And if you can prove otherwise, you have my permission to go.

187 **Milo.** Well then, with whatever Azaz agrees, you disagree.

188 **Mathemagician.** Correct.

189 **Milo.** And with whatever Azaz disagrees, you agree.

190 **Mathemagician.** [*Yawning, cleaning his nails.*] Also correct.

191 **Milo.** Then, each of you agrees that he will disagree with whatever each of you agrees with, and if you both disagree with the same thing, aren't you really in agreement?

192 **Mathemagician.** I'VE BEEN TRICKED! [*Figures it over, but comes up with the same answer.*]

193 **Tock.** And now may we go?

© Pearson Education, Inc., or its affiliates. All rights reserved.

194 **Mathemagician.** [*Nods weakly.*] It's a long and dangerous journey. Long before you find them, the demons will know you're there. Watch out for them, because if you ever come face to face, it will be too late. But there is one other **obstacle** even more serious than that.

195 **Milo.** [*Terrified.*] What is it?

196 **Mathemagician.** I'm afraid I can't tell you until you return. But maybe I can give you something to help you out. [*Claps hands. ENTER the* Dodecahedron, *carrying something on a pillow. The* Mathemagician *takes it.*] Here is your own magic staff. Use it well and there is nothing it can't do for you. [*Puts a small, gleaming pencil in* Milo's *breast pocket.*]

197 **Humbug.** Are you sure you can't tell about that serious obstacle?

198 **Mathemagician.** Only when you return. And now the Dodecahedron will escort you to the road that leads to the Castle-in-the-Air. Farewell, my friends, and good luck to you. [*They shake hands, say goodbye, and the* Dodecahedron *leads them off.*] Good luck to you! [*To himself.*] Because you're sure going to need it. [*He watches them through a telescope and marks down the calculations.*]

199 **Dodecahedron.** [*He re-enters.*] Well, they're on their way.

200 **Mathemagician.** So I see . . . [Dodecahedron *stands waiting.*] Well, what is it?

201 **Dodecahedron.** I was just wondering myself, your Numbership. What actually is the serious obstacle you were talking about?

202 **Mathemagician.** [*Looks at him in surprise.*] You mean you really don't know?

203 *BLACKOUT*

NOTES

obstacle (OB stuh kuhl) *n.* something that stands in the way or stops progress

CLOSE READ
ANNOTATE: Mark the stage direction after paragraph 202 that tells what happens after the Dodecahedron asks about the obstacle.

QUESTION: Why does the playwright include this stage direction?

CONCLUDE: How might this stage direction, if followed, affect a viewing audience?

CLOSE READ

Remind students that the stage directions refer to any text that helps actors and readers determine how the play is performed and when the scenes change. Tell them to look for a word or words that tell them what is happening onstage. You may wish to model the close read using the following think–aloud format. Possible responses to questions on the student page are included.

ANNOTATE: As I read the stage direction after paragraph 202 I notice and highlight the single word "Blackout."

QUESTION: I think the playwright includes this stage direction to show that the scene is changing. The word "Blackout" means that the lights go out and the stage goes dark, so there must be new characters or scenery appearing onstage.

CONCLUDE: A sudden blackout would be dramatic and have the effect of catching the audience's attention and signaling that the scene is ending. The audience may wonder what is next.

© Pearson Education, Inc., or its affiliates. All rights reserved.

TEACHING

© Pearson Education, Inc. or its affiliates. All rights reserved.

328 UNIT 4 • IMAGINATION

PERSONALIZE FOR LEARNING

Challenge

Stage Set Point students to the illustration of Rhyme and Reason standing in the castle window. Remind them that the play was written to be performed on a stage. Challenge students to come up with a stage set for the castle that is pictured, one that would not be too difficult to construct but that would convey the idea of a castle in the air. Explain that a stage set consists of all the scenery used to represent a place in the story. Have students create a drawing of their plan with a short explanation and then share it with the class. Discuss the different ideas and how each one represents this idea of a building that rises high into the sky.

Scene ii • The Land of Ignorance

1 *LIGHTS UP on* Rhyme *and* Reason, *in their castle, looking out two windows.*

2 **Rhyme.** *I'm worried sick I must confess*
      I wonder if they'll have success
      All others tried in vain,
      And were never seen or heard again.

3 **Reason.** Now, Rhyme, there's no need to be so **pessimistic**. Milo, Tock, and Humbug have just as much chance of succeeding as they do of failing.

4 **Rhyme.** *But the demons are so deadly smart*
      They'll stuff your brain and fill your heart
      With petty thoughts and selfish dreams
      And trap you with their nasty schemes.

5 **Reason.** Now, Rhyme, be reasonable, won't you? And calm down, you always talk in couplets when you get nervous. Milo has learned a lot from his journey. I think he's a match for the demons and that he might soon be knocking at our door. Now, come on, cheer up, won't you?

6 **Rhyme.** I'll try.

7 [*LIGHTS FADE on the* Princesses *and COME UP on the little Car, traveling slowly.*]

8 **Milo.** So this is the Land of Ignorance. It's so dark. I can hardly see a thing. Maybe we should wait until morning.

9 **Voice.** They'll be mourning for you soon enough. [*They look up and see a large, soiled, ugly bird with a dangerous beak and a* **malicious** *expression.*]

10 **Milo.** I don't think you understand. We're looking for a place to spend the night.

11 **Bird.** [*Shrieking.*] It's not yours to spend!

12 **Milo.** That doesn't make any sense, you see . . .

13 **Bird.** Dollars or cents. It's still not yours to spend.

14 **Milo.** But I don't mean . . .

15 **Bird.** Of course you're mean. Anybody who'd spend a night that doesn't belong to him is very mean.

16 **Tock.** Must you interrupt like that?

17 **Bird.** Naturally, it's my job. I take the words right out of your mouth. Haven't we met before? I'm the Everpresent Wordsnatcher.

© Pearson Education, Inc., or its affiliates. All rights reserved.

NOTES

pessimistic (pehs uh MIHS tihk) *adj.* expecting the worst, focused on the bad aspects of a situation

malicious (muh LIHSH uhs) *adj.* having or showing bad intentions

---

CLOSER LOOK

Examine Couplets

Students may have marked paragraphs 2 and 4 during their first read. Encourage them to talk about the annotations that they marked. You may want to model a close read with the class based on the highlights shown in the text.

ANNOTATE: Have students mark text that rhymes in paragraphs 2 and 4, or have students participate while you highlight it.

QUESTION: Guide students to consider what these details might tell them. Ask what a reader can infer from the rhymes that Princess Rhyme recites, and accept student responses.

Possible response: A reader can infer that Princess Rhyme is named so because she speaks in rhymes. Her rhymes indicate that she knows about Milo, Tock, and Humbug and that she is worried that they will fail in their attempt to rescue the princesses.

CONCLUDE: Help students to formulate conclusions about the importance of these details in the text. Ask students why the playwright might have included these details.

Possible response: The couplets draw readers' attention to Rhyme's concerns and also to the fact that Rhyme and Reason know about the rescue attempt. One conclusion that readers can draw is that Rhyme and Reason may be able to see what is happening from where they are or that they somehow know what is going on in Digitopolis.

Tell students that a **couplet** is a pair of rhyming lines, usually of the same meter and length. A couplet often functions as a stanza, and it generally expresses a single idea.

The Phantom Tollbooth, Act II **329**

CLOSE READ 🖉

Tell students that stage directions not only tell actors where to move and how to say their lines. They also direct lighting and sound effects. Remind students to look for the italicized text that shows that time is passing. You may wish to model the close read using the following think–aloud format. Possible responses to questions on the student page are included.

ANNOTATE: As I read paragraph 30, I notice and highlight the details in the stage directions that tell about the passage of time.

QUESTION: I think the playwright included the stage directions so that the audience and the reader will know that time has passed.

CONCLUDE: As I read the dialogue above the stage directions, I see that the Man has given Humbug a task that will take a very long time. The stage directions, then, help to emphasize just how long this task will take. It also helps create dramatic effect in the play.

NOTES

18 **Milo.** Are you a demon?

19 **Bird.** I'm afraid not. I've tried, but the best I can manage to be is a nuisance. [*Suddenly gets nervous as he looks beyond the three.*] And I don't have time to waste with you. [*Starts to leave.*]

20 **Tock.** What is it? What's the matter?

21 **Milo.** Hey, don't leave. I wanted to ask you some questions . . . Wait!

22 **Bird.** Weight? Twenty-seven pounds. Bye-bye. [*Disappears.*]

23 **Milo.** Well, he was no help.

24 **Man.** Perhaps I can be of some assistance to you? [*There appears a beautifully dressed man, very polished and clean.*] Hello, little boy. [*Shakes Milo's hand.*] And how's the faithful dog? [*Pats Tock.*] And who is this handsome creature? [*Tips his hat to Humbug.*]

25 **Humbug.** [*To others.*] What a pleasant surprise to meet someone so nice in a place like this.

26 **Man.** But before I help you out, I wonder if first you could spare me a little of your time, and help me with a few small jobs?

27 **Humbug.** Why, certainly.

28 **Tock.** Gladly.

29 **Milo.** Sure, we'd be happy to.

30 **Man.** Splendid, for there are just three tasks. First, I would like to move this pile of sand from here to there. [*Indicates through pantomime a large pile of sand.*] But I'm afraid that all I have is this tiny tweezers. [*Hands it to* Milo, *who begins moving the sand one grain at a time.*] Second, I would like to empty this well and fill that other, but I have no bucket, so you'll have to use this eyedropper. [*Hands it to* Tock, *who begins to work.*] And finally, I must have a hole in this cliff, and here is a needle to dig it. [Humbug *eagerly begins. The man leans against a tree and stares vacantly off into space. The LIGHTS indicate the passage of time.*]

31 **Milo.** You know something? I've been working steadily for a long time now, and I don't feel the least bit tired or hungry. I could go right on the same way forever.

32 **Man.** Maybe you will. [*He yawns.*]

33 **Milo.** [*Whispers to* Tock.] Well, I wish I knew how long it was going to take.

34 **Tock.** Why don't you use your magic staff and find out?

© Pearson Education, Inc., or its affiliates. All rights reserved.

© Pearson Education, Inc., or its affiliates. All rights reserved.

35 **Milo.** [*Takes out pencil and calculates. To* Man.] Pardon me, sir, but it's going to take 837 years to finish these jobs.

36 **Man.** Is that so? What a shame. Well then you'd better get on with them.

37 **Milo.** But . . . it hardly seems worthwhile.

38 **Man.** WORTHWHILE! Of course they're not worthwhile. I wouldn't ask you to do anything that was worthwhile.

39 **Tock.** Then why bother?

40 **Man.** Because, my friends, what could be more important than doing unimportant things? If you stop to do enough of them, you'll never get where you are going. [*Laughs villainously.*]

41 **Milo.** [*Gasps.*] Oh, no, you must be . . .

42 **Man.** Quite correct! I am the Terrible Trivium, demon of petty tasks and worthless jobs, ogre of wasted effort and monster of habit. [*They start to back away from him.*] Don't try to leave, there's so much to do, and you still have 837 years to go on the first job.

43 **Milo.** But why do unimportant things?

44 **Man.** Think of all the trouble it saves. If you spend all your time doing only the easy and useless jobs, you'll never have time to worry about the important ones which are so difficult. [*Walks toward them whispering.*] Now do come and stay with me. We'll have such fun together. There are things to fill and things to empty, things to take away and things to bring back, things to pick up and things to put down . . . [*They are transfixed[4] by his soothing voice. He is about to embrace them when a* Voice *screams.*]

45 **Voice.** Run! Run! [*They all wake up and run with the Trivium behind. As the voice continues to call out directions, they follow until they lose the Trivium.*] RUN! RUN! This way! This way! Over here! Over here! Up here! Down there! Quick, hurry up!

46 **Tock.** [*Panting.*] I think we lost him.

47 **Voice.** Keep going straight! Keep going straight! Now step up! Now step up!

48 **Milo.** Look out! [*They all fall into a Trap.*] But he said "up"!

49 **Voice.** Well, I hope you didn't expect to get anywhere by listening to me.

50 **Humbug.** We're in a deep pit! We'll never get out of here.

51 **Voice.** That is quite an accurate evaluation of the situation.

52 **Milo.** [*Shouting angrily.*] Then why did you help us at all?

NOTES

4. transfixed *v.* made motionless by horror or fascination.

The Phantom Tollbooth, Act II **331**

VOCABULARY DEVELOPMENT

Word Analysis Review paragraphs 42 and 44 and point to the words *worthless* and *useless*. Draw students' attention to the suffix –*less*. Explain that the suffix means "without." Then ask students what *worth* means (having value). Point out that knowing the meaning of the suffix can help them figure out the meaning of unfamiliar words. Direct students to create a two–column word chart for related word pairs in the text. For example, students can list *worthless* and *worthwhile*. Encourage them to find other word pairs that contain prefixes or suffixes, such as *important* and *unimportant,* and to add them to their word chart.

TEACHING

CLOSER LOOK

Analyze Punctuation

Students may have marked the punctuation in Milo's dialogue in paragraphs 54 and 56. Encourage students to talk about the annotations that they marked. You may want to model a close read with the class based on the highlights shown in the text.

ANNOTATE: Have students highlight the punctuation Milo uses in responding to Insincerity.

QUESTION: Guide students to think about why the playwright includes this punctuation.

Possible response: I think the playwright includes this punctuation to show how angry Milo is getting at Insincerity and how hard he is trying to avoid listening to the demon.

CONCLUDE: Help students draw conclusions about the effect of the exclamation marks.

Possible response: I can conclude that Milo is no longer bored or not paying attention. He's really annoyed at the bad advice and insincere words of the demon. The effect of the punctuation is to show Milo's anger, but it also shows that Milo is changing.

Remind students that **punctuation** in dialogue is one tool playwrights use to develop characters. Just as Milo's question marks signal the many questions Milo asks to understand his surroundings, exclamation marks help to convey his annoyance toward Insincerity.

NOTES

insincerity (ihn sihn SEHR uh tee) *n.* lack of honesty; untruthfulness

---

53 **Voice.** Oh, I'd do as much for anybody. Bad advice is my specialty. [*A Little Furry Creature appears.*] I'm the demon of **Insincerity**. I don't mean what I say; I don't mean what I do; and I don't mean what I am.

54 **Milo.** Then why don't you go away and leave us alone!

55 **Insincerity.** (VOICE) Now, there's no need to get angry. You're a very clever boy and I have complete confidence in you. You can certainly climb out of that pit . . . come on, try . . .

56 **Milo.** I'm not listening to one word you say! You're just telling me what you think I'd like to hear, and not what is important.

57 **Insincerity.** Well, if that's the way you feel about it . . .

58 **Milo.** That's the way I feel about it. We will manage by ourselves without any unnecessary advice from you.

59 **Insincerity.** [*Stamping his foot.*] Well, all right for you! Most people listen to what I say, but if that's the way you feel, then I'll just go home. [*Exits in a huff.*]

60 **Humbug.** [*Who has been quivering with fright.*] And don't you ever come back! Well, I guess we showed him, didn't we?

61 **Milo.** You know something? This place is a lot more dangerous than I ever imagined.

62 **Tock.** [*Who's been surveying the situation.*] I think I figured a way to get out. Here, hop on my back. [*Milo does so.*] Now, you, Humbug, on top of Milo. [*He does so.*] Now hook your umbrella onto that tree and hold on. [*They climb over Humbug, then pull him up.*]

63 **Humbug.** [*As they climb.*] Watch it! Watch it, now. Ow, be careful of my back! My back! Easy, easy . . . oh, this is so difficult. Aren't you finished yet?

64 **Tock.** [*As he pulls up Humbug.*] There. Now, I'll lead for a while. Follow me, and we'll stay out of trouble. [*They walk and climb higher and higher.*]

65 **Humbug.** Can't we slow down a little?

66 **Tock.** Something tells me we better reach the Castle-in-the-Air as soon as possible, and not stop to rest for a single moment. [*They speed up.*]

67 **Milo.** What is it, Tock? Did you see something?

68 **Tock.** Just keep walking and don't look back.

69 **Milo.** You *did* see something!

© Pearson Education, Inc., or its affiliates. All rights reserved.

332 UNIT 4 • IMAGINATION

HOW LANGUAGE WORKS

Word Choice Review paragraphs 53–61. As students perform their close read, explain that playwrights choose their words very carefully to enable them to convey their precise meaning and tone with a certain style. Word choice, called diction, also creates clarity. Have students complete this chart to analyze the effect of the playwright's word choice.

Words	Effect of the Words (possible response)
demon	Evokes a sense of evil
pit	Evokes a sense of despair and entrapment
clever, complete confidence, climb	The alliteration creates a sense that the demon is trying to soothe and sway Milo.
quivering	Appeals to both the sense of sight and touch

70 **Humbug.** What is it? Another demon?

71 **Tock.** Not just one, I'm afraid. If you want to see what I'm talking about, then turn around. [*They turn around. The stage darkens and hundreds of Yellow Gleaming Eyes can be seen.*]

72 **Humbug.** Good grief! Do you see how many there are? Hundreds! The Overbearing Know-it-all, the Gross Exaggeration, the Horrible Hopping Hindsight . . . and look over there! The Triple Demons of **Compromise**! Let's get out of here! [*Starts to scurry.*] Hurry up, you two! Must you be so slow about everything?

73 **Milo.** Look! There it is, up ahead! The Castle-in-the-Air! [*They all run.*]

74 **Humbug.** They're gaining!

75 **Milo.** But there it is!

76 **Humbug.** I see it! I see it!

77 [*They reach the first step and are stopped by a little man in a frock coat, sleeping on a worn ledger. He has a long quill pen and a bottle of ink at his side. He is covered with ink stains over his clothes and wears spectacles.*]

78 **Tock.** Shh! Be very careful. [*They try to step over him, but he wakes up.*]

79 **Senses Taker.** [*From sleeping position.*] Names? [*He sits up.*]

80 **Humbug.** Well, I . . .

81 **Senses Taker.** *NAMES?* [*He opens book and begins to write, splattering himself with ink.*]

82 **Humbug.** Uh . . . Humbug, Tock, and this is Milo.

83 **Senses Taker.** Splendid, splendid. I haven't had an "M" in ages.

84 **Milo.** What do you want our names for? We're sort of in a hurry.

85 **Senses Taker.** Oh, this won't take long. I'm the official Senses Taker and I must have some information before I can take your sense. Now if you'll just tell me: [*Handing them a form to fill. Speaking slowly and deliberately.*] When you were born, where you were born, why you were born, how old you are now, how old you were then, how old you'll be in a little while . . .

86 **Milo.** I wish he'd hurry up. At this rate, the demons will be here before we know it!

NOTES

compromise (KOM pruh myz) *n.* settlement of a disagreement in which each side gives up part of what it wanted

© Pearson Education, Inc., or its affiliates. All rights reserved.

The Phantom Tollbooth, Act II **333**

VOCABULARY DEVELOPMENT

Word Analysis Review paragraph 72 and point to the words *overbearing* and *know–it–all* and *hindsight*. Tell students that these are compound words, words that are made up of two or more smaller words. Explain that students can often determine the meaning of an unknown compound word by analyzing the smaller words that make up the compound word. For example, point out that *hindsight* is made up of the words *hind* and *sight*. Point out that *hind* means "backwards" and *sight* refers to seeing. Explain that by knowing the meanings of the two smaller words, you can determine that *hindsight* means "looking back." Discuss the other two words using the same method.

● CLOSE READ 🖉

Remind students to look for the actions the Senses Taker takes as well as what happens afterwards. You may wish to model the close read using the following think–aloud format. Possible responses to questions on the student page are included.

ANNOTATE: As I read paragraph 96, I notice and highlight the details that tell me what the Senses Taker does and how Milo, Tock, and Humbug react to the Senses Taker's actions.

QUESTION: I think the playwright includes these stage directions so that readers will know what's going on and so that actors who are performing the play will know what to do.

CONCLUDE: If I read the lines without the stage directions, they don't make sense. I can see that the stage directions tell the action of this part of the scene. The playwright wouldn't have been able to communicate the action without them.

NOTES

CLOSE READ
ANNOTATE: In paragraph 96, mark the stage directions that describe the Senses Taker's actions and their results.

QUESTION: Why does the playwright include these stage directions?

CONCLUDE: What is the effect of these directions? Would the playwright have been able to communicate the action without them?

---

87 **Senses Taker.** . . . Your mother's name, your father's name, where you live, how long you've lived there, the schools you've attended, the schools you haven't attended . . .

88 **Humbug.** I'm getting writer's cramp.

89 **Tock.** I smell something very evil and it's getting stronger every second. [*To* Senses Taker.] May we go now?

90 **Senses Taker.** Just as soon as you tell me your height, your weight, the number of books you've read this year . . .

91 **Milo.** We have to go!

92 **Senses Taker.** All right, all right. I'll give you the short form. [*Pulls out a small piece of paper.*] Destination?

93 **Milo.** But we have to . . .

94 **Senses Taker.** *DESTINATION?*

95 **Milo, Tock** and **Humbug.** The Castle-in-the-Air! [*They throw down their papers and run past him up the first few stairs.*]

96 **Senses Taker.** Stop! I'm sure you'd rather see what I have to show you. [*Snaps his fingers; they freeze.*] A circus of your very own. [*CIRCUS MUSIC is heard.* Milo *seems to go into a trance.*] And wouldn't you enjoy this most wonderful smell? [Tock *sniffs and goes into a trance.*] And here's something I know you'll enjoy hearing . . . [*To* Humbug. *The sound of CHEERS and APPLAUSE for* Humbug *is heard, and he goes into a trance.*] There we are. And now, I'll just sit back and let the demons catch up with you.

97 [Milo *accidentally drops his package of gifts. The Package of Laughter from* Dr. Dischord *opens and the Sounds of Laughter are heard. After a moment,* Milo, Tock, *and* Humbug *join in laughing and the spells are broken.*]

98 **Milo.** There was no circus.

99 **Tock.** There were no smells.

100 **Humbug.** The applause is gone.

101 **Senses Taker.** I warned you I was the Senses Taker. I'll steal your sense of Purpose, your sense of Duty, destroy your sense of Proportion—and but for one thing, you'd be helpless yet.

102 **Milo.** What's that?

103 **Senses Taker.** As long as you have the sound of laughter, I cannot take your sense of Humor. Agh! That horrible sense of humor.

104 **Humbug.** HERE THEY COME! LET'S GET OUT OF HERE!

© Pearson Education, Inc., or its affiliates. All rights reserved.

PERSONALIZE FOR LEARNING

Strategic Support
Unfamiliar Words For students to understand paragraph 96, they will need to know the meaning of *trance*. Have students look the word up in a dictionary and research what happens when someone goes into a trance. Lead a discussion about how and why hypnotists put

people into a trance and what it takes to get people out of a trance. Discuss what the playwright might be saying by having the Senses Taker put the characters into a trance. Ask students if Milo was in a kind of trance before he went through the phantom tollbooth.

105 [*The demons appear in nasty slithering hordes, running through the audience and up onto the stage, trying to attack Tock, Milo, and Humbug. The three heroes run past the Senses Taker up the stairs toward the Castle-in-the-Air with the demons snarling behind them.*]

106 **Milo.** Don't look back! Just keep going! [*They reach the castle. The two princesses appear in the windows.*]

107 **Princesses.** Hurry! Hurry! We've been expecting you.

108 **Milo.** You must be the Princesses. We've come to rescue you.

109 **Humbug.** And the demons are close behind!

110 **Tock.** We should leave right away.

111 **Princesses.** We're ready anytime you are.

112 **Milo.** Good, now if you'll just come out. But wait a minute—there's no door! How can we rescue you from the Castle-in-the-Air if there's no way to get in or out?

113 **Humbug.** Hurry, Milo! They're gaining on us.

114 **Reason.** Take your time, Milo, and think about it.

115 **Milo.** Ummm, all right . . . just give me a second or two. [*He thinks hard.*]

116 **Humbug.** I think I feel sick.

117 **Milo.** I've got it! Where's that package of presents? [*Opens the package of letters.*] Ah, here it is. [*Takes out the letters and sticks them on the door, spelling:*] E-N-T-R-A-N-C-E. Entrance. Now, let's see. [*Rummages through and spells in smaller letters:*] P-u-s-h. Push. [*He pushes and a door opens. The Princesses come out of the castle. Slowly, the demons ascend the stairway.*]

118 **Humbug.** Oh, it's too late. They're coming up and there's no other way down!

119 **Milo.** Unless . . . [*Looks at Tock.*] Well . . . Time flies, doesn't it?

120 **Tock.** Quite often. Hold on, everyone, and I'll take you down.

121 **Humbug.** Can you carry us all?

122 **Tock.** We'll soon find out. Ready or not, here we go! [*His alarm begins to ring. They jump off the platform and disappear. The demons, howling with rage, reach the top and find no one there. They see the Princesses and the heroes running across the stage and bound down the stairs after them and into the audience. There is a mad chase scene until they reach the stage again.*]

123 **Humbug.** I'm exhausted! I can't run another step.

124 **Milo.** We can't stop now . . .

NOTES

CLOSE READ
ANNOTATE: In the stage directions in paragraph 105, mark the word the playwright uses to refer to Milo, Tock, and Humbug.

QUESTION: Why does the playwright use this term at this point in the play?

CONCLUDE: What does this word suggest about ways in which the three characters have changed?

CLOSE READ

You may wish to model the close read using the following think-aloud format. Possible responses to questions on the student page are included.

ANNOTATE: As I read the stage directions in paragraph 105, I notice and mark the word that describes Milo, Tock, and Humbug.

QUESTION: I think the playwright uses this word to show that the characters are facing a dangerous challenge.

CONCLUDE: In the early parts of the play, these characters were bored and confused, but now they have bonded in a common purpose—to rescue the princesses.

The Phantom Tollbooth, Act II **335**

Challenge
Interview Ask students to review the rescue scene that begins in paragraph 106. Encourage interested students to create a brief video in which they imagine that they are a news crew interviewing the Princesses Rhyme and Reason after their rescue by Milo, Tock, and Humbug. The princesses tell the characters upon their arrival that they've been expecting them.

Encourage students to ask the princesses questions about how they knew Milo was coming for them and why they seemed certain that he could figure out a way to get them out of the castle. Have students write scripts upon which to base their interviews, including both the questions they will ask and the replies they imagine the princesses will give.

CLOSER LOOK

Analyze Dialogue

Students may have marked the italicized word in the dialogue in paragraph 139. Encourage students to talk about the annotations that they marked. You may want to model a close read with the class based on the highlights shown in the text.

ANNOTATE: Have students highlight the word in paragraph 139 that has been styled differently from the rest of the dialogue in the line.

QUESTION: Guide students to determine why the playwright styles the dialogue in this way.

Possible response: The word stands out as I read the line, so I think the playwright styles the word *will* this way to emphasize it.

CONCLUDE: Help students draw conclusions about the the effect of the text styling.

Possible response: I can conclude that Reason wants to stress to Milo that his intentions, or what he is willing to do, determine what he is capable of doing.

Remind students that playwrights express characterization, plot, and theme in **dialogue**, and they often use text styling such as italics to emphasize important ideas or to guide actors in their reading of lines to ensure certain ideas are conveyed.

NOTES

125 **Tock.** Milo! Look out there! [*The armies of Azaz and Mathemagician appear at the back of the theater, with the Kings at their heads.*]

126 **Azaz.** [*As they march toward the stage.*] Don't worry, Milo, we'll take over now.

127 **Mathemagician.** Those demons may not know it, but their days are numbered!

128 **Spelling Bee.** Charge! C-H-A-R-G-E! Charge! [*They rush at the demons and battle until the demons run off howling. Everyone cheers. The* Five Ministers of Azaz appear and shake Milo's hand.]

129 **Minister 1.** Well done.

130 **Minister 2.** Fine job.

131 **Minister 3.** Good work!

132 **Minister 4.** Congratulations!

133 **Minister 5.** CHEERS! [*Everyone cheers again. A fanfare interrupts. A* Page *steps forward and reads from a large scroll:*]

134 **Page.** *Henceforth, and forthwith,*

> *Let it be known by one and all.*
> *That Rhyme and Reason*
> *Reign once more in Wisdom.*

135 [*The* Princesses *bow gracefully and kiss their brothers, the* Kings.]

136 > *And furthermore,*
> *The boy named Milo,*
> *The dog known as Tock,*
> *And the insect hereinafter referred to as the Humbug*
> *Are hereby declared to be Heroes of the Realm.*

137 [*All bow and salute the heroes.*]

138 **Milo.** But we never could have done it without a lot of help.

139 **Reason.** That may be true, but you had the courage to try, and what you can do is often a matter of what you *will* do.

140 **Azaz.** That's why there was one very important thing about your quest we couldn't discuss until you returned.

141 **Milo.** I remember. What was it?

142 **Azaz.** Very simple. It was impossible!

143 **Mathemagician.** *Completely* impossible!

144 **Humbug.** Do you mean . . . ? [*Feeling faint.*] Oh . . . I think I need to sit down.

© Pearson Education, Inc., or its affiliates. All rights reserved.

PERSONALIZE FOR LEARNING

English Language Support

Formal English Direct students' attention to the words spoken by the page in paragraphs 134–136. Point out the words *henceforth*, *forthwith*, and *hereby*. Explain that these words are used in formal English. Remind students that a page, or a messenger of the king, is reading the announcement and that formal speech would be expected here. Tell students that *henceforth* means "from this time on," that *forthwith* means "immediately," and that *hereinafter* means "following this." Explain that *hereby* means "as a result of this document." Tell students that they can sometimes determine the meaning of formal words like these by the context in which they are used. **ALL LEVELS**

© Pearson Education, Inc., or its affiliates. All rights reserved.

145 **Azaz.** Yes, indeed, but if we'd told you then, you might not have gone.

146 **Mathemagician.** And, as you discovered, many things are possible just as long as you don't know they're impossible.

147 **Milo.** I think I understand.

148 **Rhyme.** I'm afraid it's time to go now.

149 **Reason.** And you must say goodbye.

150 **Milo.** To everyone? [*Looks around at the crowd. To* Tock *and* Humbug.] Can't you two come with me?

151 **Humbug.** I'm afraid not, old man. I'd like to, but I've arranged for a lecture tour which will keep me occupied for years.

152 **Tock.** And they do need a watchdog here.

153 **Milo.** Well, O.K., then. [Milo *hugs the* Humbug.]

154 **Humbug.** [*Sadly.*] Oh, bah.

NOTES

The Phantom Tollbooth, Act II **337**

PERSONALIZE FOR LEARNING

Strategic Support

Resolution Review paragraphs 138–154, a section of the play where the characters begin to reflect on their activities. Explain to students that fictional narratives contain a conflict that is developed and resolved. Ask students to think about the conflict in this story and how it is resolved on this page. Point out that in a resolution, the main character often learns something he didn't know before and loose ends are tied up. Discuss with students how they know that Milo has learned something from his experiences.

CLOSER LOOK

Analyze Theme

Students may have marked paragraphs 156–158 during their first read. Use these lines to help students understand how they can determine a theme of a fictional narrative. Encourage them to talk about the annotations that they marked. You may want to model a close read with the class based on the highlights shown in the text.

ANNOTATE: Have students mark details in paragraphs 156–158 that suggest the theme or the message the playwright wants to send to readers or have students participate while you highlight them.

QUESTION: Guide students to consider what these details might tell them. Ask what a reader can infer from Reason's advice that Milo should try to learn from mistakes and Rhyme's statement about the importance of knowledge, and accept student responses. **Possible response:** The advice that the princesses give to Milo is a sort of summary of what he has learned through his adventures in the Land of Wisdom—that he should always try and that learning is important.

CONCLUDE: Help students to formulate conclusions about the importance of these details in the text. Ask students why the playwright might have included these details.

Possible response: The playwright seems to be using the Princesses Rhyme and Reason to send a message to the readers, in case they did not infer the lessons that Milo learned during the story. This lesson is the theme of the story or the idea that the playwright wants to share with readers.

Remind students that a **theme** is the central idea, message, or insight that a literary work reveals. A theme is not the subject of the work, but rather the insight the work reveals about that subject. This central idea can usually be expressed as a generalization about people or life, and it may be directly stated or implied. Note that there is usually no single correct statement of a work's theme (though there can be numerous incorrect ones).

NOTES

155 **Milo.** [*He hugs* Tock, *and then faces everyone.*] Well, goodbye. We all spent so much time together, I know I'm going to miss you. [*To the* Princesses.] I guess we would have reached you a lot sooner if I hadn't made so many mistakes.

156 **Reason.** You must never feel badly about making mistakes, Milo, as long as you take the trouble to learn from them. Very often you learn more by being wrong for the right reasons than you do by being right for the wrong ones.

157 **Milo.** But there's so much to learn.

158 **Rhyme.** That's true, but it's not just learning that's important. It's learning what to do with what you learn and learning why you learn things that matters.

159 **Milo.** I think I know what you mean, Princess. At least, I hope I do. [*The car is rolled forward and* Milo *climbs in.*] Goodbye! Goodbye! I'll be back someday! I will! Anyway, I'll try. [*As* Milo *drives the set of the Land of Ignorance move offstage.*]

160 **Azaz.** Goodbye! Always remember. Words! Words! Words!

161 **Mathemagician.** And numbers!

162 **Azaz.** Now, don't tell me you think numbers are as important as words?

163 **Mathemagician.** Is that so? Why I'll have you know . . . [*The set disappears, and* Milo's *Room is seen onstage.*]

164 **Milo.** [*As he drives on.*] Oh, oh. I hope they don't start all over again. Because I don't think I'll have much time in the near future to help them out. [*The sound of loud ticking is heard.* Milo *finds himself in his room. He gets out of the car and looks around.*]

165 **The Clock.** Did someone mention time?

166 **Milo.** Boy, I must have been gone for an awful long time. I wonder what time it is. [*Looks at the clock.*] Five o'clock. I wonder what day it is. [*Looks at calendar.*] It's still today! I've only been gone for an hour! [*He continues to look at his calendar, and then begins to look at his books and toys and maps and chemistry set with great interest.*]

167 **Clock.** An hour. Sixty minutes. How long it really lasts depends on what you do with it. For some people, an hour seems to last forever. For others, just a moment, and so full of things to do.

168 **Milo.** [*Looks at clock.*] Six o'clock already?

169 **Clock.** In an instant. In a trice. Before you have time to blink. [*The stage goes black in less than no time at all.*] ✒

© Pearson Education, Inc., or its affiliates. All rights reserved.

Comprehension Check

Complete the following items after you finish your first read.

1. What gift does Dischord give Milo?

2. What does Dodecahedron look like?

3. What does Mathemagican give Milo before he goes to the Land of Ignorance?

4. What chases Milo, Tock, and Humbug up the stairway to the Castle-in-the-Air?

5. How does Tock help get everyone down from the Castle-in-the-Air?

6. 🗐 **Notebook** Write a summary of Act II to show your understanding.

- -

RESEARCH

Research to Clarify Choose at least one unfamiliar detail from the text. Briefly research that detail. In what way does the information you learned shed light on an aspect of the play?

Research to Explore Choose something that interested you from the text, and formulate a research question.

The Phantom Tollbooth, Act II **339**

Comprehension Check

Possible responses:

1. A package containing the sounds of laughter
2. It's a 12–sided figure with a different face on each side.
3. He gives him a magic staff that is actually a pencil.
4. demons
5. He carries them all as he flies down.
6. Students' summaries will vary but should include an account of Dischord, Dodecahedron, and the demons as well as an explanation of how Milo rescues the princesses.

Research

Research to Clarify If students struggle to come up with a detail to research, you may want to suggest that they focus on one of the following topics: geometry, Arabic numerals, censuses.

Research to Explore If students aren't sure how to go about formulating a research question, suggest that they use their findings from Research to Clarify as a starting point. For example, if students research Arabic numerals, they might formulate a question such as *What is the history of Arabic numerals?*

PERSONALIZE FOR LEARNING

Challenge

Speculate At the end of the story, Humbug says he is going on a lecture tour. A lecture tour is a trip during which a person gives speeches at various locations. Ask students to speculate what Humbug will talk about on his tour. Have them write a speech that Humbug will give, including his account of the events in the Land of Wisdom and his advice for people in the audience. Remind students to think about Humbug's character as they write and what wisdom or insight he might want to share. When students have finished their writing, encourage them to share it with the class.

TEACHING

Jump Start

CLOSE READ Ask students to consider the following prompt: *Who might have sent Milo the phantom tollbooth and why?* As students discuss the question, ask them to consider how Milo is both a hero and an ordinary boy like any other. Have them consider whether they or people they know are like Milo in some ways.

Close Read the Text 🖉

Walk students through the annotation model on the student page. Encourage them to complete items 2 and 3 on their own. Review and discuss the sections students have marked. If needed, continue to model close reading by using the Annotation Highlights in the Interactive Teacher's Edition.

Analyze the Text

Possible responses:

1. Dischord gives him a package of laughter that saves him from the Senses Taker. **DOK 2**

2. They suggest that he has changed and is learning to think. **DOK 2**

3. Learn from the mistakes you make and know what to do with information. **DOK 2**

4. **Essential Question:** I have learned that imagination can lead you to go on make-believe adventures. But it can also lead you to learn things about yourself. **DOK 3**

FORMATIVE ASSESSMENT

Analyze the Text

- **If** students fail to cite evidence, **then** remind them to support their ideas with specific information.

- **If** students struggle to identify what Milo's problem-solving skills suggest about his character, **then** tell them to consider if he showed those same skills early in the play.

340 UNIT 4 • IMAGINATION

MAKING MEANING

THE PHANTOM TOLLBOOTH, ACT II

Close Read the Text

1. This model—from paragraph 100 of Act II, scene i—shows two sample annotations, along with questions and conclusions. Close read the passage, and find another detail to annotate. Then, write a question and your conclusion.

Close Read

ANNOTATE QUESTION CONCLUDE

> **ANNOTATE:** All of these expressions use words related to size or shape but refer to types of feelings or experiences.
>
> **QUESTION:** Why does Dodecahedron refer to feelings or experiences—abstract ideas—as though they can be measured?
>
> **CONCLUDE:** In the world of the play, abstract ideas are concrete and "real."

> **ANNOTATE:** Dodecahedron repeats the words *know* and *knowing*.
>
> **QUESTION:** Why does the playwright have the character repeat these words?
>
> **CONCLUDE:** The repetition emphasizes the importance of knowledge to Dodecahedron.

> **Dodecahedron.** [*Continues shouting angrily.*] If you had high hopes, how would you know how high they were? And did you know that narrow escapes come in different widths? Would you travel the whole world wide without ever knowing how wide it was? And how could you do anything at long last without knowing how long the last was?

2. For more practice, go back into the text, and complete the close-read notes.

3. Revisit a section of the text you found important during your first read. Read this section closely, and **annotate** what you notice. Ask yourself **questions** such as "Why did the author make this choice?" What can you **conclude?**

🛠 Tool Kit
Close-Read Guide and Model Annotation

Analyze the Text

CITE TEXTUAL EVIDENCE
to support your answers.

📓 **Notebook** Respond to these questions.

1. **Analyze** How does Dischord end up helping Milo on his quest?

2. **Deduce** How do Milo's solutions for getting the princesses out of the Castle-in-the-Air show his growth since the beginning of the play?

3. **Paraphrase** In your own words, restate Rhyme and Reason's advice to Milo at the end of Act II.

4. **Essential Question:** *Where can imagination lead?* What have you learned about where imagination can lead from reading this play?

☰ STANDARDS
Reading Literature
Analyze how a particular sentence, chapter, scene, or stanza fits into the overall structure of a text and contributes to the development of the theme, setting, or plot.

340 UNIT 4 • IMAGINATION

© Pearson Education, Inc., or its affiliates. All rights reserved.

PERSONALIZE FOR LEARNING

English Language Support

Paraphrase English learners may have difficulty paraphrasing. Explain to them what it means to paraphrase. Then point out that to paraphrase, they should reread the original text until they understand its meaning. As students reread the advice of the princesses, have them describe to a partner the meaning of the lines. Once students have settled on the meaning, have them write down their paraphrase; remind them to use their own words. **ALL LEVELS**

Analyze Craft and Structure

Dramatic Structures: Stage Directions The script of a play includes both dialogue and stage directions. Lines of dialogue tell readers what the characters say. **Stage directions** are the words in the script that the characters do not say. These directions tell the performers how and where to move and how to speak. They also provide information about scenery, lighting, and sound. Stage directions are usually printed in italics and set in brackets, as in this example.

> **Dodecahedron.** [*Glaring from his upset face.*] Certainly not! They're all the wrong way! Just because you have a choice, it doesn't mean that any of them has to be right. [*Pointing in another direction.*] …

Notice how the stage directions help readers visualize, or picture, the action. They also reveal important information about how characters feel, respond, and behave.

Practice

CITE TEXTUAL EVIDENCE
to support your answers.

📓 **Notebook** Respond to these questions.

1. Read the stage directions from Act II that appear in the chart. Explain the information about the characters or action each stage direction provides.

STAGE DIRECTION	INFORMATION PROVIDED
Mathemagician. Sure. [*Opens another door.*] Here it is. It took three carts to carry it here. [*Door reveals an "8" that is as wide as the "3" was high.*]	The stage directions tell what action the Mathemagician performed and explain the prop that is on the stage.
Tock. [*Who's been surveying the situation.*] I think I figured a way to get out. Here, hop on my back. [*Milo does so.*] Now, you, Humbug, on top of Milo. [*He does so.*] Now hook your umbrella onto that tree and hold on. [*They climb over Humbug, then pull him up.*]	The stage directions tell the characters' physical actions and movement.
Bird. I'm afraid not. I've tried, but the best I can manage to be is a nuisance. [*Suddenly gets nervous as he looks beyond the three.*] And I don't have time to waste with you. [*Starts to leave.*]	The stage directions help develop the character's emotion and his movement from the stage.

2. (a) Identify and mark a point in Act II in which the stage directions are necessary to help you understand what characters are feeling or doing, or what is happening around them. (b) Find one place in the play that has no stage directions. Write your own stage directions for that section of the play. Explain how your stage directions make the action more clear.

WriteNow Express and Reflect

Stage Directions Scripts for dramas include stage directions to help the actors know what to do and how to say their lines. But scripts for television shows and movies also include stage directions. Tell students to think about a scene from a favorite television show or movie and write the stage directions. Include lighting, sound effects, props, actor's actions, and the way actors speak their lines. Students should include similar information in their stage directions and should write them in a similar style, using italicized (or underlined, if hand-written) text and brackets.

Analyze Craft and Structure

Dramatic Structures: Stage Directions Ask students to imagine that they are trying out for a part in a play and have been given a script. Explain that the script contains only dialogue and no stage directions. Display the following imaginary script and have volunteers read it:

> Laila: The creature I saw outside last night was this big!
>
> Amal: Are you sure, Laila? Take a look at this picture of a fisher cat and see if it looks like that.

Ask students what was missing from their reading. Discuss how stage directions would have told the actors how to deliver the lines, how to move, and which props to use. For more support, see **Analyze Craft and Structure: Stage Directions.** 📄

MAKE IT INTERACTIVE
Project the digital version of *The Phantom Tollbooth*, Act II, and read the end of the play, where the Mathemagician disappears and Milo arrives back in his bedroom. Model how to use the stage directions to determine what information they provide to help students understand how to complete the chart.

Practice

1. **See possible responses in chart on student page.**
2. **Possible responses:** (a) When Milo rescues the princesses and jumps out of the castle, the demons chase them. All of these actions are described in the stage directions. (b) Responses will vary.

FORMATIVE ASSESSMENT

Analyze Craft and Structure

- **If** students are unable to determine what information the stage directions provide, **then** ask them if it describes an action or an object.

- **If** students are unable to write stage directions for a place in the play with none, **then** have them identify a place with none and write stage directions that indicate that the characters do something completely different from what they have imagined.

For Reteach and Practice, see **Analyze Craft and Structure: Stage Directions (RP).** 📄

© Pearson Education, Inc., or its affiliates. All rights reserved.

Concept Vocabulary

Why These Words

Possible responses:

1. Some of the words, like *pessimistic* and *malicious*, hint at the problems the characters face by showing how they react to the problems. And others, like *obstacle* and *insincerity*, are actual problems and conflicts.

2. *dangerous, dreadful, unpleasant, unbearable*

Practice

Possible responses:

1. *skeptically, barrier, depressed, hateful, hypocrisy, agree*

2. Student sentences will vary but should incorporate context clues.

Word Network

Possible words: *wonder, marvelous, pantomime, magic*

Word Study

For more support, see **Concept Vocabulary and Word Study.** 📄

Possible responses:

1. *conformity:* the state of conforming, or being the same. *flexibility:* the state of being flexible.

2. *humanity:* the state or quality of being human; *similarity:* the state or quality of being similar or alike; *equality:* the state or quality of being equal.

FORMATIVE ASSESSMENT

Concept Vocabulary

If students have trouble listing related words for each concept vocabulary word, **then** have them use a thesaurus and determine synonyms that are closely related to the concept vocabulary words.

Word Study

If students struggle to define *conformity,* **then** have them analyze the word parts *con-* and *form.* For Reteach and Practice, see **Word Study: Latin Suffix *-ity* (RP).** 📄

THE PHANTOM TOLLBOOTH, ACT II

🔗 WORD NETWORK

Add words related to imagination from the text to your Word Network.

≔ STANDARDS

Language
• Demonstrate command of the conventions of standard English grammar and usage when writing or speaking.
• Use knowledge of language and its conventions when writing, speaking, reading, or listening.
  a. Vary sentence patterns for meaning, reader/listener interest, and style.
• Determine or clarify the meaning of unknown and multiple-meaning words and phrases based on *grade 6 reading and content,* choosing flexibly from a range of strategies.
  b. Use common, grade-appropriate Greek or Latin affixes and roots as clues to the meaning of a word.

342 UNIT 4 • IMAGINATION

Concept Vocabulary

suspiciously	pessimistic	insincerity
obstacle	malicious	compromise

Why These Words? The six concept vocabulary words relate to conflict, lack of trust, and feelings of doubt. For example, Milo *suspiciously* asks Dischord to describe the type of doctor he is. Princess Reason tells Rhyme not to be so *pessimistic.* Notice that both words relate to the characters' concerns about another character's honesty or intentions.

1. How does the concept vocabulary sharpen the reader's understanding of the conflict in the play?

2. What other words in the selection connect to this concept?

Practice

📓 **Notebook** The concept vocabulary words appear in Act II.

1. With a partner, list as many related words for each concept vocabulary word as you can. For example, for *suspiciously* you might list *suspicious.*

2. For each concept vocabulary word, write a sentence in which you use the word correctly. Include context clues that hint at the meaning of the word.

Word Study

Latin Suffix: *-ity* The Latin suffix *-ity* indicates that a word is a noun. It means "the state or quality of." The word *insincerity,* which appears in Act II of the play, means "the state of being insincere."

1. Use your understanding of the suffix *-ity* to write a definition for the following words: *conformity* and *flexibility.*

2. Identify two other words that end with the suffix *-ity.* For each word, write a definition that demonstrates the meaning of the suffix. Then, consult a dictionary to check your work.

© Pearson Education, Inc., or its affiliates. All rights reserved.

VOCABULARY DEVELOPMENT

Concept Vocabulary Reinforcement To increase familiarity with the concept vocabulary, ask students to use each of the words in a sentence. Encourage students to include context clues in their own sentences to demonstrate their knowledge of the word. If students are still struggling with the words, encourage them to identify the base word in each term, look up the base word in the dictionary, and then use the definition to come up with the meaning of the concept vocabulary word.

Conventions

Sentence Structure Sentences can be classified according to the number and kinds of their clauses. A **clause** is a group of words with its own subject and verb.

An **independent,** or **main, clause** can stand alone as a sentence because it expresses a complete thought. A **dependent,** or **subordinate, clause** cannot stand alone—it depends on the main clause. A dependent clause usually begins with a relative pronoun, such as *who, which,* or *that,* or a subordinating conjunction, such as *because, if,* or *when.* The following chart shows how clauses are used to create three types of sentence structures and gives examples of each from *The Phantom Tollbooth,* Act II.

> **TIP**
> **CLARIFICATION**
> Refer to the Grammar Handbook to learn more about these terms.

SIMPLE SENTENCE	COMPOUND SENTENCE	COMPLEX SENTENCE
Definition: a single independent clause	Definition: two or more independent clauses joined by a coordinating conjunction (such as *and, but, or*) or a semicolon	Definition: one independent clause and one or more dependent clauses (In the example, the dependent clauses are underlined.)
EXAMPLE: We want to talk to the Mathemagician.	EXAMPLE: I've been working steadily for a long time now, and I don't feel the least bit tired or hungry.	EXAMPLE: Here in Digitopolis, we have our meals when we're full and eat until we're hungry.

Read It

Mark the independent and dependent clauses. Then, label each sentence as simple, compound, or complex.

1. There are a number of ways to get to Digitopolis, if you follow the directions correctly.
2. All three roads arrive at the same place at the same time.
3. You'll take one spoonful every day, and you'll never hear another beautiful sound again.

Write It

Notebook Read the following example of a simple sentence. Notice that it has been rewritten twice. First, an independent clause was added to make a compound sentence. Then, a dependent clause was added to make a complex sentence. Do the same for sentences 1 and 2.

> **Simple:** Milo fixed the clock.
> **Compound:** Milo fixed the clock, *and he fixed the toy.*
> **Complex:** Milo fixed the clock *because it was broken.*

1. The Mathemagician mines numbers.
2. Rhyme and Reason are prisoners in the Land of Ignorance.

The Phantom Tollbooth, Act II **343**

© Pearson Education, Inc., or its affiliates. All rights reserved.

PERSONALIZE FOR LEARNING

Challenge

Building Sentences Have students create clause strips, on which they write various independent and dependent clauses related to the text, and coordinating conjunction cards. Then challenge them to mix and match the strips to create new sentences, either compound or complex. As students rearrange their clause strips, have them write the sentences down. Challenge partners to determine how many original sentences they can create using the strips.

Conventions

Sentence Structure Discuss the definition of *simple, compound,* and *complex sentences* with students and go over the information in the chart. Then discuss what *independent* and *dependent clauses* are by stressing the meaning of "independent" and "dependent." Point out that a dependent clause depends on the independent clause to give it meaning.

Explain to students that independent clauses are joined in a compound sentence by a semicolon, a colon, or by a coordinating conjunction. Share the following list of coordinating conjunctions with students: and, but, or, nor, yet, for, so. Point out that a coordinating conjunction is usually preceded by a comma. For more support, see **Conventions: Sentence Structure.**

Read It
Possible response:

1. COMPLEX: *There are a number of ways to get to Digitopolis* (independent), *if you know how to follow directions.* (dependent)
2. SIMPLE: *All three roads arrive at the same place at the same time.* (independent)
3. COMPOUND: *All you have to do is take one spoonful every day,* (independent) and *you'll never have to hear another beautiful sound again.* (independent).

Write It
Possible response:

1. The Mathemagician mines numbers, but he does not mine letters. (compound); The Mathemagician mines numbers that are big and small, long and short. (complex)
2. Rhyme and Reason are prisoners in the Land of Ignorance, but Milo will rescue them. (compound); Though Rhyme and Reason are prisoners in the Land of Ignorance, they will soon be free. (complex)

FORMATIVE ASSESSMENT

Conventions

- **If** students struggle to identify dependent clauses, **then** remind them to look for a relative pronoun or subordinating conjunction.
- **If** students fail to identify simple, compound, and complex sentences, **then** tell them to separate the sentence into clauses and determine if any of the clauses depends on another for meaning.

For Reteach and Practice, see **Conventions: Sentence Structure (RP).**

Whole-Class Learning **343**

Writing to Sources

Remind students that *perspective* refers to the lens through which story events are seen.

Tell students that to write the scene from the perspective of Tock, they really need to think about his character and determine what he might have thought or felt during the scene. Ask them to consider how Tock reacted to events and what this tells them about him. Encourage them to use Tock's way of speaking in their dialogue and to consider what Tock's role is in the story. For example, is he a teacher for Milo, a role model, a friend? For more support, see **Writing to Sources: Narrative Retelling.** 📄

Reflect on Your Writing

1. Responses will vary. If students need support, ask them to consider the insights they gained from writing from Tock's perspective.

2. Responses will vary. If students need support, ask them to think about which part of the exercise took longer.

3. **Why These Words?** Responses will vary. Have students list specific examples of words they have chosen that add power to their retelling.

FORMATIVE ASSESSMENT
Writing to Sources

• **If** students struggle to write from Tock's perspective, **then** have partners act out an event from the play from Tock's point of view. For Reteach and Practice, see **Writing to Sources: Narrative Retelling (RP).** 📄

THE PHANTOM TOLLBOOTH,
ACT II

Writing to Sources

Although *The Phantom Tollbooth* is a play, readers see events from Milo's perspective. Rewriting a scene from another character's perspective can help you understand the play in a deeper way.

> ### Assignment
> Choose a scene from *The Phantom Tollbooth,* and write a **narrative retelling** from Tock's perspective.
>
> • Reread a scene you found memorable or interesting. Note important details that reveal Tock's personality and reasons for his actions. Use these details to help develop Tock's perspective.
>
> • Present a clear sequence of events for your scene. Remember, however, that you are not writing a script with stage directions. You are retelling the scene as a story.
>
> • Write as if you were Tock. Include dialogue and description to show how Tock feels about other characters and the events taking place.

Vocabulary and Conventions Connection Consider including several of the concept vocabulary words. Also, remember to use a variety of sentence types in your writing.

suspiciously	pessimistic	insincerity
obstacle	malicious	compromise

Reflect on Your Writing

After you have written your retelling, answer the following questions.

1. How did writing from Tock's perspective help you better understand both Tock and Milo?

2. What did you find most difficult about rewriting the scene from Tock's perspective?

3. **Why These Words?** The words you choose make a difference in your writing. Which words did you specifically choose to add power to your narrative?

© Pearson Education, Inc., or its affiliates. All rights reserved.

⊟ STANDARDS

Writing
Write narratives to develop real or imagined experiences or events using effective technique, relevant descriptive details, and well-structured event sequences.
  a. Engage and orient the reader by establishing a context and introducing a narrator and/or characters; organize an event sequence that unfolds naturally and logically.
  b. Use narrative techniques, such as dialogue, pacing, and description, to develop experiences, events, and/or characters.

344 UNIT 4 • IMAGINATION

English Language Support
Narrative Retelling Ask students to work in pairs to briefly resume the selection using transition words as needed. **EMERGING**

Ask students to write a paragraph resuming the selection using transition words and phrases as needed to convey the sequential order. **EXPANDING**

Ask students to write a brief summary of the selection in sequential order and then rewrite it from Dr. Dischord's perspective. **BRIDGING**

An expanded **English Language Development Lesson** on Narrative Retelling is available in the Interactive Teacher's Edition. 📄

Speaking and Listening

A dramatic reading of a play is a performance without costumes, scenery, or movement around the stage. The presenters use their voices and gestures to act out the roles and suggest the action.

Assignment

With your class, conduct a **dramatic reading** of a scene from *The Phantom Tollbooth*.

1. **Choose a Scene** As a class, decide whether you will all work on the same scene, or whether will have two groups work on two different scenes. Make sure everyone agrees that the scene or scenes you choose are interesting and exciting.

2. **Assign Roles** Decide who will play what roles. If necessary, one person can play more than one role, or you can divide a single role among several people. So, for example, one person might play the role of Milo for a while, and then another student might take over. Also, decide who will read the stage directions.

3. **Review the Scene** Reread the scene carefully to understand the characters' feelings and thoughts and the events taking place. Try out different ways of saying the lines to see which ones work best or create an interesting effect.

4. **Deliver the Dramatic Reading** Act out your role, reading the exact words in the script clearly. Make eye contact with the actor your character is talking to, and use gestures to reflect information in the stage directions. Vary the tone and volume of your voice to express the feelings behind the character's words. If you are reading the stage directions, speak clearly and loudly. Read as a storyteller would, with liveliness and emotion.

5. **Evaluate the Reading** Use an evaluation guide like the one shown to review your class's dramatic readings.

© Pearson Education, Inc., or its affiliates. All rights reserved.

EVALUATION GUIDE

Rate each statement on a scale of 1 (not demonstrated) to 5 (demonstrated).

☐ The performers maintained appropriate eye contact.

☐ The performers delivered their lines clearly and expressively.

☐ The performers used gestures that reflected their characters and the stage directions.

☐ The performers adjusted speaking tone and volume to match their lines.

✍ EVIDENCE LOG

Before moving on to a new selection, go to your Evidence Log and record what you learned from *The Phantom Tollbooth,* Act II.

☰ STANDARDS

Speaking and Listening
Adapt speech to a variety of contexts and tasks, demonstrating command of formal English when indicated or appropriate.

The Phantom Tollbooth, Act II **345**

PERSONALIZE FOR LEARNING

Strategic Support

Dramatic Reading Help students on the autism spectrum understand and feel comfortable participating in the dramatic reading by having a short rehearsal. In the rehearsal, challenge other students to demonstrate how they might read a line from the play. Ask students to show how they might read a line in an angry way, in a sad way, in an excited way, and so on. Encourage actors to exaggerate facial expressions and gestures so that the meaning is clear. Then discuss what techniques the actors used (gestures, varied tone and volume, etc.) to convey meaning.

Speaking and Listening

1. **Choose a Scene** As students review and select scenes, you may want to remind students that they do not need the setting or props to conduct the dramatic reading. They need only to choose a scene that they think would be fun to perform. To be sure that all students are actively involved, you may want to ask students to make a list that identifies the roles they have assigned.

2. **Assign Roles** Once students have assigned roles, suggest that they go through the scene and mark their lines for review.

3. **Review the Scene** Remind students that reviewing the entire scene, including other characters' lines, ensures that they understand how to respond to or react to a given character or event. Encourage students to try out a voice for their character, one they think fits his or her personality. For example, a nervous character probably speaks quickly. A wise character may speak slowly and deliberately.

4. **Deliver the Dramatic Reading** Remind students to use the voice they adopted for their character and to follow along in the script as others are reading so they know where they are in the scene.

5. **Evaluate the Reading** Encourage students to make one supportive comment about each presentation.

For more support, see **Speaking and Listening: Dramatic Reading.** 🖹

Evidence Log Support students in completing their Evidence Log. This paced activity will help prepare them for the Performance-Based Assessment at the end of the unit.

FORMATIVE ASSESSMENT

Speaking and Listening

- **If** students are unable to decide on roles, **then** have them draw the character names from a hat.

- **If** students are unable to act out a scene without significant distress, **then** give them the task of reading stage directions.

For Reteach and Practice, see **Speaking and Listening: Dramatic Reading (RP).** 🖹

Selection Test

Administer the *The Phantom Tollbooth*, Act II, Selection Test, which is available in both print and digital formats online in Assessments. 🖹 ☑

Whole-Class Learning **345**

from The Phantom Tollbooth

🔊 **AUDIO SUMMARIES**

Audio summaries of "*from The Phantom Tollbooth*" are available online in both English and Spanish in the Interactive Teacher's Edition or Unit Resources. Assigning these summaries prior to reviewing the selection may help students build additional background knowledge and set a context for their first review.

Summary

This illustration from an animated movie of *The Phantom Tollbooth* and the excerpt from an audio performance of the play capture the beginning of Act II, Scene i, in which Milo, Tock, and Humbug are approaching Digitopolis. They encounter a wagon and then meet Dischord. He examines them and diagnoses them with suffering from a lack of noise.

Insight

Students have the opportunity to compare a scene they have read in text format with a visual image and an audio performance. In comparing the media, students will be able to consider not just the imagination captured in the story itself but also their own imaginations as readers, viewers, and listeners.

ESSENTIAL QUESTION:
Where can imagination lead?

Connection to Essential Question

With these selections, imagination leads to a self-examination of how we perceive and imagine information. Students are challenged to examine how they imagine characters, settings, and action as they read and compare their changing perceptions when they encounter the same material in different media.

WHOLE-CLASS LEARNING PERFORMANCE TASK
One day in the Kingdom of Wisdom . . .

UNIT PERFORMANCE-BASED ASSESSMENT
What might happen if a fictional character were to come into the real world?

Connection to Performance Tasks

Whole-Class Learning Performance Task The audio and image will help students to imagine the characters of the fantasy. A knowledge of the Kingdom of Wisdom will help students as they prepare their responses to the prompt.

Unit Performance-Based Assessment The play presents a story based in fantasy. Students may be able to use the imaginative elements of the plot to help them address the prompt.

LESSON RESOURCES

	Making Meaning	Language Development	Effective Expression
Lesson	First Review Close Review Analyze the Media	Media Vocabulary	Writing to Compare
Instructional Standards	**RL.10** By the end of the year, read and comprehend literature . . . **SL.2** Interpret information presented in diverse media and formats . . . **L.6** Acquire and use accurately grade-appropriate general academic and domain-specific words and phrases . . .	**L.6** Acquire and use accurately grade-appropriate general academic and domain-specific words and phrases . . .	**RL.7** Compare and contrast the experience . . . **W.2** Write informative/explanatory texts . . . **W.2.a** Introduce a topic . . . **SL.2** Interpret information presented in diverse media and formats . . .
STUDENT RESOURCES			
Available online in the Interactive Student Edition or Unit Resources	🔊 Selection Audio 📄 First-Review Guide: Multimedia 📄 Close-Review Guide: Media-Audio	📄 Word Network	📄 Evidence Log
TEACHER RESOURCES			
Selection Resources Available onlinein the Interactive Teacher's Edition or Unit Resources	🔊 Audio Summaries	📄 Media Vocabulary	📄 Writing to Compare:Comparison-and-Contrast Essay
My Resources	📄 A Unit 4 Answer Key is available online and in the Interactive Teacher's Edition.		

Media Complexity Rubric: *from* The Phantom Tollbooth

Quantitative Measures

Format and Length: Audio: 9 minutes, 4 seconds; Image

Qualitative Measures

Knowledge Demands ①—②—**❸**—④—⑤	Students will need to have read Act I of the play prior to listening to the excerpt, which begins Act II. References to medical conditions may challenge some students.
Structure ①—**❷**—③—④—⑤	The audio excerpt begins with Milo, Humbug, and Tock approaching Digitopolis. They stop and encounter Dischord.
Language Conventionality and Clarity ①—②—**❸**—④—⑤	The dialogue is fairly clear with some advanced vocabulary integrated into puns and some nonsense terminology.
Levels of Meaning/Purpose ①—②—**❸**—④—⑤	The scene has two purposes: to advance the characters from one point to another and to demonstrate the humorous and thematic points conveyed by Dischord.

Jump Start

FIRST REVIEW Ask students how they expect Milo, Tock, and Humbug to look and sound. Then have students discuss how different versions of *The Phantom Tollbooth* might portray events differently from how they are portrayed in the play.

The Phantom Tollbooth

Where are Milo, Tock, and Humbug? When will they reach Digitopolis? What other characters will they encounter on their journey? Modeling questions such as these will help students connect to "The Phantom Tollbooth" and to the Whole-Class Performance Task assignment. Selection audio and print capability for the selection are available in the Interactive Teacher's Edition.

Media Vocabulary

Encourage students to discuss the media vocabulary. Have they seen or used these terms before? Do they use any of them in their speech or writing?

⬤ FIRST REVIEW

Have students perform the steps of the first review independently:

WATCH: Encourage students to notice speakers.

NOTE: Remind students to focus on key speakers and their exchanges.

CONNECT: Encourage students to make connections beyond the media. If they cannot make connections to their own lives, have them consider other audio books or recordings they have heard that might be similar.

RESPOND: Students will answer questions to demonstrate understanding.

Point out to students that while they will always complete the Respond step at the end of the first review, the other steps will probably happen somewhat concurrently. You may wish to print copies of the **First-Review Guide: Media-Audio** for students to use. ▤

≡ STANDARDS

Reading Literature
By the end of the year, read and comprehend literature, including stories, dramas, and poems, in the grades 6–8 text complexity band proficiently, with scaffolding as needed at the high end of the range.

Language
Acquire and use accurately grade-appropriate general academic and domain-specific words and phrases; gather vocabulary knowledge when considering a word or phrase important to comprehension or expression.

⬚ MAKING MEANING

Comparing Text to Media

In this lesson, you will look at an image from an animated movie of *The Phantom Tollbooth* and listen to part of an audio performance of the play. You will then compare the image and audio with the text.

THE PHANTOM TOLLBOOTH (drama)

from THE PHANTOM TOLLBOOTH (multimedia)

from The Phantom Tollbooth

Media Vocabulary

The first two concepts will be useful as you listen to the audio. The third will be useful as you evaluate the image from the movie.

stage directions (in audio): important information that is provided by the playwright about the setting, characters, and action	• In an audio-only performance, the stage directions are spoken aloud. • The actor reads the stage directions with expression, just as a storyteller would.
dialogue (in audio): spoken conversation between or among characters	• Most plays are made up mostly of dialogue. • Because actors in an audio performance cannot be seen by listeners, they must use their voices and other clues to make their roles and the story's action clear.
light and shadow (in images): drawing techniques that add depth to an image	• Light and shadow show which parts of an image are in front or behind. • Light and shadow create a mood, or overall feeling, in an image.

First Review MEDIA: MULTIMEDIA

Apply these strategies as you conduct your first review.

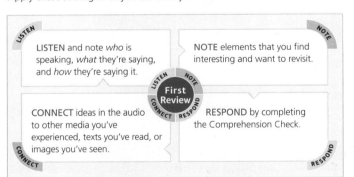

LISTEN and note *who* is speaking, *what* they're saying, and *how* they're saying it.

NOTE elements that you find interesting and want to revisit.

CONNECT ideas in the audio to other media you've experienced, texts you've read, or images you've seen.

RESPOND by completing the Comprehension Check.

© Pearson Education, Inc., or its affiliates. All rights reserved.

PERSONALIZE FOR LEARNING

English Language Support
Taking Notes Support students as they listen to the audio. Have partners listen in 20-second increments. Students should take notes on key details they hear during each segment. After listening for 20 seconds, have partners compare their notes. Repeat the process until students have listened to the entire excerpt. **ALL LEVELS**

MULTIMEDIA

from The Phantom Tollbooth

BACKGROUND

As you study the image and listen to the audio, consider how the experience of reading the play is similar to and different from the experience of viewing and listening to the multimedia.

SCAN FOR
MULTIMEDIA

NOTES

© Pearson Education, Inc., or its affiliates. All rights reserved.

from The Phantom Tollbooth (multimedia) **347**

CLOSER REVIEW

Analyze Stage Directions

Students may have noted stage directions during the first 2:50 of their first review. Use this part of the audio recording to help students understand how stage directions are utilized in an audio presentation. Encourage them to talk about what they noted. You may want to model a close review with the class.

NOTE: Have students note the stage directions during the first 2:50 of the audio recording.

QUESTION: Guide students to consider the content of the stage directions. Ask what a listener gains from the stage directions compared to the dialogue, and accept student responses.

Possible response: The stage directions tell the names of all the characters in the scene, what their movements are, and who is talking to whom. The stage directions also describe sound effects.

CONCLUDE: Help students formulate conclusions about the importance of stage directions in an audio presentation. Ask students why the artists chose to include these directions.

Possible response: The details in the stage directions help a listener understand what's going on. Without the stage directions, you would not be able to keep track of all the characters in a scene. You would not understand their movements, like Milo shaking his head. And you would not understand the setting, like all the objects in the apothecary shop.

Guide students to understand that in a scripted play, the **stage directions** are written instructions to actors and crew on how to present all aspects of the play other than the dialogue. In an audio recording, the stage directions must be read aloud by a narrator. The narrator serves a function similar to the narrator in a fictional text.

WriteNow Express and Reflect

Audio Review The audio clip of *The Phantom Tollbooth* includes the scene in which Milo, Tock, and Humbug meet Dischord. Tell students that they will write a one-page review of the clip, examining the voices of the characters and the stage directions read by the narrator. Tell them that their review should include whether they would want to listen to the rest of the story based on the audio clip they heard. Point out that they must support any opinions with reasons and evidence from the clip.

Comprehension Check

Possible responses:

1. The main characters are Milo, Humbug, and Tock.
2. They are going to Digitopolis.
3. They meet Dischord.
4. The setting is the apothecary wagon.

Comprehension Check

Complete the following items after you finish your first review.

1. Who are the main characters in this scene?

2. Where are the characters going?

3. Whom do the characters meet?

4. What is the setting?

5. 📓 **Notebook** Write a list of the characters and events featured in the audio performance.

- -

RESEARCH

Research to Explore Choose something that interests you about the audio performance or the movie image, and briefly research it. For example, you might research how an audio production or animated film is made.

© Pearson Education, Inc., or its affiliates. All rights reserved.

PERSONALIZE FOR LEARNING

Challenge

Movie Poster Challenge students to create a movie poster advertising *The Phantom Tollbooth* movie. Have them draw a scene from the audio clip they viewed on poster board and include a catchy quote, either from the video or from the play. Point out that the scene and quote they choose should aim to "sell" the movie, to make people want to see it. When students have finished their movie posters, display them in the classroom.

Close Review

Study the image and listen to the audio again. Write any new observations that seem important. What **questions** do you have? What can you **conclude**?

Close Review · REVIEW · QUESTION · CONCLUDE

THE PHANTOM TOLLBOOTH
(multimedia)

Analyze the Media

Notebook Respond to these questions.

1. (a) Describe the characters shown in the image and the expressions on their faces. (b) **Analyze** What part of the story might this image be showing? Explain your reasoning.

2. **Interpret** In the audio performance, what do Dischord's actions and the tone of his voice show about his personality? Explain.

3. **Essential Question:** *Where can imagination lead?* What have you learned about imagination by watching the video?

LANGUAGE DEVELOPMENT

Media Vocabulary

stage directions	light and shadow
dialogue	

Use these words in your responses to the questions.

1. How would actors recording an audio version of *The Phantom Tollbooth* find stage directions helpful?

2. How does dialogue play an important role in this scene from *The Phantom Tollbooth?*

3. What do you notice about light and shadow in the image from the movie version of *The Phantom Tollbooth?* How would you describe the mood, or feeling, in this image?

© Pearson Education, Inc., or its affiliates. All rights reserved.

WORD NETWORK

Add words related to imagination from the video to your Word Network.

STANDARDS

Speaking and Listening
Interpret information presented in diverse media and formats and explain how it contributes to a topic, text, or issue under study.

Language
Acquire and use accurately grade-appropriate general academic and domain-specific words and phrases; gather vocabulary knowledge when considering a word or phrase important to comprehension or expression.

from The Phantom Tollbooth (multimedia) **349**

VOCABULARY DEVELOPMENT

Domain-Specific Vocabulary Once I read the *stage directions*, I understood where I was to stand during the scene.

Then give students sentence prompts and coach them to create the clarification parts.

1. The *light and shadow* in the drawing of the three characters made them look like _____.

2. The longest section of *dialogue* in the scene was _____ by Dischord.

Jump Start

CLOSE REVIEW Ask students to discuss how the audio clip and image were similar to—or different from—what they imagined after reading the play. Have them consider the following prompts: *What are the strengths of the audio version? Its weaknesses?*

CLOSE REVIEW

If needed, model close reviewing by using the Closer Review notes in the Interactive Teacher's Edition.

Remind groups to use Accountable Talk in their discussions and to support one another as they complete the close read.

Analyze the Media

Possible responses:

1. (a) The image shows Milo, Tock, and Humbug. Their expressions look dazed. **DOK 2** (b) It might be showing their journey to Digitopolis because they seem to be on a long, endless ride. **DOK 2**

2. He sounds excited, nervous, and scatterbrained. **DOK 2**

3. People imagine characters and scenes in different ways. Everyone's imagination may lead them in different directions. **DOK 3**

Word Network

Possible words: *colorful, creature, concoction*

Media Vocabulary

For more support, see **Media Vocabulary.**
Possible responses:

1. The audience cannot see the stage, so it is important to provide descriptions of the action that isn't told through dialogue.

2. Dialogue is the most important element in an audio version of the play. The way the actors read the lines helps the listener understand the relationships between characters, as well as move the plot forward.

3. Light and shadow can add meaning to an image, so viewers will be drawn in and engage with the image.

FORMATIVE ASSESSMENT
Analyze the Media

- **If** students fail to cite evidence, **then** remind them to support their ideas with specific information from the text.

- **If** students struggle to make an inference about Dischord's personality, **then** discuss **inferences,** and illustrate with examples.

Whole-Class Learning **349**

Writing to Compare

As students prepare to compare the script of *The Phantom Tollbooth* and the excerpt from an audio performance of the play, they will evaluate the effectiveness of each.

Prewriting

Analyze the Texts Encourage students to begin by recalling the mental images they developed as they read the script of the play, and then compare those images to their immediate reactions upon hearing the audio version. Remind students that their goal during prewriting is to gather information so that they can evaluate the two versions of the selection.

Possible responses:

Responses to student chart will vary based on students' own impressions and recollections. Guide students to use this chart to record what they recall and analyze similarities and differences. In the next step they will review and evaluate.

1. Student responses will vary, but students should explain how well they were able to picture the action based on the audio version and the script version.

2. Student responses will vary, but students should support their answers with reasons and examples from the audio.

THE PHANTOM TOLLBOOTH (drama)

from THE PHANTOM TOLLBOOTH
(multimedia)

Writing to Compare

You have read and analyzed *The Phantom Tollbooth*. You have also listened to an excerpt from an audio performance of the play. Now, deepen your understanding of the play by comparing the experience of reading it and listening to it.

Assignment

Write a **comparison-and-contrast essay** in which you talk about what you "see" and "hear" in your mind when you read *The Phantom Tollbooth*. Discuss how reading the play is like or unlike the experience of listening to the audio. Use examples from Act II of the text and the audio excerpt to support your ideas. End by explaining whether you prefer the play or audio performance, and which you think tells the story better.

Prewriting

Analyze the Texts A performance of a play shows how the actors and director interpret the characters and events. As you read the text, you may have imagined the story differently than they did. Use the chart to note similarities and differences between your own imagination and the audio performance.

	SIMILARITIES	DIFFERENCES
my imagination of characters vs. actors' portrayals		
my imagination of settings vs. presentation in the audio		
my imagination of sounds vs. sound effects and music		

🔲 **Notebook** Respond to these questions.

1. Did listening to the audio help you picture the action? Or were you better able to imagine events by reading about them?

2. Were the actors' portrayals weak or strong? Why?

© Pearson Education, Inc., or its affiliates. All rights reserved.

PERSONALIZE FOR LEARNING

English Language Support

Sentence Starters Provide sentence starters to help students organize their responses to the questions in the Analyze the Texts section. For example, *Hearing the narrator read stage directions* _____ . Work with students to complete their sentence starters based on their perception of the audio performance and the play.
ALL LEVELS

Drafting

Review Your Notes Look back at the notes you took during Prewriting. Then, write a statement that summarizes your analysis of the similarities and differences between reading and listening. This statement can serve as your thesis, or main idea.

General Statement/Thesis: _____

_____

Choose a Structure Decide how best to organize your essay. Point-by-point organization and block organization are two commonly used structures. Choose the approach that will help you explain your ideas thoroughly and clearly.

Point-by-Point Organization

> I. Main Topic: Characters
>   A. How I imagined characters as I read
>   B. How characters were portrayed in the audio
> II. Main Topic: Settings and Events
>   A. How I imagined settings and events as I read
>   B. How settings and events were portrayed in the audio
> III. Evaluation: Which one I enjoyed more

Block Organization

> I. Main Topic: How I imagined the story as I read
>   A. Characters
>   B. Settings and Events
> II. Main Topic: How the audio performance presented the story
>   A. Characters
>   B. Settings and Events
> III. Evaluation: Which one I enjoyed more

Review, Revise, and Edit

Use the following checklist to review, revise, and edit your draft.

☐ Did you include details and examples from the text and media?

☐ Did you organize your essay effectively?

☐ Did you review your essay and fix any grammar or spelling errors?

© Pearson Education, Inc., or its affiliates. All rights reserved.

EVIDENCE LOG

Before moving on to a new selection, go to your Evidence Log and record what you learned from the image and audio performance of *The Phantom Tollbooth.*

STANDARDS

Reading Literature
Compare and contrast the experience of reading a story, drama, or poem to listening to or viewing an audio, video, or live version of the text, including contrasting what they "see" and "hear" when reading the text to what they perceive when they listen or watch.

Writing
Write informative/explanatory texts to examine a topic and convey ideas, concepts, and information through the selection, organization, and analysis of relevant content.
   a. Introduce a topic; organize ideas, concepts, and information, using strategies such as definition, classification, comparison/contrast, and cause/effect; include formatting, graphics, and multimedia when useful to aiding comprehension.

Speaking and Listening
Interpret information presented in diverse media and formats and explain how it contributes to a topic, text, or issue under study.

The Phantom Tollbooth (drama) • *from* The Phantom Tollbooth (multimedia) **351**

Draft

Review Your Notes Remind students that a thesis statement should express the main idea they wish to express in their essay. Their thesis may change as they continue the writing process, but it is important to establish a thesis early in the drafting stage.

Choose a Structure Encourage students to draw on their prewriting chart as they begin drafting a thesis statement. Regardless of the the structure they choose, their notes should provide plenty of examples for their evaluations.

Review, Revise, and Edit

As students revise, encourage them to review their draft to be sure they have evaluated persuasive techniques. Ask them to review their word choice. Finally, remind students to check for grammar, usage, and mechanics.

For more support, see **Writing to Compare: Comparison-and-Contrast Essay;**

Evidence Log Support students in completing their Evidence Log. This paced activity will help prepare them for the Performance-Based Assessment at the end of the unit.

FORMATIVE ASSESSMENT

Writing to Compare

- **If** students struggle to find examples from the script and audio excerpt, **then** have the students skim the text and listen again to the audio.

PERSONALIZE FOR LEARNING

Strategic Support

Comparison Some students may require more time to complete their drafts. Suggest students who are struggling to compare the play and audio excerpt look back at Act II, Scene i. If students have trouble developing a thesis statement, suggest that they write a controlling idea that tells which medium portrayed characters, settings, and events in a more interesting way.

Jump Start

Ask students to name their favorite fiction short story or book. Then have them write down all the things they like about the story. Once students have finished writing, ask them to share their ideas with the class. Discuss the features of a fictional narrative and what makes it compelling.

Write a Fictional Narrative

Make sure students understand what they are being asked to do in the assignment. Explain that the question they will answer asks them to create an imaginary story with a setting and characters similar to, but not the same as, the ones in *The Phantom Tollbooth*

Students should complete the assignment using word processing software to take advantage of editing tools and features.

Elements of a Fictional Narrative

Remind students that a good fictional narrative contains a specific setting, an interesting plot and lively characters, plus strong descriptive language that helps to create mood in the story.

MAKE IT INTERACTIVE

Project "The Great Universal Undo" from the Interactive Teacher's Edition and have students identify the elements of a fictional narrative, such as a main character, minor characters, dialogue, conflict, and plot.

Academic Vocabulary

Consider asking students for suggestions of ways they can incorporate academic vocabulary into their narratives.

WRITING TO SOURCES

- THE PHANTOM TOLLBOOTH (drama)

- from THE PHANTOM TOLLBOOTH (multimedia)

🔧 **Tool Kit**
Student Model of a Fictional Narrative

ACADEMIC VOCABULARY

As you craft your argument, consider using some of the academic vocabulary you learned in the beginning of the unit.

perspective
transform
novelty
consequently
inspire

≣ STANDARDS
Writing
• Write narratives to develop real or imagined experiences or events using effective technique, relevant descriptive details, and well-structured event sequences.
• Write routinely over extended time frames and shorter time frames for a range of discipline-specific tasks, purposes, and audiences.

352 UNIT 4 • IMAGINATION

Write a Fictional Narrative

You have read the play *The Phantom Tollbooth* and viewed media versions of the same story. In this imaginary land, Milo encounters all sorts of strange and magical creatures. After dodging demons and rescuing princesses, the boy learns that to find adventure, he simply has to notice his surroundings—and use his imagination.

> **Assignment**
>
> Think about the characters whose adventures unfold in *The Phantom Tollbooth*. Then, use your own imagination to write a new **short story** about one or more of those characters. Use this sentence opener to start your new tale:
>
> > One day in the Kingdom of Wisdom, . . .
>
> Your story should describe an imaginary setting, include interesting characters, and tell events in a clear order.

Elements of a Fictional Narrative

A **fictional narrative** is a story based on characters and events from the writer's imagination. Fictional narratives entertain, explore ideas, or send a message about life.

An effective fictional narrative includes these elements:

- a plot, or sequence of events, that make up the action of the story
- chronological order, or the order in which events occur in time
- a central conflict, or problem, that is introduced, developed, and resolved by the end of the story
- one main character, or *protagonist*, who faces and learns from a conflict
- a few minor characters who add interest to the story and help move the action along
- dialogue, or conversations between characters
- a clear setting, or the time and place in which the story occurs
- a clear point of view or perspective from which the story is told

Because a fictional narrative is brief, writers choose precise, or specific, words, and craft each element carefully.

Model Fictional Narrative For a model of a well-crafted fictional narrative, see the Launch Text, "The Great Universal Undo."

Challenge yourself to find all of the elements of an effective fictional narrative in the text. You will have an opportunity to review these elements as you prepare to write your own fictional narrative.

LAUNCH TEXT

The Great Universal Undo

© Pearson Education, Inc., or its affiliates. All rights reserved.

AUTHOR'S PERSPECTIVE | Kelly Gallagher, M.Ed.

Purposeful Editing Many students resist editing because they don't see its value. Explain that **editing**, the process of making things correct, adds power to writing. Teachers can model the process by using the Sentence of the Week (SoW) strategy. Before students enter the classroom each Monday, write three sentences with the same structural, grammatical, or style feature on the board. For example:

1. John, 14, is too young to drive.
2. My girlfriend, who is afraid of snakes, refuses to go to the zoo.
3. The player, exhausted from the long game, collapsed.

Students copy the sentences. Below the sentences, write "What do I notice?" Students might write:

- All the sentences have interruptions.
- All have two commas.
- A comma goes before and after the interruption.
- If you take out the comma, the sentences still make sense.

Teaching editing skills through sentence study helps students to generate the grammar rules organically.

Prewriting/Planning

Create a Story Map Reread the assignment. Brainstorm for ideas for characters, setting, and conflict. Remember that your narrative should feature an imaginative setting and interesting characters. Record your ideas in this chart.

CHARACTERS	SETTING	CONFLICT
Who the main character is and what the character is like:	Where the story takes place:	What the main problem is in the story:
Who the minor characters are and their role in the story:	When the story takes place:	How it is resolved:

Gather Details As you plan your story, gather important details that help your readers picture and understand how your characters look and act, where the characters are, and what they say and do. Include the following:

- **precise words:** specific words and phrases establish a clear description of characters and events
- **dialogue:** characters' conversations help move the action along. Dialogue also shows readers how the characters think, feel, and get along
- **sensory details:** words that describe how things look, sound, feel, taste, and smell help readers picture the setting and characters in the story

EVIDENCE LOG

Review your Evidence Log and identify key details you may want to cite in your fictional narrative.

STANDARDS

Writing
Write narratives to develop real or imagined experiences or events using effective technique, relevant descriptive details, and well-structured event sequences.
 b. Use narrative techniques, such as dialogue, pacing, and description, to develop experiences, events, and/or characters.
 d. Use precise words and phrases, relevant descriptive details, and sensory language to convey experiences and events.

Performance Task: Write a Fictional Narrative **353**

Prewriting/Planning

Create a Story Map Remind students that before they begin writing, they need to have a general idea of the main features of their narrative. Explain that they can flesh out these features as they write the story.

Gather Details Tell students that to spark imagination, it helps to read a good story. Encourage them to go to the library or peruse bookshelves to find a collection of short stories (fantasies would be best). Remind them that reading one or two stories, or just skimming the stories, can help give them ideas for their own story. Tell them to take notes as they go and to jot down any ideas that occur to them. Point out that discussing recent movies or television shows with friends can also provide ideas for their stories.

Remind students that although they may take inspiration from stories, and use techniques or structures from published works, the content of their own writing must be original.

Make sure students recognize that good dialogue does not have to be wordy and complicated. Point out that dialogue in fiction serves multiple purposes. It reveals details about characters by developing their voices, or perspectives, and it develops the action or plot of a story. It can even give the reader information about the setting, as characters respond to their surroundings. Remind students that their dialogue does not have to exactly mimic conversations they hear in real life.

© Pearson Education, Inc., or its affiliates. All rights reserved.

PERSONALIZE FOR LEARNING

Strategic Support

Voice Some students may require additional support in adding variety to their writing. Pair students with a partner and have them identify places in each other's narratives where adding variety might make their narrative more exciting. Have them consider the overall details and descriptive language that can improve the overall tone and clarity of the story. Finally, have students review their partner's suggestions as they revise their fiction narrative.

TEACHING

Drafting

Develop Your Plot Remind students that they must have a climax or an event that changes the course of the story. Point out that the climax is when the main character affects the outcome of the story. Explain that their story should build to this point, and that the climax often comes toward the end of the story.

Write a First Draft Explain to students that the purpose of a first draft is to get their ideas on paper. Encourage them to use their story maps, but to flesh out the details using sensory language. Remind them to use strong active verbs and to include a story beginning that captures the reader's attention and makes them want to read on.

Establish Point of View Remind students that as they write in a particular point of view, they will envision the perspective of the narrator, and they should think about what they want their narrator to see and know.

Drafting

Develop Your Plot Use a plot diagram like the one shown to organize the sequence of events in your fictional narrative. Make sure the events follow a clear chronological, or time, order that moves smoothly from one event to the next. The plot diagram here shows key events in the Launch Text. The story follows this common plot pattern:

- The exposition introduces the characters and the conflict.
- The conflict develops during the rising action.
- The rising action leads to the climax, or point of greatest tension.
- In the falling action, events and emotions should slow down.
- In the resolution, the conflict is resolved, and loose ends are tied up.

Climax: Mrs. Bieberman explains that her son Tommy likes to play video games. She gives Tommy a cookie after he demands one.

Rising Action: Alexander tries the invention again, but something goes wrong.

Falling Action: Alexander is aware of a *tap tapping* sound as the scene with Tommy and the cookie is repeated.

Rising Action: Alexander tests his invention on Mrs. Bieberman and finds that it works.

Falling Action: Alexander realizes that Tommy has also invented the Undo.

Exposition: Alexander and his invention, the Undo, are described.

Resolution: Alexander's hunch is confirmed when Tommy looks at him and taps the screen to get another cookie.

© Pearson Education, Inc., or its affiliates. All rights reserved.

STANDARDS
Writing
Write narratives to develop real or imagined experiences or events using effective technique, relevant descriptive details, and well-structured event sequences.
a. Engage and orient the reader by establishing a context and introducing a narrator and/or characters; organize an event sequence that unfolds naturally and logically.
e. Provide a conclusion that follows from the narrated experiences or events.

Write a First Draft Use your plot diagram to write your first draft. Review the elements of fictional narrative writing, as well as the story map you developed in the Prewriting/Planning section As you draft the plot events, be sure each event builds on the one before it and moves the plot toward the resolution of the conflict. The **conclusion** of your narrative should logically follow the events in the plot.

Establish Point of View Tell your story from a single point of view. Choose one of the following:

- In **first-person point of view,** your character is the one telling the story. Use first-person pronouns, such as *I, me, we,* and *us.*
- In **third-person point of view,** the story is told by a narrator who is not in the story. Use pronouns such as *he, she, they,* and *them.*

354 UNIT 4 • IMAGINATION

AUTHOR'S PERSPECTIVE   **Jim Cummins, Ph.D.**

Transfer of First Language English learners' home languages are valuable cognitive tools that can be tapped to help them improve the quality of their first drafts. Having students write in their home language often produces higher quality writing than when students write only in English because it helps them capture, express, and organize their ideas. Translation software can be useful as a starting point to help students move from their home language draft to an English draft. Obviously, the machine-translated draft will require editing but this can be done collaboratively with help from the teacher and/or the students' classmates. After students have produced their initial drafts in English, teachers can work with them on the revision process, focusing on such key areas as organization, paragraph formation, and coherence. As students revise with teacher input, teachers should encourage them to pay special attention to cognates and genre rules.

LANGUAGE DEVELOPMENT

Conventions: Combining Sentences for Variety

To add variety to your sentences and to avoid unnecessary repetition, include prepositional phrases, appositive phrases, participial phrases, and gerund phrases.

PHRASE	USE	EXAMPLE
prepositional phrase	as an adjective or as an adverb	The girl in the blue pants is my cousin. (adjective)
		I walked around the barrier to cross the street. (adverb)
appositive phrase	as a noun phrase	Winnie, the volleyball player, hugged him.
participial phrase	as an adjective	Skipping happily we laughed.
gerund phrase	as a noun	Washing clothes is necessary.

Read It

These sentences from the Launch Text reflect a variety of sentence patterns.

- **Making a working model** *was simple.* (gerund phrase)
- *That's how Alexander Dillahunt got it* **into his head** *to create the Universal Undo.* (prepositional phrase)
- *He paused,* **waiting for a response.** (participial phrase)
- *He'd read all about multiple discovery—***the idea that most inventions are made by a number of different people in different places at the same time.** (appositive phrase)

Write It

As you draft your fictional narrative, use a variety of sentence patterns. This chart provides ways to combine your sentences for variety.

ORIGINAL	ADD VARIETY	REVISION
They ate dinner. They went to bed.	Use a participial phrase.	Having eaten dinner, they went to bed.
The leaves fell. The ground was frozen.	Use a prepositional phrase.	The leaves fell onto the frozen ground.
The boy was a skilled soccer player. He was five years old.	Use an appositive phrase.	The boy, a skilled soccer player, was five years old.
We'd have to work all night. It seemed inevitable.	Use a gerund phrase.	Working all night seemed inevitable.

STANDARDS
Language
- Demonstrate command of the conventions of standard English grammar and usage when writing or speaking.
- Use knowledge of language and its conventions when writing, speaking, reading, or listening.
  a. Vary sentence patterns for meaning, reader/listener interest, and style.

© Pearson Education, Inc., or its affiliates. All rights reserved.

Conventions: Combining Sentences for Variety

Read It

Point out that writing that contains sentences of all one pattern can become monotonous or boring. In fact, it can cause readers to lose interest in the narrative. Explain that sentence variety helps add emphasis to ideas and creates rhythm in the narrative.

Write It

As students revise their drafts, they should consider combining some sentences to create variety and add emphasis to ideas and events.

Consider reviewing additional examples of different sentence patterns and how they add interest and rhythm to writing:

What happened to Sophie? The question seemed clear to Max, although the answer was anything but. Max thought about the problem for a while. He went over the last five days—who was there, what they had talked about, the family activities they all joined in. Then it hit him.

PERSONALIZE FOR LEARNING

English Language Support

Syntax Varying sentence structures may be challenging for English language learners. Pair students with a partner and have them identify places in their writing where combining sentences might add variety and interest to their writing. Have students consider the specific relationship among ideas in sentences as they consider how best to combine sentences. Then ask students to review the suggestions and determine whether or how much the suggested revision will change the meaning of the sentence. **ALL LEVELS**

Revising

Evaluating Your Draft Before students begin revising their draft, they should first evaluate their writing to make sure it contains all of the required elements and that the sequence of events makes sense and builds toward a climax and resolution.

Revising for Focus and Organization

Evaluate Point of View and Character Development Remind students that point of view usually needs to remain consistent throughout a narrative and that dialogue should be lively and engaging.

You might suggest that students read aloud their dialogue to a partner or record themselves reading as a strategy for necessary revisions.

Revising for Evidence and Elaboration

Make Logical Connections Between Events Remind students to look back at their plot diagram. Did they follow the plot they had laid out in the diagram? If so, ask them to think about how these events are connected. Do they flow from one to the other? If not, remind them to clarify how the events are connected or add transitional words and phrases.

Revising

Evaluating Your Draft

Use the following checklist to evaluate the effectiveness of your first draft. Then, use your evaluation and the instruction on this page to guide your revision.

FOCUS AND ORGANIZATION	EVIDENCE AND ELABORATION	CONVENTIONS
☐ Provides an introduction that establishes a setting and a clear point of view.	☐ Effectively uses pacing to create interest and tension in the story.	☐ Uses complete sentences and correct grammar and spelling.
☐ Presents a clear plot in chronological order.	☐ Uses sensory details and precise, descriptive language.	☐ Uses different sentence patterns for variety.
☐ Develops an interesting conflict.	☐ Uses dialogue to advance the plot and develop characters.	
☐ Provides a conclusion that follows from the narrative and resolves or wraps up the conflict.	☐ Uses transition words to signal shifts from one time frame or setting to another.	

🔗 WORD NETWORK

Include interesting words from your Word Network in your fictional narrative.

☰ STANDARDS

Writing
Write narratives to develop real or imagined experiences or events using effective technique, relevant descriptive details, and well-structured event sequences.
a. Engage and orient the reader by establishing a context and introducing a narrator and/or characters; organize an event sequence that unfolds naturally and logically.
b. Use narrative techniques, such as dialogue, pacing, and description, to develop experiences, events, and/or characters.
c. Use a variety of transition words, phrases, and clauses to convey sequence and signal shifts from one time frame or setting to another.

Revising for Focus and Organization

Evaluate Point of View and Character Development Check that the point of view you chose remains the same throughout the narrative. Have you written from a single point of view—either from a participant (first-person point of view) or an observer (third-person point of view)? How specific are your descriptions of your characters' appearances and personalities? Have you used dialogue to give your readers a strong sense of the characters and to move the plot forward?

Revising for Evidence and Elaboration

Make Logical Connections Between Events Review your narrative. Are the major events in your narrative clearly connected? If you cannot think of a clear connection between events, delete or revise one of the events. Use transitional words, phrases, and clauses, such as *meanwhile*, *back in Digitopolis*, and *while they were away*, to help show a shift in time or setting.

Adjust the Pacing Check the pacing, or the speed at which the action happens. Writers use pacing to keep readers engaged and create a desired effect. For example, speed up the pacing to build suspense. To create mystery, slow down the action.

© Pearson Education, Inc., or its affiliates. All rights reserved.

HOW LANGUAGE WORKS

Sentence Variety As students revise their narratives, remind them to use a variety of sentence patterns. Explain that using a variety of simple, complex, and compound sentences will help them create a more interesting narrative. Have students read through their narrative again and mark when they see the same sentence pattern more than three times in a row (for example, three simple sentences in a row, or three compound sentences in a row). Ask them to think about whether the paragraph seems long and boring or choppy and awkward. Then have them revise one of the sentences, perhaps adding a short, declarative sentence in the middle of two compound sentences.

PEER REVIEW

Exchange stories with a classmate. Use the checklist to evaluate your classmate's short story and provide supportive feedback.

1. Are the point of view and setting clear, and are the characters well developed through dialogue?

    ☐ yes   ☐ no   If no, suggest how the writer might improve them.

2. Do the events in the plot unfold naturally and in chronological, or time, order?

    ☐ yes   ☐ no   If no, explain what confused you.

3. Does the story's ending flow naturally from the events that came earlier?

    ☐ yes   ☐ no   If no, tell what you think might be missing.

4. What is the strongest part of your classmate's short story? Why?

_____

_____

Editing and Proofreading

Edit for Conventions Reread your draft for accuracy and consistency. Correct errors in grammar and word usage. Make sure to include a variety of sentence patterns to convey ideas clearly and keep readers engaged in your narrative.

Proofread for Accuracy Read your draft carefully, looking for errors in spelling and punctuation. Make sure that the dialogue is properly enclosed by quotation marks and that end punctuation is inside the closing quotation mark. Also, check that the speaker tag, which tells who is saying the quotation, is separated from the quotation by a comma.

Publishing and Presenting

Create a final version of your short story. Share it with your class. As you and your classmates exchange stories read each other's writing and make polite and respectful comments. Consider how each writer developed his or her plot and used techniques such as pacing, description, and dialogue. Think about how each writer introduced and resolved the main conflict, and compare it to your story.

Reflecting

Think about what you learned by writing your short story. What could you do differently the next time you write a short story to make it clearer and more interesting? What was the most difficult part of writing your short story?

STANDARDS
Writing
With some guidance and support from peers and adults, develop and strengthen writing as needed by planning, revising, editing, rewriting, or trying a new approach.

Performance Task: Write a Fictional Narrative **357**

© Pearson Education, Inc., or its affiliates. All rights reserved.

Peer Review

Remind students before they begin their peer review that they are reviewing for development of plot and characters and for clarity. Point out that they do not have to like the story or the premise but that they may point out deficiencies in the plot or in the character development or setting.

Editing and Proofreading

As students proofread, they should check for grammar, spelling, and punctuation errors. Remind them that word processing programs do not catch all mistakes and that they should review their work for errors, especially errors in the spelling of names and places.

Publishing and Presenting

Before students review their classmate's narrative, remind them to:

- Look for things their classmate did right and comment on them.
- Use formal rather than informal language when commenting.
- Support any critiques with explanations and suggestions, if possible.
- Consider how their classmate's plot development differs from their own.

Reflecting

Students should reflect not only on their narrative and the process of writing it, but also on the comments received from their peers.

PERSONALIZE FOR LEARNING

Challenge

Collection When students have finished their narratives, encourage them to combine all the narratives into a short story collection. Challenge students to illustrate some or all of the stories and to use proper formatting. Suggest that one or two students work on the cover art and that another pair of students work on the back cover blurb. You might also suggest that students write an "about the authors" piece to go on the first page. Have students agree on a name for their short story collection and add it to the front cover.

Whole-Class Learning   **357**

OVERVIEW

SMALL-GROUP LEARNING

Where can imagination lead?

Point out that many people associate the use of imagination with children and the games they play. As young adults or adults, however, people may encounter a negative connotation attached to the use of imagination. But using one's imagination can lead to creativity and inventive problem-solving. During Small-Group Learning, students will read selections that show just how useful imagination can be.

Small-Group Learning Strategies ▶

Review the Learning Strategies with students and explain that as they work through Small-Group Learning they will develop strategies to work in small-group environments.

- Have students watch the video on Small-Group Learning Strategies.
- A video on this topic is available online in the Professional Development Center.

You may wish to discuss some action items to add to the chart. For example, for "Prepare," you might solicit the following from students:

- Jot down questions so you can ask for clarification.
- Skim and scan upcoming readings to get a sense of what's ahead.

Block Scheduling

Each day in this Pacing Plan represents a 40–50 minute class period. Teachers using block scheduling may combine days to reflect their class schedule. In addition, teachers may revise pacing to differentiate and support core instruction by integrating components and resources as students require.

 OVERVIEW: SMALL-GROUP LEARNING

ESSENTIAL QUESTION:
Where can imagination lead?

Imagination can lead to new hobbies and new interests—even new adventures. You will read selections that examine how fictional characters and real-life people use their imaginations to face challenges and explore new worlds. You will work in a group to continue your exploration of the concept of imagination.

Small-Group Learning Strategies

Throughout your life, in school, in your community, and in your career, you will continue to learn and work with others.

Look at these strategies and the actions you can take to practice them as you work in teams. Add ideas of your own for each step. Use these strategies during Small-Group Learning.

STRATEGY	ACTION PLAN
Prepare	• Complete your assignments so that you are prepared for group work. • Organize your thinking so you can contribute to your group's discussion. •
Participate fully	• Make eye contact to signal that you are listening and taking in what is being said. • Use text evidence when making a point. •
Support others	• Build on ideas from others in your group. • Invite others who have not yet spoken to do so. •
Clarify	• Paraphrase the ideas of others to ensure that your understanding is correct. • Ask follow-up questions. •

SCAN FOR MULTIMEDIA

© Pearson Education, Inc., or its affiliates. All rights reserved.

Unit Introduction

Introduce Whole-Class Learning

The Phantom Tollbooth, Act I

The Phantom Tollbooth, Act II

Media: *from* The Phantom Tollbooth

Performance Task

| 1 | 2 | 3 | 4 | 5 | 6 | 7 | 8 | 9 | 10 | 11 | 12 | 13 | 14 | 15 | 16 | 17 | 18 |

CONTENTS

Overview: Small-Group Learning **359**

Contents

Selections Circulate among groups as they preview the selections. You might encourage groups to discuss any knowledge they already have about any of the selections or the situations and settings shown in the photographs. Students may wish to take a poll within their group to determine which selections look the most interesting.

Remind students that communicating and collaborating in groups is an important skill that they will use throughout their lives—in school, in their careers, and in their community.

Performance Task

Perform a Fictional Narrative Give groups time to read about and briefly discuss the fictional narrative they will create after reading. Encourage students to do some preliminary thinking about the characters and dialogue that they'll invent for their narrative. This may help focus their subsequent reading and group discussion.

© Pearson Education, Inc., or its affiliates. All rights reserved.

Introduce
Small-Group
Learning

from Alice's Adventures in Wonderland

Jabberwocky

The Importance
of Imagination

Performance
Task

Introduce
Independent
Learning

Independent
Learning

Performance-
Based
Assessment

 19 20 21 22 23 24 25 26 27 28 29 30 31 32 33 34 35 36

SMALL-GROUP LEARNING

SMALL-GROUP LEARNING

Working as a Team

1. Take a Position Remind groups to let all members share their responses. You may wish to set a time limit for this discussion.

2. List Your Rules You may want to have groups share their lists of rules and consolidate them into a master list to be displayed and followed by all groups.

3. Apply the Rules As you circulate among the groups, ensure that students are staying on task. Consider a short time limit for this step.

4. Name Your Group This task can be creative and fun. If students have trouble coming up with a name, suggest that they think of something related to the unit topic. Encourage groups to share their names with the class.

5. Create a Communication Plan Encourage groups to include in their plans agreed-upon times during the day to share ideas. They should also devise a method for recording and saving their communications.

Accountable Talk

Remind students that groups should communicate politely. You can post these Accountable Talk suggestions and encourage students to add their own. Students should:

Remember to . . .
Ask clarifying questions.

Which sounds like . . .
Can you please repeat what you said?
Would you give me an example?
Could you say more about that?

Remember to . . .
Explain your thinking.

Which sounds like . . .
I believe _____ is true because _____.
I feel _____ because _____.

Remember to . . .
Build on the ideas of others.

Which sounds like . . .
I see _____ in the text, so _____.
I think _____ is a result of _____.

Working as a Team

1. Take a Position In your group, discuss the following question:

> Can imaginary adventures be as important as real adventures?

As you take turns sharing your positions, be sure to provide reasons for your choice. After all group members have shared, discuss some specific examples of real and imaginary adventures that support each position.

2. List Your Rules As a group, decide on the rules that you will follow as you work together. Two examples are provided; add two more rules of your own. You may add or revise rules based on your experience together.

• Everyone should participate in group discussions.

• People should not interrupt.

• _____

  _____

• _____

  _____

3. Apply the Rules Practice working as a group. Share what you have learned about imagination. Make sure each person in the group contributes. Take notes, and be prepared to share with the class one thing that you heard from another member of your group.

4. Name Your Group Choose a name that reflects the unit topic.

Our group's name: _____

5. Create a Communication Plan Decide how you want to communicate with one another. For example, you might use online collaboration tools, email, or instant messaging.

Our group's decision: _____

_____

© Pearson Education, Inc., or its affiliates. All rights reserved.

FACILITATING SMALL-GROUP LEARNING

Forming Groups You may wish to form groups for Small-Group Learning so that each consists of students with different learning abilities. Some students may be adept at organizing information whereas other may have strengths related to generating or synthesizing information on the various ways to use the imagination. A good mix of abilities can make the experience of Small-Group Learning dynamic and productive.

Making a Schedule

First, find out the due dates for the Small-Group activities. Then, preview the texts and activities with your group, and make a schedule for completing the tasks.

SELECTION	ACTIVITIES	DUE DATE
from Alice's Adventures in Wonderland		
Jabberwocky		
The Importance of Imagination		

Working on Group Projects

As your group works together, you'll find it more effective if each person has a specific role. Different projects require different roles. Before beginning a project, discuss the necessary roles and choose one for each group member. Here are some possible roles; add your own ideas.

Project Manager: monitors the schedule and keeps everyone on task

Researcher: organizes research activities

Recorder: takes notes during group meetings

_____

_____

_____

_____

_____

© Pearson Education, Inc., or its affiliates. All rights reserved.

SCAN FOR
MULTIMEDIA

Making a Schedule

Encourage groups to preview the reading selections and to consider how long it will take them to complete the activities accompanying each selection. Point out that they can adjust the due dates for particular selections as needed as they work on their small-group projects, however, they must complete all assigned tasks before the group Performance Task is due. Encourage groups to review their schedules upon completing the activities for each selection to make sure they are on track to meet the final due date.

Working on Group Projects

After groups identify the roles this project will require, ask students to self-identify two or three strengths and one or two areas for improvement. Have them use this information as they work in their groups to select roles. Remind students that it is important to take on unfamiliar roles and not always work within one's comfort zone. Discuss ways to prevent favoritism, cliquishness, or stereotyping in the assignment of roles. Finally, review the roles each group assigns to its members.

AUTHOR'S PERSPECTIVE   **Ernest Morrell, Ph.D.**

Small Group Learning in Higher Education College classrooms are becoming shared discussion spaces, marked by less lecturing and more small groups. That's because college professors increasingly realize that having students work in small groups helps develop higher-level learning and problem-solving skills, increases the success of computer-based instruction, and increases retention rates. As a result, more and more college professors now have small groups lead a portion of class by sharing/presenting what the group has learned. These professors focus on the importance of each group becoming expert at something that they must teach the class. Teachers can point out to students that the project-based small group learning in colleges is increasingly common in the workplace as well, as collective production is becoming a new norm. Teachers can encourage students to collaborate and develop rubrics to assess how well students are able to work together.

from Alice's Adventures in Wonderland

🔊 **AUDIO SUMMARIES**
Audio summaries of "*from* Alice's Adventures in Wonderland" are available online in both English and Spanish in the Interactive Teacher's Edition or Unit Resources. Assigning these summaries prior to reading the selection may help students build additional background knowledge and set a context for their first read.

Summary

This selection is an excerpt from Lewis Carroll's famously whimsical novel, *Alice's Adventures in Wonderland*. Alice is sitting with her sister by a river, and she is very bored. She sees a strange rabbit pass by, one that carries a watch and seems to talk to itself. She chases after it. She follows it down a rabbit hole and finds herself somewhere strange, seemingly very deep underground. Alice has plenty of time to think as she falls, and she thinks about where she is going and what must be happening back home. Finally she lands and begins to find her way onward.

Insight

This story suggests that life can change suddenly without warning. It is also noteworthy that, bored as she has been, Alice finds the strange events more interesting than worrying. She keeps her wits about her.

ESSENTIAL QUESTION:
Where can imagination lead?

SMALL-GROUP LEARNING PERFORMANCE TASK
When Alice finally gets through the door . . .

UNIT PERFORMANCE-BASED ASSESSMENT
What might happen if a fictional character were to come into the real world?

Connection to Essential Question

Alice's imagination leads her to find excitement, meet new friends, and see extraordinary places.

Connection to Performance Tasks

Small-Group Learning Performance Task Alice is curious and fearless. Students may consider her character traits as they prepare to address the prompt.

Unit Performance-Based Assessment As students read the texts in this unit and consider the power of imagination, they can apply what they have learned to address the prompt.

LESSON RESOURCES

	Making Meaning	Language Development	Effective Expression
Lesson	**First Read** **Close Read** **Analyze the Text** **Analyze Craft and Structure**	**Concept Vocabulary** **Word Study** **Conventions**	**Research**
Instructional Standards	**RL.10** By the end of the year, read and comprehend literature . . . **L.4** Determine or clarify the meaning of unknown and multiple-meaning words and phrases . . . **L.4.a** Use context as a clue . . . **RL.1** Cite textual evidence . . . **RL.3** Describe how a particular story's or drama's plot unfolds . . .	**L.5** Demonstrate understanding of figurative language . . . **L.5.b** Use the relationship between particular words . . . **L.1** Demonstrate command of the conventions of standard English grammar . . . **L.2** Demonstrate command of the conventions of standard English capitalization . . .	**W.2** Write informative/explanatory texts . . . **W.2.a** Introduce a topic . . . **W.7** Conduct short research projects . . . **W.8** Gather relevant information from multiple print and digital sources . . .
STUDENT RESOURCES Available online in the Interactive Student Edition or Unit Resources	Selection Audio First-Read Guide: Fiction Close-Read Guide: Fiction	Word Network	Evidence Log
TEACHER RESOURCES **Selection Resources** Available online in the Interactive Teacher's Edition or Unit Resources	Audio Summaries Annotation Highlights EL Highlights *from* Alice's Adventures in Wonderland: Text Questions Analyze Craft and Structure: Characterization	Concept Vocabulary and Word Study Conventions: Conjunctions and Interjections English Language Support Lesson: Conjunctions and Interjections	Research: Report
Reteach/Practice (RP) Available online in the Interactive Teacher's Edition or Unit Resources	Analyze Craft and Structure: Characterization (RP)	Word Study: Word Relationships (RP) Conventions: Conjunctions and Interjections (RP)	Research: Report (RP)
Assessment Available online in Assessments	Selection Test		
My Resources	A Unit 4 Answer Key is available online and in the Interactive Teacher's Edition.		

Reading Support

Text Complexity Rubric: *from* Alice's Adventures in Wonderland

Quantitative Measures

Lexile: 1080   Text Length: 1,361 words

Qualitative Measures

Knowledge Demands ①—②—**❸**—④—⑤	The selection describes language, activities, and fashions typical of life in turn-of-the-century England.
Structure ①—**❷**—③—④—⑤	The selection consists of a simple, linear narrative.
Language Conventionality and Clarity ①—②—**❸**—④—⑤	The selection contains figurative language, some above-level words and formal English vocabulary as well as complex sentence structures.
Levels of Meaning/Purpose ①—**❷**—③—④—⑤	The selection consists of a singular and straightforward meaning.

DECIDE AND PLAN

English Language Support
Provide English learners with support for structure and language as they read the selection.

Structure Point out the selection's text features: the title, background, and chapter title. Explain to students how these features reveal elements of the text, including character names, author information, and setting. You may want to point out how "Chapter 1" indicates that this selection is part of a larger story about Lewis Carroll's famous Alice.

Language Help students understand complex sentences by breaking them down into parts. Model how to summarize each part and then link them together.

Strategic Support
Provide students with strategic support to ensure that they can successfully read the text.

Language Before students read, discuss the double meaning of *rabbit hole* with them. Explain the first definition: the place where rabbits burrow, and the second: a bizarre and confusing situation that is difficult to escape. Have students consider these meanings as they read.

Language Help students to unpack lengthy sentences by asking questions about each part. For example, (paragraph 2) *What was Alice wondering?* (whether she wanted to pick flowers to make a daisy-chain) *Why did she have trouble deciding?* (It was too hot.) *Who/What appeared?* (A white rabbit appeared.)

Challenge
Provide students who need to be challenged with ideas for how they can go beyond a simple interpretation of the text.

Text Analysis As students read, ask them to take note of the passages and openings that Alice experiences. Discuss the real and figurative meanings of these details.

Written Response Ask students to write a short story that involves the main character entering and departing a series of openings and other passages. When they have finished writing, have students pair up and read their stories to each other.

TEACH

Read and Respond
Have groups do their first read of the selection. Then have them complete their close read. Finally, work with them on the Making Meaning, Language Development, and Effective Expression activities.

Standards Support Through Teaching and Learning Cycle

IDENTIFY NEEDS

Analyze results of the Beginning-of-Year Assessment, focusing on the items relating to Unit 4. Also take into consideration student performance to this point and your observations of where particular students struggle.

DECIDE AND PLAN

- If students have performed poorly on items matching these standards, then provide selection scaffolds before assigning them the on-level lesson provided in the Student Edition.
- If students have done well on the Beginning-of-Year Assessment, then challenge them to keep progressing and learning by giving them opportunities to practice the skills in depth.
- Use the Selection Resources listed on the Planning pages for the excerpt from *Alice's Adventures in Wonderland* to help students continually improve their ability to master the standards.

Instructional Standards: *from* Alice's Adventures in Wonderland

	Catching Up	This Year	Looking Forward
Reading	You may wish to administer the **Analyze Craft and Structure: Characterization (RP)** worksheet to familiarize students with indirect and direct characterization, as well as personification.	**RL.3** Describe how a particular story's or drama's plot unfolds in a series of episodes as well as how the characters respond or change as the plot moves toward a resolution.	Challenge students to explain how characterization helps inform the rest of the story.
Writing	You may wish to administer the **Research: Report (RP)** worksheet to prepare students for their writing.	**W.8** Gather relevant information from multiple print and digital sources; assess the credibility of each source; and quote or paraphrase the data and conclusions of others while avoiding plagiarism and providing basic bibliographic information for sources.	Challenge students to merge the two research options, doing both historical research, as well as explaining some of the math at work in the story.
Language	You may wish to administer the **Conventions: Conjunctions and Interjections (RP)** worksheet to help students understand how to use conjunctions and interjections. You may wish to administer the **Word Study: Word Relationships (RP)** worksheet to help students consider the ways that knowledge of related words can help them build their vocabulary	**L.1** Demonstrate command of the conventions of standard English grammar and usage when writing or speaking. **L.5.b** Use the relationship between particular words to better understand each of the words.	Have students find a short story online and identify the conjunctions and interjections within it. Have students identify other word pairs that they know and challenge others to explain the relationship.

ANALYZE AND REVISE

- Analyze student work for evidence of student learning.
- Identify whether or not students have met the expectations in the standards.
- Identify implications for future instruction.

TEACH

Implement the planned lesson, and gather evidence of student learning.

Jump Start

FIRST READ Most students are likely to have some familiarity with the story of Alice in Wonderland, whether they have read the book, seen a film or TV adaptation, or simply heard references to it. Invite students to share what they already know about the story.

from Alice's Adventures in Wonderland 🔊 📄

What does Alice find when she goes down the rabbit hole? Modeling questions such as this will help students connect to the excerpt from *Alice's Adventures in Wonderland* and to the Small-Group Performance Task assignment. Selection audio and print capability for the selection are available in the Interactive Teacher's Edition.

Concept Vocabulary

Encourage groups to look at the two types of context clues discussed on the student page and discuss how these types of clues can be used to help determine meaning. Ask students to think of one other type of context clue that they might encounter in a story. Examples include elaborating details, contrast of ideas, and examples.

⬤ FIRST READ

Have students perform the steps of the first read independently:

NOTICE: Encourage students to notice how Alice reacts to the varied and strange things she encounters on her journey.

ANNOTATE: Remind students to mark passages that help develop the character of Alice.

CONNECT: Have students compare Alice's trip down the rabbit hole with other fantastical adventures that they have read, watched, or heard about.

RESPOND: Students will answer questions and write a summary to demonstrate understanding.

Point out to students that while they will always complete the Respond step at the end of the first read, the other steps will probably happen somewhat concurrently. You may wish to print copies of the **First-Read Guide: Fiction** for students to use. 📄

About the Author

Lewis Carroll (1832–1898) Charles Lutwidge Dodgson was a professor of mathematics and a talented photographer. Today, he is best remembered for two children's books he wrote under the pen name Lewis Carroll: *Alice's Adventures in Wonderland* (1865) and its sequel, *Through the Looking-Glass* (1871). Huge bestsellers almost from the moment they appeared, the Alice books have been the basis of numerous stage plays and films.

▤ STANDARDS

Reading Literature
By the end of the year, read and comprehend literature, including stories, dramas, and poems, in the grades 6–8 text complexity band proficiently, with scaffolding as needed at the high end of the range.

Language
Determine or clarify the meaning of unknown and multiple-meaning words and phrases based *on grade 6 reading and content,* choosing flexibly from a range of strategies.
  a. Use context as a clue to the meaning of a word or phrase.

362 UNIT 4 • IMAGINATION

from Alice's Adventures in Wonderland

Concept Vocabulary

As you perform your first read of this excerpt from *Alice's Adventures in Wonderland*, you will encounter these words.

| peeped | wondered | curiosity |

Context Clues To find the meaning of an unfamiliar word, look for clues in the context, which is made up of the words and phrases that surround the unknown word in a text. Here are two examples of how to use context clues to determine meaning:

Synonyms: He **stumbled**, or tripped, over a toy that had been left on the floor.

Restatement of an Idea: Tasha was **unaccompanied** in the empty room and felt lonely sitting by herself.

Apply your knowledge of context clues and other vocabulary strategies to determine the meanings of unfamiliar words you encounter during your first read.

First Read FICTION

Apply these strategies as you conduct your first read. You will have an opportunity to complete a close read after your first read.

NOTICE *whom* the story is about, *what* happens, *where* and *when* it happens, and *why* those involved react as they do.

ANNOTATE by marking vocabulary and key passages you want to revisit.

First Read

CONNECT ideas within the selection to what you already know and what you have already read.

RESPOND by completing the Comprehension Check and by writing a brief summary of the selection.

© Pearson Education, Inc., or its affiliates. All rights reserved.

AUTHOR'S PERSPECTIVE   Jim Cummins, Ph.D.

How Language Works Briefly explaining the origins of the English language will help demystify the difference between conversational and academic language. Today's English is a hybrid language, formed from a merger of Anglo-Saxon spoken in Britain from about 400–1000 and French brought by the Norman invaders in 1066. Students can see this merger in synonyms of words derived from Anglo-Saxon and Latin/Greek sources: *meet/encounter, ask/inquire, come/arrive.* The Anglo-Saxon words were used by peasants who generally didn't have much education; in contrast, Greek/Latin vocabulary was used by more educated and high-status people and became the language of written text. Today, words with Anglo-Saxon

from
Alice's Adventures in Wonderland

Lewis Carroll

© Pearson Education, Inc., or its affiliates. All rights reserved.

BACKGROUND

In 1862, a shy English mathematician entertained his colleague's three young daughters by taking them on a boat trip. As they rowed down the River Thames, he decided to tell them a story, making it up as he went along. Afterwards, one of them, a 10-year-old girl named Alice Liddell, loved his story so much that she begged him to write it down. This "golden afternoon," as Lewis Carroll called it, was the inspiration for his novel *Alice's Adventures in Wonderland*.

SCAN FOR
MULTIMEDIA

Chapter 1. Down the Rabbit-Hole

1   Alice was beginning to get very tired of sitting by her sister on the bank, and of having nothing to do: once or twice she had **peeped** into the book her sister was reading, but it had no pictures or conversations in it, "and what is the use of a book," thought Alice, "without pictures or conversation?"

NOTES

Mark context clues or indicate another strategy you used to help you determine meaning.

peeped (peept) *v.*

MEANING:

from Alice's Adventures in Wonderland **363**

PEEPED If groups are struggling to define the word *peeped,* point out the context: Alice is bored, and she describes looking into a book that has no pictures in it.

Possible response: In this context, *peeped* means "quickly looked at" or "glanced at."

Additional **English Language Support** is available in the Interactive Teacher's Edition.

---

roots are short and commonly used, while words with Greek/Latin roots tend to be low frequency and long. The most common Anglo-Saxon words in English are determiners *(the, a)*; prepositions *(of, to, for,* etc.); pronouns *(he, she, I,* etc.); conjunctions *(and, but,* etc.)*; common verbs, nouns, and adjectives *(think, little, good,* etc.)*. Because these words are high frequency and are used daily, they are generally acquired quickly by English learners.

 FACILITATING SMALL GROUP CLOSE READING

CLOSE READ: Narrative As groups perform the close read, circulate and offer support as needed.

- Remind groups that when they read a narrative, they should be sure to identify the main characters, setting, and plot.

- If a group is confused about why certain characters do certain things, remind them to

think about what they already know about the character and the setting, and to use this knowledge to make inferences about the character's motivations.

- Challenge groups to determine the theme of the story and the specific details that refine the theme.

FACILITATING

Concept Vocabulary

WONDERED If groups are struggling to define the word *wondered* in paragraph 3, point out the context of the word. Point out that Alice is questioning her behavior.

Possible response: In this context, *wondered* means "questioned" or "thought about."

CURIOSITY If groups are struggling to define the word *curiosity* in paragraph 3, point out the context of the word. Point out that Alice is reacting to something she had never seen before and wants to learn more.

Possible response: In this context, *curiosity* means "strong interest" or "desire to learn more."

NOTES

Mark context clues or indicate another strategy you used to help you determine meaning.

wondered (WUHN uhrd) *v.*
MEANING:

curiosity (kyoo ree OS uh tee) *n.*
MEANING:

---

2   So she was considering in her own mind (as well as she could, for the hot day made her feel very sleepy and stupid), whether the pleasure of making a daisy-chain would be worth the trouble of getting up and picking the daisies, when suddenly a White Rabbit with pink eyes ran close by her.

3   There was nothing so *very* remarkable in that; nor did Alice think it so very much out of the way to hear the Rabbit say to itself, "Oh dear! Oh dear! I shall be late!" (when she thought it over afterwards, it occurred to her that she ought to have **wondered** at this, but at the time it all seemed quite natural); but when the Rabbit actually *took a watch out of its waistcoat-pocket,* and looked at it, and then hurried on, Alice started to her feet, for it flashed across her mind that she had never before seen a rabbit with either a waistcoat-pocket, or a watch to take out of it, and burning with **curiosity**, she ran across the field after it, and fortunately was just in time to see it pop down a large rabbit-hole under the hedge.

4   In another moment down went Alice after it, never once considering how in the world she was to get out again.

5   The rabbit-hole went straight on like a tunnel for some way, and then dipped suddenly down, so suddenly that Alice had not a moment to think about stopping herself before she found herself falling down a very deep well.

6   Either the well was very deep, or she fell very slowly, for she had plenty of time as she went down to look about her and to wonder what was going to happen next. First, she tried to look down and make out what she was coming to, but it was too dark to see anything; then she looked at the sides of the well, and noticed that they were filled with cupboards and book-shelves; here and there she saw maps and pictures hung upon pegs. She took down a jar from one of the shelves as she passed; it was labeled "ORANGE MARMALADE," but to her great disappointment it was empty: she did not like to drop the jar for fear of killing somebody, so managed to put it into one of the cupboards as she fell past it.

7   "Well!" thought Alice to herself, "after such a fall as this, I shall think nothing of tumbling down stairs! How brave they'll all think me at home! Why, I wouldn't say anything about it, even if I fell off the top of the house!" (Which was very likely true.)

8   Down, down, down. Would the fall *never* come to an end! "I wonder how many miles I've fallen by this time?" she said aloud. "I must be getting somewhere near the center of the earth. Let me see: that would be four thousand miles down, I think—" (for, you see, Alice had learned several things of this sort in her

© Pearson Education, Inc., or its affiliates. All rights reserved.

HOW LANGUAGE WORKS

Conjunctions Call student attention to the grammar of paragraph 2. Explain that conjunctions connect sentence parts and help show the relationships between those parts. Common conjunctions include *and, or,* and *but.* Draw students' attention to these examples of conjunctions from paragraph 2:

So she was considering in her own mind (as well *as* she could, *for* the hot day made her

feel very sleepy *and* stupid), *whether* the pleasure of making a daisy-chain would be worth the trouble of getting up *and* picking the daisies, *when* suddenly a White Rabbit with pink eyes ran close by her.

Encourage groups to choose another paragraph on this page and identify all the conjunctions in that paragraph.

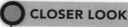

lessons in the schoolroom, and though this was not a very good opportunity for showing off her knowledge, as there was no one to listen to her, still it was good practice to say it over) "—yes, that's about the right distance—but then I wonder what Latitude or Longitude I've got to?" (Alice had no idea what Latitude was, or Longitude either, but thought they were nice grand words to say.)

9   Presently she began again. "I wonder if I shall fall right *through* the earth! How funny it'll seem to come out among the people that walk with their heads downward! The Antipathies,[1] I think—" (she was rather glad there *was* no one listening, this time, as it didn't sound at all the right word)"—but I shall have to ask them what the name of the country is, you know. Please, Ma'am, is this New Zealand or Australia?" (and she tried to curtsey as she spoke—fancy *curtseying* as you're falling through the air! Do you think you could manage it?) "And what an ignorant little girl she'll think me for asking! No, it'll never do to ask: perhaps I shall see it written up somewhere."

10   Down, down, down. There was nothing else to do, so Alice soon began talking again. "Dinah'll miss me very much tonight, I should think!" (Dinah was the cat.) "'I hope they'll remember her saucer of milk at tea time. Dinah my dear! I wish you were down here with me! There are no mice in the air, I'm afraid, but you might catch a bat, and that's very like a mouse, you know. But do cats eat bats, I wonder?" And here Alice began to get rather sleepy, and went on saying to herself, in a dreamy sort of way, "Do cats eat bats? Do cats eat bats?" and sometimes, "Do bats eat cats?" for, you see, as she couldn't answer either question, it didn't much matter which way she put it. She felt that she was dozing off, and had just begun to dream that she was walking hand in hand with Dinah, and saying to her very earnestly, "Now, Dinah, tell me the truth: did you ever eat a bat?" when suddenly, thump! thump! down she came upon a heap of sticks and dry leaves, and the fall was over.

11   Alice was not a bit hurt, and she jumped up on to her feet in a moment: she looked up, but it was all dark overhead; before her was another long passage, and the White Rabbit was still in sight, hurrying down it. There was not a moment to be lost: away went Alice like the wind, and was just in time to hear it say, as it turned a corner, "Oh my ears and whiskers, how late it's getting!" She was close behind it when she turned the corner, but the Rabbit was no longer to be seen: she found herself in a long, low hall, which was lit up by a row of lamps hanging from the roof.

NOTES

---

1. **The Antipathies** (an TIHP uh theez) Alice is trying to think of the word *Antipodes* (an TIHP uh deez), a name used by people in the northern hemisphere to refer to New Zealand and Australia.

from Alice's Adventures in Wonderland **365**

© Pearson Education, Inc., or its affiliates. All rights reserved.

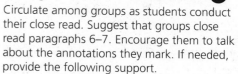

CLOSER LOOK

Analyze Characterization

Circulate among groups as students conduct their close read. Suggest that groups close read paragraphs 6–7. Encourage them to talk about the annotations they mark. If needed, provide the following support.

ANNOTATE: Have students mark details in paragraphs 6–7 that show what Alice is thinking, or work with small groups as you highlight details together.

QUESTION: Guide students to consider what these details might tell them. Ask what readers can infer about the character of Alice from these details, and accept student responses.

Possible response: She is thoughtful, introspective, proud, and prone to exaggeration. She cares what other people think of her and how her actions affect other people.

CONCLUDE: Help students formulate conclusions about the importance of these details in the text. Ask students why the author might have included these details.

Possible response: These details might explain why Alice ended up going on this imaginative journey: she seems imaginative and tends to daydream and get lost in her own head.

Tell students that **characterization** is the way a writer develops and reveals a character's personality and temperment. With **direct characterization**, a writer simply tells us what a character is like. With **indirect characterization**, the writer shows readers a character's traits by describing the character's actions and behavior, or presenting the character's words or thoughts. It's up to readers to make inferences and draw conclusions about a character based on the clues the writer provides.

PERSONALIZE FOR LEARNING

English Language Support

Commonly Confused Words Point to the word *Antipathies* in paragraph 9, and tell students that Alice uses the word incorrectly. Explain that an *antipathy* is a disgust or dislike toward something. Alice confuses *antipathies* with *antipodes*, a word that looks and sounds quite similar, but has a completely different meaning. The *antipodes* of any place on Earth are places on the exact opposite side of the globe.

The term *antipodes* is also used more generally to refer to Australia and New Zealand by people in the northern hemisphere. Provide other examples of commonly confused words, such as *stationary/ stationery, allusion/illusion, conscience/conscious,* and *capital/capitol.* Have students look up the definitions for each pair. **ALL LEVELS**

© Pearson Education, Inc., or its affiliates. All rights reserved.

NOTES

12   There were doors all round the hall, but they were all locked; and when Alice had been all the way down one side and up the other, trying every door, she walked sadly down the middle, wondering how she was ever to get out again.

13   Suddenly she came upon a little three-legged table, all made of solid glass; there was nothing on it except a tiny golden key, and Alice's first thought was that it might belong to one of the doors of the hall; but, alas! either the locks were too large, or the key was too small, but at any rate it would not open any of them.

14   However, on the second time round, she came upon a low curtain she had not noticed before, and behind it was a little door about fifteen inches high: she tried the little golden key in the lock, and to her great delight it fitted!

15   Alice opened the door and found that it led into a small passage, not much larger than a rat-hole: she knelt down and looked along the passage into the loveliest garden you ever saw. How she longed to get out of that dark hall, and wander about among those beds of bright flowers and those cool fountains, but she could not even get her head though the doorway; "and even if my head would go through," thought poor Alice, "it would be of very little use without my shoulders. Oh, how I wish I could shut up like a telescope! I think I could, if I only know how to begin." For, you see, so many out-of-the-way things had happened lately, that Alice had begun to think that very few things indeed were really impossible. ❧

DIGITAL PERSPECTIVES

Enriching the Text Call student attention to paragraph 15 which sets up Alice's adventure. *Alice's Adventures in Wonderland* has inspired several film and TV adaptations. Choose one such adaptation, and show students a section of the movie or TV version that corresponds with the excerpt from the novel. Be sure to preview the clip in advance.

After students have viewed the clip, encourage groups to compare and contrast the movie or TV version with the novel. You might suggest that they record the similarities and differences in a Venn diagram or chart. Encourage students to consider the following elements: missing or added details, characterization, and details about the setting. Finally, ask groups to discuss how or if the movie or TV version enhanced their understanding of the text.

Comprehension Check

Complete the following items after you finish your first read. Review and clarify details with your group.

1. Why does Alice decide to follow the Rabbit?

2. What does Alice see in the well?

3. What is at the bottom of the well?

4. What is the purpose of the tiny golden key?

5. Why does Alice wish she was able to "shut up like a telescope"?

6. 🔲 **Notebook** Write a summary of the excerpt from *Alice's Adventures in Wonderland* to confirm your understanding of the selection.

- -

RESEARCH

Research to Clarify Choose at least one unfamiliar detail from the text. Briefly research that detail. In what way does the information you learned shed light on an aspect of the story? Share your findings with your group.

Research to Explore Choose something that interested you from the text, and formulate a research question you might use to find out more about it.

from Alice's Adventures in Wonderland **367**

© Pearson Education, Inc., or its affiliates. All rights reserved.

Comprehension Check

Possible responses:

1. Alice decides to follow the Rabbit because she finds it very peculiar to see a rabbit taking a watch out of a waistcoat pocket.

2. Alice sees cupboards, book shelves, maps, and pictures on the sides of the well.

3. At the bottom of the well is "another long passage" that leads to "a long, low hall."

4. The tiny golden key opens a tiny door behind a curtain. The door leads to the "loveliest garden you ever saw."

5. Alice wishes she could somehow make herself smaller so she could get through the tiny door.

6. Summaries will vary but should include Alice's seeing the White Rabbit, falling down the hole, finding a key, and approaching a very small door.

Research

Research to Clarify If students struggle to come up with a detail to research, you may want to suggest that they focus on one of the following topics: waistcoats, the center of Earth, latitude and longitude.

Research to Explore If students aren't sure how to formulate a research question, suggest that they use their findings from Research to Clarify as a starting point. For example, if students researched the center of Earth, they might formulate a question such as: *What is Earth's core made of?*

PERSONALIZE FOR LEARNING

Challenge

Point of View Ask students to think about the following questions: *What might the White Rabbit have found strange about the above-ground world? What might he have found strange about Alice? What was he doing above ground? Why was he worried about being late? What might he have thought about while he was falling down the well?* Encourage students to rewrite the excerpt from the point of view of the White Rabbit. Remind students to use sensory language and descriptive details to develop the characters and events in their narrative. Have students share their narratives with members of their group and discuss how writing the story from a different point of view changes readers' experiences.

MAKING MEANING

from ALICE'S ADVENTURES IN WONDERLAND

Jump Start

CLOSE READ Ask groups to consider the following prompts: *Why do you think Alice went down the rabbit hole? What does the rabbit hole represent, or symbolize? Do you think the author meant for Alice's trip down the rabbit hole to be taken literally or figuratively?* As students discuss in their groups, remind them to refer to specific details from the selection.

Close Read the Text ✐

If needed, model close reading by using the Annotation Highlights in the Interactive Teacher's Edition.

Remind students to use Accountable Talk in their discussions and to support one another as they complete the close read.

Analyze the Text

1. **Possible response**: Paragraphs 6–10 include details that suggest that Alice is floating, or falling very slowly.
2. **Passages will vary by group.**
3. **Responses will vary by group.**

Concept Vocabulary

Why These Words? Possible response: The words all have to do with Alice's thirst for exploration and new experiences. Other words include: *trying, longed, notice,* and *opportunity*.

Practice

Paragraphs will vary.

Word Network

Possible words: *remarkable, dreamy, mind, knowledge, wander, out-of-the-way*

Word Study

For more support, see **Concept Vocabulary and Word Study.** 🖹

Possible response: elephant/vertebrate = item/category; state/republic = part/whole; thirst/quench = problem/solution

---

TIP

GROUP DISCUSSION
Reading stories can be a personal experience. Respect the fact that your classmates may have different interpretations of the selection than you do.

🔧 **WORD NETWORK**

Add words related to imagination from the text to your Word Network.

▤ **STANDARDS**

Reading Literature
• Cite textual evidence to support analysis of what the text says explicitly as well as inferences drawn from the text.
• Describe how a particular story's or drama's plot unfolds in a series of episodes as well as how the characters respond or change as the plot moves toward a resolution.
Language
Demonstrate understanding of figurative language, word relationships, and nuances in word meanings.
  b. Use the relationship between particular words to better understand each of the words.

Close Read the Text

With your group, revisit sections of the text you marked during your first read. **Annotate** details that you notice. What **questions** do you have? What can you **conclude**?

ANNOTATE · QUESTION · **Close Read** · CONCLUDE

Analyze the Text

CITE TEXTUAL EVIDENCE to support your answers.

📒 **Notebook** Complete the activities.

1. **Review and Clarify** With your group, reread paragraphs 6–10 of the excerpt. How do the details about what Alice is seeing and thinking help you to picture her experience as she falls?

2. **Present and Discuss** Discuss what you noticed in the selection, what questions you asked, and what conclusions you reached.

3. **Essential Question:** *Where can imagination lead?* What has this excerpt taught you about imagination? Discuss with your group.

LANGUAGE DEVELOPMENT

Concept Vocabulary

peeped	wondered	curiosity

Why These Words? The three concept vocabulary words from the text are related. With your group, determine what the words have in common. Write your ideas down, and add another word that relates to this concept.

Practice

📒 **Notebook** Confirm your understanding of the words from the text by using them in a paragraph about Alice's imagination. Be sure to use context clues that hint at each word's meaning.

Word Study

Word Relationships Understanding the relationship between two words can help you better understand each of the words. For example, the three concept vocabulary words have a cause-and-effect relationship. A person's *curiosity* may have caused him or her to have *wondered* about something and then *peeped* to learn more.

Work with your group to determine the relationship in each of these pairs of words: *elephant/vertebrate, state/republic, quench/thirst.* Consult a dictionary if you are unsure of a word's meaning.

© Pearson Education, Inc., or its affiliates. All rights reserved.

FORMATIVE ASSESSMENT

Analyze the Text 🖹

If students struggle to close read the text, **then** provide the *from Alice's Adventures in Wonderland: Text Questions* available online in the Interactive Teacher's Edition or Unit Resources. Answers and DOK levels are also available.

Concept Vocabulary

If students struggle to see the connection among the words, **then** suggest that they review how the words are used in the selection.

Word Study

If students have trouble identifying word relationships, **then** use simpler pairings to review types of relationships such as part/whole, cause/effect, and problem/solution.

For Reteach and Practice, see **Word Study: Word Relationships (RP).** 🖹

Analyze Craft and Structure

Characterization Authors develop characters and reveal their personalities, or character traits, through the process of **characterization.** There are two types of characterization: **direct characterization** and **indirect characterization.**

	DEFINITION	EXAMPLE
Direct Characterization	The author directly states or describes what a character is like.	Fernando is friendly.
Indirect Characterization	The author reveals a character's personality through his or her words and actions and through the thoughts, words, and actions of others.	Fernando smiled warmly and asked the new girl, "Do you want to join my friends and me for lunch?"

When an author uses indirect characterization, readers must **make inferences,** or educated guesses, about the characters based on details in the text. To make an inference, analyze the details the author provides about a character and decide what the details suggest about the character's personality.

Practice

> **CITE TEXTUAL EVIDENCE**
> to support your answers.

Work individually to analyze the passages from the excerpt identified in the chart. Use the chart to record your notes. First, decide whether the passage is an example of direct characterization or indirect characterization. Then, determine what the passage reveals about the character. Gather your notes and share them with your group.

SELECTION PASSAGE	TYPE OF CHARACTERIZATION	WHAT YOU LEARN ABOUT THE CHARACTER
Alice was beginning to get very tired of sitting by her sister on the bank, and of having nothing to do . . . (paragraph 1)	indirect characterization	This suggests that Alice is prone to boredom.
In another moment down went Alice after it, never once considering how in the world she was to get out again. (paragraph 4)	direct characterization	This shows that she is impulsive; in this case, her curiosity is stronger than her impulse control.
. . . [Alice] did not like to drop the jar for fear of killing somebody, so managed to put it into one of the cupboards as she fell past it. (paragraph 6)	indirect characterization	This shows that Alice thinks about how her actions may affect other people.

Analyze Craft and Structure

Characterization Explain that although most writers use both direct and indirect characterization, they may rely more heavily on one than the other. Ask groups to discuss which type of characterization is more effective in the excerpt from *Alice's Adventures in Wonderland.* For more support, see **Analyze Craft and Structure: Characterization.** 📄

See possible responses in the chart on the student page.

FORMATIVE ASSESSMENT
Analyze Craft and Structure

If students struggle to analyze the examples of characterization, **then** have students conduct a second close read of the relevant passages in the selection and discuss how the author develops Alice and the White Rabbit. For Reteach and Practice, see **Analyze Craft and Structure: Characterization (RP).** 📄

© Pearson Education, Inc., or its affiliates. All rights reserved.

FACILITATING

Conventions

Conjunctions and Interjections Explain to groups that there are only seven coordinating conjunctions, and they can be memorized with the help of the mnemonic device *FANBOYS* (*for, and, nor, but, or, yet, so*).

Explain that there is another type of conjunction called subordinating conjunctions, which show the relationship between a dependent clause and the rest of the sentence. Examples of subordinating conjunctions include *after*, *although*, *before*, *though*, and *while*. For more support, see **Conventions: Conjunctions and Interjections.** 📄

Read It

Possible responses:

1. <u>Oh</u>, how I wish I could shut up like a telescope! (interjection)
2. There was nothing else to do, <u>so</u> Alice soon began talking again. (conjunction)
3. "<u>Well!</u>" thought Alice to herself, "after such a fall as this, I shall think nothing of tumbling down stairs!" (interjection)

Write It

Paragraphs will vary, but make sure that students correctly use and identify conjunctions and interjections.

FORMATIVE ASSESSMENT

Conventions

If students have trouble identifying conjunctions and interjections, **then** have them look for words that connect parts of a sentence or words that express feelings. For Reteach and Practice, see **Conventions: Conjunctions and Interjections (RP).** 📄

from ALICE'S ADVENTURES IN WONDERLAND

Conventions

Conjunctions and Interjections Writers improve the flow of their writing by using **conjunctions** to connect sentence parts and show the relationships between or among those parts. **Coordinating conjunctions** are used to connect sentence parts that are of equal importance. Here are some examples.

COORDINATING CONJUNCTIONS	EXAMPLE SENTENCE
and, or, but, nor, for, yet, so	The show was sold out, **yet** there were dozens of people waiting in line.

Notice that in the example sentence, the conjunction *yet* is preceded by a comma. A conjunction that joins two independent clauses is always preceded by a comma.

Any word, phrase, or sound that expresses a sudden feeling is called an **interjection.** Writers use interjections to add liveliness and a sense of realism to their work. Here are some examples:

EXAMPLES OF INTERJECTIONS	EXAMPLE SENTENCES
ah, aha, whoa, hey, oh no, oops, shh, well, wow, whew	**Oops**, I dropped the plate! **Oh no!** I forgot my homework.

In some cases, an interjection is followed by an exclamation mark. In other cases, an interjection may be followed by a comma, and an exclamation mark may appear at the end of the sentence.

Read It

Work individually to correctly label the coordinating conjunctions or interjections in each sentence from *Alice's Adventures in Wonderland*.

1. Oh, how I wish I could shut up like a telescope!

2. There was nothing else to do, so Alice soon began talking again.

3. "Well!" thought Alice to herself, "after such a fall as this, I shall think nothing of tumbling down stairs!"

Write It

📓 **Notebook** Write a brief paragraph about an imaginary adventure. Use at least two coordinating conjunctions and two interjections in your paragraph. Then, exchange paragraphs with a group member, and label the conjunctions and interjections in your classmate's paragraph.

STANDARDS

Language
• Demonstrate command of the conventions of standard English grammar and usage when writing or speaking.
• Demonstrate command of the conventions of standard English capitalization, punctuation, and spelling when writing.

© Pearson Education, Inc., or its affiliates. All rights reserved.

PERSONALIZE FOR LEARNING

English Language Support

Conjunctions and Interjections Ask students to work in pairs to write three conjunctions and three interjections. **EMERGING**

Ask students to write two sentences including two conjunctions each, and two sentences including one interjection each. Remind them to use the appropriate punctuation. **EXPANDING**

Ask students to write a paragraph about Alice's adventure including two interjections and at least three conjunctions. Remind them to use the appropriate punctuation. **BRIDGING**

An expanded **English Language Development Lesson** on Conjunctions and Interjections is available in the Interactive Teacher's Edition. 📄

Research

Assignment

Since its publication in 1865, the characters from *Alice's Adventures in Wonderland* have been reimagined in various ways through illustrations as well as in movies. Work with your group to write a **research report** on one of the following topics:

☐ how Alice is portrayed in illustrated and animated versions of *Alice's Adventures in Wonderland,* including how these portrayals have changed over the years

☐ how Alice is portrayed in live-action movie versions of *Alice's Adventures in Wonderland,* including how these portrayals have changed over the years

Conduct Research As a group, choose your topic. Conduct research to find both textual information as well as illustrations, image stills, and other visuals to include in your report. Be sure to consult several credible print and digital sources, and record the bibliographic information for each source you use. Bibliographic information includes the title, author, and date of publication; if you are using an Internet source, you should also note the Web site address and date you accessed the information. Use this chart to keep track of your sources and the information you found in each.

SOURCE (INCLUDING BIBLIOGRAPHIC INFORMATION)	INFORMATION OR IMAGE OBTAINED FROM SOURCE

Write Your Report Work with your group to organize the information and images from your research into a report. Try different ways of sequencing the images in your report so that they highlight your main points. Each image should help readers to better understand the information you communicate in writing.

Cite Your Sources When you credit a source, you tell readers where you found your information and give them the bibliographic details necessary for locating the source themselves. Presenting someone else's ideas, research, or opinion as your own, even if you use different words, is **plagiarism**—the equivalent of academic stealing. To avoid plagiarism, review your report to be sure you have properly cited your sources, both within the text of your report and with a Works Cited list at the end. There are many different formats for citing sources; ask your teacher which one you should use in your report.

© Pearson Education, Inc., or its affiliates. All rights reserved.

✒ EVIDENCE LOG

Before moving on to a new selection, go to your Evidence Log, and record what you learned from *Alice's Adventures in Wonderland.*

☰ STANDARDS

Writing
• Write informative/explanatory texts to examine a topic and convey ideas, concepts, and information through the selection, organization, and analysis of relevant content.
  a. Introduce a topic; organize ideas, concepts, and information, using strategies such as definition, classification, comparison/contrast, and cause/effect; include formatting, graphics, and multimedia when useful to aiding comprehension.

• Conduct short research projects to answer a question, drawing on several sources and refocusing the inquiry when appropriate.
• Gather relevant information from multiple print and digital sources; assess the credibility of each source; and quote or paraphrase the data and conclusions of others while avoiding plagiarism and providing basic bibliographic information for sources.

from Alice's Adventures in Wonderland **371**

Research

If groups have trouble deciding which option to choose, encourage them to consider which option plays to their group's strengths and interests the most. If most of the group members excel in history class, then writing a historical report would be a good option. If the group is more interested in mathematics, then the explanatory report is likely to be a better choice. Remind groups that, whichever option they choose, they will need to conduct the same amount of research.

Conduct Research Encourage groups to consult several sources of information, and remind them to evaluate each source for credibility. Encourage students to look at who wrote each source and examine their credentials. Suggest that websites ending in *.gov* or *.edu* and articles written by historians and literature experts are likely to be reliable. Remind groups to consult the schedule for Small-Group activities as they create their Project Plan. Check to make sure each group has made assignments and that the work is divided evenly among group members.

Write Your Report Encourage students to consider the best organization for the images and text in their report. Students may find that chronological order is best suited to this assignment.

Cite Your Sources Encourage groups to check that they correctly cited their sources. Remind them that if they used someone else's exact words, the quote must be enclosed in quotation marks. If they reworded someone else's ideas, quotation marks are not needed, but the source still must be cited. For more support, see **Research: Report.** 📄

Evidence Log Support students in completing their Evidence Log. This paced activity will help prepare them for the Performance-Based Assessment at the end of the unit.

FORMATIVE ASSESSMENT
Research

If students have trouble finding relevant information, **then** help them refine their search terms. For Reteach and Practice, see **Research: Report (RP).** 📄

Selection Test

Administer the "*from* Alice's Adventures in Wonderland" Selection Test, which is available in both print and digital formats online in Assessments. 📄 ☑

PERSONALIZE FOR LEARNING

Strategic Support

Organizational Structures Some students may require additional support in organizing their research findings. Encourage students to think about the specific topic they chose and how information about this topic might be best organized. A historical report, for example, might be organized sequentially. An explanatory report about mathematics in *Alice's Adventures in Wonderland,* on the other hand, might be best organized by choosing a few examples from the text and explaining each one. After students have chosen an organizational structure, suggest that they organize their research findings in an outline before writing their report.

Jabberwocky

🔊 **AUDIO SUMMARIES**
Audio summaries of "Jabberwocky" are available online in both English and Spanish in the Interactive Teacher's Edition or Unit Resources. Assigning these summaries prior to reading the selection may help students build additional background knowledge and set a context for their first read.

Summary

In his poem "Jabberwocky," Lewis Carroll uses a large number of nonsense words, many of which have no specific meaning but whose emotional tone is often understandable. In the poem, a man warns his son to be careful of monsters. His son goes out in the wilderness, confronts the Jabberwock, and cuts its head off. When the son returns, his father congratulates him joyfully. The last stanza and first stanza, both describing the environment, are the same.

Insight

This poem demonstrates how onomatopoeia can express ideas. Its imaginative language tells a story even though the poem contains nonsense words.

ESSENTIAL QUESTION:
Where can imagination lead?

Connection to Essential Question

Imagination can greatly change language, and, in turn, it can change the tools readers use to interpret important texts. A number of influential authors, including Shakespeare, made up words to get their ideas across.

SMALL-GROUP LEARNING PERFORMANCE TASK
When Alice finally gets through the door . . .

UNIT PERFORMANCE-BASED ASSESSMENT
What might happen if a fictional character were to come into the real world?

Connection to Performance Tasks

Small-Group Learning Performance Task The prompt asks students to consider Alice's adventures. The fight with an imaginary beast offers one option for them to pursue.

Unit Performance-Based Assessment As this text demonstrates, creativity can lead to memorable and interesting stories and accomplishments. Students may be inspired by Carroll's work as they prepare to address the prompt.

DIGITAL
PERSPECTIVES

 Audio

 Video

 Document

 Annotation Highlights

EL Highlights

 Online Assessment

LESSON RESOURCES

	Making Meaning	Language Development	Effective Expression
Lesson	**First Read** **Close Read** **Analyze the Text** **Analyze Craft and Structure**	**Concept Vocabulary** **Word Study** **Author's Style**	**Speaking and Listening**
Instructional Standards	**RL.10** By the end of the year, read and comprehend literature . . . **L.4** Determine or clarify the meaning of unknown and multiple-meaning words and phrases . . . **L.4.a** Use context as a clue . . . **RL.4** Determine the meaning of words and phrases as they are used in a text . . .	**RL.4** Determine the meaning of words and phrases as they are used . . . **L.1** Demonstrate command of the conventions . . . **L.1.e** Recognize variations from standard English . . . **L.4** Determine or clarify the meaning of unknown and multiple-meaning words and phrases . . . **L.4.c** Consult reference materials . . . **L.4.a** Use context as a clue . . . **L.5** Demonstrate understanding of figurative language . . . **L.5.b** Use the relationship between particular words . . .	**SL.1** Engage effectively in a range of collaborative discussions . . . **SL.1.a** Come to discussions prepared . . . **SL.1.b** Follow rules for collegial discussions . . . **SL.4** Present claims and findings . . . **SL.5** Include multimedia components and visual displays . . .

⌖ STUDENT RESOURCES

Available online in the Interactive Student Edition or Unit Resources	🔊 Selection Audio 📄 First-Read Guide: Poetry 📄 Close-Read Guide: Poetry	📄 Word Network	📄 Evidence Log

⌖ TEACHER RESOURCES

Selection Resources Available online in the Interactive Teacher's Edition or Unit Resources	🔊 Audio Summaries 🖊 Annotation Highlights 💬 EL Highlights 📄 Jabberwocky: Text Questions 📄 Analyze Craft and Structure: Sound Devices	📄 Concept Vocabulary and Word Study 📄 Author's Style: Invented Language	📄 Speaking and Listening: Dramatic Reading, Multimedia Presentation 📄 English Language Support Lesson: Dramatic Poetry Reading and Multimedia Presentation
Reteach/Practice (RP) Available online in the Interactive Teacher's Edition or Unit Resources	📄 Analyze Craft and Structure: Sound Devices (RP)	📄 Word Study: Anglo-Saxon Word Origins (RP) 📄 Author's Style: Invented Language (RP)	📄 Speaking and Listening: Dramatic Reading, Multimedia Presentation (RP)
Assessment Available online in Assessments	📄 ☑ Selection Test		
My Resources	📄 A Unit 4 Answer Key is available online and in the Interactive Teacher's Edition.		

Reading Support

Text Complexity Rubric: Jabberwocky

Quantitative Measures

Lexile: NP　Text Length: 28 lines

Qualitative Measures

Knowledge Demands ①—②—❸—④—⑤	The selection consists of imaginary concepts that are partially explained in the text.
Structure ①—❷—③—④—⑤	The selection is a poem that is organized into quatrains with a simple rhyme scheme.
Language Conventionality and Clarity ①—②—③—❹—⑤	Selection contains imaginary language framed by some familiar words and ideas.
Levels of Meaning/Purpose ①—②—③—❹—⑤	The poem contains multiple meanings: to evoke imagination and to present a recognizable poetic structure.

DECIDE AND PLAN

English Language Support

Provide English Learners with support for knowledge demands and language as they read the selection.

Knowledge Demands Before students read, have them focus on the illustration of the Jabberwock and then discuss its attributes.

Language Discuss the concept of rhyming words with students. Display lines from the poem, focusing on the ending sounds. Model these sounds and ask students to repeat them with you. For example,
　'Twas brillig, and the slithy toves (OVE)
　Did gyre and gimble in the wabe; (ABE)
　All mimsy were the borogoves, (OVE)
　And the mome raths outgrabe. (ABE)

Strategic Support

Provide students with strategic support to ensure that they can successfully read the text.

Structure Review the poem's structure and rhyme scheme with students. Point out how it is arranged into quatrains—lines of four. Display a quatrain for the class and demonstrate how in most stanzas the end of every other line rhymes within it. Write A after the first line, B, after the second, A for the third, and then B for the fourth. Work with students to label other rhymes in the poem.

Language Ask students to look for examples of imagery in the poem. Explain that poets use imagery to create vivid descriptions in poems.

Challenge

Provide students who need to be challenged with ideas for how they can go beyond a simple interpretation of the text.

Text Analysis Explain the concept of assonance to students: the use of words that have the same or similar vowel sounds. Have students list examples of assonance from the poem.

Written Response First review Carroll's use of *slithy*—the combination of *lithe* and *slimy*. Then ask them to combine words to come up with their own list of invented language to describe a monster.

TEACH

Read and Respond

Have groups do their first read of the selection. Then have them complete their close read. Finally, work with them on the Making Meaning, Language Development, and Effective Expression activities.

Standards Support Through Teaching and Learning Cycle

IDENTIFY NEEDS

Analyze results of the Beginning-of-Year Assessment, focusing on the items relating to Unit 4. Also take into consideration student performance to this point and your observations of where particular students struggle.

DECIDE AND PLAN

- If students have performed poorly on items matching these standards, then provide selection scaffolds before assigning them the on-level lesson provided in the Student Edition.
- If students have done well on the Beginning-of-Year Assessment, then challenge them to keep progressing and learning by giving them opportunities to practice the skills in depth.
- Use the Selection Resources listed on the Planning pages for "Jabberwocky" to help students continually improve their ability to master the standards.

Instructional Standards: Jabberwocky

	Catching Up	This Year	Looking Forward
Reading	You may wish to administer the **Analyze Craft and Structure: Sound Devices (RP)** worksheet to help students understand how authors create musical effects, reinforce meaning, and develop tone.	**RL.4** Determine the meaning of words and phrases as they are used in a text, including figurative and connotative meanings; analyze the impact of a specific word choice on meaning and tone.	Challenge students to come up with their own versions of these sound devices.
Speaking and Listening	You may wish to administer the **Speaking and Listening: Dramatic Reading, Multimedia Presentation (RP)** worksheet to prepare students for their presentations.	**SL.1.b** Follow rules for collegial discussions, set specific goals and deadlines, and define individual roles as needed.	Challenge students to set specific goals and deadlines, and to keep track of their progress.
Language	You may wish to administer the **Author's Style: Invented Language (RP)** worksheet to help students understand how invented language in this selection comes from Standard English.	**L.1.e** Recognize variations from standard English in their own and others' writing and speaking, and identify and use strategies to improve expression in conventional language.	Have students make up their own words, making sure they are based on contemporary English.
	You may wish to administer the **Word Study: Anglo-Saxon Word Origins (RP)** worksheet to help students understand how word history can help them learn new vocabulary words.	**L.4** Determine or clarify the meaning of unknown and multiple-meaning words and phrases based on *grade 6 reading and content,* choosing flexibly from a range of strategies.	Challenge students to study the word origins of other Anglo-Saxon words.

ANALYZE AND REVISE

- Analyze student work for evidence of student learning.
- Identify whether or not students have met the expectations in the standards.
- Identify implications for future instruction.

TEACH

Implement the planned lesson, and gather evidence of student learning.

Jump Start

FIRST READ Engage students in a discussion about invented languages. Ask if any students have ever made up their own language with their friends or siblings. If so, encourage students to share how and why they made up their language.

Jabberwocky 🔊 📄

How does Lewis Carroll convey meaning through his invented language? Modeling questions readers might ask as they read "Jabberwocky" brings the text alive for students and connects it to the Small-Group Learning Performance Task question. Selection audio and print capability for the selection are available in the Interactive Teacher's Edition.

Concept Vocabulary

Encourage groups to study the two types of context clues listed on the student page and to discuss how these types of clues can be used to infer meaning. Ask students to think of one other type of context clue that they might encounter in a poem. Possibilities include antonyms and examples.

⬤ FIRST READ

Have students perform the steps of the first read independently:

NOTICE: You may want to encourage students to notice details that reveal information about the hero of the poem.

ANNOTATE: Remind students to mark any words or passages that confuse or interest them.

CONNECT: Have students compare "Jabberwocky" with the excerpt from *Alice's Adventures in Wonderland* earlier in this unit.

RESPOND: Students will answer questions and write a summary to demonstrate understanding.

Point out to students that while they will always complete the Respond step at the end of the first read, the other steps will probably happen somewhat concurrently. You may wish to print copies of the **First-Read Guide: Poetry** for students to use. 📄

About the Poet

Lewis Carroll (1832–1898) is the pen name of Charles Lutwidge Dodgson, who was a British mathematics professor at Oxford University. Under his pen name, Dodgson wrote *Alice's Adventures in Wonderland* and *Through the Looking-Glass*. Like these classic novels, his poems are noted for their clever wordplay and delightfully zany word choices.

Jabberwocky

Concept Vocabulary

As you perform your first read of "Jabberwocky," you will encounter these words.

beware	foe	slain

Context Clues If these words are unfamiliar to you, try using context clues to help you determine their meanings. **Context clues** are other words and phrases that appear in nearby text. Even if you cannot figure out a word's exact definition, you can usually determine its part of speech—whether it is a noun, a verb, an adjective, or an adverb. Here is an example of how to apply this strategy.

> **Context:** The captain countermanded the directive of the officer.
>
> **Analysis:** It is difficult to tell exactly what the underlined words mean. However, the word *countermanded* ends in *-ed* and follows the subject of the sentence, *captain*. *Countermanded* must be a verb. Similarly, the word *directive* is in between the article *the* and the preposition *of*. *Directive* must be a noun.

In the poem you are about to read, you will encounter a number of invented words. These are words that the poet made up, so you will not find them in a dictionary. You may not be able to determine exactly what they mean, but you can use context clues to figure out their parts of speech.

First Read POETRY

Apply these strategies as you conduct your first read. You will have an opportunity to complete a close read after your first read.

NOTICE *who* or *what* is "speaking" the poem and whether the poem tells a story or describes a single moment.

ANNOTATE by marking vocabulary and key passages you want to revisit.

First Read

CONNECT ideas within the selection to what you already know and what you have already read.

RESPOND by completing the Comprehension Check and by writing a brief summary of the selection.

■ **STANDARDS**

Reading Literature
By the end of the year, read and comprehend literature, including stories, dramas, and poems, in the grades 6–8 text complexity band proficiently, with scaffolding as needed at the high end of the range.

Language
Determine or clarify the meaning of unknown and multiple-meaning words and phrases based on *grade 6 reading and content*, choosing flexibly from a range of strategies.
  a. Use context as a clue to the meaning of a word or phrase.

© Pearson Education, Inc., or its affiliates. All rights reserved.

👥 FACILITATING SMALL-GROUP CLOSE READING

CLOSE READ: Poetry As groups perform the close read, circulate and offer support as needed.

- Remind groups that poets often push the boundaries of language to convey a feeling or idea. Encourage students to pay particular attention to the context of each word.

- If a group is confused about the meanings of certain words, suggest that group members try to determine the word's part of speech and that they look for similarities with words that they do know.

- Challenge group members to debate with each other the meanings of certain words and the meaning of the poem as a whole.

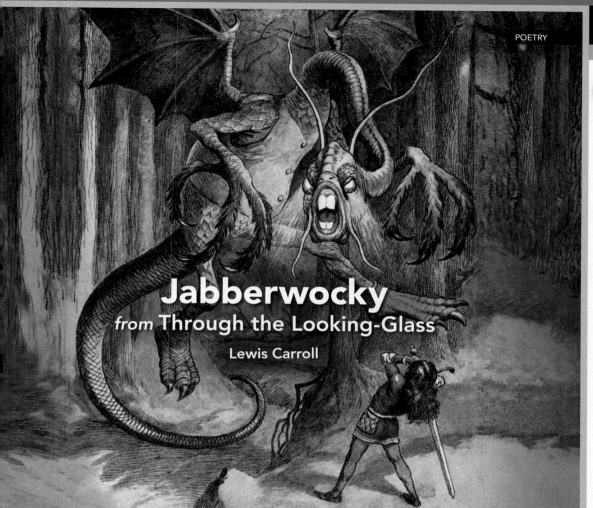

Jabberwocky
from Through the Looking-Glass
Lewis Carroll

© Pearson Education, Inc., or its affiliates. All rights reserved.

BACKGROUND
In the first chapter of *Through the Looking-Glass*, the sequel to *Alice's Adventures in Wonderland*, Alice encounters a creature called a Jabberwock. Many of the invented words in Carroll's imaginative poem are made up of two different words. For example, *brillig* is a combination of *brilliant* and *broiling*.

SCAN FOR
MULTIMEDIA

'Twas brillig, and the slithy toves
 Did gyre and gimble in the wabe;
All mimsy were the borogoves,
 And the mome raths outgrabe.

NOTES

CLOSER LOOK

Analyze Invented Language
Circulate among groups as students conduct their close read. Suggest that groups close read the first stanza. Encourage them to talk about the annotations they mark. If needed, provide the following support.

ANNOTATE: Have students mark details in the first stanza that give clues as to the meaning of the word *slithy*, or work with small groups as you highlight them together.

QUESTION: Guide students to consider what these details might tell them. Ask what a reader can infer about the word *slithy* from the other words that are used in the same sentence, and accept student responses.

Possible response: The reader can analyze the other words in the sentence to determine the meaning of the made-up word. The word *the* is always used before a noun or a noun phrase. "Slithy toves" must therefore be a noun phrase, and *slithy* must be an adjective because adjectives come before nouns in English.

CONCLUDE: Help students to formulate conclusions about the importance of these details in the text. Ask students to infer a possible meaning of the word *slithy*.

Possible response: I think *slithy* has a similar meaning to *slimy* because I know it's an adjective and it looks very similar to *slimy*.

Tell students that **invented words** may or may not follow the language patterns and grammatical rules of English. However, point out that it is very likely that the author does want the reader to understand the new words.

Additional **English Language Support** is available in the Interactive Teacher's Edition.

PERSONALIZE FOR LEARNING

English Language Support
Invented Language English learners are likely to require additional support in decoding "Jabberwocky." Explain that many of the words in the poem were made up by the author. It is nevertheless possible for the reader to get a good idea of what many of the made-up words mean. Explain that the poem uses several real English words, and that it also uses standard English grammar and syntax. Tell students that syntax is the way that words are arranged into sentences. For example, one rule of English syntax is that adjectives always come before nouns. In many other languages, including Spanish, the opposite is usually true. To help English learners decode "Jabberwocky," you may want to begin by having them watch the dramatic reading video of the poem. Then ask students to underline all the words in the poem that they do recognize and circle the words that they don't recognize. Finally, review the definitions of nouns, verbs, and adjectives and assist students in determining the part of speech and inferring the meaning of each unfamiliar word. **ALL LEVELS**

Concept Vocabulary

BEWARE If groups are struggling to define the word *beware* in line 5, point out that the word appears as a verb. Context in line 6 suggests why someone should "beware." Encourage students to use these context clues to define the word *beware*.

Possible response: The word *beware* means "be on the lookout" or "be careful."

FOE If groups are struggling to define the word *foe* in line 10, point out that the word appears as a noun. Context in line 9 includes a sword. Encourage students to use these context clues to define the word *foe*.

Possible response: The word *foe* means "enemy."

SLAIN If groups are struggling to define the word *slain* in line 21, point out that they can use context clues to help determine its meaning. Remind students to look at how the word is used in the sentence—the father asks the son if he has *slain* the Jabberwock. This occurs immediately after the son "left it dead." Encourage students to use these context clues to define the word *slain*.

Possible response: The word *slain* means "killed."

MEDIA CONNECTION ⏵

Project the media connection video in class, ask students to open the video in their interactive textbooks, or have students scan the Bounce Page icon with their phones to access the video.

Discuss It Possible response: Watching the video helps me understand the language because I see how these strange words are pronounced and emphasized. The words make more sense when you hear them.

NOTES

Mark context clues or indicate another strategy you used to help you determine meaning.

beware (bee WAIR) *v.*
MEANING:

foe (foh) *n.*
MEANING:

slain (slayn) *v.*
MEANING:

---

5 "Beware the Jabberwock, my son!
      The jaws that bite, the claws that catch!
   Beware the Jubjub bird, and shun
      The frumious Bandersnatch!"

   He took his vorpal sword in hand;
10   Long time the manxome foe he sought—
   So rested he by the Tumtum tree
      And stood awhile in thought.

   And, as in uffish thought he stood,
      The Jabberwock, with eyes of flame,
15 Came whiffling through the tulgey wood,
      And burbled as it came!

   One, two! One, two! And through and through
      The vorpal blade went snicker-snack!
   He left it dead, and with its head
20   He went galumphing back.

   "And hast thou slain the Jabberwock?
      Come to my arms, my beamish boy!
   O frabjous day! Callooh! Callay!"
      He chortled in his joy.

25 'Twas brillig, and the slithy toves
      Did gyre and gimble in the wabe;
   All mimsy were the borogoves,
      And the mome raths outgrabe.

MEDIA CONNECTION

Alice in Wonderland
(1983)—Jabberwocky

💬 Discuss It How does listening to Alice read "Jabberwocky" in the video help you to better understand the poem?

Write your response before sharing your ideas.

© Pearson Education, Inc., or its affiliates. All rights reserved.

SCAN FOR
MULTIMEDIA

VOCABULARY DEVELOPMENT

Concept Vocabulary Reinforcement Students will benefit from additional examples and practice with the concept vocabulary. Reinforce their comprehension with "show-you-know" sentences. The first part of the sentence uses the vocabulary word in an appropriate context. The second part of the sentence—the "show-you-know"

part—clarifies the first. Model the strategy with this example for *slain*:

Prince Maximanius had *slain* many dragons before; this colossal beast was proving much harder to defeat.

Then give students these sentence prompts and coach them in creating the clarification part:

1. Carlos saw his *foe* in the hallway;
   _____.

   Possible response: he quickly turned into another room.

2. *Beware* the traffic there at rush hour;
   _____.

   Possible response: it is so crowded that it will take you hours to get home.

Comprehension Check

Complete the following items after you finish your first read. Review and clarify details with your group.

1. What does the speaker say to beware of? Who is the speaker addressing?

2. What three things does the speaker warn about in lines 5–8?

3. What happens to the Jabberwock at the end of the poem?

4. ▣ **Notebook** Write 3 or 4 sentences in which you summarize what happens in the poem.

- -

RESEARCH

Research to Clarify Choose at least one unfamiliar detail from the text. Briefly research that detail. In what way does the information you learned shed light on an aspect of the poem? Share your findings with your group.

Research to Explore Choose something that interested you from the text, and formulate a research question that you might use to find out more about it.

Jabberwocky **375**

Comprehension Check

Possible responses:

1. The son's father is the speaker and says to beware of the Jabberwock, the Jubjub bird, and the Bandersnatch.
2. jaws that bite, claws that catch, and the Jubjub bird
3. It is slain.
4. A father warns his son about the Jabberwock and other dangerous creatures that live in the woods. The son goes into the woods with a sword, intending to slay the Jabberwock. Eventually, the Jabberwock appears and the son slays him. He brings the Jabberwock's head to his father, who is overjoyed to hear the news that the Jabberwock is dead.

Research

Research to Clarify If students struggle to come up with a detail to research, you may want to suggest that they focus on one of the following topics: invented languages, epic poetry, or Lewis Carroll.

Research to Explore If students aren't sure how to go about formulating a research question, suggest that they use their findings from Research to Clarify as a starting point. For example, if students researched epic poetry, they might formulate a question such as, *What are the elements of epic poetry?*

© Pearson Education, Inc., or its affiliates. All rights reserved.

PERSONALIZE FOR LEARNING

Challenge

Rewriting a Poem Challenge students to rewrite "Jabberwocky" using only standard English words. Encourage students to try to retain as much as of the original meaning as possible. This will force students to ensure that they understand each of the original words, as well as their parts of speech. Encourage students to use rich, descriptive words as much as possible. After students have written their poems, invite them to share their work with their group members. Encourage students to discuss how translating the poem into standard English enhanced their understanding of the poem's meaning.

Jump Start

CLOSE READ Remind students that although "Jabberwocky" is written in a mostly invented language, they were still able to figure out the general meaning of the poem. Point out that Carroll must have put a lot of thought into his invented words; he clearly didn't just jumble random letters together. Engage students in a discussion about the basic elements of a language. For example, students may cite the requirements of standardized spelling, grammar, and syntax.

Close Read the Text

If needed, model close reading by using the Annotation Highlights in the Interactive Teacher's Edition.

Remind students to use Accountable Talk in their discussions and to support one another as they complete the close read.

Analyze the Text

1. **Responses will vary by group.** Students may say that the repetition of *one, two,* and *through* creates a marching rhythm.

2. **Passages will vary by group.** Remind students to support their conclusions with reasons and details.

3. **Responses will vary by group.**

Concept Vocabulary

Why These Words? Possible response: All these words relate to the boy's battle victory. They show how the father reacted to his son killing the Jabberwock.

Practice

Paragraphs will vary.

Word Network

Possible words: *frabjous, manxome, snicker-snack*

Word Study

For more support, see **Concept Vocabulary and Word Study.** 📄

Possible responses: *loathsome*: repulsive, disgusting
dreadful: terrible, frightful, awful
plight: a difficult situation

MAKING MEANING

JABBERWOCKY

TIP

GROUP DISCUSSION
As you discuss "Jabberwocky" with your group, keep an open mind by considering all members' ideas about what the invented words might mean.

WORD NETWORK
Add words related to imagination from the text to your Word Network.

STANDARDS
Reading Literature
Determine the meaning of words and phrases as they are used in a text, including figurative and connotative meanings; analyze the impact of a specific word choice on meaning and tone.
Language
Determine or clarify the meaning of unknown and multiple-meaning words and phrases based on *grade 6 reading and content,* choosing flexibly from a range of strategies.
c. Consult reference materials, both print and digital, to find the pronunciation of a word or determine or clarify its precise meaning or its part of speech.

Close Read the Text

With your group, revisit sections of the text you marked during your first read. **Annotate** details that you notice. What **questions** do you have? What can you **conclude**?

ANNOTATE • QUESTION • CONCLUDE — Close Read

Analyze the Text

CITE TEXTUAL EVIDENCE to support your answers.

Complete the activities.

1. **Review and Clarify** With your group, reread lines 17–20 and underline words that are repeated. Why do you think the poet repeats these words? How does this repetition help you to better understand what is happening at this point in the poem?

2. **Present and Discuss** Discuss what you noticed in the selection, what questions you asked, and what conclusions you reached.

3. **Essential Question:** *Where can imagination lead?* What has this poem taught you about imagination? Discuss with your group.

LANGUAGE DEVELOPMENT

Concept Vocabulary

beware	foe	slain

Why These Words? The three concept vocabulary words from the text are related. With your group, determine what the words have in common. How do the concept vocabulary words deepen your understanding of the poem?

Practice

📄 **Notebook** Write a paragraph in which you describe an imaginary battle scene. Use all three of the concept vocabulary words. Be sure to use context clues that hint at each word's meaning.

Word Study

Anglo-Saxon Word Origins The three concept vocabulary words have Anglo-Saxon word origins. This means that the words or parts of the words are ancient and have been in the language since the Old English period, which ended in A.D. 1066.

Use a dictionary to look up these words that also have Anglo-Saxon word origins: *loathsome, dreadful, plight.* Discuss what you discover with your group.

© Pearson Education, Inc., or its affiliates. All rights reserved.

FORMATIVE ASSESSMENT

Analyze the Text 📄

If students struggle to close read the text, then provide the **Jabberwocky: Text Questions** available online in the Interactive Teacher's Edition or Unit Resources. Answers and DOK levels are also available.

Concept Vocabulary

If students struggle to see the connection

among the words, **then** suggest that they revisit the poem to see how they are used in context.

Word Study

If students struggle to define words with Anglo-Saxon word origins, have them use online sources. For Reteach and Practice, see **Word Study: Anglo-Saxon Word Origins (RP)**. 📄

Analyze Craft and Structure

Sound Devices Most **sound devices** are groupings of words that share certain sounds. They are sometimes called "musical devices," because they highlight the musical qualities of language. Rhyme is a sound device with which you are probably familiar. There are other types of sound devices that may be less obvious than rhyme but are no less important.

- **Onomatopoeia** is the use of a word that sounds like what it means. *Hiss* and *buzz* are onomatopoeic words.
- **Alliteration** is the repetition of the same consonant sound at the beginnings of stressed syllables in words that are close together. Here, the repeated *f* sound is alliterative: *"the white foam flew"*
- **Consonance** is the repetition of final consonant sounds in stressed syllables with different vowel sounds. Here, the repeated *n* sound creates consonance: *"dawn goes down"*

Practice

CITE TEXTUAL EVIDENCE
to support your answers.

Work on your own to complete the chart. Identify the repeated sound or sounds in the underlined groups of words in each passage from the poem. Then, state what sound device each passage presents. (Note that some passages have more than one sound device.) Share and discuss your responses with your group and answer the questions that follow.

PASSAGE	REPEATED SOUND(S)	TYPE(S) OF SOUND DEVICE(S)
The jaws that bite, <u>the claws that catch!</u> (line 6)	*aws* in jaws, claws *k* in claws; catch	consonance alliteraton
The vorpal blade went <u>snicker-snack!</u> (line 18)	*sn* in snicker-snack *k* in snicker-snack	alliteration consonance onomatopoeia
<u>Come to my arms, my beamish boy!</u> (line 22)	*b* in beamish boy.	alliteration
O frabjous day! <u>Callooh! Callay!</u> (line 23)	*k* in Callouh, Callay *l* in Callouh, Callay	alliteration alliteration

🖥 Notebook

1. Lewis Carroll is famous for inventing words. Explain what real-life sounds each of these invented words suggests: (a) *whiffling*, (b) *burbled*, (c) *galumphing*.

2. How do you think Carroll's use of sound devices adds to the poem? For example, do the sound devices make the poem seem sillier, more imaginative, more lively, or something else? Explain your thinking.

© Pearson Education, Inc., or its affiliates. All rights reserved.

Jabberwocky **377**

Analyze Craft and Structure

Sound Devices Encourage groups to discuss why sound devices may be used more often in poetry than in prose. For more support, see **Analyze Craft and Structure: Sound Devices.** 🖥

See possible responses in the chart on the student page.

Possible responses:
1. (a) the sound of something swishing through the air, (b) the sound of water bubbling, (c) the sound of someone stepping heavily.

2. Student responses will vary. Some may say the devices make the poem sound more rhythmic and musical. Others may say the words add an element of humor and fun to the lines.

FORMATIVE ASSESSMENT

Analyze Craft and Structure

If students have trouble analyzing sound devices, **then** suggest that they read the lines from the poem aloud and listen for the auditory effect of each example. For Reteach and Practice, see **Analyze Craft and Structure: Sound Devices (RP).** 🖥

WriteNow Express and Reflect

Writing With Sound Devices The poem "Jabberwocky" uses several sound devices to create musical effects and to enhance the reader's understanding of the invented language. Have students write a paragraph or a poetic stanza in which they use several sound devices. Encourage students to include at least one example of each of the sound devices discussed in this lesson. Finally, have students share their writing with their group and discuss the effects of each other's chosen sound devices.

Author's Style

Invented Language Remind groups that when it comes to the invented language in "Jabberwocky," there are no definite right or wrong answers. Students may disagree with each other about the meanings of certain words. Encourage students to discuss their differing opinions respectfully and to back up their claims with evidence from their knowledge of standard English. For more support, see **Author's Style Invented Language.** 📄

Read It

Interpretations will vary depending on the stanza chosen. Make sure that students' definitions are logical and that they demonstrate an understanding of the grammar, syntax, and thematic context of the sentence in which each word appears.

Write It

Stanzas will vary, but make sure that they:
- include English filler words
- follow standard English grammar and syntax
- make some degree of sense

JABBERWOCKY

☰ STANDARDS

Reading Literature
Determine the meaning of words and phrases as they are used in a text, including figurative and connotative meanings; analyze the impact of a specific word choice on meaning and tone.

Language
• Demonstrate command of the conventions of standard English grammar and usage when writing or speaking.
   e. Recognize variations from standard English in their own and others' writing and speaking, and identify and use strategies to improve expression in conventional language.
• Determine or clarify the meaning of unknown and multiple-meaning words and phrases based on *grade 6 reading and content*, choosing flexibly from a range of strategies.
   a. Use context as a clue to the meaning of a word or phrase.
• Demonstrate understanding of figurative language, word relationships, and nuances in word meanings.
   b. Use the relationship between particular words to better understand each of the words.

Author's Style

Invented Language In "Jabberwocky," Lewis Carroll uses **invented language**, or words that he has made up, to entertain readers and to challenge their imaginations. For example, he invents words such as *brillig* and *vorpal*. He does not explain what these words are supposed to mean, and they cannot be found in a dictionary. Instead, readers use their imaginations to fill in their meanings.

As you read "Jabberwocky," look at the **syntax** of each sentence, or how all of the words are arranged. Notice that not all of the words are invented. Carroll mixes invented words with real words such as *and, the, did, were, my,* and *that.* The arrangement of these real words helps readers determine the parts of speech of the invented words. Readers can figure out whether each invented word is a noun, a verb, an adjective, or an adverb and then imagine what the word may mean.

Consider this passage from "Jabberwocky":

> . . . the *slithy* *toves*/ Did *gyre* and *gimble* in the *wabe*. . . . (lines 1–2)

Carroll invented the four underlined words. By looking at the arrangement of the real words, you can figure out the part of speech of each invented word. Then, you can infer, or guess, what each word might mean.

- *The* at the beginning of the clause shows that a noun will follow. *Toves* must be a plural noun.

- *Slithy* must be an adjective that describes the *toves. Slithy* looks like the real word *slither,* which means "move like a snake."

- *Did* shows that *gyre* and *gimble* must be verbs. *Gyre* sounds like the real word *gyrate,* which means "rotate" or "spin."

- *In* and *the* show that *wabe* must be a noun.

Bringing all of these ideas together, you can infer that a *tove* may be a snakelike creature that spins in circles. Imagine how that would look!

Read It

As a group, choose one stanza from "Jabberwocky." First, mark all of the invented language. Then, look at the real words that you know. Use the arrangement of the words to figure out the part of speech of each of the invented words. Finally, work together to infer a possible meaning for each invented word. Discuss what you imagine is happening.

Write It

📓 **Notebook** Use invented language to write a stanza about an imaginary animal. Invent your own nouns, verbs, adjectives, and adverbs. However, also use real words such as *the, a, he, she, it, were, did,* and *with.* Arrange all of the words in such a way that a reader can infer what the invented words may mean. When you have finished, trade stanzas with a group member, and try to decipher the meanings of each other's stanzas.

FORMATIVE ASSESSMENT

Author's Style

If students struggle to write a stanza in an invented language, **then** suggest that they write their stanza in standard English first and then replace some of the words with invented words. For Reteach and Practice, see **Author's Style Invented Language (RP).** 📄

© Pearson Education, Inc., or its affiliates. All rights reserved.

PERSONALIZE FOR LEARNING

English Language Support

Invented Language English learners are likely to require additional support when writing a stanza in an invented language. Suggest that pairs of students work together to write a stanza. They can begin by making decisions about their invented animal: *What is the animal called? What does it look like? What does it eat? Is it mean or nice? Where does it live and what does it do?*

Then, they should write their stanza in standard English. Next, instruct students to circle all the nouns, adjectives, action verbs, and adverbs in their stanza: these are the words that might be more easy to replace with invented words. As students replace these words with invented words, encourage them to

create words that resemble English words of the same part of speech. Suggest that students consider incorporating other languages into their stanzas; they might combine an English word with a word from another language to create a new word.
ALL LEVELS

Speaking and Listening

Assignment

Work with your group to create and deliver an oral presentation based on the poem "Jabberwocky." Choose from the following options:

- Prepare and present a **dramatic poetry reading** of "Jabberwocky" in which you read aloud the poem with expression while acting it out so that your audience can picture and feel what is happening in the poem. Use costumes and props to enhance your performance.

- Create a **multimedia presentation** of "Jabberwocky" in which you illustrate the poem through graphics, images, artwork, music, and other multimedia displays.

Project Plan As a group, review the poem and determine what types of props, costumes, or multimedia to use in your presentation. Then, make a list of the tasks you will need to accomplish in order to complete your presentation, and assign tasks to each group member. For example, one group member could be responsible for multimedia research or costume and prop design.

TASK	GROUP MEMBER

Practice Decide which group members will be responsible for reading or narrating the different parts of the poem during your presentation. Practice delivering your presentation as a group. Use these guidelines to improve your presentation techniques:

- vary the volume, pitch, and tone of your voice to express emotion
- use appropriate pacing, speaking quickly when needed to convey excitement or suspense
- to keep listeners engaged, make eye contact with your audience regularly

Listen and Evaluate As you listen to other groups' presentations, jot down any questions you have and note interesting elements of each presentation. Wait until each group has finished their presentation before asking your questions or offering your comments.

© Pearson Education, Inc., or its affiliates. All rights reserved.

EVIDENCE LOG

Before moving on to a new selection, go to your Evidence Log, and record what you learned from "Jabberwocky."

STANDARDS
Speaking and Listening
- Engage effectively in a range of collaborative discussions with diverse partners on *grade 6 topics, texts, and issues,* building on others' ideas and expressing their own clearly.
  a. Come to discussions prepared, having read or studied required material; explicitly draw on that preparation by referring to evidence on the topic, text, or issue to probe and reflect on ideas under discussion.
  b. Follow rules for collegial discussions, set specific goals and deadlines, and define individual roles as needed.
- Present claims and findings, sequencing ideas logically and using pertinent descriptions, facts, and details to accentuate main ideas or themes; use appropriate eye contact, adequate volume, and clear pronunciation.
- Include multimedia components and visual displays in presentations to clarify information.

Jabberwocky **379**

Speaking and Listening

If groups have trouble deciding which option to choose, encourage them to consider which option plays to their group's strengths the most. If some of the group members are aspiring actors, then the dramatic poetry reading is likely to be the best choice. If the group excels at visual art, film, or technology, creating a multimedia presentation might be a better choice.

Project Plan Remind groups to consult the schedule for Small-Group activities as they create their Project Plan. Check to make sure each group has made assignments and that the work is divided evenly among group members.

Practice Suggest that one member of each group video records the group's rehearsal. Students can then watch the recording together and use it to refine their presentation techniques. For more support, see **Speaking and Listening: Dramatic Reading, Multimedia Presentation.**

Evidence Log Support students in completing their Evidence Log. This paced activity will help prepare them for the Performance-Based Assessment at the end of the unit.

FORMATIVE ASSESSMENT
Speaking and Listening

If groups struggle to assign responsibilities, **then** remind them to take into account each member's skills and interests.

For Reteach and Practice, see **Speaking and Listening: Dramatic Reading, Multimedia Presentation (RP).**

Selection Test

Administer the "Jabberwocky" Selection Test, which is available in both print and digital formats online in Assessments.

PERSONALIZE FOR LEARNING

English Language Support
Dramatic Poetry Reading and Multimedia Presentation Ask students to work in pairs to think of a poem they like and how they would dramatize it using visual displays. **EMERGING**

Ask students to summarize a poem they would like to represent. Ask them to list the media they would use, and why they would use them. **EXPANDING**

Ask students to summarize a narrative poem they have read, and describe what kind of media they would use to represent the setting and characters at different stages of the story. **BRIDGING**

An expanded **English Language Support Lesson** on Dramatic Poetry Reading and Multimedia Presentation is available in the Interactive Teacher's Edition.

The Importance of Imagination

🔊 **AUDIO SUMMARIES**
Audio summaries of "The Importance of Imagination" are available online in both English and Spanish in the Interactive Teacher's Edition or Unit Resources. Assigning these summaries prior to reading the selection may help students build additional background knowledge and set a context for their first read.

Summary

In this reflective essay, "The Importance of Imagination," Esha Chhabra describes how imagination changes as you grow older. She says that when you are young, it comes naturally, and that as you get older, your imagination has to fit within certain constraints, and you have less spare time to think. Luckily for Chhabra, her parents indulged her interest in making art and encouraged her to draw more. Chhabra argues that imagination is important in the real world. We use our imagination to solve problems and encourage creativity.

Insight

It's easy to think that imagination is only important for those people with careers as writers and artists, and that it it is of less use to those with "serious" careers, but this is wrong; solving problems in any field is about coming up with novel ideas.

ESSENTIAL QUESTION:
Where can imagination lead?

Connection to Essential Question

Chhabra gives examples of how the imagination can provide tangible benefits in some very important jobs.

SMALL-GROUP LEARNING PERFORMANCE TASK
When Alice finally gets through the door . . .

UNIT PERFORMANCE-BASED ASSESSMENT
What might happen if a fictional character were to come into the real world?

Connection to Performance Tasks

Small-Group Learning Performance Task This selection emphasizes the importance of imagination and creativity. Students must use their imagination to build upon the details about Alice and her adventures once she gets through the door.

Unit Performance-Based Assessment This selection provides background about the power of imagination to complete a host of tasks. This perspective might help students as they prepare to respond to the prompt.

LESSON RESOURCES

	Making Meaning	Language Development	Effective Expression
Lesson	**First Read** **Close Read** **Analyze the Text** **Analyze Craft and Structure**	**Concept Vocabulary** **Word Study** **Conventions**	**Writing to Sources**
Instructional Standards	**RI.1** Cite textual evidence . . . **RI.2** Determine a central idea of a text . . . **RI.3** Analyze in detail how a key individual, event, or idea . . . **RI.10** By the end of the year, read and comprehend literary nonfiction . . . **L.4** Determine or clarify the meaning of unknown and multiple-meaning words and phrases . . . **L.4.a** Use context as a clue . . .	**L.1** Demonstrate command of the conventions . . . **L.1.c** Recognize and correct inappropriate shifts . . . **L.1.d** Recognize and correct vague pronouns . . . **L.4** Determine or clarify the meaning of unknown and multiple-meaning words and phrases . . . **L.4.b** Use common, grade-appropriate Greek or Latin affixes and roots . . .	**W.2** Write informative/explanatory texts . . . **W.2.a** Introduce a topic; organize ideas . . . **W.2.b** Develop the topic with relevant facts . . . **W.2.c** Use appropriate transitions to clarify . . . **W.5** With some guidance and support from peers and adults, develop and strengthen writing . . .

⯈ STUDENT RESOURCES

Available online in the Interactive Student Edition or Unit Resources	Selection Audio First-Read Guide: Nonfiction Close-Read Guide: Nonfiction	Word Network	Evidence Log

⯈ TEACHER RESOURCES

Selection Resources Available online in the Interactive Teacher's Edition or Unit Resources	Audio Summaries Annotation Highlights EL Highlights The Importance of Imagination: Text Questions Analyze Craft and Structure: Author's Influences English Language Support Lesson: Author's Influences	Concept Vocabulary and Word Study Conventions: Pronoun-Antecedent Agreement	Writing to Sources: Essay
Reteach/Practice (RP) Available online in the Interactive Teacher's Edition or Unit Resources	Analyze Craft and Structure: Author's Influences (RP)	Word Study: Greek Prefix: *para-* (RP) Conventions: Pronoun-Antecedent Agreement (RP)	Writing to Sources: Essay (RP)
Assessment Available online in Assessments	Selection Test		
My Resources	A Unit 4 Answer Key is available online and in the Interactive Teacher's Edition.		

Reading Support

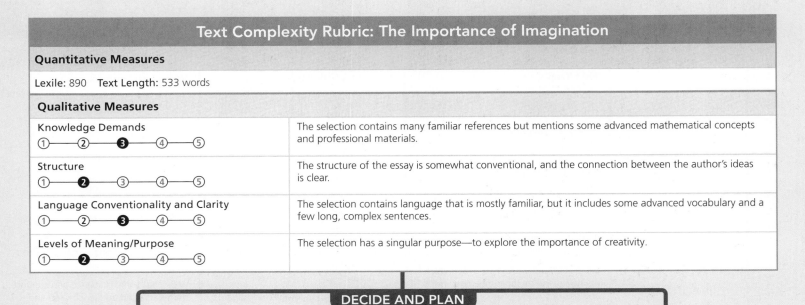

Text Complexity Rubric: The Importance of Imagination

Quantitative Measures

Lexile: 890   Text Length: 533 words

Qualitative Measures

Knowledge Demands ①—②—**❸**—④—⑤	The selection contains many familiar references but mentions some advanced mathematical concepts and professional materials.
Structure ①—**❷**—③—④—⑤	The structure of the essay is somewhat conventional, and the connection between the author's ideas is clear.
Language Conventionality and Clarity ①—②—**❸**—④—⑤	The selection contains language that is mostly familiar, but it includes some advanced vocabulary and a few long, complex sentences.
Levels of Meaning/Purpose ①—**❷**—③—④—⑤	The selection has a singular purpose—to explore the importance of creativity.

DECIDE AND PLAN

English Language Support

Provide English learners with support for knowledge demands and language as they read the selection.

Knowledge Demands Have students read the background information before reading the article. Ask them to summarize it so that you can check comprehension.

Language Help students understand longer complex sentences by rewriting them into multiple simple sentences. Have students read the shorter sentences and discuss their meanings as a class.

Strategic Support

Provide students with strategic support to ensure that they can successfully read the text.

Structure Point out the author's use of questions in the selection. Use the questions in paragraphs 1 and 7 as examples. Discuss how the author uses this device to transition from one idea to another.

Meaning For students who have difficulty understanding some of the advanced vocabulary, have them underline or list the words and phrases they don't understand. Then have them work with a partner to discuss the context in which these words and phrases appear.

Challenge

Provide students who need to be challenged with ideas for how they can go beyond a simple interpretation of the text.

Text Analysis After reading, have students discuss the author's ideas. Ask them to consider how creativity plays a role in their own lives. Have them comment on whether they might look at some of their school subjects in a new, imaginative way.

Written Response Ask students to use the Internet to research ways to promote creativity. Have them write a few paragraphs about how they can apply these ideas to their own lives.

TEACH

Read and Respond

Have groups read the selection and complete the Making Meaning, Language Development, and Effective Expression activities.

Standards Support Through Teaching and Learning Cycle

IDENTIFY NEEDS

Analyze results of the Beginning-of-Year Assessment, focusing on the items relating to Unit 4. Also take into consideration student performance to this point and your observations of where particular students struggle.

ANALYZE AND REVISE

- Analyze student work for evidence of student learning.
- Identify whether or not students have met the expectations in the standards.
- Identify implications for future instruction.

TEACH

Implement the planned lesson, and gather evidence of student learning.

DECIDE AND PLAN

- If students have performed poorly on items matching these standards, then provide selection scaffolds before assigning them the on-level lesson provided in the Student Edition.
- If students have done well on the Beginning-of-Year Assessment, then challenge them to keep progressing and learning by giving them opportunities to practice the skills in depth.
- Use the Selection Resources listed on the Planning pages for "The Importance of Imagination" to help students continually improve their ability to master the standards.

Instructional Standards: The Importance of Imagination

	Catching Up	This Year	Looking Forward
Reading	You may wish to administer the **Analyze Craft and Structure: Author's Influences (RP)** worksheet to help students determine the factors that influence an author's writing.	**RI.2** Determine a central idea of a text and how it is conveyed through particular details; provide a summary of the text distinct from personal opinions or judgments.	Have students research what influenced the writing of authors they are familiar with.
Writing	You may wish to administer the **Writing to Sources: Essay (RP)** worksheet to prepare students for their essays.	**W.2.a** Introduce a topic; organize ideas, concepts, and information, using strategies such as definition, classification, comparison/contrast, and cause/effect; include formatting, graphics, and multimedia when useful to aiding comprehension.	Challenge students to write their essays in narrative form.
Language	You may wish to administer the **Conventions: Pronoun-Antecedent Agreement (RP)** worksheet to help students understand agreement between pronouns and antecedents. You may wish to administer the **Word Study: Greek Prefix: *para-* (RP)** worksheet to help students understand the meaning and use of this prefix.	**L.1.c** Recognize and correct inappropriate shifts in pronoun number and person. **L.4.b** Use common, grade-appropriate Greek or Latin affixes and roots as clues to the meaning of a word.	Challenge students to draft a short narrative and then edit it to ensure pronoun-antecedent agreement. Have students identify words in the text that have other recognizable prefixes.

Jump Start

FIRST READ At what age do people stop being creative and imaginative? Do you know anyone who has continued to be imaginative long after childhood? In what ways does this person show imagination? Engage groups in a discussion about imaginative adults and and how imagination can influence others.

The Importance of Imagination 🔊 📄

What makes one person more imaginative than another? How does our society encourage or discourage imaginative thinking among adults? Modeling questions such as these will help students connect to "The Importance of Imagination" to the Small-Group Performance Task assignment. Selection audio and print capability for the selection are available in the Interactive Teacher's Edition.

Concept Vocabulary

Ask groups to look carefully at the context clues in the sentences to find the meaning of an unfamiliar word. Remind groups to look for examples in which the surrounding context restates the word or compares and contrasts its definition. Once students infer the preliminary meaning of the word, they can verify its definition by rereading the word in context or by checking in a dictionary.

● FIRST READ

Have students perform the steps of the first read independently:

NOTICE: You may want to encourage students to notice the comparison and contrast between examples of imaginative thought and action and those that are considered unimaginative.

ANNOTATE: Remind students to mark passages that support the main idea of the selection or a given paragraph.

CONNECT: Encourage students to begin comparing the ideas about imagination expressed in this essay to other selections and poems.

RESPOND: Students will answer questions and write a summary to demonstrate understanding.

Point out to students that while they will always complete the Respond step at the end of the first read, the other steps will probably happen somewhat concurrently. You may wish to print copies of the **First-Read Guide: Nonfiction** for students to use. 📄

MAKING MEANING

About the Author
Esha Chhabra (b. 1991) is a journalist who has written for *the New York Times, the San Francisco Chronicle,* and *the Guardian*. Chhabra is a graduate of Georgetown University and studied global politics at the London School of Economics.

☰ STANDARDS
Reading Informational Text
By the end of the year, read and comprehend literary nonfiction in the grades 6–8 text complexity band proficiently, with scaffolding as needed at the high end of the range.

Language
• Determine or clarify the meaning of unknown and multiple-meaning words and phrases based on *grade 6 reading and content*, choosing flexibly from a range of strategies.
  a. Use context as a clue to the meaning of a word or phrase.

The Importance of Imagination

Concept Vocabulary

As you perform your first read of "The Importance of Imagination," you will encounter these words.

template	parameters	model

Context Clues If these words are unfamiliar to you, try using **context clues**—other words and phrases that appear near the unfamiliar words—to help you determine their meanings. There are various types of context clues that may help you as you read. Here are two examples of how to use context clues to determine meaning.

> **Definition:** The palace was **magnificent**, grand in its size ad beauty.
>
> **Contrast of Ideas:** The winners of the race **glided** across the finish line, while the remaining competitors stumbled behind them.

Apply your knowledge of context clues and other vocabulary strategies to determine the meanings of unfamiliar words you encounter during your first read.

First Read NONFICTION

Apply these strategies as you conduct your first read. You will have an opportunity to complete a close read after your first read.

NOTICE the general ideas of the text. *What* is it about? *Who* is involved?

ANNOTATE by marking vocabulary and key passages you want to revisit.

CONNECT ideas within the selection to what you already know and what you have already read.

RESPOND by completing the Comprehension Check and by writing a brief summary of the selection.

© Pearson Education, Inc., or its affiliates. All rights reserved.

AUTHOR'S PERSPECTIVE   Kelly Gallagher, M.Ed.

Deep Reading *Deep reading* means taking the time to consider more than just what the text says by making inferences, seeing and thinking about information not literally on the page. Teachers can use the following techniques to model how to make inferences:

• Study Photographs: Have students study a photo and describe what might have happened in it. Discuss their responses, encouraging students to support their ideas.

• Complete a Say/Doesn't Say T-chart: Draw a T-chart on the board. On the left, have students write what the passage says (literal comprehension). On the right, have them record what the passage doesn't say. This helps students get at author's inference.

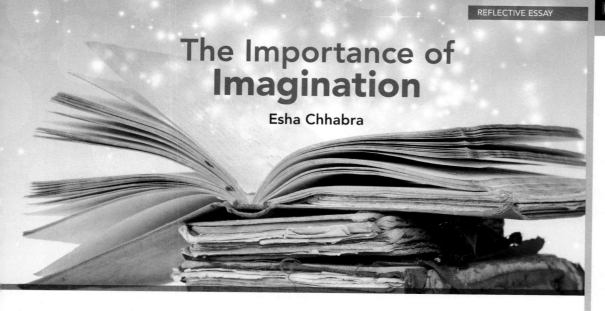

The Importance of Imagination

Esha Chhabra

Concept Vocabulary

PARAMETERS If groups are struggling to define the word *parameters* in paragraph 1, have them look for context clues. Point out the words *into* and *within* and words that describe size, such as "has to fit *into*," "*within* that little bubble."

Possible response: Based on the context clues, the word *parameters* means "boundaries, limits, or areas that control how something should be done."

TEMPLATE If groups are struggling to define the word *template* in paragraph 1, have them look for context clues. The paragraph shows the contrast between imagination and restrictions.

Possible response: Based on the context clues, the word *template* means "a document that helps writers develop text following a suggested pattern."

BACKGROUND

A curriculum vitae, or CV, is a short account of a person's background, skills, education, and work experience. In the United States, a CV is similar to a resume. Resumes are usually no longer than one page. Many employers require these documents for job applications and look at them carefully to decide who they should hire.

SCAN FOR MULTIMEDIA

1   While growing up, I'd never really considered how important it is to be imaginative. It's a childhood profession, you could say. It comes naturally. Then we hit an age when we're presented with a scantron[1] of bubble-in options, a **template** for a CV that we need to create, and Excel.[2] At that point, our learning has to fit into certain **parameters**: within that little bubble, within the one page limit, and within a tiny digital graph. So, what happens to our imagination?

2   It seems to fade.

3   Being Asian (as I am) doesn't help. The assumption that you're more apt for engineering or medicine is like a nagging tail. We have a so-called fondness for numbers apparently. If you're Asian, you must be good at math—of course.

4   Well, then I turned out to be an oddball. I developed an affinity for words and images instead. At the age of 12, my dream was to be a professional doodler, which could turn into a career as a cartoonist, if it went well. And my parents indulged me in that dream. Unlike others, who may have thought that was ridiculous,

---

NOTES

Mark context clues or indicate another strategy you used to help you determine meaning.

template (TEHM pliht) *n.*

MEANING:

parameters (puh RAM uh tuhrz) *n.*

MEANING:

---

1. **scantron** refers to a paper form used for multiple-choice tests.
2. **Excel** widely used computer program for creating spreadsheets and graphs.

Additional **English Language Support** is available in the Interactive Teacher's Edition.

© Pearson Education, Inc., or its affiliates. All rights reserved.

- Use a Positive-Negative Chart: Have students chart a character's good and bad behavior, positive and negative influence, or the highest and lowest point in a story. This technique is an excellent way to have students track specific literary elements in a novel or a play.

- Play Literary Dominoes: Start with the resolution of a narrative and have students work backwards, recording the events that led to it. This creates a chain of key events.

PERSONALIZE FOR LEARNING

English Language Support

Replacing Complex Words Some students may struggle with the meaning of the concept vocabulary or other unfamiliar words in complex nonfiction text. Encourage students to use their Word Network when reading complex text. Have students use context clues to determine the meaning of unfamiliar words. Encourage students to substitute familiar words for complex words when rereading the sentences to help them better comprehend the text. **ALL LEVELS**

Concept Vocabulary

MODEL If groups are struggling to define the word *model* in paragraph 10, point out that the writer is describing the work that economics buffs might do.

Possible response: Based on the context, *model* means "design, format, or plan." A business model is a plan that defines the way a business will run. It includes marketing, revenue, profit and product ideas.

NOTES

they got me drawing books. When my mother saw me sitting idle, or falling asleep among a pile of school books, she'd suggest, "Why don't you draw for a bit?" Over a decade later, little has changed. She still chuckles at my drawings, tells me to draw more often, and has preserved that notebook.

5 As I grew older, as the reading list of books grew longer, the assignments tougher, and jobs took up any spare time as a student in college, that ability to just sit down and pour your imagination onto a blank canvas began to disappear. Rather, that creative side had to reinvent itself.

6 My high school history teacher once told me that history is not a timeline; it's a story. She threw out the linearity of history. She made what was dry and ancient, charming, engaging, and at times, even humorous. That was her imagination at work. And it helped me develop a love for the social sciences. Our imaginations can be quite contagious, I learned.

7 But can this love for the imaginative ever find a place in the real world? Certainly.

8 Imagination creates not just fairy tales and children's books but a new vision for the way we conduct our lives. Imaginations challenge the norm, push boundaries, and help us progress.

9 We need to encourage more creativity. Forget the CV for a bit.

10 If we encourage that brilliant math student to be imaginative as well, he could use those algorithms[3] to innovate. If we encourage the biology student to be imaginative as well, she could design a new sustainable fuel source for us. If we encourage that economics buff to be imaginative as well, he could build a new people-friendly business **model**. The tools are there. You just need to reorient them towards the unexpected. That's where creativity—at home, in the classroom, and in the workplace—is so essential.

11 That's why, last week I found myself, sitting with my mom late at night, rereading Shel Silverstein's poems for children. Turns out, they're just as good for adults, maybe even better. ❧

Mark context clues or indicate another strategy you used to help you determine meaning.

model (MOD uhl) *n.*

MEANING:

---

3. **algorithms** (AL guh rihth uhmz) *n.* steps for solving a problem, usually related to math.

© Pearson Education, Inc., or its affiliates. All rights reserved.

(😊) FACILITATING SMALL-GROUP CLOSE READING

CLOSE READ: Reflective Essay As groups perform the close read, circulate and offer support as needed.

Remind groups to note that in a reflective essay, the author may:

- reflect on a specific event, a time period, or a person from his or her own life.
- use informal language that suits his or her thoughtful tone.
- include dialogue and description.

Encourage students to identify the characteristics that make "The Importance of Imagination" a reflective essay.

Challenge groups to find all the types of evidence the author uses (facts, statistics, anecdotes, quotations from authorities, or examples).

Comprehension Check

Complete the following items after you finish your first read. Review and clarify details with your group.

1. According to the author, what happens to our imagination when we grow up?

2. What was the author's dream at age 12?

3. What did the author's history teacher say about history?

4. 📓 **Notebook** Write a summary of "The Importance of Imagination" to confirm your understanding of the text.

- -

RESEARCH

Research to Clarify Choose at least one unfamiliar detail from the text. Briefly research that detail. In what way does the information you learned deepen your understanding of the essay? Share your findings with your group.

Research to Explore Choose something that interested you from the text, and formulate a research question that you might use to learn more about it.

Comprehension Check

Possible responses:

1. Our imaginations fade because we're presented with all kinds of forms and templates that our learning is expected to fit. We also do not have enough time to be imaginative because most of our time is taken up by daily routines, assignments, and jobs.
2. Her dream was to be a professional doodler, and if things went well, she would become a cartoonist.
3. The author's history teacher said that history was a story rather than a timeline.
4. Summaries will vary, but they should include the idea that imagination is beneficial for children, adults, and society as a whole—it leads to innovation and progress.

Research

Research to Clarify If groups struggle to narrow and choose one unfamiliar detail from the essay, encourage students to focus on the meaning and uses of templates.

Research to Explore If groups struggle to narrow and choose something of interest, encourage students to focus on new sustainable fuel sources.

PERSONALIZE FOR LEARNING

Challenge
Research Encourage interested students to research the innovations surrounding new sustainable fuel sources. What fuel sources are available today? How would adopting the sources influence our economy in the next ten years? What would the predicted impact be on the environment? What laws affect the research and adoption of new fuel sources? Have students create a chart or other diagram showing cause and effect and share their findings with a small group.

© Pearson Education, Inc., or its affiliates. All rights reserved.

Jump Start

CLOSE READ Ask groups to consider the following prompt: *In what ways are children's poems or stories as good or even better for adults?* As students discuss in their groups, ask them to consider the need for creativity and imagination in adult life.

Close Read the Text

If needed, model close reading by using the Annotation Highlights in the Interactive Teacher's Edition.

Remind students to use Accountable Talk in their discussions and to support one another as they complete the close read.

Analyze the Text

1. Possible response: I think the author means that, instead of using our imaginations in a more childlike way, adults need to shift their imaginations and creativity toward finding out-of-the-ordinary solutions for problems.

2. Quotes will vary by group. Remind students to explain why they chose the quote they present to the group members.

3. Responses will vary by group.

Concept Vocabulary

Why These Words? Possible response: All of these words have to do with limits. The author wants to encourage people to be creative and think outside of the expected limits.

Practice
Paragraphs will vary.

Word Network

Possible words: *imaginative, innovate, doodler, idle, creativity, vision*

Word Study

For more support, see **Concept Vocabulary and Word Study.** 📄

Possible responses:

paralegal: someone who works alongside a lawyer, offering administrative support.

paramedic: someone who works in place of doctor, offering emergency medical support.

paramilitary: someone who works alongside official military personnel, offering additional force.

MAKING MEANING

THE IMPORTANCE OF IMAGINATION

Close Read the Text

With your group, revisit sections of the text you marked during your first read. **Annotate** details that you notice. What **questions** do you have? What can you **conclude**?

Analyze the Text

CITE TEXTUAL EVIDENCE to support your answers.

Complete the activities.

1. **Review and Clarify** With your group, reread paragraph 10 of the selection. Discuss with your group what the author means when she writes, "The tools are there. You just need to reorient them towards the unexpected"?

2. **Present and Discuss** Now, work with your group to share passages from the selection that you found especially important. Discuss what you noticed in the selection, what questions you asked, and what conclusions you reached.

3. **Essential Question:** *Where can imagination lead?* What has this essay taught you about imagination? Discuss with your group.

🔧 WORD NETWORK

Add words related to imagination from the text to your Word Network.

≣ STANDARDS
Reading Informational Text
• Cite textual evidence to support analysis of what the text says explicitly as well as inferences drawn from the text.
• Determine a central idea of a text and how it is conveyed through particular details; provide a summary of the text distinct from personal opinions or judgments.
• Analyze in detail how a key individual, event, or idea is introduced, illustrated, and elaborated in a text.

Language
Determine or clarify the meaning of unknown and multiple-meaning words and phrases based on *grade 6 reading and content,* choosing flexibly from a range of strategies.
  b. Use common, grade-appropriate Greek or Latin affixes and roots as clues to the meaning of a word.

384 UNIT 4 • IMAGINATION

LANGUAGE DEVELOPMENT

Concept Vocabulary

| template | parameters | model |

Why These Words? The three concept vocabulary words from the text are related. With your group, determine what the words have in common. How do these word choices enhance the impact of the text?

Practice

📓 **Notebook** Confirm your understanding of these words from the text by using them in a paragraph. Be sure to include context clues that hint at each word's meaning.

Word Study

Greek Prefix: *para-* The Greek prefix *para-*, which means "beside" or "alongside," contributes to the meanings of many English words. For example, *parallel* lines are lines that run alongside each other. Use a dictionary to look up these words related to careers: *paralegal, paramedic, paramilitary.* Discuss with your group how the prefix *para-* contributes to the meaning of each word.

© Pearson Education, Inc., or its affiliates. All rights reserved.

FORMATIVE ASSESSMENT

Analyze the Text 📄

If students struggle to close read the text, **then** provide the **The Importance of Imagination: Text Questions** available online in the Interactive Teacher's Edition or Unit Resources. Answers and DOK levels are also available.

Concept Vocabulary

If students fail to see a connection among the words, **then** have them use each word in a sentence and think about the similarities in the sentences.

Word Study

If students struggle to define terms with the prefix *para-*, **then** share these other examples with them: *parallel, paranormal, paraphrase.* For Reteach and Practice, see **Word Study: Greek Prefix: *para-* (RP).** 📄

Analyze Craft and Structure

Author's Influences A **reflective essay,** such as "The Importance of Imagination," presents the author's thoughts, beliefs, and reflections on an idea or experience—in this case, the topic of imagination. The author's thoughts and beliefs about a topic are affected by the **author's influences,** or the factors that affect his or her writing. These influences may include historical factors, such as important or newsworthy events that happened during the author's lifetime. Authors are also influenced by cultural factors. Cultural factors may include:

- the places an author has lived
- the author's upbringing and education
- the way in which an author lives his or her life
- an author's personal experiences

An author's influences affect the issues he or she thinks are important. It is important to consider how an author's influences may have shaped the **central idea** about which he or she is writing. For example, an author may choose to focus on promoting environmental awareness because of a pollution problem in his or her own town.

As you read a reflective essay, use key details in the text to **make inferences,** or educated guesses, about the effect of the author's influences on the central ideas in his or her writing.

Practice

CITE TEXTUAL EVIDENCE to support your answers.

Use this chart to identify three of the author's influences, and explain how each influence affects the central idea of the essay. Share your responses with your group.

AUTHOR'S INFLUENCES	EFFECT ON CENTRAL IDEA
assumptions about the author's Asian heritage	helped the author realize it was okay to be herself and not worry about how she was viewed by others
the author's high school history teacher	helped the author develop a love of social sciences
the author's parents	helped the author to recognize the importance of imagination

© Pearson Education, Inc., or its affiliates. All rights reserved.

Analyze Craft and Structure

Author's Influences Discuss with groups how in this reflective essay the author explains that some of her assumptions are based on her heritage. Encourage students to find examples in which her actions contrast with the expectations that she felt were placed on her. Discuss how this influences her decisions and her writing. For more support, see **Analyze Craft and Structure: Author's Influences.**

See possible responses in the chart on the student page.

FORMATIVE ASSESSMENT
Analyze Craft and Structure

If the student struggles to identify the author's influences, **then** have them identify the anecdotes or supporting details and discuss what influenced each detail.

For Reteach and Practice, see **Analyze Craft and Structure: Author's Influences (RP).**

PERSONALIZE FOR LEARNING

English Language Support

Author's Influences Ask students to work in pairs to look for a passage in the selection where the author tells about her mother's impact on her vocation. **EMERGING**

Ask students to locate the passages where the author tells about the factors or people that had a positive impact on her vocation. **EXPANDING**

Ask students to summarize the reading by listing the factors or people that had an impact—either positive or negative—on the author's vocation. **BRIDGING**

An expanded **English Language Support Lesson** on Author's Influences is available in the Interactive Teacher's Edition.

Conventions

Pronoun-Antecedent Agreement Review with students the use of pronouns and antecedents. Encourage them to develop sentences that follow this pattern. Have other students tell whether the pronouns agree with the antecedents and whether they are clear. Have students correct the sentences where necessary.

Unclear: Mr. Smith asked Michael if he could leave. Clear: Mr. Smith asked Michael if Michael could leave. Clear: Mr. Smith asked Michael to leave.

For additional support, see **Conventions: Pronoun-Antecedent Agreement.** ⊜

Read It
Possible responses:
1. Mr. Cano gave his permission to look for a new summer job. (Agree)
2. After Olga finished doing homework, they took a walk alone. (Don't agree: *Olga* is singular, and *they* is plural.)
3. Select the books you want and put it in the box. (Don't agree: *books* is plural, and *it* is singular.)

Write It
Possible responses:
1. When the author was young, her parents encouraged her to be as creative as possible.
2. Imagination and creativity are not just about drawing and painting. They are also about progress and pushing boundaries.

FORMATIVE ASSESSMENT
Conventions

If students cannot identify the pronoun and antecedent, **then** have them identify all nouns in the sentence and ask them which word the pronoun is replacing. For Reteach and Practice, see **Conventions: Pronoun-Antecedent Agreement (RP).** ⊜

THE IMPORTANCE OF
IMAGINATION

Conventions

Pronoun-Antecedent Agreement A **pronoun** is a word takes the place of one or more nouns or other pronouns. The word that the pronoun refers to is called the **antecedent**. Follow these rules for pronoun-antecedent agreement.

PRONOUN-ANTECEDENT AGREEMENT	
Agreement in Number: A pronoun and its antecedent must agree in number (singular or plural).	**Singular:** Creativity is important because it leads to innovation. **Plural:** My stepparents said that they would pay for my art classes.
Agreement in Person: A pronoun and its antecedent must agree in person. Use a first-person pronoun with a first-person antecedent. Use a third-person pronoun with a third-person antecedent.	**First-Person:** I asked whether Li would show me how to draw. **Third-Person:** The skydivers know that they had to check their parachutes.
Clear Antecedent: Every pronoun must have a clear antecedent. Problems may arise if a pronoun has more than one possible antecedent.	**Unclear:** Juan told Frank that he was going to win the prize. **Clear:** Juan told Frank that Frank was going to win the prize.

To find and fix errors in your writing related to pronoun use, follow these steps: First, identify each pronoun/antecedent pair that you used. Second, make sure the pronoun refers to a specific antecedent. Third, decide whether the antecedent is singular or plural. Fourth, determine whether the antecedent is in the first, second, or third person. Finally, choose the pronoun that agrees with the antecedent in number and in person.

Read It

Identify the pronoun/antecedent pair in each sentence. Mark whether they agree. If they do not agree, identify the type of agreement error.

1. Mr. Cano gave his permission to look for a new summer job.

2. After Olga finished doing homework, they took a walk alone.

3. Select the books you want, and put it in the box.

Write It

📓 **Notebook** Rewrite the following sentences so that they demonstrate correct pronoun-antecedent agreement.

1. When the author was young, their parents encouraged her to be as creative as possible.

2. Imagination and creativity are not just about drawing and painting. It is also about making progress and pushing boundaries.

📋 STANDARDS
Language
Demonstrate command of the conventions of standard English grammar and usage when writing or speaking.
c. Recognize and correct inappropriate shifts in pronoun number and person.
d. Recognize and correct vague pronouns.

© Pearson Education, Inc., or its affiliates. All rights reserved.

PERSONALIZE FOR LEARNING

Challenge
Write a Poem The author of "The Importance of Imagination" references the poetry of Shel Silverstein. Encourage interested students to select a poem by Shel Silverstein as a model and write a poem with a similar pattern and theme. Do pronouns need to agree with antecedents in poems? Why or why not? Students may share their poem with groups and create a collection of class poems.

Writing to Sources

Assignment

Work individually to write an explanatory essay on one of the following topics:

☐ a **comparison-and-contrast essay** in which you compare your childhood experience with imagination with that of the author

☐ a **cause-and-effect essay** in which you explain the ways in which the author's influences caused her to develop her current views on imagination

Gather Text Evidence First, review the essay and note details that are relevant to your topic. The types of details you choose will depend on which assignment you chose:

- If you chose a comparison-and-contrast essay, note your reaction to details from the essay: Did you identify with what the author said? Or, did you feel that you couldn't relate to her experience? You may react differently to different details.

- If you chose a cause-and-effect essay, identify details that reveal what influenced the author and her views on imagination. Then, make a clear connection between each detail and her perspective.

Use this chart to record your notes.

TEXT DETAIL	WHAT IT REVEALS ABOUT MY TOPIC

Write Your Essay As you draft your essay, be sure to organize your ideas clearly. Using transitional words and phrases can help you connect your ideas in a logical way. For example, in a comparison-and-contrast essay, transitions, such as *similarly* and *however*, can highlight similarities and differences. In a cause-and-effect essay, you might include transitions, such as *since* and *therefore*, to show causes and effects.

Share and Revise After you finish drafting your essay, exchange essays with a group member. Provide feedback to your classmate by noting places in which his or her ideas are unclear or disconnected as well as any points that need more supporting details and examples. Remember to be polite and offer helpful suggestions when giving others feedback.

© Pearson Education, Inc., or its affiliates. All rights reserved.

The Importance of Imagination **387**

📝 EVIDENCE LOG

Before moving on to a new selection, go to your Evidence Log, and record what you learned from "The Importance of Imagination."

☰ STANDARDS

Writing

• Write informative/explanatory texts to examine a topic and convey ideas, concepts, and information through the selection, organization, and analysis of relevant content.

  a. Introduce a topic; organize ideas, concepts, and information, using strategies such as definition, classification, comparison/contrast, and cause/effect; include formatting, graphics, and multimedia when useful to aiding comprehension.

  b. Develop the topic with relevant facts, definitions, concrete details, quotations, or other information and examples.

  c. Use appropriate transitions to clarify the relationships among ideas and concepts.

• With some guidance and support from peers and adults, develop and strengthen writing as needed by planning, revising, editing, rewriting, or trying a new approach, focusing on how well purpose and audience have been addressed.

Writing to Sources

Explain to students that when they write to sources, they should focus on aspects of the text that allow them to say something meaningful. For example, they may want to focus on a specific moment or anecdote to which they can relate.

One way that a writer can strengthen an essay is to cite evidence from the text. Then, the writer can illustrate how his or her position compares or relates to the example. For more support, see **Writing to Sources: Essay.** 📄

Gather Text Evidence You may wish to help students create an outline by having them note key ideas that were relevant to them.

Write Your Essay Guide students to highlight the transitional words that they use in their essays. Suggest that they use a variety of transitional words and that they show the correct connection or transition. Encourage students to use charts or graphs, if appropriate, to support their essay and aid in comprehension.

Evidence Log Support students in completing their Evidence Log. This paced activity will help prepare them for the Performance-Based Assessment at the end of the unit.

FORMATIVE ASSESSMENT

Writing to Sources

If students struggle to choose which type of essay to write, **then** have them consider their own life experiences. If their experiences are similar to the author's, encourage them to write a comparison-and-contrast essay. Otherwise, encourage them to write a cause-and-effect essay. For Reteach and Practice, see **Writing to Sources: Essay (RP).** 📄

Selection Test

Administer the "The Importance of Imagination" Selection Test, which is available in both print and digital formats online in Assessments. 📄 ☑

PERSONALIZE FOR LEARNING

Strategic Support

Writing to Sources Students may struggle when identifying examples from the text to support their essays. Encourage them to use a different type of graphic organizer if it will better suit their learning style and the content. Share these options:

- Students may select a Venn diagram to begin organizing their comparison-and-contrast essay. Remind students to write differences (contrasts) in the outer circles and similarities (comparisons) in the space where the circles overlap.

- Students may select a fishbone chart for their cause-and-effect essay to organize multiple causes leading to one effect.

Small-Group Learning **387**

Perform a Fictional Narrative

Before groups begin work on their projects, have them clearly differentiate the role each group member will play. Remind groups to consult the schedule for Small-Group Learning to guide their work during the Performance Task.

Students should complete the assignment using presentation software to take advantage of text, graphics, and sound features.

Plan With Your Group

Develop Your Ideas Remind groups that authors use both direct and indirect characterization.

- Direct characterization is when an author directly states that a character has a certain trait.

- Indirect characterization is how authors develop characters through dialogue, actions, thoughts, and how other characters interact with them. Remind groups to think about how Carroll uses indirect characterization to develop Alice and the Jabberwock: What can students infer, or make a logical guess, about the characters from the details provided?

Draft Your Narrative Encourage groups to draw a rough sketch showing how they imagine the characters and the setting of "Jabberwocky" to look. This will help them synthesize their ideas and get a better sense of what types of media, costumes, and props to use.

SOURCES

- *from* ALICE'S ADVENTURES IN WONDERLAND

- JABBERWOCKY

- THE IMPORTANCE OF IMAGINATION

☰ STANDARDS

Writing
Write narratives to develop real or imagined experiences or events using effective technique, relevant descriptive details, and well-structured event sequences.
 a. Engage and orient the reader by establishing a context and introducing a narrator and/or characters; organize an event sequence that unfolds naturally and logically.
 b. Use narrative techniques, such as dialogue, pacing, and description, to develop experiences, events, and/or characters.
 d. Use precise words and phrases, relevant descriptive details, and sensory language to convey experiences and events.

Perform a Fictional Narrative

Assignment
At the end of the except from *Alice's Adventures in Wonderland,* Alice can see Wonderland through a tiny door, but cannot figure out how to fit through it. Work with your group to write and perform a **fictional narrative** in which you tell a story about where Alice goes and what happens when she gets through the door. Use this story starter to begin your narrative:

> When Alice finally gets through the tiny door…

In your performance, use costumes, props, and music to help the audience picture the characters, setting, and events in your narrative.

Plan With Your Group

Develop Your Ideas As a group, brainstorm for ideas about how to complete the story starter. As you discuss ideas with your group, allow all members to offer suggestions. You may develop a completely new story for Alice, or you may draw on parts of Lewis Carroll's story. For example, you may choose to use the setting of Wonderland, but change the characters Alice encounters and the adventures she has there. Alternatively, you could imagine a new setting for the adventures of Alice and the White Rabbit. Use the questions in the chart to guide you in this process. As you record your ideas, note words and phrases that will help you to vividly describe the setting, characters, and Alice's thoughts and feelings.

QUESTION	NOTES
How does Alice finally get through the door? What does she find when she gets there? Who does she meet?	
What happens to Alice? What adventure does she have? What challenges does she face?	
How does Alice feel? What does she want? How will she get home?	

Draft Your Narrative Once you have decided how to tell your story, use the notes from your chart to draft your fictional narrative Your written narrative will be the basis for your performance. Use narrative techniques, such as description and dialogue, to develop your characters' personalities. Include sensory details to paint an engaging picture of the setting.

© Pearson Education, Inc., or its affiliates. All rights reserved.

AUTHOR'S PERSPECTIVE **Ernest Morrell, Ph.D.**

Active Classroom Listening Teachers can help students participate in class more effectively by discussing how to ask critical questions in classroom conversations. Teachers can guide students to determine which questions are most important and will yield good answers by modeling questions that synthesizing multiple viewpoints and tap critical thinking skills. Here are some samples to use:

- What are the implications of . . . ?
- What is the difference between . . . and . . . ?
- What is the counterargument for . . . ?
- What are the strengths and weakness of . . . ?
- What is another way to look at . . . ?

Remind students to avoid yes/no questions because they cut off discussion. Teachers

can also teach students to use *critical listening*—weighing what has been said to decide if they agree with it or not. Critical listening can help students identify the salient parts of each question and integrate these parts to formulate an idea or an opinion.

Plan Your Performance Use your written narrative to plan your performance. Decide which group members will assume the roles of characters and which members will narrate the performance. Then, decide how to best use costumes, props, and music to make your narrative come to life.

Rehearse With Your Group

Practice With Your Group Practice delivering your performance with your group. Use your voice, expressions, and gestures to portray the characters and events in your narrative in an engaging way. Remember to make eye contact with your audience at appropriate intervals. Use the checklist to evaluate your first rehearsal of the performance. Then, use your evaluation and these instructions to guide your revision.

CONTENT	USE OF MEDIA	PRESENTATION TECHNIQUES
☐ The narrative responds to the prompt in a creative way.	☐ The performance includes costumes, props, and music that help the audience picture the setting and the characters.	☐ Speakers make eye contact with the audience at appropriate points in the performance.
☐ The narrative develops the characters using dialogue and description.		☐ Speakers adjust their voices and use gestures and expressions to portray characters and events in an engaging way.
☐ The narrative uses sensory details to create a vivid setting.		

Fine-Tune the Content Sometimes it is hard to describe a setting to an audience in a way that makes it seem real. If the way in which you picture the setting doesn't come through in your performance, add more sensory details to the narrated portion to ensure your audience can visualize the scene.

Brush Up on Your Presentation Techniques Performers should use voices that are expressive, and contribute to developing the characters' personalities or the setting and mood of the scene. Discuss how the characters should sound at different points in your performance. For example, when should Alice sound soft and sweet? When should she sound loud and angry? Also, consider the ways in which the narrators can adjust the tone of their voices to help convey details about the setting and mood. For example, if it the setting is a dark, threatening forest, the narrator may want to speak with a low, worried tone that conveys a sense of danger.

Present and Evaluate

Perform your group's narrative for the class. As you watch other groups perform, note differences in the ways in which you responded to the prompt. Evaluate how well other groups' presentations meet the checklist requirements.

© Pearson Education, Inc., or its affiliates. All rights reserved.

⊟ STANDARDS

Speaking and Listening
• Engage effectively in a range of collaborative discussions with diverse partners on *grade 6 topics, texts, and issues,* building on others' ideas and expressing their own clearly.
  b. Follow rules for collegial discussions, set specific goals and deadlines, and define individual roles as needed.

• Present claims and findings, sequencing ideas logically and using pertinent descriptions, facts, and details to accentuate main ideas or themes; use appropriate eye contact, adequate volume, and clear pronunciation.
• Include multimedia components and visual displays in presentations to clarify information.

Performance Task: Present a Fictional Narrative **389**

Rehearse With Your Group

Practice With Your Group Encourage performers to memorize their lines. Explain that the performance will be much more engaging if the actors are not reading from a sheet of paper. Actors will also need to be very familiar with the other performers' lines so that they know when to start speaking.

MAKE IT INTERACTIVE
Suggest that groups video record their rehearsal and then watch it together as a strategy for refining their performance.

Brush Up on Your Presentation Techniques Suggest that one group member stands at the back of the room while the performers rehearse. This student can let the performers know if they are speaking loudly enough for the whole audience to hear.

Before beginning the presentations, set the expectations for the audience. You may wish to have students consider these questions as groups present.

• How does the dialogue demonstrate an understanding of the characters?

• Which multimedia components, costumes, or props best fit the content of the narrative?

• What presentation skills did this group excel at?

As students provide feedback to the presenting group, remind them to do so respectfully and to provide praise as well as constructive criticism.

Strategic Support

Writing a Script Some groups may require additional support to write a script. Show students an example of a script for a play or movie. Ask students to identify the different elements that they see on the page (for example, the names of the characters, the dialogue, and the stage directions). Encourage students to try to write dialogue that is believable.

Suggest that students read their dialogue aloud as they are writing it to make sure that it sounds like something that the characters would actually say. Finally, remind students to include stage directions in their scripts, including any props the characters are holding, where the characters are standing, and any movements they may make.

INDEPENDENT LEARNING

Where can imagination lead?

Encourage students to think carefully about what they have already learned and what more they want to know about the unit topic of imagination. This is a key first step to previewing and selecting the text or media they will read or review in Independent Learning.

Independent Learning Strategies ▶

Review the Learning Strategies with students and explain that as they work through Independent Learning they will develop strategies to work on their own.

- Have students watch the video on Independent Learning Strategies.
- A video on this topic is available online in the Professional Development Center.

Students should include any favorite strategies that they might have devised on their own during Whole-Class and Small-Group Learning. For example, for the strategy "Create a schedule," students might include the following:

- Set intermediate deadlines as well as a final deadline.
- Review the schedule frequently to confirm that you are on track. Change intermediate deadlines if you miss them, but keep the final deadline constant.

Block Scheduling

Each day in this Pacing Plan represents a 40–50 minute class period. Teachers using block scheduling may combine days to reflect their class schedule. In addition, teachers may revise pacing to differentiate and support core instruction by integrating components and resources as students require.

📅 **Pacing Plan**

ESSENTIAL QUESTION:

Where can imagination lead?

Sometimes imaginary characters and their adventures in fantastical worlds can teach you about the real world and about yourself. In this section, you complete your study of imagination by exploring an additional selection related to the topic. You'll then share what you learn with classmates. To choose a text, follow these steps.

Look Back Think about the selections you have already studied. What more do you want to know about the topic of imagination?

Look Ahead Preview the texts by reading the descriptions. Which one seems most interesting and appealing to you?

Look Inside Take a few minutes to scan through the text you chose. Choose a different one if this text doesn't meet your needs.

Independent Learning Strategies

Throughout your life, in school, in your community, and in your career, you will need to rely on yourself to learn and work on your own. Review these strategies and the actions you can take to practice them during Independent Learning. Add ideas of your own for each category.

STRATEGY	ACTION PLAN
Create a schedule	• Understand your goals and deadlines. • Make a plan for what to do each day. •
Practice what you have learned	• Use first-read and close-read strategies to deepen your understanding. • After you read, evaluate the usefulness of the evidence to help you understand the topic. • Consider the quality and reliability of the source. •
Take notes	• Record important ideas and information. • Review your notes before preparing to share with a group. •

© Pearson Education, Inc., or its affiliates. All rights reserved.

SCAN FOR MULTIMEDIA

Unit Introduction

Introduce Whole-Class Learning

The Phantom Tollbooth, Act I

The Phantom Tollbooth, Act II

Media: *from The Phantom Tollbooth*

Performance Task

| 1 |
 2 | 3 | 4 | 5 | 6 | 7 | 8 | 9 | 10 | 11 | 12 | 13 | 14 | 15 | 16 | 17 | 18 |

Choose one selection. Selections are available online only.

CONTENTS

NOVEL EXCERPT

from The Wonderful Wizard of Oz
L. Frank Baum

A tornado may be just what you need to get carried away by your imagination.

POETRY COLLECTION

Our Wreath of Rose Buds
Corrinne

Imagination grows in the garden of one's mind.

Fantasy
Gwendolyn Bennett

Sometimes the darkness of the night is all you need to set your imagination free.

NOVEL EXCERPT

The Shah of Blah
from Haroun and the Sea of Stories
Salman Rushdie

Are stories that aren't true really worth telling?

SHORT STORY

Prince Francis
Roddy Doyle

Is Francis a real prince, or is he only a prince in his imagination?

PERFORMANCE-BASED ASSESSMENT PREP

Review Evidence for a Fictional Narrative
Complete your Evidence Log for the unit by evaluating what you have learned and synthesizing the information you have recorded.

 SCAN FOR MULTIMEDIA

© Pearson Education, Inc., or its affiliates. All rights reserved.

Contents

Selections Encourage students to scan and preview the selections before choosing the one they would like to read or review. Suggest that they consider the genre and subject matter of each one before making their decision. You can use the information on the following Planning pages to advise students in making their choice.

> Remind students that the selections for Independent Learning are only available in the Interactive Student Edition and Unit Resources. Allow students who do not have digital access at home to preview the selections or review the media selection(s) using classroom or computer lab technology. Then either have students print the selection they choose or provide a printout for them.

Performance-Based Assessment Prep
Review Evidence for a Fictional Narrative Point out to students that collecting evidence during Independent Learning is the last step in completing their Evidence Log. After they finish their independent reading, they will synthesize all the evidence they have compiled in the unit.

The evidence students collect will serve as the primary source of information they will use to complete the writing and oral presentation for the Performance-Based Assessment at the end of the unit.

Introduce
Small-Group
Learning

from Alice's Adventures in Wonderland

Jabberwocky

The Importance of Imagination

Performance Task

Introduce Independent Learning

Independent Learning

Performance-Based Assessment

| 19 | 20 | 21 | 22 | 23 | 24 | 25 | 26 | 27 | 28 | 29 | 30 | 31 | 32 | 33 | 34 | 35 | 36 |

INDEPENDENT LEARNING

Independent Learning **391**

from The Wonderful Wizard of Oz

SELECTION RESOURCES

📄 First-Read Guide: Fiction

📄 Close-Read Guide: Fiction

📄 *from* The Wonderful Wizard of Oz: Text Questions

🔊 Audio Summaries

🔊 Selection Audio

☑️📄 Selection Test

Summary

This selection is an excerpt from *The Wonderful Wizard of Oz,* a novel by L. Frank Baum. An orphan girl named Dorothy lives with her aunt and uncle in Kansas, in a small house out on the prairie. The whole prairie seems gray. There is nothing else in sight out to the horizon, nothing but sun-dried grass. Her aunt and uncle are joyless, and the only color in Dorothy's life comes from her dog, Toto. One day, a cyclone begins. Dorothy's aunt and uncle successfully take refuge in a shelter under the house, but before Dorothy can get down, the entire house is swept up into the air.

Insight

This selection focuses on how bland surroundings can dull the imagination. However, the last lines of the excerpt suggest that something very imaginative is about to begin.

Connection to Essential Question

The Essential Question is "Where can imagination lead?" Imagination and play keep Dorothy happy despite her surroundings. In the full novel, her imagination teaches her many important life lessons. Students who are familiar with the story might be surprised by the novel's gray start and its contrast with the Emerald City.

Connection to Performance-Based Assessment

The prompt is "What might happen if a fictional character were to come into the real world?" The story serves as a model for a character leaving her familiar reality behind and journeying to a new, unfamiliar place.

Text Complexity Rubric: *from* The Wonderful Wizard of Oz

Quantitative Measures

Lexile: 1030   Text Length: 24 lines; 15 lines

Qualitative Measures

Knowledge Demands ①—②—**❸**—④—⑤	The selection describes a rural existence in Kansas at the turn of the century. Some references may be unfamiliar to students.
Structure ①—②—**❸**—④—⑤	The narrative proceeds in a linear fashion with some mentions of past events.
Language Conventionality and Clarity ①—②—**❸**—④—⑤	The vocabulary of the selection is mostly explicit and on-grade level, with some above-level exceptions. Contains simple and complex sentence structures.
Levels of Meaning/Purpose ①—**❷**—③—④—⑤	The selection contains one level of meaning. Details within it are comprehensible in context. However, the last lines require interpretation.

Our Wreath of Rose Buds • Fantasy

SELECTION RESOURCES

📄 First-Read Guide: Poetry

📄 Close-Read Guide: Poetry

📄 Our Wreath of Rose Buds • Fantasy: Text Questions

🔊 Audio Summaries

🔊 Selection Audio

☑ 📄 Selection Test

Summary

"Our Wreath of Rose Buds" is a poem by a Native American woman named Corrinne. The speaker offers the reader a wreath of flowers, one that can remain eternally, grown from "the garden of the mind." They are not found outside but in internal landscapes where thoughts flow like rivers.

"Fantasy" is a poem by Gwendolyn Bennett. The speaker describes a voyage to the Land of Night. There she saw fantastic and colorful visions, including the person she addresses the poem to as queen of that land. The Queen's hair is purple, the moonlight blue, and the plants yellow-green.

Insight

These poems emphasize the beauty of imagination. It can create entire inward worlds, wondrous and magical.

Connection to Essential Question

The Essential Question is "Where can imagination lead?" In both poems, imagination leads to landscapes of splendid beauty.

Connection to Performance-Based Assessment

The prompt is "What might happen if a fictional character were to come into the real world?" Both poems provide examples of the wonderful possibilities of introducing something new in a familiar setting.

Text Complexity Rubric: Our Wreath of Rose Buds • Fantasy

Quantitative Measures

Lexile: NP; NP   Text Length: 24 lines; 15 lines

Qualitative Measures

Knowledge Demands ①—②—**❸**—④—⑤	Poems explore the familiar themes of imagination and dreams.
Structure ①—**❷**—③—④—⑤	Poems respectively contain recognizable rhyme schemes.
Language Conventionality and Clarity ①—②—**❸**—④—⑤	Selections contain figurative language with some above-level vocabulary.
Levels of Meaning/Purpose ①—②—**❸**—④—⑤	The fairly simple concepts are explored in a sophisticated manner with the use of symbolism.

The Shah of Blah

Summary

"The Shah of Blah," from the children's book *Haroun and the Sea of Stories* by Salman Rushdie, concerns a storyteller who lives in a city with many unhappy people. The storyteller, Rashid, is greatly talented. He earns money by telling stories to crowds on behalf of politicians, stories he always makes up on the spot. However, he is rarely home, and does not notice that his family is drifting from him. His son is beginning to doubt the value of fiction, and his wife leaves him. After a devastating day of realization, Rashid suddenly finds himself unable to come up with stories any longer.

Insight

Imagination can be very valuable—but also fragile. When someone pays too little attention to reality, returning to it can shake him or her terribly.

SELECTION RESOURCES

- First-Read Guide: Fiction
- Close-Read Guide: Fiction
- The Shah of Blah: Text Questions
- Audio Summaries
- Selection Audio
- Selection Test

Connection to Essential Question

The Essential Question for this unit is "Where can imagination lead?" Rashid's vivid imagination allows him to support his family and gain the esteem of many people. But a shock makes him lose his imagination and, in turn, his livelihood.

Connection to Performance-Based Assessment

The prompt is "What might happen if a fictional character were to come into the real world?" The story speaks to the power of storytelling and can help connect students to the realm of imagination.

Text Complexity Rubric: The Shah of Blah

Quantitative Measures

Lexile: 1060   Text Length: 3,350 words

Qualitative Measures

Knowledge Demands ①—②—③—❹—⑤	Selection explores complex and sophisticated themes (storytelling, freedom of speech, censorship); situations are uncommon to most readers. Reader needs some knowledge of the genre of magical realism.
Structure ①—②—③—❹—⑤	The story is in the genre of magical realism and follows a narrative structure. Organization is intricate, with complex storyline and characters. Events can be difficult to predict.
Language Conventionality and Clarity ①—②—❸—④—⑤	Language is complex and figurative. Some sentences are long with multiple clauses. Playful language is used, such as rhyme and made-up words (*glumfish, Ocean of Notions, Shah of Blah*).
Levels of Meaning/Purpose ①—②—③—❹—⑤	Multiple levels of meaning may be difficult to identify and separate; themes are implicit and complex. The story is an allegory with abundant use of symbolism within fantastical and magical situations.

Prince Francis

Summary

"Prince Francis" is a short story by Roddy Doyle. The story describes a class in Ireland during the filming of a class interview project. One by one, students are called up to be interviewed by a classmate named Alice. The questions include basic information including each student's name and place of birth. Most students are native Irish or English. Francis is anxious because he feels that he is different and has no friends, but he is ready for his turn. When Francis is interviewed, he says he was born in a place called Pikipiki. The children argue that this place does not exist, but he explains that Pikipiki is an imaginary place that he and his father invented when they lived in Africa during wartime. Francis says that he is the Prince of Pikipiki. From then on, his classmates call him Prince Francis.

Insight

This short story is told from the perspective of a young student who is coping with memories of his family's escape from a violent past and a longtime separation from his father. He finds comfort in an imaginary world he and his father had created, indicating the tremendous healing powers of the imagination.

SELECTION RESOURCES

- First-Read Guide: Fiction
- Close-Read Guide: Fiction
- Prince Francis: Text Questions
- Audio Summaries
- Selection Audio
- Selection Test

Connect to the Essential Question

The Essential Question for this unit is "Where can the imagination lead?" Francis doubts his ability to speak in front of his class, but by relying on his rich and active imagination, he discovers techniques for relating a difficult, traumatic family history.

Connect to Performance-Based Assessment

The prompt is "What might happen if a fictional character were to come into the real world?" The story provides a useful model for the insertion of an unfamiliar character in a familiar setting; only in this case the story is told from the perspective of the unfamiliar character.

Text Complexity Rubric: Prince Francis

Quantitative Measures

Lexile: 240   Text Length: 2,159

Qualitative Measures

Knowledge Demands	①—②—**❸**—④—⑤	General setting of classroom activity will be familiar, but references to Irish, UK, and African societies and conflicts may challenge readers who lack background information.
Structure	①—**❷**—③—④—⑤	The narrative structure is fairly straightforward and predictable. Readers may take time to fully understand that the scene is being filtered through one character's perspective.
Language Conventionality and Clarity	①—**❷**—③—④—⑤	Sentence structure is easy to navigate. A few names and pronunciations will challenge readers (*Daragh, Gaelic, Pikipiki*).
Levels of Meaning/Purpose	①—②—**❸**—④—⑤	Levels of meaning will be evident to most readers; themes are implicit but detectable.

MY NOTES

You may wish to direct students to use the generic **First-Read** and **Close-Read Guides** in the Print Student Edition. Alternatively, you may wish to print copies of the genre-specific **First-Read** and **Close-Read Guides** for students. These are available online in the Interactive Student Edition or Unit Resources.

● FIRST READ

Students should perform the steps of the first read independently.

NOTICE: Students should focus on the basic elements of the text to ensure they understand what is happening.

ANNOTATE: Students should mark any passages they wish to revisit during their close read.

CONNECT: Students should increase their understanding by connecting what they've read to other texts or personal experiences.

RESPOND: Students will write a summary to demonstrate their understanding.

Point out to students that while they will always complete the Respond step at the end of the first read, the other steps will probably happen somewhat concurrently. Remind students that they will revisit their first-read annotations during the close read. You may wish to print copies of the First-Read Guide for students to use.

> After students have completed the First-Read Guide, you may wish to assign the Text Questions for the selection that are available in the Interactive Teacher's Edition.

Anchor Standards

In the first two sections of the unit, students worked with the whole class and in small groups to gain topical knowledge and greater understanding of the skills required by the anchor standards. In this section, they are asked to work independently, applying what they have learned and demonstrating increased readiness for college and career.

INDEPENDENT LEARNING

First-Read Guide

🔧 **Tool Kit**
First-Read Guide and Model Annotation

Use this page to record your first-read ideas.

Selection Title: _____

NOTICE

NOTICE new information or ideas you learn about the unit topic as you first read this text.

ANNOTATE

ANNOTATE by marking vocabulary and key passages you want to revisit.

First Read

CONNECT

CONNECT ideas within the selection to other knowledge and the selections you have read.

RESPOND

RESPOND by writing a brief summary of the selection.

© Pearson Education, Inc., or its affiliates. All rights reserved.

▤ STANDARD
Reading Read and comprehend complex literary and informational texts independently and proficiently.

392 UNIT 4 • IMAGINATION

PERSONALIZE FOR LEARNING

Strategic Support
Writing a Summary Students may struggle with writing a summary for the Respond section of the First-Read Guide. Discuss the components of a successful summary, and have students create a checklist to help them review and revise their First-Read Guide entry.

• Explain that a summary should be short and should identify the title and author of a selection.

• The topic (for nonfiction selections) or genre (for literary selections) should be noted, followed by the main ideas in a nonfiction text or brief descriptions of the essential elements in literary selections (i.e., character, plot, setting, point of view, literary techniques).

Students should use their own words to describe, or restate, the ideas or elements of a selection. If they include exact words from the text, those words should be enclosed in quotation marks.

Close-Read Guide

Use this page to record your close-read ideas.

🔧 Tool Kit
Close-Read Guide and
Model Annotation

Selection Title: _____

Close Read the Text

Revisit sections of the text you marked during your first read. Read these sections closely and **annotate** what you notice. Ask yourself **questions** about the text. What can you **conclude**? Write down your ideas.

Analyze the Text

Think about the author's choices of patterns, structure, techniques, and ideas included in the text. Select one, and record your thoughts about what this choice conveys.

QuickWrite

Pick a paragraph from the text that grabbed your interest. Explain the power of this passage.

_____
_____
_____
_____
_____
_____
_____
_____

© Pearson Education, Inc., or its affiliates. All rights reserved.

⊞ STANDARD

Reading Read and comprehend complex literary and informational texts independently and proficiently.

● CLOSE READ

Students should begin their close read by revisiting the annotations they made during their first read. Then, students should analyze one of the author's choices regarding the following elements:

- **patterns,** such as repetition or parallelism
- **structure,** such as cause-and-effect or problem-solution
- **techniques,** such as description or dialogue
- **ideas,** such as the author's main idea or claim

MAKE IT INTERACTIVE
Group students according to the selection they have chosen. Then, have students meet to discuss the selection in-depth. Their discussions should be guided by their insights and questions.

PERSONALIZE FOR LEARNING

Strategic Support

QuickWrite To scaffold support for the QuickWrite, help students organize and develop their ideas about a specific paragraph in the text. Have them read aloud to a partner the paragraph they chose, summarize the main idea and supporting details, and point out specific examples in the writing that captured their interest.

Students may point to specific vocabulary, direct quotations, dialogue, descriptions, imagery, or visuals and/or captions related to the paragraph they chose. Students might also talk with their partners about something more they'd like to know. For example, they might have questions about the main idea or details in the paragraph, or they might want to know more about how the writer decided to craft the paragraph.

Share Your Independent Learning

Prepare to Share

Explain to students that sharing what they learned from their Independent Learning selection provides classmates who did not read the same selection with an opportunity to consider the text as a source of evidence during the Performance-Based Assessment. As students prepare to share, remind them to highlight how their selection contributed to their knowledge of the concept of imagination as well as how the selection connects to the question, *Where can imagination lead?*

Learn From Your Classmates

As students discuss the Independent Learning selections, direct them to take particular note of how their classmates' chosen selections align with their current position on the Performance-Based Assessment question.

Reflect

Students may want to add their reflection to their Evidence Log, particularly if their insight relates to a specific selection from the unit.

MAKE IT INTERACTIVE

To trigger ideas about imagination, provide students with a general statement, and challenge them to draw or describe in detail what they imagine after hearing it. For example, you might say, "An exciting car chase in a movie," "a monster that lives in a cave and emerges once a year to gather food," or "the most beautiful necklace ever made." After students have made their drawings or written their descriptions, ask volunteers to share their work.

Evidence Log Support students in completing their Evidence Log. This paced activity will help prepare them for the Performance-Based Assessment at the end of the unit.

✎ EVIDENCE LOG

Review your Evidence Log, and record what you learned from the text you read.

Share Your Independent Learning

Prepare to Share

Where can imagination lead?

Even when you read something independently, you can continue to grow by sharing what you have learned with others. Reflect on the text you explored independently, and write notes about its connection to the unit. In your notes, consider why this text belongs in this unit.

Learn From Your Classmates

💬 **Discuss It** Share your ideas about the text you explored on your own. As you talk with your classmates, jot down ideas that you learn from them.

Reflect

Review your notes, and mark the most important insight you gained from these writing and discussion activities. Explain how these ideas add to your understanding of the topic of imagination.

© Pearson Education, Inc., or its affiliates. All rights reserved.

AUTHOR'S PERSPECTIVE   ### Ernest Morrell, Ph.D.

Self-facing Notes Some students may not believe that they need to take notes because they'll remember what the teacher and their classmates say. However, taking notes can provide more than a memory jog. To reinforce the importance of taking good notes, teachers should remind students that they will need notes to learn effectively from their peers. In addition, self-facing notes may help students in discussion because these notes will help

them prepare the key points they want to share. Point out that the Share Your Independent Learning activity will help students in these ways:

• **Provide Feedback:** Making self-facing notes will help students give classmates useful comments about their independent reading, which will result in deeper learning.

• **Share Key Ideas:** Model how to jot down information that is essential to understanding.

Focus on identifying the main ideas and critical details.

• **Expand on Others' Ideas:** Explain to students that effective notes help them cut to the heart of the matter and so provide a scaffolding for what others may have noticed in the reading.

Review Notes for a Fictional Narrative

At the beginning of this unit, you expressed an idea about the following question:

> What might happen if a fictional character were to come into the real world?

✐ EVIDENCE LOG

Review your Evidence Log and your QuickWrite from the beginning of the unit. Did you learn anything new?

NOTES

Identify at least three key situations or events that occurred because of either the author's or character's imagination.

1.

2.

3.

Identify an interesting character from one of the selections and note some his or her character traits:

_____

_____

Identify some sensory details that you might use to develop the real-world setting of your narrative:

_____

_____

Evaluate the Strength of Your Evidence Do you have enough details and examples, both from the texts and your own experience, to write a well-developed, engaging fictional narrative? If not, make a plan.

☐ Brainstorm for details to add   ☐ Talk with my classmates

☐ Reread a selection   ☐ Ask an expert

☐ Other: _____

© Pearson Education, Inc., or its affiliates. All rights reserved.

⋮≡ STANDARDS

Writing
Write narratives to develop real or imagined experiences or events using effective technique, relevant descriptive details, and well-structured event sequences.
  d. Use precise words and phrases, relevant descriptive details, and sensory language to convey experiences and events.

Review Notes for a Fictional Narrative

Evidence Log Students should understand that their viewpoint can evolve as they learn more about the subject and are exposed to additional points of view. Point out that they initially may have felt a certain way about how they might respond to the question prompt *What might happen if a fictional character were to come into the real world?* That doesn't mean that their viewpoint can't change after careful consideration of their learning and evidence.

Evaluate the Strength of Your Evidence

Explain to students that for their fictional narratives, the "evidence" they will provide should consist of examples of how the texts they've read and the multimedia they've reviewed confirmed, challenged, or changed their initial response to the question, *How can imagination lead you to somewhere unexpected?* Here are some types of evidence they can use as support in their fictional narratives:

- examples from the texts or multimedia that support their way of thinking
- passages or anecdotes that inspired them
- passages or anecdotes that changed or challenged their way of thinking

If students are having trouble identifying how the texts or multimedia may have influenced their way of thinking, prompt them to consider the role imagination plays in each by asking the following:

- Why is using one's imagination important in this text?
- What did you learn about the use of imagination by reading this text?
- Has your thinking changed after reading this text? Why or why not?

Writing to Sources: Fictional Narrative

Students should complete the Performance-Based Assessment independently, with little to no input or feedback during the process. Students should use word processing software to take advantage of editing tools and features.

Prior to beginning the Assessment, ask students to think about how the characters in this unit's selections and how the characters' realities differ from the students' realities.

Review the Elements of a Fictional Narrative

Students can review the work they did earlier in the unit as they complete the Performance-Based Assessment. They may also consult other resources such as:

- the elements of a fictional narrative, including characters, narration, pacing, and dialogue, available in Whole-Class Learning
- their Evidence Log
- their Word Network

Although students will use evidence from the unit selections for their fictional narratives, they may need to collect additional evidence, including details of the settings in which the original works took place.

 PERFORMANCE-BASED ASSESSMENT

SOURCES

- WHOLE-CLASS SELECTIONS
- SMALL-GROUP SELECTIONS
- INDEPENDENT-LEARNING SELECTION

⛓ WORD NETWORK

As you write and revise your fictional narrative, use your Word Network to help vary your word choices.

▤ STANDARDS

Writing
- Write narratives to develop real or imagined experiences or events using effective technique, relevant descriptive details, and well-structured event sequences.
- Produce clear and coherent writing in which the development, organization, and style are appropriate to task, purpose, and audience.
- Write routinely over extended time frames and shorter time frames for a range of discipline-specific tasks, purposes, and audiences.

396 UNIT 4 • IMAGINATION

PART 1

Writing to Sources: Fictional Narrative

In this unit, you met a variety of fictional characters whose imaginations led them to unusual and fantastical places. You also considered the importance of imagination in real-life situations.

> **Assignment**
>
> Choose a character from one of the selections you read in this unit, and write a **short story** that explores the following question:
>
> > What might happen if a fictional character were to come into the real world?
>
> Use the following story starter to begin your narrative: *One day, _____ showed up on my doorstep, and. . . .*
>
> As you draft, establish a vivid setting and a clear point of view. Use narrative techniques, descriptive details, and sensory language to develop your characters and their experiences. Logically organize the events in your narrative and connect them with transitions. Your narrative should end with a conclusion that resolves the conflicts, or struggles, your characters face in the story.

Reread the Assignment Review the assignment to be sure you fully understand it. You may use the story starter provided as the first sentence of your narrative. However, if your imagination is fired up and you would like to start your story in a different way, feel free to do so.

Review the Elements of a Fictional Narrative Before you begin writing, read the Fictional Narrative Rubric. Once you have completed your first draft, check it against the rubric. If one or more of the elements is missing or not as strong as it could be, revise your narrative to add or strengthen that component.

© Pearson Education, Inc., or its affiliates. All rights reserved.

Fictional Narrative Rubric

	Focus and Organization	Evidence and Elaboration	Language Conventions
4	The introduction is engaging and clearly establishes a setting and a point of view. Events in the narrative progress logically and are connected by effectively used transitions. The conclusion is memorable and resolves the conflicts the characters face over the course of the story.	The narrative effectively uses techniques, such as dialogue, pacing, and description, to develop characters, events, and experiences in memorable way. The narrative effectively uses descriptive details and sensory language to vividly portray the characters and develop the setting.	The narrative intentionally follows standard English conventions of usage and mechanics.
3	The introduction is mostly engaging and establishes a setting and a point of view. Events in the narrative progress logically and are connected by transitions. The conclusion resolves the conflicts the characters face over the course of the story.	The narrative uses techniques, such as dialogue, pacing, and description, to develop characters, events, and experiences. The narrative uses descriptive details and sensory language to portray the characters and develop the setting.	The narrative follows standard English conventions of usage and mechanics.
2	The introduction establishes a setting and a point of view. Events in the narrative sometimes progress logically and are occasionally connected by transitions. There is a conclusion, but it does not fully resolve the conflicts the characters face over the course of the story.	The narrative sometimes uses techniques, such as dialogue, pacing, and description, to develop characters, events, and experiences. The narrative occasionally uses descriptive details and sensory language, but some word choices are vague and imprecise.	The narrative sometimes follows standard English conventions of usage and mechanics, but also contains grammar and spelling errors.
1	The introduction does not establish a setting and a point of view, or there is no introduction. Events in the narrative do not progress logically and are not connected by transitions. The conclusion does not connect to the narrative, or there is no conclusion.	The narrative does not use techniques, such as dialogue, pacing, and description, to develop characters, events, and experiences. Word choices are vague, and the narrative does not use descriptive details and sensory language to portray characters or develop the setting.	The narrative does not follow standard English conventions of usage and mechanics, and contains many grammar and spelling errors.

© Pearson Education, Inc., or its affiliates. All rights reserved.

Fictional Narrative Rubric

As you review the Fictional Narrative Rubric with students, remind them that the rubric is a resource that can guide their revisions. Students should pay particular attention to the differences between a fictional narrative that contains all of the required elements (a score of 3) and one that is thoroughly engaging and effective (a score of 4).

PERSONALIZE FOR LEARNING

English Language Support

Sequence and Pacing Review the definitions of sequence and pacing. Explain that sequence is the order in which a narrative's events happen—what happens *first, next,* and *last.* Pacing refers to how quickly or slowly they happen. Explain that good writers vary their pacing, and that readers may become overwhelmed or disinterested if the pacing is too fast or too slow.

A descriptive passage about a setting has a slow pace, while a battle scene is likely to have a very fast pace. If students have trouble sequencing the events in their narratives, encourage them to create a timeline or storyboard of events. Remind them to use transition and time words and phrases such as *this morning, later,* and *finally.*
ALL LEVELS

Speaking and Listening: Storytelling

Remind students that the effectiveness of an oral fictional narrative relies on how the speaker tells the story. If the speaker conveys the narration in a lively, expressive manner, and if the characters are portrayed as credible characters with believable thoughts and feelings, it will be easier for the audience to be caught up by the story.

Review the Rubric As you review the rubric with students, remind them that it is a valuable tool that can help them plan their presentation. They should strive to include all of the criteria required to achieve a score of 3. Draw their attention to some of the subtle differences between scores of 2 and 3.

 PERFORMANCE-BASED ASSESSMENT

PART 2
Speaking and Listening: Storytelling

Assignment
After completing the final draft of your short story, present it to the class orally during a class **storytelling** session.

STANDARDS
Speaking and Listening
• Present claims and findings, sequencing ideas logically and using pertinent descriptions, facts, and details to accentuate main ideas or themes; use appropriate eye contact, adequate volume, and clear pronunciation.
• Adapt speech to a variety of contexts and tasks, demonstrating command of formal English when indicated or appropriate.

Take the following steps to make your presentation during the storytelling session lively and engaging:

• Read your story with expression by changing your voice when reading different characters' parts and adjusting your tone to suit the events.

• As you speak, pronounce words clearly, and make eye contact with your audience regularly to keep listeners engaged.

Review the Rubric The criteria by which your presentation will be evaluated appear in the rubric below. Review these criteria before presenting to ensure that you are prepared.

	Content	Organization	Presentation Techniques
3	The introduction engages and orients listeners by establishing a clear point of view, and introducing the characters and the setting. The setting, characters, and events are brought to life through the use of narrative techniques, descriptive details, and sensory language. The conclusion resolves conflicts and provides listeners with a sense of resolution, or completion.	The speaker spends the right amount of time on each part of the story. The story includes a smooth sequence of events that is easy for listeners to follow.	The speaker makes eye contact and speaks clearly with adequate volume. The speaker adjusts his or her voice to accurately reflect different characters and events.
2	The introduction establishes the characters and the setting. The setting, characters, and events are developed through the use of some narrative techniques, descriptive details, and sensory language. The conclusion resolves conflicts in a vague way, but leaves listeners with questions.	The speaker mostly spends the right amount of time on each part of the story. The story includes a sequence of events that listeners can mostly follow.	The speaker makes some eye contact and usually speaks clearly. The speaker sometimes adjusts his or her voice to reflect different characters and events.
1	The introduction may vaguely establish the setting and the characters, or may be nonexistent. Narrative techniques, descriptive details, and sensory language are not used to develop the setting, characters, and events. The conclusion does not relate to story events, or is nonexistent.	The speaker spends too much time on some parts of the story and not enough time on others. The sequence of events is unclear and listeners have difficulty following the story.	The speaker does not make eye contact and does not speak clearly. The speaker does not adjust his or her voice to reflect different characters and events.

© Pearson Education, Inc., or its affiliates. All rights reserved.

398 UNIT 4 • IMAGINATION

DIGITAL PERSPECTIVES

Preparing for the Assignment To help students understand what effective oral storytelling looks and sounds like, find videos on the Internet of people telling stories. Preview each clip before showing it to the class. Play the clips for the class, and have students note the elements and techniques that make each storyteller successful (for example, tone of voice, facial expressions, hand gestures, different voices for different characters). Suggest that students record themselves presenting their journal entries prior to presenting to the class so that they can refine their presentations by including some of the elements from the video examples.

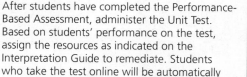

Reflect on the Unit

Now that you've completed the unit, take a few moments to reflect on your learning.

Reflect on the Unit Goals

Look back at the goals at the beginning of the unit. Use a different colored pen to rate yourself again. Think about readings and activities that contributed the most to the growth of your understanding. Record your thoughts.

Reflect on the Learning Strategies

Discuss It Write a reflection on whether you were able to improve your learning based on your Action Plans. Think about what worked, what didn't, and what you might do to keep working on these strategies. Record your ideas before a class discussion.

Reflect on the Text

Choose a selection that you found challenging, and explain what made it difficult.

Explain something that surprised you about a text in the unit.

Which activity taught you the most about imagination? What did you learn?

© Pearson Education, Inc., or its affiliates. All rights reserved.

 SCAN FOR MULTIMEDIA

Reflect on the Unit

- Have students watch the video on Reflecting on Your Learning
- A video on this topic is available online in the Professional Development Center

Reflect on the Unit Goals

Students should re-evaluate how well they met the unit goals now that they have completed the unit. You might ask them to provide a written commentary on the goal they made the most progress with as well as the goal they feel warrants continued focus.

Reflect on the Learning Strategies

Discuss It If you want to make this a digital activity, go online and navigate to the Discussion Board. Alternatively, students can share their learning strategies reflections in a class discussion.

Reflect on the Text

Consider having students share their text reflections with one another.

MAKE IT INTERACTIVE

Divide students into groups and have each group write a song in which they reflect on what they learned about imagination from this unit. They may choose to focus on a single selection or on the use of imagination generally. After students have written their songs, invite them to perform their songs for the other groups.

Unit Test and Remediation

After students have completed the Performance-Based Assessment, administer the Unit Test. Based on students' performance on the test, assign the resources as indicated on the Interpretation Guide to remediate. Students who take the test online will be automatically assigned remediation, as warranted by test results.

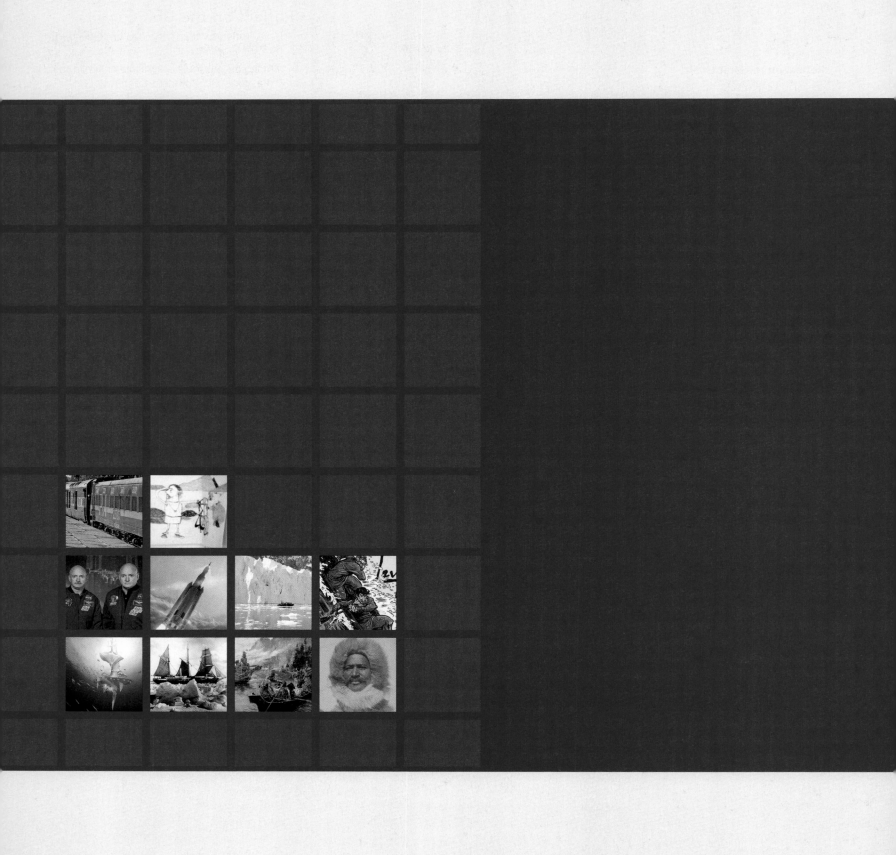

Exploration

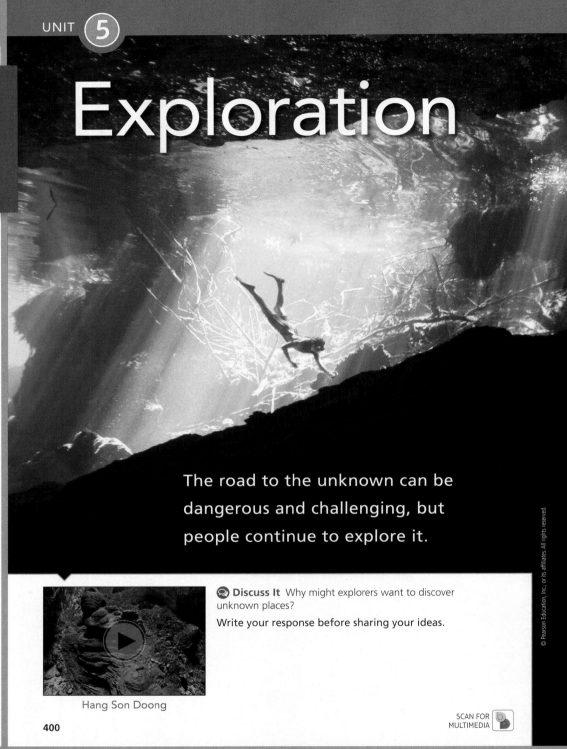

UNIT **5**

Exploration

The road to the unknown can be dangerous and challenging, but people continue to explore it.

Jump Start

Engage students in a discussion about the lure of the unknown and why some people travel to previously unexplored places. Ask them to share answers to these questions: *Where does an explorer go? Why would someone want to go "where no one has gone before"?*

Exploration

Ask students what the word *exploration* suggests to them. Point out that as they work through this unit, they will read many examples about exploration.

Video ▶

Project the introduction video in class, ask students to open the video in their interactive textbooks, or have students scan the BouncePage icon with their phones to access the video.

Discuss It If you want to make this a digital activity, go online and navigate to the Discussion Board. Alternatively, students can share their responses in a class discussion.

Block Scheduling

Each day in this pacing calendar represents a 40–50 minute class period. Teachers using block scheduling may combine days to reflect their class schedule. In addition, teachers may revise pacing to differentiate and support core instruction by integrating components and resources as students require.

💬 **Discuss It** Why might explorers want to discover unknown places?

Write your response before sharing your ideas.

Hang Son Doong

SCAN FOR MULTIMEDIA

400

© Pearson Education, Inc., or its affiliates. All rights reserved.

📅 **Pacing Plan**

Introduce Whole-Class Learning

Performance Task

Unit Introduction

from A Long Way Home

Media: BBC Science Club: All About Exploration

| 1 | 2 | 3 | 4 | 5 | 6 | 7 | 8 | 9 | 10 | 11 | 12 | 13 | 14 | 15 | 16 | 17 | 18 |

Exploration

Jump Start

Engage students in a discussion about the lure of the unknown and why some people travel to previously unexplored places. Ask them to share answers to these questions: *Where does an explorer go? Why would someone want to go "where no one has gone before"?*

Exploration

Ask students what the word *exploration* suggests to them. Point out that as they work through this unit, they will read many examples about exploration.

Video ▶

Project the introduction video in class, ask students to open the video in their interactive textbooks, or have students scan the BouncePage icon with their phones to access the video.

Discuss It If you want to make this a digital activity, go online and navigate to the Discussion Board. Alternatively, students can share their responses in a class discussion.

Block Scheduling

Each day in this pacing calendar represents a 40–50 minute class period. Teachers using block scheduling may combine days to reflect their class schedule. In addition, teachers may revise pacing to differentiate and support core instruction by integrating components and resources as students require.

📅 **Pacing Plan**

UNIT ⑤

Exploration

The road to the unknown can be dangerous and challenging, but people continue to explore it.

Discuss It Why might explorers want to discover unknown places?

Write your response before sharing your ideas.

Hang Son Doong

400

SCAN FOR MULTIMEDIA ⓑ

© Pearson Education, Inc., or its affiliates. All rights reserved.

Introduce Whole-Class Learning

Performance Task

Unit Introduction

from A Long Way Home

Media: BBC Science Club: All About Exploration

| 1 | 2 | 3 | 4 | 5 | 6 | 7 | 8 | 9 | 10 | 11 | 12 | 13 | 14 | 15 | 16 | 17 | 18 |

DIGITAL PERSPECTIVES
 Audio
 Video
 Document
 Annotation Highlights
 EL Highlights
 Online Assessment

UNIT 5

UNIT INTRODUCTION

ESSENTIAL QUESTION:

What drives people to explore?

LAUNCH TEXT
ARGUMENT MODEL
What on Earth Is Left to Explore?

WHOLE-CLASS LEARNING

ANCHOR TEXT: MEMOIR
from A Long Way Home
Saroo Brierley

MEDIA: VIDEO
BBC Science Club: All About Exploration
narrated by Dara Ó Briain

SMALL-GROUP LEARNING

NEWS ARTICLE
Mission Twinpossible
TIME For Kids

COMPARE

EPIC RETELLING
from Tales From the Odyssey
Mary Pope Osborne

BLOG
To the Top of Everest
Samantha Larson

MEDIA: GRAPHIC NOVEL
from Lewis & Clark
Nick Bertozzi

INDEPENDENT LEARNING

OPINION PIECE
Mars Can Wait. Oceans Can't.
Amitai Etzioni

NONFICTION NARRATIVE
from Shipwreck at the Bottom of the World
Jennifer Armstrong

HISTORICAL FICTION
from Sacajawea
Joseph Bruchac

EXPOSITORY NONFICTION
The Legacy of Arctic Explorer Matthew Henson
James Mills

INFORMATIVE ARTICLE
Should Polar Tourism Be Allowed?
Emily Goldberg

PERFORMANCE TASK
WRITING FOCUS:
Write an Argument

PERFORMANCE TASK
SPEAKING AND LISTENING FOCUS:
Present an Advertisement

PERFORMANCE-BASED ASSESSMENT PREP
Review Evidence for an Argument

PERFORMANCE-BASED ASSESSMENT

Argument: Essay and Speech

PROMPT:
Should kids today be encouraged to become explorers?

401

© Pearson Education, Inc., or its affiliates. All rights reserved.

What drives people to explore?

Introduce the Essential Question and point out that students will respond to related prompts.

- **Whole-Class Learning** *Is exploration a courageous act that requires a unique sense of adventure? Or, is exploration so natural to human beings that anyone can be an explorer?*

- **Small-Group Learning** *Why should we explore new frontiers?*

- **Performance-Based Assessment** *What fuels people's desire to explore?*

Using Trade Books

Refer to the Teaching with Trade Books section in this book or online in myPerspectives+ for suggestions on how to incorporate the following thematically related novels into this unit.

- *Around the World in 80 Days* by Jules Verne
- *The House of Dies Drear* by Virginia Hamilton
- *Maniac Magee* by Jerry Spinelli

Current Perspectives

To increase student engagement, search online for stories about exploration, and invite your students to recommend stories they find. Always preview content before sharing it with your class.

- **Article/Video: "Modern Day Adventure: Is There Anything Left To Discover?"** (Channel 4 News) Three adventurers discuss why they feel people should explore.

- **Video: "Bill Nye: Why We Explore"** (Big Think) A video of Bill Nye discussing the importance of space exploration, and why our curiosity drives us to learn more.

Introduce Small-Group Learning

Mission Twinpossible

from Tales From the Odyssey

To the Top of Everest

Media: from Lewis & Clark

Performance Task

Introduce Independent Learning

Independent Learning

Performance-Based Assessment

| 19 | 20 | 21 | 22 | 23 | 24 | 25 | 26 | 27 | 28 | 29 | 30 | 31 | 32 | 33 | 34 | 35 | 36 |

About the Unit Goals

These unit goals were backward designed from the Performance-Based Assessment at the end of the unit and the Whole-Class and Small-Group Performance Tasks. Students will practice and become proficient in many more standards over the course of this unit.

Unit Goals ⏵

Review the goals with students and explain that as they read and discuss the selections in this unit, they will improve their skills in reading, writing, research, language, and speaking and listening.

- Have students watch the video on Goal Setting.
- A video on this topic is available online in the Professional Development Center.

Reading Goals Tell students they will read, view, and evaluate arguments.

Writing and Research Goals Tell students that they will learn the elements of writing an argument. They will also write their own argument. Students will write for a number of reasons, including organizing and sharing ideas, reflecting on experiences, and gathering evidence. They will conduct research to clarify and explore ideas.

Language Goal Tell students that they will develop a deeper understanding of correcting errors with verb usage. They will then practice correct verb usage in their own writing.

Speaking and Listening Explain to students that they will work together to build on one another's ideas, develop consensus, and communicate with one another. They will also learn to incorporate audio, visuals, and text in presentations.

HOME Connection ✉

A Home Connection letter to students' parents or guardians is available in myPerspectives+. The letter explains what students will be learning in this unit and how they will be assessed.

Unit Goals

Throughout this unit, you will deepen your understanding of exploration by reading, writing, speaking, listening, and presenting. These goals will help you succeed on the Unit Performance-Based Assessment.

Rate how well you meet these goals right now. You will revisit your ratings later when you reflect on your growth during this unit.

SCALE	1	2	3	4	5
	NOT AT ALL WELL	NOT VERY WELL	SOMEWHAT WELL	VERY WELL	EXTREMELY WELL

READING GOALS	1	2	3	4	5
• Evaluate written arguments by analyzing how authors state and support their claims.	○—○—○—○—○				
• Expand your knowledge and use of academic and concept vocabulary.	○—○—○—○—○				

WRITING AND RESEARCH GOALS	1	2	3	4	5
• Write an essay in which you effectively incorporate the key elements of an argument.	○—○—○—○—○				
• Conduct research projects of various lengths to explore a topic and clarify meaning.	○—○—○—○—○				

LANGUAGE GOAL	1	2	3	4	5
• Correct errors with verbs.	○—○—○—○—○				

SPEAKING AND LISTENING GOALS	1	2	3	4	5
• Engage in collaborative discussions, build on the ideas of others, and express your own ideas clearly.	○—○—○—○—○				
• Integrate audio, visuals, and text in presentations.	○—○—○—○—○				

© Pearson Education, Inc., or its affiliates. All rights reserved.

≡ STANDARDS

Language
Acquire and use accurately grade-appropriate general academic and domain-specific words and phrases; gather vocabulary knowledge when considering a word or phrase important to comprehension or expression.

SCAN FOR MULTIMEDIA 🅑

AUTHOR'S PERSPECTIVE | **Ernest Morrell, Ph.D.**

How to Support Kids When They Have Trouble When setting goals with students, have them consider these questions:

1. What are the opportunities open to me if I achieve this goal?
2. What are the biggest challenges that I will face in attempting to achieve this goal?

3. What support will I need from others in order to achieve this goal and how will I ensure that I get that support?

The first question helps students see that setting goals helps them take control of their life and focus on the issues that matter to them. As a result, they are likely to make good decisions. The second

question helps students understand that achieving goals takes hard work, resilience, and determination. The third question reassures students that help is available and shows them the importance of seeking—and accepting—help when necessary.

Academic Vocabulary: Argument

Understanding and using academic terms can help you read, write, and speak with precision and clarity. Here are five academic words that will be useful in this unit as you analyze and write arguments.

Complete the chart.

1. Review each word, its root, and the mentor sentences.
2. Use the information and your own knowledge to predict the meaning of each word.
3. For each word, list at least two related words.
4. Refer to the dictionary or other resources if needed.

TIP

FOLLOW THROUGH
Study the words in this chart, and mark them or their forms wherever they appear in the unit.

WORD	MENTOR SENTENCES	PREDICT MEANING	RELATED WORDS
critical ROOT: *-crit-* "judge"	1. I don't think she liked the story because she had many *critical* comments. 2. It is *critical* to follow the steps exactly, otherwise the experiment might fail.		critic; critically
assume ROOT: *-sum-* / *-sumpt-* "take up"	1. If you get the leash, the puppy will *assume* you're taking him for a walk. 2. Jon won the election and will *assume* the role of mayor.		
compel ROOT: *-pel-* "drive"	1. His disregard of the rules may *compel* the group to dismiss him. 2. In the movie, the bad guy tries to *compel* the hero to give up.		
valid ROOT: *-val-* "strong"	1. You need a *valid* password to log in to the network. 2. If you want to convince me, you had better use *valid* reasons.		
coherent ROOT: *-here-* / *-hes-* "cling"; "stick"	1. Present your information in a clear, *coherent* order so it is easy to understand. 2. Sam's speech was *coherent* because he used clear logic and evidence.		

© Pearson Education, Inc., or its affiliates. All rights reserved.

Academic Vocabulary: Argument

Introduce the blue academic vocabulary words in the chart on the student page. Point out that the root of each word provides a clue to its meaning. Discuss the mentor sentences to ensure students understand each word's usage. Students should also use the mentor sentences as context to help them predict the meaning of each word. Check that students are able to fill the chart in correctly. Complete pronunciations, parts of speech, and definitions are provided for you. Students are only expected to provide the definition.

Possible responses:
critical *adj.* (KRIHT uh kuhl)
Meaning: disapproving; unfavorable; very important
Related words: critically; criticism
Additional words related to root *-crit-*: critic; criticize

assume *v.* (uh SOOM)
Meaning: think to be true without proof
Related words: assumption; assuming
Additional words related to root *-sum-* / *-sumpt-*: assumption; presume

compel *v.* (kuhm PEHL)
Meaning: to force someone to do something
Related words: compelling; compels
Additional words related to root *-pel-*: propel; impel

valid *adj.* (VAL ihd)
Meaning: legally acceptable; based in logic; reasonable
Related words: validity; validly
Additional words related to root *-val-*: invalidate; invalid

coherent *adj.* (koh HIHR uhnt)
Meaning: logical, clear communication
Additional words related to root *-here-* / *-hes-*: incoherent; adhere

PERSONALIZE FOR LEARNING

English Language Support
Cognates Many of the academic words have Spanish cognates. Use these cognates with students whose home language is Spanish.
ALL LEVELS

critical – crítico	stable – estable	coherent – coherente

Purpose of the Launch Text

The Launch Text provides students with a common starting point to address the unit topic. After reading the Launch Text, all students will be able to participate in discussions about exploration.

Lexile: 950 The easier reading level of this selection makes it perfect to assign for homework. Students will need little or no support to understand it.

Additionally, "What on Earth Is Left to Explore?" provides a writing model for the Performance-Based Assessment students complete at the end of the unit.

Launch Text: Argument Model

Remind students to determine the main claim of the argument and how the author supports that claim.

Have students note the structure of the text. Point out that the position statement can be inferred from the second and third paragraphs and that the rest of the text provides reasons that support this claim. Point out that the concluding paragraph restates the main claim.

Encourage students to read this text on their own and annotate unfamiliar words and sections of the text they think are particularly important.

🔊 AUDIO SUMMARIES

Audio summaries of "What on Earth Is Left to Explore?" are available in both English and Spanish in the Interactive Teacher's Edition or Unit Resources. Assigning these summaries before students read the Launch Text may help them build additional background knowledge and set a context for their reading.

LAUNCH TEXT | ARGUMENT MODEL

This selection is an example of an **argument,** a type of writing in which an author states and defends a position on a topic. This is the type of writing you will develop in the Performance-Based Assessment at the end of the unit.

As you read, look at the way that the author builds a case. Mark the text to help you answer this question: What is the author's position, and what evidence supports it?

What on Earth Is Left to Explore?

NOTES

1 At the beginning of the 1800s, the United States was a young country. Most people lived in small towns clustered on the Atlantic coast. To the west lay an entire continent, full of mystery and promise.

2 Government leaders believed that exploration of the continent was important. Exploration would bring knowledge and resources. Urged on by President Thomas Jefferson, Congress funded a small expedition to explore the lands west of the Mississippi River. The Lewis and Clark expedition became one of the most famous exploratory journeys in history.

3 In the modern world, the idea of exploration has changed. Cars, trains, and airplanes have made the world seem much smaller. People seem to be everywhere. Thousands have climbed Mount Everest, the world's highest mountain. There are even people living in Antarctica, the world's coldest continent. In addition, the Internet allows people to visit faraway places through the screens of their computers. Given these changes, some people may ask whether exploration matters anymore. Is there anything left to explore? The answer is simple: Exploration matters as much today as it ever has.

4 Let's start with ocean exploration. It is true that much of Earth has been visited and charted. However, we should remember that people actually live on less than twenty percent of the planet. We inhabit the land, but Earth is mostly ocean. Vast stretches of the

© Pearson Education, Inc., or its affiliates. All rights reserved.

SCAN FOR MULTIMEDIA

CROSS-CURRICULAR PERSPECTIVES

Social Studies Tell students that twentieth and twenty-first century explorers include Tenzig Norgay, Matthew Henson, Jacques Cousteau, Mae C. Jemison, Valentina Tereshkova, Reinhold Messner, and Sally Ride. Have students select one of these explorers and learn more about their life and exploits. Then, as a class, debate how the achievements of these modern explorers compare to the achievements of history's most renowned explorers, for example Christopher Columbus.

oceans are hidden under miles of water. The little we do know about these secret places is fascinating. For example, almost a quarter of Earth is made up of a single mountain range. It just happens to be under the sea! Consider the other wonders we might find as we explore.

5   Ocean exploration might help us solve tough problems. For example, it might lead to new food sources for the planet's growing population. It may also help us find ways to slow damage to the environment. These types of problems threaten all of us, and we need solutions. They make the need for ocean exploration more important than ever.

6   Space exploration is another area of great importance. Human beings have always been interested in the skies. We are curious about the stars and planets and the possibility that they hold other intelligent life. Satisfying that curiosity is one good reason to explore space. Another reason is that by exploring beyond Earth, we will answer essential questions about the history of our solar system and of the universe itself. This will help us understand our own planet and ourselves better. Human exploration of space also has practical benefits. According to NASA (National Aeronautics and Space Administration), space exploration pushes us to "expand technology, create new industries, and help to foster a peaceful connection with other nations."

7   Lewis and Clark did not know what they would find as they set out on their journey. They only knew that they would have an adventure. In the end, their efforts added to the country's territory and to people's knowledge and understanding. The results of exploration may not always be that impressive, but that may not be the point. The need to explore and extend the boundaries of knowledge remains vital and should continue. ❧

NOTES

Word Network for Exploration

Tell students that they can fill in the Word Network as they read texts in the unit, or they can record the words elsewhere and add them later. Point out to students that people may have personal associations with some words. A word that one student thinks is related to the concept of exploration might not be a word another student would pick. However, students should feel free to add any word they personally think is relevant to their Word Network. Each person's Word Network will be unique. If you choose to print the Word Network, distribute it to students at this point so they can use it throughout the rest of the unit.

WORD NETWORK FOR EXPLORATION

Vocabulary A Word Network is a collection of words related to a topic. As you read the selections in this unit, identify interesting words related to the idea of exploration and add them to your Word Network. For example, you might begin by adding words from the Launch Text, such as *expedition, wilderness,* and *curiosity.* Continue to add words as you complete this unit.

🔧 **Tool Kit**
Word Network Model

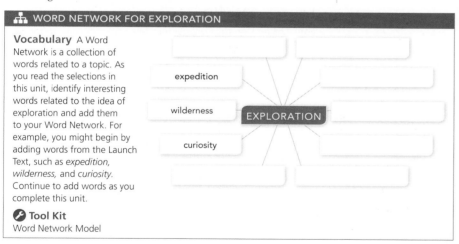

expedition

wilderness — EXPLORATION

curiosity

© Pearson Education, Inc., or its affiliates. All rights reserved.

AUTHOR'S PERSPECTIVE   Elfrieda Hiebert, Ph.D.

Rare Words Increasing reading comprehension relies on a connection between fluency and vocabulary. **Rare words** are less frequently used words that represent what might be a common idea. Instead of calling a character *nervous,* an author might use *disconcerted* or *flustered.* In reading/language arts, where many

rare unknown words pertain to known concepts, teachers should emphasize semantic connections across words. This can be achieved effectively with concept maps or word networks that help students understand the essential characteristics of a word's meaning. Here's an example for *sluggish:*

heavy	blah	indolent	inactive
comatose	inert	off	sullen

Digital tools, including online dictionaries, often have features to help demonstrate the increasing complexity of the spectrum of these words by filtering out levels of complexity.

INTRODUCTION

Summary

Have students read the introductory paragraph. Provide them with tips for writing a summary:

- Write in the present tense.
- Make sure to include the title of the work.
- Be concise: a summary should not be equal in length to the original text.
- If you need to quote the words of the author, use quotation marks.
- Don't put your own opinions, ideas, or interpretations into the summary. The purpose of writing a summary is to accurately represent what the author says, not to provide a critique.

If necessary, students can refer to the Tool Kit for help in understanding the elements of a good summary.

See possible Summary on student page.

Launch Activity

Explain to students that as they work on this unit, they will have many opportunities to discuss the topic of exploration. Remind them that there is no right or wrong position, but that they should be able to support their ideas with evidence from the material they've read, viewed, and analyzed in the unit, as well as from prior knowledge. Encourage students to listen to arguments that their classmates make and to keep an open mind.

Summary

Write a summary of "What on Earth Is Left to Explore?" A **summary** is a concise, complete, and accurate overview of a text. It should not include a statement of your opinion or an analysis.

Possible response: In this text, the author argues that although there might seem to be few unknown places left to discover on Earth, there is still much to explore. In particular, we know very little about the bottom of the oceans. The author cites the work of Robert Ballard, an underwater explorer. Using robots that can explore the ocean depths, Ballard discovers new things and shares the knowledge with everyone else. The author also includes the views of wildlife photographer Michael Nichols. He believes that part of what modern explorers should do is make notes on areas of the planet that are untouched so that they can be protected. Ballard and Nichols believe that anyone who has the interest can be a modern-day explorer.

Launch Activity

Four-Corner Debate Consider this statement: **There is nothing left on Earth to explore.** Decide your position and check one of the boxes. Then, briefly note why you feel this way.

☐ Strongly Agree ☐ Agree ☐ Disagree ☐ Strongly Disagree

_____

- Each corner of the classroom represents one position on the question. Go to the corner of the room that represents your position. Briefly discuss reasons for your position with the others in your corner. Make a list of three strong reasons.
- Start off the debate by stating your position and one reason. Then, go around the room, presenting positions and reasons.
- If you change your mind as the debate continues, move to the corner that represents your new position. Then, explain why your thinking changed.

© Pearson Education, Inc., or its affiliates. All rights reserved.

406 UNIT 5 • EXPLORATION

QuickWrite

Consider class discussions, the video, and the Launch Text as you think about the prompt. Record your first thoughts here.

PROMPT: **Should kids today be encouraged to become explorers?**

> **Possible response:** Exploration is often about curiosity, but it isn't only about curiosity. As Robert Ballard and Michael Nichols tell us, explorers care about documenting and informing other people about what they have found. They explore to satisfy their curiosity and to tell other people what they have found. Everyone likes to tell other people about interesting things he or she knows. Sharing information can be even more enjoyable than finding it in the first place; that's why many people like to write for fun.

QuickWrite

In this QuickWrite, students should present their own response to the prompt based on the material they have read and viewed in the Unit Overview and Introduction. This initial response will help inform their work when they complete the Performance-Based Assessment at the end of the unit. Students should make sure they cite reasons expressed by the explorers featured in their reading.

See possible QuickWrite on student page.

Evidence Log for Exploration

Students should record their initial thinking in their Evidence Logs along with evidence from "What on Earth Is Left to Explore?" that support this thinking.

  If you choose to print the Evidence Log, distribute it to students at this point so they can use it throughout the rest of the unit.

Performance-Based Assessment: Refining Your Thinking ▶

- Have students watch the video on Refining Your Thinking.
- A video on this topic is available online in the Professional Development Center.

✏ EVIDENCE LOG FOR EXPLORATION

Review your QuickWrite. Summarize your point of view in one sentence to record in your Evidence Log. Then, record evidence from "What on Earth Is Left to Explore?" that supports your point of view.

After each selection, you will continue to use your Evidence Log to record the evidence you gather and the connections you make. This graphic shows what your Evidence Log looks like.

🔧 **Tool Kit**
Evidence Log Model

Title of Text: _____   Date: _____

CONNECTION TO PROMPT	TEXT EVIDENCE/DETAILS	ADDITIONAL NOTES/IDEAS

How does this text change or add to my thinking?   Date: _____

© Pearson Education, Inc., or its affiliates. All rights reserved.

SCAN FOR
MULTIMEDIA

PERSONALIZE FOR LEARNING

English Language Support
Provide Context Students may not have experience with all of the Academic Vocabulary words or their related forms. If needed, provide additional examples of related words. Work with students to construct context sentences for these words. Point out the parts of speech of the related words. **ALL LEVELS**

OVERVIEW

WHOLE-CLASS LEARNING

What drives people to explore?

Engage students in a conversation about what exploration means to them. Point out that people have always had the need to explore. Ask students to consider reasons famous explorers set out to discover the unknown and to think about what might drive modern-day explorers to go out and make their own discoveries.

Whole-Class Learning Strategies ▶

Review the Learning Strategies with students and explain that as they work through Whole-Class Learning, they will develop strategies to work in large-group environments.

- Have students watch the video on Whole-Class Learning Strategies.
- A video on this topic is available online in the Professional Development Center.

You may wish to discuss some action items to add to the chart as a class before students complete it on their own. For example, for "Clarify by asking questions," you might solicit the following from students:

- When reading or listening to a presentation, take notes on information that isn't clear. Then, use your notes to form a question.
- Asking a question can lead to new questions, so ask follow-up questions as needed.

Block Scheduling

Each day in this Pacing Plan represents a 40–50 minute class period. Teachers using block scheduling may combine days to reflect their class schedule. In addition, teachers may revise pacing to differentiate and support core instruction by integrating components and resources as students require.

📅 **Pacing Plan**

OVERVIEW: WHOLE-CLASS LEARNING

ESSENTIAL QUESTION:

What drives people to explore?

Exploration may be physical, involving travel to unknown places. It may be mental, involving new ways of looking at a topic. In many cases, it requires both action and imagination. You will work with your whole class to learn more about exploration. The selections you will read present different ideas about explorers and exploration.

Whole-Class Learning Strategies

Throughout your life, in school, in your community, and in your career, you will continue to learn and work in large-group environments.

Review these strategies and the actions you can take to practice them as you work with your whole class. Add ideas of your own for each step. Get ready to use these strategies during Whole-Class Learning.

STRATEGY	ACTION PLAN
Listen actively	• Eliminate distractions. For example, put your cellphone away. • Keep your eyes on the speaker. •
Clarify by asking questions	• If you're confused, other people probably are, too. Ask a question to help your whole class. • If you see that you are guessing, ask a question instead. •
Monitor understanding	• Notice what information you already know and be ready to build on it. • Ask for help if you are struggling. •
Interact and share ideas	• Share your ideas and answer questions, even if you are unsure. • Build on the ideas of others by adding details or making a connection. •

SCAN FOR MULTIMEDIA

408 UNIT 5 • EXPLORATION

Introduce Whole-Class Learning

Unit Introduction

Media: BBC Science Club: All About Exploration

Performance Task

from A Long Way Home

| 1 | 2 | 3 | 4 | 5 | 6 | 7 | 8 | 9 | 10 | 11 | 12 | 13 | 14 | 15 | 16 | 17 | 18 |

WHOLE-CLASS LEARNING

© Pearson Education, Inc., or its affiliates. All rights reserved.

CONTENTS

ANCHOR TEXT: MEMOIR

from A Long Way Home
Saroo Brierley

Is technology the exploration vehicle of the twenty-first century?

MEDIA: VIDEO

BBC Science Club: All About Exploration
narrated by Dara Ó Briain

Throughout history, the human drive to explore has been the source of many important advances in science and engineering.

PERFORMANCE TASK

WRITING FOCUS

Write an Argument
The Whole-Class readings offer new ideas and perspectives on the topic of exploration. After reading the selection and watching the video, you will write an argument in which you make a claim as to what defines an "explorer."

© Pearson Education, Inc., or its affiliates. All rights reserved.

Contents

Anchor Texts Preview the anchor text and media with students to generate interest. Encourage students to discuss other texts they may have read or movies or television shows they may have seen that deal with the issues of exploration.

You may wish to conduct a poll to determine whether students think the anchor text or video looks more interesting and discuss the reasons for their preference. Students can return to this poll after they have read and viewed the selections to see if their preferences changed.

Performance Task

Write an Argument Explain to students that after they have finished reading and viewing the selections, they will write an argument on the topic of exploration. To help them prepare, encourage students to think about how science and technology have influenced human exploration as they progress through the selections and as they participate in the Whole-Class Learning experience.

Overview: Whole-Class Learning **409**

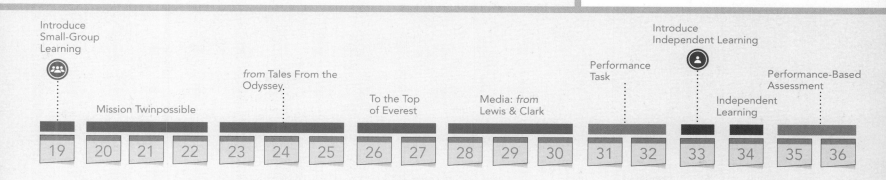

Introduce
Small-Group
Learning

Introduce
Independent Learning

Performance
Task

Performance-Based
Assessment

from Tales From the
Odyssey

To the Top
of Everest

Media: *from*
Lewis & Clark

Independent
Learning

Mission Twinpossible

| 19 | 20 | 21 | 22 | 23 | 24 | 25 | 26 | 27 | 28 | 29 | 30 | 31 | 32 | 33 | 34 | 35 | 36 |

from A Long Way Home

◄» **AUDIO SUMMARIES**
Audio summaries of the excerpt from *A Long Way Home* are available online in both English and Spanish in the Interactive Teacher's Edition or Unit Resources. Assigning these summaries prior to reading the selection may help students build additional background knowledge and set a context for their first read.

Summary

This selection is an excerpt from a memoir titled *A Long Way Home* by Saroo Brierley. In it, he talks about his attempts to find the town he was born in. Brierley got lost at a train station at the age of five, ended up in an orphanage at Kolkata, and was ultimately adopted by an Australian family. As an adult, he decided to search again for his small town using Google Earth. As he began his search, he tried to piece together his early memories of his town, but he quickly realized that trying to search through a list of towns would do him no good. Instead, he estimated how long he traveled, and he used that to figure out how far away his village could be. Several nights a week, he used satellite pictures of train lines and stations to see all the possible routes he could have taken. His focus on his search was all-consuming until he solved the mystery.

Insight

Exploration isn't only about finding new places. Brierley explores to learn about places he has been before. Brierley ultimately succeeds in finding his hometown.

ESSENTIAL QUESTION:
What drives people to explore?

Connection to Essential Question

Brierley explores to find his birth family and the town in which he was born. He is driven to find his family and to let them know what happened to him.

WHOLE-CLASS LEARNING PERFORMANCE TASK
Can anyone be an explorer?

UNIT PERFORMANCE-BASED ASSESSMENT
Should kids today be encouraged to become explorers?

Connection to Performance Tasks

Whole-Class Learning Performance Task Brierley is an ordinary person, and anyone with enough drive, determination, and patience could use online maps the way he does. Yet, few people have been separated from home the way he was, giving him an unusually intense motivation for his exploration.

Unit Performance-Based Assessment People have many different reasons for exploring. In the case of Brierley, he was motivated to explore in order to search for his roots. Students will use examples from several selections to answer this question.

LESSON RESOURCES

	Making Meaning	**Language Development**	**Effective Expression**
Lesson	First Read Close Read Analyze the Text Analyze Craft and Structure	Concept Vocabulary Word Study Author's Style	Writing to Sources Speaking and Listening
Instructional Standards	**RI.1** Cite textual evidence . . . **RI.2** Determine a central idea of a text . . . **RI.5** Analyze how a particular sentence, paragraph, chapter, or section . . . **RI.10** By the end of the year, read and comprehend literary nonfiction . . .	**RI.3** Analyze in detail how a key individual, event, or idea . . . **L.4** Determine or clarify the meaning of unknown and multiple-meaning words and phrases . . . **L.4.b** Use common, grade-appropriate Greek or Latin affixes and roots . . .	**W.1** Write arguments to support claims . . . **W.1.a** Introduce claim(s) . . . **W.1.b** Support claim(s) . . . **W.1.c** Use words, phrases, and clauses . . . **W.1.e** Provide a concluding statement . . . **SL.1** Engage effectively . . . **SL.1.a** Come to discussions prepared . . . **SL.1.d** Review the key ideas expressed . . . **SL.2** Interpret information . . . **SL.5** Include multimedia components . . .

▶ STUDENT RESOURCES

Available online in the Interactive Student Edition or Unit Resources	🔊 Selection Audio 📄 First-Read Guide: Nonfiction 📄 Close-Read Guide: Nonfiction	📄 Word Network	📄 Evidence Log

▶ TEACHER RESOURCES

Selection Resources Available online in the Interactive Teacher's Edition or Unit Resources	🔊 Audio Summaries ✏️ Annotation Highlights 💬 EL Highlights 📄 English Language Support Lesson: Technical Language 📄 Analyze Craft and Structure: Central Ideas: Autobiographical Writing	📄 Concept Vocabulary and Word Study 📄 Author's Style: Word Choice and Mood	📄 Writing to Sources: Argument 📄 Speaking and Listening: Annotated Map
Reteach/Practice (RP) Available online in the Interactive Teacher's Edition or Unit Resources	📄 Analyze Craft and Structure: Central Ideas: Autobiographical Writing (RP)	📄 Word Study: Latin Suffix –ive (RP) 📄 Author's Style: Word Choice and Mood (RP)	📄 Writing to Sources: Argument (RP) 📄 Speaking and Listening: Annotated Map (RP)
Assessment Available online in Assessments	📄 ☑️ Selection Test		
My Resources	📄 A Unit 5 Answer Key is available online and in the Interactive Teacher's Edition.		

Reading Support

Text Complexity Rubric: *from* A Long Way Home

Quantitative Measures

Lexile: 1130   **Text Length:** 4,747 words

Qualitative Measures

Knowledge Demands ①—②—**❸**—④—⑤	The selection relies on some knowledge or familiarity with India and its geography, religions, and languages. Students also need to understand Google Earth and how the author is using it for his search.
Structure ①—**❷**—③—④—⑤	The personal account is told chronologically, and it is mixed with some information about India and the author's early history.
Language Conventionality and Clarity ①—②—**❸**—④—⑤	The language has the familiar style of a personal narrative; there is some use of idiomatic expressions; sentences are sometimes lengthy, with multiple clauses; and some vocabulary is above-level.
Levels of Meaning/Purpose ①—②—**❸**—④—⑤	The author's purpose is not explained right away (selection is an excerpt), but it is explained in the background information. The descriptions include details with a wide range of information about India's geography, religions, and languages.

DECIDE AND PLAN

English Language Support

Provide English Learners with support for knowledge demands and meaning as they read the selection.

Knowledge Demands Use the background information to preview necessary content before reading. Then have students read the first paragraph to look for more information. List the information with students' help: *Brierley is searching for his hometown and birth family. The hometown is in India.* Make sure students understand the use of Google Earth for searching. Clarify if necessary.

Meaning Ask students to reread paragraph 4. As a group, make a list of what Brierley knew about his hometown. Have volunteers suggest items for the list. Clarify the meaning of any unclear phrases. For example, *in close proximity* means "near each other."

Strategic Support

Provide students with strategic support to ensure that they can successfully read the text.

Knowledge Demands Have students read the background information and the first two paragraphs. Then stop to ask questions to make sure students understand the author's basic situation. For example, *Where did he come from?* (a town in India) *How is he searching for it?* (He is using Google Earth.)

Meaning Have students stop after one or two paragraphs to list some of the relevant information they find. For example, for paragraph 4, ask them to list everything the author knows about his hometown. *(It has a train station. Hindi is spoken there. Muslims and Hindus live close to each other. The nights are warm. It isn't in the mountains.)*

Challenge

Provide students who need to be challenged with ideas for how they can go beyond a simple interpretation of the text.

Text Analysis Pair students. Have them reread the selection to make two lists: one of things the author knows about his hometown, and the other about what students learned about India. Ask them to include basics and details. For example, *(List 1) The town he is searching for is in India. There's a bridge over a river. (List 2) Muslims and Hindus live in India. The Himalayas are mountains in India.*

Written Response Ask students to imagine they are writing a similar narrative about a person searching for his or her hometown, but the person is from the student's hometown. Have students write a paragraph listing details about their own hometown that the person uses as clues.

TEACH

Read and Respond

Have students do their first read of the selection. Then have them complete their close read. Finally, work with them on the Making Meaning, Language Development, and Effective Expression activities.

Standards Support Through Teaching and Learning Cycle

IDENTIFY NEEDS

Analyze results of the Beginning-of-Year Assessment, focusing on the items relating to Unit 5. Also take into consideration student performance to this point and your observations of where particular students struggle.

ANALYZE AND REVISE

- Analyze student work for evidence of student learning.
- Identify whether or not students have met the expectations in the standards.
- Identify implications for future instruction.

TEACH

Implement the planned lesson, and gather evidence of student learning.

DECIDE AND PLAN

- If students have performed poorly on items matching these standards, then provide selection scaffolds before assigning them the on-level lesson provided in the Student Edition.
- If students have done well on the Beginning-of-Year Assessment, then challenge them to keep progressing and learning by giving them opportunities to practice the skills in depth.
- Use the Selection Resources listed on the Planning pages for the excerpt from *A Long Way Home* to help students continually improve their ability to master the standards.

Instructional Standards: *from* A Long Way Home

	Catching Up	This Year	Looking Forward
Reading	You may wish to administer the **Analyze Craft and Structure: Central Ideas: Autobiographical Writing (RP)** worksheet to help students understand the purpose of autobiography.	**RI.2** Determine a central idea of a text and how it is conveyed through particular details; provide a summary of the text distinct from personal opinions or judgments.	Challenge students to think of other autobiographical works they've read and to consider the central idea of those works.
Writing	You may wish to administer the **Writing to Sources: Argument (RP)** worksheet to help students prepare for their writing.	**W.1** Write arguments to support claims with clear reasons and relevant evidence.	Challenge students to identify and address opposing claims to their arguments.
Speaking and Listening	You may wish to administer the **Speaking and Listening: Annotated Map (RP)** worksheet to help students complete the annotated map with paraphrased descriptions of places.	**SL.2** Interpret information presented in diverse media and formats and explain how it contributes to a topic, text, or issue under study.	Challenge students to use Google Earth to identify other places Brierley mentions in the text.
Language	Review the **Word Study: Latin Suffix –ive (RP)** worksheet with students to ensure they understand the suffix -*ive* means "pertaining to," "tending to," or "serving to do." You may wish to administer the **Author's Style: Word Choice and Mood (RP)** worksheet to ensure students understand that analogies allow authors to compare two or more things that are similar in some ways.	**L.4.b** Use common, grade-appropriate Greek or Latin affixes and roots as clues to the meaning of a word. **L.4** Determine or clarify the meaning of unknown and multiple-meaning words and phrases based on *grade 6 reading and content,* choosing flexibly from a range of strategies.	Have students identify words in the selection that use other suffixes they recognize. Have students think about other works they've read in which an author uses descriptive language to create a certain mood.

Jump Start

FIRST READ What does it mean to be an explorer? Is an explorer someone who goes into unknown territory for the first time, or is it someone who embarks on a journey of discovery? Engage students in a discussion about what it takes to be an explorer to set the context for reading the excerpt from *A Long Way Home*.

from *A Long Way Home* 🔊 📄

How can Brierley find his hometown using Google Earth? How does Brierley's story connect to the concept of exploration? Modeling the questions that readers might ask as they read the excerpt from *A Long Way Home* for the first time brings the text alive for students and connects it to the Whole-Class Performance Task assignment. Selection audio and print capability for the selection are available in the Interactive Teacher's Edition.

Concept Vocabulary

Support students as they rank their words. Ask if they've ever heard, read, or used them. Reassure them that the definitions for these words are listed in the selection.

FIRST READ

As they read, students should perform the steps of the first read:

NOTICE: You may want to encourage students to notice what Brierley is looking for and how he is conducting his search.

ANNOTATE: Remind students to mark passages that they feel are particularly evocative or worthy of analysis in their close read. For example, students may want to focus on passages that have descriptive language or contain dialogue.

CONNECT: Encourage students to make connections beyond the text. If they cannot make connections to their own lives or to other texts, have them think about connections they can make to television shows or movies they've seen.

RESPOND: Students will answer questions and write a summary to demonstrate understanding.

Point out to students that while they will always complete the Respond step at the end of the first read, the other steps will probably happen somewhat concurrently. You may wish to print copies of the **First-Read Guide: Nonfiction** for students to use. 📄

About the Author

Saroo Brierley (b. 1981) was born in a tiny village in India. At around the age of 5, he accidentally boarded a train alone and was whisked away from his family, hopelessly lost. He ended up at an orphanage in the West Bengal capital of Kolkata, formerly known as Calcutta. Brierley was eventually adopted by an Australian family and was raised in Tasmania. After twenty-five years of separation, Brierley finally succeeded in his quest to find his Indian family.

🔧 **Tool Kit**
First-Read Guide and Model Annotation

📋 **STANDARDS**
Reading Informational Text
By the end of the year, read and comprehend literary nonfiction in the grades 6–8 text complexity band proficiently, with scaffolding as needed at the high end of the range.

---

from A Long Way Home

Concept Vocabulary

You will encounter the following words as you read the excerpt from *A Long Way Home*. Before reading, note how familiar you are with each word. Then, rank the words in order from most familiar (1) to least familiar (6).

WORD	YOUR RANKING
deliberate	
quest	
thorough	
obsessive	
intensity	
relentlessly	

After completing the first read, come back to the concept vocabulary and review your rankings. Mark changes to your original rankings as needed.

First Read NONFICTION

Apply these strategies as you conduct your first read. You will have an opportunity to complete the close-read notes after your first read.

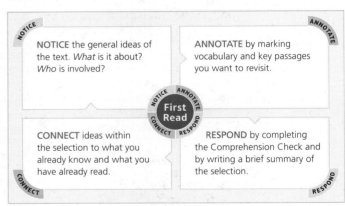

NOTICE the general ideas of the text. *What* is it about? *Who* is involved?

ANNOTATE by marking vocabulary and key passages you want to revisit.

CONNECT ideas within the selection to what you already know and what you have already read.

RESPOND by completing the Comprehension Check and by writing a brief summary of the selection.

© Pearson Education, Inc., or its affiliates. All rights reserved.

Kelly Gallagher, M.Ed.

Reading Reasons Students often ask "Why should I read?" Increasingly, teachers see students who often give up easily when confronted with challenging reading material such as a biology textbook or a state-mandated exam. They are unable, or unwilling, to tackle difficult text. How do teachers turn around this apathy? How do teachers shelter fragile adolescent readers and help them grow into people for whom reading matters?

Building reading motivation is complex, as there isn't a single correct motivational tool, but together, many of these techniques send the message that reading is rewarding.

- Give students access to high-interest reading material, which is provided in this program.
- Give students a time and place to read.

from
A Long Way Home
Saroo Brierley

© Pearson Education, Inc., or its affiliates. All rights reserved.

BACKGROUND
In his memoir *A Long Way Home*, Saroo Brierley shares his memories of searching for his hometown and his birth family. He describes the detailed method he used to locate them after decades of separation. At this point in the memoir, Brierley has recently graduated from college and moved in with his friend Byron.

SCAN FOR
MULTIMEDIA

1   Alas, the new search didn't start out as an obsession.

2   If Byron wasn't home, I might spend a couple of hours musing over the various "B" towns[1] again. Or I might make a casual sweep down the east coast, to see what was there. I even checked out a Birampur in Uttar Pradesh, near Delhi, in the central north of India, but that was a ridiculously long way from Kolkata, and I couldn't have traveled that far in twelve or so hours. It turned out it doesn't even have a train station.

3   These occasional forays showed the folly of searching by town, particularly when I wasn't sure about the names. If I was going to do this, I needed to be strategic and methodical about it.

NOTES

1. **"B" Towns** Brierley remembers that the name of the train station near his hometown begins with a "B." This is the station at which he boarded a train and became lost.

from A Long Way Home **411**

- Model the value of reading. Read with students, so they see you enjoying reading. Start a student book club in school.
- Build in an element of choice.
- Build in time to confer with students to discuss their reading progress.
- Establish reading goals.
- Provide structure to the reading program by logging the number of words, pages, and time that students read.

CLOSER LOOK

Analyze First-Person Narrative ⊘

Students may have marked paragraph 4 during their first read. Use this paragraph to help students understand some of the elements that make up a first-person narrative. You may want to model a close read with the class based on the highlights shown in the text.

ANNOTATE: Have students mark words in paragraph 4 that indicate that this narrative is written in the first person.

QUESTION: Guide students to consider what these details might tell them. Ask what a reader can infer from what was marked, and accept student responses.

Possible response: The use of the words *I* and *my* show that the author himself is describing events from his life. He is detailing the process of his search as he remembers it.

CONCLUDE: Help students to formulate conclusions about the importance of the details in the text. Ask students why the author might have included these details.

Possible response: The use of the first person gives the author's account a directness and power that might otherwise be missing. Readers learn of his struggle and how he worked through portions of the problem of finding his home in his own words.

Remind students that the **first-person** is a point of view in which an author is directly involved in the events that he or she describes. The first-person point of view is indicated through the use of words such as *I* and *my*.

NOTES

4   I went over what I knew. I came from a place where Muslims and Hindus lived in close proximity and where Hindi was spoken. Those things were true of most of India. I recalled all those warm nights outside, under the stars, which at least suggested it wouldn't be in the colder regions of the far north. I hadn't lived by the sea, although I couldn't rule out that I'd lived near it. And I hadn't lived in the mountains. My hometown had a railway station—India was riddled with train lines, but they didn't run through every single village and town.

5   Then there was the opinion of the Indians at college that I looked like someone from the east, perhaps around West Bengal. I had my doubts: in the eastern part of the country, the region took in some of the Himalayas,[2] which wasn't right, and part of the Ganges Delta, which looked much too lush and fertile to be my home. But as these were people who had firsthand experience of India, it seemed silly to dismiss their hunch.

6   I also thought I could remember enough landmark features to recognize my hometown if I came across it, or to at least narrow the field. I clearly recalled the bridge over the river where we played as kids and the nearby dam wall that restricted the river's flow below it. I knew how to get from the train station to our house, and I knew the layout of the station.

7   The other station I thought I remembered quite well was the "B" one, where I'd boarded the train. Although I'd been there quite a few times with my brothers, they'd never let me leave it, so I knew nothing of the town outside the station—all I'd ever seen beyond the exit was a sort of small ring road for horse carts and cars, and a road beyond it that led into the town. But still, there were a couple of distinguishing features. I remembered the station building and that it only had a couple of tracks, over the other side of which was a big water tank on a tower. There was also a pedestrian overpass across the tracks. And just before the train pulled into town from the direction of my home, it crossed a small gorge.

8   So I had some vague thoughts on likely regions, and some ways of identifying "Ginestlay"[3] and the "B" place if I found them. Now I needed a better search method. I realized that the names of places had been a distraction, or were at least not the right place to start. Instead, I thought about the end of the journey. I knew that train lines linked the "B" place with Kolkata. Logic dictated, then, that if I followed all the train lines out of Kolkata, I would eventually find my starting point. And from there, my hometown was itself up the line, not far away. I might even come upon my

---

2. **Himalayas** (hihm uh LAY uhz) tallest mountain range in the world.
3. **"Ginestlay"** Brierley remembered this as the name of his hometown, but no one asked had heard of it and he could not find it on a map.

© Pearson Education, Inc., or its affiliates. All rights reserved.

CROSS-CURRICULAR PERSPECTIVES

Social Studies Have students research the geography of India and create a map. They should label regions and the major geographical features mentioned in the selection, such as the Himalayas and the Ganges Delta, which are mentioned in paragraph 5. Once students have finished their maps, discuss the geography of India. Elicit from students that India is made up of deserts, mountains, rainforests, and flat, rolling plains. Explain that India is approximately one third the size of the United States with about 1.25 billion people, roughly four times the population of the United States. Ask students to consider how the size and the population of the country affected Brierley's search.

home first, depending on how the lines linked up. This was an intimidating prospect—there were many, many train lines from the national hub of Kolkata's Howrah Station, and my train might have zigzagged across any of the lines of the spider's web. It was unlikely to be a simple, straight route.

9   Still, even with the possibility of some winding, irregular paths out of Howrah, there was also a limit to how far I could have been transported in the time frame. I'd spent, I thought, a long time on the train—somewhere between twelve and fifteen hours. If I made some calculations, I could narrow the search field, ruling out places too far away.

10   Why hadn't I thought of the search with this clarity before? Maybe I had been too overwhelmed by the scale of the problem to think straight, too consumed by what I didn't know to focus on what I did. But as it dawned on me that I could turn this into a painstaking, **deliberate** task that simply required dedication, something clicked inside. If all it took were time and patience to find home, with the aid of Google Earth's[4] god's-eye view, then I would do it. Seeing it almost as much an intellectual challenge as an emotional **quest**, I threw myself into solving it.

11   First, I worked on the search zone. How fast could India's diesel trains travel, and would that have changed much since the eighties? I thought my Indian friends from college might be able to help, especially Amreen, whose father would likely have a more educated guess, so I got in touch with them. The general consensus was around seventy or eighty kilometers an hour. That seemed like a good start. Figuring I had been trapped on the train for around twelve to fifteen hours, overnight, I calculated how many kilometers I might have traveled in that time, which I put at around a thousand, or approximately 620 miles.

12   So the place I was looking for was a thousand kilometers along a train line out of Howrah Station. On Google Earth you can draw lines on the map at precise distances, so I made a circular boundary line of a thousand kilometers around Kolkata and saved it for my searches. That meant that as well as West Bengal, my search field included the states of Jharkhand, Chhattisgarh, and nearly half of the central state of Madhya Pradesh to the west, Orissa to the south, Bihar and a third of Uttar Pradesh to the north, and most of the northeastern spur of India, which encircles Bangladesh. (I knew I wasn't from Bangladesh, as I'd have spoken Bengali, not Hindi. This was confirmed when I discovered

4. **Google Earth** computer program that displays satellite images of the world.

NOTES

CLOSE READ
ANNOTATE: In paragraph 8, mark details that describe the challenges Brierley faces in finding his hometown.

QUESTION: Why does Brierley provide so much detail about his thought process?

CONCLUDE: What can you conclude about Brierley and his mission from these details?

deliberate (dih LIHB uhr iht) *adj.* carefully thought over in advance; planned

quest (kwehst) *n.* long search undertaken in order to find or realize something

from A Long Way Home **413**

 CLOSE READ

Remind students to focus on the comparison of the train lines and something not made by humans. You may wish to model the close read using the following think-aloud format. Possible responses to questions on the student page are included. You may also want to print copies of the **Close-Read Guide: Nonfiction** for students to use.

ANNOTATE: As I read paragraph 8, I notice and mark two things that are being compared: the train lines and something that isn't made by humans and appears in the natural world.

QUESTION: The author may have made the comparison to show that although the two things being compared may not seem to have much in common at first, they share some qualities. If viewed from above, many train lines extending out from a central point, or hub, might look like a spider's web, which also has lines extending out from a central point.

CONCLUDE: There are many train lines extending out from the hub—just like there are many lines in a spider's web. This shows that the author's task will be difficult because there are many possible train destinations.

Additional **English Language Support** is available in the Interactive Teacher's Edition.

PERSONALIZE FOR LEARNING

English Language Support
Idioms Idioms can be confusing to English learners. Explain that the term *I threw myself into* in paragraph 10 is an idiom. To help them understand its usage in the paragraph, explain that to throw oneself into something means to do it with a lot of energy and commitment. For example, tell them if they threw themselves

into studying for a test, they would be studying eagerly and with enthusiasm. Point out that here, the author is saying that once he figured out how to do the search, he became eager and enthusiastic about it—he began searching with great energy and commitment. **ALL LEVELS**

© Pearson Education, Inc., or its affiliates. All rights reserved.

NOTES

that a rail connection between the two countries had only been established a few years ago.)

13   It was a staggering amount of territory, covering some 962,300 square kilometers, over a quarter of India's huge landmass. Within its bounds lived 345 million people. I tried to keep my emotions out of the exercise, but I couldn't help but wonder: Is it possible to find my four family members among these 345 million? Even though my calculations were reliant on guesswork and were therefore very rough, and even though that still presented me with a huge field within which to search, it felt like I was narrowing things down. Rather than randomly throwing the haystack around to find the needle,[5] I could concentrate on picking through a manageable portion and set it aside if it proved empty.

Image from Google Earth.

14   The train lines within the search zone wouldn't all simply stretch out to the edge in a straight radius, of course—there would be a lot of twists, turns, and junctions, as they wound around and traveled much more than a thousand kilometers before they

---

5. **haystack . . . needle** the saying "finding a needle in a haystack" means looking for something almost impossible to find.

© Pearson Education, Inc., or its affiliates. All rights reserved.

DIGITAL PERSPECTIVES

Enriching the Text Beginning in paragraph 8, the author mentions how many train lines ran to and from Kolkata. To help students visualize these many train lines and what an enormous task Brierley had, find and show Indian railway maps on the Internet, especially aerial images of the lines that run in and out of Kolkata. Ask students to locate Kolkata on the maps and discuss how the maps help them understand the difficulties the author faced. Guide students to match the details from the maps to the author's written description.

reached the boundary edge. So I planned to work outward from Kolkata, the only point of the journey I was certain about.

15   The first time I zoomed in on Howrah Station, looking at the rows of ridged gray platform roofs and all the tracks spilling out of it like the fraying end of a rope, I was amazed and shocked that I'd once trod barefoot along these walkways. I had to open my eyes wide to make sure what I was looking at was real. I was about to embark on a high-tech version of what I'd done in my first week there, twenty years ago, randomly taking trains out to see if they went back home.

16   I took a deep breath, chose a train line, and started scrolling along it.

17   Immediately, it became clear that progress would be slow. Even with broadband, my laptop had to render the image, which took time. It started a little pixelated, then resolved into an aerial photograph. I was looking for landmarks I recognized and paid particular attention to the stations, as they were the places I remembered most vividly.

18   When I first zoomed out to see how far I'd gone along the track, I was amazed at how little progress the hours of scrolling and studying had brought me. But rather than being frustrated and impatient, I found I had enormous confidence that I would find what I was looking for as long as I was **thorough**. That gave me a great sense of calm as I resumed my search. In fact, it quickly became compelling, and I returned to it several nights a week. Before I turned in each night, I'd mark how far I'd gone on a track and save the search, then resume from that point at the next opportunity.

19   I would come across goods yards, overpasses and underpasses, bridges over rivers and junctions. Sometimes I skipped along a bit but then nervously went back to repeat a section, reminding myself that if I wasn't methodical, I could never be sure I'd looked everywhere. I didn't jump ahead to look for stations in case I missed a small one—I followed the tracks so I could check out anything that came along. And if I found myself reaching the edge of the boundary I'd devised, I'd go back along the train line to a previous junction and then head off in another direction.

20   I remember one night early on, following a line north, I came to a river crossing not far outside a town. I caught my breath as I zoomed in closer. The dam wall was decaying, but maybe the area had since been reconstructed? I quickly dragged the cursor to roll the image along. Did the countryside look right? It was quite green, but there were a lot of farms on the outskirts of my town. I watched as the town unpixelated before my eyes. It was quite small. Too small, surely. But with a child's perspective . . .

NOTES

CLOSE READ
ANNOTATE: A **simile** compares two unlike things using the word *like* or *as*. Mark the simile in paragraph 15.

QUESTION: Why might the author have used a simile to describe what he was viewing on his computer screen?

CONCLUDE: How does the simile help the reader to better understand the challenges the author is facing?

thorough (THUR oh) *adj.* including everything possible; careful and complete

© Pearson Education, Inc., or its affiliates. All rights reserved.

CLOSE READ

Remind students to look for two things that are being compared using the word *like*. You may wish to model the close read using the following think-aloud format. Possible responses to questions on the student page are included.

ANNOTATE: As I read paragraph 15, I notice and mark two things that are being compared using the word *like*.

QUESTION: The author may have included the simile as a way of describing what he was viewing on his screen. The image of the frayed rope end helps readers visualize the train lines extending out from the station.

CONCLUDE: The simile helps readers get a sense of how many train lines the author has to trace. It will be a long, slow process.

VOCABULARY DEVELOPMENT

Domain-Specific Words Reinforce students' comprehension of the technical vocabulary in the selection with "show-you-know" sentences. The first part of the sentence uses the vocabulary word in an appropriate context. The second part—the "show-you-know" part—clarifies the first. Model the strategy with this example for the word *pixelated* from paragraph 17:

The image was *pixelated*, so I had trouble recognizing people and objects because they were grainy.

Then give students these sentence prompts and coach them to create the clarification parts.

1. When I *zoomed* in on the image, it showed _____.

2. She had *broadband*, which helped with homework because it _____.

3. Dragging the *cursor* allowed her to _____.

NOTES

And there was a high pedestrian overpass across the tracks near the station! But what were the large blank areas dotted around the town? Three lakes, four or five even, within the tiny village's bounds—and it was suddenly obvious that this wasn't the place. You didn't clear whole neighborhoods to put in lakes. And of course, many, many stations were likely to have overpasses, and many towns would be situated near life-giving rivers, which the tracks would have to cross. How many times would I wonder if all the landmarks aligned, only to be left with tired, sore eyes and the realization that I was mistaken again?

21   Weeks and then months passed with my spending hours at a time every couple of nights on the laptop. Byron made sure I spent other nights out in the real world so I didn't become an Internet recluse. I covered the countryside of West Bengal and Jharkhand in these early stages without finding anything familiar, but at least it meant that much of the immediate vicinity of Kolkata could be ruled out. Despite the hunch of my Indian friends, I'd come from farther away.

22   Several months later, I was lucky enough to meet someone with whom I started a new relationship, which made the search less of a priority for a while. Lisa and I met in 2010 through a friend of Byron's and mine. We became friends on Facebook, and then I asked her for her phone number. We hit it off immediately; Lisa's background is in business management and she is smart, pretty, and can hold a great conversation. However, we had an unsettled start together, with a couple of breakups and reunions, which meant there was a similar inconsistency in the periods I spent looking on the Internet, before we finally settled into the lasting relationship we have today.

23   I didn't know how a girlfriend would take to the time-consuming quest of her partner staring at maps on a laptop. But Lisa understood the personal and growing importance of the search, and was patient and supportive. She was as amazed as anyone about my past, and wanted me to find the answers I was looking for. We moved into a small flat[6] together in 2010. I thought of the nights I spent there on the laptop as being a pastime, like playing computer games. But Lisa says that even then, with our relationship in full swing, I was **obsessive**. Looking back, I can see that this was true.

24   After all the years of my story being in my thoughts and dreams, I felt I was closing in on the reality. I decided this time I wasn't going to listen to anybody who said, "It might be time to move on," or "It's just not possible to find your hometown in

obsessive (uhb SEHS ihv) *adj.* tending to think or worry so much about something that you cannot think about anything else

© Pearson Education, Inc., or its affiliates. All rights reserved.

---

6. **flat** *n.* apartment.

416 UNIT 5 • EXPLORATION

WriteNow   Express and Reflect

Description In paragraph 23, the author describes how his girlfriend Lisa encouraged his search. Have students write a one-page description of a time when someone encouraged them to do something that was important to them. For example, perhaps they decided they wanted to learn tae kwon do and were unsure if they could do it before receiving support and encouragement from a friend or family member. Have them explain what the person said or did and how it affected them. Draw students' attention to the way the author describes Lisa's encouragement of his search in paragraph 23, and direct students to include similar details in their descriptions.

all of India like this." Lisa never said those things, and with her support, I became even more determined to succeed.

25   I didn't tell many people what I was doing anyway. And I decided not to tell my parents. I was worried they might misunderstand my intentions. I didn't want them to think that the **intensity** of my search revealed an unhappiness with the life they'd given me or the way they'd raised me. I also didn't want them to think that I was wasting time. So even as it took up more and more of my life, I kept it mostly to myself. I finished work with Dad at five p.m., and by five-thirty I would be back at the laptop, slowly advancing along train tracks and studying the towns they led to. This went on for months—it had been over a year since I started. But I reasoned that even if it took years . . . or decades . . . it was possible to eventually sift completely through a haystack. The needle would have to show up if I persisted.

26   Slowly, over several more months, I eliminated whole areas of India. I traced all the connections within the northeastern states without finding anything familiar, and I was confident that I could rule out Orissa, too. Determined to be thorough, no matter how long it took, I started following lines farther out than my original thousand-kilometer zone. South beyond Orissa, I eliminated Andhra Pradesh, five hundred kilometers farther down the east coast. Jharkhand and Bihar didn't offer up anything promising, either, and as I wound up in Uttar Pradesh, I thought I'd keep going to cover most of the state. In fact, the states eventually replaced my zone boundary as a way of marking my progress. Ruling out areas state by state provided a series of goals that spurred me on.

27   Unless I had something pressing to do for work, or some other unbreakable commitment, I was on the laptop seven nights a week. I went out with Lisa sometimes, of course, but the moment we got home I was back on the computer. Sometimes I caught her looking at me strangely, as though she thought I might have gone a bit crazy. She'd say, "You're at it again!" but I would reply, "I have to . . . I'm really sorry!" I think Lisa knew she simply had to let me exhaust myself of the interest. I became distant during that time, and although Lisa would have been within her rights to feel alone in this still-new relationship, we worked through it. Perhaps to some extent sharing something so fundamental to me strengthened our connection—and that came through when we sometimes talked about what it all meant. It wasn't always easy for me to articulate,[7] especially as I was trying to keep a lid on my expectations, trying to convince myself it was a fascinating exercise, not a deeply meaningful personal quest. Talking to Lisa

_____
7. **articulate** (ahr TIHK yuh layt) *v.* express clearly using words.

NOTES

intensity (ihn TEHN suh tee) *n.* great focus or concentration; strong commitment

CLOSE READ
ANNOTATE: In paragraph 27, mark details that show how often Brierley is searching for his hometown at this point.

QUESTION: What do these details reveal about how his search is progressing?

CONCLUDE: How do these details help the reader to better understand Brierley's state of mind?

from A Long Way Home **417**

CLOSE READ

Remind students to look for words or phrases that indicate how the author is spending his time. You may wish to model the close read using the following think-aloud format. Possible responses to questions on the student page are included.

ANNOTATE: As I read paragraph 27, I notice and mark words that show when the author was at his computer searching for his hometown.

QUESTION: The details show that the author is making progress. He is eliminating areas, and those results encourage him. The encouragement he feels makes him want to press on even more.

CONCLUDE: The details show how determined the author is. He is willing to make a huge effort to achieve his goal.

© Pearson Education, Inc., or its affiliates. All rights reserved.

PERSONALIZE FOR LEARNING

English Language Support
Idioms Explain to students that *keep a lid on* in paragraph 27 is an idiomatic expression—the words used are not meant literally. If students struggle to understand idioms, encourage them to look for context clues. Instruct students to keep reading to get clues about the meaning of this expression. (Context clue: "trying to

convince myself it was a fascinating exercise, not a deeply meaningful personal quest.") Make sure students understand that *keep a lid on my expectations* means to control his expectations, to make sure they don't grow too much and set him up for disappointment later. **ALL LEVELS**

NOTES

sometimes revealed the underlying importance of the search to me: that I was looking for my home to provide closure and to understand my past and perhaps myself better as a result, in the hope that I might somehow reconnect with my Indian family so they would know what had happened to me. Lisa understood all this and didn't resent it, even if there were times when she wanted to ban me from staring at the screen for my own sake. Once in a while she would simply come over and shut my laptop and place it on the floor because I was becoming so obsessive about my search.

28   At times Lisa admitted her own greatest fear: that I would find what I thought I was looking for, go back to India, and somehow be wrong or fail to find my family there. Would I return to Hobart[8] and simply start again, obsessively searching online? I couldn't answer her questions any more than I could allay her fears. I couldn't allow myself to think about failure.

29   If anything, I became more intense about my search as 2010 drew to a close, and the speed of our newly acquired broadband connection made it quicker to refresh the images and zoom in and out. But I still had to take it slowly—if I rushed, I'd leave myself open to wondering later if I'd missed anything and then going back in an endless cycle. And I had to try not to bend my memories to fit what I was looking at.

30   By early 2011, I was concentrating more on areas within India's center, in Chhattisgarh and Madhya Pradesh. I spent months poring over them, **relentlessly**, methodically.

relentlessly (rih LEHNT lihs lee) *adv.* without stopping; with determination

31   Of course, there were times when I doubted the wisdom, and even the sanity, of what I was doing. Night after night, with the day's last reserves of energy and willpower, I sat staring at railway lines, searching for places my five-year-old mind might recognize. It was a repetitive, forensic[9] exercise, and sometimes it started to feel claustrophobic, as if I were trapped and looking out at the world through a small window, unable to break free of my course in a mind-twisting echo of my childhood ordeal.

32   And then one night in March around one in the morning, in just such a mood, spent with frustration, I took a wild dive into the haystack, and it changed everything.

33   As always, on March 31, 2011, I had come home from work, grabbed my laptop, opened Google Earth, and settled in for a session on the sofa, stopping only briefly for dinner when Lisa got home. I was examining the central west at this time, so I picked up there, "traveling" a train line near my former search zone

---

8. **Hobart** capital of Tasmania, an island state of Australia, where Brierley lives.
9. **forensic** (fuh REHN sihk) *adj.* careful and detailed, similar to the scientific methods used to solve a crime.

© Pearson Education, Inc., or its affiliates. All rights reserved.

418 UNIT 5 • EXPLORATION

boundary. Even with quicker broadband, it was still slow going. I continued for what seemed like ages, looking at a few stations, but as usual, when I zoomed out, I found I'd only covered a tiny area. I thought that the countryside looked a bit green for my dusty old town, but I knew by now that India's landscape changed appearance regularly as you moved across it.

34   After a few hours, I had followed a line to a junction. I took a break, checking Facebook for a while before rubbing my eyes, stretching my back, and returning to my task.

35   Before zooming in, I idly flicked the map along to get a quick picture of where the westerly line out of the junction headed, and watched hills, forests, and river sweep by, a seemingly endless terrain of reasonably similar features. I was distracted by a large river that fed into what looked like a massive, deep blue lake called Nal Damayanti Sagar, which was surrounded by some lush country and had mountains to its north. For a while, I enjoyed this little exploration, indulgently unrelated to my search, like a recreational hike of grand proportions. It was getting late, after all, and I'd turn in soon.

36   There didn't seem to be any train lines in this part of the country, which might have been why it was relaxing to look at. But once I'd noticed that, I found myself almost subconsciously looking for one. There were villages and towns dotted around here and there, and I wondered how the people traveled without rail—perhaps they didn't move around much? And farther west, still no tracks! Then as the countryside flattened out into farmland, I finally came across a little blue symbol denoting a train station. I was so attuned to looking for them, I was somehow relieved to find this one, and I checked out the tiny wayside station, just a few buildings to the side of a reasonably major train line with several tracks. Out of habit, I started tracing the route as it wound southwest. I quickly came across another station, a bit bigger, again with a platform on only one side of the tracks, but some areas of the township on either side. That explained the overpass, and was that . . . was that a water tower just nearby?

37   Holding my breath, I zoomed in for a closer look. Sure enough, it was a municipal water tank just across from the platform, and not far from a large pedestrian overpass spanning the railway line. I scrolled over to the town side and saw something incredible—a horseshoe-shaped road around a square immediately outside the station. Could it be—perhaps it was the ring road I used to be able to see from the platform! Was it possible? I closed my

> Could it be—perhaps it was the ring road I used to be able to see from the platform! Was it possible?

from A Long Way Home **419**

© Pearson Education, Inc. or its affiliates. All rights reserved.

CLOSER LOOK

Analyze Description

Students may have marked paragraph 36 during their first read. Use this paragraph to help students understand how the author's description helps the reader see what he sees. Encourage them to talk about the annotations that they marked. You may want to model a close read with the class based on the highlights shown in the text.

ANNOTATE: Have students mark details in paragraph 36 that describe what the author sees as he looks at the images on Google Earth, or have students participate while you highlight them.

QUESTION: Guide students to consider what these details might tell them. Ask what a reader can infer from the descriptions of the countryside and the town with a railway station, and accept student responses.

Possible response: The author describes exactly what he sees as he follows the railway tracks along the countryside and into a village. As he zooms in and describes more specific details of the place, such as the station with a platform on only one side of the tracks and the nearby water tower, the author allows readers to see what he is seeing.

CONCLUDE: Help students to formulate conclusions about the importance of these details in the text. Ask students why the author might have included these details.

Possible response: As the author's details become more specific, he builds suspense. The reader follows the description and wonders if the author has finally found his childhood home.

Remind students that a **description** is a portrait in words of a person, place, or thing. Descriptive writing uses images that appeal to the senses: sight, hearing, taste, smell, and touch. Point out that in this case, the writer is mostly appealing to the reader's sense of sight, allowing the reader to follow the rail line along with the author.

PERSONALIZE FOR LEARNING

English Language Support

Domain-Specific Vocabulary Students may need help interpreting the vocabulary related to transportation. Support them in understanding the text by reviewing the following terms:

Pedestrian: a person who is walking

Overpass: a bridge that crosses over a road or railway

Route: road or path

Wayside: roadside

Have students locate these terms in paragraphs 36 and 37 and read the sentences containing the terms. Then, have them paraphrase the sentences, replacing the transportation term with its definition.

For example:

I checked out the tiny *wayside* station, just a few buildings to the side of a reasonably major train line with several tracks.

I checked out the tiny *roadside* station, just a few buildings to the side of a reasonably major train line with several tracks.

ALL LEVELS

 CLOSE READ ✎

Remind students to look for the words that have been italicized. You may wish to model the close read using the following think-aloud format. Possible responses to questions on the student page are included.

ANNOTATE: As I read paragraph 37, I notice and highlight the words that are set in italics.

QUESTION: The author emphasizes these words to let the reader know that they are important and that special attention should be given to them.

CONCLUDE: The emphasis placed on the sentence *"This is unique..."* helps readers understand the suspense that the author himself is feeling, and the emphasis placed on the word *Burhanpur*, which is italicized and is punctuated with an exclamation mark, shows his excitement.

NOTES

CLOSE READ
ANNOTATE: In paragraph 37, mark the words the author emphasizes with italics.

QUESTION: Why does the author choose to emphasize these words?

CONCLUDE: How does this emphasis help the reader understand Brierley's thoughts and emotions?

eyes and went back twenty four years in time to when I would walk to the station's exit and see the ring road with an island in the middle. I thought to myself, *This is unique; I haven't seen this before.* I zoomed out, discovering that the train line skimmed the northwestern edge of a really large town. I clicked on the blue train station symbol to reveal its name . . . Burhanpur. My heart nearly stopped. *Burhanpur!*

38   I didn't recognize the town itself, but then I'd never been in it—I'd never left the platform. I zoomed back in and re-examined the ring road, the water tower, the overpass, and they were all positioned where I remembered them. That meant that not far away, just up the line, I should find my hometown, "Ginestlay."

39   Almost afraid to do so, I dragged the cursor to pull the image north along the train line. When I saw that the track crossed a gorge just on the edge of the built-up area, I was flooded with adrenaline—I remembered in a flash that the train I took with my brothers traveled on a small bridge over a gorge like that before pulling into the station. I pushed on more urgently, east then northeast, in just moments zooming over seventy kilometers

© Pearson Education, Inc., or its affiliates. All rights reserved.

VOCABULARY DEVELOPMENT

Multiple Meanings Tell students that the word *gorge* has multiple meanings. Discuss the following sentence with students.

1. The children stood on the bridge and looked down into the *gorge*. (a narrow valley between hills or mountains)

2. He *gorged* himself on apple pie at Thanksgiving. (ate large amounts of food)

3. The bend in the river was blocked by an ice *gorge*. (a mass that blocks the way)

Have students reread the following sentence in paragraph 39: *When I saw that the track crossed a gorge just on the edge of the built-up area, I was flooded with adrenaline . . .* Guide them to identify which meaning is used in the sentence. Discuss how to use context clues to define a word with multiple meanings.

of green farms, forested hills, and small rivers. Then I passed across some dry, flat land, broken up by a patchwork of irrigated farmland and the occasional small village, before I hit a bridge over a substantial river. Ahead I was able to see the town's outskirts. The river's flow was significantly reduced below the bridge by dam walls on either side. If this was the right place, this was the river I used to play in, and there should be a bigger concrete dam wall to my right a little farther from the bridge . . .

40   There it was!

41   I sat staring at the screen for what seemed like an eternity. What I was looking at matched the picture in my head exactly. I couldn't think straight; I was frozen with excitement, terrified to go on.

42   Finally, after a couple of minutes, I forced myself to take the next step, slowly, nervously. I tried to calm myself so I didn't jump to any rash conclusions. If I really was looking at "Ginestlay" for the first time in twenty-four years, then I should be able to follow the path I remembered from the river back to the train station, only a short way up ahead. I began to drag the cursor again, slowly rolling the map to trace the course of the path, which wound gently alongside a tributary stream, left and right, around a field, under a street overpass and then . . . the station. I clicked on the blue symbol and the name came up on the screen: Khandwa Railway Station.

43   The name meant nothing to me.

44   My stomach knotted. How could this be?

45   Things had looked so right all the way from Burhanpur, which had to be the "B" town I had tried to remember. But if the bridge and the river were correct, where was "Ginestlay"? I tried not to despair. I had spent a lot of time in and around our local train station as a boy, so I checked off what I remembered—the three platforms, the covered pedestrian overpass that connected them, an underpass road beneath the tracks at the northern end. But it wasn't so much the existence of these reasonably common features but their position in relation to each other that would identify the specific place that I was looking for. It all checked out. I also remembered a huge fountain in a park near the underpass, and I went looking. Sure enough, it was a little indistinct, but I thought I detected its familiar circular shape in a central clearing, surrounded by trees.

46   From here, I knew the route to where my home should be. This was why I'd gone over and over it in my head since I was a little boy: so that I would never forget it.

47   Now, as a man, I followed the road up from the fountain and along the route of the underpass, and then the streets and alleys I had walked as a child—the way I used to imagine myself walking

NOTES

CLOSE READ

ANNOTATE: In paragraph 41, mark the words that show Brierley's reaction to the image on his screen.

QUESTION: Why might Brierley react with these feelings?

CONCLUDE: How does the description of his reaction add suspense to Brierley's narrative?

© Pearson Education, Inc., or its affiliates. All rights reserved.

CLOSE READ

Remind students to look for words that describe the author's reaction. You may wish to model the close read using the following think-aloud format. Possible responses to questions on the student page are included.

ANNOTATE: As I read paragraph 41, I notice and mark the words that show Brierley's reaction to the image on his screen.

QUESTION: Brierley might have reacted the way he did because he realized that after so much time and effort spent in searching, he might be very close to finding his hometown.

CONCLUDE: The phrases "frozen with excitement" and "terrified to go on" add suspense because the author is hopeful that he is close to finding his hometown, but if he is wrong, the disappointment would be great. Readers are meant to share in the author's excitement and fear of being wrong.

from A Long Way Home **421**

HOW LANGUAGE WORKS

Troublesome Verbs Explain to students that some verb pairs can be confusing. Point to the first sentence in paragraph 47: *. . . the way I used to imagine myself walking when I lay in bed at night . . .* Explain that the verb pairs *lie* and *lay* are often confused. Point out that *lie* means "to recline" and that it usually refers to a person. (She wants to *lie* on the beach towel.) Then point out that the past tense of *lie* is *lay*, which is what is used in the sentence in paragraph 47. Explain that *lay* is also the present tense of the verb *to lay*, which means "to place something."

Provide students with the following chart, which shows how the words are conjugated.

Present Tense	Past Tense	Past Participle	Present Participle
lie	lay	have lain	Is lying
lay	laid	have laid	Is laying

CLOSER LOOK

Analyze Tone 🌐

Students may have marked paragraphs 48 and 49 during their first read. Use these paragraphs to help students understand tone. Encourage students to talk about the annotations that they marked. You may want to model a close read with the class based on the highlights shown in the text.

ANNOTATE: Have students mark details in paragraphs 48 and 49 that reveal tone, or have students participate while you highlight them.

QUESTION: Guide students to consider what these details might tell them. Ask what a reader can infer from the author's description of when he first realized he had found his home, and accept student responses.

Possible response: The author's use of the words *astonished* and *excitement* and his exclamations ("I've found my hometown! You've gotta come and see this!") help set a tone of amazement and joy.

CONCLUDE: Help students to formulate conclusions about the importance of these details in the text. Ask students why the author might have included these details.

Possible response: The happy, excited tone helps readers realize both what a huge accomplishment this was for the author and also how life-changing this discovery is for him. It helps the reader feel the joy that the author felt in finding his home.

Remind students that the **tone** of a literary work is the writer's attitude toward his or her audience and subject. This tone can often be described by a single adjective, such as formal or informal, serious or playful, gentle or bitter, naive or ironic, sympathetic or scathing, friendly or distant, breezy or pompous. Tone almost always affects the **mood** of a literary work—the overall feeling that it evokes in the reader.

NOTES

when I lay in bed at night, in the safe comfort of my house in Hobart, trying to project myself back to my village home to let my mother know I was okay. Before I realized I'd gone far enough, I was looking down at the neighborhood I knew as a boy.

48 Still, nothing like "Ginestlay" came up on the map. It was the strangest feeling, and one that I became familiar with over the next year or so—part of me was certain, but still another part of me doubted. I was sure this was the right place, but for all this time I'd also been sure of the name "Ginestlay." Khandwa rang no bells whatsoever. Maybe "Ginestlay" was a part of Khandwa? A suburb? That seemed possible. I looked through the maze of alleys where my family lived, and although the image wasn't as clear as what I would get when I looked at where I lived in Hobart, I was sure I could see the little rectangular roof of my childhood home. Of course, I'd never seen the place from above, but the building was the right shape and in precisely the correct location. I hovered over the streets for a while, astonished, trying to take it all in. Finally I couldn't contain my excitement any longer.

49 I called out to Lisa, "I've found my hometown! You've gotta come and see this!" It was only then that I realized the time. I'd been at the computer for over seven hours nonstop, except for dinner.

50 Lisa poked her head around the corner, yawning, in her nightie. It took her a moment to wake up properly, but even half-asleep she could see my excitement. "Are you sure?" she asked.

51 "This is it, this is it!" I replied.

52 In that moment, I was convinced. "This is my hometown!"

53 It had taken eight months of intense searching, and it was nearly five years since I'd first downloaded Google Earth.

54 Lisa grinned and hugged me tightly. "That's so great! You did it, Saroo!" ❧

© Pearson Education, Inc., or its affiliates. All rights reserved.

PERSONALIZE FOR LEARNING

Strategic Support

Key Ideas Point out the beginning of paragraph 48 to students—specifically, where the author writes, "It was the strangest feeling, and one that I became familiar with over the next year or so—part of me was certain, but still another part of me doubted." If students have difficulty understanding why the author still had doubts, remind them that the selection is an excerpt of a book, and explain that in the remaining chapters, the author describes in detail how he determined for certain that this was his home.

Comprehension Check

Complete the following items after you finish your first read.

1. What is the goal of Saroo Brierley's search?

2. What is the main resource Brierley uses to conduct his search?

3. According to the author, what is Lisa's greatest fear?

4. What is "Ginestlay"? Does Brierley ever find it?

5. 📓 **Notebook** Write a summary of the memoir to show your understanding.

- -

RESEARCH

Research to Clarify Choose at least one unfamiliar detail from the text. Briefly research that detail. In what way does the information you learned shed light on an aspect of the text?

Research to Explore Choose something that interests you from the text, and formulate a research question.

from A Long Way Home **423**

© Pearson Education, Inc., or its affiliates. All rights reserved.

Comprehension Check

Possible responses:

1. He is looking for his hometown in India.
2. Brierley uses Google Earth to follow train tracks until he finds a place that looks like his hometown.
3. According to the author, Lisa's greatest fear is that he will travel to India thinking he will find his family—only to not find them, return home, and continue his obsessive online search.
4. "Ginestlay" is what Brierley remembers as the name of his hometown. He finds what he believes is his hometown using Google Earth, but he doesn't see the name "Ginestlay" on the map.
5. Summaries will vary but should include a description of the process Brierley used and how he eventually located his hometown.

Research

Research to Clarify If students struggle to come up with a detail to research, you may want to suggest that they focus on one of the following topics: Kolkata, rail travel, or Google Earth.

Research to Explore If students aren't sure how to go about formulating a research question, suggest that they use their findings from Research to Clarify as a starting point. For example, if students researched Kolkata, they might formulate a question such as *Where is the city of Kolkata, and what is it like there?*

PERSONALIZE FOR LEARNING

Challenge

Speculate Ask students to speculate on what happened when he went to his home and saw his family. Remind students of his commitment to finding his family and letting them know he is okay. Then have students write a one-page description from the point of view of Brierley of what they think happened. Explain that they should try to use Brierley's descriptive writing style as they describe what he thought when he visited his home, how he reacted upon seeing his family, and how they reacted upon seeing him.

Jump Start

CLOSE READ Provide students with the following prompts: *Why do you think Brierley finally succeeded in finding his home? Was his success a result of dedication, skill, good luck, or a combination?* As students discuss the prompt in groups, ask them to consider the role that Google Earth played in Brierley's search and whether he would have found his home without it.

Close Read the Text

Walk students through the annotation model on the student page. Encourage them to complete items 2 and 3 on their own. Review and discuss the sections students have marked. If needed, continue to model close reading by using the Annotation Highlights in the Interactive Teacher's Edition.

Analyze the Text

Possible responses:

1. (a) Brierley emphasizes how painstaking and thorough he was in his search and how this meticulousness required a great deal of his time and energy. **DOK 2** (b) The text details suggest that Brierley is focused, patient, detail-oriented, and hard-working. **DOK 2**

2. He means that it would be tempting to deceive himself and tell himself that he recognized a place just so that his long search would end. **DOK 3**

3. People often explore to find new places, but the author explored to find out where he came from and to let his family know what happened to him. **DOK 3**

FORMATIVE ASSESSMENT

Analyze the Text

- **If** students fail to cite evidence, **then** remind them to support their ideas with specific information.

- **If** students struggle to understand the importance of Brierley's search method, **then** have them consider whether he would have found his hometown if he had not stuck to his method or if he had used another method.

MAKING MEANING

from A LONG WAY HOME

🔧 Tool Kit
Close-Read Guide and Model Annotation

≣ STANDARDS
Reading Informational Text
• Cite textual evidence to support analysis of what the text says explicitly as well as inferences drawn from the text.
• Determine a central idea of a text and how it is conveyed through particular details; provide a summary of the text distinct from personal opinions or judgments.
• Analyze how a particular sentence, paragraph, chapter, or section fits into the overall structure of a text and contributes to the development of the ideas.

Close Read the Text

1. This model, from paragraph 13, shows two sample annotations, along with questions and conclusions. Close read the passage, and find another detail to annotate. Then, write a question and conclusion.

ANNOTATE QUESTION CONCLUDE Close Read

ANNOTATE: The author has included numbers and statistics in this passage.

QUESTION: What information is provided by these details?

CONCLUDE: The data reveal how difficult Brierley's search will be.

> It was a staggering amount of territory, covering some 962,300 square kilometers…. Within its bounds lived 345 million people. I tried to keep my emotions out of the exercise, but I couldn't help but wonder: Is it possible to find four family members among these 345 million?

ANNOTATE: The author asks himself a question.

QUESTION: What purpose does this question serve?

CONCLUDE: This question creates suspense and reveals Brierley's doubt.

2. For more practice, go back into the text and complete the close read sections.

3. Revisit a section of the text you found important during your first read. Read this section closely and **annotate** what you notice. Ask yourself **questions** such as "Why did the author make this choice?" What can you **conclude**?

Analyze the Text

CITE TEXTUAL EVIDENCE to support your answers.

📓 **Notebook** Respond to these questions.

1. (a) **Connect** How does Brierley emphasize the importance of his search method and process throughout the excerpt? (b) **Infer** What do those text details suggest about Brierley's personality?

2. **Interpret** Review paragraph 29. What does Brierley mean when he says "And I had to try not to bend my memories to fit what I was looking at"?

3. **Essential Question:** *What drives people to explore?* What has this text revealed about what drives people to explore?

© Pearson Education, Inc., or its affiliates. All rights reserved.

WriteNow Analyze and Interpret

Reflection Have students write a short reflection about the role of family in Brierley's search. Direct students to answer questions such as the following in their reflections:

- Why is family so important for so many people?

- Why might Brierley have spent so much time searching for his family?

- Do you think Brierley's efforts were worth it? Why or why not?

Encourage students to use text details and provide examples from their own lives as they respond to the questions.

Analyze Craft and Structure

Central Ideas: Autobiographical Writing An **autobiography** is a true account of events and experiences written by the person who directly experienced them. A **memoir** is a type of autobiography that focuses on a specific period in the author's life or an experience that holds particular significance for the author.

Autobiographical writing relates an author's thoughts, feelings, and reflections on the events and experiences he or she describes. Autobiographies and memoirs can communicate a variety of insights including:

- what the author learned from the event or experience
- what the author values and his or her goals in life
- how the author feels about other people in his or her life
- how the author relates to his or her environment and the world
- how the author responds to the **conflicts,** or struggles, with which he or she is faced

These insights help to develop the author's **central ideas,** or main points. To determine an author's central ideas in a text, analyze and connect details that reveal the author's reflections and insights.

Practice

CITE TEXTUAL EVIDENCE
to support your answers.

📓 **Notebook** Review the excerpt from *A Long Way Home.* Use the chart to identify the author's central ideas in each passage. Then, answer the questions that follow.

PARAGRAPH(S)	DETAILS THAT REVEAL REFLECTIONS AND INSIGHTS	CENTRAL IDEA OF PASSAGE
10	a. See sample answers in the Teacher's Edition.	b.
17–18	c.	d.
31	e.	f.

1. Review your completed chart. What inference can you make about the central idea of the text as a whole, based on the central ideas you identified for each passage?
2. (a) Review paragraphs 48–51. What conflicting feelings does Brierley express in this passage? (b) How does the method and process of Brierley's search create inner conflict?
3. What comparisons does Brierley make between his childhood journey and his quest to find his hometown as an adult?
4. (a) What role do Brierley's childhood memories play in his search? (b) What do they reveal about Brierley's goals?

from A Long Way Home **425**

Analyze Craft and Structure

Central Ideas: Autobiographical Writing Discuss with students that autobiographical writing can be thought of as all or part of the author's life story that he or she tells. The events and experiences that the author relates are true, and autobiographies are usually written so that the author can reflect on the importance of those events and experiences. Point out to students that an author may relate only a part of his or her life, such as a period that was especially important, or he or she may try to relate a summary of his or her life up to the point of writing. For more support, see **Analyze Craft and Structure: Central Ideas: Autobiographical Writing.** 📄

Practice

Possible responses:

(a) "Why hadn't I...before?"; Maybe I had been too overwhelmed..."; "it dawned on me..." (b) The author discovers a method that might allow him to find his hometown. (c) "it became clear that progress would be slow"; "I was amazed at how little progress..."; "That gave me a great sense of calm" (d) The author realizes that his task will be slow and tedious, but he believes his method will work if he is thorough. (e) "I doubted ...what I was doing"; "sometimes it started to feel claustrophobic..." (f) The process of searching wears on the author and causes him to question himself.

1. The author is determined to find his family, and he won't be discouraged by how tedious and time-consuming the task is.
2. (a) The author feels certain that he has found his hometown, but he also has doubts. (b) The author's search relies on images taken from high above. Such images aren't always clear, so they add to the author's uncertainty.
3. The author traces the same path he took when he became lost as a child—but in reverse and using the technology of Google Earth.
4. (a) Brierley's childhood memories help him in his task—he tries to recall landmarks that will aid him in his search. (b) Brierley wants closure and to make a connection to the person he was.

FORMATIVE ASSESSMENT

Analyze Craft and Structure

- **If** students are unable to identify reflections and insights, **then** have them look for details that show the author gaining clarity or coming to a realization about something.

- **If** students struggle to identify the central idea of a passage, **then** have them ask themselves

what the passage is about and what message the author is trying to express.

For Reteach and Practice, see **Analyze Craft and Structure: Central Ideas: Autobiographical Writing (RP).** 📄

© Pearson Education, Inc., or its affiliates. All rights reserved.

Concept Vocabulary

Why These Words?

Possible responses:

1. They help show that the author was driven to find his hometown.

2. *painstaking, challenge, strategic, methodical*

Practice

Students' paragraphs will vary but should include three concept vocabulary words other than *quest*.

Word Network

Possible words: *search, landmarks, advancing, progress, expectations*

Word Study

For more support, see **Concept Vocabulary and Word Study.** 📄

Possible responses:

1. supportive: tending to give help or encouragement

2. active: tending to be part of a physical activity; inclusive: tending to include or cover everything; possessive: tending to not share

---

FORMATIVE ASSESSMENT

Concept Vocabulary

If students fail to see a connection among the words, **then** have them use each word in a sentence and think about what is similar about the sentences.

Word Study

If students struggle to identify words with the suffix *-ive*, **then** have them think of common verbs and determine if the suffix can be added to the verb to form an adjective. For Reteach and Practice, see **Word Study: Latin Suffix *-ive* (RP).** 📄

from A LONG WAY HOME

🗂 WORD NETWORK

Add words related to exploration from the text to your Word Network.

☰ STANDARDS

Reading Informational Texts
Analyze in detail how a key individual, event, or idea is introduced, illustrated, and elaborated in a text.
Language
Determine or clarify the meaning of unknown and multiple-meaning words and phrases based on *grade 6 reading and content*, choosing flexibly from a range of strategies.
  b. Use common, grade-appropriate Greek or Latin affixes and roots as clues to the meaning of a word.

Concept Vocabulary

deliberate	thorough	intensity
quest	obsessive	relentlessly

Why These Words? The concept vocabulary words relate to the idea of searching or exploring. Saroo Brierley uses these words as he describes his search for his hometown in India. For example, Brierley discusses how his search must be *deliberate*, or carefully planned, if he has any chance of succeeding.

1. How does the concept vocabulary sharpen the reader's understanding the author's experiences while on his mission?

2. What other words in the selection connect to this concept?

Practice

📝 **Notebook** Demonstrate your understanding of the concept vocabulary words by writing a paragraph in which you describe an imaginary quest. For example, you may write about a quest to find a mythical creature or a hidden treasure. Include three concept vocabulary words, other than *quest*, in your paragraph.

Word Study

Latin Suffix: *-ive* The Latin suffix *-ive* means "pertaining to," "tending to," or "serving to do." Words that contain this suffix are usually adjectives. In *A Long Way Home*, Brierley describes his behavior and attitude as *obsessive* because he tended to think about his search so much that he neglected his personal relationships.

1. Find another word in paragraph 23 that contains the Latin suffix *-ive*, and write a brief definition of it.

2. Explain how the suffix *-ive* contributes to the meanings of the following words: *active, inclusive, possessive.*

© Pearson Education, Inc., or its affiliates. All rights reserved.

AUTHOR'S PERSPECTIVE Elfrieda Hiebert, Ph.D.

Digital Tools As students develop and expand their word networks, remind them of the digital tools available and of their value. Explain what digital tools offer—pronunciation; audio; word families; definitions; links to synonyms and antonyms; interactive levels of complexity of synonyms and antonyms; words in context sentences. Using digital tools to access word families is especially helpful in a cross-cultural context. A word family for science, for instance, might include the words *botanist, chemist, geneticist, neurologist, nutritionist, physicist, zoologist,* as they all end with the suffix *–ist.* A word family for westward expansion might be organized around the common concept, and so include the words *settler, heritage, mission,* and *manifest destiny.* To conclude, help students understand that digital tools also have drawbacks. For instance, the word family feature doesn't show how the words are related in meaning, only in sound.

Author's Style

Word Choice and Mood Saroo Brierley's memoir contains rich descriptive details. In his narrative he introduces people, events, and ideas and then provides additional details to further illustrate and elaborate. The depth of description enables readers to fully engage in Brierley's journey, along with him. Here are some descriptive examples from *The Long Way Home*:

- **Description of Actions:** *I traced all the connections within the northeastern states without finding anything familiar, and I was confident that I could rule out Orissa, too.*
- **Description of Places:** *I zoomed back in and re-examined the ring road, the water tower, the overpass, and they were all positioned where I remembered them.*
- **Description of Emotions:** *Finally, after a couple of minutes, I forced myself to take the next step, slowly, nervously. I tried to calm myself so I didn't jump to any rash conclusions.*

Writers' word choices also help to create **mood,** or atmosphere. Mood can be described using adjectives such as *gloomy, upbeat, eerie,* and *lighthearted.* Sometimes the mood of a narrative shifts to match the main character's experiences and observations; sometimes the mood of a story stays the same throughout.

Practice

Complete the chart by marking descriptive words in the passages provided from the memoir. Then, in the column to the right, describe the mood of the passage.

PASSAGE FROM TEXT	MOOD OF PASSAGE
I recalled all those warm nights outside, under the stars, which at least suggested it wouldn't be in the colder regions of the far north. I hadn't lived by the sea, although I couldn't rule out that I'd lived near it. And I hadn't lived in the mountains. My hometown had a railway station—India was riddled with train lines, but they didn't run through every single village and town. (paragraph 4)	a. See sample answers in teacher's edition.
If anything, I became more intense about my search as 2010 drew to a close, and the speed of our newly acquired broadband connection made it quicker to refresh the images and zoom in and out. But I still had to take it slowly—if I rushed, I'd leave myself open to wondering later if I'd missed anything and then going back in an endless cycle. (paragraph 29)	b.
I thought to myself, *This is unique; I haven't seen this before.* I zoomed out, discovering that the train line skimmed the northwestern edge of a really large town. I clicked on the blue train station symbol to reveal its name . . . Burhanpur. My heart nearly stopped. *Burhanpur!* (paragraph 37)	c.

from A Long Way Home **427**

Author's Style

Author's Style: Word Choice and Mood

Discuss with students how authors create mood by choosing certain words. Authors of nonfiction likewise use certain words to build a mood—sometimes in a specific section of a text and sometimes in the overall work.

Relate to students that they likely create mood in their writing all of the time without even realizing it. For instance, have them consider the mood created if they were writing an e-mail to a friend on one of the following subjects. What words might they use, and what mood would be created?

- planning a surprise birthday party
- having to take a test they forgot to study for
- having to work instead of hanging out with friends

For more support, see **Author's Style: Word Choice and Mood.**

Practice

Possible responses:

(a) The mood is reflective and dreamy, as the author recalls memories of his childhood.

(b) The mood is one of tenseness and eagerness.

(c) The mood is one of anticipation and great excitement.

FORMATIVE ASSESSMENT

Author's Style

- **If** students struggle to understand the connection between word choice and mood, **then** have them consider the language they might use to write for different occasions.

- **If** students have difficulty completing the chart, **then** have them identify the descriptive words used by the author and consider what they have in common and the overall feeling they help create. For Reteach and Practice, see **Author's Style: Word Choice and Mood (RP).**

PERSONALIZE FOR LEARNING

English Language Support

Creating Mood To reinforce the connection between word choice and mood, have students provide descriptive words or phrases that they might use to create mood in, for example, a mystery or work of science fiction. Then, discuss how these words would contribute to the overall feeling of the mystery or work of science fiction. **EMERGING**

Have students write a sentence or two that could serve as the beginning of a mystery, a work of science fiction, or another work of their choosing. They should use descriptive words to help set the mood. **EXPANDING**

Have students write the first paragraph of a mystery, a work of science fiction, or another work of their choosing. They should determine the mood they want to create and use descriptive words to help set that mood. **BRIDGING**

An expanded **English Language Support Lesson** on Mood is available in the Interactive Teacher's Edition.

© Pearson Education, Inc., or its affiliates. All rights reserved.

TEACHING

Writing to Sources

Make sure students understand what they are being asked to do. Explain that they will write an essay in which they answer the question about whether Saroo Brierley is an explorer and that they will support their answer with evidence from the text. Remind students that every paragraph in their argument should directly support their claim or position statement and that the argument should be written in a formal and objective tone. For more support, see **Writing to Sources: Argument.** 📄

Vocabulary Connection As students write their arguments, they should include several of the concept vocabulary words and, where appropriate, technical language. If students have difficulty generating technical language, encourage them to think of terms that might be related to geography or technology or travel.

Reflect on Your Writing

1. Responses will vary. If students need support, ask them to consider which part took the most time.

2. Responses will vary. Be sure that students have included all the elements of an argument.

3. **Why These Words?** Responses will vary. Have students list specific examples of words they have chosen that help them convey ideas clearly and accurately.

FORMATIVE ASSESSMENT

Writing to Sources

If students struggle to identify support for their claim, **then** have them look up the definition of *explorer* in the dictionary and determine if Brierley fits the definition. For Reteach and Practice, see **Writing to Sources: Argument (RP).** 📄

EFFECTIVE EXPRESSION

from A LONG WAY HOME

☰ STANDARDS

Writing
Write arguments to support claims with clear reasons and relevant evidence.
  a. Introduce claim(s) and organize the reasons and evidence clearly.
  b. Support claim(s) with clear reasons and relevant evidence, using credible sources and demonstrating an understanding of the topic or text.
  c. Use words, phrases, and clauses to clarify the relationships among claim(s) and reasons.
  e. Provide a concluding statement or section that follows from the argument presented.

428 UNIT 5 • EXPLORATION

Writing to Sources

In an **argument**, an author makes a claim in which he or she states an opinion on a topic or an issue. Then, the author tries to persuade readers to adopt this opinion by providing reasons and supporting evidence for it.

> **Assignment**
>
> When we think of explorers, we often think of pioneers who travel to new and unknown places. Write an **argument** in which you state a claim in response to the following question:
>
> **Is Saroo Brierley an explorer? Why, or why not?**
>
> Consider Brierley's search and how he conducted his search, as well as what you think an explorer should try to accomplish.
>
> - Begin your argument by clearly stating whether or not you think Brierley is an explorer—this is your claim.
>
> - Support your claim by providing logical reasons and evidence from the text.
>
> - Organize your reasons and evidence clearly, and use transition words and phrases to clarify and connect your ideas.
>
> - Include a strong conclusion that restates your claim in a new way and provides an additional idea or insight.

Vocabulary Connection You may want to use some concept vocabulary words and descriptive details in your writing.

deliberate	thorough	intensity
quest	obsessive	relentlessly

Reflect on Your Writing

After you have written your argument, answer the following questions.

1. What do you think was the most challenging part of the assignment?

2. How would you revise your argument to improve it?

3. **Why These Words?** The words you choose make a difference in your writing. Which words did you choose to help you convey precise ideas?

© Pearson Education, Inc., or its affiliates. All rights reserved.

PERSONALIZE FOR LEARNING

English Language Support
Define Key Terms Ask students to write key terms used in the lesson, such as *argument, claim,* and *evidence.* Then have them reread the instructions to find the definitions of these terms: *argument*—a claim that is supported by evidence; *claim*—a position; *evidence*—examples or ideas that support a claim. Discuss aspects of the words that will help students understand their meanings. Explain that *argument* comes from *argue* and that *claim* can also be a verb.
ALL LEVELS

Speaking and Listening

An annotated map is a type of map that includes descriptions and explanations of map locations. Annotated maps enable viewers to quickly and easily find information.

> **Assignment**
>
> As a class, create an **annotated map** in which you trace the route Brierley follows on March 31, 2011, when he finally finds his childhood home.

1. **Prepare for the Activity** Work individually to review the excerpt, and take notes on the specific locations Brierley describes in paragraphs 33–54. Use print or online resources to locate a map of India to familiarize yourself with the locations he discusses.

2. **Find the Locations** As a class, use your notes to mark the locations from the March 31st search on a map of India, print or digital, that your teacher provides.

3. **Paraphrase Descriptions** Once you have identified the locations on the map, take turns with classmates to **paraphrase,** or restate Brierley's descriptions of the area. Include details about what he remembers as well as what he sees as he approaches and zooms in on his hometown.

4. **Annotate the Map** Annotate the map with the paraphrased descriptions. When you **annotate,** you add notes that give additional information or explain something. If you are using a print map, use sticky notes or notecards with pins to add your annotations. If you are using a digital map, create text boxes and enter your paraphrases there.

5. **Discuss** Once your map is complete, discuss the map as a class. Use these questions as a guide for your discussion:

   - How does the map help you to visualize Brierley's search?
   - How does seeing a map of India enable you to grasp the enormous scope of his search?
   - How did the process of annotating the map deepen your understanding of the excerpt?

© Pearson Education, Inc., or its affiliates. All rights reserved.

✎ EVIDENCE LOG

Before moving on to a new selection, go to your Evidence Log and record what you learned from *A Long Way Home.*

☰ STANDARDS

Speaking and Listening
- Engage effectively in a range of collaborative discussions with diverse partners on *grade 6 topics, texts, and issues,* building on others' ideas and expressing their own clearly.
  a. Come to discussions prepared, having read or studied required material; explicitly draw on that preparation by referring to evidence on the topic, text, or issue to probe and reflect on ideas under discussion.
  d. Review the key ideas expressed and demonstrate understanding of multiple perspectives through reflection and paraphrasing.
- Interpret information presented in diverse media and formats and explain how it contributes to a topic, text, or issue under study.
- Include multimedia components and visual displays in presentations to clarify information.

from A Long Way Home **429**

PERSONALIZE FOR LEARNING

Strategic Support

Identify Key Ideas Some students may struggle to identify the relevant descriptors in the text that they should locate on the map and paraphrase. Pair students and have them highlight place names in the text. Then have one student read aloud the text that surrounds or describes that place name while the other listens. Ask students to work together to jot down ideas about the place and then locate it on the map. Then have them team up with another pair of students and compare the locations and annotations they made.

Speaking and Listening

1. **Prepare for the Activity** After students review paragraphs 33–54 and jot down the names of places mentioned, they might, if resources allow, use online maps to find these places quickly and get a sense of the geography of the area.

2. **Find the Locations** Point out that the map of India will be divided into states and that they should find the name of the state from the March 31, 2011, search. Explain to students that the author was searching in the state of Madhya Pradesh when he found the clues that led him to his hometown.

3. **Paraphrase Descriptions** Remind students that before they paraphrase the descriptions, they should reread them to make sure they understand fully what the author was saying.

4. **Annotate the Map** Tell students that they must attach the annotation to the place it describes.

5. **Discuss** Lead students in a class discussion about the process. Ask them to discuss how difficult locating the specific places on the map was and how it helped them understand the difficulty of Brierley's quest.

For more support, see **Speaking and Listening: Annotated Map.** 📄

Evidence Log Support students in completing their Evidence Log. This paced activity will help prepare them for the Performance-Based Assessment at the end of the unit.

FORMATIVE ASSESSMENT

Speaking and Listening

- **If** students struggle to paraphrase, **then** have them jot down ideas about the description as they read it and then paraphrase based on their notes.

- **If** students fail to note how the annotations helped them visualize Brierley's quest, **then** ask them to compare what they did to what Brierley did.

For Reteach and Practice, see **Speaking and Listening: Annotated Map (RP).** 📄

Selection Test

Administer the "*from* A Long Way Home" Selection Test, which is available in both print and digital formats online in Assessments. 📄 ☑

BBC Science Club: All About Exploration

Summary

The animated video "BBC Science Club: All About Exploration" is an overview of the history of exploration from the BBC. Narrated by Dara Ó Briain, it discusses tricks that past explorers used, such as the Vikings' use of birds to find land, the refinement of star-based navigation in medieval Islamic countries, and the invention of the compass in China. It explains that Columbus mistook America for India because he sailed before clocks worked accurately aboard traveling ships. The video then moves to later periods, when people found ways to reach the sky and, ultimately, space.

Insight

This video illustrates how exploration is not limited to any one part of the world or even one part of the universe. People everywhere have made contributions to our collective knowledge.

AUDIO SUMMARIES
Audio summaries of "BBC Science Club: All About Exploration" are available online in both English and Spanish in the Interactive Teacher's Edition or Unit Resources. Assigning these summaries prior to viewing the selection may help students build additional background knowledge and set a context for their first viewing.

ESSENTIAL QUESTION:
What drives people to explore?

Connection to Essential Question

In the examples in the video, curiosity and the desire to possess more land are the main motivations.

WHOLE-CLASS LEARNING PERFORMANCE TASK
Can anyone be an explorer?

UNIT PERFORMANCE-BASED ASSESSMENT
Should kids today be encouraged to become explorers?

Connection to Performance Tasks

Whole-Class Learning Performance Task Rather than a common sense of adventure, the video indicates that curiosity is the shared element in the human urge to explore. From the ancient Greeks to modern astronauts, anyone with determination and drive can explore the universe.

Unit Performance-Based Assessment The video shows that curiosity is a common factor in people's desire to explore the world and the universe.

LESSON RESOURCES

	Making Meaning		**Effective Expression**
Lesson	**First Review**	**Analyze the Media**	**Research**
	Close Review	**Media Vocabulary**	
Instructional Standards	**RI.1** Cite textual evidence to support analysis of what the text says . . . **RI.10** By the end of the year, read and comprehend literary nonfiction . . . **L.6** Acquire and use accurately grade-appropriate general academic and domain-specific words and phrases . . .		**W.2** Write informative/explanatory texts . . . **W.2.b** Develop the topic . . . **W.7** Conduct short research projects . . . **SL.5** Include multimedia and visual displays . . .
⇗ **STUDENT RESOURCES**			
Available online in the Interactive Student Edition or Unit Resources	🔊 Selection Audio 📄 First-Review Guide: Media-Video 📄 Close-Review Guide: Media-Video 📄 Word Network		📄 Evidence Log
⇗ **TEACHER RESOURCES**			
Selection Resources Available online in the Interactive Teacher's Edition or Unit Resources	🔊 Audio Summaries 📄 Media Vocabulary		📄 Research: Storyboard
My Resources	📄 A Unit 5 Answer Key is available online and in the Interactive Teacher's Edition.		

Media Complexity Rubric: BBC Science Club: All About Exploration

Quantitative Measures

Format and Length: Video, 4 minutes 16 seconds

Qualitative Measures

Knowledge Demands ①—②—③—**④**—⑤	The video covers a wide range of topics that are all related to exploration (for example, Greeks, Vikings, stellar navigation, air balloons, first flights, rockets, moon landing).
Structure ①—②—**③**—④—⑤	The video covers a wide range of content. At times, there is one-to-one correspondence of images and audio, but there are also topics that are not shown visually.
Language Conventionality and Clarity ①—②—**③**—④—⑤	The language is somewhat complex, with lengthy sentences and above-level vocabulary. At some moments, speech can be difficult to understand due to the fast pace and the accent of the speaker.
Levels of Meaning/Purpose ①—②—③—**④**—⑤	Although the progression of ideas is logical, the main ideas of the video are not explicitly stated. Many details are described but not summarized.

Jump Start

FIRST REVIEW Did you ever wish you could "watch" history that took place before the time of videos and photos? Filmmakers can use many tools, including animation, to make modern media about the past. Animation not only tells stories, but it can also bring events and people from history to life.

BBC Science Club: All About Exploration ▶ ◀))

What tools do filmmakers use to bring historical events to life? Why do filmmakers choose to portray certain events? How do filmmakers use humor to describe events? Modeling the questions students might ask as they review "BBC Science Club: All About Exploration" brings the video to life and connects it to the Whole-Class Performance Task question. Selection audio is available in the Interactive Teacher's Edition.

Media Vocabulary

Encourage students to discuss the media vocabulary. Have they seen the terms in texts before? Do they use any of them in their speech and writing? For more support, see **Media Vocabulary.** 📄

● FIRST REVIEW

As they watch and listen, students should perform the steps of the first review:

WATCH: Remind students to notice which pieces of history the filmmakers chose to animate.

NOTE: Encourage students to notice how the filmmakers chose to share the history.

CONNECT: Encourage students to make connections beyond the video. If they cannot make connections to their own lives, have them consider other videos or books, as well as stories or historical events they have learned in school.

RESPOND: Students will answer questions and write a summary to demonstrate understanding.

Point out to students that while they will always complete the Respond step at the end of the first review, the other steps will probably happen somewhat concurrently. You may wish to print copies of the **First-Review Guide: Media-Video** for students to use. 📄

About the Narrator

The Irish comedian **Dara Ó Briain** (b. 1972) is a self-described "geek." He attended University College, Dublin, and studied math and theoretical physics. Ó Briain is best known, however, for his comedy and for his hosting of many popular television shows, including the British version of *The Apprentice: You're Fired* and *Mock the Week*.

STANDARDS

Reading Informational Text
By the end of the year, read and comprehend literary nonfiction in the grades 6–8 text complexity band proficiently, with scaffolding as needed at the high end of the range.

Language
Acquire and use accurately grade-appropriate general academic and domain-specific words and phrases; gather vocabulary knowledge when considering a word or phrase important to comprehension or expression.

BBC Science Club: All About Exploration

Media Vocabulary

The following words or concepts will be useful to you as you analyze, discuss, and write about animated videos.

cut-out animation: technique that uses flat characters, backgrounds, and props cut from materials such as paper, cardboard, and fabric	Cut-out animation involves moving cut-out objects in small steps to imitate natural movement while taking a picture at each step.
object animation: form that involves the movement of non-drawn objects, such as a book or a pen	• The objects used in this type of animation are generally not designed to look like a recognizable human or animal character. • Animated objects are not made of flexible materials, such as clay or wax.
real-time animation: style in which animated events or objects are reproduced so that they appear to be occurring or moving at the same speed they would in real life	• Interactive video games commonly use real-time animation to mimic the pace of natural movements. • Animated movies also use real-time animation to give viewers the impression of real life.

First Review MEDIA: VIDEO

Apply these strategies as you watch the video. As you watch, note the time codes of sections so that you can easily revisit them.

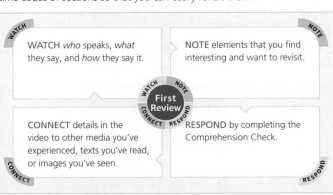

WATCH who speaks, what they say, and how they say it.

NOTE elements that you find interesting and want to revisit.

CONNECT details in the video to other media you've experienced, texts you've read, or images you've seen.

RESPOND by completing the Comprehension Check.

First Review

© Pearson Education, Inc., or its affiliates. All rights reserved.

PERSONALIZE FOR LEARNING

English Language Support

Humor The filmmakers chose to use humor to animate the stories. Ask students, *Did humor make the film more interesting?* Then, discuss the challenges of separating the humor from the important information. Ask students to cite examples of humor in the film. Was the humor meant to be an accurate depiction of events? Did it have any impact on their understanding of the events? **ALL LEVELS**

MEDIA | VIDEO

BBC Science Club: All About Exploration

BACKGROUND

In the video, the narrator mentions the pioneering scientist Dr. Robert Goddard, who invented liquid-fueled rockets in the early 20th century. Goddard devoted his life to researching and developing rockets, laying the groundwork for space exploration. An insightful physicist and inventor, Goddard envisioned the possibility of space flight, and his contributions were essential to making space travel a reality. The Goddard Space Flight Center in Maryland, a major NASA research laboratory, was established in his memory.

SCAN FOR MULTIMEDIA

NOTES

© Pearson Education, Inc., or its affiliates. All rights reserved.

BBC Science Club: All About Exploration **431**

CLOSER REVIEW

Analyze Information

Students may have noted the section of the video from 1:04 to 1:40 during their first review. Encourage them to talk about what they noted. You may want to model a close review with the class based on the notes below.

NOTE: Have students note details in the video from 1:04 to 1:40 that describe Columbus's mistake, focusing on the animation of the Native American, or have students participate while you note them together.

QUESTION: Guide students to consider what these details might tell them. The Native American in the excerpt from 1:04 to 1:40 changes his expression. Have students infer why he does this.

Possible response: Columbus plants a flag that reads "India" on the Native American.

CONCLUDE: Help students to formulate conclusions about the importance of this detail in the video. Ask students why the filmmakers might have included this detail.

Possible response: The filmmakers may have included this detail to show that Columbus mistakenly named a place that he thought he "discovered" without regard to the native people who were living there. The Native American's expression of displeasure shows that he doesn't appreciate being named by a newly arrived European.

CROSS-CURRICULAR PERSPECTIVES

Humanities Have students select an exploration event or explorer, from either the video (such as Samuel Langley at 2:13 of the video) or from independent research. Then have each student create a comic strip telling about the explorer or an event from the explorer's experiences. Offer examples of comic strips if needed. Students' comic strips should contain at least five boxes and tell a story using words and pictures. Remind students that they can use humor as long as they stay true to the story. Display comic strips in class.

Comprehension Check

Possible responses:

1. The ancient Greeks used stars to navigate.

2. He didn't know how far he had gone.

3. People couldn't control where they went.

4. Reporters said a rocket could not fly in a vacuum.

Close Review

If needed, model close reviewing by using the Closer Review notes in the Interactive Teacher's Edition.

Remind groups to use Accountable Talk in their discussions and to support one another as they complete the close review. You may wish to print the **Close-Review Guide: Media-Video** for students to use.

Analyze the Media

Possible responses:

1. (a) Advancements in navigation have allowed people to broaden areas of exploration. **DOK 2** (b) Students' responses will vary but should be supported by details from the video. **DOK 2**

2. He means that people need the right tools to determine where they are going, how far they have traveled, and how they get there. **DOK 2**

3. People long ago went to new places themselves, but we explore space mostly by sending robots and probes to do it for us. **DOK 2**

4. I have learned that people explore because they want to travel and because they want to discover new places and try new things. **DOK 3**

Word Network

Encourage students to add words about exploration from the selection to their Word Networks.

Possible words: *wanderlust, voyaging, navigation, probing*

FORMATIVE ASSESSMENT

Analyze the Media

If students struggle to analyze the events in the video, **then** have them watch the video again, pausing the video after each segment to take notes and jot down questions they still have about the segment.

MAKING MEANING

Comprehension Check

Complete the following items after you finish your first review.

1. How did ancient Greeks navigate?

2. Why didn't Columbus know he wasn't in India?

3. What was the problem with the early balloons used for air travel?

4. Why didn't the *New York Times* initially believe that it was possible to go to the moon?

MEDIA VOCABULARY

Use these words as you discuss and write about the video.

cut-out animation
object animation
real-time animation

STANDARDS

Reading Informational Texts
Cite textual evidence to support analysis of what the text says explicitly as well as inferences drawn from the text.

Close Review

Watch the video or parts of it again. Write any new observations that seem important. What questions do you have? What can you conclude?

Analyze the Media

CITE TEXTUAL EVIDENCE
to support your answers.

Notebook Respond to these questions.

1. (a) **Draw Conclusions** What conclusions can you draw about the ways in which exploration has been influenced by advancements in navigation? (b) **Make a Judgment** Do you think that navigational advancements or technological advancements were more important to expanding our ability to explore? Explain.

2. **Interpret** At the beginning of the video, the narrator says that people need "effective means and methods" to explore. What does he mean by this statement?

3. **Evaluate** How effective is the use of animation in conveying information about exploration?

4. **Essential Question: *What drives people to explore?*** What have you learned about what drives people to explore from watching the video?

© Pearson Education, Inc., or its affiliates. All rights reserved.

PERSONALIZE FOR LEARNING

English Language Support
Drawing Conclusions The filmmakers provided information about exploration through time. Have students draw a conclusion about the filmmakers' message or purpose in making this video. Have each student write down the conclusion on a slip of paper. Read several conclusions aloud and decide as a class which most accurately explains the filmmakers' purpose. **ALL LEVELS**

Research

The video "All About Exploration" provides a humorous but factual look at the history of exploration.

**BBC SCIENCE CLUB:
ALL ABOUT EXPLORATION**

Assignment

Perform research to identify an explorer whose accomplishments could be added to the "All About Exploration" video. Then, create a **storyboard** in which you provide information about the explorer and his or her exploration activities.

Research and Plan Begin by performing research on an explorer from history. Once you have identified the explorer, consult various sources and take careful notes about his or her mission, the dates of the mission, and the success of the mission. Strive to find facts, explanations, quotations, or other interesting information that will bring your explorer to life.

Draft a Storyboard Once your research is completed, use a storyboard template like this one to present your ideas. Draw or find images that depict key events of the exploration. Style the images to match the style in "All About Exploration." Then, add captions to images in which you indicate the voiceover narration that would accompany the images. Challenge yourself to create a humorous tone as in the original video.

STORYBOARD

Present Once you are happy with your storyboard, share it with your classmates. If you are comfortable using digital tools, consider animating your images and recording the voiceover narration. If you prefer, simply present your storyboard on an overhead projector and read the voiceover narration as classmates listen.

EVIDENCE LOG

Before moving on to a new selection, go to your Evidence Log and record what you learned from the video.

STANDARDS

Writing
• Write informative/explanatory texts to examine a topic and convey ideas, concepts, and information through the selection, organization, and analysis of relevant content.
  b. Develop the topic with relevant facts, definitions, concrete details, quotations, or other information and examples.

• Conduct short research projects to answer a question, drawing on several sources and refocusing the inquiry when appropriate.

Speaking and Listening
Include multimedia components and visual displays in presentations to clarify information.

Research

Discuss with students that storyboards are often used by filmmakers as a way to get a visual representation of ideas. They help with planning and organizing, too, as they often show scenes in sequence.

Research and Plan Once students have chosen a historical figure to research, encourage them to look for information about him or her that will make the figure come alive and interest viewers. This information will help them to potentially see something humorous in the person.

Draft a Storyboard Explain to students that their drawing skills are not being judged. They can make simple representations of people—even stick figures are fine. The point is to translate their research into something visual.

For more support, see **Research: Storyboard.**

FORMATIVE ASSESSMENT

Research

If students struggle to think of a historical figure to research, **then** have them consider a scientist, an explorer, or a world leader they've read about or seen a documentary about.

Selection Test

Administer the "BBC Science Club: All About Exploration" Selection Test, which is available in both print and digital formats online in Assessments.

PERSONALIZE FOR LEARNING

Strategic Support

Taking Notes Taking notes while watching a film can be challenging and might lead to students missing the humor. Point out that if they have trouble remembering details, they can revisit the film. To organize the information they note in their second viewing, draw a chart and have students copy it and fill it in.

Event	Obstacle	Turning Point

© Pearson Education, Inc. or its affiliates. All rights reserved.

Jump Start

What would it take to be an explorer? Would you need to be unusually bright or courageous? Would it take great wealth or just the will to explore new places? Have students write answers to these questions and share them with the class.

Write an Argument

Tell students that in order to complete this assignment and write an effective argument, they need to choose a side. It is possible to feel that there is truth to both sides, but to be successful in constructing an argument, they are going to have to choose and support one perspective.

Students should complete the assignment using word processing software to take advantage of editing tools and features.

Elements of an Argument

Remind students to choose their position, list reasons for their position, and provide evidence to support it. Finally, they will write a conclusion in which they convince others of the validity of their argument.

MAKE IT INTERACTIVE

Project "What on Earth Is Left to Explore?" from the Interactive Teacher's Edition. Have students identify the elements of an argument and identify the writer's claim. Next, ask volunteers to identify evidence that supports the author's claim.

Academic Vocabulary

Have students use each of the academic vocabulary words to make a statement about their arguments. Provide an example, such as the following: *To be an explorer, curiosity is critical.*

WRITING TO SOURCES

• *from* A LONG WAY HOME

• BBC SCIENCE CLUB: ALL ABOUT EXPLORATION

ACADEMIC VOCABULARY

As you craft your argument, consider using some of the academic vocabulary you learned in the beginning of the unit.

critical
assume
compel
valid
coherent

≣ STANDARDS

Writing
• Write arguments to support claims with clear reasons and relevant evidence.
• Draw evidence from literary or informational texts to support analysis, reflection, and research.
  b. Apply *grade 6 Reading standards* to literary nonfiction.
• Write routinely over extended time frames and shorter time frames for a range of discipline-specific tasks, purposes, and audiences.

Write an Argument

You have read an excerpt from a memoir and watched a video that discuss different aspects of exploration. In *A Long Way Home*, the author describes how he used Google Earth to search for his childhood home in India. In "BBC Science Club: All About Exploration" viewers learn about the history of exploration.

> **Assignment**
>
> Use your knowledge of both the memoir and the video to take and defend a position on the topic of exploration. Write a brief **argumentative essay** in which you state and support your position on this question:
>
>   Can anyone be an explorer?
>
> Include examples and details from the memoir and the video, as well as your own observations to support your reasoning.

Elements of an Argument

An **argumentative essay** is a short work in which a writer presents a position and supports it with reasons and evidence. The purpose is to persuade readers to think a certain way about the topic. An effective argumentative essay contains these elements:

• a claim, or statement of a position
• clear, convincing reasons that relate to the claim
• evidence, or facts and examples that support the claim
• a clear organization, including an introduction, a body, and a conclusion
• transitional words and phrases that make the relationships among claims and reasons clear
• a concluding statement or section that follows from the ideas presented earlier in the essay
• a formal style that takes the subject and reader seriously
• error-free grammar, including accurate use of verbs

Model Argument For a model of a well-crafted argument, see the Launch Text, "What on Earth Is Left to Explore?"

Challenge yourself to find all of the elements of an effective argument in the text. You will have an opportunity to review these elements as you prepare to write your own argument.

© Pearson Education, Inc., or its affiliates. All rights reserved.

AUTHOR'S PERSPECTIVE   Kelly Gallagher, M.Ed.

Read, Analyze, Emulate Teachers can use scaffolding to help students grow as writers by studying good writing with them. When students recognize the qualities of good writing, they begin producing it.

Step 1: Read Provide students with excellent narratives from the text and direct them to "read like a writer" by paying attention to ideas, style, voice, and organization. Encourage students to look for the moves the writer made to elicit a response in readers.

Step 2: Analyze Focus on the ideas by asking students questions such as "What is the writer's theme? How did the writer develop it?" Then turn to style and voice, asking, "How did the writer develop the characters?" "What effect did the dialogue have?" "What sensory details did the writer use?" and "Where do you hear the author's distinctive voice?" Finally, ask questions about organization, such as "How did the writer pace events?" "What do you notice about the writer's paragraphing decisions?"

Step 3: Emulate Select one or two of the writer's moves to practice. Guide students to follow the models they studied as they write.

Prewriting / Planning

Write a Working Claim A working claim is a statement of your main idea that will help you get started with your writing. It allows you to try out your ideas and evidence. Depending on how your essay develops, you may wind up keeping your working claim or you may change it completely. Write a working claim here.

Working Claim: _____

_____

Consider Other Opinions Considering how other people feel or think about a topic can strengthen your argument. Think about questions readers might have about your position, or opinions that might differ from yours. Plan to answer those questions or address those opinions in your essay. Use these sentence starters to pull your ideas together.

A different opinion is _____

The reason someone might think this is because _____

The reason this idea is not convincing is _____

Collect Evidence The most important evidence you will use comes from the memoir and video. However, you may want to support your position with other types of details, as well. Consider using these types of evidence:

- **facts:** statements that can be proved true
- **statistics:** facts presented in the form of numbers
- **anecdotes:** brief stories that can be used as examples
- **quotations from authorities:** statements from experts
- **examples:** specific people, situations, or events that support a general idea

Using a variety of evidence can make your argument stronger. In the Launch Text, the writer includes a variety of examples to support the point that "people seem to be everywhere."

> *Thousands have climbed Mount Everest, the world's highest mountain. There are even people living in Antarctica, the world's coldest continent. In addition, the Internet allows people to visit faraway places through the screens of their computers.*
> —from "What on Earth Is Left to Explore?"

Connect Across Texts As you write your essay, you will use evidence from both the video and the memoir to support your ideas. Include that evidence in different ways. For example, use **exact quotations** if the exact words are important. Otherwise, **paraphrase**, or restate ideas in your own words.

© Pearson Education, Inc., or its affiliates. All rights reserved.

EVIDENCE LOG

Review your Evidence Log and identify key details you may want to cite in your argument.

STANDARDS
Writing
Write arguments to support claims with clear reasons and relevant evidence.
  a. Introduce claim(s) and organize the reasons and evidence clearly.
  b. Support claim(s) with clear reasons and relevant evidence, using credible sources and demonstrating an understanding of the topic or text.

Performance Task: Write an Argument **435**

Prewriting/Planning

Write a Working Claim Is exploration a courageous act? Or, is it something that is natural to human beings? Ask students to raise their hands to show which argument they think is most valid. Have a few volunteers share a thought or two as to why they chose the sides they did. Remind students to think about each other's ideas as they formulate their own claims.

Collect Evidence Have students review their Evidence Log to find possible support for their claim. They may have sufficient evidence in their Evidence Log, but they may want to go back and review the selections to identify additional or stronger evidence for their argument. Point out to students that they can also use other sources to support their claim and should remember to identify and cite evidence used from theses sources.

Connect Across Texts When students write their arguments, they should draw on information from the selections in this unit. Remind them of the structure they need to use to make an exact quote, including quotation marks. For paraphrasing, select a quote from one of the selections and ask for volunteers to paraphrase the quote.

PERSONALIZE FOR LEARNING

Strategic Support
Graphic Organizer In preparing to write a cohesive argument, organization of ideas will help students more effectively write their essays. Suggest that students create a chart like the one here to help organize their thoughts before they begin to write.

Claim		
Reason	Evidence	Type of Evidence

Drafting

Organize Ideas Explain to students the difference between the *elements* of an argument (claim, counterclaims, valid reasoning and evidence, and concluding statement) and the *organization* of an argument (introduction, body, and conclusion). Students should use their working claim, possible counterclaims, and evidence to complete an Argument Outline of their own.

Write a First Draft Remind students to begin their argument with an interesting point that will engage the reader. Students should remember to include sufficient details to ensure that a reader with no knowledge of the subject can understand their claim and reasoning.

Drafting

Organize Ideas Argumentative essays include three sections: an **introduction,** a **body,** and a **conclusion.** Each section should build on the one that came before it, and every point should support your main claim. Look at the guidelines for each section given in the chart. Then, add notes about the ideas and evidence you will include in each part of your essay. This outline will help you plan a logical order for your ideas and evidence.

SECTION	GUIDELINES	PLAN FOR EACH SECTION
Introduction Present the topic and claim.	• Engage readers with interesting information. • Clearly state the claim.	
Body Give supporting reasons and evidence.	• Use one paragraph for each reason. • Include a topic sentence, or main idea, in each paragraph. • Use strong evidence.	
Conclusion Sum up the argument.	• Restate the claim in different words. • End with a strong, statement.	

Write a First Draft Use your outline to write your first draft. Be sure to write an introduction that will grab the reader's attention. Then, present your supporting reasons in a logical order. Provide a strong conclusion that ends your argument with a clear statement.

⊞ STANDARDS

Writing
Write arguments to support claims with clear reasons and relevant evidence.
  e. Provide a concluding statement or section that follows from the argument presented.

© Pearson Education, Inc., or its affiliates. All rights reserved.

AUTHOR'S PERSPECTIVE **Jim Cummins, Ph.D.**

Working in Pairs There is an important sense in which the development of academic expertise on the part of English learners is a process of socialization rather than simply instruction. As a result, English writing development will be enhanced when students can work in pairs to create texts to share with others. That's because the process of collaboration and communication entails social interaction, which fosters language development.

• First, teachers can partner students to read, discuss, and react to a reading in the unit. Select a text, such as a nonfiction article, poem, or narrative.

• Have partners discuss the text, make notes about their ideas, and together write a response that highlights what they found important, or responds to a prompt teachers provide.

Encourage students to include specific details from the text in their drafts.

• Then, teachers can invite partners to share their writing with the whole class. Guide students to explain how working together helped them express their ideas more effectively than working alone.

Word Choice for Style and Tone

In an argument, your writing style should be formal. Your **tone,** or attitude, should be serious. These two qualities help make your ideas believable, which strengthens your argument. To create and maintain the right style and tone, pay careful attention to your word choice throughout your essay.

Read It

These sentences from the beginning, middle, and end of the Launch Text are both formal and serious.

Passage 1 (beginning): *To the west lay an entire continent, full of mystery and promise.*

Passage 2 (middle): *Vast stretches of the oceans are hidden under miles of water.*

Passage 3 (end): *The need to explore and extend the boundaries of knowledge remains vital and should continue.*

Write It

As you draft your essay, avoid using slang, people's first names, and contractions. In addition, apply the following strategies to choose words that create the formal style and serious tone you need:

- **Choose accurate words.** Informal or exaggerated expressions may be fun, but they may not say exactly what you mean. In an argument, avoid exaggeration. Choose accuracy over excitement.

  Original Sentence: The number of tourists has <u>gone through the roof</u>.
  Revised Sentence: The number of tourists has <u>increased</u>.

- **Avoid absolute words.** Words such as *all, always, never,* and *only* may lead to statements that are too broad. Replace them with words you can defend.

  Original Sentence: Climbing Mount Everest is not as special because <u>everyone</u> has done it.
  Revised Sentence: Climbing Mount Everest is not as special because <u>many people</u> have done it.

- **Use reasonable words.** Charged words can capture readers' interest, but make sure you focus more on facts. Always avoid name-calling.

  Original Sentence: Exploring a cave without proper equipment is <u>stupid</u>.
  Revised Sentence: Exploring a cave without proper equipment is <u>risky</u>.

STANDARDS

Writing
- Write arguments to support claims with clear reasons and relevant evidence.
  d. Establish and maintain a formal style.

Language
Use knowledge of language and its conventions when writing, speaking, reading, or listening.
  b. Maintain consistency in style and tone.

Word Choice for Style and Tone

Read It

Provide examples to help students grasp the idea of formal versus informal tone when writing. For instance, if a person were writing an e-mail to a close friend about going to see a movie, the tone would be casual and informal. The purpose of such writing is simply to organize a meeting and share the anticipation of doing something fun—and the tone reflects the familiarity of the reader and the overall purpose of writing.

But, if a person were writing a cover letter for a job or a proposal to a community organization seeking change, the tone would be serious and formal. The writer would likely not know the reader, and the purpose is to achieve a goal—either to get hired or to affect some sort of change. The seriousness of the intended outcome is reflected in the tone.

Write It

Remind students that a formal tone will help them be taken seriously by readers. If a writer makes careless jokes and refers to people by their first names, readers may think that he or she doesn't have respect for his or her subject. Likewise, all of the claims in an argument should be supported, and generalizations should be avoided, so that readers get the sense that the writer has prepared the argument carefully.

© Pearson Education, Inc., or its affiliates. All rights reserved.

Revising

Evaluating Your Draft As students draft, remind them to avoid using phrases such as "I think" or "I know." Using a formal style and making a convincing argument in the third-person point of view, backed by evidence and facts, will be more effective than an argument that uses a first-person point of view.

Show Connections Remind students that transition words help connect two thoughts. Words such as *because, in fact, therefore, such as,* and *including* are transitions. Have the students suggest other transitions and create a list accessible to students to aid them as they write their arguments.

Revising

Evaluating Your Draft

Use the following checklist to evaluate the effectiveness of your first draft. Then, use your evaluation and the instruction on this page to guide your revision.

FOCUS AND ORGANIZATION	EVIDENCE AND ELABORATION	CONVENTIONS
☐ Introduces a clear claim.	☐ Provides clear reasons and strong evidence that supports them.	☐ Observes the conventions of standard English grammar.
☐ Provides a conclusion that follows from the argument.	☐ Uses words, phrases, and clauses that clarify the relationships among ideas.	
☐ Establishes a logical organization and develops a clear progression.	☐ Establishes and maintains a formal style and serious tone.	

🔲 WORD NETWORK

Include words from your Word Network in your narrative.

Revising for Focus and Organization

Show Connections Reread your argument. Revise your sentences to clarify the relationships between the claim you make and the evidence you provide. Use transition words such as *because, in fact,* or *therefore* to show the connections among ideas.

Revising for Evidence and Elaboration

Check Your Evidence Make sure that you have stated your ideas with authority and supported them with relevant evidence from the texts. Also consider *how* you have presented evidence. Make sure you have chosen the approach that gives readers information in the most effective way.

- **Summarize,** or briefly restate ideas, to give readers information quickly.
- **Paraphrase,** or restate ideas in your own words, when you wish to help readers understand a complicated idea.
- **Quote** a writer's or a speaker's exact words when they are especially interesting or powerful.

Make sure to clearly introduce each piece of evidence you use. Explain why it is important and how it connects to your ideas.

☰ STANDARDS

Writing
Write arguments to support claims with clear reasons and relevant evidence.
a. Introduce claim(s) and organize the reasons and evidence clearly.
b. Support claims with clear reasons and relevant evidence, using credible sources and demonstrating an understanding of the topic or text.
c. Use words, phrases, and clauses to clarify the relationships among claim(s) and reasons.

© Pearson Education, Inc., or its affiliates. All rights reserved.

PEER REVIEW

Exchange essays with a classmate. Use the checklist to evaluate your classmate's essay and provide supportive feedback.

1. Is the claim clear?

☐ yes ☐ no   If no, explain what confused you.

2. Is the organization logical?

☐ yes ☐ no   If no, explain what was confusing about the organization.

3. Does the conclusion logically wrap up the essay?

☐ yes ☐ no   If no, point out what is missing.

4. What is the strongest part of your classmate's essay?

_____

_____

Editing and Proofreading

Edit for Conventions Reread your draft for accuracy and consistency. Correct errors in grammar and word usage. Make sure you have used words that accurately reflect your meaning. Avoid using any words that you are uncertain about. Check a dictionary, glossary, or other reference to make sure you have used every word correctly.

Proofread for Accuracy Read your draft carefully, looking for errors in spelling and punctuation. Make sure that you have not confused words that sound the same. For example, ships *sail* across the *sea*, they don't *sale* across the *see*.

Publishing and Presenting

Use technology to create a slide show to accompany your essay. Find images that support the claims you make, and add explanations of the images to your essay. Record a presentation of the slide show with audio of your essay and post it online to a school or class website. Share your presentation with your classmates and offer polite feedback in the comments section of the website.

Reflecting

Think about what you learned by writing your argument. What could you do differently to make writing an argument simpler or easier?

© Pearson Education, Inc., or its affiliates. All rights reserved.

≡ STANDARDS

Writing
• With some guidance and support from peers and adults, develop and strengthen writing as needed by planning, revising, editing, rewriting, or trying a new approach.
• Use technology, including the Internet, to produce and publish writing as well as to interact and collaborate with others; demonstrate sufficient command of keyboarding skills to type a minimum of three pages in a single sitting.

Language
• Demonstrate command of the conventions of standard English grammar and usage when writing or speaking.

e. Recognize variations from standard English in their own and others' writing and speaking, and identify and use strategies to improve expression in conventional language.

Performance Task: Write an Argument **439**

Peer Review

Remind students that the purpose of peer review is to help the writer. Constructive, respectful input can give the writer ideas about how to strengthen his or her argument. When students point out the strongest part of the argument, they should explain why they chose that point.

Editing and Proofreading

Suggest that students edit each other's essays for conventions and accuracy. Explain that when writers spend a lot of time developing an essay, they can often miss their own errors. Having another person edit their work can help catch an overlooked mistake.

Publishing and Presenting

Before students review their classmates' arguments, remind them to keep comments positive, use formal language, and disagree respectfully. Constructive and thoughtful comments will help polish the arguments before they are presented.

Reflecting

Remind students to take a few notes on what they learned from constructing and presenting an argument.

PERSONALIZE FOR LEARNING

Challenge

Prepare an Argument Arrange students into pairs and select several topics that are relevant to students. The topics can be serious or fun. Have the pairs select a topic. Each student in the pair will take one side of the argument and prepare a brief presentation supporting that side. Students will discuss the effectiveness of each argument. Remind students to review the important components of an argument they employed in this unit as they work on this assignment.

SMALL-GROUP LEARNING

What drives people to explore?

Discuss with students how many attempts were made to cross the Atlantic Ocean before explorers arrived in the Americas. Does this compare to the attempts to travel to the moon and beyond? During Small-Group Learning, students will read about explorers and exploration.

Small-Group Learning Strategies ⊙

Review the Learning Strategies with students and explain that as they work through Small-Group Learning, they will develop strategies to work in small-group environments.

- Have students watch the video on Small-Group Learning Strategies.
- A video on this topic is available online in the Professional Development Center.

You may wish to discuss some action items to add to the chart as a class before students complete it on their own. For example, for "Support others," you might solicit the following from students:

- Encourage others in your group to elaborate on an opinion or idea.
- Ask group members questions to show that you are interested in what they have to say.

Block Scheduling

Each day in this Pacing Plan represents a 40–50 minute class period. Teachers using block scheduling may combine days to reflect their class schedule. In addition, teachers may revise pacing to differentiate and support core instruction by integrating components and resources as students require.

👥 OVERVIEW: SMALL-GROUP LEARNING

ESSENTIAL QUESTION:

What drives people to explore?

Explorers of faraway places, the ocean depths, and outer space must adapt to and survive in new and extremely challenging conditions. In this section, you will read about some of those conditions. You will work in a group to examine the concept of exploration.

Small-Group Learning Strategies

Throughout your life, in school, in your community, and in your career, you will continue to learn and work with others.

Review these strategies and the actions you can take to practice them as you work in teams. Add ideas of your own for each step. Use these strategies during Small-Group Learning.

STRATEGY	ACTION PLAN
Prepare	• Complete your assignments so that you are prepared for group work. • Organize your thinking so you can contribute to your group's discussion. •
Participate fully	• Make eye contact to signal that you are listening and taking in what is being said. • Use text evidence when making a point. •
Support others	• Build on ideas from others in your group. • Invite others who have not yet spoken to join the discussion. •
Clarify	• Paraphrase the ideas of others to ensure that your understanding is correct. • Ask follow-up questions. •

SCAN FOR
MULTIMEDIA 🄱

© Pearson Education, Inc., or its affiliates. All rights reserved.

📅 Pacing Plan

Introduce Whole-Class Learning 🄯

Unit Introduction

from A Long Way Home

Media: BBC Science Club: All About Exploration

Performance Task

| 1 | 2 | 3 | 4 | 5 | 6 | 7 | 8 | 9 | 10 | 11 | 12 | 13 | 14 | 15 | 16 | 17 | 18 |

CONTENTS

COMPARE

© Pearson Education, Inc., or its affiliates. All rights reserved.

Overview: Small-Group Learning **441**

Contents

Selections Circulate among groups as they preview the selections. You might encourage groups to discuss any knowledge they already have about any of the selections or the situations and settings shown in the photographs. Students may wish to take a poll within their group to determine which selections look the most interesting.

Remind students that communicating and collaborating in groups is an important skill that they will use throughout their lives—in school, in their careers, and in their community.

Performance Task

Present an Advertisement Give groups time to read about and briefly discuss the advertisement they will create after reading. Encourage students to do some preliminary thinking about the types of media they may want to use. This may help focus their subsequent reading and group discussion.

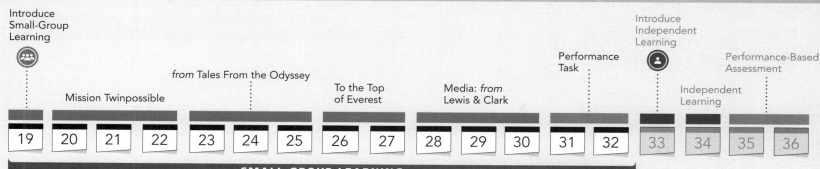

Introduce
Small-Group
Learning

Introduce
Independent
Learning

Performance
Task

Performance-Based
Assessment

Mission Twinpossible

from Tales From the Odyssey

To the Top
of Everest

Media: *from*
Lewis & Clark

Independent
Learning

| 19 | 20 | 21 | 22 | 23 | 24 | 25 | 26 | 27 | 28 | 29 | 30 | 31 | 32 | 33 | 34 | 35 | 36 |

SMALL-GROUP LEARNING

SMALL-GROUP LEARNING

Working as a Team

1. **Take a Position** Remind groups to let all members share their responses. You may wish to set a time limit for this discussion.

2. **List Your Rules** You may want to have groups share their lists of rules and consolidate them into a master list to be displayed and followed by all groups.

3. **Apply the Rules** As you circulate among the groups, ensure that students are staying on task. Consider a short time limit for this step.

4. **Name Your Group** This task can be creative and fun. If students have trouble coming up with a name, suggest that they think of something related to the unit topic. Encourage groups to share their names with the class.

5. **Create a Communication Plan** Encourage groups to include in their plans agreed-upon times during the day to share ideas. They should also devise a method for recording and saving their communications.

Accountable Talk

Remind students that groups should communicate politely. You can post these Accountable Talk suggestions and encourage students to add their own. Students should:

Remember to . . .
Ask clarifying questions.

Which sounds like . . .
Can you please repeat what you said?
Would you give me an example?
I think you said _____. Did I understand you correctly?

Remember to . . .
Explain your thinking.

Which sounds like . . .
I believe _____ is true because _____.
I feel _____ because _____.

Remember to . . .
Build on the ideas of others.

Which sounds like . . .
When _____ said _____, it made me think of _____.

Working as a Team

1. **Take a Position** In your group, discuss the following question:

   Would you rather explore an ancient civilization in the middle of a desert or an island in the middle of the ocean?

   As you take turns sharing your positions, be sure to provide reasons for your choices. After all group members have shared, come to a consensus, or agreement, as to the pros and cons of each option.

2. **List Your Rules** As a group, decide on the rules that you will follow as you work together. Samples are provided; add two more of your own. You may add or revise rules based on your experience together.

   • Everyone should participate in group discussions.
   • People should not interrupt.

   • _____

     _____

   • _____

     _____

3. **Apply the Rules** Practice working as a group. Share what you have learned about exploration. Make sure each person in the group contributes. Take notes and be prepared to share with the class one thing that you heard from another member of your group.

4. **Name Your Group** Choose a name that reflects the unit topic.

   Our group's name: _____

5. **Create a Communication Plan** Decide how you want to communicate with one another. For example, you might use online collaboration tools, email, or instant messaging.

   Our group's decision: _____

   _____

© Pearson Education, Inc., or its affiliates. All rights reserved.

FACILITATING SMALL-GROUP LEARNING

Forming Groups You may wish to form groups for Small-Group Learning so that each consists of students with different learning abilities. Some students may be adept at organizing information whereas others may have strengths related to generating or synthesizing information. A good mix of abilities can make the experience of Small-Group Learning dynamic and productive.

Making a Schedule

First, find out the due dates for the Small-Group activities. Then, preview the texts and activities with your group and make a schedule for completing the tasks.

SELECTION	ACTIVITIES	DUE DATE
Mission Twinpossible		
from Tales From the Odyssey		
To the Top of Everest		
from Lewis & Clark		

Working on Group Projects

As your group works together, you'll find it more effective if each person has a specific role. Different projects require different roles. Before beginning a project, discuss the necessary roles and choose one for each group member. Here are some possible roles; add your own ideas.

Project Manager: monitors the schedule and keeps everyone on task

Researcher: organizes research activities

Recorder: takes notes during group meetings

_____

_____

_____

_____

_____

© Pearson Education, Inc., or its affiliates. All rights reserved.

 SCAN FOR MULTIMEDIA

Overview: Small-Group Learning **443**

Making a Schedule

Encourage groups to preview the selections and to consider how long it will take them to complete the activities accompanying each selection. Point out that they can adjust the due dates for particular selections as needed as they work on their small-group projects. However, they must complete all assigned tasks before the group Performance Task is due. Encourage groups to review their schedules upon completing the activities for each selection to make sure they are on track to meet the final due date.

Working on Group Projects

Point out to groups that the roles they assign can also be changed later. Students might have to make changes based on who is best at doing what. Try to make sure that there is no favoritism, cliquishness, or stereotyping by gender or other means in the assignment of roles.

Also, you should review the roles each group assigns to its members. Based on your understanding of students' individual strengths, you might find it necessary to suggest some changes.

AUTHOR'S PERSPECTIVE   Kelly Gallagher, M.Ed.

Accountability in Group Work The teacher's role during group work is to serve as the facilitator rather than as the leader. This means that the teacher should support the thinking and discussion, but not provide the answers or content direction. Problems can arise if a group is unfocused, if the task is not meaningful, or if there is no accountability. To help groups work together well, achieve their goals, and ensure accountability, teachers can follow these three steps:

1. First, define and clarify the task. Explain why it is valuable, and make sure students know what they are expected to do.

2. Let each group know that one student will be selected randomly to share the group's thinking. This randomness builds in accountability.

3. Pull the whole class back together to share back information and to check learning.

If groups struggle, teachers can prod them with questions that support how they will get to the answer. For example, if they are unable to find the main point of the essay, ask them: *"In this type of text, where might a reader look to find the main idea?"*

Small-Group Learning   **443**

Mission Twinpossible

Summary

The *TIME For Kids* news article "Mission Twinpossible" describes a NASA mission with identical twins Scott and Mark Kelly. Scott Kelly will go to the International Space Station while Mark Kelly will stay on Earth. Over the course of one year, scientists will study both twins to help them understand more about how living and working in space affects the human body.

Insight

NASA is looking for ways that humans can travel beyond the moon to explore more of space. In order to do that, scientists must first understand how space travel and living in space affects the human body. With this knowledge, future astronauts will be better prepared for exploration.

🔊 AUDIO SUMMARIES

Audio summaries of "Mission Twinpossible" are available online in both English and Spanish in the Interactive Teacher's Edition or Unit Resources. Assigning these summaries prior to reading the selection may help students build additional background knowledge and set a context for their first read.

ESSENTIAL QUESTION:
What drives people to explore?

SMALL-GROUP LEARNING PERFORMANCE TASK
Why should we explore new frontiers?

UNIT PERFORMANCE-BASED ASSESSMENT
What fuels people's desire to explore?

Connection to Essential Question

This selection will give students a sense of how medical exploration is used for the sake of space exploration. Investigating how space affects health will enable scientists to help plan for longer missions in space.

Connection to Performance Tasks

Small-Group Learning Performance Task Exploring new frontiers, such as long-term space travel, helps us expand on what we already know about the universe.

Unit Performance-Based Assessment Sometimes, people explore to test their limits—to see what they are capable of and what they can endure. In this news article, scientists explore the effects of space travel to determine what humans might be capable of doing in space during long-term exploration.

DIGITAL PERSPECTIVES

 Audio

 Video

 Document

Annotation Highlights

EL Highlights

 Online Assessment

LESSON RESOURCES

Lesson	Making Meaning	Language Development	Effective Expression
	First Read **Analyze Craft and Structure** **Close Read** **Analyze the Text**	**Concept Vocabulary** **Word Study** **Conventions**	**Research**
Instructional Standards	**RI.1** Cite textual evidence . . . **RI.2** Determine a central idea of a text . . . **RI.3** Analyze in detail . . . **RI.5** Analyze how a particular sentence . . . **RI.10** By the end of the year, read . . . **L.4** Determine or clarify the meaning . . . **L.5** Demonstrate understanding of . . . **L.5.b** Use the relationship between . . . **L.6** Acquire and use accurately . . .	**L.1** Demonstrate command . . . **L.4** Determine or clarify the meaning . . . **L.4.b** Use common, grade-appropriate . . . **L.4.c** Consult reference materials . . . **L.6** Acquire and use accurately . . .	**W.2** Write informative/explanatory . . . **W.2.a** Introduce a topic . . . **W.2.b** Develop the topic . . . **W.2.c** Use appropriate transitions . . . **W.7** Conduct short research projects. . . **W.8** Gather relevant information . . .

STUDENT RESOURCES

Available online in the Interactive Student Edition or Unit Resources	Selection Audio First-Read Guide: Nonfiction Close-Read Guide: Nonfiction	Word Network	Evidence Log

TEACHER RESOURCES

Selection Resources Available online in the Interactive Teacher's Edition or Unit Resources	Audio Summaries Annotation Highlights EL Highlights Mission Twinpossible: Text Questions Analyze Craft and Structure: Central Idea: Make Inferences	Technical Vocabulary and Word Study Conventions: Prepositions and Prepositional Phrases English Language Support Lesson: Prepositions and Prepositional Phrases	Research: How-To Essay
Reteach/Practice (RP) Available online in the Interactive Teacher's Edition or Unit Resources	Analyze Craft and Structure: Central Idea: Make Inferences (RP)	Word Study: Latin Root -dur- (RP) Conventions: Prepositions and Prepositional Phrases (RP)	Research: How-To Essay (RP)
Assessment Available online in Assessments	Selection Test		
My Resources	A Unit 5 Answer Key is available online and in the Interactive Teacher's Edition.		

Reading Support

Text Complexity Rubric: Mission Twinpossible

Quantitative Measures

Lexile: 980   Text Length: 445 words

Qualitative Measures

Knowledge Demands ①——②——**❸**——④——⑤	Readers will need to be familiar with the International Space Station (ISS) and NASA.
Structure ①——**❷**——③——④——⑤	Organization is clear and straightforward; connection between ideas is apparent. Use of subheadings helps clarify content of sections.
Language Conventionality and Clarity ①——**❷**——③——④——⑤	Language is straightforward, with journalistic style. Sentences mostly have simple construction; vocabulary is mostly on-level, with some more difficult words.
Levels of Meaning/Purpose ①——②——**❸**——④——⑤	Events and situations described in article are not immediately apparent, but are eventually explained.

DECIDE AND PLAN

English Language Support

Provide English Learners with support for knowledge demands and language as they read the selection.

Knowledge Demands Write the acronym NASA and what it stands for: *National Aeronautics and Space Administration*. Clarify that NASA is the U.S. government agency in charge of the space program and research. Write *ISS* and ask students to read the background to find what it is (*International Space Station*). Explain that it is a spacecraft orbiting Earth. Astronauts live in it and it is used as a lab. It is international because several countries worked together to build it.

Language Have students read aloud parts of the text. After listening to each part, have students identify unfamiliar words. Guide them to figure out meanings or look them up.

Strategic Support

Provide students with strategic support to ensure that they can successfully read the text.

Knowledge Ask students to tell you what they know about ISS and NASA. Refer them to the background information to read what ISS stands for. Then ask them what they think the *S* in NASA could be for (*space*). Say the name *National Aeronautics and Space Administration* and ask students what they know about it. If necessary, explain more about NASA and ISS.

Meaning After students read each section of the text, pause to confirm their understanding of the events described. For example, after reading the section "Star Twins," ask, *Are both twins going to go to space together?* (No—one is going to space and the other will stay on the ground.)

Challenge

Provide students who need to be challenged with ideas for how they can go beyond a simple interpretation of the text.

Text Analysis Ask students to think about the roles of the two twins—one in space and one on the ground. Ask what factors would be important in choosing which should go to space, such as desire, family, and health.

Written Response Ask students to imagine that they are astronauts, each with a twin as in the article. Have them choose if they would rather be on the ground or in the space station for the experimental year. Have them write a paragraph in the voice of that astronaut, describing their feelings about going into space or being on the ground, explaining why they prefer that choice, and sharing what other plans they have for the year.

TEACH

Read and Respond

Have groups read the selection and complete the Making Meaning, Language Development, and Effective Expression activities.

Standards Support Through Teaching and Learning Cycle

IDENTIFY NEEDS

Analyze results of the Beginning-of-Year Assessment, focusing on the items relating to Unit 5. Also take into consideration student performance to this point and your observations of where particular students struggle.

DECIDE AND PLAN

- If students have performed poorly on items matching these standards, then provide selection scaffolds before assigning them the on-level lesson provided in the Student Edition.
- If students have done well on the Beginning-of-Year Assessment, then challenge them to keep progressing and learning by giving them opportunities to practice the skills in depth.
- Use the Selection Resources listed on the Planning pages for "Mission Twinpossible" to help students continually improve their ability to master the standards.

Instructional Standards: Mission Twinpossible

	Catching Up	This Year	Looking Forward
Reading	You may wish to administer the **Analyze Craft and Structure: Central Idea: Make Inferences (RP)** worksheet to help students understand how to determine a work's central idea.	**RI.2** Determine a central idea of a text and how it is conveyed through particular details; provide a summary of the text distinct from personal opinions or judgments.	Challenge students to determine whether the selection may have more than one central idea, or sub-themes. If not, then refer to a prior text.
Writing	You may wish to administer the **Research: How-To Essay (RP)** worksheet to help students prepare for their writing.	**W.2** Write informative/explanatory texts to examine a topic and convey ideas, concepts, and information through the selection, organization, and analysis of relevant content.	Challenge students to write "How-Not-To" essays after they have written their "How-To" essays.
Language	Review the **Word Study: Latin Root -dur- (RP)** worksheet with students to ensure they understand the Latin root -dur- means "to harden," "to hold out," or "to last." You may wish to administer the **Conventions: Prepositions and Prepositional Phrases (RP)** worksheet to ensure students understand that a preposition relates a noun or a pronoun that follows it to another word in the sentence.	**L.4.b** Use common, grade-appropriate Greek or Latin affixes and roots as clues to the meaning of a word. **L.1** Demonstrate command of the conventions of standard English grammar and usage when writing or speaking.	Have students identify words in the selection that use other Latin roots they recognize. Have students find examples of prepositions in other selections they have read.

ANALYZE AND REVISE

- Analyze student work for evidence of student learning.
- Identify whether or not students have met the expectations in the standards.
- Identify implications for future instruction.

TEACH

Implement the planned lesson, and gather evidence of student learning.

Jump Start

FIRST READ Ask students to consider the following prompts: *How is exploring space similar and different from other exploration? Why might the urge to explore run in families?* As students discuss in groups, ask them to consider why identical twins might be able to provide important information during exploration.

Mission Twinpossible 🔊 🖹

How can Scott and Mark Kelly each improve our understanding of the effects of space travel? Modeling the questions readers might ask as they read "Mission Twinpossible" brings the text alive for students and connects it to the Small-Group Performance Task assignment. Selection audio and print capability for the selection are available in the Interactive Teacher's Edition.

Technical Vocabulary

Ask groups to look closely at the technical vocabulary. Have they seen the terms in texts before? Do they use any of them in their speech or writing?

Then, ask students to consider how clues can help them understand the term *genetic makeup.* Have groups discuss how words surrounding an unknown word help them narrow down possibilities of meaning, especially when the unknown word has multiple meanings.

⬤ FIRST READ

Have students perform the steps of the first read independently:

NOTICE: You may want to encourage students to notice the basic meaning of the informational text, including the main idea of the selection.

ANNOTATE: Remind students to mark passages that include important details that support the main idea of the selection.

CONNECT: Students can increase their understanding of the selection by connecting it to other articles or stories they have read or media they have viewed about space or about identical twins.

RESPOND: Students will answer questions and write a summary to demonstrate understanding. Point out to students that while they will always complete the Respond step at the end of the first read, the other steps will probably happen somewhat concurrently. You may wish to print copies of the **First-Read Guide: Nonfiction** for students to use. 🖹

About the Source

TIME For Kids is a weekly classroom news magazine for kids. Real-world topics are explored both in the magazine and on the website. Science, technology, and social issues are discussed in a way that is easy for young readers to understand. Many *TIME For Kids* articles are actually written by kid reporters and deal with subjects that kids enjoy, such as sports, travel, and entertainment.

☰ STANDARDS

Reading Informational Text
By the end of the year, read and comprehend literary nonfiction in the grades 6–8 text complexity band proficiently, with scaffolding as needed at the high end of the range.

Language
• Determine or clarify the meaning of unknown and multiple-meaning words and phrases based on *grade 6 reading and content,* choosing flexibly from a range of strategies.
• Demonstrate understanding of figurative language, word relationships, and nuances in word meanings.
  b. Use the relationship between particular words to better understand each of the words.
• Acquire and use accurately grade-appropriate general academic and domain-specific words and phrases; gather vocabulary knowledge when considering a word or phrase important to comprehension or expression.

Mission Twinpossible

Technical Vocabulary

As you perform your first read, you will encounter these words.

program manager	sample group	endurance test

Infer Meaning Technical terms are often made up of two familiar words that combine to have a specialized meaning. If a technical term is unfamiliar to you, try using your knowledge of the individual words to make an **inference,** or an educated guess, about the term's meaning.

> **Unfamiliar Term:** *genetic makeup*
>
> **Familiar Individual Words:** *genetic* and *makeup*
>
> **Inferred Meaning:** *Genetic* relates to genes, the parts of your DNA that you inherit from your parents and that determine your personal traits. *Makeup* is the way something is made, or put together. Using your knowledge of these words, you can make an inference that *genetic makeup* means "the way in which a person's inherited traits come together."

Make inferences and use other vocabulary strategies to determine the meanings of unfamiliar words and technical terms you encounter during your first read.

First Read NONFICTION

Apply these strategies as you conduct your first read. You will have an opportunity to complete a close read after your first read.

NOTICE the general ideas of the text. *What* is it about? *Who* is involved?

ANNOTATE by marking vocabulary and key passages you want to revisit.

First Read

CONNECT ideas within the selection to what you already know and what you have already read.

RESPOND by completing the Comprehension Check and by writing a brief summary of the selection.

© Pearson Education, Inc., or its affiliates. All rights reserved.

AUTHOR'S PERSPECTIVE **Jim Cummins, Ph.D.**

Language Awareness Vocabulary knowledge is an extremely robust predictor of students' reading comprehension. The Frayer model is an effective tool for enabling students to extend their vocabulary knowledge in a systematic way.

The tool aims to deepen students' knowledge of words and concepts by focusing their attention not only on simple definitions but also on characteristics of the concept and examples and nonexamples of it.

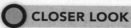

Mission Twinpossible

BACKGROUND

So far, human participation in space exploration has been limited to missions close to Earth. Astronaut crews have been living and working in the International Space Station in Earth's orbit since 2000. The farthest a person has gone is to the moon, but the next step may be landing on Mars, Earth's nearest planet.

SCAN FOR MULTIMEDIA

NOTES

1   When Scott Kelly calls home from the International Space Station (ISS) sometime this year, whoever answers the phone might simply hang up on him. The call will be welcome, but the connection can be bad. That can happen when you're placing your call from 229 miles above the Earth. "When someone answers, I have to say, 'It's the space station! Don't hang up!'" says Scott.

2   But his brother, Mark, knows the crackle of an extraterrestrial[1] signal in his ear. Mark is a former astronaut who has been to space four times. Mark is also known for being married to former congresswoman Gabrielle Giffords, who was hurt in an assassination attempt in 2011.

3   Mark and Scott, 50, are identical twins. They have the same genetic makeup. Though they have served a combined seven missions, the brothers have never gone to space together.

---

1. **extraterrestrial** (ehks truh tuh REHS tree uhl) *adj.* not from Earth.

© Pearson Education, Inc., or its affiliates. All rights reserved.

Mission Twinpossible **445**

CLOSER LOOK

Analyze Key Details

Circulate among groups as students conduct their close read. Suggest that groups close read paragraph 1. Encourage them to talk about the annotations they mark. If needed, provide the following support.

ANNOTATE: Have students mark details in paragraph 1 that seem important, or work with small groups as you highlight them together.

QUESTION: Guide students to consider what these details might tell them. Ask what a reader can infer from the details about Scott Kelly and where he will be.

Possible response: Scott Kelly will be living in the International Space Station and will be trying to call home.

CONCLUDE: Help students to formulate conclusions about the importance of these details in the text. Ask students why the author might have included these details.

Possible response: Scott Kelly is one of the twins who is part of a study. He is the one who will be traveling to the space station. These key details help support the main idea of the text.

Remind students that **key details** tell about the topic of the text and support the central idea. In this case, the details about Scott Kelly—who he is and where he will be—are more important than the details about a possible bad phone connection.

Create an electronic template and have students work in groups of "language detectives" to enter new and interesting words onto the group's template. If time allows, encourage students to compile two to five words each day. Where multiple home languages are represented in a group, students could take turns entering words in their home language, and all members of the group could learn that word. At the end of each week, the teacher could compile the words into a class quiz.

Definition	Image
TARGET WORD	
Synonym and/or Antonym	Sentence

Concept Vocabulary

PROGRAM MANAGER If groups are struggling to define the term *program manager* in paragraph 5, point out that they should look at each individual word. For example, students should think about what *program* means and what *manager* means. Have them use that understanding to define the term *program manager*.

Possible response: In this case, *program manager* means "project director."

SAMPLE GROUP If groups are struggling to define the term *sample group* in paragraph 6, point out that they should look at each individual word. That is, students should think about what *sample* means and what *group* means. Have them use their understanding of both words to define the term *sample group*.

Possible response: In this case, *sample* means "selection" and *group* means "a set of people," so a *sample group* is a "selection of a set of people."

ENDURANCE TEST If groups are struggling to define the term *endurance test* in paragraph 9, point out that they should look at each individual word. That is, students should think about what *endurance* means and what *test* means. Have them use that understanding to define the term *endurance test*.

Possible response: An *endurance test* is "a trial of one's ability to go on."

> 🗨 Additional **English Language Support** is available in the Interactive Teacher's Edition.

NOTES

Make an inference or indicate another strategy you used that helped you determine meaning.

program manager (PROH gram man ih juhr) *n.*
MEANING:

sample group (SAM puhl groop) *n.*
MEANING:

endurance test (ehn DUR uhns tehst) *n.*
MEANING:

A Year in Space

4   In March,[2] Scott will leave his family in Houston, Texas, for a one-year stay aboard the ISS. It will set a single-mission record for a US astronaut. Scott will share his marathon mission with Russian cosmonaut Mikhail Kornienko. A rotating cast of 13 other crew members will join them for shorter visits.

5   The US has long dreamed of sending astronauts to Mars. The biggest problem with reaching this goal is, simply, the human body. We are designed for Earth. In space, bones get brittle, eyeballs lose their shape, hearts beat less efficiently, and balance goes awry. "There's quite a bit of data [on human health] for six months in orbit," says space-station **program manager** Mike Suffredini. "Do things change at one year?"

6   NASA needs subjects to test the long-term effects of space. In a perfect experiment, every subject would have a control subject on Earth with the exact same genes. This would help scientists separate the changes that come from being in space from those that are a result of growing the same year older on Earth. In the Kelly brothers—and only the Kelly brothers—NASA has that two-person **sample group**.

Star Twins

7   Scott's days on the ISS will be packed with science experiments, exercise, and monitoring and fixing the station's systems. The station is stocked with movies and books, and the crew can surf the Internet.

8   On this flight, Scott and Kornienko will be very closely monitored with medical and psychological tests. Mark will undergo similar study on the ground. Scientists hope that comparing the data will shed light on the impact of spending a long time in space.

9   Scott's upcoming mission may be equal parts science experiment, **endurance test**, and human drama. To the Kelly brothers, it is just the latest mile in a journey they've shared for half a century. 🐾

---

2. **March** This article was written in 2015.

© 2015 Time Inc. All rights reserved. Reprinted/Translated from *TIME* and published with permission of Time Inc. Reproduction in any manner in any language in whole or in part without written permission is prohibited. *TIME* and the *TIME* logo are registered trademarks of Time Inc. used under license.

© Pearson Education, Inc., or its affiliates. All rights reserved.

CROSS-CURRICULAR PERSPECTIVES

Science Have students reread paragraph 6. Then, pose the following questions:

• Why are identical twins such as Mark and Scott Kelly so important to scientific research?

• What are some other scientific studies that have involved identical twins?

Next, have groups conduct research on identical-twin studies in science, including some of the results of the studies. Lastly, have each group share its findings with the class.

Comprehension Check

Complete the following items after you finish your first read. Review and clarify details with your group.

1. According to the selection, what is the biggest problem with reaching the goal of sending astronauts to Mars?

2. What happens to the human body in space?

3. How long will Scott Kelly stay at the International Space Station?

4. What will Mark Kelly do while his brother is on the International Space Station?

5. 📓 **Notebook** Write a summary of the news article.

- -

RESEARCH

Research to Clarify Choose at least one unfamiliar detail from the text. Briefly research that detail. In what way does the information you learned shed light on an aspect of the article?

Research to Explore Choose something that interests you from the article, and formulate a research question.

Mission Twinpossible **447**

Comprehension Check

Possible responses:

1. The biggest problem with sending astronauts to Mars is that the human body is designed for Earth, not space.

2. In space, according to the selection, "bones get brittle, eyeballs lose their shape, hearts beat less efficiently, and balance goes awry."

3. Scott Kelly will stay at the International Space Station for one year.

4. Mark Kelly will undergo medical and psychological tests similar to what his brother is receiving.

5. Summaries will vary but should include the facts that Scott Kelly will be at the International Space Station for one year and scientists will study the effects of living in space on his body. At the same time, scientists will study his identical twin brother, Mark Kelly, so that they can compare changes in Mark's health on Earth with changes in Scott's health on the International Space Station.

Research

Research to Clarify If groups struggle to come up with an unfamiliar detail, have them reread the selection and notice something that might be new to them, such as the International Space Station or data on humans in orbit.

Research to Explore If groups struggle to narrow their research topic, you may want to suggest that they focus on one of the following ideas: the missions of Mark and Scott Kelly, the Russian cosmonaut's role in the mission, or the known effects of space travel on the human body.

© Pearson Education, Inc., or its affiliates. All rights reserved.

PERSONALIZE FOR LEARNING

Challenge

Space Travel Encourage interested students to research past space missions. What have scientists learned about the effects of long space travel on the human body? What about the effects on personality? Students may choose to research one astronaut who has spent a long time in space, such as Russian cosmonaut Valeri Polyakov, who spent 438 days on the former *Mir* space station, or Spanish American astronaut Michael López-Alegría, who spent 215 days in space. Students should write a short informational report, sharing what they learn.

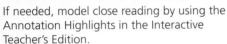

Jump Start

CLOSE READ Ask groups to consider the following prompt: *What would it be like to live and work in space for long periods of time? What would it be like to wait at home while your identical twin got to live and work in space?* As students discuss in their groups, ask them to consider the contribution that each of the Kelly twins is making to science.

Close Read the Text

If needed, model close reading by using the Annotation Highlights in the Interactive Teacher's Edition.

Remind students to use Accountable Talk in their discussions and to support one another as they complete the close read.

Analyze the Text

Possible responses:

1. A *control subject* is a person or group in a scientific study that is not subjected to the particular treatment or condition that is being studied. Without them, researchers wouldn't know whether results are caused by the treatment or by other factors.

2. Remind students to explain why they chose the passage they shared with their group members.

3. Responses will vary by group.

Technical Vocabulary

Why These Words? Possible response: A *program manager* means "project director." A *sample group* is "a selection of a set of people used in a study to represent a larger group." An *endurance test* is "a trial of one's ability to go on under difficult conditions." Understanding precise meanings helps me understand the relationship between what scientists will find by studying Scott and Mark Kelly.

Word Network

Possible words: *International, Space, extraterrestrial*

Word Study

For more support, see **Technical Vocabulary and Word Study.**

Possible responses:

Endurance means "the ability to stay strong under difficult conditions," and Scott Kelly will face difficult conditions. *Durable* describes an object that stays tough and lasts. *Duress* describes a situation when someone is being coerced into doing something he or she does not want to do. *Duration* is a period of time that something lasts.

MAKING MEANING

MISSION TWINPOSSIBLE

Close Read the Text

With your group, revisit sections of the text you marked during your first read. **Annotate** details that you notice. What **questions** do you have? What can you **conclude**?

Analyze the Text

CITE TEXTUAL EVIDENCE
to support your answers.

📝 **Notebook** Complete the activities.

1. **Review and Clarify** Reread paragraph 6 of the article. Use a dictionary of scientific terms to determine the meaning of the term *control subject*. Why might having a control subject be important when conducting a science experiment? Discuss with your group.

2. **Present and Discuss** Now, work with your group to share the passages from the text that you found especially important. Discuss what you noticed in the article, what questions you asked, and what conclusions you reached.

3. **Essential Question: *What drives people to explore?*** What has this article taught you about why people are driven to explore?

💡 TIP

GROUP DISCUSSION
If you disagree with a classmate, it is okay to voice your disagreement, as long as you do so respectfully. Wait for your classmate to finish speaking, and then politely explain why your opinion differs. Some of the best discussions emerge from differing opinions!

⬡ WORD NETWORK

Add words related to exploration from the text to your Word Network.

▤ STANDARDS

Language
• Determine or clarify the meaning of unknown and multiple-meaning words and phrases based on *grade 6 reading and content*, choosing flexibly from a range of strategies.
   b. Use common, grade-appropriate Greek or Latin affixes and roots as clues to the meaning of a word.
   c. Consult reference materials, both print and digital, to find the pronunciation of a word or determine or clarify its precise meaning or its part of speech.
• Acquire and use accurately grade-appropriate general academic and domain-specific words and phrases; gather vocabulary knowledge when considering a word or phrase important to comprehension or expression.

LANGUAGE DEVELOPMENT

Technical Vocabulary

program manager	sample group	endurance test

Why These Words? Many fields of study have specialized vocabularies. Although you may recognize some of the individual words, they combine to form technical terms that have specific meanings. Use a dictionary of scientific terms to determine the precise meaning of each of these technical terms. How does understanding each term's precise meaning deepen your understanding of the text?

Word Study

Latin Root: *-dur-* The word *endurance* is part of the technical vocabulary term *endurance test*. The Latin root *-dur-* in *endurance* means "hard," "to hold out," or "to last."

Explain how the root *-dur-* contributes to the meaning of the technical vocabulary term *endurance test*. Then, find the definition of each of the following words, and explain how the root *-dur-* contributes to the its meaning: *durable, duress, duration*.

FORMATIVE ASSESSMENT

Analyze the Text

If students struggle to close read the text, **then** provide the **Mission Twinpossible: Text Questions** available online in the Interactive Teacher's Edition or Unit Resources. Answers and DOK levels are also available.

Technical Vocabulary

If students have difficulty understanding the technical meaning of the vocabulary, **then** review the meanings as a group, asking students to try to use the words in a sentence.

Word Study

If students have difficulty understanding how the root *-dur-* is important to each word's meaning, **then** model how the root contributes to the meaning of the word *endurance*. For Reteach and Practice, see **Word Study: Latin Root: *-dur-* (RP).**

© Pearson Education, Inc., or its affiliates. All rights reserved.

Analyze Craft and Structure

Central Idea: Make Inferences The **central idea** is the most important point in a text. Sometimes, the central idea is stated directly, but more often it is implied, or suggested. When a central idea is implied, the reader must make inferences to identify it. An **inference** is a logical conclusion that you develop about information that is not directly stated. To make inferences about a central idea, combine your prior knowledge, or what you already know, with the key details that the author provides. Remember that the details in a text are not equal. The key details are the ones that support or tell more about the central idea. Follow these guidelines to distinguish key details from unimportant ones:

- Key details often reveal the topic or subject of the text.
- Key details are sometimes repeated throughout the text in different ways or in different words.
- Key details are related to other details in the text.
- Together, key details support the central idea.

As you make inferences to determine the central idea of a text, ask yourself questions about the details the author included, such as *Why did the author include this detail?*, *Does this detail help readers understand the central idea?*, and *How does this detail support the central idea?*

STANDARDS
Reading Informational Text
- Cite textual evidence to support analysis of what the text says explicitly as well as inferences drawn from the text.
- Determine a central idea of a text and how it is conveyed through particular details; provide a summary of the text distinct from personal opinions or judgments.
- Analyze in detail how a key individual, event, or idea is introduced, illustrated, and elaborated in a text.
- Analyze how a particular sentence, paragraph, chapter, or section fits into the overall structure of a text and contributes to the development of the ideas.

Practice

With your group, reread the paragraphs from the selection that are identified in the chart. Use the key details in each paragraph to make inferences about the central idea of the paragraph. Then, combine your inferences to infer the central idea of the news article as a whole.

CITE TEXTUAL EVIDENCE to support your answers.

PARAGRAPH	INFERENCES ABOUT CENTRAL IDEA
Paragraph 5	Scientists want to study the effects of one year of space travel on a human body.
Paragraph 7	Scott will be active and will communicate with people on Earth.
Paragraph 8	Scientists will use Mark Kelly's data to help understand the effects of space on Scott Kelly and Kornienko.

Central Idea of "Mission Twinpossible":
Scott and Mark Kelly are each playing an important role in helping scientists understand the effects of long-term space travel on the human body.

Mission Twinpossible **449**

Analyze Craft and Structure

Central Idea: Make Inferences Explain to students that when they are trying to identify key details in a news article, they should pay attention to important information about the people described in the article. Information that tells more about what these people are doing and why may help readers understand the central idea of the text. For more support, see **Analyze Craft and Structure: Central Idea: Make Inferences.**

See possible responses in the chart on the student page.

FORMATIVE ASSESSMENT

Analyze Craft and Structure

If students have difficulty making inferences, **then** have them summarize each paragraph of the selection and tell what the key details help them figure out. For Reteach and Practice, see **Analyze Craft and Structure: Central Idea: Make Inferences (RP).**

DIGITAL PERSPECTIVES

Enriching the Text To help students understand more about the International Space Station, show photographs and video of the space station. You may be able to find video of Scott Kelly checking in from the space station or of another astronaut or cosmonaut who is currently there. Discuss with students how viewing the photographs or video sheds light on the selection.

© Pearson Education, Inc., or its affiliates. All rights reserved.

Conventions

Prepositions and Prepositional Phrases
Review the following prepositions from the selection with students. Consider providing additional examples to reinforce their understanding of prepositions and objects of prepositions.

- Paragraph 2: "in his ear"; Preposition: in; Object of preposition: ear
- Paragraph 4: "for shorter visits"; Preposition: for; Object of preposition: visits
- Paragraph 7: "with movies and books"; Preposition: with; Object of preposition: movies and books

For more support, see **Conventions: Prepositions and Prepositional Phrases.**

Read It
Possible responses:
1. Paragraph 1: "*above* the Earth"; Object of preposition: *Earth*
2. Paragraph 4: "*with* Russian cosmonaut Mikhail Kornienko"; Object of preposition: *Mikhail Kornienko*
3. Paragraph 5: "*at* one year"; Object of preposition: *year*
4. Paragraph 4: "*for* a U.S. astronaut"; Object of preposition: *astronaut*
5. Paragraph 1: "*from* the International Space Station"; Object of preposition: *International Space Station*
6. Paragraph 9: "*To* the Kelly brothers"; Object of preposition: *Kelly brothers*

Write It
Paragraphs will vary, but make sure that students use common prepositions and write prepositional phrases correctly.

FORMATIVE ASSESSMENT
Conventions
If students are unable to identify prepositions, **then** return to the list of common prepositions and work together to find prepositional phrases within the text. For Reteach and Practice, see **Conventions: Prepositions and Prepositional Phrases (RP).**

MISSION TWINPOSSIBLE

LANGUAGE DEVELOPMENT

Conventions

Prepositions and Prepositional Phrases A **preposition** relates a noun or a pronoun that follows it to another word in the sentence. In the sentence *The book is on the table,* the preposition *on* relates the noun *table* to another word in the sentence, *book.*

A **prepositional phrase** begins with a preposition and ends with a noun or pronoun—called the **object of the preposition.** In the prepositional phrase *on the table,* the preposition is *on,* and the object of the preposition is *table.* This chart shows a number of commonly used prepositions.

COMMONLY USED PREPOSITIONS			
above	below	in	over
across	beneath	into	through
after	between	near	to
against	by	of	toward
along	down	on	under
at	during	onto	until
before	for	out	up
behind	from	outside	with

Read It

Notebook In the selection, find a prepositional phrase that contains each of these prepositions. Then, determine the object of each preposition.

1. above	**3.** at	**5.** from
2. with	**4.** for	**6.** to

Write It

Write a short paragraph in which you explain whether you would like to go on a yearlong space mission. In your paragraph, correctly use at least three of the commonly used prepositions. Then, exchange paragraphs with a member of your group. Identify each prepositional phrase in your classmate's paragraph.

STANDARDS
Language
Demonstrate command of the conventions of standard English grammar and usage when writing or speaking.

© Pearson Education, Inc., or its affiliates. All rights reserved.

PERSONALIZE FOR LEARNING

English Language Support
Prepositions and Prepositional Phrases Have English learners take turns using prepositional phrases in sentences. Encourage students to emphasize each preposition and its object. For example, "The space station orbits *above* the Earth." As students gain confidence, you might wish to challenge them to construct sentences with two or more prepositional phrases.

Then, have pairs of students work together to use prepositional phrases in a summary of the news article "Mission Twinpossible." **ALL LEVELS**

Research

Assignment

Work with your group to write a **how-to guide.** Choose from the following options:

☐ **Option 1:** The article mentions the negative effects that the lack of gravity in space has on the human body. Conduct research to learn more about how astronauts minimize these negative effects while they are traveling in space. Write a how-to guide for keeping fit in space.

☐ **Option 2:** Astronauts must go through years of training and preparation before traveling to space. Conduct research to find out more about the training and preparation required to become an astronaut. Write a how-to guide for people who want to become astronauts.

Conduct Research As you conduct your research, keep in mind that your purpose is to explain a specific process. In order to create a clear explanation, identify the following:

- important steps
- the order in which the steps should be completed
- any materials required to complete the task—for example, exercise equipment

Take care to include only essential information about staying fit in space or becoming an astronaut. Unnecessary information will distract readers and make the steps of the process you are explaining difficult to follow.

Organize Your Information A clear organizational format is an important part of any successful how-to essay. Make sure you explain and order the steps in the process clearly and precisely. Use transitional words, such as *first, next, after, then,* and *finally,* to keep the order clear. Use visuals, such as illustrations and diagrams, to help your readers understand information that might be complicated or confusing.

Cite Your Sources Include a **works-cited list,** also called a **bibliography,** at the end of your guide. This list should include bibliographic information for all the sources that you used to write your guide. Ask your teacher what citation style you should use when creating your list of sources. Failure to properly credit your sources can be considered **plagiarism** because you are using the ideas, words, or work of someone else as if it is your own.

© Pearson Education, Inc., or its affiliates. All rights reserved.

✎ EVIDENCE LOG

Before moving on to a new selection, go to your Evidence Log and record what you learned from "Mission Twinpossible."

☰ STANDARDS

Writing

- Write informative/explanatory texts to examine a topic and convey ideas, concepts, and information through the selection, organization, and analysis of relevant content.
  a. Introduce a topic; organize ideas, concepts, and information, using strategies such as definition, classification, comparison/contrast, and cause/effect; include formatting, graphics, and multimedia when useful to aiding comprehension.
  b. Develop the topic with relevant facts, definitions, concrete details, quotations, or other information and examples.
  c. Use appropriate transitions to clarify the relationships among ideas and concepts.

- Conduct short research projects to answer a question, drawing on several sources and refocusing the inquiry when appropriate.

- Gather relevant information from multiple print and digital sources; assess the credibility of each source; and quote or paraphrase the data and conclusions of others while avoiding plagiarism and providing basic bibliographic information for sources.

Mission Twinpossible **451**

Research

If students have difficulty in choosing a topic, point out that the first option has to do with the effects of space travel on human beings, including unpleasant physical effects that some students may find unsettling. Students who are very interested in space travel may find this topic particularly intriguing. Explain that the second option includes the physical and mental preparation that astronauts undergo. For more support, see **Research: How-To Essay.** 📄

Conduct Research Once students have decided on their topic, make sure that they conduct research using credible sources. Explain to them that information from NASA and other government websites is most likely trustworthy.

Organize Your Information As students work on organizing their information, point out that they may simply number the steps of the process they are describing. Before describing the steps of the process, however, they should include an introduction that tells what the process is and why it is important.

Cite Your Sources Explain to students that it is important to use more than one source and to provide full information about the sources they use.

Evidence Log Support students in completing their Evidence Log. This paced activity will help prepare them for the Performance-Based Assessment at the end of the unit.

FORMATIVE ASSESSMENT

Research

If students have difficulty in researching a topic, **then** have them work with their group to review effective search terms. For Reteach and Practice, see **Research: How-To Essay (RP).** 📄

Selection Test

Administer the "Mission Twinpossible" Selection Test, which is available in both print and digital formats online in Assessments. 📄 ☑

PERSONALIZE FOR LEARNING

Strategic Support

Research Help students find trustworthy online sources for their research by pointing out the following information about the last three letters of an internet URL, which identify the domain of the site.

- .gov – Government sites are created and maintained by the United States federal government and are considered reliable.

- .edu – Information from an educational research center or department is likely to be carefully checked but may also include student pages that are not edited or monitored.

- .org – Groups with organization domains are nonprofit groups. Nonprofit groups usually maintain credibility, but their sites may reflect strong biases.

from Tales from the Odyssey

🔊 **AUDIO SUMMARIES**
Audio summaries of the excerpt from *Tales from the Odyssey* are available online in both English and Spanish in the Interactive Teacher's Edition or Unit Resources. Assigning these summaries prior to reading the selection may help students build additional background knowledge and set a context for their first read.

Summary

This excerpt from *Tales from the Odyssey* by Mary Pope Osborne tells part of the story of Odysseus. Based on a famous ancient Greek epic called the *Odyssey*, readers of Osborne's myth meet the Greek king and war hero Odysseus and his men as they are trying to get home after fighting in the Trojan War. They face challenges and dangers on their journey, and Odysseus must show bravery, intelligence, and leadership if he is to get his men home safely.

Insight

Sometimes, unexpected or unplanned journeys can lead to opportunities for exploration and learning. For example, in the section from the excerpt from *Tales from the Odyssey* called "The Mysterious Shore," it is Odysseus' curiosity that leads him to suspend his journey home long enough to explore the mysterious shore. Curiosity and the desire to learn are characteristics shared by many explorers, though in Odysseus' case, they may lead to unexpected dangers.

ESSENTIAL QUESTION:
What drives people to explore?

Connect to the Essential Question

Although Odysseus' journey was not a planned journey of exploration, his sense of curiosity leads him to explore. This curiosity links him to other explorers throughout history who are driven by a desire to learn and discover.

SMALL-GROUP LEARNING PERFORMANCE TASK
Why should we explore new frontiers?

UNIT PERFORMANCE-BASED ASSESSMENT
What fuels people's desire to explore?

Connection to Performance Tasks

Small-Group Learning Task By exploring new frontiers, we expand the limits of our knowledge. For example, the knowledge that Odysseus gains by exploring would have remained obscured had he simply focused on his journey home and not explored.

Unit Performance-Based Assessment Part of what drives people to explore is curiosity and the desire to know something new. In Odysseus' case, knowledge gained through exploration might simply satisfy his curiosity, but it might also expedite his journey home.

LESSON RESOURCES

	Making Meaning	**Language Development**
Lesson	**First Read** **Close Read** **Analyze the Text** **Analyze Craft and Structure**	**Concept Vocabulary** **Word Study** **Conventions**
Instructional Standards	**RL.2** Determine a theme or central idea of a text . . . **RL.5** Analyze how a particular sentence, chapter, scene, or stanza . . . **RL.10** By the end of the year, read and comprehend literature . . . **L.4** Determine or clarify the meaning of unknown and multiple-meaning words and phrases . . . **L.4.a** Use context as a clue . . .	**RL.4** Determine the meaning of words and phrases . . . **L.1** Demonstrate command of the conventions . . . **L.4** Determine or clarify the meaning of unknown and multiple-meaning words and phrases . . . **L.4.b** Use common, grade-appropriate Greek or Latin affixes and roots . . . **L.4.c** Consult reference materials . . .
⬈ STUDENT RESOURCES		
Available online in the Interactive Student Edition or Unit Resources	🔊 Selection Audio 📄 First-Read Guide: Fiction 📄 Close-Read Guide: Fiction	📄 Word Network
⬈ TEACHER RESOURCES		
Available online in the Interactive Teacher's Edition or Unit Resources	🔊 Audio Summaries ✏️ Annotation Highlights 💬 EL Highlights 📄 English Language Support Lesson: Acronyms 📄 Analyze the Text Questions 📄 Analyze Craft and Structure: Universal Theme	📄 Concept Vocabulary and Word Study 📄 Conventions: Participial and Gerund Phrases
Reteach/Practice (RP) Available online in the Interactive Teacher's Edition or Unit Resources	📄 Analyze Craft and Structure: Universal Theme (RP)	📄 Word Study: Latin Root: *-vad-* (RP) 📄 Conventions: Participial and Gerund Phrases (RP)
Assessment Available online in Assessments	📄 ✅ Selection Test	
My Resources	📄 A Unit 5 Answer Key is available online and in the Interactive Teacher's Edition.	

Reading Support

Text Complexity Rubric: *from* Tales from the Odyssey

Quantitative Measures

Lexile: 710   Text Length: 1,318 words

Qualitative Measures

Knowledge Demands ①—②—③—❹—⑤	The selection requires background knowledge of who Odysseus is and why he and his men are on a journey. Some knowledge of Greek mythology is also required, though some references to the Greek gods are explained.
Structure ①—❷—③—④—⑤	Fairly straightforward order of events and narrative structure.
Language Conventionality and Clarity ①—②—❸—④—⑤	Short to moderate-length sentences; some formal diction and terms that will be unfamiliar to students.
Levels of Meaning/Purpose ①—②—❸—④—⑤	Myth contains some fantastic elements, and the concept of gods who act like humans and are vengeful may be challenging.

DECIDE AND PLAN

English Language Support

Provide English Learners with support for language and meaning as they read the selection.

Language Point out to students that the author uses some words and phrases that will likely be unfamiliar to them, such as the word *valiantly* in paragraph 9 or the phrase "Why did they tarry?" in paragraph 18. Ask students to skim the text and pick out an example of a word or phrase that is unfamiliar to them. Help students to define these to foster reading comprehension.

Meaning As they read, have students jot down words or phrases that they don't understand. Then, as a class, define unfamiliar words and phrases and discuss them in the context of the narrative.

Strategic Support

Provide students with strategic support to ensure that they can successfully read the text.

Knowledge Demands Review what students know about Greek mythology. Explain that the ancient Greeks believed in hundreds of gods and goddesses and that each one had his or her realm of influence. These gods were thought to share human traits, such as jealousy and anger.

Meaning Have students skim the text and note references to specific gods. Then, provide background information on these gods. For example, you might explain that Poseidon is god of the sea, and then ask why offending him would have consequences for Odysseus and his men, who are traveling by sea.

Challenge

Provide students who need to be challenged with ideas for how they can go beyond a simple interpretation of the text.

Text Analysis Have students work in pairs to identify the relationship between the gods and humans in the selection. They should consider why Odysseus is so concerned about offending the gods and how his concerns shape the narrative.

Written Response Ask students to conduct research on Greek gods, listing several of the most well known and noting their characteristics. Then, challenge them to write a paragraph in which they explain how these gods might help or hurt Odysseus and his men if they chose to intervene in his journey.

TEACH

Read and Respond

Have the groups read the selection and complete the Making Meaning and Language Development activities.

Standards Support Through Teaching and Learning Cycle

IDENTIFY NEEDS

Analyze results of the Beginning-of-Year Assessment, focusing on the items relating to Unit 5. Also take into consideration student performance to this point and your observations of where particular students struggle.

DECIDE AND PLAN

- If students have performed poorly on items matching these standards, then provide selection scaffolds before assigning them the on-level lesson provided in the Student Edition.
- If students have done well on the Beginning-of-Year Assessment, then challenge them to keep progressing and learning by giving them opportunities to practice the skills in depth.
- Use the Selection Resources listed on the Planning pages for the excerpt from *Tales from the Odyssey* to help students continually improve their ability to master the standards.

Instructional Standards: *from* Tales from the Odyssey

	Catching Up	This Year	Looking Forward
Reading	You may wish to administer the **Analyze Craft and Structure: Universal Theme (RP)** worksheet to help students better understand the theme of this work.	**RL.5** Analyze how a particular sentence, chapter, scene, or stanza fits into the overall structure of a text and contributes to the development of the theme, setting, or plot.	Challenge students to think of other myths they know and consider what the themes of those myths might be.
Language	Review the **Word Study: Latin Root: -vad- (RP)** worksheet with students to ensure they understand the Latin root -vad- means "to go." You may wish to administer the **Conventions: Participial and Gerund Phrases (RP)** worksheet to ensure students understand how participles and gerunds function.	**L.4.b** Use common, grade-appropriate Greek or Latin affixes and roots as clues to the meaning of a word. **L.1** Demonstrate command of the conventions of standard English grammar and usage when writing or speaking.	Have students identify other words that contain the root -vad-. Have students find examples of participles and gerunds in the selection.

ANALYZE AND REVISE

- Analyze student work for evidence of student learning.
- Identify whether or not students have met the expectations in the standards.
- Identify implications for future instruction.

TEACH

Implement the planned lesson, and gather evidence of student learning.

Jump Start

FIRST READ Tell students that they will read about some of the adventures of a hero from Greek mythology named Odysseus. Explain that Odysseus and his men are trying to return home after fighting in the Trojan War, but they face dangers and challenges and are thrown off course on their journey. Ask students to speculate on how searching for ways to get home might lead to exploration.

from Tales from the Odyssey 🔊 📄

What makes an explorer? Is it a desire to find new places? Is it a sense of curiosity? A desire for adventure? Modeling the questions readers might ask as they read the excerpt from *Tales from the Odyssey* for the first time brings the text alive for students and connects it to the Small-Group Performance Task assignment. Selection audio and print capability for the selection are available in the Interactive Teacher's Edition.

Concept Vocabulary

Have groups discuss the concept vocabulary words and share their knowledge of the words. Then, ask students to study the modeling of context clues, and have groups discuss how nearby words can help them understand an unfamiliar word.

🔘 FIRST READ

Have students perform the steps of the first read independently:

NOTICE: Encourage students to note Odysseus' characteristics and to pay attention to the way that the characters view the gods.

ANNOTATE: Remind students to mark passages that include vivid details or that seem important in advancing the narrative.

CONNECT: Encourage students to go beyond the text to make connections to their own personal experiences or to other stories they've read or movies and TV shows they've seen.

RESPOND: Students will answer questions and write a summary to demonstrate understanding. Point out to students that while they will always complete the Respond step at the end of the first read, the other steps will probably happen somewhat concurrently. You may wish to print copies of the **First-Read Guide: Fiction** for students to use. 📄

TO THE TOP OF EVEREST

Comparing Texts

from TALES FROM THE ODYSSEY

In this section, you will read and compare two works about adventure and challenges. First, you will complete the first-read and close-read activities for the excerpt from *Tales From the Odyssey.*

About the Author

Mary Pope Osborne (b. 1949) has lived an adventurous life. Her father was in the military, and her family moved seven times before Osborne was fifteen. As a young adult, she explored sixteen Asian countries with friends. Osborne began to write in her thirties. Today, she is best known for her series *The Magic Tree House.* "There is no career better suited to my eccentricities, strengths, and passions than that of a children's book author," Osborne says.

📋 STANDARDS

Reading Literature
By the end of the year, read and comprehend literature, including stories, dramas, and poems, in the grades 6–8 text complexity band proficiently, with scaffolding as needed at the high end of the range.

Language
Determine or clarify the meaning of unknown and multiple-meaning words and phrases based on *grade 6 reading and content,* choosing flexibly from a range of strategies.
a. Use context as a clue to the meaning of a word or phrase.

from Tales From the Odyssey

Concept Vocabulary

As you perform your first read, you will encounter these words.

invaded	violent	offended	wrath

Context Clues If these words are unfamiliar to you, try using **context clues**—other words and phrases that appear in nearby text—to help you determine their meanings. There are various types of context clues that may help you as you read.

> **Synonyms:** Tourism depends on visitors who participate in **leisure** and <u>entertainment</u> activities.
>
> **Contrast of Ideas:** Once a **sullen** girl, Elena had grown into a <u>bright, cheerful</u> young woman.

Apply your knowledge of context clues and other vocabulary strategies to determine the meanings of unfamiliar words you encounter during your first read.

First Read FICTION

Apply these strategies as you conduct your first read. You will have an opportunity to complete a close read after your first read.

NOTICE *whom* the story is about, *what* happens, *where* and *when* it happens, and *why* those involved react as they do.

ANNOTATE by marking vocabulary and key passages you want to revisit.

First Read

CONNECT ideas within the selection to what you already know and what you have already read.

RESPOND by completing the Comprehension Check and by writing a brief summary of the selection.

© Pearson Education, Inc., or its affiliates. All rights reserved.

👥 FACILITATING SMALL-GROUP CLOSE READING

Myths Explain that a myth is a type of fictional story that involves gods, goddesses, heroes, and heroines. Myths reflect the values and beliefs of the culture that originated them, and they sometimes explain or teach a lesson.

One of the functions of a myth was to teach the people who heard it—myths of this type were part of the oral storytelling tradition—a lesson about life. It was also meant to teach listeners how their society or culture thought a person should behave or what qualities a person should have.

EPIC RETELLING

from
TALES
From the
ODYSSEY

Mary Pope Osborne

SCAN FOR MULTIMEDIA

BACKGROUND

In *Tales From the Odyssey*, Mary Pope Osborne adapts the famous Greek epic by Homer called the *Odyssey*. Homer's prequel to the *Odyssey* was called the *Iliad*, which tells the story of the Trojan War, a ten year war between the Greeks and the people of Troy. In the *Odyssey*, Homer tells the story of Odysseus, a Greek king and war hero, and the long, dangerous journey he and his men make on their way home from the Trojan War. The excerpt from Osborne's retelling starts at the beginning of the their ten year journey.

The Odyssey Begins

1 Soon after the Greek ships left Troy, the skies began to blacken. Lightning zig-zagged above the foamy sea. Thunder shook the heavens.

2 Mighty winds stirred the water. The waves grew higher and higher, until they were rolling over the bows of the ships.

3 "The gods are punishing us!" the Greek warriors shouted. "We shall all drown!"

4 As his men frantically fought the storm, Odysseus felt bewildered. Why was Zeus, god of the skies, hurling his thunderbolts at them? Why was Poseidon, lord of the seas, sending great waves over the waters?

5 Odysseus turned to his men. "What has happened to anger the gods?" he shouted. "Tell me!"

NOTES

from Tales From the Odyssey **453**

© Pearson Education, Inc., or its affiliates. All rights reserved.

CLOSER LOOK

Analyze Conflict

Circulate among groups as students conduct their close read. Suggest that groups close read paragraph 4. If needed, provide the following support.

ANNOTATE: Have students reread paragraph 4 and mark the names of the two gods, where they rule, and what Odysseus thinks they are doing to him and his men.

QUESTION: Guide students to consider what these details might tell them. Ask what a reader can infer from these details, and accept student responses.

Possible response: Odysseus thinks that he and his men must have done something to offend the gods because they appear to be causing the thunder and waves of the storm.

CONCLUDE: Help students to formulate conclusions about the importance of the details in the text. Ask students why the author might have included these details.

Possible response: The details tell us that ancient Greeks believed in gods who took an active role in their lives. In this case, Odysseus believes that he and his men must have offended the gods and are therefore being punished by the storm they created.

Remind students that **conflict** is a struggle between opposing forces. In this case, the conflict is between the gods and Odysseus and his men.

VOCABULARY DEVELOPMENT

Dictionary Use Students may not be familiar with some of the above-level and multiple-meaning words used in the selection. Working in their groups, have students use a dictionary to determine the definition and part of speech for the following words from paragraphs 2 and 4 of the selection. For the word *bows,* students should use the context of the narrative to determine which meaning fits.

- **bows:**
- **frantically:**
- **hurling:**

After students have determined the definitions and parts of speech, direct them to use each word in a sentence. Or, challenge students to use all three words in one sentence about Odysseus and his men in the storm. Have groups share their sentences with the class.

Concept Vocabulary

INVADED If groups struggle to define the word *invaded* in paragraph 6, point out that they can use context clues to help determine the word's meaning. Draw students' attention to the fact that Odysseus and his men fear they are being punished by the gods, and in paragraph 6, Odysseus' men tell him what Greek warriors did.

Possible response: Based on context clues, the word *invaded* means "entered by force."

VIOLENT If groups struggle to define the word *violent* in paragraph 6, work with them to use context clues to uncover the word's meaning. For example, readers know that Odysseus asks his men why the gods might be angry with them. And, in paragraph 6, his men tell him what the Greek warriors did to Athena's temple—it was something *disrespectful*.

Possible response: Based on these clues, the word *violent* means "using physical force to damage or harm."

OFFENDED If groups struggle to define the word *offended* in paragraph 7, work with them to define it using context clues. Point out that readers learn in paragraph 6 that Greek warriors were *disrespectful* at Athena's temple. In paragraph 7, readers learn that her anger is behind the storm that threatens Odysseus and his men.

Possible response: Based on these clues, the word *offended* means "hurt or upset through speech or action."

WRATH If groups struggle to define the word *wrath* in paragraph 12, direct them to use context clues to help uncover the word's meaning. In paragraph 12, Odysseus and his men encounter another storm because Athena's *wrath* had not been satisfied, and readers know from paragraph 6 that the Greeks did something to her temple that was *disrespectful* and caused her to act against Odysseus and his men.

Possible response: Based on these clues, the word *wrath* means "anger; rage."

NOTES

Mark context clues or indicate another strategy you used that helped you determine meaning.

invaded (ihn VAYD ihd) *v.*
MEANING:

violent (VY uh luhnt) *adj.*
MEANING:

offended (uh FEHND ihd) *v.*
MEANING:

wrath (rath) *n.*
MEANING:

---

6   "Before we left Troy,[1] Greek warriors **invaded** Athena's[2] temple!" said one of his men. "They were **violent** and disrespectful."

7   Odysseus was stunned. The Greeks had **offended** the goddess who had helped them to victory! And now her anger might drown them all.

8   The wind grew stronger. It whipped the sails of the Greek ships and slashed them to rags. "Lift your oars!" Odysseus shouted to his men. "Row! Row to shore!"

9   The Greeks struggled valiantly against the mighty wind and waves. Fighting for their lives, they finally rowed their battered ships to a strange shore. There they found shelter in a rocky cave.

10   The storm raged for two more days and nights. Then, on the third day, a fair wind blew, the sun came out, and the wine-dark sea was calm at last.

11   "Now we can continue on our way," Odysseus said to his men. "Athena is no longer angry." In the rosy dawn, he ordered them to raise their tattered sails and set off again for Ithaca.[3]

12   But, alas, the **wrath** of Athena had not been fully spent. Hardly had Odysseus reached the open sea than another gale began to blow.

13   For many days, Odysseus and his men fought the wind and the waves, refusing to surrender to the storm. Finally, on the tenth day, there was sudden calm.

14   Odysseus ordered his fleet to sail into the cove of a leafy green island. There he hoped to find food and drink for his hungry, weary men.

15   The Greeks dropped anchor. Then they dragged themselves ashore. They drank cool, fresh water from a spring and collapsed onto the sand.

16   As Odysseus rested, he ordered three of his men to explore the island and look for provisions.

18   When the three had not returned by late afternoon, Odysseus grew angry. Why did they tarry? he wondered.

18   Odysseus set out in search of the men. He moved through the brush and brambles, calling their names.

19   He had not gone far when he came upon a group of peaceful islanders. They greeted him with warm, friendly smiles. And they offered him their food—lovely bright flowers.

---

1. **Troy** site of the Trojan War in the Greek oral and literary tradition.
2. **Athena's** In Greek mythology, Athena is the daughter of Zeus and the goddess of wisdom and victory in war.
3. **Ithaca** Greek island that is Odysseus's home.

© Pearson Education, Inc., or its affiliates. All rights reserved.

PERSONALIZE FOR LEARNING

Strategic Support

Research Call students' attention to the words "Before we left Troy..." in paragraph 6. Then, explain that in the excerpt from *Tales from the Odyssey*, the hero Odysseus and his men are trying to return home after fighting in the Trojan War. Have students perform research to learn more about the basics of the Trojan War in Greek mythology, including the following:

- the combatants (the Greeks and the Trojans)
- the role of Helen of Troy
- the Trojan Horse
- Odysseus' role in the war

You may wish to assign a specific point of research to each group and then have groups report their findings to the class, which can be assembled into a more complete picture of events.

© Pearson Education, Inc., or its affiliates. All rights reserved.

20 Odysseus was famished. But just as he was about to eat the flowers, he caught sight of his missing men. The three were lying on the ground with dreamy smiles on their faces.

21 Odysseus called each man by name, but none of them answered. They did not even look at him.

22 "What have you done to them?" he asked the islanders.

23 "We have given them our flowers to eat," an islander answered. "This is our greatest gift. The gods would be angry if we did not offer to feed our guests."

24 "What sort of flowers are these?" Odysseus asked.

25 "They come from the lotus tree," the islander said. "They have the magical power of forgetfulness. They make a man forget the past."

26 "Forget his memories of home?" asked Odysseus. "And his memories of his family and friends?"

NOTES

from Tales From the Odyssey **455**

○ CLOSER LOOK

Infer Key Ideas ✐

Circulate among groups as students conduct their close read. Suggest that groups close read paragraph 23. If needed, provide the following support.

ANNOTATE: Have students reread paragraph 23 and mark what the islanders say would make the gods angry.

QUESTION: Guide students to consider what this detail might tell them. Ask what a reader can infer from this detail, and accept student responses.

Possible response: In Greek mythology, the gods took an active role in humans' lives and had human-like emotions, such as anger.

CONCLUDE: Help students to formulate conclusions about the importance of this detail in the text. Ask students why this detail was included in the myth.

Possible response: This detail reveals that ancient Greeks valued hospitality in their culture, and including it in this narrative strengthens the importance of that belief.

Remind students that **key ideas** are those that are central to the meaning of a text. In this case, the author doesn't state explicitly that ancient Greeks valued hospitality. Readers must make an inference, or a logical conclusion based on details in the text.

CLOSER LOOK

Analyze Suspense 🌐

Circulate among groups as students conduct their close read. Suggest that groups close read paragraph 32. If needed, provide the following support.

ANNOTATE: Have students reread paragraph 32 and mark the words that show how Odysseus feels and the sentence that builds suspense.

QUESTION: Guide students to consider what these details might tell them. Ask what a reader can infer from these details, and accept student responses.

Possible response: Based on Odysseus feeling "troubled and anxious" and the unanswered question that ends the paragraph, readers can infer that Odysseus and his men will face more dangers and challenges on their journey home.

CONCLUDE: Help students to formulate conclusions about the importance of these details in the text. Ask students why these details were included in the myth.

Possible response: The question the author poses is intentionally left unanswered so that readers will want to read on and find out what happens next.

Remind students that **suspense** is a feeling of anxious uncertainty about the outcome of events. Authors create suspense by raising questions about what will happen, and delaying the answers.

NOTES

27   The lotus-eaters only smiled. They again offered Odysseus their sweet, lovely flowers. But he roughly brushed them away. He pulled his three men to their feet and commanded them all to return to their ships at once.

28   The men began to weep. They begged to be left behind so they could stay on the island and eat lotus flowers forever.

29   Odysseus angrily herded the men back to the ships. As they drew near the shore, the three tried to escape. Odysseus called for help.

30   "Tie their hands and feet!" he shouted to his crew. "Make haste! Before others eat the magic flowers and forget their homes, too!"

31   The three flailing men were hauled aboard and tied to rowing benches. Then Odysseus ordered the twelve ships to push off from shore.

32   Once more, the Greeks set sail for Ithaca, sweeping the gray sea with their long oars. As they rowed past dark islands with jagged rocks and shadowy coves, Odysseus felt troubled and anxious. What other strange wonders lurked on these dark, unknown shores?

The Mysterious Shore

33   Soon the Greek ships came upon a hilly island, thick with trees. No humans seemed to live there. Hundreds of wild goats could be heard bleating from the island's gloomy thickets.

34   Odysseus ordered his men to drop anchor in the shelter of a mist-covered bay. By the time the Greeks had lowered their sails, night had fallen. The moon was hidden by clouds. In the pitch dark, the men lay down on the sandy shore and slept.

35   When daylight came, the men woke to see woodland nymphs,[4] the daughters of Zeus, driving wild goats down from the hills. The hungry Greeks eagerly grabbed their bows and spears and slew more than a hundred goats.

36   All day, the Greeks lingered on the island, feasting on roasted meat and drinking sweet wine. As the sun went down, they stared at a mysterious shore across the water. Smoke rose from fires on the side of a mountain. The murmur of deep voices and the bleating of sheep wafted through the twilight.

37   *Who lives there? Who stokes those fires?* Odysseus wondered silently. *Are they friendly or lawless men?*

38   Darkness fell, and the Greeks slept once more on the sand. When he was wakened by the rosy dawn, Odysseus stared again

---

4. **woodland nymphs** female spirits of the natural world and nurses to the Greek gods.

© Pearson Education, Inc., or its affiliates. All rights reserved.

DIGITAL PERSPECTIVES

Enriching the Text Review the lotus-eaters scene which begins in paragraph 27. There is a long history of artists and filmmakers creating depictions of scenes from the *Odyssey*. With their groups, have students review the scene. Then, have groups do research online for images that show Odysseus and his men among the lotus-eaters. Students can research paintings, illustrations, stills from movies, and so on.

Have students record their thoughts on the images they found and share their findings with the rest of the class. If they have trouble getting started, you may wish to prompt them with questions such as the following:

• How did the images you found compare to what you imagined as you read?

• Which did you find more powerful—the descriptions in the text, or the images? Why?

at the mysterious shore in the distance. Though he was yearning to set sail for Ithaca, a strange curiosity had taken hold of him.

39 Odysseus woke his men. "I must know who lives on that far shore," he said. "With a single ship, I will lead an expedition to find out whether they are savages or civilized humans. Then we will continue our journey home."

40 Odysseus chose his bravest men to go with him. They untied a ship from their fleet and pushed off from the island.

41 Soon the Greeks were swinging their long oars into the calm face of the sea, rowing toward the mysterious shore. When they drew close, they dropped anchor beneath a tall, rocky cliff.

42 Odysseus filled a goatskin with the best wine he had on board, made from the sweetest grapes. "This will be our gift to repay the hospitality of anyone who welcomes us into his home," he said.

43 He ordered some of this men to remain with the ship, then led the rest up the side of the cliff. On a ledge high above the water, they discovered a large, shady clearing. On the other side of the clearing, creeping vines hung over the mouth of a cave. The Greeks pushed past the vines and stepped inside.

44 The cave was filled with young goats and lambs. Pots of cheese and pails of goat's milk were everywhere. But there was no sign of a shepherd.

45 "Hurry!" said one of Odysseus's men. "Let us grab provisions and leave!"

46 "Yes! We should drive the lambs down to our ship before their master returns!" said another.

47 "No," said Odysseus. "We will wait awhile. . . . I am curious to see who lives here."

48 The Greeks made a fire and gave an offering to the gods. Then they greedily took their fill of milk and cheese. Finally, in the late afternoon, they heard whistling and bleating.

49 "Ah, the shepherd returns," Odysseus said. "Let us step forward and meet this man."

50 But when they peered out of the cave, the Greeks gasped with horror—for the shepherd was no a man at all. He was a monster. 🐚

NOTES

CLOSER LOOK

Analyze Character

Circulate among groups as students conduct their close read. Suggest that groups close read paragraphs 38, 39, and 47. If needed, provide the following support.

ANNOTATE: Have students reread paragraphs 38, 39, and 47 and mark the words that show that Odysseus has a desire to know something.

QUESTION: Guide students to consider what these details might tell them. Ask what a reader can infer from these details, and accept student responses.

Possible response: Readers can infer that Odysseus is by nature a curious person. The details also show his persistence—he doesn't want to continue the journey home until he finds out who lives on the mysterious shore.

CONCLUDE: Help students to formulate conclusions about the importance of these details in the text. Ask students why these details were included in the myth.

Possible responses: Odysseus' curiosity shows that despite his desire to get home, he is still an explorer at heart. His desire for knowledge outweighs his desire to resume his journey.

© Pearson Education, Inc., or its affiliates. All rights reserved.

from Tales From the Odyssey **457**

Comprehension Check

Possible responses:

1. The gods are punishing Odysseus and his men, who are Greek, because Greek warriors invaded and disrespected the goddess Athena's temple.

2. The islanders give Odysseus' men lotus flowers to eat.

3. Odysseus and his men find a monster in the cave.

4. Summaries will vary, but they should include the main events described in the narrative.

Research

Research to Clarify If students struggle to come up with a detail to research, you may want to suggest they choose a detail from the text that provides evidence that the ancient Greeks believed that the gods played an active role in their lives.

Research to Explore If students struggle to generate a research topic, you may want to suggest that they focus on one of the following topics: the Trojan War, Odysseus' journey, or the gods and goddesses of Greek mythology.

Comprehension Check

Complete the following items after you finish your first read. Review and clarify details with your group.

1. At the beginning of the epic retelling, why are the gods punishing Odysseus and his men?

2. What do the islanders give Odysseus' men at the first place they stop?

3. At the second place Odysseus and his men stop, what do they find in the cave?

4. 🗐 **Notebook** Confirm your understanding of the excerpt from *Tales From the Odyssey* by writing a brief summary.

- -

RESEARCH

Research to Clarify Choose at least one unfamiliar detail from the text. Briefly research that detail. In what way does the information you learned shed light on an aspect of the retelling?

Research to Explore Choose something that interests you from the text, and formulate a research question that you might use to find out more about it.

Close Read the Text

With your group, revisit sections of the text you marked during your first read. **Annotate** details that you notice. What **questions** do you have? What can you **conclude**?

from TALES FROM THE ODYSSEY

Analyze the Text

CITE TEXTUAL EVIDENCE
to support your answers.

Complete the activities.

1. **Review and Clarify** If events in a story are the opposite of what you expect, the effect is called **situational irony**. Reread paragraphs 33–50 of the epic retelling. Why is the ending ironic? What effect does the situational irony have on you as a reader?

2. **Present and Discuss** Now, work with your group to share passages from the excerpt that you found especially interesting. Discuss what you noticed in the text, what questions you asked, and what conclusions you reached.

3. *Essential Question:* **What drives people to explore?** What has this retelling taught you about what drives people to explore?

LANGUAGE DEVELOPMENT

Concept Vocabulary

invaded	violent	offended	wrath

Why These Words? The concept vocabulary words from the text are related. With your group, determine what the words have in common. How does the author's word choice help develop the characters and settings in the myth?

Practice

Notebook With your group, write a brief paragraph predicting what will happen to Odysseus and his men after they meet the monster mentioned at the end of the selection. Use all four concept vocabulary words in your paragraph.

Word Study

Latin Root: -vad- In the epic retelling, the gods are angry because the Greek warriors invaded Athena's temple. The word *invaded* is formed from the Latin prefix *in-*, which means "in" or "into," and the Latin root *-vad-*, which means "go." Write a sentence or two in which you explain how knowing the meaning of the root *-vad-* helps you understand the meaning of *invaded*. Then, use a dictionary to find the definitions of the words *evade* and *pervade*. Discuss with your group how these words are related to the word *invaded*.

 WORD NETWORK

Add words related to exploration from the text to your Word Network.

STANDARDS

Reading Literature
Determine the meaning of words and phrases as they are used in a text, including figurative and connotative meanings; analyze the impact of a specific word choice on meaning and tone.
Language
Determine or clarify the meaning of unknown and multiple-meaning words and phrases based on *grade 6 reading and content,* choosing flexibly from a range of strategies.
b. Use common, grade-appropriate Greek or Latin affixes and roots as clues to the meaning of a word.
c. Consult reference materials, both print and digital, to find the pronunciation of a word or determine or clarify its precise meaning or its part of speech.

from Tales From the Odyssey **459**

Jump Start

CLOSE READ Ask students to consider the following prompt: *Should Odysseus have insisted on finding out who lived on the mysterious shore? Why or why not?* As students discuss the prompt in their groups, have them consider what chances are sometimes necessary to take in order to explore, and whether the risks are worth it.

Close Read the Text

If needed, model close reading by using the Annotation Highlights in the Interactive Teacher's Edition. Remind students to use Accountable Talk in their discussions and to support one another as they complete the close read.

Analyze the Text

1. **Possible response:** The end of the myth is ironic because Odysseus insists on finding out who lives on the mysterious shore, and it turns out to be a monster.

2. **Passages will vary by group.** Remind students to explain why they chose specific passages.

3. **Responses will vary by group.**

Concept Vocabulary

Why These Words? Possible response: All of these words relate to the goddess Athena in some way and the revenge she takes on Odysseus and his men.

Practice

Paragraphs will vary, but students should correctly use the concept vocabulary words.

Word Network

Possible words: *ships, shelter, provisions, curiosity, bewildered, valiantly*

Word Study

For more support, see **Concept Vocabulary and Word Study.**

Possible responses:
evade: avoid; escape from
pervade: spread throughout

FORMATIVE ASSESSMENT
Analyze the Text

If students struggle to close read the text, **then** provide the *from* Tales from the Odyssey: Text Questions available online in the Interactive Teacher's Edition or Unit Resources. Answers and DOK levels are also available.

Concept Vocabulary

If students struggle to make a connection among the concept vocabulary words, **then** encourage them to revisit the selection and review how they are used in context.

Word Study

If students have trouble explaining how the Latin root *-vad-* relates to the meaning of each word, **then** work as a class to break the words down and see how the root contributes to the meaning of each.

For Reteach and Practice, see **Word Study: Latin Root: *-vad-* (RP).**

© Pearson Education, Inc., or its affiliates. All rights reserved.

Analyze Craft and Structure

Universal Theme Explain to groups that themes aren't always expressed directly by an author. Often, readers have to make inferences, or conclusions based on details in the text, to determine a theme.

For more support, see **Analyze Craft and Structure: Universal Theme.** 📄

Practice

Possible responses:

1. (a) The Greek warriors who invaded Athena's temple cause problems for Odysseus. The Greek gods Zeus and Poseidon and the goddess Athena cause problems for Odysseus. (b) Odysseus struggles with a keen sense of curiosity—he needs to know who lives on the mysterious shore.

2. (a) The characters are curious, and in Odysseus' case, this brings him face to face with "a monster." (b) Odysseus is clever, as when he figures out the effect of eating lotus flowers and saves the men who have eaten them by having them tied to the rowing benches of the ship.

3. (a) Odysseus overcomes these problems by being clever, resourceful, and confident. (b) Odysseus overcomes such problems by trusting his instincts.

4. Reponses will vary.

FORMATIVE ASSESSMENT

Analyze Craft and Structure: Universal Theme

If students have trouble identifying themes in the selection, **then** suggest they reread the selection and look for larger messages about life or the culture of ancient Greeks.

For Reteach and Practice, see **Analyze Craft and Structure: Universal Theme (RP).** 📄

👥 MAKING MEANING

from TALES FROM THE ODYSSEY

Analyze Craft and Structure

Universal Theme Stories of Odysseus have been around, in some form, for thousands of years. One reason they have lasted so long is that people still connect with their messages and with their portrayals of human nature. In other words, their themes are universal. A **universal theme** is a message or insight about life that is expressed in the literature and art of all cultures and time periods. Examples include the importance of courage, the power of love, and the danger of greed.

The ancient version of the *Odyssey* is an **epic**—a long poem about heroes. Even though the version you read was adapted for our times, the universal themes remain. To find universal themes in the epic retelling, focus on the main character, analyze the problems he faces, and notice how he responds or changes as a result.

Practice

CITE TEXTUAL EVIDENCE to support your answers.

📓 **Notebook** Work together to examine how this universal theme is expressed in the epic retelling: *We are all tested by life's challenges.* Complete the activity and answer the questions.

1. Use the chart to identify details from the text that show specific types of challenges Odysseus faces.

CHALLENGES FROM OTHERS	CHALLENGES FROM HIMSELF
Which people and gods create problems for Odysseus?	What feelings or thoughts does Odysseus struggle with?
a. See possible responses in the teacher's edition.	b.

2. **(a)** In what ways do the characters' personalities make their problems worse? **(b)** In what ways do their personalities make them better?

3. **(a)** How does Odysseus overcome problems with others? **(b)** How does Odysseus overcome problems that arise from his own thoughts or feelings? Explain.

4. What might the ways in which Odysseus responds to problems suggest about how people can or should deal with challenges? Explain.

STANDARDS

Reading Literature
• Determine a theme or central idea of a text and how it is conveyed through particular details; provide a summary of the text distinct from personal opinions or judgments.
• Analyze how a particular sentence. chapter, scene, or stanza fits into the overall structure of a text and contributes to the development of the theme, setting, or plot.

© Pearson Education, Inc., or its affiliates. All rights reserved.

Conventions

Participial and Gerund Phrases A **participle** is a verb form that acts as an adjective. The **present participle** of a verb ends in -*ing*: *relaxing music*. The **past participle** of a regular verb ends in -*ed*: *a relaxed position*. For irregular verbs, you must memorize the past participle form: *broken promises*.

A **participial phrase** combines a present or past participle with other words; the entire phrase acts as an adjective:

> *Relaxing on the patio*, Jo fell asleep. **(The participial phrase modifies *Jo*.)**

> *The small ship, beaten by the winds, couldn't manage to reach the shore.* (The participial phrase modifies **ship**.)

A **gerund** is a verb form that also ends in -*ing* but is used as a noun: *I like relaxing*.

A **gerund phrase** combines a gerund with other words; the entire phrase acts as a noun:

> *Relaxing in your spare time is important.* **(The gerund phrase is the subject of the sentence.)**

> *The sailors tried anchoring the ship.* **(The gerund phrase is the object of the verb *tried*.)**

Read It

Identify and label all the participles, gerunds, participial phrases, and gerund phrases in each of these sentences from the excerpt from *Tales From the Odyssey*.

1. Fighting for their lives, they finally rowed their battered ships to a strange shore.

2. The murmur of deep voices and the bleating of sheep wafted through the twilight.

3. The three flailing men were hauled aboard and tied to rowing benches.

Write It

📓 **Notebook** Think of a fictional adventure at sea that you could write as a story. Then, write the first paragraph of that story. Include at least one participial phrase and at least one gerund phrase.

📝 **EVIDENCE LOG**

Before moving on to a new selection, go to your Evidence Log and record what you have learned from the excerpt from *Tales from the Odyssey*.

☰ **STANDARDS**
Language
Demonstrate command of the conventions of standard English grammar and usage when writing or speaking.

from Tales From the Odyssey **461**

© Pearson Education, Inc., or its affiliates. All rights reserved.

Conventions

Participial and Gerund Phrases As you review the participles and gerunds in the selection with students, consider providing additional examples to reinforce the differences between the different types.

- Present participles: *a refreshing beverage, a flourishing business*
- Past participles: *a ruined cake, a stuffed animal, a broken glass*. (Explain that since *to break* is an irregular verb, it does not end in -*ed* like the others.)
- Participial phrase: *Singing quietly to herself, Becky was beginning to miss her best friend.*
- Gerund: *Tony is afraid of flying.*
- Gerund phrase: *Flying to the moon would be an awesome experience.*

For more support, see **Conventions: Participial and Gerund Phrases.** 🖹

Read It

1. Participial phrase: *Fighting for their lives*
2. gerund: *bleating*
3. participle: *flailing*

Write It

Paragraphs will vary, but make sure that students answer the prompt and correctly use all the required elements.

Evidence Log Support students in completing their Evidence Logs. This paced activity will help prepare them for the Performance-Based Assessment at the end of the unit.

FORMATIVE ASSESSMENT

Conventions

If students have trouble determining whether a word that ends in -*ing* is a gerund or a present participle, **then** remind them to look at whether it is being used as a noun or an adjective. For Reteach and Practice, see **Conventions: Participial and Gerund Phrases (RP).** 🖹

Selection Test

Administer the "*from* Tales from the Odyssey" Selection Test, which is available in both print and digital formats online in Assessments. 🖹 ☑

PERSONALIZE FOR LEARNING

English Language Support

Participles and Gerunds Review the definitions of the parts of speech referenced in this lesson (*participles, present participles, past participles, participial phrases, gerunds,* and *gerund phrases*). Give students a list of examples of these parts of speech (you can use the additional examples in the side column or create your own) and ask them to sort them or label them with the correct part of speech. Then, ask students to think of their own example of each part of speech and use it in a sentence. **ALL LEVELS**

An expanded **English Language Development Lesson** on Participles and Gerunds is available in the Interactive Teacher's Edition. 🖹

To the Top of Everest

🔊 **AUDIO SUMMARIES**
Audio summaries of "To the Top of Everest" are available online in both English and Spanish and can be assigned to students in the Interactive Teacher's Edition or Unit Resources. Assigning these summaries prior to reading the selection may help students build additional background knowledge and set a context for their first read.

Summary

"To the Top of Everest" is a series of blog entries by Samantha Larson that follows her successful climb to the top of the world's tallest mountain at age 18. She describes the process of getting used to high elevations, which involves hiking between camps at different elevations on the mountain. She also describes the Puja ceremony, in which a Tibetan spiritual leader asks the mountain gods for permission to climb the mountain. Details related to getting to the top of the mountain are shared—as is Larson's return home.

Insight

This selection shows that being an explorer is more about a certain mindset than it is about age. Samantha Larson shows that the desire to seek out something new makes facing the obstacles worthwhile.

ESSENTIAL QUESTION:
Should kids today be encouraged to explore?

Connection to Essential Question

Reaching the summit of Mount Everest requires time, energy, and sacrifice. When Samantha Larson was 18, her devotion to her goal drove her to achieve it. Students may argue that her drive supports a positive answer to the Essential Question.

SMALL-GROUP LEARNING PERFORMANCE TASK
Why should we explore new frontiers?

UNIT PERFORMANCE-BASED ASSESSMENT
What fuels people's desire to explore?

Connection to Performance Tasks

Small-Group Learning Performance Task This selection describes a teenager's ascent of the world's tallest mountain. As she does so, she pushes the boundaries of her own personal frontiers.

Unit Performance-Based Assessment Larson's writing will help students consider the prompt. This selection suggests that people explore because they are seeking a unique experience. In this case, that unique experience is exploring a remote environment.

LESSON RESOURCES

	Making Meaning	Language Development	Effective Expression
Lesson	**First Read** **Close Read** **Analyze the Text** **Analyze Craft and Structure**	**Concept Vocabulary** **Word Study** **Conventions**	**Writing to Compare**
Instructional Standards	**RI.2** Determine a central idea of a text . . . **RI.3** Analyze in detail . . . **RI.10** By the end of the year, read and comprehend literary nonfiction . . . **L.4** Determine or clarify the meaning of unknown and multiple-meaning words and phrases . . .	**L.1** Demonstrate command . . . **L.4** Determine or clarify the meaning of unknown and multiple-meaning words and phrases . . . **L.4.b** Use common, grade-appropriate Greek or Latin affixes and roots . . . **L.4.c** Consult reference materials . . . **L.4.d** Verify the preliminary determination . . .	**RL.9** Compare and contrast texts in different forms or genres . . **W.2** Write informative/explanatory texts . . . **W.2.b** Develop the topic . . . **W.9** Draw evidence from literary or informational texts . . . **W.9.a** Apply *grade 6 Reading standards* . . .

▷ STUDENT RESOURCES

Available online in the Interactive Student Edition or Unit Resources	🔊 Selection Audio 📄 First-Read Guide: Nonfiction 📄 Close-Read Guide: Nonfiction	📄 Word Network	📄 Evidence Log

▷ TEACHER RESOURCES

Selection Resources Available online in the Interactive Teacher's Edition or Unit Resources	🔊 Audio Summaries 🖊 Annotation Highlights 💬 EL Highlights 📄 To the Top of Everest: Text Questions 📄 Analyze Craft and Structure: Central Idea 📄 English Language Support Lesson: Central Idea	📄 Concept Vocabulary and Word Study 📄 Conventions: Subject Complements	📄 Writing to Compare: Compare-and-Contrast Essay
Reteach/Practice (RP) Available online in the Interactive Teacher's Edition or Unit Resources	📄 Analyze Craft and Structure: Central Idea (RP)	📄 Word Study: Latin Root: *-ped-* (RP) 📄 Conventions: Subject Complements (RP)	
Assessment Available online in Assessments	📄 ☑ Selection Test		
My Resources	📄 A Unit 5 Answer Key is available online and in the Interactive Teacher's Edition.		

Reading Support

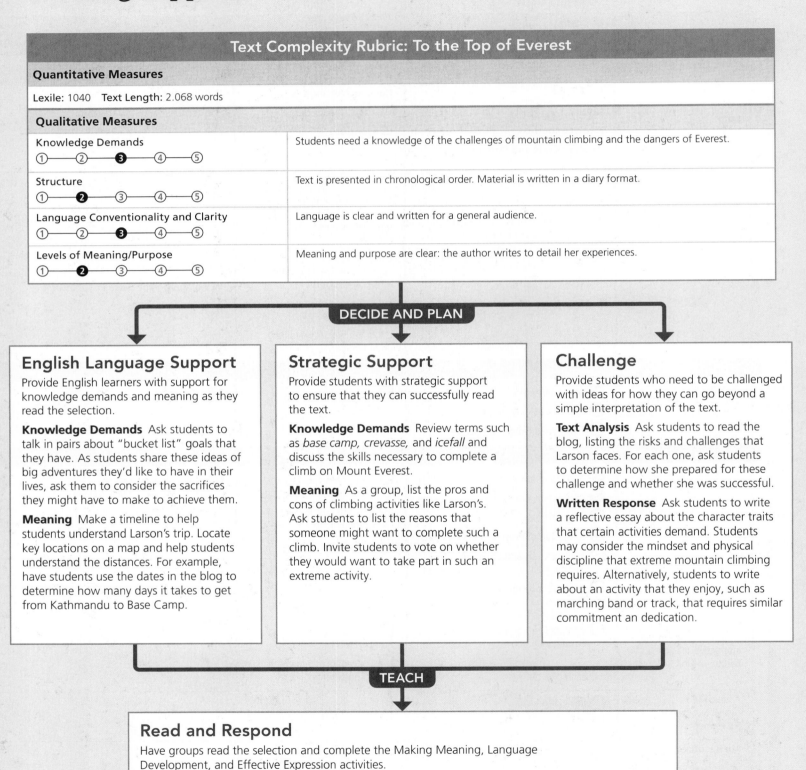

Text Complexity Rubric: To the Top of Everest	
Quantitative Measures	
Lexile: 1040 **Text Length:** 2.068 words	
Qualitative Measures	
Knowledge Demands ①——②——**❸**——④——⑤	Students need a knowledge of the challenges of mountain climbing and the dangers of Everest.
Structure ①——**❷**——③——④——⑤	Text is presented in chronological order. Material is written in a diary format.
Language Conventionality and Clarity ①——②——**❸**——④——⑤	Language is clear and written for a general audience.
Levels of Meaning/Purpose ①——**❷**——③——④——⑤	Meaning and purpose are clear: the author writes to detail her experiences.

DECIDE AND PLAN

English Language Support

Provide English learners with support for knowledge demands and meaning as they read the selection.

Knowledge Demands Ask students to talk in pairs about "bucket list" goals that they have. As students share these ideas of big adventures they'd like to have in their lives, ask them to consider the sacrifices they might have to make to achieve them.

Meaning Make a timeline to help students understand Larson's trip. Locate key locations on a map and help students understand the distances. For example, have students use the dates in the blog to determine how many days it takes to get from Kathmandu to Base Camp.

Strategic Support

Provide students with strategic support to ensure that they can successfully read the text.

Knowledge Demands Review terms such as *base camp, crevasse,* and *icefall* and discuss the skills necessary to complete a climb on Mount Everest.

Meaning As a group, list the pros and cons of climbing activities like Larson's. Ask students to list the reasons that someone might want to complete such a climb. Invite students to vote on whether they would want to take part in such an extreme activity.

Challenge

Provide students who need to be challenged with ideas for how they can go beyond a simple interpretation of the text.

Text Analysis Ask students to read the blog, listing the risks and challenges that Larson faces. For each one, ask students to determine how she prepared for these challenge and whether she was successful.

Written Response Ask students to write a reflective essay about the character traits that certain activities demand. Students may consider the mindset and physical discipline that extreme mountain climbing requires. Alternatively, students to write about an activity that they enjoy, such as marching band or track, that requires similar commitment an dedication.

TEACH

Read and Respond

Have groups read the selection and complete the Making Meaning, Language Development, and Effective Expression activities.

Standards Support Through Teaching and Learning Cycle

IDENTIFY NEEDS

Analyze results of the Beginning-of-Year Assessment, focusing on the items relating to Unit 5. Also take into consideration student performance to this point and your observations of where particular students struggle.

DECIDE AND PLAN

- If students have performed poorly on items matching these standards, then provide selection scaffolds before assigning them the on-level lesson provided in the Student Edition.
- If students have done well on the Beginning-of-Year Assessment, then challenge them to keep progressing and learning by giving them opportunities to practice the skills in depth.
- Use the Selection Resources listed on the Planning pages for "To the Top of Everest" Allowed?" to help students continually improve their ability to master the standards.

Instructional Standards: To the Top of Everest

	Catching Up	This Year	Looking Forward
Reading	You may wish to administer the **Analyze Craft and Structure: Central Idea (RP)** worksheet to help students understand how nonfiction texts are organized.	**RI.3** Analyze in detail how a key individual, event, or idea is introduced, illustrated, and elaborated in a text.	Challenge students to break the blog into sections to find details that support the central ideas.
Language	Review the **Word Study: Latin Root: -ped- (RP)** worksheet to ensure students recognize this root. You may wish to administer the **Conventions: Subject Complements (RP)** worksheet to ensure students understand how predicate nouns and predicate adjectives work.	**L.4** Determine or clarify the meaning of unknown and multiple-meaning words and phrases based on *grade 6 reading and content,* choosing flexibly from a range of strategies. **L.1** Demonstrate command of the conventions of standard English grammar and usage when writing or speaking.	Encourage students to find other words that have this root. Have students find examples of predicate nouns and adjectives in the selection.

ANALYZE AND REVISE

- Analyze student work for evidence of student learning.
- Identify whether or not students have met the expectations in the standards.
- Identify implications for future instruction.

TEACH

Implement the planned lesson, and gather evidence of student learning.

Jump Start

FIRST READ Engage students in a discussion about Mount Everest. Ask students to share what they know about the people who work to climb it. Use this prompt: *Would you want to climb to the top of Mount Everest if you could? Why or why not?* Ask: *Would you visit Antarctica or the Arctic if you had the chance? Why or why not?*

To the Top of Everest

Why would someone want to visit the top of Mount Everest? What are some of the challenges climbers face? Modeling the questions readers might ask as they read "To the Top of Everest" brings the text alive for students and connects it to the Small-Group Performance Task question. Selection audio and print capability for the selection are available in the Interactive Teacher's Edition.

Concept Vocabulary

Ask groups to look closely at the type of context clues described on the student page. Discuss how these types of clues can help clarify meaning. Encourage groups to think of two other types of context clues that they might encounter in a blog written in an informal writing style. Possibilities include examples, antonyms, and synonyms.

FIRST READ

Have students perform the steps of the first read independently.

NOTICE: Encourage students to notice the types of details that seem important to Larson.

ANNOTATE: Remind students to mark passages that provide specific details that show the challenges of the adventure.

CONNECT: Encourage students to connect mountain climbing to other activities that require a big commitment.

RESPOND: Students will answer questions and write a summary to demonstrate understanding.

Point out to students that while they will always complete the Respond step at the end of the first read, the other steps will probably happen somewhat concurrently. You may wish to print copies of the **First-Read Guide: Nonfiction** for students to use.

MAKING MEANING

Comparing Texts

from TALES FROM THE ODYSSEY

You will now complete the first-read and close-read activities for "To the Top of Everest." Then, you will compare the blog with the excerpt from *Tales From the Odyssey*.

TO THE TOP OF EVEREST

About the Author

In 2007, American **Samantha Larson** (b. 1988) became the youngest person to climb the "Seven Summits"—the highest mountains on each of the seven continents. Larson climbed her first, Mount Kilimanjaro in Africa, at the age of 12. She finished her quest when she successfully reached the top of Mount Everest at age 18. Larson calls Everest "much harder, longer, and higher" than the other peaks. "It was one big challenge," she recalls, but adds, "Deep down, I thought I would make it."

STANDARDS

Reading Informational Text
By the end of the year, read and comprehend literary nonfiction in the grades 6–8 text complexity band proficiently, with scaffolding as needed at the high end of the range.

Language
Determine or clarify the meaning of unknown and multiple-meaning words and phrases based on *grade 6 reading and content*, choosing flexibly from a range of strategies.

462 UNIT 5 • EXPLORATION

To the Top of Everest

Concept Vocabulary

As you perform your first read, you will encounter these words.

expedition	trek	journeys	destination

Context Clues If these words are unfamiliar to you, try using **context clues** other words and phrases that appear in nearby text—to help you determine their meanings. There are various types of context clues that may help you as you read.

> **Definition: Cygnets**, or young swans, tend to be larger than ducklings or chicks of the same age.
>
> **Elaborating Details:** As the **acrobat**, performed the crowd cheered at every leap, flip, and somersault

Apply your knowledge of context clues and other vocabulary strategies to determine the meanings of unfamiliar words you encounter during your first read.

First Read NONFICTION

Apply these strategies as you conduct your first read. You will have an opportunity to complete a close read after your first read.

NOTICE the general ideas of the text. *What* is it about? *Who* is involved?

ANNOTATE by marking vocabulary and key passages you want to revisit.

First Read

CONNECT ideas within the selection to what you already know and what you have already read.

RESPOND by completing the Comprehension Check and by writing a brief summary of the selection.

© Pearson Education, Inc., or its affiliates. All rights reserved.

FACILITATING SMALL-GROUP CLOSE READING

CLOSE READ: Blog As groups perform the close read, circulate and offer support as needed.

• Remind groups that when they read a blog, they are reading an online diary that may be more informal than other types of nonfiction. Ask students to look for details that reveal Larson's personality.

• Most blogs are written for a very specific purpose. Encourage students to review the content to determine why Larson is writing.

• Ask students to discuss the tone of the blog's writing. Is it humorous, serious, informal, lighthearted? Challenge students to discuss how the tone of the work suits its purpose.

BLOG

To the Top of Everest

Samantha Larson

Concept Vocabulary

EXPEDITION If groups are struggling to define *expedition* in paragraph 2, point out that they can use context clues to infer the meaning of the word. Details in paragraph 2 indicate that Larson is doing physical training. Details in paragraph 1 and 3 indicate that she is going on a trip. Encourage students to use this information to define the word.

Possible response: *Expedition* means "a trip." More specifically, an *expedition* is "a trip taken with a specific purpose, often to explore or to conduct research."

BACKGROUND

Mount Everest is the highest mountain in the world, rising approximately 29,000 feet above sea level. It is part of the Asian mountain range called the Himalayas, and is located on the border between Nepal and Tibet. Tibetans refer to the mountain as Chomolunga, or "Mother Goddess of the Earth." In 1953, Sir Edmund Hillary of New Zealand and Sherpa Tenzing Norgay of Nepal became the first people to reach Mount Everest's summit. Sherpas are an ethnic group that is native to the highest regions in Nepal and are known for their abilities in mountaineering. Sherpas are still valued today for their key role in successful attempts to climb Mount Everest.

SCAN FOR MULTIMEDIA

Friday, March 30, 2007
Here we go ⟶ Kathmandu!

1 Today is the day! Our bags are (nearly) packed and we're (just about) ready to go. I've got eleven hours to run around doing last minute errands before our plane takes off.

2 I arrived back in Long Beach from New York last Saturday, where I've been since our return from Cho Oyu. When I wasn't training by running, swimming at the pool, taking dance classes, or rock climbing, I was taking oboe lessons, French, and photography classes. Hopefully I'll be able to take some great pictures on this **expedition!**

3 It has been a very exciting week in all our general trip preparation mayhem, filled with lots of gear sorting and FedEx package arrivals. But now my dad and I are pretty much all set to go.

4 See you in Kathmandu!

NOTES

Mark context clues or indicate another strategy you used that helped you determine meaning.

expedition (ehks puh DIHSH uhn) *n.*

MEANING:

Additional **English Language Support** is available in the Interactive Teacher's Edition.

To the Top of Everest **463**

VOCABULARY DEVELOPMENT

Concept Vocabulary Reinforcement If groups are struggling with the definition of *remote*, remind them that the word has multiple meanings. Point out four of the most common definitions:

1. far apart
2. out-of-the-way or secluded
3. controlled from a distance
4. distant in relationship or connection

Explain to groups that in the selection, *remote* refers to the second definition. The Arctic and Antarctica are out-of-the-way and secluded because they are difficult to access and they have very little human settlement. Have groups brainstorm example sentences for the other definitions of the word *remote*.

Small-Group Learning **463**

© Pearson Education, Inc., or its affiliates. All rights reserved.

Concept Vocabulary

TREK If groups are struggling to define *trek* in paragraph 6, point out that they can use context clues to infer the meaning of the word. Details in paragraph 5 indicate that the group is planning its route. In paragraph 7, details like *porters* and *loads* also provide context. Encourage students to use this information to define the word.

Possible response: *Trek* means "a trip taken on foot."

JOURNEYS If groups are struggling to define *journeys* in paragraph 7, point out that they can use context clues to infer the meaning of the word. Details in paragraph 7 include a four-hour hike through several villages. Encourage students to use this information to define the word.

Possible response: *Journeys* means "trips from one place to another."

DESTINATION If groups are struggling to define *destination* in paragraph 12, point out that they can use context clues to infer the meaning of the word. Paragraph 12 uses a contrasting piece of information to help define the word. The group would turn around at a specific time, not a specific destination. Encourage students to use this information to define the word.

Possible response: *Destination* means "a specific ending place."

Mark context clues or indicate another strategy you used that helped you determine meaning.

trek (trehk) *n.*
MEANING:

journeys (JUR neez) *n.*
MEANING:

destination (dehs tuh NAY shuhn) *n.*
MEANING:

Monday, April 2, 2007
Kathmandu

5 After nearly 24 hours of travel we finally arrived in Kathmandu yesterday afternoon. Doug, my dad, and I met up with the rest of the team (Victor, James, and Wim) at our hotel in Kathmandu. We had a group meeting where we went over the route we are going to take to base camp, and then we picked up some odds and ends at one of the dozens of local climbing stores.

6 The team is flying to Lukla to begin the **trek** to base camp early tomorrow morning.

Wednesday, April 4, 2007
Namche Bazaar

7 Yesterday after a very scenic flight and a heart-stopping landing on a small airstrip perched on the side of a mountain, we arrived in Lukla to begin the trek to base camp. Lukla was filled with excitement as porters organized their loads and trekkers began their **journeys**. From Lukla, we hiked for about 4 hours through the beautiful Nepalese countryside, passing through several villages until we reached the village of Monjo, where we stayed the night in the Monjo Guesthouse. I think my dad and I got the big sleep that we needed to catch up on our jetlag; around 4 in the afternoon, we decided to take a "nap" that lasted until 7 the next morning!

Thursday, April 12, 2007
Base Camp

8 We made it to base camp yesterday afternoon. Today we are going to practice crossing the ladders over the Khumbu Icefall. We are well and safe.

9 En route here we visited Lama Gesa and he blessed our journey. It was an amazing experience!

10 I am going to try and connect my laptop and charge it with my solar charger—we will see if that works.

11 More to follow. . . .

Monday, April 16, 2007
Rest Day

12 Yesterday we got an early start for our first time through the icefall. We left around 6:30 in the morning, with the idea that we would turn around 11—we did not necessarily have a **destination** in mind, it was more for acclimatization[1] and to get an idea of

---

1. **acclimatization** (uh kly muh tuh ZAY shuhn) *n.* process of allowing the body to adjust to the climate, especially at high altitude.

© Pearson Education, Inc., or its affiliates. All rights reserved.

PERSONALIZE FOR LEARNING

Challenge

Ecosystem Research Call student attention to paragraphs 5–8. Encourage interested students to research the geographic locations named in the text. Students can annotate a map to indicate the dates and places of the groups' travel. Ask students to continue to update the map based on the information they read in the rest of the blog.

what the icefall was like. However, at 11 we were about half an hour from the top of the icefall, so we decided to just continue to the top.

13 It was quite fun climbing up the icefall. The ladders that we had to cross over crevasses[2] were especially exciting. I was pretty tired by the time we got back to base camp, but today was a rest day (our first), so I've had plenty of time to recover.

14 Tomorrow we are going up to camp one to spend the night. Camp one is about an hour further than we went yesterday. The next day we will go up to tag camp two and then come back down to base camp.

Thursday, April 19, 2007
Puja

15 The day before yesterday we all made it up to camp one to spend the night. This time we were able to get through the Khumbu Icefall an hour quicker than the last. We had a pretty good night at camp one; my dad and I both had a bit of a headache at first, but we were both able to eat and sleep well.

16 Camp one is at the start of the Western Cwm.[3] Yesterday, from camp one we continued up the Cwm to camp two. The Cwm is infamous for being very uncomfortably hot, but yesterday it was actually really nice. It was very beautiful, and we could see the summit of Everest, which we haven't been able to see since before we got to base camp. After we tagged camp two we came all the way back down to base camp. It was a long day, and we all returned pretty tired. However, it was nice to be back in base camp, and after dinner we watched *Mission Impossible III* on Ben's laptop (from the London Business School team). Unfortunately the power ran out about halfway through, but I have been asked to charge up my laptop so we can finish tonight.

17 Today was the Puja, which is a ceremony that the Sherpas organize. A Lama comes up and performs many chants to ask the mountain gods for permission to climb the mountain, and to ask for protection. I had my ice ax and my crampons[4] blessed in the ceremony. As part of the ceremony, they also put out long lines of prayer flags coming out from the stupa where the ceremony was performed. Afterwards, they passed out lots of yummy treats.

---

2. **crevasses** (kruh VAS ihz) *n.* deep cracks in ice or a glacier.
3. **Western Cwm** broad valley at the base of Mount Everest.
4. **crampons** (KRAM puhnz) *n.* metal plates with spikes that are attached to boots to provide greater traction.

© Pearson Education, Inc., or its affiliates. All rights reserved.

CLOSER LOOK

Analyze Conflict With Nature

Circulate among groups as students conduct their close read. Suggest that groups close read paragraphs 19 and 20. Encourage them to talk about the annotations they mark. If needed, provide the following support.

ANNOTATE: Have students mark details in paragraphs 19 and 20 that indicate the risks of the adventure or work with small groups as you highlight them together.

QUESTION: Guide students to consider what these details might tell them. Ask what a reader can infer from these details, and accept student responses.

Possible response: These risks are serious. If the climbers are not careful, they could endure critical injury or death. As an example, students might be interested to read that the group plans to rest for a few days before their next climb.

CONCLUDE: Help students to formulate conclusions about the importance of these details in the text. Ask students why the author might have included these details.

Possible response: The author probably included these details in order to explain the challenges of the climb and to help readers understand the seriousness of the adventure.

Remind students that a **conflict with nature** pits people against the elements such as wind, rain, cold, and natural danger.

NOTES

18 While we were up at camp one, the shower tent was set up here at base camp. It's just a little bucket of water with a hose attached to it, but definitely 15 minutes of heaven.

Saturday, April 28, 2007
Base Camp

19 We are back at base camp! We came down from camp two yesterday, and arrived just in time for lunch. We were delayed a bit in the morning because we were radioed from base camp that there was a break in the icefall, and we didn't want to leave until we knew that the "ice doctors" had fixed up the route. As we came down, we found that the break was in a flat area known as the "football field" that we had previously designated as a "safe" area to take a little rest. And the whole shelf just collapsed!

20 Now that we have spent a night at camp three, we are done with the acclimatization process. We are going to take a few days for rest and recovery, and then we just wait for good weather to make a summit bid. We plan to go back down to Pengboche tomorrow so we can really get a good rest at lower altitude before our summit attempt.

21 Here is what we have been up to these past few days:

© Pearson Education, Inc., or its affiliates. All rights reserved.

4/23/07

22 Yesterday we all made it up to camp one for the night. We were joined by Tori from the London Business School team, because she wasn't feeling 100% when her team went up the day before.

23 Today we all came up to camp two. It was very hot coming up the Cwm this time, and we all had heavy packs because we had to bring up what we had left at camp one the last time we stayed there. It certainly made it a lot harder work!

4/24/07

24 Despite the fact that I caused us to get a later start than planned this morning (I had a particularly hard time getting out of my warm sleeping bag into the cold air) we accomplished our goal for the day. We went up the very first pitch of the Lhotse Face, and are now back at camp two for the evening.

4/26/07

25 Yesterday we went about halfway up the Lhotse Face to camp three to spend the night. This was a new record for my dad and me, as our highest night ever! Camp three is at about 23,500 feet, and our previous highest night was at camp two on Cho Oyu, at 23,000 feet. We arrived at camp three around noon, and then had a lot of time to kill in our tents, as it wasn't really safe to go more than five feet outside the tent without putting on crampons and clipping into the fixed ropes. Thankfully, I had not yet reached a hypoxic[5] level where I couldn't enjoy my book.

26 Coming up the Lhotse Face was a bit windy, and some parts were pretty icy. It gets fairly steep, so I was glad to have my ascender, which slides up the rope, but not back down, so you can use it as a handhold to pull yourself up.

Sunday, May 6, 2007
Back from Holiday

27 We're back at base camp from our little holiday down the mountain.

28 Now that we are back in base camp, we are just waiting till we can go for our summit attempt. The ropes are not yet fixed to the summit. Once the ropes are fixed, we hope there will soon be a good weather window.

Friday, May 11, 2007
Base Camp

29 We're still at base camp. Hopefully we'll be able to go up soon though.

NOTES

---

5. **hypoxic** (hy POK sihk) *adj.* having too little oxygen.

To the Top of Everest **467**

© Pearson Education, Inc., or its affiliates. All rights reserved.

PERSONALIZE FOR LEARNING

English Language Learners

Analyzing Supporting Details Call student attention to paragraphs 25 and 26. Larson describes the conditions at camp three as a rest stop at a very high altitude. Encourage students to work with partners to mark details in these paragraphs that show what it was like to spend time there. (Students should note that they had to stay in tents, that it was windy and icy, and that moving around without crampons was not safe.)

Ask students to note the meaning of *hypoxic,* and then to generate a list of adjectives that describe the conditions at camp three. Finally, ask students to write a paragraph that expresses the main idea of these paragraphs and uses the supporting details they found. **ALL LEVELS**

NOTES

30 We've tried to hold on to our fitness these past few days by doing some sort of activity each day. We've been ice climbing in a really neat cave near base camp, and we've also been on hikes up Pumori to Pumori base camp, and then up to camp one. Pumori is a 7145-meter mountain near Everest.

Saturday, May 12, 2007
Still at Base Camp

31 It looks like we're going to be able to go up soon for our summit attempt. Fingers crossed!

32 We've gotten our oxygen masks and tested them out. I was able to get my oxygen saturation back up to 100% this morning! After I turned off the oxygen, I only had a few seconds of being at pseudo sea level before it went back down, though.

33 We're all getting a little restless hanging around base camp.

Monday, May 14, 2007
Camp 2

34 We finally started our summit push yesterday, making our way from base camp to camp two. We don't have Internet access up here, but we were able to relay this information to our correspondents in New York via satellite phone. We're taking a rest day today, and plan to press on tomorrow. If all goes well, we should summit on the 17th.

Thursday, May 17, 2007
Summit!

35 We made it to the top! Now all we have to do is get back down . . .

Wednesday, May 23, 2007
Back Home!

36 We've been in a big rush getting back home, and I haven't been able to update for a while, as I have not had Internet access. We woke up this morning at 16,000 feet in a village called Lobuche, and this evening my dad and I arrived back at sea level in Long Beach! The rest of the team are celebrating in Kathmandu—my dad and I skipped out on the celebration to make it back in time for my brother Ted's college graduation in New York.

37 The day after we summited, we came down from the South Col (camp four) to camp two. I was very tired at that point, but glad that we had all made it back safely lower on the mountain. It was amazing how after being to almost 30,000 feet, 20,000-foot camp two felt like it was nearly at sea level!

38 The day after that, we came back down to base camp, where we received lots of warm hugs and congratulations.

© Pearson Education, Inc., or its affiliates. All rights reserved.

PERSONALIZE FOR LEARNING

Strategic Support

Using Graphic Organizers Call student attention to paragraphs 31–34. Help students track the risks and difficulties that the group faced during the expedition. Prepare a two-column chart. In the first column, ask students to write the challenges the text describes. In the second column, ask students to explain why it is a challenge. Ask students to discuss these risks in a group discussion.

NOTES

© Pearson Education, Inc., or its affiliates. All rights reserved.

39 We only had one night back at base camp, as the next day (the 20th), we packed up our bags and headed down the valley. Base camp had a strange, empty feeling—it was sad to leave my little tent that had been my home for the past 2 months! My dad, Doug, Wim, and I were hoping to get a helicopter out of Lobuche on the 21st to save a little time, but Victor and James decided to walk down to the Lukla airstrip to fly out to Kathmandu on the 23rd. However, even though we awoke on the 21st to a beautiful, clear day in Lobuche, apparently there were clouds lower down the valley, so the helicopter couldn't fly in until the 23rd either. It was kind of hard waiting those two days in Lobuche. We were just an hour away from a hot shower and a big meal, if only those clouds would clear!

40 Once the helicopter landed in Kathmandu, I was greeted by a mob of journalists and cameramen. I was so surprised! After nearly 20 hours of travel, my dad and I landed at LAX[6] and were greeted by my family, and some more news people. Now we only have a few hours before we jump back on a plane to go to New York! I am very excited to see my mom and brother though.

41 Thank you everyone for all of your wonderful comments and your support!!! ◆

6. **LAX** *n.* Los Angeles International Airport.

CLOSER LOOK

Analyze Descriptive Language

Circulate among groups as students conduct their close read. Suggest that groups close read paragraph 39. Encourage them to talk about the annotations they mark. If needed, provide the following support.

ANNOTATE: Have students mark details in paragraph 39 that describe how Larson felt about leaving the camp or work with small groups as you highlight them together.

QUESTION: Guide students to consider what these details might tell them. Ask what a reader can infer from these details, and accept student responses.

Possible response: These details show that she feels sad to leave a place that has become somewhat of a home to her.

CONCLUDE: Help students to formulate conclusions about the importance of these details in the text. Ask students why the author might have included these details.

Possible response: The author expresses her emotions. So much of the text has been details about the climb, but this information gives some insight into how she feels.

Remind students that **descriptive language** helps writers convey feelings to readers. Words like *strange* and *empty* help paint a picture for readers.

Comprehension Check

Possible responses:

1. Lama Gesa blessed the journey.

2. A Puja is a ceremony run by the Sherpas. A leader asks for the blessings of the mountain gods for the safety of the group that will climb.

3. Camp three is 23,500 feet high.

4. She reached the summit on Thursday, May 17, 2007.

5. Summaries should include details of the trip including leaving the United States, arriving in Kathmandu, traveling to base camp, working to get acclimatized, reaching the summit, and going home.

RESEARCH

Research to Clarify If students struggle to find a detail to research, suggest they learn more about crampons, icefalls, crevasses, Sherpas, and other Mount Everest climbs.

Research to Explore If students struggle to devise research questions, suggest that the start with the detail they identified in the previous activity.

Comprehension Check

Complete the following items after you finish your first read. Review and clarify details with your group.

1. Who blessed Larson's journey before she began?

2. What is a Puja?

3. How high is camp three?

4. On what day did Larson reach the top of Mount Everest?

5. 📓 **Notebook** Confirm your understanding of the blog posts by writing a brief summary.

- -

RESEARCH

Research to Clarify Choose at least one unfamiliar detail from the text. Briefly research that detail. In what way does the information you learned shed light on an aspect of the blog posts?

Research to Explore Choose something that interests you from the text, and formulate a research question that you might use to find out more about it.

PERSONALIZE FOR LEARNING

Challenge

Research Student may want to learn more about Samantha Larson and her life after her climb. Invite students to go online to find out more about Larson's life and work. Use these questions to guide research: *Does she still have a blog? Does she continue to climb? How has she incorporated her climbing experience into her life?* Ask students to share their findings with the class.

Close Read the Text

With your group, revisit sections of the text you marked during your first read. **Annotate** details that you notice. What **questions** do you have? What can you **conclude**?

Analyze the Text

Complete the activities.

> CITE TEXTUAL EVIDENCE
> to support your answers.

1. **Review and Clarify** With your group, review paragraphs 35–41. Discuss with your group the reasons for the six-day gap between blog posts. Consider reasons Larson gives, and speculate about others.

2. **Present and Discuss** Now, work with your group to share passages from the blog that you found especially important. Discuss what you noticed in the selection, what questions you asked, and what conclusions you reached.

3. **Essential Question: What drives people to explore?** What has this blog taught you about what drives people to explore?

LANGUAGE DEVELOPMENT

Concept Vocabulary

| expedition | trek | journeys | destination |

Why These Words? The concept vocabulary words from the blog are related. With your group, determine what the words have in common. Add another word that fits the concept.

Practice

Notebook Confirm your understanding of the concept vocabulary words by using each one in a sentence. Include context clues that hint at each word's meaning.

Word Study

Latin Root: -ped- The Latin root -ped- in expedition means "foot." Use this information to answer these questions.

1. Which of these words containing -ped- have a meaning connected to feet? Use a dictionary to check your answers.
   a. pediatrician   c. pedal
   b. pedestal   d. peddler

2. What other words related to "feet" are formed from the root -ped-? Use a dictionary to check your answers.

TO THE TOP OF EVEREST

> **TIP**
> **GROUP DISCUSSION**
> In a group discussion, listening is just as important as speaking. When others are speaking, be sure to give them your full attention.

> **WORD NETWORK**
> Add words related to exploration from the text to your Word Network.

> **STANDARDS**
> **Language**
> Determine or clarify the meaning of unknown and multiple-meaning words and phrases based on *grade 6 reading and content*, choosing flexibly from a range of strategies.
> b. Use common, grade-appropriate Greek or Latin affixes and roots as clues to the meaning of a word.
> c. Consult reference materials, both print and digital, to find the pronunciation of a word or determine or clarify its precise meaning or its part of speech.
> d. Verify the preliminary determination of the meaning of a word or phrase.

To the Top of Everest **471**

Jump Start

CLOSE READ Ask groups to consider the following prompt: *What are the unique challenges to mountain climbing as a teenager?* As students discuss the prompt in their groups, remind them to refer to specific details from the selection and from any additional research they have conducted.

Close Read the Text

Students may speculate that the climb down was just as tough as the climb up, that the oxygen level was challenging, or that Larson needed to rest and recover.

Remind students to use Accountable Talk in their discussions and to support one another as they complete the close read.

Analyze the Text

1. **Possible response:** Larson may have been too busy or been too excited to write.

2. **Passages will vary by group.** Remind students to explain why they chose the passage they are presenting to the group members.

3. **Responses will vary by group.**

Concept Vocabulary

Why These Words? Possible response: These words describe the difficult trip that Larson and the group take. Other words include *travel, hike, climb, exploration*.

Practice

Possible response: The **expedition** took 42 days in difficult conditions. The group planned to **trek** across the desert. After days of travel, group members could see their **destination** in the distance. Some of my favorite **journeys** happen when I travel away from home.

Word Network

Possible words: *route, accomplish, summit*.

Word Study

1. Answer choices b. (*pedestal*) and c. (*pedal*) derive from the Latin root meaning "foot." are related to -*ped*-. *Pediatrician* is related to -*ped*-, meaning "child." *Peddler* may derive from a root meaning "basket."

2. Possible response: *pedestrian, biped*.

FORMATIVE ASSESSMENT

Analyze the Text

If students struggle to close read the text, **then** provide the **To the Top of Everest: Text Questions** available online in the Interactive Teacher's Edition or Unit Resources. Answers and DOK levels are also available.

Concept Vocabulary

If students struggle to identify the concept, **then** encourage them to review the selection to see how the concept vocabulary words are used in context.

Word Study

If students fail to find words related to -*ped*-, **then** help students to use online sources that indicate word origins. For Reteach and Practice, see **Word Study: Latin Root: -ped- (RP).**

© Pearson Education, Inc., or its affiliates. All rights reserved.

FACILITATING

Analyze Craft and Structure

Central Idea Explain to students that a blog is a special type of writing that usually is written for a very specific purpose—to convey information about a narrow topic. Each blog post is a self-contained essay about a focused topic that expresses a central idea. For more support, see **Analyze Craft and Structure: Central Idea.** 📄

Possible responses

1. a. training at home; practicing crossing ladders; acclimatization work; Puja ceremonies.
   b. 24-hour travel to Kathmandu; long days of rest and recovery; difficulty of showers; issues with oxygen.
   c. excitement of packing; excitement of meeting Lama Gesa; happiness over seeing the view; the thrill of the summit; sadness of leaving.

2. (a) There were long hikes and lots of time without activity. The climb was dangerous. The weather was very challenging. There was very little electricity. (b) Larson had a good attitude and seemed able to manage these difficulties.

3. Responses will vary. Some students will say that she focuses more on the preparation and training.

4. Responses will vary. Some students may say that she is an explorer. She was very focused on her goal.

FORMATIVE ASSESSMENT

Analyze Craft and Structure

If students have trouble identifying the central idea of the text, **then** remind them think about the message they got from reading the blog. For Reteach and Practice, see **Analyze Craft and Structure: Central Idea (RP).** 📄

TO THE TOP OF EVEREST

Analyze Craft and Structure

Central Idea A **central idea** is an important point that is supported by other details and examples in the text. Certain types of informal writing, such as blogs, friendly letters, or diary entries, are not necessarily written with one central idea in mind. Authors are simply writing about their daily life experiences. However, by grouping together particular details and determining what is repeated or emphasized, you can identify a central idea.

The blog entries you read offer numerous details about Samantha Larson's trip to and ascent of Mount Everest. Some of the details revolve around preparation and training, others around the physical effort required to climb the world's highest mountain, and still others about the emotions—from excitement to boredom—that Larson experiences during her trip. The central idea of this blog is an overarching statement that can tie together these diverse collections of details.

Practice

CITE TEXTUAL EVIDENCE to support your answers.

📝 **Notebook** Work together to complete the activity and answer the questions.

1. Identify details from the blog entries that fit into the categories listed in the chart. Then, work together to state a central idea that ties these details together.

TYPES OF DETAILS	EXAMPLES FROM BLOG
preparation and training	a. See possible responses in Teacher's Edition.
effort required to climb Everest	b.
thoughts and feelings	c.
Central Idea:	

2. **(a)** What were some of the difficulties that Larson experienced on her trip to and up Mount Everest? **(b)** Did these difficulties seem hard for her to overcome? Explain.

3. Which type of detail does Larson emphasize in her blog? Why do you think that is?

4. Do you think Larson possesses the qualities of an explorer? Why, or why not?

📋 STANDARDS

Reading Informational Text
• Determine a central idea of a text and how it is conveyed through particular details; provide a summary of the text distinct from personal opinions or judgments.
• Analyze in detail how a key individual, event, or idea is introduced, illustrated and elaborated in a text.

472 UNIT 5 • EXPLORATION

© Pearson Education, Inc., or its affiliates. All rights reserved.

PERSONALIZE FOR LEARNING

English Language Support

Central Idea Ask students to choose a nonfiction topic that they would like to explore in a short blog entry. For example, students might want to explain something they have learned in after-school activities, a tip for getting around school, or an idea for using smartphones or other digital devices.

Ask students to list the central idea they would develop, and then ask them to list several details that support the main idea. **EMERGING**

Have students write a one-paragraph blog entry. They should introduce the central idea and then include details that build the idea. **EXPANDING**

Ask students to write a multi-paragraph blog entry that develops the central idea with several details that explore it. **BRIDGING**

An expanded **English Language Support Lesson** on Central Ideas is available in the Interactive Teacher's Edition. 📄

Conventions

Subject Complements Writers use subject complements to provide more information about their subjects. A **subject complement** is a noun, a pronoun, or an adjective that appears after a linking verb, such as *be, become, remain, look, seem,* or *feel.*

There are two kinds of subject complements. A **predicate nominative** is a noun or pronoun that renames or identifies the subject. A **predicate adjective** is an adjective that describes the subject.

PREDICATE NOUN OR PRONOUN	PREDICATE ADJECTIVE
I am *she.*	That popcorn looks *delicious.*
Cindy *will become* a doctor.	You have seemed *cheery* all week.
He *remains* a fool.	My legs felt *exhausted.*

Read It

Identify the subject complement(s) in each of these sentences from "To the Top of Everest." Label each one as a predicate noun or a predicate adjective.

1. We are well and safe.

2. I was pretty tired by the time we got back to base camp, but today was a rest day. . . .

3. It has been a very exciting week. . . .

Write It

Complete each sentence with a subject complement. Use either a predicate adjective or a predicate noun, as indicated in parentheses.

1. People who travel to remote regions are _____.
(predicate adjective)

2. Climbing the peak of Mount Everest could be a great
_____. (predicate noun)

© Pearson Education, Inc., or its affiliates. All rights reserved.

▤ STANDARDS

Language
Demonstrate command of the conventions of standard English grammar and usage when writing or speaking.

To the Top of Everest **473**

Conventions

Subject Complements If necessary, remind students that the subject of a sentence is the person, place, thing, or idea that is doing (or being) something.

For each example in the chart, encourage students to think of another subject complement that could replace the one shown in italics. For more support, see **Conventions: Subject Complements.** 📄

Read It

Possible responses:
1. We are <u>well</u> and <u>safe</u>. (predicate adjectives)
2. I was <u>pretty tired</u> by the time we got back to base camp, but today was a rest <u>day</u>. (predicate adjective/predicate noun)
3. It has been a very exciting <u>week</u>. (predicate noun)

Write It

Possible responses:
1. adventurous
2. adventure

FORMATIVE ASSESSMENT

Conventions

If students have trouble identifying subject complements, **then** remind them to look for linking verbs, such as *to be, to feel, to become, to seem,* and *to look*. For Reteach and Practice, see **Conventions: Subject Complements (RP).** 📄

Selection Test

Administer the "To the Top of Everest" Selection Test, which is available in both print and digital formats online in Assessments. 📄 ☑

PERSONALIZE FOR LEARNING

English Language Support

Subject Complements English learners may be confused by the various terms used in this lesson. Review the definitions of *nouns, pronouns, linking verbs,* and *adjectives.* Explain that predicate nouns and predicate adjectives are two types of subject complements. Point out that predicate nouns and predicate adjectives are nouns and adjectives but that not all nouns and adjectives are subject complements. Explain that predicate nouns and predicate adjectives are *always* preceded by a linking verb. In phrases such as "the soft pillow" and "the cute puppy," the adjectives are not subject complements because there is no linking verb. Ask students how they could turn these phrases into complete sentences with subject complements. (**Possible response:** The pillow is soft. The puppy is cute.) **ALL LEVELS**

Writing to Compare

As students prepare to compare the excerpt from *Tales From the Odyssey* with the blog entry "To the Top of Everest," they will consider how each selection presents the risks and rewards of exploration.

Planning and Prewriting

Analyze the Texts

Remind students that a "reward" is not necessarily something of monetary value. For explorers, a reward might simply be the sense of satisfaction that comes from achieving a personal goal. Or, it might take the form of overcoming a struggle.

To reinforce this concept of a personal, non-material reward, you might provide examples that students can relate to, such as the following:

- studying for a test and feeling great when you get an A
- seeing a friend's reaction to a thoughtful act or gift

See possible responses in chart on student page.

Possible responses:

1. In the excerpt from *Tales From the Odyssey*, Odysseus and his men are in danger because Greek soldiers have offended the Greek goddess Athena, and she, Zeus, and Poseidon are punishing them. In "To the Top of Everest," the author is choosing to take risks to achieve her goal of summiting Mount Everest.

2. Odysseus takes action to lead his men out of danger, but he ends up unwittingly putting them in danger when he decides to explore the mysterious shore. The author of "To the Top of Everest" knows that she has to take risks to achieve her goal, but the risks don't prevent her from continuing her climb.

FORMATIVE ASSESSMENT

Write to Compare

If students are unable to compare the two selections, **then** have them first write a brief summary of the main points in each selection.

from TALES FROM THE ODYSSEY

TO THE TOP OF EVEREST

STANDARDS

Reading Literature
Compare and contrast texts in different forms or genres in terms of their approaches to similar themes and topics.

Writing
- Write informative/explanatory texts to examine a topic and convey ideas, concepts, and information through the selection, organization, and analysis of relevant content.
  b. Develop the topic with relevant facts, definitions, concrete details, quotations, or other information and examples.
- Draw evidence from literary or informational texts to support analysis, reflection, and research.
  a. Apply *grade 6 reading standards* to literature.

474 UNIT 5 • EXPLORATION

Writing to Compare

Both the excerpt from Mary Pope Osborne's *Tales From the Odyssey* and Samantha Larson's blog suggest that exploration and adventure offer both risks and rewards. Deepen your understanding of the two texts and the nature of exploration by comparing and writing about them.

Assignment

Write a **comparison-and-contrast essay** in which you discuss how these two selections present the risks and rewards of exploration and adventure. Consider the risks and dangers the Greek warriors face in the *Odyssey*. Explain the rewards they experience or expect. Also, discuss the risks and dangers Larson faces as she climbs Mount Everest. Consider the rewards she experiences or hopes to receive. At the end of your essay, express your opinion about which selection better shows the risks and rewards of exploration.

Planning and Prewriting

Analyze the Texts Work with your group to discuss the tale and blog entries. Identify specific events and details related to risk or danger. Then, identify other details or events related to rewards. Make sure to consider different types of risks and rewards. For example, risks might involve physical, emotional, or mental dangers. In the same way, rewards can be material—involving money or comfort, for example—or emotional. Capture your observations and notes in the chart.

	from TALES FROM THE ODYSSEY	TO THE TOP OF EVEREST
Risks and Dangers	Odysseus ventures into the unknown to find out who lives on the mysterious shore.	The author endures a "heart-stopping landing" on a plane to get to base camp.
Rewards	Odysseus' curiosity is satisfied.	The author eventually has the satisfaction of summiting Mount Everest.

Notebook Respond to these questions.

1. In the two selections, why are characters or people in risky situations? Was it their choice or was it their fate?

2. Do the reasons characters or people are in risky situations affect how their feelings and actions? Explain.

© Pearson Education, Inc., or its affiliates. All rights reserved.

PERSONALIZE FOR LEARNING

Strategic Support

Setting The excerpt from *Tales From the Odyssey* has multiple settings, which may confuse students. Tell students to focus on one setting at a time and take notes on what happens there. Then, they can note the risks that Odysseus and his men face there. After they have identified the risks, students can then discuss potential rewards.

Similarly, because it is a blog, "To the Top of Everest" contains multiple settings and may appear disjointed. Have students consider the action of one entry at a time and decide if risks are being taken and what rewards these risks might lead to.

Drafting

Write a Main Idea Write two or three sentences that sum up your ideas. State how the two selections show risks and rewards in ways that are the same and different. Use compare and contrast key words such as those underlined in the frames.

Sentence Frames: <u>Both</u> the excerpt from *Tales From the Odyssey* and Larson's blog posts show _____

_____

<u>However</u>, the stories from the *Odyssey* show _____

_____

<u>In contrast,</u> the blog entries _____

_____

Organize Ideas Consider using one of these two ways to organize your essay.

Block Organization	Point-by-Point Organization

I. *Tales From the Odyssey*
    A. risks characters face
    B. reasons they face the risks
    C. rewards they receive
 II. To the Top of Everest
    A. risks people face
    B. reasons they face the risks
    C. rewards they receive
	I. Risks Characters/People Face
	    A. *Tales From the Odyssey*
	    B. To the Top of Everest
	 II. Risks
	    A. *Tales from the Odyssey*
	    B. To the Top of Everest
	 III. Rewards They Receive
	    A. *Tales from the Odyssey*
	    B. To the Top of Everest

Use Transitions When you write a comparison-and-contrast essay, you will need to shift from one topic to another. Use transition words and phrases, such as the ones shown here, to make shifts in your ideas clear.

COMPARISON	CONTRAST
and, also, additionally, likewise, in the same way, both, similarly	but, however, on the other hand, in a different way, in contrast, although

Review, Revise, and Edit

Reread your draft, and ask yourself these questions:

- Have I used words that say exactly what I mean?
- Did I leave out any details that I want to include?
- Does the order of my ideas make sense?

Swap drafts with group members and give feedback on one another's work. Discuss the changes your peers recommend and make the ones you feel are important. Fix any spelling or grammar errors you find.

© Pearson Education, Inc., or its affiliates. All rights reserved.

from Tales From the Odyssey • *To the Top of Everest* **475**

☑ EVIDENCE LOG

Before moving on to a new selection, go to your Evidence Log and record what you learned from "To the Top of Everest."

≣ STANDARDS

Writing
• Write informative/explanatory texts to examine a topic and convey ideas, concepts, and information through the selection, organization, and analysis of relevant content.
  a. Introduce a topic; organize ideas, concepts, and information, using strategies such as definition, classification, comparison/contrast, and cause/effect; include formatting, graphics, and multimedia when useful to aiding comprehension.
  c. Use appropriate transitions to clarify the relationships among ideas and concepts.

Drafting

Write a Main Idea Remind students that their main idea will need to be supported. So, if they jot down a brief summary of their ideas and find that they can't provide support, they will need to change the main idea of their essay.

Organize Ideas Explain that proper paragraphing is a key to a good organizational plan. Main ideas should appear in separate paragraphs. Each paragraph should also include supporting evidence.

Use Transitions Relate to students that writing without transitions will be confusing to readers. Transitions signal to readers that a new thought is being expressed or a new point is being made.

Review, Revise, and Edit

As students revise, have them make sure they have included supporting evidence that involves the risks and rewards of exploration. Ask students to review their word choice to be sure they are saying exactly what they want to say, and remind students to check for grammar, usage, and mechanics.

For more support, see **Writing to Compare: Compare-and-Contrast Essay.** 📄

Evidence Log Support students in completing their Evidence Log. This paced activity will help prepare them for the Performance-Based Assessment at the end of the unit.

FORMATIVE ASSESSMENT
Writing to Compare

If groups struggle to identify risks and rewards in the selections, **then** ask them to think about times when the characters or people are in danger and what they achieve that's positive.

Selection Test

Administer the "To the Top of Everest (*with the excerpt from* Tales From the Odyssey)" Selection Test, which is available in both print and digital formats online in Assessments. 📄 ☑

Small-Group Learning **475**

from Lewis & Clark

🔊 **AUDIO SUMMARIES**
An excerpt from *Lewis & Clark* is available online in both English and Spanish in the Interactive Teacher's Edition or Unit Resources. Assigning these summaries prior to reading the selection may help students build additional background knowledge and set a context for their first read.

Summary

This selection is a graphic novel by Nick Bertozzi. It begins with workers on the Lewis and Clark expedition constructing a fort to spend the winter in. Once it is complete, they honor the Native Americans who have helped them with a dance. The weather outside becomes miserable and rainy, and there is little food to find. A hunter, Mister Ordway, speaks with York, a skilled scout who grew up in slavery. Ordway suggests that York run away, but York says he will earn his freedom rather than running. York then knocks away a local who tries to touch his hair.

Insight

Exploration can seem like a great expression of freedom. However, explorers do not leave society behind when they strike out into the unknown. Power, legal structures, and values can limit people no matter where they go.

ESSENTIAL QUESTION:
What drives people to explore?

Connection to Essential Question

The excerpt from *Lewis & Clark* provides a clear-cut connection to the Essential Question, "What drives people to explore?" The members of the expedition face great challenges in surviving the winter. Although they manage to have at least one celebration, they also spend a lot of time working hard to get, make, and maintain food, clothing, and shelter. Each member of the party may have a different experience of the drive to explore.

SMALL-GROUP LEARNING PERFORMANCE TASK
Why should we explore new frontiers?

UNIT PERFORMANCE-BASED ASSESSMENT
What fuels people's desire to explore?

Connection to Performance Tasks

Small-Group Learning Performance Task Exploration provides opportunities to meet new people, and to find freedom.

Unit Performance-Based Assessment Early on, we see that Lewis is more interested in doing research than in anything else. Clark and Ordway seem partly motivated by the power they can have on the expedition. York seems motivated to stay on the expedition rather than run away due to his strong sense of responsibility.

LESSON RESOURCES

	Making Meaning	Effective Expression
Lesson	**First Review** **Close Review** **Analyze the Media** **Media Vocabulary**	**Research**
Instructional Standards	**RL.10** By the end of the year, read and comprehend literature . . . **L.6** Acquire and use accurately grade-appropriate general academic and domain-specific words and phrases . . .	**RI.7** Integrate information presented in different media or formats . . . **W.7** Conduct short research projects . . . **W.8** Gather relevant information . . . **SL.2** Interpret information presented in diverse media and formats. . . **SL.5** Include multimedia components and visual displays . . .
⤷ STUDENT RESOURCES Available online in the Interactive Student Edition or Unit Resources	🔊 Selection Audio 📄 First-Review Guide: Media: Art/Photography 📄 Close-Review Guide: Media: Art/Photography	📄 Evidence Log 📄 Word Network
⤷ TEACHER RESOURCES **Selection Resources** Available online in the Interactive Teacher's Edition or Unit Resources	🔊 Audio Summaries 📄 Media Vocabulary	📄 Research: Annotated Timeline
My Resources	📄 A Unit 5 Answer Key is available online and in the Interactive Teacher's Edition.	

Media Complexity Rubric: *from* Lewis & Clark

Quantitative Measures

Format and Length   graphic novel excerpt

Qualitative Measures

Knowledge Demands ①—②—③—❹—⑤	At the center of the selection are situations about which students will have little prior knowledge. Familiarity with the Lewis and Clark expedition is helpful (some information is given in the background).
Structure ①—②—③—❹—⑤	Both text and graphics are used to convey meaning and events. Some illustrations are complex and show story developments without the support of text.
Language Conventionality and Clarity ①—②—❸—④—⑤	Language is conversational but as it is meant to show scenes in the early 1800s, language is more formal sounding and does not follow contemporary style. Language is supported by images.
Levels of Meaning/Purpose ①—②—❸—④—⑤	Reader needs to infer meanings and events by following the text and interpreting events that are shown only in illustrations.

Jump Start

FIRST REVIEW Ask students to consider the following prompts: *What type of person would volunteer to travel into unknown territory on a journey that could take months or even years? Would you? Why or why not?* Engage students in a discussion of the kinds of people who become explorers.

About the Author

Nick Bertozzi (b.1970) was introduced to comics by his father before he could read. As an adult, he developed his own mini-comic while working in the marketing department at DC Comics. Besides being an illustrator and an author of graphic novels, Bertozzi is also a computer programmer and an educator who has taught his craft at several prestigious art schools.

from Lewis & Clark

Media Vocabulary

The following words or concepts will be useful to you as you analyze, discuss, and write about graphic novels.

penciler: artist who sketches the basic layout for each panel	• A penciler shows the figures, expressions, objects, and backgrounds in each panel. • The amount of detail in the drawings varies from penciler to penciler.
inker: artist who goes over the penciled art in ink	• An inker uses pen and brush with ink to create an image that will print well. • The amount of detail left for the inker to fill in depends on how much detail was done by the penciler.
letterer: artist who letters the dialogue and captions	• A letterer fills in the speech ballons and may also place them in the panel. • Different weights, shapes, and sizes of letters can convey different emotions and meanings.

from Lewis and Clark

What is the point of undertaking a dangerous journey into unknown territory? What are the possible benefits to the explorer and to his or her society? Modeling the questions readers might ask as they read "Lewis & Clark" brings the text alive for students and connects it to the Small-Group Performance Task question. Selection audio for the selection is available in the Interactive Teacher's Edition.

Media Vocabulary

Encourage students to discuss the media vocabulary. Have they seen or used these terms before? Do they use any of them in their speech or writing?

Ask groups to look closely at the terms to see what they have in common. Students will notice that each identifies a specific type of artist and the role that artist plays in creating a graphic novel.

● FIRST REVIEW

Have students perform the steps of the first review independently.

LOOK: Encourage students to focus on the basic elements of each panel of the graphic novel to ensure they know who is pictured, what the setting is, and what is happening.

NOTE: Students should mark any panels they have questions about or wish to revisit during the close review.

CONNECT: Encourage students to make connections beyond the images. If they cannot make connections to their own lives, have them consider films or TV shows they may have seen or selections they have read in this unit.

RESPOND: Students will answer questions to demonstrate understanding. Point out to students that while they will always complete the Respond step at the end of the first review, the other steps will probably happen concurrently. You may wish to print copies of the **First-Review Guide: Media: Art / Photography** for students to use. ⓔ

First Review MEDIA: GRAPHIC NOVEL

Apply these strategies as you conduct your first review. You will have an opportunity to complete a close review after your first review.

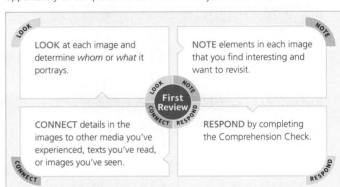

STANDARDS
Reading Literature
By the end of the year, read and comprehend literature, including stories, dramas, and poems, in the grades 6–8 text complexity band proficiently, with scaffolding as needed at the high end of the range.
Language
Acquire and use accurately grade-appropriate general academic and domain-specific words and phrases; gather vocabulary knowledge when considering a word or phrase important to comprehension or expression.

476 UNIT 5 • EXPLORATION

VOCABULARY DEVELOPMENT

Domain-Specific Words Help students understand the media vocabulary by making sure they understand domain-specific words surrounding the media vocabulary as needed. For instance, explain the meanings of *layout, panel, dialogue,* and *captions,* and point out examples in the graphic novel. Making things as concrete as possible and engaging their senses will help students understand and learn these words.

© Pearson Education, Inc., or its affiliates. All rights reserved.

© Pearson Education, Inc., or its affiliates. All rights reserved.

BACKGROUND
The Lewis and Clark expedition (1804–1806) was a major exploration of the northwestern United States that allowed the government to later claim the area. The band of explorers and their co-leaders, Captain Meriwether Lewis and Lieutenant William Clark, were known as the Corps of Discovery.

SCAN FOR
MULTIMEDIA

from Lewis & Clark **477**

CLOSER REVIEW

Analyze the Image

Circulate among groups as students conduct their close review. Suggest that groups close review the cover art. Encourage them to analyze and discuss the scene depicted. What does the image suggest about the story to follow? What does it suggest about Lewis and Clark and about their journey? Does the cover image make you want to read the graphic novel? Why or why not?

NOTE: Have students note details in the graphic novel that emphasize color, line, shape, and perspective, or work with small groups to have students participate while you note them together.

QUESTION: Guide students to consider the artist's purpose by asking: Based on the colors, lines, shapes, and perspective, what do you think was the artist's purpose?

Possible response: The artist uses bright contrasting colors; strong, dark lines; simple shapes; and a dramatic perspective to engage and focus the readers' attention.

CONCLUDE: Help students to formulate conclusions about the importance of design elements in a graphic novel.

Possible response: Design elements are very important in a graphic novel because the author is using pictures, as well as words, to tell a story.

Remind students that **images** in Graphic Novels are critical to the storytelling. Colors, textures, and details are all important to presenting the narrative.

CROSS-CURRICULAR PERSPECTIVES

Social Studies Have students work in their small groups to research a specific aspect of Lewis and Clark's journey. Students can choose their own specific topics for research or you can provide topics. Here are some possible topics: purpose of the expedition, method of travel, geography of the expedition, about Lewis, about Clark, interactions with Native Americans, the winter of 1804–05, arrival at the Pacific, results of expedition. Guide each group to research a different topic and have groups present their findings to the class.

FACILITATING

CLOSER REVIEW

Analyze the Image

Circulate among groups as students conduct their close review. Suggest that groups close review panel 8. What does the image suggest about what wintering at Fort Clatsop was like? What design elements does the artist use to suggest this impression?

NOTE: Have students note details about line, shape, and perspective.

Possible response: The artist uses lots of black ink; sharp, diagonal lines; and a distant perspective.

QUESTION: Guide students to consider the artist's purpose by asking: Based on the lines, shapes, and perspective, what impression of wintering at Fort Clatsop did the artist want to create?

Possible response: The artist wanted to suggest that wintering at Fort Clatsop was wet, cold, dreary, isolated, and difficult.

CONCLUDE: Help students to formulate conclusions about the effectiveness of images in establishing setting and mood.

Possible response: Design elements can be used to create images that establish the setting and mood of a story.

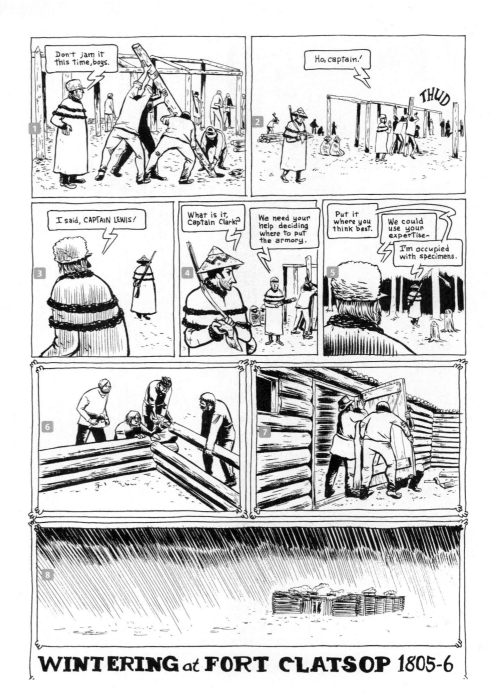

© Pearson Education, Inc., or its affiliates. All rights reserved.

478 UNIT 5 • EXPLORATION

VOCABULARY DEVELOPMENT

Domain-Specific Words Have groups work together to use context clues and word parts to determine the meanings of any unfamiliar words, such as *armory* in panel 4 and *specimens* in panel 5. You can guide students through this process by providing these sentence prompts.

1. *Arms* is another word for *weapons*. An armory is a room in which you store _____.

2. Captain Lewis is famous for collecting, identifying, and identifying many plant _____.

© Pearson Education, Inc., or its affiliates. All rights reserved.

from Lewis & Clark **479**

PERSONALIZE FOR LEARNING

Challenge

Dialogue and Captions Have students write dialogue and captions for panels 10–14. Challenge groups to keep the purpose, mood, and tone of the dialogue and captions that they write consistent with the purpose, mood, and tone of the images and the existing captions. Afterward, have groups share their dialogue and captions with the class.

FACILITATING

© Pearson Education, Inc., or its affiliates. All rights reserved.

DIGITAL PERSPECTIVES

Enriching the Text Call students' attention to panel 18, and note that York was an African-American man enslaved by Clark's family. He was a valuable member of the expedition, and he is reputed to have facilitated relations with Native Americans and saved several lives, including Clark's. Recordings of radio interviews with experts discussing York, his interactions with Native Americans, and how he felt at the end of the expedition can be found online. Be sure to listen to each recording first. Have students listen to the interviews and then reread the excerpt from the graphic novel. Ask students how knowing more about York can help them better understand this section of the graphic novel.

from Lewis & Clark **481**

© Pearson Education, Inc., or its affiliates. All rights reserved.

CLOSER REVIEW

Analyze the Image

Circulate among groups as students conduct their close review. Suggest that groups close review panels 29–32.

NOTE: Have students note details in panels 29–32 that show what actions the people take and how they feel.

QUESTION: Who is depicted in these panels? What actions do they take? What can we infer about their thoughts?

Possible response: The characters depicted in the panels are York and a Native American. York sews a moccasin. He might be thinking about his conversation with Ordway on freedom. The Native American, after observing the conversation, reaches out to touch York's hair. York scowls and knocks the hand away.

CONCLUDE: What does the final panel of the selection suggest about York, his relationship to the people around him, and how he feels?

Possible response: The final panel shows York sitting alone in the dark with his head down. This suggests he does not feel like part of a group, is isolated, and feels sad and lonely.

FACILITATING SMALL-GROUP CLOSE REVIEWING

CLOSE REVIEW: Graphic Novels As groups perform the close review, circulate and offer support as needed.

- Remind groups that when they view each panel, they should decide who is depicted, what the setting is, and what the people are doing.
- Tell students to consider the mood and tone created by design elements such as shading,

shape, and line. For example, you might call students' attention to panel 32 and ask how the lines, shading, and perspective add to the mood.

- Suggest that trying to write captions and dialogue for a panel can help them understand it more fully.

Comprehension Check

Possible responses:

1. The men are building a fort.
2. Captain Lewis prefers to collect plant and animal specimens.
3. The Clatsop are Native Americans. The fort is named after them.
4. Ordway says this because a single squirrel was the result of his hunting trip. There is not much to eat around the fort.

Close Review

If needed, model close reviewing by using the Closer Review notes in the Interactive Teacher's Edition.

Remind students to use Accountable Talk in their discussions and to support one another as they complete the close review.

Analyze the Media

1. **Students' responses will vary.** Make sure students identify what they noticed and what questions were raised, and explain the conclusions they reached.

2. **Students' responses will vary.** Groups should notice that most of the story is told by the illustrations and that there are few words. Groups might also note that sometimes pictures can convey mood and feelings better than words. For instance, the last panels on several of the pages are illustrations that effectively convey isolation and loneliness.

3. **Students' responses will vary.** Require that they support their opinions with specific evidence from the graphic novel.

Media Vocabulary

For more support, see **Media Vocabulary.** 📄

Word Network

Possible words: *specimens, wintering, optimism, expertise*

👥 MAKING MEANING

Comprehension Check

Complete the following items after you finish your first review. Review and clarify details with your group.

1. What are the men building?

2. Why doesn't Captain Lewis help with the construction of the building?

3. Who or what are the Clatsop?

4. Why does Ordway say, "It's no wonder you're all such a scrawny bunch"?

MEDIA VOCABULARY

Use these words as you discuss and write about the graphic novel.

penciler
inker
letterer

 WORD NETWORK

Add words related to exploration from the text to your Word Network.

Close Review

Revisit the graphic novel and your first-review notes. Write down any new observations that seem important. What **questions** do you have? What can you **conclude**?

Analyze the Media

CITE TEXTUAL EVIDENCE
to support your answers.

Complete the activities.

1. **Present and Discuss** Choose the section of the graphic novel you found most interesting or powerful. Discuss what you noticed, what questions you asked, and what conclusions you reached.

2. **Review and Synthesize** With your group, review the illustrations in the selection. How do the illustrations add to your understanding of what it was like to be a member of the Lewis and Clark expedition? What do they tell you that the words do not?

3. **Essential Question:** *What drives people to explore?* What has this graphic novel taught you about exploration? Discuss with your group.

© Pearson Education, Inc., or its affiliates. All rights reserved.

Research

A timeline is a way of displaying events in the order in which they actually occurred over time.

Assignment

As a group, conduct research to learn more about the Lewis and Clark expedition, including the events and people presented in the graphic novel. Then, create and present an **annotated timeline** of important events in the expedition. You may present your timeline digitally, as a poster, or through another method of visual display.

Conduct Research Work with your group to find credible print and digital sources of information about the Lewis and Clark expedition. As you research, note the specific dates and locations of important events as well as the source from which you obtained the information. Pick five or six key events to highlight in your timeline. Then, find images to accompany at least three events; for example, you might use a map to accompany the arrival of the expedition in a new location, or an illustration of Lewis or Clark to highlight an event in which the explorer played an important role.

Organize Your Timeline First, arrange the events you will include in your timeline in **chronological order**, or the order in which the events actually happened. The first event on your timeline should have the earliest date, and the last should have the latest date.

Create Your Annotations To annotate your timeline, use the information and images from your research to create a brief explanatory note for each event. In each note, write a sentence or two in which you summarize what happened and why it was important. If you are including an image in an annotation, you should provide a short caption in which you describe the image and explain how it connects to the event it illustrates.

Assemble and Present Once you have finished your annotations, assemble your timeline to display in your presentation. Assign group members to explain the information about each event during the presentation.

from LEWIS & CLARK

✒ EVIDENCE LOG

Before moving on to a new selection, go to your Evidence Log, and record what you learned from the graphic novel *Lewis & Clark*.

▤ STANDARDS

Reading Informational Text
• Integrate information presented in different media or formats as well as in words to develop a coherent understanding of a topic or issue.

Writing
• Conduct short research projects to answer a question, drawing on several sources and refocusing the inquiry when appropriate.
• Gather relevant information from multiple print and digital sources; assess the credibility of each source; and quote or paraphrase the data and conclusions of others while avoiding plagiarism and providing basic bibliographic information for sources.

Speaking and Listening
• Interpret information presented in diverse media and formats and explain how it contributes to a topic, text, or issue under study.
• Include multimedia components and visual displays in presentations to clarify information.

from Lewis & Clark **483**

Research

Explain to students that a timeline graphically represents a sequence of events in chronological order, or time order. Tell groups that their timelines should include the date of each event, a very brief description of the event, and, if space permits, a photo or an illustration that depicts the event. Tell groups to begin their timelines with the start of the expedition and end with the homecoming. Have groups also include at least five events in between. Students will have to work together to decide which are the most important events to include in their group's timeline. For more support, see **Research: Annotated Timeline.** ▤

Evidence Log Support students in completing their Evidence Log. This paced activity will help prepare them for the Performance-Based Assessment at the end of the unit.

© Pearson Education, Inc., or its affiliates. All rights reserved.

PERSONALIZE FOR LEARNING

English Language Support

Graphic Novels English learners will be on a level playing field with native speakers when it comes to interpreting illustrations in the graphic novel. If students enjoy reading this graphic novel, suggest that they look for other graphic novels that depict historical events, classic literature, epic poems, or traditional tales. Being familiar with these stories will help students understand allusions and other cultural references and will generally improve their cultural literacy.

Present an Advertisement

Before groups begin work on their projects, have them clearly differentiate the role each group member will play. Remind groups to consult the schedule for Small-Group Learning to guide their work during the Performance Task.

Students should complete the assignment using presentation software to take advantage of text, graphics, and sound features.

Plan With Your Group

Analyze the Text Discuss with groups the attributes of good advertising. For example, a convincing advertisement is memorable, entertaining, attention-grabbing, and clear, while effectively targeting a specific audience. Point out that "less is more" when it comes to advertising—it is better to deliver one clear, concise message than to overload the target audience with too much information.

Gather Evidence and Media Examples Remind groups to choose media that makes the expedition look safe, rewarding, and fun. Any people in the images should look like they are happy to be there. Suggest to students that using too much media could overwhelm their presentation and cause their audience to lose interest. Students should choose one or two powerful images that effectively communicate the message of the advertisement.

SOURCES

- MISSION TWINPOSSIBLE
- *from* TALES FROM THE ODYSSEY
- TO THE TOP OF EVEREST
- *from* LEWIS & CLARK

Present an Advertisement

Assignment

You have read about expeditions to remote places. Now, write and present an argument in the form of an **advertisement** that answers this question:

> **Why should we explore new frontiers?**

You may imagine and advertise an upcoming expedition on Earth, in space, or to an imagined location. It can take place in the past, the present, or the future.

Plan With Your Group

Analyze the Text As a group, review the selections in this section and analyze the ways in which the selections would make exploration seem exciting to potential tourists. Record your notes in the chart shown. Then, when the chart is complete, decide what kind of expedition to advertise, as well as the location, time, and purpose of the expedition.

TITLE	NOTES
Mission Twinpossible	
from Tales From the Odyssey	
To the Top of Everest	
from Lewis & Clark	

Discuss Advertising Elements With your group, discuss what you know about advertising. How do advertisers convince customers to buy their products? Then, decide whether to make your advertisement a poster or a digital graphic.

Gather Evidence and Media Examples Scan the selections to record specific examples that would add interest and strengthen your argument for participating in the imagined expedition. Brainstorm for types of media that would make the advertisement more enticing. Consider photographs, illustrations, music, charts, graphs, and video clips. Allow each group member to make suggestions.

▤ STANDARDS

Writing
- Write arguments to support claims with clear reasons and relevant evidence.
  b. Support claim(s) with clear reasons and relevant evidence, using credible sources and demonstrating an understanding of the topic or text.
- Produce clear and coherent writing in which the development, organization, and style are appropriate to task, purpose, and audience.

484 UNIT 5 • EXPLORATION

© Pearson Education, Inc., or its affiliates. All rights reserved.

AUTHOR'S PERSPECTIVE   Ernest Morrell, Ph.D.

Digital Speech Since "a picture is worth a thousand words," help students find and use effective images for oral presentations. Remind students to give full credit to visual sources, as they would for print ones. Teachers can guide students to create rhetorically powerful digital presentations such as slideshows, blogs, and online forums using these suggestions:

- *Keep it simple.* Choose one striking image rather than several smaller ones. Position the visual carefully, allowing "white space" to make the image stand out.
- *Go for quality.* Choose clear, high-quality images or take high-resolution photos.
- *Limit bullet points and text.* The most effective slideshows have limited text. Suggest that slides should have no more than six words across and six lines down of text.
- *Choose color and font carefully.* Cool colors (blues, greens) work best for backgrounds; warm colors (orange, red) work best for objects in the foreground. Use a simple, standard font, such as Arial or Helvetica. Last, teachers can help students create a rubric to assess presentations.

Create a Draft As a group, design and create your advertisement. Assign roles to each member—for instance, finding media, organizing examples, writing text, and advertisement design. Also, decide which group member or members will be presenting the advertisement to the class.

Rehearse With Your Group

Practice With Your Group Practice presenting your ad to the class. Use this checklist to evaluate the effectiveness of your group's first run-through. Then, use your evaluation and these instructions to guide your revision.

CONTENT	USE OF MEDIA	PRESENTATION TECHNIQUES
☐ The ad presents a convincing argument for joining the expedition.	☐ Media components are relevant and well chosen.	☐ Speakers make eye contact and speak clearly with adequate volume.
☐ The ad maintains consistency in style and tone.	☐ Media components add to the excitement of the expedition.	☐ Speakers sound enthusiastic and persuasive.

Fine-Tune the Content Reread your advertisement. If it is not convincing, find places where you can strengthen your argument. If necessary, review your notes and add evidence to support your claim. Use engaging, precise language to draw attention to exciting adventures that await potential explorers. Consider listing the benefits of joining the expedition someplace in your advertisement.

Improve Your Use of Media Review your media components. Do your visuals provide enough relevant evidence to convince thrill-seekers to join your expedition? If not, carefully choose vivid photographs or graphics to provide a dramatic illustration of the claim you make in your argument.

Present and Evaluate

When you present your advertisement, be sure to pronounce words clearly and maintain appropriate eye contact. As your classmates deliver their group presentations, consider whether they have been successful in convincing you to participate in their expeditions. Listen attentively and evaluate their content, use of media, and presentation skills.

© Pearson Education, Inc., or its affiliates. All rights reserved.

≡ STANDARDS

Speaking and Listening
• Delineate a speaker's argument and specific claims, distinguishing claims that are supported by reasons and evidence from claims that are not.
• Present claims and findings, sequencing ideas logically and using pertinent descriptions, facts, and details to accentuate main ideas or themes; use appropriate eye contact, adequate volume, and clear pronunciation.
• Include multimedia components and visual displays in presentations to clarify information.
Language
Maintain consistency in style and tone.

Performance Task: Present an Advertisement **485**

Create a Draft Encourage students to be creative in their use of materials and media, and remind them to play to their strengths. For example, if one student is a talented painter, that student might paint an illustration for the advertisement.

Rehearse With Your Group

Fine-Tune the Content Encourage students to read their advertisement from the perspective of a potential adventure-seeker. Ask them to think about what would make them, personally, want to join the expedition.

Improve Your Use of Media Remind groups to consider whether they have used too many media components (does the advertisement appear cluttered?) and to make sure that the media is large enough to be easily viewed by the class.

Present and Evaluate

Before beginning the presentations, set the expectations for the audience. You may wish to have students consider these questions as groups present.

• What expedition is being advertised?
• What are the advertisement's most convincing claims?
• How do the media components strengthen the advertisement's argument?
• What presentation skills did this group excel at?

As students provide feedback to the presenting group, remind them to balance constructive criticism with praise.

PERSONALIZE FOR LEARNING

Strategic Support
Advertisements If some groups have trouble planning and creating their advertisements, suggest that they look for examples of advertisements both online and in newspapers and magazines. Encourage students to sort the examples they find into two categories: *Effective Advertisements* and *Ineffective Advertisements*.

Then ask students to discuss what elements make each advertisement effective or ineffective. Finally, encourage students to make a list of elements that they want to include in their own advertisement. They might also use one of the advertisements they found as a design template for their own advertisement.

INDEPENDENT LEARNING

What drives people to explore?

Encourage students to think carefully about what they have already learned and what more they want to know about the unit topic of exploration. This is a key first step to previewing and selecting the text they will read in Independent Learning.

Independent Learning Strategies ▶

Review the Learning Strategies with students and explain that as they work through Independent Learning they will develop strategies to work on their own.

- Have students watch the video on Independent Learning Strategies.
- A video on this topic is available online in the Professional Development Center.

Students should include any favorite strategies that they might have devised on their own during Whole-Class and Small-Group Learning. For example, for the strategy "Create a schedule," students might include:

- Understand the goals and deadlines.
- Make a schedule for what to do each day.

Block Scheduling

Each day in this Pacing Plan represents a 40–50 minute class period. Teachers using block scheduling may combine days to reflect their class schedule. In addition, teachers may revise pacing to differentiate and support core instruction by integrating components and resources as students require.

ESSENTIAL QUESTION:

What drives people to explore?

What challenges do explorers face in unfamiliar environments? In this section, you will complete your study of exploration by studying an additional selection related to the topic. You'll then share what you learn with classmates. To choose a text, follow these steps.

Look Back Think about the selections you have already studied. What more do you want to know about the topic of exploration?

Look Ahead Preview the texts by reading the descriptions. Which one seems most interesting and appealing to you?

Look Inside Take a few minutes to scan through the text you chose. Make another selection if this text doesn't meet your needs.

Independent Learning Strategies

Throughout your life, in school, in your community, and in your career, you will need to rely on yourself to learn and work on your own. Review these strategies and the actions you can take to practice them during Independent Learning. Add ideas of your own for each category.

STRATEGY	ACTION PLAN
Create a schedule	• Understand your goals and deadlines. • Make a plan for what to do each day. •
Practice what you have learned	• Use first-read and close-read strategies to deepen your understanding. • After you read, evaluate the usefulness of the evidence to help you understand the topic. • Consider the quality and reliability of the source. •
Take notes	• Record important ideas and information. • Review your notes before preparing to share with a group. •

© Pearson Education, Inc., or its affiliates. All rights reserved.

SCAN FOR MULTIMEDIA

📅 **Pacing Plan**

Introduce Whole-Class Learning

Unit Introduction

from A Long Way Home

Media: BBC Science Club: All About Exploration

Performance Task

| 1 | 2 | 3 | 4 | 5 | 6 | 7 | 8 | 9 | 10 | 11 | 12 | 13 | 14 | 15 | 16 | 17 | 18 |

CONTENTS

Choose one selection. Selections are available online only.

 SCAN FOR MULTIMEDIA

Overview: Independent Learning **487**

DIGITAL PERSPECTIVES

Contents

Selections Encourage students to scan and preview the selections before choosing the one they would like to read. Suggest that they consider the genre and subject matter of each one before making their decision. You can use the information on the following Planning pages to advise students in making their choice.

> Remind students that the selections for Independent Learning are only available in the Interactive Student's Edition. Allow students who do not have digital access at home to preview the selections or review the media selection(s) using classroom or computer lab technology. Then either have students print the selection they choose or provide a printout for them.

Performance Based-Assessment Prep
Review Evidence for an Argument Point out to students that collecting evidence during Independent Learning is the last step in completing their Evidence Log. After they finish their independent reading, they will synthesize all the evidence they have compiled in the unit.

The evidence students collect will serve as the primary source of information they will use to complete the writing and oral presentation for the Performance-Based Assessment at the end of the unit.

© Pearson Education, Inc., or its affiliates. All rights reserved.

Introduce Small-Group Learning

Mission Twinpossible

from Tales From the Odyssey

To the Top of Everest

Media: *from* Lewis & Clark

Performance Task

Introduce Independent Learning

Independent Learning

Performance-Based Assessment

| 19 | 20 | 21 | 22 | 23 | 24 | 25 | 26 | 27 | 28 | 29 | 30 | 31 | 32 | 33 | 34 | 35 | 36 |

INDEPENDENT LEARNING

Independent Learning **487**

Mars Can Wait. Oceans Can't.

SELECTION RESOURCES

- 📄 First-Read Guide: Nonfiction
- 📄 Close-Read Guide: Nonfiction
- 📄 Mars Can Wait. Oceans Can't: Text Questions
- 🔊 Audio Summaries
- 🔊 Selection Audio
- ☑ 📄 Selection Test

Summary

In "Mars Can Wait. Oceans Can't," an opinion piece, Amitai Etzioni argues that exploring the oceans should be a higher priority than exploring space. He says that sending humans into space is more expensive than sending robots. He points out that space exploration is helpful in inspiring the next generation of scientists. However, he says that ocean exploration could be just as inspirational for a much lower cost. He argues there are many more valuable things in the oceans than in space. He says that the oceans can teach us about climate control and water scarcity. Also, he says that studying ocean animals has helped us solve many problems in human biology, including developing better medicines. Etzioni argues that technologies that come from ocean exploration tend to be more practical than those that come from space exploration.

Insight

This argument makes the case that exploring the oceans is more urgent and useful than sending people to space.

Connection to Essential Question

Etzioni provides many answers to the Essential Question, "What drives people to explore?" In this opinion piece, the author emphasizes discovering things that can help humanity, such as new medicines and ways to mitigate global warming.

Connection to Performance-Based Assessment

The prompt is "What fuels people's desire to explore?" This text offers strong evidence to support students' responses. Some students may say that the author suggests that hope of finding something that will be useful back home is a strong motivator.

Text Complexity Rubric: Mars Can Wait. Oceans Can't.

Quantitative Measures

Lexile: 1400   Text Length: 1,063 words

Qualitative Measures

Knowledge Demands ①—②—③—❹—⑤	Selection contains multiple details about which students will have very little prior knowledge. Numerous references are made to people, processes, and events that will be unfamiliar.
Structure ①—②—❸—④—⑤	Text covers a wide range of ideas; organization is clear, but many examples and elaboration techniques may challenge some readers.
Language Conventionality and Clarity ①—②—③—❹—⑤	Language is very complex, but also has an informal, conversational style at times. Many sentences are lengthy, with complex construction, multiple ideas and clauses, and above-level vocabulary.
Levels of Meaning/Purpose ①—②—❸—④—⑤	Main idea and opinion are explicitly stated up front. However, multiple details back up main concepts, and readers must be able to understand difficult language in order to understand meaning.

DIGITAL PERSPECTIVES

Audio   Video   Document   Online Assessment   EL Highlights   Online Assessment

from Shipwreck at the Bottom of the World

SELECTION RESOURCES

- 📄 First-Read Guide: Nonfiction
- 📄 Close-Read Guide: Nonfiction
- 📄 *from* Shipwreck at the Bottom of the World: Text Questions
- 🔊 Audio Summaries
- 🔊 Selection Audio
- ☑ 📄 Selection Test

Summary

The excerpt from *Shipwreck at the Bottom of the World* is a nonfiction narrative by Jennifer Armstrong. It details the experiences of the crew of *The Endurance,* a ship that was exploring Antartica in 1915. At the time—before radios and satellites—the only ways to track location were through navigational strategies that relied on clocks, the stars, and the sun. When these strategies failed because of inclement weather, the ship wound up in completely frozen waters. The men struggled to survive through freezing Antarctic temperatures.

Insight

This selection helps students understand how technological change made exploration easier. But it also shows how nature's whims can overwhelm our ability to solve problems with technology. The description of the men's survival experience is gripping.

Connection to Essential Question

The Essential Question is "What drives people to explore?" The men's motivation to explore was quickly diverted into a deep desire to survive despite very difficult challenges.

Connection to Performance-Based Assessment

This text describes the challenges of exploration in the days of limited technology. It provides background for the prompt, "What fuels people's desire to explore?" The challenge of crossing Antarctica was immense. That difficulty and danger may have been what motivated Shackleton to do it.

Text Complexity Rubric: *from* Shipwreck at the Bottom of the World

Quantitative Measures

Lexile: 1110   Text Length: 2,280 words

Qualitative Measures

Knowledge Demands ①—②—③—**④**—⑤	The text includes information about navigation, voyage by ship, and survival on ice. Students may not have prior knowledge of these topics. Background information about the expedition is provided.
Structure ①—②—③—**④**—⑤	Text includes both scientific explanation and narration which may present a challenge. Story is told chronologically; text is dense with multiple details; quotations are included.
Language Conventionality and Clarity ①—②—③—**④**—⑤	Language is concrete, but dense and complex; some language is not contemporary. Many sentences are complex and include above-level vocabulary.
Levels of Meaning/Purpose ①—②—**③**—④—⑤	Purpose of text is to account the experiences of *The Endurance* crew. Information about means of navigation provides background, but may challenge some readers.

from Sacajawea

SELECTION RESOURCES

📄 First-Read Guide: Fiction

📄 Close-Read Guide: Fiction

📄 *from* Sacajawea: Text Questions

🔊 Audio Summaries

🔊 Selection Audio

☑ 📄 Selection Test

Summary

Told from the point of view of Sacajawea, this excerpt from the novel *Sacajawea* by Joseph Bruchac describes the Lewis and Clark Expedition. In this selection, the group approaches Sacajawea's homeland. Captain Clark is ill, but insists on scouting ahead for Sacajawea's people. She expects to find them soon, and recognizes the landscape the group travels through. She worries that they may not recognize her, and tries not to show emotion to the group. When she tells the captains that her people are nearby, they give her a string of beads as a present. She explains the customs of her people, and how to greet them, and what Europeans would be called in her language. The party continues along the river, hoping to make contact soon.

Insight

While the party does not encounter Sacajawea's people in this selection, it raises the question of European contact with Native American nations.

Connection to Essential Question

The Essential Question is "What drives people to explore?" This selection describes both the expedition led by Lewis and Clark, and Sacajawea's own drive to return to her people. In that sense, the exploration is itself in question, as Sacajawea is returning to a place she knows better than any other.

Connection to Performance-Based Assessment

Students may use this text to prepare to address the prompt, "What fuels people's desire to explore?" In this selection, Sacajawea's motivation is made very clear, as she desires to explore both to return to her homeland and to prove her worth to the expedition. Sacajawea does not explain the motivations of Lewis and Clark, but she does describe their habit of taking notes and making careful drawings, which suggest they wanted to learn.

Text Complexity Rubric: *from* Sacajawea

Quantitative Measures

Lexile: 790   Text Length: 1,613 words

Qualitative Measures

Knowledge Demands ①—②—❸—④—⑤	Prior knowledge or familiarity is needed of Sacajawea, Lewis and Clark's expedition, and Native American culture. Students may have some of this background information from previous studies and selections.
Structure ①—②—❸—④—⑤	Story is told chronologically in a narrative style. Students may struggle to identify First Born Son, the person that Sacajawea addresses in the text. Some dialogue is included.
Language Conventionality and Clarity ①—②—❸—④—⑤	Language is descriptive, with some figurative phrases and symbols. Sentences mostly have simple construction, though some may have unfamiliar syntax and non-contemporary style.
Levels of Meaning/Purpose ①—②—❸—④—⑤	Text includes plot events with levels of cultural meaning. Story events are clear and explicit, but readers need to infer meaning related to the cultural understanding of past events.

The Legacy of Arctic Explorer Matthew Henson

SELECTION RESOURCES

- 📄 First-Read Guide: Nonfiction
- 📄 Close-Read Guide: Nonfiction
- 📄 The Legacy of Arctic Explorer Matthew Henson: Text Questions
- 🔊 Audio Summaries
- 🔊 Selection Audio
- ☑️ 📄 Selection Test

Summary

This article by James Mill describes the life of an often-overlooked American explorer, Matthew Henson. As a member of the Peary 1909 expedition, Henson is the first person to reach the North Pole. An African American man from Maryland, Henson first takes a job aboard a sailing ship at the age of twelve. Returning to Washington, D.C., to take a job as a shop clerk, he meets Robert Peary, an explorer. The pair travel across Central America and later explore Greenland's northern shore. They make a number of famous scientific discoveries, and after eight attempts, they are the first team to reach the North Pole. The team of four Inuit guides, Henson, and Peary, return to great acclaim. The men's long-term friendship ends because of a dispute about whether Peary or Henson arrived at the North Pole first. Henson is only received as a hero in 1937, many years after his historic expedition.

Insight

This article raises one of the fundamental questions of exploration: the question of credit. Not only do others question the group's success, but also within the group Henson and Peary are divided by questions of credit.

Connection to Essential Question

The Essential Question is "What drives people to explore?" Henson's biography is laid out in the article, and shows that he pursued exploration and adventure throughout his life. From a young age, he traveled great distances and took dangerous jobs.

Connection to Performance-Based Assessment

Students may decide to use Henson's life story to help them address the prompt, "What fuels people's desire to explore?" Henson's career, and Peary's support, allowed him to turn his drive to explore into action. The article outlines how the infrastructure of exploration meant that Henson, an excellent explorer, was unable to continue without that support.

Text Complexity Rubric: The Legacy of Arctic Explorer Matthew Henson

Quantitative Measures	
Lexile: 1240 **Text Length:** 2,491 words	

Qualitative Measures	
Knowledge Demands ①——②——③——**④**——⑤	Selection presents information about Arctic exploration that will be unfamiliar to most readers.
Structure ①——②——**❸**——④——⑤	Events are explained chronologically; organization is evident; multiple intricate events and details are included.
Language Conventionality and Clarity ①——②——**❸**——④——⑤	Language is concrete and straightforward; some sentences are lengthy or complex, with multiple clauses and ideas; some vocabulary is above-level.
Levels of Meaning/Purpose ①——**❷**——③——④——⑤	Main idea is clearly explained at beginning of selection and at end; multiple concepts and ideas are explored in detail and fully explained.

Should Polar Tourism Be Allowed?

SELECTION RESOURCES

📄 First-Read Guide: Nonfiction

📄 Close-Read Guide: Nonfiction

📄 Should Polar Tourism Be Allowed?: Text Questions

🔊 Audio Summaries

🔊 Selection Audio

☑️📄 Selection Test

Summary

Emily Goldberg's article "Should Polar Tourism Be Allowed?" makes an argument that tourism to the Arctic and Antarctica may be a bad idea. Transporting tourists to the poles puts fragile ecosystems at risk. Tourists can damage plants, and vehicles can disturb animals. But Goldberg also presents the pro-tourism side of the debate, noting that some people argue that polar tourism offers economic benefits and encourages people to support conservation efforts.

Insight

"Should Polar Tourism Be Allowed?" shows how exploration can put ecosystems at risk. Even if people don't build anything, their presence might disrupt the environment. Still, there is value in seeing new places, and tourism does provide an incentive to keep these places intact.

Connection to Essential Question

This selection connects to the Essential Question by suggesting that some people explore to impress others or to make their nation look impressive, and others want the experience of exploring the environment of a remote area.

Connection to Performance-Based Assessment

This selection connects to the Performance-Based Assessment by noting that some people explore because of a sense of competition, and others seek an experience outside of everyday life.

Text Complexity Rubric: "Should Polar Tourism Be Allowed?"

Quantitative Measures

Lexile: 1210   Text Length: 338 words

Qualitative Measures

Knowledge Demands ①—②—**❸**—④—⑤	Some knowledge of the Arctic and Antarctica is required.
Structure ①—**❷**—③—④—⑤	Text is organized clearly and logically.
Language Conventionality and Clarity ①—②—**❸**—④—⑤	Language in text is concrete and straightforward.
Levels of Meaning/Purpose ①—②—**❸**—④—⑤	In the text, the two sides of the issue/argument are clearly explained.

DIGITAL PERSPECTIVES

 Audio

 Video

 Document

 Annotation Highlights

EL Highlights

 Online Assessment

MY NOTES

You may wish to direct students to use the generic **First-Read** and **Close-Read Guides** in the Print Student Edition. Alternatively, you may wish to print copies of the genre-specific **First-Read** and **Close-Read Guides** for students. These are available online in the Interactive Student Edition or Unit Resources.

● FIRST READ

Students should perform the steps of the first read independently.

NOTICE: Students should focus on the basic elements of the text to ensure they understand what is happening.

ANNOTATE: Students should mark any passages they wish to revisit during their close read.

CONNECT: Students should increase their understanding by connecting what they've read to other texts or personal experiences.

RESPOND: Students will write a summary to demonstrate their understanding.

Point out to students that while they will always complete the Respond step at the end of the first read, the other steps will probably happen somewhat concurrently. Remind students that they will revisit their first-read annotations during the close read. You may wish to print copies of the First-Read Guide for students to use.

After students have completed the First-Read Guide, you may wish to assign the Text questions for the selection that are available in the Interactive Teacher's Edition.

Anchor Standards

In the first two sections of the unit, students worked with the whole class and in small groups to gain topical knowledge and greater understanding of the skills required by the anchor standards. In this section, they are asked to work independently, applying what they have learned and demonstrating increased readiness for college and career.

● INDEPENDENT LEARNING

First-Read Guide

Tool Kit
First-Read Guide and
Model Annotation

Use this page to record your first-read ideas.

Selection Title: _____

NOTICE new information or ideas you learn about the unit topic as you first read this text.

ANNOTATE by marking vocabulary and key passages you want to revisit.

First Read

CONNECT ideas within the selection to other knowledge and the selections you have read.

RESPOND by writing a brief summary of the selection.

© Pearson Education, Inc., or its affiliates. All rights reserved.

▤ STANDARD
Reading Read and comprehend complex literary and informational texts independently and proficiently.

488 UNIT 5 • EXPLORATION

PERSONALIZE FOR LEARNING

Challenge
Additional Questions To help students reflect on their first read and prepare for the close read, encourage them to think about what more they would like to know about a text. Ask students to write two to three questions they have about the text. Then, students can meet in small groups with others who have read the same selection. Each group can share First-Read Guides and their additional questions before proceeding to the Close Read.

Close-Read Guide

Use this page to record your first-read ideas.

🔧 **Tool Kit**
Close-Read Guide and
Model Annotation

Selection Title: _____

Close Read the Text

Revisit sections of the text you marked during your first read. Read these sections closely and **annotate** what you notice. Ask yourself **questions** about the text. What can you **conclude**? Write down your ideas.

Analyze the Text

Think about the author's choices of patterns, structure, techniques, and ideas included in the text. Select one, and record your thoughts about what this choice conveys.

QuickWrite

Pick a paragraph from the text that grabbed your interest. Explain the power of this passage.

_____
_____
_____
_____
_____
_____
_____
_____
_____
_____

© Pearson Education, Inc., or its affiliates. All rights reserved.

≣ STANDARD
Reading Read and comprehend complex literary and informational texts independently and proficiently.

Independent Learning **489**

CLOSE READ

Students should begin their close read by revisiting the annotations they made during their first read. Then, students should analyze one of the author's choices regarding the following elements:

- **patterns,** such as repetition or parallelism
- **structure,** such as cause-and-effect or problem-solution
- **techniques,** such as description or dialogue
- **ideas,** such as the author's main idea or claim

MAKE IT INTERACTIVE
Group students according to the selection they have chosen. Then, have students meet to discuss the selection in-depth. Their discussions should be guided by their insights and questions.

PERSONALIZE FOR LEARNING

Challenge

Group Review Have students who have read the same selection collaborate to write a group review of the entire text. The review should include a summary and excerpts from each group member's Close-Read Guide. Group members should agree on contributions, the order in which the excerpts will appear, and how the excerpts will fit into paragraphs within the review. Together, group members should revise and edit the writing for coverage of the entire text, and make sure ideas are logically organized and expressed clearly. They can use signal words and transitions to connect the ideas and writing of all the contributors. After editing and proofreading, the completed reviews may be posted in a blog or printed and distributed to the class.

Share Your Independent Learning

Prepare to Share
Explain to students that sharing what they learned from their Independent Learning selection provides classmates who read a different selection with an opportunity to consider the text as a source of evidence during the Performance-Based Assessment. As students prepare to share, remind them to highlight how their selection contributed to their knowledge of the concept of survival, as well as how the selection connects to the question *What drives people to explore?*

Learn From Your Classmates
As students discuss the Independent Learning selections, direct them to take particular note of how their classmates' chosen selections align with their current position on the Performance-Based Assessment question.

Reflect
Students may want to add their reflection to their Evidence Log, particularly if their insight relates to a specific selection from the unit.

MAKE IT INTERACTIVE
With students, create a game of "Concentration" with the names of explorers and the places they explored. The explorers can be from this unit, or students can research for names and data on famous explorers from history. Make up 15 three-inch by five-inch index cards with an explorer and the place they explored written on each card. Then, make a matching set of cards. (You will have 30 cards altogether.) Shuffle all of the cards. Place the cards face down in five rows of 6 each. Each student then takes a turn by turning over two cards. The student must explain how they match. Other students may disagree. If they match, the cards remain right side up. If they do not match, they are placed face down again, and the next student takes a turn. The game continues until all of the cards are matched and face up.

You can increase the difficulty of this game by having 15 cards with explorers' names and 15 cards with the names of the places they explored. Students must match each explorer to a place.

Evidence Log Support students in completing their Evidence Log. This paced activity will help prepare them for the Performance-Based Assessment at the end of the unit.

📝 EVIDENCE LOG

Go to your Evidence Log and record what you learned from the text you read.

📋 STANDARDS
Speaking and Listening
Engage effectively in a range of collaborative discussions with diverse partners on *grade 6 topics, texts, and issues,* building on others' ideas and expressing their own clearly.

Share Your Independent Learning

Prepare to Share

What drives people to explore?

Even when you read something independently, your understanding continues to grow when you share what you have learned with others. Reflect on the text you explored independently, and write notes about its connection to the unit. In your notes, consider why this text belongs in this unit.

Learn From Your Classmates

💬 **Discuss It** Share your ideas about the text you explored on your own. As you talk with your classmates, jot down ideas that you learn from them.

Reflect

Review your notes, and mark the most important insight you gained from these writing and discussion activities. Explain how this idea adds to your understanding of the topic of exploration.

© Pearson Education, Inc., or its affiliates. All rights reserved.

AUTHOR'S PERSPECTIVE | Ernest Morrell, Ph.D.

Powerful Speaking in Small Groups Explain to students that learning how to speak with confidence, without over-compensating, will help them make and/or defend an argument and point of view in a small group. Point out that their goal is to be convincing, but not argumentative. To help build this skill, provide students with the following guidelines:

1. **Earn credibility.** Speakers who are prepared with evidence tailored to their audience's needs will sway their audience with the power of their proof. As a result, these speakers will have no need to try to harass or intimidate their listeners.

2. **Choose words carefully.** Effective speakers use the exact words they need, words that

---

Review Evidence for an Argument

At the beginning of this unit you took a position on the following question:

Should kids today be encouraged to become explorers?

✏ EVIDENCE LOG

Review your Evidence Log and your QuickWrite from the beginning of the unit. Has your position changed?

☐ YES	☐ NO
Identify at least three pieces of evidence that convinced you to change your mind.	Identify at least three pieces of evidence that reinforced your initial position.
1.	1.
2.	2.
3.	3.

State your claim now: _____

_____

_____

Identify a possible counterclaim, or opposing position: _____

_____

_____

Evaluate the Strength of Your Evidence Consider your argument. Do you have enough evidence to support your claim? Do you have enough evidence to disprove possible counterclaims? If not, make a plan.

☐ Do more research ☐ Talk with my classmates

☐ Reread a selection ☐ Ask an expert

☐ Other: _____

© Pearson Education, Inc., or its affiliates. All rights reserved.

☰ STANDARDS
Writing
Write arguments to support claims with clear reasons and relevant evidence.
b. Support claim(s) with clear reasons and relevant evidence, using credible sources and demonstrating an understanding of the topic or text.

Review Evidence for an Argument

Evidence Log Students should understand that their position on an issue can evolve as they learn more about the subject and are exposed to additional points of view. Point out that just because they took an initial position on the question *What fuels people's desire to explore?* doesn't mean that their position can't change after careful consideration of their learning and evidence.

Evaluate the Strength of Your Evidence

Encourage students to keep in mind that their written argument should include evidence. The evidence they provide should support their position, or their side of the argument. Evidence may include facts (such as statistics and physical details), personal anecdotes (personal experience of the student or others), and expert opinions. The evidence that they provide in their written argument should support and strengthen their position.

convey their precise meaning. Further, effective speakers avoid "loaded words" that attempt to sway an audience by appealing to stereotypes.

3. **Be audible, not loud.** Speakers who avoid shouting convey their point with greater confidence than those who do raise their voices.

Writing to Sources: Argument

Students should complete the Performance-Based Assessment independently, with little to no input or feedback during the process. Students should use word processing software to take advantage of editing tools and features.

Prior to beginning the Assessment, ask students to think about what might make people want to explore.

Review the Elements of Effective Argument

Students can review the work they did earlier in the unit as they complete the Performance-Based Assessment. They may also consult other resources such as:

- the elements of an effective argument, including language, tone, and grammar, as well as how to organize an argument, available in Whole-Class Learning

- their Evidence Log

- their Word Network

Although students will use evidence from unit selections for their argument, they may need to collect additional evidence, including facts, statistics, anecdotes, quotations from authorities, or examples that support their position.

 PERFORMANCE-BASED ASSESSMENT

SOURCES

- WHOLE-CLASS SELECTIONS

- SMALL-GROUP SELECTIONS

- INDEPENDENT-LEARNING SELECTION

© Pearson Education, Inc., or its affiliates. All rights reserved.

PART 1

Writing to Sources: Argument

In this unit, you read about a variety of explorers and considered different perspectives on important issues related to exploration.

Assignment

Write an **argument** in which you state and defend a claim in response to the following question:

> Should kids today be encouraged to become explorers?

First, state your claim, and then develop a coherent argument to support that claim. Organize your argument logically, and support your claim with valid evidence from credible sources. Use precise words to clarify the relationships among the reasons and the claim. Include a conclusion that follows from your argument. Strive to maintain a formal tone throughout your writing.

Reread the Assignment Review the assignment to be sure you fully understand it. The task may reference some of the academic words presented at the beginning of the unit. Be sure you understand each of the words given below in order to complete the assignment correctly. Also, consider using the academic vocabulary words in your argument. These words may help you to clarify your claims with precise word choices.

critical	compel	coherent
assume	valid	

Review the Elements of Effective Argument Before you begin writing, read the Argument Rubric. Once you have completed your first draft, check it against the rubric. If one or more of the elements is missing or not as strong as it could be, revise your essay to add or strengthen that element.

⬥ WORD NETWORK

As you write and revise your argument, use your Word Network to help vary your word choices.

≡ STANDARDS

Writing
- Write arguments to support claims with clear reasons and relevant evidence.
- Write routinely over extended time frames and shorter time frames for a range of discipline-specific tasks, purposes, and audiences.

Language
Use knowledge of language and its conventions when writing, speaking, reading, or listening.
  b. Maintain consistency in style and tone.

Argument Rubric

© Pearson Education, Inc., or its affiliates. All rights reserved.

	Focus and Organization	Evidence and Elaboration	Conventions
4	The introduction is engaging and states the claim in a compelling way. The claim is supported by clear reasons and relevant evidence. Words, phrases, and clauses are used to clarify the relationships among the claim and reasons. The conclusion clearly follows from the argument.	Sources are credible and support the claim. The tone of the argument is formal and objective. Words are carefully chosen and suited to purpose and audience.	The argument correctly uses standard English conventions of usage and mechanics.
3	The introduction is mostly engaging and states the claim. The claim is mostly supported by clear reasons and relevant evidence. Words, phrases, and clauses are mostly used to clarify the relationships among the claim and reasons. The conclusion mostly follows from the argument.	Sources are mostly credible and mostly support the claim. The tone of the argument is mostly formal and objective. Words are mostly suited to purpose and audience.	The argument mostly demonstrates accuracy in standard English conventions of usage and mechanics.
2	The introduction somewhat states the claim. The claim is supported by some reasons and evidence. Words, phrase, and clauses are occasionally used to clarify relationships among the claim and reasons. The conclusion somewhat follows from the argument.	Sources are somewhat credible and somewhat support the claim. The tone of the argument is occasionally formal and objective. Words are somewhat suited to purpose and audience.	The argument demonstrates some accuracy in standard English conventions of usage and mechanics.
1	The introduction does not clearly state the claim. The claim is not supported by reasons and evidence. Words, phrase, and clauses are not used to clarify relationships among the claim and reasons. The conclusion does not follow from the argument.	Sources are not credible nor do they support the claim. The tone is informal. Words are not suited to purpose or audience.	The argument contains mistakes in standard English conventions of usage and mechanics.

Argument Rubric

As you review the Argument Rubric with students, remind them that the rubric is a resource that can guide their revisions. Students should pay particular attention to the differences between an argument that contains all of the required elements (a score of 3) and one that is compelling, well-organized, and strongly supported by logical reasons and relevant evidence (a score of 4).

PERSONALIZE FOR LEARNING

English Language Support
Sentence starters Provide sentence starters to help students organize their claim and their supporting reasons and evidence. For example, *I think that _____ and _____ fuels people's desire to explore because _____ and*

_____. Pair students and have them work together to complete the answers. Ask them to read their responses aloud to each other and to help each other correct any errors. Then have them write their arguments independently.
ALL LEVELS

Speaking and Listening: Speech

Students should annotate their written argument in preparation for the oral presentation, marking the important elements (claim, reasons, and evidence) as well as critical facts, quotations, or statistics.

Remind students that the effectiveness of an oral argument relies on how the speaker establishes credibility with his or her audience. If a speaker comes across as confident and authoritative, it will be easier for the audience to give credence to the speaker's claim.

Review the Rubric As you review the rubric with students, remind them that it is a valuable tool that can help them plan their presentation. They should strive to include all of the criteria required to achieve a score of 3. Draw their attention to some of the subtle differences between scores of 2 and 3.

PERFORMANCE-BASED ASSESSMENT

PART 2

Speaking and Listening: Speech

Assignment
After completing the final draft of your argument, use it as the foundation for a brief **speech.**

Do not simply read your argument aloud. Take the following steps to make your presentation lively and engaging.

- Review your argument and annotate the most important reasons and evidence. Refer to the annotations to guide your presentation.
- Keep your audience in mind, and adapt the wording of your speech as needed to appeal to them.
- Use appropriate eye contact. Make sure to pronounce words clearly and speak loudly enough for people to hear you. Vary your volume and your talking speed to emphasize key points.

Review the Rubric Before you deliver your presentation, check your plans against this rubric. If one or more of the elements is missing or not as strong as it could be, revise your presentation.

STANDARDS

Speaking and Listening
• Present claims and findings, sequencing ideas logically and using pertinent descriptions, facts, and details to accentuate main ideas or themes; use appropriate eye contact, adequate volume, and clear pronunciation.
• Adapt speech to a variety of contexts and tasks, demonstrating command of formal English when indicated or appropriate.

	Content	Organization	Presentation Techniques
3	The introduction is engaging and establishes the claim in a compelling way. The presentation includes strong, clear reasons and relevant evidence to support the claim. The conclusion clearly follows from the argument.	Ideas progress logically, with clear transitions so that the argument is easy to follow. Important ideas are given emphasis and are well supported.	The speaker maintains effective eye contact and speaks clearly with adequate volume.
2	The introduction establishes the claim. The presentation includes some clear reasons and relevant evidence to support the claim. The conclusion somewhat follows from the argument.	Ideas progress logically with some transitions between ideas.that the argument is easy to follow. Important ideas are sometimes emphasized and are supported.	The speaker sometimes maintains effective eye contact and speaks somewhat clearly and with adequate volume.
1	The introduction does not clearly establish the claim. The presentation does not include reasons or evidence to support the claim. The conclusion does not follow from the argument.	Ideas do not progress logically. Important ideas are not emphasized and may lack support.	The speaker does not maintain effective eye contact or speak clearly with adequate volume.

© Pearson Education, Inc., or its affiliates. All rights reserved.

494 UNIT 5 • EXPLORATION

DIGITAL PERSPECTIVES

Preparing for the Assignment To help students prepare for their presentation, suggest that they pair up with another student and video record each other's presentation rehearsals. The student doing the recording should time the other student's presentation to make sure it stays within the allotted time limit. Afterward, students should watch the recordings together and use the rubric to evaluate the rehearsals. Remind students to incorporate feedback from their partner into their final presentation.

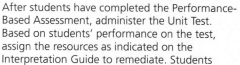
Reflect on the Unit

Now that you've completed the unit, take a few moments to reflect on your learning.

Reflect on the Unit Goals

Look back at the goals at the beginning of the unit. Use a different-colored pen to rate yourself again. Then, think about the readings and activities that contributed the most to the growth of your understanding. Record your thoughts.

Reflect on the Learning Strategies

Discuss It Write a reflection on whether you were able to improve your learning based on your Action Plans. Think about what worked, what didn't, and what you might do to keep working on these strategies. Record your ideas before participating in a class discussion.

Reflect on the Text

Choose a selection that you found challenging, and explain what made it difficult.

Explain something that surprised you about a text in the unit.

Which activity taught you the most about exploration? What did you learn?

SCAN FOR
MULTIMEDIA

Reflect on the Unit

- Have students watch the video on Reflecting on Your Learning.
- A video on this topic is available online in the Professional Development Center.

Reflect on the Unit Goals

Students should re-evaluate how well they met the unit goals now that they have completed the unit. You might ask them to provide a written commentary on the goal they made the most progress with as well as the goal they feel warrants continued focus.

Reflect on the Learning Strategies

Discuss It If you want to make this a digital activity, go online and navigate to the Discussion Board. Alternatively, students can share their learning strategies reflections in a class discussion.

Reflect on the Text

Consider having students share their text reflections with one another.

MAKE IT INTERACTIVE

Have students write a blog post reflecting on what they learned from the units in the selection. Then encourage them to share their posts with their classmates, and to comment on each other's posts.

Unit Test and Remediation

After students have completed the Performance-Based Assessment, administer the Unit Test. Based on students' performance on the test, assign the resources as indicated on the Interpretation Guide to remediate. Students who take the test online will be automatically assigned remediation, as warranted by test results.

© Pearson Education, Inc., or its affiliates. All rights reserved.

RESOURCES

TABLE OF CONTENTS

© Pearson Education, Inc., or its affiliates. All rights reserved.

Marking the Text: Strategies and Tips for Annotation

When you close read a text, you read for comprehension and then reread to unlock layers of meaning and to analyze a writer's style and techniques. Marking a text as you read it enables you to participate more fully in the close-reading process.

Following are some strategies for text mark-ups, along with samples of how the strategies can be applied. These mark-ups are suggestions; you and your teacher may want to use other mark-up strategies.

✱	Key Idea
!	I love it!
?	I have questions
◯	Unfamiliar or important word
----	Context Clues

Suggested Mark-Up Notations

WHAT I NOTICE	HOW TO MARK UP	QUESTIONS TO ASK
Key Ideas and Details	• Highlight key ideas or claims. • Underline supporting details or evidence.	• What does the text say? What does it leave unsaid? • What inferences do you need to make? • What details lead you to make your inferences?
Word Choice	• Circle unfamiliar words. • Put a dotted line under context clues, if any exist. • Put an exclamation point beside especially rich or poetic passages.	• What inferences about word meaning can you make? • What tone and mood are created by word choice? • What alternate word choices might the author have made?
Text Structure	• Highlight passages that show key details supporting the main idea. • Use arrows to indicate how sentences and paragraphs work together to build ideas. • Use a right-facing arrow to indicate foreshadowing. • Use a left-facing arrow to indicate flashback.	• Is the text logically structured? • What emotional impact do the structural choices create?
Author's Craft	• Circle or highlight instances of repetition, either of words, phrases, consonants, or vowel sounds. • Mark rhythmic beats in poetry using checkmarks and slashes. • Underline instances of symbolism or figurative language.	• Does the author's style enrich or detract from the reading experience? • What levels of meaning are created by the author's techniques?

© Pearson Education, Inc., or its affiliates. All rights reserved.

TOOL KIT: CLOSE READING

CLOSE READING

First Read
NOTICE · ANNOTATE · CONNECT · RESPOND

* Key Idea
! I love it!
? I have questions
◯ Unfamiliar or important word
---- Context Clues

In a first read, work to get a sense of the main idea of a text. Look for key details and ideas that help you understand what the author conveys to you. Mark passages which prompt a strong response from you.

Here is how one reader marked up this text.

NOTES

MODEL

INFORMATIONAL TEXT

from **Classifying the Stars**

Cecilia H. Payne

*

1 Sunlight and starlight are composed of waves of various lengths, which the eye, even aided by a telescope, is unable to separate. We must use more than a telescope. In order to sort out the ? component colors, the light must be dispersed by a prism, or split up by some other means. For instance, sunbeams passing through rain drops are transformed into the (myriad) tinted rainbow. The familiar rainbow spanning the sky is Nature's most ! glorious demonstration that light is composed of many colors.

*

2 The very beginning of our knowledge of the nature of a star dates back to 1672, when Isaac Newton gave to the world the results of his experiments on passing sunlight through a prism. To describe the beautiful band of rainbow tints, produced when sunlight was dispersed by his three-cornered piece of glass, he took from the Latin the word *spectrum*, meaning an appearance. The rainbow is the (spectrum) of the Sun. . . .

*

3 In 1814, more than a century after Newton, the spectrum of the Sun was obtained in such purity that an amazing detail was seen and studied by the German optician, Fraunhofer. He saw that the multiple spectral tints, ranging from delicate violet to deep red, were crossed by hundreds of fine dark lines. In other words, there were narrow gaps in the spectrum where certain shades were wholly blotted out. We must remember that the word spectrum is applied not only to sunlight, but also to the light of any glowing substance when its rays are sorted out by a prism or a (grating.)

© Pearson Education, Inc., or its affiliates. All rights reserved.

First-Read Guide

Use this page to record your first-read ideas.

You may want to use a guide like this to organize your thoughts after you read. Here is how a reader completed a First-Read Guide.

Selection Title: _Classifying the Stars_

NOTICE new information or ideas you learned about the unit topic as you first read this text.

Light = different waves of colors. (Spectrum)

Newton - the first person to observe these waves using a prism.

Faunhofer saw gaps in the spectrum.

ANNOTATE by marking vocabulary and key passages you want to revisit.

Vocabulary
  myriad
  grating
  component colors

Different light types = different lengths

Isaac Newton also worked theories of gravity.

Multiple spectral tints? "colors of various appearance"

Key Passage:
Paragraph 3 shows that Fraunhofer discovered more about the nature of light spectrums: he saw the spaces in between the tints.

First Read

CONNECT ideas within the selection to other knowledge and the selections you have read.

I remember learning about prisms in science class.

Double rainbows! My favorite. How are they made?

RESPOND by writing a brief summary of the selection.

Science allows us to see things not visible to the naked eye. What we see as sunlight is really a spectrum of colors. By using tools, such as prisms, we can see the components of sunlight and other light. They appear as single colors or as multiple colors separated by gaps of no color. White light contains a rainbow of colors.

© Pearson Education, Inc., or its affiliates. All rights reserved.

TOOL KIT: CLOSE READING

CLOSE READING

* Key Idea
! I love it!
? I have questions
◯ Unfamiliar or important word
---- Context Clues

In a close read, go back into the text to study it in greater detail. Take the time to analyze not only the author's ideas but the way that those ideas are conveyed. Consider the genre of the text, the author's word choice, the writer's unique style, and the message of the text.

Here is how one reader close read this text.

MODEL

TOOL KIT: CLOSE READING

NOTES

explanation of sunlight and starlight

What is light and where do the colors come from?

This paragraph is about Newton and the prism.

What discoveries helped us understand light?

Fraunhofer and gaps in spectrum

INFORMATIONAL TEXT

from Classifying the Stars
Cecilia H. Payne

1   Sunlight and starlight are composed of waves of various lengths, which the eye, even aided by a telescope, is unable to separate. We must use more than a telescope. In order to sort out the component colors, the light must be dispersed by a prism, or split up by some other means. For instance, sunbeams passing through rain drops are transformed into the myriad-tinted rainbow. The familiar rainbow spanning the sky is Nature's most glorious demonstration that light is composed of many colors.

2   The very beginning of our knowledge of the nature of a star dates back to 1672, when Isaac Newton gave to the world the results of his experiments on passing sunlight through a prism. To describe the beautiful band of rainbow tints, produced when sunlight was dispersed by his three-cornered piece of glass, he took from the Latin the word *spectrum*, meaning an appearance. The rainbow is the spectrum of the Sun. . . .

3   In 1814, more than a century after Newton, the spectrum of the Sun was obtained in such purity that an amazing detail was seen and studied by the German optician, Fraunhofer. He saw that the multiple spectral tints, ranging from delicate violet to deep red, were crossed by hundreds of fine dark lines. In other words, there were narrow gaps in the spectrum where certain shades were wholly blotted out. We must remember that the word spectrum is applied not only to sunlight, but also to the light of any glowing substance when its rays are sorted out by a prism or a grating.

© Pearson Education, Inc., or its affiliates. All rights reserved.

Close-Read Guide

Use this page to record your close-read ideas.

You can use the Close-Read Guide to help you dig deeper into the text. Here is how a reader completed a Close-Read Guide.

Selection Title: _Classifying the Stars_

Close Read the Text

Revisit sections of the text you marked during your first read. Read these sections closely and **annotate** what you notice. Ask yourself **questions** about the text. What can you **conclude?** Write down your ideas.

Close Read (ANNOTATE · QUESTION · CONCLUDE)

Paragraph 3: Light is composed of waves of various lengths. Prisms let us see different colors in light. This is called the spectrum. Fraunhofer proved that there are gaps in the spectrum, where certain shades are blotted out.

More than one researcher studied this and each built off the ideas that were already discovered.

Analyze the Text

Think about the author's choices of patterns, structure, techniques, and ideas included in the text. Select one, and record your thoughts about what this choice conveys.

The author showed the development of human knowledge of the spectrum chronologically. Helped me see how ideas were built upon earlier understandings. Used dates and "more than a century after Newton" to show time.

QuickWrite

Pick a paragraph from the text that grabbed your interest. Explain the power of this passage.

The first paragraph grabbed my attention, specifically the sentence "The familiar rainbow spanning the sky is Nature's most glorious demonstration that light is composed of many colors." The paragraph began as a straightforward scientific explanation. When I read the word "glorious," I had to stop and deeply consider what was being said. It is a word loaded with personal feelings. With that one word, the author let the reader know what was important to her.

© Pearson Education, Inc., or its affiliates. All rights reserved.

TOOL KIT: CLOSE READING

WRITING

Argument

When you think of the word *argument,* you might think of a disagreement between two people, but the word has another meaning, too. An argument is a logical way of presenting a belief, conclusion, or stance. A good argument is supported with reasoning and evidence.

Argument writing can be used for many purposes, such as changing a reader's opinion or bringing about an action or a response from a reader.

Elements of an Argumentative Text

An **argument** sets forth a belief or stand on an issue. A well-written argument may convince the reader, change the reader's mind, or motivate the reader to take a certain action.

An effective argument contains these elements:

- a precise claim
- consideration of alternate claims, or opposing positions, and a discussion of their strengths and weaknesses
- logical organization that makes clear connections among claim, reasons, and evidence
- valid reasoning and evidence
- a concluding statement or section that follows from and supports the argument
- formal and objective language and tone
- error-free grammar, including accurate use of transitions

© Pearson Education, Inc., or its affiliates. All rights reserved.

ARGUMENT: SCORE 1

Celebrities Should Try to Be Better Role Models

A lot of Celebrities are singers or actors or actresses or athletes. Kids spend tons of time watching Celebrities on TV. They listen to their songs. They read about them. They watch them play and perform. No matter weather the Celebrities are good people or bad people. Kids still spend time watching them. The kids will try to imitate what they do. Some of them have parents or brothers and sisters who are famous also.

Celebrities don't seem to watch out what they do and how they live. Some say, *"Why do I care? It's none of you're business"*! Well, that's true. But it's bad on them if they do all kinds of stupid things. Because this is bad for the kids who look up to them.

Sometimes celebrity's say they wish they are not role models. *"I'm just an actor!" "I'm just a singer"*! they say. But the choice is not really up to them. If their on TV all the time, then kids' will look up to them, no matter what. It's stupid when Celebrities mess up and then nothing bad happens to them. That gives kids a bad lesson. Kids will think that you can do stupid things and be fine. That is not being a good role model.

Some Celebrities give money to charity. That's a good way to be a good role model. But sometimes it seems like Celebrities are just totally messed up. It's hard always being in the spotlight. That can drive Celebrities kind of crazy. Then they act out.

It is a good idea to support charities when you are rich and famous. You can do a lot of good. For a lot of people. Some Celebrities give out cars or houses or free scholarships. You can even give away your dresses and people can have an auction to see who will pay the most money for them. This can help for example the Humane Society. Or whatever charity or cause the celebrity wants to support.

Celebrities are fun to watch and follow, even when they mess up. I think they don't realize that when they do bad things, they give teens wrong ideas about how to live. They should try to keep that under control. So many teens look up to them and copy them, no matter what.

The claim is not clearly stated in the introduction or elsewhere.

Some of the ideas in the essay do not relate to the stated position or focus on the issue.

The word choice in the essay is not effective and lends it an informal tone.

The progression of ideas is not logical or well-controlled.

Errors in spelling, capitalization, punctuation, grammar, usage, and sentence boundaries are frequent. The fluency of the writing and effectiveness of the essay are affected by these errors.

The conclusion does not clearly restate the claim.

TOOL KIT: WRITING

© Pearson Education, Inc, or its affiliates, All rights reserved.

WRITING

TOOL KIT: WRITING

MODEL

ARGUMENT: SCORE 2

Celebrities Should Try to Be Better Role Models

Most kids spend tons of time watching celebrities on TV, listening to their songs, and reading about them. No matter how celebrities behave—whether they do good things or bad—they are role models for kids. They often do really dumb things, and that is not good considering they are role models.

The introduction does not state the argument claim clearly enough.

Sometimes celebrity's say they wish they were not role models. "*I'm just an actor!*" or, "*I'm just a singer!*" they say. But the choice is not really up to them. If they are on TV all the time, then kids' will look up to them. No matter what. It's really bad when celebrities mess up and then nothing bad happens to them. That gives kids a false lesson because in reality there are bad things when you mess up. That's why celebrities should think more about what they are doing and what lessons they are giving to kids.

Errors in spelling, grammar, and sentence boundaries decrease the effectiveness of the essay.

Some celebrities might say, "*Why do I care? Why should I be bothered?*" Well, they don't have to. But it's bad on them if they do all kinds of stupid things and don't think about how this affects the kids who look up to them. Plus, they get tons of money, much more even than inventors or scientists or other important people. Being a good role model should be part of what they have to do to get so much money.

The word choice in the essay contributes to an informal tone.

When you are famous it is a good idea to support charities. Some celebrities give out cars, or houses, or free scholarships. They even sometimes give away their dresses and people have an auction to see who will pay the most money for them. This can help for example the Humane Society, or whatever charity or cause the celebrity wants to support.

The writer does not make use of transitions and sentence connections.

Sometimes it seems like celebrities are more messed up than anyone else. That's in their personal lives. Imagine if people wanted to take pictures of you wherever you went, and you could never get away. That can drive celebrities kind of crazy, and then they act out.

Some of the ideas in the essay do not relate to the stated position or focus on the issue.

Celebrities can do good things and they can do bad things. They don't realize that when they do bad things, they give teens wrong ideas about how to live. So many teens look up to them and copy them, no matter what. They should make an effort to be better role models.

The essay has a clear conclusion.

© Pearson Education, Inc., or its affiliates. All rights reserved.

ARGUMENT: SCORE 3

Celebrities Should Try to Be Better Role Models

Kids look up to the celebrities they see on TV and want to be like them. Parents may not *want* celebrities to be role models for their children, but they are anyway. Therefore, celebrities should think about what they say and do and live lives that are worth copying. Celebrities should think about how they act because they are role models.

"I'm just an actor!" or, *"I'm just a singer!"* celebrities sometimes say. *"Their parents and teachers are the ones who should be the role models!"* But it would be foolish to misjudge the impact that celebrities have on youth. Kids spend hours every day digitally hanging with their favorite stars. Children learn by imitation, so, for better or worse, celebrities are role models. That's why celebrities should start modeling good decision-making and good citizenship.

With all that they are given by society, celebrities owe a lot back to their communities and the world. Celebrities get a lot of attention, time, and money. Often they get all that for doing not very much: acting, singing, or playing a sport. It's true; some of them work very hard. But even if they work very hard, do they deserve to be in the news all the time and earn 100 or even 1000 times more than equally hard-working teachers, scientists, or nurses? I don't think so. After receiving all that, it seems only fair that celebrities take on the important job of being good role models for the young people who look up to them.

Celebrities can serve as good role models is by giving back. Quite a few use their fame and fortune to do just that. They give scholarships, or even build and run schools; they help veterans; they visit hospitals; they support important causes such as conservation, and women's rights. They donate not just money but their time and talents too. This is a great way to be a role model.

Celebrities should recognize that as role models, they have a responsibility to try to make good decisions and be honest. Celebrities should step up so they can be a force for good in people's lives and in the world.

The writer's word choice is good but could be better.

The introduction mostly states the claim.

The ideas relate to the stated position and focus on the issue.

The sentences are varied and well controlled and enhance the effectiveness of the essay.

The progression of ideas is logical, but there could be better transitions and sentence connections to show how ideas are related.

The conclusion mostly follows from the claim.

© Pearson Education, Inc., or its affiliates. All rights reserved.

TOOL KIT: WRITING

WRITING

TOOL KIT: WRITING

MODEL

ARGUMENT: SCORE 4

Celebrities Should Try to Be Better Role Models

Like it or not, kids look up to the celebrities they see on TV and want to be like them. Parents may not *want* celebrities to be role models for their children, but the fact is that they are. With such an oversized influence on young people, celebrities have a responsibility to think about what they say and do and to live lives that are worth emulating. In short, they should make an effort to be better role models.

Sometimes celebrities say they don't want to be role models. "I'm just an actor!" or "I'm just a singer!" they protest. "Their parents and teachers are the ones who should be guiding them and showing them the right way to live!" That is all very well, but it would be foolish to underestimate the impact that celebrities have on children. Kids spend hours every day digitally hanging out with their favorite stars. Children learn by imitation, so for better or worse, celebrities act as role models.

Celebrities are given a lot of attention, time, and money. They get all that for doing very little: acting, singing, or playing a sport very well. It's true some of them work very hard. But even if they work hard, do they deserve to be in the news all the time and earn 100 or even 1,000 times more than equally hardworking teachers, scientists, or nurses? I don't think so.

With all that they are given, celebrities owe a lot to their communities and the world. One way they can serve as good role models is by giving back, and quite a few celebrities use their fame and fortune to do just that. They give scholarships or even build and run schools; they help veterans; they entertain kids who are sick; they support important causes such as conservation and women's rights. They donate not just money but their time and talents too.

Celebrities don't have to be perfect. They are people too and make mistakes. But they should recognize that as role models for youth, they have a responsibility to try to make good decisions and be honest about their struggles. Celebrities should step up so they can be a force for good in people's lives.

The writer has chosen words that contribute to the clarity of the essay.

The writer clearly states the claim of the argument in the introduction.

The essay is engaging and varied.

There are no errors to distract the reader from the fluency of the writing and effectiveness of the essay.

The writer uses transitions and sentence connections to show how ideas are related.

The writer clearly restates the claim and the most powerful idea presented in the essay.

© Pearson Education, Inc., or its affiliates. All rights reserved.

Argument Rubric

	Focus and Organization	Evidence and Elaboration	Conventions
4	The introduction is engaging and states the claim in a compelling way. The claim is supported by clear reasons and relevant evidence. Reasons and evidence are logically organized so that the argument is easy to follow. The conclusion clearly restates the claim and the most powerful idea.	Sources are effectively credible and accurate. The argument demonstrates an understanding of the thesis by providing strong examples. The tone of the argument is formal and objective.	The argument intentionally uses standard English conventions of usage and mechanics. The argument effectively uses words, phrases, and clauses to clarify the relationships among claim(s) and reasons.
3	The introduction is mostly engaging and states the claim. The claim is mostly supported by logical reasons and evidence. Reasons and evidence are organized so that the argument is mostly easy to follow. The conclusion mostly restates the claim.	Sources are mostly credible and accurate. The argument mostly demonstrates an understanding of the thesis by providing adequate examples. The tone of the argument is mostly formal and objective.	The argument mostly demonstrates accuracy in standard English conventions of usage and mechanics. The argument mostly uses words, phrases, and clauses to clarify the relationships among claim(s) and reasons.
2	The introduction somewhat states the claim. The claim is supported by some reasons and evidence. Reasons and evidence are organized somewhat logically with a few transitions to orient readers. The conclusion somewhat relates to the claim.	Some sources are relevant. The argument somewhat demonstrates an understanding of the thesis by providing some examples. The tone of the argument is occasionally formal and objective.	The argument demonstrates some accuracy in standard English conventions of usage and mechanics. The argument somewhat uses words, phrases, and clauses to clarify the relationships among claim(s) and reasons.
1	The claim is not clearly stated. The claim is not supported by reasons and evidence. Reasons and evidence are disorganized and the argument is difficult to follow. The conclusion does not include relevant information.	There is little or no reliable, relevant evidence The argument does not demonstrate an understanding of the thesis and does not provide examples. The tone of the argument is informal.	The argument contains mistakes in standard English conventions of usage and mechanics. The argument does not use words, phrases, and clauses to clarify the relationships among claim(s) and reasons.

© Pearson Education, Inc., or its affiliates. All rights reserved.

Informative/Explanatory Texts

Informative and explanatory writing should rely on facts to inform or explain. Informative writing serves several purposes: to increase readers' knowledge of a subject, to help readers better understand a procedure or process, or to provide readers with an enhanced comprehension of a concept. It should also feature a clear introduction, body, and conclusion.

Informative/explanatory texts present facts, details, data, and other kinds of evidence to give information about a topic. Readers turn to informative and explanatory texts when they wish to learn about a specific idea, concept, or subject area, or if they want to learn how to do something.

An effective informative/explanatory text contains these elements:

- a topic sentence or thesis statement that introduces the concept or subject
- relevant facts, examples, and details that expand upon a topic
- definitions, quotations, and/or graphics that support the information given
- headings (if desired) to separate sections of the essay
- a structure that presents information in a direct, clear manner
- clear transitions that link sections of the essay
- precise words and technical vocabulary where appropriate
- formal and objective language and tone
- a conclusion that supports the information given and provides fresh insights

© Pearson Education, Inc., or its affiliates. All rights reserved.

MODEL

INFORMATIVE: SCORE 1

Kids, School, and Exercise: Problems and Solutions

In the past, children ran around and even did hard physical labor. Today most kid's just sit most of the time. They don't know the old Outdoor Games. Like tether ball. and they don't have hard chores to do. Like milking the cows. But children should be Physically Active quite a bit every day. That doesn't happen very much any more. Not as much as it should anyway.

Even at home when kid's have a chance to run around, they choose to sit and play video games, for example. Some schools understand that it's a problem when students don't get enough exercise. Even though they have had to cut Physical Education classes. Some also had to make recess shorter.

But lots of schools are working hard to find ways to get kid's moving around again. Like they used to long ago.

Schools use volunteers to teach kid's old-fashioned games. Old-fashioned games are an awesome way to get kid's moving around like crazy people.

Some schools have before school activities. Such as games in the gym. Other schools have after school activities. Such as bike riding or outdoor games. They can't count on kid's to be active. Not even on their own or at home. So they do the activities all together. Kids enjoy doing stuff with their friends. So that works out really well.

If you don't exercise you get overweight. You can end up with high blood pressure and too much colesterol. Of course its also a problem if you eat too much junk food all the time. But not getting enough exercise is part of the problem too. That's why schools need to try to be part of the solution.

A break during class to move around helps. Good teachers know how to use exercise during classes. There are all kinds of ways to move in the classroom that don't mean you have to change your clothes. Classes don't have to be just about math and science.

Schools are doing what they can to get kids moving, doing exercise, being active. Getting enough exercise also helps kid's do better in school. Being active also helps kids get strong.

There are extensive errors in spelling, capitalization, punctuation, grammar, usage, and sentence boundaries.

Many of the ideas in the essay do not focus on the topic.

The word choice shows the writer's lack of awareness of the essay's purpose and tone.

The essay's sentences are not purposeful, varied, or well-controlled. The writer's sentences decrease the effectiveness of the essay.

The essay is not well organized. Its structure does not support its purpose or respond well to the demands of the prompt.

The essay is not particularly thoughtful or engaging.

© Pearson Education, Inc., or its affiliates. All rights reserved.

TOOL KIT: WRITING

WRITING

MODEL

INFORMATIVE: SCORE 2

Kids, School, and Exercise: Problems and Solutions

In the past, children ran around a lot and did chores and other physical work. Today most kid's sit by a TV or computer screen or play with their phones. But children should be active for at least 60 minutes a day. Sadly, most don't get nearly that much exercise. And that's a big problem.

Some schools understand that it's a problem when students don't get enough exercise. Even though they have had to cut Physical Education classes due to budget cuts. Some also had to make recess shorter because there isn't enough time in the schedule. But they are working hard to find creative ways that don't cost too much or take up too much time to get kid's moving. Because there's only so much money in the budget, and only so much time in the day, and preparing to take tests takes lots of time.

Schools can use parent volunteers to teach kid's old-fashioned games such as kick-the-can, hopscotch, foursquare, tetherball, or jump rope. Kid's nowadays often don't know these games! Old-fashioned games are a great way to get kid's moving. Some schools have before school activities, such as games in the gym. Other schools have after school activities, such as bike riding or outdoor games. They can't count on kid's to be active on their own or at home.

A break during class can help students concentrate when they go back to work. There are all kinds of ways to move in the classroom. And you don't have to change your clothes or anything. Wiggling, stretching, and playing a short active game are all good ideas. Good teachers know how to squeeze in time during academic classes like math and language arts.

Not getting enough exercise is linked to many problems. For example, unhealthy wait, and high blood pressure and colesterol. When students don't' get enough exercise, they end up overweight.

Physical activity also helps kid's do better in school. Kids who exercise have better attendance rates. They have increased attention span. They act out less. They have less stress and learn more. Being active also helps muscles and bones. It increases strength and stamina.

Schools today are doing what they can to find a solution by being creative and making time for physical activity before, during, and after school. They understand that it is a problem when kid's don't get enough exercise.

Not all the ideas in the essay focus on the topic.

The writer uses some transitions and sentence connections.

Some of the ideas in the essay are reasonably well developed. Some details and examples add substance to the essay.

Some ideas are well developed. Some examples and details are well chosen and specific and add substance to the essay.

Some details are specific and well chosen.

There are errors in spelling, punctuation, grammar, usage, and sentence boundaries that decrease the effectiveness of the essay.

The essay is not well organized. Its organizing structure does not support its purpose well or respond well to the demands of the prompt.

© Pearson Education, Inc., or its affiliates. All rights reserved.

INFORMATIVE: SCORE 3

Kids, School, and Exercise: Problems and Solutions

A 2008 report said school-age children should be physically active for at least 60 minutes a day. Sadly, most children don't get nearly that much exercise. Lots of schools have cut Physical Education classes because of money and time pressures. And there's less recess than there used to be. Even at home when kids have a chance to run around, many choose screen time instead. No wonder so many of us are turning into chubby couch potatoes!

Not getting exercise is linked to many problems, for example unhealthy weight, and high blood pressure and cholesterol. Studies show physical activity also helps students do better in school: it means better attendance rates, increased attention span, fewer behavioral problems, less stress, and more learning. Being active helps develop strong muscles and bones. It increases strength and stamina.

Many schools around the country get that there are problems when students are inactive. They are working hard to find creative solutions that don't cost too much or take up precious time in the school schedule.

Some schools are using parent volunteers to teach kids active games such as kick-the-can, hopscotch, foursquare, tetherball, or jump rope. These games are more likely to get kids moving than just sitting gossiping with your friends or staring at your phone. Some schools have before school activities such as run-around games in the gym. Other schools have after school activities such as bike riding or outdoor games. They can't count on kids to be active on their own.

There are all kinds of fun and healthy ways to move in the classroom, without changing clothes. An active break during class can help students concentrate when they go back to work. Creative teachers know how to squeeze in active time even during academic classes. Wiggling, stretching, and playing a short active game are all good ideas.

Schools today understand that it is a problem when kids don't get enough exercise. They are doing what they can to find a solution by being creative and making time for physical activity before, during, and after school.

The essay is fairly thoughtful and engaging.

Almost all the ideas focus on the topic.

The ideas in the essay are well developed, with well-chosen and specific details and examples.

The writer uses transitions and connections, such as "Not getting exercise is linked…" "Many schools …" "Some schools…" "Other schools…"

Ideas in the essay are mostly well developed.

Words are chosen carefully and contribute to the clarity of the essay.

TOOL KIT: WRITING

© Pearson Education, Inc., or its affiliates. All rights reserved.

WRITING

MODEL

INFORMATIVE: SCORE 4

Kids, School, and Exercise: Problems and Solutions

In 2008, the U.S. Department of Health and Human Services published a report stating that all school-age children need to be physically active for at least 60 minutes a day. Sadly, most children don't get nearly the recommended amount of exercise. Due to budget cuts and time pressure, many schools have cut Physical Education classes. Even recess is being squeezed to make room for more tests and test preparation.

Lack of exercise can lead to many problems, such as unhealthy weight, high blood pressure, and high cholesterol. Physical activity helps develop strong muscles and bones, and it increases strength and stamina. Studies show physical activity leads to better attendance rates, increased attention span, fewer behavioral problems, less stress, and more learning. When kids don't get enough physical activity, a lot is at stake!

Many schools around the country are stepping up to find innovative solutions—even when they don't have time or money to spare. Some have started before-school activities such as active games in the gym. Others have after-school activities such as bike riding or outdoor games. Just a few extra minutes a day can make a big difference!

Some schools try to make the most of recess by using parent volunteers to teach kids active games such as kick-the-can, hopscotch, foursquare, tetherball, or jump rope. Volunteers can also organize races or tournaments—anything to get the kids going! At the end of recess, everyone should be a little bit out of breath.

Creative educators squeeze in active time even during academic classes. It could be a quick "brain break" to stretch in the middle of class, imaginary jump rope, or a game of rock-paper-scissors with legs instead of fingers. There are all kinds of imaginative ways to move in the classroom, without moving furniture or changing clothes. And research shows that an active break during class can help students focus when they go back to work.

Schools today understand the problems that can arise when kids don't have enough physical activity in their lives. They are meeting the challenge by finding opportunities for exercise before, during, and after school. After all, if students do well on tests but end up unhealthy and unhappy, what is the point?

The writer explains the problem and its causes.

The writer clearly lays out the effects of the problem.

The writer turns to the solution. The essay's organizing structure supports its purpose and responds to the demands of the prompt.

The writer includes specific examples and well-chosen details.

The progression of ideas is logical and well controlled.

Details and examples add substance to the essay.

The essay is thoughtful and engaging.

© Pearson Education, Inc., or its affiliates. All rights reserved.

TOOL KIT: WRITING

Informative Rubric

	Focus and Organization	Evidence and Elaboration	Conventions
4	The introduction is engaging and sets forth the topic in a compelling way. The ideas progress logically. A variety of transitions are included to show the relationship among ideas. The conclusion follows from the rest of the essay.	The topic is developed with relevant facts, definitions, details, quotations, and examples. The tone of the essay is formal. The vocabulary is precise and relevant to the topic, audience, and purpose.	The essay uses standard English conventions of usage and mechanics.
3	The introduction is somewhat engaging and sets forth the topic in a way that grabs readers' attention. The ideas progress somewhat logically. Some transitions are included to show the relationship among ideas. The conclusion mostly follows from the rest of the essay.	The topic is developed with some relevant facts, definitions, details, quotations, and other examples. The tone of the essay is mostly formal. The vocabulary is generally appropriate for the topic, audience, and purpose.	The essay demonstrates general accuracy in standard English conventions of usage and mechanics.
2	The introduction sets forth the topic. More than one idea is presented. A few transitions are included that show the relationship among ideas. The conclusion does not completely follow from the rest of the essay.	The topic is developed with a few relevant facts, definitions, details, quotations, or other examples. The tone of the essay is occasionally formal. The vocabulary is somewhat appropriate for the topic, audience, and purpose.	The essay demonstrates some accuracy in standard English conventions of usage and mechanics.
1	The topic is not clearly stated. Ideas do not follow a logical progression. Transitions are not included. The conclusion does not follow from the rest of the essay.	The topic is not developed with reliable or relevant evidence. The tone is informal. The vocabulary is limited or ineffective.	The essay contains mistakes in standard English conventions of usage and mechanics.

© Pearson Education, Inc., or its affiliates. All rights reserved.

WRITING

Narrative

Narrative writing conveys an experience, either real or imaginary, and uses time order to provide structure. Usually its purpose is to entertain, but it can also instruct, persuade, or inform. Whenever writers tell a story, they are using narrative writing. Most types of narrative writing share certain elements, such as characters, setting, a sequence of events, and, often, a theme.

Elements of a Narrative Text

A **narrative** is any type of writing that tells a story, whether it is fiction, nonfiction, poetry, or drama.

An effective nonfiction narrative contains these elements:

- an engaging beginning in which characters and setting are established
- characters who participate in the story events
- a well-structured, logical sequence of events
- details that show time and place
- effective story elements such as dialogue, description, and reflection
- a narrator who relates the events from a particular point of view
- use of language that brings the characters and setting to life

An effective fictional narrative usually contains these elements:

- an engaging beginning in which characters, setting, or a main conflict is introduced
- a main character and supporting characters who participate in the story events
- a narrator who relates the events of the plot from a particular point of view
- details that show time and place
- narrative techniques such as dialogue, description, and suspense
- use of language that vividly brings to life characters and events

© Pearson Education, Inc., or its affiliates. All rights reserved.

NARRATIVE: SCORE 1

Mind Scissors

There's a bike race. Right away people start losing. But me and Thad were winning. Thad is the kid who always wins is who is also popular. I don't like Thad. I pumped pumping hard at my pedals, I knew the end was coming. I looked ahead and all I could see was Thad, and the woods.

I pedaled harder and then I was up to Thad. That was swinging at me, I swerved, I kept looking at him, I was worried!

That's stick had untied my shoelace and it was wrapped around my pedal! But I didn't know it yet.

We were out of the woods. I still wanted to win, I pedaled even faster. than my pedals stopped!

I saw with my mind the shoelace was caught in my pedal. No worries, I have the superpower of mind scissors. That's when my mind looked down and I used my mind scissors. I used the mind scissors to cut the shoelace my right foot was free.

That's how I became a superhero. I save people with my mind scissors now.

The story's beginning is not clear or engaging.

The narrative does not include sensory language and precise words to convey experiences and to develop characters.

Events do not progress logically. The ideas seem disconnected, and the sentences do not include transitions.

The narrative contains mistakes in standard English conventions of usage and mechanics.

The conclusion does not connect to the narrative.

TOOL KIT: WRITING

© Pearson Education, Inc., or its affiliates. All rights reserved.

WRITING

TOOL KIT: WRITING

MODEL

NARRATIVE: SCORE 2

Mind-Scissors

When I was a baby I wound up with a tiny pair of scissors in my head. What the doctors couldn't have predicted is the uncanny ability they would give me. This past summer that was when I discovered what I could do with my mind-scissors.

Every summer there's a bike race. The kid who always wins is Thad who is popular.

The race starts. Right away racers start losing. After a long time pumping hard at my pedals, I knew the end was coming. I looked ahead and all I could see was Thad, and the woods.

I pedaled harder than ever. I was up to Thad. I turned my head to look at him. He was swinging a stick at me, I swerved, I kept looking at him, boy was I worried.

We were now out of the woods. Still hopeful I could win, I pedaled even faster. Suddenly, my pedals stopped!

Oh no! Thad's stick had untied my shoelace and it was wrapped around my pedal!

I was going to crash my bike. That's when my mind looked down. That's when I knew I could use my mind-scissors. I used the mind scissors to cut the shoelace my right foot was free.

That's how I won the race.

The story's beginning introduces the main character.

Events in the narrative progress somewhat logically, and the writer use some transition words.

The writer uses some description in the narrative.

The narrative demonstrates some accuracy in standard English conventions of usage and mechanics.

The words vary between vague and precise. The writer uses some sensory language.

The conclusion is weak and adds very little to the narrative.

© Pearson Education, Inc., or its affiliates. All rights reserved.

MODEL

NARRATIVE: SCORE 3

Mind-Scissors

When I was a baby I wound up with a tiny pair of scissors in my head. Lots of people live with pieces of metal in their heads. We just have to be careful. What the doctors couldn't have predicted is the uncanny ability they would give me.

Every summer there's a bike race that ends at the lake. The kid who always wins is Thad Thomas the Third, who is popular. This past summer that was about to change. It's also when I discovered what I could do with my mind-scissors.

The race starts. Right away racers start falling behind. After what seemed an eternity pumping hard at my pedals, I knew the end had to be in sight. I looked ahead and all I could see was Thad, and the opening to the woods—the last leg of the race.

I felt like steam was coming off my legs. I could see Thad's helmet. I turned my head to flash him a look. Only, Thad was the one who was gloating! And then I saw it—he was holding a stick he had pulled off a low-hanging branch.

He jabbed it toward me. I swerved out of the way. I kept pedaling, shifting my eyes to the right, to see what he was going to do.

But I waited too long. Then Thad made a slashing motion. Then he tossed the stick aside, yelled, "Yes!" and zoomed forward.

What happened? I felt nothing. We were now out of the woods and into the clearing before the finish line. Still hopeful I could win, I pedaled even faster. Suddenly, there was a jerk. My pedals had stopped!

I looked down. Oh no! My shoelace was wrapped around my pedal! Thad's stick had untied it!

I looked for a place to crash. That's when my head started tingling. I looked down at the shoelace. I concentrated really hard. I could see the scissors in my mind, floating just beside the pedal. Snip! The shoelace broke and my foot was free.

Thad was too busy listening to his fans cheer him on as I rode past him. Thanks to the mind-scissors, I won.

The story's beginning is engaging and clearly introduces the main character and situation.

Events in the narrative progress logically, and the writer uses transition words frequently.

The writer uses precise words and some sensory language to convey the experiences in the narrative and to describe the characters and scenes.

The writer uses some description and dialogue to add interest to the narrative and develop experiences and events.

The narrative demonstrates accuracy in standard English conventions of usage and mechanics.

The conclusion follows from the rest of the narrative.

© Pearson Education, Inc., or its affiliates. All rights reserved.

TOOL KIT: WRITING

WRITING

MODEL

NARRATIVE: SCORE 4

Mind-Scissors

As long as I wear my bike helmet, they say I'll be okay. Lots of people live with pieces of metal in their heads. We just have to be careful. When I was a baby I wound up with a tiny pair of scissors in mine. What the doctors couldn't have predicted is the uncanny ability they would give me.

Every summer there's a bike race that ends at the lake. The kid who always wins is Thad Thomas the Third, who is popular, but if you ask me, it's because he knows how to sweet-talk everyone. This past summer that was about to change. It's also when I discovered what I could do with my mind-scissors.

The race starts. Right away, racers start falling behind. After what seemed an eternity pumping hard at my pedals, I knew the end had to be in sight. I looked ahead and all I could see was Thad and the opening to the woods—the last leg of the race.

I put my stamina to the test—pedaling harder than ever, I felt like steam was coming off my legs. Thad's red helmet came into view. As I could sense I was going to overtake him any second, I turned my head to flash him a look. Only, to my befuddlement, Thad was the one who was gloating! And then I saw it—he was holding a stick he had pulled off a low-hanging branch.

He jabbed it toward me. I swerved out of the way. Was he trying to poke me with it? I kept pedaling, shifting my eyes to the right, to see what he was going to do.

But I waited too long. Thad made a slashing motion. Then he tossed the stick aside, yelled, "Yes!" and zoomed forward.

What happened? I felt nothing. We were now out of the woods and into the clearing before the finish line. Still hopeful I could win, I pedaled even faster. Suddenly, there was a jerk. My pedals had stopped!

I looked down. Oh no! My shoelace was wrapped around my pedal! Thad's stick had untied the shoelace!

I coasted as I looked for a place to crash. That's when my head started tingling. I got this funny notion to try something. I looked down. I had the tangled shoelace in my sights. I concentrated really hard. I could see the scissors in my mind, floating just beside the pedal. Snip! The shoelace broke and my right foot was free.

Thad was busy motioning his fans to cheer him on as I made my greatest effort to pedal back up to speed. Guess who made it to the finish line first?

The story's beginning is engaging and introduces the main character and situation in a way that appeals to a reader.

The writer uses techniques such as dialogue and description to add interest to the narrative and to develop the characters and events.

Events in the narrative progress in logical order and are linked by clear transitions.

Writer uses vivid description and sensory language to convey the experiences in the narrative and to help the reader imagine the characters and scenes.

The writer uses standard English conventions of usage and mechanics.

Writer's conclusion follows from the events in the narrative.

© Pearson Education, Inc., or its affiliates. All rights reserved.

Narrative Rubric

	Focus and Organization	Development of Ideas/Elaboration	Conventions
4	The introduction is engaging and introduces the characters and situation in a way that appeals to readers. Events in the narrative progress in logical order and are linked by clear transitions. The conclusion effectively follows from and reflects on the narrated experiences or events.	The narrative effectively includes techniques such as dialogue and description to add interest and to develop the characters and events. The narrative effectively includes precise words and phrases, relevant descriptive details, and sensory language to convey experiences and events. The narrative effectively establishes voice through word choice, sentence structure, and tone.	The narrative intentionally uses standard English conventions of usage and mechanics. The narrative effectively varies sentence patterns for meaning, reader interest, and style.
3	The introduction is somewhat engaging and clearly introduces the characters and situation. Events in the narrative progress logically and are often linked by transition words. The conclusion mostly follows from and reflects on the narrated experiences or events.	The narrative mostly includes dialogue and description to add interest and develop experiences and events. The narrative mostly includes precise words and sensory language to convey experiences and events. The narrative mostly establishes voice through word choice, sentence structure, and tone.	The narrative mostly demonstrates accuracy in standard English conventions of usage and mechanics. The narrative mostly varies sentence patterns for meaning, reader interest, and style.
2	The introduction occasionally introduces characters. Events in the narrative progress somewhat logically and are sometimes linked by transition words. The conclusion adds very little to the narrated experiences or events.	The narrative includes some dialogue and descriptions. The words in the narrative vary between vague and precise, and some sensory language is included. The narrative occasionally establishes voice through word choice, sentence structure, and tone.	The narrative demonstrates some accuracy in standard English conventions of usage and mechanics. The narrative occasionally varies sentence patterns for meaning, reader interest, and style.
1	The introduction does not introduce characters and an experience or there is no clear introduction. The events in the narrative do not progress logically. The ideas seem disconnected and the sentences are not linked by transitions. The conclusion does not connect to the narrative or there is no conclusion.	Dialogue and descriptions are not included in the narrative. The narrative does not incorporate sensory language or precise words to convey experiences and to develop characters. The narrative does not establish voice through word choice, sentence structure, and tone.	The narrative contains mistakes in standard English conventions of usage and mechanics. The narrative does not vary sentence patterns for meaning, reader interest, and style.

© Pearson Education, Inc., or its affiliates. All rights reserved.

TOOL KIT: WRITING

RESEARCH

Conducting Research

You can conduct research to gain more knowledge about a topic. Sources such as articles, books, interviews, or the Internet have the facts and explanations that you need. Not all of the information that you find, however, will be useful—or reliable. Strong research skills will help you find accurate information about your topic.

Narrowing or Broadening a Topic

The first step in any research is finding your topic. Choose a topic that is narrow enough to cover completely. If you can name your topic in just one or two words, it is probably too broad. Topics such as mythology, hip hop music, or Italy are too broad to cover in a single report. Narrow a broad topic into smaller subcategories.

When you begin to research, pay attention to the amount of information available. If there is way too much information on your topic, you may need to narrow your topic further.

You might also need to broaden a topic if there is not enough information for your purpose. A topic is too narrow when it can be thoroughly presented in less space than the required size of your assignment. It might also be too narrow if you can find little or no information in library and media sources. Broaden your topic by including other related ideas.

Generating Research Questions

Use research questions to focus your research. Specific questions can help you avoid wasting time. For example, instead of simply hunting for information about Peter Pan, you might ask, "What inspired J. M. Barrie to write the story of Peter Pan?" or "How have different artists shown Peter Pan?"

A research question may also lead you to find your topic sentence. The question can also help you focus your research plan. Write your question down and keep it in mind while you hunt for facts. Your question can prevent you from gathering unnecessary details. As you learn more about your topic, you can always rewrite your original question.

© Pearson Education, Inc., or its affiliates. All rights reserved.

Consulting Print and Digital Sources

An effective research project combines information from multiple sources. It is important not to rely too heavily on a single source. The creativity and originality of your research depends on how you combine ideas from many places. Plan to include a variety of these resources:

- **Primary and Secondary Sources:** Use both primary sources (firsthand or original accounts, such as interview transcripts and newspaper articles) and secondary sources (accounts that are not created at the time of an event, such as encyclopedia entries).

- **Print and Digital Resources:** The Internet allows fast access to data, but print resources are often edited more carefully. Plan to include both print and digital resources in order to guarantee that your work is accurate.

- **Media Resources:** You can find valuable information in media resources such as documentaries, television programs, podcasts, and museum exhibitions.

- **Original Research:** Depending on your topic, you may wish to conduct original research to include among your sources. For example, you might interview experts or eyewitnesses or conduct a survey of people in your community.

Evaluating Sources It is important to evaluate the credibility and accuracy of any information you find. Ask yourself questions such as these to evaluate other sources:

- **Authority:** Is the author well known? What are the author's credentials? Does the source include references to other reliable sources? Does the author's tone win your confidence? Why or why not?

- **Bias:** Does the author have any obvious biases? What is the author's purpose for writing? Who is the target audience?

- **Currency:** When was the work created? Has it been revised? Is there more current information available?

Using Online Encyclopedias

Online encyclopedias are often written by anonymous contributors who are not required to fact-check information. These sites can be very useful as a launching point for research, but should not be considered accurate. Look for footnotes, endnotes, or hyperlinks that support facts with reliable sources that have been carefully checked by editors.

© Pearson Education, Inc., or its affiliates. All rights reserved.

TOOL KIT: RESEARCH

RESEARCH

Using Search Terms

Finding information on the Internet is easy, but it can be a challenge to find facts that are useful and trustworthy. If you type a word or phrase into a search engine, you will probably get hundreds—or thousands—of results. However, those results are not guaranteed to be relevant or accurate.

These strategies can help you find information from the Internet:

- Create a list of topic keywords before you begin using a search engine. Use a thesaurus to expand your list.
- Enter six to eight keywords.
- Choose unique nouns. Most search engines ignore articles and prepositions. Verbs may lead to sources that are not useful. Use modifiers, such as adjectives, when necessary to specify a category. For example, you might enter "ancient Rome" instead of "Rome."
- Use quotation marks to focus a search. Place a phrase in quotation marks to find pages that include exactly that phrase. Add several phrases in quotation marks to narrow your results.
- Spell carefully. Many search engines correct spelling automatically, but they cannot catch every spelling error.
- Scan search results before you click them. The first result isn't always the most useful. Read the text and notice the domain before make a choice.
- Consult more than one search engine.

Evaluating Internet Domains

Not everything you read on the Internet is true, so you have to evaluate sources carefully. The last three letters of an Internet URL identify the site's domain, which can help you evaluate the information of the site.

- **.gov**—Government sites are sponsored by a branch of the United States federal government and are considered reliable.
- **.edu**—Information from an educational research center or department is likely to be carefully checked, but may include student pages that are not edited or monitored.
- **.org**—Organizations are nonprofit groups and usually maintain a high level of credibility but may still reflect strong biases.
- **.com** and **.net**—Commercial sites exist to make a profit. Information might be biased to show a product or service in a good light.

© Pearson Education, Inc., or its affiliates. All rights reserved.

Taking Notes

Use different strategies to take notes:

- Use index cards to create notecards and source cards. On each source card, record information about each source you use—author, title, publisher, date of publication, and relevant page numbers. On each notecard, record information to use in your writing. Use quotation marks when you copy exact words, and indicate the page number(s) on which the information appears.
- Photocopy articles and copyright pages. Then, highlight relevant information. Remember to include the Web addresses of printouts from online sources.
- Print articles from the Internet or copy them directly into a "notes" folder.

You will use these notes to help you write original text.

Source Card

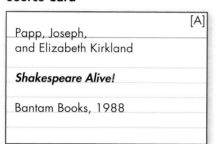

[A]
Papp, Joseph,
and Elizabeth Kirkland

Shakespeare Alive!

Bantam Books, 1988

Notecard

Only the upper classes could read.

Most of the common people in Shakespeare's time could not read.
Source Card: A, p. 5.

Quote Accurately Responsible research begins with the first note you take. Be sure to quote and paraphrase your sources accurately so you can identify these sources later. In your notes, circle all quotations and paraphrases to distinguish them from your own comments. When photocopying from a source, include the copyright information. Include the Web addresses of printouts from online sources.

© Pearson Education, Inc., or its affiliates. All rights reserved.

▶ RESEARCH

Reviewing Research Findings

You will need to review your findings to be sure that you have collected enough accurate and appropriate information.

Considering Audience and Purpose

Always keep your audience in mind as you gather information. Different audiences may have very different needs. For example, if you are writing a report for your class about a topic you have studied together, you will not need to provide background information in your writing. However, if you are writing about the topic for a national student magazine, you cannot assume that all of your readers have the same information. You will need to provide background facts from reliable sources to help inform those readers about your subject. When thinking about your research and your audience, ask yourself:

- Who am I writing for?
- Have I collected enough information to explain my topic to this audience?
- Do I need to conduct more research to explain my topic clearly?
- Are there details in my research that I can leave out because they are already familiar to my audience?

Your purpose for writing will also affect your research review. If you are researching to satisfy your own curiosity, you can stop researching when you feel you understand the answer completely. If you are writing a research report that will be graded, you need to think about your assignment. When thinking about whether or not you have enough information, ask yourself:

- What is my purpose for writing?
- Will the information I have gathered be enough to achieve my purpose?
- If I need more information, where might I find it?

Synthesizing Sources

Effective research writing is more than just a list of facts and details. Good research synthesizes—gathers, orders, and interprets—those elements. These strategies will help you synthesize effectively:

- Review your notes. Look for connections and patterns among the details you have collected.
- Organize notes or notecards to help you plan how you will combine details.
- Pay close attention to details that emphasize the same main idea.
- Also look for details that challenge each other. For many topics, there is no single correct opinion. You might decide to conduct additional research to help you decide which side of the issue has more support.

© Pearson Education, Inc., or its affiliates. All rights reserved.

Types of Evidence

When reviewing your research, also think about the kinds of evidence you have collected. The strongest writing combines a variety of evidence. This chart describes three of the most common types of evidence.

TYPE OF EVIDENCE	DESCRIPTION	EXAMPLE
Statistical evidence includes facts and other numerical data used to support a claim or explain a topic.	Statistical evidence are facts about a topic, such as historical dates, descriptions about size and number, and poll results.	Jane Goodall began to study chimpanzees when she was 26 years old.
Testimonial evidence includes any ideas or opinions presented by others. Testimonies might be from experts or people with special knowledge about a topic.	Firsthand testimonies present ideas from eyewitnesses to events or subjects being discussed.	Goodall's view of chimps has changed: "When I first started at Gombe, I thought the chimps were nicer than we are. But time has revealed that they are not. They can be just as awful."
	Secondary testimonies include commentaries on events by people who were not directly involved.	Science writer David Quammen points out that Goodall "set a new standard, a very high standard, for behavioral study of apes in the wild."
Anecdotal evidence presents one person's view of the world, often by describing specific events or incidents.	An anecdote is a story about something that happened. Personal stories can be part of effective research, but they should not be the only kind of evidence presented. Anecdotes are particularly useful for proving that broad generalizations are not accurate.	It is not fair to say that it is impossible for dogs to use tools. One researcher reports the story of a dog that learned to use a large bone as a back scratcher.

© Pearson Education, Inc., or its affiliates. All rights reserved.

TOOL KIT: RESEARCH

RESEARCH

Incorporating Research Into Writing

Avoiding Plagiarism

Whether you are presenting a formal research paper or an opinion paper on a current event, you must be careful to give credit for any ideas or opinions that are not your own. Presenting someone else's ideas, research, or opinion as your own—even if you have phrased it in different words—is *plagiarism*, the equivalent of academic stealing, or fraud.

Do not use the ideas or research of others in place of your own. Read from several sources to draw your own conclusions and form your own opinions. Incorporate the ideas and research of others to support your points. Credit the source of the following types of support:

- Statistics
- Direct quotations
- Indirectly quoted statements of opinions
- Conclusions presented by an expert
- Facts available in only one or two sources

When you are drafting and revising, circle any words or ideas that are not your own. Follow the instructions on pages R32 and R33 to correctly cite those passages.

Reviewing for Plagiarism Take time to review your writing for accidental plagiarism. Read what you have written and take note of any ideas that do not have your personal writing voice. Compare those passages with your resource materials. You might have copied them without remembering the exact source. Add a correct citation to give credit to the original author. If you cannot find the questionable phrase in your notes, think about revising your word choices. You want to be sure that your final writing reflects your own thinking and not someone else's work.

Quoting and Paraphrasing

When including ideas from research into your writing, you will decide to quote directly or paraphrase.

Direct Quotation Use the author's exact words when they are interesting or persuasive. You might decide to include direct quotations in these situations:

- to share a strong statement
- to reference a historically significant passage
- to show that an expert agrees with your position
- to present an argument to which you will respond

Include complete quotations, without deleting or changing words. If you need to leave out words for space or clarity, use ellipsis points to show where you removed words. Enclose direct quotations in quotation marks.

© Pearson Education, Inc., or its affiliates. All rights reserved.

Paraphrase A paraphrase restates an author's ideas in your own words. Be careful to paraphrase accurately. Beware of making sweeping generalizations in a paraphrase that were not made by the original author. You may use some words from the original source, but a good paraphrase does more than simply rearrange an author's phrases, or replace a few words with synonyms.

Original Text	"Some teens doing homework while listening to music and juggling tweets and texts may actually work better that way, according to an intriguing new study performed by two high-school seniors." *Sumathi Reddy, "Teen Researchers Defend Media Multitasking"*
Patchwork Plagiarism phrases from the original are rearranged, but they too closely follow the original text.	An intriguing new study conducted by two high-school seniors suggests that teens work better when they are listening to music and juggling texts and tweets.
Good Paraphrase	Two high-school students studied homework habits. They concluded that some people do better work while multitasking, such as studying and listening to music or checking text messages at the same time.

Maintaining the Flow of Ideas

Effective research writing is much more that just a list of facts. Maintain the flow of ideas by connecting research information to your own ideas. Instead of simply stating a piece of evidence, use transitions to connect information you found from outside resources and your own thinking. The transitions in the box on the page can be used to introduce, compare, contrast, and clarify.

Choosing an effective organizational strategy for your writing will help you create a logical flow of ideas. Once you have chosen a clear organization, add research in appropriate places to provide evidence and support.

Useful Transitions

When providing examples:

for example   for instance   to illustrate   in [name of resource], [author]

When comparing and contrasting ideas or information:

in the same way   similarly   however   on the other hand

When clarifying ideas or opinions:

in other words   that is   to explain   to put it another way

© Pearson Education, Inc., or its affiliates. All rights reserved.

RESEARCH

ORGANIZATIONAL STRUCTURE	USES
Chronological order presents information in the sequence in which it happens.	historical topics; science experiments; analysis of narratives
Part-to-whole order examines how several categories affect a larger subject.	analysis of social issues; historical topics
Order of importance presents information in order of increasing or decreasing importance.	persuasive arguments; supporting a bold or challenging thesis
Comparison-and-contrast organization presents similarities and differences.	addressing two or more subjects

Formats for Citing Sources

When you cite a source, you acknowledge where you found your information and you give your readers the details necessary for locating the source themselves. Within the body of a paper, you provide a short citation, a footnote number linked to a footnote, or an endnote number linked to an endnote reference. These brief references show the page numbers on which you found the information. Prepare a reference list at the end of a research report to provide full bibliographic information on your sources. These are two common types of reference lists:

- A bibliography provides a listing of all the resources you consulted during your research.
- A works-cited list indicates the works your have referenced in your writing.

The chart on the next page shows the Modern Language Association format for crediting sources. This is the most common format for papers written in the content areas in middle school and high school. Unless instructed otherwise by your teacher, use this format for crediting sources.

Focus on Citations When you revise your writing, check that you cite the sources for quotations, factual information, and ideas that are not your own. Most word-processing programs have features that allow you to create footnotes and endnotes.

Identifying Missing Citations These strategies can help you find facts and details that should be cited in your writing:

- Look for facts that are not general knowledge. If a fact was unique to one source, it needs a citation.
- Read your report aloud. Listen for words and phrases that do not sound like your writing style. You might have picked them up from a source. If so, use you notes to find the source, place the words in quotation marks, and give credit.
- Review your notes. Look for ideas that you used in your writing but did not cite.

© Pearson Education, Inc., or its affiliates. All rights reserved.

MLA (8th Edition) Style for Listing Sources

Book with one author	Pyles, Thomas. *The Origins and Development of the English Language.* 2nd ed., Harcourt Brace Jovanovich, 1971. [Indicate the edition or version number when relevant.]
Book with two authors	Pyles, Thomas, and John Algeo. *The Origins and Development of the English Language.* 5th ed., Cengage Learning, 2004.
Book with three or more authors	Donald, Robert B., et al. *Writing Clear Essays.* Prentice Hall, 1983.
Book with an editor	Truth, Sojourner. *Narrative of Sojourner Truth.* Edited by Margaret Washington, Vintage Books, 1993.
Introduction to a work in a published edition	Washington, Margaret. Introduction. *Narrative of Sojourner Truth,* by Sojourner Truth, edited by Washington, Vintage Books, 1993, pp. v–xi.
Single work in an anthology	Hawthorne, Nathaniel. "Young Goodman Brown." *Literature: An Introduction to Reading and Writing,* edited by Edgar V. Roberts and Henry E. Jacobs, 5th ed., Prentice Hall, 1998, pp. 376–385. [Indicate pages for the entire selection.]
Signed article from an encyclopedia	Askeland, Donald R. "Welding." *World Book Encyclopedia,* vol. 21, World Book, 1991, p. 58.
Signed article in a weekly magazine	Wallace, Charles. "A Vodacious Deal." *Time,* 14 Feb. 2000, p. 63.
Signed article in a monthly magazine	Gustaitis, Joseph. "The Sticky History of Chewing Gum." *American History,* Oct. 1998, pp. 30–38.
Newspaper article	Thurow, Roger. "South Africans Who Fought for Sanctions Now Scrap for Investors." *Wall Street Journal,* 11 Feb. 2000, pp. A1+. [For a multipage article that does not appear on consecutive pages, write only the first page number on which it appears, followed by the plus sign.]
Unsigned editorial or story	"Selective Silence." Editorial. *Wall Street Journal,* 11 Feb. 2000, p. A14. [If the editorial or story is signed, begin with the author's name.]
Signed pamphlet or brochure	[Treat the pamphlet as though it were a book.]
Work from a library subscription service	Ertman, Earl L. "Nefertiti's Eyes." *Archaeology,* Mar.–Apr. 2008, pp. 28–32. *Kids Search,* EBSCO, New York Public Library. Accessed 7 Jan. 2017. [Indicating the date you accessed the information is optional but recommended.]
Filmstrips, slide programs, videocassettes, DVDs, and other audiovisual media	*The Diary of Anne Frank.* 1959. Directed by George Stevens, performances by Millie Perkins, Shelley Winters, Joseph Schildkraut, Lou Jacobi, and Richard Beymer, Twentieth Century Fox, 2004. [Indicating the original release date after the title is optional but recommended.]
CD-ROM (with multiple publishers)	Simms, James, editor. *Romeo and Juliet.* By William Shakespeare, Attica Cybernetics / BBC Education / Harper, 1995.
Radio or television program transcript	"Washington's Crossing of the Delaware." *Weekend Edition Sunday,* National Public Radio, 23 Dec. 2013. Transcript.
Web page	"Fun Facts About Gum." ICGA, 2005–2017, www.gumassociation.org/index.cfm/facts-figures/fun-facts-about-gum. Accessed 19 Feb. 2017. [Indicating the date you accessed the information is optional but recommended.]
Personal interview	Smith, Jane. Personal interview, 10 Feb. 2017.

All examples follow the style given in the MLA Handbook, 8th edition, published in 2016.

© Pearson Education, Inc., or its affiliates. All rights reserved.

TOOL KIT: RESEARCH

TOOL KIT: PROGRAM RESOURCES

MODEL

Evidence Log

Unit Title: Discovery

Perfomance-Based Assessment Prompt:
Do all discoveries benefit humanity?

My initial thoughts:
Yes - all knowledge moves us forward.

As you read multiple texts about a topic, your thinking may change. Use an Evidence Log like this one to record your thoughts, to track details you might use in later writing or discussion, and to make further connections.

Here is a sample to show how one reader's ideas deepened as she read two texts.

Title of Text: Classifying the Stars   Date: Sept. 17

CONNECTION TO THE PROMPT	TEXT EVIDENCE/DETAILS	ADDITIONAL NOTES/IDEAS
Newton shared his discoveries and then other scientists built on his discoveries.	Paragraph 2: "Isaac Newton gave to the world the results of his experiments on passing sunlight through a prism." Paragraph 3: "In 1814 . . . the German optician, Fraunhofer . . . saw that the multiple spectral tints . . . were crossed by hundreds of fine dark lines."	It's not always clear how a discovery might benefit humanity in the future.

How does this text change or add to my thinking? This confirms what I think.   Date: Sept. 20

Title of Text: Cell Phone Mania   Date: Sept. 21

CONNECTION TO THE PROMPT	TEXT EVIDENCE/DETAILS	ADDITIONAL NOTES/IDEAS
Cell phones have made some forms of communication easier, but people don't talk to each other as much as they did in the past.	Paragraph 7: "Over 80% of young adults state that texting is their primary method of communicating with friends. This contrasts with older adults who state that they prefer a phone call."	Is it good that we don't talk to each other as much? Look for article about social media to learn more about this question.

How does this text change or add to my thinking?   Date: Sept. 25
Maybe there are some downsides to discoveries. I still think that knowledge moves us forward, but sometimes there are negative effects.

© Pearson Education, Inc., or its affiliates. All rights reserved.

Word Network

A word network is a collection of words related to a topic. As you read the selections in a unit, identify interesting theme-related words and build your vocabulary by adding them to your Word Network.

Use your Word Network as a resource for your discussions and writings. Here is an example:

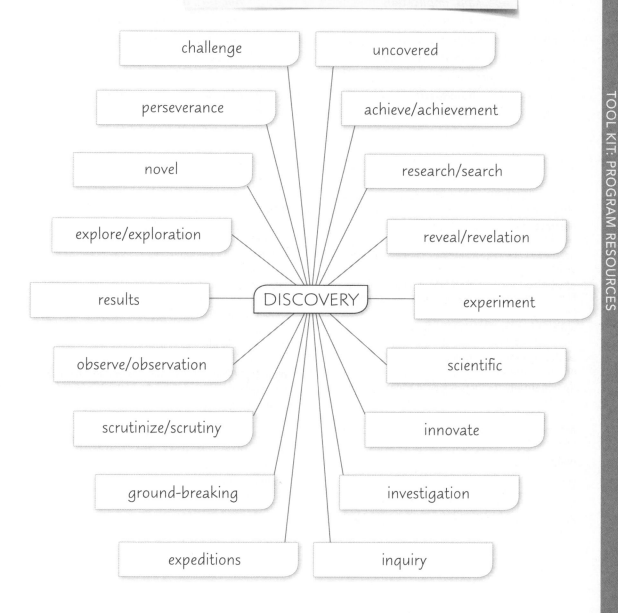

© Pearson Education, Inc., or its affiliates. All rights reserved.

ACACDEMIC / CONCEPT VOCABULARY

Academic vocabulary appears in **blue type**.

Pronunciation Key

Symbol	Sample Words	Symbol	Sample Words
a	*at, catapult, Alabama*	oo	*boot, soup, crucial*
ah	*father, charms, argue*	ow	*now, stout, flounder*
ai	*care, various, hair*	oy	*boy, toil, oyster*
aw	*law, maraud, caution*	s	*say, nice, press*
awr	*pour, organism, forewarn*	sh	*she, abolition, motion*
ay	*ape, sails, implication*	u	*full, put, book*
ee	*even, teeth, really*	uh	*ago, focus, contemplation*
eh	*ten, repel, elephant*	ur	*bird, urgent, perforation*
ehr	*merry, verify, terribly*	y	*by, delight, identify*
ih	*it, pin, hymn*	yoo	*music, confuse, few*
o	*shot, hopscotch, condo*	zh	*pleasure, treasure, vision*
oh	*own, parole, rowboat*		

A

absorbing (ab ZAWR bihng) *v.* learning; fully taking in

abstract (AB strakt) *adj.* expressed in a way that is not specific or realistic

aesthetic (ehs THEHT ihk) *adj.* having to do with beauty or art

animation (an uh MAY shuhn) *n.* process of making films or cartoons from drawings, computer graphics, or photos

antagonism (an TAG uh nihz uhm) *n.* hostility; state of being opposed to someone

anxiously (ANGK shuhs lee) *adv.* in a worried, uneasy manner; nervously

apologetically (uh pol uh JEHT ihk lee) *adv.* in a way that shows someone is sorry for having done or said something; regretfully

assume (uh SOOM) *v.* take for granted; take on, as a role or responsibility

audio (AW dee oh) *n.* recorded sound

B

blossom (BLOS uhm) *n.* state of bearing flowers

beware (bee WAIR) *v.* act carefully in case there is danger

C

certain (SUR tuhn) *adj.* without a doubt; reliable; particular

clenched (klehncht) *adj.* gripped tightly

coherent (koh HIHR uhnt) *adj.* logical; clearly communicated

community (kuh MYOO nuh tee) *n.* people or animals who exist together in a place

compel (kuhm PEHL) *v.* force; command

compromise (KOM pruh myz) *n.* settlement of a disagreement in which each side gives up part of what it wanted

compulsory (kuhm PUHL suhr ee) *adj.* that must be done; required

consequently (kon suh KWEHNT lee) *adv.* as a result; therefore

consumed (kuhn SOOMD) *adj.* absorbed; occupied

consideration (kuhn sihd uh RAY shuhn) *n.* careful thought

continuation (kuhn tihn yoo AY shuhn) *n.* state of going on without interruption; unbroken action

© Pearson Education, Inc., or its affiliates. All rights reserved.

contribute (kuhn TRIHB yoot) *v.* give or provide along with others

convince (kuhn VIHNS) *v.* persuade

critical (KRIHT uh kuhl) *adj.* disapproving or having a negative opinion about; very important

cultivate (KUHL tuh vayt) *v.* prepare the soil for planting crops

curiosity (kyoo ree OS uh tee) *n.* eager desire to know

cut-out animation (KUHT owt) (an uh MAY shuhn) *n.* technique that uses flat characters, backgrounds, and props cut from materials such as paper, cardboard, and fabric

D

declare (dih KLAIR) *v.* make a statement; announce

deliberate (dih LIHB uhr iht) *adj.* carefully thought over in advance; planned

desperate (DEHS puhr iht) *adj.* suffering extreme need or frustration; with little hope

destination (dehs tuh NAY shuhn) *n.* place where someone or something is going

devouring (dih VOW rihng) *v.* taking in greedily

dialogue (DY uh log) *n.* spoken conversation between or among characters

digesting (dih JEH stihng) *v.* thinking over; mentally taking in

disgusted (dihs GUHS tihd) *adj.* feeling a strong dislike; annoyed

distraught (dihs TRAWT) *adj.* very troubled and unhappy

distressed (dih STREHST) *adj.* troubled; upset

domesticated (duh MEHS tuh kay tihd) *adj.* changed from a wild state to a tame state

dominate (DOM uh nayt) *v.* rule or control

E

elaborate (ih LAB uh rayt) *v.* explain by adding more details

enactment (ehn AKT muhnt) *n.* state of being made into law

encapsulation (ehn kap suh LAY shuhn) *n.* choice of important scenes to display in each panel

endurance test (ehn DUR uhns) (tehst) *n.* test to measure the ability of a person to deal with physical activity

entitled (ehn TY tuhld) *v.* had certain rights given to; earned certain rights

exclude (ehk SKLOOD) *v.* shut out; keep from entering, happening, or being

expedition (ehks puh DIHSH uhn) *n.* journey or trip made for a special purpose

F

feathery (FEH<u>TH</u> uhr ee) *adj.* light and airy, like the touch of a feather

foe (foh) *n.* enemy

G

gradually (GRAJ oo uhl ee) *adv.* in a way that is little by little

H

host (hohst) *n.* someone who introduces and talks to the guests on a television or radio program

humming (HUHM ihng) *v.* singing with closed lips and without words

I

ignorance (IHG nuhr uhns) *n.* state of lacking knowledge, learning, or information

illustrate (IHL uh strayt) *v.* provide pictures, diagrams or maps that explain or decorate; provide an example that demonstrates an idea

images or graphics (IHM uh jihz) (GRAF ihks) *n.* representations of a person or thing

impetuous (ihm PEHCH yoo uhs) *adj.* acting suddenly with little thought

inker (IHNGK uhr) *n.* artist who goes over the penciled art in ink

insincerity (ihn sihn SEHR uh tee) *n.* lack of honesty; untruthfulness

inspire (ihn SPYR) *v.* influence; stimulate creative effort

intensity (ihn TEHN suh tee) *n.* great focus or concentration; strong commitment

interview (IHN tuhr vyoo) *n.* recorded conversation in which someone is asked questions about his or her life, experiences, or opinions

invaded (ihn VAYD ihd) *v.* attacked; entered with force

irritable (IHR uh tuh buhl) *adj.* easily annoyed or angered

J

journeys (JUR neez) *n.* trips from one place to another

L

lamented (luh MEHN tihd) *v.* said in a way that showed sadness or sorrow

letterer (LEHT uhr uhr) *n.* artist who letters the dialogue and captions

light and shadow (lyt) (SHAD oh) drawing techniques that add depth to an image

loftily (LAWF tih lee) *adv.* in a superior manner

loneliness (LOHN lee nihs) *n.* feeling of being alone or isolated from others

© Pearson Education, Inc., or its affiliates. All rights reserved.

M

malicious (muh LIHSH uhs) *adj.* having or showing bad intentions

memorize (MEHM uh ryz) *v.* learn well enough to later recall; learn by heart

microchips (MY kroh chihps) *n.* small pieces of computer technology that have integrated circuits

milled (mihld) *v.* moved about in a confused way

misapprehension (mihs ap ree HEHN shuhn) *n.* incorrect understanding; wrong idea

miserable (MIHZ uhr uh buhl) *adj.* extremely unhappy or uncomfortable

model (MOD uhl) *n.* set of ideas to be followed as a plan or an example

mournfully (MAWRN fuh lee) *adv.* in a way that expresses grief or sadness

N

narrator (NA ray tuhr) *n.* person who tells a story

nonchalantly (non shuh LONT lee) *adv.* done in an unconcerned way

nostalgic (nuhs TAL jihk) *adj.* longing for the past

notable (NOHT uh buhl) *adj.* worthy of notice; remarkable; important

novelty (NOV uhl tee) *n.* something new, fresh, or unusual

O

object animation (OB jehkt) (an uh MAY shuhn) *n.* form that involves the movement of non-drawn objects, such as a book or a pen

objective (uhb JEHK tihv) *n.* aim or goal

obsessive (uhb SEHS ihv) *adj.* tending to think or worry so much about something that you cannot think about anything else

obstacle (OB stuh kuhl) *n.* something that stands in the way or stops progress

offended (uh FEHND ihd) *v.* hurt the feelings of someone; affected in an unpleasant way

P

panel (PAN uhl) *n.* individual frame of a comic, depicting a single moment

parameters (puh RAM uh tuhrz) *n.* boundaries; characteristics

pathetically (puh THEHT ihk lee) *adv.* in a way that causes someone to feel pity

patiently (PAY shuhnt lee) *adv.* bearing annoyance, hardship, or pain calmly and without complaint or anger

peeped (peept) *v.* looked through a small hole or crack; looked without being noticed

penciler (PEHN suhl uhr) *n.* artist who sketches the basic layout for each panel

perspective (puhr SPEHK tihv) *n.* point of view; ability to see how ideas relate to one another

pessimistic (pehs uh MIHS tihk) *adj.* expecting the worst; focused on the bad aspects of a situation

pixels (PIHK suhlz) *n.* smallest elements of an image that can be individually processed in a video display system

podcast (POD kast) *n.* digital audio or video file or recording, usually part of a series, that can be downloaded from the Internet

presume (prih ZOOM) *v.* take for granted; assume something to be the case

process (PROS ehs) *v.* gain an understanding of

program manager (PROH gram) (MAN ih juhr) *n.* person who is in charge of a project

purist (PYOOR ihst) *n.* someone who is strict about following traditional ways

Q

quest (kwehst) *n.* long search undertaken in order to find or realize something

quivering (KWIHV uhr ihng) *n.* trembling; shivering

R

real-time animation (REEL tym) (an uh MAY shuhn) *n.* style in which animated events or objects are reproduced so that they appear to be occurring or moving at the same speed they would in real life

recognize (REHK uhg nyz) *v.* identify something from memory or description; acknowledge as worthy of appreciation; honor

reflect (rih FLEHKT) *v.* think carefully

refugee (rehf yoo JEE) *n.* person who flees to another country to escape danger, as in time of war

relentlessly (rih LEHNT lihs lee) *adv.* without stopping; with determination

respected (rih SPEHK tihd) *adj.* honored; treated with esteem

S

sample group (SAM puhl) (groop) *n.* group of people that are taken from a larger group and studied

shushes (SHUHSH ihz) *v.* tells or signals someone to be quiet

shyly (SHY lee) *adv.* in a shy manner; in a bashful way

silently (SY luhnt lee) *adv.* without noise

skittered (SKIHT uhrd) *v.* moved lightly or quickly

slain (slayn) *v.* killed

sorrowfully (SAWR oh fuhl ee) *adv.* done with sadness

speculate (SPEHK yuh layt) *v.* guess, using information that is uncertain or incomplete

speech balloon (speech) *(buh* LOON) *n.* display of what a character is speaking or thinking

© Pearson Education, Inc., or its affiliates. All rights reserved.

squish (skwihsh) *n.* spongy, cushioned feeling when walking on a flexible surface

stage directions (stayj) (duh REHK shuhnz) important information that is provided by the playwright about the setting, characters, and action

stubborn (STUB uhrn) *adj.* refusing to give in, obey, or accept

sufficient (suh FIHSH uhnt) *adj.* as much as needed

surmise (suhr MYZ) *v.* guess, using only intuition or imagination

suspiciously (suh SPIHSH uhs lee) *adv.* based on a lack of trust or belief; disbelievingly; cautiously

T

template (TEHM pliht) *n.* pattern or shape to be used as an example

tenseness (TEHNS nihs) *n.* tightness in the muscles of the body

thorough (THUR oh) *adj.* including everything possible; careful and complete

thoughtfully (THAWT fuhl lee) *adv.* showing careful consideration or attention

threateningly (THREHT uhn ihng lee) *adv.* in a frightening or alarming way

timidly (TIHM ihd lee) *adv.* in a shy or fearful way; cautiously

transform (trans FAWRM) *v.* convert or change

trek (trehk) *n.* difficult, slow, or long journey

trigonometry (trihg uh NOM uh tree) *n.* field of math that deals with the relationships between the sides and angles of triangles

twirl (twurl) *v.* turn around and around quickly

twist (twihst) *v.* wind or spin around one another

V

valid (VAL ihd) *adj.* acceptable; based on and supported by facts

vanished (VAN ihsht) *v.* disappeared

various (VAIR ee uhs) *adj.* different from one another

violent (VY uh luhnt) *adj.* using strong, rough force that causes injury

voiceover (VOYS oh vuhr) *n.* voice commenting on the action or narrating a film off-camera

W

wild (wyld) *adj.* living in nature without human control; not tame

wondered (WUHN duhrd) *v.* thought about; questioned

wrath (rath) *n.* intense anger

© Pearson Education, Inc., or its affiliates. All rights reserved.

VOCABULARIO ACADÉMICO / VOCABULARIO DE CONCEPTOS

El vocabulario académico está en **letra azul**.

A

absorbing / asimilando *v.* aprendiendo; adquiriendo conocimientos por completo

abstract / abstracto *adj.* expresado de manera no específica ni realista

aesthetic / estético *adj.* relacionado con la belleza o el arte

animation / animación *s.* proceso de crear películas o caricaturas a partir de dibujos, gráficas de computadora o fotos

antagonism / antagonismo *s.* hostilidad; estado de oponerse a una persona

anxiously / ansiosamente *adv.* de manera estresada y nerviosa

apologetically / arrepentido *adv.* de una manera que muestra sentimiento de pesar por haber hecho o dicho algo

assume / suponer *v.* dar por hecho; conjeturar; sostener

assumption / suposición *s.* consideración de algo como cierto

audio / audio *s.* sonido grabado

B

beamish / radiante *adj.* resplandeciente; que siente optimismo y alegría

blossom / flor *s.* brote de las plantas del que se formará el fruto

beware / cuidarse de *v.* actuar con cuidado por si hay peligro

C

caption / leyenda *s.* título o explicación breve

certain / incuestionable *adj.* que no presenta dudas; fiable

character design / diseño del personaje *s.* proceso de desarrollar el papel y la personalidad de un personaje mediante ilustraciones y gráficos

clenched / contraído *v.* apretado; constreñido

coherent / coherente *adj.* que se comunica con claridad y lógica

community / comunidad *s.* las personas o los animales que viven en un lugar determinado

compel / obligar *v.* forzar; ordenar

compromise / mutuo acuerdo *s.* acuerdo alcanzado por partes distintas o enfrentadas en el que cada parte cede en algo

compulsory / obligatorio *adj.* que se debe hacer; exigido

consequently / por consiguiente *adv.* en consecuencia; por lo tanto

consumed / abstraído *adj.* absorto en, ocupado con

consideration / consideración *s.* pensar sobre algo y analizarlo con atención

continuation / continuación *s.* acción de seguir sin interrupción; acción que no se detiene

contribute / contribuir *v.* dar o aportar junto con otras personas

convince / convencer *v.* persuadir

critical / crítico crucial *adj.* que suele estar en contra de hechos e ideas / muy importante

cultivate / cultivar *v.* preparar la tierra para plantar cultivos

curiosity / curiosidad *s.* anhelo de saber algo

cut-out animation / animación con recortes *s.* técnica que utiliza figuras planas, fondos y objetos recortados de materiales tales como papel, cartón y tela

D

declare / declarar *v.* decir algo públicamente; anunciar

deliberate / meditado *adj.* pensado de antemano; que se ha reflexionado qué hacer atenta y detenidamente

desperate / desesperado *adj.* que sufre necesidad o frustración extrema y con poca esperanza

destination / destino *s.* lugar al que se dirige alguien o algo

devouring / devorando *v.* consumiendo de manera voraz

dialogue / diálogo *s.* conversación oral entre dos o más personajes

digesting / digiriendo *v.* pensando con concentración para entender algo bien

disgusted / indignado *adj.* con un fuerte sentimiento de desaprobación; molesto

distraught / desconsolado *adj.* muy preocupado y triste

distressed / consternado *adj.* apenado; molesto

domesticated / domesticado *adj.* que cambió de un estado salvaje a uno manso

dominate / dominar *v.* dirigir o controlar

E

elaborate / profundizar *v.* explicar incluyendo muchos detalles

enactment / promulgación *s.* acto de publicar oficialmente una ley

encapsulation / encapsulación *s.* selección de las escenas importantes que van a aparecer en cada viñeta

endurance test / prueba de resistencia *s.* prueba que mide la capacidad física de una persona

entitled / tener derecho *v.* disfrutar de algún derecho, ya sea otorgado o logrado

© Pearson Education, Inc., or its affiliates. All rights reserved.

exclude / excluir *v.* dejar fuera; impedir que entre, que ocurra o que esté

expedition / expedición *s.* excursión o viaje que tiene un propósito determinado

F

feathery / ligero *adj.* que no pesa mucho y es vaporoso, como una pluma de ave

foe / rival *s.* enemigo

G

gradually / gradualmente *adv.* que ocurre poco a poco

H

host / presentador *s.* persona que presenta y habla con los invitados en un programa de televisión o de radio

humming / tatareo *s.* acción de cantar con los labios cerrados y sin palabras

I

ignorance / ignorancia *s.* falta de conocimiento, educación o información

illustrate / ilustrar *v.* hacer dibujos, diagramas o mapas para explicar o decorar una historia; proveer un ejemplo que demuestre una idea

images or graphics / imágenes o gráficas *s.* representaciones de una persona o cosa

impetuous / impulsivo *adj.* que actúa repentinamente y con poca reflexión

inker / entintador *s.* artista que repasa con tinta un dibujo hecho a lápiz

insincerity / insinceridad *s.* falta de honestidad; falsedad

inspire / inspirar *v.* influenciar; animar al esfuerzo creativo

intensity / intensidad *s.* cualidad de concentrarse o comprometerse del todo

interview / entrevista *s.* conversación grabada en la cual se hacen preguntas a una persona sobre su vida, sus experiencias o sus opiniones

invaded / invadió *v.* atacó; entró por la fuerza

irritable / irritable *adj.* que se enoja o indigna fácilmente

J

journeys / travesías *s.* viajes de un lugar a otro

L

lamented / lamentó *v.* expresó pena o tristeza

letterer / rotulista *s.* artista que escribe los textos de los diálogos y las leyendas

light and shadow / luces y sombras *s.* técnica de dibujo mediante la cual se le da profundidad a una imagen

loftily / altivamente *adv.* con aire de superioridad

loneliness / soledad *s.* sentimiento de aislamiento y de abandono

M

malicious / malicioso *adj.* que tiene o demuestra malas intenciones

memorize / memorizar *v.* aprender algo de manera que pueda recordarse perfectamente luego

microchips / microchips *s.* pequeñas piezas utilizadas en la informática y que tienen circuitos integrados

milled / vagó *v.* se movió desplazándose sin orden ni dirección

misapprehension / malentendido *s.* confusión

miserable / miserable *adj.* profundamente infeliz e incómodo

model / modelo *s.* conjunto de ideas que se deben seguir como plan de acción o ejemplo

mournfully / tristemente *adv.* de una manera que manifiesta pena y desconsuelo

N

narrator / narrador *s.* persona que cuenta una historia

nonchalantly / con aire despreocupado *adv.* hecho de manera indiferente

nostalgic / nostálgico *adj.* que extraña el pasado

notable / notable *adj.* digno de atención; destacado; señalado

novelty / novedad *s.* algo nuevo, fresco o inusual

O

object animation / animación de objetos *s.* técnica que utiliza los movimientos de objetos que no han sido dibujados, como un libro o una pluma

objective / objetivo *s.* finalidad o meta

obsessive / obsesivo *adj.* que se preocupa tanto por algo que no puede pensar en otra cosa

obstacle / obstáculo *s.* algo que se cruza en nuestro camino o nos impide progresar

offended / ofendió *v.* hirió los sentimientos de alguien; afectó de manera desagradable

P

panel / viñeta *s.* cada uno de los recuadros de un cómic, mostrando un momento individual

parameters / parámetros *s.* límites; características

pathetically / patéticamente *adv.* de manera que provoca pena a una persona

patiently / pacientemente *adv.* que aguanta dificultades o dolor de manera voluntaria y calmada

peeped / miró furtivamente *v.* miró por un pequeño agujero o a través de una grieta; miró sin que nadie se diera cuenta

penciler / dibujante *s.* artista que bosqueja las viñetas en una página

perspective / perspectiva *s.* efecto de la distancia en la apariencia de un objeto

© Pearson Education, Inc., or its affiliates. All rights reserved.

pessimistic / pesimista *adj.* que espera que pase lo peor, que se fija en los inconvenientes

pixels / píxels *s.* elementos más pequeños de los que se compone una imagen y que pueden controlarse individualmente en un sistema de video

podcast / podcast *s.* archivo digital o de audio o de video, que forma normalmente parte de una serie y se puede descargar de Internet

presume / presumir *v.* suponer que algo es cierto; asumir

process / procesar *v.* lograr el entendimiento de información

program manager / director de programas *s.* persona que está a cargo de un proyecto

pungent / acre *adj* que tiene un olor fuerte y áspero

purist / purista *s.* alguien que hace las cosas de manera estrictamente tradicional

Q

quest / búsqueda *s.* acción de ir en busca de algo, expedición larga

quivering / temblando *s.* estremecimiento o temblor

R

real-time animation / animación en tiempo real *s.* técnica que consiste en simular que eventos u objetos animados ocurran o se muevan a la misma velocidad que en la vida real

recognize / reconocer *v.* identificar algo a través de la memoria o mediante una descripción

reflect / reflexionar *v.* pensar detenidamente

refugee / refugiado *s.* persona que huye de su país natal, por ejemplo durante un período de guerra

relentlessly / implacablemente *adv.* sin detenerse; con determinación

remember / recordar *v.* evocar o traer a la memoria; no olvidarse

respected / respetado *adj.* venerado; tratado con aprecio

S

sample group / grupo de muestra *s.* grupo de personas provenientes de un grupo más grande que son sometidas a un estudio

sensation / sensación *s.* sentimiento de emoción e interés

shushes / hace callar *v.* manda o señala a alguien que guarde silencio

shyly / tímidamente *adv.* de manera tímida; de manera vergonzosa

silently / silenciosamente *adv.* de manera silenciosa; sin ruido

skittered / se escabulió *v.* se movió sutil y rápidamente

slain / asesinado *v.* ha matado

solid drawing / dibujo sólido *s.* técnica para hacer que una imagen parezca tridimensional

sorrowfully / tristemente *adv.* hecho con pena

speculate / especular *v.* pensar sobre algo y formar una idea sin tener información definitiva

speech balloon / globo de diálogo *s.* espacio donde se escribe lo que el personaje dice o piensa

squish / blandura *s.* sensación suave y esponjosa que se tiene al caminar en una superficie flexible y mullida

stage directions / acotaciones *s.* información importante que provee el dramaturgo sobre el escenario, los personajes y la acción

stubborn / terco *adj.* que se niega a ceder, obedecer o aceptar algo

surmise / conjeturar *v.* adivinar; pensar algo sin tener datos definitivos en que basarse

sufficient / suficiente *adj.* bastante para cubrir lo necesario

suspiciously / sospechosamente *adv.* con recelo, que causa desconfianza

T

template / patrón *s.* plantilla o forma fija que se usa como ejemplo

tenseness / tensión *s.* tirantez de los músculos del cuerpo

thorough / riguroso *adj.* meticuloso; completo; incluyendo cada detalle posible

thoughtfully / atentamente *adv.* de manera considerada y atenta

threateningly / amenazadoramente *adv.* de manera que da miedo o alarmante

timidly / tímidamente *adv.* con timidez o de manera temerosa

transform / transformar *v.* convertir o cambiar

trek / caminata *s.* excursión larga o difícil

trigonometry / trigonometría *s.* campo de las matemáticas que trata de las relaciones entre los lados y ángulos de los triángulos

twirl / dar vueltas *v.* girar sobre sí mismo rápidamente

twist / girar *v.* enrollarse o dar vueltas alrededor de sí mismo

V

valid / válido *adj.* aceptable; que se basa o respalda con hechos

vanished / desapareció *v.* se esfumó, dejó de estar a la vista

various / variados *adj.* diferentes los unos de los otros

violent / violento *adj.* con fuerza y brusquedad que causa daño

voiceover / voz en off *s.* voz que comenta sobre la acción o narra una película detrás de la cámara

W

wild / salvaje *adj.* que vive en la naturaleza sin control humano

wondered / se preguntó *v.* pensó; reflexionó

wrath / furia *s.* rabia intensa

© Pearson Education, Inc., or its affiliates. All rights reserved.

LITERARY TERMS HANDBOOK

ALLEGORY An *allegory* is a story or tale with two or more levels of meaning—a literal level and one or more symbolic levels. The events, setting, and characters in an allegory are symbols for ideas and qualities.

ALLITERATION *Alliteration* is the repetition of initial consonant sounds. Writers use alliteration to draw attention to certain words or ideas, to imitate sounds, and to create musical effects.

ANALOGY An *analogy* makes a comparison between two or more things that are similar in some ways but otherwise unalike.

ANECDOTE An *anecdote* is a brief story about an interesting, amusing, or strange event. Writers tell anecdotes to entertain or to make a point.

ARGUMENT An *argument* is a logical way of presenting a belief, conclusion, or stance. A good argument is supported with reasoning and evidence.

ASSONANCE *Assonance* is the repetition of similar vowel sounds in stressed syllables that end with different consonants, as in seal and meet.

AUTHOR'S INFLUENCES An *author's influences* are things that affect his or her writing. These include *historical factors*, such as world events that took place during the author's lifetime, and *cultural factors*, such as the author's upbringing, education, lifestyle, and personal experiences.

AUTHOR'S PURPOSE An *author's purpose* is his or her main reason for writing. Texts are written to inform, to persuade, to entertain, to describe, and to express the author's point of view. In many cases, an author has more than one purpose, or reason, for writing.

AUTHOR'S STYLE *Style* is an author's typical way of writing. Many factors determine an author's style, including diction; tone; use of characteristic elements such as figurative language, dialect, rhyme, meter, or rhythmic devices; typical grammatical structures and patterns; typical sentence length; and typical methods of organization.

AUTOBIOGRAPHY An *autobiography* is the story of the writer's own life, told by the writer. Autobiographical writing may tell about the person's whole life or only a part of it.

Because autobiographies are about real people and events, they are a form of nonfiction. Most autobiographies are written in the first person.

BIBLIOGRAPHY A list of sources used at the end of an essay is a *bibliography*. Also called a *works-cited list*, a bibliography can have different citation styles, such as MLA. Failure to properly cite sources is considered *plagiarism* because you are using someone else's work without giving proper credit.

BIOGRAPHY A *biography* is a form of nonfiction in which a writer tells the life story of another person. Most biographies are written about famous or admirable people. Although biographies are nonfiction, the most effective ones share the qualities of good narrative writing.

CENTRAL IDEA Sometimes a writer will state the *central idea* of a text *directly*, but other times the central idea is implied. An *implied* central idea is identified by *making an inference*.

CHARACTER A *character* is a person or an animal that takes part in the action of a literary work. The main, or *major*, character is the most important character in a story, poem, or play. A *minor* character is one who takes part in the action but is not the focus of attention.

CHARACTERIZATION *Characterization* is the act of creating and developing a character. Authors use two major methods of characterization—*direct* and *indirect*. When using *direct* characterization, a writer states the *character's traits*, or characteristics.

When describing a character *indirectly*, a writer depends on the reader to draw conclusions about the character's traits. Sometimes the writer tells what other participants in the story say and think about the character.

CHARACTER TRAITS *Character traits* are the qualities, attitudes, and values that a character has or displays—for example, dependability, intelligence, selfishness, or stubbornness.

CHRONOLOGICAL ORDER In a nonfiction narrative, the writer often sequences events in *chronological order*, so that one event proceeds to the next in the order in which they actually happened, from first to last.

CLAIM A *claim* is an statement in a text that can be called into question. Claims can be facts or *opinions*.

CLIMAX The *climax*, also called the turning point, is the high point in the action of the plot. It is the moment of greatest tension, when the outcome of the plot hangs in the balance.

COMPARISON-AND-CONTRAST ESSAY A *comparison-and-contrast essay* analyzes the similarities and differences between two texts. Comparison-and-contrast essays can be written using different methods of organization. Using *block organization*, one subject is discussed completely, then the other subject is discussed. *Point-by-point* organization discusses one point at a time of both subjects before moving on to the next.

CONFLICT A *conflict* is a struggle between opposing forces. Conflict is one of the most important elements of

© Pearson Education, Inc., or its affiliates. All rights reserved.

stories, novels, and plays because it causes the action. There are two kinds of conflict: external and internal. An *external conflict* is one in which a character struggles against some outside force, such as another person. Another kind of external conflict may occur between a character and some force in nature.

An *internal conflict* takes place within the mind of a character. The character struggles to make a decision, take an action, or overcome a feeling.

CONSONANCE *Consonance* is the repetition of final consonant sounds in stressed syllables with different vowel sounds, as in sit and cat.

CONNOTATIONS The *connotation* of a word is the set of ideas associated with it in addition to its explicit meaning. The connotation of a word can be personal, based on individual experiences. More often, cultural connotations—those recognizable by most people in a group—determine a writer's word choices.

DEBATE A *debate* is a formal discussion in which opposing sides of a question are argued.

DENOTATION The *denotation* of a word is its dictionary meaning, independent of other associations that the word may have. The denotation of the word *lake,* for example, is "an inland body of water." "Vacation spot" and "place where the fishing is good" are connotations of the word *lake.*

DESCRIPTION A *description* is a portrait, in words, of a person, place, or object. Descriptive writing uses images that appeal to the five senses—sight, hearing, touch, taste, and smell.

DIALOGUE A *dialogue* is a conversation between characters. In poems, novels, and short stories, dialogue is usually set off by quotation marks to indicate a speaker's exact words.

In a play, dialogue follows the names of the characters, and no quotation marks are used.

DRAMA A *drama* is a story written to be performed by actors. Although a drama is meant to be performed, one can also read the *script*, or written version, and imagine the action. The *script* of a drama is made up of dialogue and stage directions. The *dialogue* is the words spoken by the actors. The *stage directions,* usually printed in italics, tell how the actors should look, move, and speak. They also describe the setting, sound effects, and lighting.

Dramas are often divided into parts called *acts.*

The acts are often divided into smaller parts called *scenes.*

DRAMATIC READING A *dramatic reading* is an oral presentation that includes powerful dramatic expression, gestures, and body language to help express feelings and ideas.

EDITORIAL An editorial is a type of argument in which the writer presents a viewpoint on an issue.

ELEMENTS In organizing an essay, a writer needs to put together various *elements* to explain ideas in a logical way.

ENJAMBMENT An *enjambment*, or run-on line, is the continuation of a sentence between lines of poetry without end punctuation. It is the opposite of an *end-stopped line*.

ESSAY An *essay* is a short nonfiction work about a particular subject. Most essays have a single major focus and a clear introduction, body, and conclusion.

There are many types of essays. An *informal essay* uses casual, conversational language. A *historical essay* gives facts, explanations, and insights about historical events. An *explanatory essay* is a short piece of nonfiction in which the author explains, defines, or interprets ideas, events, or processes. A *reflective essay* is a brief prose work in which an author presents his or her thoughts or feelings—or reflections—about an experience or an idea. An *expository essay* explains an idea by breaking it down. A *narrative essay* tells a story about a real-life experience. A *how-to essay* explains a process. A *persuasive essay* offers an opinion and supports it.

EVIDENCE Effective arguments and persuasive essays use *evidence* to support claims. Facts, statistics, anecdotes, examples, and quotations from authorities are forms of evidence used by writers.

EXPOSITION In the plot of a story or a drama, the *exposition,* or introduction, is the part of the work that introduces the characters, setting, and basic situation.

EXPOSITORY WRITING *Expository writing* is writing that explains or informs.

FANTASY A *fantasy* is highly imaginative writing that contains elements not found in real life. Examples of fantasy include stories that involve supernatural elements, stories that resemble fairy tales, stories that deal with imaginary places and creatures, and science-fiction stories.

FICTION *Fiction* is prose writing that tells about imaginary characters and events. Short stories and novels are works of fiction. In *historical fiction*, real events, places, or people are adapted into a fictional story. Other writers rely on imagination alone.

FIGURATIVE LANGUAGE *Figurative language* is writing or speech that is not meant to be taken literally. The many types of figurative language are known as *figures of speech.* Common figures of speech include metaphor, personification, and simile. Writers use figurative language to state ideas in vivid and imaginative ways.

© Pearson Education, Inc, or its affiliates. All rights reserved.

FLASHBACK A *flashback* is a scene within a story that interrupts the sequence of events to relate events that occurred in the past.

FREE VERSE *Free verse* is poetry not written in a regular, rhythmical pattern, or meter. The poet is free to write lines of any length or with any number of stresses, or beats. Free verse is therefore less constraining than *metrical verse,* in which every line must have a certain length and a certain number of stresses.

GENRE A *genre* is a division or type of literature. Literature is commonly divided into three major genres: poetry, prose, and drama. Each major genre is, in turn, divided into lesser genres, as follows:

1. *Poetry:* lyric poetry, concrete poetry, dramatic poetry, narrative poetry, epic poetry
2. *Prose:* fiction (novels and short stories) and nonfiction (biography, autobiography, letters, essays, and reports)
3. *Drama:* serious drama and tragedy, comic drama, melodrama, and farce

IDIOMS *Idioms* are expressions that have different meanings from the literal meanings

IMAGERY *Imagery* is the use of vivid word pictures writers use to appeal to one or more of the five senses. Writers use images to describe how their subjects look, sound, feel, taste, and smell. Poets often paint images, or word pictures, that appeal to your senses. These pictures help you experience the poem fully.

INFER To *infer* is to make an educated guess about *implied* information in a text.

INFERENCE An *inference* is a logical assumption made about information in a text that is not directly stated. *Prior knowledge* and *key details* are used to make inferences about *implied* ideas.

IRONY *Irony* is a contradiction between what happens and what is expected. The three main types of irony are *situational irony, verbal irony,* and *dramatic irony.*

MEDIA ACCOUNTS *Media accounts* are reports, explanations, opinions, or descriptions written for television, radio, newspapers, and magazines. While some media accounts report only facts, others include the writer's thoughts and reflections.

MEMOIR A *memoir* is a type of autobiography that focuses on a particularly meaningful period or series of events in the author's life. A memoir is typically written from the *first-person point of view* in which the author, or narrator, takes part in the story's events. The author will refer to himself or herself using the pronoun *I.*

METAPHOR A *metaphor* is a figure of speech in which something is described as though it were something else. A metaphor, like a simile, works by pointing out a similarity between two unlike things.

MYTH A *myth* is a fictional tale that describes the actions of heroes or gods.

MYTHOLOGY *Mythology* is the system of myths belonging to a culture.

NARRATION *Narration* is writing that tells a story. The act of telling a story is also called narration. Each piece is a *narrative.* A story told in fiction, nonfiction, poetry, or even in drama is called a narrative.

NARRATIVE A *narrative* is a story. A narrative can be either fiction or nonfiction. Novels and short stories are types of **fictional narratives**. Biographies and autobiographies are **nonfiction narratives**. Poems that tell stories are also narratives.

NARRATOR A *narrator* is a speaker or a character who tells a story. The narrator's perspective is the way he or she sees things. A *third-person narrator* is one who stands outside the action and speaks about it. A *first-person narrator* is one who tells a story and participates in its action.

NONFICTION *Nonfiction* is prose writing that presents and explains ideas or that tells about real people, places, objects, or events. Autobiographies, biographies, essays, reports, letters, memos, and newspaper articles are all types of nonfiction.

NOVEL A *novel* is a long work of fiction. Novels contain such elements as characters, plot, conflict, and setting. The writer of novels, or novelist, develops these elements. In addition to its main plot, a novel may contain one or more subplots, or independent, related stories. A novel may also have several themes.

ONOMATOPOEIA *Onomatopoeia* is the use of words that imitate sounds. *Crash, buzz, screech, hiss, neigh, jingle,* and *cluck* are examples of onomatopoeia. *Chickadee, towhee,* and *whippoorwill* are onomatopoeic names of birds.

Onomatopoeia can help put the reader in the activity of a poem.

OPINION An *opinion* is a belief that cannot be proven as fact and appeals to reader's emotions.

ORGANIZED STRUCTURE The body of an essay presents ideas in an *organized structure*, such as comparison-and-contrast or cause-effect. The writer should provide *support* for the ideas in the form of evidence, examples, or quotations.

OUTLINE An *outline* lists the main ideas of an essay or presentation and helps to organize ideas in a logical sequence. A typical outline structure is:

I. Thesis Statement

II. Body of Presentation

   A. First Idea

© Pearson Education, Inc., or its affiliates. All rights reserved.

B. Second Idea

C. Third Idea

III. Conclusion: Importance of Ideas

OXYMORON An *oxymoron* (pl. *oxymora*) is a figure of speech that links two opposite or contradictory words, to point out an idea or situation that seems contradictory or inconsistent but on closer inspection turns out to be somehow true.

PACING Writers use *pacing* to slow down or speed up the action in a scene. Action is slowed down by adding more description and longer sentences. Action speeds up by using shorter sentences. Pacing helps you draw attention to an important idea or build suspense.

PERSONIFICATION *Personification* is a type of figurative language in which a nonhuman subject is given human characteristics.

PERSUASION *Persuasion* is used in writing or speech and attempts to convince the reader or listener to adopt a particular opinion or course of action. Newspaper editorials, letters to the editor, political campaign speeches, and advertisements use persuasion.

PERSUASIVE TECHNIQUES *Persuasive techniques* are used to strengthen an argument. *Repetition*, or repeating a word or phrase so that it makes an impact, is one persuasive technique. *Appeals to authority* show that a higher power supports an idea. *Appeals to emotion* influence readers by using words that create positive or negative feelings. *Appeals to reason* use logical arguments backed by facts.

PLAYWRIGHT A *playwright* is a person who writes plays. William Shakespeare is regarded as the greatest playwright in English literature.

PLOT *Plot* is the sequence of events in which each event results from a previous one and causes the next. In most novels, dramas, short stories, and narrative poems, the plot involves both characters and a central conflict. The plot usually begins with an *exposition* that introduces the setting, the characters, and the basic situation. This is followed by the *inciting incident,* which introduces the central conflict. Events then increase the tension of the conflict with *rising action* until it reaches a high point of interest or suspense, the *climax.* The climax is followed by the *falling action,* or end, of the central conflict. Any events that occur during the *falling action* make up the *resolution,* or *denouement.*

Some plots do not have all of these parts. Some stories begin with the inciting incident and end with the resolution.

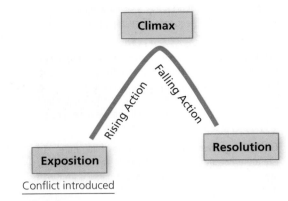

Conflict introduced

POETRY *Poetry* is one of the three major types of literature, the others being prose and drama. Most poems make use of highly concise, musical, and emotionally charged language. Many also make use of imagery, figurative language, and sound devices such as rhythm, rhyme, repetition, and onomatopoeia. Major types of poetry include lyric poetry, narrative poetry, and concrete poetry.

POINT OF VIEW *Point of view* is the perspective, or vantage point, from which a story is told. The storyteller is either a narrator outside the story or a character in the story. *First-person point of view* describes a story told by a character who uses the first-person pronoun "I."

The two kinds of *third-person point of view,* limited and omniscient, are called "third person" because the narrator uses third-person pronouns such as "he" and "she" to refer to the characters. There is no "I" telling the story.

In stories told from the *omniscient third-person point of view,* the narrator knows and tells about what each character feels and thinks.

In stories told from the *limited third-person point of view,* the narrator relates the inner thoughts and feelings of only one character, and everything is viewed from this character's perspective.

PROSE *Prose* is the ordinary form of written language. Most writing that is not poetry, drama, or song is considered prose. Prose is one of the major genres of literature and occurs in two forms—fiction and nonfiction.

PROTAGONIST The *protagonist* is the main character in a literary work. Often, the protagonist is a person, but sometimes it can be an animal.

REPETITION *Repetition* is the use, more than once, of any element of language—a sound, word, phrase, clause, or sentence. Repetition is used in both prose and poetry.

RESOLUTION The *resolution* is the outcome of the conflict in a plot.

RHYTHM *Rhythm* is the pattern of stressed and unstressed syllables in spoken or written language.

© Pearson Education, Inc., or its affiliates. All rights reserved.

SCENE A *scene* is a section of uninterrupted action in the act of a drama.

SCIENCE FICTION *Science fiction* combines elements of fiction and fantasy with scientific fact. Many science-fiction stories are set in the future.

SENSORY LANGUAGE *Sensory language* is writing or speech that appeals to one or more of the five senses.

SETTING The *setting* of a literary work is the time and place of the action. The setting includes all the details of a place and time—the year, the time of day, even the weather. The place may be a specific country, state, region, community, neighborhood, building, institution, or home. Details such as dialects, clothing, customs, and modes of transportation are often used to establish setting. In most stories, the setting serves as a backdrop—a context in which the characters interact. Setting can also help create a feeling, or atmosphere.

SHORT STORY A *short story* is a brief work of fiction. Like a novel, a short story presents a sequence of events, or plot. The plot usually deals with a central conflict faced by a main character, or protagonist. The events in a short story usually communicate a message about life or human nature. This message, or central idea, is the story's theme.

SIMILE A *simile* is a figure of speech that uses *like* or *as* to make a direct comparison between two unlike ideas. Everyday speech often contains similes, such as "pale as a ghost," "good as gold," "spread like wildfire," and "clever as a fox."

SOUND DEVICES Poets use *sound devices* to create musical effects, reinforce meaning, develop tone, and emphasize the sound relationships among words. Sound devices include *repetition, onomatopoeia, alliteration, consonance,* and *assonance.*

SPEAKER The *speaker* is the imaginary voice a poet uses when writing a poem. The speaker is the character who tells the poem. This character, or voice, often is not identified by name. There can be important differences between the poet and the poem's speaker.

STAGE DIRECTIONS *Stage directions* are notes included in a drama to describe how the work is to be performed or staged. Stage directions are usually printed in italics and enclosed within parentheses or brackets. Some stage directions describe the movements, costumes, emotional states, and ways of speaking of the characters.

STAGING *Staging* includes the setting, lighting, costumes, special effects, music, dance, and so on that go into putting on a stage performance of a drama.

STANZA A *stanza* is a group of lines of poetry that are usually similar in length and pattern and are separated by spaces. A stanza is like a paragraph of poetry—it states and develops a single main idea.

SYMBOL A *symbol* is anything that stands for or represents something else. Symbols are common in everyday life. A dove with an olive branch in its beak is a symbol of peace. A blindfolded woman holding a balanced scale is a symbol of justice. A crown is a symbol of a king's status and authority.

SYMBOLISM *Symbolism* is the use of symbols. Symbolism plays an important role in many different types of literature. It can highlight certain elements the author wishes to emphasize and also add levels of meaning.

SYNTAX The organization of words into sentences is *syntax*. Poets often play with syntax to highlight ideas.

TECHNICAL LANGUAGE *Technical language* is words or language specific to a particular topic, process, or industry.

THEME The *theme* is a central idea, concern, or purpose in a literary work. A theme can usually be expressed as a generalization, or a general statement, about human beings or about life. The theme of a work is not a summary of its plot. The theme is the writer's central idea.

Although a theme may be stated directly in the text, it is more often presented indirectly. When the theme is stated indirectly, or implied, the reader must figure out what the theme is by looking carefully at what the work reveals about people or about life.

THESIS A *thesis* is a sentence that states the controlling idea of an essay.

TONE The *tone* of a literary work is the writer's attitude toward his or her audience and subject. The tone can often be described by a single adjective, such as *formal* or *informal, serious* or *playful, bitter,* or *ironic.* Factors that contribute to the tone are word choice, sentence structure, line length, rhyme, rhythm, and repetition.

TOPIC SENTENCE Each paragraph of an essay should have a *topic sentence* that states the main idea of the paragraph. The paragraph also has facts and examples to support the main idea.

UNIVERSAL THEME A *universal theme* is a message about life that is expressed regularly in many different cultures and time periods. Folk tales, epics, and romances often address universal themes such as the importance of courage, the power of love, or the danger of greed.

VERSE *Verse* is a form of literature also called poetry. *Free verse* is not written in a regular, rhythmical pattern, or meter. The poet is free to write lines of any length or with any number of stresses, or beats. Free verse is therefore less constraining than *metrical verse*, in which every line must have a certain length and a certain number of stresses.

VOICE *Voice* describes a writer's distinct style. A writer's voice can be influenced by *word choice,* the writer's choice and use of specific words; *sentence structure,* or the way the writer constructs a sentence; and *tone,* or the writer's attitude toward the subject.

© Pearson Education, Inc., or its affiliates. All rights reserved.

MANUAL DE TÉRMINOS LITERARIOS

ALLEGORY / ALEGORÍA Una *alegoría* es una historia o un cuento con dos o más niveles de significado (un nivel literal y uno o más niveles simbólicos). Los eventos, escenarios y personajes de una alegoría son símbolos de ideas y cualidades.

ALLITERATION / ALITERACIÓN Una *aliteración* es la repetición de sonidos consonánticos iniciales. Los escritores usan la aliteración para dirigir la atención de los lectores hacia ciertas palabras o ideas, imitar sonidos o crear efectos musicales.

ANALOGY / ANALOGÍA Una *analogía* establece una comparación entre dos o más cosas que presentan similitudes, pero son distintas en todo lo demás.

ANECDOTE / ANÉCDOTA Una *anécdota* es un cuento corto sobre un evento extraño, interesante o divertido. Los escritores cuentan anécdotas para entretener o explicar algo importante.

ARGUMENT / ARGUMENTO Un *argumento* es una manera lógica de expresar una opinión, una conclusión o una postura. Un buen argumento contiene razonamientos y pruebas.

ASSONANCE / ASONANCIA Una *asonancia* es la repetición de sonidos vocálicos similares a partir de la última sílaba acentuada, como en *foca* y *nota*.

AUTHOR'S INFLUENCES / INFLUENCIAS DEL AUTOR Las *influencias del autor* son cosas que influyen en su escritura. Algunas de estas influencias incluyen *factores históricos*, como los sucesos mundiales en la vida del autor, y *factores culturales*, como la niñez, educación, estilo de vida y experiencias personales del autor.

AUTHOR'S PURPOSE / PROPÓSITO DEL AUTOR El *propósito del autor* es la razón principal por la que este autor o autora escribe. Los textos se escriben para informar, persuadir, entretener, describir y expresar el punto de vista del autor. En muchos casos, un autor tiene varios propósitos o razones por los que escribir.

AUTHOR'S STYLE / ESTILO DEL AUTOR El *estilo* es la forma de escribir típica de un autor. Hay muchos factores que determinan el estilo del autor: la dicción, el tono, el uso de elementos característicos como el lenguaje figurativo, el dialecto, la rima, la métrica o los distintos recursos rítmicos; las estructuras y patrones gramaticales típicos, el tamaño típico de la frase; y los métodos típicos de organización textual.

AUTOBIOGRAPHY / AUTOBIOGRAFÍA Una *autobiografía* es la historia de la vida del propio autor. Los textos autobiográficos pueden hablar de la vida completa del autor o solo de una parte.

Como las autobiografías tratan sobre gente y acontecimientos reales, se les considera no ficción. La mayoría de las autobiografías están escritas en primera persona.

BIBLIOGRAPHY / BIBLIOGRAFÍA Se conoce como *bibliografía* a la lista que se incluye al final de un ensayo con las fuentes que se utilizaron. También llamada *lista de obras citadas*, para su elaboración se sigue una guía de estilo como, por ejemplo, la de MLA. No citar las fuentes se considera *plagio* porque se usa el trabajo de otra persona sin reconocerle el mérito al autor.

BIOGRAPHY / BIOGRAFÍA Una *biografía* es un tipo de texto de no ficción donde el escritor explica la historia de la vida de otra persona. La mayoría de las biografías son sobre gente famosa y admirable. Aunque las biografías se consideran libros de no ficción, las de mayor calidad suelen compartir cualidades con los textos narrativos.

CENTRAL IDEA / IDEA CENTRAL En ocasiones el escritor expone la *idea central* de un texto *directamente*, pero en otros casos la idea central está *implícita*. Una idea central implícita se identifica al *hacer una inferencia*.

CHARACTER / PERSONAJE Un *personaje* es una persona o un animal que participa en la acción de una obra literaria. El personaje *principal* o protagonista es el más importante de una historia, poema u obra teatral. El personaje *secundario* participa también en la acción pero no es el centro de atención.

CHARACTERIZATION / CARACTERIZACIÓN *Caracterización* es la acción de crear y desarrollar un personaje. Los autores utilizan dos métodos principales de caracterización: *directa* e *indirecta.*

Cuando se utiliza la caracterización *directa*, el escritor describe los *rasgos del personaje* o sus características.

En cambio, cuando se describe a un personaje *indirectamente*, el escritor depende del lector para que se puedan extraer conclusiones sobre los rasgos del personaje. A veces el escritor cuenta lo que otros personajes que participan en la historia dicen o piensan sobre el personaje en cuestión.

CHARACTER TRAITS / RASGOS DEL PERSONAJE Los *rasgos del personaje* son cualidades, actitudes y valores que un personaje tiene o manifiesta, por ejemplo la fiabilidad, inteligencia, egoísmo o terquedad.

CHRONOLOGICAL ORDER / ORDEN CRONOLÓGICO En una narrativa de no ficción, el escritor suele ordenar los sucesos en *orden cronológico*, es decir, los sucesos se describen en el orden que tuvieron lugar, del primero al último.

© Pearson Education, Inc., or its affiliates. All rights reserved.

CLAIM / AFIRMACIÓN Una *afirmación* es una declaración que puede cuestionarse. Las afirmaciones pueden ser hechos u *opiniones*.

CLIMAX / CLÍMAX El *clímax,* también llamado momento culminante, es el punto más elevado de acción de una trama. Es el momento de mayor tensión, es decir, cuando el desenlace de la trama pende de un hilo.

COMPARISON-AND-CONTRAST ESSAY / ENSAYO DE COMPARACIÓN Y CONTRASTE Un *ensayo de comparación y contraste* analiza las semejanzas y diferencias entre dos textos. Los ensayos de comparación y contraste pueden tener distintos métodos de organización. En una *organización de método de bloques*, se trata primero uno de los asuntos y después el otro. En una *organización de punto por punto* se trata un aspecto de cada asunto antes de pasar al siguiente aspecto.

CONFLICT / CONFLICT Un *conflicto* es una lucha entre fuerzas opuestas. El conflicto es uno de los elementos más importantes de los cuentos, novelas y obras de teatro porque provoca la acción. Hay dos tipos de conflictos: externos e internos.

Un *conflicto externo* se da cuando un personaje lucha contra una fuerza ajena a él, como por ejemplo otra persona. Otro tipo de conflicto externo puede ocurrir entre un personaje y una fuerza de la naturaleza.

Un *conflicto interno* tiene lugar en la mente de un personaje. El personaje lucha por tomar una decisión, llevar a cabo una acción o frenar un sentimiento.

CONNOTATION / CONNOTACIÓN La *connotación* de una palabra es el conjunto de ideas que se asocian con esta más allá de su significado explícito. La connotación de una palabra puede ser personal, basada en una experiencia individual. Con frecuencia son las connotaciones culturales, aquellas que son reconocibles por la mayoría de las personas de un grupo, las que determinan la elección de un autor.

CONSONANCE / CONSONANCIA La *consonancia* es la repetición desde de la última sílaba acentuada de las mismas vocales y consonantes. Por ejemplo: *zapato* y *gato*.

DEBATE / DEBATE Un *debate* es una discusión formal en la que se argumentan puntos de vista opuestos sobre un mismo asunto.

DENOTATION / DENOTACIÓN La *denotación* de una palabra es su significado del diccionario, independientemente de otras asociaciones que se le puedan otorgar. La denotación de la palabra *lago* sería "una masa de agua que se acumula en un terreno". "Un lugar de vacaciones" o "un lugar adonde se puede ir de pesca" son connotaciones de la palabra *lago*.

DESCRIPTION / DESCRIPCIÓN Una *descripción* es un retrato en palabras de una persona, lugar u objeto. Los textos descriptivos usan imágenes que se relacionan con los cinco sentidos: vista, oído, tacto, gusto y olfato.

DIALOGUE / DIÁLOGO Un *diálogo* es una conversación entre personajes. En los poemas, novelas y cuentos en inglés, los diálogos se indican normalmente entre comillas para señalar que estas son las palabras exactas que dice un personaje.

En una obra de teatro, los diálogos se colocan detrás de los nombres de los personajes y no se utilizan comillas.

DRAMA / DRAMA Un *drama* es una historia escrita para ser representada por actores. Aunque está destinada a ser representada, también se puede, únicamente, leer el guión o texto e imaginar la acción. El *guión* está compuesto de diálogos y acotaciones. Los *diálogos* son las palabras que dicen los personajes. Las *acotaciones* aparecen normalmente en cursiva e indican qué apariencia deben tener los personajes, y cómo deben moverse o hablar. También describen la escenografía, los efectos de sonido y la iluminación.

Los dramas suelen estar divididos en distintas partes denominadas *actos.*

Los actos aparecen a menudo divididos en partes más pequeñas denominadas *escenas*.

DRAMATIC READING / LECTURA DRAMATIZADA Una *lectura dramatizada* es una presentación oral que incluye gran expresividad dramática, gestos y lenguaje corporal para transmitir sentimientos e ideas.

EDITORIAL / EDITORIAL Un *editorial* es un tipo de argumento en el que el escritor presenta un punto de vista sobre un asunto.

ELEMENTS / ELEMENTOS Al organizar un ensayo, el escritor debe reunir diversos *elementos* para explicar las ideas de una manera lógica.

ENJAMBMENT / ENCABALGAMIENTO En un *encabalgamiento*, o verso encabalgado, la oración continúa de un verso al siguiente. Es lo opuesto a un *verso no encabalgado*.

ESSAY / ENSAYO Un *ensayo* es un texto de no ficción corto sobre un tema particular. La mayoría de los ensayos se concentran en un único aspeco fundamental y tienen una introducción clara, un desarrollo y una conclusión.

Hay muchos tipos de ensayos. Un *ensayo informal* emplea lenguaje coloquial y conversacional. Un *ensayo histórico* nos presenta hechos, explicaciones y conocimientos sobre acontecimientos históricos. Un *ensayo explicativo* aclara, define e interpreta ideas, acontecimientos o procesos. En un *ensayo reflexivo* el autor presenta sus pensamientos y sentimientos o reflexiones sobre una experiencia o idea. Un *ensayo expositivo* expone una idea desglosándola. Un *ensayo narrativo* cuenta una historia sobre una experiencia real. Un *ensayo de proceso* explica cómo hacer algo. Un *ensayo argumentativo* ofrece una opinión y la argumenta.

© Pearson Education, Inc, or its affiliates. All rights reserved.

EVIDENCE / EVIDENCIA Los argumentos efectivos y los ensayos persuasivos utilizan *evidencia* para respaldar sus afirmaciones. Los datos, estadísticas, anécdotas, ejemplos y citas de fuentes fiables son algunas de las evidencias que emplean los escritores.

EXPOSITION / PLANTEAMIENTO En el argumento de una historia o drama, el *planteamiento* o introducción es la parte de la obra que presenta a los personajes, el escenario y la situación más básica.

EXPOSITORY WRITING / TEXTO EXPOSITIVO Un *texto expositivo* es un texto que explica e informa.

FANTASY / LITERATURA FANTÁSTICA La *literatura fantástica* son textos con elementos muy imaginativos que no pueden encontrarse en la vida real. Algunos ejemplos de literatura fantástica incluyen historias que contienen elementos supernaturales, historias que recuerdan a los cuentos de hadas, historias que tratan de lugares y criaturas imaginarias e historias de ciencia ficción.

FICTION / FICCIÓN La *ficción* son obras en prosa que hablan de sucesos y personajes imaginarios. Los relatos y las novelas son obras de ficción. En la *ficción histórica* se incluyen eventos, lugares o personas reales en la obra de ficción. Otros escritores se sirven únicamente de la imaginación.

FIGURATIVE LANGUAGE / LENGUAJE FIGURADO El *lenguaje figurado* es un texto o diálogo que no se debe interpretar literalmente. Los numerosos tipos de lenguaje figurado son conocidos como *figuras retóricas.* Algunas de las más comunes son las metáforas, las personificaciones y los símiles. Los escritores utilizan el lenguaje figurado para expresar ideas de una manera imaginativa y vívida.

FLASHBACK / ESCENA RETROSPECTIVA Una *escena retrospectiva* es una escena dentro de una historia que interrumpe la secuencia temporal de los acontecimientos para contar un acontecimiento que ocurrió en algún momento del pasado.

FREE VERSE / VERSO LIBRE El *verso libre* es poesía que no está escrita en un patrón rítmico ni métrico corriente. El poeta es libre de escribir versos del tamaño que prefiera con un número libre de acentos. Por consiguiente, el verso libre es menos limitador que el *verso métrico*, en el que cada verso debe contener acentos y un número concreto de sílabas.

GENRE / GÉNERO Un *género* es una clase o tipo de literatura. La literatura se divide normalmente en tres géneros principales: poesía, prosa y drama. Cada uno de estos géneros está, a su vez, dividido en otros géneros más pequeños:

    1 *Poesía:* poesía lírica, poesía concreta, poesía dramática, poesía narrativa, poesía épica

    2 *Prosa:* ficción (novelas y cuentos) y no ficción (biografías, autobiografías, cartas, ensayos y reportajes)

    3 *Drama:* drama serio y tragedia, comedia, melodrama y farsa

IDIOMS / MODISMOS Los *modismos* son expresiones idiomáticas que tienen un significado diferente a su significado literal.

IMAGERY / IMAGINERÍA La *imaginería* es el uso que le da el escritor al lenguaje para crear descripciones visuales vívidas que se relacionan con uno o varios de los cinco sentidos. Los escritores utilizan imágenes para describir qué apariencia tienen, cómo suenan, sienten, saben y huelen los personajes u objetos descritos. Los poetas suelen dibujar imágenes o hacer una descripción visual que se vincule con los sentidos. Estas descripciones visuales nos ayudan a experimentar el poema en su totalidad.

INFER / INFERIR *Inferir* es hacer una deducción lógica acerca de la información que está *implícita* en un texto.

INFERENCE /INFERENCIA Una *inferencia* es una suposición lógica que se hace acerca de la información que no se detalla directamente en un texto. Se usan el *conocimiento previo* y los *detalles clave* para hacer inferencias sobre las ideas *implícitas*.

IRONY / IRONÍA Una *ironía* es una contradicción entre lo que ocurre realmente y lo que se espera que pase. Los tres tipos principales de ironía son: *ironía situacional*, *ironía verbal* e *ironía dramática.*

MEDIA ACCOUNTS / REPORTAJES PERIODÍSTICOS Los *reportajes periodísticos* son relatos, explicaciones, opiniones o descripciones escritas para televisión, radio, periódicos o revistas. Si bien algunos reportajes periodísticos solo relatan hechos, otros incluyen también las opiniones y reflexiones del autor.

MEMOIR / MEMORIAS Unas *memorias* es un tipo de autobiografía que se concentra en un período particular y significativo, o en una serie de acontecimientos de la vida del autor. Las memorias se suelen escribir en *primera persona* dado que el autor o narrador participa en los acontecimientos de la historia. El autor se refiere a sí mismo con el pronombre "yo" y la conjugación en primera persona del singular.

METAPHOR / METÁFORA Una *metáfora* es una figura retórica que se utiliza para identificar una cosa con algo distinto. Una metáfora, al igual que un símil, se obtiene identificando las similitudes que comparten dos cosas distintas.

MYTH / MITO Un *mito* es un relato de no ficción que describe las acciones de héroes o dioses.

© Pearson Education, Inc., or its affiliates. All rights reserved.

MYTHOLOGY / MITOLOGÍA La *mitología* es el sistema de mitos de una cultura determinada.

NARRATION / NARRACIÓN Una *narración* es un texto que cuenta una historia. También se denomina narración a la acción de contar una historia. Cada una de estas creaciones son *textos narrativos*. Una historia contada en ficción, no ficción, poesía o incluso en drama es conocida como narración.

NARRATIVE / TEXTO NARRATIVO Un *texto narrativo* es una historia. Un texto narrativo puede ser de ficción y de no ficción. Las novelas y los cuentos son tipos de *textos narrativos de ficción*. Las biografías y las autobiografías son *textos narrativos de no ficción*. Los poemas que cuentan una historia pueden ser también textos narrativos.

NARRATOR / NARRADOR Un *narrador* es la persona o personaje que cuenta una historia. El punto de vista del narrador es la manera en la que él o ella ve las cosas. Un *narrador en tercera persona* es aquel que solo habla de la acción sin implicarse en ella. Un *narrador en primera persona* es aquel que cuenta una historia y toma parte en su acción.

NONFICTION / NO FICCIÓN Una *no ficción* es un texto en prosa que presenta y explica ideas, o que habla sobre gente, lugares, objetos o acontecimientos reales. Las autobiografías, biografías, ensayos, reportajes, cartas, memorandos y artículos periodísticos son todos diferentes tipos de no ficción.

NOVEL / NOVELA Una *novela* es una obra larga de ficción. Las novelas contienen elementos tales como los personajes, la trama, el conflicto y los escenarios. Los escritores de novelas o novelistas desarrollan estos elementos. Aparte de tu trama principal, una novela puede contener una o varias subtramas, o narraciones independientes o relacionadas con la trama principal. Una novela puede contener también diversos temas.

ONOMATOPOEIA / ONOMATOPEYA Una *onomatopeya* es el uso de palabras que imitan sonidos. *Cataplam, zzzzzz, zas, din don, glu glu glu, achís* y *crag* son ejemplos de onomatopeyas. El *cuco,* la *urraca* y el *pitirre* son nombres onomatopéyicos de aves.

La onomatopeya puede ayudar al lector a sumergirse en la descripción de un poema.

OPINION / OPINIÓN Una *opinión* es una creencia que no se puede corroborar y que apela a las emociones del lector.

ORGANIZED STRUCTURE / ESTRUCTURA ORGANIZATIVA En el cuerpo de un ensayo se presentan las ideas mediante una *estructura organizativa*, como comparación y contraste o causa y efecto. El escritor debe *respaldar* las ideas mediante el uso de evidencia, ejemplos o citas.

OUTLINE / BOSQUEJO Un *bosquejo* es una lista de las ideas principales de un ensayo o presentación y ayuda a organizar las ideas en una secuencia lógica. La estructura típica de los bosquejos es la siguiente:

I. Planteamiento

II. Cuerpo de la presentación

A. Primera idea

B. Segunda idea

C. Tercera idea

III. Conclusión: importancia de las ideas

OXYMORON / OXÍMORON Un *oxímoron* (pl. *oxímoron*) es una figura retórica que vincula dos palabras contrarias u opuestas con el fin de indicar que una idea o situación, que parece contradictoria o incoherente a simple vista, encierra algo de verdad cuando la analizamos detenidamente.

PACING / RITMO LITERARIO Los escritores usan el *ritmo literario* para hacer más lenta o más rápida la acción en una escena. La acción se hace más lenta al agregar descripciones y usar oraciones más largas. La acción se acelera al usar oraciones más cortas. El ritmo literario destaca una idea importante o crea suspenso.

PERSONIFICATION / PERSONIFICACIÓN La *personificación* es una figura retórica con la que se atribuyen características humanas a un animal o una cosa.

PERSUASION / PERSUASIÓN La *persuasión* se utiliza cuando escribimos o hablamos para convencer a nuestro lector o interlocutor de que debe adoptar una opinión concreta o tomar un rumbo en sus decisiones. Los editoriales periodísticos, las cartas al editor, los discursos de las campañas políticas y los anuncios utilizan la persuasión.

TÉCNICAS PERSUASIVAS Las *técnicas persuasivas* se utilizan para reforzar un argumento. La *repetición*, es decir, repetir una palabra o frase para que tenga más efecto, es una técnica persuasiva. Las *apelaciones a la autoridad* indican que alguien poderoso respalda una idea. Las *apelaciones a las emociones* influencian a los lectores mediante el uso de palabras que crean sentimientos positivos o negativos. Las *apelaciones a la razón* utilizan argumentos lógicos respaldados por hechos.

PLAYWRIGHT / DRAMATURGO Un *dramaturgo* es una persona que escribe obras de teatro. A William Shakespeare se le considera el mejor dramaturgo de la literatura inglesa.

PLOT / TRAMA La *trama* es la secuencia de acontecimientos en la cual cada uno de estos acontecimientos es el resultado de otro acontecimiento anterior y la causa de uno nuevo que lo sigue. En la mayoría de novelas, dramas, relatos y poemas narrativos, la trama contiene personajes y un conflicto central. La trama suele comenzar con un *planteamiento* o introducción

© Pearson Education, Inc., or its affiliates. All rights reserved.

que presenta los escenarios, los personajes y la situación básica. Los sucesos aumentan la tensión del conflicto mediante la **acción ascendente** hasta que alcanza el punto más elevado de interés o suspenso, el **clímax.** El clímax va seguido de una **acción descendente** del conflicto central. Todos los acontecimientos que ocurren durante la **acción descendente**, o final, forman el **desenlace**.

Algunas tramas no tienen todas estas partes. Algunas historias comienzan con la acción ascendente y acaban con un desenlace.

Presentación del conflicto

POETRY / POESÍA La **poesía** es uno de los tres géneros más importantes de la literatura junto con la prosa y el drama. La mayoría de los poemas utilizan lenguaje muy conciso, musical y cargado de emoción. Muchos también emplean imágenes, lenguaje figurado y recursos sonoros como la rima, el ritmo, la repetición y la onomatopeya. Los tipos de poesía más importante son la poesía lírica, la poesía narrativa y la poesía concreta.

POINT OF VIEW / PUNTO DE VISTA El **punto de vista** es la perspectiva, el punto de observación, desde el que se cuenta una historia. Puede tratarse de un narrador situado fuera de la historia o un personaje dentro de ella. El **punto de vista en primera persona** corresponde a un personaje que utiliza la primera persona "yo" o la conjugación de los verbos en primera persona del singular.

Los dos tipos de **punto de vista en tercera persona**, parcial y omnisciente, son conocidos como "tercera persona" porque el narrador utiliza los pronombres de tercera persona como "él" y "ella" y la conjugación de los verbos en tercera persona para referirse a los personajes. Por el contrario, no se utiliza el pronombre "yo".

En las historias contadas desde el **punto de vista en tercera persona omnisciente**, el narrador sabe y cuenta todo lo que sienten y piensan los personajes.

En las historia contadas desde el **punto de vista en tercera persona limitado**, el narrador relata los pensamientos y sentimientos de solo un personaje, y se cuenta todo desde la perspectiva de este personaje.

PROSE / PROSA La **prosa** es la forma más corriente del lenguaje escrito. La mayoría de los textos escritos que no se consideran poesía, drama ni canción son textos en prosa. La prosa es uno de los géneros más importantes de la literatura y puede ser de ficción o de no ficción.

PROTAGONIST / PROTAGONISTA El **protagonista** es el personaje principal de una obra literaria. Aunque suele ser una persona, a veces puede tratarse también de un animal.

REPETITION / REPETICIÓN La **repetición** se da cuando se utiliza más de una vez cualquier elemento del lenguaje (un sonido, una palabra, una expresión, un sintagma o una oración). La repetición se emplea tanto en prosa como en poesía.

RESOLUTION / DESENLACE El **desenlace** es la resolución del conflicto en una trama.

RHYTHM / RITMO El **ritmo** es el patrón de sílabas acentuadas y átonas en el lenguaje hablado o escrito.

SCENE / ESCENA Una **escena** es una sección de acción ininterrumpida dentro de alguno de los actos de un drama.

SCIENCE FICTION / CIENCIA FICCIÓN La **ciencia ficción** combina elementos de ficción y fantásticos con hechos científicos. Muchas historias de cienca ficción están situadas en el futuro.

SENSORY LANGUAGE / LENGUAJE SENSORIAL El **lenguaje sensorial** es texto o diálogo que tiene relación con uno o varios de los cinco sentidos.

SETTING / ESCENARIO El **escenario** de una obra literaria es el tiempo y lugar en los que ocurre la acción. El escenario incluye todos los detalles sobre el tiempo y el lugar: el año, el momento del día o incluso el tiempo atmosférico. El lugar puede ser un país concreto, un estado, una región, una comunidad, un barrio, un edificio, una institución o el propio hogar. Los detalles como los dialectos, ropa, costumbres y medios de trasporte se emplean con frecuencia para componer el escenario. En la mayoría de historias, los escenarios sirven de telón de fondo, es decir, de contexto en el que los personajes interactúan. El escenario también puede contribuir a crear una cierta sensación o un ambiente.

SHORT STORY / CUENTO Un **cuento** es una obra corta de ficción. Al igual que sucede en una novela, los cuentos presentan una secuencia de acontecimientos o trama. La trama suele contener un conflico central al que se enfrenta un personaje principal o protagonista. Los acontecimientos en un cuento normalmente comunican un mensaje sobre la vida o la naturaleza humana. Este mensaje o idea central es el tema de la historia.

SIMILE / SÍMIL Un **símil** es una figura retórica que utiliza **como** o **igual que** para establecer una comparación entre dos ideas distintas. Las conversaciones que mantenemos a diario también contienen símiles como, por ejemplo, "pálido como un muerto", "se expande igual que un incendio" y "listo como un zorro".

© Pearson Education, Inc., or its affiliates. All rights reserved.

SOUND DEVICES / RECURSOS SONOROS Los poetas usan *recursos sonoros* para crear efectos musicales, enfatizar el mensaje, desarrollar el tono y resaltar la relación sonora entre las palabras. Algunos de los recursos sonoros son: *repetición, onomatopeya, aliteración, consonancia* y *asonancia.*

SPEAKER / YO POÉTICO El *yo poético* es la voz imaginaria que emplea un poeta cuando escribe un poema. El yo poético es el personaje que dice el poema. Este personaje o voz no suele identificarse con un nombre. Hay notables diferencias entre el poeta y el yo poético.

STAGE DIRECTIONS / ACOTACIONES Las *acotaciones* son notas que se pueden encontrar en un texto dramático en las que se describe como se debe interpretar o escenificar la obra. Las acotaciones suelen aparecer en cursiva y encerradas entre paréntesis o corchetes. Algunas acotaciones describen los movimientos, el vestuario, los estados de ánimo y el modo en el que deben hablar los personajes.

STAGING / ESCENOGRAFÍA La *escenografía* engloba la ambientación, iluminación, vestuario, efectos especiales, música y baile que deben aparecer en el escenario donde se representa un drama.

STANZA / ESTROFA Una *estrofa* es un grupo de versos de un poema que suelen tener el mismo tamaño y patrón, y están separadas por espacios entre ellas. Una estrofa es como un párrafo en poesía: presenta y desarrolla una única idea principal.

SYMBOL / SÍMBOLO Un *símbolo* es algo que simboliza o representa una cosa diferente. Los símbolos son muy comunes en nuestra vida diaria. Una paloma con una rama de olivo en el pico es un símbolo de la paz. Una mujer con los ojos vendados sujetando una balanza es un símbolo de la justicia. Una corona es un símbolo del poder y la autoridad de un rey.

SYMBOLISM / SIMBOLISMO El *simbolismo* es el uso de los símbolos. El simbolismo juega un papel importante en muchos tipos de literatura. Puede ayudar a destacar algunos elementos que el autor quiere subrayar y añadir otros niveles de significado.

SYNTAX / SINTAXIS El orden de las palabras en una oración es la *sintaxis*. Los poetas suelen jugar con la sintaxis para resaltar las ideas.

TECHNICAL LANGUAGE / LENGUAJE TÉCNICO El *lenguaje técnico* son las palabras o terminología que se usa para hablar de un tema, proceso o industria en particular.

THEME / TEMA El *tema* es la idea central, asunto o propósito de una obra literaria. Un tema se expresa comúnmente como una generalización o declaración general sobre los seres humanos o la vida. El tema de una obra no es el resumen de su trama. El tema es la idea central del escritor.

Aunque el tema puede ser expuesto directamente en el texto, a menudo se suele presentar indirectamente. Cuando se expone el tema indirecta o implícitamente, el lector podrá deducirlo observando lo que se muestra en la obra sobre la vida y las personas.

THESIS / TESIS La *tesis* es una oración que expresa la idea principal de un ensayo.

TONE / TONO El *tono* de una obra literaria es la actitud del escritor hacia sus lectores o aquello sobre lo que escribe. El tono puede ser descrito con un único adjetivo como, por ejemplo, *formal* o *informal, serio* o *jocoso, amargo* o *irónico.* Los factores que contribuyen a crear el tono son la elección de las palabras, la estructura de la oración, el tamaño de un verso, la rima, el ritmo y la repetición.

TOPIC SENTENCE / ORACIÓN TEMÁTICA Cada uno de los párrafos de un ensayo debe tener una *oración temática* que expresa la idea principal del párrafo. El párrafo debe también tener datos y ejemplos que respalden la idea principal.

UNIVERSAL THEME / TEMA UNIVERSAL Un *tema universal* es un mensaje sobre la vida que se expresa habitualmente en muchas culturas y períodos históricos diferentes. Los cuentos populares, epopeyas y romances suelen abordar temas universales como la importancia de la valentía, el poder del amor o el peligro de la avaricia.

VERSE / VERSO El *verso* es un tipo de literatura también conocida como poesía. El *verso libre* no sigue un patrón regular y rítmico, es decir, no sigue la métrica. El poeta es libre para escribir versos de distintas extensiones o con diferente cantidad de acentos. Por lo tanto, el verso libre es menos restrictivo que el *verso métrico*, en el cual los versos deben tener una extensión determinada y un número particular de acentos.

VOICE / VOZ La voz describe el estilo particular del escritor. La voz del escritor se ve influenciada por la *elección de palabras*, es decir, la preferenica y uso que el escritor hace de ciertas palabras; la *estructura de las oraciones* o manera en la que el escritor construye las oraciones; y el *tono* o actitud del escritor hacia aquello sobre lo que escribe.

© Pearson Education, Inc., or its affiliates. All rights reserved.

GLOSARIO: MANUAL DE TÉRMINOS LITERARIOS

GRAMMAR HANDBOOK

PARTS OF SPEECH

Every English word, depending on its meaning and its use in a sentence, can be identified as one of the eight parts of speech. These are nouns, pronouns, verbs, adjectives, adverbs, prepositions, conjunctions, and interjections. Understanding the parts of speech will help you learn the rules of English grammar and usage.

Nouns A **noun** names a person, place, or thing. A **common noun** names any one of a class of persons, places, or things. A **proper noun** names a specific person, place, or thing.

Common Noun	Proper Noun
writer, country, novel	Charles Dickens, Great Britain, *Hard Times*

Pronouns A **pronoun** is a word that stands for one or more nouns. The word to which a pronoun refers (whose place it takes) is the **antecedent** of the pronoun.

A **personal pronoun** refers to the person speaking (first person); the person spoken to (second person); or the person, place, or thing spoken about (third person).

	Singular	Plural
First Person	I, me, my, mine	we, us, our, ours
Second Person	you, your, yours	you, your, yours
Third Person	he, him, his, she, her, hers, it, its	they, them, their, theirs

A **reflexive pronoun** reflects the action of a verb back on its subject. It indicates that the person or thing performing the action also is receiving the action.

I keep *myself* fit by taking a walk every day.

An **intensive pronoun** adds emphasis to a noun or pronoun.

It took the work of the president *himself* to pass the law.

A **demonstrative** pronoun points out a specific person(s), place(s), or thing(s).

this, that, these, those

A **relative pronoun** begins a subordinate clause and connects it to another idea in the sentence.

that, which, who, whom, whose

An **interrogative pronoun** begins a question.

what, which, who, whom, whose

An **indefinite pronoun** refers to a person, place, or thing that may or may not be specifically named.

all, another, any, both, each, everyone, few, most, none, no one, somebody

Verbs A **verb** expresses action or the existence of a state or condition.

An **action verb** tells what action someone or something is performing.

gather, read, work, jump, imagine, analyze, conclude

A **linking verb** connects the subject with another word that identifies or describes the subject. The most common linking verb is *be.*

appear, be, become, feel, look, remain, seem, smell, sound, stay, taste

A **helping verb,** or **auxiliary verb,** is added to a main verb to make a verb phrase.

be, do, have, should, can, could, may, might, must, will, would

Adjectives An **adjective** modifies a noun or pronoun by describing it or giving it a more specific meaning. An adjective answers the questions:

What kind?	*purple* hat, *happy* face, *loud* sound
Which one?	*this* bowl
How many?	*three* cars
How much?	*enough* food

The articles *the, a,* and *an* are adjectives.

A **proper adjective** is an adjective derived from a proper noun.

French, Shakespearean

Adverbs An **adverb** modifies a verb, an adjective, or another adverb by telling *where, when, how,* or *to what extent.*

will answer *soon, extremely* sad, calls *more* often

Prepositions A **preposition** relates a noun or pronoun that appears with it to another word in the sentence.

Dad made a meal *for* us. We talked *till* dusk. Bo missed school *because of* his illness.

Conjunctions A **conjunction** connects words or groups of words. A **coordinating conjunction** joins words or groups of words of equal rank.

bread *and* cheese, brief *but* powerful

Correlative conjunctions are used in pairs to connect words or groups of words of equal importance.

both Luis *and* Rosa, *neither* you *nor* I

© Pearson Education, Inc., or its affiliates. All rights reserved.

PARTS OF SPEECH continued

Subordinating conjunctions indicate the connection between two ideas by placing one below the other in rank or importance. A subordinating conjunction introduces a subordinate, or dependent, clause.

> We will miss her *if* she leaves. Hank shrieked *when* he slipped on the ice.

Interjections An **interjection** expresses feeling or emotion. It is not related to other words in the sentence.

> ah, hey, ouch, well, yippee

PHRASES AND CLAUSES

Phrases A **phrase** is a group of words that does not have both a subject and a verb and that functions as one part of speech. A phrase expresses an idea but cannot stand alone.

Prepositional Phrases A **prepositional phrase** is a group of words that begins with a preposition and ends with a noun or pronoun that is the **object of the preposition.**

> before dawn   as a result of the rain

An **adjective phrase** is a prepositional phrase that modifies a noun or pronoun.

> Eliza appreciates the beauty **of a well-crafted poem.**

An **adverb phrase** is a prepositional phrase that modifies a verb, an adjective, or an adverb.

> She reads Spenser's sonnets **with great pleasure.**

Appositive Phrases An **appositive** is a noun or pronoun placed next to another noun or pronoun to add information about it. An **appositive phrase** consists of an appositive and its modifiers.

> Mr. Roth, **my music teacher,** is sick.

Verbal Phrases A **verbal** is a verb form that functions as a different part of speech (not as a verb) in a sentence. **Participles, gerunds,** and **infinitives** are verbals.

A **verbal phrase** includes a verbal and any modifiers or complements it may have. Verbal phrases may function as nouns, as adjectives, or as adverbs.

A **participle** is a verb form that can act as an adjective. Present participles end in *-ing;* past participles of regular verbs end in *-ed.*

A **participial phrase** consists of a participle and its modifiers or complements. The entire phrase acts as an adjective.

> Jenna's backpack, **loaded with equipment,** was heavy.
> **Barking incessantly,** the dogs chased the squirrels out of sight.

A **gerund** is a verb form that ends in *-ing* and is used as a noun.

A **gerund phrase** consists of a gerund with any modifiers or complements, all acting together as a noun.

> **Taking photographs of wildlife** is her main hobby. [acts as subject]
> We always enjoy **listening to live music.** [acts as object]

An **infinitive** is a verb form, usually preceded by *to,* that can act as a noun, an adjective, or an adverb.

An **infinitive phrase** consists of an infinitive and its modifiers or complements, and sometimes its subject, all acting together as a single part of speech.

> She tries **to get out into the wilderness often.** [acts as a noun; direct object of *tries*]
> The Tigers are the team **to beat.** [acts as an adjective; describes *team*]
> I drove twenty miles **to witness the event.** [acts as an adverb; tells why I drove]

Clauses A **clause** is a group of words with its own subject and verb.

Independent Clauses An independent clause can stand by itself as a complete sentence.

> George Orwell wrote with extraordinary insight.

Subordinate Clauses A subordinate clause cannot stand by itself as a complete sentence. Subordinate clauses always appear connected in some way with one or more independent clauses.

> George Orwell, **who wrote with extraordinary insight,** produced many politically relevant works.

An **adjective clause** is a subordinate clause that acts as an adjective. It modifies a noun or a pronoun by telling *what kind* or *which one.* Also called relative clauses, adjective clauses usually begin with a **relative pronoun:** *who, which, that, whom,* or *whose.*

> "The Lamb" is the poem **that I memorized for class.**

An **adverb clause** is a subordinate clause that, like an adverb, modifies a verb, an adjective, or an adverb. An adverb clause tells *where, when, in what way, to what extent, under what condition,* or *why.*

GLOSSARY: GRAMMAR HANDBOOK

© Pearson Education, Inc., or its affiliates. All rights reserved.

The students will read another poetry collection **if their schedule allows.**
When I recited the poem, Mr. Lopez was impressed.

A **noun clause** is a subordinate clause that acts as a noun.

William Blake survived on **whatever he made as an engraver.**

SENTENCE STRUCTURE

Subject and Predicate A **sentence** is a group of words that expresses a complete thought. A sentence has two main parts: a *subject* and a *predicate*.

A **fragment** is a group of words that does not express a complete thought. It lacks an independent clause.

The **subject** tells *whom* or *what* the sentence is about. The **predicate** tells what the subject of the sentence does or is.

A subject or a predicate can consist of a single word or of many words. All the words in the subject make up the **complete subject.** All the words in the predicate make up the **complete predicate.**

Complete Subject   Complete Predicate
Both of those girls | have already read *Macbeth*.

The **simple subject** is the essential noun, pronoun, or group of words acting as a noun that cannot be left out of the complete subject. The **simple predicate** is the essential verb or verb phrase that cannot be left out of the complete predicate.

Both of those girls | **have** already **read** *Macbeth*.
[Simple subject: *Both*; simple predicate: *have read*]

A **compound subject** is two or more subjects that have the same verb and are joined by a conjunction.

Neither the horse nor the driver looked tired.

A **compound predicate** is two or more verbs that have the same subject and are joined by a conjunction.

She **sneezed and coughed** throughout the trip.

Complements A **complement** is a word or word group that completes the meaning of the subject or verb in a sentence. There are four kinds of complements: *direct objects, indirect objects, objective complements,* and *subject complements.*

A **direct object** is a noun, a pronoun, or a group of words acting as a noun that receives the action of a transitive verb.

We watched the **liftoff**.
She drove **Zach** to the launch site.

An **indirect object** is a noun or pronoun that appears with a direct object and names the person or thing to which or for which something is done.

He sold the **family** a mirror. [The direct object is *mirror.*]

An **objective complement** is an adjective or noun that appears with a direct object and describes or renames it.

The decision made her **unhappy**.
[The direct object is *her.*]
Many consider Shakespeare the greatest **playwright.** [The direct object is *Shakespeare.*]

A **subject complement** follows a linking verb and tells something about the subject. There are two kinds: *predicate nominatives* and *predicate adjectives.*

A **predicate nominative** is a noun or pronoun that follows a linking verb and identifies or renames the subject.

"A Modest Proposal" is a **pamphlet.**

A **predicate adjective** is an adjective that follows a linking verb and describes the subject of the sentence.

"A Modest Proposal" is **satirical.**

Classifying Sentences by Structure

Sentences can be classified according to the kind and number of clauses they contain. The four basic sentence structures are *simple, compound, complex,* and *compound-complex.*

A **simple sentence** consists of one independent clause.

Terrence enjoys modern British literature.

A **compound sentence** consists of two or more independent clauses. The clauses are joined by a conjunction or a semicolon.

Terrence enjoys modern British literature, but his brother prefers the classics.

A **complex sentence** consists of one independent clause and one or more subordinate clauses.

Terrence, who reads voraciously, enjoys modern British literature.

A **compound-complex sentence** consists of two or more independent clauses and one or more subordinate clauses.

Terrence, who reads voraciously, enjoys modern British literature, but his brother prefers the classics.

Classifying Sentences by Function

Sentences can be classified according to their function or purpose. The four types are *declarative, interrogative, imperative,* and *exclamatory.*

© Pearson Education, Inc, or its affiliates. All rights reserved.

A **declarative sentence** states an idea and ends with a period.

An **interrogative sentence** asks a question and ends with a question mark.

An **imperative sentence** gives an order or a direction and ends with either a period or an exclamation mark.

An **exclamatory sentence** conveys a strong emotion and ends with an exclamation mark.

PARAGRAPH STRUCTURE

An effective paragraph is organized around one **main idea,** which is often stated in a **topic sentence.** The other sentences support the main idea. To give the paragraph **unity,** make sure the connection between each sentence and the main idea is clear.

Unnecessary Shift in Person

Do not change needlessly from one grammatical person to another. Keep the person consistent in your sentences.

> **Max** went to the bakery, but **you** can't buy mints there. [shift from third person to second person]

> **Max** went to the bakery, but **he** can't buy mints there. [consistent]

Unnecessary Shift in Voice

Do not change needlessly from active voice to passive voice in your use of verbs.

> Elena and I **searched** the trail for evidence, but no clues **were found.** [shift from active voice to passive voice]

> Elena and I **searched** the trail for evidence, but we **found** no clues. [consistent]

AGREEMENT

Subject and Verb Agreement

A singular subject must have a singular verb. A plural subject must have a plural verb.

> **Dr. Boone uses** a telescope to view the night sky.
> The **students use** a telescope to view the night sky.

A verb always agrees with its subject, not its object.

> *Incorrect:* The best part of the show were the jugglers.
> *Correct:* The best part of the show was the jugglers.

A phrase or clause that comes between a subject and verb does not affect subject-verb agreement.

> His **theory,** as well as his claims, **lacks** support.

Two subjects joined by *and* usually take a plural verb.

> The **dog** and the **cat are** healthy.

Two singular subjects joined by *or* or *nor* take a singular verb.

> The **dog** or the **cat is** hiding.

Two plural subjects joined by *or* or *nor* take a plural verb.

> The **dogs** or the **cats are** coming home with us.

When a singular and a plural subject are joined by *or* or *nor,* the verb agrees with the closer subject.

> Either the **dogs** or the **cat is** behind the door.
> Either the **cat** or the **dogs are** behind the door.

Pronoun and Antecedent Agreement

Pronouns must agree with their antecedents in number and gender. Use singular pronouns with singular antecedents and plural pronouns with plural antecedents.

> **Doris Lessing** uses **her** writing to challenge ideas about women's roles.
> **Writers** often use **their** skills to promote social change.

Use a singular pronoun when the antecedent is a singular indefinite pronoun such as *anybody, each, either, everybody, neither, no one, one,* or *someone.*

> Judge **each** of the articles on **its** merits.

Use a plural pronoun when the antecedent is a plural indefinite pronoun such as *both, few, many,* or *several.*

> **Both** of the articles have **their** flaws.

The indefinite pronouns *all, any, more, most, none,* and *some* can be singular or plural depending on the number of the word to which they refer.

> **Most** of the *books* are in **their** proper places.
> **Most** of the *book* has been torn from **its** binding.

© Pearson Education, Inc., or its affiliates. All rights reserved.

USING VERBS

Principal Parts of Regular and Irregular Verbs

A verb has four principal parts:

Present	Present Participle	Past	Past Participle
learn	learning	learned	learned
discuss	discussing	discussed	discussed
stand	standing	stood	stood
begin	beginning	began	begun

Regular verbs such as *learn* and *discuss* form the past and past participle by adding *-ed* to the present form. **Irregular verbs** such as *stand* and *begin* form the past and past participle in other ways. If you are in doubt about the principal parts of an irregular verb, check a dictionary.

The Tenses of Verbs

The different tenses of verbs indicate the time an action or condition occurs.

The **present tense** expresses an action that happens regularly or states a current condition or general truth.

> Tourists **flock** to the site yearly.

Daily exercise **is** good for your heallth.

The **past tense** expresses a completed action or a condition that is no longer true.

> The squirrel **dropped** the nut and **ran** up the tree.
> I **was** very tired last night by 9:00.

The **future tense** indicates an action that will happen in the future or a condition that will be true.

> The Glazers **will visit** us tomorrow.
> They **will be** glad to arrive from their long journey.

The **present perfect tense** expresses an action that happened at an indefinite time in the past or an action that began in the past and continues into the present.

> Someone **has cleaned** the trash from the park.
> The puppy **has been** under the bed all day.

The **past perfect tense** shows an action that was completed before another action in the past.

> Gerard **had revised** his essay before he turned it in.

The **future perfect tense** indicates an action that will have been completed before another action takes place.

> Mimi **will have painted** the kitchen by the time we finish the shutters.

USING MODIFIERS

Degrees of Comparison

Adjectives and adverbs take different forms to show the three degrees of comparison: the *positive*, the *comparative*, and the *superlative*.

Positive	Comparative	Superlative
fast	faster	fastest
crafty	craftier	craftiest
abruptly	more abruptly	most abruptly
badly	worse	worst

Using Comparative and Superlative Adjectives and Adverbs

Use comparative adjectives and adverbs to compare two things. Use superlative adjectives and adverbs to compare three or more things.

> This season's weather was **drier** than last year's.
> This season has been one of the **driest** on record.
> Jake practices **more often** than Jamal.
> Of everyone in the band, Jake practices **most often.**

USING PRONOUNS

Pronoun Case

The **case** of a pronoun is the form it takes to show its function in a sentence. There are three pronoun cases: *nominative, objective,* and *possessive.*

Nominative	Objective	Possessive
I, you, he, she, it, we, you, they	me, you, him, her, it, us, you, them	my, your, yours, his, her, hers, its, our, ours, their, theirs

Use the **nominative case** when a pronoun functions as a *subject* or as a *predicate nominative.*

> **They** are going to the movies. [subject]

The biggest movie fan is **she.** [predicate nominative]

Use the **objective case** for a pronoun acting as a *direct object,* an *indirect object,* or the *object of a preposition.*

> The ending of the play surprised **me.** [direct object]
> Mary gave **us** two tickets to the play. [indirect object]
> The audience cheered for **him.** [object of preposition]

Use the **possessive case** to show ownership.

> The red suitcase is **hers.**

© Pearson Education, Inc., or its affiliates. All rights reserved.

Diction The words you choose contribute to the overall effectiveness of your writing. **Diction** refers to word choice and to the clearness and correctness of those words. You can improve one aspect of your diction by choosing carefully between commonly confused words, such as the pairs listed below.

accept, except

Accept is a verb that means "to receive" or "to agree to." *Except* is a preposition that means "other than" or "leaving out."

> Please **accept** my offer to buy you lunch this weekend.
>
> He is busy every day **except** the weekends.

affect, effect

Affect is normally a verb meaning "to influence" or "to bring about a change in." *Effect* is usually a noun meaning "result."

> The distractions outside **affect** Steven's ability to concentrate.
>
> The teacher's remedies had a positive **effect** on Steven's ability to concentrate.

among, between

Among is usually used with three or more items, and it emphasizes collective relationships or indicates distribution. *Between* is generally used with only two items, but it can be used with more than two if the emphasis is on individual (one-to-one) relationships within the group.

> I had to choose a snack **among** the various vegetables.
>
> He handed out the booklets **among** the conference participants.
>
> Our school is **between** a park and an old barn.
>
> The tournament included matches **between** France, Spain, Mexico, and the United States.

amount, number

Amount refers to overall quantity and is mainly used with mass nouns (those that can't be counted). *Number* refers to individual items that can be counted.

> The **amount** of attention that great writers have paid to Shakespeare is remarkable.
>
> A **number** of important English writers have been fascinated by the legend of King Arthur.

assure, ensure, insure

Assure means "to convince [someone of something]; to guarantee." *Ensure* means "to make certain [that something happens]." *Insure* means "to arrange for payment in case of loss."

> The attorney **assured** us we'd win the case.
>
> The rules **ensure** that no one gets treated unfairly.
>
> Many professional musicians **insure** their valuable instruments.

bad, badly

Use the adjective *bad* before a noun or after linking verbs such as *feel, look,* and *seem.* Use *badly* whenever an adverb is required.

> The situation may seem **bad**, but it will improve over time.
>
> Though our team played **badly** today, we will focus on practicing for the next match.

beside, besides

Beside means "at the side of" or "close to." *Besides* means "in addition to."

> The stapler sits **beside** the pencil sharpener in our classroom.
>
> **Besides** being very clean, the classroom is also very organized.

can, may

The helping verb *can* generally refers to the ability to do something. The helping verb *may* generally refers to permission to do something.

> I **can** run one mile in six minutes.
>
> **May** we have a race during recess?

complement, compliment

The verb *complement* means "to enhance"; the verb *compliment* means "to praise."

> Online exercises **complement** the textbook lessons.
>
> Ms. Lewis **complimented** our team on our excellent debate.

compose, comprise

Compose means "to make up; constitute." *Comprise* means "to include or contain." Remember that the whole comprises its parts or is composed of its parts, and the parts compose the whole.

> The assignment **comprises** three different tasks.
>
> The assignment is **composed** of three different tasks.
>
> Three different tasks **compose** the assignment.

different from, different than

Different from is generally preferred over *different than,* but *different than* can be used before a clause. Always use *different from* before a noun or pronoun.

> Your point of view is so **different from** mine.
>
> His idea was so **different from** [or **different than**] what we had expected.

farther, further

Use *farther* to refer to distance. Use *further* to mean "to a greater degree or extent" or "additional."

> Chiang has traveled **farther** than anybody else in the class.
>
> If I want **further** details about his travels, I can read his blog.

GLOSSARY: GRAMMAR HANDBOOK

© Pearson Education, Inc., or its affiliates. All rights reserved.

fewer, less

Use *fewer* for things that can be counted. Use *less* for amounts or quantities that cannot be counted. *Fewer* must be followed by a plural noun.

Fewer students drive to school since the weather improved.

There is **less** noise outside in the mornings.

good, well

Use the adjective *good* before a noun or after a linking verb. Use *well* whenever an adverb is required, such as when modifying a verb.

I feel **good** after sleeping for eight hours.

I did **well** on my test, and my soccer team played **well** in that afternoon's game. It was a **good** day!

its, it's

The word *its* with no apostrophe is a possessive pronoun. The word *it's* is a contraction of "it is."

Angelica will try to fix the computer and **its** keyboard.

It's a difficult job, but she can do it.

lay, lie

Lay is a transitive verb meaning "to set or put something down." Its principal parts are *lay, laying, laid, laid. Lie* is an intransitive verb meaning "to recline" or "to exist in a certain place." Its principal parts are *lie, lying, lay, lain.*

Please **lay** that box down and help me with the sofa.

When we are done moving, I am going to **lie** down.

My hometown **lies** sixty miles north of here.

like, as

Like is a preposition that usually means "similar to" and precedes a noun or pronoun. The conjunction *as* means "in the way that" and usually precedes a clause.

Like the other students, I was prepared for a quiz.

As I said yesterday, we expect to finish before noon.

Use **such as,** not **like,** before a series of examples.

Foods **such as** apples, nuts, and pretzels make good snacks.

of, have

Do not use *of* in place of *have* after auxiliary verbs such as *would, could, should, may, might,* or *must.* The contraction of *have* is formed by adding *-ve* after these verbs.

I **would have** stayed after school today, but I had to help cook at home.

Mom **must've** called while I was still in the gym.

principal, principle

Principal can be an adjective meaning "main; most important." It can also be a noun meaning "chief officer of a school." *Principle* is a noun meaning "moral rule" or "fundamental truth."

His strange behavior was the **principal** reason for our concern.

Democratic **principles** form the basis of our country's laws.

raise, rise

Raise is a transitive verb that usually takes a direct object. *Rise* is intransitive and never takes a direct object.

Iliana and Josef **raise** the flag every morning.

They **rise** from their seats and volunteer immediately whenever help is needed.

than, then

The conjunction *than* is used to connect the two parts of a comparison. The adverb *then* usually refers to time.

My backpack is heavier **than** hers.

I will finish my homework and **then** meet my friends at the park.

that, which, who

Use the relative pronoun *that* to refer to things or people. Use *which* only for things and *who* only for people.

That introduces a restrictive phrase or clause, that is, one that is essential to the meaning of the sentence. *Which* introduces a nonrestrictive phrase or clause—one that adds information but could be deleted from the sentence—and is preceded by a comma.

Ben ran to the park **that** just reopened.

The park, **which** just reopened, has many attractions.

The man **who** built the park loves to see people smiling.

when, where, why

Do not use *when, where,* or *why* directly after a linking verb, such as *is.* Reword the sentence.

Incorrect: The morning is when he left for the beach.

Correct: He left for the beach in the morning.

who, whom

In formal writing, use *who* only as a subject in clauses and sentences. Use *whom* only as the object of a verb or of a preposition.

Who paid for the tickets?

Whom should I pay for the tickets?

I can't recall to **whom** I gave the money for the tickets.

your, you're

Your is a possessive pronoun expressing ownership. *You're* is the contraction of "you are."

Have you finished writing **your** informative essay?

You're supposed to turn it in tomorrow. If **you're** late, **your** grade will be affected.

© Pearson Education, Inc., or its affiliates. All rights reserved.

Capitalization

First Words

Capitalize the first word of a sentence.

Stories about knights and their deeds interest me.

Capitalize the first word of direct speech.

Sharon asked, "**D**o you like stories about knights?"

Capitalize the first word of a quotation that is a complete sentence.

Einstein said, "**A**nyone who has never made a mistake has never tried anything new."

Proper Nouns and Proper Adjectives

Capitalize all proper nouns, including geographical names, historical events and periods, and names of organizations.

Thames **R**iver	**J**ohn **K**eats	the **R**enaissance
United **N**ations	**W**orld **W**ar II	**S**ierra **N**evada

Capitalize all proper adjectives.

Shakespearean play	**B**ritish invaision
American citizen	**L**atin **A**merican literature

Academic Course Names

Capitalize course names only if they are language courses, are followed by a number, or are preceded by a proper noun or adjective.

Spanish	**H**onors **C**hemistry	**H**istory 101
geology	**a**lgebra	**s**ocial **s**tudies

Titles

Capitalize personal titles when followed by the person's name.

Ms. Hughes   **D**r. Perez   **K**ing George

Capitalize titles showing family relationships when they are followed by a specific person's name, unless they are preceded by a possessive noun or pronoun.

Uncle Oscar   Mangan's **s**ister   his **a**unt Tessa

Capitalize the first word and all other key words in the titles of books, stories, songs, and other works of art.

Frankenstein   "**S**hooting an **E**lephant"

Punctuation

End Marks

Use a **period** to end a declarative sentence or an imperative sentence.

We are studying the structure of sonnets.
Read the biography of Mary Shelley.

Use periods with initials and abbreviations.

D. H. Lawrence	Mrs. Browning
Mt. Everest	Maple St.

Use a **question mark** to end an interrogative sentence.

What is Macbeth's fatal flaw?

Use an **exclamation mark** after an exclamatory sentence or a forceful imperative sentence.

That's a beautiful painting!   Let me go now!

Commas

Use a **comma** before a coordinating conjunction to separate two independent clauses in a compound sentence.

The game was very close, but we were victorious.

Use commas to separate three or more words, phrases, or clauses in a series.

William Blake was a writer, artist, and printer.

Use commas to separate coordinate adjectives.

It was a witty, amusing novel.

Use a comma after an introductory word, phrase, or clause.

When the novelist finished his book, he celebrated with his family.

Use commas to set off nonessential expressions.

Old English, of course, requires translation.

Use commas with places and dates.

Coventry, England   September 1, 1939

Semicolons

Use a **semicolon** to join closely related independent clauses that are not already joined by a conjunction.

Tanya likes to write poetry; Heather prefers prose.

Use semicolons to avoid confusion when items in a series contain commas.

They traveled to London, England; Madrid, Spain; and Rome, Italy.

Colons

Use a **colon** before a list of items following an independent clause.

Notable Victorian poets include the following: Tennyson, Arnold, Housman, and Hopkins.

Use a colon to introduce information that summarizes or explains the independent clause before it.

She just wanted to do one thing: rest.
Malcolm loves volunteering: He reads to sick children every Saturday afternoon.

Quotation Marks

Use **quotation marks** to enclose a direct quotation.

"Short stories," Ms. Hildebrand said, "should have rich, well-developed characters."

An **indirect quotation** does not require quotation marks.

Ms. Hildebrand said that short stories should have well-developed characters.

Use quotation marks around the titles of short written works, episodes in a series, songs, and works mentioned as parts of collections.

"The Lagoon"   "Boswell Meets Johnson"

© Pearson Education, Inc., or its affiliates. All rights reserved.

GLOSSARY: GRAMMAR HANDBOOK

Italics

Italicize the titles of long written works, movies, television and radio shows, lengthy works of music, paintings, and sculptures.

Howards End   *60 Minutes*   *Guernica*

For handwritten material, you can use underlining instead of italics.

<u>The Princess Bride</u>   <u>Mona Lisa</u>

Dashes

Use **dashes** to indicate an abrupt change of thought, a dramatic interrupting idea, or a summary statement.

I read the entire first act of *Macbeth*—you won't believe what happens next.

The director—what's her name again?—attended the movie premiere.

Hyphens

Use a **hyphen** with certain numbers, after certain prefixes, with two or more words used as one word, and with a compound modifier that comes before a noun.

seventy-two

self-esteem

president-elect

five-year contract

Parentheses

Use **parentheses** to set off asides and explanations when the material is not essential or when it consists of one or more sentences. When the sentence in parentheses interrupts the larger sentence, it does not have a capital letter or a period.

He listened intently (it was too dark to see who was speaking) to try to identify the voices.

When a sentence in parentheses falls between two other complete sentences, it should start with a capital letter and end with a period.

The quarterback threw three touchdown passes. (We knew he could do it.) Our team won the game by two points.

Apostrophes

Add an **apostrophe** and an *s* to show the possessive case of most singular nouns and of plural nouns that do not end in -*s* or -*es*.

Blake's poems   the mice's whiskers

Names ending in *s* form their possessives in the same way, except for classical and biblical names, which add only an apostrophe to form the possessive.

Dickens's   Hercules'

Add an apostrophe to show the possessive case of plural nouns ending in -*s* and -*es*.

the girls' songs   the Ortizes' car

Use an apostrophe in a contraction to indicate the position of the missing letter or letters.

She's never read a Coleridge poem she didn't like.

Brackets

Use **brackets** to enclose clarifying information inserted within a quotation.

Columbus's journal entry from October 21, 1492, begins as follows: "At 10 o'clock, we arrived at a cape of the island [San Salvador], and anchored, the other vessels in company."

Ellipses

Use three ellipsis points, also known as an **ellipsis,** to indicate where you have omitted words from quoted material.

Wollestonecraft wrote, "The education of women has of late been more attended to than formerly; yet they are still . . . ridiculed or pitied. . . ."

In the example above, the four dots at the end of the sentence are the three ellipsis points plus the period from the original sentence.

Use an ellipsis to indicate a pause or interruption in speech.

"When he told me the news," said the coach, "I was . . . I was shocked . . . completely shocked."

Spelling

Spelling Rules

Learning the rules of English spelling will help you make **generalizations** about how to spell words.

Word Parts

The three word parts that can combine to form a word are roots, prefixes, and suffixes. Many of these word parts come from the Greek, Latin, and Anglo-Saxon languages.

The **root word** carries a word's basic meaning.

Root and Origin	Meaning	Examples
-leg- (-log-) [Gr.]	to say, speak	*legal, logic*
-pon- (-pos-) [L.]	to put, place	*postpone, deposit*

A **prefix** is one or more syllables added to the beginning of a word that alter the meaning of the root.

Prefix and Origin	Meaning	Example
anti- [Gr.]	against	*antipathy*
inter- [L.]	between	*international*
mis- [A.S.]	wrong	*misplace*

© Pearson Education, Inc, or its affiliates. All rights reserved.

A **suffix** is a letter or group of letters added to the end of a root word that changes the word's meaning or part of speech.

Suffix and Origin	Meaning and Example	Part of Speech
-ful [A.S.]	full of: *scornful*	adjective
-ity [L.]	state of being: *adversity*	noun
-ize (-ise) [Gr.]	to make: *idolize*	verb
-ly [A.S.]	in a manner: *calmly*	adverb

Rules for Adding Suffixes to Root Words

When adding a suffix to a root word ending in *y* preceded by a consonant, change *y* to *i* unless the suffix begins with *i*.

ply + -able = pliable   happy + -ness = happiness

defy + -ing = defying   cry + -ing = crying

For a root word ending in *e*, drop the *e* when adding a suffix beginning with a vowel.

drive + -ing = driving   move + -able = movable

SOME EXCEPTIONS: traceable, seeing, dyeing

For root words ending with a consonant + vowel + consonant in a stressed syllable, double the final consonant when adding a suffix that begins with a vowel.

mud + -y = muddy   submit + -ed = submitted

SOME EXCEPTIONS: mixing, fixed

Rules for Adding Prefixes to Root Words

When a prefix is added to a root word, the spelling of the root remains the same.

un- + certain = uncertain   mis- + spell = misspell

With some prefixes, the spelling of the prefix changes when joined to the root to make the pronunciation easier.

in- + mortal = immortal   ad- + vert = avert

Orthographic Patterns

Certain letter combinations in English make certain sounds. For instance, *ph* sounds like *f*, *eigh* usually makes a long *a* sound, and the *k* before an *n* is often silent.

pharmacy   n**eigh**bor   **k**nowledge

Understanding **orthographic patterns** such as these can help you improve your spelling.

Forming Plurals

The plural form of most nouns is formed by adding -*s* to the singular.

computer**s**   gadget**s**   Washington**s**

For words ending in *s, ss, x, z, sh,* or *ch,* add -*es.*

circus**es**   tax**es**   wish**es**   bench**es**

For words ending in *y* or *o* preceded by a vowel, add -*s.*

key**s**   patio**s**

For words ending in *y* preceded by a consonant, change the *y* to an *i* and add -*es.*

cit**ies**   enem**ies**   troph**ies**

For most words ending in *o* preceded by a consonant, add -*es.*

echo**es**   tomato**es**

Some words form the plural in irregular ways.

women   oxen   children   teeth   deer

Foreign Words Used in English

Some words used in English are actually foreign words that have been adopted. Learning to spell these words requires memorization. When in doubt, check a dictionary.

sushi   enchilada   au pair   fiancé

laissez faire   croissant

© Pearson Education, Inc., or its affiliates. All rights reserved.

GLOSSARY: GRAMMAR HANDBOOK

INDEX OF SKILLS

Boldface numbers indicate pages where terms are defined.

© Pearson Education, Inc., or its affiliates. All rights reserved.

consonance, 377
onomatopoeia, 377
repetition, 142
stage directions, 341
stanza structure, 148
couplet, 148
octave, 148
quatrain, 148
sestet, 148
structure, 47
theme, 74, 123, 201
implied theme, 201
science fiction, 245
universal, 460
tone, 142, 377
poetry, 142
word choice
poetry, 142
Drama, 282, 283, 312, 313
acts, 309
dialogue, 309
point of view, 309
scene, 309
script, 309
stage directions, 341
Draw conclusions, 30, 112, 200, 308, 432
Essay, 153
explanatory essay, 93, 94
reflective essay, 253, 381
Essential question, 10, 20, 30, 80, 98, 112, 122, 134, 174, 192, 210, 218, 226, 234, 262, 280, 308, 340, 349, 358, 390, 424, 440, 476
Evaluate, 200, 210, 218, 226
Explanatory essay, 93, 94
Fiction, 194, 238, 362
short story, 195, 238, 239
Fictional narrative, 275, 276
First read
drama, 282, 312
fiction, 194, 238, 362
first-read guide, 82, 176, 264, 392, 478
nonfiction, 42, 100, 206, 214, 248, 380, 410, 444, 452, 458
blog post, 118
informational text, 50, 60
short story, 162
poetry, 68, 138, 144, 372
First review media
art and photography, 26, 152, 466
audio, 256
video, 224, 346, 430
Independent learning, 174

close-read guide, 83, 177, 265, 393, 479
first-read guide, 82, 176, 264, 392, 478
share learning, 84, 178, 266, 394, 480
strategies
create a schedule, 80, 174, 262, 390, 476
practice what you have learned, 80, 174, 262, 390, 476
take notes, 80, 174, 262, 390, 476
Infer, 200
Interpret, 112, 122, 210, 226, 308, 349, 424
Magazine article, 51
Make a judgment, 20, 122, 200
Make inferences, 20, 30, 424
Media
analyze, 30, 226, 349
describe, 432
essential question, 160, 258, 432
evaluate, 432
infer, 432
interpret, 432
present and discuss, 160, 258
review and synthesize, 160, 258
audio, 256
comic strip, 27
graphic novel, 467
podcast, 257
video, 54, 121, 224, 346, 347, 430
visual essay, 153
Memoir, 12, 60, 61, 68, 101, 113, 411
Metaphor, 207
Narrative
fictional, 275, 276
nonfiction, 5, 6
News article, 445
Nonfiction
memoir, 12
short story, 163
Nonfiction narrative, 5, 6
Novel excerpt, 363
Paraphrase, 210, 340
Plot, 169
climax, 169
conflict, 169
external, 169
internal, 169
exposition, 169
falling action, 169
resolution, 169
rising action, 169
Podcast, 257

Poetry, 60, 68, 69, 138, 139, 144, 145, 149, 372, 373
figurative language, 142
sound devices, 142
speaker, 148
stanza, 148
structure, 148
word meanings, 148
Problem/solution, 340
Public document, 43
Reflective essay, 381
Science fiction, 245
Short story, 162, 163, 195, 239
Speculate, 20, 30, 112, 200, 210, 218, 308, 424
Support, 20, 30
Symbolism, 18
Symbolize, 308
Synthesize, 200
Tense
future tense, 143
past tense, 143
present tense, 143
Verbs
action verbs, 143
linking verbs, 143
Visual essay, 153

Assessment

Speaking and listening
oral presentation, 88, 182, 270, 398, 484
Writing to sources
argument, 268, 482
explanatory essay, 180
fictional narrative, 396
nonfiction narrative, 86

Language Conventions

Adjectives, 67
comparative, 254
predicate adjective, 463
Adverbs, 67
comparative, 254
Antecedents, 386
pronoun-antecedent agreement, 386
Appositive phrases, 213
Appositives, 213
Capitalization, 125
Clauses
dependent (subordinate) clauses, 221, 343
independent clauses, 221, 343
relative clauses, 221
Compound words, 203

© Pearson Education, Inc., or its affiliates. All rights reserved.

Research

Speaking and Listening

© Pearson Education, Inc., or its affiliates. All rights reserved.

take a position, 40, 136, 236, 360, 442
Talking points, 227
Theatrical performance, 473
Whole-class learning strategies
    clarify by asking questions, 10, 98, 192, 280, 408
    interact and share ideas, 10, 98, 192, 280, 408
    listen actively, 10, 98, 192, 280, 408
    monitor understanding, 10, 98, 192, 280, 408
Whole-group discussion, 117

Vocabulary

Academic vocabulary
    assume, 403, 434, 492
    certain, 187, 228, 268
    coherent, 403, 434, 492
    community, 93, 128, 180
    compel, 403, 434, 492
    consequently, 275, 352
    contribute, 5, 32, 86
    convince, 187, 228, 268
    critical, 403, 434, 492
    declare, 187, 228, 268
    elaborate, 93, 128, 180
    exclude, 93, 128, 180
    illustrate, 93, 128, 180
    inspire, 275, 352
    memorize, 5, 32, 86
    notable, 5, 32, 86
    novelty, 275, 352
    objective, 93, 128, 180
    perspective, 275, 352
    propel, 403, 434, 482
    recognize, 5, 32, 86
    reflect, 5, 32, 86
    sufficient, 187, 228, 268
    transform, 275, 352
    valid, 403, 434, 492
    various, 187, 228, 268
Concept vocabulary
    absorbing, 214, 215, 220
    abstract, 152, 158, 160
    aesthetic, 152, 156, 160
    antagonism, 50, 52, 56
    anxiously, 118, 120, 124
    apologetically, 194, 197, 202, 204
    beware, 372, 374, 376
    blossom, 138, 140, 141
    clenched, 68, 69, 73
    compromise, 312, 333, 342, 344
    compulsory, 42, 44, 46
    consumed, 214, 215, 220

consideration, 238, 293, 310
continuation, 248, 251, 252
cultivate, 144, 146, 147
curiosity, 362, 364, 368
deliberate, 410, 413, 426, 428
desperate, 60, 62, 65
destination, 462, 464, 471
devouring, 214, 215, 220
digesting, 214, 216, 220
disgusted, 60, 63, 65
distraught, 50, 52, 56
distressed, 194, 197, 202
domesticated, 144, 146, 147
dominate, 100, 109, 114, 116
enactment, 42, 44, 46
entitled, 42, 43, 46
expedition, 462, 463, 471
feathery, 12, 18, 22, 24
foe, 372, 374, 376
gradually, 248, 250, 252
humming, 12, 14, 22, 24
ignorance, 238, 284, 310
impetuous, 100, 108, 114, 116
insincerity, 312, 332, 342, 344
intensity, 410, 417, 426, 428
invaded, 452, 454, 459
irritable, 100, 107, 114, 116
journeys, 462, 464, 471
lamented, 194, 197, 202, 204
loftily, 238, 241, 244
loneliness, 138, 139, 141
malicious, 312, 329, 342, 344
milled, 162, 166, 168
misapprehension, 238, 296, 310
miserable, 100, 107, 114, 116
model, 380, 382, 384
mournfully, 194, 197, 202, 204
nonchalantly, 238, 241, 244
nostalgic, 248, 250, 252
obsessive, 410, 416, 426, 428
obstacle, 312, 327, 342, 344
offended, 452, 454, 459
parameters, 380, 381, 384
pathetically, 194, 197, 202, 204
patiently, 118, 120, 124
peeped, 362, 363, 368
pessimistic, 312, 329, 342, 344
presume, 238, 289, 310
process, 214, 215, 220
purist, 152, 156, 160
quest, 410, 413, 426, 428
quivering, 162, 166, 168
refugee, 50, 52, 56
relentlessly, 410, 418, 426, 428

respected, 60, 61, 65
shushes, 12, 16, 22, 24
shyly, 138, 139, 141
silently, 118, 120, 121, 124
skittered, 162, 166, 168
slain, 372, 374, 376
sorrowfully, 238, 240, 244
speculate, 238, 289, 310
squish, 12, 13, 22, 24
stubborn, 68, 71, 73
surmise, 238, 289, 310
suspiciously, 312, 315, 342, 344
template, 380, 382, 384
tenseness, 68, 71, 73
timidly, 118, 119, 120, 124
thorough, 410, 415, 426, 428
thoughtfully, 118, 120, 121, 124
threateningly, 100, 107, 114, 116
trek, 462, 464, 471
twirl, 12, 15, 22, 24
twist, 12, 15, 22, 24
vanished, 100, 102, 114, 116
violent, 452, 454, 459
wild, 144, 146, 147
wondered, 362, 364, 368
wrath, 452, 454, 459
Media vocabulary
    animation, 224, 226
    audio, 224, 226
    character design, 430, 432
    cut-out animation, 430, 432
    encapsulation, 26, 30
    graphics, 224, 226
    host, 256, 258
    images, 224, 226
    inker, 466, 472
    interview, 256, 258
    letterer, 466, 472
    light and shadow, 346, 349
    narrator, 224, 226
    object animation, 430, 432
    panel, 26, 30
    podcast, 256, 258
    real-time animation, 430, 432
    speech balloon, 26, 30
    stage directions, 346, 349
    dialogue, 346, 349
    voiceover, 224, 226
Technical vocabulary
    endurance test, 444, 446, 448
    microchips, 206, 207, 212
    pixels, 206, 208, 212
    program manager, 444, 446, 448
    sample group, 444, 446, 448

© Pearson Education, Inc., or its affiliates. All rights reserved.

© Pearson Education, Inc., or its affiliates. All rights reserved.

© Pearson Education, Inc., or its affiliates. All rights reserved.

INDEX OF AUTHORS AND TITLES

The following authors and titles appear in the print and online versions of Pearson Literature.

© Pearson Education, Inc., or its affiliates. All rights reserved.

T

Teen Researchers Defend Media Multitasking, 263
Teens and Technology Share a Future, 207
TIME For Kids, 444, 445
Turner, Pamela S., 118, 119

U

United Nations (UN), 42
United Nations General Assembly, 43

V

Villanueva, Alma Luz, 68, 69

W

Watterson, Bill, 26, 27
Wind in the Willows, The, from, 175
Wonderful Wizard of Oz, The, from, 391
Woodson, Jacqueline, 12, 13
Wright, James, 138, 139

© Pearson Education, Inc., or its affiliates. All rights reserved.

INDEX: INDEX OF AUTHORS AND TITLES

ADDITIONAL SELECTIONS: AUTHOR AND TITLE INDEX

The following authors and titles appear in the Online Literature Library.

© Pearson Education, Inc., or its affiliates. All rights reserved.

ACKNOWLEDGMENTS AND CREDITS

ACKNOWLEDGMENTS

The following selections appear in this grade level (Grade 6) of *my*Perspectives. Some selections appear online only.

3D Systems. *Dog Receives Prosthetic Legs Made by 3D Printer,* courtesy of 3D Systems, Inc.

BBC News Online. "Michaela DePrince: The War Orphan Who Became a Ballerina" from BBC, October 15, 2012. Used with permission; "The Girl Who Gets Gifts From Birds" from BBC, February 25, 2015. Used with permission.

BBC Worldwide Americas, Inc. *The Secret Life of the Dog*-BBC ©Two BBC Worldwide Learning; Animation of the history of exploration ©BBC Worldwide Learning.

Bloomsbury Publishing Plc. "Eleven" from *Woman Hollering Creek* by Sandra Cisneros. Copyright ©Sandra Cisneros. Used with permission of Bloomsbury Publishing.

Bolinda Publishing. Excerpted from *A Long Way Home* by Saroo Brierley with Larry Buttrose. Copyright ©2013 Saroo Brierley. Used with permission of Bolinda Publishing.

Candlewick Press and Amnesty International. "Prince Francis" from *Free? Stories about Human Rights*, edited by Roddy Doyle. Copyright ©2009 by Amnesty International. Published by Candlewick Press.

Charles Scribner's Sons. *The Wind in the Willows* by Kenneth Grahame (1908).

Chhabra, Esha. "The Importance of Imagination" by Esha Chhabra, from *The Importance of Imagination*, http://www.dailygood.org/story/207/the-importance-of-imagination/. Used with permission of the author.

Chronicle Books. "Oranges" from *New and Selected Poems* ©1995 by Gary Soto. Used with permission Chronicle Books LLC, San Francisco. Visit ChronicleBooks.com.

Column Five Media. "The Age of Exploration: Life on the Open Seas" ©2015, A&E Television Networks, LLC. All Rights Reserved.

Creative Book Services. Audio of text for "Lewis and Clark" courtesy of the author, Nick Bertozzi.

Deboodt, Ryan. *Hang Son Doong Largest Cave* ©Ryan Deboodt

DePrince, Michaela. "Michaela DePrince: Ballet Dancer" courtesy of Michaela DePrince.

Discovery Communications, LLC. "Dolphins Talk Like Humans" by Jennifer Viegas, posted on the Discovery News website on September 6, 2011. Courtesy of Discovery Communications, LLC.

Disney-Hyperion Books. *Tales of the Odyssey* by Mary Pope Osborne. Text copyright ©2002 by Mary Pope Osborne. Used by permission of Disney-Hyperion Books.

ESPN Magazine, LLC. "Best of the Spelling Bee" ©ESPN.

Etienne, Stefan. "Teens and Technology Share a Future" by Stefan Etienne, from *Huffington Post*, March 6, 2014. Copyright ©2014. Used with permission of the author.

Hanging Loose Press. "Sonnet, Without Salmon" reprinted from *What I've Stolen, What I've Earned* ©2014 by Sherman Alexie, by permission of Hanging Loose Press.

HarperCollins Publishers. *Tales of the Odyssey* by Mary Pope Osborne. Text copyright ©2002 by Mary Pope Osborne. Used by permission of HarperCollins Publishers.

Henry Holt & Company. From *Lewis & Clark* ©2011 by Nick Bertozzi. Reprinted by permission of First Second, an imprint of Roaring Book Press, a division of Holtzbrinck Publishing Holdings limited Partnership. All rights reserved.

Hogan, Linda E. "Predators" by Linda E. Hogan, from *9 Poems*. Used with permission of the author.

Houghton Mifflin Harcourt Publishing Co. *Hachiko: The True Story of a Loyal Dog* by Pamela S. Turner. Text copyright ©2004 by Pamela S. Turner. Reprinted by permission of Houghton Miffilin Harcourt Publishing Company. All rights reserved; "All Watched Over by Machines of Loving Grace" from *The Pill Versus the Springhill Mine Disaster* by Richard Brautigan. Copyright ©1968 by Richard Brautigan. Reproduced by permission of Houghton Mifflin Harcourt Publishing Company. All rights reserved; Excerpt from *Sacajawea: The Story of Bird Woman and the Lewis and Clark Expedition* by Joseph Bruchac. Copyright ©2000 by Joseph Bruchac. Reprinted by permission of Houghton Mifflin Harcourt Publishing Company. All rights reserved.

IBM Corporation. "The Internet of Things" ©IBM External Submissions.

J. Boylston & Company, LLC. From *My Life with the Chimpanzees* by Jane Goodall. Used with permission of J. Boylston & Company Publishers.

K-MB CREATIVE NETWORK NY, Inc. "Michaela DePrince: Ballet Dancer" ©K-MB Creative Network NY.

Khan, Leena. "The Black Hole of Technology" by Leena Khan, from *Huffington Post*, January 20, 2015. Used with permission of the author.

Larson, Samantha. "To the Top of Everest" by Samantha Larson. Used with permission of the author.

Loesch, Cailin. "Is Our Gain Also Our Loss?" by Cailin Loesch, from *Huffington Post*, November 14, 2014. Used with permission of the author.

MacMillan. *White Fang* by Jack London (1906).

Mountaineers Books. "The Legend of Artic Explorer Matthew Henson" ©2014. Reprinted with permission from *The Adventure Gap: Changing the Face of the Outdoors* by James Edward Mills, Mountaineers Books, Seattle.

National Geographic Creative. "People of the Horse: Special Bond" by National Geographic ©National Geographic Creative.

New York Public Radio. NPR "Bored…and Brilliant?": A Production of WNYC Studios.

NPR (National Public Radio). ©2012 National Public Radio, Inc. News report titled "Pet Therapy: How Animals And Humans Heal Each Other" by Julie Rovner was originally published on NPR.org on March 5, 2012, and is used with the permission of NPR. Any unauthorized duplication is strictly prohibited.

PARS International Corporation. "Mars Can Wait. Oceans Can't" from CNN.com, August 17, 2012 ©2012 Turner Broadcast Systems, Inc. All rights reserved. Used by permission and protected by the Copyright Laws of the United States. The printing, copying, redistribution, or retransmission of this Content without express written permission is prohibited.

Penguin Books, Ltd. (UK). "Monday, March 30, 1992," "Sunday, April 12, 1992," "Tuesday, April 14, 1992," "Saturday,

© Pearson Education, Inc., or its affiliates. All rights reserved.

May 2, 1992," "Tuesday, May 5, 1992," "Thursday, May 7, 1992," "Monday, June 29, 1992," "Thursday, October 29, 1992," "Monday, November 2, 1992," "Thursday, December 3, 1992," "Tuesday, July 27, 1993," "Thursday, October 7, 1993," "Tuesday, October 12, 1993," "Epilogue: December 1993," from *Zlata's Diary: A Child's Life in Sarajevo* by Zlata Filipovic, translated by Christina Pribichevich-Zoric, copyright ©1993 by Fixot et Editions Robert Laffont; translation copyright ©1994 by Fixot et Editions Robert Laffont. Used by permission of Viking Books, an imprint of Penguin Publishing Group, a division of Penguin Random House LLC.; "The Shah of Blah" from *Haroun and The Sea of Stories* by Salman Rushdie (Granta/Penguin Books, 1990) Copyright ©Salman Rushdie, 1990. Reproduced by permission of Penguin Books Ltd.; *A Long Way Home* by Saroo Brierley. Copyright ©2013 by Sarco Brierley. Reproduced with permission by Penguin Books Ltd.

Penguin Group (Australia). *A Long Way Home* by Saroo Brierley. Reproduced with permission by Penguin Australia Pty Ltd.

Penguin Publishing Group. "another way," "believing," "brooklyn rain," "gifted," "sometimes," "uncle robert" and "wishes" from *Brown Girl Dreaming* by Jacqueline Woodson, copyright ©2014 by Jacqueline Woodson. Used by permission of Nancy Paulsen Books, an imprint of Penguin Young Readers Group, a division of Penguin Random House LLC.; "Monday, March 30, 1992," "Sunday, April 12, 1992," "Tuesday, April 14, 1992," "Saturday, May 2, 1992," "Tuesday, May 5, 1992," "Thursday, May 7, 1992," "Monday, June 29, 1992," "Thursday, October 29, 1992," "Monday, November 2, 1992," "Thursday, December 3, 1992," "Tuesday, July 27, 1993," "Thursday, October 7, 1993," "Tuesday, October 12, 1993," "Epilogue: December 1993," from *Zlata's Diary: A Child's Life in Sarajevo* by Zlata Filipovic, translated by Christina Pribichevich-Zoric, copyright ©1993 by Fixot et Editions Robert Laffont; translation copyright ©1994 by Fixot et Editions Robert Laffont. Used by permission of Viking Books, an imprint of Penguin Publishing Group, a division of Penguin Random House LLC.; From *Black Cowboy, Wild Horses: A True Story* by Julius Lester, copyright ©1998 by Julius Lester. Used by permission of Dial Books for Young Readers, an imprint of Penguin Young Readers Group, a division of Penguin Random House LLC.; "The Shah of Blah," from *Haroun and The Sea of Stories* by Salman Rushdie, copyright ©1990 by Salman Rushdie. Used by permission of Viking Books, an imprint of Penguin Publishing Group, a division of Penguin Random House LLC.; From *A Long Way Home* by Saroo Brierley, copyright ©2013 by Saroo Brierley. Used by permission of G. P. Putnam's Sons, an imprint of Penguin Publishing Group, a division of Penguin Random House LLC.

Penguin Random House Canada Limited (McClelland & Stewart). Excerpted from *A Long Way Home* by Saroo Brierley with Larry Buttrose. Copyright ©2013 Saroo Brierley. Reprinted by permission of Penguin Canada, a division of Penguin Random House Canada Limited.

Random House, Inc. "Raymond's Run," copyright © 1971 by Toni Cade Bambara; from *Gorilla, My Love* by Toni Cade Bambara. Used by permission of Random House, an imprint and division of Penguin Random House LLC. All rights reserved. Any third party use of this material, outside of this publication, is prohibited. Interested parties must apply directly to Penguin Random House LLC for permission; "Into the Boats" from *Shipwreck at the Bottom of the World: The Extraordinary True Story of Shackleton and the Endurance* by Jennifer Armstrong, copyright ©1998 by Jennifer M. Armstrong. Used by permission of Crown Publishers, an imprint of Random House Children's Books, a division of Penguin Random House LLC. All rights reserved. Any third party use of this material, outside of this publication, is prohibited. Interested parties must apply directly to Penguin Random House LLC for permission.

Ringgold, Faith. "The Boy Nobody Knew" by Faith Ringgold ©1998.

Samuel French, Inc. *The Phantom Tollbooth* by Susan Nanus and Norton Juster ©1977 by Susan Nanus and Norton Juster. CAUTION: Professionals and amateurs are hereby warned that "THE PHANTOM TOLLOOTH" being fully protected under the copyright laws of the United States of America, the British Commonwealth countries, including Canada, and the other countries of the Copyright Union, is subject to a royalty. All rights, including professional, amateur, motion picture, recitation, public reading, radio, television and cable broadcasting, and the rights of translation into foreign languages, are strictly reserved. Any inquiry regarding the availability of performance rights, or the purchase of individual copies of the authorized action edition, must be directed to Samuel French Inc., 235 Park Avenue South, Fifth Floor, New York, NY 10003, with other locations in Hollywood and London.

Scholastic, Inc. From *Freak the Mighty* by Rodman Philbrick. Copyright ©1993 by Rodman Philbrick. Reprinted by permission of Scholastic Inc.

Scovil Galen Ghosh Literary Agency, Inc. "Feathered Friend" reprinted by permission of the author's estate and the author's agents, Scovil Galen Ghosh Literary Agency, Inc.

Shotarov, Vasil. "Yo Ho Ho and a Rubber Ducky" ©Vasil Shotorov.

Simon & Schuster, Inc. Reprinted with the permission of Simon & Schuster Books for Young Readers, an imprint of Simon & Schuster Children's Publishing Division from *My Life With the Chimpanzees* by Jane Goodall. Copyright 1988, 1996 Byron Preiss Visual Publications, Inc. Text copyright ©1998, 1996 Jane Goodall; Reprinted with the permission of Atheneum Books for Young Readers, an imprint of Simon & Schuster Children's Publishing Division from *Out of My Mind* by Sharon M. Draper. Copyright ©2010 Sharon M. Draper.

Society for Science & the Public. "Screen Time Can Mess With the Body's Clock" Source: Student Science, Science News for Students, February 9, 2015, used with permission.

Susan Bergholz Literary Services. "Eleven" from *Woman Hollering Creek*. Copyright ©1991 by Sandra Cisneros. Published by Vintage Books, a division of Penguin Random House, and originally in hardcover by Random House. By permission of Susan Bergholz Literary Services, New York, NY, and Lamy, NM. All rights reserved; "Dusting" from *Homecoming*. Copyright ©1984, 1996 by Julia Alvarez. Published by Plume, an imprint of Penguin Random House, and originally by Grove Press. By permission of Susan Bergholz Literary Services, New York, NY, and Lamy, NM. All rights reserved.

Susanna Lea Associates. "Monday, March 30, 1992," "Sunday, April 12, 1992," "Tuesday, April 14, 1992," "Saturday, May 2, 1992," "Tuesday, May 5, 1992," "Thursday, May 7, 1992," "Monday, June 29, 1992,, "Thursday, October 29, 1992,, "Monday, November 2, 1992," "Thursday, December 3, 1992,, "Tuesday, July 27, 1993," "Thursday, October 7, 1993," "Tuesday, October 12, 1993," "Epilogue: December 1993," from *Zlata's Diary: A Child's Life in Sarajevo* by Zlata Filipovic, translated by Christina Pribichevich-Zoric, copyright ©1993 by Fixot et Editions Robert Laffont; translation copyright ©1994 by Fixot et Editions Robert Laffont. Used by permission

© Pearson Education, Inc., or its affiliates. All rights reserved.

of Viking Books, an imprint of Penguin Publishing Group, a division of Penguin Random House LLC.

The Times Online. "Congo the Chimpanzee" from *The Times*, September 25, 2005. Copyright ©2005 News Syndication.

Time-Life Syndication. "Mission Twinpossible" ©2005 Time Inc. All rights reserved. Reprinted/Translated from *Time for Kids* and published with permission of Time Inc. Reproduction in any manner in any language in whole or in part without written permission is prohibited.

United Nations Publications. Declaration of the Rights of the Child, ©United Nations. Reprinted with the permission of the United Nations.

University of Pennsylvania Press. "Our Wreath of Rosebuds," from *Changing Is Not Vanishing: A Collection of American Indian Poetry to 1930* by Corinne, edited by Robert Dale Parker. Copyright ©2011. Reprinted with permission of the University of Pennsylvania Press.

Villanueva, Alma Luz. "I Was a Skinny Tomboy Kid" by Alma Luz Villanueva. Used with permission of the author.

Wall Street Journal. "Teen Researchers Defend Media Multitasking" republished with permission of Dow Jones, Inc, from *Wall Street Journal*, October 13, 2014; permission conveyed through Copyright Clearance Center, Inc.

Wesleyan University Press. Wright, James. "A Blessing" from *Above the River* ©1990 by James Wright. Reprinted with permission of Wesleyan University Press, www.wesleyan.edu/wespress.

William Morris Endeavor. "another way," "believing," "brooklyn rain," "gifted," "sometimes," "uncle robert" and "wishes" from *Brown Girl Dreaming* by Jacqueline Woodson, copyright ©2014 by Jacqueline Woodson. Used by permission William Morris Endeavor Entertainment, LLC.

William Morris Endeavor Entertainment, LLC. "The Fun They Had" from *Isaac Asimov: The Complete Stories of Vol. 1* by Isaac Asimov. Copyright ©1951 by Isaac Asimov. Used with permission of William Morris Endeavor Entertainment, LLC.

WNET. "Jabberwocky" from *Through the Looking Glass* by Lewis Carroll ©WNET.

Wylie Agency. "The Shah of Blah" from *Haroun and The Sea of Stories* by Salman Rushdie. Copyright ©1990 by Salman Rushdie, used by permission of The Wylie Agency LLC.

YGS Group. "7-Year-Old Girl Gets New Hand From 3-D Printer" ©The Associated Press, Reprinted with permission of the YGS Group.

© Pearson Education, Inc., or its affiliates. All rights reserved.

ACKNOWLEDGMENTS AND CREDITS

ACKNOWLEDGMENTS AND CREDITS

Credits

Photo locators denoted as follows Top (T), Center (C), Bottom (B), Left (L), Right (R), Background (Bkgd)

Cover: (L) Efks/123RF, (R) Robert F. Balazik/Shutterstock

vi Jacob Maentz/Terra/Corbis; **viii–ix** 1stGallery/Shutterstock; **x** Jewel Samad/AFP/Getty Images; **xii** Jamesteohart/Shutterstock; **xiv** Paul Nicklen/National Geographic/Getty Images; **2** Jacob Maentz/Terra/Corbis; **3** (BC) Mettus/Shutterstock, (BCR) Maridav/Shutterstock, (BL) C.H. Pete Copeland/The Plain Dealer/AP Images, (BR) Vadim.Petrov/Shutterstock; (BCL) Ekaphon Maneechot/Shutterstock, (BCR) AMERICAN STOCK/Historical/Corbis, (TC) Gallo Images/Alamy, (T) Solarseven/Shutterstock, (C) Rana Sajid Hussain/Pacific Press/LightRocket/Getty Images, (TCR) Magnus Agren/Alamy, (TL) Maigi/Shutterstock, (TR) Kathy Quirk Syvertsen/Masterfile/Corbis; **6** Solarseven/Shutterstock; **11** (T) Maigi/Shutterstock, (B) C.H. Pete Copeland/The Plain Dealer/AP Images; **12** Robin Marchant/Stringer/Getty Images; **13, 20, 22, 24** Maigi/Shutterstock; **17** David Lichtneker/Alamy; **25, 26, 27, 30** C.H. Pete Copeland/The Plain Dealer/AP Images; **32** Solarseven/Shutterstock; **39** (B) Mettus/Shutterstock, (BC) Ekaphon Maneechot/Shutterstock, (TC) Gallo Images/Alamy, (T) Rana Sajid Hussain/Pacific Press/LightRocket/Getty Images; **43, 46, 48** Rana Sajid Hussain/Pacific Press/LightRocket/Getty Images; **51, 56, 58** Gallo Images/Alamy; **60** (TR) Mettus/Shutterstock, (BL) New York Daily News Archive/Getty Images, (TL) Ekaphon Maneechot/Shutterstock; **61, 65, 66** Ekaphon Maneechot/Shutterstock; **68** (BL) Alma Luz Villanueva, (TL) Ekaphon Maneechot/Shutterstock, (TR) Mettus/Shutterstock; **69, 73, 74** Mettus/Shutterstock; **76** (B) Mettus/Shutterstock, (T) Ekaphon Maneechot/Shutterstock; **90** 1stGallery/Shutterstock; **81** (C) AMERICAN STOCK/Historical/Corbis; **81** (B) Vadim.Petrov/Shutterstock, (TC) Magnus Agren/Alamy, (T) Kathy Quirk Syvertsen/Masterfile/Corbis; **91** (BC) Lisa Dearing/Alamy, (BCR) Renata Fedosova/Shutterstock, (BR) Herbert Me/Fotolia, **91** (B) Image Asset Management Ltd, (CL) Pictures From History/The Image Works, (CT) Jannis Tzimopulos/Alamy, (T) ZUMA Press, Inc./Alamy, (TC) Bootsandbling/iStock/Getty Images, (TCR) Svetlana Foote/Shutterstock, (TL) Animal Planet/Everett Collection; **94** ZUMA Press, Inc./Alamy; **99** (B) Pictures From History/The Image Works, (T) Animal Planet/Everett Collection; **100** British primatologist, ethologist, anthropologist Jane Goodall, c. 1976./PVDE/Bridgeman Art Library; **101, 112, 114, 116** Animal Planet/Everett Collection; **106** Jeryl Tan/Getty Images; **110** Everett Collection Inc/Alamy; **118** Jamie Westdal; **119, 122, 124, 126** Pictures From History/The Image Works; **128** ZUMA Press, Inc./Alamy; **135** (B) Lisa Dearing/Alamy, (BC) Image Asset Management Ltd, (TC) Jannis Tzimopulos/Alamy, (T) Bootsandbling/iStock/Getty Images, (CL) Douglas Kent Hall/ZUMA Press/Corbis; **138** (TL) Bootsandbling/iStock/Getty Images, (TR) Jannis Tzimopulos/Alamy; **139, 141, 142** Bootsandbling/iStock/Getty Images; **144** (CL) Chris Felver/Archive Photos/Getty Images, (TL) Bootsandbling/iStock/Getty Images, (TR) Jannis Tzimopulos/Alamy; **145, 147, 148** Jannis Tzimopulos/Alamy; **150** (T) Bootsandbling/iStock/Getty Images, (B) Jannis Tzimopulos/Alamy; **153–160** Image Asset Management Ltd; **163, 168, 170** Lisa Dearing/Alamy; **175** (B) Herbert Me/Fotolia, (BC) Renata Fedosova/Shutterstock, (TC) Svetlana Foote/Shutterstock; **184** Jewel Samad/AFP/Getty Images; **185** (BC) Bikeriderlondon/Shutterstock, (BCL) Karinkamon/Shutterstock, (BCR) David Crockett/Shutterstock, (BR) Dgmata/Shutterstock; **185** (CL) H. Armstrong Roberts/ClassicStock/Getty Images, (CR) R. Gino Santa Maria/Shutterstock, (T) Van1981Roo/Shutterstock, (TC) Kirill_Makarov/Shutterstock, (TCL) Sergey Nivens/Shutterstock, (TCR) Junpinzon/Shutterstock, (TL) Eric Isselee/Shutterstock, (TR) Damian Dovarganes/AP Images; **188** Van1981Roo/Shutterstock; **193** (T) Eric Isselee/Shutterstock, (TC) Sergey Nivens/Shutterstock, (BC) Karinkamon/Shutterstock; **194** Sanka Vidanagama/Stringer/Getty Images; **195, 200, 202, 204** Eric Isselee/Shutterstock; **206** (BL) ©Stefan Etienne, (TL) Sergey Nivens/Shutterstock, (TR) Karinkamon/Shutterstock; **207, 210, 212** Sergey Nivens/Shutterstock; **214** (BL) ©Leena A. Khan, (TL) Sergey Nivens/Shutterstock, (TR) Karinkamon/Shutterstock; **215, 218, 220** Karinkamon/Shutterstock; **222** (B) Karinkamon/Shutterstock, (T) Sergey Nivens/Shutterstock; **235** (B) Bikeriderlondon/Shutterstock, (CL) H. Armstrong Roberts/ClassicStock/Getty Images, (CR) R. Gino Santa Maria/Shutterstock, (T) Kirill_Makarov/Shutterstock; **238** Marty Lederhandler/AP Images; **239, 244, 246** Kirill_Makarov/Shutterstock; **248** Robin Platzer/Twin Images/LFI/Photoshot/Newscom; **249, 252, 254** (L) H. Armstrong Roberts/ClassicStock/Getty Images; **249, 252, 254** (R) R. Gino Santa Maria/Shutterstock; **257, 259** Bikeriderlondon/Shutterstock; **263** (B) Dgmata/Shutterstock, (T) Damian Dovarganes/AP Images, (BC) David Crockett/Shutterstock, (TC) Junpinzon/Shutterstock; **272** Jamesteohart/Shutterstock; **273** (BC) Melis/Shutterstock, (BCR) Kristin Smith/Shutterstock, (C) Duncan1890/iStock/Getty Images, (T) Dotshock/Shutterstock, (TC) Duncan Walker/iStock/Getty Images, (TCR) Painting/Alamy, (TR) Ryan Etter/Ikon Images/Superstock; **276** Dotshock/Shutterstock; **352** Dotshock/Shutterstock; **359** (B) Melis/Shutterstock, (C) Duncan1890/iStock/Getty Images, (T) Duncan Walker/iStock/Getty Images; **362, 272** New York Public Library/Science Source/Getty Images; **363, 368, 370** Duncan Walker/iStock/Getty Images; **373, 376, 378** Duncan1890/iStock/Getty Images; **380** Esha Chhabra; **381, 384, 386** Melis/Shutterstock; **400** Paul Nicklen/National Geographic/Getty Images; **391** (BC) Kristin Smith/Shutterstock, (T) Ryan Etter/Ikon Images/Superstock, (TC) Painting/Alamy; David Levenson/Getty Images; **401** (BCR) Lewis & Clark on the Lower Columbia River, 1905 (oil on canvas), Russell, Charles Marion (1865–1926)/Private Collection/Peter Newark American Pictures/Bridgeman Art Library, (BR) PhotoQuest/Archive Photos/Getty Images, (BC) Matt Berger/Shutterstock, (CR) Royal Geographical Society/Alamy, (TC) NG Images/Alamy, (T) Universal Images Group/DeAgostini/Alamy, (TCL) NASA Photo/Alamy, (TCR) Agencja Fotograficzna Caro/Alamy; **401** (TL) Pjhpix/fotolia, (TR) SeaOrbiter/Jacques Rougerie Architect; **404** Universal Images Group/DeAgostini/Alamy; **409** (B) BBC Worldwide Learning, (T) Pjhpix/fotolia; **410** Saroo Brierly; **411** Pjhpix/fotolia; **414** Universal Images Group Limited/Alamy; **420** Pep Roig/Alamy; **424, 426, 428** Pjhpix/fotolia; **431, 433** BBC Worldwide Learning; **434** Universal Images Group/DeAgostini/Alamy; **441** (BC) Matt Berger/Shutterstock, (T) NASA Photo/Alamy, (TC) NG Images/Alamy; **445, 448, 450** NASA Photo/Alamy; **452** (L) NG Images/Alamy, (R) Matt Berger/Shutterstock; **453, 455, 456** NG Images/Alamy; **458** (L) NG Images/Alamy, (R) Matt Berger/Shutterstock; **458** Scott Smeltzer/The Press Telegram/AP Images; **459, 461, 462** Matt Berger/Shutterstock; **464** (B) Matt Berger/Shutterstock, (T) NG Images/Alamy; **466** ©Creative Book Services, Peter Connolly/akg images/Newscom; **477** (B) PhotoQuest/Archive Photos/Getty Images, (BC) Lewis & Clark on the Lower Columbia River, 1905 (oil on canvas), Russell, Charles Marion (1865–1926)/Private Collection/Peter Newark American Pictures/Bridgeman Art Library, (T) SeaOrbiter/Jacques Rougerie Architect, (TC) Agencja Fotograficzna Caro/Alamy.

Credits for Images in Interactive Student Edition Only

Unit 1

AP Images; ASSOCIATED PRESS/AP Images; David Livingston/Contributor/Getty Images; Kathy Willens/AP Images; Kevin Weaver/REX/Newscom; Les Stone/Sygma/Corbis; Print Collector/Getty Images; Ryan McVay/Ocean/Corbis;

Unit 2

Julie Rovner/Doby; Frederick Hollyer/Hulton Archive/Getty Images;

Unit 3

©Chapelo Photography; Andrew Bridges; Chris Felver/Archive Photos/Getty Images; LeshaBu/Shutterstock; Michael Ochs Archives/Moviepix/Getty Images; Nikkytok/Shutterstock;

Unit 4

David Levenson/Getty Images; Fotomaster03/Shutterstock; Interim Archives/Archive Photos/Getty Images; Levon Biss/Getty Images; Piumadaquila/Fotolia;

Unit 5

©Chapelo Photography; AP Images; Nick Berard; Royal Geographical Society/Alamy.

© Pearson Education, Inc., or its affiliates. All rights reserved.